W9-BLT-020

THE GREAT BOOK OF
MODERN
WARPLANES

THE GREAT BOOK OF
MODERN WARPLANES

Featuring full technical descriptions, and battle action from Baghdad to Belgrade
Over 1,000 artworks, diagrams, and photographs

EDITED BY MIKE SPICK

PUBLISHED BY
SALAMANDER BOOKS LIMITED
LONDON

A SALAMANDER BOOK
Published by Salamander Books Ltd.,
8 Blenheim Court,
Brewery Road,
London N7 9NT,
United Kingdom.
© Salamander Books Ltd., 2000

ISBN 1 84065 156 3
1 2 3 4 5 6 7 8 9 10

All rights reserved. No part of this publication may be
reproduced, stored in a retrieval system
or transmitted in any form or by any means, electronic,
mechanical, photocopying, recording
or otherwise, without the prior permission of Salamander Books.

All correspondence concerning the content of this volume
should be addressed to Salamander Books Ltd.

Author

Mike Spick, who has extensively revised and updated this
work from the original published in 1987, and has written
several new entries, is a leading commentator on military
aviation with over 25 books to his credit, including
*Modern Air Combat, Modern Fighters, Illustrated Guide to
Modern Attack Aircraft,* and *Classic Warplanes.* He is a
consultant to *AirForces Monthly* and a contributor to *Air
International* and *Air Enthusiast.*

Credits

Project Manager: Ray Bonds
Designers: Interprep
Cutaway drawings: Mike Badrocke (© Pilot Press Ltd),
and © Salamander Books.
Color profiles: © Pilot Press Ltd.,
© Salamander Books Ltd., and © Pegasus Publishing Ltd.
Line three-view and side-view drawings:
© Pilot Press Ltd., and © Salamander Books Ltd.
Color reproduction: Studio Tec
Printed and bound in Spain

Contents

(The authors of the original works are shown in parenthesis.)

Acknowledgements

The publishers wish to thank the aircraft and systems manufacturers, the
various armed services, and private individuals who have provided
illustrations for this book, and in particular *AirForces Monthly* magazine
for providing many of the photographs.

Introduction

The first edition of *The Great Book of Modern Warplanes* had its origins in the *Aviation Fact File* series published between 1983 and 1986, ten selected volumes of which were combined in 1987 to form a single work. Of these, nine were single aircraft subjects; the other dealt with the products of the Mikoyan Design Bureau. During the past 17 years, since the first individual titles were published, a great deal has happened in the world of military aviation. Some major aircraft types covered then have been withdrawn from service; others have replaced or are about to replace them; while virtually every other type dealt with in the combined volume has undergone major upgrades. Looking into the future, radically new fighter types should and, bureaucracy and funding permitting, will enter service within the next two decades.

In the introduction to the first edition of *Modern Warplanes*, my friend and sometime mentor Bill Gunston wrote: "This book tells the story of many of the most important combat aircraft flying today. Each story is told in considerable depth, and was written in close collaboration with the manufacturer of the aircraft concerned. The quality of the results is obvious from the fact that some chapters of this book are used by the relevant manufacturer as the official all-embracing description, purchased from the publisher in order to be given to anyone from a five-star general to a potential foreign customer."

That this is no mere hyperbole the present writer can attest from experience. Shortly after the publication of the *Fact File* on the B-1B, I called in to see Rockwell's B-1B programme manager Scott White at Farnborough Air Show 1986 to thank him for his assistance. I was then hauled in front of Rockwell President "Buzz" Hello who, in addition to being extremely complimentary about the book, asked if I could arrange for the immediate delivery of 50 copies!

The first edition of *The Great Book of Modern Warplanes* contained a unique record of advanced Western technology, and fascinating, little-known facts about the Soviet MiGs. Since then, three factors have combined to alter the situation. The intervening years have seen massive technological advances, mainly in the fields of low observables and avionics. The Soviet Union has been dissolved, diminishing the major threat which drove Western combat aircraft requirements and design. Finally, Russia, the great aeronautical unknown, driven to export its latest and greatest by economic considerations, has become much more forthcoming about its latest projects.

Only a handful of nations have the expertise and the funding to produce truly modern warplanes: the USA and Russia, the four-nation European consortium of Britain, Germany, Italy and Spain; and the two loners, France and Sweden, although the latter has received considerable outside help. The People's Republic of China is trying hard, currently with Israeli assistance, but with little success, as evidenced by their recent purchases of Sukhoi Flankers from Russia. Many other nations are updating older aircraft, mainly by installing more modern avionics and weapons systems, but, while combat capability can be improved, the aerodynamic limitations of the original design remain.

This brings us back to the subject of this work. Many of the greatest fighters in service today, which are included here, were conceived in a previous era, to operate against a threat which no longer exists. The genesis of these is still relevant, and for this reason, and the fact that the other four authors of the series are well respected in the aviation world, the original text has been left largely unmodified. Upgrades and service history of the past 17 years has generally been included in the final parts of each section.

Parts of this second edition are of course totally new. In 1986, "stealth" was a black art in the open literature. The only section in which it was briefly touched upon was the B-1B. Now we have a complete section on US stealth warplanes, starting with the B-1B and encompassing the F-117A Nighthawk, the B-2A Spirit, the F-22A Raptor, and the Joint Strike Fighter, which will be developed from either the Boeing X-32 or the Lockheed Martin X-35. This is the future.

Below: Due to become operational in 2005, the F-22A Raptor's combination of supercruise, agility, and stealth, mark it as the world's most potent fighter for decades to come. AAMs are carried internally.

Below right: The MiG-29SM Fulcrum is a potent but unstealthy fighter. Fast and extremely agile, it has however achieved nothing air combat despite its formidable reputation. Pilot workload is high.

European fighters of the near future now have their own new section: the Mirage 2000 and Rafale from Dassault, the Eurofighter Typhoon, and the Swedish JAS 39 Gripen are all covered in detail. A point of interest here is that the final three are all of tail-less delta configuration with canard foreplanes, a layout that the USA and Russia have largely (but not entirely) ignored.

One of Bill Gunston's comments in 1987 was that many of the latest Russian combat aircraft appeared to be very strongly influenced by Western designs. It would be strange if this was not the case. Combat aircraft design is based on threat and counter-threat, and given that the USA possessed a technological lead, Russia was always trailing.

Classic examples were the Su-24 Fencer, a variable-sweep wing interdictor closely comparable to the F-111; the MiG-29 Fulcrum, a high performance and highly manoeuvrable fighter evidently intended as a counter to the F-16 and F/A-18; the Su-25 Frogfoot, almost a mirror-image of the A-10 Warthog; and the excellent Su-27 Flanker, which was very much the counterpart of the F-15 Eagle.

It was not entirely a one-way street. The specification for the F-15 was based on a very erroneous intelligence appreciation of the capabilities of the MiG-25 Foxbat, while the F-16 was designed to counter the extremely agile if basic MiG-21 Fishbed.

For many years before 1986, the "worst case" scenario was an all-out conflict between the Warsaw Pact and NATO in Western Europe. Individually inferior though the Eastern Bloc aircraft were at that time, they had a tremendous numerical advantage which might have given them aerial victory over the West. The American approach had been to make every fighter pilot an ace via superior technology, but this had an inherent flaw. In a one versus one encounter, American pilots had a decided advantage, which persisted even in a four versus four encounter. But in a close combat, multi-bogey fight, with each pilot basically dependent on what he could see "out of the window", the numerical superiority of the Warsaw Pact air forces could have been simply overwhelming.

Numbers create confusion, and confusion degrades technology very quickly indeed. The ideal solution for the West was the "invisible man" concept. How does one fight someone that one cannot see? Low observables, more usually known as stealth, had been around for decades. Germany had attempted to produce an "invisible" fighter in 1916, using transparent Cellon skinning, but only during the so-called "Cold War" period, when invisibility to radar became of increasing importance, did the concept, and the technology, come of age.

Stealth aircraft could penetrate hostile air defences and put ordnance on target without being intercepted. In the fighter world, a stealth aircraft could detect earlier than its opponent, and get a missile in the air first. Even if this missed, the opposition would immediately be put on the defensive, ceding the all-important initiative.

In the shape of the current F-117 and B-2, and the future F-22, the USAF has nailed its colours firmly to the stealth mast, while the Joint Strike Fighter, currently proposed for the USN and USMC as well as for the USAF, is also stealthy. Highly successful stealth is very costly, however, and the Europeans – with their Rafale, Typhoon and Gripen – have compromised, opting for high agility coupled with reduced radar cross-section.

What of the Russians? They have produced the superbly agile MiG-29 and the ever-proliferating Sukhoi Flanker family which, although magnificent fighters, are non-stealthy. It is known that they have been experimenting with plasma shielding for many years, but the semi-stealthy Mikoyan I.42 which was to have demonstrated this remains grounded for lack of funds.

Other trends are supercruise (the ability to maintain speeds of the order of Mach 1.5 without recourse to afterburning) and supermanoeuvrability (the ability to manoeuvre hard under full control at speeds below the aerodynamic stall by using vectored thrust). Supercruise will of course aid stealth in medium range combat, while supermanoeuvrability is a close combat attribute. Another trend is towards high off-boresight missile capability. Which of these evolving systems will be most effective remains to be seen. In the meantime, the descriptions of the great warplanes featured in this book make fascinating reading.

Mike Spick

A-10 Thunderbolt II

Contents

Top: A USAF A-10 of 1st TFW, armed with AGM-65B scene-magnification Maverick air-to-surface missile, and equipped with the Westinghouse ALQ-19(V) ECM pod.

Above: Four A-10s of 917th TFG, based at Barksdale AFB, Louisiana, participating in AFRES Aerials exercises over Texas in the 1980s.

Above right and left: Two fine studies of USAF 52nd Wing, 81st TFS Panthers, based in Spangdahlem, Germany, and operating from Aviano, Italy, in March 1999, during the Serbian conflict.

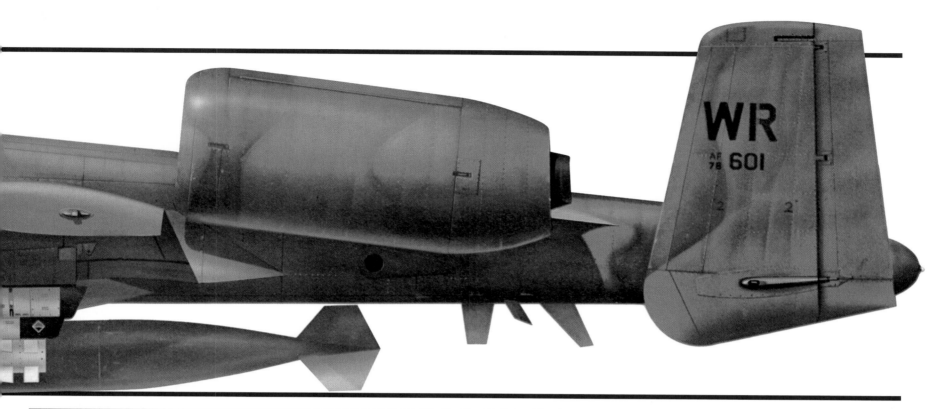

Introduction

The A-10 is most unusual among modern American combat aircraft. Built in a single model, in strictly limited numbers, for one specialized role, and without a single export order to its name, it is the antithesis of such predecessors as the Phantom or the nearly contemporary F-15 and F-16, which are notable for their popularity and versatility.

Critics would explain the A-10's lack of sales by pointing to its apparently outdated performance figures, its lack of sophisticated avionics and its airliner engines, all of which add up to no more than an absence of spurious glamour. In fact, for its uniquely demanding role of visual-range tank-busting, the A-10 Thunderbolt II – 'Warthog' to its intimates – is uniquely well-suited.

Down on the deck, under the cloud and in visibility that would ground almost any of its contemporaries, it can hide from missile and AA radars for all but the few seconds needed for a devastating gun or Maverick attack; it can out-turn high-speed interceptors; and its gun is as deadly against aircraft as against main battle tanks.

Paradoxically, the Warthog's strengths are a principal reason for the limit on numbers built. Hard to break, easy to mend, with a unique capability to fight, take punishment, regenerate their strength and fight again, A-10s simply do not suffer the kind of attrition associated with other modern fighters.

And other aspects of the design are equally original and impressive. The engines, unique among modern combat aircraft, are ideally suited to the role; the GAU-8/A Avenger cannon gives it a positively awesome punch; and in an era of supersophisticated fighters with appallingly accident-prone systems, an aircraft that has to be flown from the cockpit, rather than by means of a battery of black boxes, is one of the most sought-after assignments the Air Force has to offer.

Development

The requirements of the close air support mission could not be met by the big, complex supersonic jets developed for Tactical Air Command during the 1950s: in Vietnam, they were met instead by slow, propeller-driven aircraft whose virtues were long endurance, good weapon-carrying ability, low-speed manoeuvrability and good visibility. All the latter qualities are embodied in the A-10, which originated in the Attack Experimental programme initiated, at least partly as a result of pressure from the US Army, in 1966, and which has found its main role as a tank-killer on NATO's Central Front.

Close support is one of the least standardized missions in military aviation. It can, perhaps, be best defined as the use of air power to attack hostile ground forces which are already in contact with friendly troops, or are on the point of engaging them. Some air forces do not even use the term 'close air support' (CAS), preferring phrases that emphasise offensive strike slightly to the rear of the battlefield. The former Soviet Union's tacticians believed that the most intimate forms of close support should be the province of the ground forces' own helicopters.

The infantry commander cares little for such fine distinctions. He wants some friendly firepower to deal with an imminent attack by a superior force, and he wants it without delay.

The Fairchild Republic A-10A, officially named Thunderbolt II and universally known as the Warthog, is the only Western fixed-wing aircraft which has been designed without compromise for the CAS mission. All of its many unique characteristics stem from CAS requirements. These include its low speed, its long endurance, its unparalleled protection and its awesome built-in armament. However, its dedication to the CAS mission has also been the reason why it has been overshadowed by its sinuous supersonic contemporaries.

The basic controversy over CAS is over half a century old and still kicking. Is it best handled by a specialized aircraft, or by a fighter with bomb racks?

Advocates of the CAS type argue that the 'fast-mover' fighter can hardly perform the mission at all. Its relative delicacy and poor low-speed handling tend to confine it to a single run against a previously identified or designated target. Their opponents argue that it is foolish to design any aircraft to the requirements of land warfare, to the detriment of its ability to fight and survive in the air.

The Western Allies' experience in the 1939-45 war was decisive. The Luftwaffe's favoured CAS weapon, the Ju 87 dive-bomber, won high renown in the early stages of the war, but the Royal Air Force found its measure and defeated it. The RAF and the US Army Air Force had already ordered quite large numbers of dive-bombers, but hardly any of them were used in action. Instead, the most successful CAS weapons in Northern Europe were Typhoons, Tempests, P-51 Mustangs and P-47 Thunderbolts, second-generation fighters armed with newly developed rocket projectiles and heavy gun armament.

The 1944-45 campaign was to influence planning into the 1960s. Its lessons were fresh in mind when Tactical Air Command was formed in 1947, and when the independent US Air Force followed later that year. One of the first things that the USAF did was to eliminate the 'Attack' category from its designation system, along with the obsolete 'Pursuit'. The fighter-bomber became the backbone of TAC. At the same time, though, the concept of close support began to melt into the 'strike' mission. TAC's main new project for the 1950s was an aircraft designed to fly at supersonic speed at low level, to navigate to a known ground target in bad weather and hit it with a nuclear bomb: the Republic F-105 Thunderchief.

Fighter design trends

The F-105 typified a great many trends in fighter design. It was bigger and more complex than its predecessors and cost a great deal more to buy and maintain, so there would be fewer of the new aircraft built. Because of its great complexity, it would demand more maintenance, so each aircraft would fly fewer missions and each mission would be preceded by many hours of preparation and equipment checks. The F-105 would operate only from well-equipped bases, safely in the rear of the war zone. Its range was excellent, at a high cruising speed; its endurance, in hours, was poor. In brief, there was no way in which an F-105 unit could respond to a call for immediate support.

By 1960, TAC's less sophisticated fighter-bomber types were getting older. Far from planning a replacement, TAC was busily working on SOR-183, a requirement which defined an aircraft much bigger and more sophisticated than the F-105. Nobody appreciated the implications of this trend more clearly than the customers for close air support in the US Army. For a time, the Army seriously considered acquiring its own

CAS aircraft, and the Northrop N-156F (which had not yet received its first Air Force order) and the Fiat G.91 were both evaluated in 1961. The Army also received presentations on a quaint British machine called the Hawker P.1127. The sight of jet fighters in Army insignia touched off an inter-service dispute over the roles and missions split between the USAF and Army. Finally, the Army had to accept tight restrictions on the types of fixed-wing aircraft which it could operate, but the US Air Force was told by the Defense Secretary, Robert McNamara, to rebuild its ability to provide battlefield air support to the Army.

To begin with, CAS was closely linked to the 'limited war' theories of the time, and to the perceived US need to contain Soviet-inspired 'insurgencies' directed at allied states. The revival of CAS within TAC was originally directed at defeating guerrilla-type forces, using limited effort in an unsophisticated air environment. The first practical application of new 'counter-insurgency' (COIN) air power was to be Vietnam, where air of the USAF's COIN detachments arrived in late 1961.

COIN operations against concealed ground troops called for the accurate delivery of small weapon loads, and with the weapon-aiming technology of 1961 this meant using an aircraft with good manoeuvrability at low speed. Such a light combat aircraft had been conceived in the late 1950s by North American: a strengthened, re-engined

Left: The A-X specification that gave rise to the A-10 was the product of a long process of analysis of close air support requirements: the resulting prototype is seen here with instrument boom attached to its nose.

Right: Slow, but tough and manoeuvrable at low speeds, and able to loiter for long periods with a heavy weight of ordnance, the A-1E Skyraider proved to be the most useful CAS aircraft available in Vietnam.

adaptation of a surplus T-28A trainer. The French had produced the conversion in quantity, as the Fennec, for use in Algeria, and TAC's Special Air Warfare Center at Eglin AFB, Florida, created the similar T-28D for use by Vietnamese forces and the rapidly growing force of US 'advisors'. A three-service requirement was issued for a successor aircraft: a highly versatile, carrier-capable machine of about the same size, power, warload and speed as the T-28D. This was the Light Armed Reconnaissance Aircraft (LARA), and was to be built in huge numbers for the USAF, Navy and Marines and for US allies.

But plans for LARA were upset by the Viet Cong, who began to demonstrate disturbing proficiency with their Soviet-supplied light anti-aircraft artillery (AAA), mostly of 14mm calibre. T-28D losses mounted steadily in 1963-64, and TAC's COIN experts attributed many losses to the type's modest speed. Even before the LARA contest winner – Rockwell's OV-10 Bronco – made its first flight, TAC had decided that it was to be confined to the forward air control mission. By late 1964, there were references to a Super-COIN aircraft with a minimum speed – at low level, with a full weapons load – around 315kt (580km/h).

But the need to replace the increasingly vulnerable T-28D was urgent, and the situation became worse in early 1964 when the heavy-lift contingent of the Vietnam-based attack force – Douglas

B-26s – was grounded en masse by structural problems. Fortunately, a replacement was at hand in the burly shape of the A-1 Skyraider, which had been under evaluation at Eglin AFB since the previous year. The A-1 was not fast, but it was reasonably tough, it was manoeuvrable at low speeds – its massive divebrakes were an asset – and it had a long

endurance with a heavy weapon load, thanks to the efficiency of its piston engine.

The A-1 proved to be by far the most successful CAS improvisation in Vietnam, and one even shot down a MiG-17 which strayed in front of its four 20mm cannon. It was a decisive participant in many rescue operations, because it

could remain on station and continue to fire long after any jet would have turned for home, out of fuel and ammunition. In the CAS mission, its endurance allowed it to loiter just behind the battle area and respond to a call for support faster than any jet. The A-1's low-speed manoeuvrability, and the all-round visibility from its high-perched bubble canopy (infinitely better than that of any contemporary fighter) meant that its pilot saw targets that a jet pilot would miss, and could keep them in sight as he swung the A-1 around to attack. A small turning radius allowed the A-1 to manoeuvre and turn among hills and low cloud, in conditions where jets were confined to a single pass at the target.

Endurance at a premium
The USAF did use other aircraft for CAS in Vietnam – such as the F-100 and the A-37, a version of the T-37 jet trainer – but none had the A-1's endurance, so they had to be kept on the ground until needed. Too often, they arrived too late, or found the tactical situation had changed, and their pilots could not see targets quickly enough to attack on a single pass. Experience in Vietnam convinced the USAF that a manoeuvrable, long-endurance aircraft, primarily relying on the 'Mark One Eyeball' for target acquisition, was the only way to provide effective CAS. The payload and endurance of the A-1 became the baseline for the Super-COIN studies.

Another piece of the jigsaw dropped into place in 1966, when the USAF ordered the A-7D development of the Navy's Corsair II. This was an aircraft about the same size as the Skyraider, but had a longer range, higher operating speeds and much more sophisticated equipment. Its presence in the TAC inventory would help fight the temptation to upgrade a COIN aircraft into another fast, expensive long-range strike type.

Meanwhile, the increasing strength of the Viet Cong was making the early-

Below left: The A-10's World War II namesake, the P-47 Thunderbolt. Shown here with 2,000lb (907kg) bombs, the P-47 was also a useful tank-buster with guns and rockets.

Below: Another Republic product, the F-105 Thunderchief was designed as a supersonic strike aircraft, but spent much of its career delivering iron bombs over Vietnam.

Bottom: The T-28D attack version of the T-28A trainer, seen here in 1962 at Bien Hoa AB, South Vietnam, with gun pods, rockets and bombs, proved too vulnerable to ground fire.

Below: The USAF's acquisition of the A-7D Corsair II in the late 1960s provided a capable long-range attack bomber and cleared the way for a dedicated COIN aircraft.

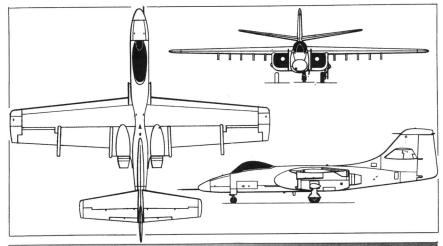

Top: Northrop's A-X contender, the YA-9A, was of conventional layout, with shoulder-mounted wing, single fin, and engines faired neatly into the fuselage sides.

Above: The first YA-9A on an early flight in June 1972. Although the fly-off results were close, the Northrop design lost out in terms of maintainability and survivability.

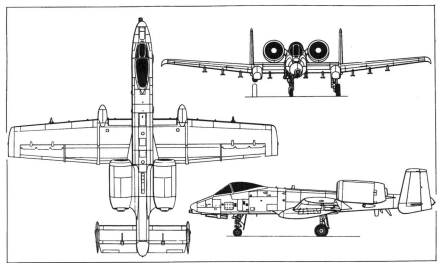

Above left: In complete contrast to the YA-9A, Fairchild's A-10 design was thoroughly unconventional in layout, with low wings, twin fins and podded engines high on the rear fuselage.

Left: The first YA-10A after roll-out from Fairchild's Farmingdale, Long Island, plant. Concern over the company's future, with no major order on its books, was an important factor in the USAF's choice.

Below: Airborne on a test flight, the first YA-10A demonstrates its ordnance-carrying capability.

1960s image of a limited war look positively peaceful. Radar-directed AAA was encountered over Laos in 1964, and was expected to spread elsewhere. On the ground, North Vietnamese Army regular forces were encountered in late 1965, in the Ia Drang Valley. The possibility of encountering hostile armour could no longer be ruled out. Any future CAS aircraft, it was clear, would have to be able to destroy heavier targets and survive against more sophisticated defences than had been envisaged a few years earlier.

In the course of 1964, the US Army began to talk about an Advanced Aerial Fire Support System (AAFSS). The non-specific programme title masked the fact that AAFSS was to be a 220kt (410km/h) all-weather strike aircraft, which the Army could pursue and develop because it would be a compound helicopter. While the USAF would have produced a CAS aircraft in any case, the timing and details were certainly influenced by the constant pressure from the Army aviators.

The A-X programme

In mid-1966, these factors came together with the launching of the Attack, Experimental (A-X) programme by USAF Chief of Staff Gen. John P. McConnell. A request for proposals (RFP) was issued to 21 companies in March 1967, outlining the current state of USAF thinking on the new aircraft and seeking the views of the industry. The RFP was couched in broad terms, and it was not expected to lead directly to full-scale development. However, it laid out the most significant features which had been deemed necessary by the USAF experts.

The A-X was to combine A-1-type endurance and weapon load with a minimum speed of 350kt (650km/h) – the old A-1 was limited to 240kt (444km/h) with a heavy load. Despite its increased speed, it was to be able to manoeuvre hard at low airspeeds; the USAF wanted an aircraft which could turn in a limited amount of space, in order to attack an objective without overflying its defences, or make a complete turn in poor visibility without losing sight of the target.

The speed of A-X would not be enough to avoid ground fire completely, so it would be designed to survive when hit. In Vietnam, too many US fighters were being lost to small-calibre or frag-

ment strikes in vulnerable areas, revealing design flaws in most of the service types. Although systems were duplicated, they were seldom protected, and the two channels often ran close together where a single hit would destroy both. In parallel with the A-X programme, several companies were placed under contract to study the specific question of combat aircraft vulnerability.

In addition to its external armament, A-X was to carry a heavy internal gun. Vietnam experience had led the USAF back to the gun as a fighter weapon, and it was the only class of weapon with which a low-cost CAS aircraft could hit a small moving target. A scaled-up version of the very successful General Electric M61 was the obvious starting point. A-X would also have to be cheap, compared with supersonic fighters, and as simple as possible to maintain and operate. It would be designed to use short, unprepared strips, and to function with the limited maintenance facilities available at such bases. The type's low-speed manoeuvrability, and the heavy gun, were intended to eliminate the need for costly automated weapon-aiming systems.

All in all, the A-X requirement was a great deal more difficult than the updated Skyraider which many people thought it was at the time. With the jet engines available at that time, it would not be possible to match the Skyraider's endurance. A low-bypass-ratio engine (such as a Pratt & Whitney TF30 or Rolls-Royce/Allison TF41) has poor propulsive efficiency at low speeds. The A-7, which uses those engines, has excellent range at Mach 0.75-0.8, but will burn fuel almost as fast at half the airspeed. Its loiter capability is therefore limited. Improving propulsive efficiency at lower

Above: Tanker's eye view of a bomb-laden YA-10A during in-flight refuelling trials. The dummy slipway was not connected to the fuel system.

Left: The two YA-10As in formation. Comparative evaluation was carried out at Edwards AFB, California, during the last three months of 1972.

While the industry worked on responses to the RFP, the USAF worked on refining the A-X requirement, to minimize the size and cost of the aircraft while ensuring that all the service's essential needs were met, and on setting up the programme structure to avoid the risk of delays and cost escalation. The USAF was in deep political trouble over two major programmes, the F-111 and the C-5, and had no desire to add A-X to the list. Moreover, while cost increases could be tolerated for an advanced-technology aircraft, they would be the end of the road for A-X, which was billed as a low-cost, low-risk concept.

A-X was beginning to gain even greater importance in Air Force planning. Shocked by the lack-lustre performance of its F-4s against obsolescent MiG-17s and boy-racer MiG-21s over Vietnam, and by the sudden advent of the (apparently) awesome Mach 3 Mikoyan Foxbat, the USAF had directed its FX advanced fighter programme towards maximum performance in air-to-air combat. To suggest compromise for CAS or strike was heresy. From 1968-69 onwards, the entire Air Force CAS mission was riding on the A-X; if the A-X did not materialise, the plans for the new fighter would have to be changed, to add some strike capability, and the Army would demand and get all the money it wanted for the AAFSS, which had now

materialised as the amibitious, sophisticated and expensive Lockheed AH-56A Cheyenne.

Four years elapsed between the first A-X discussions and the issue of a final RFP: a long interval, certainly, but understandable in the light of the fact that A-X was a completely new type of aircraft. The most important change during this initial development period came about as a result of improved engine technology. High-bypass-ratio turbofan engines were being run by all the major engine manufacturers, and were proving capable of everything claimed for them. While they had initially been designed for huge freighters and airliners, the technology turned out to be readily 'scaleable'. Small high-BPR engines for a variety of aircraft – airliners as well as military types – were soon under development and seemed to offer modest risks. On the A-X, the high-BPR engines were efficient enough to meet the endurance requirement. They could be mounted close to the centreline, easing the one-engine-out design case, and the adverse stability and trim effects associated with large propellers were absent. The turbofan, with a single fan stage driven directly by a turbine, is also inherently much simpler than the turboprop, with its gearbox and variable-pitch propeller.

Two other changes were related to the adoption of turbofans by nearly all the companies participating in the A-X programme. The speed of the A-X increased toward 400kt (740km/h), closer to the optimum for the turbofan, and the USAF set its final runway-length objective at a somewhat greater value than had been expected earlier: A-X was to operate from a 4,000ft (1,200m) strip at maximum weight. This was a fairly

speeds means imparting a lesser acceleration to a larger mass of air, and in 1967 the only established way of doing so was the propeller.

Propellers, however, bring their own problems. Because of the survivability requirements, A-X would have to have two engines, and the speed and short-takeoff-and-landing (Stol) capability desired by the USAF meant that the A-X would have to be quite powerful for its size. The Stol and low-speed manoeuvrability requirements would demand large propellers, so the engines would be well out from the centreline of the aircraft. It became difficult to design the

A-X so that it would be controllable if one engine failed at low speed, just after takeoff. Northrop looked at the possibility of coupling two turboprops in the tail, as on the Learfan business aircraft, but this would have made the entire aircraft vulnerable to a hit on the single propeller and gearbox. An alternative proposal was to install a cross-shaft between the two engines, but this added weight and complexity. The overall effect was that the turboprop-powered A-X became steadily bigger, approaching 60,000lb (27,200kg) maximum takeoff weight, and accordingly more expensive.

modest aim. With the thrust/weight ratio and the wing loading already dictated by the low-speed manoeuvre requirements, the field-length target could be met without complex high-lift devices or thrust reversal. Again, this helped reduce the weight and cost of the aircraft.

Another significant change of emphasis began to enter the programme in 1967-68. The North Vietnamese Army had, by that time, made their first use of tanks against US forces, and conventional warfare in Europe was once more being considered now that the 'nuclear trip-wire' philosophy had been abandoned. The anti-armour capability of A-X began to be considerably more important. Meanwhile, in June 1967, the Israeli Air Force had succeeded in knocking out a large number of tanks with the 30mm cannon fitted to their Dassault Mystères. What had happened was that while tank guns and frontal armour had made considerable advances since 1945, tanks remained, inevitably, more vulnerable at the rear, on the sides and, particularly, on the top. The 20mm M61 would not suffice though, so the USAF began to draw up requirements for a new gun for A-X, of larger calibre and with a higher muzzle

velocity. This would be a destructive and very accurate weapon, but it would also be a great deal larger than the M61, and it would only fit in a specially designed aircraft. Quietly, and with very little public attention, the A-X turned from a general-purpose bomb truck into a cannon-armed 'tankbuster', a breed which had been considered extinct since 1945.

Specific requirements

The final RFP was issued in May 1970. Performance requirements included a speed of 350-400kt (650-740km/h). The maximum external load was to be 16,000lb (7,250kg), but this could be traded for internal fuel or for 1,350 cannon rounds. The A-X was to be able to carry 9,500lb (4,300kg) of external ordnance and internal ammunition over a 250nm (460km) radius, and loiter for two hours in the target area. Low-speed manoeuvrability was identified as the route to adverse-weather operations. The A-X, according to the USAF, would be so manoeuvrable that it could operate safely and effectively under a ceiling of 1,000ft (305m) with one nm (1.85km) visibility. "Weather conditions worse than this exist only 15 per cent of the

time," noted an official USAF statement, without specifying to what part of the world this figure applied.

Contestants would be assessed on three other requirements. Survivability, or the ability to avoid or survive hits from a range of current and projected Soviet AAA weapons, was the most novel. Fuel system protection, duplicated and dispersed system runs and armour were basic requirements, but the USAF was keen to have an aircraft which could lose large segments of itself and stay airborne.

Simplicity, another prime requirement, was related to survivability in one respect; a survivable aircraft is of little use if it cannot be quickly repaired. But it was also important from the point of view of reducing the unit and operating cost – and saving money for the sophisticated FX. A-X was to use no new or untried technology, both to reduce costs and to eliminate, as far as possible, the danger of problems in the programme. 'Design to cost' was the watchword: if necessary, weight increases would be accepted and performance sacrificed to meet cost targets. Simplicity was also part of the last main requirement, for rapid response. The A-X might be based at

forward operating bases, close to the battle line, for quicker response to any calls for support, and maintenance facilities would be limited.

The programme was novel in another respect; it would be the first in 15 years to involve a head-on, competitive evaluation between two prototypes. This reversion in policy stemmed from the problems with the F-111 programme, which had been launched simultaneously into production and development. Technical problems were encountered, and by the time they were fixed a great many aircraft had been built. It had also been necessary to modify many aircraft on the production line, and costs had escalated enormously.

The revived 'fly-before-buy' philosophy would avoid such problems, because the new aircraft would be flown and thoroughly tested before a production decision was taken. In the case of A-X, which was to be a low-risk design, this aspect of fly-before-buy was perhaps less important than the psychological factor. The manufacturers would be kept under strong competitive pressure until a much later stage in the programme, and by the time they had built and flown prototypes they would have a much greater stake in success.

Six companies responded to the 1970 RFP by the August 10 deadline: Cessna, Fairchild, Boeing-Vertol, Lockheed, General Dynamics and Northrop. The programme was significant, in that the USAF and US Navy had already selected contractors for their other important new aircraft. The A-X was – at that time – the last major combat aircraft programme in sight for many years. The field of contenders was strong. Lockheed and GD were among the most capable of aerospace companies, even if both were in the Pentagon's doghouse over the C-5 and F-111. Cessna had experience with the A-37 Dragonfly. Northrop had shown great expertise in building effective combat aircraft with comparatively low purchase and operating costs. Boeing-Vertol, a helicopter manufacturer, was an unexpected participant, with the only remaining propeller-driven design.

Fairchild – to be more precise, the Republic Aviation Division of Fairchild-Hiller – had learned a great deal from the performance of its F-105 in combat, but had produced no new aircraft since then. Thunderchief production had been terminated prematurely in favour of the F-4C Phantom; Republic had been involved in two separate efforts to develop highly advanced, supersonic, variable-sweep V/Stol fighters, in collaboration with European countries, but neither had borne fruit; and the company had been a finalist in the F-X competition, losing to McDonnell Douglas. Of all the A-X contenders, the Republic organisation was the only one which risked disappearing from the scene as a prime contractor if its bid did not succeed, and its best people were assigned to the preparation of the A-X proposal.

Weapon for the A-X

Also in 1970, the USAF issued an RFP couched in similar terms for what would now be the primary weapon, the internal gun. Designated GAU-8, it was to be a 30mm weapon with a 4,000 rounds/min rate of fire; the latter requirement effectively dictated that it would be a Gatling-type weapon, with multiple barrels. While the calibre was not as large as that of earlier airborne anti-tank guns, the weapon would make up the lost impact energy in muzzle velocity: 3,500ft/sec (1,067m/sec), equal to the best 20mm weapons in service and considerably better than most heavy cannon. It should be remembered, too, that the size of a

Right: This mock-up of the A-10 forward fuselage was mounted on a rocket-powered sled and used to test the McDonnell Douglas Escapac IE-9 ejection seat at Holloman AFB, New Mexico, in August 1974. Later A-10s were fitted with the Escapac II.

Below: The ejection seat saved the life of this pilot, who banged out after experiencing control problems. One of a batch of six Development, Test and Evaluation machines, the A-10 is carrying Air Force Systems Command markings; the incident occurred during filming of gun firing as part of the successful programme to eradicate the dangerous build-up of explosive gases from the gun barrel experienced with early GAU-8/As.

Below: The second YA-10A with its port outer wing and tailfin painted white for spin and recovery testing at **Edwards in November 1974. This aircraft was retired in June 1975 after logging 548.5hr in 354 flights.**

Above: The spin chute container installed on the tail of the second YA-10A, serial 71-1370, to help recovery during spin trials.

gun increases rapidly with greater calibre. The mass of each round rises with the cube of the calibre, and the loads on the breech, the barrel and the feed systems follow suit. Barrel length increases with the calibre and the velocity. By the time the RFPs were issued, it was clear that the GAU-8 would be among the largest guns ever mounted on an aircraft, eclipsing even the 75mm weapons which had been tried in the 1940s. As in the case of A-X itself, the gun was to be selected after a competitive prototype evaluation. Four companies responded to the GAU-8 RFP – General Electric, which had built the original M61, Philco-Ford, Hughes and General American Transportation.

Above: Early firing trials with a prototype of the GAU-8/A 30mm cannon were carried out by the first YA-10A at Edwards AFB from September 1974. The fireballs formed by unburnt gun gas are apparent.

Left: Heavy-duty nose installation used to dispel the gun gases during early GAU-8/A firing trials.

After so many studies of the A-X requirement, the USAF's needs were quite clear, and the final evaluation was quick. Four months after the closing date for proposals, the USAF announced that Northrop and Fairchild would each build two A-X prototypes. Northrop's contract for the YA-9A was worth $28.9 million, and Fairchild would receive $41.2 million for the YA-10A. The main reason for the difference was that Fairchild planned to build an aircraft close to production standards, while Northrop preferred to build something closer to a classic prototype, which would show what the production aircraft could do, but would not necessarily resemble it internally. The decision on the gun was announced later: General Electric and Philco-Ford were to build competing prototypes under $12.1 million contracts. The gun prototypes would thus cost one-third as much as the four A-X contenders themselves. The prototypes would be armed with the trusty M61 while GAU-8 development continued.

A common characteristic of all the USAF competitive flight evaluations or 'fly-offs' in the early 1970s was that the finalists were very different from each

15

Above: The first DT & E A-10, serial 73-1664, with three fuel tanks and instrumented nose boom during testing at Edwards in mid-1975.

Right: Underside view of the same aircraft carrying 18 1,000lb (907kg) bombs and reflecting the golden rays of the setting sun.

other. This was contrived quite deliberately, because one advantage of the fly-off approach was that a promising, but unconventional configuration or solution could be tested without risking the entire programme if it turned out to have some inherent and unacceptable flaw. The A-X finalists were different in many ways, and gave the USAF a very real choice of design philosophies; the contest was, however, the closest of all the fly-off evaluations.

The differences between the two aircraft started with their external shape. Where the Northrop design followed conventional fighter practice, with a shoulder wing, single fin and engines mounted close to the fuselage, the YA-10A resembled no previous combat aircraft apart from a few last-days-in-the-bunker German projects from 1945. The engines were mounted on the rear fuselage, airliner-style, there were twin fins and rudders and the main landing gear retracted into pods under the wing. The low-slung YA-9A was a design of elegant solidity, with its engines faired smoothly into the fuselage and the fin sweeping upwards from the aft body; its rival was a gangly beast, its long, skinny fuselage and broad wing improbably mated atop a stalky undercarriage.

Another material difference between the two aircraft was the choice of engine. Two high-bypass turbofans in the right thrust bracket were available in the USA. Fairchild selected the General Electric TF34, already under development for the US Navy's Lockheed S-3A anti-submarine warfare aircraft. Northrop chose a smaller engine, the Avco Lycoming ALF 502, which had been launched as a private venture in 1969. It received the military designation YF102-LD-100. It delivered 15 per cent less thrust than the TF34, but was 23 per cent lighter and only just over half as long. It was based on the world's first high-bypass turbofan, the PLF1, which had run in late 1963. The main selling point of the F102 was that it was derived from the T55 turboshaft, which had a long and distinguished record of peacetime and combat service in military helicopters. The YA-9A's cleaner shape largely made up for its lower installed thrust; the mission performance of the two aircraft was very similar, both meeting the

specification, but the YA-10A would do so at slightly higher weights. Both contestants, though, were required to provide performance data with either engine.

Control surfaces

Both A-X contenders featured combined aileron/speedbrake surfaces on their outer wings; these resembled conventional ailerons, but were split into upper and lower panels. When opened, they produced a powerful deceleration effect with virtually no trim change, unlike a fighter-type dorsal or ventral brake. The YA-9A went somewhat further than its rival, featuring a unique side-force control (SFC) system. This linked the speedbrakes and the very large rudder, and could be engaged or disengaged from the cockpit. If the pilot commanded a move to the left, the SFC system would deflect the rudder to the right, opposite

to the usual direction. At the same time, the left speedbrake would open, preventing the aircraft from turning to the right. Instead, the thrust of the rudder would move the aircraft bodily to the left, without turning or banking. With SFC, the pilot could track a ground target without constantly worrying about the bank angle and fuselage direction changes that accompany a conventional turn; Northrop estimated that SFC could double the tracking accuracy of a typical attack.

Before either design left the ground, the entire A-X programme had to survive the first of many critical reviews by Congress. By the end of 1970, there were no fewer than three very active CAS programmes under way in the USA: A-X, the Army's Cheyenne, and the US Marine Corps' acquisition of the Hawker Siddeley Harrier. Congressional critics demanded to know why all three types

were needed. The Department of Defense – which, of course, oversaw all three services – launched its own extensive study of CAS doctrine, tactics and requirements in February 1971. At about the same time, the USAF was working on its own study, TAC 85, which covered the entire spectrum of tactical missions. One of the most significant aspects of these studies was that they marked a break from Vietnam-oriented attitudes, and concentrated instead on the situation in Europe.

Emphasis on Europe

The DoD told Congress that the US military simply did not have anything in service which could perform CAS effectively. Delivery accuracy, acquisition of small tactical targets and response times were all inadequate to a greater or lesser extent. For the first time, the report referred to the imbalance of ground armoured forces in Europe, and to the potency of new and forthcoming Soviet air defence systems (such as the SA-6 missile and the ZSU-23 mobile anti-aircraft gun system, although these were not specifically mentioned in the unclassified version of the report). The DoD argued that the extent of the threat made CAS a critically important mission, and also a very complex one. Each of the three CAS types, in the DoD's view, was best suited to some part of the requirement: "Cheyenne in discrete, responsible, highly mobile units, operating as part of the ground manoeuvre force;

Left: Line-up of early A-10s at Edwards in mid-1975. The two prototypes (furthest from camera) were retired in May and June as soon as three of the six DT & E aircraft (foreground) were available.

reported on both contestants. The evaluation was planned to include 123hr flying for each type, but eventually the YA-9As flew 146hr in 92 sorties, while the Fairchild aircraft logged 138.5hr in 87 sorties. Just under half the time was spent firing 20,000 rounds from the M61 cannon and releasing 700 'iron' bombs – no guided weapons were used at this stage – while about a third of the flying hours were devoted to performance and handling tests. Flight tests were followed by a week of maintenance demonstrations.

While the fly-off was unquestionably important, it was certainly not the only factor in the evaluation. Systems Command carried out its own theoretical assessment of the competing aircraft in parallel with the fly-off, covering areas which flight-testing could not be expected to explore. These included operational aspects, such as the degree of protection provided against gun and missile attack in the two aircraft; industrial considerations, such as the amount of work needed to set up production, and future concerns, including the potential of each type for development. The two engines were the subject of a parallel evaluation. An unprecedented series of tests was carried out at Systems Command's headquarters at Wright-Patterson AFB, Ohio, where representative components of both A-X designs were set up on stands, blasted with a simulated slipstream from a jet engine, and bombarded with 23mm shells from a Soviet-built anti-aircraft gun, to determine whether their foam-filled fuel tanks would withstand such hits without ignition.

Political pressure

Politically, there was pressure on the Air Force to select Fairchild. The aircraft industry in New York State had historically been dominated by Republic and Grumman. The latter, in 1972, was in serious trouble with the F-14 programme, and there were doubts about its future. Fairchild's Republic division had also been the largest single subcontractor on the Boeing SST programme, scrapped the previous year. Unless Fairchild was awarded the A-X, Long Island's aerospace industry might suffer permanent damage. It was not exactly possible to say the same about Northrop and Los Angeles.

Congressional pressure alone would not be enough to swing an Air Force decision against the service's own assessment, but neither was it in the USAF's interest to let a major contractor lose its capability to design and build a complete military aircraft. Competition was – and remains – a key element in the USAF procurement system, and the service had come to expect at least half-a-dozen responses from qualified suppliers to any of its RFPs. Other things being equal, this factor would tend to favour Fairchild.

Results from the fly-off competition were close. The Northrop type displayed better handling qualities in some respects; the YA-10A proved slightly superior from the maintenance viewpoint; but both aircraft improved on the specification. Systems Command's analysis showed a significant advantage for the Fairchild aircraft in the important area of survivability. The YA-10A, due partly to its unconventional configuration, appeared to be better protected against attack. The most important difference, though, was that the YA-10A was much more representative of a production-type A-X than the YA-9A, something which had been reflected in the higher price quoted and paid for the Fairchild prototypes. This would mean an easier transition to production, with lower risks and smaller learning costs.

Harrier in rapid response to urgent firepower requirements during amphibious operations; and A-X in concentrating heavy firepower, matching selected munitions to different targets, at threatened sectors from dispersed bases". The DoD conceded that the capabilities of the three types might overlap "in less demanding situations", but concluded that all three would be needed for the full spectrum of operations.

The A-X programme survived this first brush with politics, but with some conditions. The A-X would not be launched into full production as soon as a winner emerged from the fly-off. Further testing would have to prove the type's prowess in the CAS role, including its ability to survive against defensive systems and the lethality of its internal gun against armoured vehicles. As the initial development of the GAU-8 was not due to be completed until mid-1973, there

would clearly be some delay to the programme, but the DoD regarded lethality and survivability as essential to the A-X and would not release the type for production until it had proved itself.

The fly-off competition called for both A-X candidates to be delivered by road to Edwards AFB, where they would make their first flights in the hands of company test pilots before being handed over to a specially formed USAF joint test force (JTF). The Air Force evaluation was to start in late October 1972. The YA-10A was the first to fly, taking to the air in the hands of Howard 'Sam' Nelson on May 10, 1972. Its Northrop rival followed 20 days later. The second YA-10A flew on July 21, and the second YA-9A joined the programme on August 23. The manufacturers had five months to unearth and fix any operationally significant problems in the design, because the rules of the

Above: Seen from the cockpit of an A-37, a DT & E A-10 without ordnance but with eight pylons installed, rolls to port over a gun range where M48 and T-62 tanks will be attacked.

contest prohibited any design changes during the JTF evaluation unless safety was in jeopardy. The only externally visible change concerned the YA-10A. Not surprisingly, stalling the aircraft sent turbulent airflow into the TF34s, which responded by stalling themselves. A fixed slot was fitted to the inboard wing to smooth out the airflow. The second YA-10A, too, was involved in the only incident of the test programme, blowing both main tyres in a heavy landing and sustaining minor damage to its nosewheel.

JTF evaluation

These and other problems had all been taken care of by the time the JTF took the four aircraft over, on October 24. The JTF was a new type of organisation, designed specifically to handle the competitive evaluation. It comprised test pilots from USAF Systems Command, which is responsible for the engineering and procurement of all USAF aircraft, and from TAC, which would use the A-X. Other experts were assigned to the JTF from the USAF Logistics Command and the Air Training Command, and their task would be to assess the maintenance requirements of the competing aircraft. All JTF team members worked and

Left: The second DT &E A-10, 73-1665, armed with Hobo and Paveway guided bombs, fires a burst from its cannon during the weapons test programme which it shared with the third preproduction aircraft.

Above: For trials with Paveway laser-guided bombs and the Pave Penny laser seeker pod, 73-1665 – showing the effects of a strenuous test programme – is equipped with cameras under the nose and tail.

Left: The ability to fly from forward bases close to the battle area was a prime A-X requirement: one of the first production batch of 52 A-10As kicks up the dust as it comes in to land on the dry lake bed at Edwards.

Barely two weeks after the close of the fly-off and maintenance comparison, on January 18, 1973, the USAF announced the selection of the Fairchild aircraft. In the following weeks, the USAF and Fairchild negotiated a $159 million contract, covering ten development, test and evaluation (DT & E) aircraft for further testing. (This batch was later cut to six aircraft by Congress, and the remaining four pre-production aircraft were completed under the first production contract.) The contract included an option for initial production of 48 aircraft, but the A-10 would not be ordered in quantity until further tests of the aircraft had been completed, and the effectiveness of the GAU-8 had been demonstrated.

At the same time, the General Electric TF34 was selected to power the new aircraft. This was not a foregone conclusion, because an Avco-powered A-10 and a GE-powered A-9 had both been studied, and Avco Lycoming was offering a developed version of the F102 with greater power and growth potential. While the F102 was being offered at a considerably lower price than the TF34, the GE engine had one tremendous advantage: it was three years into a full-scale development programme for a military aircraft. The USAF also planned to use eight TF34s to power the Boeing AWACS (the idea was dropped a few weeks later) and large-scale orders held the prospect of lower unit costs in the future. Moreover, Fairchild and GE had worked together on a package of low-risk modifications to the TF34 which would reduce its cost without degrading its performance in the A-X.

Three days before the decision on the airframe and engine was announced, the two GAU-8A prototypes began side-by-side ground firing trials at the Armament Development and Test Center at Eglin AFB, Florida. Initial trials concerned the accuracy and general functioning of the guns; the advanced family of ammunition types was tested from a single-barrel stand in March, and tests proceeded with both guns until a firing rate of 4,000 rounds/min was attained. GE's experience with Gatlings, and the company-funded research on advanced 30mm weapons which it had started in 1968, told heavily in its favour, and it was selected for Phase 2 GAU-8 development in June 1973. GE was awarded a $23.7 million contract for 11 pre-production models, three for quality testing, and eight for installation in the pre-production A-10s.

Unofficial name
A less official event in the history of the programme can also be traced to Eglin AFB and the summer of 1973. Discussing the A-10 in the Tactical Air Warfare Center's *TAWC Review*, Major Michael G. Major closed his article by proposing a name for the new aircraft. Republic's first jet fighter, the F-84, had a less-than-sparkling take-off performance which earned it the nickname 'Groundhog' or just 'Hog'. Its swept-wing development, the F-84F, became the 'Super-Hog', and the concrete-hungry F-105 was christened 'Ultra-Hog'. "What do you suppose the A-10 will be called?" wondered Major. "The 'warthog'?" The name was

Right: Carrying its Paris Air Show number on the engine pod, a 355th TTW A-10 en route back to its base at Davis-Monthan in June 1977.

too appropriate not to stick to an ugly beast with a thick hide and dangerous tusks.

The two YA-10As flew from Edwards throughout the rest of 1973 and 1974, although at a slightly lower rate than in 1972. The main thrust of the programme was the definition and completion of the pre-production aircraft, the first of which was due to be delivered at the end of 1974. The No 2 aircraft tested refinements to the design, including a package of aerodynamic changes which reduced drag both in cruising and manoeuvring flight: the wingspan was increased by 30in (76cm), cutting induced drag, the canopy and windscreen shapes were refined, the engine pylons were shortened and streamlined and the landing gear pods were reduced in cross-section. The temporary fixed slats were replaced by automatic retractable slats. All of these were to be incorporated on the pre-production aircraft. The second YA-10A explored the spinning and recovery envelope in late 1974.

Another series of trials took place as a result of Congressional pressure to replace the A-10 with the A-7D. After scaling down the pre-production programme in mid-1973, as mentioned above, the Senate Armed Services Committee threatened to make further cuts and divert the money into additional A-7D orders. In September 1973, it was agreed that the A-10 programme could continue, provided that a second fly-off contest was arranged between a YA-10A and an A-7D. This took place in April-May 1974 at Fort Riley, Kansas. The A-10 was found to offer significant advantages, particularly in less-than-perfect visibility where targets might merge into a dull background. Air Force testimony to Congress after the trials was unanimous: the A-10 was the only aircraft for the short-range CAS mission.

Operationally related testing included the installation of a standard 'slipway' for the USAF flying-boom refuelling system in the nose of the No 1 YA-10. This was a departure from normal fighter practice – most US fighters have receptacles behind the cockpit – but was found to be an improvement. The slipway was not plumbed into the fuel system on the prototypes, which instead took off at high gross weights to simulate the behaviour of the aircraft towards the end of the fuel transfer operation. The refuelling tests were concluded in August; in the same month, a mock-up forward fuselage, attached to a rocket-powered sled, was used for successful tests of the Escapac IE9 ejection seat at Holloman AFB, New Mexico. August 1974 also saw the start of

Above: A formation flight of four early production A-10s assigned to the 355th TTW. The wing's 333rd Tactical Fighter Training Squadron received its first A-10s in March 1976, and was the first operational unit to be equipped with the type, training pilots for service with combat wings.

Left: While two of its aircraft visited the Paris Air Show before going on to tour USAFE bases, three of the 355th TTW's A-10s carried out a series of demonstrations of their capabilities at PACAF bases, including this one in Korea, during June and July, 1977.

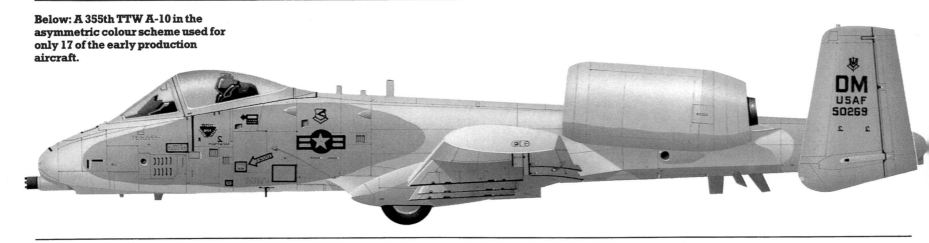

Below: A 355th TTW A-10 in the asymmetric colour scheme used for only 17 of the early production aircraft.

a series of unguided launches of the Hughes AGM-65A Maverick television-guided 'fire-and-forget' missile. Along with the GAU-8/A, Maverick was to be a standard weapon for the A-10. Eleven missiles were launched during the first evaluation flights.

Development of the gun and its three types of ammunition – armour-piercing incendiary (API), high-explosive incendiary (HEI) and target practice (TP) – continued in parallel with that of the aircraft. By September 1974, a prototype GAU-8/A was installed in the first YA-10A for preliminary trials. These disclosed a potentially serious problem. The explosive gases generated by the propellant were not being fully burned in the barrel, and the remnants were being expelled and ignited in front of the aircraft, forming a large and dangerous fireball. This was the most serious technical problem facing the A-10 programme towards the end of 1974, but was solved by adding a potassium nitrate additive to the propellant: a technique borrowed from the US Navy's

battleship guns. This change also increased the projectile velocity to some degree. The gun itself passed its Critical Design Review in September 1974.

Production problems
Completion of the Critical Design Review on the production-standard airframe, with its aerodynamic changes, provision for the GE gun and other operational equipment, had been announced in May 1974. USAF people at Fairchild's Farmingdale plant, however, were growing concerned about the progress of production. The company had not run a major programme since the F-105 line had closed ten years before; many of its management people lacked experience in production, and the plant's machinery was outdated. (Some of it, one USAF officer asserted, had been used to build P-47s.) Both the cost and schedule targets of the programme were in danger. An Air Force inquiry led to a series of changes in Fairchild production management and organisation, and the USAF increased its staff at

Farmingdale. Fairchild acquired new numerically-controlled machine tools to replace equipment from the F-105 era, and, on the recommendation of the Air Force, placed more of the A-10's critical machined components – the first parts to be assembled in any aircraft, which have the greatest potential to delay or disrupt production – with subcontractors.

Generally, progress with the A-10 was considered to be encouraging by mid-1974, and the GAU-8/A was also going well, although it had yet to be fired from the A-10. The Department of Defense accordingly gave the production programme an amber light at the end of July, releasing $39 million to start production of 52 production A-10As: the 48 aircraft which the USAF had taken on option at the start of the programme, plus the four aircraft which Congress had cut from the original DT & E contract. However, options to buy a smaller quantity were to be kept open. Five months later, with more aircraft and weapon trials completed and the DT & E fleet in final assembly, production of the A-10 was

unconditionally authorized by the DoD.

The first DT & E aircraft was completed at Farmingdale in late 1974, and after preliminary ground tests it was stripped of its wing and empennage and flown to Edwards AFB in a C-5A transport, where it made its first flight on February 15, 1975. (On the previous day, the 1,000th YA-10 flight hour had been recorded.) The first DT & E aircraft was 'heavily instrumented' – that is to say, packed with sensors to measure temperature, vibration and strain in every component, and warrened with wiring runs linking all the gauges to a central digital recording system. It was not fitted with a gun, and its task was to measure and evaluate performance, handling, aerodynamic efficiency, loads and flutter.

The second of the pre-production batch was the first A-10 to make its first

Below: With the wing's old A-7Ds parked in the background, A-10s of the 355th TTW form up on the runway at Davis-Monthan AFB, Arizona.

Left: During 1977 the 354th TFW at Myrtle Beach began to convert to the A-10: here one of the wing's new aircraft refuels from a KC-135.

Below: A pair of 354th TFW A-10s in the new European camouflage scheme in flight with Mk bombs (foreground) and Maverick missiles.

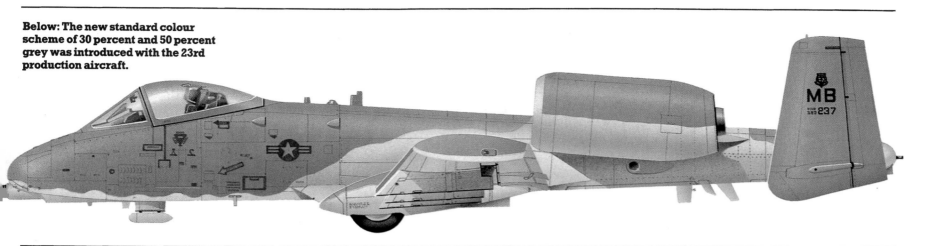

Below: The new standard colour scheme of 30 percent and 50 percent grey was introduced with the 23rd production aircraft.

flight from Farmingdale, on April 26; it was also the first new aircraft to fly from Farmingdale since the last F-105 was completed. Fairchild, however, had sold the company airfield for general-aviation use some years before, and it was too crowded to be used for acceptance-test flying once the production programme got into its stride. By April, it had been decided to move A-10 final assembly and testing to another Fairchild facility at Hagerstown, Maryland, after the completion of the 10th aircraft.

The second DT & E aircraft was to share weapons and systems testing with the third of the batch, which flew on June 10. Both had GAU-8/A cannon installed. From June onwards, one A-10 joined the test programme every month. The fourth DT & E aircraft backed up the first for performance tests, and like the first, it did not have a gun. The fifth would lead

Below: Specifications of the A-10A production aircraft, first flight, October 1975, alongside salient features of its A-X programme competitor, the YA-9A.

the initial operational test and evaluation programme, and the sixth would be used for climate testing.

As the second DT & E aircraft joined the test programme in April 1975, the first YA-10A was retired and placed in 'flyable storage' after 467 flights and 590hr. Likewise, the second YA-10A was withdrawn from the programme in June, once the third pre-production aircraft was available. It had flown a total of 548.5hr in 354 flights.

Testing progressed with few problems. By the end of the year, it was revealed that the original weight estimates for the DT & E aircraft – including a 2,000lb (907kg) weight saving compared with the YA-10s – had been optimistic, and that the type was somewhat overweight. The USAF, however, decided that the resulting degradation of overall performance was not critical. One failure occurred during static testing of the fatigue-test airframe at Farmingdale; a minor redesign of a forged fuselage/wing fitting was carried out to solve the problem.

Snags were overshadowed, though, by the performance of the second DT & E aircraft in the first live gun-firing tests, conducted against surplus US M-48 tanks and Soviet T-62s obtained via Israel. The A-10/GAU-8 combination confounded the sceptics, and clearly demonstrated that design aims had been achieved. Accuracy, range and destructive firepower were incomparably superior to anything achieved before. Strikes against the side and top armour of the T-62s, not only with the API ammunition but also with the HEI shells – which had been designed originally for use against softer-skinned vehicles – penetrated the heavy tanks' protection and set off secondary explosions of internal fuel and ammunition. The targets were totally destroyed, by what was effectively point-blank shooting: even at long ranges, the GAU-8/A's velocity was such that ballistic drop and windage could be ignored.

The first production A-10 flew in October 1975, and was delivered to the USAF on November 5. Along with the

next three aircraft off the line – numbers 7 to 10 of the originally planned DT & E batch – it joined the test programme at Edwards AFB, but subsequent aircraft, starting in March 1976, were delivered to the first operational unit. This was the 333rd Tactical Fighter Training Squadron (333 TFTS), which had been designated as the first A-10 squadron in November 1974; part of the 354th Tactical Fighter Trianing Wing, it was based at Davis-Monthan AFB, Arizona.

Production build-up at Hagerstown was steady, rather than spectacular, and it was April 3, 1978, before the USAF accepted the 100th production A-10A. Present at the handover ceremony were two retired USAF officers: Brig. Gen. Francis S. Gabreski and Col. Robert S. Johnson. Both had distinguished themselves by destroying more than two dozen enemy aircraft in an earlier Republic product, so it was only fitting that the USAF should choose the occasion to give the A-10 a name, one that had ben proposed unofficially four years earlier: Thunderbolt II.

Specifications

Fairchild A-10A				Northrop YA-9A
Dimensions	Wingspan	57ft 6in/17.53m		58ft/17.67m
	Length overall	53ft 4in/16.62m		56ft 6in/17.22m
	Height overall	14ft 8in/4.47m		16ft 11in/5.16m
	Wing area	506sq ft/47.01sq m		580sq ft/53.9sq m
Powerplant		Two GE TF34-GE-100A		Two Avco-Lycoming YF102-LD-100
	Thrust (each)	9,065lb/40.3kN		7,500lb/33.3kN
	Bypass ratio	6.2:1		
			Definition	
Weights	Operating empty	24,959lb/11,321kg	Pilot, oxygen, unusable fuel and oil, gun and six pylons	
	Basic design weight	30.384lb/13,782kg	Maximum weight at 7.33 g	
	Internal fuel	10,700lb/4,853kg		
	Max external load	16,000lb/7,250kg		
Take-off weights	Clean			26,000lb/11,800kg
	Maximum	50,000lb/22,680kg		42,000lb/19,051kg
	CAS mission	47,094lb/21,362kg	18 565lb (256kg) Mk 82 bombs, 750 rounds of ammunition and full internal fuel	
	Anti-armour mission	42,071lb/19,083kg	Six Mavericks on triple launchers, 1,174 rounds of ammunition, ALQ-119, 480 flare/chaff cartridges and full internal fuel	
	Ferry	49,774lb/22,577kg	Full internal fuel and three US gal (2.271 litre) external tanks	
Performance	Never-exceed speed	450kt/834kmh		390kt/723kmh
	Max level speed at sea level, clean	381kt/706kmh		
	Combat speed at 5,000ft (1,525m) with six Mk 82 bombs	380kt/704kmh		
	Cruising speed at sea level	300kt/555kmh		270kt/500kmh
	Sea-level rate of climb at design weight	6,000ft/min/1.828m/min		
	Service ceiling	45,000ft/13,715m		
Combat radii	Anti-armour configuration, 30min combat, 40nm (74km) sea-level penetration and exit	252nm/467km		250nm/463km with 2hr loiter
	CAS configuration, 1.88hr single-engine loiter at 5,000ft (1,525m), 10min combat	250nm/463km		
	Ferry range, 50kt (93km) headwinds, 20min reserve	2,240nm/4,148km		

Structure

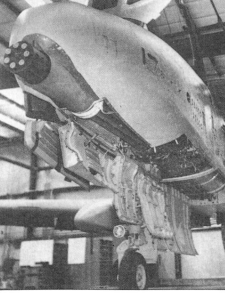

Those who describe the A-10 as the world's ugliest combat aircraft are unjust. The Soviet Mil Mi-24 Hind-D helicopter gunship is the clear winner in this category, by two warts and a proboscis, but the A-10 runs a respectable second. Standing high on its landing gear, its fins and engines reaching out toward the clouds, it is an imposing machine. Its weights and dimensions set it well above most Western support and attack types: it is similar in overall length to the formidable Tornado interdiction-strike aircraft, and its wing span is almost equal to that of the F-111A.

Basic dimensions, though, are misleading; the A-10 may be large, and its maximum take-off weight is considerable, but its normal in-service operating weights are considerably lower. Its configuration springs from the fact that it is designed to excel in a unique flight regime: constant manoeuvre at low speed and low altitudes. Its size is a product of its flight regime and its intended warload.

A heavy weapon load was one of the best features of the A-1, and it was carried over into the A-X requirement. A lesson of Vietnam was that effective intervention in the ground battle called for heavy firepower; dug-in troops or armour were generally unimpressed by the loads delivered by adapted fighters. Endurance requirements also drove the weight upward. The use of external fuel for the normal mission was ruled out from the survivability standpoint, and this meant all the fuel had to be accommodated internally. Morover, the need to protect the internal fuel compromised the conventional fighter-design approach, which is to use every available cubic inch in the air-frame for fuel.

The need for long endurance, and the low operating speeds, ruled out that great weight-saver, the afterburner. The result was higher engine weight for a given thrust level. The advent of the high-BPR turbofan was a major breakthrough, because its low fuel consumption helped make up for that weight penalty.

A-X also set standards for protection around vital areas – the pilot, the fuel system, and the internal ammunition – so that part of the empty weight was virtually independent of the overall size of the aircraft. Given a certain 'defeat level' – the maximum strike which the aircraft must survive – the amount of armour around the cockpit, for example, was the same however large or small the aircraft might be.

These requirements in themselves would have driven A-X beyond the size

Below: Although of unconventional layout, the A-10 prototype, seen here during final assembly, was built using conventional materials and straightforward techniques.

and weight of the Skyraider. As the requirement evolved toward tank-busting, however, the weight of a phenomenally large cannon installation, several times as heavy as an M61, had to be figured into the equation. So did the added air-frame size, weight and drag incurred by carrying such a weapon internally, together with the large quantity of ammunition needed for even tens of seconds of firing time. While the A-10 may look large and beefy, its armour, its gun and its ammunition amount to some 25 per cent of its empty weight. It is no larger than an effective platform for the GAU-8/A, armoured to the levels specified by A-X, needs to be.

Wing design
Given the size and weight of an aeroplane, the next feature to be defined is the wing. In the case of the A-10, as with most combat aircraft, the main factors behind the wing design are speed and manoeuvre; other factors, such as range and field performance, tend to fall into place.

The high end of the speed envelope in

Above: The size and weight of the A-10 were largely dictated by the requirement for the massive cannon installation, and the need for sufficient protection to enable it to survive close-quarter tank-busting.

the A-X requirement was not demanding. The maximum operating speed was to be only 400kt (740km/h), and the Fairchild designers selected a maximum design speed (VD) of 450kt (833km/h), allowing a normal safety margin in case a pilot allowed his aircraft to overspeed in combat. Wing designers care more about Mach number, or the relation of speed to the speed of sound, than pure airspeed; in the case of the A-10, the maximum speeds are to be attained at sea level, where the local speed of sound is higher than at medium altitude, so the wing does not have to be designed for more than Mach 0.68. It is possible to encounter high-Mach buffet at such speeds, particularly if the aircraft has to manoeuvre, but the A-10 is not required to manoeuvre tightly at its top speeds.

Right: The large Fowler flaps and split-aileron airbrakes, displayed here by the second DT & E A-10, form the key to the A-10's low-speed manoeuvrability, and are readily accommodated on the large wings.

USAF tactics of the late 1960s were another important factor in the wing design. Attack aircraft, including the A-X, were not generally required to fly for long periods at high speed and low level. 'Ingress' profiles were invariably flown more than 1,000ft (305m) above ground level, in level flight above the roughest air. This, combined with the modest speed, meant that there was no need for the A-10 to have the short, swept, highly loaded wing that were required by contemporary Royal Air Force tactics, for example.

The peak performance of the A-X specification, instead, called for the ability to turn in a small radius and short elapsed time, at modest airspeeds; the A-10, pulling a 3.25g turn at 275kt (510km/h), can manoeuvre in a smaller radius than a fast-jet fighter, and can actually change heading more quickly. The implications of low speed and high g are important. The total drag generated by any aircraft is made up of a number of components, most of which increase with the square of the airspeed. A major exception is induced drag, or the drag due to lift, which increases with the lifting force generated by the wing. In a 3g turn at 275kt, the lift and the induced drag are at three times their normal value, but the other components of airframe drag are still modest. The main thrust of the A-X aerodynamic design, therefore, was to cut down the induced drag in a medium-speed manoeuvre, and the best way to do this was to increase the wingspan.

The A-10 design benefited from the steady advance in the basic design of wing sections. Classic wing sections of

Above: Tufts attached to a YA-10's wings to monitor the airflow, and the stall slats fitted to smooth turbulence at high angles of attack.

Right: Assembly of the A-10 port, starboard and centre wing sections prior to mating with the fuselage.

the 1950s produced most of their lift close to the leading edge; this was to say that the airflow over the wing underwent a single rapid acceleration at this point. This made the wing prone to buffet at even modest Mach numbers, and the only way to delay the buffeting was through the use of sweepback or a thinner section. Thin-section wings are heavier for a given strength, because the spars are not as deep (think of the way beams are placed in a building) and are less efficient at low speeds. In the 1960s, though, the use of computers enabled aerodynamicists to improve their mathematical 'models' of the airflow over the wing. This allowed them to design new

sections in which the lift was more evenly distributed along the chord; they were called 'rooftop' sections, because a chart showing chordwise lift distribution was more symmetrical, like a house roof. Rooftop-section wings could be deeper, and hence lighter, for an equivalent Mach number.

The A-10 accordingly has a long-span, lightly loaded wing, which allows excellent low- to medium-speed turning performance with low drag and a low power requirement. The wing has a rooftop section and a 16 per cent thickness/chord ratio. The deep section makes it possible to build a wing which is reasonably light, has a long span and a high

aspect ratio, and can withstand high g loadings. The depth of the wing, and its bluff leading edge, make for high lift and efficiency at low speeds. Another drag reduction is provided by the down-turned Hoerner wingtips, which act as small, lightweight endplates, reduce vortex flow at the tips and improve aileron effectiveness near the stall.

The big, thick wing also provides ample lift for take-off and landing, meeting all the A-X field-length requirements without the use of complex high-lift devices. The A-10 has classic area-increasing Fowler flaps, driven out along curved tracks to increase the area and camber of the wing. Fairchild did study

alternative wing designs, with less area and double- or triple-slotted flaps, but the increased complexity and cost more than cancelled out the reduction in weight, while straight-line drag and manoeuvrability would have been somewhat worse. The simple Fowler flaps create little additional drag when extended, and can be partially lowered for manoeuvre at very low speeds.

Another advantage of the generously sized wing is that the flaps need extend over only part of the span, leaving room on the trailing edge for large ailerons for effective low-speed roll control; the A-10 has no wing spoilers. The ailerons also incorporate the only unconventional feature of the mainly straightforward aerodynamic control system. Each aileron is split on the horizontal plane, aft of its leading edge. An actuator and linkage in the aileron leading edge drive the two sections apart to form a powerful airbrake. This arrangement gives effective deceleration with virtually no trim change, unlike a dorsal or ventral brake, and does not interfere aerodynamically with the empennage as fuselage-side brakes can do. Similar airbrakes were used on the Northrop YA-9A; in fact, the devices were originally invented by Northrop in the 1940s for its flying-wing designs.

Low-wing advantages

While most contemporary attack aircraft, including the Northrop YA-9A, had shoulder-mounted wings, Fairchild chose a low-wing configuration for the A-10, for a number of reasons. The most important was that the A-X requirement called for at least ten separate weapons pylons under the aircraft. With a low wing it is possible to put the most highly loaded pylons under the fuselage itself, and, generally, to concentrate the heaviest stores near the centreline. This substantially reduces the rolling inertia of the aircraft with a maximum weapon load, and improves its handling. The low wing also provides for a wide-track landing gear with a simple retraction sequence. Some aspects of ground handling are simplified; it is easier to work around the aircraft with the engines running, for instance. On the debit side, all the maintenance has to be done with ladders and platforms.

The wing design is the key to the A-10's performance in the most important flight regime, sustained low- to medium-speed manoeuvre. This regime dictates the installed thrust, so there is plenty of excess thrust available to meet the comparatively relaxed straight-line speed requirement. Reducing drag by the classic means – streamlining, blending and fairing, and reducing surface area - was not necessary to meet the specification and was therefore not considered worthwhile. It can also be argued that achieving, say, a five per cent reduction in clean airframe drag is a futile exercise

Above: A-10 fuselage assembly line. Long and deep, the fuselage accommodates the pilot and gun forward, fuel tanks above the wings, and engine aft.

Above: The fuselage shell, showing the massive gun compartment and smaller nosewheel well, with the pilot's armoured 'bathtub' above, is hoisted along the line.

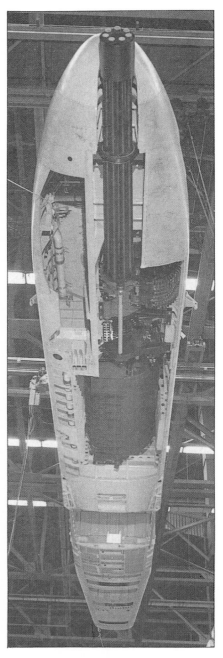

Above: One stage further along, the fuselage, with nose cone in place, gun installed and nose gear hydraulics fitted, is moved into position for mating with the wing assembly.

Above: The imposing, long-legged aspect of the A-10 on the ground is a result of the low-mounted wing and wide-track landing gear.

Right: The second DT & E A-10 with avionics and armament bay doors open for final installation of equipment prior to roll-out.

on an aircraft which will spend most of its life carrying a very large, drag-evoking external payload. Recognizing these factors, Fairchild designed the A-10 fuselage, engine location and empennage according to the demands of utility as well as those of aerodynamics.

The first requirement in the fuselage design is capacity. In most aircraft, a big, thick wing provides the natural home for the fuel, but it was clear from the start of the A-X programme that large wing tanks presented an unacceptably large vulnerable area to the enemy. Instead, the A-10 carries most of its fuel in fuselage tanks, which have a much higher ratio of volume to surface area. To minimize changes in trim as the fuel was used, the tanks were located in the centre fuselage, above the wing.

The forward fuselage is designed around the GAU-8/A cannon and its ammunition drum. The weight of the latter can drop by more than 1,000lb (454kg) as propellant and projectiles are expended (the cartridge cases are recycled back into the drum) so it is located to the rear of the gun, just ahead of the fuel tanks and close to the centre of gravity. The sheer power of the gun itself defines its position. The mass of its shells, its muzzle velocity and its rate of fire generate a constant recoil thrust of 9,000lb (40kN). Unless the recoil thrust vector was aligned precisely on the aircraft's centreline, this would make accurate shooting impossible.

Blast from the gun means that the muzzle must be well clear of any structure, so the only possible location is the nose of the aircraft, right on the centreline. The gun is set below the centre of gravity, so the firing angle is very slightly depressed (by about 2deg) to eliminate any pitch change. The YA-10As featured an automatic elevator compensator, to counter any pitch effects from firing the gun, but this was found to be unnecessary. The seven-barrel rotary gun is offset slightly to the left, and its mechanism is arranged so that the firing barrel is in the nine o'clock position, placing it exactly on the centreline. This makes room for the nose landing gear, which retracts into the right side of the fuselage.

The A-10's long forward fuselage provides room for the 21ft (6.4m) weapon, and the pilot occupies a lofty perch above the feed and breech mechanism. The narrow, flat-sided fuselage, the short nose and the bubble canopy, set well above the wing plane, give the A-10 pilot an all-round view matched by few other aircraft. The forward fuselage design also provides ample room for a second cockpit, which can be accommodated by rearranging some of the internal avionics. (Otherwise, the only change in the design of the two-seater is a slight increase in the size of the tailfins, to compensate for the added side area.)

The rear fuselage is the controversial part of the A-10 design, aesthetically and functionally. The skinny tail section carries the two engines, mounted high on the rear fuselage in airliner style, and the twin-fin tail assembly. It looked strange in the extreme to anyone used to fighter design, but Fairchild had sound reasons in its favour.

The only basic requirement affecting the location of the A-X's engines was that they should be far enough apart that a single hit would not disable both. To Fairchild's designers, it seemed that a conventional installation, with the engines under the wings, eliminated too much of the stores-carrying space on the

Left: The finished product, its bluff lines betraying few concessions to aesthetic considerations, but with an air of purpose and aggression in its strictly functional design.

aircraft. This was particularly true with the fat high-bypass engines, which were being used for the first time on a combat type. Neither were these engines very suited to being built into the fuselage, because of their large airflow requirements and their bulk. It seemed less risky, aerodynamically speaking, to house the engines in straightforward pods with short inlets. Fairchild studied overwing pods, as used on the unsuccessful German VFW 614 jet feederliner, but it would have proved difficult to change the engines without using special lifting equipment, particularly in the confines of a standard concrete hangarette.

The high-mounted rear-fuselage location which was finally chosen has a number of advantages. The engines are well out of the way of any dirt or foreign objects thrown up from the nosewheel when operating from unimproved strips; this is important, because high-bypass engines make superb vacuum-cleaners when placed too close to the ground and their high-pressure cores are very sensitive to erosion caused by dirt and grit. The inlets are also well to the rear, allowing gun gases more time to disperse. Also, as noted earlier, the engines can be kept running while the aircraft is being served and re-armed. One drawback of this arrangement, the fact that changes in thrust could change the trim of the aircraft in pitch, has been avoided by canting the engine nozzles 9deg upwards relative to the rest of the engine.

Tail layout
Rear-engined airliners have mid-set or high tail units, but the risk of a 'deep stall' – a condition in which the wing is stalled, the aircraft is sinking, and the tailplane, trapped in the turbulent wake of the wing and engine pods, has no power to recover the aircraft – immediately ruled out such a layout for the A-10, so the tail is low. Twin fins are partly a result of the engine location. It was felt that the engines could create some odd airflows around the rear fuselage, and might cause spin-recovery problems by shedding turbulent wakes on to a conventional single fin. The complexity of a twin-fin layout is justified, because it is almost impossible for both fins to be rendered ineffective at the same time.

Where the resulting layout scored very high points was in survivability. Control power in pitch and yaw can be retained even if one side of the entire empennage is shot away. More important, though, is the protection afforded to the engines. The fuselage and wing tend to conceal one or both of the engines from groundfire, from many different angles. The vertical and horizontal tail surfaces form what is almost a shroud around the engine exhausts, helping protect the aircraft against early-technology infra-red homing missiles: these weapons, such as the SA-7 Strela, need to 'see' the hot metal of the jetpipe before they will lock on to a target.

Testing of the YA-10s revealed some not unexpected problems with the engine installation. When the wing stalled, turbulent airflow from the wing-fuselage junction entered the inlets and stalled the compressors. The solution was to fit a flow-smoothing slat to the wing, inboard of the landing gear pods, which extended automatically under hydraulic power when the angle of attack exceeded the stall angle. A stall strip – a small spanwise fence, a few inches long

Right: The capacious forward fuselage proved readily capable of accommodating a second cockpit, and the second DT & E A-10 was converted to two-seat configuration for evaluation purposes.

Fairchild A-10A Thunderbolt II cutaway

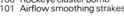

1 Cannon muzzles
2 Forward radar warning antenna (one each side)
3 ILS antenna
4 Air refuelling ramp door
5 Air refuelling receptacle
6 AAS-38 Pave Penny laser seeker pod
7 Rudder pedals
8 Hinged windscreen panel (for instrument access)
9 Head-up display
10 Control column
11 Pilot's intrument display
12 Engine throttle levers
13 McDonnell Douglas ACES II ejection seat
14 Canopy jettison strut
15 Canopy actuator
16 Leading edge stall strip
17 Starboard wing stores pylons
18 Cockpit canopy cover
19 Pitot tube
20 Starboard navigation and strobe lights
21 Starboard aileron
22 Split aileron/airbrake
23 Airbrake operating jack
24 Aileron hydraulic actuator
25 Aileron tab
26 Cockpit air valves
27 IFF antenna
28 Tab balance weight
29 Anti-collision light
30 UHF/Tacan antenna
31 Starboard single slotted Fowler flaps
32 Flap guide rail
33 Flap hydraulic actuator
34 Fuselage fuel cells
35 Conditioned air delivery duct
36 General Electric TF34-GE-100 turbofan engine
37 Engine oil tank
38 Engine accessory equipment gearbox
39 Bleed air ducting
40 Air conditioning system intake and exhaust duct
41 Heat exchanger
42 Fire extinguisher bottle
43 Starboard tailfin
44 X-band antenna
45 Rudder mass balance
46 Rudder
47 Fan air exhaust duct
48 Core engine exhaust duct
49 Trim tab actuator
50 Elevator tab
51 Starboard elevator
52 Elevator hydraulic activators
53 Rear radar warning receiver
54 Tail navigation light
55 Port elevator
56 Port tailfin
57 Rudder hydraulic actuator
58 Formation light
59 IFF antenna
60 Elevator mechanical linkage
61 UHF/Tacan antenna
62 VHF/AM antenna
63 Fuel jettison
64 Air system ground connection
65 Hydraulic reservoir
66 VHF antenna
67 Hydraulic system ground connectors
68 APU exhaust
69 Auxiliary power unit (APU)
70 Air conditioning unit
71 Port Fowler flaps
72 Flap self-aligning torque shaft
73 Trim tab control rod
74 Aileron trim tab
75 Split aileron/airbrake
76 Strobe light
77 Port navigation light
78 Port aileron
79 Cambered wing tip fairing
80 Airbrake operating jack
81 Aileron hydraulic actuator
82 ECM pod
83 Aileron mechanical linkage
84 Flap hydraulic actuators
85 Hydraulic retraction jack
86 Main undercarriage pivot bearing
87 Chaff/flare dispenser
88 Forward-retracting mainwheel
89 Leading edge stall strip
90 Port wing stores pylons
91 Maverick air-to-ground missile
92 Wing centre section integral fuel tank
93 Main undercarriage wheel housing
94 Inboard wing stores pylon
95 Pressure refuelling connection
96 Slat hydraulic actuators
97 Inboard leading edge slat
98 Fuselage stores pylons (3)
99 Multiple ejector rack
100 Rockeye cluster bomb
101 Airflow smoothing strakes

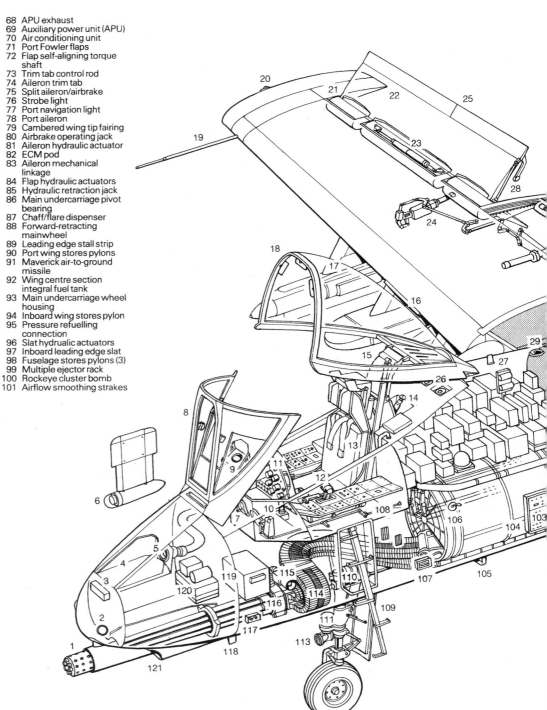

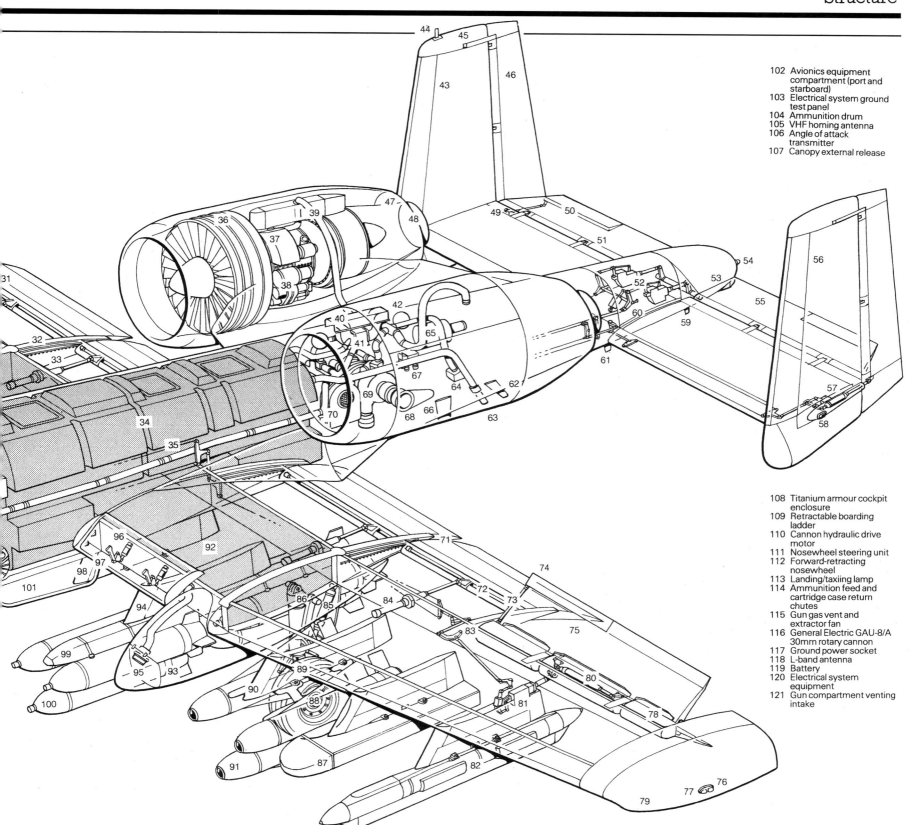

102 Avionics equipment compartment (port and starboard)
103 Electrical system ground test panel
104 Ammunition drum
105 VHF homing antenna
106 Angle of attack transmitter
107 Canopy external release

108 Titanium armour cockpit enclosure
109 Retractable boarding ladder
110 Cannon hydraulic drive motor
111 Nosewheel steering unit
112 Forward-retracting nosewheel
113 Landing/taxiing lamp
114 Ammunition feed and cartridge case return chutes
115 Gun gas vent and extractor fan
116 General Electric GAU-8/A 30mm rotary cannon
117 Ground power socket
118 L-band antenna
119 Battery
120 Electrical system equipment
121 Gun compartment venting intake

Above: The short nose and high-mounted cockpit with bubble canopy give the A-10 pilot a superb view, readily apparent in this phothograph of an 18th TFS pilot preparing for a mission from Eielson AFB, Alaska.

– was attached to the outboard leading edge to restore the natural stall warning. Two other devices were also added to cure the wing-engine interaction: prominent vertical strakes, fitted to the fuselage beneath the leading-edge wing root, and a trailing-edge fillet. Otherwise, the A-10 is aerodynamically straightforward, devoid of ventral fins, strakes, vortex generators and other fixes.

The final element in the A-10's unusual shape is provided by the main landing gear, which retracts forward into prominent underwing pods. This arrangement has a number of advantages, and the extra drag which it creates is not critical to the A-10. Unlike a sideways-retracting gear, it takes up little stores-carrying space beneath the wing. (The A-1 had a rearwards-retracting gear, for the same reason.) The entire landing-gear mechanism is attached beneath the wing itself, and the wheel is stowed ahead of the front spar, so there are no cut-outs in the structure.

The retraction mechanism is simple, and all three of the undercarriage legs retract forward; this is the ideal arrangement if the hydraulics are gone and the

Above: The A-10's forward-retracting landing gear legs, simple and rigid, with single wheels and low-pressure tyres, were designed to lower under gravity and wind resistance in the event of hydraulics failure, and the main gear and wheels are stowed in pods to maximize stores loading.

Right: Even in the event of landing gear collapse, the configuration should ensure that the main airframe structure sustains minimum damage.

gear must free-fall into the locked position, because gravity and the airstream both help to extend the gear. If even this next-to-last resort fails, the A-10 gear is designed, like those of the DC-3 or B-17, so that the mainwheels protrude from the gear pods and are free to rotate in a belly-landing. The A-10, in theory, will come to rest on its mainwheels and the lower tips of the fins with barely a bent antenna.

The landing gear itself is simple. The A-10 is designed to use short strips of prepared concrete, of the type that would be left on an airfield where the main runway had been cut in two by bombs, but is not really a rough-field aircraft. The landing gear, therefore, has simple rigid legs rather than more complex levered-suspension units, and there is only one wheel to each leg, carrying a single low-pressure tyre.

Odd as the A-10 may appear, its design has avoided any trace of unusual or unexpected handling qualities. This was a fundamental A-X requirement, and was one of the most important factors in the original fly-off competition; the USAF's view as that the A-X pilot, flying, navigating and acquiring targets at low level with a minimum of artificial help, would have no time to deal with any idiosyncratic handling behaviour.

A-10 pilots report that the aircraft feels much smaller than it looks, to the point where it is necessary to bear in mind that

Left: Preparing for takeoff during Operation Gunsmoke '81 at Nellis AFB, A-10 pilots enjoy an unmatched all-round view from their cockpits, while only minimal ground support equipment clutters the flight line.

the wingtip may be nearly 30ft (9.15m) closer to the ground than the pilot in a steep turn over rolling terrain. The aircraft will tolerate a great deal of abuse, and gives plenty of notice when the limits of its tolerance are approached. The A-10 will remain controllable after the stall, and will only spin if pro-spin controls – full nose-up pitch and full rudder – are applied and held for several seconds; it will recover as soon as the controls are released.

Overall, the aircraft has been summed up as an 'easy aircraft to fly safely, but difficult to fly precisely'.

A-10 production manufacturing plan

Fuselage aft section

Fuselage centre section

Fuselage forward section

Fuselage mating

Empennage assembly

Nacelle assembly

Wing centre section

Wing outboard panel

Wing assembly

Engine assembly

Final assembly

Flight operations

Delivery

Below: By the time Fairchild secured a production order for the A-10, it was ten years since the end of its last major programme – the F-105 – and substantial modernization was required. However, the design-to-cost philosophy which had governed detail design meant that manufacturing processes were kept as simple as possible: 95 percent of the airframe is of aluminium, compound curves were avoided, and straightforward manufacturing techniques such as riveting were the rule. Interchangeability of many components also helped simplify production, and the modular construction of fuselage, empennage, engine nacelles, centre wing box and outer wing panels enabled final mating to be carried out in a single eight-hour shift.

Left: From the 11th aircraft onward, final assembly of A-10s was transferred to Fairchild's facility at Hagerstown, Maryland, where the company was able to conduct flight testing, its old airfield at Farmingdale having become too cluttered to permit such activity. Here one of the first production batches reaches the end of the assembly line, where the engines are installed and final checks are carried out on the structure and systems, though the line has been cleared for the photographer.

Fairchild selected a very similar configuration for the T-46A, which was initially selected for the US Air Force's Next Generation Trainer (NGT). However, the order for this was later cancelled, possibly due to the lack of precision handling.

Internal arrangement

Beneath the skin, the design of the A-10 reflects two main considerations: survivability and design-to-cost. The ability to take hits from a variety of weapons, and survive, pervades both the structure and the systems of the A-10; design-to-cost mainly affects the construction and manufacture of the aircraft.

Design-to-cost was a new philosophy for military aircraft, but has always been a way of life for the designers of light aircraft and, to a limited extent, the airliner industry. While military aircraft, even the most exotic types, were never

designed and built with total disregard for cost, the importance of price decreased rapidly with the move from basic to detailed design. The manufacturing cost would be estimated before any of the detail drawings were prepared, on the basis of the manufacturer's experience with earlier aircraft and the relative complexity of the new aircraft's structure and systems. The customer would base his procurement plan on that estimate.

Once detail design started, however, performance took priority over cost. If a part proved more highly loaded than had been expected, the normal practice was to make it from a higher-grade material and to accept the resulting cost increase. The same would be true if an assembly procedure was more complex than expected. On the other hand, there was no strong incentive to look for ways

in which components could be made more simply, or manufactured from cheaper material than had been envisaged. It was therefore inevitable that costs would increase during the design and development stage.

Under the design-to-cost approach, the manufacturing cost was to be estimated, as usual, as part of the basic design: the A-X requirement set a $1.5 million cost target for the entire aircraft. What was new was that the cost was to be held down to the design level, even if it meant increasing weight and degrading performance. This policy was easier to implement on the A-10 than on a high-performance fighter, because a given mass of excess weight at 3g saps only one-third as much performance as the same mass at 9g. Nevertheless, the cost target was not easy to reach, and fundamentally affected the design.

Cost considerations

Design-to-cost, to begin with, ruled out the use of promising advanced composite materials. Closely contemporary designs such as the F-15 and F-18 used such materials to save weight, but, at the time, the costs of mass-producing composite components could not be safely predicted. A-X would be a conventional light-alloy aircraft, with the exception of some specialized components. The well-proven 7075 and 2024 alloys were chosen, due to their known resistance to stress and chemical corrosion.

During development, any proposed weight-saving was examined for its effect on manufacturing costs. A yardstick of $75/lb ($165/kg) empty weight was used, and if a proposed change cost more per unit saved, it was automatically discarded. Conversely, if a design change would add weight, but save more than $75/lb of extra weight, it would stand a chance of being implemented. This was the first time in a military aircraft programme that an actual dollar value had been put on empty weight.

Another basic principle, followed throughout the design and apparent in the external shape of the A-10, was the avoidance of 'double curvature': as far as possible, the A-10's shape is composed of flat planes or cylindrical or conical sections, reducing the need for slow and costly stretch-forming processes in the manufacturing stage. The fuselage sides are flat; the engine nacelles are cylindrical, rather than teardrop-shaped. Fuselage panels are overlapped and riveted, avoiding the smoother but more complex butt-jointing.

The A-10 is also unique in the degree to which components are interchangeable between the left and right sides of the aircraft: the fins and rudders, main landing gear, wing-root slats, inboard flaps, many fuselage skin panels and all pylons are examples. It was the first twin-jet USAF aircraft on which the engines were not 'handed', and this has now become a requirement for other new USAF types.

The advantages of this philosophy are two-fold: it cuts production cost, by doubling the output of a single part, and it simplifies spares support. In wartime, it may be critical, because the only spares that are any use at all are those that can be found on the base, whether in the normal supply system or aboard a damaged or otherwise inactive aircraft.

A related thrust in the production engineering of the A-10 was to ensure that components would be interchangeable between individual aircraft. This is not always the case: some aircraft have major components which are individually fitted at the factory, and a piece from another aircraft or an 'out of the crate' spare may fit only after precise, time-consuming adjustments, if at all.

Ultimately, the A-10 taught the USAF a lesson in manufacturing economics. After all the effort put into reducing the designed-in cost of the airframe, the Department of Defense revised its budget plans and authorised initial production of only 15 A-10s a month, rather than the 20 aircraft originally planned. This raised the price of the aircraft from the target of $1.5 million to $1.8 million. The USAF itself requested some changes in the avionics fitted to the aircraft, further increasing the price to $2 million. (These figures are compared to the target price and expressed in the same 1970 values; the dollar cost of A-10s as finally delivered was, of course, much higher due to general economic inflation.) Against this 33 per cent increase in the basic cost of the aircraft, the cost savings made through detail design seemed rather insignificant.

Survivability

The other major influence on the internal design, survivability, was equally new as a philosophy. It is strange but true that, before 1968, the ability of an aircraft to absorb battle damage and survive – specifically, to regain its base, with its pilot unharmed, and be repaired to fight again – had never been systematically studied. It was known that some aircraft were good in this respect (such as the B-17) and some were bad (the B-24), but there was no telling, or even guessing, which was the better aircraft until they were committed to combat.

Part of the reason for this state of affairs was a lack of basic data. Vietnam changed the situation. A great many modern aircraft, of a great many types, were used. The defensive fire was more intense, and more dangerous, than anything encountered since 1944-45, and came from a wide range of contemporary weapons. Modern ejection seats were more reliable under a wider range of circumstances; pilots were more easily tempted to stay with a damaged aircraft, if only to increase their chances of rescue by friendly units, and came back to report how they had been shot down.

F-105 experience

Survivability data began to arrive in quantity: the picture was mixed and confusing. One F-105 survived a direct hit on the wing from a 85mm AAA shell, and another was perforated in 87 places by an SA-2 missile and regained its base. But other F-105s were felled in seconds by small-calibre or fragment strikes. The same paradoxical situation applied to other types; Fairchild, however, had an early start in the field, because its F-105 bore the brunt of the Rolling Thunder operations in 1965-68, and F-105 experience was the first large single body of data. Before the A-X programme was initiated, too, Fairchild was upgrading and hardening the surviving F-105s.

It was soon found that the inconsistency of the hit-survival record stemmed directly from the fact that the question had never been seriously investigated. Structural design was driven by strength requirements, and systems design by reliability. While the F-105, designed for supersonic low-level flight, was structurally tough, and would stay together at reduced airspeeds after suffering quite serious damage, the designers had seen no reason not to run the two independent hydraulic systems close together in the belly of the aircraft. A minor strike in this area could knock out the F-105's hydraulics and, in consequence, its flying controls.

The positive lesson drawn from this experience was that survivability could be dramatically increased by attention to a few key areas, and by improvements which added only a modest amount to the empty weight; there was no need to encase the entire aircraft in an armoured carapace.

Guns were the main cause of losses in Vietnam, particularly in the close support mission. Often, the main function of

the SA-2 missile was to force the attackers to use low altitude, within the range of AAA. Cannon projectiles were taken as the measure of the A-10's survivability. Among the most dangerous of these was the 23mm armour-piercing incendiary shell, lethal against fuel tanks; direct hits from 57mm guns were also encountered, but these, like SAMs, were more dangerous as fragments. Since then, the defensive armoury has been modernized; however, studies of vulnerability have shown that the effectiveness of protection does not decline abruptly as the calibre of the threat increases.

Another batch of combat data concerned the vulnerability of the aircraft to damage in different areas. No fewer than 62 per cent of losses of single-engined aircraft, in Vietnam and the Middle East, were caused by damage to the fuel system; 18 per cent to pilot incapacitation; 10 per cent to flying-control damage; 7 per cent to loss of engine power; and 3 per cent to structural damage. These losses reflected heavy missile kills as well as gunfire; however, the A-X operational envelope would be biased towards heights and speeds where AAA would be more effective. The A-X also embodied a new vulnerable zone, in the shape of a very large drum of ammunition. The loss statistics were an indication of what to do on A-X, but not a complete guide.

Survivability has been taken into

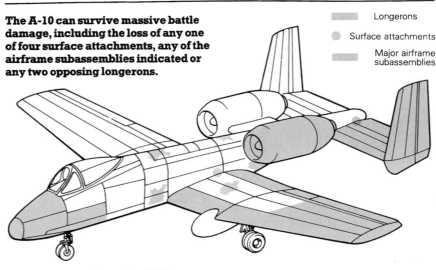

The A-10 can survive massive battle damage, including the loss of any one of four surface attachments, any of the airframe subassemblies indicated or any two opposing longerons.

Longerons
Surface attachments
Major airframe subassemblies

A-10 structural survivability

account in every area of the A-10 design. Important features of the basic configuration include the widely separated engines, the duplicated tail surfaces, and large and powerful controls in all three axes. The combination of these features is intended to allow the A-10 to stay airborne even after sustaining gross airframe damage such as the loss of half the tail assembly, a complete engine or part of the wing.

Internally, the A-10 structure is de-

signed so that any member can be severed by impact without causing a total failure. The wing and the tail surfaces are all designed around three spars of approximately equal size and strength, any two of which can absorb all anticipated air loads. Both the tailplane and the wing are continuous one-piece structures from tip to tip and, as noted above, the landing gear configuration was chosen partly because it eliminated structural breaks in the wing. The fusel-

Above: The effects of 7.62mm armour-piercing projectiles on the bullet-proof/bird-proof front windshield fitted to the A-10.

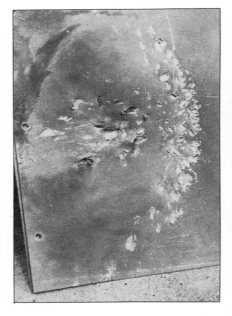

Above: A panel of the armour used for the GAU-8/A ammunition drum after being hit by a 23mm high-explosive projectile during tests.

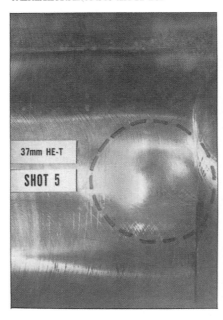

Above: Further tests were carried out on the titanium armour panels used for the pilot's 'bathtub': the back of one is shown after a 37mm HE hit.

Above: The front of the same panel — used for the bathtub side — showing the effects of one 37mm and two 23mm rounds hitting at 90 deg.

age incorporates four main longerons, any three of which can take the full structural loads. Most of the skin area is unstressed, greatly simplifying the repair task.

The structure would have presented no problems had the A-10 been used as it was intended, spending most of its time above the worst turbulence. In Europe, however, the A-10 was routinely flown at high speed and low level for most of its training missions. After cracks began to appear around fastener holes in the lower wing skin (which carries the peak tension loads in high-g flight) USAF fitted accelerometers to some operational aircraft and found that they were experiencing high g loadings more than three times as often as had been expected. The simplicity of the aircraft, too, means that it spends a great deal of time in the air. A-10s are being fitted with thicker lower wing skins, during routine maintenance, to extend their useful lives to 8,000 hours.

Unique protection

Dealing with the cause of the majority of losses called for action to make the internal components less vulnerable to damage, and to protect them when this was not possible. It is this sort of protection which is unique to the A-10. It exceeds in degree anything applied to any helicopter, with the possible exception of the Mi-24, and is different in nature from the

protection accorded to any fighter aircraft.

The fuel system had proved the weakest spot on the aircraft used in Vietnam. This was, perhaps, not surprising. Self-sealing fuel tanks had been developed before the 1939-45 war; they had an intermediate lining made from a rubber compound, which expanded when a puncture in the inner wall allowed it to be soaked with fuel. They had proved to be a vital feature in com-

Above: Warthog pilots – this one is wearing the badge of the 354th TFW – have expressed great confidence in their aircraft, and they are certainly as well protected as any.

Below: The wide separation of critical systems and control runs, as well as the ready access for maintenance, is apparent in this view of an 81st TFW A-10 in the hangar at RAF Bentwaters/Woodbridge.

bat, but were abandoned in the early 1950s in favour of integral tanks, which were much more efficient and were almost essential to the design of a supersonic fighter with a useful range. It was argued that future air combats would involve missile strikes, which would be lethal regardless of fuel system design, and that jet fuel was less inflammable than the high-octane gasolines used in 1939-45.

In the Vietnam environment, unprotected fuel tanks were as dangerous as ever. Operating altitudes were low, speeds were high, and oxygen-rich air would swirl into any perforation in the airframe, scouring up any fuel leakages in the structural cavities and creating an instantly explosive atmosphere. The high fuel flows of jet engines meant that the fuel would spill more quickly from broken lines.

The A-10 fuel system is fundamentally different from the usual fighter system. For every USAF mission, apart from ferry flights, all the fuel is carried internally. (For ferry purposes, the centreline station and two wing pylons are plumbed, and can each carry a 600US gal (2,271lit) tank.) The 10,700lb (4,853kg) internal tankage is concentrated around the centre-section, so that the vulnerable area presented to hostile weapons is as small as possible, and the fuel lines are short. (This also effectively eliminates trim change with fuel use, making the aircraft simpler and easier to fly.) Most of the fuel is housed in true tanks, rather than integral cells formed by the aircraft skin and structure, although the inner wings include integral tanks.

The tanks are protected in several ways. The fuselage tanks, supplied by the Goodyear Tire & Rubber Company, are tear-resistant, and self-sealing in the event that they are perforated. All the tanks are filled with 'reticulated' rubber foam – that is to say, foam panels folded to fill the tanks. The foam serves several purposes: it slows the spillage of fuel, keeps airflows out of a punctured tank and inhibits the movement of flame fronts through the cavity. Protective firewalls and panels of rigid foam are installed between the individual tanks, and between the tank compartments and the remainder of the airframe, and more foam is fitted between the tanks and the fuselage sides; the object is to prevent any fuel which escapes from the tanks from flooding other airframe cavities.

Fuel provision

Fuel lines and valves are protected, as far as possible, by running them through the tanks. The final stages of the fuel lines are located in the upper section of the fuselage and on top of the engine pylons, where they are protected from damage by the rest of the airframe. The pipes are self-sealing, and the system is fitted with check valves which prevent fuel from flowing into a damaged tank. The single long fuel line leading to the flight-refuelling point in the nose is provided with its own purging system to clean out any remnants of fuel after use. If all else fails, the entire main tank system can be cut off, and two small, self-sealing sump tanks between the engines will provide a 200nm (370km) reserve for a safe return to base.

Equal attention is given to the flight control system, which has some unusual features for a modern combat aircraft. Control signals are transmitted to the hydraulic actuators by cables, rather than rods, because cables are less likely to be jammed by airframe damage. The cable system is duplicated, and either channel can be cut off from the cockpit if it jams. To provide greater protection for the critical pitch and roll axes, the control channels are completely separate

from the control surface to the point where they enter the protected cockpit enclosure.

Dual hydraulic systems power the controls in normal operations, but if all power fails, the elevators and rudders can be moved directly by the pilot, through the control cables. Electrically powered trim tabs are fitted to the elevators, and help reduce the considerable control forces needed to fly the A-10 without hydraulic boost. The ailerons are too heavy for direct manual control; instead, if hydraulic power is lost, the control cables move small 'servo-tabs' attached to each aileron, which deflect in the opposite direction to the control input. Aerodynamic forces move the ailerons the other way, creating the desired rolling force. The A-10 is the only Western combat aircraft since the 1950s to be designed with this 'manual reversion' feature.

Each complete control channel runs through one of a pair of accessory tunnels built into opposite sides of the fuselage. These tunnels also carry duplicate hydraulic, electric and pneumatic runs, so that no single hit on one side can deprive the aircraft of any of its services. However, the manual back-up in the control system, and the fact that the landing gear is designed to free-fall into the locked position, means that the A-10 can, in theory, regain its base and land without further damage as long as at least one engine and one flight control channel remain operational.

Conventional systems

Other systems are largely conventional. Each engine powers one of the two 3,000lb/sq in (211kg/m^2) hydraulic circuits, which provide power to the controls, airbrakes, flaps, landing gear, brakes and gun mechanism. Engine bleed air is used for pressurization, air-conditioning and windshield anti-icing and rain clearance (the rest of the airframe is not de-iced) and is also used to clear gases from the gun compartment after firing. A Garrett auxiliary power unit (APU) is installed in a titanium firewall box in the rear fuselage, between the engines, and provides power for engine starting and 'ground loitering'.

The other major areas for specialized protection are in the forward fuselage. One of these is the ammunition drum, which presents a unique potential for catastrophic damage; a single hostile round exploding in the ammunition drum could set off the A-10's magazine and destroy the aircraft instantly. The solution is to provide a layered protection system, designed to protect the drum from the direct impact of an armour-piercing explosive shell. The drum is placed at mid-height in the fuselage, as far from the skin as possible, and is armoured against fragments. The fuselage around it is not armoured in the normal sense, but is provided with trigger plates of various thicknesses to detonate any incoming round, whether armour-piercing, explosive or incendiary, before it reaches the drum.

The pilot himself is protected by a unique structural assembly called 'the bath-tub'. This is a bolted-together box, made of heavy titanium sheets – ranging from 0.5in (12.7mm) to 1.5in (38.1mm) in thickness – and built into the forward fuselage, the sides of the box forming the upper sides of the airframe. It extends up to the canopy and windscreen frame, and provides side, front, rear and ventral protection. It accommodates the pilot, on his ejection seat, the flying controls and the instruments.

The sides of the bathtub are intended to defeat a direct hit from a 23mm API shell; the impact is likely to cause 'spalling' or the shedding of titanium frag-

Above: A ground crewman checks the pressure refuelling panel of a 355th TFS, 354th TFW, A-10 prior to takeoff on a training mission.

ments at high velocity from the inner surface of the armour, so the tub is lined internally with layers of ballistic nylon. Weighing some 1,200lb (544kg), the tub is the heaviest single piece of protection in the aircraft. Overall, it is estimated that 2,887lb (1,310kg), or 14 per cent of the A-10's empty weight, goes strictly to protection, without counting the survivability features of the structure and the configuration.

The final layer of protection is provided by the pilot's ejection seat. Initial production A-10s used the then-standard McDonnell Douglas IE-9 Escapac seat, one of the first to feature zero-height, zero-speed capability. However, the same company's ACES II (Advanced Concept Ejection Seat) has since been substituted; it provides better performance, considerably improved pilot comfort (an important factor, given the A-10's long endurance), and is common to the F-15 and F-16.

While it was clearly not practical to verify the effectiveness of the protection system by shooting an A-10 to pieces, the USAF carried out a unique programme of static tests in the course of development. Representative wing and fuselage sections, complete with their fuel loads, were placed on ground rigs and subjected to a 400kt (740km/h) airstream generated by a turbofan engine. Tests with a Soviet 23mm AAA gun, firing API and HEI ammunition – the most dangerous types against fuel cells – demonstrated the fire-suppressing qualities of the foam system around the tanks, and advantages of the foamed tanks. The same weapon was used to evaluate the effectiveness of the titanium armour, in comparison with ceramics and aluminium.

All in all, 707 rounds of 23mm API and HEI were fired at A-10 structural specimens: 430 at the cockpit, 250+ into the fuel tanks, and nearly 60 into the ammunition drum. Among 108 rounds of other calibres was a burst of 7.62mm API fired into the windscreen. It was concluded that the area within which a single 23mm HEI/API strike would be lethal

Above: Studies of aircraft losses over Vietnam showed that a principal cause was the concentration of fuel, hydraulic and electrical systems in small volumes, increasing their vulnerability to a single round: in the A-10 all systems are well protected and widely separated.

Left: Quick turnaround between sorties is vital to the effectiveness of close air support: here an A-10 of the 174th TFW, New York Air National Guard, is supplied with liquid oxygen during Exercise Sentry Castle '81.

Below: Realistic training is an essential part of TAC and reserve force readiness: chemical warfare clothing is worn by an ANG Technical Sergeant of the 104th TFG during an A-10 rescue exercise at Phelps-Collins ANG Base, Michigan.

Bottom: Refuelling an A-10 during Exercise Coronet Sail at Lechfeld AB, Germany. The fuel in the inner wing tanks should be used up by the time an A-10 reaches the battle area, further reducing its vulnerability.

Flight control separation

Aircraft used in Vietnam had duplicate flight control systems, but these were provided to guard against system failure: they were not physically separated, so that a single **hit could disable both primary and back-up systems. The A-10s has duplicate, spatially separated control channels, and a manual back-up, indicated by the broken lines.**

was one-tenth the equivalent area on a smaller, but unhardened, aircraft.

The idea that the A-10 can survive the physical loss of half a wing, half the tail, one engine or all its hydraulics, and even survive several such losses, may appear far-fetched. Consider, though, the case of a certain F-15. The Eagle is a close contemporary of the A-10, and its design drew upon very similar combat experience; while survivability was not a prime requirement in the F-15 design, McDonnell Douglas certainly incorporated many hard lessons from F-4 experience.

In the summer of 1983, an Israeli F-15 was engaged in mock combat with an A-4 when the two aircraft collided. The impact tore off 90 per cent of the Eagle's starboard wing, leaving an 8in (20cm) stump. The A-4 crashed. The Eagle survived thanks to lift from the wide body, survivable hydraulics, jam-resistant control circuits and its powerful tail surfaces. The F-15 was repaired and back in service within weeks.

The tactical value of such toughness is considerable, particularly when it is combined with the structural and systems simplicity of the A-10. Because of

the A-10's design, strikes which might require major repair on another aircraft may simply call for a non-structural patch on the A-10. A heavier hit might destroy a conventional aircraft, but leave the A-10 able to regain its base. An A-10 in such a condition might well be beyond repair, and would almost certainly be too badly damaged to be returned to combat status at a front-line base, but, in wartime, that is not the whole story. The aircraft has recovered its irreplaceable pilot, and now represents a large stockpile of spares; the basic simplicity of the aircraft makes it easier to use the undamaged parts to restore other aircraft to fighting condition.

The A-10's aerodynamic and structural design has proved successful. Like the rest of the weapon system, it accomplishes what it set out to do at the estimated cost. Its design, incomprehensible in terms of pure fighter engineering or aesthetics, represents an uncompromised approach to a clearly defined requirement, and every feature of its gnarled and complex configuration responds to some part of the A-X specification.

Powerplant

In the definition of the A-X programme, the specific requirement which caused most problems was for endurance, or the ability to remain airborne behind the battlefield, ready to deliver a rapid response to any call for support. The reason that it was a problem was that the classic fighter engine is a poor way of providing endurance. The solution was to use a type of engine which had evolved to meet the payload and range requirements of passenger aircraft: the high-bypass-ratio turbofan. The A-10 was and remains unique among combat aircraft in using these inherently efficient and quiet engines.

Jet engines, turbofan engines and propellers all drive in the same way: they seize the air through which the aircraft flies and accelerate it rearwards, and Newton's 'equal and opposite reaction' forces the engine to accelerate forwards. This acceleration is transmitted to the airframe through steel-tube or forged engine mountings, and pulls it through the air.

The difference between the jet and the propeller is that the jet takes a smaller quantity of air, and accelerates it to a much greater degree. The effect on performance and efficiency is fundamental. A good analogy is an oarsman, who is also developing thrust by accelerating a fluid. He rows efficiently when the tips of the oars are almost static in the water with each sweep; he is imparting the smallest possible amount of acceleration to a large mass of water. If he moves his oars twice as fast with the same amount of energy, he will simply move a smaller mass with each stroke. His style will be inelegant and much of his energy will be dissipated in splashes and vortices. The same principle of propulsive efficiency – that the ideal is to apply the minimum acceleration to the maximum mass, disturbing the working fluid as little as possible – applies to aircraft engines.

There is one other basic point to consider. It is impossible for the rower to go faster than he can move the ends of his sculls. When the speed of the boat equals that of the fastest stroke, thrust equals zero. Likewise, each aircraft engine has a theoretical maximum speed at which it will no longer produce thrust – although most have practical speed limits which are lower, for other reasons. At lower speeds, though, the engine will no longer produce thrust equal to its own drag.

Selecting the right type of engine for an aircraft is a matter of defining the desired performance profile, and choosing the type of engine which is best suited to the most critical performance regime. The problem, in the early stages of the A-X programme, was that no engine had yet flown which possessed the desired characteristics.

Jet engine characteristics

The most important attribute of early jet engines was that they could operate at speeds well above the normal limits for propellers. Their main disadvantage was their poor fuel consumption, due to their low pressure ratio – a measure of how much air had to be moved to generate a given amount of power – compared to highly refined piston engines. During the 1950s this disadvantage was reduced by increasing jet pressure ratios through improved high-temperature materials and better compressor design. Higher exhaust velocities went hand-in-hand with increased pressure ratios – the engine drew in less air, squeezed it harder and expelled it faster. At subsonic speeds, the oars were skating over the water, and the gains in efficiency within the engine were wiped out by propulsive losses.

By the mid-1960s, there were two alternatives to the pure-jet engine. One was the turboprop, in which a high-pressure turbine engine was coupled to a conventional propeller through a power turbine and reduction gearbox. The other was the turbofan engine; this had been created by modifying a pure-jet engine with oversized forward compressor stages. Roughly half the air taken in by the engine 'bypassed' the compressor and turbine. The high-velocity exhaust from the compressor and high-pressure turbine was fed to a second turbine, and drove the fan. The turbofan produced a higher-mass, lower-speed exhaust than the pure jet, and was much more efficient at high subsonic speed: it powered the first jet airliners which could match the range capability of propeller-driven aircraft.

In 1963 the US Navy ordered the LTV A-7, a long-range light attack aircraft designed around a single TF30 turbofan. But this 'low-bypass' engine, although it represented a great advance over the pure-jet, was well out of its element at speeds under 350-400kt (650-740km/h). At higher speeds, fuel flows were too high to provide the endurance needed for the A-X mission.

Above: Twin engine pods, mounted high on the rear fuselage, form one of the principal elements in the A-10's startlingly original appearance.

The turboprop was much better adapted to low-speed cruising, and its maximum speed was acceptable to the USAF. Its disadvantages, outlined in the first chapter, were mainly concerned with the difficulty of integrating two powerful turboprops and their large propellers into a combat aircraft with a wide speed range, and making the resulting aircraft survivable.

Interestingly, a turboprop aircraft in the A-X class had been extensively tested more than a decade before the USAF formulated its requirement. This was the US Navy's Douglas A2D-1 Skyshark, which had started its development life as a turbine-powered version of the A-X's forebear, the Skyraider, and evolved into a different aircraft with a thinner wing and almost exactly the same top speed as the ultimate A-10.

The Skyshark was aimed at achieving twin-engine performance without the engine-out handling problems of a conventional twin. Like some of the early A-X studies, it had two engines deliver-

Below: The General Electric TF34 engine selected for the A-10 was only developed after the original A-X specification had been written.

Right: Originally developed for the US Navy's S-3A, the TF34 was operated for 400 hours under the wing of this B-47 test aircraft.

ing their power along the centreline – the coupled powerplant was the Allison T40, consisting of two T38s with a common gearbox. It was the powerplant that proved the Skyshark's undoing; the Skyshark's designer, Ed Heinemann, likened it to a chronic toothache. One prototype crashed when one turbine unit failed; the dead engine, still coupled to the live powerplant, acted as a huge air pump and drained all the power from the system. Other problems – with the separate engine and propeller control systems, with the reduction gear and overheating of the entire installation – prevented the engine from reaching its projected 5,500shp output.

In 1954 the Skyshark programme was cut back to purely experimental status, and replaced by Heinemann's far simpler Skyhawk. Its significance to the A-X programme lay not only in the similarity of its design goals to those established for the later aircraft, but in the fact that the Skyshark represented the last serious attempt, before A-X, to design a high-performance combat aircraft around turboprop power. The fundamental problem, as before, would be to steer a path between the conventional twin-turboprop installation, with its drag, weight and engine-out-condition penalties, and the risks and complexity of some type of coupled layout. The latter offered better performance, but it would be hard to ensure or demonstrate that it would not be vulnerable to a single hit.

High-bypass turbofans
The arrival of the classic compromise, the high-bypass turbofan, was entirely unexpected; neither of the engines eventually tested under the A-X programme had been designed with it in mind. The concept originated independently with several manufacturers in the early 1960s. Rolls-Royce and Pratt & Whitney approached it through extrapolation from their existing large commercial engines. Lycoming saw it as a means to break into the fixed-wing turbine power market, making the maximum use of its existing T55 turbine engine; the company was the first to run a true high-bypass engine, in late 1963.

General Electric's route into the market was different again. In the late 1950s GE had started work on a design for a vertical takeoff fighter using lift fans. These resembled enlarged jet engine rotors, and were designed to be buried within the wing of a small aircraft; they were driven by exhaust from small jet engines, impinging on small turbine blades fixed to the outside of the lift fan.

Very early in the 1960s the lift-fan research spawned a demonstration programme for a cruise fan – essentially, a lift fan turned through 90deg to give propulsive thrust. The biggest test rig comprised an 80in (205cm) fan driven by the exhaust of a J79. Results showed that the big fan could operate at high subsonic speeds with much greater efficiency than previous turbofans. Data from these tests was passed to the USAF in 1962, while the service was in the early stages of formulating its requirement for a huge strategic freighter.

In 1962-63, GE moved from the cruise fan, in which the fan and the gas generator were separate, to a more integrated concept in which the fan was driven by a conventional turbine, via a shaft running through the engine. Up to eight times as much air passed through the fan as went through the compressor, combustor and turbines (the 'core engine'); that was to say, the engine had an 8:1 bypass ratio.

This was the basis for the GE1/6 demonstrator engine, the foundation for GE's August 1965 victory in the contest to provide power for the USAF's new C-5.

This early experience and background set the pattern for GE high-bypass engines. GE's fortunes in jet propulsion had been founded on the J79, a single-shaft engine with a large number of stages and a great deal of internal variable geometry, and its later turbojet engines featured similar configurations. Its new high-bypass fan engines sustained the family tradition. They had long, many-staged 'cores', resembling GE's single-shaft turbojets, with the fan added to the front and the fan turbine at the rear. Unlike its rivals' engines, GE's big-fan engines did not have low-pressure compressors, although one or two 'booster' stages might be attached to the fan shaft behind the fan.

While GE's heavy brigade worked on the TF39 for the C-5, the company's small-engine group at Lynn, Massachusetts, was looking at smaller high-bypass engines. As Lycoming had done, GE started with a proven turbine core; the first high-bypass test engine built at Lynn was based on a T64 turboshaft engine, fitted with a scaled-down version of the TF39 fans and a new multi-stage power turbine. Otherwise, the geometry was unchanged. There was no booster

Above: The TF34 test installation on the Navy's B-47, with the associated wiring runs carried along the leading edge of the wing.

stage, although the overall pressure ratio was slightly increased by the presence of the fan stage.

The existence of engines such as the Lycoming and GE demonstrators was to bring about a decisive change in the A-X programme. The new engines were not as efficient as turboprops in the A-X speed range, but they had many other advantages. They were easier to install; with no propellers, they could be located close to the centreline where engine-out

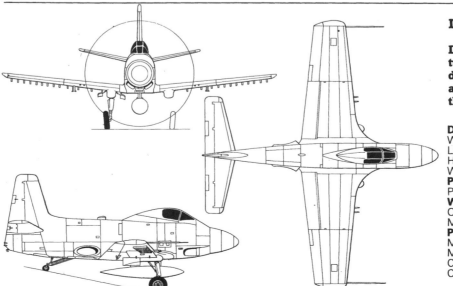

Douglas A2D-1 Skyshark

Designed in the early 1950s, the twin-turboprop Skyshark illustrated the difficulties of using such engines in an aircraft with performance similar to that proposed for the A-X.

Dimensions
Wing span	50ft 2in (15.28m)
Length overall	41ft 2in (12.54m)
Height	17ft (5.18m)
Wing area	400sq ft (37.2m²)

Powerplant
	Allison XT40-A-2
Power	5,500shp (4,105kW)

Weights
Operating empty	12,994lb (5,894kg)
Max takeoff	21,764lb (9,872kg)

Performance
Max speed	435kt (806km/h)
Max speed at SL	406kt (752km/h)
Cruising speed	249kt (461km/h)
Combat range	553nm (1,024km) at 320kt (593km/h)

Above: The first DT & E A-10 was the first to have the USAF-standard T34-100, the prototypes having flown with US Navy development engines.

Below: TF34 cutaway, showing the single-stage fan, 14-stage compressor derived from GE's T64, and high- and low-pressure turbines.

Right: A-10s with external tanks form up before a ferry mission. Despite doubts in some quarters about the advisability of using a high-bypass turbofan on a combat aircraft, the high mounting keeps the intakes well clear of runway debris, and upward-pointing exhausts reduce the risk of FOD in a stream takeoff.

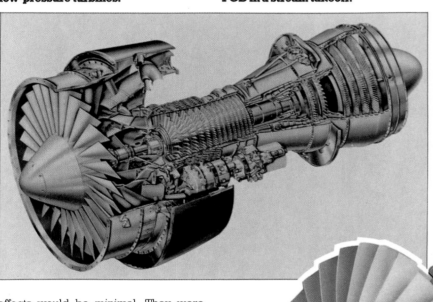

Below: The five basic modular components of the TF34: (from left) titanium-blade fan and casing; axial compressor; annular combustor of

effects would be minimal. They were simpler, dispensing with complex and critical components such as the propeller and reduction gear. (While the Lycoming engine did have a reduction gear, it had a much smaller ratio than a turboprop's gear and was much less complicated.) All in all, their advantages were overwhelming.

While the A-X requirement was still being refined, the US Navy followed a similar line of reasoning, and specified high-bypass turbofans for its new VSX – the replacement for the S-2 Tracker carrier-based antisubmarine warfare aircraft. GE based its proposed VSX engine on data from the test engine run at Lynn, although it would be a basically different engine from the T64. In late 1966 the Navy awarded design contracts for the GE engine, now designated TF34, and the Allison TF32, and definitive proposals were submitted in January 1968. In April GE was announced the winner, and Lockheed was awarded the contract to build the S-3A airframe. According to a GE official history, the victory came as a complete surprise to many of those associated with the programme.

Development of the TF34 moved ahead smoothly, and the engine made its first run in May 1969. In January 1971 it started a 200-hour test programme beneath the port wing of an obsolete Boeing B-47 bomber, leased by GE as a test-bed and operated from the company's flight test centre at Edwards AFB. Meanwhile, development of the S-3A Viking proceeded smoothly, and the compact ASW aircraft made its first flight in January 1972; the engine was qualified for US Navy use in August of that year.

There were several factors favouring the TF34 over any other engine proposed in the A-X competition. The most important was that the development of the engine, and initial production, were already fully funded under the S-3A programme, and USAF development expenditures would be confined to any changes needed for the A-X mission; none of these would be fundamental, whereas the production version of the Lycoming F102 would combine a higher-powered core, based on the T55-L-11B, with a redesigned fan. The TF34 was also at the beginning of its development life, and GE had identified a series of changes which could make extra thrust available if it were needed. The USAF

already planned to use eight TF34s to power the new airborne warning and control system (Awacs) under development by Boeing, so there was some potential for commonality. Lastly, GE was an established supplier of combat engines to the USAF (unlike Lycoming, for instance) and already had the facilities and resources to develop the A-X engine.

GE's main disadvantage was cost. The TF34 was not a particularly simple engine, and had been developed for a quite demanding Navy mission; it would cost almost $140,000 more than the proposed production version of the Lycoming F102. (Both Fairchild and Northrop were required to provide data for both en-

gines in their final proposals to the USAF, so in that sense the two engines were in direct competition.) However, it proved possible to reduce the cost of the TF34 by eliminating some features which were unnecessary for the A-X mission, and the GE engine emerged victorious.

Since that time, the TF34 has done steady rather than spectacular business for GE. Just after the A-10 decision was announced, Boeing and the USAF decided to use the older TF33-P-7 for the Awacs, to save the cost of developing a new version of the TF34 and its twin nacelle. Production of 187 S-3A Vikings ended in 1978, and A-10 production has also ceased. The basic engine is now in low-rate production in a commercially

Above: Large access doors allow the TF34 to be maintained 'on condition', removal of modules only being necessary when a problem arises.

Below: Ladders are needed to reach the engines, but the pod mounting makes them readily accessible when the access doors are opened.

nickel alloy with low-pressure fuel injection system; two-stage high-pressure tubine; and four-stage low-pressure turbine.

certified version, the CF34, for the Canadair Challenger 601 business jet, and a marine turboshaft version, the LM500, has been demonstrated.

An engine *aficionado* would immediately recognise the TF34 as a GE engine. There is no low-pressure compressor, although incoming air is slightly compressed by the fan before being split into bypass and core flows. The mechanical layout of the compressor is similar to that of the T64, with 14 axial stages, and the stators, or static blades, in the first five stages can be varied in pitch. Variable stators were developed by GE for the J73 and J79, and their use in large numbers is a GE trademark. Their function is to vary the airflow through the

engine, making it easier to start a single high-pressure-ratio spool and improving handling; other manufacturers generally split such a long compressor into two spools. The compressor is driven by a conventional two-stage turbine.

Titanium fan blades
Aerodynamically, the fan is based on TF39 technology, although the design is modified to cater for the lower bypass ratio of the TF34 – 6:1, versus 8:1 for the C-5 engine – and does not feature the complex and unique one-and-a-half-stage configuration of the TF39. The fan has a single stage, with no booster stage. Each blade is forged and machined to shape from a solid piece of titanium alloy,

the only material available at that time with sufficient lightness, tensile strength and rigidity to meet the requirements of a high-bypass engine.

Mechanically, the fan was different from that of the TF39. Because of its smaller size, it was not necessary to brace the blades by linking them together, so the annular mid-span shroud could be eliminated. The TF34 is also designed so that each blade can be removed individually by pulling out a securing pin, rotating the fan and withdrawing the blade through a slot in the fan case. The fan is driven by a conventional four-stage turbine.

Perhaps the most technically important feature of the TF34, at the time of its appearance, was the combustor section. Previous combustors had comprised sheet metal assemblies, called 'liners', built into the engine case. These promoted good combustion, and were cheap; the snag was that they had limited lives and needed frequent maintenance, and any work on the combustor called for dismantling the entire engine. The TF34, however, was the first engine to feature a more durable combustor, which was machined from a nickel alloy originally developed for turbine blades.

The TF34's fuel-injection system was also novel, relying on a two-stage swirler to generate powerful aerodynamic shearing forces which would vaporize the fuel before ignition. While these caused development problems in late 1971, they were fixed before they could delay the entire programme, and the Navy engine was qualified on schedule.

Later in the decade, GE's advanced combustor technology was to be a major factor in the success of its F404 and F110 fighter engines. Not only did the combustor prove efficient and durable, but the injector/burner system proved to be virtually free of visible smoke emission. GE, of course, had good reasons for working in this area: not for nothing was the twin-J79-powered F-4 nicknamed

'Ol' Smokey'. Smokeless exhaust is a tactically important feature of the A-10.

Modular maintennce
The TF34 is one of the first service engines to be designed with easy maintenance as a major consideration. It is a 'modular' engine, designed so that the main mechanical components can be separated from each other without disconnecting and stripping all the accessories. All the compressor blades can be individually removed and replaced by opening the engine carcass – which is split along the centreline – without dismantling the entire engine. The TF34 is also supplied with strategically located borescope ports, which allow the mechanic to insert a fibre-optic probe and survey the engine's interior for damage while it is still 'on the wing' (although that expression does not apply to the A-10).

Generally, the TF34 is designed to be maintained 'on condition': that is to say, the engine is only removed or serviced when regular performance checks, metal chip detectors in the oil system, or external and borescope inspections indicate that there is a problem. If the difficulty can be traced to a given module, it can be replaced without removing the engine from service, and, in some cases, without pulling the engine off the aircraft. (In the case of the A-10, though, it is probably easier to bring the engine down to ground level.) This is a great advance on earlier engines, which had to be removed, disassembled and inspected every few hundred hours, the intervals being determined on the basis of service experience.

Approaching the A-X competition, the GE engineers determined that they could easily match the opposition on performance, but were vulnerable to price comparisons. There was little point, therefore, in making changes to the basic aerodynamic and thermodynamic characteristics of the engine, which

Above: A 355th TFW A-10 makes a low pass over the Gila Bend range, Arizona. The turbofan's high thrust at low speeds formed the key to the A-10's low-level manoeuvrability.

Left: A Warthog touches down on the runway. Landing distance, even at maximum weight, is an economical 2,500ft (762m), while a fully-loaded A-10 can take off in 4,500ft (1,372m).

Right: A-10s of the 917th TFG refuelling from a 78th Air Refuelling Squadron KC-10 during an AFRES Aerials exercise held at Carswell AFB, Texas, in September 1983.

would accomplish little in terms of useful performance and add to the overall cost of the engine to the USAF. Instead, GE concentrated on cutting the manufacturing cost of the engine, without making extensive changes that would add to its development cost.

The only mission-related changes to the TF34 for the A-X concerned its installation. Even these were quite small. The main thrust and support bearings for the engine remained on top, as they had been designed for the S-3A's underwing engine installation; in the A-10, the engines were to be hung from dual forged outriggers projecting from the top of the fuselage. Some accessories were moved, to facilitate maintenance and satisfy the USAF requirement for left-to-right interchangeability.

The engine installation itself was conventional, except for the near-full length fan cowlings, the first on a high-bypass engine. They were chosen so that the exhaust nozzles could be angled slightly upwards, reducing changes of trim with changes of engine power. The engines were set higher than was ideal for maintenance purposes; by way of compensation, the cowlings, including the inner wall of the fan duct, were split and top-hinged, providing easy access to most of the engine without removing a single component. Provisions for hoisting the engines were built into the engine mounts, eliminating the need for external lifting devices.

Most of the differences between the Navy and USAF engines were the result of GE's effort to identify and implement savings in production costs. These were possible because the USAF requirement was, in some ways, less severe than that of the USN. The S-3, for example, was required to loiter for long periods at low speed in icing conditions. Because of the low speed the engines would not be at maximum power, and the icing bleed air would be cooler than normal. The Navy

TF34 needed a complex, large-volume de-icing system to cope with these conditions; the USAF, however, had no icing requirement for the A-X, and the entire system could be eliminated.

Another specific Navy requirement was to operate at low thrust, but with high power being drawn from the engine to feed the S-3A's complex systems; draining power from the compressor caused aft-end temperatures to rise higher than they would on the A-X, at least in sustained operation. In some cases, it proved possible to use cheaper materials for the A-X engine. Other changes simply involved eliminating machining operations such as the removal of excess material and the drilling of lightening holes, trading a slight weight increase for lower cost. The USAF engine also required, and received, a simpler and cheaper control system.

The first YA-10s flew with Navy-standard development engines. The modified USAF engine, designated TF34-GE-100, made its first run in July 1973. Production-configured engines were put through 2,181 hours of testing on GE and USAF ground-testing facilities, including two 150-hour endurance cycles. The engine was declared qualified for military use in November 1974, and flew on the first pre-production A-10 early in the following year.

Reliability in service

The TF34 has posed few problems in development and service, and had logged two million flight hours by the end of 1982. The service environment has been more strenuous than was envisaged at the start of the programme, mainly because the lower-flying, higher-energy tactics now used keep the engines close to their full-power ratings much of the time. Largely for this reason, hot-section wear and tear has caused some 10 per cent of TF34s to need main-base overhaul and repair only 500 hours after

being rebuilt in the field. To correct this situation A-10 powerplants are being upgraded to the new TF34-GE-100A model by the introduction of a modified combustor and high-pressure turbine module.

The most important change is the introduction of 'directionally solidified' DSR80 material in the first-stage turbine blades. DS blades are cast in a special furnace and are allowed to cool from the root to the tip. The metal forms long, uniform crystals instead of a random crystal structure: this means that some of the elements in a conventional casting alloy, which are added to bond the crystal boundaries and which are otherwise undesirable, can be removed. The DSR blades are more costly to produce than conventional blades, but the longer life more than makes up for the cost difference.

The -100A update includes a number of other changes: combustor modifications, to reduce 'hot spots' in the gas flow striking the turbine, changes to shrouds and seals and other new materials. The hot-section life of the -100A should be 2,000 hours, including 360 hours at maximum power, both figures being twice those attained by the -100 engine. The TF34-GE-100A was qualified for service in August 1983.

The TF34 has proved resistant to foreign-object damage (FOD) in service, despite those who doubted the wisdom of using a high-bypass engine on a combat-type aircraft. The high engine mounting keeps the inlets well clear of runway FOD, while the high exhaust position and upward-pointing exhaust reduce the problems of FOD in a stream takeoff. In 1982, A-10s involved in exercises in Egypt flew through heavy sandstorms with no problems, and the engines did not even need to be washed. Neither has the A-10 suffered unduly from birdstrikes, even in Northern Europe.

Above: Post-flight inspection of an A-10's TF34. The titanium fan blades have proved highly resistant to bird strikes over Europe, and have shrugged off heavy sandstorms during exercises in Egypt.

Non-problems are rarely investigated, but the most likely reason for the toughness of the TF34 lies in its basic front-end layout. The fan itself, with solid titanium blades and a modest 7,800rpm speed, is unlikely to suffer much damage from a birdstrike. The inlet to the core, where FOD can do far more damage, is not very prominent, being flush with the inner wall of the duct, and is well behind the fan. If a bird hits the fan, the heavier fragments will be thrown outwards, well clear of the core inlet. The same applies for any objects denser than the inlet air, including sand and water. Some other high-bypass engines, which have encountered more serious problems with ingestion and erosion, feature core inlets immediately behind the fan.

Operating their engines at constant full power in combat, A-10 pilots have

encountered no serious handling problems. In 1980 some engine stalls were being reported during prolonged gunfiring; this is understandable, since the GAU-8/A spits out 24lb (10.9kg) of used propellant every second when firing at its maximum rate. Usually this is not too much of a problem: there are few targets which can absorb more than a short burst from the A-10.

Another feature of the TF34 is that it is inherently much quieter than any other fighter engine. The advantage of this attribute in the tactical arena may be in dispute, but it has certainly been welcome to the people in the neighbourhood of the A-10's operating bases in Europe.

A higher-powered version of the TF34 was to have been developed for the Awacs programme, and would have improved A-10 performance in some respects, but GE's plans for uprated engines have not yet been implemented. Using the same fan as the existing version, the TF34 could be taken up to 10,000lb (4,540kg) thrust by increasing the turbine entry temperature; the standard core, mated to a larger fan and operating at the same temperatures, would yield around 11,500lb (5,100kg) thrust. There is no current requirement for an engine in this class, however: the only active development programme for a TF34-powered aircraft is the US Navy's S-3B, and modifications to this improved version of the Viking are likely to centre on the aircraft's avionics rather than the powerplant.

Engine change proposal

Briefly, in 1976, alternative engines were studied for the A-10, in an effort to generate more interest in the A-10 among Western European customers. Although the European F-16 programme was under way by that time, the Tornado was still several years away from service and its future was by no means assured. The prevailing view among Western European air forces was that the A-10 was too slow, and that airborne loiter was, in European conditions, a costly and unnecessary tactic. Fairchild therefore investigated a version of the A-10 in which some endurance would be traded for higher speed by installing different engines.

At the 1976 Farnborough Air Show Fairchild showed a model of an A-10 with longer, slimmer cowlings, and suggested that the aircraft could be powered by unreheated versions of two current fighter engines: General Electric's own J101, a very-low-bypass engine developing more than 10,000lb (4,540kg), and Europe's Turbo-Union RB.199. Either engine would generate more net thrust than the TF34 at higher airspeeds, and the modified aircraft would have been some 30-50kt (55-93km/h) faster than the standard A-10 in level flight, with weapons carried. The A-10's airframe limit of 450kt (830km/h) was, however, too slow for the taste of European commanders, who continued to regard the A-10 as something of a curiosity, and no serious discussions took place as a result.

The engines of the A-10 are unique among the world's fighter and attack aircraft, and the key to its unusual performance. Their basic configuration is more akin to the typical modern airliner engine than to the normal fighter powerplant: for the mission which the A-10 was designed to perform, though, they are ideal.

Below: A fuel tank is fitted under the wing of an A-10 in JAWS (Joint Attack Weapon System) colour scheme ready for deployment to Europe in 1978.

Above: Even without air refuelling, the A-10 has a ferry range of 2,240nm (4,148km) with a 20min reserve against 50kt (93km/h) headwinds.

Above: the unusual nose position for the refuelling receptable proved to be an improvement on the more normal location to the rear of the cockpit.

Left: An A-10 of the 174th TFW, New York Air National Guard, its refuelling panel open, is de-iced with warm air during a deployment to Lechfeld AB, Germany, in 1981.

Weapons and Avionics

No other aircraft approaches the A-10 in its ability to carry a heavy load of hard-target ordnance; a single Warthog can carry enough weaponry to disable 16 main battle tanks. The primary weapon, unique to the A-10, is the massive GAU-8/A Avenger Gatling cannon, and this powerful gun is backed up by the highly accurate fire-and-forget Maverick missile, which offers a choice of television, scene-magnification TV or – soon – infra-red guidance. With these weapons the A-10 accomplishes its mission without the need for sophisticated – and costly and unreliable – weapon-aiming avionics. Meanwhile, the navigation and ECM systems have been upgraded as a result of operational experience.

If the infantry commander has one recurrent nightmare, it is the unexpected rumble of armour. It signifies that he is about to be engaged by a force which his defensive weapons may blunt, but which they will probably not neutralize, and that it is too late to call for friendly armour to support his unit. In a ground-only battle, the options are immediate retreat, or destruction.

The nightmare came true more than once in Vietnam, and it can happen to a front-line unit at almost any time, even

Below: 354th TFW ground crew prepare to reload a GAU-8/A's ammunition drum, using the Ammunition Loading System.

with the best reconnaissance and intelligence. Its importance for the A-10 is that it represents the most critical test for close air support (CAS). Only air power can rescue the unit under attack, and it can do so only if it arrives quickly, can distinguish friend and enemy, and can engage and defeat the attackers. This leads to a few basic requirements for effective CAS.

It can be taken for granted that the CAS aircraft will be outnumbered by main battle tanks (MBTs) and their escorts and support vehicles. Almost by definition, the CAS aircraft is responding to an emergency, and there will be no time to muster a superior force. The first essential for an effective CAS system is

the ability to kill several targets in a single sortie.

The primary target is the MBT, a notoriously difficult machine to kill. Its resistance to blast weapons is sufficient to make their use uneconomical, and light cluster weapons, dispensing a shower of submunitions over a wide area, are also ineffective. Another basic requirement for CAS, therefore, is an airborne weapon that can guarantee a direct, lethal hit on a tank under operational conditions. Modern armoured formations, particularly in Soviet practice, carry their own defensive systems, so the weapon must have sufficient range to be fired from a position of relative security. Finally, even the fastest-

Above: The 9,000lb (40kN) recoil thrust of the GAU-8/A cannon demanded a centreline location, and the forward fuselage was designed around the gun and its ammunition.

responding CAS may not reach the fight before the attacking armour has engaged the friendly force. Telling friend from foe, when the position of the target is no help, is a great deal more difficult than simply acquiring, tracking and shooting a target which is known to be hostile.

General Electric GAU-8/A Avenger 30mm armament system

Easily the biggest gun carried by any combat aircraft, the GAU-8/A is based on General Electric's proven range of Gatling type cannon. The ammunition drum holds 1,350 rounds which are forced into the feed chute by the rotary motion of the helical inner drum. Each of the seven barrels has its own breech and bolt, with integral firing and locking mechanism, and as a round is fed into the breech the bolt rams it home and locks. The firing pin is compressed by a cocking pin and released by a trigger; after firing, the bolt is unlocked and withdraws the empty cartridge case, which is returned to the ammunition drum. As in the original Gatling, the rotation of the barrels and their individual firing mechanisms on a single rotor synchronize the firing sequence through a system of cam tracks on the inside of the rotor casing, though hydraulic power is used rather than the manual crank of its nineteenth-century ancestor.

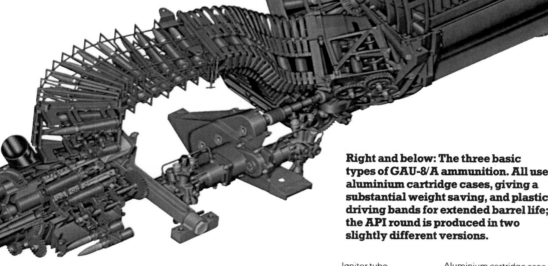

GAU-8/A ammunition

Aluminium nose
Steel body
Training practice

Heavy metal penetrator
Aluminium positioning ring
Aluminium base
Steel windscreen
Armour-piercing incendiary

Igniter tube
Aluminium cartridge case
Plastic rotating bands
High-explosive/incendiary mix
Steel fragmenting body
M505A3 impact fuze
Single base nitrocellulose extruded propellant or double base nitrocellulose/nitroglycerine ball propellant
High-explosive/incendiary

Right and below: The three basic types of GAU-8/A ammunition. All use aluminium cartridge cases, giving a substantial weight saving, and plastic driving bands for extended barrel life; the API round is produced in two slightly different versions.

Looking at these basic requirements in the mid-1960s, the USAF planners realised that there was no combination of weapons and sensors in the inventory, or even envisaged, which could meet the requirement. Unguided weapons and iron bombs were not accurate at safe ranges. Autonomous air-to-surface missiles guided by TV cameras were under study, but even if they worked as advertised, they would not kill a tank with every shot (the air-to-air battles over Vietnam had been a cold shower for those who believed in theoretical kill probabilities, as defined in the early 1960s). The cost-per-kill numbers, placed against the relatively low cost of the cheap, unrefined Soviet MBT, were not encouraging.

Reviewing the history of aircraft-versus-tank battles in the 1939-45 war, the USAF came across a few successes for the aircraft. Most of these involved the use of a heavy-calibre gun: the British Hurricane IID in the North African desert, with its two 40mm cannon; the German Ju 87G, with two 37mm weapons; and the Soviet Il-2, with 23mm or 37mm cannon. There was also the German Hs 129, with its massive 75mm gun, designed to tackle the huge Josef Stalin MBT.

The gun became the standard weapon of the A-X by a process of elimination: there was simply no other weapon in sight that could kill a tank from a fast-moving aircraft at a reasonable cost. The encouraging lesson from history, and from experience and tests with the more modern 30mm calibre weapons used by Britain and France, was that a tank could be destroyed by an airborne gun of moderate calibre, because the aircraft could attack the more lightly armoured sides and top of the tank. The tanks of the 1960s were a great deal better protected than those of the 1940s, but the design of guns, and, to a greater extent, the design of ammunition, had made advances as well.

Gun design

The design of an airborne anti-tank cannon had barely been considered since the mid-1940s. The principles of gun design, though, are constant regardless of the intended use of the weapon. Since the modern gun was conceived, in the mid-1880s, these principles have become fairly well established.

The gun has been likened to a piston engine, with the barrel as the cylinder and the shell as the piston. Its power is proportional to the pressure generated by the expansion of the burning gases inside the barrel, and there are physical and practical limits, such as gun strength and durability, to that pressure. The power of the gun, and the speed of the shell, can be increased by adding more propellant without increasing calibre. But if the peak pressure is to be held constant, the propellant gases must have more time, and more room, to expand. This means a longer barrel, and is the reason why the ratio of barrel length to calibre is a basic parameter in gun design.

The speed of the shell – muzzle velocity – is a contributor to absolute range, but it is a vital quality in two specific types of gunnery. These, conveniently, are airborne gunnery and shooting tanks.

In airborne gunnery accuracy is the main requirement. No system, including a gun, is absolutely consistent in operation. Rounds may vary – to a tiny degree – in the burning rate of their propellant. Firing from a warm barrel is not quite the same as firing from a cold barrel. Outside the barrel, the weight of the shell and the wind take effect, and cause the shell to deviate from the straight and narrow path. An added factor in an aircraft is the varying speed and g loading when the gun is fired. All these add up to 'dis-

Right: Hand-loading 30mm rounds for early firing trials with the GAU-8/A. Each round is 11.4in (290mm) long, and the complete API round weighs an impressive 2.05lb (930g).

Above and top: An M47 tank shows the effects of the GAU-8/A's HEI and API ammunition. The gun's accuracy is such that even at 4,000ft (1,800m), 80 percent of the rounds fired will hit within a 20ft (8.1m) radius.

persion', the fact that shells diverge slightly in flight. Dispersion cannot be eliminated, but most of the factors that cause it are reduced by higher muzzle velocity.

The importance of velocity to antitank gunnery is in the nature of the target. Tanks are invulnerable to blast explosives, except in extremely large quantities. The common feature of all antitank munitions is that they concentrate their force on a single point, either in the form of a solid piece of hard metal or, in the case of a hollow-charge warhead, as a high-velocity jet of vaporized metal. The hollow charge is too bulky to be fired from a gun; the effectiveness of the solid penetrator is proportional to its impact velocity, and thus to its muzzle velocity.

Finally, antitank and airborne gunnery share a common feature. The fighter or attack pilot has neither the means nor the time to consider the ballistic drop of the shell with distance, and it is certainly impractical to fire and observe a ranging shot before firing for effect. While it may be possible for a ground-based antitank gun to fire a ranging shot before engaging a tank, it is definitely inadvisable. The effective range, in both cases, is the maximum range at which ballistic drop can be ignored: 'point-blank' shooting, in the original and accurate sense of the term. This range is almost directly proportional to muzzle velocity.

Given the basic principles of gun design and gunnery, and the state of the art

in projectile design and propellant composition, the shape of the A-X gun became a factor of the operational requirements. These could be summarized as the need to assure the destruction of a T-62 tank at 4,000ft (1,200m) range. However, the phrase 'assure the destruction' introduced a new parameter into the requirement: rate of fire.

High muzzle velocity could reduce dispersion, but not eliminate it, particularly in airborne firing. It was reasonable to expect the new gun to put half its shots within an approximately tank-sized area from a given point at maximum effective range. The problem was that no two shells would be fired from the same point, because the aircraft would be moving. Again, this was a factor which could never be eliminated. It could, however, be reduced. The key was a very high rate of fire, so that the movement of the firing point between each round would be as small as possible.

The requirement for the A-X gun took shape in 1968-69. It soon became clear that the weapon would be of awesome size, and would utterly dwarf any aircraft gun since the 75mm freaks of 1939-45. Its shells would be more than twice as heavy as those of any gun with a comparable muzzle velocity or rate of fire, and the rest of the weapon would naturally grow in proportion. The multiple-target-kill capability required by the USAF, together with the high rate of fire, also meant that the A-X would carry more

Right: During trials, pilots found a quick method of estimating target ranges based on the HUD gun cross: the upper and lower views show a T62 as it appears at 2,000ft (610m) and 4,000ft (1,220m).

rounds of its heavy ammunition than other aircraft.

The rate of fire demanded by the USAF determined the basic configuration of the gun. It would be a design which dated back two decades or a century, depending on your historical perspective. It was in 1861 that Richard Jordan Gatling patented the first operable machine gun, a weapon which could load, cock and fire itself at a far faster

rate than any human operator could attain. The Gatling gun consisted of six independent barrels and breeches, arranged in a circle and revolving around a common axis under the power of a hand crank, and it was used in the American Civil War, and later by the British Army. Its limitation was its need for external power, and by the turn of the century it had been replaced by weapons such as the Maxim, which used

Range estimation

Above: The GAU-8/A expels 24lb (10.9kg) of used propellant a second, causing occasional engine stalls, but few targets can withstand more than a very short burst.

Below: An M48 on the receiving end of a burst of fire from the GAU-8/A: as the rounds penetrate the tank armour, ammunition and fuel inside ignite to cause secondary explosions.

Above: An armoured column like this would be meat and drink to the Warthog, though both tanks and aircraft are on the same side during the 1978 series of Reforger exercises.

recoil energy to operate the mechanism.

The Gatling remained a museum piece until 1946, when the US Army Air Force began serious investigations of a new type of aircraft gun. In 1939-45 German aircraft cannon had proved superior in most respects to the Anglo-French Hispano, and vastly more effective than the USAAF's standard .5in (12.7mm) machine gun. The invading Allies also discovered prototypes of the Mauser MG 213 revolver cannon, which could fire twice as fast as any previous weapon for a modest increase in weight.

Post-war development of aircraft guns followed two parallel tracks. The development of the MG 213 was completed independently in Britain, France and the USA. The other route was started by the USAAF, which intended to create an ultimate aircraft gun, combining high velocity with an unheard-of rate of fire: the aim was to arm a fighter or defend a bomber with a single gun.

This was Project Vulcan, and a development contract was awarded to General Electric's Armament Systems Department in 1946. GE's response to the USAAF requirement was to resurrect the Gatling. There were a number of reasons for this apparent throwback to the past. The most important was that the Gatling, coupled with a modern-technology feed system, could reach and sustain otherwise unthinkable rates of fire. The MG 213, firing at 1,400rds/min, was close to the limits on barrel life and barrel heating. A six-barrel Gatling, by contrast,

could fire at 6,000rds/min, but each barrel would be firing at little more than two-thirds the rate of the MG 213 barrel.

The Gatling's need for external power was no longer a problem, now that fighter aircraft carried their own reliable electrical power supplies; in fact, it could be seen as a positive advantage. While a recoil-powered gun might run out of power if a round failed to fire, the Gatling's external power provided a number of options for clearing a misfired round from the cycle. A final mechanical advantage of the Gatling was that many of its functions were driven by the rotary movement of the barrel assembly; rotary movements are inherently more reliable, and impose fewer loads on the rest of the system, than the reciprocating motions of a conventional gun.

GE ground-tested its first T-171 20mm Gatling in 1949, successfully firing up to 6,000rds/min. The cannon's only real drawback was its unusual, bulky shape, which made it very difficult to install in an aircraft not specifically designed to carry it; it did not enter service until early 1958, first on the Lockheed F-104 and later on the Republic F-105, under the military designation M61A1. It proved its worth on the F-105 over North Vietnam, was squeezed into the nose of the F-4, fired in the USAF A-7 and fired in broadsides from AC-119 and AC-130 gunships. GE had developed a 7.62mm baby Gatling, the Minigun, which was fitted to helicopters, AC-47 'Puff-Ships' and the A-37B. By the time the A-X requirement emerged, the USAF was thoroughly convinced of the merits of the Gatling.

The fact that GE had designed every operational Gatling gun in the world gave it something of a head start in the

succeeding competition. The company's own efforts at research and development, aimed at expanding its family of Gatling weapons, also told in its favour; a six-barrel, 30mm demonstrator designated T-212 was tested in 1967-68, before the formal USAF requirement was issued. As outlined in the first chapter, the contest to produce the GAU-8/A weapon for the A-10 led to a 'shoot-off' between rival prototypes from GE and Philco-Ford, which had developed the MG 213-based M39 for the F-100 and F-5. GE was announced the winner in mid-1973, and the production cannon was first fired from the A-10 in 1975.

GAU-8/A Avenger

The GAU-8/A Avenger is more than a scaled-up M61. Such a weapon could have been designed and built, but would have been unacceptably heavy. The first of many design differences is that the heavier weapon has seven barrels, instead of six. The maximum firing rate is lower (4,200rds/min versus 6,000), and the firing rate per barrel is lower again; each GAU-8/A barrel fires a maximum of 10rds/sec, while the M61 barrel fires nearly 17. Essentially, maximum firing rate has been traded for a heavier, more accurate and more lethal round; each shell is far heavier than the M50 round fired by the older weapon, and the more modest firing rate per barrel is necessary to ensure a long barrel life. The USAF specified a minimum 21,000-round life for each set of barrels. The GAU-8/A also has an improved and more compact bolt design which reduces the overall length and weight of the gun. The GAU-8/A is relatively compact, being only fractionally larger in diameter than the much less powerful M61.

The basic GAU-8/A gun closely follows the philosophy of Richard Gatling's original. Each of the seven 30mm barrels is a simple non-repeating rifle, with its own breech and bolt; the cocking and firing mechanism is built into the bolt. The bolt rams the shell into the breech and locks into position; a cocking pin compresses the firing spring, and a trigger releases it. The bolt is unlocked, and slides back to withdraw the empty cartridge case.

None of the barrels, though, can fire without some force to move and lock the bolt, and cock and release the trigger. The genius of the original Gatling concept is that all these operations are carried out and synchronized through the movement of a single component: the multiple barrels, built into one rotating assembly (which GE calls the 'rotor') and revolving on a common axis inside the gun casing. The firing mechanisms for each individual barrel are located on the outside of the rotor, and engage fixed cam tracks on the inside of the casing. As the rotor spins, the curving cam tracks engage and move the bolt, the locking mechanism and the firing pin, and take the barrel through a complete, perfectly synchronized firing sequence for each revolution of the rotor. This, essentially, is what happens in all the GE weapons.

Each GAU-8/A barrel is some 80 calibres in length. The muzzle velocity of the GAU-8/A is about the same as that of the M61, but the heavier, more advanced ammunition is not only more destructive but has better ballistic properties. It decelerates much less rapidly after leaving the barrel, so that its time of flight to 4,000ft (1,200m) is 30 per cent less than that of an M61 round, and the projectile drops a negligible distance – barely 10ft

AGM-65 Maverick

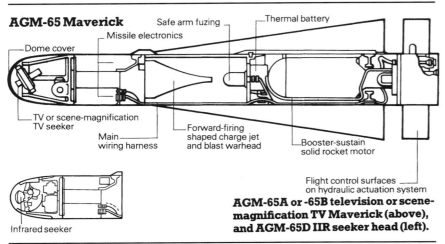

AGM-65A or -65B television or scene-magnification TV Maverick (above), and AGM-65D IIR seeker head (left).

Maverick launch zones

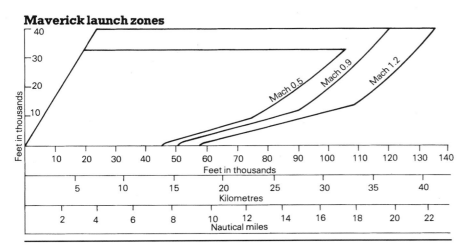

Above left: The Maverick's launch envelope varies with the speed and altitude of the launch aircraft, and with target range, though the Warthog pilot will be most concerned with the bottom left-hand corner.

Left: Preparing to load an AGM-65B scene-magnification Maverick onto an A-10 at Cairo West AB during a Bright Star exercise in 1981.

Below: After being loaded onto LAU-88 launchers, Mavericks are transferred to the special launcher rack, seen here at RAF Bentwaters, ready for mounting on the aircraft.

(3m) – in the process. The accuracy of the GAU-8/A, installed in the A-10, is rated at '5mil, 80 per cent', meaning that 80 per cent of rounds fired at 4,000ft (1,800m) will hit within a circle of 20ft (6.1m) radius; the M61 is rated at 8mil.

A very important innovation in the design of the GAU-8/A shells is the use of aluminium alloy cases in place of the traditional steel or brass. This alone adds 30 per cent to ammunition capacity for a given weight. The shells also have plastic driving bands to improve barrel life. They are imposing to examine and handle, measuring 11.4in (290mm) in length and weighing 1.53lb (694g) or more. There are four types in service. Two are common to most aircraft cannon: a practice round, and a general-purpose shell loaded with high-explosive/incendiary (HEI) compound. Specially developed for the A-10, however, are two armour-piercing incendiary (API) rounds. The USAF chose two companies, Aerojet and Honeywell, to develop and produce API shells for the A-10 under its 'second-source' philosophy: when items are acquired in large quantities, the USAF buys them from two organizations, and lets them bid competitively for each year's order.

The two API rounds are slightly different in detail, but basically are similar. Neither contains any explosive. Instead, they consist of a lightweight aluminium body, cast around a small 'penetrator' of smaller calibre than the shell. (The calibre is about 15mm.) It projects from

the blunt body section, and the shell has a thin aluminium 'windscreen' to keep the shape aerodynamic. The penetrator is made of depleted uranium, a by-product of the enrichment process used to make nuclear fuel. The material has an extremely high density, comprising roughly two-thirds of the projectile's weight.

The result is that two-thirds of the total impact energy is concentrated in the small-calibre penetrator: enough energy to lift a thirty-ton weight one foot, delivered instantly to a penny-sized area. Not only is this ammunition capable of penetrating the top and side armour of an MBT, but the depleted uranium ignites on impact, sending a jet of flame into the vehicle.

Ammunition and feed system

The GAU-8/A ammunition is linkless, reducing weight and avoiding a great deal of potential for jamming. The feed system is double-ended: the spent cases are not ejected from the aircraft (which takes a great deal of force if the possibility of severe airframe damage is to be eliminated) but are cycled back into the ammunition drum. The feed system is based on that developed for later M61 installations, but uses more advanced design techniques and materials throughout, to save weight.

Inside the cylindrical outer drum is a rotating inner drum, resembling a huge, deeply cut worm gear. The helical channel which winds around this rotor holds the 1,350 shells; they are stored radially, with their tips toward the axis of the drum, and their bases are held in channels running the length of the fixed, outer drum. As the rotor turns, the shells are forced forward along the drum and into the complex of turning mechanisms and chutes leading to the gun.

Power for the gun and its feed mechanism is drawn from the A-10's dual hydraulic systems. Two hydraulic motors provide the total 77hp (57.4kW) needed to drive the system at its maximum firing rate. If either hydraulic system fails, the remaining motor can sustain the alternative 2,100rds/min rate.

Loading the linkless ammunition is the function of the only specialized piece of ground equipment used by the A-10. The Ammunition Loading System (ALS) resembles a trailer-mounted version of the GAU-8/A ammunition drum and feed system, and operates on the same principle, loading rounds and extracting empty cases simultaneously. A full load can be changed in less than 13 minutes.

GAU-8/A derivatives

Some of the GAU-8/A technology has been transferred into the smaller 25mm GAU-12/U Equalizer developed for the AV-8B, which is about the same size as the M61 but is considerably more lethal. GE has also developed the GAU-13, a four-barrel weapon using GAU-8A components, which has been tested in podded form, and the Avenger forms the basis for the Dutch-developed Goalkeeper naval air-defence gun. No current or contemplated aircraft other than the A-10, however, carries the full-up Avenger system. The weapon is simply too large. It measures 19ft 10.5in (5.06m) from the muzzle to the rearmost point of the ammunition feed system, and the ammunition drum alone is 34.5in (87.6cm) in diameter and 71.5in (181.6cm) long. With full ammunition, the system weighs 4,029lb (1,830kg).

In short, the GAU-8/A system, fully armed and ready to fire, is just about as long and as heavy as a Rolls-Royce or a full-size Cadillac. At its maximum firing rate, its average recoil force of 9,000lb (40kN) thrust is equal to the power of one of the A-10's engines. Operationally, the

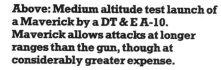

Above: Medium altitude test launch of a Maverick by a DT & E A-10. Maverick allows attacks at longer ranges than the gun, though at considerably greater expense.

Left: Unlike earlier command-guided air-to-surface missiles such as Bullpup, Maverick is a fire-and-forget weapon: the pilot designates the target as seen by the TV or infrared seeker head and displayed on his cockpit CRT, launches the missile and takes evasive action while it homes automatically on the selected target. This sequence shows the destruction of an M113 APC.

performance of the gun makes it as vital to the A-10's mission as the wings and engines. It has many unique attributes, and no other weapon, in service or under study, can take its place.

The gun gives the A-10 the ability to attack multiple targets in one mission. It is designed to fire its full ammunition load in ten two-second bursts, with one minute to cool down between bursts; in normal use, the bursts and the cool-down time would be much shorter. A one-second burst from 4,000ft (1,220m) will put 40 shells into a circle little bigger than the length of a tank, and half-a-dozen hits are considered to be a lethal strike. With the theoretical ability to deliver 15-20 such bursts, the A-10 is unlikely to have to abort an attack for want of firepower.

The gun also eliminates the need for many of the systems which have been considered standard on other attack aircraft since the late 1960s. Its shells travel at Mach 3; from 4,000ft (1,220m) they are on target in 1.2 seconds. This means that the movement of an MBT is irrelevant to the aiming problem; to the A-10, all ground targets are fixed. Because of the flat trajectory of the shells, too, the distance to the target does not have to be accurately estimated or measured. Within the normal maximum range, the trajectory is a straight line in front of the aircraft, represented by a fixed dot on the head-up display. The absence of inertial platforms, laser rangefinders and

other systems from the weapon-aiming loop not only simplifies the aircraft, but makes the pilot's workload less as well. Without the point-and-fire simplicity of the GAU-8/A, the A-10 concept of manoeuvring, medium-speed CAS with visual navigation and target acquisition would probably collapse due to excessive pilot workload.

The gun is extremely reliable. Stoppages are predicted to occur once in 150,000 rounds, or once in more than 100 missions when every round is fired. Even then, the weapon can often be cleared in flight by reversing the gun and feed mechanism and trying again. There is no guidance system to fail and nothing to be jammed or deceived. All this adds up to the fact that the kill probability of a GAU-8 burst is high: tests have shown that as many as half the bursts may be effective in a diving attack on the rear of a tank, and one third in side attacks.

AGM-65 Maverick

The gun is not only the primary weapon of the A-10, but it is one of only two weapons generally used by the aircraft. The other, the Hughes AGM-65 Maverick air-to-surface missile, complements the gun; it is also designed for attacks against hard, mobile precision targets, but from rather greater standoff distances. On the other hand, the Maverick does not give the A-10 the same sustained firing capability as the gun, and is not as fast-acting, and its cost per kill is very much greater. The cost of an early-model Maverick was quoted at $60,000 in 1981, versus $1,800 in ammunition and maintenance costs for a two-second burst from the cannon. The two systems, however, had a very similar kill probability (Pk) per pass, so the gun was far more economical.

Maverick was developed after the miserable failure of the command-guided Bullpup to accomplish anything in Vietnam. It was a very advanced concept for its day: a compact missile, designed for multiple carriage, which could guide itself autonomously to a precision target and destroy it with a large shaped-charge warhead. Its guidance system was based on television technol-

Alternative mission loads

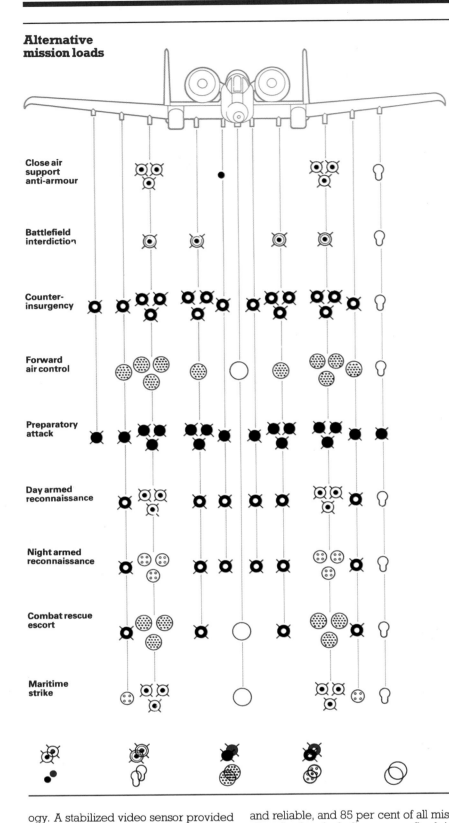

Close air support anti-armour

Battlefield interdiction

Counter-insurgency

Forward air control

Preparatory attack

Day armed reconnaissance

Night armed reconnaissance

Combat rescue escort

Maritime strike

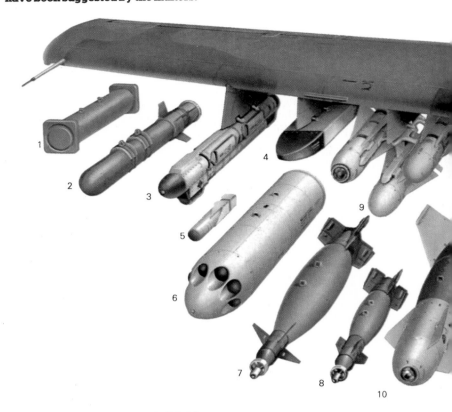

Left: During operational evaluation, the USAF found the A-10 well-suited to the preparatory role, and unmatched as an escort; FAC capability was judged satisfactory, while other roles have been suggested by the makers.

Below: 333rd TFTS, 355th TTW A-10 en route to the Gila Bend range, with 25lb (11kg) BDU-33 practice bombs on wing-mounted triple and fuselage multiple ejection racks.

ogy. A stabilized video sensor provided a picture to a cockpit display, and fed a simple image-processing system in the missile. The pilot pointed the camera at the target using cockpit controls, commanded the seeker to lock on and launched the missile. The guidance system sensed relative movement by analyzing the video signal, and generated correction signals to keep the missile on target.

Two production versions of Maverick were built in the 1970s. The first was the basic AGM-65A, with an optical system designed to cover a 5deg cone in front of the aircraft – equivalent to the field of view of a 200mm lens on a 35mm camera. It was replaced in production by the AGM-65B, originally known as the Scene Magnification Maverick, which has a 2.5deg field of view, and is carried as a standard weapon by the A-10. Underwing pylons 3 and 9, immediately outboard of the landing gear pods, are each fitted to carry the LAU-88/A triple launcher for the AGM-65. Maverick is controlled from its own panel in the cockpit, consisting of a video screen and controls for slewing the seeker, switching from low to high magnification and locking the missile on to the target.

Maverick has proven to be successful and reliable, and 85 per cent of all missiles fired – including some fired in anger, in Southeast Asia and the Middle East – are claimed to have hit their targets. More than 30,000 Mavericks have been built for the USAF and export customers. The weapon has only one serious drawback: it has to be fired from a point uncomfortably close to the target. The AGM-65B has a theoretical range of 6-7nm (11-13km) even under the most unfavourable conditions – launch from a slow aircraft, such as an A-10, at low level. However, its TV tracker will not normally lock on to a target outside 2-3nm (3.7-5.5km). This is because air is not perfectly transparent, and the attenuation of optical wavelengths with distance prevents the guidance circuitry from getting the clear, high-contrast image that it needs. Maverick takes 4-8 seconds to lock on, which is a long time in air combat, and particularly so when the launch sequence takes place within the envelope of standard air-defence systems such as the SA-8 Gecko. Multiple launches in a single attack pass are not practicable.

Right: A powered hoist is used to load a Mk 83 1,000lb (454kg) GP bomb under the wing of a 354th TFW A-10.

1 Typical glassfibre weapon storage container
2 Matra Durandal anti-runway penetration bomb
3 Westinghouse ALQ-119(V) ECM pod
4 ALE-37 high-capacity chaff dispenser
5 Hughes Aircraft Wasp anti-armour missile (fins folded)
6 10-round Wasp pod
7 Texas Instruments GBU-10E/B Paveway II Mk 84 2,000lb (907kg) laser-guided bomb
8 Texas Instruments GBU-12D/B Paveway II Mk 82 500lb (227kg) laser-guided bomb
9 Hughes Aircraft AGM-65A TV-guided, AGM-65B scene-magnification TV and AGM-65D imaging infra-red Maverick air-to-surface missiles on LAU-88/A triple launcher
10 Rockwell International GBU-15 guided glide bomb, 2,000lb (907kg) Mk 84 warhead
11 600US gall (500 Imp gall/2,273lit) fuel tank
12 Martin Marietta Lantirn navigation
13 Martin Marietta AAS-35 Pave Penny laser tracking pod
14 General Electric GAU-8/A Avenger 30mm cannon with hydraulic feed system and 1,174-round ammunition drum
15 Rockwell International Hobo electro-optically guided Mk 84 2,000lb (907kg) smart bomb
16 Martin Marietta Lantirn targeting pod
17 Mk 84 2,000lb (907kg) general-purpose bomb
18 Rockwell International Hellfire anti-tank missiles
19 Stores container
20 Mk 83 1,000lb (454kg) general-purpose bomb
21 Honeywell Mk 20 Rockeye cluster bomb
22 Mk 82 500lb (227kg) Snakeye high-drag general-purpose bomb
23 Mk 82 low-drag general-purpose bomb
24 CBU-52 cluster bomb

Above: Despite the wide range of weapons which the A-10 has carried, its standard armament remains the potent antitank combination of GAU-8/A cannon and Maverick air-to-surface missile. Other combat aircraft can deliver all the other weapons shown here, but none is even capable of mounting the lethal gun. Moreover, the Warthog's standard low-level tactics preclude the use of most conventional weapons, which depend to a large extent on energy gained from the aircraft, and the aircraft lacks the sophisticated weapon-aiming systems carried by aircraft such as the F-16, Harrier and Jaguar.

The introduction of the AGM-65D Maverick, which uses infra-red (IR) homing, made a significant difference for the A-10 force. IR video technology has been available for many years, but it has taken new advances in electronics to create missile-sized and missile-priced image-processing systems which will cull guidance data from IR images. Because IR wavelengths are relatively little affected by attenuation in 'clear air', the AGM-65D can lock on at twice the stand-off range possible with the AGM-65B. This is close to the maximum range of the SA-8, and brings multiple launches within the realms of possibility. These are being facilitated by the development of a rapid-fire modification for the LAU-88/A, incorporating a circuit which slews the seeker of the second missile on to the target area as the seeker of the first is locked-on.

The IR weapon is also less affected by dust and smoke on the battlefield, and the better-quality image allows the pilot to discriminate between different types of vehicle according to their characteristic IR 'signatures'. The weapon requires no mandatory modifications to any aircraft already fitted to fire the AGM-65B. However, it is equipped to receive targeting data from the aircraft's

weapon-aiming systems, and this capability can be used if the necessary control channel is installed.

The IR weapon's most important attribute is, for the time being, of limited use to the A-10: it operates identically by day and by night, the quality of the IR image being basically the same. This was a major factor in giving the A-10 a limited night-operating capability.

Photographs of the A-10 loaded from wingtip to wingtip with weapons have helped to spread the impression that the aircraft was designed as an ordnance truck, primarily intended to carry a massive external load. This is not exactly true. The A-10 can lift a large warload because it was designed to use short fields, manoeuvre and fight while carrying a more moderate load. If the man-

oeuvring requirements are less severe, and a longer runway is available, the aircraft can lift a larger load. For an anti-tank mission from a forward operating base, however, six Mavericks and ammunition for the GAU-8/A constitute a full offensive load. Between them, the missiles and the gun are well suited to the A-10's primary mission, like most other aspects of the design.

In service with the USAF, the A-10 has been cleared to drop and fire a wide variety of weapons. These include the straightforward Mk 82 '500lb' bomb (which actually weighs 565lb/256kg); the A-10 can carry 28 such weapons. For use against troops or soft-skinned vehicles, the A-10 can carry cluster weapons such as Rockeye, CBU-52/58/71 and the British BL755. More sophisticated weapons include the GBU-12 laser-guided glide bomb, based on the 3,000lb Mk 84.

The A-10, however, is not particularly suited to deliver many of these weapons

Left: Bomb-carrying trials with the first DT & E A-10. Maximum load is 16,000lb, distributed between 11 pylons, though the extreme outboard wing pylons, limited to 1,000lb (454kg), are rarely used for anything but an ALQ-119 ECM pod.

A-10 Thunderbolt II

Standard and INS HUD symbology and control units

The A-10 was designed for visual navigation and target acquisition, and the original avionics suite was as simple as possible, the head-up display using only the basic symbology shown below. The switch to low-level tactics, especially in poor visibility, made an inertial navigation system necessary, resulting in the expanded symbology shown right.

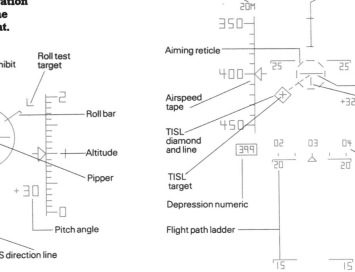

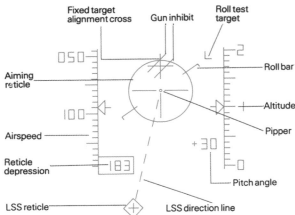

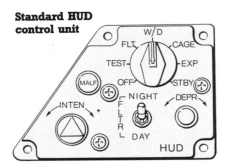

Standard HUD control unit

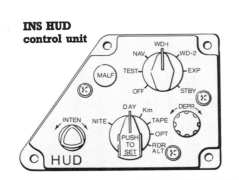

INS HUD control unit

Above: The head-up display unit developed by Kaiser Electronics specially for the A-10 has been improved to incorporate inputs from the inertial navigation system.

in the face of intense defences. As noted earlier, it does not possess many of the features which are standard on other light strike types, such as the F-16, Harrier and Jaguar. All these aircraft have some sort of weapon-aiming system which can measure the velocity of the aircraft relative to the ground and the distance to the target, compute the trajectory of whatever ordnance may be on board and indicate the precise moment to release the weapon. The A-10 has no means of measuring ground velocity, such as a high-accuracy inertial platform; it has no means of measuring range to the target and no weapons-release computer. Accurate attack with any weapon other than Maverick and the GAU-8/A is possible only in a steep, low-airspeed dive from medium altitude, a somewhat foolhardy tactic in the presence of SAMs or AAA.

It is not that the A-10 is deficient in its relative inability to use such weapons safely and effectively; just that it is a specialized aircraft, and is used as such. In the GAU-8/A and Maverick, it carries two proven and reliable precision-attack weapons which operate without complex aiming systems. The aircraft can dispense with them, and is thereby made more reliable and less costly.

Avionic systems

The original concept of the A-10 was for an aircraft that would be as devoid of avionics as the original Skyraider: no inertial navigation system, no complex displays, and no automatic flight control system or other pilot aids. It would be equipped with communications equipment, simple beacon-type navigation gear, and a straightforward head-up display with limited weapon-aiming symbology. While the A-10 is still closer to the Skyraider than any other aircraft in the USAF

inventory, contact with reality has, as usual, changed plans to some extent.

The changing threat and the changing tactics needed to meet it have been the main motivations behind additions to the A-10's equipment list. More mobile missile systems, and the need to fly the entire mission at low altitude, are among them. The basic system has been little changed, though. The instrument panel facing the pilot is simple, with standard flight instruments and dual sets of gauges for the TF34 engines. To the pilot's right is the video display for the Maverick missile. The primary flight instrument is the Kaiser Electronics head-up display. This is a specially developed, uncomplicated unit which displays aircraft pitch and roll attitude, airspeed and altitude. Weapon-aiming systems on the initial production aircraft amounted to a fixed gunsight reticle on the HUD and the Maverick control panel.

The only addition to the weapon-aiming system to date is the Martin Marietta AAS-35 Pave Penny laser target-identification set, introduced to squadron use in early 1978. Pave Penny

Above: The cockpit reflects the absence of sophisticated avionics, with standard flight instruments and the Maverick TV display to the right.

acts as a link between the attack aircraft and a forward air controller (FAC), who may be in a ground vehicle, a helicopter or an OV-10 reconnaissance aircraft. It is a low-cost, compact and lightweight device, 32in (81cm) long and weighing 32lb (14.5kg), which scans the area ahead of the aircraft for laser radiation. The FAC designates a target with his own laser equipment; Pave Penny picks up the reflection of the coded beam, and places a HUD symbol over the target. The A-10 pilot then takes over and attacks in the usual way. Pave Penny is carried on an unusual pylon mounting, attached to the starboard side of the forward fuselage; the usual nose installation is ruled out by the proximity of the gun muzzle with its associated shockwaves and vibration.

Defensive avionics on the first A-10s were confined to the Itek ALR-46 radar-warning receiver (RWR) system, a fairly simple piece of equipment with anten-

nae built into the nose and tail of the aircraft. This has since been upgraded to the improved ALR-64 and ALR-69 models, to cope with the changing frequencies of Soviet air-defence radars. All the systems feed a simple plan-position indicator (PPI) scope in the cockpit, and show the bearing and approximate range of threatening radars. The system is most useful against the Shilka air-defence gun; the RWR shows the Shilka's position before the A-10 gets within range of its quad-barrelled 23mm cannon.

ECM protection

For active ECM protection in a high-threat environment, the A-10 normally carries a single Westinghouse ALQ-119 electronic countermeasures (ECM) pod on the outermost starboard pylon. The ALQ-119 has been superseded by the same company's ALQ-131 on later USAF aircraft such as the F-16. This is not to say that the older pod is ineffective or obsolete, but the newer system is effective against a wider range of threats, and can jam a greater number of frequencies.

The A-10 does, however, carry a very comprehensive internal decoy system, in the shape of the Tracor ALE-40. Built into formerly empty space in the landing gear pods and wingtips, the ALE-40 consists of 16 batteries of small tubes – 30 tubes to a battery – housing a total of 480 pyrotechnically-fired decoys. Some of these are flares, designed to lead an infra-red homing missile away from the A-10; the rest contain chaff, or thin strips of aluminium foil, and deploy into a loose cloud of metal after being ejected from the aircraft. Chaff is the oldest form of ECM, and under certain circumstances is still one of the most effective deception techniques and one of the hardest to counter. Decoys are a last-ditch defence

Typical head-up displays

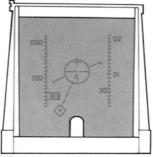

Test mode

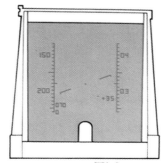

Cage mode

Flight mode

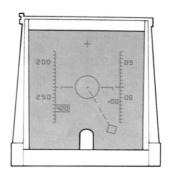

Expanded mode

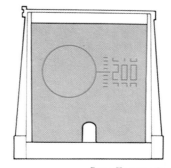

Weapon delivery mode

Standby mode

1984, and the entire fleet was upgraded prior to the Gulf War.

In the original A-10, the HUD gave the pilot basic flight information – speed, altitude and aircraft pitch and roll angle. The new system adds a wealth of data: vertical speed and flightpath (the angle at which the aircraft is climbing or diving), actual heading, the direction to steer to a pre-programmed waypoint or target location, and the distance and time to go to the next waypoint. Essentially, it relieves the pilot of the need to map-read and fly evasively at the same time. Navigation inputs can be made when convenient, and appear as clear directions on the HUD. The new equipment calls for little change to the cockpit; the HUD control unit is modified to control the new functions and an INS panel is added.

Because INS data would be projected on to the head-up display, Kaiser was made responsible for devising the INS installation. The chosen solution was to improve the HUD, and link it to the existing central air-data computer and the INS through a digital data-handling system or 'bus'. The existing HUD projection system is retained, but a completely new symbol generator of much greater power is installed. It is still fed with data from the conventional heading, attitude and reference system, but this pitch and roll information is used for back-up purposes only. The most important data is fed to the HUD through dual digital buses.

Another improvement accompanies the introduction of INS. The A-10 was originally fitted with a conventional pressure altimeter, providing readings above sea level, but this was soon found to be inadequate on prolonged low-level flights over Europe's rolling hills. A standard APN-194 radar altimeter replaced it on late-production and retrofitted A-10s.

against missile attack; the pilot fires his decoys and simultaneously pulls a hard break, hoping that the missile's tendency to assume that the aircraft will continue in a straight path will lead it to follow the decoys rather than the real target.

Essentially, the USAF considers that tactics are more important than ECM to the close-support mission. This is why the A-10's equipment is relatively unsophisticated, and why the aircraft is not scheduled to receive the ALQ-165 advanced self-protection jammer (ASPJ), when it becomes available later in the 1980s. ECM is most necessary when an aircraft is exposed for long periods of time to the larger and more sophisticated missile systems: A-10 tactics are geared to avoiding such systems. Also, the A-10 is intended to carry the attack to close quarters, where large and complex systems are close to their minimum range and increasingly cumbersome. In brief, the A-10 is designed and used to need less help from sophisticated ECM than an F-16 or F-15.

Flight control and navigation

The A-10 has no automatic flight control system (AFCS), but is fitted with a stability augmentation system (SAS). The primary function of the SAS is to improve the stability of the aircraft as a weapons platform, and to make the aircraft respond more consistently to the controls; it is a simple, single-channel system and has been upgraded since the aircraft entered service. The SAS also provides warning of an excessive angle of attack, and impending stall, via a stick-shaker.

In one major respect, it was soon discovered, the philosophy of austerity had been taken too far: the A-10's lack of a built-in, autonomous navigation system. Like many features of the aircraft, this went back to the original A-X concept, and to US tactics of the late 1960s. The A-10 was expected to cruise to its loitering point at low-to-medium altitude, where the pilot would not have to follow terrain and Tacan beacons would provide necessary navigational data. But at low level Tacan is of limited use because its line-of-sight transmissions are usually blocked by terrain or the curvature of the earth. A-10 pilots in Europe found themselves navigating with 1/50,000-scale maps across their knees, while

trying to avoid both the defences and the ground.

The solution was to add an inertial navigation system (INS) to the A-10. While some critics charged that installing INS ran counter to the basic philosophy of the A-10, there was nothing else to be done: in sustained low-level flight, the need to map-read pushed the pilot's workload to unacceptably high levels, while the need to pull up periodically to search for landmarks compromised the security of the formation.

A standard USAF INS, the ASN-141, was incorporated in the last 283 A-10s, starting in 1980, and the INS-equipped aircraft were first delivered to Europe, where the need was greatest. As production of new A-10s ran down, modification kits were produced for earlier aircraft; a contract covering the last batch of these was announced in April

Above: the AAS-38 Pave Penny laser seeker pod allows the A-10 to acquire targets designated by forward air controllers, who may be airborne or with the troops on the ground. The pod detects the reflected radiation from the target and indicates it on the HUD, and the pilot then manoeuvres into position for a standard gun or Maverick attack.

Right: External avionics pods on a 354th TFW A-10 at Myrtle Beach AFB. The Pave Penny is offset from the usual nose position to avoid the gun blast; the ALQ-119 jamming pod is normally carried on the outboard starboard wing pylon.

Deployment

By the late 1980s, almost every tactical command in the USAF had at least one A-10 unit on strength. Largest of all was the 108-aircraft superwing, based at RAF Bentwaters and Woodbridge, England, which in the event of war would have deployed immediately to Germany. But the effectiveness of the A-10 was by now in question, and replacement with F-16s seemed very probable.

As a rule, unless things go badly wrong, the USAF buys more of every type of aircraft than it originally planned. As the end of planned production approaches a number of factors conspire to keep the line open. The aircraft is cheap to buy, compared with new types: newer aircraft are seldom ready as soon as had been envisaged, and there may be gaps in the front line to fill. New versions of the type may have been developed to carry out different missions, expanding the service's requirement.

At the same time, US combat aircraft nearly always find export markets. While US aircraft manufacturers often bewail the advantageous terms offered by foreign competitors in the commercial aircraft market, they are less vocal about the excellent credit facilities provided to their military customers through the Pentagon's FMS (foreign military sales) organization.

The A-10 has been an exception. Production ceased in 1984 after the exact quantity planned had been delivered. The last aircraft off the line was the same subtype as the first – in this respect, the A-10 was unique among US combat aircraft. Nor have any A-10s been sold for export. A disappointing outcome for Fairchild, this has been no fault of the

aircraft or those who developed it; the programme has been trouble-free, and what cost overruns did occur were due to outside circumstances such as production-rate cutbacks and inflation. The aircraft does exactly what it was designed to do, and does it well.

The A-10's real problem came from outside the programme; it was fast, it was manoeuvrable, it was everything that a fighter should be, and it was called the F-16. It did not even exist, except as General Dynamics' Model 401 design study, when the USAF ordered the YA-10A prototypes, and it was a year away from its first flight when the A-10 was selected for production. At that time, in early 1973, the YF-16/YF-17 fly-off was not expected to lead to a production programme. Within just over a year, the two types were competing for a massive USAF order. The change had come about under pressure from Secretary of Defense James Schlesinger, and was motivated by two factors: concern over the cost of replacing all the USAF's fighters with the costly and sophisticated F-15, and the prospect of securing a massive order from Europe. The latter could, and did, assure US dominance of the international fighter scene for a decade or more.

The F-16 emerged victorious in the fly-off, and won the European order. It was not intended as a substitute for the A-10, but as a running-mate for the F-15; however, the simple laws of manufacturing economics put the GD and Fairchild aircraft in a kind of competition. Like any manufactured object, aircraft are cheaper if built in the largest possible quantities. Moreover, the graph of unit cost versus production rate is not a straight line, but a curve, and the price for each aircraft increases very rapidly at low rates. In the second half of the 1970s the USAF was in the middle of a post-Vietnam budgetary squeeze. There was simply not enough money available to buy three types of fighter – F-15s, F-16s and A-10s – at economical production rates. If the USAF continued indefinitely to buy all three types at the low rates it could afford, it would get far fewer aircraft at much higher prices.

Losing to the F-16

The F-15 was sacrosanct. The Air Force wanted, and still wants, as many F-15s as possible from every year's budget. Between the A-10 and the F-16 there was very little room for choice. Four NATO allies were committed to the F-16, and if the USAF was to stop after buying, say,

Above: Checking the gun on a Warthog of the 23rd TFW at England AFB, Louisiana. The original 23rd Tactical Fighter Group was formed in China in 1942, and the present unit perpetuates the nose markings of the American Volunteer Group.

650 aircraft, they would be faced with a massive price increase for any future batches of F-16s. The Europeans were relying on USAF partnership in upgrading and improving the aircraft. Neither should it be forgotten that TAC, more than any other air command in the world, has a built-in aversion to an aircraft that cannot chase MiGs.

The F-16 was also a dual-role fighter/strike aircraft, a concept which had been poison when the A-10/F-15 requirements were drafted, but which was now returning to favour thanks to economic pressure and new technology. Improved radar, better HUDs and accurate INS were making it possible for a relatively simple fighter to deliver ordnance with acceptable accuracy. There was no clear point at which the USAF decided to stop the A-10 programme; all purchases are negotiated independently, year by year. By the late 1970s, however, it was

Above: An 81st TFW A-10 ready for collection alongside a Virginia ANG F-105. The pilots of the 91st collected new Warthogs as their old ones fell due for maintenance.

Below: An 81st TFW pilot prepares for a mission during a Reforger '82 exercise. Despite the addition of an inertial system, maps are still important for visual navigation.

Left: Although based in England, the 81st regularly deploys to Germany for training: one of the wing's aircraft waits for takeoff clearance at a dispersal point during Reforger '82.

becoming increasingly clear that the USAF would stop production of the A-10 after buying the 700+ aircraft which had been set as the necessary force level to handle a strictly defined CAS mission. All other air-to-ground tasks would be handled by the dual-purpose F-16.

The A-10's technical and operational success helped to bring production to a close. This sounds paradoxical, but consider the cumulative impact of the following facts. At any time, the USAF's frontline A-10s have a mission-capable rate around 75 per cent – that is to say, three-quarters of the aircraft in the squadrons are fit to fly under wartime conditions. Despite being used almost exclusively in low-altitude, visual close-support missions, the A-10 has one of the lowest accident rates of any USAF fighter in history. It can be turned round between missions faster than any other USAF aircraft, and it can sustain operations from dispersed locations close to the front; for these reasons, it can sustain the kind of sortie rates which other aircraft only reach in an all-out surge. Lastly, its toughness, simplicity and ease of repair give the operating units a unique capability to 're-generate' after taking hits in action. Unfortunately for Fairchild, the foregoing adds up to one conclusion: a few A-10s go a long way.

Deliveries of the A-10 to operational units began in March 1977, a few months after the first aircraft had reached the designated training wing. As is normal practice, a unit based in the continental USA (CONUS) was assigned the first aircraft: the 354th Tactical Fighter Wing (TFW) at Myrtle Beach AFB, South Carolina. One reason for the choice of base was its proximity to a large gunnery test and training range. The first of its squadrons to be declared fully operational was the 356th Tactical Fighter Squadron (TFS), in October 1977.

Deployment proceeded steadily rather than rapidly, because the production decision had been delayed until flight tests were well advanced, and Congress had repeatedly reduced the number of A-10s to be bought each year. By mid-1977 the USAF still had only 55 A-10s, divided among the 354th TFW at Myrtle Beach, the designated training organisation – the 355th Tactical Fighter Training Wing (TFTW) at Davis-Monthan AFB, Arizona – and the 57th Tactical Training Wing at Nellis AFB, which was tasked with developing A-10 tactics.

From 1977, however, USAF priority was to field the A-10 in Europe. In August

six A-10s of the 355th TFTW flew to Sembach, in then-West Germany, to participate in the Autumn Forge series of exercises. Together with the JAWS tests carried out in late 1977, this experimental deployment provided a great deal of information on the best way to use the A-10 against typical Warsaw Pact targets in European weather.

81st TFW

In February 1978 the USAF announced that the 81st TFW, based at RAF Bentwaters/Woodbridge (the two bases are so close together that, administratively, they are a single unit) and equipped with F-4C and F-4D Phantoms, would use the A-10 in Europe. Instead of deploying two wings, as had been planned, the 81st would be expanded into a 'superwing' with six 18-aircraft operating squadrons instead of the usual four. From early 1978, the main thrust of USAF A-10 activity was to get the 81st operational as soon as possible. The 355th TFTW took a leading role in the programme, using experience gained in the European tests and JAWS trials, and processing pilots and new aircraft – the 81st was to receive only factory-fresh A-10s to the latest build standard – at Davis-Monthan.

Pilots for the 81st TFW were drawn from four groups, in roughly equal numbers: new graduates from T-38 training; T-38 instructor pilots, ready for their first operational wing; the 81st's own F-4D pilots, with European experience; and pilots returning to flight status from other assignments. The balance worked well: the F-4 pilots and the last-mentioned group included a great deal of combat support and FAC experience, but the unit was not so loaded with experience that the younger pilots would be denied any chance of leadership.

The first squadron to complete training was the 92nd TFS, which ferried its 18 aircraft to Bentwaters on January 25, 1979. Thanks to specialized training by the 355th TFTW, with the help of senior 81st TFW personnel, the 92nd was considered mission-ready as soon as it arrived. By late 1979 four squadrons were operational and two forward operating locations (FOLs) had been activated, at Sembach and Ahlhorn. The remaining two squadrons arrived at Bentwaters by mid-1980, and the two remaining FOLs became operational.

The 81st continued to be the priority A-10 unit. As its aircraft became due for major maintenance, the pilots would ferry them back to the Air Logistics Center at McClellan AFB, Sacramento, the centre of all A-10 overhaul and modification, and then travel to Hagerstown and pick up a factory-fresh replacement for the squadron. In this way the 81st became the first unit to have INS and other important features on all its aircraft.

Tactical Air Command added only one CONUS-based A-10 unit after 1978 – the 23rd TFW at England AFB, Louisiana. Together with the 354th TFW, then still at Myrtle Beach, the 23rd was assigned to TAC's primary role of rapid reinforcement worldwide. The 355th TTW was at Davis-Monthan and conducted all basic A-10 training for the USAF. Completing the regular A-10 force were three independent squadrons: one at Nellis AFB, one in Korea and one in Alaska.

AFRES and ANG
The balance of the A-10 force in CONUS was assigned to the US Air Force Reserve (AFRES), with four squadrons, and the Air National Guard (ANG) with five. With its moderate maintenance requirements, the A-10 was a logical choice for these forces. Both were manned by part-time volunteers and operated in a similar way, training on a regular schedule and participating in frequent exercises and other operations with regular USAF units. ANG and AFRES A-10 units were assigned to reinforce the 81st TFW in Europe in time of need, and deployed to Europe as often as budgets would permit.

Additionally, the 81st regularly exchanged pilots with the part-time units; the AFRES/ANG pilots directly involved gained experience in Europe, the pilots at the home bases gained by contact with the European-trained 81st TFW pilots, and the programme also gave the 81st TFW pilots the chance to take part in major exercises such as Red Flag.

The USAF had planned to acquire some 750 A-10As, and production reached a peak rate of 13 aircraft a month in 1980. However, Congressional budget cuts in 1982 reduced the service's production orders to 707 aircraft, excluding the two non-standard YA-10A prototypes and the six development aircraft. Fairchild completed its last contract for A-10As in February 1984.

The end of production came about despite efforts to expand the A-10 market. Fairchild leased an A-10 from the USAF in September 1976, to make the type's first appearance outside the USA at the Farnborough Air Show. An appearance at the Paris show in the following year ended disastrously on the opening day, when the A-10 failed to complete a loop under a low cloudbase and crashed, killing its pilot. But the USAF itself had not yet devised satisfactory tactics for the A-10, and although professional observers were impressed by the power of the GAU-8/A, little serious interest was forthcoming.

Two-seat A-10s
The longest and most costly campaign was aimed at developing the A-10 into a specialized night/adverse weather (N/AW) attack aircraft. While the USAF had no stated requirement for such an aircraft, there was enough interest to persuade Fairchild that a full-scale demonstration programme would be worthwhile. In late 1977 the company began to discuss such a programme with the USAF and avionics suppliers, and work started in April 1978, supported by USAF research and development money, Fairchild company funds and contributions of time and materiel from interested avionics suppliers.

The demonstrator was based on the first of the A-10 development aircraft, and the modification took only 13 months, the N/AW aircraft making its first flight on May 4, 1979. Provision for a second seat had been made in the original design: the second cockpit occupied the space above the ammunition drum, displacing a few avionics boxes, which were relocated in the fairing behind the canopy. The fins were increased in height by 20in (51cm) to compensate for the extra

Right: The shark's mouth nose markings made famous by the American Volunteer Group in China were adopted by the 23rd TFG that replaced it, and are still used by the 23rd TFW, one of only two A-10 combat wings based in the continental United States. The 23rd and 354th TFWs, along with the rest of TAC's combat wings, constitute the USAF's ready reserve element.

Above: The 118th TFS, 103rd TFG, Connecticut ANG, based at Bradley Field, is one of five Air National Guard squadrons equipped with the A-10.

Right: The USAF's other part-time volunteer element, the Air Force Reserve, has one training and four regular A-10 squadrons: the distinctive Warthog nose marking is the trademark of the 917th TFG.

side area, but the airframe was otherwise unchanged. The two-seater could be flown from either cockpit, with the elevated rear seat and back-up flight controls.

The most important feature of the aircraft, though, was a pair of pods housing a suite of avionic subsystems. Assembled from proven and available components, these were designed to allow precision attacks at night, en route navigation in weather at low level and, to some extent, precision attacks in adverse weather.

Equipment on the N/AW demonstrator included a modified Westinghouse WX-50 radar in an underwing pod. Based on a standard weather radar, it was modified to act as a short-range, multi-mode navigation and attack radar. It had three functions: simple mapping, terrain-avoidance and attack, and as an attack radar it was capable of picking out small moving targets on the ground. The second pod, on the centreline pylon, contained a Texas Instruments AAR-42 Flir and a Ferranti 105 laser designator, on a single mounting which could be steered to search for targets. A forward-

looking low-light TV system was mounted in place of the Pave Penny sensor, and a Litton LN-39 inertial navigation system completed the suite. The avionics fed a modified Kaiser A-10 HUD and a pair of cathode-ray-tube (CRT) displays in the rear cockpit.

The system was much simpler than that on a fast-mover night strike aircraft such as the F-111, because it was not automatic; with only half the speed, it did not need to be. And because it was not directly controlling the aircraft, the navigation/attack system did not have to be designed to be fully operational after a major failure, the single biggest complicating factor in the F-111 systems. The pilot flew the aircraft at all times, with the help of terrain-following radar (TFR) and Flir data, superimposed on the HUD to give a single picture with limited depth cues. The back-seat weapons system operator (WSO) would use the INS for en route navigation, and could use the Flir to search for targets to either side of the track; in that case, the pilot would use LLTV in place of Flir.

The WSO would operate guided weapons, and the pilot would carry out gun attacks. The concept of the two-seat aircraft was that the WSO would search for a second target as the pilot attacked

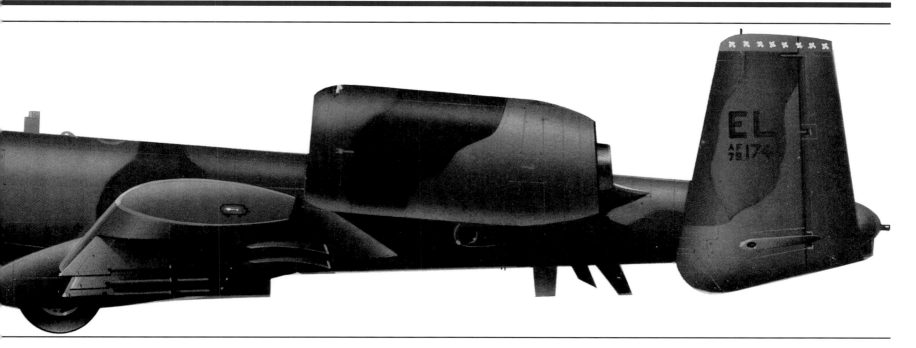

the first. The WSO would enter its exact coordinates on the INS, and the pilot would follow INS instructions for an accurate, first-pass attack. The laser would be used for accurate ranging and to designate targets for laser-guided bomb attacks.

The demonstrator was extensively evaluated during 1979-82, and just under 300 hours of testing proved that precision night attack was possible with the simple sensor fit. Fairchild proposed a production version, with the Flir and radar built into the landing gear pods, and the laser and LLTV installations buried in the wing leading edge. Avionics integration would have been more refined than on the 'breadboard' prototype. The N/AW aircraft would also have had a cleaner one-piece windshield and a single clamshell canopy, and the rear cockpit would have been protected by alloy/titanium/nylon side panels.

Night attack options

The N/AW A-10 would have cost $1.5 million more than the standard A-10A, and in 1979 Fairchild was offering new-built aircraft for delivery in early 1983. In retrospect, it is clear that this would have provided the USAF with a versatile nocturnal interdiction type much more quickly than any other programme. Fairchild also offered a number of cheaper options based on the demonstrator programme. One of these was a single-seat night attack (SSNA) configuration, with underwing Flir/laser and radar pods, as on the demonstrator, modified HUD and two head-down multifunction CRTs. There was also an 'austere' SSNA version with no radar, but with Flir/laser pod and INS for night attack on targets of known location, and an austere two-seater.

Unfortunately, all these A-10 variants were designed to do the same job as Lantirn, which was still scheduled to be available before 1985. Lantirn promised a great many advantages. Its high-technology features, such as its automatic target recognition system and advanced HUD, would provide all the performance of the fully-equipped two-seater, through a simple modification of the single-seat aircraft; one of the USAF's biggest reservations about the N/AW programme was that the WSO represented superfluous weight and cost on daytime missions and in some night operations in clear air. Lantirn, too, could be applied to the F-16 and F-15 as well as to the A-10.

Most of the USAF's testing of the de-

Left: Four A-10s of the 917th TFG, based at Barksdale AFB, Louisiana, participating in AFRES Aerials exercises over Texas.

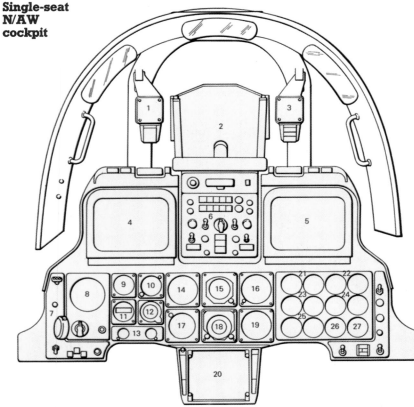

Single-seat N/AW cockpit

N/AW mission profile

Airbase or airborne orbit: crew given target description and location or general area

En route navigation checkpoints: navigation by INS, coordinates, map references and INS updates

Low-level penetration: INS updated, planned route adjusted if necessary in light of latest threat location information

Conversion to attack: pilot manoeuvres aircraft, using FLIR, Electronic Systems Operator monitors ground clearance and operates countermeasures systems

Minimum altitudes for N/AW low-level navigation: 300ft (90m) with two crew, FLIR and WX-50 multi-mode radar; 500ft (150m) with single crew, FLIR and WX-50 multi-mode radar; 650ft (200m) with FLIR and radar altimeter only

Target area search and target acquisition using FLIR and moving target indication radar

The cockpit proposed by Fairchild for the radar-equipped single-seat night attack A-10 would have allowed both fixed and moving targets to be attacked at night in low to moderate threat areas; an austere version without radar was also offered, as well as the two-seater.

1 Acceleration indicator
2 Head-up display
3 Standby compass
4 Left multifunction display
5 Right multifunction display
6 Display controls
7 Landing controls
8 Fuel quantity indicator
9 Angle of attack indicator
10 Clock
11 Channel frequency indicator
12 Standby attitude indicator
13 Hydraulics systems indicators
14 Airspeed indicator
15 Attitude director indicator
16 Barometric altitude indicator
17 Radar warning receiver azimuth indicator
18 Horizontal situation indicator
19 Vertical velocity indicator
20 Armament control panel
21 Engine temperature indicators
22 Engine fan RPM indicators
23 Engine core RPM indicators
24 Engine fuel flow indicators
25 Engine oil pressure indicators
26 Auxiliary power unit RPM indicator
27 Auxiliary power unit temperature indicator

Top: The two-seat night/adverse weather A-10 conversion prepares for a night takeoff with FLIR/laser pod under the fuselage and WX-50 radar pod under the port wing.

Above: Typical mission profile for a night/adverse weather attack in the A-10, with the avionics pods facilitating penetration, target acquisition and attack.

monstrator was dedicated to proving the service's contention that such a type could be operated successfully by a single pilot, as would be the case with

Lantirn. It was not until late 1981 that the DoD decided to delay production of Lantirn until the basic principles had been proven, and by that time the opportunity for the all-weather two-seat A-10 had passed. The USAF did order 30 two-seat A-10Bs in 1981, but these were to have been combat trainers with standard cockpits. They would have been used by AFRES and ANG units, but Congress cancelled funding for these aircraft and no A-10Bs were built. Fairchild did try to find export markets for the A-10 – such as Morocco, the target of extensive presentations – but the type was hampered by specialization; with fighter unit costs

climbing towards $20 million, few potential customers could afford economically sized fleets unless they standardized on a single type. The A-10's inability to take on the air-to-air role was apparent, while its sleek supersonic competitors could, at least, make an impressive show of putting bombs or A-model Mavericks on to simulated targets.

Soviet counterpart
The Su-25 was originally hailed as a copy of the A-10, but in fact it is a much faster aircraft, powered by two Soyuz R-955h turbojets. The aerodynamic configuration is very similar to that of the YA-

9A, with fuselage-mounted engines and a single fin and rudder. Dimensionally slightly smaller than the A-10, the Su-25 has a much lighter maximum takeoff weight, with similar installed power. Both wing and power loading are better than those of the A-10 at normal combat weights, and its combat cruising speed is considerably higher.

Frogfoot has no equivalent to the monster GAU-8 cannon of the Warthog; it carries a 30mm twin-barrel GSh-2-30 cannon with 250 standard API and HEI rounds. Typically it carries laser-guided air-to-surface missiles, cluster weapons, and iron bombs, with two R-60 AAMs for

Right: The first of the development batch of A-10s was converted to the two-seat configuration, making its first flight in May 1979. Although the extended capabilities of the N/AW version were impressive, the Air Force expected Lantirn to enable one man to do the job, and the A-10B made no further progress. The production version would have had the avionics incorporated in the landing gear pods and wing leading edge.

Above: First flying in February 1975, the Su-25 was at first thought to be a Soviet copy of the A-10, but is more similar aerodynamically to the YA-9A, and its mission is more focused on close air support than on tankbusting.

Above right: The N/AW A-10 was tested for nearly 300 hours between and 1982, successfully demonstrating its ability to carry out precision attacks at night.

self-defence.

Interestingly, Frogfoots in Afghanistan were observed practising joint tactics with Mi-24 Hind attack helicopters, just as A-10s practise with US Army gunships.

Export attempt

The last battle to save the A-10 was mounted in 1982-83, when the type was proposed to several nations as a multi-role 'flying artillery' system, useful against many targets other than tanks. Following the Falklands war, Fairchild pushed the use of the A-10 as a maritime strike aircraft, particularly in areas such as South-East Asia. Equipped with the WX-50 radar, already tested on the N/AW demonstrator, and exploiting its long endurance, the A-10 could have proved a useful maritime strike weapon, carrying missiles such as Harpoon or Exocet. Air battles in the Falklands and Middle East, too, had shown the effectiveness of the new 'point-and-shoot' AIM-9L missile, and Fairchild's simulations demonstrated that the A-10 would defeat most opponents if armed with a weapon in that class.

At the 1983 Paris Air Show, Fairchild salesmen did their best to sound optimistic. Three customers, two in the Middle East and one in South-East Asia, were

Air Combat Command			
Unit	Name	Base	Tailcode
23rd Wing	74th FS Tigers	Pope, NC	FT
	75th FS Sharks		
57th Wing	FWS	Nellis, NV	
347th Wing	70th FS White Knights	Moody, GA	MY
355th Wing	354th FS Eagles	Davis - Monthan, AX	DM
	357th FS Dragons		
	358th FS Lobos		
Air Force Materiel Command			
46th Test Wing		Eglin, FL	ET
Air Force Reserve Command			
	47th FS Terrible Termites	Barksdale, LO	BD
	303rd FS	Whiteman, Mo	KC
Air National Guard			
	103rd FS Black Hogs	Willow Grove, Penn	PA
	104th FS Liberati in Promptu	Baltimore, MD	MD
	118th FS Flying Yankees	Bradley, CN	CT
	131st FS Death Vipers	Barnes, Mass	MA
	172nd FS	Battle Creek, Mi	BC
Pacific Air Forces			
51st Wing	75th FS Dragons	Osan, RoK	OS
354th Wing	355th FS Falcons	Eielson, AK	AK
USAFE			
52nd Wing	81st FS Panthers	Spangdahlem, GY	SP

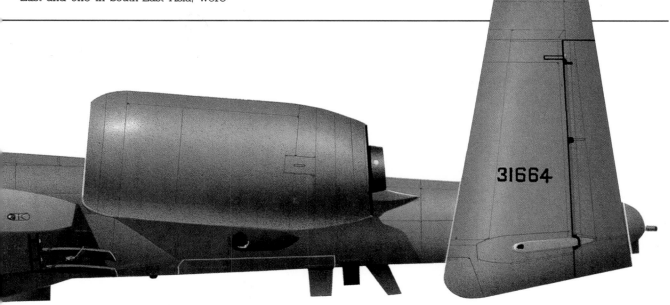

leading candidates for A-10 sales. The type was seen as a useful complement to an interceptor such as the F-5E, and Fairchild expected to sell 70-80 aircraft in 1983-85. At the same time, in Washington, the company and its Congressional friends were making a final and unsuccessful attempt to reverse the 1982 production cutback and keep the line open until export orders could be secured.

One Fairchild man at Paris gave a penetrating analysis of the factors favouring and hampering his company's sales efforts. "Essentially, our competitors are fighters which could cost twice as much as an A-10," he told Dave Griffiths of the US publication *Defense Week*, but went on to define what was probably the A-10's biggest negative in the export market: "Of course, a Mach 2 plane is sexier, and some pilots may think hitting ground targets is a grunt's job." Even more accurately, the executive added: "If there were any armies in the world that had their own tactical aviation, they'd love the A-10." Unhappily for Fairchild, and, perhaps, unhappily for the 'grunt' in the field, soldiers seldom if ever have any say in buying fighters.

Performance and Tactics

Although the A-10 concept was born of the Vietnam experience, its tactics were amended to suit conditions in the projected "worst case" scenario: a massive armoured attack across Western Europe by Warsaw Pact forces. This involved making the greatest possible use of cover – hills, trees, buildings etc.— and carefully coordinating attacks with battlefield helicopters. It therefore came as a culture shock when in 1991, A-10s found themselves operating over the flat wastes of the Iraqi desert.

January 25, 1979, was an English winter day like most others. There was a penetratingly damp chill in the air, and the overcast hung over RAF Bentwaters like an inverted bowl of frozen porridge. It was on this uncompromisingly European day that the A-10A arrived in Europe as an operational fighting aircraft.

It is not considered gentlemanly to cast aspersions upon an ally's newest weapon system, but concern over the effectiveness of the A-10 in Europe had reached very high levels in the NATO command structure. The USAF A-10s would replace McDonnell Douglas F-4C/D Phantoms. These were not the newest types in service, and were certainly not designed for blind precision attacks, but they had two seats, inertial navigation systems and secondary air-

Below: An 81st TFW pilot demonstrates the Warthog's surprising agility: the same degree of manoeuvrability, translated to low levels, is the key to the A-10's ability to survive combat in high-threat areas.

defence capability, and the back-seater was available to operate the whole range of first-generation targeting pods and guided weapons.

All NATO's senior air officers had seen films of A-10s delivering deadly, accurate anti-tank attacks from the gin-clear skies of Nevada, and most of them were not convinced that the same effect could be achieved in Europe, which is dark for 19 hours of the day in winter and overcast more often than not. The same officers had been briefed on the A-10's ability to withstand multiple hits from 23mm shells; they were also well aware of the existence of the Soviet SA-8 Gecko missile system, which had made its public debut in 1975. Generally, the feeling was that the European air forces had managed to prevent the USAF from fielding the F-16 in a form ideally suited to a central front in Vietnam or, preferably, Nevada, but that they might have failed to do so in the case of the A-10.

The controversy over the A-10 has remained active, and has kept the pressure on TAC to devise effective tactics

against the changing threat, and demonstrate how they would be used in action. Certainly, the way in which the A-10 is used in training and exercises today is very different from the projections of the A-X planners. But it is also true that current A-10 tactics exploit virtually all the unique features of the aircraft; and even if some things might have been done differently had the present mission been envisaged from the outset, the A-10 is available, works well and is no sense inadequate for its mission.

The threats

The concept and design of the A-10 were based on an accurate perception of Soviet military equipment and tactics in the late 1960s. (In this, at least, the Warthog is one up on the aristocratic F-15 Eagle, which was strongly influenced by an immensely flattering assessment of the MiG-25 Foxbat). The primary attack weapon was the tank, used in large concentrations and dedicated to the advance. Unlike contemporary Western tank units, Soviet armoured

Above: Although ostensibly lacking in glamour, the A-10 mission is one of the most demanding in the USAF – and one of the most sought-after by pilots.

Flight envelope

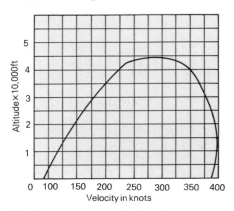

Performance graph for the A-10 in standard day conditions, at a design weight of 31,170lb (14,138kg), with six pylons fitted and at maximum thrust.

Turn performance

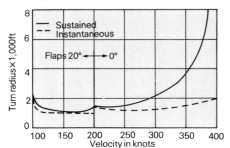

Standard day sustained and instantaneous turn rates for an A-10 with six Mk 82 bombs for a weight of 31,000lb (14,061kg) at 5,000ft (1,524m).

Load factors

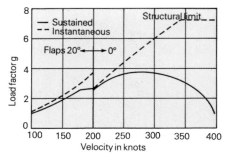

Maximum load factors in standard day conditions at an altitude of 5,000ft with six Mk 82 bombs for a gross weight of 31,000lb (14,061kg).

formations carried their own air defence systems. The most formidable of these was the ZSU-23-4 Shilka, a close-range defence weapon with no direct equivalent in the West.

The Shilka is designed to run with the tanks, on a PT-76 tracked amphibious chassis. It is armed with four 23mm cannon, with a total firing rate of 4,000 rounds/min, carries a great deal of ammunition and features liquid-cooled gun barrels, so it can sustain high rates of fire over a relatively long period. Considering the effectiveness of much less sophisticated light AAA over Vietnam, it was understandable that TAC perceived the Shilka system as a prime threat in the CAS arena long before its combat debut in 1973.

The threat from Soviet aircraft was not considered to be much of a problem for A-X in the late 1960s. Soviet air-to-air fighters were used defensively, to protect airbases and rear-area assets. TAC's fighter squadrons were equipped to keep the skies cleared over friendly ground all the time, and over hostile ground where necessary. A-X was not intended to penetrate far beyond the FLOT (forward line of own troops), and any encounters with MiGs would be accidental. However, the threat of aircraft or missile attack on airbases, particularly those closest to the battle line, was certainly present.

Tactical concepts
The A-10 was designed and equipped with European weather in mind, contrary to some opinion. But it was designed to cope with weather in a com-

pletely different way from an F-111 or Tornado. The theory was that zero-zero weather – no ceiling and no horizontal visibility – was not only rare but would halt all military operations, so there was no need for such extreme in-weather capability in a CAS type. Instead, the A-X was planned to operate under, rather than in, the weather and in reduced visibility.

Low ceilings and poor visibility are a cage for the fighter pilot. Unknown terrain lurks beyond the limits of visibility, and, as pilots say, the ground has a kill probability of 1.0. The ceiling is not dangerous in itself, but is a one-way exit from the air-to-ground fight. The pilot loses his target, and has to find a hole in the cloud if he is to descend and rejoin battle. The A-10 was designed to manoeuvre and fight visually within this confined space.

The A-10 is not a high-g, high-powered aircraft, but the one thing that it can do better than any supersonic fighter is turn at low speeds. A fighter like the F-16 is designed to catch a victim or lose an attacker in a turn, and does it with brute power installed in the lightest possible airframe. Low speeds represent loss of energy, and are avoided at all costs. The A-10 is different in concept. Low turning airspeeds are accepted, because air combat capability is not required. Because the airspeed is low, the

Above: Medium-altitude Maverick launch from the lead ship of a standard two-aircraft formation. The threat level in Europe forced a revision of the tactical concepts.

Below: From target recognition to Maverick launch takes the same time, during which the fast-mover gets much closer to the target and its associated defensive systems.

A-10/F-16 Maverick attack ranges

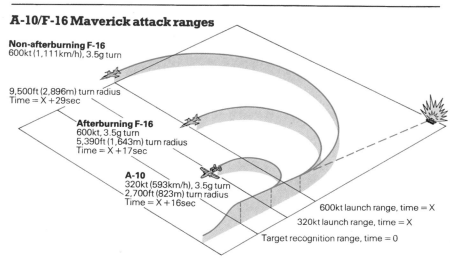

Non-afterburning F-16
600kt (1,111km/h), 3.5g turn

9,500ft (2,896m) turn radius
Time = X +29sec

Afterburning F-16
600kt, 3.5g turn
5,390ft (1,643m) turn radius
Time = X +17sec

A-10
320kt (593km/h), 3.5g turn
2,700ft (823m) turn radius
Time = X +16sec

600kt launch range, time = X
320kt launch range, time = X
Target recognition range, time = 0

A-10 can attain a high rate of turn, in degrees/sec, without the high g forces that would be associated with the same rate at higher speeds. Low airspeed and high turn rate combine to give a small turning radius; the first lesson in geometry states that the circumference of the turn, the distance which the aircraft actually travels, is smaller too. The aircraft will therefore take less time to complete its turn.

Translating theory into fact, it is paradoxical but true that the A-10 will out-turn even an F-16 in full afterburner when the two aircraft are carrying similar loads. At 320kt (590km/h) and 3.5g, the A-10 can complete a half-turn, radius 2,700ft (824m), in 16 seconds. The F-16, at 600kt (1,110km/h) and 6g, makes a 3,620ft (1,043m) turn, and takes 17 seconds.

It is because of this emphasis on a quick turn rather than a fast turn that the A-10 can fight in the cage – the limited volume defined by ceiling and visibility. Early operational tests with the A-10 showed that this concept worked, and that the A-10 pilot could run into the target area, identify a pinpoint target, turn and attack it under a 1,000ft (305m) ceiling, with 1.5-2 miles (2.4-3.2km) visibility. Even in a European midwinter, TAC's records showed, similar or better

conditions could be expected, on average, for eight hours a day.

By contrast, the apparently better equipped F-4D could not venture below the clouds unless the ceiling was at least 3,000ft (915m) and visibility 3 miles (4.8km). Conditions that good are encountered, on average, only four hours a day in midwinter, and only six hours a day from the beginning of November to the end of February. And as any European knows, the daily weather pattern does not conform to some arbitrary seasonal average. The difference between the A-10 and the fast mover could amount to weeks on end in which the A-10 would be the only aircraft that could attack ground targets at all.

Another objective set down by the original A-X philosophy was quick reaction, to be attained by a number of means. Airborne loiter was among the most important. The A-10 was designed to be launched from a relatively safe base, 250nm (460km) behind the battle line, and loiter for two hours before carrying out an attack. This meant that the A-10 could, in theory, be used on the 'cabrank' principle developed by the 2nd Tactical Air Force in Western Europe in 1944-45. A-10s would be launched at regular intervals and join a loose traffic pat-

Below: Medium-altitude loiter, World War II style, was out of the question in the context of NATO's Central Front, but could still have applications in low-threat environments.

Designed close air support mission

1.88hr loiter
174kt (322km/h)
5,000ft (1,524m)

Return cruise at 286kt (530km/h) and 35,000ft (10,668m)

20min sea level loiter at 130kt (241km/h)

Cruise out at 296kt (549km/h) and 25,000ft (7,620m)

10min combat 300kt (556km/h) at sea level

250nm (463km)

Takeoff weight 46,196lb (20,954kg)
18 Mk 82 LDGP bombs, max 30mm ammunition

Terrain following at high and low speeds

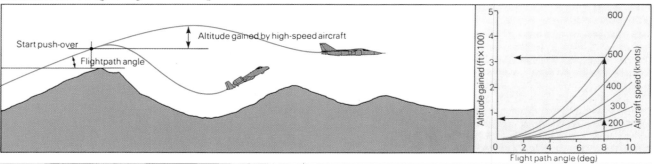

Above: While the A-10 at 300kt (555km/h) gains a modest 80ft (24m) in the push-over, an F-111 in hard-ride terrain-following mode climbs a dangerous 330ft (100m).

SA-8 avoidance tactics

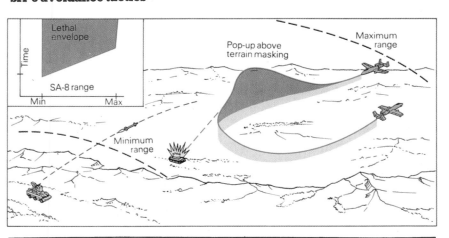

Left: The deployment of the Soviet SA-8 surface-to-air-missile with armoured columns contributed to a major rethink of CAS tactics.

Above: The A-10 returns to terrain masking after the attack in less time than it takes the SA-8 to acquire its target, lock on and launch.

tern, the 'cab-rank', behind the battle line. They could respond immediately to any call for support, while other A-10s would be launched to relieve aircraft on the rank after their two hours on station expired.

In combat, the A-10 was designed to be relatively invulnerable to light AAA or shoulder-fired SAMs. Heavier SAMs presented a different type of threat. In the late 1960s these did not travel with the main armoured force, and if they were encountered in the CAS zone, would have been emplaced in a hurry. Moreover, the A-10's manoeuvrability would enable it to stay below the minimum altitudes of such weapons, and inside their minimum range, as it roamed around the battlefield shooting tanks.

The foregoing represents a brief summary of A-10 tactics as they were envis-

ZSU-23-4 avoidance tactics

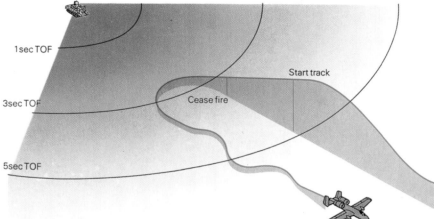

3sec linear flight path from
start track to cease fire;
open fire after 1.5sec

1sec TOF

3sec TOF

Start track

Cease fire

5sec TOF

TOF: Time of flight of ZSU-23-4 projectile

Left: At GAU-8/A range, the Warthog can carry out its attack and be back under the Shilka's minimum elevation before the deadly stream of 23mm projectiles can reach it.

Below left: The ZSU-23-4, seen here in Polish army service, was always considered a major threat, but its lethality was not fully appreciated until the 1973 Arab-Israeli war.

(1,110km/h); the A-10 attacks at barely more than half that speed, being capable of 325kt (602km/h) with a typical weapons load. TAC and Fairchild contended, however, that when the A-10 was properly used it could survive against Soviet-built defensive systems, and fare better than any other aircraft. Tactics were presumably evaluated not only against simulated former Soviet systems on the USAF's Nevada ranges, but also against the real thing: captured SA-8s and Shilkas, and clandestinely obtained MiG-23s, were all available at this time.

The first point made by the A-10's advocates is that in the battle area, where the A-10s operate, the air defence system is not operating at peak efficiency. Firing positions will have been selected under pressure, on unfamiliar ground, and fields of fire of the different systems will not overlap in the optimum pattern. Communications, command and control will all be degraded to some extent. Even the advancing second echelon is subject to similar pressures.

Another important observation is that a Mach 0.9 speed is not a primary defence against a Mach 2.3 missile, let alone a Mach 3 shell. The only benefit of speed itself is to reduce the time in which an aircraft is exposed to defensive systems on a given flightpath. It is also a factor in generating high crossing rates relative to the defensive weapon's sightline.

Under some circumstances, higher speed may actually militate against the best defensive tactic, which is to interpose a hill between the gun or SAM system and the target. TAC has been a late but enthusiastic convert to the doctrine of very-low-level flight, and A-10 units are the command's leading exponents of the tactic. Once again, it is the A-10's ability to manoeuvre hard at low airspeeds that is important. Cruising at its normal and most efficient speed, the A-10 can make sharp flightpath changes without incurring as much g as a faster aircraft following the same trajectory. Clearing the top of a hill, the A-10 will have less upward momentum than the faster aircraft, and can descend more rapidly on the other side without en-

Below: Warthog pilots do not consider MiGs a major threat: they can turn more quickly, and their guns are very effective against aircraft.

Above: Manoeuvrability at low altitudes allows the A-10 to exploit natural cover to the full, allowing air defences only the briefest glimpse of its armoured form.

aged in the early days of the programme. It is probably fair to say that most of them were completely invalidated by the time the A-10 came to Europe at the beginning of 1979. There were at least three critical factors which were not anticipated in the formulation of the A-X requirement, and between them they have made life a great deal more difficult for the A-10.

New threats

One factor was the performance of the ZSU-23-4. It was known to be a dangerous system, but its lethality was not fully appreciated until the Arab-Israeli war of 1973. The projectile is nearly twice as heavy as that of the M61A-1 Vulcan, at 0.41lb (0.19kg), and muzzle velocity is a respectable 3,200ft/sec (970m/sec). More importantly, however, the barrel cooling and other features give the four-barrel mount a very low dispersion. Combined with the sustained 4,000rds/min rate of fire, this makes the ability to withstand one or two 23mm strikes more or less academic. Like the GAU-8/A, the Shilka tends to hit its targets more than once or twice, and the effects have been compared to those of a rotary saw. The Shilka's effectiveness drops off very sharply beyond about 3,000-3,300ft (920-1,000m), but this certainly does not mean that the threat which it poses can be ignored.

The West got another unpleasant surprise in 1975, with the unveiling of the Soviet SA-8 Gecko mobile SAM system. Western experts had expected the Soviet Union to field a new short-range SAM. It would be much more effective

than a pursuit-course heat-seeking weapon, but it would be more mobile than the bigger SA-6 system, which is carried on two vehicles, and it would have a shorter minimum range and lower minimum altitude. Everyone assumed, though, that the Soviets would design a small, simple system like the Roland or Rapier. Instead, they adapted the design of a sophisticated naval missile, the SA-N-4.

The SA-8 is a heavy, complex system, indicating its importance in Soviet planning and tactics. Mounted on a specially developed 25-30 ton (27.5-33 tonne) wheeled vehicle, the SA-8 system is complete with surveillance and tracking radar, and two independent high-power, narrow-beam radio command links. If radar is jammed or ineffective for other reasons, SA-8 has an electro-optical tracking and guidance system which can launch two missiles at a target, each with its own guidance frequency. The round is considerably larger than those used by Western fully mobile systems, and carries a 110lb (50kg) blast-fragmentation warhead. The initial SA-8 configuration carried four missiles, but the improved SA-8B carries six, in sealed box launchers.

A third unexpected development was the extremely rapid introduction into service of the MiG-23 Flogger B/G fighter. The MiG-23 itself had been seen in 1967, but Western intelligence – hypnotised by the MiG-25 – failed to appreciate its importance to Soviet tactical air power. Production accelerated at breakneck speed in 1972-75, in parallel with development of its new radar and missile armament. Not a dogfighter, but fast, heavily armed and comprehensively equipped, Flogger B/G was the first Soviet fighter designed to carry the air war into NATO's territory, beyond the reach of ground control.

The effect of these three developments on planned A-10 tactics was profound. The A-10 pilot was supposed to identify and select his target on the first pass, keep it in sight in a tight turn and attack on a second pass. Against Shilkas and SA-8s, this would be suicide. The aggressive MiG-23, meanwhile, put an end to the absolute security of airspace over friendly ground: so much for loiter and transit at medium altitudes. Between 1975 and 1979 the ground rules of A-10 operation were completely rewritten to cope with the changing threats while still exploiting the unique attributes of the aircraft. The changes affected survival and defensive tactics, attack profiles and targeting, and operational deployment.

Tactics for survival

Survivability has been at the centre of the A-10 controversy. The aircraft has most often been criticized on account of its speed. Most NATO strike aircraft are designed to attack at speeds of 600kt

Survival against interceptors

A-10 Thunderbolt II

Battlefield air support mission

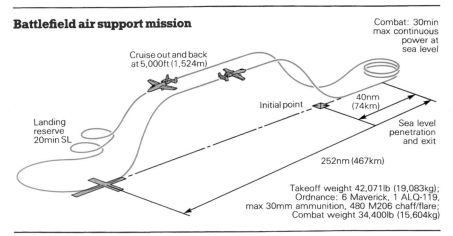

Cruise out and back at 5,000ft (1,524m)

Landing reserve 20min SL

Initial point

Combat: 30min max continuous power at sea level

40nm (74km)

Sea level penetration and exit

252nm (467km)

Takeoff weight 42,071lb (19,083kg); Ordnance: 6 Maverick, 1 ALQ-119, max 30mm ammunition, 480 M206 chaff/flare; Combat weight 34,400lb (15,604kg)

Above: Revised A-10 tactics emphasise sea-level penetration and combat in the face of the intense air defenses likely to be encountered.

Right: In battle, this would almost certainly be an opposing tank commander's last view of an A-10 – or anything else.

countering excessive levels of negative g. (Faster aircraft can, of course, roll inverted and pull their way around the top of the hill under positive g, but this tactic is only recommended if you are absolutely certain that the terrain does fall away on the opposite side of the crest.)

The A-10's small turning radius gives it a wider choice of tracks across uneven terrain which may not give a faster aircraft room to change course, and its low speed gives the pilot more time to plan the next manoeuvre. Light and natural handling takes a further weight off the pilot's mind.

At these low speeds, the A-10 can actually pull higher g than an F-16 in similar trim. When both aircraft are loaded for anti-armour operations, the A-10 can sustain a 3.25g turn at 250-300kt (460-555km/h). The F-16 can only match this performance with the use of reheat, and on dry thrust can manage only 2-2.5g in the same speed range. On dry thrust it can match the A-10's performance only by speeding up above 400kt (740km/h) and accepting a larger turning radius.

It is true that a fast-mover attack aircraft can follow terrain at reduced speeds and emulate some of the A-10's tactics. The snag is that only the A-10 and its engines are designed for such speeds. Fast-movers do not usually reduce their speed, because by doing so they drop out of their efficient cruising regime and suffer unacceptable warload/radius penalties. It is this consideration that makes the A-10's performance unique.

A-10s have been operated successfully by service pilots at average altitudes of 100ft (30m) above ground level, although most training is carried out at higher altitudes, mainly because of peacetime restrictions. Slightly higher altitudes are acceptable where the threat comes from Floggers rather than SAMs, but on the final run to the target the A-10s fly substantially lower than any other fixed-wing aircraft.

Low-level operation protects the A-10 in a number of ways. Simply concealing the aircraft for as long as possible from the sightline of the defensive system is one of them. Fairchild studies show that in hilly terrain, such as the Fulda Gap in West Germany, a ZSU-23-4 can engage targets in just 22 per cent of the area covered by its effective range if the target stays below 200ft (61m).

Again, one of the defender's advantages is the ability to see and identify the attcking aircraft before its pilot can pick out a SAM or gun system among ground clutter and other targets, but this 'first-look' advantage can be wiped out if the aircraft breaks cover at close quarters. With radar-guided or command-guided systems such as the SA-8, low flying also reduces the SAM's advantage due to

greater maximum range. Also, such weapons are not 'fire and forget' – they need a certain amount of time to lock on, fire a missile and guide it to the target. Breaking ground cover at the last moment, and returning to it as soon as possible, gives the operator the shortest possible time to engage the target.

Even with a target in sight, extremely low altitudes present problems for SAMs. Simple IR-homing SAMs have to be launched at a minimum elevation angle, because of their short range and their tendency to fly into the ground. Their effective envelope is shaped like an inverted cone with its apex at the launch point, and the lower an aircraft flies, the shorter its flightpath through the cone. An aircraft flying at 300kt (555km/h), 100ft (30m) over a SAM with a 20deg minimum launch elevation – typical of unsophisticated weapons – will be in and out of the operator's launch window in less than one second.

Radar-guided SAMs have other limitations, and can be confused by a very-low-altitude target. Radar signals bounce off a target in all directions, and will be reflected again when they strike the ground. Usually, such echoes will be well outside the narrow cone of a missile tracking beam, and will not be detected by the radar's receiver. But if the aircraft's altitude is less than twice the width of the beam, the ground echoes will be close enough to create false targets on the radar screen. Multiple echoes are another problem which increases with low altitude.

Operation at very low altitudes also protects the A-10, to some extent, from 'snapdown' attacks by MiG-23s or similar aircraft firing IR or semi-active radar-guided missiles from higher altitudes. The latest Flogger G variant is considered to have "some look-down/shoot-down capability" according to the US Department of Defense, and this implies that its High Lark radar and AA-7 Apex missile would be of limited use against a small target 100ft (30m) off the ground.

IR missiles such as the AA-8 Aphid, also carried by the MiG-23, are probably of little use against an A-10 at a lower altitude than the launch aircraft. Such all-aspect IR missiles home on the heat energy generated by friction between an airframe and the air. The A-10 is slow and relatively small, and is therefore a weak target, and the sensitivity of an IR missile is limited; if the seeker is too sensitive, it will lock on to false targets on the ground. While low-level operation does not provide a complete defence against fighters, it does mean that if the MiG-23s want to shoot down the A-10s they probably have to come down to the A-10's level to do it.

The main disadvantage of low-level operation is probably the great stress

Low-level gunnery

Above: Spending most of its time less than 100ft (30m) above the ground, the A-10 pops up to between 200ft (60m) and 500ft (150m) to destroy tanks with brief bursts of gunfire.

Below: The same terrain-masking and three-dimensional jinking are employed in the run-up to a Maverick delivery from 500ft (150m); a cloud base of 1,000ft (300m) is no problem.

Low-level Maverick delivery

which it places on the pilot. This has been a major factor in the abandonment of the cab-rank loiter concept. Loitering at medium altitudes is unsafe, but the physical and mental demands of flight among the treetops at 300kt (555km/h) make it inadvisable to add two hours to the mission. At that point, pilot fatigue could become a limiting factor on a squadron's ability to sustain its readiness to fight.

In combat, the A-10 is to survive partly by means of its manoeuvrability, and partly by its ability to counter-attack, with the help of its built-in and podded EW and decoys. The basic attack manoeuvre in the SA-8 era is the pop-up, or, in TAC argot, the 'bunt-up', in which the aircraft emerges from the protection of terrain, engages its target, attacks and dives back into cover.

Once again, the most important characteristic is not high speed, but low exposure time; if it is shorter than the time that the SA-8 takes to engage and hit the target, the missile operator can do nothing. The A-10's ability to manoeuvre in small radii and short time is its main asset here. Its lower speed means that it can drop back into cover at a higher descent rate than a fast jet: in a bunt, or negative-g pushover, the limiting factor is pilot tolerance rather than aircraft power, so the g force will be the same, and the slower aircraft will follow a steeper and shorter downward trajectory.

Speed is also of secondary importance in avoiding hits after a weapon has been fired at the aircraft, because any sophisticated defensive system can measure speed accurately and compensate for it. (In deference to the fast mover, it should be noted that sheer speed does reduce the time in which the target is within the lethal envelope, all other things being equal.) In the case of guns and radar-guided SAMs, however, it is possible to 'generate miss distance'. Translated, this means that when the projectile arrives where the fire-control system says the target ought to be, it is safest for the target to be somewhere else.

A common weakness of both guns and command-guided SAMs is that they work on a projection of where the target will be in one or two seconds' time, rather than shooting at its present position. This is commonsense in the case of the gun, with its dumb, unguided projectile, and less obvious in the case of the missile; but even the missile system takes a finite amount of time to detect the movement of the target, process the movement into a command signal and transmit it to the missile. Then, the missile control surfaces move, and – not quite immediately – the missile's flight-path will begin to change according to the target's motion. Unless some degree of prediction is built into the system, the combined delay will be enough to guide the missile behind the target.

The Shilka's fire-control system assumes that the aircraft will continue on a straight path at constant speed, and the SA-8 system probably does the same. The rate at which the target can diverge from that straight path is largely a matter of the g force which it can generate: in this case, the important parameter is instantaneous, short-period g rather than sustained g, because evading instant destruction is a great deal more important than preserving energy or avoiding a stall. Loaded for air-to-ground operations, the A-10 can pull as much instantaneous g as most other aircraft.

In the case of the gun, the miss distance will be a function of g and the firing

Left: Even during the brief periods when the A-10 might be exposed to fire, its structure makes it uniquely able to survive major damage.

range. At 300kt (460km/h), and with a five-second flight time for the shell, the gun will miss by 1,310ft (400m). In a missile attack, the important factors are g and the distance between the aircraft and the missile when the manoeuvre starts. According to Fairchild figures, apparently based on SA-8 characteristics, a 4g manoeuvre, initiated when the missile is 12,000ft (3,660m) away, will cause the weapon to miss by 500ft (150m); not much, but better than nothing.

Tactics such as these would be used in conjunction with the A-10's countermeasure systems. Chaff would be dropped during a bunt-up manoeuvre, to keep multiple false returns coming into the hostile radar as the A-10 itself leaves the safety of the low-level confusion zone. The ALQ-119 pod and the chaff clouds can degrade the SA-8 command link, even if the system reverts to electro-optical tracking. Flares would be used during the bunt-up, to create similar multiple-target problems for IR missiles.

The A-10 carries no specifically defensive armament, although trials have shown that an advanced IR missile such as the AIM-9L Sidewinder would be a formidable addition to its armoury. The AIM-9L is a particularly good match for the A-10. Its critical advantage over earlier weapons is that it can lock on to a target from almost any direction. This eliminates the need for the classic tail-chase, in which the attacker tries to manoeuvre into the enemy's rear quarter. Instead, the advantage goes to the aircraft which can swing its nose on to the target most rapidly, and at low altitude this will usually be the A-10. Even without

the AIM-9L, though, the instant fire-power of the GAU-8/A, coupled with the A-10's rapid turn ability, make the Warthog a dangerous beast to tackle.

In particular, the effective range of the GAU-8/A has been shown to be greater than that of the Shilka, and the USAF's A-10 weapons school at Nellis AFB teaches the use of the GAU-8/A to suppress the Soviet gun in a classic High Noon shoot-out. The attack starts with a bunt-up, which takes the A-10 to the Shilka's maximum range. The Shilka starts tracking and fires, while the A-10 simultaneously enters a three-second diving attack, including a two-second burst from the cannon. At the point which the Shilka's projectiles will reach three seconds after firing, and just before the first rounds arrive, the A-10 breaks and heads for cover, and the shells miss. By that time, the first of the 130-plus shells

fired by the A-10 will be hitting the vehicle. This tactic was first demonstrated at Nellis AFB in February 1979 against a simulated Soviet tank battalion array, including four Shilkas. Two pairs of A-10s from 422 TFW attacked the formation, killed the Shilkas and, in four minutes, killed 23 tanks.

In the air-to-air regime the A-10 is, technically speaking, unarmed, because it has no way of aiming the cannon against a rapidly crossing target. But the first A-10 pilots to engage in dissimilar air combat training simply disregarded this factor and followed their instincts, pulling the quickest possible turn and spraying the adversary with simulated GAU-8/A fire. The 'Warthog stomp' has since proved extremely effective. In 57 sorties flown by the USAF's Aggressor unit at Nellis against A-10s, the A-10s survived as long as they saw their attack-

ers. Only once, when an A-10 was attacked by two F-5Es, did an A-10 pilot even have to jettison external weapons.

In more recent Red Flag exercises, even the most manoeuvrable fighters have found it advisable to avoid close-quarters engagements with the A-10s, preferring a less effective but safer shoot-down pass from above. A-10s enjoy a special exception from the Red Flag safety rule which prohibits close-quarters head-on attacks, and are permitted to close to 1,000ft (305m) before breaking off.

In action, the A-10s would usually have the advantage of sighting the enemy first. The MiG-23's High Lark radar would give advance warning of an attack and its direction, via the A-10's radar-warning system, while the A-10 itself has no emitting devices to give its location away to a Sirena 3 or similar Soviet radar-warning

Right: Conus-based A-10 units train for worldwide deployment and a variety of threat levels: the 354th TFW uses a 300 acre (120 hectare) wooded area of its South Carolina base for realistic training for Europe.

device. The aircraft are difficult to spot against the ground in their subfusc green finish – one operational problem is that A-10 pilots have been known to lose sight of their wingmen – while any attacker will be outlined against the sky. The problems presented by snap-down attacks against the A-10 have already been mentioned, so any combat will take place at low level. In all, according to Brig.Gen.Rudolph Wacker, the commander of the Europe-based A-10 force in August 1979, "At the altitudes we expect to fly, enemy interceptors pose almost a negligible threat. Interestingly,' he continued, "a careless interceptor pilot quickly changes from the hunter to hunted, and generally will find himself outmanoeuvred by the A-10, and always outgunned."

Trained in low-level tactics, schooled to take advantage of every chink in the defences, and equipped with their jamming and decoy suites, the A-10 units have become confident that their ability to survive is as great as that of any other system in clear air above a European battlefield. The controversy over the A-10 has receded, and its unique place within the NATO Central Region line-up is beginnng to be appreciated.

In current thinking, the most important of the A-10's attributes is its ability to sustain combat. Against armour, its firepower is more than twice that of any other aircraft in the TAC inventory. With 1,174 GAU-8/A rounds and six Mavericks, the A-10 can deliver 16 lethal anti-armour attacks in a single mission, or even more given efficient use of the GAU-8/A. No other type can deliver more than six Mavericks, or is armed with an effective anti-armour gun.

The A-10 can also stay in combat longer than other types, even though they may appear to have a superior range on paper. As noted earlier, an A-10 can sustain a higher turn rate than an F-16 with a comparable ordnance load, unless the

Above: During annual Thunderhog exercises, the 354th TFW uses its 'European' environment to simulate deployment, complete with all supporting elements, to austere forward operating locations.

Right and below: A-10s are also based in Alaska with the 18th TFS, 343rd Composite Wing, at Eielson AFB. During Exercise Cool Snow Hog 82-1, held at Kotzebue Air Station, this Warthog was given an unusual black and white paint scheme for evaluation purposes. The A-10s of Alaskan Air Command, along with a squadron of O-2A forward air control aircraft, provide the primary air support for the US Army's ground forces stationed in the Alaska defence region.

F-16 uses reheat; but the use of reheat is highly demanding of fuel. Again, with a comparable ordnance load and the same mission profile, the F-16 comes close to the A-10's radius of action, but only if it uses dry thrust exclusively in the combat area. Two minutes of combat afterburner are enough to cut the F-16's operational radius to 60 per cent of the A-10's. Four minutes of afterburner, and the F-16 can go only 40 per cent as far. With its typical anti-armour ordnance load, an ALQ-119 pod, a full load of 480 decoys and full internal fuel, the A-10 can fly 252nm (466km) to the target, including 40nm (74km) at low level, and remain in the fight, on full power, for 30 minutes.

While that mission is an indicator of the A-10's performance, it is not typical of the way the A-10 would be used in service, because one of the type's other attributes – an unusual one, but not quite unique – gives the commander a better option. The quality in queston is the A-10's ability to operate from short strips and rudimentary bases. Supersonic fighters, in general, still need 8,000-10,000ft (2,440-3,050m) of concrete for normal operations. The A-10, with full fuel and weapons, can take off in 3,600ft (1,097m) and land in 1,140ft (347m).

The landing distance is particularly significant. Combined with the A-10's slow approach speed and docile handling, it means that the aircraft can be recovered safely on a short strip with a large safety margin. Even with reduced hydraulic power, no flaps or a fatigued pilot, the A-10 can recover to a 4,000ft (1,200m) strip with no trouble at all, and without using an emergency arrester hook.

Forward operating locations
At the same time, the A-10's simplicity, and the absence of any critical non-mechanical systems, means that the aircraft can not only operate from dispersed bases, which most aircraft can do, but can also sustain operations from such bases, which is a rare ability indeed. In Europe, the A-10s are based at RAF Bentwaters, well behind the battle line, in an efficient, consolidated organisation. They would operate in wartime, however, from a group of six bases 100nm (185km) from the West German border: from north to south, Ahlhorn, Noervenich, Sembach and Leipheim, plus two more bases which are not revealed. These forward operating locations (FOLs) have stocks of fuel, ammunition and Mavericks, together with a few of the most important spares.

With most aircraft, an attempt to sustain operations from an austere base would rapidly result in an airfield full of damaged and defective airframes 250nm (463km) nearer the battle line than the spares and people needed to repair them. The A-10's simplicity and survivability features change the picture. A hit, or close miss, which would send a more complex and less resilient aircraft down for extensive repairs may well simply pepper the A-10's secondary structure, calling for nothing more than a few temporary patches. Again, a less survivable aircraft might regain a friendly base after being hit, but might not be airworthy enough to be flown back to its home base. A maintenance team must be dispatched, to fix it for the flight home, before the main work of repair can even start. Experience has shown that the A-10 can, under the same circumstances, often ferry itself back from the FOL to the main base.

The FOL has several major advantages. It is an effective and more efficient substitute for airborne loiter in decreasing reaction time; not only are the FOLs close to the front line, but the force is spread out so that no part of the line is very far from A-10 support. Because the FOL is closer to the front line than any main base, it takes less time for the A-10s to return to base, rearm and rejoin the fight, so more sorties can be flown in a day. A related benefit is a reduction of pilot flying time and fatigue for each mission.

FOL basing also makes the force less vulnerable to counter-airfield attack, for a number of reasons. Splitting the fleet among a number of FOLs forces the enemy to carry out several raids against less valuable targets. Not only that, but it is more difficult to deny an airfield to A-10s than it is to close it to fast-mover operations. The A-10s can operate from half a runway, or from a long taxiway, while their lower landing and take-off speeds mean that runway repairs need not be completed to the same standard.

Also, the FOLs can, if necessary, be covertly changed and concealed. The A-10 is an easy aircraft to fly, and operations from an unfamiliar field would present no prblems. It uses only one piece of specialized ground equipment, the ammunition loader, and supplies held at the FOL are, in general, compact and limited. Changing the position of a FOL does not, for example, call for the movement of dozens of spare engines.

Using FOLs close to the battle line, A-10 units have demonstrated their ability to fly more sorties per aircraft per day than any other type in the inventory. In early tests of the FOL concept, in April 1978, A-10s averaged nearly 15 missions per day over a three-day period and surge rates above 10 sorties have been attained in later exercises. The average sortie surge rate, though, is above six missions per day, greater than that of any other USAF aircraft.

Firepower, endurance, short reaction time, resistance to counter-air attacks and high sortie rates make the A-10 force a unique asset. Live exercises and studies have repeatedly shown that the A-10 not only performs better than other systems in its own specialized arena, but does many things which no other weapon can do at all. For example, a secondary mission assigned to the 81st TFW is to escort the USAF's combat rescue helicopters, should they have to penetrate hostile territory in the daytime. Armed with cluster weapons and the cannon to suppress groundfire, the A-10's endurance and speed make it a much more suitable escort than any other fighter.

To the ground commander or forward air controller (FAC) the A-10's 'combat persistence' is, perhaps, its salient advantage. The fast-mover strike aircraft, with its limited endurance, may be able to respond quickly to a call for help, but the support which it can offer is not only limited in duration, but also tied to a certain time. The FAC knows that the F-16 strike requested some time ago will arrive at 1543 hours precisely, and the activities of other systems on the battlefield must be geared to that time. The A-10, by contrast, can be held in reserve until another weapon has had time to attack, or can be vectored to another part of the engagement zone after completing one effective attack.

Top: Pilots of the 511st TFS, one of the six squadrons that make up the 81st TFW, are briefed before a mission during the Cold Fire 83 exercise at Wiesbaden Air Base, Germany, in September 1983.

Above: Off-loading a Maverick from a 511st TFS A-10 after a Cold Fire 83 training mission. A total of 18 aircraft were deployed to Wiesbaden in support of the German army's Brave Lion exercise.

Left: A 511st TFS pilot at the end of a Cold Fire mission. Cold Fire and Brave Lion both formed part of the annual Autumn Forge series of combined NATO manoeuvres in Germany.

One way of using the A-10, which has been practised to the limited extent possible in peacetime, is 'ground loiter', a technique otherwise confined to the Harrier. If the A-10s are required to wait near the battle for any extended period, they can alight easily on a good stretch of road – and Germany's autobahns are the best in the world – and wait for a call to action. The APU keeps all the systems running while using a minimal amount of fuel, so the aircraft can start engines and take off at shorter notice than any other type.

The A-10 is the only weapon which offers this sort of performance without sacrificing the full mobility of airpower; this is one of the factors which distinguishes the A-10 from the tank-killing helicopter. The helicopter is slow and short-legged, and the commander at the scene is, for practical purposes, limited to the helicopter force in his immediate vicinity. The available helicopter resources have to be spread out along the entire battle line, so the numbers available at any one spot will not be large enough to mount a strong counterattack. The A-10, however, is available for rapid reinforcement at any point.

Another attribute of the A-10 versus the helicopter is the ability of the faster fixed-wing aircraft to survive at close quarters with enemy SAM and AAA units. The helicopter is, essentially, an ambush weapon, unparalleled in its ability to find and exploit cover and attack from concealment. Its limitation is that it is most effective against the front and forward flanks of an advancing unit, and that it is unable to strike targets deep within the formation. Apart from the new AH-64, too, no helicopter has more than half the A-10's firepower, measured in effective anti-armour weaponry.

The tasks assigned to the A-10 in each phase of the battle reflect the type's strengths. In the early stages, as the advancing enemy spreads out through the van of the defences, the A-10s are available to respond quickly as advance ground forces engage the first enemy units. The ground forces delay the advance, and provide targeting information for effective attacks by A-10s.

Once the main force is engaged, the A-10 force can be used to provide 'firehose' CAS, a constant flow of sorties to the battle area which the commander can direct as necessary. The aircraft may support a unit in danger of being broken through, or exploit the brief opportunity offered by a new unit joining battle, and not yet fully deployed. In the case of a breakthrough, the A-10 force can be rapidly concentrated to slow the advancing force, attack the flanks of forces moving through the breach, and disrupt the movement of forces to the front. The last-named mission is not regarded as CAS but is termed 'battlefield air interdiction' or BAI.

Warthog at war

The A-10 played a peripheral role in the invasion of Grenada in 1983, but its baptism of fire was yet to come. As the 1980s drew to a close, several Warthog units re-equipped with the F-16. This was only partially due to doubts about the A-10's survivability; the Fort Worth fighter was a multi-role aircraft, and therefore of greater utility. At much the same time, many Warthogs were redesignated OA-10As, and assigned to Forward Air Control. The USAF's plans for the A-10's future were also affected by the dissolution of the Warsaw Pact, and eventually of the Soviet Union itself, which effectively removed the main threat.

Just when it seemed that the A-10 was due for premature retirement, it was given a reprieve. Operation Desert Shield saw five Warthog units, a total of 194 aircraft, deploy to various bases in Saudi Arabia. The Iraqi Army was one of the largest in the world, and deployed literally thousands of main battle tanks and other armoured vehicles. One thing was certain, there would be no lack of targets.

There is an old saying that one never fights the war for which one is equipped and has trained. And so it proved. The flat and treeless desert was a far cry from the cluttered terrain of Western Europe. The Warthog pilots had been trained to fly down among the weeds, taking advantage of every scrap of cover, in what was essentially a close-range slugging match, in which their survival depended on minimising their exposure to enemy fire. But in the desert, they now found themselves out in the open.

The alternative was to stay as far as possible out of reach of the defences at low to medium altitudes, picking off targets with the AGM-65D IR-guided Maverick. Medium altitudes were also sought when using the Rockeye cluster bomb or old fashioned iron bombs against soft targets.

This of course put them in fighter territory, and for self defence they were armed with two AIM-9L Sidewinders under the starboard outboard wing pylon, with the port pylon occupied by a self-protection jammer. As it proved, Coalition air superiority was so overwhelming that no Iraqi fighters were encountered by A-10s, and no Sidewinders were used. The nearest occasion came when an A-10 driver tried to use a Sidewinder against a helicopter at low level. Unfortunately the seeker failed to acquire the target.

On the other hand, a total of 5,013 Mavericks were launched by Warthogs during the brief war. A-10 pilots claimed the destruction of 987 Iraqi tanks and other armoured vehicles, although not all with AGM-65. This was disappointing when compared to prewar projections, and makes the "own goal" scored on a British Warrior AFV appear even more unfortunate. As in all forms of air warfare, overclaiming was a feature, and the kill total was later reduced to 330, probably due to faulty battle damage assessment. A considerable number of casualties may have been counted, or even attacked, more than once. The complexity of the battlefield, and the huge numbers involved, overextended an inefficient recording system.

On February 25, 1991, Warthogs of the 23rd TFW were scrambled to engage a large column of Iraqi tanks moving southwards from a Republican Guard area. Eric 'Fish' Salomonson and John 'Karl' Marks, arrived in the area at sunrise. They were not the first to arrive; several tanks were already burning, and the column had scattered. Surprisingly, no anti-aircraft fire greeted them.

They were cleared to fire by an OA-10 FAC, and went in. In the space of 10 minutes, the pair knocked out six tanks with Mavericks and another two with cannon fire. After refuelling and rearming at a forward operating location, they were ordered off again to support the US Marines near Kuwait City. Two missions in this area saw the destruction of another 15 tanks, again mainly with Mavericks. This total of 23 tanks in six sorties proved to be the zenith of Warthog operations in the Gulf War.

The fighting was not without loss, however: five Hogs were lost to ground fire and many more were badly damaged. For example, on February 15, two Hogs of the 354th TFW were shot down over north-west Kuwait killing one pilot while the other was taken prisoner.

The USAF, sensitive to losses, restricted A-10s to night attacks only on heavily defended areas until the start of the ground war some nine days later. This was largely made possible by the AGM-65D Maverick, the heat-sensing seeker of which could detect targets in darkness.

The losses have been held in some quarters to demonstrate that the A-10A was not as survivable as it was claimed to be, but this assessment is unfair. Five losses in more than 8,000 sorties is hardly proof of vulnerability. What must be remembered is that the featureless Iraqi desert lacked any form of cover, thus denying the A-10s their main means of defence, and largely forcing them to make stand-off attacks.

Warthogs also ranged deep into Iraqi-held territory to seek out their prey. This was another departure from training; over Europe they were not expected to penetrate more than a mile or two behind the FEBA (Forward Edge of Battle Area). The fact was that the wide-open spaces were an invitation to roam, in order to hit the enemy from an unexpected direction. In this they were often directed by OA-10A Forward Air Controllers, somewhat ironically referred to as Fast Movers. They were however considerably faster than the Rockwell OV-10A.

Another role which they fulfilled admirably was that of Sandy, locating downed aircrew, then directing and escorting search and rescue helicopters to the scene. A notable instance occurred on January 21. A-10 Sandy pilots Paul Johnson and Randy Goff of the 354th TFW managed to gain radio contact with downed Navy pilot Devon Jones, who talked them into his position. But the Iraqis had also been listening. Jones was 150 miles (240km) inside hostile territory, and reaching him took time. It turned into a race; as the A-10s brought the rescue helicopter in, an Iraqi truck came barrelling down the road towards Jones. Against the GAU-8/A it stood no chance; two passes from close range and it was reduced to flaming pieces. The pickup made, the return trip took an hour, escorted by the A-10s, who by then had been aloft for eight hours.

The big gun claimed two helicopters during the course of the War. On February 6, Bob Swain of the 926th TFW knocked down an unidentified machine. Two passes and it 'fell to pieces!' Then, on February 15, Todd Sheehy of the 10th TFW gunned down an Iraqi Mi-8.

Even before the Gulf War, a Ground Collision Avoidance system had been projected for the A-10. It finally emerged as LASTE (Low Altitude Safety and Targeting Enhancement), which makes constant calculations based on altitude, wind, temperature, and other variables, and is stated to double aiming accuracy. It also gives a voice warning of ground proximity.

Radical changes in the USAF – the merging of SAC and TAC to form Air Combat Command, with Composite Wings consisting of several aircraft types – have seen reductions of the A-10 fleet, despite commitments of the type to the Balkan theatre in recent years. At present the active duty USAF fields 210 OA-10As, the USAF Reserve 51, and the Air National Guard 100 – barely more than 50 per cent of the number acquired.

This notwithstanding, the future looks bright. The fleet is to undergo a series of upgrades. These will include a new GPS/INS and missile warning system, and avionics which will make it compatible with modern air-to-surface ordnance, including JSOW (Joint Stand-Off Weapon). A life extension programme will enable it to remain in service until 2020.

Left: An A-10 in JAWS markings outside its aircraft shelter at Ramstein AB. Testing of IIR missiles concentrated on performance in bad weather and battlefield smoke.

F-14 Tomcat

Contents

Top: US Navy fighter squadron VF-102 flew the F-14A Tomcat from May 1982, initially aboard USS *America* as part of the Atlantic Fleet. VF-102 was called the Diamondbacks after a rattlesnake of the same name.

Above: A Tomcat refuels from a USAF tanker during the Gulf War. Fitted with a probe rather than the USAF receptacle, the boom of the tanker had to be modified with a drogue, which complicated matters a bit.

Above right: A rather worn-looking F-14A of VF-41 Black Aces engaged in AMRAAM missile trials in 1987. VF-41 Tomcats first deployed in December 1977. By 1999 they were one of only five F-14A squadrons.

Left: The final Tomcat variant is the F-14D, with much more powerful and reliable engines, and a greatly improved radar. But few were built, and only one operational squadron, VF-213, is equipped with it.

Introduction

The aircraft carrier has a vital part to play both in keeping the peace and in time of war. Seven-tenths of our planet is covered by salt water, the greater part of which is a neutral area in terms of air power. This is where the aircraft carrier comes into its own, as wherever it goes it converts roughly half a million square miles of surrounding air space into a friendly air defence zone, which a potential assailant must penetrate.

The huge United States Navy carriers are equipped with well balanced Air Wings which typically consist of two squadrons of fighters, two of attack aircraft and one of all-weather attack aircraft, supported by four tankers, four airborne early warning and four electronic warfare aircraft, plus a sizable complement of fixed and rotary wing anti-submarine machines. They are therefore capable of packing an enormous punch, both in offence and defence – and by the same token, they are prime targets for an enemy.

The vulnerability of land-based airfields is a matter of extreme concern to the military. Some degree of protection against conventional attack can be given to airfields by dispersal, coupled with hardened shelters, but no such alternative exists for an aircraft carrier, which perforce must cram over 90 aircraft, with their fuel, munitions and servicing requirements, into the smallest usable volume. In comparison with an airfield, a carrier can afford to absorb very little damage. Its survival depends on its own integral air defences and those of its accompanying ships, and the key is defence in depth: an attacking force must be detected, intercepted, and destroyed as far away as possible, so that if the first interception is only partially successful there is still time and space to effect another.

Synonymous with US carriers during the last quarter-century has been the F-14 Tomcat. Since its first flight 30 years ago, the specific threat it was designed to counter has largely vanished, while its original technology has become dated. The current need is for greater flexibility. Many A-models reached the end of their useful lives and were retired; a few were re-engined to become B-models; while a mere handful of the very potent D-models, with advanced avionics, were produced. These will remain in service until 2008.

Development

In March 1972 Admiral Elmo R. Zumwalt, Jr., Chief of Naval Operations, outlined the importance of the F-14 to the US Navy: "The F-14 weapon system is one of the highest-priority items in the Navy budget . . . It will be capable of tracking and evaluating multiple targets and of controlling up to six independent Phoenix missiles simultaneously. This multiple-shot capability is precisely what the Navy must possess if it is to survive and operate forces in the face of enemy air and missile concentrations. The increase in effectiveness over the single-shot F-4, or any single-shot fighter, is more than 4:1 when outnumbered by even moderately high-performance threats."

Historical perspective shows that wars are won by offensive action, but one of the cardinal principles of war is that the base of such action must be secure enough to allow the striking forces freedom of action. Total security is of course impossible, and in the limited space of an aircraft carrier a balance between offensive and defensive forces must be struck.

Defence against air attack has traditionally been a process of attrition, breaking up attacks and degrading their effectiveness while striving to inflict unacceptable casualties on the attackers. Today, the defences form two layers: point defence; consisting of surface-to-air missiles (SAMs) and guns, plus fighters operating outside the SAM zone. Any attempt to operate defending fighters in the SAM zone is bound to lead to a degradation of the effectiveness of both, so the fighters must operate away from the carrier, but within the range of an effective detection and reporting system.

The 1950s saw fundamental advances in military aviation. Aircraft speeds increased greatly, reducing the time available for interception. More sinister still, stand-off weapons began to be developed that could be released at very long distances from the target. The requirement for a fleet air defence interceptor that emerged in 1955 stipulated an aircraft that could launch from the carrier, cruise out to a distance of 250nm (463km), stay on patrol at that radius, intercept and destroy intruders with AIM-7 Sparrow semi-active radar homing (SARH) missiles, then return to the carrier three hours after takeoff. This requirement resulted in the F-4 Phantom, which became operational in 1962.

Having initiated the programme that led to the Phantom, the US Navy immediately looked to the future. The projected threat appeared to be an aircraft that would approach at high speed to within about 200nm (368km) of the fleet, launch cruise missile type guided weapons, and retire to safety. Just one aircraft attacking in this manner would be difficult to counter, but a formation, each armed with two missiles . . . The missiles, once launched, would become the priority targets, but they were small and difficult to acquire on radar.

All in all, the larger, more readily detectable aircraft with its weapons still on board would be in many ways the easier target, but this entailed detection and interception at previously unheard-of distances. Excellent weapon system though the Phantom was, it would have to be in the right place at the right time to even attempt to cope with the problem. A permanent barrier of standing patrols appeared to be the only feasible solution, but with a total carrier complement of two Phantom squadrons (24 aircraft), this was hardly practicable. Something new was needed.

The answer proposed was to let the missiles rather than the interceptor do the work. There was nothing particularly outrageous about the idea; the Bomarc surface-to-air missile was already under development for just this purpose. Initially considered to be a pilotless interceptor (the propulsion test vehicle was given the experimental fighter designation XF-99), Bomarc A had a range of 200nm (370km) and a speed of between Mach 3 and Mach 4. Initial and midcourse guidance was from the ground, and active radar homing was used for the terminal guidance stage. Provided that a suitable missile could be developed, the main requirements for the aircraft were

that it should carry a useful number of them, be capable of a long loiter (patrol) time and have excellent target detection and multiple target engagement capability, while at the same time being small enough to fit the lift on an aircraft carrier and light enough to land aboard without wrecking the arrestor gear.

Formal Requests for Proposals (RFPs) were issued in the summer of 1957. Fifteen companies competed for the missile contract, which was won by the Bendix Corporation Systems Division, of Ann Arbor, Michigan, with its AAM-N-10 Eagle proposal. Eagle was a large missile, 16.125ft (4.91m) long and with a launch weight of 1,284lb (852kg). Using

Above: Three of the 12 F-14 prototypes in flight. BuAer 157981 (nearest camera) demonstrates minimum sweep, 157983 (centre) has wings swept to 45deg, and 157991, the renumbered prototype 1X, has its wings fully swept.

tandem stages with solid-fuel motors, its maximum range was 110nm (204km), with a top speed of Mach 4. Westinghouse derived the pulse-Doppler seeker from its DPN-53 developed for the Bomarc B, which gave active homing over the final 10nm (16km), while Grumman was responsible for the airframe and propulsion system integration.

Above: An F-111B prototype equipped with four AIM-54 Phoenix missiles. The underwing missile pylons had to swivel to match the wing sweep, a problem not shared by the Tomcat with its fixed wing-glove pylons.

Below: (From left) Fleet Readiness Manager Emerson Fawkes, DCNO(AIR) Vice Admiral Tom Connolly, Programme Director Mike Pelehach, and Product Manufacturing Director Larry Mead.

The aircraft selected to carry Eagle was the Douglas Model D-766 Missileer, naval designation F6D. With an all-up weight not exceeding 50,000lb (22,680kg), it was to have been powered by two Pratt and Whitney TF-30-P2 unaugmented turbofans. Its high, un-swept wing was optimized for economic cruise, and figures released at the time credited it with a maximum speed of Mach 0.8 and an endurance of between four and six hours. A Hughes high power pulse-Doppler and track-while-scan detection and missile control system was fitted. Three Eagles could be carried under each wing, and a further two could be fitted to the lower front fuselage.

The idea of an aircraft optimized to carry the heaviest possible air-to-air armament at the expense of performance and agility was far from new. Early in 1915, Lieutenant Colonel (later Marshal of the Royal Air Force Lord) Trenchard, then commanding 1st Wing, Royal Flying Corps, had recommended the development of a three-seat pusher-propelled fighter to carry two machine gunners. During the 1920s the Italian General Guilio Douhet postulated the use of 'battleplanes' – bombers fitted with extra guns and armour protection instead of a bombload. And in 1943 the US Army Air Forces put theory into practice by converting a handful of Boeing B-17 bombers into YB-40 gun-ships. For various reasons they were a failure. But the Missileer, with its battery of long-range Eagles, looked to be a

Above: Grumman's response to the Navy's VFX Request for Proposals ran to a massive 37 volumes which occupied 54 binders, including a 42-page guide. Mike Pelehach (left) and President Llew Evans (in jacket) have something to smile about.

Below: The Tomcat as it nearly was – a mock-up of design 303E, submitted by Grumman in response to the Navy's VFX specification. In this rare picture, the single dorsal fin and one of the two ventral folding fins are clearly visible. The ventral folding fins would almost certainly have hampered quick engine changes.

feasible proposition for the simple reason that it would vastly outrange any possible opponent.

Interestingly enough, also under study at the same time was a USAF air defence concept codenamed 'Project Aerie'. This took the 'flying battleship' idea a stage further and was to have consisted of Boeing C-135As acting as airborne command centres and armed with no less than 24 Eagles. Project Aerie was stillborn, but the US Navy placed a study contract for the F6D in 1959.

The concept of a fighter that was no more than a slow, unwieldy missile carrier worried many people. Certainly it could fly the basic fleet air defence

mission, which was to patrol at about 150nm (275km) out from the carrier at an altitude of 35,000ft (10,700m) while carrying at least six large missiles, detect and track bandits from ultra-long range, then kill them from a distance which rendered the Missileer safe from counter-attack. There were, however, certain disadvantages. Once the Missileer had expended its weapons, its only form of defence lay in flight, and it was comparatively slow – and lacking any self-defence capability, once overhauled, it would be hacked from the sky with relative ease.

Comparisons with the McDonnell Douglas F-4 Phantom, shortly to enter service in the fleet air defence role, were inevitable. The Phantom could not carry Eagle missiles, nor could it remain on station for more than a fraction of the time of the Missileer, but its tremendous rate of climb and Mach 2 capability enabled it to get out on station much faster, and to evade interception with ease once it had expended its missiles. It could also act as an escort fighter for the carrier's attack squadrons, which was totally beyond the capability of the Missileer.

The two horns of the dilemma can be summarized as follows: firstly, could an aircraft carrier, with its limited deck and hangar space, afford the luxury of a single-role aircraft, however capable it was in that role? Secondly, could the Navy afford to be without the undoubted interception capability of the Missileer/

Eagle combination? The uncertainty, generated in part by the lack of a historical precedent, lingered on until December 1960, when Thomas S. Gates, Jr., Secretary of Defense in the outgoing Eisenhower Administration, cancelled the Missileer. The flying battleship concept was once more put back on the shelf, although the Eagle and the weapon control system were allowed to continue for a while longer.

The administration of President John F. Kennedy took office on January 20, 1961, bringing with it a new Defense Secretary, Robert S. McNamara, and a new buzz-word, commonality. The idea of commonality had been around the DoD for a good few years, but its practical application was difficult. As applied to aircraft procurement, it implied an all-singing, all-dancing aeroplane that could perform many roles with equal facility, for both Air Force and Navy.

The advantage of such a multi-role machine was largely financial. The ability to carry out interception, air superiority, battlefield support, interdiction and reconnaissance missions, and to operate with equal ease from aircraft carriers or land bases, was bound to lead to large production runs, with attendant low unit costs. Spares, support, and training would also be greatly simplified. In other words, it meant either cheaper aeroplanes, or more aeroplanes for a

fixed sum. The real irony was the fact that the only aircraft type ever to approach these goals, the Phantom, was entering service at precisely that moment.

Under the Kennedy administration, the new ideas and vigorous approach of comparatively young men was supposed to revitalize the nation, sweeping aside the caution of the older generation and the entrenched bureaucracy, compensating for experience with innovation and energy. McNamara was of this new breed. As a Vice-President of the Ford Motor Company, he had reorganized and streamlined the ailing industrial giant and generally knocked it into shape. Now he prepared to give the DoD the same treatment.

Defence costs generally defy comprehension; there are so many noughts as to make the figures meaningless. To McNamara, the scope for savings appeared almost limitless and commonality appeared to be the tool for the purpose, so one of his first acts was to examine the major new programmes.

It so happened that there were two major requirements for the near future. The first was the USAF specification SOR-183, issued in June 1960 and calling for a tactical strike fighter, later referred to as the TFX. The specification was demanding, including a low-level speed of Mach 1.2, a high-level speed of Mach 2.5, a radius of action with internal

weapons of 800nm (1,475km), good short-field performance, and a ferry range sufficient to cross the Atlantic unrefuelled. The second requirement was, as we have seen, for a fleet air defence fighter (FADF) to fill the slot left vacant by the Missileer cancellation.

Meanwhile, the National Aeronautics and Space Administration (NASA) had been conducting studies in variable geometry. In mid-1959 they briefed

Above: Escalating costs caused by rocketing inflation forced radical alternatives to be considered, among them these two single-seat designs. The model on the right is still recognizable as a Tomcat and at this stage retains the glove vanes, while that on the left not only has a fixed wing, but also features narrower engine intakes, a revised canopy and more closely spaced fins.

Design 303-60

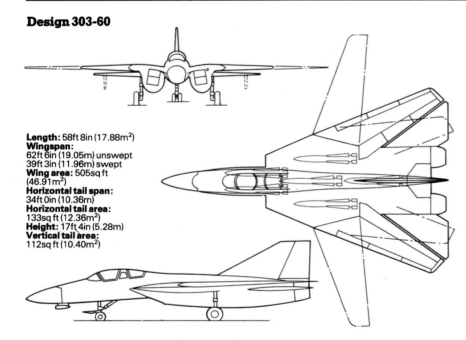

Length: 58ft 8in (17.88m²)
Wingspan:
62ft 6in (19.05m) unswept
39ft 3in (11.96m) swept
Wing area: 505sq ft
(46.91m²)
Horizontal tail span:
34ft 0in (10.36m)
Horizontal tail area:
133sq ft (12.36m²)
Height: 17ft 4in (5.28m)
Vertical tail area:
112sq ft (10.40m²)

Design 303C

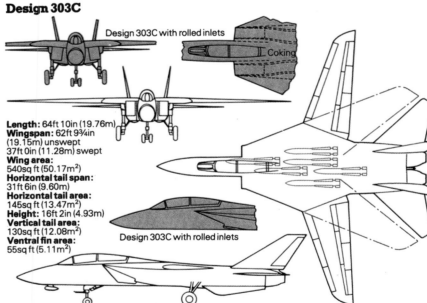

Design 303C with rolled inlets

Coking

Design 303C with rolled inlets

Length: 64ft 10in (19.76m)
Wingspan: 62ft 9¾in
(19.15m) unswept
37ft 0in (11.28m) swept
Wing area:
540sq ft (50.17m²)
Horizontal tail span:
31ft 6in (9.60m)
Horizontal tail area:
145sq ft (13.47m²)
Height: 16ft 2in (4.93m)
Vertical tail area:
130sq ft (12.08m²)
Ventral fin area:
55sq ft (5.11m²)

Design 303E

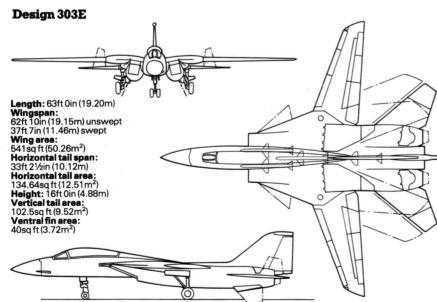

Length: 63ft 0in (19.20m)
Wingspan:
62ft 10in (19.15m) unswept
37ft 7in (11.46m) swept
Wing area:
541sq ft (50.26m²)
Horizontal tail span:
33ft 2½in (10.12m)
Horizontal tail area:
134.64sq ft (12.51m²)
Height: 16ft 0in (4.88m)
Vertical tail area:
102.5sq ft (9.52m²)
Ventral fin area:
40sq ft (3.72m²)

Design 303D

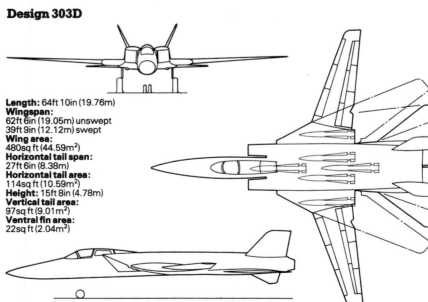

Length: 64ft 10in (19.76m)
Wingspan:
62ft 6in (19.05m) unswept
39ft 9in (12.12m) swept
Wing area:
480sq ft (44.59m²)
Horizontal tail span:
27ft 6in (8.38m)
Horizontal tail area:
114sq ft (10.59m²)
Height: 15ft 8in (4.78m)
Vertical tail area:
97sq ft (9.01m²)
Ventral fin area:
22sq ft (2.04m²)

Top: Design 303-60 was an assembly of reasonable goals rather than a mature design. A very high degree of oversweep was considered which entailed the outboard portions of the tailerons folding downwards.

Above: Design 303E emerged through 303A and B. Radical changes include the canopy, dorsal fin and taileron shape, and the addition of glove vanes and folding ventral fins. Main armament was to be four Sparrows.

Top: Design 303C featured twin fins and an orthodox submerged engine layout. A modification of this proposal envisaged the use of inlets rolled to the sides and intakes trunked inward in a 'coked', or area-ruled, fuselage.

Above: Design 303D combined a low-set variable-sweep wing with canted twin fins and submerged engines. Wind tunnel tests soon established that it would have been inferior to Design 303E in almost all areas.

senior US Navy officials on state-of-the-art variable-sweep configuration technology, and, applying it to a hypothetical naval fighter of the same weight as the proposed Missileer, demonstrated a performance potential sufficient to outclass any project then under consideration. NASA then repeated the exercise for the staff of USAF Tactical Air Command, but related to the then still only partially formulated SOR-183 requirement. Both Navy and Air Force issued study contracts to industry.

This was the situation when McNamara became Defense Secretary. It appeared to him that the two sets of requirements had much in common. The load-carrying ability of the TFX could be equated with the heavy load of large AAMs for the FADF, while the long ferry range of the TFX would match the extended patrol time of the Navy fighter. Both needed high speed at all altitudes, and the short-field performance of the TFX tallied with a slow carrier approach speed. The one really important point overlooked was that SOR-183 called for an attack aircraft: TFX should really have been TAX.

Convinced that a single type of tactical fighter could do both jobs, McNamara issued a formal recommendation on February 14, 1961, that both the Air Force and the Navy study a single basic design, to be developed in two versions to meet the needs of both services, but with maximum commonality. Naturally there were objections. Both requirements could be met by a twin-engined, two-seat swing-wing design, but there the resemblance ended, and on August 22, 1961, McNamara was told that a compromise aircraft capable of fulfilling both missions was not technically feasible. He reacted with a directive that it would be done, even going so far as to delineate certain design aspects, and instructed the Air Force to proceed with the development. With his Ford Motors background in mind, one cannot help but recall the saying attributed to the late Henry Ford: "You can have any colour you want so long as it's black!"

Naval TFX

After protracted hassles, General Dynamics was awarded the TFX contract in December 1962, with Grumman as principal subcontractor. Grumman, with a string of successful carrier fighters to its credit, and also previous swing-wing experience with the XF10F Jaguar, was to take primary responsibility for the development of the naval version. The Air Force variant was designated the F-111A, that for the Navy F-111B, and the two aircraft retained a high degree of commonality – the principal reason why the General Dynamics proposal had been accepted. The main difference between the F-111A and B was one of length, which in the naval version had to be held down to a size that could be accommodated by the carrier lifts.

The weapon system naturally varied according to the role, and the weapon control system developed for the Missileer, refined and designated AWG-9, was to be fitted to the F-111B. Meanwhile, the Eagle missile had been cancelled in what appears to have been part of the commonality purge. The Navy opposed this decision violently, and the technology was transferred from Bendix to Hughes, who began developing their own long-range missile, the AIM-54 Phoenix. The advantages of the same contractor developing both the missile and the detection/guidance/launch system were obvious, and Phoenix was the weapon selected for the new fleet air defence fighter.

The F-111B was in trouble from the outset. The concept of commonality dictated that the special needs of carrier operations, such as the ability to withstand repeated stresses of catapult launches and arrested landings, be incorporated into the basic design. This ensured a heavy aeroplane from the outset, and as development proceeded, so the weight increased. As if this were not enough, severe compressor stalls were experienced with the engines.

The first flight of the F-111B took place on May 18, 1965, and NPE 1 (Naval Preliminary Evaluation) was held during the following October. The findings were uniformly unfavourable, the F-111B proving inferior to the F-4 in almost every department. The windshield angle caused a serious reflection problem, and this, coupled with a high angle of attack (AOA) on the approach, caused pilots to lose sight of the carrier. Carrier landings are exciting enough without such problems. Further problems were experienced both with propulsion and in manoeuvrability, especially at supersonic speeds. It rapidly became obvious that despite the F prefix, the F-111B was not and never would be a fighter, nor was it suited for carrier operations.

Continued attempts to remedy the deficiencies were made, but despite Grumman's best efforts the problems, particularly that of excess weight, proved intractable. In May 1968 Congress refused further funding for the project. Work was halted in July and the contract officially terminated in December of that year. Ten years of effort had left the Navy no nearer acquiring the fighter it wanted. Or so it seemed.

Spurred on by the disastrous NPE 1 in October 1965, the Navy funded Grumman to prepare advanced fighter studies. Preliminary work began in January 1966, with more than 6,000 configurations being studied, and a process of elimination reduced these to a handful collec-

Design 303F

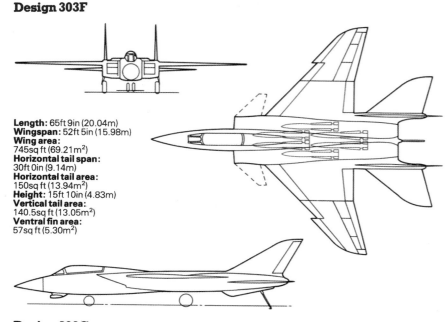

Length: 65ft 9in (20.04m)
Wingspan: 52ft 5in (15.98m)
Wing area:
745sq ft (69.21m²)
Horizontal tail span:
30ft 0in (9.14m)
Horizontal tail area:
150sq ft (13.94m²)
Height: 15ft 10in (4.83m)
Vertical tail area:
140.5sq ft (13.05m²)
Ventral fin area:
57sq ft (5.30m²)

Design 303G

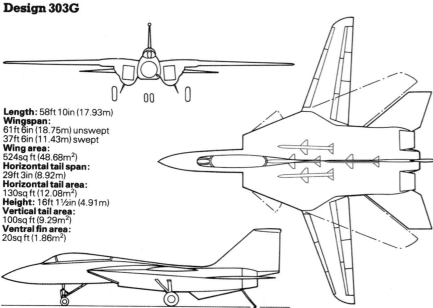

Length: 58ft 10in (17.93m)
Wingspan:
61ft 6in (18.75m) unswept
37ft 6in (11.43m) swept
Wing area:
524sq ft (48.68m²)
Horizontal tail span:
29ft 3in (8.92m)
Horizontal tail area:
130sq ft (12.08m²)
Height: 16ft 1½in (4.91m)
Vertical tail area:
100sq ft (9.29m²)
Ventral fin area:
20sq ft (1.86m²)

Top: Design 303F was a fixed-wing, submerged-engine proposal which, interestingly for 1968, considered the use of canard foreplanes. It was developed primarily to prove the advantages of variable sweep.

Above: Design 303G was studied to determine the extent to which the Phoenix requirement penalized the 303E as a fighter. The result was a smaller and lighter aircraft, but performance gains were marginal.

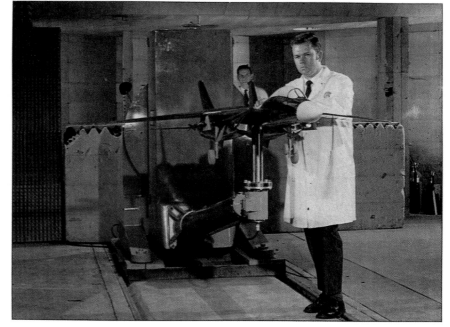

Above: A scale model of the Tomcat, now in its final form, is prepared for low-speed wind tunnel testing. Many thousands of hours of tests with models ranging from 1/7 to 1/48 scale were carried out.

Below: A 1/48 scale supersonic test model with a typical combat load of missiles. Surprisingly, the carriage of Phoenix in the tunnel between the engines is reported to cause no interference drag.

tively known as Project 303. The Admirals were encouraging, and in October 1967 Grumman made a formal proposal to the Navy. In essence, this consisted of a new airframe designed around the weapon control system and engines intended for the F-111B.

The Navy responded by forming Fighter Study Group II to examine the proposal, which became known as VFX-1. There also existed a second proposal called VFX-2 which was the same airframe and weapon control system wrapped around two Advanced Technology Engines (ATE) that were under development at that time. But more of VFX-2 later. Fighter Study Group II concluded that Project 303 was potentially vastly superior to the F-111B. For a start it was carrier-compatible, and it promised to have excellent close combat capability, a quality sadly lacking in the F-111B. It could therefore be used in the escort fighter role as well as fleet defence, and would obviously possess a 'fallout' capability for ground attack.

VFX-1 was Grumman Design No. 303-60. It has been described by the company as "more an assemblage of reasonable goals than a mature blend of aerodynamics, structures, electronics, and subsystems." This was soon to change.

As at January 1968, Design 303-60 featured a shoulder-mounted variable-sweep wing and widely spaced engines in pods. The undersides of the fuselage and engine pods were smoothly curved, and a single vertical tail surface of low aspect ratio was featured. Notwithstanding the other trouble encountered by the F-111B, the variable-sweep wing had functioned well and offered considerable advantages over a more orthodox layout. The concept was therefore adopted by Grumman for their new fighter.

The widely spaced engine pods were a direct result of experience with the F-111B. The Pratt & Whitney TF30 had proved to be very sensitive to high AOA and the quarter-cone inlet situated well downstream on the fuselage was less than ideal. Grumman's answer was to place the engines as far out from the fuselage nacelle as possible to minimize airflow interference, with the airstream running in a straight line from the front of the intake to the nozzle.

Original armament

The weapon control system was to be a modified Hughes AWG-9, but contrary to popular belief, the basic weaponry was to be Sparrow rather than Phoenix. The design philosophy was to produce an air superiority fighter first and a missile carrier second. Grumman's Robert W. Kress summed it up in June 1984: "We were totally preoccupied with producing a fighter, with a basic weapon fit of four AIM-7s and two AIM-9s. Then we sat back and figured how to screw six AIM-54s onto it without messing it up in its basic fighter role. That led to the palletized Phoenix carriage." (Phoenix missiles are carried on external flush-mounted low-drag racks, referred to as pallets). Design 303-60 was a large aeroplane and consequently heavy; the extensive use of exotic materials such as titanium and boron composites were to be incorporated into the structure to minimize the weight as far as possible.

Between January and September 1968 the design moved fast, and eight final configurations were in turn developed, examined, and discarded, with the exception of the one that was destined to emerge as the F-14. A minor nacelle modification turned 303-60 into 303A, then further modifications produced 303B the following month. By the end of

June, enough further developments had occurred for a redesignation to 303E.

Other variants were running in parallel. Design 303C featured submerged engines and a shoulder-mounted variable sweep wing, while 303D also had submerged engines but with a low-set variable-sweep wing. Interestingly, both featured twin fins and ventral strakes. Wind tunnel tests and further studies revealed that 303D would have poor longitudinal stability, excessive drag due to lift at subsonic speeds, reduced maximum thrust in supersonic flight, and high fuel consumption at cruising speed. It was eliminated during April. A few weeks later, 303C was also eliminated as having a lower supersonic combat ceiling, and less growth potential than 303E.

As these two fell by the wayside, attention was turned to 303F, a submerged-engine design with a shoulder-mounted fixed wing, and 303G, a 'fighter only' variant whose AWG-10 weapon control system had no Phoenix capability. Designed to have the same mission capability as 303E, 303F had an empty weight calculated to be 2,520lb (1,143kg) heavier while takeoff gross weight (TOGW) panned out at 4,920lb (2,232kg) heavier than its variable-sweep rival. Most of the extra weight came from the need for a much larger wing – 745sq ft (69.24m^2) compared with 541sq ft (50.28m^2). In addition, the fixed wing had to be equipped with various trim and high lift devices to suit it for carrier operations. Even then it could not have met carrier suitability requirements when carrying six Phoenix and it was terminated in July of that year.

Design 303G was studied to establish the degree to which the Phoenix-armed fleet air defence mission requirement penalized the design as a pure fighter. Overall dimensions were smaller and

both empty and TOGW weights were reduced, by 1,615lb (733kg) and 2,230lb (1,012kg) respectively. Calculations showed that only marginal gains in acceleration, combat ceiling, etc., were possible. As the Navy had been pushing for the long-range kill capability for many years, yet another Sparrow-armed fighter was hardly what it wanted. Furthermore, 303E had greater growth potential and greater attack capability.

Design evolution

Fighter design is a process of evolution, and it is instructive to examine the steps which led from 303-60 to 303E, and the reasons for them.

1) An increase in wing area from 505sq ft (46.93m^2) to 541sq ft (50.28^2) improved manoeuvrability, and also allowed a single-slotted hinged flap to be used rather than a complicated double-slotted extending flap.

2) A Grumman-designed convergent-divergent (con-di) iris nozzle increased maximum supersonic thrust.

3) The distance between the engine pods was reduced and forward fuselage depth increased. This improved area distribution, reduced wetted area and thus drag, and gave better single-engined control due to a reduction in the asymmetry of the thrust.

4) A revised trailing edge to the 'pancake' area between the nacelles reduced supersonic trim drag.

5) Wing aspect ratio was reduced from 8.15 to 7.28, yielding the minimum takeoff gross weight (TOGW).

6) The addition of a 'Mach Sweep Programmer' gave the pilot maximum combat agility and allowed the wing to be designed for a much lower static bending moment, thus making a considerable weight saving while reducing the flutter weight penalty.

Left: Round-the-clock working was needed to prepare the first Tomcat prototype for its maiden flight before Christmas 1970. Here it is being towed from the paint shop at dawn, masking still in place, for the next stage of preparation.

Above: The ill-fated first prototype, BuAer 147980, seen in the early part of its disastrous second flight on December 30, 1970. Minutes after this picture was taken, a series of hydraulic failures occurred.

Right: Flames and smoke erupt from the trees as Tomcat 1 crashes just short of the Calverton runway. Test pilots Miller and Smythe used their Martin Baker ejection seats – their parachutes can be seen above and in front of the fireball.

7) The addition of Direct Lift Control (DLC) for carrier approach gave a more stable glide path and a more consistent touch-down attitude.

8) A glove vane was incorporated to destabilize the aircraft in supersonic flight, thus reducing supersonic trim drag and improving supersonic manoeuvrability.

9) The addition of a 'speed bump' at the base of the vertical tail reduced supersonic drag.

10) Wing dihedral inboard and anhedral outboard produced better sealing at the sweep joint.

11) Wing thickness was revised from a constant 9 per cent to 10.65 tapering to 7 per cent, reducing structure weight and improving the buffet boundary.

12) The pallet concept for carrying Phoenix enabled the aircraft to operate at a lower weight when carrying Sparrows than would have been the case with a fixed mounting.

13) A revised horizontal tail planform as suggested by NASA to improve longitudinal stability also allowed the wing to be placed further to the rear to eliminate balance problems.

14) Improved external lines to upper and lower surfaces of the forward inlet reduced both drag and negative zero-lift moments at supersonic speeds.

15) Improved nose and canopy lines gave better supersonic cross-sectional area distribution, as well as better visibility from the cockpit. The F-14 was a trend-setter in the latter respect.

16) A lower positioning of the horizontal tail, another NASA suggestion to improve longitudinal stability, also insured against pitch-up at transonic speeds.

17) Revisions to the main landing gear fairing and horizontal tail actuator bump improved area ruling and lessened supersonic drag.

18) Deletion of the high-lift device on the glove leading edge reduced weight and complexity with no adverse effect on performance.

19) Cross-sectional area was redistributed to reduce wave drag.

20) A redesigned vertical tail similar in shape to that of the A-6 Intruder with an area reduction from 112sq ft (10.41m^2) on 303-60 to 102.5sq ft (9.53m^2) on 303E, plus sideways-retracting ventral fins totalling 40sq ft (3.73m^2) in area, were added.

At first sight the list seems formidable, but closer examination reveals it to be almost entirely a process of improvement, refining a basically sound design rather than seeking fixes because something was wrong.

The Navy issued a Request for Proposals for the VFX Specification to the aerospace industry in July 1968. The basic VFX requirements were a two-man crew seated in tandem, two engines

Below: Tomcat 12 (BuAer 157991) was redesignated 1X to replace the first prototype in the high-speed test and performance envelope exploration programme. Its first flight was made on August 30, 1971.

(the TF30-P-412 was expected to be used), an advanced weapon control system, and an air-to-air weapon load of either six Phoenix, or a combination from six AIM-7E or F Sparrows and four AIM-9 Sidewinders. An internal M61A 20mm multi-barrel cannon was mandatory. The 303E, by now a mature design, formed the basis of Grumman's submission.

Grumman's competitors for the VFX contract were General Dynamics, Ling-Temco-Vought, McDonnell Douglas, and North American Rockwell. By December, Grumman and McDonnell Douglas had emerged as the front runners, and on January 14, 1969, the DoD announced the award of the contract for the VFX fighter, now designated F-14, to Grumman. The contract was negotiated on a basis of six R&D aircraft and 463 production F-14As and Bs, although at that time, to update the fighter force of the USN and USMC would have required a total of 716 production aircraft. The Grumman proposal had at first been considerably more expensive than that of McDonnell, but had been negotiated downwards to within acceptable limits. Projected procurement was as follows: Lot I: 6 aircraft; Lot II: 6 aircraft; Lot III: 30 aircraft; Lots IV, V, VI, and VII: 96 aircraft each; and Lot VIII: 43 aircraft. On this basis, the unit cost per aircraft worked out at $12.4 million in FY 1970 terms.

Twin fins

One final major change occurred before the design was frozen in March 1969. Up to this point, Design 303E had featured a single fin, with two folding ventral fins to give the required directional stability and control. Early wind tunnel tests, performed on the 303B model, had confirmed the superiority of the single fin, particularly at high AOA, and it also possessed better wave drag qualities than twin fins, as well as weight and simplicity advantages.

However, at a very late date, the Navy objected to the complex ventral folding fins as being unsuitable for carrier operations. A further objection arose from the widely spaced engine thrust lines. In the event of a dynamic engine failure in high Mach number flight, at the critical external loading, a single fin might not have given sufficient directional stability without the extra area provided by the folding fins. As a direct result, the twin fins familiar to us today were adopted.

By this time, the need for the F-14 had become urgent. Three main factors were involved. Firstly, the abortive Missileer and F-111B projects had caused years of delay. Secondly, experience over North Vietnam had exposed the shortcomings of the F-4 Phantom in the close combat arena against the far from new Soviet-built MiG-17s and -21s. Thirdly, the nature of the threat was changing.

The Soviet Union was now producing a series of new fighters, among them the MiG-25 Foxbat. During the late 1960s the Foxbat had set a whole range of world records for speed, altitude, and rate of climb. Its very existence was interpreted to mean that the Soviets had made astounding technical advances, and as a result the Foxbat was credited with capabilities far in excess of those it actually possessed. For the next few years, the Foxbat was to become a sort of aerial bogeyman to the West. Something was needed to counter it.

That something was the Grumman F-14 Tomcat. The name had arisen fortuitously from a combination of the Grumman practice of naming its fighters after felines, and the enthusiasm for the project of Vice Admiral Tom Connolly, who at the time held the post of Deputy Chief of Naval Operations, Air (DCNO-AIR).

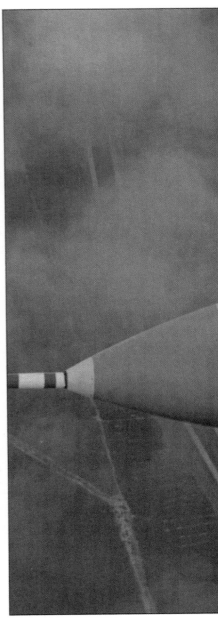

Above: The second prototype Tomcat, BuAer 147981, was assigned to low-speed, high AOA and spin testing. It is seen here in high AOA flight, in which the Tomcat excels. (Note the angle of the horizontal tails.)

Right: A close-up view of Tomcat 2 showing the canard surfaces fitted before spin trials commenced in the spring of 1972. In the event, the Tomcat proved to be extremely resistant to spinning.

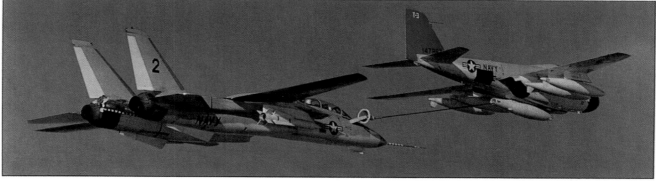

Left: With wings fully spread and everything – gear, flaps, slats and speedbrake – hanging out, Tomcat 2 flies slowly past the camera. The prominent ribs on the upper surface and the shape of the trailing edge of the pancake were later modified.

Right: In-flight refuelling played a large part in keeping the test programme on schedule by extending the duration of each flight. Here Tomcat 2 takes on fuel from a KA-6 equipped with a 'buddy pack'.

The project had been referred to from an early stage as 'Tom's Cat', and this was eventually formalized into Tomcat. Other names had been suggested, among them Alley Cat, rejected as being in questionable taste, and Seacat.

Meanwhile, an advanced technology engine known as the ATE was under development. Funded jointly by the USAF and US Navy, this was expected to produce a thrust of 28-30,000lb (12,700-13,600kg), for a weight saving of 800lb (363kg) per engine, and have a specific fuel consumption calculated to be 30 per cent better. The Tomcat was designed to accept the ATE with minimal modifications – the new engine promised considerable performance improvements, but to wait for it was to accept yet further postponement of the in-service date, which was scheduled for April 1973.

The decision was taken to proceed with all haste, using the flight-proven TF30-P-412 engines for the prototypes and early production models, a total of 67 aircraft. After this point, Tomcats were to be fitted with the ATE, with the designation F-14B, and the earlier model F-14As were to be retrofitted with the new engine. On the horizon was the F-14C,

which was to feature advanced multi-mission avionics. The need for growth had been foreseen: what Grumman was tooling up to build was the world's most advanced fighter, designed to counter any present or projected threat, and capable of being progressively updated as required. It was a large aeroplane – "a big fighter to do a big job" was Grumman's comment – and it represented the pinnacle of technological achievement at that time.

Two years to first flight
Grumman, confident in its ability to win the VFX contract, had initiated fabrication of certain parts late in 1968. Now it was faced with the tremendous task of producing flyable hardware in just two years, successfully completing the flight test programme, and getting production aircraft into service by 1972.

The 'Ironworks', as Grumman was affectionately known to the Navy, tooled up to get the first prototype into the air in double-quick time, organized the production, including the extensive use of the expensive and intractable titanium, and set out to streamline the flight test programme. Under the terms of the

contract, the maiden flight had to take place on or before January 31, 1971, while the US Navy Board of Inspection and Survey (BIS) trials were scheduled to take place just 17 months later – a very short time into which to compress a full flight test programme.

As the Tomcat project gathered momentum, the detractors were seizing upon it as a new duty scapegoat. Coming along, about two years behind in terms of an in-service date (and about level with the USAF's new F-15 fighter), was the USAF's new F-15 fighter. Civilian experts at the Pentagon started predicting that the F-14 could be out-manoeuvred by the MiG-21, while once again the familiar question arose as to why the two services could not agree on a common design, in this case inferring that the lighter and cheaper F-15 should be selected. Again the historical lesson that the process of converting a land-based fighter for carrier operations involved so much structural redesign as to make the exercise self-defeating, was being ignored. But both Secretary of Defense Melvin R. Laird and DCNO-AIR Vice Admiral Tom Connolly remained adamant that not only was the Tomcat the aircraft that the Navy wanted, but it was

needed as soon as possible. The first Navy order, for 26 production aircraft, was placed in October 1970, and with this the possibility of cancellation faded.

The first prototype, BuAer (Bureau of Aeronautics number) 157980, was intended for high-speed testing and exploration of the flight performance envelope. Taxi trials started on December 14, 1970, and high-speed taxi runs were made six days later. The weather was not good on the following day (December 21) but the forecast for the next few days was worse. After consultation with high-ranking Navy observers, the test pilots took the decision to go.

With Grumman Chief Test Pilot Robert Smythe at the controls and Project Test Pilot William Miller in the rear seat, the big fighter lifted off the runway at Grumman's Calverton Field at 16:18. After circling the airfield twice at moderate speed and at low level, it touched down exactly at sunset after just ten minutes in the air. No attempt was made to vary the wing sweep on this flight, during which four dummy Sparrows were carried.

The next flight was scheduled as a test flight proper, with Miller at the controls and Smythe in the back seat, monitoring the instruments. The weather was bright and sunny on December 30, 1970, and the Tomcat lifted off the runway at 10:08. Accompanied by three chase aircraft, it headed southeast toward the test area over the Atlantic. Stability and control tests were carried out with the wheels down, then the gear was retracted and the speed gently increased from 133kt (245km/h) to 180kt (332km/h).

Twenty-five minutes into the flight, at an altitude of 14,000ft (4,270m), the pilot of a chase aircraft noticed what looked like smoke coming from the F-14. Simultaneously, Bill Miller reported a failure of the primary hydraulic system and announced that he was aborting the mission and returning, using the back-up flight system. The 'smoke' was actually leaking hydraulic fluid.

The early stages of the return flight were uneventful. At a distance of 4 miles (6km) out from Calverton, at an altitude of 2,500ft (750m), Miller blew down the landing gear with the nitrogen bottle and confirmed to the tower that both nose and main gears were down and locked. By this time he was within sight of the runway, but just when the emergency appeared to be over, the flight hydraulic system also failed, and in a last-ditch attempt to save the aircraft, Miller switched to the Combat Survival System. Designed to give enough control to allow a battle-damaged F-14 to egress from the combat zone and reach a safe area for the crew to eject, this system powered the rudders and tailerons only, but extremely skilful piloting might allow the valuable prototype to be landed safely.

On the final approach, however, the big fighter began a gentle longitudinal oscillation. Miller realized that he was no longer able to control it and decided to eject. The Martin Baker zero/zero seats worked as advertised, and the crew escaped unhurt from just above the treetops a split second before the F-14 impacted the ground about a mile short of the runway and caught fire.

Crash investigators were quickly on the scene, and on February 12 their findings were announced. Two ¼in (6.5mm) titanium hydraulic lines, one on each side of the fuselage, had both ruptured just behind the main landing gear, and loss of fluid had caused a catastrophic failure of both systems. The Navy Accident Review Board concluded that the failures had been caused by "a highly improbable set of simultaneous conditions." At low engine settings used during the flight, the vibration frequency of the tubing matched

that of the hydraulic pumps, setting up a resonance that caused the lines to fracture. This condition had been aggravated by a loose mounting connection. Shortly after, the pump in the combat survival system had become unserviceable, rendering this emergency system useless. The remedy for the fractured pipes was simple: the titanium tubes were replaced by heavier gauge stainless steel pipes.

Second prototype

After undergoing exhaustive ground testing of its hydraulic systems, the second prototype took to the air from Calverton on May 24, 1971. This flight, with Robert Smythe at the controls and Bill Miller in the back seat, lasted 58 minutes. It was uneventful, as was the second flight, lasting more than two hours, two days later. Only moderate speeds and altitudes were recorded on these flights, as this aircraft, BuAer 157981, was assigned to low speed, high AOA, and spin testing, and was specially instrumented and equipped for this task. To replace the crashed high speed test aircraft, No. 12, BuAer 157991, was accelerated through production and redesignated No. 1X, making its first flight on August 31 of that year, and going supersonic on September 16.

Although only the first dozen Tomcats were preproduction aircraft, a total of around 20 took part in the accelerated flight test programme, which had inevitably suffered some slippage as a result of the loss of the first prototype. Nine Tomcats had flown by the end of 1971, and all 20 by the following November.

The programme itself was very intensive. Calverton possessed an Automated Telemetry System (ATS), first used for the A-6 programme and consisting of a Control Data System CDC 6400 computer, with three CDC 1700 pre-processors. Each pre-processor could be linked to an individual aircraft, so that three Tomcats could undergo flight testing simultaneously. Also linked into the system was a laser ranging theodolite, used for tracking to an extreme degree of accuracy, and IFF. Flight test instruments on board each aircraft recorded literally hundreds of readings which were relayed to the ATS, processed by the computer and displayed to engineering test staff on the ground, either in real time or after a very short delay. Previously, the aircraft on test had to land back before the data could be retrieved and analysed.

Using ATS, most of the information was available in real time, while the remainder could be processed and made

available before the end of the flight debrief. Real-time data gave quite startling advantages. Tests for thrust/drag, static and dynamic stability and structural flutter could be carried out simultaneously, and the real-time data enabled engineers on the ground to clear the aircraft for the next test sequence immediately, or alternatively rerun the test on the spot if necessary. No longer could adverse weather or a minor component failure negate a test flight; the flight could be immediately rescheduled to cover a new aspect. For weapon and avionic systems testing, the broadly comparable Systems Integration Test Station (SITS) was installed at the Pacific Missile Range at Point Mugu.

This dynamic flight testing at Calverton, involving Tomcats 1X, 2, 3, and 8, was backed up to a tremendous degree by in-flight refuelling (IFR). In particular, IFR made a large contribution to the high-speed flight tests, allowing up to three protracted afterburner runs per flight instead of the usual one. The endurance of a test flight thus became limited by weather or pilot fatigue rather than fuel, as in the past, while the proportion of takeoffs and landings to flight hours was dramatically reduced. Test flying on previous aircraft without IFR had produced an average of 1.3 hours

Above: Tomcat 3 (BuAer 157982) was the structural test aircraft. Comprehensively instrumented, it was responsible for proving both interceptor and fighter envelopes.

Below: Tomcat 4 (BuAer 157983) was the first Tomcat to be fitted with AWG-9 and AIM-54 missiles. The low-drag pallets and cranked wing pylon are clearly visible from this angle.

Right: Tomcat 5 (BuAer 157984) was the systems instrumentation aircraft, tasked with testing communication, navigation and weapon systems, as well as data link and countermeasures.

Typical test flight profile

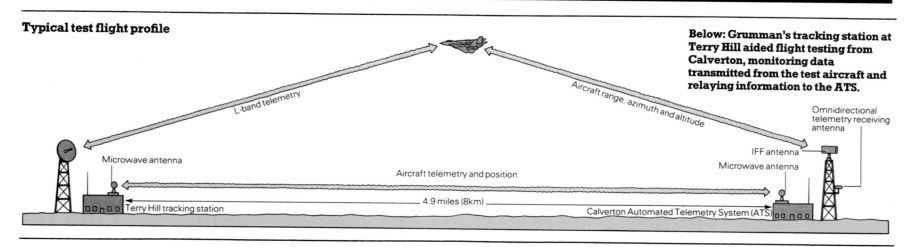

L-band telemetry

Aircraft range, azimuth and altitude

Microwave antenna

Omnidirectional telemetry receiving antenna

IFF antenna

Microwave antenna

Aircraft telemetry and position

4.9 miles (8km)

Terry Hill tracking station

Calverton Automated Telemetry System (ATS)

per flight. The F-14 programme, with IFR, averaged 2.9 hours per flight, more than 200 per cent better.

The pace was hectic. The accelerated flight test programme was aimed at completing 3,600 flight test hours by the end of 1972, with the object of getting the F-14 into fleet service during the following year. In the course of 1971, the maximum number of flying hours in one day reached 12.5, while one single mission involved five in-flight refuellings. On one occasion, five test flights were made in one day.

The back-up effort required was prodigious. Three F-4 Phantoms were employed as high-speed chase aircraft, while low-speed chase duties were performed by three Grumman A-6s. A fourth A-6 augmented the low-speed chase aircraft and also dispensed smoke for high-speed, high-altitude airspeed calibration. The A-6s also acted as tankers, equipped with McDonnell Douglas 'buddy packs', holding 20,000lb (9,000kg) of transferable fuel; they were positioned where required by the IFF tracking station that augmented the ATS.

NPE 1 took place between December 2 and 16, 1971. The flight envelope that had been cleared by Grumman prior to the evaluation ranged from Mach 0.9 at sea level to Mach 1.8 at 35,000ft (10,700m).

The functions of the aircraft used in the flight test programme were as follows. No. 1, BuAer 157980, was assigned to high-speed testing and exploration of the flight performance envelope. As we have seen, it did not survive its second flight. No. 2, BuAer 157981, performed the low-speed and high AOA tests, followed later by stall/spin testing. For

the latter, the variable geometry wings were at first fixed at a sweep angle of 20deg while the variable engine inlets were locked fully open, and an anti-spin parachute was fitted.

Intended to operate at low airspeeds and high AOA, No. 2 was the test aeroplane most likely to lose both engines in flight, so it was fitted with an emergency power unit. To provide power for the flight controls and an emergency electrical generator, a hydraulic pump driven by a Sundstrand hydrazine-powered turbine was fitted.

Grumman had set out to design and build a spinproof aeroplane, but early tests in NASA's Langley Research Center spin tunnel had shown a tendency for the scale models to enter a fast flat spin. Further tests with 1/10 scale radio-controlled models dropped from a helicopter failed to confirm this tendency, but Grumman was taking no chances. Before the spin test programme started in the Spring of 1972, Tomcat No. 2 was fitted with 6ft×2ft (1.83m×0.61m) canard surfaces on each side of the cockpit, as a precautionary measure. Later in 1972, this Tomcat was used for gun trials, firing the 20mm M61A multi-barrel cannon at speeds up to Mach 1.8. No. 2 was instrumented to record and transmit 325 different measurements via the ATS.

Replacement for Tomcat 1

Tomcat No. 12, BuAer 157991, was the next to take to the air. Redesignated No. 1X, it replaced 157980 in the flight test programme. Hydraulically powered shakers were attached to the wing and tail surfaces for flutter testing, and by December 1972 it had exceeded Mach 2.25. The most comprehensively instrumented of all the test aircraft, it could record and transmit no fewer than 647 different measurements via ATS.

Next off, on October 7, 1971, was No. 4, BuAer 157983. On October 30 it was flown to the Navy Missile Center (NMC) at Point Mugu, where it was fitted by Hughes with the AWG-9 fire control system and AIM-54 Phoenix missiles for evaluation. Also to Point Mugu on December 12 went No. 5, BuAer 157984, for systems instrumentation and compatibility testing. This covered navigation, communications, air-to-air and air-to-ground weapon systems, electronic countermeasures and data link.

No. 5 was followed to Point Mugu on January 15, 1972, by No. 6, BuAer 157985, which was scheduled take part in missile separation and weapon system compatibility tests. This aircraft was lost through an unfortunate accident on June 20, 1973, when an unarmed AIM-7E-2 Sparrow pitched up after launch and struck it, causing the Tomcat to catch fire. Both crew members ejected and were rescued from the sea. As a result of this accident, more powerful cartridges were used for missile ejection.

Tomcat No. 3, BuAer 157982, was the structural test vehicle, and first flew on December 28, 1971. Comprehensively fitted with strain gauges, it measured bending moments, torsion, and shear loads on the wings, fuselage and tail over the fighter interceptor envelope of 6.5g and weapons delivery envelope of 7.5g. A total of 477 different measurements could be recorded and transmitted.

No. 7, BuAer 157986, was the F-14B prototype, to test the new ATE engines. Holdups with the ATE delayed the first flight, which was made with the proven TF30-P-412 on one side and the new F401-PW-400 on the other, on September 12, 1973. No. 8, BuAer 157987, first flew on December 31, 1971, and was scheduled to provide contractual guarantee data for a production configuration aircraft. The first Tomcat to exceed an altitude of 56,000ft (17,000m), it was instrumented to record and transmit 164 different measurements. No. 9, BuAer 157988, went to Point Mugu to be used by Hughes to assist in the evaluation of the AWG-9 fire control system.

No. 10, BuAer 157989, was slated to undertake the carrier suitability proving programme. First flown on February 29, 1972, it was ferried to Naval Air Test Center (NATC) Patuxent River on April 6 for initial trials. These completed, it made the first Tomcat catapult launch from USS Forrestal on June 15, and its first arrested deck landing on the same carrier on June 28. It was lost on the following day in an unfortunate accident which claimed the life of test pilot Bill Miller. The annual air show at Patuxent River was to be held on June 30 and the Tomcat was scheduled to make two passes across the airfield at 1,000ft (300m), the first with the wings spread and the second with them swept back. On June 29, Miller was rehearsing for the show. It was a hazy day, and eyewitnesses saw the Tomcat flying low over Chesapeake Bay, then suddenly attempt to pull up. The big fighter mushed in, hitting the water tail first. Fortunately, the rear seat was unoccupied.

No. 11, BuAer 157990, joined the growing Tomcat contingent at Point Mugu for avionics systems compatibility testing on March 24, 1972. This included air-to-air evaluation, air-to-ground gunnery, automatic carrier landing system (ACLS), and antenna patterns. The ACLS, which had been successfully tested and used operationally by the F-4 Phantom, was designed to aid the recovery of aircraft at night or in marginal weather conditions. In such circumstances, the pilot couples his ACLS to the ACLS on the carrier, while the carrier ACLS acquires the aircraft on radar and tracks it, trans-

F-14 development milestones

Jan 1966	Preliminary studies started
Oct 1967	VFX concept formulated
May 1969	Funds for F-111B refused by Congress
Jun 21, 1968	RFP released to industry
Dec 13, 1968	Evaluation of proposals completed
Dec 15, 1968	Grumman and MCAIR proposals short-listed
Jan 5, 1968	Grumman and MCAIR final revisions submitted
Jan 14, 1968	Announcement of VFX award to Grumman
Feb 3, 1969	RTD&E contract signed
Mar 1969	Design frozen
Sep 16, 1969	Performance characteristics validated by NASA
Nov 1969	Engineering mockup and manufacturing assembly (EMMA) started
Feb 2, 1970	AWG-9 computer and development test equipment delivered to SITS, Point Mugu
Feb 27, 1970	ATE engine contract awarded to Pratt & Whitney; F-14B proposal submitted
May 18, 1970	XTF-30-P-412 ground test engine received from Pratt & Whitney and inlet compatibility testing started
Jul 9, 1970	Engine and inlet tests concluded
Jul 23, 1970	EMMA demonstration completed
Sep 30, 1970	F-14B contract signed
Dec 21, 1970	First flight
Sep 16, 1971	First supersonic flight
Dec 2-16, 1971	NPE I
Jun 15, 1972	First catapult launch from carrier
Jun 28, 1972	First arrested landing on carrier
Jul 6-Aug 15, 1972	NPE 2
Sep 28, 1972	First operational evaluation begun by test squadron VX-4
Dec 31, 1972	First delivery to RAG squadron VF-124
Oct 14, 1972	VF-1 and VF-2 commissioned at NAS Miramar
Oct 1973	BIS trials concluded
Sep 17, 1974	VF-1 and VF-2 deploy to sea aboard USS Enterprise
Jul 5, 1977	BuAer 157988 becomes the first Tomcat to reach 1,000 flight hours

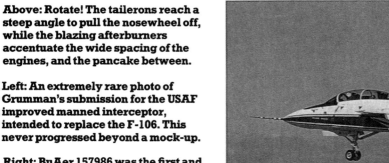

Above: Rotate! The tailerons reach a steep angle to pull the nosewheel off, while the blazing afterburners accentuate the wide spacing of the engines, and the pancake between.

Left: An extremely rare photo of Grumman's submission for the USAF improved manned interceptor, intended to replace the F-106. This never progressed beyond a mock-up.

Right: BuAer 157986 was the first and only F-14B, although it was intended as the definitive Tomcat. It flew just 33 hours with the F401-PW-400 Advanced Technology Engine.

Below: Only the paint job and the tail markings distinguish the F-14B from the F-14A. It was later used as the test airframe for the F101 Derivative Fighter Engine.

mitting signals to the aircraft's auto-pilot which guide the aircraft straight onto the deck, making due allowance for the motion of the carrier. The frontal radar cross-section of the Tomcat causes 'glint' which leads to inaccuracies; consequently the ACLS is carried but not used operationally. Tomcat No. 12 was redesignated 1X as related earlier.

No. 13, BuAer 158612, made its maiden flight on May 2, 1972, then on August 2 entered Grumman's anechoic chamber at Calverton for intensive radiation and electro-magnetic compatibility tests. No. 14, BuAer 158613, was assigned to maintenance and reliability work at Calverton, while Nos 15 to 19, BuAer 158614 to 158618, were allotted to pilot training, although No. 17 was reassigned to Patuxent River to replace No. 10 on carrier suitability work. The final Tomcat to take part in the test programme, No. 20, BuAer 158620, was intended for climatic testing at Point Mugu, where it was to be 'cycled through the weather hangar' – an intriguing prospect! It later finished up at Patuxent River.

Meanwhile, cost problems were appearing. Grumman's original bid had been considerably higher than that of its main rival, McDonnell Douglas, and although it had been pared down subsequently it still remained higher. In evaluating the two fighters, cost had not been the only consideration for the Navy, and the contract had been awarded after an overall appraisal of the qualities of the two contenders on a value for money basis. Obviously, fleet air defence capability had weighed heavily with the assessors. The Tomcat was expensive, but it was clearly capable, and in time of war the loss of an aircraft carrier which might have been saved by better defensive equipment would be difficult to justify in terms of peacetime savings on aircraft procurement.

Cost escalation

Apart from the high initial cost of the Tomcat, however, other factors were emerging to boost the cost still higher. One was a reduction in company turnover, which meant that the Tomcat programme had to carry a higher proportion of the overheads than had originally been anticipated, but the main factor was inflation, which in the early 1970s started going through the roof. The contract for the F-14 contained set options to buy over a period of years, with an inflation content of 3 per cent on labour and 2 per cent on materials built in. This was the so-called total procurement package, and was one of the last such contracts to be issued.

The inflation percentages were insufficient to cover the true increases. This was not something that applied solely to Grumman, the aerospace industry, or even the United States: it was a world-wide trend, as readers in any country and any industry who were involved with fixed-price contracts during this period will remember with a shudder. To summarize the story, Grumman chairman E. Clinton Towl testified to the Senate Air Power Tactical Subcommittee that if the contract was enforced, the company would be compelled to close down. The importance to the security of the nation of Grumman products was such that a compromise was reached and production continued.

NPE 2 took place between July 6 and August 15, 1972, in two phases. Phase 2A was conducted at Calverton by a team from Patuxent River, headed by Commander George White. Aircraft Nos 2 and 8 were put through a demanding series of tests while configured with various combinations of Phoenix, Sparrow, Sidewinder, and drop tanks. The M61A cannon was also evaluated. Phase 2B was carried out at Point Mugu by a team led by Commander Frank Schluntz. Using aircraft Nos 5 and 9, they checked out the avionics and weapon system. A total of 178 flight hours in 72 flights was logged, and the final report contained this verdict: "Displayed outstanding performance characteristics and potential to accomplish the air superiority fighter and fleet air defence missions".

Flaws and modifications
Flight testing proceeded apace, with over 3,500 flight test hours recorded by June 1, 1973. Inevitably, problems were encountered. Initially it was found that buffetting was caused with the flaps down: a gap between the spoilers on the upper wing sections and the flaps was responsible, and closing the gap cured the problem. Fatigue cracks occurred in the beaver tail structure, and a minor redesign was necessary, while fibreglass skins in this area had to be replaced by metal. Vibration and fatigue caused the fin caps to be reinforced.

As had been feared, problems with spinning also began to be encountered. The Tomcat was a relatively vice-free aeroplane to fly; it was often described by its pilots as a pussycat in the air. It appeared to have no AOA limitations, and during tests had reached angles exceeding 90deg and negative angles of over 50deg. The negative angle was attained by a hard pull-up followed by a roll inverted. It remained controllable when well outside the normal flight envelope. But it could enter an irrecoverable flat spin, something which was to remain a vexed question for years.

The original Tomcat was designed

Top: Tomcats wearing a jagged rectilinear disruptive camouflage scheme reminiscent of the Luftwaffe in World War II. All identification has been painted over, but these are from VX-4 and are participants in AIMVAL/ACEVAL at Nellis in 1977.

with an Automatic Rudder Interconnect (ARI), which had been developed for use on aircraft which did not have leading edge wing flaps. The production machines featured manoeuvring wing slats which deployed automatically during hard manoeuvres. Like many other high-performance fighters, the Tomcat suffers from wing rock at high AOA. To roll the aircraft in this condition, the pilot must either use the rudder into the roll, or use rudder into but stick opposite to the direction of roll. The original ARI would command a large rudder input which could, and sometimes did, cause a flat spin. Once the spin was established, the crew had no option but to eject.

After an early loss of a production aircraft to this cause, the decision was taken to uncouple the signal inputs on AOA to the ARI, thus disabling the system. This still left the Tomcat with a wing rock and roll reversal problem, although to be fair, the Grumman fighter was more tractable than either the F-4 Phantom or F-8 Crusader that it was designed to replace.

The method of using rudder into the roll but with opposite stick gave the fastest rate of roll, but in essence it was a pro-spin input, and if coupled with an engine stall, would easily turn into a flat spin. This had two consequences, both bad. The first was a small but steady attrition rate in fleet service attributable to this cause. The second was that inexperienced pilots tended to play safe, and did not handle the aircraft to the extremes of its capability. This was a problem that the Navy simply had to learn to live with, as they had lived with the unforgiving departure tendencies of

Above: An F-14 attached to the Naval Air Test Center at Patuxent River goes off the ski jump. While it would appear to have little application for carrier operations other than with vertical landing aircraft, the ski jump, which can be erected in just two hours, could be used to assist short takeoffs from a damaged airfield.

the Phantom, but testing to overcome the problem continued.

New ARI
In 1980, a joint US Navy/NASA programme was instituted involving a new ARI. Tomcat 1X was extensively modified with spin prevention systems to carry out the flight testing. Modifications involved a spin chute, battery-driven hydraulic pumps to maintain pressure to the control surfaces in the event of a double engine stall, and extending canards. In a flat spin, a jettisoned canopy tends to remain in the vicinity of the aircraft, so an eject-through canopy and compatible seat were also fitted. Fitted with the new ARI, 1X carried out a three-year test programme at the Dryden Flight Research Facility at Edwards AFB, California.

Gradually, the system was evolved. The new ARI activates only when the AOA reaches about 33deg coupled with an excessive yaw rate. If the controls are set in a pro-spin direction, the ARI washes them out, allowing only 2deg of rudder input in a pro-spin direction; however, if they are against the spin, they are not modified. Roll reversal is reportedly eliminated, while wing rock has been suppressed. The handling qualities throughout the ACM envelope are significantly improved.

The flight test programme also produced engine stalling problems at high AOA. The TF30 had proved to be rather sensitive when used in the F-111, hence the widely spaced engine pods on the F-14. But provided that the power settings were left high, the engines appeared to be relatively stall-free at high AOA, although stalls did occur. It should

however be noted that the TF30 had never previously flown in a real manoeuvring-type fighter, and that exploration of the high AOA regime came as a distinct culture shock to it. But as the ATE engine was scheduled to replace it as the definitive engine for the F-14, the TF30 was regarded as an interim measure and its shortcomings consequently seemed less significant.

In the long term, the question of powerplants for the Tomcat proved troublesome. The prototype F-14B, which first flew on September 12, 1973, was put through what was described as a reasonably successful test programme. The ATE, the powerful F401-PW-400, offered significant increases in thrust and improved fuel consumption, but it was pushing the technology of the times fairly hard, and two engines were reported to have exploded on the test rig prior to the first flight. With a large financial question mark hanging over the F-14 itself at this time, extra funds for further development were hard to come by, and tests with the F401 were finally suspended in April 1974. The F-14A, with its interim TF30 engine, was to be the definitive in-service model.

By 1974, as the number of F-14As in fleet service built up, the problems became really serious. During simulated combat missions flown by Navy pilots it was found that the compressor stalling was more serious than had been thought. This was coupled with a serious lack of reliability that on occasion caused catastrophic failure followed by fire. Much of the unreliability stemmed from the fact that the TF30-P-412 contained parts with short fatigue lives. To counter this, Pratt and Whitney developed the P-414, which among other design changes had a belt of armour around the fan section to contain the pieces of broken blade in the event of a failure.

The P-412 was gradually replaced by the P-414 in fleet service from February 1977 onwards. Further modifications resulted in the P-414A, the first of which was delivered in December 1982. However, the stall problem could only partially be dealt with using the existing engine or its derivatives. At the time that the TF30 had been conceived, the constant high AOA work combined with the continual throttle movements used in modern fighter operations had not been foreseen, and the basic powerplant was just not designed to be worked that hard.

To return to the flight test programme, on the Pacific Missile Range, a dazzlingly successful series of AWG-9/AIM-54 Phoenix demonstrated both single and multi-shot capability against a wide variety of targets, details of which are given in the Avionics and Armament chapter. As an aeroplane, the Tomcat had demonstrated that it was a major advance on previous fleet fighters; now it showed an unparalleled capability as a weapon system in the fleet air defence role that remains unequalled.

Tomcats in service
BIS trials were successfully completed during October 1973, and the second batch of sea trials were flown from USS Forrestal off the Virginian Capes at the end of November. Three F-14s participated, notching up 54 catapult launches, 124 bolters and 56 traps during a seven day period, during which minimum wind over deck (WOD) requirements were evaluated, in addition to the approach power compensator (APC) and weapon systems. The first two Tomcat squadrons, VF-1 and VF-2, were commissioned at NAS Miramar on October 14, 1972, although the first production aircraft to be allocated to them, BuAer 158983, did not reach them until a year later. Also formed at Miramar was the

first fleet training and Replacement Air Group (RAG) squadron, VF-124, previously equipped with F-8s. They received their first Tomcat, BuAer 158620, on the last day of 1972.

Although the Tomcat had been demonstrated to be a first class fighter and an unequalled weapon system, its escalating costs were still a source of worry. One of the arguments used against it was that four Phantoms could be purchased for the cost of one Tomcat. This argument, which overlooked the added crew, fuel and support costs of four Phantoms, was invalid for other reasons. It was doubtful whether four Phantoms could do the work of just one Tomcat in the fleet air defence role, while both aircraft occupied a comparable amount of deck space. Twenty-four Tomcats could therefore only be replaced by the same number of Phantoms, which would mean that the defensive capability of the carrier would be greatly reduced. The Navy's prime argument was that they really could not afford to be without the Tomcat.

As early as July 1971, the Secretary of Defense requested the Navy to examine the possibility of a navalized Eagle, the F-15N. McDonnell Douglas, makers of the F-15, the prototype of which had not at this time flown, produced a modification study which, not surprisingly, resulted in a considerable weight increase. The Navy's Fighter Study Group III, formed to carry out an independent examination of the project, concluded that even greater weight increases would result, and once Phoenix missiles were added, performance would fall while costs would increase, both to unacceptable levels.

New discussions were initiated in March 1973. This time the idea was to compare the F-15N, an austere variant of the F-14, an upgraded F-4, and proposals from other aerospace companies. Also under consideration was a return to the time-honoured method of selecting fighter aircraft – building rival prototypes then conducting a competitive flyoff. At this time the F-14B was still six months away from its first flight, and the projected F-14C lay still further in the future. The austere Tomcat proposal was therefore at first referred to as the F-14D.

The proposed changes gave it what can only be described as a negative improved capability. Among the modifications considered were four new weapon control systems, three of which had no Phoenix capability, and a modified Hughes AWG-9A, with the simultaneous tracking capability halved from 24 to 12, and the simultaneous engagement capability reduced from six Phoenix to four. The glove vane, DLC, and APC were to be deleted and the avionics made more austere.

By the following year, the F-14 Optimod, or F-14X, had emerged as a design study, with 38 airframe alterations, reduced avionics and modified engines. Also projected was the F-14T, so basic that it was regarded as a 'Model T' aeroplane. The whole idea was dropped in May 1974, one of the major influences being the high attrition rate of US-designed aircraft in the previous October's Arab-Israeli war. In a nutshell, the carrier air groups could not afford high attrition rates, so it made little sense to equip them with anything less than the very best, although one thing which did emerge from the discussions was the F/A-18 Hornet, a true dual-role fighter that could if necessary assist the Tomcat in the fleet air defence role, while largely supplanting it as an escort.

As with any other fighter, various updates took place over the years, although nothing of sufficient magnitude to warrant a redesignation. At sea, water

intrusion caused electronic failures, and sealers, baffles and drain holes had to be incorporated. A Garrett AiResearch central air data computer was fitted in manufacturing batches from 1976 onward, along with a new ARC-159 UHF radio, both offering greatly improved reliability. And the manoeuvre flaps, previously controlled manually, were automated, operating as a function of Mach number, wing sweep angle, and AOA. This not only reduced the pilot's workload, but improved the sustained turning performance.

In the early 1970s, a dedicated reconnaissance variant, the RF-14, had been considered. Studies had been made, but the idea was dropped in 1974. Finally, the Tactical Airborne Reconnaissance Pod System (TARPS) was adopted. The TARPS was originally developed for the A-7, but no problems were encountered in fitting it on a modified F-14, although it neutralizes two Phoenix stations, and requires a control panel in the rear cockpit. F-14 TARPS can be modified back to carry six Phoenix, but the standard F-14A cannot be modified to carry TARPS. It is planned that one squadron on each carrier will have three TARPS

F-14s. The pod has little effect on performance, just slightly increased buffet at high speeds and low altitudes. In all, 49 Tomcats have been modified.

New engines for the long-overdue F-14B were still under development in 1980. In 1981, the F-14B prototype was fitted with the new General Electric F101 DFE engines for a 25-flight test programme, held between July and September of that year. The results were promising, and the F110-GE-400 augmented turbofan was developed from the DFE. The decision to use this engine in the F-14D (the B and C designations by now having been bypassed), and to retrofit the F-14A, was taken by the Navy in February 1984. The first engine was delivered to Grumman in 1986, and flown in the original F-14B Super Tomcat on 29 September of that year.

Meanwhile Grumman was pressing on with the F-14D, with a new digital avionics fit to replace the analogue systems of the original bird, including the APG-71 radar. But after more than 10 years in service, the need for

Top: The last of the many. Super Tomcat BuNo 164604 was the last F-14 off the production line. Seen here in December 1995, it was operated by VX-9 Evaluators at Point Mugu.

Above: The prototype Super Tomcat was used to prove the F110-GE-400 engines. It used the same airframe, BuNo 357986, which had been used for the earlier F-14B.

better performance was pressing. This was provided by the F110 engine at little expense.

The final F-14A rolled off the production line in March 1987, to be replaced by an interim variant, the F-14A+, which varied from the original only in having GE engines and minor avionics and systems changes. The first F-14A+ was delivered to the US Navy in the autumn of 1987. Initial requirements were for 38 new-build aircraft with a further 32 low-mileage airframes upgraded to F-14A+ standard. Ironically the F-14A+ designation proved incompatible with the USN computer system, and on 1 May, 1991, it officially became the F-14B!

The first F-14D was delivered to the US Navy in May 1990. But by this time, the end of the Cold War and the demand for cutbacks intervened. Instead of the planned 127, only 37 F-14Ds were built, the last of them was completed on July 20, 1992. They were supplemented by 18 F-14D(R)s, upgraded from A models, the last of which was delivered in November 1994.

F-14A
Dimensions
Length: 62ft 8in (19.10m)
Wingspan: 64ft 1½in (19.55m) unswept
         38ft 2½in (11.65m) swept
         33ft 3½in (10.15m) overswept
Gross wing area: 565sq ft (15.49m²)
Aspect ratio: 7.28 unswept
Height: 16ft 0in (4.88m)
Weights
Empty: 39,921lb (18,108kg)
Normal takeoff: 58,571lb (26,567kg)
Maximum: 74,349lb (33.724kg)
Power
Engines: 2 Pratt & Whitney TF30-P-412A or -414A
Maximum thrust: 20,900lb (93kN)
Internal fuel: 16,200lb (7,348kg)
External fuel: 3,800 (1,724kg)
Performance
Vmax: Mach 2.34 at altitude
      Mach 1.2 at sea level
Sea level rate of climb: 30,000ft/min (9,140m/min)
Service ceiling: 56,000ft (17,070m)

F-14D

Dimensions: as for F-14A	
Weights	
Empty	41,780lb (18,951kg)
Normal takeoff	61,200lb (27,760kg)
Maximum	74,349lb (33,724kg)
Power	
Engines:	2 General Electric F110-GE-400
Maximum thrust	27,080lb (12,283kg)
Military thrust	16,610lb (7,534kg)
Internal fuel	16,200lb (7,350kg)
External fuel	3,800lb (1,724kg)
Performance	
V_{max}	Mach 1.88 at altitude. NB: this is an operational rather than a physical limit
	Mach 1.2 at sea level
Sea level rate of climb	c48,000ft/min (14,630m/min)
Service ceiling	c60,000ft (18,290m)
Maximum range	1,600nm (2,965km)

Structure

In the period leading up to 1970, the technologically advanced nations demanded ever greater capability from their new jet fighters. They were expected to be able to operate with equal facility in fair weather or foul, as interceptors, air superiority fighters or tactical fighters with a strike capability, and these requirements resulted in ever-increasing size, complexity and cost. The F-14 Tomcat represented the apogee of this trend, being obviously large, undeniably complex and almost (but fortunately not quite) prohibitively expensive. Only its unique capabilities saved it from cancellation, but with a high proportion of exotic concepts in its design and advanced materials demanding new fabrication techniques in its structure, it represented the summit of the fighter designer's art.

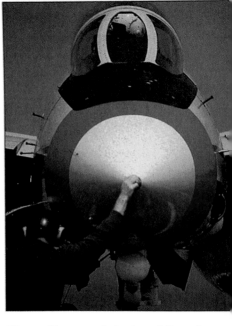

It is many years since I first set eyes on a Tomcat, but my initial impressions have remained fresh. The general appearance was pleasing; from the side it looked sleek despite its size, the enormous, sharply raked intakes suggested immense power, and the large cockpit canopy gave the crew an excellent all-round view, something that had been missing from fighters for a long time. The twin fins were unusual in those days, but after all, this was supposed to be the shape of the future, and to support this view were the then very exotic variable sweep wings.

On walking round to view it from the rear, however, it suddenly looked a very strange bird indeed. For many years, twin-engined jet fighters had had the engines situated close together in the rear fuselage and the cockpit situated up in the front portion. Here was something very different. The huge engine nozzles

were spaced many feet apart, connected by a flat area generally known as the pancake, with an oddly shaped beavertail trailing edge. Looking up toward the front, the cockpit just seemed to grow out of this flat area. A rapid walk round to the front confirmed this: there was no orthodox fuselage, just two rectangular intakes fronting engine pods that ran from front to back in straight lines, with a nacelle between them housing the radar and cockpit which tapered away smoothly into the pancake, while underneath, between the engine pods, was a very pronounced tunnel. This was all so different that it really did look like the shape of the future.

The fleet air defence role carrying Phoenix missiles demanded a large aircraft, and the F-14 is dimensionally large. It therefore could hardly help being fairly heavy, and there are weight constraints involved in carrier operations.

Furthermore, the weight of any fighter has a habit of increasing during its service life as new bits are screwed on, and this can quickly exceed acceptable limits unless sufficient margin is allowed from the outset. Sheer weight had been one of the prime causes of the failure of the F-111B.

The structural design of the F-14 was therefore based on saving as much weight as possible by the use of advanced materials, in particular titanium alloy. By weight, this material accounts for approximately 25 per cent of the structure of the F-14, with 15 per cent steel, only 36 per cent of aluminium alloy, and 4 per cent of non-metallics, which last is made up of boron epoxy composites on the horizontal tail surfaces, fibreglass epoxy in the radome and ventral strakes, and acrylics in the windshield and canopy. This compares with the slightly later McDonnell

Above: Grumman's design philosophy for the Tomcat was to space the engines well away from the fuselage, as seen here. The dielectric cone over the antenna hinges upwards.

Douglas F-15 Air Force fighter, which contains 26 per cent of titanium alloy, just over 37 per cent of aluminium, and 5.5 per cent of steel.

The desirable characteristics of titanium are its high strength to weight ratio, resistance to corrosion, which is essential in a maritime environment, and ability to withstand high temperatures. The alloy mostly used in the F-14 is Ti 6A1 4V, which contains 6 parts of aluminium and 4 parts of vanadium by weight. This alloy has very good welding characteristics, but is expensive and difficult to work. It had been used in fairly small quantities on many aircraft over the years, but a combination of cost and

Above: Instead of using pins, as on the F-111, the wing of the F-14 pivots on two spherical bearings, each held in a pair of lugs. One bearing can support the wing if the other fails.

difficulties in fabrication had restricted its use.

Titanium has a very high yield strength and a low modulus of elasticity. Consequently, it is difficult to shape cold, as it has a tendency to warp, wrinkle, or spring back, while tight bends or radii cause cracking. In the early 1960s, however, a major technological breakthrough increased fabrication potential and reduced costs. The method evolved was to preform individual parts with partially formed contours and flanges. They were then placed in a hot-forming press and creep-formed to their final size and shape at temperatures of 600-800deg C (1,050-1,470deg F), after which

Left: The Tomcat begins to take shape. An abundance of precision measuring equipment is in evidence: theodolite and level in the foreground, and another level on the left wing box.

Right: Titanium alloy was widely used in the construction of the Tomcat – in the wing skins, for example, as well as in structural applications. The F-14's tailerons involved the first major structural use of composites.

Below: The widely separated engine pods and fuselage nacelle form a distinct tunnel. The extra keel area provided by this layout contributes to directional stability.

Below right: Seen from the rear, the Tomcat is unlike any other aircraft. The fuselage nacelle tapers away into the pancake, with its unique beaver tail between the nozzles.

they were held in position for between 10 and 25 minutes to relieve the stress, thereby preventing wrinkling.

This was a tremendous advance, but it did not lend itself to efficient mass production. Grumman engineers decided that they could do better. They incorporated a die-cushion system in each of two conventional four-column presses, and added an electrically heated platen. This created a hot-forming process that allowed titanium sheet parts to be developed from flat pattern blanks in just the one operation, giving considerable savings in time, money, and equipment. Chem-milling is also used for shaping titanium sheets in some applications, and the old bogey of hydrogen embrittlement has been eliminated.

Hot isostatic pressing is also used to reduce wastage, which with titanium tends to be very high. In this process, titanium powder is poured into a mould,

which is then sealed and pressurized with a chemically inert gas, before being heated to very high temperatures to produce a preformed part which is very close to the final shape required. This minimizes waste due to machining.

Titanium wing box
One of the most obvious applications of titanium in a variable sweep wing aeroplane is the wing carry-through box, which holds the pivots. This is inevitably a large and heavy structure which needs great strength to carry the in-flight loads. The corresponding item in the F-111 had been made of steel, part welded and part bolted together. Bolting is an excellent way of connecting things, but it does introduce discontinuities, as the stresses and strains are taken by the bolts and the areas surrounding the bolt holes. Suffice it to say that the F-111 experienced a few problems with its wing box assembly,

and to avoid this, Grumman elected not only to manufacture the structure from titanium, but to produce an all-welded assembly. So large a component had never before been made from titanium, but the rewards, in the form of a 900lb (408kg) weight saving over the same product in steel, was great. The weight reduction also reduced the fuel load needed to meet mission requirements.

The wing box assembly was a large structure, 22ft (6.71m) long, made up of 35 sub-assemblies, which had to be carefully aligned before being placed in a vacuum chamber for electron-beam (EB) welding. For the production of the F-14, Grumman invested heavily in EB welding machines, five in all, including two of the biggest in the Western world. The largst was 32ft × 10ft (9.76m × 3.05m) and was capable of welding titanium wing planks 26ft (7.93m) long, while the machine used to weld the wing carry-

Materials distribution

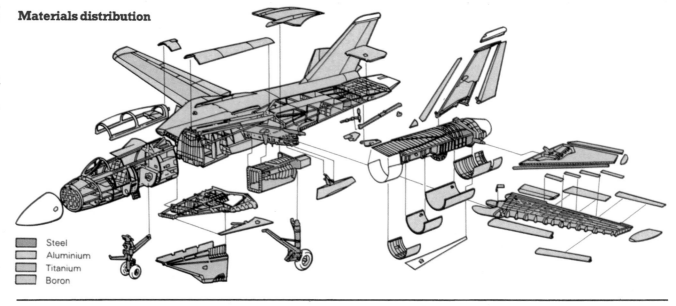

- Steel
- Aluminium
- Titanium
- Boron

through boxes measured 25ft × 11ft × 9ft (7.62m × 3.35m × 2.74m). The vacuum chamber is necessary to maintain the high energy levels needed (60,000 volts), and to prevent atmospheric contamination of the weld. With the components in position, the chamber is closed and evacuated, and the machine operator uses a telescope to track the thin seam line of the joint.

Seventy welds are needed on each wing box assembly, and the machine is capable of operating at speeds of up to 60in (152.4cm) per minute. The energy of the electron beam is focussed on a spot roughly ⅛in (3mm) wide, and can penetrate up to 2½in (63.5mm) of titanium at a single pass. The resulting weld is very narrow, very strong, causes hardly any distortion, and needs little cleaning up on completion. The F-14 has had its share of problems, but the wing box was not one of them. So strong is it, that following the crash of the first prototype, the component was recovered intact from the wreck and put to use as a test fixture.

Wing design

No component of the airframe of a fighter affects its performance and flying characteristics as much as the wing. A wing of fixed shape and size is inevitably a compromise, optimized for a particular point in the flight envelope, and growing increasingly inefficient as the flight regimes diverge from that point. Wing design is therefore an attempt to meet the aerodynamic needs of widely varying flight conditions and operational requirements by building for the design point which gives the best results at contradictory extremes.

The Tomcat was designed to fulfil both the interceptor and the air superiority fighter functions. An interceptor needs endurance, economic cruise, then rapid

Above: Some idea of how much of the wing area is taken up with flaps and slats can be gained from this picture of a prototype Tomcat under construction. Also seen are the original beaver tail and speedbrake.

Below: To meet the varying demands of different flight regimes, the wing reconfigures itself using leading edge slats and trailing edge flaps. The manoeuvre flap setting is only used at subsonic and transonic speeds.

Wing control surfaces

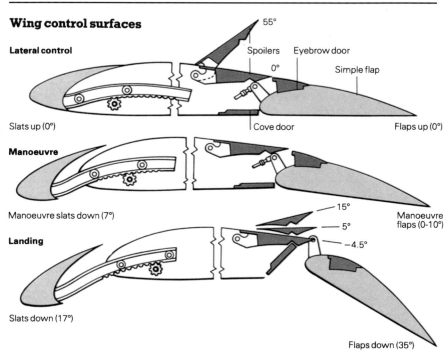

acceleration to give its missiles maximum energy at launch, which extends their range and reduces their time of flight to the target, and consequently increases the probability of a kill. In passing, this little refinement seemed to have escaped the advocates of the subsonic Missileer.

An air superiority fighter also needs sparkling acceleration, both to catch an opponent and to disengage from the fight, and at the time when the Tomcat was designed it was also thought that a top speed exceeding Mach 2 was desirable. It also needs to be able to haul its nose around the horizon as fast as possible, both to bring its weaponry to bear on an evading target, and to crimp in the missile envelope of an assailant. If caught in a big multi-bogey dogfight – the

furball, as American pilots call it – disengagement will be fraught with peril, and under certain circumstances it may well be preferable to stay and fight it out. This calls for two more desirable qualities, the ability to fly a slow-speed, high AOA engagement effectively, and combat persistence, which is the ability to outlast the enemy in the fight and force him to break off through fuel shortage.

While many of these qualities depend partially on the powerplant, all of them are influenced by the wing design to a greater or lesser degree. The precise requirements will also be conditioned by the altitude at which the engagement takes place. Many of these requirements aerodynamically oppose each other, while others occupy a middle ground. This is why the F-14 was designed with a variable-sweep wing, so that each need was met by the best possible solution.

To see why this is so, we need to briefly examine the nature of lift and drag. Lift is created by the movement of air over the lifting surface, or wing, which creates a low pressure area. The pressure underneath the wing will either remain normal, or be higher than normal, which creates a tendency for the wing to move vertically, into the area of low pressure. The amount of lift created depends on three factors: the velocity of the airflow, the cross-sectional shape of the lifting surface, and the angle at which the lifting surface meets the airflow, which is known as the angle of attack (AOA). As AOA increases, so does lift, but only up to a certain point. If the AOA gets too steep, the smooth flow of 'air across the lifting surface will break down, destroying the lift completely.

The final factor affecting lift is wing loading. There is a limit to the amount of lift that any surface can provide. Hard turns cause accelerations, usually

Above: The transparent mockup shown here taking shape is used to sort out the routings of hydraulic and fuel lines, also electric wiring. With large moving parts such as the wings, contact is to be avoided. The integral

wing fuel tanks, shown here in forward and swept positions by time-lapse photography, are formed of aluminium frames with titanium alloy fuel-tight skin panels fixed with oversized rivets.

measured in terms of multiples of the force of gravity, or g forces. A wing area which is lifting an aeroplane weighing 40,000lb (18,144kg) suddenly finds itself having to cope with a weight of 160,000lb (72,576kg) if the aeroplane enters a 4g turn. It therefore has to find four times the lift, and high lift devices apart, it can only do that by increasing the AOA.

Drag comes basically in three forms: parasite, or profile drag, induced drag, and wave drag. In level flight, the profile drag of a wing is directly proportionate to its surface area. Profile drag also increases in direct proportion to the square of the speed (V^2). Thus the difference in profile drag at speeds of 200kt (370km/h) and 400kt (741km/h) is a factor of four – the velocity has doubled, but the drag has quadrupled. Induced drag is caused by creating lift with the wing, and is proportional to the span loading squared.

The best measurement of the aerodynamic efficiency of the wing is called the lift/drag (L/D) ratio. The obvious way of improving the L/D ratio is to decrease the span loading by increasing the ratio of the span squared to the wing area. This is known as the aspect ratio, and wings are often described as being either high or low aspect ratio. To illustrate the point, the long slender wing of the Lockheed U-2 is of high aspect ratio, while the short, broad wing of the Saab Viggen, for example, is of low aspect ratio. The final form of drag is called wave drag, which manifests itself only in the transonic speed region, dying away at about Mach 1.2.

The high aspect ratio wing is most advantageous at high lift, and the maximum L/D ratio is reached at increasingly high lift as the aspect ratio increases. High sustained and transient turn rates are best achieved by high aspect ratio

Above: The surrounding workstands convey something of the size of the big fighter as the first prototype takes shape. The speed bumps at the bases of the fins recommended by NASA are clearly apparent.

Lift/drag control surfaces

Below: The wings of the Tomcat have no ailerons. Lateral control is by differentially moving tail surfaces assisted at subsonic speeds by the spoilers, which also give direct lift control for carrier landings.

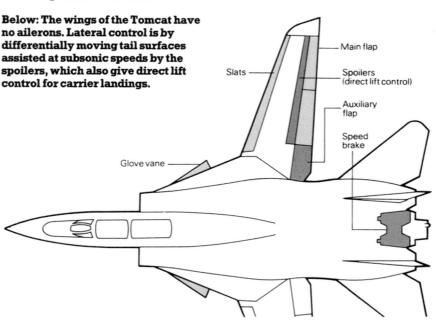

wings. Sustained turn rate is in effect thrust-limited g, and is the product of thrust/weight (T/W) ratio and L/D ratio. All else being equal, the higher L/D ratio of the high aspect ratio wing gives a higher level of sustained manoeuvrability down to lower speeds than a fixed wing. It also permits transient turning out to the very edge of lift with a smaller loss of energy, than a low aspect ratio wing.

Above: A Tomcat of VF-124 showing the wings in the oversweep position. This is used to reduce the parking space required in the confines of a carrier. Despite early design studies, tail folding was not required.

If we examined two wings of equal area, each creating equal lift, we would find that the higher aspect ratio wing has a lower AOA, and consequently less induced drag. The direct result of this is that the high aspect ratio wing needs less thrust to maintain both its lift, and the energy level of its aircraft. The reduction in drag also means that less thrust is needed to achieve the same perform-

ance than with a low aspect ratio wing, and by the same token, less fuel.

The beauty of a variable sweep wing is that it permits a fighter to have either a high or a low aspect ratio wing to suit the demands of the moment, and it converts from high to low aspect ratio by the simple process of sweeping the wings back. Now under some circumstances, a swept wing can be a desirable asset for a fighter. It reduces profile drag to assist rapid acceleration, and also delays the onset of compressibility and wave drag in the transonic region. An aircraft with a variable sweep wing can therefore redesign itself in flight, both in sweep angle and aspect ratio.

Wing control surfaces

The movable part of the Tomcat's wing is fitted with leading edge slats, trailing edge flaps, and spoilers on the top surface. Ailerons are not fitted, and lateral control is achieved primarily by means of differentially moving tawhilerons. The slats are in two sections, which run the full length of the leading edge from the wingtip cap to the trim line of the wing glove. They are simple slotted extending devices which operate at 7deg in the manoeuvre setting, and 17deg for the high-lift landing position.

The flaps are also in two sections and occupy the entire trailing edge. They are the single-slotted type, with a simple hinge, and have a maximum deflection angle of 35deg. Only the inboard flap section is used for take-off and landing. The flaps can be used to improve manoeuvrability by using a 'manoeuvre flap' setting of 10deg, combining with the slats to form wing camber and increase usable lift coefficient. This is used in subsonic and transonic flight only, as the air data computer monitors the flap deflection and prevents the Mach

Sweep Programmer (MSP) from sweeping the wings beyond 50deg when the manoeuvre flap setting is selected.

The spoilers, which are in four sections mounted on the upper surface of the wing, augment lateral control at subsonic speeds, operating only at sweep angles of less than 55deg. They are also used for direct lift control (DLC) on the final approach, and as lift dumpers after touchdown. DLC is pilot-activated by means of a switch on the throttle which deflects the spoilers to a neutral position of 7deg. Using a thumbwheel on the stick, the pilot can then command corrections to altitude while maintaining the same attitude. Deflections of the spoilers by this means give vertical accelerations of roughly 0.13g upwards and 0.07g downwards. In the event of a waveoff, retraction of the speed brakes automatically deactivates DLC and retracts the spoilers. As lift dumpers, the spoilers automatically deflect to a 55deg angle when the weight comes on the main gear. This kills lift and helps to shorten the landing run.

Combat agility

The airfoil selected for the wings was the NACA 64 A2, with a spanwise thickness ratio of 10.2 per cent at the pivot and 7 per cent at the tip. The wing area of 541sq ft (50.28m^2) was sized to achieve maximum combat agility through a combination of low wing loading and manoeuvre flaps and slats. The simple flap system was a design objective, and one which saved sufficient weight to offset the penalty of increasing the wing area. Originally, the aspect ratio at minimum sweep had been in excess of 8, which was absolutely out of sight for a fighter. Optimizing the aspect ratio at minimum sweep at 7.28 also reduced weight, and at this point shifted the determining factor for the six-Phoenix fleet air defence mission from available lift to single-engined rate of climb.

Another factor here is the pancake, which provides additional lifting area.

The total lifting area of the F-14 is roughly 40 per cent greater than the defined wing area, which reduces bending moments in both the wings and the fuselage. It also produces an effective wing loading vastly lower than the reference wing loading, and for all practical purposes constitutes a third, low aspect ratio wing. This makes a significant contribution to the Tomcat's ability to fly at very high AOA, and remain under control at speeds outside the normal performance envelope. The lift on a high aspect ratio wing runs out quite suddenly at around 16deg AOA, whereas with a low aspect ratio surface such as the lifting body of the Tomcat, the lift curve gradually goes flat, with no abrupt break. Pilots have actually been in situations where the Tomcat has been flying on body lift alone, with the wings completely stalled!

In flight, the wing sweeps from the minimum of 20deg to the maximum of 68deg at a rate of 7.5deg/sec in level flight which reduces to just over 4deg/sec at a loading of 7.5g. To ease parking and general space problems in the limited confines of an aircraft carrier, there is an oversweep position of 75deg, which reduces the space occupied. In flight, there are four wing sweep modes. The most important of these is automatic, which is used in almost all flight conditions. It is controlled by the MSP, which uses outputs from the Central Air Data Computer (CADC) to give the optimum wing sweep angle for the flight conditions pertaining at the time.

In automatic mode, the sweep angle for takeoff and landing is 20deg, and at speeds of less than Mach 0.4 the wing sweeps through a mere 2deg. It then remains constant at 22deg up to Mach 0.75. Wing sweep really begins at this point, and the maximum sweep angle of 68deg is reached at Mach 1.2. The MSP was designed not only to improve agility, but also to reduce structural weight. It was obvious that a manual sweep mode would have to be provided, but in manual mode the MSP automatically limits the sweep angle as a function of Mach number and altitude. As this prevents the pilot from overstressing the airframe, the pivot bending moments design limit could be reduced by 30 per cent, or from 14.4×10^6in/lb, down to 11×10^6in/lb. This produced a substantial weight saving.

Manual sweep mode can therefore over-ride automatic mode. For example, if the pilot wants maximum acceleration, he can sweep the wings right back regardless of speed, but the electrons prevent him from over-extending them,

Below: Variable-sweep wings give a low AOA on finals and a good view over the nose for the pilot. The revised speedbrakes are evident as this Tomcat approaches the carrier.

Below: In-flight pictures of the Tomcat with the wings fully swept and the glove vanes extended are rare, but this Iranian formation is at high speed for the camera.

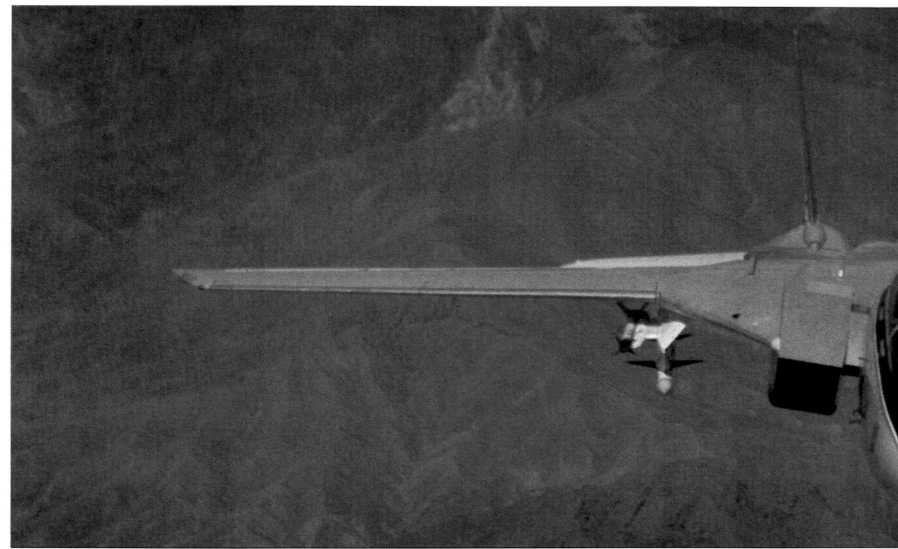

although there is a third mode, emergency, that allows the pilot to spread the wings as he wants them. Generally, the Tomcat is always flown in automatic mode. Manually optimizing the wing sweep during a manoeuvring combat would call for extremely fine judgement, adding considerably to the pilot's workload. In practice, MSP is always better.

The fourth and final mode is ground attack, which locks the wings at an angle of 55deg for bombing or strafing runs. A 55deg sweep angle provides a high-g load factor for heavy manoeuvring with a load of ordnance, and fixing the sweep removes one rapidly changing variable from the weapon release calculation.

Early experiments with variable sweep wings showed pronounced changes in what is called the static margin – the difference between the aircraft's centre of gravity and its aerodynamic centre. This was no problem when designing a fixed wing aeroplane, but with a variable sweep design both the lift and the weight were moving around. It

was found that static margin changes could be minimized by locating the wing pivot well outboard of the aircraft centreline, which suited the widely spaced pod configuration chosen for the F-14 very nicely indeed, and the pivots are set 8.92ft (2.72m) out from the centreline.

Unlike the enormous wing pins used in the F-111 and Tornado, the Tomcat uses two spherical annular bearings for each wing. They are made of titanium alloy, and have Teflon-type and silver rhenium bearing surfaces. One bearing in each wing can fail without compromising the structural integrity of the wing. The loads on the pivot are focussed at a point which roughly corresponds to the centre of pressure of the wing, so that differential tension and compression in the lugs relieves to a certain extent the shear loads acting on the bearing.

The wing movement is powered by a pair of ball screw actuators which are coupled to keep the movement synchronized, while the closure between the fixed wing glove and moving wing

section is done by a fairing assembly which 'breathes' as the wing moves back and forth. An air bag maintains the smooth contour of the aircraft when the wing is in the forward position, and is compressed as it sweeps aft, while the overwing fairing has external stiffeners.

As the wings sweep back, a high proportion of the lift also moves rearward, but very little of the weight, so that the centre of lift is well to the rear of the centre of gravity. This produces a nose-down moment which must be counterbalanced by a download on the horizontal tail surfaces to trim the aircraft as the wings sweep. At supersonic speeds, this produces excessive stability, which incidentally, is not confined to variable sweep fighters. It is most undesirable, because it reduces supersonic manoeuvrability. The F-111B had been described as 'absolutely awful' in this respect, unable to pull more than 2-3g at 35,000ft (10,670m) at high Mach numbers.

Glove vane

The solution was the brainchild of F-14 Project Manager Robert Kress, and consisted of a small, retractable triangular surface called a glove vane located in the leading edge of the wing glove. Controlled by the CADC, it automatically extends at speeds exceeding Mach 1.4. Its function is to destabilize the forward area of the aircraft, and relieve the downloads on the tail caused by trimming. As an example of its effect, at 68deg sweep angle and 4g acceleration, the net loading is reduced from 6,000lb to 4,000lb (2,721kg to 1,814kg). This reduces the airframe bending moments by some 12.5 per cent and permits a lighter structure. The glove vanes also enabled the F-14 to pull a 7½g turn at Mach 2, maintaining the loading as the speed wound down through Mach 1. At the time, this was practically unheard of, but a high premium had been placed on supersonic manoeuvre capability, partly because the F-111 had been so poor.

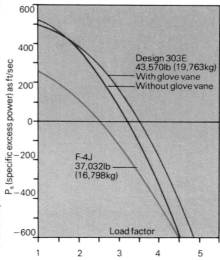

Above: The glove vane improves supersonic manoeuvrability by a considerable margin. These figures are for Mach 1.65 at 35,000ft (10,670m) with 50 per cent fuel.

Glove vane

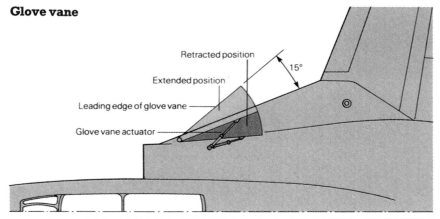

Below: The flattened pancake behind the cockpit acts virtually as a third, low aspect ratio wing, and greatly increases the lifting area. F-14A of VF-211 Checkmates.

Above: A unique feature of the Tomcat is the glove vane, which improves supersonic manoeuvrability by destabilizing the forward area of the aircraft, reducing trim drag.

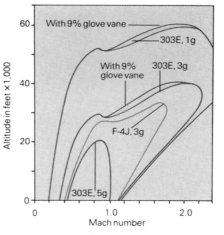

Above: The glove vane increases the flight performance envelope appreciably, as shown by the steady state boundaries for 1g and 3g (weights as in upper graph).

The glove vane can be manually extended at speeds between Mach 1 and Mach 1.4, but is prevented from operating at sweep angles below 35deg at subsonic speeds as it would make the aircraft unstable in pitch. However, when the ground attack sweep mode is used, the vanes extend automatically to their full travel of 15deg at speeds exceeding Mach 0.35. The glove vane is hydraulically actuated, and pivots about its foremost angle at a maximum rate of about 10.5deg/sec.

Each wing is an integral fuel tank, although no special sealants are used. The wing skins are titanium alloy, Ti 6A1 4V on the upper surface and the slightly different Ti 6A1 4V 2Sn, with two parts of tin added, on the lower. The skins are creep-formed, and drilled by computerized methods. Oversized rivets are used and punched into the holes with such force and accuracy that they fuse into the metal, making a fuel-tight joint.

The fuselage is of semi-monocoque construction, with machined main frames and titanium longerons. The inlet duct support frame and engine support beams are also of titanium, while both the main gear support frame and the spectacle-shaped beam which carries the engine mounts and taileron connections are of steel. The stressed skin is generally of aluminium. The huge dielectric cone at the nose which houses the radar antenna is unusual in that it hinges upwards. The spacious cockpit, equipped with two Martin Baker GRU-7A ejection seats, rocket assisted to give a zero altitude, zero speed escape capability, is reached by means of an integral boarding ladder, which retracts into the left hand side of the nacelle, midway between the seats.

The speed brakes are situated well aft, extending above and below the pancake. They were deliberately over-sized at the design stage for use in air combat manoeuvring. The dorsal speed brake has a total area of 8.6sq ft ($0.8m^2$) and operates in phase with the ventral brake, of 7.4sq ft ($0.69m^2$) area. The ventral speed brake is in two parts to operate around the arrester hook. Hydraulically operated, their maximum extension angle is 60deg, and the operating time to full extension is two seconds. Balancing the speed brakes in this under and over manner minimizes trim change when they are actuated. When the gear is lowered for landing, an interlock restricts the extension angle of the ventral speed brake to 18deg to provide sufficient ground clearance.

In the period when the F-14 was designed, there were no such luxuries as artificial stability and fly-by-wire, so the flight control system is largely mechanical. The F-111B had a considerable quantity of electronics in the flight control system, but early in the F-14 design stage, the decision was taken to use the proven spring and bobweight system. The wing sweep, slats, flaps, tailerons and rudders all have direct mechanical linkage, and only the spoilers are electrically driven. The result is a basically stable aeroplane which possesses flying qualities good enough to complete most missions even when stability augmentation and automatic systems operation are not functioning.

One of the obvious reactions to the unusual fuselage shape of the F-14 is, "Whatever happens to the airflow in the tunnel between the engine pods?" In fact, it was so obvious that it was the first question I put to Grumman when starting this work. Naturally Grumman had thought of it first, and NASA had been hard on their heels, but very extensive testing in all flight regimes, with and without external stores carried in the tunnel, failed to reveal any adverse flow

Grumman F-14A Tomcat cutaway

1 Pressure sensor
2 Radar target horn
3 Radome
4 Flight refuelling probe
5 Automatic direction finding antenna
6 Windshield rain dispersal air ducts
7 Angle of attack probe
8 Rudder pedals
9 Pilot's instrument displays
10 Head-up display combiner glass (no longer fitted)
11 Control column
12 Wing sweep control
13 Throttle levers
14 Pilot's Martin Baker GRU-7A ejection seat
15 Naval Flight Officer's instrument console
16 'Kick-in' boarding step
17 Radar hand controller
18 Cockpit canopy cover
19 Naval Flight Officer's ejection seat
20 Canopy jack
21 Glove vane hydraulic jack
22 Starboard glove vane
23 Navigation light
24 UHF/Tacan antenna
25 Forward fuselage fuel tanks
26 Intake bleed door and hydraulic jack
27 Leading edge slat
28 Starboard wing integral tank
29 Starboard navigation light
30 Formation light
31 Spoilers
32 Outboard manoeuvre flaps
33 Flap sealing vane
34 Wing pivot box integral fuel tank
35 Inboard high-lift flap
36 Manoeuvre flap and slat drive motor and gearbox
37 Emergency hydraulic generator
38 UHF/IFF antenna
39 Wing sweep actuating screw jack
40 Inflatable wing seal
41 Engine bleed air ducting
42 Flight control rod linkages
43 Wing fully swept position
44 Wing oversweep position (for carrier stowage)
45 Aft fuselage fuel tanks
46 Starboard taileron
47 Rudder hydraulic actuator
48 Airbrake hydraulic jack
49 Upper airbrake
50 Tail navigation light
51 ECM antenna
52 Starboard rudder
53 Fully variable convergent/divergent exhaust nozzle
54 Anti-collision light
55 Formation lighting strip
56 ECM antenna
57 Port rudder
58 Fuel jettison pipe
59 ECM antenna
60 Arresting hook
61 Chaff/flare dispensers
62 Exhaust nozzle control jacks
63 Radar warning antenna
64 Port taileron
65 Taileron pivot bearing
66 Taileron hydraulic actuator
67 Arresting hook dashpot
68 Pratt & Whitney TF30-P-412 augmented turbofan
69 Formation lighting strip
70 Hydraulic system filters
71 Oil cooler intake
72 Formation light
73 Port navigation light
74 Manoeuvre flap rotary actuators and pushrods
75 Port leading edge slat
76 Port wing integral fuel tank
77 Spoiler hydraulic actuators
78 Slat drive shaft
79 Flap drive shaft
80 Slat rotary actuators and guide rails
81 Hydraulic reservoirs
82 Engine accessory equipment gearbox
83 Inboard flap hydraulic jack
84 Main undercarriage hydraulic retraction jack
85 Undercarriage leg pivot bearing
86 Forward retracting mainwheel
87 Wing pivot bearing
88 Sparrow missile adapter
89 AIM-7 Sparrow AAM
90 Wing glove pylon
91 AIM-9 Sidewinder air-to-air missile
92 Flap and slat bevel drive gearbox
93 Telescopic drive shaft
94 Variable area intake ramps
95 External fuel tank
96 Hydraulic brake accumulators
97 Intake ramp hydraulic actuators
98 Air conditioning system heat exchanger
99 Air data computer
100 Electrical relay panel

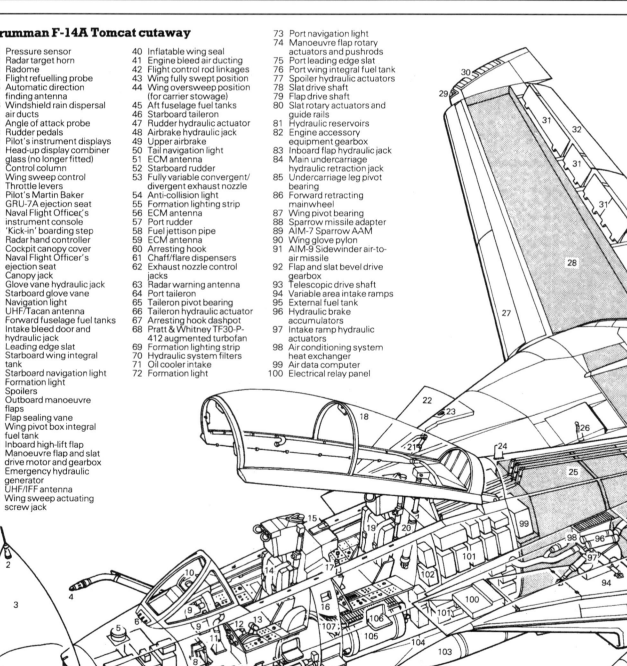

phenomena at all, not even interference drag when Phoenix missiles are carried. The increased wetted area caused by the podded configuration was responsible for a little extra drag, but this was considered to be offset by the improved stability of the layout, stability in pitch being enhanced by the aerofoil-like pancake, while extra stability in the directional plane was due to the keel area of the engine nacelles.

Tail configuration

As we saw in the previous chapter, twin fins replaced a single fin at a very late stage in the design. Twin fins do have one great advantage in that they reduce the adverse effects of body vortices at high AOA. A secondary advantage is, of course, systems redundancy in the event of battle damage.

The outward-canted ventral fins are in some flight conditions better than extra main fin area, as they are situated in a position where cross-flow induced by sideslip accelerates under the rear fuselage, which increases their effectiveness, while their low aspect ratio makes them very stiff and resistant to flexing. In sideslip conditions, the loading on them eases the torsion which the main fin loading exerts on the fuselage, while the rolling moment caused by sideslip opposes the rolling moment of the dorsal

fins, thus reducing dihedral effect. Being situated in an undisturbed airflow, the ventral fins retain effectiveness at high AOA, and also help directional stability at high speeds. As recounted in the Development chapter, an automatic rudder interconnect was incorporated in the design from the outset, but handling problems caused it to be disconnected, although the hardware is still in position.

The horizontal tail surfaces are fully powered, all-moving surfaces with differential movement to provide control both in pitch and in roll. At wing sweep angles of more than 50deg these tailerons are the sole source of roll control, while at lower sweep angles the are augmented by the spoilers. The size of the tail surfaces was determined by the control requirements only. Stability was not a factor, since the wing and pivot were already located to provide this. The horizontal tail arm was determined by supersonic roll acceleration requirements, and the podded engine layout has an inherent lateral tail arm advantage, which resulted in a tail area 10 per cent smaller than that required for an equivalent submerged engine design. In this respect, it is interesting to compare the horizontal tail layout with that of the much more recent F-18 Hornet.

The F-14's tailerons are of multi-spar construction with 5 per cent thickness at the root, tapering to 3 per cent at the tip, with honeycomb leading edges and trailing edges, skinned with the very expensive boron epoxy composite. The F-14 was the first aircraft to employ advanced composites in a major structural application from the outset. Like other advanced composites, boron epoxy has outstanding strength and stiffness for a comparatively light weight, and is highly tolerant of damage, though in common with all advanced composite materials, damage repair is a problem area, research into which is still going on. Grumman developed a 'Band-Aid' answer, consisting of fibreglass and titanium discs as patches, hot-applied with a structural adhesive.

Providing air for the TF30 engines are two massive rectangular two-dimensional inlets, which rake back at a very acute angle. These inlets are placed 8in (20.3cm) out from the fuselage nacelle, which effectively isolates them from the forebody effect and obviates the need for a fuselage boundary layer air removal system, saving both weight and drag. The external compression type inlet is optimized for fighter operation and provides a stable airflow with low distortion levels. The upper intake surface is extended farther forward than the lower to improve high AOA performance.

The state of the art in jet engine design is that they cannot run using a supersonic airflow, and the air must be slowed down to subsonic speeds in the duct before it reaches the engine face. This is done by applying Bernouli's principle, which states that a moving fluid (in this case a gas) will slow down as it expands to occupy a greater volume. A movable hydraulic ramp system is used to adjust the volume of air entering the duct.

Two ramps are used, one hinged forward, the other hinged downstream to the airflow. The ramp movements are automatic, and are controlled by their own air data computer and hydraulic system which are independent of the CADC and main hydraulics. Air entering the inlet is compressed by the forward ramp. At transonic speeds this forms a shockwave, while at supersonic speeds four shocks are formed which decelerate and compress the air entering the inlet. Behind the forward ramp is a variable-size throat bleed slot, which cleans up the airflow by removing the

Left: Once quantity production commenced, the main gear was fitted at an early stage to allow the Tomcats to move down the assembly line on their own wheels. Here the right main gear is being fitted.

Above: Block 90 aircraft, including some destined for Iran, move down the assembly line at Calverton in 1975. This assembly building is also used for A-6s, as is evidenced by the Intruder in the right foreground.

101 Avionics equipment bays
102 Electrical system equipment
103 AIM-54 Phoenix air-to-air missile
104 Phoenix missile pallet
105 Ammunition drum
106 Boarding step
107 Ammunition feed and link return chutes
108 Retractable boarding ladder
109 Forward retracting nosewheels
110 Nosewheel steering actuator
111 Carrier approach lights
112 Catapult launch strop
113 M61A-1 20mm six-barrel rotary cannon
114 Canopy emergency release
115 Pitot head
116 Formation lighting strips
117 Radar equipment bay
118 ECM antenna
119 AWG-9 pulse-Doppler flat plate radar scanner

Below: Cutaway drawing of what was arguably the world's most complex and certainly the world's most expensive fighter at the time. The construction of the wing carry-through box, and the wing fuel tanks, which are skinned with titanium fixed with oversized rivets, and the main frame details, are all works of art in their way.

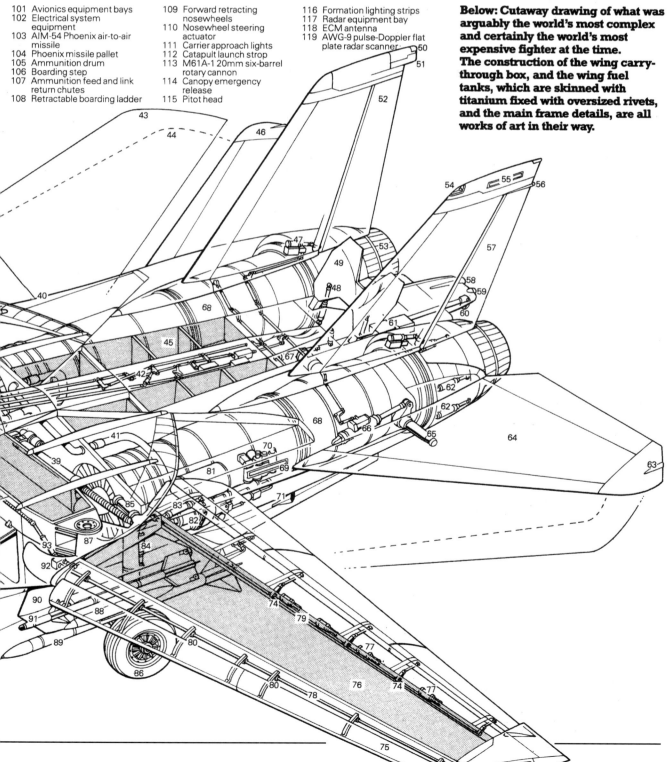

boundary layer, directs air down the face of the aft ramp and handles the bypass of excess air when necessary. Without the slot, flow separation would occur at ramp angles of 10-15deg.

Further compression takes place downstream of the ramp, in the subsonic diffuser duct. Because the air is clean (no boundary layer flow) and its local flow angle is optimized, rapid diffusion rates are possible, and the air which reaches the engine is of high quality. At speeds of up to Mach 0.5, the forward, external compression ramp is overcollapsed, while the aft, subsonic compression ramp collapses forward to contact the forward ramp and closes the bleed slot.

This configuration provides a 7.08sq ft ($0.66m^2$) capture area for takeoff and slow speed flight. Between Mach 0.5 and 1.2, the forward ramp deploys to form a

continuous compression ramp at an angle of 3deg, while the aft ramp positions itself to match the forward ramp to provide a pre-scheduled throat bleed area. As the aft ramp is actuated, the bypass exit door on top of the duct opens, discharging any surplus air rearward with a low pressure drop, thus recovering most of the momentum as thrust. At velocities exceeding Mach 2, the operation of both ramps is scheduled according to a function of flight Mach number and AOA, but is biased by the duct exit Mach number to deliver the correct volume of air to the engine at the correct velocity. If the highly automated system fails at speeds of Mach 1.2 or higher, the ramps lock in position, while if a failure occurs at below this speed, they deploy into the fully open position.

At the other end of the engines are the

nozzles. These are of the convergent/divergent type (con-di), and vary in area from 7.5sq ft ($0.7m^2$) in the fully open afterburning position, to 3.6sq ft ($0.33m^2$) when fully closed. Considered to be a significant breakthrough in fighter nozzle design when they were developed, the nozzles feature translating flaps, moving on curved rails which are attached to the rear of the afterburner shell. This layout, which produces some really graceful curves, passed a higher thrust than previous designs, and saved weight because it did not need a supply of cooling air.

The undercarriage, stressed for arrested landings on the heaving deck of a carrier at sea, accounts for a high proportion of the steel used in the structure. It consists of a twin-wheel steerable nose gear and single-wheel main gears, all of

which retract forward. The nosewheel is housed under the cockpit and the main gears in the underside of the wing glove.

Launch procedure

Attached to the nosewheel strut is the catapult launch bar. Once it is in position over the shuttle, the Tomcat is made to 'kneel' by compressing the gear. Shortening it by 1.17ft (0.36m), gives the strut added strength for the launch, as well as eliminating any tendency the aircraft might have to lift off during the acceleration phase. As the fighter leaves the catapult, the compression is released, thrusting the nose up as the aircraft leaves the deck.

An early modification, introduced from BuAer 157981 on, is an automatic centering device for the nosewheel, which is actuated when the arrester hook is lowered. This prevents castoring as the aircraft rolls backwards from the arrester wires after landing. The brakes were originally of beryllium, but after an exhaustive test programme at Patuxent River in 1981, they have been replaced by carbon composite fitments. Carbon composites give high strength, low weight, and, most important, excellent thermal stability.

The airframe of the Tomcat has a design fatigue life of 6,000 flight hours, which at the current rate represents approximately 20 years. It has an induction cycle of 30 months, which means that after every 2½ years of operational usage it is returned to the Naval Air Rework Facility at Norfolk, Virginia. There it is refurbished, updated as required, and returned to service.

To achieve this long service life, a comprehensive structural test programme was carried out, the idea being to get the main design concepts structurally verified before the production line really got under way. In all, three aircraft and many individual components were assigned to the static and fatigue

Above: It was simpler to mount a stores pylon on the fixed portion of the wing, but the pylon had to be cranked to clear the main gear doors. The missile is an AIM-7F.

Below: Propelled by explosive bolts, the canopy goes up and back a split second before the ejection sequence is initiated in this static test. The crew are, of course, dummies.

Below: As it was known from the start that the TF30 was a rather sensitive engine, design of the inlets was given careful thought. Three basic flight regimes had to be catered for:

subsonic, transonic and supersonic, each of which demands high quality, non-turbulent air to be delivered to the compressor at subsonic speed. Three ramps and a bleed door are employed.

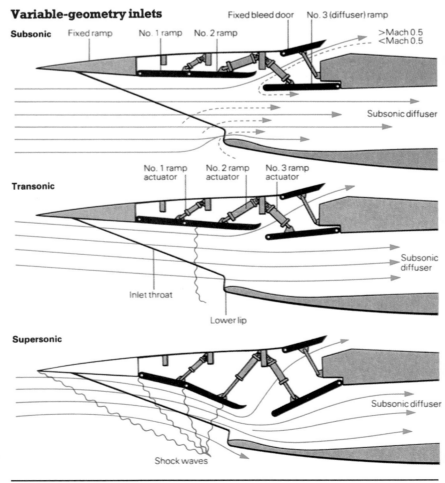

Variable-geometry inlets

Subsonic — Fixed ramp — No. 1 ramp — No. 2 ramp — Fixed bleed door — No. 3 (diffuser) ramp — >Mach 0.5 <Mach 0.5 — Subsonic diffuser

Transonic — No. 1 ramp actuator — No. 2 ramp actuator — No. 3 ramp actuator — Subsonic diffuser — Inlet throat — Lower lip

Supersonic — Subsonic diffuser — Shock waves

Above: Close view of the tunnel between the engine pods showing the large lifting area. Also clearly visible are three of the four Phoenix pallets, designed to carry the big missile without compromising the Tomcat in its Sparrow-armed fighter role. The front ends of the forward pallets are turned down to reduce drag when the missiles are carried.

Above: The widely spaced engine pods set well out from the forward fuselage, and their straight lines from intake to nozzle, are apparent in this shot of a Gunfighters F-14.

Below: A perfectly judged arrival, as this VF-2 Bountyhunters Tomcat returns to the *Enterprise* in 1974. The smoke seems to indicate that the pilot is using full dry thrust.

test programme. To relate them all would be tedious, but we can pick out some of the more important ones.

Qualification of the wing carry-through box and pivot structure started early in 1970. Both static and dynamic tests were carried out, with loadings reaching 128 per cent of the design limits, which were applied at wing sweep angles varying between 25deg and 68deg. To ensure that the friction levels of the pivot were acceptably low, the bearing was tested during wing sweeps at temperatures of −43deg C (−45deg F).

Next, a fatigue test was initiated on the structure, scheduled to last twice the anticipated life, or 12,000 equivalent flight hours (EFH). At 9,700 EFH, one of the lower lugs on the pivot structure failed. All the lugs on all the pivot structures were increased in thickness as a result of this mishap, and the assembly was then tested to destruction. This occurred at 23,760 EFH, nearly four times the design life. Also tested to more than twice the design life was the boron epoxy taileron. In this case, it was the test rig and not the component that failed, fully justifying Grumman's faith in this material.

Drop tests

The most structurally demanding part of the life of a carrier fighter is the continual series of arrested deck landings. A series of drop tests were run, up to the design limit sink rate of 24.7ft/sec (7.53m/sec). Over 500 drop tests were scheduled, culminating in a planned drop to failure in September 1972.

In the 1950s and 1960s, the complexity of modern aircraft tended to cause production tailbacks at the final assembly stage. To avoid this, the Ironworks used what they called the 'colony' concept. In essence, this was modular construction, with each major structural unit – wings, forward fuselage, and so on – completed as a module, then stuffed with all its plumbing and wiring and tested in its own area. Only at the final assembly stage did the completed modules come together on a final assembly line.

Powerplant

Technically, the most troubled aspect of the F-14 programme has been the engine. The TF30-P-412 augmented turbofan originally used was intended only as a stopgap until the new Advanced Technology Engine became available, but for various reasons the ATE was a non-starter and the Tomcat has soldiered on with two TF30 developments, the P-414 and the P-414A. Neither was ever entirely satisfactory, but a replacement was a long time in evolving: only in 1984 was the matter finally settled, with the selection of the F110-GE-400, but the new powerplant did not enter fleet service until 1987.

The design of the Pratt & Whitney JTF-10A turbofan, military designation TF30, was started on April 1, 1958. One of its first applications was to have been to power the Missileer; later, equipped for afterburning, or more correctly for a turbofan, augmentation, it was selected to propel the F-111, with a variant, the TF30-P-12, designed specifically for the Navy F-111B. The TF30 was the world's first augmented turbofan engine, and when the naval F-111B was cancelled, was the only suitable choice to power its successor.

It was recognized that the TF30 was not ideal; it was a bit short on thrust for the job that it was expected to do, and in the F-111 had suffered severely from compressor stalling. On the horizon was the new ATE, funded jointly by the Navy and the Air Force, which was expected to have less sensitivity, about 40 per cent greater thrust and a 30 per cent improvement in specific fuel consumption (sfc), as well as offering a considerable weight saving. The temptation surely existed for the Navy to wait for the new engine, but the existence of new Soviet fighter types, including the MiG-25 Foxbat, gave the F-14 programme added urgency. Consequently, the decision was taken to proceed with the TF30-powered F-14A, with the ATE-powered F-14B following about two years later. At the earliest reasonable moment (not the earliest possible: TF30s were too expensive to just throw away), the F-14A was to be retrofitted with the new engine.

The early definitive engine for the F-14A was the Pratt & Whitney TF30-P-412, a modified P-12. It produced 12,350lb (5,600kg) thrust in military power, increased to 20,900lb (9,480kg) at full augmentation, for a weight of 3,969lb (1,800kg); overall length was 19ft 7in (5.97m), and maximum diameter 4ft 2in (1.27m).

The P-412 was an axial flow turbofan, with the fan and low pressure compressor stages driven by the low pressure turbine stage. The three-stage fan had a pressure ratio of 2.14:1, and both the rotor and stator stages were of titanium.

The six-stage low pressure compressor was also built of titanium, but with steel stator blades, while the high pressure compressor, made mainly of nickel alloy, had seven stages. The combustion chamber was can-annular with a steel casing, and contained eight Hastelloy X flame cans, with four dual-orifice burners in each. Behind this came the single-stage high pressure turbine, whose rotor blades and stators were of cobalt-based alloy to combat temperatures typically exceeding 1,000deg C (1,832deg F). The three-stage low pressure turbine was constructed of nickel-based alloy, while the augmentor consisted of a double wall outer duct, and an inner liner holding the five-zone burner system.

Turbofan advantages

The difference between a turbofan and a turbojet is that the turbofan's low pressure turbine takes energy from the hot jet to power large fan stages at the front of the engine. The fan stages take air from the inlet duct and pass it round the

Above: Seen here at full thrust on the test rig is an example of the Pratt & Whitney TF30 turbofan. At the front is a FOD screen intended to prevent birds being ingested.

Right: The TF30-P-412 turbofan was intended as an interim measure only. Its unreliability constrained its pilots in action, and caused far too many accidents.

hot core of the engine proper, which reduces the average velocity of the core jet and the surrounding fan air combined, effectively reducing fuel consumption. In a turbojet, the afterburner operates in the engine exhaust gases, which have already had a high proportion of their oxygen burned, while the turbofan supplies a constant stream of oxygen-rich unburnt air through to the augmentation stage. The greater amount of oxygen allows more fuel to be used, which gives increased thrust. The ratio of air passing through the annular fan duct to that passing through the engine

core is known as the bypass ratio, and in the case of the TF30-P-412, is 0.9.

Experience with the F-111 programme had demonstrated that the TF30 family of engines were prone to compressor stalls. The blades of a compressor have sections like miniature air foils, and these will stall if the airflow meets them at more than a certain angle. It was known, however, that much of the compressor stalling problem encountered by General Dynamics arose from the design and position of the inlets. Aware of the difficulties, Grumman had done everything possible to get the

engine inlets and ducts right, to the extent that, as described in the Development chapter, the engine airflow requirements influenced the layout of the airframe.

Early flight testing soon confirmed that Grumman had got it right, and compressor stalling, which could not reasonably have been expected to be eliminated entirely, seemed to have been confined to acceptable levels, even in high AOA flight, provided that the power levels were kept high. Specific fuel consumption was higher than had been anticipated when using augmentation, while

more thrust would have been useful, even though the F-14 outperformed the Phantom in almost every department. The thrust to weight (t/w) ratio was only about 0.78, quite a low figure compared with the slightly later F-15's ratio of greater than unity. T/w ratio affects rate of climb, acceleration, and specific excess power (P_s) for manoeuvring flight. With more powerful engines all of these could be considerably improved, although the automatic wing sweep compensated to some extent by reducing drag, and the F-14 actually has much better performance than its modest t/w

ratio implies. But apart from all these factors, it should be remembered that the TF30 was regarded merely as an interim solution pending the arrival of the ATE about two years later.

The ATE had arisen from an Air Force-funded technology demonstration programme in 1968, with Pratt & Whitney and General Electric as contenders, and

Below: With nozzles dilated an F-14 blasts off using all five stages of augmentation. Despite continual improvement the engine has proved to be unreliable in service.

a contract was awarded to Pratt & Whitney on February 27, 1970, for development of the ATE, in the shape of the F401-PW-400. Incidentally, the F100 powering the Air Force F-15 and F-16 was developed from the same base. The F401 and F100 were each optimized for their respective missions, and were therefore cousins rather than brothers, despite their common ancestry. The F401 was pushing the technology of the times pretty close to its limits, but the potential benefits were considerable. Rated at 28,000lb (12,700kg) augmented thrust, it would have raised the t/w ratio of the F-14 at combat weight to just over unity, with commensurate improvements in performance. Sfc was also claimed to be considerably better, especially with augmentation.

A mockup of the F401 was made, and a fit check accomplished in the nacelle of the EMMA mockup on September 15, 1970. This was followed by an installation and removal demonstration on April 28, 1971. Progress was slow, and the first ground test engine was not received by Grumman until November 22, 1972, by which time 19 Tomcats had flown. The first flight of the F401 took place on September 12, 1973, in BuAer 157986. It was mounted in one pod only, with a standard TF30-P-412 in the other. Meanwhile, the escalating costs of the F-14 were causing raised eyebrows, voices, and blood pressure. Even more money to improve it, when all the indications were that it was doing very nicely with its existing engines, was hard to obtain. The F401 had technical problems, as did its Air Force cousin, the F100, although these were not insoluble, but caught between the Scylla of technology and the Charybdis of cost, the F401 programme was suspended in April 1974.

This left the TF30-P-412 as the definitive Tomcat engine for the immediate future. As related, it had performed quite adequately during the flight test programme, but as the Tomcat entered fleet service and the numbers of aircraft in the squadrons mounted, problems with the powerplant slowly began to emerge. They did not manifest themselves quickly, for the simple reason that the numerical build-up was slow, and this made patterns hard to identify at first.

Problems emerge

The basic TF30 could, after years of service in the F-111, be considered a mature engine, but in the F-111 it had led a relatively easy life. Then, during the Tomcat test programme, the F-14 had been flown by both Grumman and Navy pilots of above average ability, on a careful and premeditated exploration of the flight performance envelope. But when the operational squadrons got their hands on it and started to amass flight hours at a high rate, it was a very different story, especially in air combat manoeuvring flights: excursions to 50deg AOA became a daily event, with the throttles being worked back and forward, in and out of afterburner.

Part of the trouble lay in the aerodynamic excellence of the Tomcat, which permitted manoeuvring that the Phantom or Crusader driver could only dream of. Both of these fighters, good though they undoubtedly were, were of the previous generation. The Phantom in particular tended to bleed off energy rapidly in a turning fight; the normal procedure was to keep the loud pedal firmly down to keep the energy levels up. The Tomcat, on the other hand, was so good in this respect that often pilots were forced to throttle back to maintain a good attacking position, then throttle up again. All this meant hard work for the engines, and they frankly didn't like it: they just had not been designed for such hard usage.

TF30-P-414 exhaust nozzle

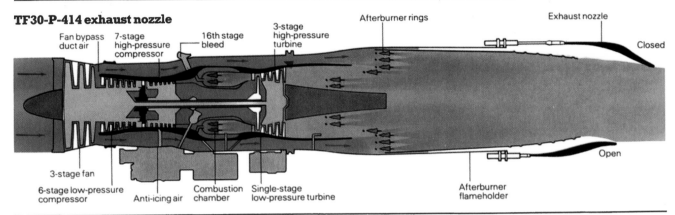

Fan bypass duct air | 7-stage high-pressure compressor | 16th stage bleed | 3-stage high-pressure turbine | Afterburner rings | Exhaust nozzle | Closed

3-stage fan | 6-stage low-pressure compressor | Anti-icing air | Combustion chamber | Single-stage low-pressure turbine | Afterburner flameholder | Open

Left: Essentially a -412 modified to improve reliability and safety, the TF30-P-414 incorporated a certain amount of redesign plus steel containment casing around the first three fan stages. This increased the weight but provided no extra thrust.

Below: The -414 was unsatisfactory and further fixes produced the -414A seen here. A total of 31 further engine mods were made, and kits to modify the -414 were produced in addition to new engines. Less prone to compressor stalling than earlier models, the -414 suffered from the disadvantage of being smoky.

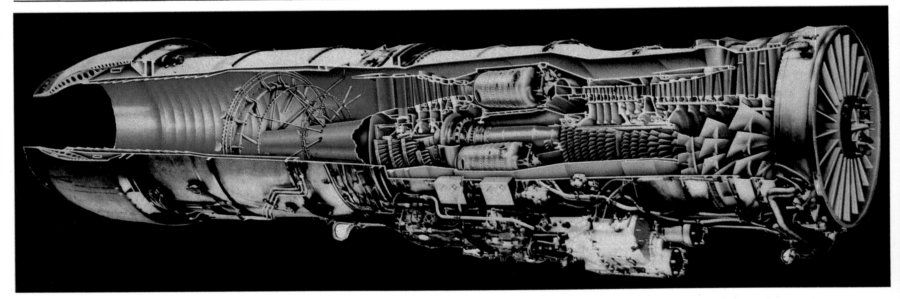

Below: The nozzles of jet engines are designed to expand the exhaust gases to reduce their pressure to roughly that of the outside air, which demands that their area should be variable. The nozzle designed for the TF30 as used in the Tomcat is a delicately engineered system of hydraulically actuated leaves mounted on rollers and sliding on a track.

Right: Tomcat variable nozzles. The upper illustration shows the normal military power setting, while the lower shows the nozzle fully dilated for afterburning.

Exhaust nozzle positions

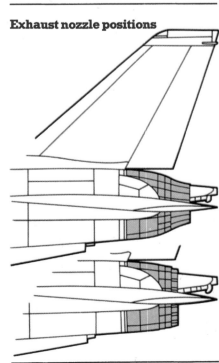

TF30-P-414 internal layout

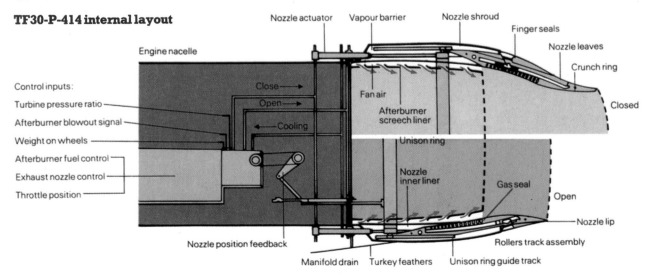

Engine nacelle | Nozzle actuator | Vapour barrier | Nozzle shroud | Finger seals | Nozzle leaves | Crunch ring

Control inputs:
Turbine pressure ratio
Afterburner blowout signal
Weight on wheels
Afterburner fuel control
Exhaust nozzle control
Throttle position

Close | Open | Cooling | Fan air | Afterburner screech liner | Unison ring | Nozzle inner liner | Gas seal | Closed | Open | Nozzle lip

Nozzle position feedback | Manifold drain | Turkey feathers | Unison ring guide track | Rollers track assembly

It had been thought that the hardest part of an engine's life was in prolonged full power running, but in fact these continued throttle transients took a far greater toll, and compressor stalls became frequent. Some were caused by high AOA at low power settings; others by afterburner 'pop', which is a result of delay in afterburner light-up: fuel momentarily accumulates in the tailpipe, where it is ignited by the hot core exhaust, causing a small explosion, which in turn causes pressure to back up through the engine, stalling the fan, the compressor, or both. The risk increased in proportion to the number of times that afterburner was either engaged or cancelled.

Back in 1972, the Navy anticipated that 1,000 flight hours would involve 597 afterburner lights, and 1,165 engine cycles, the definition of a cycle being a transition through all the power settings. These figures were subsequently shown

to be way short of the mark: in 1979 the Naval Air Test Center installed low cycle fatigue monitors in the engines of 30 F-14As, and the results, gathered by late 1981, showed the true requirements to be no fewer than 2,250 afterburner lights, and 10,549 engine cycles, increases of 277 and 805 per cent respectively!

With these unanticipated stress levels, it was little wonder that the TF30 had component failures, the most frequent of which, and potentially the most damaging, were failures of the fan blades. Unfortunately, at the design stage, no requirement had been laid down for blade containment. When a failure occurred, the broken blades sliced through almost everything in their path, causing considerable damage and rupturing fuel lines and tanks, which all too often resulted in fires. Several Tomcats were lost to this cause.

A programme of fixes was put in hand. Steel containment cases were installed

around the first three fan stages, and the radius of the fan blade leading edges was increased, while the blades themselves were manufactured from a different titanium alloy which was less susceptible to stress corrosion cracking, the second to third stage fan air seal was modified, and the third stage fan rotor was redesigned. Fire containment measures also featured in the fixes. Titanium sheets were installed over the engine nacelles, while thin steel plates coated with an ablative substance helped to protect the flight control rods from the effect of engine fires. The flight control rods had been found to be particularly vulnerable to fires, and a fire extinguisher bottle was added to the centreline trough area as well as to the engine nacelles.

Various fixes, plus a certain amount of redesign, led to a new engine variant, the TF30-P-414, essentially the P-412 with the fixes described in the previous

paragraph. It was slightly heavier, turning the scales at just over 4,000lb (1,800kg), and it produced no extra thrust. A test programme, although resulting in the loss of the aircraft, cleared the new engine for installation in production machines. The accident happened during stall tests flown from NATC Patuxent River on February 22, 1977, when the test vehicle, fitted with one P-412 and one P-414 engine, stalled the P-414 at high AOA as intended while cutting the afterburner on the P-412 in and out. The stall occurred when the P-412 engine was at full power, causing a violent yaw, and the Tomcat immediately entered a fast, flat, irrecoverable spin, forcing the crew to eject. The pilot was picked up with minor injuries, but the NFO did not survive. We shall return to this point later.

The P-414 showed no performance advantages, providing the same thrust as its predecessor, but it did offer slightly

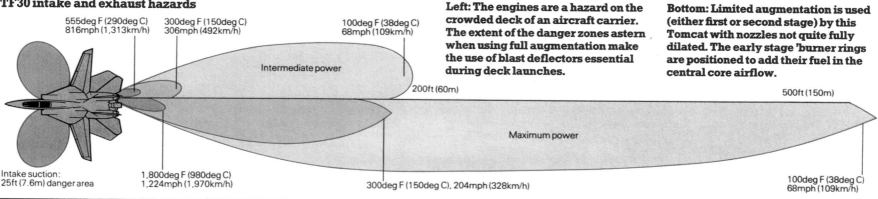

TF30 intake and exhaust hazards

555deg F (290deg C) 816mph (1,313km/h) | 300deg F (150deg C) 306mph (492km/h) | 100deg F (38deg C) 68mph (109km/h)

Intermediate power

200ft (60m)

Intake suction: 25ft (7.6m) danger area

1,800deg F (980deg C) 1,224mph (1,970km/h)

Maximum power

300deg F (150deg C), 204mph (328km/h)

500ft (150m)

100deg F (38deg C) 68mph (109km/h)

Left: The engines are a hazard on the crowded deck of an aircraft carrier. The extent of the danger zones astern when using full augmentation make the use of blast deflectors essential during deck launches.

Bottom: Limited augmentation is used (either first or second stage) by this Tomcat with nozzles not quite fully dilated. The early stage 'burner rings are positioned to add their fuel in the central core airflow.

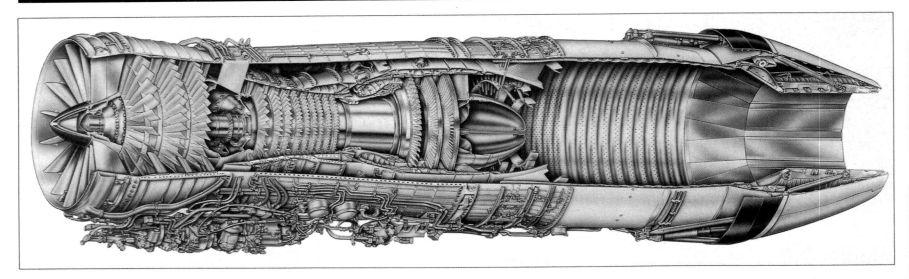

greater safety and reliability. The full extent of the problem would not become apparent until the figures were produced, although the loss statistics were bad enough. In the 35 months between January 1975 and November 1978, 31 Tomcats were lost to all causes. Of these, over 35 per cent were due to engine-related causes, and had it not been for the fan blade containment and fire prevention measures adopted, this figure might well have been higher. In two cases, *both* engines failed. The P-412 was replaced in fleet service between February 1977 and June 1979.

While the P-414 was a definite improvement over its predecessor, it was still far from satisfactory, a fact underlined by an engine up-grade programme consisting of 31 changes that was instituted by the Navy as early as October 1978, barely two-thirds of the way through the P-414 replacement programme. This had a fourfold purpose. It was intended to increase the low cycle fatigue life of all rotating components, to extend the inspection period for the hot section of the engine from 550 hours to 1,000 hours, to double the time between engine overhauls from 1,200 hours to 2,400 hours, and to reduce the stall rate. In the event, the inspection and overhaul targets were not achieved due to a vane in the third turbine disc burning through during testing in May 1981. Finding the cause of the failure and developing a cure would have caused unacceptable delays to the modification programme. The 31 changes were proved in two

2,400 hour accelerated simulated mission endurance tests, and were sufficient to warrant a change to the engine suffix: the P-414 now became the P-414A.

Sufficient kits to upgrade 1,007 engines from P-414 to P-414A configuration were issued to the Navy, the first being delivered to the Naval Air Rework Facility at Norfolk in October 1982. As the aircraft came in for their 30-month overhaul, so the modifications were made. At the same time, new production engines to P-414A standard replaced the P-414 on the production lines, the first of 158 new-build engines reaching the Navy during the following December.

The P-414A was more durable, and less prone to compressor stalling at low power settings than the P-414, but yet another problem was emerging: the exhaust was leaving a smoky trail. The F-14 is a big aeroplane and relatively easily spotted from a distance. Smoke made it even more visible and was one thing that it could really have done without. Pratt & Whitney instituted a programme to find a fix, but by mid-1984 no firm proposals had been made. Also in mid-1984, the manufacturers were still wrestling with the compressor stall problem, and were in the process of developing an automatic recovery system, but the real answer was the F110 engine that started to become available from 1987.

In spite of numerous fixes, engine durability is still not all it might be, while the latest TF30 produces exactly the same thrust as it did 25 years ago. It is

Above: The US Air Force General Electric F110-GE-100 was developed from the B-1's F101 via the F101DFE. Internally it is simpler than the TF30, and although more powerful, it is substantially smaller.

Below: The main difference between the -100 for the USAF and the -400 for the F-14 is the length. The basic F110 is shorter than the TF30 and has a 50in (127cm) steel tailpipe extension fitted to suit the F-14.

F110-GE-100/-400 profile section

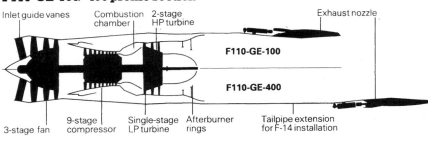

Inlet guide vanes — Combustion chamber — 2-stage HP turbine — Exhaust nozzle — F110-GE-100 — F110-GE-400 — 3-stage fan — 9-stage compressor — Single-stage LP turbine — Afterburner rings — Tailpipe extension for F-14 installation

difficult not to be critical, and in a statement to the House Appropriations subcommittee of Congress in 1984, Navy Secretary John F. Lehman, Jr., pulled no punches. Referring to the TF30/F-14 combination, he called it "probably the worst engine/airframe mismatch we have had in many years. The TF30 is just a terrible engine and has accounted for 28.2 per cent of all F-14 crashes . . . the F-14 can perform its mission, but it has to be flown very carefully. You have to fly

Below: With a FOD screen and funnel fitted over the intake an F110 is tested at full thrust. The exhaust gases are drawn off through a noise and heat baffle at the rear.

the engine, and cannot fly it in certain parts of the upper left-hand corner of the flight envelope (i.e., low speed, high altitude), without high risk."

Lehman, it should be pointed out, is not just a politician; he is also a pilot in the Navy Reserve, and therefore better qualified than most to make a statement of this kind. On the other hand, it does seem a trifle harsh. On the evidence, Pratt & Whitney were at least as much victims as villains of the piece. At the time of the Tomcat design inception the TF30 was the only engine in sight that appeared to be capable of doing the job, and the Navy expected that it would be used in the VFX competition by all tenderers. It was not foreseen that the flight performance of the airframe would be such as to make unprecedented demands on the engines, while if the problem was foreseeable, the user service was as well equipped as anyone to see it coming. In this context it should be remembered that both the F-15 and F-16 suffered engine problems arising from the same mission-related cause. And the final word on the subject must surely be that the TF30 was originally intended as a stopgap engine pending the availability of the ATE.

Replacement needed

Development of the advanced technology F401-PW-400 had been suspended in April 1974, but the need for more thrust, and incidentally, more dollars for development, lingered on. As the Tomcat entered fleet service, so the needs for greater durability, better sfc and stall-free performance were added to the shopping list. All of this pointed to a new engine, but as the Tomcat was committed to the TF30 for the time being, it was reasonable to hope that engine fixes could be devised to cover at least the durability and stalling problems. As we have seen, this was not to be, but there was no way of knowing that at the time.

By 1976 three new engines were emerging as possible TF30 replace-

ments. These were the Pratt & Whitney F401-PW-26C, which offered increased performance over the F-400, General Electric's F101-X, of which more later, and variants of the Allison TF41 as used in the A-7: the TF41-912-B31, an unaugmented engine offering approximately 18,000lb (8,165kg) of dry thrust, and the -B32, the same engine fitted with a variety of afterburners. No real action was taken, because although the Navy had $15m in the FY 1977 budget for a hardware competition for a follow-on engine, no money was available in the FY 1978 budget to continue the programme. It therefore seemed pointless to engage the manufacturers in a competition with no future.

At the time, Pratt & Whitney were widely regarded as the most advanced of all the engine manufacturers. This caused some misgivings in government circles, partly due to the competition aspect, and partly because problems were being experienced with another Pratt & Whitney product, the F100 used to power the F-15 and F-16.

It was only sensible that both the USAF and the USN should pool their limited resources to develop a common powerplant which could be used as a replacement for both the TF30 and F100. Air Force Systems Command was directed

to define a limited development programme by November 5, 1978, and a 30-month development contract was awarded to General Electric in March 1979. This would achieve two stated aims: to produce a fall-back engine for both services should such become essential; and to bring General Electric to a state of technical parity with Pratt & Whitney, thus solving the problem of future competition. The chosen engine was the F101-X, or, as it was to become known, the F101DFE (Derivative Fighter Engine). Its origins lay in the core of the F101, then under development for the Rockwell B-1 supersonic bomber, coupled with a scaled-up fan and augmentation from the F404 turbofan used to power the F-18 Hornet. In passing, it is interesting to note that the F404 was an exceptionally reliable and stall-free unit, in contrast to the TF30.

The development programme was unusual in that only three engines were to be built and tested, although two earlier 'boilerplate' F101-X demonstrators had logged 350 hours of test running in 1977-78. The first engine, No. 003, underwent systems and operability testing at General Electric's Evendale, Ohio, facility, while 004 was used for accelerated mission testing, also at Evendale. This involved 1,000 equivalent

Above: The original F-14B prototype is fitted with General Electric F101DFE engines prior to flight testing. Performance improvements justified the Super Tomcat label.

flight hours using the mission profile of the F-16, for which it was also under consideration, after which it was stripped down and inspected, then put back together for another 1,000 equivalent flight hours test using the mission profile of the Tomcat. This was completed in June 1981. The third engine, 005, was put through exhaustive altitude testing in the Naval Air Propulsion Test Center at Trenton, New Jersey, completing the schedule by February 1981. These three engines were then scheduled to be fitted into aircraft and flight tested, a procedure described by George H. Ward of General Electric as "pretty sporty."

Super Tomcat

The prototype F-14B, BuAer 157986, which had only flown for 33 hours in the development programme before being stored, was the obvious choice for this task. Dusted off, with F101 DFEs fitted and the legend 'Super Tomcat' blazoned across both fins, it lifted off from Calverton on July 14, 1981 for a flight test lasting

an hour and a half. This was the start of a limited development programme of flight testing that lasted into late September. Actually, 24 flights were scheduled, 24 flights were recorded, but 30 takeoffs and landings were made. Odd? You bet, but if one returns and hot refuels, i.e., refuels with the engines running, then goes off again, it apparently only counts as one flight! Results were favourable, and a further 20 flights, involving some 70 flight hours, were carried out in the period ending March 1982.

The data obtained justified the Super Tomcat title. Time on station for CAP missions was increased by 34 per cent and combat radius for deck-launched intercepts was up by a staggering 62 per cent, while significantly better acceleration rates were achieved throughout the entire envelope. Thrust was up, sfc was down, and the engines had demonstrated remarkably stall-free performance. One tremendous advantage was that the available thrust was sufficient to allow the Tomcat to be catapult-launched at military power settings, as the use of full augmentation at takeoff from the carrier had led to a number of accidents directly attributable to compressor stalling. One of the few unfavourable test results was in airstarting the engines: a speed ex-

ceeding 450kt (830km/hr) was needed, which was too high to be practicable.

The Navy was very impressed, and by the summer of 1982 a re-engining programme was definitely on the cards, the only remaining question being the choice of engine. Pratt & Whitney had by this time taken their F100 and developed it into the PW1130, the thrust of which, at 27,410lb (12,430kg), was comparable to the DFE for a lighter installed weight. The PW1130 lagged the DFE in development by about 18 months, but the Navy was still interested in keeping competition between the two companies open. Meanwhile, full scale development of the F101DFE began in October 1982.

Finally, General Electric was selected by the Air Force to supply 120 DFEs, now designated F110-GE-100, for the F-16, with a proposed follow-on of more than 3,000 engines over the next few years. The announcement was made on February 3, 1984, and this strongly influenced the Navy. The Air Force order meant that economy would be achieved through large-scale production, also that most of the research and development

Above: The F110-GE-400, showing its steel tailpipe extension. The nozzle is based on that of the F404, while the gearbox and some components are rearranged to fit the Tomcat.

costs had been met by the Air Force. The F110 was therefore chosen as the engine to power the F-14D, due to enter production in 1988. Apart from the economic factors, the F110 seemed a very suitable engine for the purpose. At the same time, a feasibility study was also put in hand to examine the possibility of retrofitting the F-14A with the new engine.

The designation of the new engine for Navy service became F110-GE-400. It varies slightly from the Air Force -100 in having a 50in (127cm) long steel tailpipe extension, and the gearbox and some components are rearranged to fit the Tomcat. It was also "navalised" to withstand the corrosive effect of salt spray.

The -400 has a bypass ratio of 0.85, with a three-stage fan, the blades of which are solid titanium, while the inlet guide vanes have variable trailing edge flaps.

With a pressure ratio exceeding 3, the fan is the key to the engine's stall resistance, which is such that there are no restrictions on throttle movement throughout the entire operational range. For ease of repair, both the guide vanes and the fan blades are individually replaceable. The HP compressor has nine stages, the first three of which are variable. The blades are made of titanium in the front stages, changing to stainless steel towards the rear, where both temperature and pressure increase. The maximum pressure ratio developed is 11:1. The combustor is annular, with dual-cone nozzles which inject fuel into 20 scroll cups. These give a contra-rotating swirl effect to the airflow which ensures a satisfactory fuel/air mix in a very short distance.

The HP turbine is a single stage, with hollow airfoil section blades and vanes which are convection- and film-cooled

Below: The 'Super Tomcat' shows its paces for the camera during tests with the F101DFE engines in 1981. The extra power allows catapult launches without using 'burner.

by bleed air from the compressor, while the stationary shroud is segmented, being designed for cooling in such a way that the temperature expansion is compatible with that of the blades. In this way, constant clearance is provided for the blade tips. The LP turbine has two stages and is uncooled, driving the fan through the inner shaft which is concentric with the engine core. The blades in both are all individually replaceable.

F100 augmentation
The augmentation uses a convoluted flow mixer to mingle and burn flows from both the core and the fan. The flows mix in the plane of the flameholder, so that initial augmentation takes place in the hot, high-energy core stream, which gives much more reliable initial light-up than has been achieved on many turbofans, which in turn lessens the possibility of 'burner pop. Ignition is begun on the inner ring of the radial flameholder, and only when 90 per cent of the core flow is being burned is any fuel injected into the fan stream. This provides a relatively smooth increase in temperature over the augmentation range.

Left: The carrier wings take their IFR
tankers to sea with them. Here a
Tomcat of VF-41 Black Aces takes on
fuel from a Grumman KA-6D tanker of
VF-355, also based on *Nimitz.*

A different exhaust nozzle is needed
for the F110; this is a scaled-up version of
the type used with the F404, with convergent-divergent flaps and seals, and
outer flaps. If the F110-GE-400 lives up to
its early promise, and there is no obvious
reason why it should not, it will make the
F-14D a very superior fighter in the air
combat manoeuvring regime.

The fuel for the F-14 is generally JP-5,
although JP-4 and -7 are both compatible. A total of 16,200lb (7,348kg) is
carried internally in six areas: 4,700lb
(2,132kg) is located in the forward fuselage, behind the cockpit; 4,400lb
(1,996kg) is situated in the aft fuselage,
where, incidentally, it was directly in
line with stray blades from a disintegra-
ting fan, a contributory factor to many
in-flight fires; 2,000lb (907kg) is carried
in each wing, utilizing telescopic fuel
lines to accommodate changes in the
angle of wing sweep; and the left and
right feed tanks, mounted inside the
wing carry-through box, contain 1,500lb
(680kg) and 1,600lb (726kg) respectively.

The fuel dump outlet is situated on the
trailing edge of the pancake, and connects to the aft fuselage tank. For in-flight
refuelling, a retractable probe is located
on the right-hand side of the fuselage
nacelle, just ahead of the cockpit, while
for ground refuelling a single point set
low down beneath the IFR probe is used.

Information released at the time of the
F-14 prototype's first flight stated that to
achieve the Sparrow-armed air superiority mission radius of 500nm (921km),
only 14,250lb (6,464kg) of fuel would be
needed, but the additional capacity
would be needed for the F-14B. The
additional tankage was therefore included in all aircraft to save conversion
at a later date; although the F-14B did not
proceed, this proved to be a sound
decision. The internal fuel load can also

be supplemented by two external tanks,
each holding 1,800lb (816kg) and carried
on store stations 2 and 7.

Before we leave the subject of the
Tomcat's propulsion, we should take a
look at a question that has arisen quite
frequently during the service life of the
aircraft. The wide spacing of the engines
resulted in a 4ft 6in (1.37m) moment arm
between the centreline of the aircraft
and the centreline of each engine. What
was unarguable was that the dynamic
failure of one engine while at full bore
would cause a considerable asymmetric
thrust loading, inducing a yawing
moment. This appeared to have been a
contributory factor in some F-14 accidents, although the precise degree to
which it affected loss of control was
unknown.

The loss of an F-14 during air combat
manoeuvres at MCAS Yuma in 1983 was
the final straw, and a test programme
was instituted to investigate yaw characteristics under these conditions. A total of
22 sorties was made over the Edwards
AFB test range, using the NASA Dryden
facilities. The aircraft used was the early
prototype Tomcat 1X, which was already
equipped with many spin recovery aids.
The tests were carried out at an altitude
of 10,000ft (3,050m), but the engine
functions were modified to simulate an
altitude of 3,000ft (915m).

The final, and most demanding test in
the series was flown by Grumman Chief
Test Pilot Charles Sewell. It called for an
AOA of 41deg, an airspeed of 150kt
(276km/h) and both engines at maximum
power. The right engine was then deliberately stalled by chopping the throttle
to idle. The Tomcat pitched up to an
angle of 72deg and developed a yaw
rate of approximately 47deg/sec, while
airspeed fell to a mere 25kt (46km/hr).
Recovery was initiated and the effect
was described as very positive, the
Tomcat returning to normal controlled
flight after about ten seconds. From this
test, and the preceding flights in the
series, it was concluded that the yawing
moment was not a significant factor in
causing loss of control.

Fuel tank locations

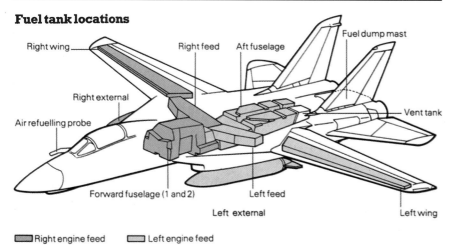

**Above: A total of 16,200lb (7348kg) of
fuel is carried internally in six tanks,
including 2,000lb (907kg) in each
wing; telescopic fuel lines adjust as
the wing sweeps. The feed tanks are
located in the wing box, and a further
3,800lb (1,724kg) can be carried in
'jugs', or external tanks.**

**Below: In-flight refuelling is standard
to all Tomcats, allowing patrol time to
be extended and combat radius to be
increased. The retractable IFR probe
is situated just below and in front of
the cockpit, as this close-up of an
Iranian machine shows; the ground
refuelling point is below it.**

Avionics and Armament

Writing in the spring of 1982, Commander John R. Wilson, Jr., Flight Test Officer of the F-14 Joint Evaluation Team, gave his verdict on the Tomcat's capabilities: "The F-14A is the most formidable and versatile fighter weapon system flying today. There are aircraft that fly faster or slower, but not both. Some fly higher, turn tighter, are better in the one-on-one visual ACM arena, but there is none, repeat none, that compares across the entire spectrum of fighter roles and missions, and *none* that can track 24 targets and selectively engage six targets simultaneously in the all-weather environment. It is the Phoenix/AWG-9 that really makes the F-14 unique among fighter aircraft."

The unique stand-off kill capability of the Tomcat against virtually any known or predicted type of target, from the ultra-high altitude, high speed Foxbat type, to tiny, wave-hugging cruise missiles, is conferred by the combination of the AIM-54 Phoenix missile and the Airborne Weapons Group Nine (AWG-9) avionic system for attack and detection, both produced by the Hughes Aircraft Company. AWG-9 is not just a radar. It is an integrated detection and weapon control system comprising a long-range, high-power multi-mode radar, an advanced fire control system, infra-red detection, computers and cockpit displays, and it also has a two-way data-link capability to enable it to transmit and receive information from surface ships and other aircraft.

The origins of AWG-9, like those of the Tomcat, date back to the Missileer, and were developed through the F-111B programme, though the design philosophy for AWG-9 as fitted to the Tomcat differs in principle from that developed for the F-111B. The F-14 was designed to be flown by the pilot rather than the black boxes, which was not the case in the earlier aircraft. Advanced technology (for the late 1960s) permitted a sizeable reduction in both weight and volume while increasing capability and giving more systems redundancy and back-up modes. In particular, a new generation of lightweight solid state computers provided major advantages, including the ability to simultaneously track up to 24 contacts while engaging six of them.

All weapons readiness is combined in a single control panel which, using the data from the sensors and/or the data link, advises the crew of the most effective weapon usage for the tactical situation. In addition, the computers permit extensive in-flight monitoring during non-critical phases of the mission, informing the crew of any malfunctions in the equipment, while all critical navigational functions are performed by the single Airborne Missile Control System (AMCS) computer. This eliminates the need for a separate navigational computer. Air-to-ground weapon release calculations are also made as required. AWG-9 was probably the most complicated airborne avionics system developed prior to the advent of databus technology.

As developed for the F-111B, AWG-9 had no Sparrow or Sidewinder capability and these had to be added, along with a tracking facility for the Vulcan cannon. New fighter attack modes were also incorporated. AWG-9 for the F-14 was more capable, cheaper, and 600lb (272kg) lighter than that for the F-111B. The first flight test of the reconfigured system took place in April 1970, in an adapted TA-3B.

While AWG-9 is an integrated system, it cannot be examined that way. To explain how it works, it must be considered unit by unit. The primary detection unit is the radar, which was based on the ASG-18 developed for the Mach 3 F-108 Rapier. Radar works rather like an echo sounder. It sends out a pulse, or stream of pulses, of electro-magnetic energy. The pulses weaken as the distance increases. If a pulse hits a solid object it bounces back, and can be 'heard' by the radar receiver.

Above: Tomcat 9 (BuAer 157988) launches a Phoenix missile in the first simulated Foxbat interception, in July 1972. This machine was bailed to the Hughes Aircraft Company during 1972-73; returned to the Navy in January 1974, it was assigned to PMTC and became the first Tomcat to reach 1,000 flight hours in June 1977.

The pulse attenuates in inverse proportion to the square of the distance covered, so that the echo is very faint by comparison with the pulse from which it emanated. For this reason, radar transmitters need to be very strong while the receivers should be extremely sensitive. AWG-9 has a very powerful radar, with a capacity of 10.2kW. This tremendous power is a great asset in long range detection, and also renders the radar less susceptible to electronic countermeasures (ECM), or jamming as it is generally known. Many jamming systems, particularly of the airborne type, are of relatively low power, and are unable to counter the AWG-9 emissions, which 'burn through' their signals.

Antenna performance

The radar antenna is a slotted planar array type, of 36in (914mm) diameter, the largest ever carried by a fighter. This type of antenna provides a higher gain than a parabolic dish antenna of comparable size, and is less vulnerable to certain types of jamming. Furthermore, the sidelobes, which are excess energy spilling over the side of the dish and causing erroneous returns, are much smaller. The planar array is also convenient for the location of interferometer identification/friend foe (IFF) antennas, which can also be used to obtain angular information.

The radiated energy is focussed into a narrow beam and pulses are trans-

mitted, the number of pulses per second being referred to as the pulse repetition frequency (PRF). The antenna scans hydraulically and the echoes are received back while it is still aligned in pretty much the same direction as it was when the pulse was transmitted. From the received return a bearing angle can be obtained, and by measuring the time

Above: The radar components of AWG-9 are easily accessible for maintenance, as a Hughes technician demonstrates. They are all line replaceable units and the lifting handles can be seen. This enables faulty units to be quickly replaced. AWG-9 is self-testing and monitors itself in flight and on the ground.

lapse between the emission and the return a distance can be established. In this connection, we are dealing with a time scale measured in microseconds.

The primary purpose of AWG-9 was to provide an ultra-long range detection and guidance facility for the Phoenix missile. For this it needed high power, and to achieve high power a high PRF is used. The greater the number of pulses transmitted per second, the higher the average power that is radiated, and the greater the detection range possible. High PRFs can be defined as exceeding 100,000 pulses a second.

So far we have described radar operating in the basic pulse mode. In the fleet air defence role, the Tomcat is likely to spend much of its time on station at medium and high altitudes, with the radar looking at or below the horizon. The pulses reflect back not only from aircraft, but also from the ground. In consequence, the radar picks up a multiplicity of echoes from the surface, generally referred to as 'clutter', amid which the return from a low flying aircraft would be lost. This poses a problem which is solved by the use of coherent pulse-Doppler radar.

Pulse-Doppler radar makes use of the Doppler shift, which is a frequency shift caused by relative speed, the time-honoured example of which is the change in pitch of the whistle of a locomotive as it rushes toward, past, then away from the listener. Exactly the same

Left: AWG-9 and Phoenix are the eyes and the claws of the Tomcat. The slotted planar array antenna, on which the IFF dipoles can be seen, is less vulnerable to jamming than a parabolic dish of comparable size. It is hydraulically actuated.

Right: Some idea of the complexity of AWG-9 can be gained from this simplified block diagram layout, in which can be seen the interplay of data and commands centred around the computer. Databus technology will streamline the system.

Below: AWG-9 components on display. The scale is given by the antenna, which is 36in (914mm) in diameter. Top right are controls and displays, top left are radar components. The upgraded AWG-9 system is digital and features four fewer units. The radar has a 10.2kW capacity.

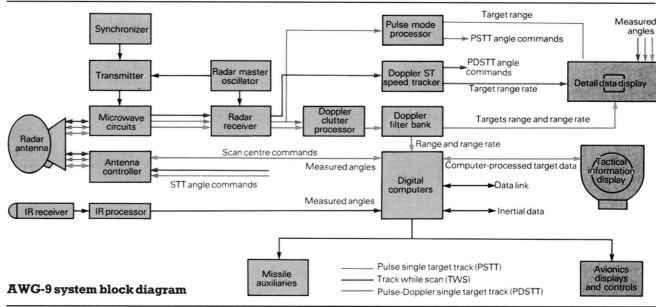

AWG-9 system block diagram

effect occurs with radar returns; the frequency of the returns from a moving object will vary from that of a stationary object, the variation in frequency being directly related to the relative speeds of the two objects.

Pulse-Doppler radar was made possible by the development of the gridded travelling wave tube (TWT) during the 1950s. The effect of the TWT is to increase the power level of a signal that is fed into it. It is very important to have each pulse exactly in phase with its neighbours, which is called coherence, and the TWT is pulsed with signals from a continuously running, ultra-stable coherent oscillator. In this manner, each pulse is transmitted precisely in phase with its fellows, so that any shift in frequency of the return can be detected and measured, giving the radar its lookdown capability.

Returns from the ground naturally show a frequency shift as a result of the motion of the transmitting aircraft, but a moving contact will demonstrate a slightly different shift in almost all cases, and the ground returns can be filtered out by a bank of filters with graduated thresholds. These filters also grade the amount of shift, and by doing so determine the range rate, or speed differential, between the two aircraft. The ground returns having been eliminated, only moving objects are shown, which are almost certainly aircraft, and potential targets. Exceptions to this occur when a contact is moving at or close to right angles to the flight path of the transmitting fighter, or co-speed, heading away on the same flight path. In both cases, the contact's frequency shift will conform to that of the echoes received from the ground and will be filtered out with them, there being insufficient relative movement for detection.

High PRF is needed to give ultra-long distance detection, but it has one disadvantage. The time interval between pulses is so short that with distant contacts, several pulses will have been transmitted before the first echo is received, resulting in ambiguity as to which echo was engendered by which pulse. Frequently the radar return could be from a small contact at relatively close range, or a much larger and more distant contact. This difficulty is overcome by impressing a frequency modulation (FM) on a proportion of the pulses as a positive identifier.

Enhanced resolution

The change in the FM rate is detected by the computer by comparing the frequency difference between the modulated and unmodulated portions of the signal, while filters give improved range resolution to match the inherent resolution of the IFF system. At the same time, monopulse techniques and data processing are used to improve angular resolution which in normal search modes is rather coarse. The high PRF waveform is also limited in its ability to accurately measure range, while its ability to detect low closure rate contacts (i.e., tail-on, nearly co-speed) is poor.

On the other hand, AWG-9 radar is very versatile, and using the broad band gridded TWT it has 19 transmission channels available for pulse-Doppler search signals. Six of these channels are dedicated to Phoenix guidance, while a further five are used to provide semi-active guidance for Sparrows. The sheer number of channels permits adequate cover to minimize the effects of hostile ECM, while the TWT can accept different forms of modulation from the oscillator, allowing low as well as high PRFs to be used as circumstances dictate.

Vital parts of AWG-9 are the two cathode ray tube (CRT) displays in the NFO's cockpit. At the top of the panel is the 5in (12.4cm) Detail Data Display (DDD), which presents basic target data, while below it is situated the 10in (25.4cm) Tactical Information Display (TID). The TID presents processed information on a clutter-free screen showing the tactical situation with alpha-numeric notation. Contacts are depicted together with their altitude and heading, identified as friendly or hostile, and, if hostile, assigned a firing priority as recommended by the computer, calculated on a pre-programmed 'greatest threat' basis. The NFO can override the computer-provided firing priority at his discretion.

The TID picture can be presented in two ways, either aligned with the F-14 with the fighter at the bottom of the scope pointing upwards, which depicts target motion in relation to the movement of both aircraft; or geostabilized with true north at the top of the screen and both the Tomcat and its targets shown. With a target on the TID, the NFO can instruct the computer to show its range, altitude, heading, and speed over the ground. The TID can also accept and display up to eight additional contacts from the ASW-27 two-way data link.

To ensure that the computer is tracking all targets, and to aid in the positive location of targets using ECM, the NFO monitors the information displayed on the DDD. The pilot also has a target display which is coupled into his Horizontal Situation Display (HSD) so that he has access to basically the same information as the NFO. Phoenix and Sparrow can be fired by either the pilot or the NFO, but only the pilot can launch Sidewinders.

The radar antenna of AWG-9 has a maximum scan pattern of 65deg to either side of the aircraft's centreline in azi-

AWG-9 pulse modes

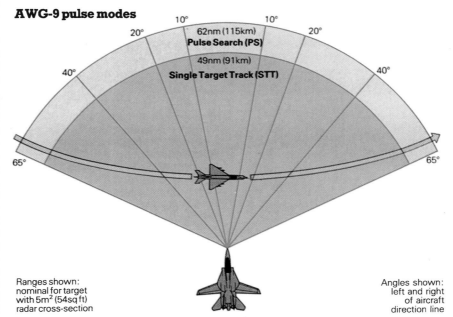

Ranges shown: nominal for target with 5m² (54sq ft) radar cross-section

Angles shown: left and right of aircraft direction line

Above: Both pulse search and single target track modes utilise the same scan patterns as pD (see below) but with reduced range. They are both effective against contacts at 90deg angle-off or with low closure rates.

Below: The pulse-Doppler modes give better range capability than pulse and also a look-down capability, but are ineffective against targets crossing at 90deg (see bottom right) due to lack of Doppler shift.

AWG-9 pulse-Doppler modes

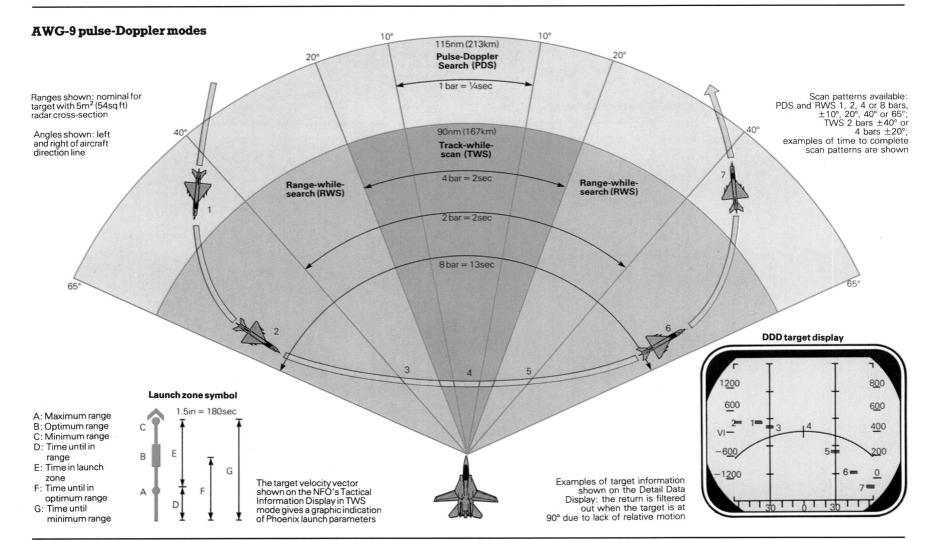

Ranges shown: nominal for target with 5m² (54sq ft) radar cross-section

Angles shown: left and right of aircraft direction line

Scan patterns available: PDS and RWS 1, 2, 4 or 8 bars, ±10°, 20°, 40° or 65°; TWS 2 bars ±40° or 4 bars ±20°; examples of time to complete scan patterns are shown

Launch zone symbol

A: Maximum range
B: Optimum range
C: Minimum range
D: Time until in range
E: Time in launch zone
F: Time until in optimum range
G: Time until minimum range

1.5in = 180sec

The target velocity vector shown on the NFO's Tactical Information Display in TWS mode gives a graphic indication of Phoenix launch parameters

Examples of target information shown on the Detail Data Display: the return is filtered out when the target is at 90° due to lack of relative motion

DDD target display

muth, and eight bars in elevation, the time cycle for the full scan being 13 seconds. The radar operates in six basic modes, four of which are pulse-Doppler, while the other two, used primarily for backup, are pulse only. The pulse-Doppler modes are: pulse-Doppler search (PDS), range while search (RWS), track while scan (TWS), and pulse-Doppler single target track (PDSTT).

PDS is used for long-range search and detection, using either the full antenna capability, or various reduced antenna programmes of 10deg, 20deg or 40deg to either side of the aircraft centreline coupled with one, two or four bars in elevation. The nominal detection range

Right: The NFO in the rear seat of a Tomcat is at the centre of a barrage of information, which can approach saturation point. Cockpit layout was designed by NFOs.

Below: Every inch of space is used. This view shows the left side console and the armament panel, on which can be seen various weapon switches and a clearly marked launch button.

Bottom: The NFO is the human end of AWG-9. His cockpit is dominated by the large circular TID and its hand control stick, with the smaller DDD just above. The NFO has a vital role to play in formulating tactics.

NFO's instrument panel and consoles

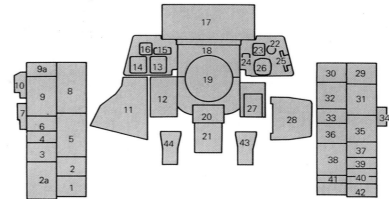

Left side console
1 G valve pushbutton
2 Oxygen vent airflow controls
2a Data stowage
3 Communications and navigation command control panel
4 Intercommunications system control panel
5 Integrated control panel
6 Tacan control panel
7 Liquid cooling controls
8 Computer address panel
9 Radar/infra-red/TV control panel
9a UHF communications selection panel
10 Eject command panel
Left vertical console
11 Armament panel
Left knee panel
12 System test/system power panel

Left instrument panel
13 Servopneumatic altimeter
14 Airspeed Mach indicator
15 UHF remote indicator
16 Standby attitude indicator
Centre panel
17 Detail data display panel
Centre console
18 Navigation control and data readout
19 Tactical information display
20 Tactical information control panel
21 Hand control unit
Right instrument panel
22 Fuel quantity totalizer
23 Clock
24 Threat advisory lights
25 Canopy jettison handle
26 Bearing distance heading indicator
Right knee panel
27 Caution advisory panel

Right vertical console
28 Multiple display indicator
Right side console
29 Digital data indicator
30 ECM display control panel
31 Data link reply and interior light control panel
32 ECM control panel
33 Defensive ECM controls
34 Defog control level
35 IFF transponder controls
36 ALE-39 programmer
37 AA1 control panel
38 Chaff/flare dispense panel
39 IFF antenna deployment and test panel
40 Radar beacon controls
41 KY-28 cryptographic system control panel
42 Electrical power test panel
Left and right foot wells
43 Microphone foot button
44 ICS foot button

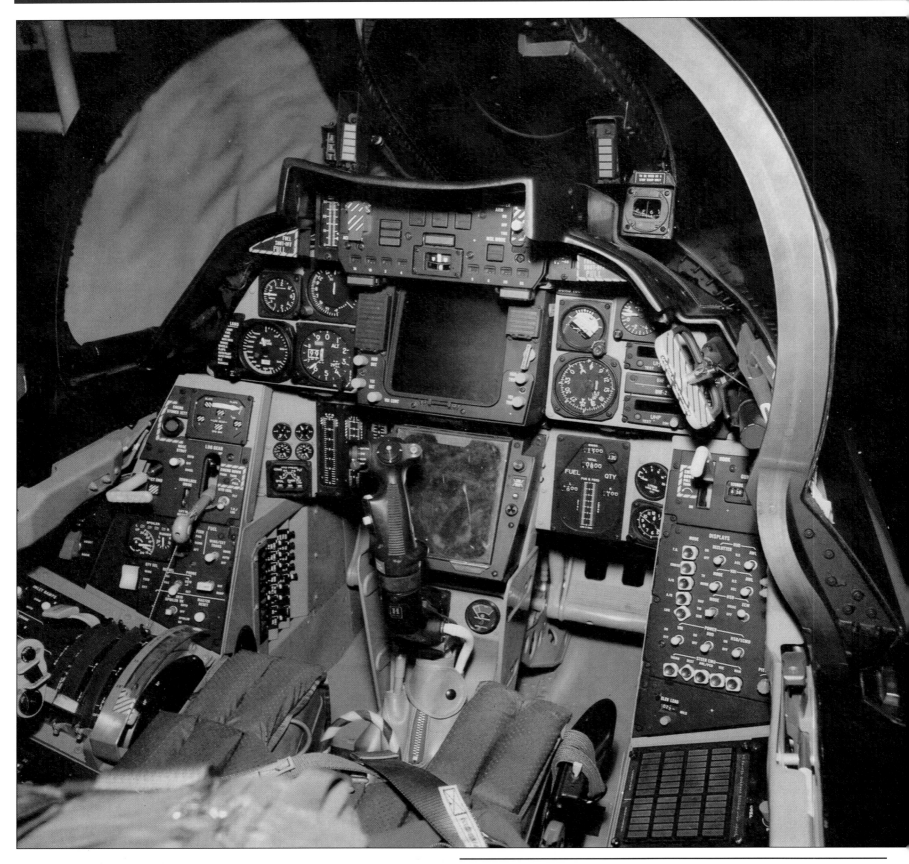

is given as 115nm (212km) against fighter-sized targets with a 54sq ft (5m^2) radar cross-sectional area, though it is reported that jumbo-sized contacts can be detected as far away as 200nm (368km), and small cruise missiles at over 65nm (120km). Contact data is displayed on the DDD in terms of azimuth, elevation, and range rate, but not range. Boresight missile modes can be used in PDS.

RWS mode adds ranging to the long range search and detection by using FM techniques as described earlier, for a slight penalty in maximum detection range, which reduces to 90nm (166km) for a fighter-sized contact. The antenna programmes are the same as for PDS. The data is displayed on both the DDD and the TID.

TWS is the mode which sets AWG-9 apart from all other systems, with its ability to track 24 targets simultaneously. Ground testing has confirmed this capability, while a flight test has been carried out that successfully monitored seventeen, which was more of a headache for the ground controllers than for AWG-9.

In order to allow the computer to function correctly, contact data must be updated every two seconds; to achieve this, the field of scan has to be reduced to give coverage within this timescale. Two antenna patterns are compatible: plus and minus 40deg in azimuth combined with 2 bars elevation; and plus and minus 20deg in azimuth with 4 bars elevation. These enable the computer to store look angles, range, and range rate for each contact in a separate track file.

Intercept parameters
After a series of returns, the computer predicts where each contact should be and where the antenna should point on each subsequent scan. It then calculates missile intercept parameters based on stored launch envelopes, also launch priorities which are based primarily on the degree of threat indications. The designated targets are displayed on the TID, with a number indicating Phoenix launch order to their right. When the optimum launch position is achieved, the target symbol on the TID begins to flash, telling the crew they can launch.

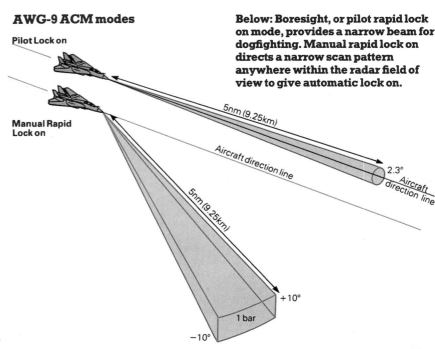

AWG-9 ACM modes

Pilot Lock on

Manual Rapid Lock on

5nm (9.25km)

Aircraft direction line

2.3°

Aircraft direction line

5nm (9.25km)

+10°

−10°

1 bar

Below: Boresight, or pilot rapid lock on mode, provides a narrow beam for dogfighting. Manual rapid lock on directs a narrow scan pattern anywhere within the radar field of view to give automatic lock on.

Pilot's instrument panel and consoles

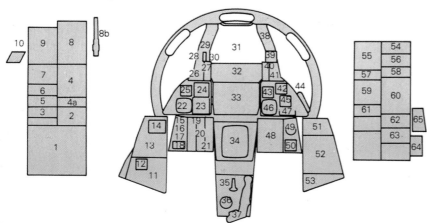

Left side console
1 G valve pushbutton
2 Oxygen vent airflow control panel
3 Communications and navigation command control panel
4 UHF (AN/ARC-159)
4a UHF communications selector panel
5 Tone/volume controls
6 Intercommunications system control panel
7 AFCS control panel
8 Throttle quadrant
8a Hydraulic hand pump
9 Inlet ramps/throttle controls
10 Target designate switch
Left vertical console
11 Fuel management panel
12 Control surface position indicator
12a Launch bar abort
13 Landing gear control panel
14 Wheels/flaps position indicator
Left knee panel
15 Engine pressure ratio indicator
16 Exhaust nozzle position indicator
17 Oil pressure indicator
18 Hydraulic pressure indicator

19 Electrical tachometer indicator
20 Thermocouple temperature indicator
21 Rate of flow indicator
Left instrument panel
22 Servopneumatic altimeter
23 Radar altimeter
24 Airspeed Mach indicator
25 Vertical velocity indicator
26 Left engine fuel shut-off
27 Angle of attack indicator
Left front windshield frame
28 Approach indexer
29 ACLS/AP/nosewheel steering engaged warning lights
30 Wheels/brakes warning lights
Centre panel
31 Head-up display
32 ACM panel
33 Vertical display indicator
34 Horizontal situation display
35 Pedal adjust handle
36 Brake pressure indicator
37 Control stick
Right front windshield frame
38 ECM warning light
39 Standby compass
Right instrument panel
40 Wing sweep indicator
41 Right engine fuel shutoff

42 Accelerometer
43 Standby attitude indicator
44 Canopy jettison handle
45 Clock
46 Bearing distance heading indicator
47 UHF remote indicator
Right knee panel
48 Fuel quantity indicator
49 Liquid oxygen quantity indicator
50 Cabin pressure altimeter
Right vertical console
51 Arresting hook panel
52 Displays control panel
53 Elevation lead panel
Right side console
54 Compass control panel
55 Caution advisory indicator
56 Tacan control panel
57 Master generator control panel
58 ARA-63 receiver-decoder control panel
59 Air conditioning controls
60 Master light control panel
61 External environmental control panel
62 Master test panel
63 Hydraulic transfer pump switch
64 Defog control panel
65 Windshield defog switch

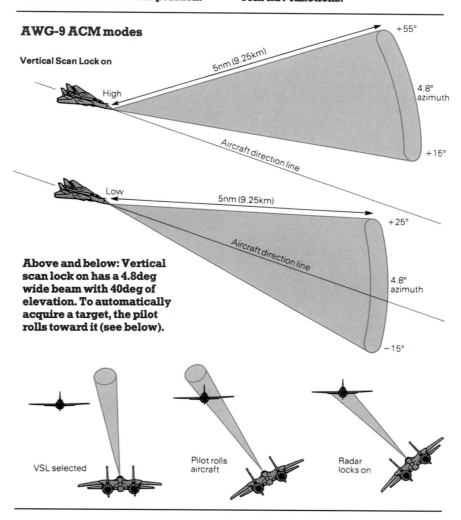

Left: The pilot's cockpit differs considerably from that of the NFO. The flight controls are in evidence, and the CRT displays are less dominant than in the rear position.

Above: The left console in the front cockpit is much simpler than that in the back, containing mainly engine controls plus Tacan and some other com/nav functions.

AWG-9 ACM modes

Vertical Scan Lock on

+55°
5nm (9.25km)
High
4.8° azimuth
Aircraft direction line
+15°

Low
5nm (9.25km)
+25°
Aircraft direction line
4.8° azimuth
−15°

Above and below: Vertical scan lock on has a 4.8deg wide beam with 40deg of elevation. To automatically acquire a target, the pilot rolls toward it (see below).

VSL selected

Pilot rolls aircraft

Radar locks on

Left: The pilot's cockpit looks dated by modern standards, but in 1970 the air combat manoeuvre panel was an innovation, and some dials were replaced by tape instruments.

Above: Unlike more recent American fighters, the Tomcat is a two-seater. Each crewman has a well defined role and teamwork is the keynote, particularly for interception work.

Multiple Phoenix launches carried out in this manner are generally described as simultaneous attacks; this description is correct insofar as setting up the attack goes, but the missiles are necessarily fired one after the other in a predetermined order. TWS retains the nominal 90nm (166km) detection range for fighter-sized targets, but the maximum launch range for Phoenix in a multi-shot attack is stated as 52nm (96km). Mid-course guidance for Phoenix is provided by SARH until the terminal homing stage is reached, when the missile's active radar is used. In a multiple attack time-sharing is used to guide all the missiles.

TWS mode has one unusual advantage. With more conventional radars, the radar goes into attack mode, or locks on to the target prior to weapon release. Radar warning receivers in the target aircraft can detect the difference quite readily between a search scan, which simply indicates that someone is looking at them, and lock on, which indicates that a missile may very soon be on its way with hostile intent, but the TWS scan emissions are more difficult to identify as

they appear to have the characteristics of a search mode rather than an attack mode. Warning of an inbound Phoenix is therefore minimal.

PDSTT is the mode used for the spectacular long-range Phoenix tests. It gives maximum range for tracking and also maximum range for a Phoenix launch. The antenna locks onto the target and the presented data includes range, range rate, and angle. PDSTT is also used for launching Sparrow and Sidewinder missiles. It employs a velocity track process, but it also incorporates a jamming angle track facility, for use against targets employing ECM, which provides range rate and angular data. Against standard fighter-sized targets, PDSTT provides a stated maximum launch range of 63nm (116km) for Phoenix, 38nm (70km) for AIM-7F Sparrow, and 10nm (16km) for Sidewinder. The earlier AIM-7E Sparrow needs continuous wave (CW) illumination on which to home; this is provided by a supplementary TWT in the transmitter.

Two pulse modes are used, mainly as backup for the pulse-Doppler modes.

Pulse search is used for air-to-air search or for ground mapping. The antenna scan combinations are the same as for PDS, but naturally have no Doppler effect; range rate is therefore not available, just range and azimuth. Detection range reduces to 62nm (114km) for a fighter-sized target, but pulse search does have the advantage of being able to detect in the two blind areas of pD and can acquire bogeys at 90deg crossing angles or those with negligible closure rates.

Single target tracking

Pulse single target track is the other mode and is used in the conventional manner to lock on. It is compatible with all weapons, including the Vulcan cannon. Once acquired, the contact is displayed on the DDD together with its range. Phoenix can be used as a short range weapon using its active terminal homing, while CW illumination is provided for Sparrows, giving a maximum launch range of 18nm (33km) for the AIM-7E version and 29nm (53km) for the improved AIM-7F.

For close combat three modes are provided which give automatic lock on at ranges up to 5nm (9km). These are boresight, used in short-range attack or dogfight, which projects a 2.3deg wide beam along the axis of the Tomcat; vertical scan lock on, which is used to acquire a turning target; and a manual lock on mode. Vertical scan projects a narrow vertical beam in one of two positions, variable according to the needs of the moment. The first extends from 15deg to 55deg above the Tomcat datum line, while the second is from 15deg below datum to 25deg above, datum being a reference to the level axis of the Tomcat in the pitching plane. Above-datum acquisition permits missile launch without the nose being pointed directly at the target, while below-datum acquisition would be used for pulling lead on a hard-turning target.

Manual lock on uses a 20deg, 1-bar scan which gives lock on anywhere within the radar field of view to a range of 5nm (9km). Operated by the NFO, its use appears to require a high degree of communication and co-operation between the crew members, and for this reason it is unlikely to be used often. In all the close combat modes, the computer projects continuously updated weapon launch solutions through the Kaiser Aerospace Head Up Display (HUD) onto the windshield, which is used instead of a combiner glass.

An invaluable adjunct to the detection equipment of AWG-9 is its gimbal-mounted infra-red (IR) sensor, mounted in a pod beneath the nose of the aircraft. It possesses inherently better angular resolution than radar and can thus be used to confirm target azimuth and elevation. As it is a passive sensor, its use is undetectable, and it is sufficiently sensitive to gather data, including a rough assessment of range, to be used for either Phoenix or Sidewinder launch.

The IR detector can be used independently of the radar, for example to scan high while the radar searches downwards; or it can be slaved to the radar or vice versa so that the systems complement each other. It is especially effective in detecting high altitude after-burning targets, or rocket-propelled cruise missiles at long ranges, and in a heavy ECM environment it is an invaluable backup.

Weapon firing is actually performed by a separate computer, the AWG-15, while the problems inherent in using four different weapons, possibly in rapid succession and not in any particular order, are solved by using an integrated armament control system. A control and display indicator in the cockpit indicates, firstly, what selections a pilot should make for a particular weapon; secondly, when all necessary selections have been made; and thirdly, if an erroneous selection has been made. As an alternative, all weapon options can be pre-programmed and stored prior to takeoff, in which case a weapon is instantly prepared for launch at the touch of a switch.

A unique item for its time was the air combat manoeuvre panel, which consists of a single master panel mounted within the pilot's cone of vision. This contains the controls for rapid selection of all short-range weapons and was designed to be operated without the pilot risking losing visual contact with an opponent. This panel also gives the status of all remaining weapons, including the rounds remaining for the gun. Compared with the latest breed of fighter cockpit displays this sounds old hat, but in 1970 it was a major advance.

Another advance made possible in AWG-9 by computer technology was built-in test (BIT) capability. This provides both ground and in-flight monitoring of the equipment and, in the event of a malfunction in any of the 31 sub-assemblies that comprise AWG-9, can isolate the fault and at the same time advise the crew of the serviceable modes remaining, this enabling them to complete the mission using alternative means provided by systems redundancy. The bulk storage magnetic tape in the main AWG-9 computer has a capacity of about 70,000 words, of which nearly half are dedicated to BIT.

The computer network in the Tomcat would need a book of its own to describe its workings in full. Virtually all on-board computers, including AWG-9, are linked by the Computer Signal Data Converter (CSDC). It links AWG-9 data to the displays and their subsystems, and presents data from other systems, such as the Central Air Data Computer (CADC), which among other functions controls wing sweep, to AWG-9. It controls the two-way data link, the HUD, the cockpit displays, which are themselves computers, the INS, and data exchange between the cockpits.

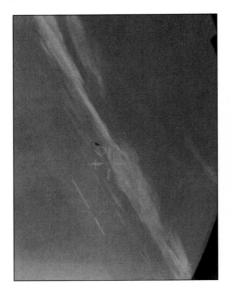

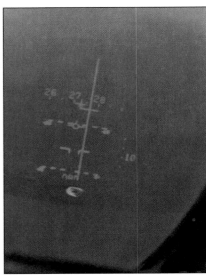

Above: The HUD projects data in symbolic and numeric format onto the windshield. It is focussed at infinity to aid the pilot in his visual search. Often, as seen here, contact is beyond visual distance.

Above: Close combat! A Tomcat turns hard to keep out of the sights of a fellow squadron member. The long oblique line gives the horizon and the intersecting symbol the angle of bank of the attacking fighter.

Above: An unseen opponent bores in but is detected and displayed on the pilot's windshield. The weapon is selected ready for use and the seconds tick away while the optimum firing solution is achieved.

Above: The Northrop TCS, mounted in place of the IR sensor, can provide positive identification at well beyond visual distance. Capable of working by nothing more than starlight, it gives cats' eyes to the Tomcat.

Below: Part of the update for AWG-9 is this digital display which is replacing the old analogue unit. The new DDD is much larger than the original and has a full range of brightness control, with greatly improved image quality.

It incorporates a computer keyboard with software programmable switches – the key to future updates is seen as software changes using the flexibility provided by the new programmable signal processor.

New radar

However good AWG-9 was by the standards of its day, by the mid-1980s that day was long gone. Its weaknesses were apparent. For example, it was not very good in a tail-chase against a co-speed target, whilst the processing speed of its analogue computers had been left far behind by the modern digital variety.

The slightly later Hughes APG-63 developed for the F-15 was already in the throes of being supplanted by the APG-70, which not only had greater fighter capability, it had air-to-ground modes developed for the F-15E Strike Eagle. Not too much modification was needed to turn this into the APG-71, which was compatible with Tomcat weapons systems. This, with other avionics updates, was scheduled for the F-14D Super Tomcat.

At the heart of the new digital avionics suite were two MIL-STD-1553G multi-processors, which essentially link the black boxes together. APG-71 itself was designed to operate in a severe ECM environment, with improved (over AWG-9) detection and tracking modes. New capabilities included monopulse angle tracking, which gives greater accuracy, and beyond visual range target identification. Radar returns have always contained more information than technology is able to extract from them; the six-fold processing increment of APG-71 went some way towards rectifying this.

In addition, the radar works in conjunction with the Northrop Television Camera System (TCS), an optical low-light system believed to allow visual identification of a Jumbo Jet at more than 50nm (93km), and an Infra-Red Search and Track (IRST) sensor, of which more later.

The Tomcat's new-found air-to-surface mission called for multi-function ground mapping modes, using Doppler beam-sharpening and synthetic aperture techniques, aided by navigation and ground target detection. Terrain avoidance is yet another obviously valuable attribute.

APG-71 has a maximum power output of 5kW, which provides long range detection, with a practical maximum acquisition range of 200nm (370km). However, this distance can be doubled on the cockpit tactical display by using contacts handed off from other aircraft via secure data link, thus giving increased situational awareness. "More than" 24 targets can be tracked simultaneously, while digital processors analyse contacts and assign priorities.

Software is of course the key to the whole thing, and in the early 1980s the attitude was that most problems could be solved by reprogramming. The buzzword was, "It's only a software change!" In practice this was torpedoed by improved computer capacity and processing speeds which made possible programmes of extraordinary complexity. This made software changes so difficult, and so time-consuming, as to become virtually anathema!

Getting the information around AWG-9 had been a major problem, with literally hundreds of miles of wiring connecting the various analogue components. For the new digital Tomcat, the information is carried by databus. A databus can be pictured as a circular railway, with components as stations. Passengers are data, each one carrying a ticket (electronic code) to a specific component (station). In this way, all pieces of coded data arrive at the correct component for processing.

Other sensors

Other sensors are the TCS and IRST. The first is an old idea which will not go away. In the form of TISEO it was used by F-14s in the AIMVAL/ACE-VAL exercise at Nellis AFB in 1977/78. It was judged a success in the cloudless skies of Nevada, but when deployed to cloud-laden Europe with Phantoms, it proved rather less effective.

TCS, developed by Northrop, is a closed-circuit television with the camera mounted on a gimbal platform stabilized in both azimuth and elevation. Two modes are selectable by the NFO: wide angle for search, and close-up for identification.

A separate lens system is used for each mode, with two cameras and two vidicons, which are detectors which convert light impulses into electronic signals. The vidicons are very sensitive and reportedly give satisfactory results even in starlight. The cameras are normally slaved to the radar, and automatically lock onto the first contact acquired, although the identification camera can also be operated manually by the NFO. The target images, which are stabilized automatically, can be shown on the radar displays in either cockpit. On 4 January, 1989, two Tomcats shot down two Libyan MiG-23s. Afterwards, what were described as gun camera pictures were released. But at least one, showing the armament of one of the MiGs, apparently taken from very close range, was almost certainly from a TCS.

An IR sensor was originally fitted to the F-14A, but in practice this was found wanting, and it was replaced with the TCS. Since then, advances in IR technology have once more made it a valid option.

The new IRST is by Lockheed Martin, and is a different piece of kit altogether. Operating in both the mid (3-5 micron) and long (8-12 micron) wavebands, it is a "two-colour" sensor, able to detect exhaust plumes and aerodynamic hotspots with equal facility. The sensor head houses the IR optics, and can be either steered by the NFO or set to scan automatically. All "hot spots" are automatically processed, using complex algorithms, and false alarms (hopefully including those caused by IRCM) are screened out. The IRST can detect and track multiple targets at extreme ranges – up to 100nm (185km) according to some sources. Like the TCS, contacts identified by IRST are displayed in the cockpit.

Both TCS and IRST are located in a common chin pod under the nose of the F-14D. The other thing they have in common is that they are both passive sensors and, unlike radar, their use cannot betray the presence of the Tomcat. Of course, neither the TCS nor the IRST can see through cloud, making the advantages they confer reliant on clear weather. But, having said that, many potential theatres of conflict have decent visibility much of the time, while the sky is quite often clear at high altitudes. Given these circumstances, TCS and IRST are both potential combat assets.

Target identification has already been touched upon. Another area where both TCS and IRST have potential is raid assessment. Aircraft flying in very close formation often show up on a radar screen as a single blip. Various techniques can be used to overcome this but, as both TCS (optical) and IRST operate at much shorter wavelengths than radar, they have inherently better angular discrimination. This often enables them to resolve what is apparently a single contact into several components, so that Tomcat pilots may know the odds beforehand, and select their tactics accordingly.

Defensive sensors

Threat detection is of course essential, and this is largely accomplished by the Litton ALR-76(V) processor-controlled radar warning and countermeasures system. This detects hostile radar emissions, identifies them by comparing them to a stored library of signatures, and assigns priorities in terms of threat (in a high-threat area more signals will be received than can be displayed). An audible warning is then given, with

Below: A technician fine-tunes the AN/ALQ-165 Advanced Self-Protection Jammer. A Northrop Grumman product, it is used by many Navy and Marine Hornets as well as the Tomcat.

visual presentation of identity together with range and angular data. Remarkably, the advanced ALR-67(V) gives coverage not only in the conventional radar spectrum, but into millimetric and laser frequencies. It is coupled with chaff and IRCM dispensers. It was also designed to be compatible with the ALQ-165 Advanced Self-Protection Jammer (ASPJ).

Active countermeasures were originally provided by the ALQ-100, but by the mid-1980s this was perceived as lacking the flexibility to cope with future projected threats. To replace it, ITT/Westinghouse combined to produce the ALQ-165 ASPJ. A pod, it consisted of two receivers and two transmitters, using high speed digital processing to counter future threat radars via constantly upgraded software.

As noted earlier, the weakness of this approach was the increasing complexity of software. Development was protracted, but low-rate production finally started in 1989. Failure to meet certain objectives coupled with the demand for a "peace dividend" led to its cancellation in 1992. However, rumour control has it that operations over Bosnia a year or two later resulted in a few pods being taken out of store for use, although not on the F-14.

Recce bird

While reconnaissance is a task of the utmost importance, the limited space aboard a carrier makes a dedicated machine rather a luxury, as the US Navy had discovered with the RA-5C Vigilante, a huge machine familiarly known as the Elephant. The Navy decided it was preferable to have a dual role aircraft.

The Tactical Airborne Reconnaissance Pod System (TARPS) had been developed for the A-7 Corsair II. This subsonic attack aircraft was hardly ideal for the a mission involving penetration of hostile air space, and the task then fell to the F-14A, 49 of which were adapted to carry a TARPS pod on the rear left Phoenix station. Little modification was required for the aircraft: this included some wiring, air conditioning, and controls for the NFO in the rear cockpit. As it could be fitted or dismounted in just 30 minutes, TARPS caused no reduction to the strength of the main fighter defence of the carrier.

The TARPS pod is 17.3ft (5.27m) long and weighs 1,760lb (798kg). It contains a KS-87B frame camera for forward oblique or vertical views, a KA-99 panoramic camera, and an AAD-5 Infra-Red Line Scanner (IRLS),

which records the terrain along the route. This last has one tremendous advantage. Conventional cameras can record only what is there at the time, but IRLS can detect where they were even after they have gone by recording the heat footprint on the hardstanding. Finally there is the ASQ-172 data display system, which is used to provide identifiable event marks on the film to aid interpretation. The first TARPS Tomcat entered service in November 1981, and three were assigned to one squadron in each carrier air group.

Claws of the Tomcat

The superb performance and capability demonstrated by the Tomcat in its designated role has tended to obscure the fact that it was designed as an uncompromised air superiority fighter, and only then adapted for fleet air defence. Even more so, it has obscured the fact that it has significant low-level capability, although the "Bombcat" emerged only late in its career. But, having said that, the most important aspect of the Tomcat has always been, and probably always will be, as an interceptor.

The weapon with which the Tomcat is mainly associated is the AIM-54

Phoenix. Carried by no other fighter in the world, Phoenix conferred a long-range kill capability which is only now, at the beginning of the 21st Century, beginning to be exceeded, and only by weapons which are still in the project development stage. It was expensive; not for nothing did it earn the soubriquet of "the million dollar missile".

The origins of the Phoenix lay in the Bendix Eagle, as outlined in the Development chapter, and also in the Hughes GAR-9, which was later redesignated AIM-47A. A member of the Falcon family, AIM-47A had a maximum range of 115nm (213km) and a maximum speed of Mach 6. Designed to be carried by the Mach 3.2-capable Rapier interceptor, it used SARH midcourse guidance coupled with IR terminal homing. This ambitious programme proved to be rather beyond the state of the art (1958-1960), and both Rapier and AIM-47A were cancelled.

The extreme range of the AIM-47A missile made extraordinary demands on the detection, tracking, and SARH system. This was meant to have been provided by the Hughes ASG-18 pulse-Doppler radar,

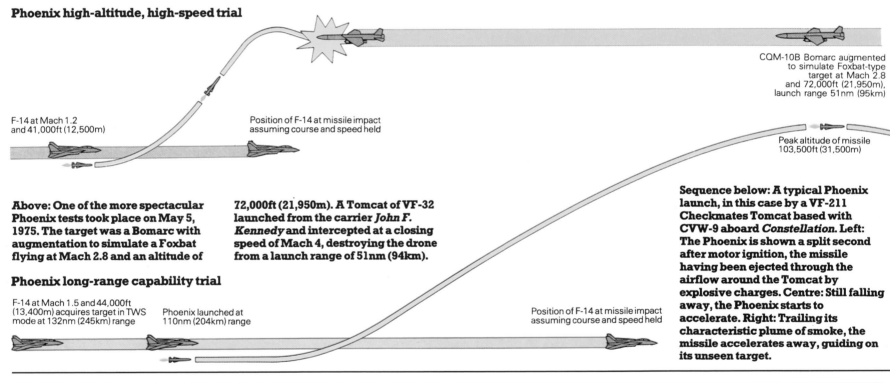

Phoenix high-altitude, high-speed trial

F-14 at Mach 1.2 and 41,000ft (12,500m)

Position of F-14 at missile impact assuming course and speed held

CQM-10B Bomarc augmented to simulate Foxbat-type target at Mach 2.8 and 72,000ft (21,950m), launch range 51nm (95km)

Peak altitude of missile 103,500ft (31,500m)

Above: One of the more spectacular Phoenix tests took place on May 5, 1975. The target was a Bomarc with augmentation to simulate a Foxbat flying at Mach 2.8 and an altitude of

72,000ft (21,950m). A Tomcat of VF-32 launched from the carrier *John F. Kennedy* and intercepted at a closing speed of Mach 4, destroying the drone from a launch range of 51nm (94km).

Sequence below: A typical Phoenix launch, in this case by a VF-211 Checkmates Tomcat based with CVW-9 aboard *Constellation*. Left: The Phoenix is shown a split second after motor ignition, the missile having been ejected through the airflow around the Tomcat by explosive charges. Centre: Still falling away, the Phoenix starts to accelerate. Right: Trailing its characteristic plume of smoke, the missile accelerates away, guiding on its unseen target.

Phoenix long-range capability trial

F-14 at Mach 1.5 and 44,000ft (13,400m) acquires target in TWS mode at 132nm (245km) range

Phoenix launched at 110nm (204km) range

Position of F-14 at missile impact assuming course and speed held

AIM-54A Phoenix

Below: AIM-54A Phoenix differs from the later AIM-54C version only in the digital avionics and radar. Its manoeuvre capability is reported as being up to 25g.

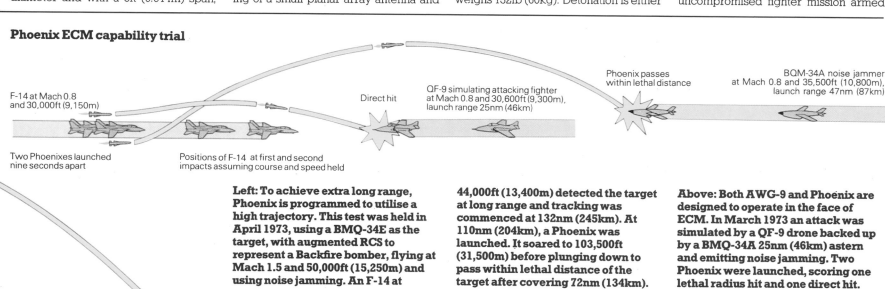

Labels (clockwise): Aircraft mounting lug · Multi-pin umbilical · Fixed cruciform wings · Motor nozzle · Proximity fuze antenna · Fuzing unit · Aircraft mounting lug · Transceiver · Planar array radar scanner · Radome · Radar avionics · Proximity radar target detector · Annular blast fragmentation warhead · Solid fuel propellant · Electrical converter · Autopilot controller · Tailfin hydraulic actuator · Rear detection antenna · Control fins

from which AWG-9 was developed. About 80 AIM-47As were built before cancellation.

AIM-54 Phoenix, reportedly so named because it arose from the ashes of its two predecessors, was selected to arm the F-111B, and Hughes received a contract in 1962. Originally designated AAM-N-11, Phoenix is a big, heavy air-to-air missile, 13ft (3.96m) long, 1.25ft (0.38m) in diameter and with a 3ft (0.914m) span,

and the A variant weighs 975lb (443kg). Resembling its Falcon ancestor in shape and aerodynamic layout, it has cruciform wings and is controlled by hydraulically operated tail fins. This layout has low induced drag and gives excellent sustained manoeuvrability, even towards the end of its run.

For guidance, Phoenix has the battery-powered DSQ-26 system, consisting of a small planar array antenna and

electronics for terminal homing using active radar; a transmitter/receiver electronics suite for semi-active midcourse guidance from AWG-9, which is used on a time-share basis in a multiple launch; and the autopilot. Phoenix can lose the Doppler return for up to 14 seconds, and still re-acquire its target.

The warhead is of the annular blast fragmentation type (continuous rod) and weighs 132lb (60kg). Detonation is either

on impact with a DA fuze, or by the Downey Mk 334 proximity fuze, or, as a third option, a Bendix IR fuze. The propulsion unit is either a Rocketdyne Mk 47 or Aerojet Mk 60 long-burning motor, which gives an all-burnt speed of Mach 3.8, although some sources give a maximum speed of Mach 5 at very high altitude. In the design of the propulsion unit the trade-off was burn time against thrust; in the event, a single burn time and total impulse was selected.

To provide maximum range capability without incurring unacceptable size and weight penalties in the missile, it was decided to adopt a high midcourse trajectory, using altitudes where the rocket motor was at its most efficient and drag at a minimum. This had the added advantage that extra positional energy was gained in the form of altitude which could be converted back into kinetic energy for manoeuvre towards the end of the flight path. The active radar terminal homing has an approximate range of 10nm (18.5km), while maximum range is stated to be in excess of 100nm (185km).

Up to six Phoenix missiles are carried by the F-14: two on pylons situated on the wing gloves, and another four carried on semi-conformal pallets under the fuselage. The Tomcat was designed for the uncompromised fighter mission armed

Phoenix ECM capability trial

F-14 at Mach 0.8 and 30,000ft (9,150m)

Direct hit

QF-9 simulating attacking fighter at Mach 0.8 and 30,600ft (9,300m), launch range 25nm (46km)

Phoenix passes within lethal distance

BQM-34A noise jammer at Mach 0.8 and 35,500ft (10,800m), launch range 47nm (87km)

Two Phoenixes launched nine seconds apart

Positions of F-14 at first and second impacts assuming course and speed held

Missile impacts 72.5nm (134km) from launch point

Position of target at Phoenix launch

Left: To achieve extra long range, Phoenix is programmed to utilise a high trajectory. This test was held in April 1973, using a BMQ-34E as the target, with augmented RCS to represent a Backfire bomber, flying at Mach 1.5 and 50,000ft (15,250m) and using noise jamming. An F-14 at

44,000ft (13,400m) detected the target at long range and tracking was commenced at 132nm (245km). At 110nm (204km), a Phoenix was launched. It soared to 103,500ft (31,500m) before plunging down to pass within lethal distance of the target after covering 72nm (134km).

Above: Both AWG-9 and Phoenix are designed to operate in the face of ECM. In March 1973 an attack was simulated by a QF-9 drone backed up by a BMQ-34A 25nm (46km) astern and emitting noise jamming. Two Phoenix were launched, scoring one lethal radius hit and one direct hit.

BQM-34E augmented to simulate radar cross-section of Backfire-type target at Mach 1.5 and 50,000ft (15,250m)

Phoenix cruise missile interception trial

Below: Sea-skimming cruise missiles are among the most dangerous threats surface ships have to counter. Hugging the waves at high subsonic speed, their small size makes them difficult to detect. In this test, an unaugmented BMQ-34A flying at Mach 0.75 and just 50ft (15m) was shot down by a Tomcat 22nm (41km) away from 10,000ft (3,050m).

Phoenix manoeuvring target trial

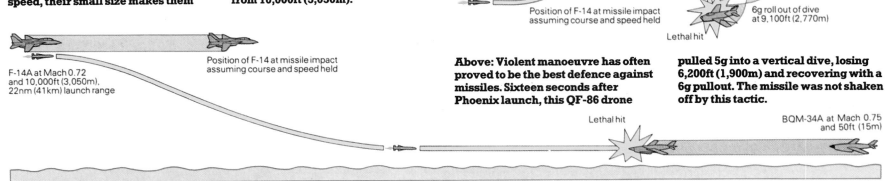

F-14 at Mach 0.75 and 10,000ft (3,050m), 9.5nm (17.6km) launch range

Position of F-14 at missile impact assuming course and speed held

5g roll into vertical dive

QF-86 at Mach 0.8 and 15,300ft (4,660m)

6g roll out of dive at 9,100ft (2,770m)

Lethal hit

Above: Violent manoeuvre has often proved to be the best defence against missiles. Sixteen seconds after Phoenix launch, this QF-86 drone pulled 5g into a vertical dive, losing 6,200ft (1,900m) and recovering with a 6g pullout. The missile was not shaken off by this tactic.

F-14A at Mach 0.72 and 10,000ft (3,050m), 22nm (41km) launch range

Position of F-14 at missile impact assuming course and speed held

Lethal hit

BQM-34A at Mach 0.75 and 50ft (15m)

---

with Sparrows semi-recessed into the underside of the fuselage for minimum drag. Phoenix needs a frequency decoder, wiring, and coolant lines as well as a launcher, and these were all incorporated into the pallets, which are only fitted when Phoenix are to be carried. The removal of these pallets saves both weight and drag when the Sparrow-armed fighter mission is flown, and does not compromise the recesses in which the Sparrows are carried.

Flight testing of Phoenix began at PMTC Point Mugu in 1965, using an A-3A Skywarrior as the trials aircraft, and the first interception was made on May 12, 1966, when a direct hit on a drone target was scored. The first multiple launch was made in March 1969 from an F-111B against two drones.

F-14 Phoenix trials

The Phoenix/Tomcat programme began in April 1972 with a jettison test. From this point, progress was rapid, and a dazzlingly successful series of tests, mainly with inert warheads but including some live, followed. Full details of Phoenix testing are impossible to give as between May 1972 and October 1980, in tests and in operational readiness exercises, no less than 155 production models of AIM-54A were launched, with a claimed success rate of 92 per cent. The success rate does not include failures in the equipment of the launching aircraft, nor failures in the augmentation of the drone targets. We can pick out some of the more spectacular tests – and not only those that were 100 per cent successful.

One of the reasons why the Navy had been so insistent on the Phoenix/Tomcat combination had been the need to counter the threat posed by the Soviet MiG-25, codenamed Foxbat by NATO. In July 1972, the first anti-Foxbat test took place at the PCMR. An AQM-37A Stiletto drone with radar augmentation to simulate the signature of the Foxbat was flown at an altitude of 82,000ft (25,000m) and a speed of Mach 2.2, and the intercepting Tomcat, flying at 47,000ft (14,300m) and Mach 1.2, launched a single Phoenix from a range of just under 35nm (64km). The big missile climbed unerringly and passed within lethal range of the target drone.

The first multiple launch from a Tomcat came during the following December, when BuAer 157983 launched two Phoenix at drones representing an aircraft and its previously-launched cruise missile. The cruise missile target was destroyed, but an anomaly in the second Phoenix caused one of its few failures.

A few days later, on December 20, the target was a simulated fighter wave consisting of three QT-33 drones, and two BQM-34s with their radar cross-sectional areas electronically augmen-

ted to the 32-54sq ft (3-5m²) typical of the MiG-21 Fishbed. The five drones were staggered across a front 20nm (37km) wide at altitudes between 20,000ft and 25,000ft (6,100-7,600m), and their mean velocity was Mach 0.6, a reasonable fighter cruising speed. Higher up, at 31,500ft (9,600m), a single Tomcat armed with six AIM-54As moved to intercept at Mach 0.7. Using the pulse-Doppler radar to look down, detection was achieved at over 60nm (110km), and tracking, in the TWS mode, began at 50nm (92km). From a distance of 30nm (56km) the first missile was launched, followed during the next 45 seconds by three more. One QT-33 was destroyed by a direct hit, while the other three missiles all passed within the lethal distance of their targets. This was a most promising beginning.

Both AWG-9 and AIM-54 had been designed to operate in the face of electronic countermeasures. This ability was first put to the test in March 1973 when a raid was simulated by a QF-9 flying at Mach 0.8 and 30,600ft (9,300m), trailed by a BQM-34A 25nm (46km) astern, co-speed and at an altitude of 35,500ft (10,800m), which was emitting noise jamming to cover the lead drone. A Tomcat moved to intercept, and detected both targets at long range. Closing in at 30,000ft (9,150m) and Mach 0.8, it launched a Phoenix at the QF-9 from 25nm (46km) away, then just nine seconds later launched a second at the jamming drone from a distance of 47nm (87km). The QF-9 was destroyed by a direct hit, while the second Phoenix passed within lethal distance of its target.

Phoenix has what has been quaintly described as a 'home on jam' capability: its sensors tell it that it is being jammed; it then promptly homes on the source of the interference. Incidentally, it should be noted that most tests were carried out with inert warheads; drones are too expensive to merely throw away and are recovered for re-use when possible.

Air-to-air world record

The next test was to set a world record for air-to-air missiles. The new Soviet bomber codenamed Backfire was about to enter service, so in April 1973 a Backfire-type target was simulated by an augmented BQM-34E, flying at a speed of Mach 1.5 and an altitude of 50,000ft (15,250m), and using intermittent noise jamming. From 44,000ft (13,400m) the F-14 moved to intercept. It should be noted that the highest possible speed should be attained by all fighters engaging long-range targets in order to impart the maximum possible kinetic energy (in the form of their own velocity) to the missile on launch.

The Tomcat detected the oncoming target at very long range and started accelerating to Mach 1.5. Tracking

Below: The most spectacular test of all was the simultaneous six-on-six held on November 21, 1973. The targets were three unaugmented QT-33s and three augmented BMQ-34As flying in no discernable formation, staggered over a 15nm (27km) front at altitudes of 22-24,000ft (6,700-7,300m) and at speeds ranging from Mach 0.6 to 1.1. The opposing Tomcat ripple-fired six Phoenix in 38 seconds, scoring three direct hits, a lethal radius hit, one miss, and one no-test, giving an overall success rate of 80 per cent.

Phoenix simultaneous six-target capability trial

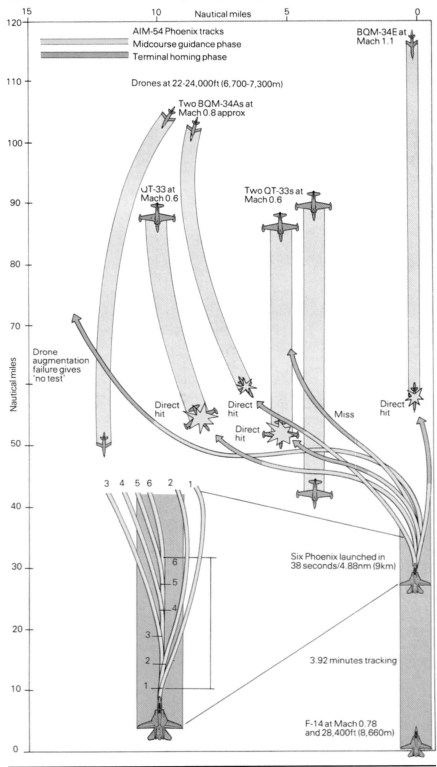

Above: Typical Tomcat armament in Desert Storm was four AIM-7 Sparrows carried semi-conformally, and four AIM-9 Sidewinders carried on the wing glove pylons as shown. Here the wings are fully swept.

Right: Wings at intermediate sweep, an F-14D of the Point Mugu Test Centre launches an AIM-9 Sidewinder. Sidewinders accounted for two Libyan Fitters over the Gulf of Sidra.

began at 132nm (245km), and at a range of 110nm (204km) the Tomcat launched a single missile. Using its pre-programmed high trajectory to gain the required range, the big Phoenix soared up to a maximum altitude of 103,500ft (31,500m) before swooping down to pass within lethal distance of the target after a flight time of 2.62 minutes, during which time it covered a total horizontal distance of 72.5nm (134km). No other air-to-air missile has ever flown so high and so far to intercept.

The simultaneous six-target attack capability has been tested only once, on November 21, 1973. The simulated raid

consisted of three QT-33s and three BQM-34s, augmented to fighter size and spread over a 15nm (27km) frontage, at altitudes ranging from 22,000 to 24,000ft (6,700-7,300m) and at speeds of between Mach 0.6 and Mach 1.1. Confronting them was an F-14 flown by Commander John R. Wilson Jr., Flight Test Officer of the F-14 Joint Evaluation Team, with Lieutenant Commander Jack Hawver in the back seat. At an altitude of 28,400ft (8,660m) and a speed of Mach 0.78, they detected the drones from ranges varying between 85 and 115nm (157-212km). The crew selected the first three targets, while the second three priorities were as

recommended by the AWG-9 computer.

The first Phoenix was launched from a distance of 31nm (57km) and the other five followed within the space of 38 seconds, the shortest interval between launches being 3.5 seconds. In what must be one of the most expensive air-to-air missile tests ever conducted, four direct hits were scored, while a missile antenna malfunction caused one miss, and the failure of the augmentation in one of the drones caused both the Tomcat's AWG-9 and the AIM-54 aimed at it to break lock. This last was subsequently declared a 'no-test', which gave an 80 per cent success rate for the test.

Various other tests were carried out, some with live warheads. In one, a cruise missile type target skimming the waves at 50ft (15m) and Mach 0.75, was knocked down from a range of 22nm (41km). And in one of a number involving violently manoeuvring targets, a QF-86 drone pulled a 6g turn just four seconds after the Phoenix had been launched to try and break the radar lock. After

Below: Six Phoenix is the design load for the fleet air defence role. There is also provision for a Sidewinder to be carried on each wing pylon for close-range combat.

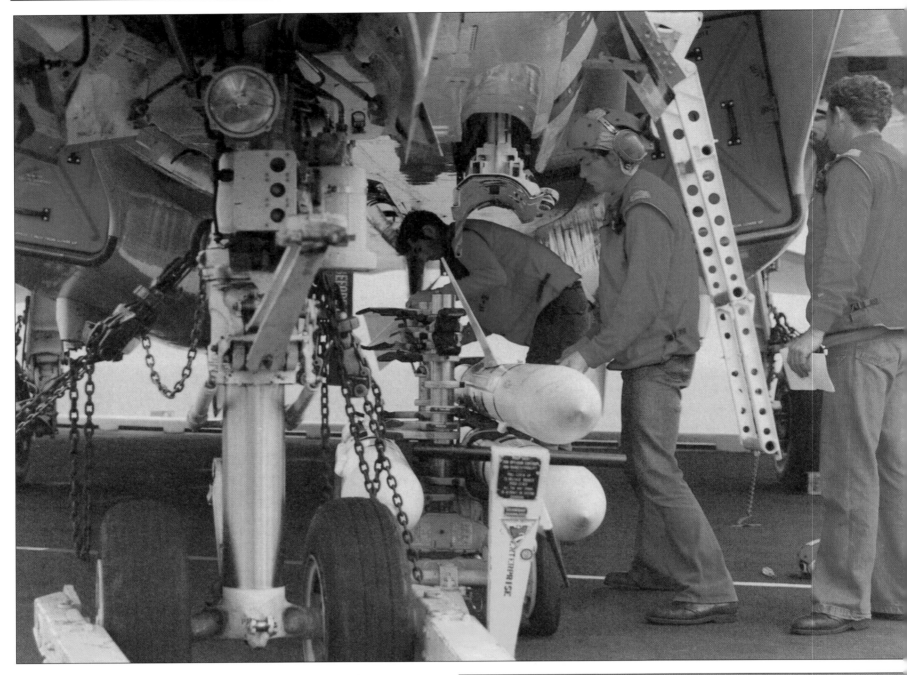

Above: Phoenix is the weapon most commonly associated with the Tomcat, but the F-14 was designed as a Sparrow-armed fighter. Here, Sparrows on their trolley have their fins fitted prior to loading.

Right: A Sparrow is launched from an F-14A of VF-41 Black Aces. The Sparrow has been much criticised for requiring its launching fighter to provide continuous illumination of the target during the homing phase.

174deg of turn, the missile caught up with it, having pulled 16g in the attempt. Also tested was a very short-range, tail-on aspect, active mode Phoenix launch.

Service evaluation

Most of the missile tests had been carried out either by test pilots or by the very experienced fliers of the Navy evaluation squadron VX-4, begging the question: how would the average squadron pilots and NFOs, often first-tour men, fare? The question was answered on May 5, 1975, during a three-day exercise by the squadrons of Carrier Air Wing One, based aboard USS *John F. Kennedy*, at sea off the coast of Jacksonville. A CQM-10B Bomarc missile augmented to represent a Foxbat was launched from Eglin AFB, Florida. Flying at a speed of Mach 2.8 and an altitude of 72,000ft (21,950m), it was intercepted by an F-14A of VF-32 Swordsmen. Piloted by Lieutenant Commander Andrews, with Lt(jg) Earl Kraay as his NFO, the Tomcat intercepted from 41,000ft (12,500m) at a speed of Mach 1.2, and launched an AIM-54A with a live warhead from a distance of 51nm (95km). In this test, an F-14A flown by a fleet squadron crew destroyed an ultra-fast, very high altitude target at a distance of 450nm (830km) from their carrier.

Impressive as the performance of Phoenix is, technology does not stand

still, and it was a safe bet that any potential enemy would be busy trying to find the means to counter it. Since late 1977, many production models of Phoenix have been the AIM-54B version. This features sheet metal wings and fins instead of the previous honeycomb structure, digital guidance utilizing some micro-circuitry, non-liquid hydraulic and environmental conditioning systems, and generally simplified engineering. Production of the AIM-54A ceased in 1980 after more than 2,500 had been built, including a total of 484 which were supplied to the Imperial Iranian Air Force.

Development of the AIM-54C was begun by Hughes in 1977. Their philosophy was to upgrade selected components of the missile while retaining the basics, with only those modifications showing the greatest capability improvements to be adopted; 'nice to have' modifications were eliminated on cost grounds. The main focus was on improved reliability, better ECCM capability, and enhanced performance to cope with the projected threats through the 1990s.

The use of a programmable digital computer gives many advantages, including better high-altitude performance, increased ECCM logic, greater reliability, and the flexibility to accept further development through software

rather than expensive hardware changes, while a digital autopilot and a strapdown inertial reference system improve accuracy and range, and enhanced target discrimination is provided by a new solid-state transmitter/receiver. The overall dimensions of Phoenix have not altered, but the weight has increased slightly to 1,008lb (457kg).

First AIM-54C launch

The first 15 engineering models of the AIM-54C were delivered from early 1980, and the first launch, against a supersonic QF-4 target, was made on June 2 of that year. The test, which used SARH throughout from a launch range believed to exceed 60nm (110km), was successful. The first pilot production model, from an initial batch of 30, was delivered on October 27, 1981, with full production starting in 1982.

Meanwhile, the search for better performance goes on, funded by Hughes rather than the Navy. At present under consideration are: a new low-sidelobe antenna to improve ECCM properties; a transmitter with higher power to give better burn-through capability against jamming; a lower noise level receiver to give greater sensitivity; and a rapid reprogramming capability.

We have spent a great deal of time describing the AIM-54 Phoenix. This is because it is a unique weapon. But while it inevitably overshadows the other weapons carried by the F-14, it should not do so to the point of exclusion.

Possible weapon combinations for the F-14 are: six AIM-54 and two AIM-9; four AIM-54 and four AIM-9; four AIM-54, two AIM-7 and two AIM-9; two AIM-54, three AIM-7 and two AIM-9; two AIM-54, one AIM-7 and four AIM-9; six AIM-7 and two

Stores options

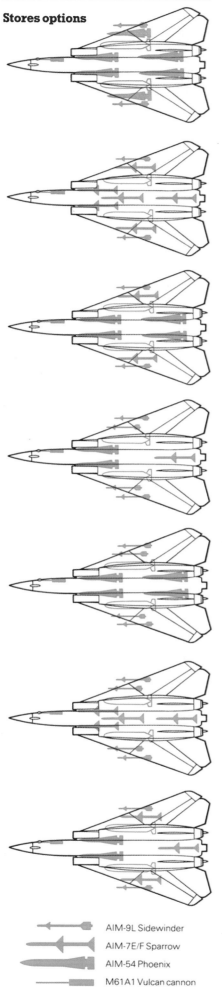

Above: Procurement of Phoenix has not been very high, and the full load of six is rarely carried. A typical external load for fleet air defence would be that shown here: four Phoenixes, two Sparrows (and later AMRAAM) and two Sidewinders. With the gun and two drop tanks, this will meet most foreseeable contingencies.

Right: Criticism of the Sparrow led to the development of the launch and leave AIM-120 AMRAAM (Advanced Medium Range Air-to-Air Missile), seen here on the left pylon of this Pacific Missile Test Center F-14 just prior to a test launch over the range during August 1982.

⬤ AIM-9L Sidewinder
⬤ AIM-7E/F Sparrow
⬤ AIM-54 Phoenix
⬤ M61A1 Vulcan cannon
⬤ Fuel tank

Above: Combat persistence depends on two factors – fuel status, and on-board kills – while the weapon load is also influenced by the mission. Here are shown some of the permutations of weapons available to the Tomcat, each providing either seven or eight on-board missile kills, while the gun provides backup for short-range work. Two external fuel tanks can be carried to increase range or patrol endurance without compromising weaponry or performance.

AIM-9; or four AIM-7 and four AIM-9. From this it is clear that Tomcat can be configured for a wide variety of counter-air missions according to the needs of the moment. The M61A Vulcan cannon is carried with all the above combiations, while AIM-120A AMRAAM is interchangeable with Sparrow.

If Phoenix is the long-range weapon of the Tomcat, then the AIM-7 Sparrow covers the middle ground. At first sight it is difficult to justify the use of Sparrow as it does nothing that Phoenix does not do a great deal better, but on reflection it can be seen that Sparrow has virtues of its own. At 503lb (228kg) the AIM-7F is less than half the weight of Phoenix; it does not require the use of special pallets; and, carried semi-submerged, it has but a small fraction of the drag of the bigger missile. In consequence, the fighter performance of the Tomcat is not pena-

lized by carrying a full bag of Sparrows, while the same cannot be said of the full six-Phoenix load.

Sparrow is also considerably cheaper, and therefore more cost-effective against heart-of-the-envelope targets. Finally, partly because it is cheaper, it is available in much larger numbers. One has only to consider the Phoenix procurement figures and match them with the number of F-14s in service to wonder how long Phoenix stocks would last if the necessity to use them arose.

Sparrow variants
Two main types of Sparrow are used by the Tomcat, the AIM-7E and the AIM-7F, while the AIM-7M may well be used in the future. AIM-7E is the more prolific of the two types, with a total production of 25,000. Lighter than the F variant, it weighs 452lb (205kg). It uses SARH with

continuous wave illumination, has a 66lb (30kg) continuous-rod warhead, and is propelled by a Rocketdyne solid motor which gives it an all-burnt speed of Mach 3.7 and a range of 24nm (44km).

AIM-7E and earlier Sparrow variants were widely used in Vietnam, where its users were not very happy. Inadequate IFF techniques caused restrictions in use to visually identified targets in most cases, whereas Sparrow is essentially a beyond-visual-range (BVR) weapon, at its best against a non-manoeuvring target approaching from head-on. It also suffered from doubtful reliability so that pilots tended to launch it in pairs, which did nothing for its kill rate. When it worked, it worked very well, and in fact, all the kills of USAF Phantom aces Ritchie and Debellevue were scored with Sparrows. Notwithstanding, when at visual distance, pilots in Vietnam preferred to use the simpler and more reliable Sidewinder. Consequently Sparrow was in many cases used for the more difficult shots, which in part accounts for the fact that its probability of kill (PK) in Vietnam was much lower than that of Sidewinder.

AIM-7F, introduced in 1977, has improved solid-state electronics; a conical-scan slotted aerial which renders it less vulnerable to ECM; a larger, 88lb (40kg) continuous-rod warhead; and a Hercules Mk 58 high-impulse motor giving the missile a maximum velocity of about Mach 4 and a greatly increased range of 54nm (100km). A total of 19,000 F models are expected to have been produced by 1985. AIM-7F is compatible with pulse-Doppler as well as CW SARH.

A new model, AIM-7M, entered production in 1982. It features an inverse-process digital monopulse seeker which gives greater accuracy under adverse conditions. All Sparrows are 8in (20cm) in diameter and both E and F models are 12ft (3.66m) long, while AIM-7M is slightly longer. The control surfaces are triangular moving wings situated halfway along the body, with fixed fins at the tail.

Sparrow has come in for considerable criticism in recent years. Its SARH homing demands that the launching fighter illuminate the target all the way to impact, making it predictable for far too long. When Sparrow is used for a head-on attack, it is sometimes possible for the target to sight the illuminating fighter approaching in the distance and let fly with a launch-and-leave missile of its own, just seconds before it is destroyed by the oncoming Sparrow. This is a particularly valid point for the Tomcat, which by no stretch of the imagination could be described as a small fighter, and can be spotted at longer ranges than most. Swapping one for one is of course, no way to fight a war, but while the risk certainly exists, it appears to have been overstated.

A launch and leave missile has always been preferable to SARH, and AIM-120A AMRAAM (Advanced Medium Range Air-to-Air Missile) is the chosen successor to Sparrow. Its overall dimensions are the same as Sparrow to enable it to fit the same recessed missile wells, but at 345lb (156.5kg) it is 162lb (73.5kg) lighter. Its brochure speed is Mach 4, while maximum range is between 30 and 40nm (55-75km). It uses inertial midcourse guidance with periodic updating from its parent fighter, with active radar terminal homing. It is therefore compatible with the weapons system of the F-14A, B and D. Its warhead is a 49lb (22kg) HE fragmentation type, rather lighter than that of the AIM-7M/P.

AIM-9 Sidewinder
The short-range weapon in the Tomcat's armoury is the AIM-9 Sidewinder. Able to home on both exhaust plumes and aerodynamic hot spots, the Sidewinder has evolved into an all-aspect missile from its AIM-9B rear attack variant. A small and cheap weapon, it is just 9ft 4in (2.85m) long, with a diameter of 5in (12.7cm). The weight of the latest AIM-9R and AIM-9S variants is 192lb (87km). Brochure range is 9.5nm (17km); brochure speed is Mach 2.5, and time of flight is typically about 60 seconds.

A launch and leave weapon, Sidewinder can be fitted to almost any aircraft, needing little more than launch rails, some wiring and switches, and earphones for the pilot. Once selected, Sidewinder announces that it has acquired a target by a noise described as a growl, rising to a strident singing tone as it locks on. An IR homer is more accurate than a radar missile, as it can "see" the target much more clearly.

The seeker head uses argon-cooled indium antimonide, which is very sensitive to heat emissions. There is one alternative: a visual wavelength imaging seeker, used by the AIM-9R Sidewinder produced by Loral for the USN since late 1991. Otherwise, the usual Sidewinder carried by the F-14 is the AIM-9L/M.

M61A1 Vulcan
Back in the 1960s, guns were often considered to be redundant in air combat. This was shown to be erroneous by American, and, dare we say it, North Vietnamese experience in Southeast Asia, and by Israeli experience in the Middle East. During the gestation stage of the F-14, Admiral John S. Thach, a US Navy tactician and fighter ace who had commanded a Wildcat squadron at the Battle of Midway in June 1942, commented that a fighter without a gun was terrible.

Unlike its fleet air defence predecessor the Phantom, the Tomcat was fitted with a gun from the outset. This was the 20mm M61A1 Vulcan cannon, which is located low on the port side of the forward fuselage. A six-barrelled Gatling-style weapon, it fires 100 rounds of 20mm M50 ammunition a second. This colossal rate of fire gives an excellent chance of scoring hits on a rapidly crossing, high angle-off target. The Tomcat carries 675 rounds, enough to give a seven-second burst, although since the Vulcan takes about one third of a second to wind up to its full firing rate, under combat conditions it gives about 10 one-second bursts.

The six rifled barrels of the Vulcan rotate anti-clockwise, and a linkless ammunition feed is used. It is an exceptionally reliable weapon; the stoppage rate is about once in every 10,000 rounds, while the six rotating barrels minimise wear and increase life. It must however be said that the M50 round has very poor ballistic qualities; new ammunition would increase effectiveness. The gun will rarely be used in air combat; it is essentially a weapon of the last resort, but having said that, it is the one weapon that is resistant to all countermeasures except manoeuvre. It is also a multi-shot weapon.

Bombcat
Whereas the Phantom had gone on to become a multi-mission aircraft with not only the US Navy but the USAF and US Marine Corps as well, the Tomcat remained a specialised interceptor and air superiority fighter for almost two decades. It had of course been checked out as a low-level attack aircraft in its early days, dropping conventional and low-drag (slick) bombs, and Snakeye retarded bombs. But such was the Cold War need to provide security of base, which is one of the cardinal points of any form of warfare, that this capability had been allowed to lapse.

With the end of the Cold War, it was once more revived. Bomb-dropping trials were resumed, aided in the case of the F-14D by the air-to-ground modes of its APG-71 radar. Apart from Mk 82, Mk 83 and Mk 84 "dumb" bombs, CBUs were also carried and tested. The move towards smart weapons, fuelled by the *Desert Storm* experience, led naturally on to the use of Paveway III laser guided bombs (LGBs): GBU-22, 23 and 24, armed with Mk 82, Mk 84, and BLU-109 warheads.

AGM-65F Maverick was a contender in the stand-off weapons arena. This variant, developed specifically for the US Navy, combined the imaging infra-red (IIR) seeker of AGM-65D, with the 300lb (136kg) blast/penetration fragmentation warhead of AGM-65E, which was developed for the US Marines. The tracker is

F-14A Tomcat weapons

Below: The number of different stores carried by the F-14A was unusually low for a modern fighter, but until the end of the Cold War the Tomcat was considered too vital for fleet air defence against sophisticated modern threats to risk it being squandered as an attack aircraft.

Although it was designed to have a secondary attack capability, this was allowed to lapse. But with the end of the Cold War this was revived, and later Tomcats have carried a variety of bombs and missiles, the latter including advanced versions of Maverick, and AGM-84 Harpoons.

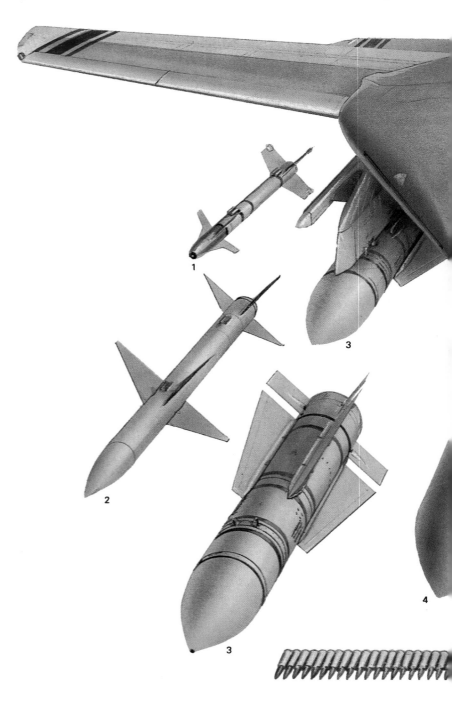

fine-tuned to increase effectiveness against ships at sea, while fuzing is selectable by the flight crew according to whether impact or penetration is required.

The AGM-84 Harpoon anti-shipping missile was an obvious choice for the carrier-borne Tomcat. Although elderly in concept, it is one of the most effective anti-shipping missiles extant. Launched from more than 67nm (124km) away, it is a subsonic (Mach 0.75) sea-skimmer, staying below the radar horizon for as long as possible, using strap-down inertial navigation. When its active radar seeker detects the target, it pops up, then swoops down in an almost vertical attack which is very difficult to defend against.

A Harpoon derivative is SLAM ER (Stand-off Land Attack Missile, Expanded Response), which combines the Maverick IIR seeker with a Walleye data link (for man-in-the-loop control) and Global Positioning System (GPS) for navigation. The first production SLAM was delivered to the US Navy in November 1988.

1 Ford AIM-9J Sidewinder infra-red homing air-to-air missile
2 Raytheon AIM-7E/F Sparrow semi-active radar homing air-to-air missile
3 Hughes AIM-54A Phoenix semi-active radar guided/ active radar terminal homing air-to-air missile
4 292 US gal (243Imp gal, 1,106lit) external fuel tank
5 20mm ammunition
6 General Electric M61A1 Vulcan 20mm cannon
7 675-round ammunition drum
8 Tactical Airborne Reconnaissance Pod System (TARPS), incorporating KS-87B serial frame camera, KA-99 panoramic camera and AAD-5 infra-red linescanner
9 Hughes Aircraft AIM-120 Advanced Medium Range Air-to-air Missile (AMRAAM) with inertial mid-course guidance and active radar terminal homing
10 Ford/Raytheon AIM-9L Sidewinder infra-red homing air-to-air missile
11 AIM-7 Sparrow training round

Below: The laser boresighting system is used to align an F-14's M61 cannon. In view of the long and medium range kill capability of the F-14's missile armament, a gun appears to be an anachronism, but experience in limited wars has shown that a gunless fighter is disadvantaged in close combat. The maximum rate of fire of the M61 is 6,000rds/min.

Performance and Handling

Set down in black and white, the performance figures for the F-14 Tomcat appear to offer little if any advantage over those for its predecessor, the F-4 Phantom. Maximum speed, service ceiling and rate of climb are all broadly similar, and only the AWG-9/Phoenix combination seems to offer any real gain. Yet air fighting consists of much more than long-range sniping, and the Tomcat is much more than a mere missile carrier. Once close combat is joined speed and height bleed off rapidly, and in this regime the Tomcat enjoys almost as great an advantage over the Phantom as it does at long ranges.

The Tomcat seems to have fallen into semi-obscurity during recent years. The reasons are not hard to find, but are as much to do with fashions and images as with logic. It has been followed into US service by the F-15 Eagle, F-16 Fighting Falcon and F/A-18 Hornet, all of which were designed as air superiority fighters with a one-man crew, a thrust/weight ratio of unity or slightly better, and fixed wings. The F-16 and F-18 also represented a trend toward a simple, austere and cheap fighter, a reaction against the relentless increases in size, cost and complexity which had reached their apogee with the F-14.

To deal with these points in reverse order, the small austere fighters were simply not capable of carrying out the fleet air defence role. Moreover, both, particularly the Hornet (described in a companion volume), have had new equipment added to increase their capability. No longer can either be described as either austere or cheap, particularly if measured against the yardstick of the F-5E.

Only one other Western fighter uses variable-sweep wings, and that is the Tornado F.3, which flies a long-range interception mission broadly comparable to that of the Tomcat. The Russians have of course introduced many variable-sweep wing types into service, notably the MiG-23 Flogger, but they were primarily influenced by the need to operate from short, semi-prepared airfields. This is not to say that variable sweep was an aberration; for the Tomcat it was an adequate solution to a problem, but it has since been superseded by computerized variable camber, a different form of variable geometry.

The relatively low thrust/weight ratio of the F-14A was of course the main shortcoming of what was otherwise a fine fighter, but as we have seen, this should have been corrected at a very early stage. When after nearly 20 years a new engine was finally made available, performance and handling were transformed, and what had been a fine fighter became superb!

The main reason why the Tomcat has been overshadowed is that it was the first of a new generation, and those that followed were, originally at least, designed as air superiority fighters. Both the media and the public can more readily understand the concept of the air superiority fighter, and the spurious glamour of the dogfight has an instant appeal, unlike the cold-blooded sniper type killing ability of the Tomcat: the duellist always attracts more attention than the ambusher.

AWG-9 and Phoenix are an undoubtedly fearsome combination, but the publicity that they have attracted, while well earned, has tended to be counterproductive in that the Tomcat is all too often presented as a mere missile carrier, whereas it is also a remarkably fine close combat fighter in its own right. As an F-15 driver recently commented, "We think that we have the best dogfighter in the world, but we don't get slow against the gents in F-14s".

The 1970s trend towards single-seat fighters was not followed in the F-14, which is a two-holer. The reasons for this are partly technical and partly tactical. On the technical side, the complexity of the AWG-9 system requires a second crewman to obtain maximum results, particularly in a multi-target engagement or in an ECM environment. Detecting the launching of small air-to-surface missiles by a hostile radar contact demands full-time attention to the dis-

Above: A VF-84 Jolly Rogers Tomcat in a vertical climb. If the speed drops to zero at this angle, the aircraft slides backward before pitching nose-down. Recovery is simple.

Below: In the Korean war fighters had excellent rearward visibility, but the quest for greater speeds curtailed it badly. The Tomcat was the first modern fighter to reverse the trend and restore the rear view.

plays, as the launch indications may be of very brief duration and can easily be missed.

Again, as with all electronic gadgetry, part of the equipment will occasionally decide to sulk, invariably at the most inopportune moment. The NFO is then called upon to correct the problem, or to select alternative modes which will allow the mission to proceed. He also makes a valuable contribution to flight safety. A high proportion of accidents are caused by pilot error, often involving incorrect procedures. By monitoring procedures the second crewman provides a safeguard against error. It is very possible that Tomcat No. 10 might not have been lost had an NFO been aboard.

NFO's function

Tactically, the NFO performs many vital functions. It is his responsibility to structure the initial intercept and decide on the tactics to be used, basing his decisions on the information displayed as an all-round picture on his TID, although as the pilot is the aircraft commander, he can presumably exercise his own judgement, taking into account the different experience levels of himself and his NFO. Having said this, the NFO is hardly along for the ride; with information from two radios, data link and AWG-9 to deal with, he can get very close to saturation point.

In addition to all this, he must remain in constant communication with his pilot. If the fight closes to knife range, he then takes his head out of the office and becomes a spare pair of eyes checking 6

F-14 dogfight performance

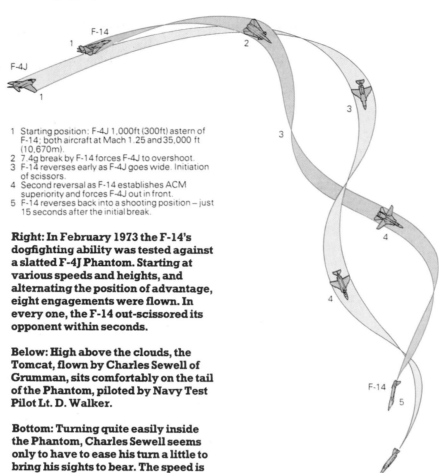

1 Starting position: F-4J 1,000ft (300ft) astern of F-14; both aircraft at Mach 1.25 and 35,000 ft (10,670m).
2 7.4g break by F-14 forces F-4J to overshoot.
3 F-14 reverses early as F-4J goes wide. Initiation of scissors.
4 Second reversal as F-14 establishes ACM superiority and forces F-4J out in front.
5 F-14 reverses back into a shooting position – just 15 seconds after the initial break.

Right: In February 1973 the F-14's dogfighting ability was tested against a slatted F-4J Phantom. Starting at various speeds and heights, and alternating the position of advantage, eight engagements were flown. In every one, the F-14 out-scissored its opponent within seconds.

Below: High above the clouds, the Tomcat, flown by Charles Sewell of Grumman, sits comfortably on the tail of the Phantom, piloted by Navy Test Pilot Lt. D. Walker.

Bottom: Turning quite easily inside the Phantom, Charles Sewell seems only to have to ease his turn a little to bring his sights to bear. The speed is still quite high.

o'clock. Vietnam experience in 1972 showed that the NFOs made around 40 per cent of the visual MiG sightings, and this from the Phantom, with its notoriously poor rearward visibility. The all-round view from the F-14 makes sightings much easier, and with the rear arc under surveillance by his NFO, the pilot is relieved of a major chore and so able to concentrate much more on offensive action.

Combat formation

Back in World War II and Korea, fighters flew in basic sections of two aircraft, spaced roughly 900ft (275m) apart and, although circumstances varied, usually with the wingman, whose function it was to protect the leader, stepped back slightly. In this way, mutual cross-cover against gun attacks was maintained, but with the emergence of the relatively long-range homing missile such close spacing became redundant, as effective cover could no longer be given.

Fighters still operate in pairs, but the lateral spacing between them generally exceeds 5,000ft (1.5km) and is often combined with vertical separation. Visual cross-cover can still be given, but rapid intervention in a critical situation has become difficult (the previous close spacing made intervention totally impossible). What, in effect, the two-seat fighter does in close combat is provide the pilot with a wingman in very close formation, roughly 6ft (1.83m) behind him, as a lookout.

Pilot descriptions of flying the Tomcat are full of adjectives such as "amazingly controllable", "easy", and "vice-free". This praise comes from experienced pilots who have converted from the F-8 Crusader and the F-4 Phantom. The Phantom in particular had to be treated with care at low speeds, high weights, high AOA, or any combination of these three. By contrast, the Tomcat driver can generally "keep tugging on the pole 'til it hurts" as long as the engine settings are left high, without the risk of undue problems arising.

The Tomcat is very forgiving when flown into out-of-control manoeuvres and is highly spin-resistant except for a small region around 17 units AOA when not using slats. It will spin if pushed hard enough – a very fast, flat spin, with loadings nearing 6g, which is extremely difficult to get out of. The following observations of handling have been condensed from an article by Grumman Chief Test Pilot Charles Sewell written in 1973.

High AOA flight. The F-14 does not stall in the accepted sense as there is no g break or minimum control speed at any wing sweep. From the pilot's point of view, the airplane does not stall, and little change in flight characteristics in this condition is observable when carrying external stores, or with the speed brakes or manoeuvre flaps extended. At 22deg wing sweep and deceleration to a fully aft stick position, buffet commences at 14 units AOA, reaching moderate levels at 17 units and decreasing in intensity at about 24 units. Less buffet is experienced in proportion to the angle of wing sweep.

Above 24 units AOA, lateral stick deflection causes opposite yaw, which is countered by centering the stick and using opposite rudder. Above 24 units AOA, the stick should be kept centred, and the rudders used to control yaw and bank angle. With full aft stick, the actual AOA is about 38deg. The maximum rate of descent can reach 9,000ft (2,745m) per minute.

Yawing motion will, if unchecked, lead to roll, owing to dihedral effect. Recovery to normal flight needs about 5,000ft (1,500m) of height, and is effected

by pushing the stick forward to decrease the AOA while maintaining lateral and directional control with the rudders, then pulling out into level flight when 17 units AOA is reached, holding 17 units with the engines in full military thrust, although if the afterburner is already engaged, it should be retained until the recovery is completed.

Vertical stall. If the Tomcat is allowed to decelerate to zero airspeed in a vertical or near-vertical position, it will slide backward before pitching down into a near-vertical dive. The nose-down pitch rate is about 20deg/sec with the wing sweep angle up to 50deg, increasing to about 30deg/sec at full sweep. At sweep angles exceeding 60deg the Tomcat will pitch down through the vertical before returning to it. Yaw and/or roll may sometimes be evident, but will damp out automatically as the airplane accelerates.

The Tomcat responds in pitch to control movements at all AOA and at airspeeds down to 100kt (184km/h) indicated. Recovery from the point of pitchover usually takes less than 10,000ft (3,050m) of altitude, and from zero airspeed is safely made 'hands-off', with the controls centralized. The pullout should be commenced at 200kt (368km/hr) indicated, maintaining 17 units AOA with full military thrust.

Inverted stall. Moderate application of full forward stick while flying inverted results in an AOA of about minus 30deg, which is off the AOA indicator. During inverted negative-g flight, the oil pressure indicators will drop to zero and the caution light will illuminate, but will return to normal on regaining positive-g flight. A caution here is that the load factor can exceed −2.5g. Recovery from the inverted stall is made by pulling the nose down, then rolling into a normal position with either rudder or lateral stick as the F-14 returns to positive-g flight.

In passing, the structural integrity of the Tomcat was convincingly demonstrated on September 11, 1980, when an aircraft of VF-24 flown by Lieutenants Blake Stichter and Chris Berg suffered a double malfunction, losing power to the flight controls. The fighter rolled nose-low inverted, and negative g pinned the crew against the canopy. In his effort to recover control, Stichter broke the grip clean off the stick. The negative g and high speed precluded ejection, but Stichter pushed forward on the remainder of the stick and succeeded in arresting the dive after a bunt during which negative acclerations of 7-8 g were experienced. While climbing away, still inverted, the malfunction righted itself and control was regained. Despite the broken control column, the aircraft was successfully recovered aboard USS *Constellation*.

Takeoff or landing configuration stalls. With gear and flaps extended the F-14 exhibits divergent wing rock and yaw at about 28deg AOA. If the high AOA is maintained, yaw angles may reach 25deg and roll angles 90deg within six seconds. At the first sign of wing rock, the AOA should be reduced to less than 15 units. Recovery from a stall with gear and flaps down requires about 1,000ft (300m) of altitude, maintaining 15 to 16 units AOA at full military thrust.

Departing controlled flight. This can occur during manoeuvres in which roll is combined with increasing AOA, and is caused by the adverse yaw generated by the differentially moving tailerons. Warning of departure is given by adverse yaw combined with a decrease in the turn rate, and the Tomcat will sometimes 'hang up', the rate of turn practically ceasing while the angle of bank remains constant. The cure is to centralize the stick laterally and use rudder to continue the turn.

During air combat manoeuvres and all high AOA manoeuvring, the F-14 should be handled with generous use of the rudders, either leading or simultaneously with lateral stick movement. If the Tomcat 'hangs up' and the stick is not centralized laterally, roll reversal occurs at an AOA of about 25 units. The departure takes the form of a snap roll or series of snap rolls opposite to the direction of turn, acceleration occurring about all three axes, with roll rates of up to 120deg/sec and yaw rates of up to 60deg/sec, while the AOA increases to at least 45deg and the positive g loading almost doubles.

Recovery is effected by neutralizing rudders and lateral stick, then pushing

Above: A Tomcat destined for Iran is put through its paces. Contrails stream from the wingtips in a tight turn, and water vapour can be seen near the wing sweep junction.

the stick slowly forward to reduce the AOA to 17 units or less. If the yaw and roll motion does not cease, it should be controlled by using the stick in the direction of, and the rudders opposite to, the direction of the roll/yaw, neutralizing both controls when the motion stops. Level flight is then regained by holding 17 units AOA until the speed increases enough to permit a harder pullout.

Compressor stalls

As Naval Secretary John F. Lehman stated in 1984, with the Tomcat you have to fly the engine and not just the airframe. Charles Sewell addressed this problem also, although at the time the article was written much exploration of the flight envelope remained to be done. His conclusions were that compressor stalls could occur at thrust settings of less than 85 per cent rpm, and sideslip at high AOA was found to increase the probability of an engine stall. About half the stalls encountered were self-clearing, reducing the throttle to the idle setting and reducing the AOA to 14 units or less. It was recommended that for high AOA operations, engine revolutions should be maintained at 88 per cent or above.

One problem encountered was that the engine stalls were often inaudible to the pilot, and could only be detected by monitoring the engine instruments – and at subsonic speeds the temperature in a stalled engine could quickly rise to destruction point if the throttle was not retarded in time. The handling procedures recommended to avoid engine stalls in a nose-high attitude with rapidly decreasing airspeed were: 1) if above 40,000ft (12,200m) in afterburner, slowly retard the throttles to full military thrust; 2) at less than 40,000ft (12,200m) in afterburner, leave the throttles well alone; 3) at any altitude and at any power setting less than full military, slowly advance the throttles to full military.

The pilots of the F-14D Super Tomcat do not have these problems, the F110 being almost completely stall-free at high AOA and high yaw rates, while throttle "slams" are possible throughout the entire flight regime.

In combat air patrol (CAP) configuration, with four AIM-54 Phoenix, two AIM-

Below: Afterburners blazing, a Tomcat of VF-84 blasts off the deck of *Nimitz* during the Teamwork 80 exercise, while a VF-41 aircraft is prepared for a catapult launch.

The acceleration time achieved on test was just two minutes. The maximum speed is generally quoted as Mach 2.34 at altitude and Mach 1.2 at sea level, although naturally these figures vary with the load. Maximum rate of climb at sea level exceeds 30,000ft/min (152m/sec) and the combat ceiling is better than 56,000ft (17,000m).

Takeoff and landing

From a land base, a fully augmented takeoff is achieved in 1,300ft (396m), the nosewheel liftoff speed varying between 95kt and 110kt (175-203km/h). The minimum landing roll is 2,700ft (823m). Landing can if necessary be accomplished with the wings fully swept, with the approach speed increased to about 160kt (295km/h), while single-engined bolters without augmentation and with the wings fully swept at an all-up weight of 57,000lb (25,855kg) have been demonstrated. Maximum takeoff weight is 74,349lb (33,724kg) and the design landing weight is 51,830lb (23,510kg).

Catapult launch from a carrier is regarded as easy: the Tomcat flies 'hands off' accelerating to 150kt (276km/h) in the space of 2.5sec. With a load of four Sparrows it can launch with a negative wind over deck of between 10 and 20kt (18-37km/h), while at maximum launch weight 10kt (18km/h) of wind over deck is needed.

For carrier landings the normal approach speed is 123kt (227km/h), although at light weights this can be reduced to 115kt (212km/h). In fact, the Tomcat can fly considerably more slowly than this, but the increased AOA necessary would ground the rear end before the wheels if a landing were attempted. The AOA on approach is a constant 10.8deg, held using DLC. This gives the pilot a visibility line over the nose of 15.5deg, which means that the waterline on the carrier is always in sight. On touchdown, the throttles are advanced to full military power, and if the hook fails to take a wire the big fighter flies straight past and off the deck again. The six-Phoenix CAP mission is rarely if ever flown from the deck of a carrier in training, as the weight of the missiles and their pallets makes recovery aboard rather marginal.

Below: Despite its size and weight, the Tomcat has a landing speed considerably slower than that of the Phantom: a Bounty Hunters F-14 about to land aboard *Enterprise*.

Above: A Tomcat of VF-142 Ghost Riders about to take the third wire aboard *Dwight D. Eisenhower* during Distant Drum in 1982. Along with VF-143, VF-142 forms part of CVW-7.

7 Sparrow and two AIM-9 Sidewinder, and carrying two 280US gal (1,060lit) drop tanks, the F-14A can remain approximately 50 minutes on station at a distance of ,300nm (550km) from the carrier, the time on station increasing as the distance from the carrier decreases. This involves a fully augmented takeoff and climbout, with the cruise out to the CAP station and the return conducted at an economic speed and altitude.

With the same load, the F-14A has a combat radius of 134nm (247km) in the deck-launched intercept mission (DLI), using an augmented takeoff and an intercept run-out at Mach 1.5. The greater power and lower SFC of the F110-GE-400 engines gave an increase of 62 per cent on mission radius, in part because catapult launches could be made without afterburning, and a 61 per cent reduction in time to altitude.

The original specification called for a maximum speed of Mach 2.4 and an acceleration time from Mach 0.8 to Mach 1.8 of 2.2 minutes. On an early test flight a Tomcat attained Mach 2.41 and was still accelerating when, the objective having been achieved, the test was curtailed.

Below: At low speeds, with the gear, flaps and slats down and the spoilers, rudders and differentially moving tail surfaces all working, the F-14 has been likened to a turkey.

Combat and Deployment

At its peak, the Tomcat equipped 22 operational squadrons and two Replacement Air Groups, plus four USN Reserve squadrons. As airframes became time-expired and were withdrawn from service, these have reduced to eight. The remaining F-14As are scheduled for replacement by the Super Hornet before 2004, while the handful of F-14Bs and Ds will soldier on until 2008. Tomcat has seen little air combat; two brushes with Libyan fighters are a matter of record, while it had virtually no opportunities during Desert Storm. Although it is known to have been used by Iran against Iraq, little hard information is available.

The first United States Navy unit to fly the Tomcat was the test and evaluation squadron VX-4 Evaluators, based at NMC Point Mugu. Charged with evaluating systems and developing tactics, at one time the Evaluators had no less than nine Tomcats on charge. The first Tomcat squadron proper was the training unit, usually known as a Replacement Air Group (RAG), VF-124 Gunfighters, based at NAS Miramar. They were assigned as the west coast – and initially the only – F-14 training squadron in August 1972, receiving their first Tomcat, BuAer 158620, on the last day of that year.

The first fleet squadrons to be assigned were VF-1 Wolfpack and VF-2 Bounty Hunters, which were officially reactivated on October 14, 1972, at Miramar, under Commanders Rene W. Leeds and Richard L. Martin respectively. The crews functioned as part of VF-124 for the training period, which for Tomcat conversion typically lasts about ten months. The F-14 has no provision for flight controls in the rear cockpit and dual-control flying instruction in the accepted sense is not possible. Simulators are widely used in the initial instruction period, and few if any problems seem to have been met.

VF-1 and VF-2 were assigned to Carrier Air Wing (CVW) 14, aboard USS

Enterprise. On completion of their training period with the Gunfighters, delivery of their aircraft began on October 31, 1973, with BuAer 158979, the 40th Tomcat to be built, while the 24th and last arrived at Miramar on April 26, 1974. The working up period and carrier qualifications completed, the two squadrons, now led by Commanders Edward J. Thaubald (VF-1) and Joseph A. Brantuas (VF-2), embarked aboard *Enterprise* at NAS Alameda, where the aircraft were unceremoniously hoisted aboard by crane. On the morning of September 17, 1974, the 75,700-ton nuclear powered carrier took the first operational Tomcat squadrons to sea.

The deployment, into the western Pacific and the Indian Ocean, was not uneventful. Besides covering the evacuation of Saigon for a brief period, Wolfpack and Bounty Hunters logged more

Above: First deployment, and the Tomcats of CVW-14 are hoisted on board *Enterprise* at Alameda in September 1974. A VF-1 aircraft is in midair and one from VF-2 waits.

Below: Aircraft of VF-143 Pukin' Dogs (at rear) and VF-142 Ghost Riders show off their bright paint schemes on their first deployment aboard *America* in 1976.

F-14 Tomcat Deployment		
Unit/Name	Fleet	Comments
VF-1 Wolfpack	Pacific	decommissioned
VF-2 Bounty Hunters	Pacific	decommissioned
VF-11 Red Rippers	Atlantic	decommissioned
VF-14 Top Hatters	Atlantic	F-14A
VF-21 Freelancers	Pacific	decommissioned
VF-24 Renegades	Pacific	Checkertails/decommissioned
VF-31 Tomcatters	Atlantic	decommissioned
VF-32 Swordsmen	Atlantic	F-14B
VF-33 Starfighters	Atlantic	was Tarsiers/decommissioned
VF-41 Black Aces	Atlantic	F-14A
VF-51 Screaming Eagles	Pacific	decommissioned
VF-74 Bedevilers	Atlantic	decommissioned
VF-84 Jolly Rogers	Atlantic	decommissioned
VF-101 Grim Reapers	Atlantic	was RAG/now F-14A
VF-102 Diamondbacks	Atlantic	decommissioned
VF-103 Jolly Rogers	Atlantic	was Sluggers/decommissioned
VF-111 Sundowners	Pacific	decommissioned
VF-124 Gunfighters	Pacific	was RAG/decommissioned
VF-142 Ghost Riders	Atlantic	decommissioned
VF-143 Pukin' Dogs	Atlantic	decommissioned
VF-154 Black Knights	Pacific	F-14A
VF-201 Hunters	Atlantic	F-14A, USN Reserve
VF-202 Superheats	Atlantic	USN Reserve/decommissioned
VF-211 Checkmates	Pacific	F-14A
VF-213 Black Lions	Pacific	F-14D
VF-301 Devil's Disciples	Pacific	USN Reserve/decommissioned
VF-302 Stallions	Pacific	USN Reserve/decommissioned
VX-4 Evaluators	Test	now VX-9

than 2,900 flight hours and 1,600 traps between them, 460 of the traps being at night. Lieutenant Commanders Grover Giles and his NFO, Roger McFillen, of VF-1, had gained the distinction of being the first squadron F-14 crew to become carrier qualified for day operations in March 1974. They now achieved the more dubious distinction of being the first active duty Naval aviators to take a Martin-Baker departure from the Tomcat when their fighter caught fire over the South China Sea on January 2, 1975. They survived their enforced bath, McFillen going on to command his own F-14 squadron at a later date. The fire was the first of far too many that led to F-14 losses. The deployment ended back at base in May 1975.

Meanwhile, other F-14 squadrons were forming. VF-14 Tophatters and VF-32 Swordsmen, sometimes called the Gypsies, were next, deploying aboard USS *John F. Kennedy* as CVW-1 on June 28, 1975, for a Mediterranean cruise. It was immediately prior to this deployment that the simulated Foxbat kill described in the Avionics and Armament chapter took place. Of particular interest during this trip was Exercise Lafayette. The French Air Force, using Mirage IIIs and Jaguars, launched 91 sorties against JFK, with the advantage of French ground control. The Tomcats of CVW-1, working with Grumman E-2C Hawkeyes for the first time, achieved a 100 per cent interception rate. The F-14 had started to prove itself as a fleet defence interceptor.

Tophatters and Swordsmen were followed into service by VF-142 Ghost

Riders and VF-143 Pukin' Dogs. This unsalubrious name is an irreverent reference to the appearance of their unit emblem, a griffon. Forming CVW-6, VF-142 and 143 deployed to the Mediterranean aboard USS *America* in April 1976. In July of that year VF-1 and VF-2 returned to the Pacific aboard *Enterprise*, while VF-14 and VF-32, now reassigned to CVW-8 but still aboard *John F. Kennedy*, sailed out into the Atlantic for a NATO exercise between September and November.

Headline news
This was the deployment that made headlines around the world when a Phoenix-carrying Tomcat went berserk on the flight deck and dived headlong overboard, the crew just managing to eject in time. As with all NATO exercises, units of the Soviet fleet had been hovering nearby; it was essential that the US Navy's latest air weapon was not compromised by being recovered by the wrong side. The efforts to recover both the aircraft and the much smaller

Above: Huge though the USN fleet carriers are, with a complement of more than 80 aircraft, space, both on deck and in the hangar, is at a premium, and inches count. Wing-folding is widely used, but this adds weight and complexity. With the Tomcat, Grumman took advantage of variable wing sweep to introduce oversweep for parking, reducing the span to less than that of the F-4. This is CV-67 John F Kennedy, with 17 F-14s of VF-14 and VF-32 on deck.

Left: In close combat the Tomcat is disadvantaged by its size, which makes it easy to see, and the original bright unit markings have been replaced by low visibility finish. The Pukin' Dogs transferred to *Eisenhower* in 1979.

missile were as costly as they were protracted, but were crowned with success after nearly eight weeks.

As Tomcats rolled off the production line, new squadrons continued to be formed, including the promised east coast RAG, based at Oceana, Virginia. VF-101 Grim Reapers were first tasked for this role in January 1976, their official designation as a Tomcat training squadron coming in July 1977. Details of the Tomcat squadrons deployed to date are given in the accompanying table.

The Tomcat has seen considerable action in USN service. TARPS Tomcats flew reconnaissance missions over Lebanon from USS *Independence* in December 1983, but the only combat involving the type took place in the Gulf of Sidra on August 19, 1981. This came during a two-day missile firing exercise in international waters of the southern Mediterranean. Despite the usual warning notices (NOTAMs) issued several days in advance, the first day of the exercise was marred by continual incursions of the Libyan Arab Air Force (LAAF). No fewer than 35 patrols of LAAF fighters approached the area, six of them actually entering it. In each case they were intercepted by the Tomcats from *Nimitz* and Phantoms from *Forrestal* operating in conjunction with E-2C Hawkeyes, and turned away without incident, apart from a certain amount of jockeying for position, which generally amounted to unscheduled dissimilar ACM training.

Fitter combat

The fatal encounter came early in the morning of the second day. Shortly after 0600, two Tomcats of VF-41 Black Aces launched from *Nimitz*. They were flown by the CO, Commander Henry Kleemann, with Lieutenant Dave Venlet as his NFO, and Lieutenant Larry Muczynski, with Lieutenant James Anderson in his back seat. Initially the two aircraft were assigned to different CAP stations, but as F-14s usually operate in pairs and Muczynski was on his own, Kleemann was sent to join him. They set up a north-south oriented racetrack pattern on the CAP station and waited, not really expecting anything to happen in this area, which had been quiet the previous day.

At about 0715 Venlet picked up a radar contact to the south, heading toward them. The contact climbed to the same altitude as the Black Aces pair, 20,000ft (6,100m), and accelerated to 540kt (995km/h), coming right at them. The Tomcats had been flying in combat spread, 5-10,000ft (1,500-3,000m) apart and in line abreast, with the section lead, Kleemann, on the left.

As they headed towards the contact, Muczynski gained some 6-8,000ft (1,800-2,400m) of altitude to obtain a better position from which to begin the interception, which was expected to be a repeat of the previous day's manoeuvring tussles. On the way, the Tomcats tried to 'sidestep' to gain lateral separation in order to be well placed to turn in behind the bogeys, but each time this was attempted the bogeys, obviously directed from the ground, turned into them and neutralized the angle. It became obvious that no advantage could be gained, so the Tomcats continued to close from nearly head-on. By this time, Muczynski had dropped back slightly, even though using stage five augmentation.

In Commander Kleemann's own words: "At approximately 8 miles (13km) I saw the section of two Su-22 Fitters on the nose (i.e., dead ahead). They were flying a formation we refer to as welded wing, within about 50ft (150m) of each other. The pass (was) nose to nose, with No. 102 (Kleemann's Tomcat) very

nearly on the flight path with the two Fitters . . . I rolled my wings and began a (left) turn to keep the Fitters in sight and turn around and rendezvous on them. About 500ft (150m) above them and 1,000ft (300m) out in front, I observed a missile being fired from the right station of the Fitter." (Muczynski remembers it as the left side, launching with a bright orange flash and a smoke trail).

"As I saw the missile come off, I communicated to my wingman that we had been fired at. I then continued a very hard turn across their tails to come back and find them. I kept both of them in sight through this area. The lead Fitter did a climbing left-hand turn in the general direction of my wingman. I was initially turned around to go after the man who

had fired, as I saw my wingman come in. He came into view in front of me, starting to come into a position behind the lead Fitter as he continued off in that direction. Since I saw that he had him under control, I switched my attention to the wing Fitter who had done a climbing right-hand turn.

"My Fitter was approaching the sun; as I intended to use a Sidewinder heat-seeking missile, I realised that that was not a good position to shoot. I waited about ten seconds until he cleared the sun, (then) fired my missile. The missile guided, struck him in his tailpipe area causing him to lose control of the airplane and he ejected within about five seconds."

Meanwhile, Lieutenant Muczynski

had latched on to the leader and also launched a Sidewinder. It guided, and went straight up the Fitter's tailpipe. Muczynski, a bare half-mile astern, performed a 6g pull-up into the vertical to clear the debris. The encounter had lasted just 45 seconds.

In retrospect, it seems unlikely that the Libyan pilot had intended to open fire – missiles have been accidentally pooped off before now – but once done it could not be recalled, and the Black Aces gave him no further chance. This combat was a historic first, with all aircraft involved being variable geometry types.

Action replay against Libya

On 4 January, 1989, the nuclear-powered carrier USS *John F.Kennedy* was fissioning

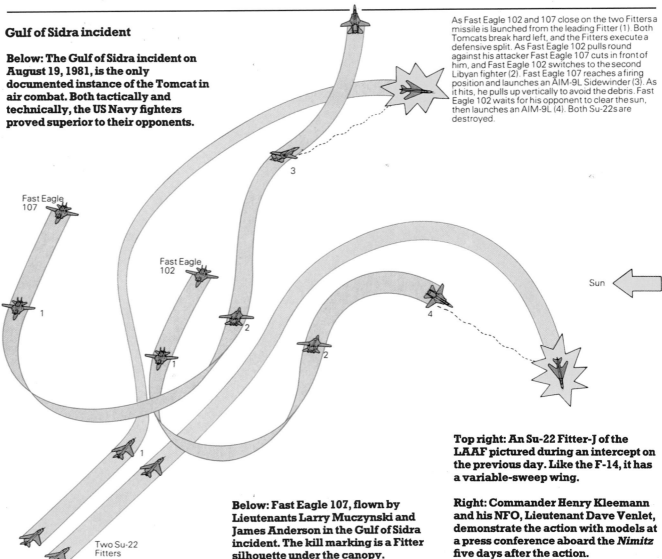

Gulf of Sidra incident

Below: The Gulf of Sidra incident on August 19, 1981, is the only documented instance of the Tomcat in air combat. Both tactically and technically, the US Navy fighters proved superior to their opponents.

Fast Eagle 107

Fast Eagle 102

Two Su-22 Fitters

Sun

As Fast Eagle 102 and 107 close on the two Fitters a missile is launched from the leading Fitter (1). Both Tomcats break hard left, and the Fitters execute a defensive split. As Fast Eagle 102 pulls round against his attacker Fast Eagle 107 cuts in front of him, and Fast Eagle 102 switches to the second Libyan fighter (2). Fast Eagle 107 reaches a firing position and launches an AIM-9L Sidewinder (3). As it hits, he pulls up vertically to avoid the debris. Fast Eagle 102 waits for his opponent to clear the sun, then launches an AIM-9L (4). Both Su-22s are destroyed.

Top right: An Su-22 Fitter-J of the LAAF pictured during an intercept on the previous day. Like the F-14, it has a variable-sweep wing.

Below: Fast Eagle 107, flown by Lieutenants Larry Muczynski and James Anderson in the Gulf of Sidra incident. The kill marking is a Fitter silhouette under the canopy.

Right: Commander Henry Kleemann and his NFO, Lieutenant Dave Venlet, demonstrate the action with models at a press conference aboard the *Nimitz* five days after the action.

(sounds terrible, but is more accurate than "steaming") eastwards through the Mediterranean, and was almost level with the Egyptian/Libyan border. In accordance with standard practice, it was escorted by a CAP (Combat Air Patrol) consisting of two F-14As and an E-2C Hawkeye AEW aircraft.

In the late morning, two Libyan MiG-23 Floggers lifted off from their base at Al Bumbah, and were detected by the Hawkeye climbing out in the general direction of the USN battle group. At this stage they could only be identified as bogeys. The pair of Tomcats, flying at 20,000ft (6,100m), gained radar contact with the MiGs, which were at half this altitude, and which descended to 8,000ft (2,400m) shortly after.

The Gulf of Sidra incident more than seven years earlier had established a precedent. Since then, directly AWG-9 locked onto a Libyan aircraft, it was reported to the controller, who promptly recalled it. For years the closest a Libyan aircraft has come to a Tomcat is 30nm (56km). But on this occasion there was no recall; the Libyan fighters, boring along at 430kt (797kmh), kept coming. The Tomcats jinked, but the MiGs turned into them every time.

The Tomcats descended to 3,000ft (914m), to give a look-up aspect to their radars and force the MiGs to look down. A decision was imminent; the Floggers carried the Vympel R-23 SARH missile, which is most effective from head-on. Waiting for the Libyan pilots to launch first

would be arrant folly. It was later established that the MiGs also carried the Molniya R-60 heat homer.

Little more than four minutes after the Tomcats first gained radar contact, with the bogeys accelerating through 550kt (1,020kmh), the Tomcat leader launched a Sparrow and called "Fox One" from a range of 12nm (22km). Twelve seconds later and two miles nearer, he launched a second Sparrow. At exactly the same time, the pilot of the second Tomcat called a visual on two bogeys from 5-6nm (9-11km) away. Wherever Tomcat 2 had got to, he was certainly not flying fighting wing!

The second Sparrow also missed, and at much the same time the Libyans spotted the second Tomcat and broke hard into it even as it launched another Sparrow. This one connected. Shortly after, the Tomcat leader, clawing around to the left in an almost vertical bank, squeezed off an AIM-9L Sidewinder at a range of about 1.5 to 2nm (3-4km). It also connected. Both Libyan pilots were seen to eject.

Iranian Tomcats

A full-scale war between Iran and Iraq erupted in September 1980, and continued for the next eight years. An embargo on spares had been implemented after the overthrow of the Shah, and many Tomcats were grounded. At the same time, and for the same reason, AIM-54

Below: Interception! A Tomcat of VF-111 Sundowners pulls alongside a Soviet Tu-95 Bear for a close look. The weapon fit appears to be a single Phoenix and one Sparrow.

Phoenix capability appears to have been lost. Iraqi pilots claimed the destruction of several F-14s during the war, but the accuracy of their claims is suspect. Iranian Tomcats were probably used in the AEW role, directing Phantoms and F-5Es onto incoming raids. Just one thing is certain: some 25 Tomcats were seen at an Iranian flypast in 1985. On the other hand, there is a tremendous difference between flyable and operational aircraft!

Other ventures

Tomcats flew combat air patrols over Lebanon in the second half of 1983, fending off Syrian fighters which might have tried to interfere with carrier-borne strike forces. Reconnaissance by TARPS Tomcats was also a feature. Then later in the same year, Tomcats played a peripheral role in the invasion of Grenada.

Desert Shield/Desert Storm

Following the invasion of Kuwait in August 1990, there was little to stop the Iraqi Army rolling on down into Saudi Arabia and gaining a stranglehold on much of the world's oil supplies. The USN carrier battle groups were soon on the scene. The USS *Independence*, with two squadrons of F-14As – VF-21 and VF-154 – was in the Gulf of Oman, and entered the Persian Gulf on 8 August. That same day, the USS *Dwight D. Eisenhower* arrived in the Red Sea with two squadrons of F-14Bs – VF-142 and VF-143.

They were relieved by USS *Saratoga*, which had sailed on 7 August with VF-74 and VF-103, both with F-14Bs, followed by USS *John F. Kennedy*, which sailed from Norfolk, Virginia, on 15 August, with VF-14 and VF-32, both with F-14As,

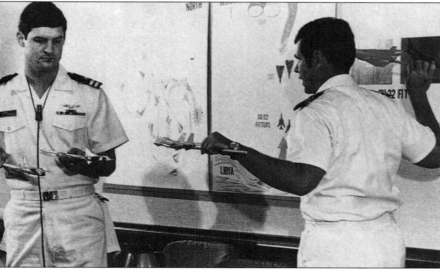

aboard. Other carriers with Tomcat squadrons were USS *Ranger* with VF-1 and VF-2 (F-14As), which sailed on 8 December, while two carriers followed on 28 December: USS *America* with VF-33 and VF-102, and USS *Theodore Roosevelt* with VF-41 and VF-84, all with F-14As.

When the shooting war finally started, the high hopes of Tomcat pilots were dashed. Most missions were CAPs, some lasting several hours with multiple in-flight refuellings, or escort, but air combat eluded them. There were several reasons for the lack of contact. Firstly, targets were few and far between. Secondly, the majority of fighter control over Kuwait and Iraq was handled by E-3 Sentries of the USAF, and these naturally handed off contacts to the air superiority F-15 squadrons, rather than to the F-14s. Thirdly, due to the previous conflict with Iran, the Iraqi pilots were familiar with the radar signature of AWG-9. As David Parsons, commanding Tomcat Squadron VF-32 recalled, as soon as they got a sniff of AWG-9 on their RWRs, they "skedaddled in every direction! Our radar was so powerful that it could saturate their warning gear and would not give them a definite location of the F-14; only an indication that it was out there somewhere....

"It was very frustrating or us not to get kills, but we were too disciplined to strip off and go after the MiGs. That was not our job. We were supposed to stay with the attack guys." Parsons also stated that the Iraqis did not react in the same way to the APG-63 emissions of the F-15, which allowed the USAF fighters to get in close.

The only air-to-air kill scored in the Gulf War by a Tomcat was a Mil Mi-8 helicopter, downed with a Sidewinder by Stuart Broce and Ron McElraft of VF-1. A single Tomcat was lost in the conflict: an F-14B of VF-103 was shot down during an escort mission on 21 January. There have been rumours that it fell to an AAM launched by an Iraqi MiG-25 Foxbat, but both Tomcat crewmen sighted what was later identified as an "old-fashioned" SA-2 Guideline coming up through the clouds. As they were operating at between 26,000 and 30,000ft (7,900-9,150m), which is where the SA-2 is at its best, they had little time to react.

A hard inverted break towards the big missile failed to gain sufficient clearance, and it detonated just astern of the Tomcat, sending it into a fast flat spin. When recovery proved impossible, the crew ejected. Pilot Devon Jones was rescued from deep inside Iraqi territory, but his NFO, Larry "Rat" Slade, was taken prisoner. He was released shortly after the end of the war.

TARPS Tomcats were active from the first day of war, with damage assessment quickly added to the primary reconnaissance task. On the evening of 18 January, the "Great Scud Hunt" commenced, and TARPS Tomcats were also assigned to this. Each day search areas were assigned, but the mobile launchers proved elusive. It was a serious diversion of effort, but attempts were made to minimise the effect by combining pre and post-strike damage assessment with the Scud search. This was only possible if the diversion for damage assessment was fairly minor. But with at most three TARPS Tomcats assigned to each carrier, there were never enough.

One final factor – for TARPS to be effective, the Tomcat had to fly more or less straight and level, and in a high-threat area at medium or low altitude, this took a lot of doing, even with an EA-6B Prowler defence suppression aircraft in attendance.

Flight refuelling was an integral part of every mission, but this caused problems with USAF KC-135 tankers, which were of course more used to topping up fixed wing fighters such as the F-15 and F-16. With its wings set at minimum sweep, the optimum tanking speed of the F-14A is a

comparatively slow 250kt (463kmh). Much faster than this, at high weights and altitude, it needed to plug in 'burner to stay in position. This was self-defeating, but a quick talk to the tanker drivers soon corrected matters.

Postwar progress

Despite work having been initiated on the "Bombcat" well before the Gulf War, no air-to-surface weapons were used by F-14s in that conflict. However, progress continued, and in June 1996 the first night attack-capable Tomcats joined the fleet with VF-103 Jolly Rogers. These carried LANTIRN pods, GPS receivers for precision navigation and target finding, and night vision goggles with NVG-compatible cockpit lighting. For defence suppression, AGM-88 HARM (High-Speed Anti-Radiation Missile) has been cleared for use.

The proposed successor was Tomcat 21. This variant had a high-lift wing system with an extendable Fowler flap and an increased chord leading edge slat, giving a third more lift at typical approach speeds and allowing an all-up weight increase of about 5,500lb (2,495kg). It also carried an extra 2,500lb (1,134kg) of fuel in a redesigned wing glove, increasing range and endurance. It was planned to use F110-GE-129 engines to give a supercruise speed of Mach 1.3 (the F-14D supercruises at Mach 1.1), and a new fixed phased array radar operating at twice the power of APG-71. But with a naval version of the Advanced Tactical Fighter (ATF) in the offing, Tomcat 21 stood little chance of adoption.

Left top: An F-14A Tomcat of VF-102 Diamondbacks shortly after launch from the USS America. It carries two AIM-54 Phoenix, two AIM-7 Sparrow, and two AIM-9 Sidewinder missiles.

Left bottom: A VF-32 Swordsmen F-14 from the carrier John F Kennedy is seen escorting an A-6E Intruder of VA-75, low over the desert during the Gulf War of 1991.

Above: Hook down, a Tomcat comes in to land aboard USS Saratoga during Operation Desert Storm. They had no opportunities to score in air combat during the conflict.

Below: The TCS under the nose shows up well on this VF-84 Jolly Rogers Tomcat on the deck of USS Theodore Roosevelt (CVN-71) during Operation Provide Comfort in May 1991.

F-15 Eagle

Contents

Top: 71-0289 was the tenth and final Category I single-seater development F-15 Eagle. These proved the concept of a world-beating fighter.

Above: Afterburners blazing and laden with three external fuel tanks, this F-15E Strike Eagle was from the 4th Fighter Wing based at Seymour Johnson.

Above right: Heavily laden with 250lb (113kg) "slick" (i.e. low drag) bombs, this F-15E from the 58th TFTW, based at Luke, Arizona, heads for the range.

Left: The F-15E Strike Eagle proved itself in the Gulf War of 1991. Later, this 48th FW F-15E, based at Lakenheath, UK, is seen leaving Aviano in March 1999 to attack Serbian targets.

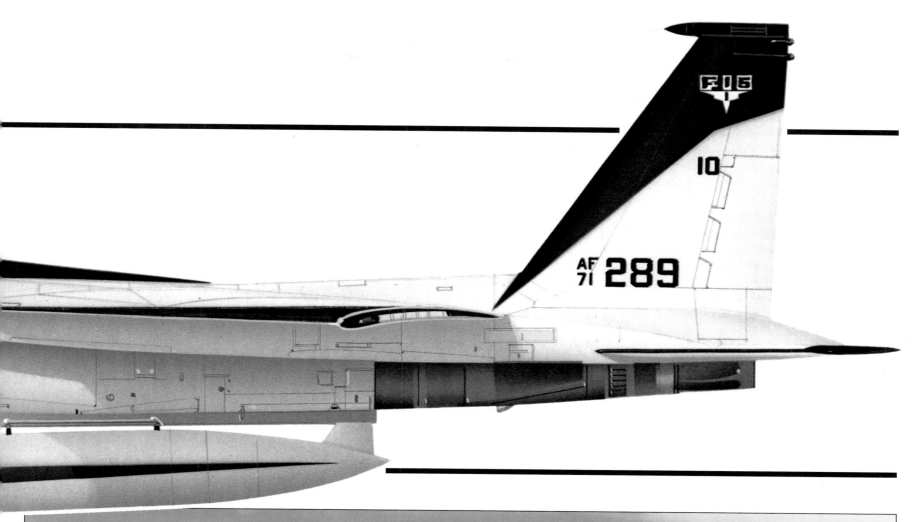

Introduction

For more than two decades the F-15 Eagle was widely acknowledged as the world's greatest fighter. Conceived in the days before low observable technology (stealth) was considered important, it was designed to outfly and outfight not only its contemporaries, but the next generation of Soviet fighters too. Its thrust/weight ratio exceeding unity enabled it to remove itself vertically from the furball, as anyone will attest who has experienced the chest-vibrating thunder of its twin turbofans during a "Viking" takeoff: pulling into a vertical climb straight from the runway.

Combined with moderate wing loading, this gave the F-15 a previously unmatched agility. This was combined with a new and very sophisticated radar; the APG-63, a multi-mode type combining long range detection with excellent close combat capability. A ground-breaking innovation to keep pilot workload to manageable proportions was Hands On Throttles And Stick (HOTAS), in which all controls needed for critical flight conditions, notably combat and landing, were positioned where the pilot could reach them without moving his hands from the main controls.

The gestation period of the F-15 coincided with a time of galloping inflation, with the result that even the USAF could not acquire it in the numbers needed. This naturally restricted the export market, and to date only Israel, Japan and Saudi Arabia have been able to afford it; Israel of course deemed it essential at any price. The Israelis were first to use it in combat, followed by the Saudis against Iran. Not until the Gulf War of 1991 did the USAF take its greatest fighter into action.

At the design stage, the motto was: "Not a pound for air to ground!" This is ironic when one considers that the latest variant, the F-15E, is a two-seater configured for the delivery of air-to-surface ordnance. This concept was proven in the Gulf War.

Alarmed by the air combat capability of the F-15, the former Soviet Union had developed a counter: the Su-27 Flanker. After a false start, this became a rival for the title of the greatest; whether it is or not will hopefully never be known. One thing is certain: the combat record of the F-15 will be hard to beat.

Development

Confronted with a new generation of Soviet combat aircraft in 1967, while it was fighting in Vietnam with the "second-hand" F-4 Phantom, the US Air Force began serious work on a new fighter of its own. Designated FX, and intended to provide air superiority in friendly and hostile airspace alike, the new design was to be optimized for combat, with the power and agility to overcome any current or projected Soviet opponent. In the resulting F-15 Eagle, with its unequalled combination of performance, firepower and sophisticated avionics, the USAF for many years had such a machine.

There are two adages which apply to the McDonnell Douglas F-15 Eagle: "if it looks good, it is good" and "if you design a good fighter, it can be adapted to other roles successfully". The basic objective of the F-15 programme was, according to Majoir General Benjamin N. Bellis, F-15 System Program Director, "to efficiently acquire a fighter capable of gaining and maintaining air superiority through air-to-air combat". Although the Eagle was not flown in action by the USAF until 1991, it had fulfilled its purpose of being a high performance, extremely agile aircraft, well able to meet the projected threat of the 1980s and 1990s, as demonstrated by Israeli pilots over Lebanon prior to and including the Beka'a action of 1982. Even before this, the type was developed into the F-15E Strike Eagle, and at the same time adopted for continental air defence to replace the F-106 Delta Dart.

The F-15 Eagle was the first air superiority fighter to stem from USAF requirements since the F-86 Sabre of

Below: Silhouetted against the setting sun, a pair of F-15As in the skies they were designed to dominate.

1948. The previous TAC (Tactical Air Command) fighter was the F-4 Phantom II, designed for the US Navy and, together with the A-7D Corsair II, forced on the USAF by the circumstances of the Vietnam War. Having to procure Navy aircraft was anathema to the Air Force, and despite the success of both Phantom and Corsair, when the time came for a new tactical fighter the Air Force was determined that it should be of their own choosing.

New Soviet fighters

The genesis of the Eagle can, perhaps, be traced back to a Russian airfield at Domodevodo, near Moscow, in July 1967. At an air show there, in front of the world's press, the Soviet Union unveiled a new generation of combat aircraft. Of particular note were a swing-wing fighter, codenamed Flogger by NATO, and a high-speed, twin-fin fighter codenamed Foxbat, both from the famous Mikoyan-Gurevich (MiG) design bureau. Later information was to identify the Flogger as the MiG-23 and the Foxbat as the MiG-25, while a later ground-attack version of the MiG-23 was designated MiG-27 Flogger D by NATO.

The MiG-23 Flogger was a single-

seat air combat fighter powered by a single Khachaturov R-23-300 afterburning turbojet with a Mach 2.35 capability. Armed with a twin-barrelled 23mm GSh-23 cannon, two R-23R SARH missiles and two R-23T heat homers, its ferry range of 1,300 miles (2,081km) and service ceiling of 59,040ft (18,000m) made it a potent interceptor. It was to supplement the MiG-21 Fishbed series of fighters, which was by then reaching its third stage of development.

The MiG-25 Foxbat was also a single seater, but powered by a pair of Tumansky R-15BD-300 afterburning turbojets. It carried two R-40R SARH and two R-40T heat homing missiles, plus at need two R-60Rs and two R-60Ts. Its high power, if crude and basic, radar was the Smerch-A. It had a top speed of Mach 2.83 and a service ceiling of 67,900ft (20,700m), but its supersonic intercept radius was a mere 160nm (296km), even with more than 14 tons of special high-density fuel. Designed to counter the US A-12 and SR-71, it was a pure interceptor. But the Pentagon assumed that it was an air superiority fighter which far outperformed their current F-4 Phantom.

Above: Air superiority blue and dayglo orange paint scheme on one of the pre-production F-15s during the flight test programme.

The FX study

Work on a new air superiority fighter had begun within the USAF as a general feeling of need for an aircraft in the best traditions of the P-51 Mustang and F-86 Sabre. This was in the early 1960s, and by April 1965 the USAF fighter lobby were looking at a Fighter Experimental (FX) type. In October 1965 the USAF asked for funding of full scale studies, and two months later issued a Request for Proposals (RFP) for a Tactical Support Aircraft. The Concept Formulation Study (CSF) which came out of the RFP went to Boeing, Lockheed and North American Rockwell in March 1966, the McDonnell Aircraft Company (MCAIR) being one of the losers at this stage. However, none of the submitted designs was considered further, mainly due to the aerodynamic configurations and bypass ratio of the powerplants.

From mid-1966 to autumn 1967, activity on the FX was minimal, although the USAF maintained its own CFS team in being until autumn 1968. The impact of

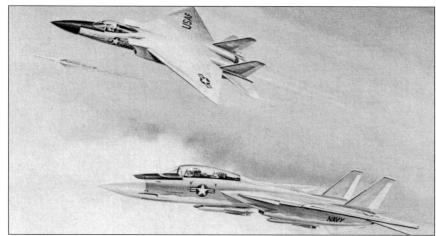

the Domodevodo revelations was felt, and in August 1967 a second RFP for a CFS was issued. This time the words "Tactical Support Aircraft" were changed to one – "Fighter" – and MCAIR, and General Dynamics were awarded the six-month study.

Among the objectives set by the USAF was a maximum speed of Mach 3. General Dynamics offered both a variable geometry and a fixed-wing FX; MCAIR recommended a fixed wing, twin engines and a single crewman. The second CFS was completed in May 1968, and in September of that year the FX Concept Development was authorized. In the same month the RFP for Contract Definition stage was offered to the aerospace industry, and MCAIR, along with Boeing, Fairchild Hiller, General Dynamics, Grumman, Lockheed, Ling Temco Vought and North American, bid for the contract. By

Right: The first F-15A prototype airborne for the first time from Edwards AFB on July 27, 1972.

Below: A month earlier, the same aircraft was photographed before the roll-out ceremony at St Louis.

December 1968 only MCAIR, Fairchild Hiller and North American were in the running.

By now the FX was designated F-15 and the three contenders were hard at work. A Development Concept Paper issued by the USAF defined the overall parameters of the design, and justified it against pressure from the US Navy to take a modified version of their VFAX/F-14 on four counts: it would be a single-seat, fixed-wing, twin-engined fighter of approximately 40,000lb (18,000kg);

Top left: The 60,000lb (27,000kg) variable-geometry proposal produced by MCAIR in early 1968.

Above left: slightly later design study with fixed delta wing.

there would be no competitive fly-off, as this was not thought desirable; the VFAX was not considered a suitable replacement for the F-4E Phantom, nor could the F-4E be modified to meet the threat; and no air-to-ground capability

Top: Variable-camber leading edges were envisaged for this wing form developed in early 1969.

Above: Wooden mock-up of the F-15 used for NASA wind-tunnel tests.

was to be considered if it would in any way prejudice air-to-air capability.

Initiated under the Total Procurement Package, the programme therefore left a large volume of work for the contractors bidding. Lack of a hardware competition

Above: The third development F-15A, used to test the avionics, is seen here in the markings of the USAF Flight Dynamics Laboratory Advanced Environmental Control System.

Above: The second development TF-15, later redesignated F-15B, was flown for the first time on October 18, 1973, and has subsequently been seen in a variety of configurations.

F-15 Project demonstration milestones

Preliminary design review	Sep 70
Radar contractor selection	Sep 70
Critical design review	Apr 71
Avionics review	June 71
Major sub-assembly tests	Jun 72
Engine inlet compatibility	Mar 72
First flight	Jul 72
Bench avionics complete	Sep 72
First aircraft performance demonstration	Sep 72
First airborne avionics performance	Dec 72
Fatigue test to reach one lifetime	Jan 73
Static test 2 critical concluded	Jan 73
Armament ground test	Jun 73
1g flight envelope	Aug 73
Fatigue test to reach 3 lifetimes	Dec 73
USAF evaluation summary	Dec 73
Equipment qualified	Mar 74
Category II aircraft and equipment in place	Mar 74
Training equipment in place	Oct 74
Fatigue test to reach 4 lifetimes	Oct 74
External stores flutter and release	Aug 74
AGE equipment in place	Oct 74
Category I flight tests complete	Nov 74
First aircraft delivered to TAC	Nov 74

meant an enormous amount of paper studies and documentation, while the contract itself had to include tooling, development, testing and production. Later, in response to criticism from Congress and the public over cost over-runs on the C-5A Galaxy and F-111 programmes, the USAF worked in de-monstration milestones which the con-tractor had to meet before receiving the next stage of funding. These are listed in the accompanying table.

The bids were made by June 1969, and from July to December the USAF's Aeronautical Systems Division made their evaluation. Selection of the McDonnell Douglas bid was announced on December 23, 1969. Major General Bellis announced in Washington the next day that in the technical, oper-ational, management and logistic areas McDonnell Douglas had been placed first. In addition he went on to say that the MCAIR price had been lowest of the three. Selection of the winning contrac-tor was the responsibility of Secretary of

the Air Force Robert G. Seamans Jr, after hearing presentations from the F-15 source selection evaluation board and the source selection advisory coun-cil, neither of which made specific rec-ommendations. Secretary Seamans' choice was favourably received throughout the USAF.

The initial contract called for 20 de-velopment aircraft: a preliminary batch of 10 single-seat F-15A (71-0280–71-0289) and a pair of two-seat trainer TF-15A (71-0290 and 71-0291, later re-designated F-15B) Category I versions; and eight Category II full scale develop-ment (FSD) aircraft in single seat F-15A form (72-0113–72-0120). The FSD batch were closely matched to the production configuration.

The first F-15 was rolled out officially at MCAIR's plant at St Louis on June 26, 1972 with due ceremony. In July it was taken apart, loaded into a USAF C-5A Galaxy transport and airlifted to Ed-wards AFB, California. There it was re-assembled, checked out and prepared

for its maiden flight. On a typical Califor-nian clear day, with blazing sunshine, MCAIR's Chief Test Pilot Irving Burrows took the first Eagle (USAF serial 71-0280) into the air on July 27, 1972.

The Eagle's missions

In the terms of the FX Development Concept Paper (DCP), the F-15 is "op-timized for counter-air missions" operat-ing as part of TAC. These missions, which come under the general heading of air superiority, include escorting friendly strike forces over enemy air-space, making fighter sweeps ahead of such a strike force, combat air patrol between friendly strike aircraft and enemy bases, and tactical air defence of friendly territory.

According to the DCP, the most dif-ficult of these roles is combat over enemy airspace, where "the counter-air fighter must protect the strike force from enemy fighters while under the disadvantage of being in the enemy's GCI network and exposed to potential attack from his fighters, SAMs and AAA". It is no surprise, therefore, to learn that the DCP calls for the F-15 to be "superior in air combat to any pre-sent or postulated Soviet fighters both in close-in, visual encounters and in stand-off or all-weather encounters".

According to the DCP assessment, neither an improved F-4E, with new wings and engines, or a version of the VFX (F-14 Tomcat) for which a contract was placed in February 1969, were considered able to meet the FX re-quirement. USAF politics aside, the con-figuration as a carrier aircraft for the basic role of fleet air defence and its consequent cost ruled out the VFX. However, an 'escape clause' was writ-ten into the DCP, which considered a

Left: An August 1975 view of the second F-15B, seen here carrying out trials with the Fuel and Sensor Tactical (FAST) pack conformal fuel tanks on the intake sides.

Below: F-15B 71-0291 in the
Bicentennial paint scheme worn by
this much repainted Eagle during
1976 as part of the celebrations of 200
years of American independence.

F-15 pre-production aircraft flight test roles

Serial	First flight	Function	Serial	First flight	Function
71-0280	Jul 27, 1972	Open flight envelope; explore handling qualities; external stores carriage	71-0285	May 23, 1973	Avionics tests; flight control evaluation; missile fire control
71-0281	Sep 26, 1972	F100 engine tests	71-0286	Jun 14, 1973	Armament and fuel stores tests
71-0282	Nov 4, 1972	Avionics development; calibrated air speed tests	71-0287	Aug 25, 1973	Spin recovery, high AOA and fuel system tests
71-0283	Jan 13, 1973	Structural test airframe	71-0288	Oct 20, 1973	Integrated aircraft/engine performance tests
71-0284	Mar 7, 1973	Internal gun, external fuel jettison and armament tests	71-0289	Jan 16, 1974	Tactical EW system, radar and avionics evaluation

further examination when "revised, detailed information on the tradeoffs between VFX-2 (with new engines and lighter avionics) and FX will be available to enable a decision as to whether to pursue one or both of these aircraft".

It is further interesting to note that the Eagle itself was later considered for adoption by the US Navy. This occurred in July 1971, when the Secretary of Defense asked the Navy to investigate the possibility of an F-15N, via the Systems Program Office. A minimum modification study by MCAIR to equip the Eagle for carrier operations increased the weight of the aircraft by some 2,300lb (1,043kg). The Navy Fighter Study Group III then did their own appreciation, disregarding the MCAIR data, which resulted in further weight increases and the addition of AIM-54 Phoenix AAM. In this configuration the weight and drag sent the performance down and the costs up to a level where the F-15N was deemed unacceptable.

The navalized Eagle made one more appearance before being finally rejected. Investigative testimony before the Senate Armed Services Committee's ad hoc Tactical Air Power subcommittee started new discussions on a modified Eagle for the Navy. This was in March 1973, at a time when the F-14 Tomcat programme was under pressure. Deputy Secretary of Defense Packard wanted to look at a lower-cost F-14, the F-15N and improved F-4s as alternatives for the Navy mission. The result was the formation of Navy Fighter Study IV, where these alternatives were discussed, and out of it came the concept of the Naval Air Combat Fighter to partner the F-14 in a maritime equivalent of the Air Force F-15/F-16 hi-lo mix. Ironically, MCAIR was selected as prime contractor on this programme, which involved navalizing the Northrop YF-17 as the F-18 Hornet.

Each of the ten pre-production Eagles was allocated a specific task in the flight test programme. Their roles were as outlined in the table. The first two-seater, 71-0290, was first flown on July 7, 1973, and was used for the two-seater evaluation. The second two-seater was flown on October 18, 1973. The first two-seater was slotted between the seventh and eighth aircraft, and since then every seventh aircraft built has been in two-seat configuration.

Right: The Bicentennial Eagle in flight, sporting the flags of the many countries where it had been demonstrated below the canopy.

Below: Back to a more familiar colour scheme, but still sporting an array of flags below the canopy, 71-0291 touches down with speed brake deployed.

The first 12 Eagles were allocated to Category I of the test programme (now known as Contractor Development, Test and Evaluation) under the manufacturer's test pilots. The eight FSD aircraft allocated to Category II testing (now the Air Force Development, Test and Evaluation) were flown by a USAF Joint Test Force of Air Systems Command test pilots and Tactical Air Command fighter pilots. Category III of the test programme (now the Follow-on Operational Test and Evaluation) was conducted by the USAF. Later some of the Category I aircraft were passed on to the USAF.

By October 29, 1973, when the 1,000th test flight was flown by an F-15, 11 of the 12 Category I airframes were flying. Those aircraft had expanded the flight envelope of the Eagle to a speed of Mach 2.3 and a height of 60,000ft (18,300m). While development proceeded reasonably smoothly, it was not without its problems, and MCAIR Chief Test Pilot Irving Burrows and Colonel Wendell Shawler, the USAF's Director of the Joint Test Force 'went public' on a number of these in a joint lecture to the Society of Experimental Test Pilots in 1973.

The first problem discussed related to the stick force per g value. As a result of simulator experience prior to the first flight, it was thought that the aircraft might not be as nimble as expected, simply because of the stick forces. As designed, it was thought that these stick forces would be comfortable for manoeuvring, while not being so low as to suggest the chance of a pilot-induced oscillation or aggravate high g sensitivity. There are two sets of controls: a conventional hydromechanical system, and a Control Augmentation System (CAS). Both are capable of flying the aircraft, though the former was considered a back-up system in the event of the CAS failing.

The hydromechanical system determines the basic control deflections,

Below: An early production F-15A in the markings of the 58th Tactical Fighter Training Wing, based at Luke AFB, Arizona, and wearing the standard Compass Gray two-tone paint scheme.

Above: Underside view of the 43rd production F-15A, the 61st of all single-seat Eagles.

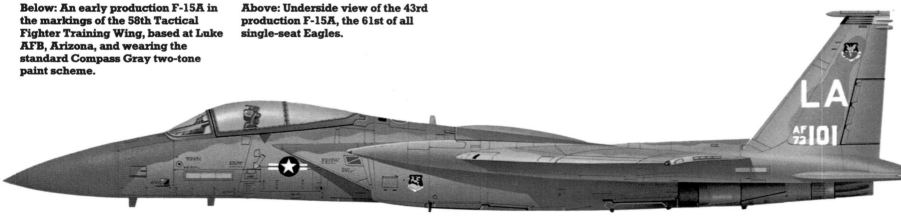

Below: One of two F-15Bs which, along a pair of F-15As, all from the 58th TFTW, were painted in a special attitude-deception three-tone grey camouflage scheme devised by aviation artist Keith Ferris.

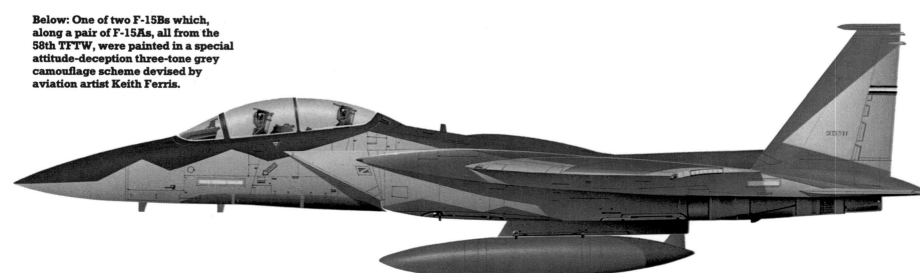

Right: F-15Cs on the McDonnell Douglas production line in June 1981, when over 600 Eagles had been delivered to the USAF.

while the CAS operates over the hydro-mechanical system and modifies the control surface deflections which provided aircraft response in line with the stick position. In the mechanical longitudinal system a spring cartridge provided the linear force gradient. There was much debate as to what was the optimum setting for the cartridge, but as the evidence was based on simulator experience only there was some reluctance to make changes. Besides, it was thought unwise to lighten the stick forces too much in case the aircraft was accidentally overstressed. Thus with a stick force (ie the pressure required to be applied to the control column in order to move the control surfaces) of 3.75lb (1.7kg) per g, manoeuvres in excess of 6.5g required some 25lb (11.3kg) of stick force to initiate a response to control demand. In such high-g situations this meant some considerable strain on the pilot.

Modified stick forces

Early flight testing confirmed the initial simulation findings. With the CAS off the manoeuvring forces were too heavy for a fighter with the inherent capability of the F-15. With the CAS on these forces were more comfortable, but there was room for improvement. A dual-gradient longitudinal spring cartridge was evaluated, and found to be an improvement, while modifications were also made to the CAS pitch computer, enabling a satisfactory match between the CAS and the hydromechanical system. Flight testing of these fixes confirmed their suitability, and were incorporated in production aircraft. Forces around the neutral position are considered 'comfortable' at all speeds within the flight envelope, and there was no excessive longitudinal sensitivity or trend towards oscillation with the CAS either on or off. Pilots can now fly 6g manoeuvres one-handed with no trouble.

The lateral sensitivity of the Eagle also came in for some criticism. Although, again, it was recognized on the simulator, it was partially masked by the lack of physiological cues. The original specifications called for rolling capabilities in excess of previous accelerations. These could only be achieved by using a large amount of lateral control – quickly. This meant that lateral control surface deflections were 'sudden and big'. While the ailerons, with plus or minus 20deg of travel, are mechanically served, the differential stabilator (all-moving tailplane) is connected to both the mechanical and CAS circuits.

Normal smooth manoeuvring was highly responsive, but comfortable. However, any sudden small lateral movements of the stick, such as might be expected during formation flying, gun-tracking or air-to-air refuelling, caused an undesirable jerkiness resulting in a possible pilot-induced oscillation. While not as simple to correct as was the longtitudinal system, a two-point solution was arrived at. A dual-gradient force system coupled with a higher setting on the CAS transducer prevented the CAS from augmenting roll commands at small stick deflections was the first fix; the second involved a modification to the CAS in order to

Right: Tanker's eye view of a two-seat Eagle, with the refuelling boom positioned in the F-15's receptacle. In-flight refuelling has enabled Eagles to fly non-stop the 7,000 miles (9,620km) between Okinawa and Florida.

Above: Three brand new F-15As in flight early in 1976 before delivery to the 1st TFW at Langley AFB.

Below right: Streak Eagle easily beat the F-4's climb records, and was faster than an Apollo moonshot to 15,000m.

negate some of the roll rate demanded by small sharp deflection of the stick.

The need to retract the undercarriage into the fuselage led to a rather narrow track of 9ft 0¼in (2.75m) and a wheelbase of 17ft 9½in (5.42m). To have considered another configuration would have incurred an unacceptable weight penalty. The narrow track promised to produce a few problems, and these duly appeared during the flight testing. During crosswind landings the upwind wing would come up, causing the aircraft to tend to weathervane into the wind, and again drift downwind. Holding the nose up on landing only accentuated the problems, and so pilots always tried to get the nosewheel on the ground as quickly as possible.

The causes of the problems were soon identified. The first involved the aileron-rudder interconnect (ARI) system: as the stick was moved laterally (assuming a neutral or aft longitudinal position) rudder movement was initiated in sympathy. So, if the right wing came up and the stick was moved to the right to counteract it, the rudder motion would make the aircraft yaw to the right, and thus aggravate the tendency to weathervane. The second problem occurred with the stick aft, as if to hold the

nose up, when the aircraft systems washed out some lateral control. This had been designed into the controls so as to mimimize lateral deflections of the stick at high angles of attack. As the pilots said, "Rolling out on the runway was not the place to reduce lateral control, particularly in a very lightly wing-loaded fighter with a narrow gear".

In these circumstances, the wind would blow the wing up, and the aircraft would start weathervaning. The normal response by the pilot would be to move the stick into wind, but this did nothing to level the wings, and succeeded only in worsening the yaw into wind, giving the pilot the impression that the aircraft wanted to tip up and over onto the downwind forward quarter. Once the nosewheel was down, the situation improved slightly, but all the characteristics remained to a lesser degree, and the resultant roll-out was described as 'uncomfortable'. The whole problem was exacerbated by the oleo struts on the mainwheels tending to stroke at different times in the roll-out and on a calm day, there could be a 2 or 3deg difference until the up-wing oleo would stroke. A further weak point was the low-gain steering on the nosewheel.

Streak Eagle world time-to-height records

Altitude	Time	Date	Previous time	Margin
3,000m (9,843ft)	27.57sec	Jan 16, 75	34.52sec (F-4B)	20 per cent
6,000m (19,685ft)	39.33sec	Jan 16, 75	48.79sec (F-4B)	19 per cent
9,000m (29,528ft)	48.86sec	Jan 16, 75	61.68sec (F-4B)	21 per cent
12,000m (39,370ft)	59.38sec	Jan 16, 75	77.14sec (F-4B)	23 per cent
15,000m (49,212ft)	77.02sec	Jan 16, 75	114.50sec (F4-B)	33 per cent
20,000m (65,617ft)	122.94sec	Jan 19, 75	169.80sec (MiG-25)	28 per cent
25,000m (82,021ft)	161.02sec	Jan 26, 75	192.60sec (MiG-25)	16 per cent
30,000m (98,425ft)	207.80sec	Feb 1, 75	243.86sec (MiG-25)	15 per cent

Above: The record-breaking Streak Eagle, 72-0119, over the familiar St Louis skyline.

The full plus or minus 15deg steering should have assisted three-point directional control, but because of the pedal-to-wheel deflection, long, strong legs were required to get positive response.

Considerable effort went into fixing the whole dilemma of cross-wind landing, and the Eagle can now accept such landings in 25–30kt crosswinds. To begin with, the ARI was all but eliminated on touch-down, as it had no essential function on the ground. The mechanical ARI was made to deactivate on sensing wheel-spin on the ground, which was almost instantaneous after touch-down. This effectively eliminated the effects of the ARI, but did retain it in a static condition until the ground checks were made. The CAS ARI was also largely eliminated during the roll-out in a similar fashion.

The mechanical lateral control wash-out with the stick aft was eliminated with the undercarriage down, while the gain was increased on the nosewheel steering so that the response was swifter.

Right: Major D.W. Peterson, who piloted the Streak Eagle to the 15,000m and 25,000m records on January 16 and 26, 1975, by the nose of the specially prepared F-15A.

Above: An early production F-15C refuels from a KC-135A tanker with an example of MCAIR's previous USAF fighter, the F-4, in attendance.

This fix was primarily to improve the taxying qualities of the Eagle, but the benefits to directional control on the runway were welcomed. The main-wheel oleo struts were significantly modified, so as to achieve a greater load stroke quicker on touchdown, while the remainder was taken up at lower speeds. Overall the Eagle had a

Below: One of the virtues of the F-15 is the minimal amount of ground support equipment needed, as illustrated in this view of pre-flight checks at a snow-covered base.

more solid feel following touch-down.

The time and effort expended on this series of fixes have paid dividends for Eagle operations. The 25–30kt cross-wind component allows crab angles of up to 12deg to be used on landing. With the nose held at 12deg pitch, for maximum braking effect, the Eagle's velocity vector is simply held straight down the runway with the rudder until the nose is lowered at about 80kt, where the nose-wheel steering takes over. All the pilot needs do is to fly down the runway using normal aerodynamic control until the nosewheel is lowered to contact with the ground.

The handling qualities of the F-15 Eagle in flight are described as 'excellent' using either the conventional hydro-mechanical system or the CAS to fly the

aircraft. However, several modifications known as Engineering Change Proposals (ECPs) were made, though by autumn 1974 only 36 had been recommended, of which 13 did not involve the Eagle itself. Of the 23 ECPs made to the aircraft, only three are externally visible: the raked wing tips, the dog-tooth stabilator, and the enlarged speed brake.

Early in the test programme MCAIR discovered a buffet and wing-loading problem at certain altitudes. After attempting to solve the problem with wing fences, the solution adopted was to remove 4sq ft (0.37sq m) diagonally from the wing tip to create a raked appearance. The cutting of the dog-tooth into the leading edge of the stabilator was the solution to a flutter

problem discovered in wind tunnel testing. This produced a minor shift in the coefficient of pressure and a change in the moment of inertia sufficient to remove the flutter. The enlargement of the speedbrake from 20 to 31.5sq ft (1.86 to 2.93sq m) allowed the required drag to be produced from lower extension angles, and removed a buffet caused by the original brake at the desired drag configurations (and higher extension angles).

Radio-controlled models

One of the more interesting aspects of the F-15's flight test programme was the use of large glider models of the Eagle, which were dropped from a Boeing B-52 of the NASA Flight Research Center flying at 45,000ft (13,700m) at 175kt. Termed 'remotely piloted research vehicles', these models were built of aluminium and glass fibre to three-eights scale, having a wing span of 16ft 1¼in (4.91m) and a length of 23ft 10¾in (7.28m) and weighing some 2,000lb (907kg). Radio-controlled from the ground, they performed their manoeuvres, deployed a parachute and were recovered in mid-air by a helicopter. Among their tasks were to conduct high angles of attack, stalling and spinning manoeuvres ahead of the live flight tests performed by the eighth development Eagle.

All these ECPs, many of a minor nature, have contributed to making a good flying aircraft into a fighter with excellent handling qualities. Following its first flight, the F-15 Eagle met all its milestones on time with one exception: because of technical problems concerned with F100 engine durability tests, this part was some months late. The test programme's deliberately slow pace was, according to Major General Bellis, able to provide "a significant capability to profit from information derived from the initial and intensive ground-test programme and the current joint Air Force and contractor F-15 flight test activities". Such a pace is totally in keeping with the 'test before fly' and 'fly before buy' attitude adopted by the USAF in their procurement procedure.

Final proof of the new fighter's capabilities was provided by Operational Streak Eagle, a joint USAF/MCAIR operation to break a number of time-to-height world records, previously held

Specifications

	F-15A	F-15C	F-15E
Length	63ft 9in/10.43m	63ft 9in/10.43m	63ft 9in/10.43m
Wingspan	42ft 9¾in/13.05m	42ft 9¾in/13.05m	42ft 9¾in/13.05m
Height	18ft 5½in/5.63m	18ft 5½in/5.63m	18ft 5½in/5.63m
Weights			
Empty	28,000lb/12,700kg	28,000lb/12,700kg	32,000lb/14,515kg
Takeoff (air-to-air)	41,500lb/18,824kg	44,500lb/20,185kg	c72,000lb/32,659kg
Maximum takeoff	56,000lb/25,401kg	68,000lb/30,844kg	81,000lb/36,742kg
Wing area	608sq ft/56.5sq m	608sq ft/56.5sq m	608sq ft/56 5sq.m
Load factor	+9g/−3g	+9g/−3g	+9/-3g
Combat thrust: weight ratio	1.4:1	1.3:1	0.65
Maximum speed	>Mach2.5	>Mach2.5	>Mach 2.5
Service ceiling	65,000ft/19,813m	65,000ft/19,813m	65,000ft/19813m
Range			
Ferry (with external tanks)	>2,500nm/4,630km	>2,500nm/4,630km	>2,500nm/4,630km
Ferry (with FAST Packs)	—	>3,000nm/5,556km	>3,000nm/5,566km
Internal fuel	11,635lb/5,278kg	13,455lb/6,103kg	22,904lb/10,389kg
Number of hardpoints	5	5	10
Maximum ordnance load	16,000lb/7,257kg	16,000lb/7,257kg	26,096lb/11,837kg

by the F-4 Phantom and Soviet MiG-25 Foxbat. The 19th pre-production aircraft (the 17th single-seater) was totally stripped down: radar, cannon, missiles, tail hook, utility hydraulic system, one of the generators, and several actuators were removed, along with the paint finish, leaving a bare metal aircraft. Between January 16 and February 1, 1975, Majors W. R. Macfarlane, D. W. Peterson and R. Smith established a total of eight new time-to-climb records flying from Grand Forks AFB. The Eagle was some 2,800lb (1,270kg) lighter than a standard production aircraft and only sufficient fuel was carried for the specific flight and return to the airfield.

The Category I and II flight test programme was completed by the delivery of the first production Eagle, a TF-15A (F-15B) to the USAF's Tactical Air Command at Luke AFB on November 14, 1974. On July 1, 1975, the first operational F-15 Eagle squadron within Tactical Air Command – the 1st Tactical Fighter Wing (TFW) – was formed at Langley AFB, and six months later, on January 9, 1976, this wing received its first aircraft.

As with most aircraft in production, improvements and refinements are constantly emerging. The current production models of the Eagle are the F-15C and F-15D, which replaced the single-seat F-15A and twin-seat F-15B respectively from mid-1979, when a total of 443 had been produced.

Externally there is no major difference between the two sets of Eagles. Internally, the APG-63 radar has been improved by the addition of a programmable signal processor (PSP), details of which are given in Chapter 4; the fuel capacity has been increased by some 312.5USgal (260Imp gal/1,188 litre); and the aircraft has been modified to accept two conformal Fuel and Sensor Tactical (FAST) packs on either side of the fuselage, enabling the internal fuel capacity to be increased by a further 1,523US gal (1,268Imp gal/5,788 litre) altogether.

The first F-15C Eagle flew on February 27, 1979, with the first F-15D following on June 19, 1979. These versions entered service with the USAF in September 1979, when the 18th TFW at Kadena AB, Okinawa, Japan, received their first squadron. The F-15C/D model represented the baseline from which the F-15 Multi-Stage Improvement Programme (MSIP) began. In addition to the enhancements already noted, the MSIP encompassed a new programmable weapon control set, with provision for the AIM-120 Amraam, AIM-7M Sparrow and AIM-9M Sidewinder missiles; expanded electronic warfare (EW) equipment, including an enhanced radar warning receiver (RWR), an internal ECM system and the addition of chaff/flare launchers; and expanded communications facilities, Seek Talk, HF radio and other provisions. Although the F-15E Strike Eagle was under development at the time, the F-15C/D variant of the Eagle was the final production air combat fighter version, and has remained so thus far.

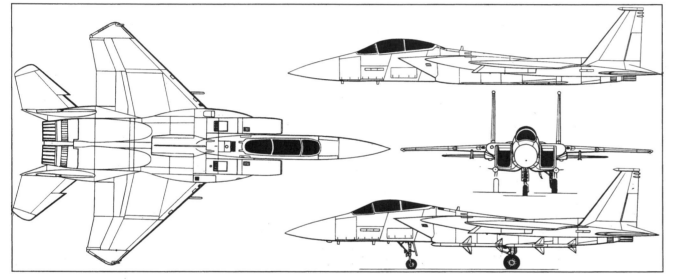

Above left: Three-view drawing of the production F-15C; the upper side profile shows the two-seat F-15D. Without the FAST packs, the F-15C is externally identical to the A.

Left: St Louis again forms the background for this February 1979 view of the first F-15C before its delivery to TAC.

Structure

Thousands of hours of computer studies and wind-tunnel tests went into the F-15's design; billions of dollars have been spent on building the aircraft and its essential systems. Much of this effort and expense was devoted to keeping the basic structure as simple as possible, for maximum survivability in combat and ease of maintenance on the ground. In service, the Eagle may not have quite matched its designers' expectations, but an outstanding safety record and an improving rate of availability demonstrated by Tactical Air Command Squadrons are testimony to its basic soundness.

By mid-1967 the early conception of the FX as a 60,000lb (27,000kg) variable-sweep multirole aircraft had been rejected in favour of a 40,000lb (18,000kg) fixed-wing fighter, and by September 1968, when the Contract Definition RFP was issued, a number of design criteria had been established. Several of these were directly concerned with structural features, while others involving specific operational requirements imposed their own indirect constraints on the physical details of the resulting aircraft.

Since the Eagle was to be used for air combat, a combination of high thrust-to-weight ratio and low wing loading were stipulated, within the overall gross weight limit of 40,000lb. A high degree of survivability was called for in structure and subsystems, involving comprehensive testing of components used, along with extended component life and reduced maintenance requirements. And the single crew member, who would be provided with a comprehensive suite of automated avionics to enable him to carry out his mission unaided, was to be given all-round visibility.

Computer evaluations

During the preliminary FX design studies – which ultimately involved some 2,500,000 man-hours and resulted in 37,500 pages of documentation – MCAIR engineers carried out extensive computer evaluations comparing the weights of hypothetical aircraft of given cost resulting from a variety of basic design features. For example, if a two-man, all weather avionic suite were installed, the gross weight of the aircraft was calculated as 46,000lb (20,865kg), while single-seat, clear-air avionics required a gross weight of only 31,500lb (14,290kg). Similar comparisons were made between theoretical aircraft with varying degrees of energy manoeuvrability and maximum speeds ranging from Mach 0.8 sea-level dash to a sustained Mach 2.7.

The parameters for the structural component of the computer evaluation were represented by an upper limit of 8g with 100 per cent fuel and a lower capacity for 6.5g with only 60 per cent fuel, giving respective gross weight figures of 41,500lb (18,825kg) and 38,000lb (17,235kg). The actual design limitation of 7.33g was achieved within the specified 40,000lb weight limit.

Considering that the external dimensions of the F-15 are marginally greater than those of the F-4 Phantom, it is remarkable that the maximum takeoff weight of the newer fighter should be nearly 6,000lb (2,700kg) less than that of its predecessor. Part of this reduction is a result of the lighter internal fuel load, which with the Eagle's more efficient

Above: Viewed from above, the contours of the Eagle fuselage clearly show the central pod and twin boom structural configuration.

Below: June 1981, and among the F-15Cs and Ds on the MCAIR assembly line is the distinctive tail of an F/A-18 Hornet.

engines still gives a longer range, and the rest is accounted for by the higher percentage of titanium and advanced composite materials used in its construction. As originally designed the F-4 was built with more titanium than any previous fighter, but even in its later versions this only amounted to some 9 per cent by weight of the total structure, whereas the Eagle airframe includes 25.8 per cent titanium, only 5.5 per cent steel and 37.3 per cent aluminium.

The titanium is largely concentrated around the engines and the inboard sections of the wings. The fuselage itself is of conventional semi-monocoque construction, and its pod and twin boom configuration is apparent in the contours of the upper surfaces. The frames of the central pod and of the air intakes on either side and their skin are of machined aluminium, as is the front wing spar, but the three main wing spars and the bulkheads connecting them and the frames of the engine pods are of titanium, also machined. Aft of the forward main wing spar the fuselage skin is also of titanium, and the same metal forms the cantilever booms outboard of each engine which carry the twin fins and horizontal stabilators, the stabilator attachments and the spars of the fins.

Titanium strength

There are several advantages to the use of titanium in these areas. The resulting structure is strong enough to transmit the control forces from the tail surfaces, and the strength of the twin engine bays, with titanium firewalls between them, reduces the risk of a fire or explosion in one engine damaging or incapacitating the other. Similarly, the titanium skin of the inboard underwing skin covers the integral fuel tanks, which are filled with sealant foam injected through channels in the joints between the spars and the aluminium upper skin. Moreover, the titanium wing spars and supporting bulkheads are strong enough to allow the aircraft to keep flying with any one spar in each wing completely severed.

Further weight savings are achieved by the use of composite materials over honeycomb cores for the wing flaps and ailerons and the tailfins and stabilators. The central sections of the tail surfaces, where the titanium structural members form torque boxes, as well as the rudders, are covered with boron composite skins with aluminium and Nomex honeycomb between, while aluminium skins cover the honeycomb flaps and ailerons and the raked outboard sections of the wings. The speedbrake, similarly, has a graphite composite skin

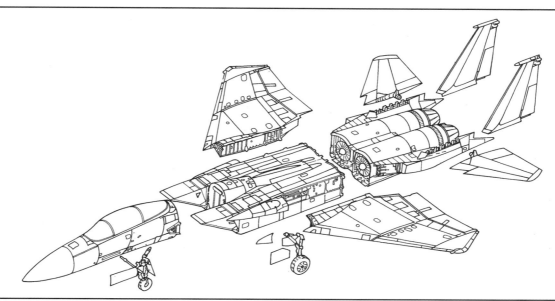

Below: The bubble canopy is the only external feature of the Eagle to interrupt the aerodynamically clean contours of the airframe.

Above: Major structural assemblies of the F-15 airframe. Tail surfaces and wings are interchangeable between aircraft.

Top: Automatic drilling machines in action, forming the attachment holes around the edges of the acrylic windshield destined for an F-15.

over a core of aluminium honeycomb.

The wing torque box assembly is based on the three titanium spars, extended by aft and outer spars of aluminium, and the wings are attached to the titanium bulkheads by pin joints which allow interchangeability between aircraft. The flaps and ailerons are similarly interchangeable, as are the windshield, canopy, speedbrake and fibreglass nose radome, while the vertical stabilizers, rudders and stabilators are interchangeable between right and left sides of the aircraft.

The aircraft is constructed in stages, with individual assemblies built up separately and progressively integrated. The main assemblies are the rear, centre and forward fuselage sections, the vertical and horizontal stabilizers and the wings, and various techniques are used in forming the multitude of sub-assemblies involved.

Sheet aluminium parts are drilled and routed automatically, with more sub-

stantial aluminium sections formed in a two-storey press exerting a pressure of 7,000 tons. Titanium forgings are also finished by computer-controlled milling machinery, and titanium sheets are formed in a furnace at temperatures of 1,650deg F (900deg C) and pressures of 250psi (45kg/sq cm). Graphite skins for the speedbrake are shaped by a high-speed laser cutter, while the honeycomb core is mechanically carved to match. Other automated processes include computerized pipe bending and robot drilling of the attachment holes for the acrylic windshield.

Meanwhile, sheets of the boron epoxy composites used for the tail surfaces are assembled by hand before being bonded by high-pressure steam in an autoclave. Metallic parts are spray-painted individually to protect them from corrosion, and critical sub-assemblies such as the engine intake ducts and wing leading edges are drilled and riveted by hand. Another job for

Above: Ground crew work under floodlights to prepare a 49th TFW F-15A for a sortie during Red Flag exercises at Nellis AFB in 1980.

Below: A ground crewman sporting an 'Eagle Keeper' badge takes advantage of the ready accessibility of the F-15's internal systems.

skilled technicians is the assembly of the 290 bundles of electric wiring: these are installed during the build-up of the fuselage sections, as are fuel and hydraulic systems.

The final assembly stage brings together the three fuselage sections and the wings, and the final connections of all the power, control and environmental systems. These are checked before the final stage, which involves the installation of engines and avionics, and after a final checkout the aircraft is flown by a company test pilot to ensure that all systems are functioning.

As well as the parts fabricated in MCAIR's own plant, the F-15 involves the use of parts supplied by some 1,200 sub-contractors whose value is approximately half that of the total aircraft cost. By 1980 total cost of the F-15 programme had amounted to $16.58 billion, giving an average unit cost for the 749 aircraft involved of rather more than $22 million (in FY 1980 dollars). The 60 F-15s sold to Saudi Arabia cost a total of $1.92 billion, while Israel's first 40 Eagles were worth $907 million.

Design rationale

The wing configuration is relatively straightforward, though it was only selected after several hundred had been analysed and more than 100 were tested in almost a year of solid wind-tunnel trials. Ultimately, variable camber, with movable surfaces on both leading and trailing edges as used on the F-16, was rejected, since an alternative design with a fixed leading edge employing conical camber was found to offer only slightly higher supersonic drag and marginally reduced subsonic performance, both of which were more than offset by advantages in terms of

weight, simplicity of manufacture and ease of maintenance. The chosen design has a straight leading edge swept at an angle of 45deg, an aspect ratio of 3, zero incidence and 1deg of anhedral.

As outlined in the previous chapter the wingtips were modified from their original shape, a total of 3sq ft (0.28sq m) being removed from each tip to reduce excessive lift at the wingtips and consequent severe buffeting at high g loads and high subsonic speed at altitudes of 30,000ft (9,000m) or so. Another change made as a result of flight testing was the increase in chord of the outer portions of the horizontal stabilators, creating the characteristic notched leading edges of these surfaces, to eliminate flutter. At the same time, the original speedbrake was increased in size by more than 50 per cent, again to eliminate a buffet problem.

Overall, the F-15 profile is designed to minimize wave drag at high speeds, with the single exception of the bubble canopy, which is a feature of both the Eagle and the USAF's other new fighter, the F-16 Fighting Falcon. The aerodynamic penalties imposed by such a canopy are regarded as unavoidable if the pilot is to be enabled to perform his air superiority mission effectively.

The canopy itself is a single transparency with only one transverse frame, hinged at the rear and counterbalanced by a single strut, with a second strut immediately behind the pilot's seat for emergency jettison of the canopy. The size of the canopy is the only external difference between single-seat and two-seat Eagles: the latter have a longer canopy to accommodate the rear crew member, while the single-seater has an avionics bay behind the pilot's seat. This

Left: An F-15B from Nellis AFB's 57th TTW in its hangar for routine servicing during a Red Flag desert warfare simulation.

Right: For maximum maintainability the F-15 airframe features a total of 570sq ft (53sq m) of access doors and panels, as demonstrated here.

houses several avionics 'black boxes' associated with the Tactical Electronic Warfare System in current models but is largely empty and offers ample room for additional avionic equipment; it is un-pressurized, and when the canopy is lowered it is isolated by an integral seal.

Directly behind the avionics bay are the fuselage fuel tanks, and between the forward and aft tanks, below the speed-brake, are the ammunition drum and feed system for the M61 cannon. The gun itself is housed in the starboard wing root fairing, while the equivalent fairing at the port wing root contains the flight refuelling receptacle.

The only examples of variable geometry in the F-15's structure are the engine air inlets on either side of the forward fuselage. Because the aircraft was designed to be flown at high angles

Right: Extending steps built into the fuselage side of the F-15 can be used instead of the normal ladder for cockpit access.

of attack in combat, the intakes are able to 'nod' up or down to keep the aperture facing directly into the airflow in order to maintain an adequate supply of air to the engines. The intakes are pivoted at their lower edge and adjusted to angles of 4deg above or 11deg below the horizontal by hydraulic actuators controlled by the air data computer. The intake angle can also be adjusted to prevent more air than necessary being

Below: An 8th TFW Eagle is given an automatic wash at Kwang Ju air base in Korea, during Exercise Cope North in June 1982.

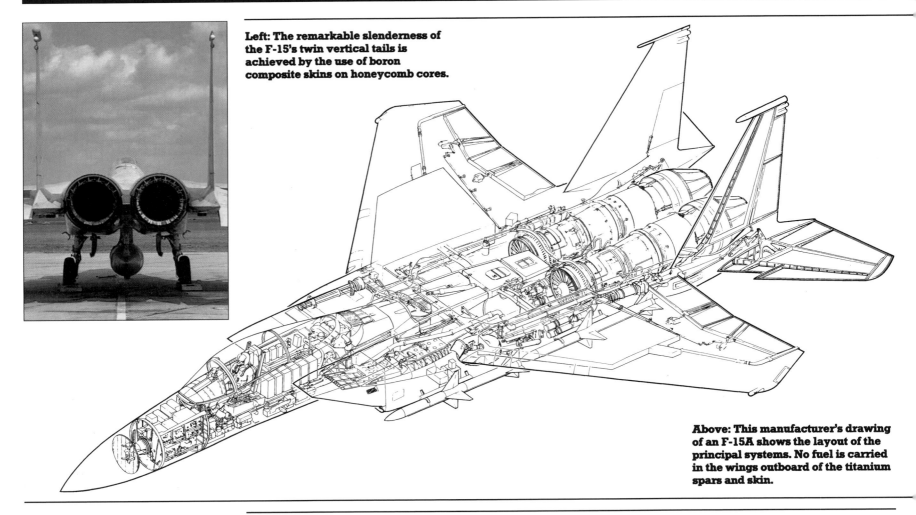

Left: The remarkable slenderness of the F-15's twin vertical tails is achieved by the use of boron composite skins on honeycomb cores.

Above: This manufacturer's drawing of an F-15A shows the layout of the principal systems. No fuel is carried in the wings outboard of the titanium spars and skin.

Right: Wing leading and trailing edge tanks, and additional tanks in the centre fuselage, allow the F-15C to carry an extra 1,855lb (880kg) of fuel internally.

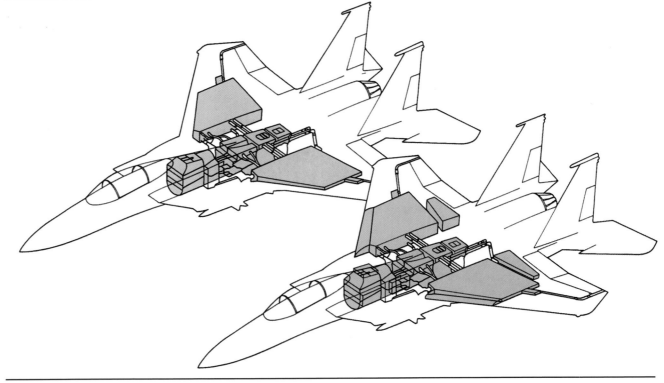

taken in, and the intake surfaces have a further function in providing additional manoeuvring control in a similar manner to canard foreplanes. At supersonic speeds their effectiveness is almost a third as great as that of the stabilators, whose size and weight were enabled to be reduced in consequence. Immediately aft of the intakes themselves are twin mechanically linked ramps to control the shockwaves created in the incoming air.

Of course, structural and aerodynamic efficiency are prerequisites in any aircraft, but a combat aircraft must also be designed to survive the inevitable wear and tear of battle. In this respect the Eagle's main assets are reckoned to be its overall superiority in such areas as pilot visibility, radar detection ability, weapons systems and performance, but a number of less obvious safety features were included, largely as a result of experience with the F-4 in Vietnam, in addition to the basic structural elements described above.

Hydraulics and fuel

As well as twin engines, the F-15 has three separate hydraulic systems which can detect and isolate leaks in their associated subsystems and each of which is capable of sustaining the flight control system on its own. Similarly, twin electrical systems, powered by 40/50kVA AC generators operating through DC conversion units, are capable independently of fulfilling the aircraft's power requirements, while a standby hydraulic generator is fitted to supply critical systems in an emergency. Either the electronic control augmentation system or the hydromechanical system can provide independent flight control should one or the other be put out of action.

Fuel supply is another vital system, and this too is designed to cope with

various emergencies. The fuel tanks themselves are filled with foam, and the fuel lines are also self-sealing. In the event of electrical failure, the fuel system will continue to operate on standby power, providing fuel flow adequate for engine operation up to the mid-afterburner range.

Additional protection against fire is provided in the form of a fire-suppression system. A pressurized bottle containing a non-corrosive agent is located between the engine bay firewalls, with three nozzles able to release the agent into either engine or in the space between them. The provision of this fire suppression system is one of the direct results of the F-4's experiences in Vietnam, and the Eagle is one of the few fighter aircraft to be fitted with such equipment. The physical separation of the fuel tanks from the engine bays is another precaution against fire.

Another aspect of the F-15 design

intended to maximize its efficiency in combat is the emphasis placed on ease of maintenance and relative independence of ground support equipment. The airframe features a total of 570sq ft (53sq m) of access panels, allowing most routine maintenance to be carried out without the use of work stands. The overall simplicity of the airframe is a major factor in reducing maintenance requirements: by comparison with the F-4E, the F-15 has only 202 lubrication points against the earlier fighter's 510; seven hydraulic filters, all of which are interchangeable and which incorporate visual indications of the need for replacement, are used in place of the Phantom's 21; plumbing connections in the fuel system are reduced from 281 to only 97, and the interchangeable fuel pumps are of a plug-in design that allows them to be changed in only 30 minutes; and whereas the F-4E had 905 potted electrical connectors, whose

waterproof compounds were subject to deterioration, the F-15 has a total of 809 silicone grommet connectors to avoid this problem.

The digital avionic systems used also help to reduce the maintenance workload. No routine servicing is needed for these: they are line replaceable units (LRUs), readily removable in the event of failure for testing and repair, and faulty units can be located by means of a built-in test panel located in the nose-wheel well. The cockpit is also equipped with a caution light panel to indicate system failures and a built-in test (BIT) panel for the avionic systems. To reduce dependence on support equipment the secondary power system which provides power for the jet fuel starters can also power the electrical and hydraulic systems for up to 30 minutes while maintenance work is carried out or for munitions loading.

Power for the electrical generators

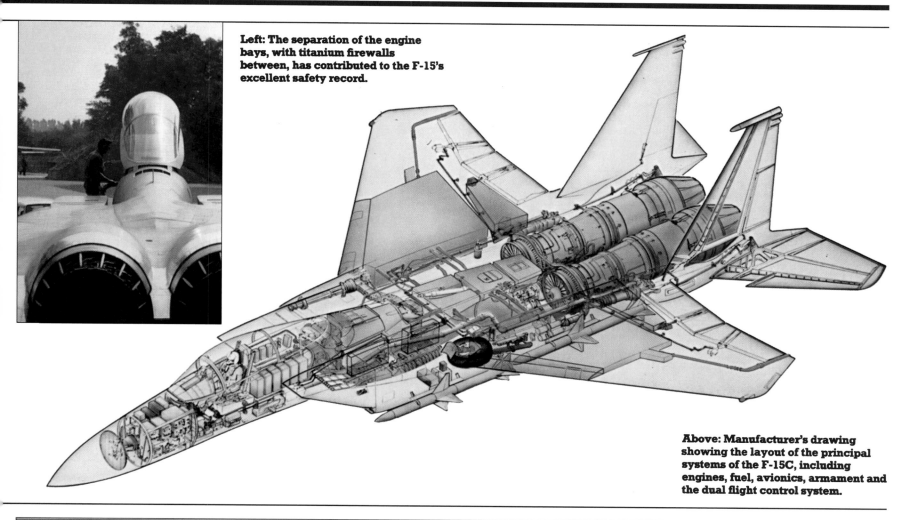

Left: The separation of the engine bays, with titanium firewalls between, has contributed to the F-15's excellent safety record.

Above: Manufacturer's drawing showing the layout of the principal systems of the F-15C, including engines, fuel, avionics, armament and the dual flight control system.

Left: The increased maximum takeoff weight of the F-15C necessitated strengthening of the undercarriage, tyres and brakes. A 36th TFW F-15C shows its landing gear.

and hydraulic pumps is derived from the main powerplant via an aircraft-mounted accessory drive shaft. Being mounted on the aircraft rather than in the engines themselves, this allows the engines to be interchangeable between right and left. To simplify engine maintenance, each F100 turbofan can be broken down into five main modules, consisting of the inlet and fan, the gearbox, the fan drive, the engine core and the augmentor (afterburner) duct and nozzle. Any of these can be removed for maintenance while another module is substituted, so that a malfunction in one part of the engine does not put the whole powerplant out of action while it is repaired. The engines themselves are removed quickly and easily, sliding out of the rear of the bays on integral rails onto a cart with matching rails, and with only ten disconnections necessary before removal. Complete engine change can be accomplished well

inside the 30 minutes minimum specified by the Air Force. And with the engines installed internal inspections can be carried out by means of 12 borescope ports on each engine.

The overall intention behind this careful planning of maintenance features was to meet a USAF requirement for a maximum of 11.3 maintenance man-hours per flight hour (MMH/FH), just under half the requirement of the F-4E, which would allow a 15 per cent reduction in the number of maintenance personnel. In practice, however, this figure has not been achieved: reduced to 19 by the time type testing was complete, the MMH/FH figure had risen to around 35 by 1980. One reason for this was the continuing difficulties with the engine, as described in the following chapter, with the powerplant absorbing nearly half the total maintenance effort. Another was the continuing shortage of skilled maintenance personnel, partly

as a result of the comparatively low rates of pay which such personnel received compared with those available elsewhere.

An equally serious problem was the difficulties encountered with the Avionics Intermediate Shops (AIS), the second of three stages in the F-15 planned maintenance programme. The first level of maintenance takes place on the flight line, where routine servicing is carried out and line-replaceable units are removed as necessary. The second stage, of which the AIS forms part, is the repair on base of faulty units, and the third is depot repair at Air Logistic Centres.

Among the problems encountered with this system was the difficulty of repairing LRUs on base, with nearly half of the avionics LRUs being returned to the depots. This in turn meant that stocks of replacement LRUs were quickly exhausted. The principal reason

for this state of affairs was the repeated failures of the automated testing stations which comprise the AIS, to the extent that only half the AISs were operational at any time. And the problem was compounded by the failure of the AIS to agree in its diagnosis of the fault with the indications of the on-board BIT equipment in a large percentage of cases.

The natural consequence of all these problems was a high rate of cannibalization, with parts being removed from one aircraft to keep another flying. Consequently, by 1979 availability of the F-15 within TAC had fallen to an alarmingly low 56 per cent. On the other hand, a high degree of readiness has been achieved on numerous exercises, and the Eagle has compiled an impressive safety record. Overall availability by 1983 had risen to more than 65 per cent, and an official inspection of the 1st TFW at Langley in August 1982 found a record 98.6 per cent of aircraft operational: this compares with an availability of only 35 per cent of the same wing's aircraft three years earlier.

New model

Meanwhile, the original F-15A and B production models were replaced by the improved C and D from June 1979. Again, external differences between the single and two-seat version are limited to the slightly longer canopy fitted to the F-15D, and the principal external distinguishing feature of the later models is the provision of the conformal fuel tanks (CFTs).

The CFTs are attached to the outside of each air intake, and can carry an additional 4,875lb (2,211kg) of fuel. Alternatively, sensors such as reconnaissance cameras or infra-red equipment, radar warning receivers and jammers, laser designators and low-light TV cameras, or a combination of such sensors with reduced quantities, can be carried, although this is seldom the case. When the CFTs are fitted, the four Sparrow missiles are mounted on their corners, and bombs or air-to-surface missiles weighing up to 4,400lb (1,995kg) can be carried as an alternative.

Internal fuel capacity of the F-15C/D is also increased by 1,885lb (880kg), with additional tanks located in the centre fuselage and in the wing leading and trailing edges. The effect of this increased fuel capacity is to raise the potential gross weight of the F-15C to 68,000lb (30,845kg) with full internal fuel, CFTs and three external tanks. As a result, tyres, wheels and brakes

have been strengthened to cope with the increased weight.

The CFTs alone carry slightly less fuel than the normal three external tanks, but allow the aircraft to be flown at considerably higher speeds. Compared with the clean configuration, an F-15 equipped with CFTs experiences only slightly increased profile drag at subsonic speeds, and compared with the standard external tanks the conformal tanks contribute only a fraction of the former's drag at supersonic speeds. Ferry range with the increased internal fuel, CFTs and wing and fuselage tanks is increased to 3,450 miles (5,560km). According

to the manufacturers, unused space in the outboard sections of the wings could accommodate a further 90lb (400kg) of fuel.

The manufacturers have also proposed to exploit currently unused internal space, particularly in the

rear of the cockpit and in the tail booms, to equip the Eagle for other roles. As much as 56cu ft (1.6cu m) of growth space is claimed to be available for avionics, and in the F-15E Strike Eagle variant, the rear cockpit was developed into a station for the Weapons Systems operator. The latter version involved a greatly strengthened structure and landing gear in order to accommodate an enormously increased takeoff and, to a lesser degree, landing weight. Efforts to replace the Wild Weasel defence suppression Phantom with a dedicated F-15 were abortive. The Panavia Tornado was superior in this role, but was similarly not selected.

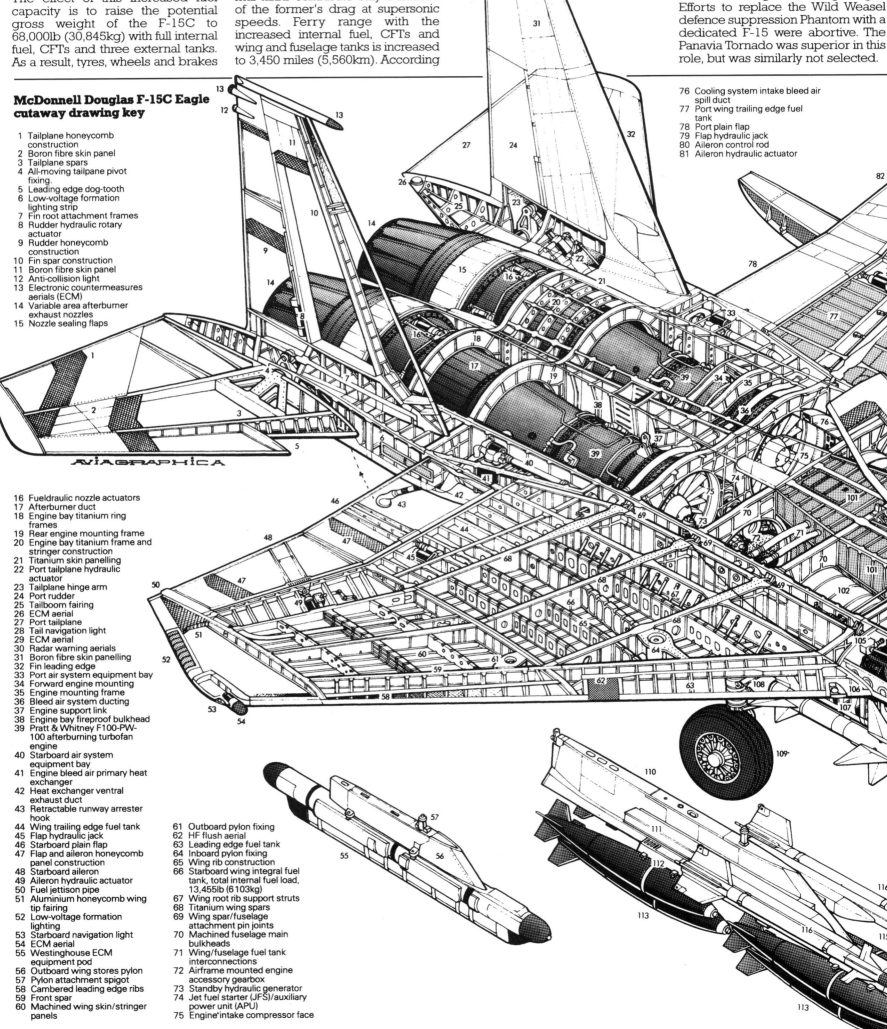

McDonnell Douglas F-15C Eagle cutaway drawing key

1 Tailplane honeycomb construction
2 Boron fibre skin panel
3 Tailplane spars
4 All-moving tailpane pivot fixing
5 Leading edge dog-tooth
6 Low-voltage formation lighting strip
7 Fin root attachment frames
8 Rudder hydraulic rotary actuator
9 Rudder honeycomb construction
10 Fin spar construction
11 Boron fibre skin panel
12 Anti-collision light
13 Electronic countermeasures aerials (ECM)
14 Variable area afterburner exhaust nozzles
15 Nozzle sealing flaps
16 Fueldraulic nozzle actuators
17 Afterburner duct
18 Engine bay titanium ring frames
19 Rear engine mounting frame
20 Engine bay titanium frame and stringer construction
21 Titanium skin panelling
22 Port tailplane hydraulic actuator
23 Tailplane hinge arm
24 Port rudder
25 Tailboom fairing
26 ECM aerial
27 Port tailplane
28 Tail navigation light
29 ECM aerial
30 Radar warning aerials
31 Boron fibre skin panelling
32 Fin leading edge
33 Port air system equipment bay
34 Forward engine mounting
35 Engine mounting frame
36 Bleed air system ducting
37 Engine support link
38 Engine bay fireproof bulkhead
39 Pratt & Whitney F100-PW-100 afterburning turbofan engine
40 Starboard air system equipment bay
41 Engine bleed air primary heat exchanger
42 Heat exchanger ventral exhaust duct
43 Retractable runway arrester hook
44 Wing trailing edge fuel tank
45 Flap hydraulic jack
46 Starboard plain flap
47 Flap and aileron honeycomb panel construction
48 Starboard aileron
49 Aileron hydraulic actuator
50 Fuel jettison pipe
51 Aluminium honeycomb wing tip fairing
52 Low-voltage formation lighting
53 Starboard navigation light
54 ECM aerial
55 Westinghouse ECM equipment pod
56 Outboard wing stores pylon
57 Pylon attachment spigot
58 Cambered leading edge ribs
59 Front spar
60 Machined wing skin/stringer panels
61 Outboard pylon fixing
62 HF flush aerial
63 Leading edge fuel tank
64 Inboard pylon fixing
65 Wing rib construction
66 Starboard wing integral fuel tank, total internal fuel load, 13,455lb (6103kg)
67 Wing root rib support struts
68 Titanium wing spars
69 Wing spar/fuselage attachment pin joints
70 Machined fuselage main bulkheads
71 Wing/fuselage fuel tank interconnections
72 Airframe mounted engine accessory gearbox
73 Standby hydraulic generator
74 Jet fuel starter (JFS)/auxiliary power unit (APU)
75 Engine intake compressor face
76 Cooling system intake bleed air spill duct
77 Port wing trailing edge fuel tank
78 Port plain flap
79 Flap hydraulic jack
80 Aileron control rod
81 Aileron hydraulic actuator

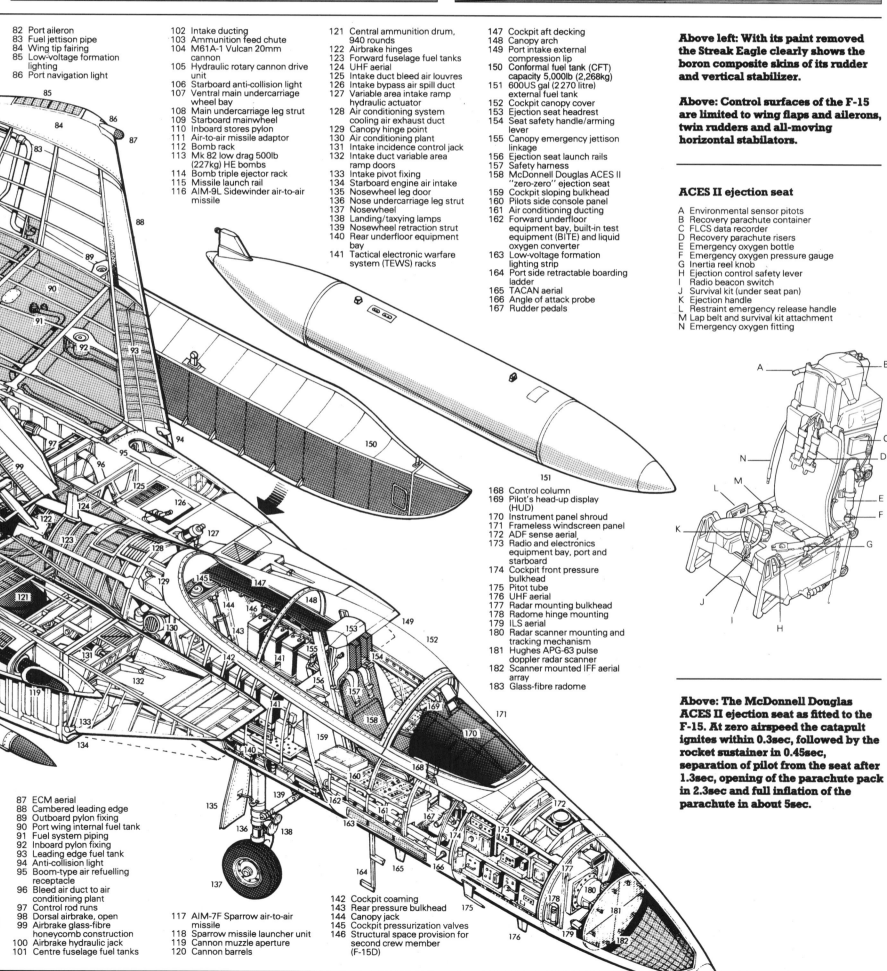

82 Port aileron
83 Fuel jettison pipe
84 Wing tip fairing
85 Low-voltage formation lighting
86 Port navigation light

102 Intake ducting
103 Ammunition feed chute
104 M61A-1 Vulcan 20mm cannon
105 Hydraulic rotary cannon drive unit
106 Starboard anti-collision light
107 Ventral main undercarriage wheel bay
108 Main undercarriage leg strut
109 Starboard mainwheel
110 Inboard stores pylon
111 Air-to-air missile adaptor
112 Bomb rack
113 Mk 82 low drag 500lb (227kg) HE bombs
114 Bomb triple ejector rack
115 Missile launch rail
116 AIM-9L Sidewinder air-to-air missile

121 Central ammunition drum, 940 rounds
122 Airbrake hinges
123 Forward fuselage fuel tanks
124 UHF aerial
125 Intake duct bleed air louvres
126 Intake bypass air spill duct
127 Variable area intake ramp hydraulic actuator
128 Air conditioning system cooling air exhaust duct
129 Canopy hinge point
130 Air conditioning plant
131 Intake incidence control jack
132 Intake duct variable area ramp doors
133 Intake pivot fixing
134 Starboard engine air intake
135 Nosewheel leg door
136 Nose undercarriage leg strut
137 Nosewheel
138 Landing/taxying lamps
139 Nosewheel retraction strut
140 Rear underfloor equipment bay
141 Tactical electronic warfare system (TEWS) racks

147 Cockpit aft decking
148 Canopy arch
149 Port intake external compression lip
150 Conformal fuel tank (CFT) capacity 5,000lb (2,268kg)
151 600US gal (2 270 litre) external fuel tank
152 Cockpit canopy cover
153 Ejection seat headrest
154 Seat safety handle/arming lever
155 Canopy emergency jettison linkage
156 Ejection seat launch rails
157 Safety harness
158 McDonnell Douglas ACES II "zero-zero" ejection seat
159 Cockpit sloping bulkhead
160 Pilots side console panel
161 Air conditioning ducting
162 Forward underfloor equipment bay, built-in test equipment (BITE) and liquid oxygen converter
163 Low-voltage formation lighting strip
164 Port side retractable boarding ladder
165 TACAN aerial
166 Angle of attack probe
167 Rudder pedals

168 Control column
169 Pilot's head-up display (HUD)
170 Instrument panel shroud
171 Frameless windscreen panel
172 ADF sense aerial
173 Radio and electronics equipment bay, port and starboard
174 Cockpit front pressure bulkhead
175 Pitot tube
176 UHF aerial
177 Radar mounting bulkhead
178 Radome hinge mounting
179 ILS aerial
180 Radar scanner mounting and tracking mechanism
181 Hughes APG-63 pulse doppler radar scanner
182 Scanner mounted IFF aerial array
183 Glass-fibre radome

87 ECM aerial
88 Cambered leading edge
89 Outboard pylon fixing
90 Port wing internal fuel tank
91 Fuel system piping
92 Inboard pylon fixing
93 Leading edge fuel tank
94 Anti-collision light
95 Boom-type air refuelling receptacle
96 Bleed air duct to air conditioning plant
97 Control rod runs
98 Dorsal airbrake, open
99 Airbrake glass-fibre honeycomb construction
100 Airbrake hydraulic jack
101 Centre fuselage fuel tanks

117 AIM-7F Sparrow air-to-air missile
118 Sparrow missile launcher unit
119 Cannon muzzle aperture
120 Cannon barrels

142 Cockpit coaming
143 Rear pressure bulkhead
144 Canopy jack
145 Cockpit pressurization valves
146 Structural space provision for second crew member (F-15D)

Above left: With its paint removed the Streak Eagle clearly shows the boron composite skins of its rudder and vertical stabilizer.

Above: Control surfaces of the F-15 are limited to wing flaps and ailerons, twin rudders and all-moving horizontal stabilators.

ACES II ejection seat

A Environmental sensor pitots
B Recovery parachute container
C FLCS data recorder
D Recovery parachute risers
E Emergency oxygen bottle
F Emergency oxygen pressure gauge
G Inertia reel knob
H Ejection control safety lever
I Radio beacon switch
J Survival kit (under seat pan)
K Ejection handle
L Restraint emergency release handle
M Lap belt and survival kit attachment
N Emergency oxygen fitting

Above: The McDonnell Douglas ACES II ejection seat as fitted to the F-15. At zero airspeed the catapult ignites within 0.3sec, followed by the rocket sustainer in 0.45sec, separation of pilot from the seat after 1.3sec, opening of the parachute pack in 2.3sec and full inflation of the parachute in about 5sec.

Powerplant

A fighter pilot needs as much power as he can get, so a fighter designed to be the best in the world needs most power of all. The thrust demanded for the F-15 pushed US engine technology to its limits, and the F100 turbofan has had its share of problems. But when a principal source of engine wear turns out to be pilots flying aircraft in ways that were never possible before the manufacturers have reason to congratulate themselves. Meanwhile, the F100 has formed the basis for newer powerplants, and new second generation turbofans were developed to offset the huge weight growth of the most recent F-15s.

Development of the Pratt & Whitney F100 turbofan started in August 1968, when the USAF awarded development contracts to P&W and General Electric for engines suitable for use in the planned FX fighter. In view of the high thrust-to-weight ratio planned for the new fighter, the resulting engines would have to push the technology of the time to its limits. P&W faced the daunting task of developing a powerplant producing 25 per cent more thrust per unit of weight than the then-current TF30 turbofan used in the F-111, and twice that of the J75 turbojet used in the F-105 Thunderchief and F-106 Delta Dart.

Both companies built and ran demonstration engines whose light weight, high thrust and low fuel consumption were well in advance of previous designs. The P&W engine was selected by the USAF for further development, contracts being awarded in 1970. Two versions were originally planned – the F100 for the USAF and the F401, intended to power later models of the US Navy's

Below: An F-15A of the 32nd TFS, its engines in full afterburner, accelerates down the runway at Camp New Amsterdam.

F-14 Tomcat, but the latter was cancelled when the USN was ordered by the Department of Defense to cut back the size of the planned F-14 fleet.

The F100 is an axial-flow turbofan with a bypass ratio of 0.7:1. It has two shafts – one carrying a three-stage fan driven by a two-stage turbine, the other carrying the ten-stage main compressor and its two-stage turbine. The completed engine is 191in (4.85m) long and 34.8in (0.88m) in diameter at the inlet, and weighs 3,068lb (1,391kg).

Powder metallurgy
New technologies used in the F100 included powder metallurgy. Instead of forming some metal components in the traditional manner, P&W reduced the raw material to a powder. This could be heated and formed under high pressure to create engine components better able to tolerate the high temperatures planned for the F100 core.

Operating temperature of the F100 turbine was far above that of earlier engines. Successful turbojets of earlier vintage, such as the GE F85 which powers the F-5E, or the GE J79 used in the F-4 and F-104, had turbine inlet temperatures of around 1,800deg F

(982deg C). P&W had achieved figures of just over 2,000deg F (1,093 deg C) in the TF30 turbofan, but to meet the demanding requirements of the F100 specification involved temperatures of 2,565deg F (1,407deg C).

Use of such advanced technology resulted in an engine capable of providing the high levels of thrust required. Maximum thrust is normally described as being 'in the 15,000lb (6,800kg) thrust class' when running without afterburner, and 'in the 25,000lb (11,340kg) class' when full augmentation is selected.

Normal dry (non-afterburning) rating is 12,420lb (5,634kg), rising to a maximum of 14,670lb (6,654kg) at full Military Intermediate rating – the maximum attainable without afterburning. Specific fuel consumption (sfc) – the amount of thrust produced for each pound of fuel burned per hour – is 0.69 at normal rating and 0.71 at Military Intermediate. At full afterburning power, the F100 develops 23,830lb (10,809kg) of thrust at an sfc of 2.17. At this rating, the engine swallows an impressive 860lb (390kg) of fuel per minute.

By the time the F-15 was ready for its first flight in July 1972, the F100 had

Above: The convergent/divergent nozzles of an F-15's twin Pratt & Whitney F100s fully open in the afterburning position.

completed most of its test programme, meeting 23 out of 24 critical 'project milestones'. Between February and October of the following year, a series of turbine failures dogged attempts to complete the 150-hour running trial which formed part of the formal Qualification test. The latter was the most punishing series of tests to which any US military jet engine had ever been subjected, according to P&W. It included 30 hours of running at a simulated speed of Mach 2.3, and 38 hours of running at a simulated Mach 1.6.

Following completion of this test, the F100 was subjected to a further series of intensive trials, including 150 hours of running at over-temperature conditions, and a long series of accelerated Mission Tests. Conducted on the ground, but designed to simulate the stresses of operational service, these were intended to build up running time and detect potential problems. The latter were not serious enough to delay the start of production. The powerplant is

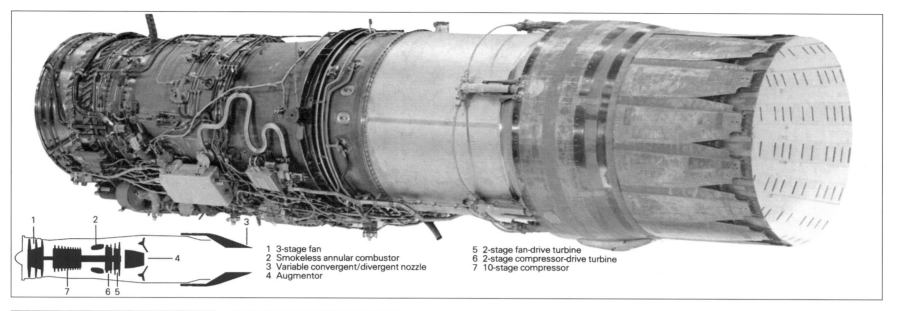

1 3-stage fan
2 Smokeless annular combustor
3 Variable convergent/divergent nozzle
4 Augmentor

5 2-stage fan-drive turbine
6 2-stage compressor-drive turbine
7 10-stage compressor

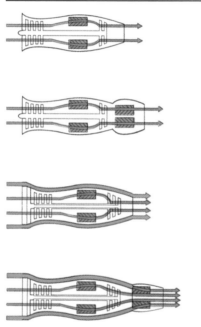

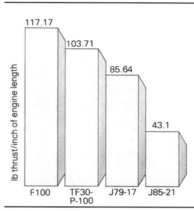

Above: Comparison of the thrust available per inch of engine length from powerplants of (left to right) the F-15, F-111F, F-4E and F-5E.

Top: Exterior of the F100, with diagram of its principal components. Nearly half its length is occupied by the augmentor chamber and nozzle.

Above: Evolution of the afterburning turbofan (bottom) via the turbojet (top), afterburning turbojet and straight turbofan.

designated F100-PW-100 by the company and JTF22A-25A by the USAF.

USAF hopes that the F100 would be a fully-reliable powerplant by the time the F-15 entered service were confounded by a series of technical and operational problems. Strikes at two major subcontractors delayed the delivery of engines, while service experience showed that the F100 was wearing out twice as fast as had been predicted. By the end of 1979 the USAF was being forced to accept engineless F-15 airframes, and by the spring of the following year around 30 were in storage. A massive effort by P&W brought the delivery situation under control, but for a long time the F-15 fleet remained short of engines.

A modification introduced into the fuel pump of the F100 created problems for the F-15 early in its career. In cruising flight, cavitation could begin in the pump, badly damaging the pump vanes. The solution adopted was simple – revert to the original design. In the case of the single-engined F-16 Fighting Falcon, which also uses the F100, a pump failure would be more serious, so Sunstrand developed an alternative dual-element pump for this aircraft. This runs at a lower speed, and should one section fail, the other can continue to deliver fuel at a lower rate.

The electronic engine control unit uses the fuel as a coolant. This technique for obtaining 'free' cooling led to problems when the F-15 first entered

Above: Factory inspection of an F100. The engine weighs 3,068lb (1,391kg) and has a thrust-to-weight ratio of nearly 8:1 at full augmentation.

service. During training missions at Luke AFB, aircraft sometimes had to wait for 45 minutes or more before takeoff, with engines running at idle settings. This gradually heated the mass of fuel in the Eagle's tanks to the point where it was no longer cold enough to cool the engine control unit.

Modified fuel flow

Given the high temperature of the desert environment at Luke, the unit could not radiate the excess heat away, so tended to overheat. This resulted in engine overspeed problems and turbine failures. The fix in this case, according to the Burrows/Shawler paper presented to the Society of Experimental Test Pilots in 1975, was to cut back the fuel flow rate of the electronic engine control, based on the rate of temperature increase, just prior to full military power. Acceleration time was reduced by this modification to less than 50 per cent of the original time.

Another early problem was that the afterburner light-up envelope was considered too restrictive. Among the more important changes was one involving the five-segment afterburner range (practically mandatory for all fan engines) designed to make a smooth transition between segments, where the

Right: Test equipment is positioned on an F100 at Pratt & Whitney's Government Products Division, West Palm Beach, Florida.

main problems were either too rich a mixture causing a light and then a blow-out, or too lean a mixture preventing a relight at all.

The spray-ring of each segment of the afterburner has a quick-fill capability which controls the light-up of each segment. The amount of fuel in each segment was the same for all altitudes and speeds, resulting in insufficient fuel at sea level and too much at high altitudes. The solution was the provision of a barometric sensor to reduce the amount of fuel fed into the quick-fill area as altitude was increased. The improvement is described as 'the biggest increment' on this problem.

The other major afterburner change

was to reduce fuel flow in full reheat mode, which countered the effects of excess fuel for airflow and afterburner size. By reducing the total fuel flow by a nominal 4,000lb/hr (1,814kg/hr), the blow-out difficulty at full reheat was eliminated. An additional benefit was equal or greater thrust for less fuel flow.

The limited throttle movement came in for some criticism at this stage of the flight testing. Originally, the rpm was to be kept to a minimum at all altitudes, thus allowing 65 per cent rpm at 40,000ft (12,000m). This caused problems in getting the engine out of idle, due to low fuel flow, while requiring a slow throttle movement for acceptable acceleration. The fix was simple enough, involving

increasing the idling rpm in line with increasing altitude.

On the air intakes, which incorporate a variable-geometry ramp to adjust the airflow at varying speeds and heights to the optimum required by the engine, months of wind-tunnel research paid off. The amount of travel provided for the ramp was found to be more than necessary, and the engine inlet compatibility testing was completed in four months. Similar testing with the F-4 Phantom took 22 months, and with the F-101 Voodoo some 30 months.

Early operational and durability problems with the F100 during the late 1970s were largely overcome by modifications plus improvements in materials, maintenance and operating procedures. Production of spare parts was accelerated, and field maintenance teams were increased in size.

Part of the problem lay in the fact that the USAF had underestimated the number of cycles which engines aboard such high-performance types as the F-15 and F-16 would actually undergo. (A cycle is defined as the temperature variation experienced in a mission from engine start to maximum power and afterburner, then back to the lower settings used for landing). In 1977 the service estimated that each engine would undergo 1.15 cycles per flight hour. In practice the rate was 2.2 for the F-15 and 3.1 for the F-16.

At one time, designers had assumed that the most arduous duty which a jet engine had to face was running for long periods at high power levels. By the late 1960s, research had shown that this was simply not the case. Many failures were due to this type of running, but others were created by the heating and cooling resulting from an engine being run up to high power then throttled back.

Technicians dubbed this 'low-cycle fatigue', but had to admit that it was difficult to measure. To aid the design of future engines such as the F100, estimates were made of the average number of thermal cycles to which an engine would be exposed per flying hour. Unfortunately for the F100 programme, these estimates were wrong. In practice, engines were being subjected to far more thermal cycles than the designers had allowed for.

Overworked engines

Paradoxically, the additional stress which the engines were receiving was largely due to the F-15 and F-16 being such good aircraft. Given the high manoeuvrability of their new mounts, pilots were flying in a manner not possible on earlier types, pushing the aircraft to high angles of attack and making full use of the extended performance envelope. In the heat of a dogfight, the throttle setting would be changed much more often than on earlier fighters. All this spelled hard work for the engine.

Critical components such as first-stage turbine blades showed signs of

Below: The titanium frames of an F-15 engine bay, with the powerplant about to be installed, as seen by the wide-angle lens.

distress, condemnation rate during repair being 60 per cent instead of the predicted 20 per cent. Maximum gas temperature was reduced to conserve component life, while R&D funding was concentrated on improvements to reliability rather than increasing thrust. Despite these problems, the F-15 had a better engine related safety record by the end of the 1970s than any other USAF fighter at a comparable point in its service career.

Another problem which was to dog the F100 during the first years of its service career was stagnation stalling. The compressor blades in a jet engine are of aerofoil section, and, like the

Above: The split tail of the F-15 allows the stabilators and vertical stabilizers to be kept well clear of the efflux from the engines.

wing of an aircraft, can be stalled if the angle at which the airflow strikes them exceeds a critical value. Powerplant stalls are occasional occurrences in most jet engines, particularly in the early stages of development, and the F100 was to prove excessively vulnerable to stagnation stalling during its first few years of operational service.

Turbofans are prone to a particularly severe type of stall from which recovery is not possible. As the flow of air through

the compressor is disturbed, the engine core loses speed, while the combustor section of the engine continues to pass hot gas to the turbine, causing the latter to overheat. If this condition is not noticed, the turbine may be damaged.

Experience with the F-15 showed that in the event of a mild hard start, the pilot might not notice that a stall had occurred, as the loss of acceleration on the twin-engined aircraft was often not sharp enough to indicate to the pilot that one engine had failed. Unless he checked the temperature gauge, low-pressure turbine entry temperature could reach the point were damage might occur. To avoid this problem, an audible-warning system was devised.

Some stagnation stalls were found to be due to component failures, but most were linked with afterburner problems. The latter usually took the form of 'hard starts' – virtually mini-explosions within the afterburner. In some cases the afterburner failed to light on schedule; in other instances the burner extinguished. In either event, large amounts of unburned fuel were sprayed into the jetpipe, creating a momentary build-up of fuel. When this was ignited by the hot efflux from the engine core, a pressure pulse was created – the aerospace equivalent of a car backfiring.

Deliberate hard start

A reporter from the journal *Aviation Week* gave this account of a deliberately-induced hard start on a test stand: "The force of the auto-ignition was sufficient to rock the heavily sound-insulated concrete test building. A large gout of flame at the afterburner exhaust was seen on the closed-circuit color-television system."

The pressure in the afterburner resulting from a hard start sent a shock wave back up through the fan duct. When this reached the front section of the engine, it could cause the fan to stall, the high-pressure compressor to stall, or, in the worst case, both. It was sometimes possible for a series of stagnation stalls to occur, with each resulting in the afterburner hard start needed to trigger off another.

Stagnation stalls usually took place at altitude and at high Mach numbers, but rarely below 20,000ft (6,100m). Normal recovery method was for the pilot to shut down the engine, and allow it to spool down. Once the tachometer showed that engine rpm had fallen below the 50 per cent mark, the throttle could safely be reopened to the idle position, and the F100 would carry out its automatic relight sequence. Critical factor in restarting the engine after a stagnation stall is the low-pressure turbine-inlet temperature. This must fall to 450deg F (232deg C) before the engine can be restarted.

Several modifications were devised to reduce the frequency of stagnation stalls. The first approach taken was to try to prevent pressure build-ups in the afterburner. A quartz window in the side of the afterburner assembly allowed a flame sensor to monitor the pilot flame of the augmentor. If this went out, the flow of fuel to the outer sections of the burner was stopped.

When the F100 engine-control system was originally designed, P&W engineers allowed for the possibility that ingestion of efflux from missiles might stall the engine. A 'rocket fire' facility was designed into the controls in order to cope with such an eventuality. When missiles were fired, an electronic signal could be sent to the unified fuel control system which supplies fuel to the engine core and to the afterburner. The angle of the variable stator blades in the engine could be altered to avoid a stall,

while the fuel flow to the engine was momentarily reduced, and the afterburner exhaust was increased in area to reduce the magnitude of any pressure pulse in the afterburner.

Tests had shown that the 'rocket fire' facility was not needed, but P&W engineers were able to use it as a means of preventing stagnation stalls. Engine shaft speed, turbine temperature and the angle of the compressor stator blades are monitored on the F100 by a digital electronic engine control unit. This normally serves to 'fine-tune' the engine throughout flight to ensure optimum performance.

By monitoring and comparing HP spool speed and fan exhaust temperature, the engine control unit is able to sense that a stagnation stall is about to take place, and send a dummy 'Rocket Fire' signal to the unified fuel control system to initiate the anti-stall measures described above. At the same time, a second modification to the fuel control system reduces the afterburner setting to zone 1 – little more than a pilot light – in order to help reduce pressure within the jetpipe.

In an attempt to prevent any pulses coming forward through the fan duct from affecting the core, P&W engineers devised a modification known as the 'proximate splitter'. This is a forward extension to the internal casing which

Below: Eagles rendezvous with a KC-10A tanker. Specific fuel consumption of the F100 is 2.17 with full augmentation.

splits the incoming airflow coming from the engine compressor fan, passing some to the core of the engine and diverting the remainder down the fan duct, past the core and into the afterburner. By closing the gap between the front end of this casing and the rear of the fan to just under half an inch (1.3cm), the engine designers reduced the size of the path by which the high-pressure pulses from the burner had been reaching the core.

Engines fitted with the proximate splitter were test-flown in the F-15, but this modification was not embodied in the engines of production Eagles, whose twin engines made the loss of a

Above: The 'nodding' air intakes on either side of the F-15's forward fuselage are necessary to maintain the optimum rate of airflow to the engines, and for operation at high angles of attack.

single engine less hazardous. It was, however, fitted to engines destined for the single-engined F-16.

The improvement in reliability as a result of the modifications to the fuel control system and nozzle was dramatic. Back in 1976, the F-15 fleet experienced a stagnation stall rate of 11–12 per 1,000 flying hours; by the end of 1981 this had dropped to 1.5 per 1,000 hours.

Above: A two-seat F-15 approaches a tanker boom for refuelling. Economical at normal ratings, the F100 consumes 860lb (390kg) of fuel per minute in full afterburner.

Efforts are under way to further reduce the smoke output of the F100 as part of a planned component-improvement programme. For example, the combustor has been modified to increase the velocity of the airflow in its front end, resulting in improved mixing of air and fuel and leading to more complete combustion and less residual smoke.

Traditional engine-servicing techniques involve replacing critical components at the end of a statistically-calculated lifetime. This often results in components being removed and scrapped while still perfectly servicable, giving good safety margins, but at a high cost to the operator. The USAF now wants engine designers to develop

parts with greater tolerance to crack damage so that these may be left in the engine until inspection by non-destructive test (NDT) methods shows that cracks are starting to develop and a replacement is needed. Life-cycle costs may be cut by up to 60 per cent.

The service's Damage Tolerant Design (DTD) programme involved both Pratt & Whitney and General Electric, and focussed much of its attention on the F100. One of the programme's first achievements was a new pattern of F100 fan disc having five times the life of the original component. Key design elements under DTD are high quality control of the raw material, and the avoidance of shapes and configurations such as sharp radii which cause stress concentrations.

The Air Force plans to begin testing engine discs currently under development as part of the DTD programme in 1984, and hopes to fit these into operational engines before the end of that

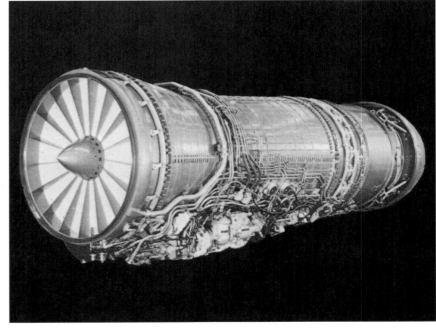

Below left: The General Electric F110 has been test-flown in an F-15, and is one candidate to power future variants of the Eagle.

Top: The P&W PW1120 is based on the core of the F100: smaller and lighter, it is to be used in the Israel Aircraft Industries Lavi fighter.

Above: The other potential replacement for the F100 is P&W's own PW1128, which began test-flying in March 1983.

year. By 1985 or 1986 the F100 may be fitted with second and third-stage turbine blades and vanes manufactured using a single-crystal technique. Although more expensive than components made from traditional materials, these will probably have a lifetime at least twice that of current vanes and blades.

The USAF was the first F100 user to take advantage of a warranty scheme offered by P&W in 1980. The company undertook to repair or replace certain high-pressure turbines unserviceable as a result of wear or mechanical failure at no extra cost to the USAFD. Engines covered by the deal were from production Lot IX and were delivered during 1981 and 1982.

To qualify for free treatment, faulty engines would have to have carried out less that 900 equivalents of the TAC engine operating cycle (about two years of normal use) or develop the fault

within three and a half years of delivery. If the HP failure had caused secondary damage to the engine, P&W undertook to cover costs up to 75 per cent of that of a new engine.

Pratt & Whitney are continuing research into new engines based on the F100 and its technology. During a series of tests carried out in late summer of 1982, the company ground-tested an F100 fitted with a two-dimensional nozzle. Rectangular in cross-section, this is a convergent/divergent design featuring moveable upper and lower surfaces which could be used to vector the thrust. This design was developed under a USAF contract, and while no production applications were planned, vectored thrust nozzles were to become essential for the next generation of air combat fighters.

Angles of up to 20deg were demonstrated, but P&W was confident that the design would be good for up to 30deg. Coupled with the use of thrust reversing, this technique could greatly in-

crease the agility of current aircraft, and could cut the take-off run to 1,200ft (366m) or less. Earlier attempts to design axisymmetric nozzles with vectoring and thrust-reversing have resulted in complex and heavy units which paid a high penalty in thrust loss. The latest P&W design could be offered as an add-on modification, weighing only a few hundred pounds, to the standard F100 gas generator section.

Using experience gained from the F100 programme, P&W was able to begin development of the cropped-fan PW1120 afterburning turbofan. Based on the core of the earlier engine, this is a low-risk development with 60 per cent commonality, but incorporating a new low-pressure compressor and turbine and a simplified afterburner. Operating temperatures have been slightly reduced, and the PW1120 has a slightly lower thrust-to-weight ratio of 7.25:1 instead of 7.9:1. The PW1120 is some 20in (51cm) shorter than the F100 and

7in (18cm) narrower in diameter. It is rated at 20,620lb (9,342kg) and was planned to fly early in 1984. The first application of the PW1120 to be announced was the planned Israel Aircraft Industries Lavi air combat fighter.

Two other engines were proposed for retrofitting to the F-15, and to power later variants of the F-14 and the F-16. These were the General Electric F110 and the Pratt & Whitney F100-PW-220. The latter was selected, and began to enter service in 1986.

The thrust of this version was slightly less than that of the original, but while performance and manoeuvrability were slightly reduced this was more than compensated by far greater durability. Engine failures became largely a thing of the past.

Greater power was needed by the F-15E Strike Eagle, to compensate for its massive all-up weight of 81,000lb (36,741kg). The F100-PW-229 provided 17,800lb (8,074kg) of thrust in dry power and 29,100lb (13,200kg) with full augmentation. The -229 is obviously a candidate for re-engining the F-15C/D, but even with the -220 this is a match for most contemporary fighters.

Avionics

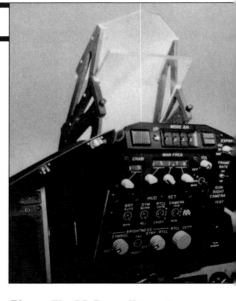

The key to the Eagle's combat capability is its sophisticated suite of avionics: long-range, look-down radar that can detect even low-flying targets at ranges of up to 100 miles (160km); a tactical electronic warfare system to warn of any threat; and displays and controls that present the pilot with almost all the information he needs and allow him to control weapon systems and radar without looking inside the cockpit. The addition of programmable signal processing has further increased the radar capability, and for the ground-attack role still more improvements are planned.

When considering the anatomy of a modern aeroplane the airframe can be likened to the skeleton and flesh, the engines provide muscle and the on-board computers and avionics can be considered as the brain and nervous system. For many years the avionic systems were relatively simple and were purely add-on items to assist in communication and navigation: failure of any one item did not create any great problem, and the aeroplane could fly quite happily under human control and judgement. Then came the great electronic revolution and the emergence of the silicon chip.

The evolution of the integrated circuit – an entire microelectronic system embodied in a chip of semiconductive material, normally crystalline silicon – brought immediate gains to the designers of avionic equipment. The size and weight of 'black boxes' could be drastically reduced; power consumption fell, the associated need for complicated cooling systems; reliability increased; and, perhaps most significantly, the new devices allowed for a considerable expansion of functions.

Computers that had once required large storage space shrank to shoe-box size, offered great reliability and could be programmed for a variety of complex tasks. With programming came the new word 'software', denoting an arcane, subjective art that can achieve the apparently impossible.

Generally, software can be considered as the process of telling a computer what to do and how to do it, while making the process understandable to the computer itself. This last consideration is crucial to efficient operation, since a computer totally lacks judgement and intuition and cannot relate in any useful manner to past experience. Consequently, the software must be able to dictate behaviour under all operating conditions including abnormal situations.

High-speed operation

A major advantage of electronic systems is that they operate at the speed of light, allowing a considerable number of operations to take place in a very short space of time. If a pilot operates a switch which affects a circuit under computer control and at that point the computer is working hard it may introduce a delay of perhaps one tenth of a second. This is a valuable breathing space for the computer, yet so short as to be entirely unnoticeable to the pilot.

As well as operational functions, software programs can be used to carry out automatic test and system monitoring, constantly evaluating the health of the associated hardware and providing an indication of malfunction to the pilot. This is an extremely important part of a modern avionic system, usually referred to as built-in test equipment (BITE). It enables failures to be identified and isolated, allowing the pilot to carry on with the operation by selecting alternate systems. One manufacturer of such equipment is on record as saying that a typical system with 100,000 computer instructions may use almost three quarters of this capacity for diagnostic purposes.

As the electronic revolution gained pace so avionic equipment became more complex. By the early 1970s systems were evolving with considerable computational powers, and with digital computers forming an integral part. Reliability had improved and maintenance had been simplified by the use of self-checking systems. More and more critical functions came under the control of electronic systems and the avionic suite now ranked alongside airframe and engine as an essential and fundamental element. Integration of these three areas has reached the point where it is now inconceivable that any part of a modern military aircraft should not be under some form of electronic control of influence.

A modern aeroplane such as the F-15 depends upon electronic systems for communication, navigation, flight management, weapons management, automatic flight control (auto-pilot), systems control and management (eg hydraulics and pressurization), control and management of electronic warfare (EW) systems and the continual monitoring of all aspects of engine and airframe operation and maintenance. Indeed, the pace of change in modern technology and military tactics to meet evolving threats is such that any simple list of electronic devices is necessarily incomplete. Although the aeroplane appears externally unchanged, its black boxes can undergo constant evolution and refinement, and the practised eye can sometimes note the addition of certain lumps, bulges and antennas on the external surface of the airframe.

Above: The McDonnell Douglas head-up display present all essential navigation and attack information to the Eagle pilot.

Below: Nose radars, HUDs and bubble canopies give these F-15s unmatched target detection ability.

Air-to-air gun mode

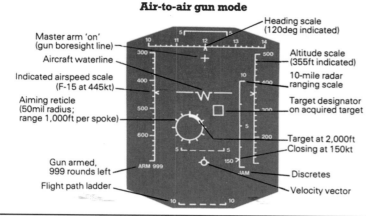

- Master arm 'on' (gun boresight line)
- Aircraft waterline
- Indicated airspeed scale (F-15 at 445kt)
- Aiming reticle (50mil radius; range 1,000ft per spoke)
- Gun armed, 999 rounds left
- Flight path ladder
- Heading scale (120deg indicated)
- Altitude scale (355ft indicated)
- 10-mile radar ranging scale
- Target designator on acquired target
- Target at 2,000ft
- Closing at 150kt
- Discretes
- Velocity vector

Air-to-air medium range missile mode

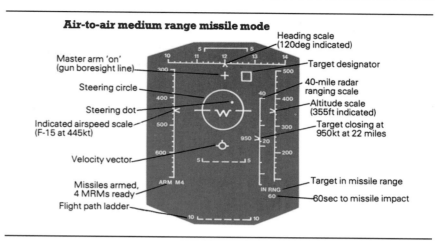

- Master arm 'on' (gun boresight line)
- Steering circle
- Steering dot
- Indicated airspeed scale (F-15 at 445kt)
- Velocity vector
- Missiles armed, 4 MRMs ready
- Flight path ladder
- Heading scale (120deg indicated)
- Target designator
- 40-mile radar ranging scale
- Altitude scale (355ft indicated)
- Target closing at 950kt at 22 miles
- Target in missile range
- 60sec to missile impact

Air-to-ground automatic mode

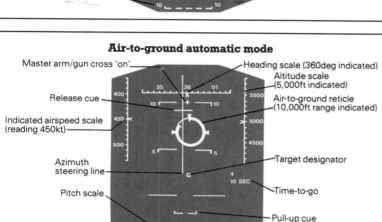

- Master arm/gun cross 'on'
- Release cue
- Indicated airspeed scale (reading 450kt)
- Azimuth steering line
- Pitch scale
- Heading scale (360deg indicated)
- Altitude scale (5,000ft indicated)
- Air-to-ground reticle (10,000ft range indicated)
- Target designator
- Time-to-go
- Pull-up cue

Air-to-ground CDIP mode

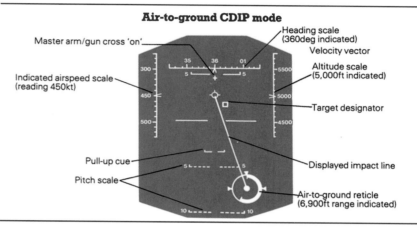

- Master arm/gun cross 'on'
- Indicated airspeed scale (reading 450kt)
- Pull-up cue
- Pitch scale
- Heading scale (360deg indicated)
- Velocity vector
- Altitude scale (5,000ft indicated)
- Target designator
- Displayed impact line
- Air-to-ground reticle (6,900ft range indicated)

Above: Typical displays presented by the F-15 HUD showing the symbology used in various air-to-air and air-to-ground attack modes.

This is an important aspect of avionic innovation as it can enhance abilities and performance even though the aircraft is still restricted by its own basic dynamic performance. In other words, the power/weight ratio tends to remain constant, but its electronic eyes and brain can become more far-seeing and powerful so that it can be a more effective fighting machine.

The basic electrical power of the F-15 is provided by engine driven generators manufactured by the Lear Siegler Power Equipment Division. These feature a 40/50kVA generator constant speed drive unit, produced by the Sundstrand Corporation, which ensures that the generator itself is always driven at a constant speed regardless of engine speed or revolutions. This in turn ensures a constant, steady output of closely controlled electrical power in terms of voltage, frequency and phase and does away with the need for additional on-board devices to ensure such

basic integrity of power supplies. Power is then distributed throughout the aircraft via other control systems, circuit breakers, distribution boards and transformer-rectifiers to ensure adequate power, of the correct type, for each sequence of operation. For instance, certain switched selection circuits can accept fairly brutal power sources while other types of instrumentation require highly accurate and sensitive power inputs.

Much of the flight information can be presented to the pilot on a cathode ray tube (CRT) display, which can accept

inputs from radar or electro-optical sensors. This is in line with the current trend for information to be presented in visual terms, often supported by colour. The pilot can assimilate more information more efficiently and ambiguity is reduced. An IBM on-board digital air data computer is used to process information from other sensors such as al-

Below: View through the head-up display following the launch of a medium-range AIM-7 Sparrow. The missile itself is visible in the target designator box.

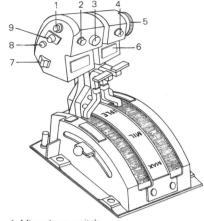

1 Microphone switch
2 IFF interrogate button
3 Target designate control
4 Gunsight reticle stiffen/reject short-range missile
5 Radar antenna elevation control
6 ECM dispenser switch
7 Weapon selection switch (gun, short-range missile or medium-range missile)
8 Spare
9 Speed brake switch

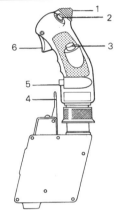

1 Trim button
2 Weapon release button
3 Radar auto acquisition switch
4 Autopilot/nose gear steering release switch
5 SRM/EO weapon seeker head cage/uncage control
6 HUD camera and gun trigger

Above: The throttles (top) and control stick carry all the weapons and radar controls needed in combat, enabling the pilot to keep his eyes attention on the target or HUD.

The F-15 carries such a system in the Northrop ALQ-135, which is part of the aircraft's tactical electronic warfare system (TEWS) and is associated with the active jamming role.

More readily apparent is the Loral ALR-56 radar warning receiver, four external antennas mounted at each wing tip and on top of each fin give them a distinctive, easily recognizable shape. A fifth blade-shaped antenna is mounted under the forward fuselage. Associated equipment includes receivers, power supply, receiver controls and a display of an alpha-numeric type which indicates the degree of lethality and range of the emerging threat. The all-solid-state ALR-56 is based on a digitally controlled dual channel receiver which scans from H-band through to J-band (6-20GHz), while changes in the perceived threat can be accommodated by changes in software.

The APG-63 radar

While it is invidious to suggest that any one part of the avionic system is more important than any other in these days of integrated and interrelated systems, it is hard not to admit that the awesome capability of the Hughes APG-63 radar is really the heart of the F-15 and the

timeters, and this too is presented on the CRT display.

Communication is usually through VHF/UHF links, which essentially form a line-of-sight system. In other words, the range of the equipment is directly proportional to the aircraft's height above the ground. For long-distance flights, therefore, the communications system is supplemented by HF to provide the necessary range. Interference by the enemy is always a problem in communications and several programmes have been undertaken to overcome the problem. Typically, the signal can be spread over a wide spectrum to reduce the chances of detection and require a widely spread jamming signal with consequent dissipation of power and loss of effectiveness.

The aircraft's Litton ASN-109 navigation system is based upon inertial navigation techniques. This is a completely

passive, on-board system which does not have to rely on ground-based aids and is largely automatic in operation. It depends upon highly sensitive gyroscopes which are used to accurately align a platform in relation to true North. The pilot tells the computer the start point and can add several desired destinations or waypoints, and as the aircraft moves off, accelerometers on the platform detect rates of movement. All the information is then processed by a digital computer, which comes up with a variety of answers which are displayed to the pilot. This information includes position, time to go to next waypoint and wind conditions.

The high degree of accuracy of platform stabilization can give attitude information for the aircraft's flight instruments providing pitch, roll and heading data at all times. This navigation system is backed up by ground-based navaids

such as TACAN, ADF and ILS allowing the F-15 to integrate with any type of traffic pattern. In a cross-country mode these aids can be used to update the inertial system.

Among the most classified equipment is that concerned with aspects of electronic warfare (EW). This is also likely to be the system most often modified, changed and reprogrammed. EW systems can be used to detect radars, notify the pilot of various types of hostile EW and allow a degree of offensive reaction such as jamming enemy signals. Such is the state of modern electronics that many of these devices act completely automatically and can recognize the difference between friendly and hostile emissions. They are capable of reacting to rapid changes in the enemy scenario and can fire off decoys such as chaff or infra-red (IR) flares to confuse the seeker of enemy missiles.

EMERGENCY
AIR REFUELING
HANDLE

T PANEL

IFF

RADAR

FUEL

COMMUNICATIONS

EXTERIOR LIGHTS

Left: A feature of the left console is the BIT (built-in-test) equipment panel, allowing the pilot to locate faults in the avionics.

Below left: Adjusting the head-up display controls of an F-15D during pre-flight checks at Kadena Air Base, Okinawa.

foundation of its air combat efficiency.

When the F-15 was designed its primary mission of air superiority depended on an advanced fire control radar. The daunting specification numbered among its requirements: use in a single-seat aircraft to track targets at extremely long ranges; close-in and look-down operation that would blind other radars; a clutter-free radar display which would show all target information; the ability to provide tracking and steering data on a head up display (HUD) allowing the pilot to keep his eyes on the target; ease of operation; weapons control and coordination; and selected air-to-ground capabilities. In addition it was expected to reach high standards of reliability and maintainability.

Such a requirement would have been unthinkable a few years earlier and showed just how much influence the new electronics could have on the capabilities of a new aircraft. Even so, to meet the specification certain compromises had to be reached and innovative techniques employed to the full.

Most airborne radars work in the X-band (8–12.5GHz) and choice of frequency is the first area of compromise. The critical factor in an aircraft is the size of the antenna: in a fighter the most convenient position is in the nose, where space is restricted by aerodynamic considerations. It so happens that X band produces a good compromise antenna size. Dropping to S band demands a larger antenna, while going further up, say to K band, offers a small and neater antenna but a signal which is adversely affected by meteorological conditions such as rain – hardly a good choice for a modern fighter aircraft.

Pulse repetition frequency

Another fundamental choice is that of the pulse repetition frequency (PRF) which refers to the number of transmitted pulses per second. This is often classed as high or low, with high considered to be energy transmitted at 100,000 or more pulses per second while low is only some 1,000 pulses per second. In general terms, the use of a high PRF in the pulse-Doppler radars common in fighters gives good long-range detection of head-on targets, but a restricted detection of tail-on targets and a tendency to lose track of manoeuvring targets.

In comparison, the low-PRF radars then commonly employed for air combat proved to be good for ground mapping but could not detect targets in a look-down mode. It seemed that the compromise choice of a medium PRF would offer improved performance against manoeuvring targets, but at the expense of long range detection.

Hughes overcame the difficulty by developing a radar that had all three PRF modes. High and medium operate together, while low is used for ground mapping. So emerged the APG-63 multi-mode pulse-Doppler radar with an all-altitude, all-aspect attack capability and a maximum detection range in excess of 100 miles (160km). It can also guide radar-controlled missiles against all

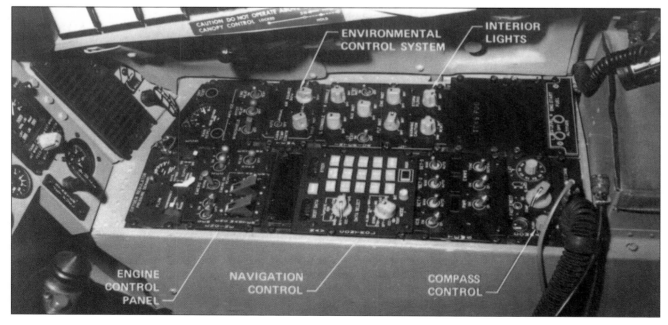

CAUTION DO NOT OPERATE
CANOPY CONTROL

ENVIRONMENTAL
CONTROL SYSTEM

INTERIOR
LIGHTS

ENGINE
CONTROL
PANEL

NAVIGATION
CONTROL

COMPASS
CONTROL

Left: Layout of the navigation, engine and environmental system controls on the F-15 cockpit's right console.

Below: The radar display format used in the Strike Eagle includes a window which can be moved to select enlarged patch maps.

Bottom: Comparative effective ranges of the F-15's APG-63 and the MiG-25's Fox Fire radars, showing the former's clear advantage.

Above: Scott AFB, Illinois, as seen by the camera (right) and as an 8.5ft (2.6m) resolution ground map produced by the F-15 AFCD radar.

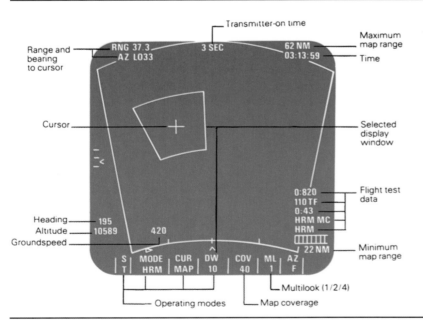

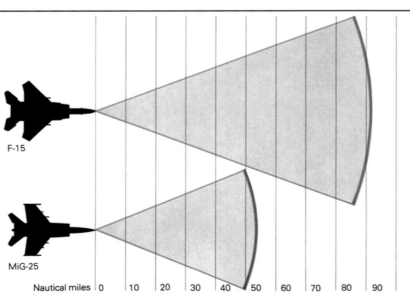

types of target. The primary radar controls are mounted on the aircraft's throttle so allowing the pilot to keep his head up during combat. The HUD shows target positioning, steering, range data and weapons release data.

The radar display provides a clear, clutter-free presentation and look-down view of any target aircraft even in the presence of heavy ground clutter. This ability is the result of a combination of both high and low PRF; digital processing of data, and the use of Kalman filtering in the tracking loops. The last process is a computer technique which continually compares the relative errors of the on-board equipment and data from the external sensors – in other words, a form of averaging of available data. In addition, the radar uses a gridded travelling wave tube that permits variation of the radar waveform to suit the prevailing situation.

Another problem with radar is that of false alarms. These are eliminated by the use of a low-sidelobe antenna – which is a good preventative against enemy EW – a guard receiver and frequency rejection of ground clutter and ground moving targets. Air-to-ground modes include target ranging for automated weapon release, a mapping mode for navigation and, thanks to the Doppler element, a velocity update for the INS. The nose-mounted antenna is a planar array that is hydraulically driven and gimballed in three axes.

Combat evaluation

When the radar first came into operation in the F-15 a series of air combat evaluations were carried out by USAF pilots flying the aircraft against seven different types of aircraft modified to simulate leading threats, and the F-15 won by a handsome margin. More significantly, perhaps, it took part in a series of exercises in which an E-3A Sentry AWACS faces attack by a large force. The F-15 proved to be successful in 38 out of 39 intercepts and its radar overcame the effects of jamming techniques.

Further improvement came with the

development of a programmable signal processor (PSP). This is a feature of all new AN/APG-63s and is available as a retrofit item to earlier models. When it appeared, in 1979, this was the only known deployed PSP and was considered to be a key element in expanding the F-15's tactical air interdiction role while enhancing its tactical air superiority capability. The PSP is a high-speed, special-purpose computer which controls the radar modes through its software rather than through a hard wired circuit design; this allows rapid switching of modes for maximum operational flexibility. PSP-modified radar is fitted to the 420th and subsequent Eagles, which are designated F-15C (single-seat) and F-16D (two-seat).

The use of the PSP paved the way for the modification of an ANAPG-63 to provide synthetic aperture radar (SAR). The modification followed on from earlier SAR work in the USAF Forward-looking Advanced Multimode Radar (FLAMR) programme. The PSP in this instance is a fourth-generation model which performs over seven million operations per second.

SAR imagery sharpens mapping details and provides the pilot with an overhead view, as if he were flying directly over the target, when in fact he can be 100 miles (160km) away. Previously, such imagery had to be processed on the ground because suitable equipment was too large to be easily fitted into an aircraft and processing speed was too slow for real time display.

The first flight of the new radar in an F-15 took place in November 1980, and initially a radar mapping resolution of 127ft (39m) was obtained. Within a month it was down to 60ft (18m) – still not good enough for the recognition of small tactical targets. By the 40th test flight, however, resolution was down to the stipulated level of just 10ft (3m).

This degree of resolution means that at a distance of 20–30 miles (30–50km) from the target street patterns, power lines and field boundaries are visible. At 10 miles (16km) from an airfield a ⅔-mile (1km) square radar map can be displayed and aircraft as little as 8ft 6in (2.6m) apart can be clearly recognized. Other targets may be seen equally clearly, making target selection easy and unambiguous. The radar maps are updated every few seconds and linked to the navigation systems and weapons modes for ground attack preparations.

By this time, too, MCAIR had developed low-drag fuel pallets to increase the F-15's ferry range. These are two close fitting packs known as fuel and sensor tactical (FAST) packs. In addition to increased fuel tankage, the FAST packs allow a greater range of electronic sensors to be carried, including optical cameras, low light level TV cameras and a laser designator.

Enhanced Eagles

Coincident with this development, the manufacturers suggested that the USAF needed an all-weather fighter capable of performing long-range, air-to-ground interdiction missions while maintaining its air-to-air capabilities, and suggested than an enhanced Eagle would fulfil these requirements.

Two-seater F-15 Eagles had been built and were externally identifiable only by their larger cockpit canopy. This allowed them to function as trainers as well as being combat capable. The manufacturer used one of these two-seaters in a company-funded project known as Strike Eagle to create an all-weather, day/night ground attack aircraft using the new SAR radar integrated with forward looking infra-red (FLIR) system of the Pave Tack pod. The rear cockpit was modified to allow a specialist crew member to handle the radar and FLIR inputs.

The rear cockpit was fitted with four electronic displays and two hand controllers which allow the crew member to focus his attention on the displays while operating systems and controlling

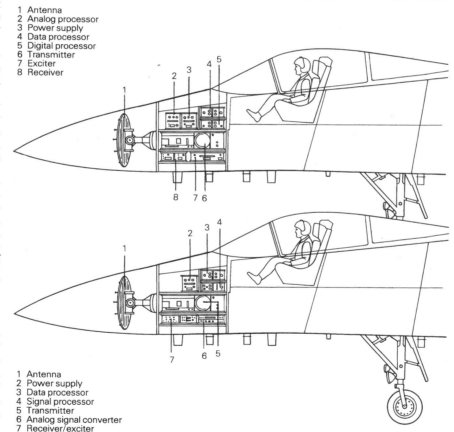

1 Antenna
2 Analog processor
3 Power supply
4 Data processor
5 Digital processor
6 Transmitter
7 Exciter
8 Receiver

1 Antenna
2 Power supply
3 Data processor
4 Signal processor
5 Transmitter
6 Analog signal converter
7 Receiver/exciter

Above: Comparison of the standard APG-63 (top) and the PSP-modified equipment carried by the F-15C.

display content. Two of the displays are used for navigational purposes, one for weapon selection and one to monitor enemy tracking systems.

At the same time, improving electronic systems had created more sensitive electronic countermeasures sensors and the manufacturers proposed an Advanced Wild Weasel F-15. The outcome of these projects is described elsewhere in this book though they deserve mention in the evolution of the aircraft's avionic systems.

In 1981, another advanced avionic feature became linked with the F-15,

when the Integrated Flight/Fire Control (IFFC) and Firefly III programmes were initiated. The IFFC 1 programme, being undertaken by MCAIR under a $14 million contract from the Air Force Flight Dynamics Laboratory, is for the design, development, integration and flight testing of a system which couples the Eagle's fire control and flight control systems to accept dual control inputs and tailor flight control response to the various weapons delivery modes. The Firefly III programme, being conducted by the General Electric Aircraft Equipment Division under a $7 million Air Force Avionics Laboratory contract for the further development of the fire control system.

The IFFC/Firefly III coupling will

Above: Routine maintenance on an F-15A's APG-63 radar. All the equipment is readily accessible, and individual components are easily removable for repair.

allow automatic positioning of the aircraft to attack targets detected by an electro-optical target designation pod. This is expected to shorten engagement times and enable the aircraft to drop its bombs or stores without having to overfly the target. The F-15 in the Firefly programme carries a Martin Marietta-built Atlis II designator pod in the port forward missile well and this is linked to the aircraft's fly-by-wire system via an intermediate additional digital computer.

The USAF had become aware of its need to have a long-range all-weather interdiction aircraft, preferably a multi-role type to replace the aging Phantom. The Panavia Tornado IDS was considered, and USAF Chief of Staff General Allen examined this (including a flight demonstration at RAF Wittering) before it was rejected. USAF doctrine of the day called for medium-level ingress and egress under cover of intensive ECM and defence suppression. Tornado IDS, with its ultra low level attack profile, ran counter to this. Tornado would of course have been ideal for the Phantom Wild Weasel replacement, but the NIH (not invented here) syndrome blocked it.

Rather than designing a new aircraft from scratch, the obvious answer was to modify an existing type, mainly with improved avionics. Two contenders were chosen: the F-15 and the F-16. It soon emerged that a two-seater was needed, with a back-seater to handle all the electronic magic. This made the F-15, which had the greatest growth capability, and was easily adapted for the two-man strike mission, the front-runner. A new radar, APG-70, with additional air to ground modes, and other avionics, was easily accommodated in the F-15, which eventually emerged as the F-15E Strike Eagle.

Possibly the greatest operational

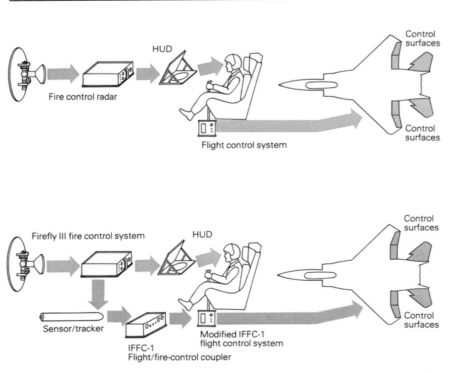

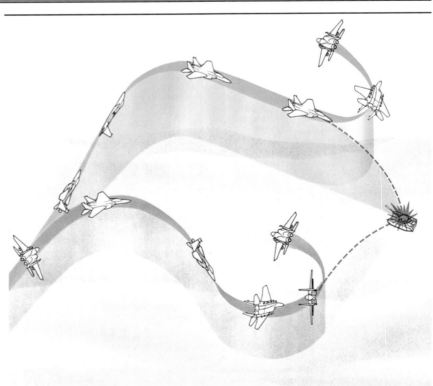

Left: The blue bar below the cockpit of this F-15E Echo is a station-keeping light, invisible at all but close range as it cruises out into the gathering darkness.

Below left: The Strike Eagle's APG-63 was modified to use synthetic aperture radar techniques for high resolution ground mapping.

Right: Illuminated indicators on the front panel include fire warning (top left), canopy unlocked (top right), air-to-ground mode button and beacon light (centre) landing gear (bottom left) and caution panel (bottom right).

Below right: The IFFC/Firefly III F-15B, with Martin Marietta ATLIS II optical sensor and tracker pod on the port wing missile pylon.

problem that had to be overcome in the advanced role was that of survivability. This has been achieved with the use of advanced sensors and more capable avionics, with a two-man crew, while forward-looking infra-red (FLIR) was needed for low altitude flight at night or in poor visibility, using terrain-avoidance radar and a radar altimeter. Some of this innovation has evolved as part of the Multi-Stage Improvement Programme (MSIP), which has included the introduction of Seek Talk (a programme to reduce the vulnerability of UHF radios to enemy jamming by modifying existing radios with the addition of spread spectrum techniques and the use of a null steering antenna) and other sensors.

Global Positioning System

The next event in the evolving avionics scene was the introduction of the Global Positioning System (GPS), which was expected to revolutionize navigation, although it required satellites which could be vulnerable in war. Two F-15s conducted GPS trials, and the complete system, consisting of a network of Navstar satellites orbiting the Earth, was operational by 1990.

It has developed into a network of Navstar satellites circling the earth. Thousands of ground receivers mounted in all types of military vehicles and even carried by foot soldiers translate satellite signals into navigation information that is accurate to within 10-20m anywhere in the world, day or night and regardless of weather. The information includes altitude, longitude, velocity to 0.1m/sec and a precise time in nanoseconds.

The Navstar satellites orbit the earth at an altitude of 12,500 miles (20,000km), each one continuously broadcasting time and position messages. This information greatly enhances tactical air operations and is a potent all-weather navigation system. Advanced anti-jamming techniques are built into the system to permit continuing operation under the most stringent of enemy EW operations.

The GPS tactical air configuration provides continuous signal tracking under all flight conditions and the system is integrated with other on-board avionics so that the GPS-derived data can be used to refine other flight systems.

Far Left: Modifications introduced on the IFFC/Firefly III flight and fire control system, compared with the standard F-15 system.

Left: Typical manoeuvring attack made possible by the IFFC system (bottom) compared with the conventional pop-up attack profile.

Armament

The missiles-only fighters produced for the USAF in the late 1950s and early 1960s were found to be at a severe disadvantage over Vietnam, and the Eagle weapon system was planned from the outset to include a gun. At the same time, improved versions of the medium-range, radar-guided Sparrow and short-range, heat-seeking Sidewinder were provided. New weapons planned for the Eagle include the AIM-120 AMRAAM, while the type has also proved able to deliver air-to-ground weapons with a high degree of accuracy, which led to the dual-role F-15E Strike Eagle.

The basic requirements of the Eagle weapons system, as outlined in the Development Concept fall into three distinct categories: guns, air-to-air missiles and air-to-ground weaponry. In addition, we must also consider the use of external fuel and EW pods to enhance the basic capability of the Eagle.

During the late 1950s and early 1960s air combat with guns was thought by many to have had its day, and the latest American fighters had no guns, relying solely on air-to-air missiles. Air combat during the Vietnam War, however, revealed such an urgent need for gun armament that a new version of the F-4

Phantom, TAC's principal fighter, had to be developed with an internal 20mm gun.

From the beginning, therefore, the FX was planned with an internal gun as an integral part of its weapons system. Initial production models were to rely on the tried and true M61A1 20mm Vulcan cannon, produced by the Aircraft Equipment Division of the General Electric Company. Later models of the Eagle were to have a new 25mm cannon, using a new type of caseless ammunition, which would have the advantage of eliminating cartridge extraction and ejection systems, resulting in a

simpler mechanism. General Electric and Philco-Ford (now Ford Aerospace and Communications) both submitted designs, and after evaluation in December 1971 Philco-Ford was awarded the contract for the new gun, designated the GAU-7.

Although potentially a simpler weapon, the advantages mentioned above were offset by other problems, basically involving the ammunition. With caseless ammunition there is no spent cartridge to be wasted (or collected) after the round is fired, promising potentially enormous savings. However, the US Army had been trying to get caseless ammunition right for the previous 15 years with a continuing lack of success. (The world's first weapon designed with a successful caseless ammunition is the Heckler & Koch G-11 rifle, with ammunition from H&K in collaboration with Dynamit Nobel.)

The GAU-7 ammunition was being developed by the Brunswick Corporation. The propellent half of the 25mm round was covered with a flame retardant covering, which was stripped off mechanically as the rounds entered a

conveyor which took them to the five barrels of the weapon. This stripping mechanism was causing the ammunition conveyor to jam. Another problem involved the development of a moisture-protective material for use with the ammunition, whose final drawback was inconsistent ballistic action. In theory the higher muzzle velocity of 4,000ft/sec (1,200m/sec), compared with the 3,200ft/sec (975m/sec) of the M61, meant that not only did the projectile reach the target sooner than an M61 round, but also that it had a flatter trajectory, producing a more concentrated hit pattern on the target and giving a higher probability of kill. Unfortunately, the whole system proved too unreliable.

By September 1973, with over $100 million spent on development, the problems with the GAU-7 had still to be overcome, and with other new-technology items on the Eagle running reasonably smoothly, the Air Force decided to

Above: F-15 in standard air superiority configuration, with four AIM-7s and four AIM-9s.

Left: Armourers use a conveyor belt to load 20mm ammunition into an F-15 ammunition drum. The links are stripped during the loading process.

Below: Radar-guided Sparrow for BVR engagements and short-range Sidewinders form a potent combination.

Right: Missile launch as seen from the back of a two-seat F-15. At one stage the USAF switched to an all-missile armament, but during the Vietnam war the F-4 had to be revised to accommodate a gun, since many engagements took place at ranges too short for a missile to be launched effectively.

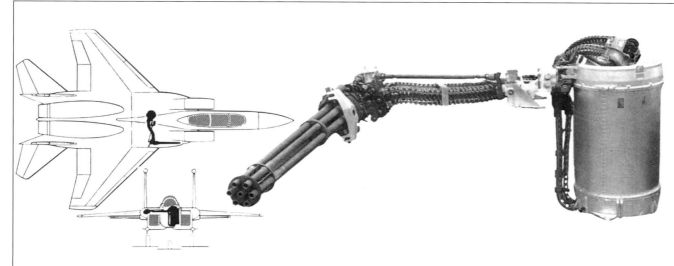

Left: The General Electric M61 Vulcan 20mm gun system, and details of its location in the F-15 airframe. The gun could not be mounted in the nose, since this would interfere with the radar, and the wing root alternative was found to be eminently satisfactory. The ammunition drum, housing 940 rounds, is mounted in the centre fuselage; a linkless feed system transports the rounds to the gun and carries the spent cartridge cases back again. This system has proved extremely reliable in operation.

cut its losses. Although Philco-Ford proposed a year's delay on the programme, it was cancelled and replaced by the M61, of 1954 vintage.

. The M61A1 is an exceptionally reliable system. Its rotary action allows a rate of fire of some 6,000 rounds per minute (although only 940 rounds are carried on the Eagle). The use of six barrels minimizes erosion, thus ensuring long life for the weapon. The high rates of fire dictate a special linkless feed for the M61, and while some aircraft systems expel the used cases, others collect them. The ammunition used is in the M50 series, and includes armour piercing (with or without tracer elements) and incendiary types. The rotary action of the weapon as installed in the F-15 is provided by hydraulic/electrical power.

Locating the gun

The choice of location for the internal gun was not easy. Ideally it should have been placed as close to the fighter's cg as possible in order to reduce aiming errors when the weapon was fired, but a nose mounting was ruled out because the vibration of the weapon firing would upset the microcircuitry of the APG-63 radar. A second location, further aft on the fuselage centreline, was rejected because of possible gun-gas ingestion problems. The final solution, approached with some trepidation, was to mount the gun in the starboard wing root, where there was plenty of room for the weapon and its ammunition drum and feed system. Tests later showed that the comparatively large separation of the gun from the fore-and-aft axis of the aircraft produced no aiming or recoil problems. In addition, the gun alignment could more easily be varied to give maximum tracking time on target, a facility initially demonstrated in simulation, and later proved in practice.

For the future, there was the new General Electric 25mm cannon, the GAU-12/U, under development for the AV-8B Harrier II/Harrier GR.5. This was considered for the F-15E, but rejected. Another suggestion for the F-15E was the carriage of three General Electric GE 430 GEPOD-30 30mm gun pods on fuselage and underwing pylons. The GEPOD-30 was a lightweight four-barrel variant of the GAU-8/A used in the A-10A Thunderbolt II, which fires the same depleted uranium ammunition. After due consideration, it was

Below: The view from the rear seat of an F-15D as a missile is launched at a high crossing target. This is obligingly contrailing, so that we can all see where it is!

F-15 Eagle

Right: The rocket motor fires as an AIM-7 Sparrow is launched from the first F-15C Eagle. The aircraft has an instrumented nose probe.

deemed that risking a $30 million fighter in strafing surface targets was not an economically viable proposition.

Although the gun has been restored, the missile remains the Eagle's primary air-to-air weapon. The new fighter's missile armament was originally to consist of the AIM-7F Sparrow for beyond visual range (BVR) engagements, and a new short-range IR-homing missile, designated AIM-82. The latter missile was cancelled well before it reached the hardware stage, and the AIM-9L Sidewinder took over. The AIM-120 AMRAAM has since replaced the Sparrow, while the advanced AIM-9X Sidewinder has been selected as the close combat weapon, rather than the European AIM-132 ASRAAM.

AIM-7 Sparrow

The AIM-7 Sparrow originated as Sperry Gyroscope's Project Hot Shot in 1946, and by 1955 it was in service as the beam-riding AAM-N-2 Sparrow I with the US Navy. The active-radar Sparrow II was cancelled in 1957 and the AIM-7F comes from the third generation of Sparrow, the Raytheon AAM-N-6 Sparrow III, which became the AIM-7C when the US services changed nomenclature in 1962. The AIM-7C introduced semi-active radar homing with continuous wave (CW) guidance and was in service by 1958. The AIM-7E, later versions of which armed early Eagles, featured a continuous-rod warhead, consisting of a 66lb (30kg) explosive charge enclosed in a tight drum made from a continuous rod of stainless steel. On detonation, this rod shatters into some 2,500 lethal fragments. The more manoeuvrable AIM-7E2 was developed to reduce the missile's minimum range as a result of experience in Vietnam, when the demand for visual identification of targets inhibited its use, and this version armed the initial batches of F-15 Eagles.

The AIM-7F, designated missile for the Eagle, brought the Sparrow into the solid-state electronic age. Reducing the size and weight of the guidance package, still CW, allowed a more powerful motor, the Hercules Mk 58, to be used, resulting in an increased range of 62 miles (100km), and enabling a larger 88lb (40kg) warhead to be carried. Introduced in 1977, the AIM-7F is claimed to be able to lock-on to a target against clutter up to 10dB.

The most recent version of the Sparrow is the AIM-7M, which has an inverse monopulse seeker, a digital signal processor, a new autopilot and a new fuze. It is expected to offer greatly

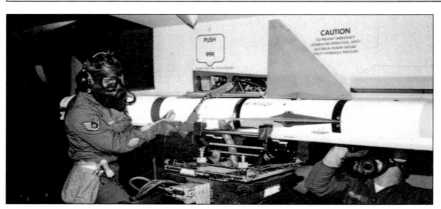

Above: The Sparrow accelerates towards its maximum speed of approximately Mach 4. Range of the AIM-7F is 62 miles (100km).

Left: Armourers in protective clothing and respirators install a Sparrow on its fuselage mounting.

Below: In its air superiority configuration, the F-15 can have its fuel, oil and liquid oxygen replenished, and Sparrows and ammunition reloaded, in a turnaround time of only 12 minutes.

improved results in adverse weather conditions, as well as in an ECCM environment, and starting with the FY 1981 budget funding, Sparrow production has been concentrated on this variant.

AIM-9 Sidewinder

The Sidewinder is the original simple, low-cost air-to-air missile, capable of being carried by practically any combat aircraft. Since its development in 1949 by a team of scientists at the Naval Ordnance Test Station (now the Naval Weapons Centre) at China Lake, it has been produced in seven major variants, with at least one further derivative under consideration. US production of the initial AIM-9B variant reached a total of 80,900 missiles, while a European consortium produced about 15,000. The usefulness of the missile is exemplified by the fact that during the Falklands conflict of 1982 the RAF modified their Nimrod maritime patrol and ASW aircraft to carry four Sidewinders in a matter of weeks in order to give them a measure of self-defence capability.

Sidwinder has an infra-red seeker which homes onto heat emissions from the jet efflux of the target. A variety of guidance heads, and six major forward fin configurations have been used, and many of the later versions combined older airframes with new seekers and fins. The AIM-9L, which represents the third generation of the missile, features a new double-delta forward fin configuration of larger span than previous missiles and a new seeker head. Part of the DSQ-29 guidance and control system, the new head uses AM-FM conical scan, with a fixed-reticle, tilted-mirror system, and is cooled by Argon gas. The new seeker offers greater sensitivity and improved tracking stability, while lethality is increased by the use of the DSU-15B active optical laser fuze, allied to the WDU-17B annular blast fragmentation warhead.

The latest Sidewinder variant in service is the AIM-9M, the improvements of which include greater resistance to countermeasures and a rocket motor that is less smokey than its predecessors. But in recent years the AIM-9 has been outclassed by the Russian Vympel R-73, and a replacement for it, which could possibly be the proposed AIM-9X, is urgently needed.

AIM-120 AMRAAM

Despite all the advances made over the years with the Sparrow AAM, it retains one basic drawback – its semi-active radar guidance system requires the target to be continuously illuminated throughout an engagement, so that the pilot can only deal with one target at a time. Consequently, the prime require-

ment during development of the Advanced Medium Range Air-to-Air Missile (AMRAAM) was that it should be a launch-and-leave missile, allowing several targets to be engaged simultaneously beyond visual range without monopolizing the fire-control radar and leaving the pilot blind to other threats. AMRAAM was also required to be

usable in all weathers, fired from or at all aspects and with a look-down/shoot-down capability. With the proliferation of Sparrow throughout the US Air Force, Navy and Marine Corps, it had to be able to integrate with existing fighters and fire control radar, and physically fit where a Sparrow was previously located. The final requirement was con-

siderably higher reliability than that of Sparrow.

This was a demanding specification, and in 1976 a joint USAF/US Navy project office was set up at Elgin AFB to organize the development of the new missile. By February 1979 the conceptual studies had been narrowed down to submissions from Hughes Aircraft and Raytheon, who were awarded contracts for ten prototype missiles each to be fired from F-14, F-15 and F-16 aircraft in a competitive evaluation.

After only three firings of each contender the trials were halted, with the Hughes entry a clear winner, and in December 1981 the company received a 50-month full scale development contract valued at some $421 million. The resulting missile, designated AIM-120 but still known as AMRAAM at the time of writing, is some two-thirds of the weight of the Sparrow, and similar in configuration, though the main fins are somewhat smaller. It has an estimated speed of Mach 4, and an active X-band radar terminal seeker using a high-power solid-state transmitter with a low-sidelobe, wide-gimbal antenna, and a built-in radio-frequency processor. Navigation, autopilot, radar, datalink, fuzing, sequencing and self-test functions are all handled by a single 30MKz microprocessor.

The last two of the Hughes test firings were from an F-15, following one from an F-16, and the second launch, on November 23, 1981, scored a direct hit on a QF-102 target drone. The F-15 was flying at 6,000ft (1,830m) at Mach 0.75, and the missile was launched in a look-down/shoot-down mode at the QF-102 flying at 1,000ft (300m) at Mach 0.7. The missile was cued by the APG-63 radar and launched by the aircraft's stores

Top left: A fully armed F-15 stands ready for takeoff, with safety tags on missiles and airframe and cockpit canopy open.

Centre left: An armourer removes the cover from the seeker head of a Sidewinder as the aircraft is prepared for a sortie.

Left: Mock-up of the Hughes AIM-120 AMRAAM is assembled on the fuselage station of an F-15.

Below left: First captive flight test of a Hughes AMRAAM Instrumented Measurement Vehicle, used to test the new missile's aerodynamic compatibility with the F-15.

Below: During the firing trials that resulted in its selection, a prototype of the Hughes AMRAAM is launched from an F-15B.

control system. It demonstrated inertial midcourse guidance and then acquired its target against ground clutter.

The final prototype firing came late in 1982 and demonstrated the missile's ability to intercept a low-flying aircraft using self-screening ECM. It was launched from an F-15 flying at 16,000ft (4,900m) some 10.8nm from a QF-102 drone flying towards the launch aircraft at 400ft (120m). It was launched with command-inertial guidance and then switched to active radar in order to acquire and intercept the target, which passed within lethal range of the AMRAAM's warhead.

AIM-120A Amraam was scheduled to enter service in 1986, but a series of problems followed. The arming system was unreliable, while carry trials caused the fuselage-mounted missiles to flex

under extreme flight conditions, damaging the flight control surfaces and some electronic connectors.

Problems were due to incompatibility with the software of the radar and fire control system of the F-15, which provided faulty targeting and tracking information. In a multi-target trial in August 1989, all four AIM-120s missed. Reprogramming, and fine-tuning the guidance software in the missile, finally cured that problem, and in May of the following year an F-15 from Eglin AFB "killed" four drones nearly simultaneously against heavy ECM. Full-rate production did not commence until April 1991.

Air-to-ground weapons
While primarily an air superiority fighter, the Eagle possess a substantial

air-to-ground secondary capability. The need to replace the F-111 in the adverse weather interdiction role also resulted in the F-15E Strike Eagle, a two-seater optimised for the task.

The basic stores capability of the F-15A/C has five weapons pylons, in addition to the four Sparrow missiles, capable of carrying up to 16,000lb (7,257kg) of bombs, rockets, ECM equipment or external fuel tanks.

The Strike Eagle demonstrator, on which the F-15E was based, could carry up to 24,000lb (10,886kg) of stores.

Among the stores compatible with the Eagle in this role are the AGM-88A High-Speed Anti-Radiation Missile (HARM), AGM-84A Harpoon anti-ship-missile, Mk 20 Rockeye bombs on MER-200 multiple ejection racks, Matra Durandal runway denial weapons, 500lb (227kg) Mk 82 bombs in slick (low-drag) and Snakeye (retarded) configuration, 2,000lb (907kg) Mk 84 bombs in slick, laser, electro-optical and infra-red homing versions, ALQ-131 ECM pods and 600US gal (500Imp gal/2,280 litre) drop tanks.

1 ECM antenna
2 ALQ-119(V) jammer pod
3 600US gal (500Imp gal/2,273 litre) fuel tank
4 MER (multiple ejector rack) carrying three Mk 82 500lb (227kg) slick (low-drag) general-purpose bombs (one with a stand-off contact fuze) plus one AIM-9J and one AIM-9L Sidewinder AAMs
5 Conformal fuel tank (CFT)
6 MK 20 Rockeye cluster bomb
7 Tactical nuclear bomb
8 MK 82 Snakeye high-drag bomb
9 M61 cannon with 940 rounds of 20mm ammunition
10 GBU-10E/B (Mk 84 2,000lb) Paveway II laser-guided bomb
11 AVQ-26 Pave Tack sensor pod
12 GBU-12D/B (Mk 82 500lb) Paveway II laser-guided bomb
13 CBU-52B/B cluster bomb dispenser
14 AIM-7F/M Sparrow AAM
15 AGM-84A Harpoon anti-ship missile
16 SUU-20 practice bomb dispenser
17 MK 84 2,000lb (907kg) general-purpose bomb
18 GBU-15(V)-4-B modular guided glide bomb
19 AGM-88A Harm anti-radar missile
20 AGM-65D IIR (imaging infra-red) Maverick air-to-surface missile
21 Two AGM-65A (TV) or AGM-65C (laser) Mavericks
22 General Electric GPU-5/A gun pod housing 30mm GAU-13/A gun, ammunition and drive system
23 AIM-120 AMRAAM (advanced medium-range air-to-air missile)

The MER-200 multiple ejection bomb rack is designated BRU-26A/A, and allows the Eagle a high degree of flexibility in its weapons carriage. It is in production to equip all Eagles assigned to the US Rapid Deployment Joint Task Force, as well as for the Japanese Air Self Defense Force F-15Js. Its main advantage is that it allows supersonic carriage and release of up to six weapons, and can jettison them in any loading configuration. It is strong enough to allow the pilot to pull 7.3g during combat manoeuvres, and has been flight tested to Mach 1.4, although MCAIR, the manufacturers, claim carriage, jettison and release of stores up to Mach 2. Production of this low drag multiple ejection rack was running at 40 units per month by mid-1983.

In addition, the Eagle can enhance its range by the use of the CFTs mounted on the fuselage sides, and these retain the ability to mount Sparrow or AMRAAM missiles on the lower corners, or carry some 4,400lb (1,996kg) of air-to-ground stores. Each of the CFTs can carry 849US gal (707Imp gal/3,228 litres) of fuel. Alternatively, or in combinatioin with fuel, they can house cameras and IR sensors for reconnaissance; low-light television (LLTV), forward-looking IR (FLIR) and laser designators for the strike role; or Wild Weasel equipment for defence suppression.

CFTs were first flown on an F-15B on July 27, 1974. MCAIR claimed that carriage of the conformal tanks only slightly increased the subsonic profile drag relative to the clean aircraft and represented only a fraction of the supersonic drag of the three standard drop tanks, which between them carry 20 per cent more fuel that the CFTs. Installation of the CFTs is possible in 15 minutes, despite their complex shape and size. With CFTs and the three drop tanks, the F-15C has demonstrated an unrefuelled ferry range of 2,660nm (4,903km). In this configuration, the F-15C has a maximum gross weight of 68,000lb (30,840kg), while the F-15D model is only some 800lb (363kg) heavier with the same internal fuel.

Weapons configurations
In the basic air-to-air role, the F-15A/C Eagle carries four AIM-7F Sparrows, four AIM-9L Sidewinders and the internal 20mm gun. In addition, it usually carries a 600US gal drop tank on the centre-line pylon, and the inner wing pylon can also carry a similar drop tank without sacrificing the Sidewinder capability.

The basic attack configuration of the non-dedicated Eagle retains the basic air-to-air configuration, possibly including the centre-line tank, and adds extra stores. Any range enhancements required can be provided by air-to-air refuelling. The prime requirement was for the attack mission not to detract from the basic air-to-air combat mission, which is certainly the case.

Below: The second F-15B in early 1976, before its development into the Strike Eagle. Even at this stage MCAIR were keen to demonstrate the F-15's ground-attack capability, and 71-0291 is seen here armed with 18 500lb (227kg) Mk 82 slicks.

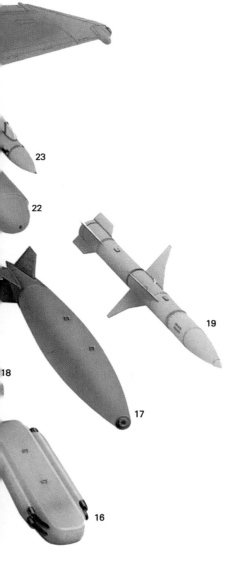

Left: The impressive array of stores that have been launched by the Eagle or are designed to be compatible with the aircraft's delivery system.

23

22

19

18

17

16

Right: A USAF F-15E armed with AIM-120 AMRAAM over Aviano, Italy, in March 1999, during the conflict against Serbian forces. The AIM-120 replaced the Sparrow.

Deployment and Combat

Following its service introduction with the 'Triple Nickel' 555th TFTS, the Eagle achieved operational status in 1976 with the 1st Tactical Fighter Wing. Subsequently the type has been deployed with USAF units in Europe, the Far East and Alaska, as well as equipping selected units of TAC's Air Defense Command, while export customers have included Israel, Japan and Saudi Arabia. Israeli pilots were the first to take the Eagle to war, achieving predictably impressive results, the Saudis next, and finally the USAF in *Desert Storm* and over Yugoslavia and Bosnia.

The operational career of the F-15 effectively began on November 14, 1974, at Luke AFB, Arizona, when President Gerald Ford accepted TF-15A 73-0108 on behalf of Tactical Air Command (TAC). The Eagle had been flying in full USAF insignia for some time by then, but the handful of Air Force units which had used the type prior to November 1974 were essentially test organizations, unlike the 58th Tactical Fighter Training Wing (TFTW), the unit which was to operate the first TF-15A. This aircraft, incidentally, was christened 'TAC 1' during the ceremonies that marked the type's introduction to service.

The first F-15 squadron was the 555th Tactical Fighter Training Squadron

Below: Ready to get airborne on an interception in less than five minutes, a fully-armed F-15A waits in its hardened shelter.

(TFTS). This unit, the famed 'Triple Nickel', had racked up an impressive air combat record in Vietnam when, equipped with another MCAIR product, the F-4 Phantom. It accounted for no less than 40 MiGs. The 555th quickly set about the task of qualifying instructor pilots and formulating a training syllabus, a process which was largely completed by about the middle of 1975 when personnel earmarked to serve with the first fully operational wing were present in some considerable numbers at Luke.

Mission-ready status

The responsibility of bringing TAC's newest piece of hardware to mission-ready status was entrusted to the 1st Tactical Fighter Wing (TFW), which shared Langley AFB, Virginia, with TAC headquarters, and the next 18 months or so proved to be a period of

intense activity at this base as more and more personnel were posted in to join the team.

As with most modern combat aircraft, introduction of the Eagle did not go entirely according to plan. One of the most significant difficulties concerned delays in the output of qualified pilots by the 58th TFTW, this arising directly from the rather lower than anticipated sortie production rate (SPR). In fact, low SPR levels affected the entire project for quite some time, and although the decision in November 1975 to eliminate the air-to-ground portion of the training syllabus went some way towards alleviating the pilot shortage, the situation was compounded by the AIMVAL/ACEVAL (Air Intercept Missile Evaluation/Air Combat Evaluation) test programme of 1976-77 which called for the 58th TFTW to surrender six aircraft to the 57th Fighter Weapons Wing (FWW) at

Above: An unarmed 36th TFW F-15A on deployment over Norway. The 36th was the first USAFE unit to be equipped with the Eagle.

Nellis. An example of the effect that these difficulties had on the overall pace of the project is provided by the fact that the 1st TFW was still some 18 pilots short of its authorized level in May 1976, about five months after it had been fully equipped with 72 Eagles.

A key factor in the SPR shortfall was the low rate of aircraft serviceability during the early stages of the Eagle's career mainly because of difficulties involving the F100 engine and the fire control system and its associated APG-63 radar. Engine-related problems such as compressor stalls, slow acceleration and stagnation with a corresponding loss of thrust have continued to cause concern and were certainly not helped

by the production difficulties experienced by Pratt & Whitney in the late 1970s.

As far as the avionics are concerned, the picture is somewhat brighter. Most early problems resulted from poor performance of on-base Avionics Intermediate Shop (AIS) test equipment and the consequent need to send many defective LRUs (Line Replaceable Units) back to the contractor for repair and rectification work. This, in turn, brought about a 'domino' effect as cannibalization became necessary to maintain aircraft in an 'up' condition, the situation eventually reaching a point where, when engine difficulties were taken into account, the expected degree of reliability was being missed by in excess of 50 per cent. Hardware and software fixes incorporated in the latter half of the 1970s have gone some way toward improving avionics performance but AIS test equipment is still causing more than a few headaches for maintenance personnel.

Despite these trials and tribulations, training of 1st TFW personnel forged ahead steadily, being highlighted by delivery of the first F-15A (74-0083 'Peninsula Patriot') to the 27th TFS at Langley on January 9, 1976. By the end of that year two further squadrons, the 71st and 94th TFSs, had also received their allotted number of aircraft and the 1st TFW was fully equipped if not yet fully operational.

Not surprisingly, the pilots spent most of 1976 familiarizing themselves with their new mounts and exploring the capabilities of the F-15 in the air combat role. This involved extensive training exercises against each other and against dissimilar types such as the T-38 Talon, A-4 Skyhawk, F-4 Phantom, F-5E Tiger II and F-106 Delta Dart. The opportunity to participate in Red Flag exercises at Nellis was also taken: during September and October no less than 24 aircraft deployed to Nevada for Red Flag VIII. They performed credit-

ably, the SPR rising significantly along with pilot confidence in the aircraft and its systems.

By the end of 1976 both the 27th TFS and the 71st TFS were adjudged to be mission-ready but the emphasis was already shifting toward Europe, home of the next wing to convert. This was the 36th TFW, then operating the F-4E Phantom from Bitburg AB, West Germany. However, rather than accomplish transition at Bitburg it was decided that a new concept would be used in an attempt to curtail the 'down-time' which is usually associated with major re-equipment programmes. Accordingly, the 1st TFW was tasked with assisting the 36th TFW to attain operational read-

iness on the F-15 under the code name Ready Eagle.

36th TFW build-up

Maintenance personnel for the 36th TFW duly began training at Langley in September 1976 while aircrew for the first squadron – a mix of experienced F-15 pilots from Luke and Langley plus some former F-4E pilots from Bitburg – gradually accumulated at Langley. Responsibility for overseeing the Langley-based phase of flying training rested with the 94th TFS and was highlighted by the first pilot achieving mission-ready status in mid-January of 1977. On January 5, the first two Eagles had reached Bitburg for maintenance

Above: A trio of F-15As from the famous 555th 'Triple Nickel' TFTS, 58th TFTW, based at Luke AFB, Arizona.

familiarization training, where they were joined by two more during March.

In the meantime, delivery of those Eagles earmarked for service with the 36th TFW was being effected to Langley and it was from here that some 20 F-15As and a trio of TF-15As left for the first mass transatlantic migration to Bitburg on April 27, these all reaching Germany safely during the afternoon of the same day. Within 12 hours of arrival the 525th TFS was in business, some of the new arrivals already standing 'Zulu'

Below: A pair of F-15As from the 1st Tactical Fighter Wing, the first operational Eagle unit, based at TAC's Langley HQ.

Below: A 1st TFW F-15A banks over one of the world's most expensive flight lines at Langley AFB, Virginia, also home of the 48th FIS.

Bottom: Three F-15As and a two-seat F-15B of the 57th Fighter Weapons Wing, based at Nellis AFB, Arizona, in formation.

alert duty and providing a fitting testimonial to the success of the initial phase of Ready Eagle.

Back in the USA, training of the second 36th TFW squadron, the 53rd TFS, followed similar lines. Deployment of the 53rd to Bitburg followed in July, while the third squadron – the 22nd TFS – brought the re-equipment process to a successful conclusion when it took up residence at Bitburg in October. It should be noted that transatlantic ferry flights of aircraft for these two squadrons were made over a fairly lengthy period, groups of half-a-dozen or so being deployed at a time during the summer and autumn of 1977 until the planned level of about 80, including several spares, was achieved.

Holloman AFB in New Mexico was the next base to welcome the Eagle, re-equipment of the resident 49th TFW's three squadrons being accomplished during 1977-78. Another new procedure, code-named Ready Team, was employed on this occasion, the intention being to permit some existing fighters – in this case F-4D Phantoms – to remain combat-ready during the initial phases of conversion. The process of transition got under way in June 1977 when the first pilots for the 7th TFS reported to Luke for training with the 58th Tactical Training Wing (TTW) as it had become known during 1977. The 58th TTW had itself been expanded in June 1976 when the 461st TFTS was organized as the second F-15 training squadron, and it grew still further while the 49th TFW was undergoing conversion, gaining the 550th TFTS in September 1977. Initial qualification of the 7th TFS was managed by the 461st and 555th TFTSs, and was followed by a brief assignment to the 550th TFTS for mission-ready checkout, culminating in reassignment to Holloman where F-15s began to arrive in October 1977. Re-equipment of the 8th TFS was accomplished with effect from January 1978.

The F-15C/D was first deployed to join the 18th TFW at Kadena, on the Japanese island of Okinawa, and has remained the type operated by this unit for some 20 years. Even as the Phantom had been supplanted in the air superiority and air defence roles by the F-15A/B, so in time the early Eagles were replaced in their turn by the superior F-15C/D and handed down, not to the Air Force Reserve, as might have been expected, but to the Air National Guard squadrons, the "week-end flyers". Only the ANG still fly the F-15A/B, secure in the knowledge that, part-timers or no, they have a fighter which is still the equal of almost anything in the world.

Israeli Eagles

Ever since its foundation in 1948, Israel had lived under permanent threat from its Arab neighbours. Border skirmishes were frequent, and had on three occasions erupted into full-scale war. Beset on all sides, and heavily outnumbered, the Israelis needed the best fighter they could get, to match quantity with quality.

The October War of 1973 was a close-run thing, and Israeli aircraft losses, albeit mainly to ground fire, had been high. Their best fighter at that time was the F-4E Phantom II, a good workhorse, but lacking manoeuvrability in the air combat arena. Only superb pilot quality had seen the Israelis through, and they knew it. But what of the future?

Having evaluated the F-15 in 1974, the Israel Defense Force/Air Force (IDF/AF), to give it its proper name, soon made up its collective mind. "Peace Fox", as the US Foreign Military Sales (FMS) programme was codenamed, provided for the export of Eagles to Israel, where it

entered service as the Baz (Falcon).

Many, both in Israel and outside, questioned the wisdom of acquiring such an expensive and complex fighter. But there was really no alternative. The next generation of light fighters – represented by the F-16 and F/A-18 – was still in the future, while the homebrew Kfir was no more than a stopgap. For greater close combat capability, it was the Eagle or nothing.

The first four, drawn from a batch of development aircraft, were delivered in December 1976. This was followed during 1977 by 19 new-build F-15As and two F-15Bs. Eighteen F-15Cs and eight F-15Ds joined the fleet in 1981. Five attrition replacements, all F-15Ds, joined them in 1989. Then, during the Gulf War of 1991, 17 non-MSIP F-15As and five F-15Bs were delivered as an inducement not to join in.

The air-to-ground capability of the Phantom had always been one of its greatest attractions for the IDF/AF. While the F-15 was acquired for air superiority, it was not long before it began to be used as a bomb truck. Its most spectacular mission was the long range strike against PLO headquarters in Tunis on October 1, 1985 – a round trip of 2,400nm (4,450km), which involved three in-flight refuellings.

Given this, it was hardly surprising that the Israelis were interested in the Strike Eagle, and ordered 25 examples of the export F-15I variant. Deliveries of the Raam (Thunder) began on January 19, 1998. It differs from the F-15E in having an Israeli-designed Elisra SPS-2100 defensive aids package with active ECM, radar warning, and missile approach warning. Radar is the upgraded APG-70I, and a helmet-mounted sight is standard.

F-15's first victory

The first Israeli F-15 operational sorties were flown in March 1978, but it was not until June 27, 1979, that the F-15 recorded its first victory. A flight of F-15s patrolled high over Lebanon with a flight of Kfirs. Two or three flights of Syrian MiGs (8-12 fighters) rose to oppose

Left: A trio of 36th TFW F-15As during the Arctic Express exercise held in 1978 to test combat readiness in Arctic conditions.

Above: One of the 36th TFW's Bitburg-based F-15As parked outside its hardened aircraft shelter for routine maintenance.

Below left: An F-15C of the 18th TFW is the centre of attention after flying from Okinawa to Florida for the William Tell 82 meet.

Below: An F-15A of the 49th TFW, from Holloman AFB, New Mexico, demonstrates its ability to climb vertically.

USAF F-15 Units			
Wing/Tail Codes	**Squadrons**	**Types**	**Bases**
1st "FF"	27th Fighting Eagles	F-15C/D	Langley AFB, VA
	71st Ironmen	F-15C/D	
	94th Hat in the Ring	F-15C/D	
3rd "AK"	19th Fighting Gamecocks	F-15C/D	Elmendorf AFB, Alaska
	54th Leppards	F-15C/D	Seymour Johnson
	90th Pair o'Dice	F-15E	AFB, NC
4th "SJ"	333rd Lancers	F-15E	
	334th Eagles	F-15E	
	335th Chiefs	F-15E	
	336th Rocketeers	F-15E	
18th "ZZ"	12th Dirty Dozen	F-15C/D	Kadena AFB,
	44th Vampires	F-15C/D	Okinawa, Japan
	67th Fighting Cocks	F-15C/D	
33rd "EG"	58th Gorillas	F-15C/D	Eglin AFB, FL
	60th Fighting Crows	F-15C/D	
48th "LN"	492nd Bowlers	F-15E	RAF Lakenheath,
	493rd Grim Reapers	F-15C/D	UK
	494th Panthers	F-15E	
53rd "OT"	85th TES	F-15C/D	Eglin AFB, FL
	422nd TES	F-15C/D/E	Nellis AFB, NV
57th "WA"	Weapons School	F-15C/D/E	Nellis AFB, NV
325th "TY"	1st Griffins	F-15C/D	Tyndall AFB, FL
	2nd Second to None	F-15C/D	
	95th Mr Bones	F-15C/D	
366th "MO"	390th Wild Boars	F-15C/D	Mountain Home
	391st Bold Tigers	F-15E	AFB, ID
412th Test "ED"	420th FLTS	F-15B/C/D/E	Edwards AFB, CA
Air National Guard F-15 Units			
	101st	F-15A/B	Otis ANGB, MA
	110th Lindbergh's Own	F-15A/B	St.Louis IAP, MO
	114th Eager Beavers	F-15A/B	Klamath Falls, OR
	122nd Coonass Militia	F-15A/B	New Orleans, LA
	123rd Red Hawks	F-15A/B	Portland, OR
	159th	F-15A/B	Jacksonville, FL
	199th	F-15A/B	Hickam AFB, HI

Above: Israel was the first export customer for the Eagle, receiving its first three in December 1976. Here four IDF-AF F-15s fly over the historic Masada fortress.

Top right: Four F-15s from 1st FW at Langley. Deployed to the Gulf in 1991, the 1st had so many lieutenant colonels that many missed out on the action.

them, and two Sparrows were launched. Both missed. Six-victory Phantom ace Colonel M (who is still serving, so his name cannot be released) then scored a direct hit on a MiG, breaking it in two, for his seventh victory. Three more F-15s and a Kfir claimed victories. The Eagle had commenced what was to be an outstanding score.

MiG-25 Foxbats fell to Sparrows on March 13 and July 29, 1981, as they tried to intercept Israeli RF-4Es. Then on June 6, 1982, Operation Peace for Galilee was launched over the Beka'a. Drones were used to bring Syrian detection and SAM guidance radars on line; these were then taken out by attack aircraft. When Syrian MiGs rose to oppose the Israeli incursions, they were detected and tracked by E-2C Hawkeye AEW aircraft. Meanwhile the Israeli fighters lurked in the radar shadows cast by the mountains until directed into action by the Hawkeyes. The F-15 was credited with

"about" 40 victories in this conflict. Yet another Foxbat fell to Sparrows launched by F-15s on August 31 of that year. It is of course no surprise to find that in Israeli service, Sidewinder has largely been replaced by the indigenous Shafrir and Python.

Saudi Arabian Eagles
Prior to 1981, Saudi air defence fighters consisted of a mix of potent but elderly BAe Lightnings and austere Northrop F-5Es. Having backed Israel in the Middle East, the USA was reluctant to supply F-15s to an Arab nation but, as Saudi Arabia had not been involved in any hostile actions, finally agreed, with the proviso that no more than 60 could be incountry at any one time.

First deliveries, of F-15C/Ds, commenced in August 1981. Like all exported machines, they did not have the ALQ-128 radar warning receiver (RWR). Another dozen were ordered in

1989, but the Iraqi invasion of Kuwait intervened, and 20 F-15Cs were hurriedly despatched. For Desert Shield/Desert Storm operations, all Saudi Eagles were fitted with the ALQ-135 RWR. After the Gulf War, 12 more F-15C/Ds were ordered as attrition replacements.

Saudi Eagles are credited with four air combat victories. Two of these were Iranian F-4Es, which violated Saudi air space on June 5, 1984. Then, during the Gulf War, Ayed Salah al-Shamrani accounted for two Iraqi Mirage F.1s with Sidewinders. It must however be said that this encounter was carefully stage-managed, with a fighter controller in an E-3 leading him into position.

Right: Demonstration of rescue methods for Japanese ground crew is rehearsed during a USAF F-15 deployment to the Nyutabaru AFB as part of Exercise Cope North 81-3.

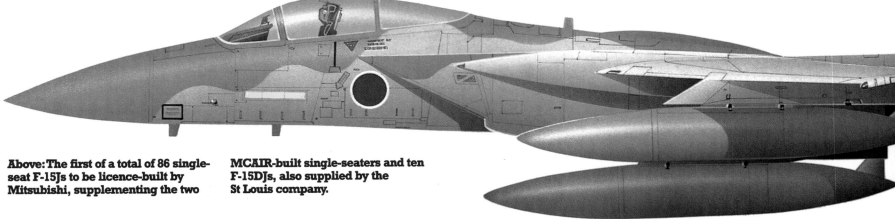

Above: The first of a total of 86 single-seat F-15Js to be licence-built by Mitsubishi, supplementing the two **MCAIR-built single-seaters and ten F-15DJs, also supplied by the St Louis company.**

Above: One of the 15 F-15Ds which Saudi Arabia has bought along with 47 single-seaters.

ROYAL SAUDI AIR FORCE

Above: Israeli deployment is shrouded in secrecy, but it is known that the country's initial order for 25 F-15A and B Eagles went to equip No 133 Squadron of the IDF-AF.

Below: One of the MCAIR-built F-15J Eagles arrives at Gifu air base in Japan after a ferry flight from St Louis.

F-15 Eagles, offshore nations		
Israel		
69 Sqn, The Hammers	F-15I	Hatzerim
106 Sqn, Second Baz	F-15C/D	Tel Nof
133 Sqn, Double Tails	F-15A/B	Tel Nof
Saudi Arabia		
5 Sqn	F-15C/D	Taif
6 Sqn	F-15C/D	Khamis Mushait
13 Sqn	F-15C/D	Dhahran
42 Sqn	F-15C/D	Dhahran
55 Sqn	F-15S	Khamis Mushait
Japan		
2nd Kokudan	F-15J/DJ	Chitose
5th Kokudan	F-15J/DJ	Nytabaru
6th Kokudan	F-15J/DJ	Komatsu
7th Kokudan	F-15J/DJ	Hykuri
8th Kokudan	F-15J/DJ	Tsuiki
Hiko Kyodotai	F-15J/DJ	Nyutabaru
Hiko Kaihatsu Jikkendan	F-15J/DJ	Gifu

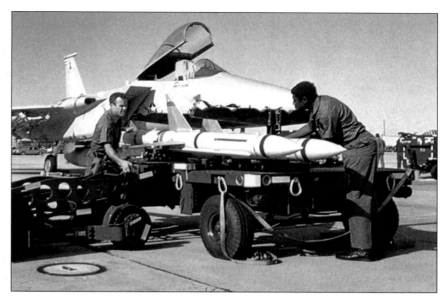

The Saudis next wanted a single-seat variant of the Strike Eagle, the F-15F, but this was not approved by the US Congress. Instead they settled for the F-15S, a Strike Eagle lacking some of the more sensitive equipment, and with the resolution of the APG-70 radar degraded from 2.4m to 18m. Of the 72 ordered, 24 will be used as interceptors while the remainder are employed for air-to-ground missions. The CFTs of all aircraft are modified to prevent the tangential carriage of weapons, leaving only two wing and one centreline hardpoints available for ordnance – unless of course the CFTs are removed, in which case range is severely restricted.

Japanese Eagles
As the bulwark of the Western democracies in the Far East, and its location within easy flying distance of both the then Soviet Union, North Korea, and the People's Republic of China, Japan was an obvious candidate for the F-15. Under the FMS programme "Peace Sun", the Japanese Air Self-Defense Force (JASDF) has acquired a total of 213 F-15CJ/DJ Eagles. Unusually, all except 14 were assembled in Japan by Mitsubishi, the company which produced the infamous Zero fighter in World War II.

The first (US-built) F-15 arrived in Japan in March 1981, while the first indigenous article first flew some six months later. Replacing the F-104J Starfighter, and some years later the F-4EJ Phantom II, it has been deployed to protect the northern, central and western regions of the country. The JASDF operates a dedicated Aggressor unit, the Hiko Kyodotai, which unlike any other F-15 outfit worldwide flies camouflaged Eagles.

The F-15J is very similar to the F-15C, but lacking the nuclear strike capability and many of the ECM systems of the American variant. Currently it is fitted with the ALQ-8, and the APR-4 RWR. Since 1996 F100-PW-220E engines have been retrofitted.

USAF Eagles at war
When Iraq invaded Kuwait in August 1990, two squadrons of F-15C/D Eagles of the 1st TFW, were soon on the scene. They flew non-stop from Langley, Virginia, to Dhahran in Saudi Arabia, a squadron at a time. First to arrive was the 71st TFS, on August 7, followed by the 27th TFS. The trip lasted more than 14 hours, and included six or seven inflight refuellings. The Eagles flew fully armed, with four Sparrows and four Sidewinders, and were prepared to fight on arrival if need be.

Top left: "Nodding" intakes down, an F-15C of the 1st FW prepares to take off on a combat air patrol during the Gulf War of 1991. Steve Tate of this unit scored the first air kill.

Bottom left: A Saudi Arabian Air Force F-15. Saudi Eagles accounted for two Iranian Phantoms, then in the Gulf War two Iraqi Mirage F.1s were downed by Ayed Al-Shamrani.

Top right: In competitive spirit, AIM-7 Sparrow mssiles are brought out to arm a US Air Force 36th Tactical Fighter Wing F-15C during the William Tell 82 weapons meet.

Above right: A backseater's view from an F-15D of the 27th FS, 1st FW, during the Gulf War. The 1st FW, from Langley AFB, Virginia, were first to arrive in the Gulf.

The first task of the squadrons was to familiarise themselves with the area, working with Saudi E-3 Sentry AWACS aircraft and setting up defensive patrols to guard against Iraqi attack. In this they were of course assisted by Saudi F-15 squadrons. Other F-15C units deployed were the 58th TFS (33rd TFW) from Eglin AFB to Tabuk, and the 53rd TFS (36th TFW) from Bitburg in Germany. Two more F-15C squadrons deployed to Incirlik in Turkey. They were the 525th TFS, also from Bitburg, and the 32nd TFS from Soesterberg in Holland. Most of these units had been preceded by the F-15E Strike Eagles of the 4th TFW from Seymour Johnson, which deployed to Al Kharj on August 12/13.

Desert Shield gave way to Desert Storm on January 17, 1991. During the hours of darkness, Eagles guided by E-3 Sentries ranged the length and breadth of Kuwait and Iraq, hunting down the few Iraqi aircraft which tried to oppose them. Meanwhile, Strike Eagles, widely known as "Mud Hens", used their LANTIRN (Low Altitude Navigation and Targeting Infra-Red) pods to make precision attacks on selected targets.

First blood of the war fell to F-15C pilot Steve "Tater" Tate of the 71st TFS, who downed a Mirage F.1 with an AIM-7M Sparrow just hours after hostilities commenced. The Iraqis, their detection, reporting and communication system in tatters from a very early stage, put up only a token resistance. The Coalition chose to make much of their early bid for air supremacy at night, where the superior avionics and weapons systems of the F-15s, backed by AWACS and

Above: With no hostiles in sight, two Saudi Arabian F-15 Eagles fly low over the inhospitable desert between Iraq and Saudia, accompanied by a Saudi F-5E Tiger II.

Below: Laden with CBUs, this F-15E Strike Eagle (Mud Hen) of the 48th FW, based at Lakenheath in the UK, but operating out of Aviano in Italy, heads for Serbian targets.

dedicated EW aircraft, provided a significant advantage. As the Iraqi fighters took off, they were ruthlessly hunted down. As one wag put it, an Iraqi fighter sortie consisted of "gear up, flaps up, blown up!"

The predominance of night action caused one long-established trend to be reversed. Whereas the majority of victories had previously fallen to heat-homers, 25 of the USAF F-15 victories were scored with Sparrows, only six with Sidewinders. The much-vaunted MiG-29 came off badly with five losses, one of which flew into the ground after having been outma-noeuvred. No F-15C/Ds were lost to any cause.

The F-15E Mud Hens equally proved their worth. Initially they were allotted three main missions. Firstly, Scud-busting against fixed launch sites and missile storage bunkers. Secondly, attacks on strategic targets such as communications centres, air-fields, and power stations deep inside Iraq. Thirdly, against Republican Guard tanks and artillery positions in occupied Kuwait. They carried LAN-TIRN pods on the right intake, while a handful of aircraft were fitted with laser target designators on the left intake. The latter were at first in short supply; one aircraft had to designate for the others in the flight. Only later was this remedied.

Something like 90 per cent of F-15E sorties took place at night. At first penetration took place at low level, but when it emerged that the air threat was minimal they reverted to medium altitudes where they were above the reach of light AAA and SAMs. Typical weapons loads were up to 12 GBU-12 Paveway II LGBs; six Rockeye CBUs (Cluster Bomb Units), each dispensing up to 247 bomblets; coupled with two AIM-7 Sparrow and/or AIM-9 Sidewinder missiles for self-defence.

At an early stage, Iraqi mobile Scuds were used to attack targets in Saudi Arabia and Israel. Israeli inter-vention could at that time have caused the breakup of the Coalition, and to prevent this, massive resources were diverted to what became known as "The Great Scud Hunt". Mud Hens were at the fore-front, patrolling likely roads in pairs at about 15,000ft (4,500m). The lead aircraft carried four GBU-10 2,000lb

(907kg) LGBs, while the wingman carried either six CBU-87s or 12 Mk 82 500lb (227kg) iron bombs. Where flat, hard terrain would have allowed Scud launchers to operate off-road, these areas were liberally seeded with area denial mines.

Two main difficulties were encoun-tered. It was virtually impossible to tell the difference between a Scud launcher vehicle and an ordinary fuel tanker. Then, unless the Mud Hen patrols were exceptionally well placed at the time of detection, the time lag involved meant that the sus-pected mobile Scud launchers slipped the net. Many optimistic claims were made, but long after the war it was revealed that the number of mobile launchers destroyed was a big fat zero. But their efforts kept Israel out of the war!

It is however probable that Mud Hen attacks had one unexpected effect on the course of the air war. Whereas the Iraqi air force appeared to have been held back, presumably for use once the ground war started, precision attacks on their hardened aircraft shelters on the airfields con-vinced them that if they stayed in situ they would soon have no air assets left. On January 26, Iraqi combat air-craft commenced an exodus to Iran, although only Allah knows why they thought they would be welcome there. A fair proportion of F-15C/D victories were scored against Iraqi aircraft in transit to interment in Iran!

As Desert Storm progressed, air superiority became air supremacy. With this, AAMs on F-15Es were reduced in favour of air-to-ground munitions. Typical loads became 12 CBUs or 12 Mk 82 iron bombs, var-ied occasionally with Mk 84 2,000lb (907kg) bombs for specific targets.

Although Mud Hens had full air-to-air capability, their only victory in the conflict came on February 15 when an F-15E sighted an Iraqi Hughes 500 helicopter in a low-level hover over Kuwait. A laser-guided GBU-10 bomb was used to despatch it. Two F-15Es fell to Iraqi ground fire, on January 18 and 21, while a non-com-bat loss occurred during Desert Shield on September 30, 1990.

After the Iraqi withdrawal from Kuwait, no-fly zones were set up over northern and southern Iraq. In March 1991, two Su-22 Fitters fell to F-15Cs, while a Pilatus PC-9 trainer pilot decided that he was outmatched, and ejected without a shot being fired. Operation Desert Fox has seen F-15Es attacking Iraqi SAM sites and command and control centres. Since then a few more Eagle victories have been scored. The Eagle's current air combat record in all air arms is 96 1/2 victories for no losses.

Eagles were used extensively over Bosnia during Operation Deny Flight, and more recently the 48th FW flew missions with its F-15Es over Yugoslavia and Bosnia, delivering a huge amount of ordnance, including, it is believed, the BLU-116B advanced Unitary Penetrator, designed for use against deep underground bunkers.

Far left: The F-15 Raam (Thunder) is the Eagle in Israeli service. Seen here with a sensor pod under the port wing, it has largely replaced the F-4 Phantom in Israel's air force.

Left: The F-15I Raam is seen here with a dozen practice bombs on its underwing stations. This was the configuration used for the attack on PLO headquarters in Tunis.

Performance and Handling

The fundamental aim of the FX programme was to produce a fighter capable of outflying and outfighting any real or projected Soviet opponent. While this was at first achieved, three decades have now passed, and the opposition has since caught up. While this was only to be expected, given the time lapse, the Eagle remains in most departments at least the equal of anything it is likely to encounter. Its air combat record is exemplary – 96.5 victories for no losses – while the F-15E is no less impressive.

The performance requirements embodied in the FX Request for Proposals were intended to equip the resulting fighter to better all existing and projected Warsaw Pact opponents. As of the late 1960s these were represented by the small, agile MiG-21 and the rather bigger but less manoeuvrable MiG-23, expected to be encountered at all altitudes; the fast, high-altitude MiG-25; and the Su-24 interdictor, for which the look-down radar capability was likely to be needed.

At the same time, some compromises had to be accepted, so that the USAF's original requirement for a maximum speed of Mach 2.7 at high altitudes, for example, was reduced to Mach 2.3, with a Mach 2.5 minimum burst capability. The higher speed would not only have prevented the use of a bubble canopy, added up to 3,000lb (1,360kg) to gross weight and reduced dash radius, it would also use up fuel at a rate of 65,000lb/hr (29,480kg/hr), equivalent to consuming the entire internal fuel load of an F-15A in about 11 minutes. The fuel flow at Mach 2.3 was estimated at a significantly lower 45,000lb/hr (20,400kg/hr). It was also argued that

higher speeds were in any case irrelevant to most missions.

Other performance figures specified included a top speed of Mach 1.2 at sea level, which it was felt would provide a useful margin of superiority over potential opponents. The wing was to be optimized for buffet-free performance at Mach 0.9 and 30,000ft (9,100m). More generally, performance was to be a consequence of high thrust-to-weight ratio and low wing loading, which had been recognized as the fundamental elements in providing the desired degree of superiority in performance and agility.

Wing loading

In its production form, at a takeoff weight of 41,500lb (18,820kg) with full internal fuel, the F-15A's 608sq ft (56.5sq m) of wing area gives a loading figure of just over 68lb/sq ft (333kg/sq m), and with half internal fuel this figure falls to 57lb/sq ft (279kg/sq m). Similarly, thrust-to-weight ratio at takeoff, with the F100s in full afterburner and full internal fuel, is 1.15:1, and by the time half the fuel has been used the ratio increases to nearly 1.4:1. By comparison, wing load-

ing of the F-4E at combat weight is 80lb/sq ft (390kg/sq m), with a thrust-to-weight ratio of approximately 0.85:1.

When translated into actual flying qualities these figures have important consequences. The four forces acting on an aircraft in flight are thrust, drag, weight and lift, and all are inter-related. Lift and drag increase as airspeed rises; both lift and drag are increased by increasing the angle of attack, and increasing the angle of bank in a turn also increases drag. Lift is considered as acting perpendicularly to the surface of a wing, and in a steep turn it has to counteract both the weight of the aircraft and the centrifugal force acting on it. Lift can be increased by increasing the angle of attack, but this also results in more drag, which in turn demands more power if the turn is to be sustained.

It is in this context that the theories of former fighter instructor Major John Boyd assume such importance. By the time Boyd was assigned to the FX programme in October 1966 he had already developed his theory of energy manoeuvrability in conjunction with Tom Christie, a mathematician working

Above: The F-15's thrust to weight ratio allows it to remove itself vertically from the furball, something that few other fighters can match.

at Eglin AFB. By subtracting drag from thrust and multiplying the residue by velocity, Boyd realized, it was possible to express the 'energy rate': when drag exceeds thrust the energy rate becomes negative, so that either more thrust must be made available or the aircraft will lose altitude, airspeed or both. This in turn gives rise to the concept of specific excess power (Ps), or the amount of 'spare' thrust available in a turn, and explains the importance of the F-15's unprecedentedly high thrust-to-weight ratio.

Wing loading also has an important effect on turning performance. As an aircraft banks, the amount of life needed to counteract the combination of gravity and centrifugal force increases as the bank angle increases; and since the

Below: A 32nd TFS F-15A leaves the Camp New Amsterdam runway at a speed of 135kt after a takeoff run of only 900ft (274m).

radius of turn at a given airspeed depends on the bank angle, it follows that the turn radius of which an aircraft is capable is dependent on the extent to which it can continue to develop lift with increasing bank angles. The high available thrust enables the Eagle to maintain or increase speeds in high banked turns, thus enabling it to fly turns at high rates. Thus the F-15's low wing loading and high thrust-to-weight ratio combine to give it outstanding performance. Compared with the F-4, the F-15 can take off in a shorter distance, accelerate faster to a higher maximum speed, turn with a reduced radius and at a higher

rate and fly higher; alternatively, it can climb at a lower airspeed.

To allow pilots to make maximum use of the Eagle's power and agility a dual flight control system was developed. The conventional hydromechanical system operates through push rod linkages acting on the valves of hydraulic actuators which deflect the control surfaces. The pitch-roll control assembly is a mechanical system which modifies the response of the system and the aileron-rudder interconnect couples the rudders and stabilators so that the former are operated automatically in conjunction with the stabilators, allowing ma-

noeuvres to be carried out using the stick alone.

Meanwhile, the automatic control augmentation system (CAS) forms a separate fly-by-wire system using electrical signal signals and servo motors to operate the hydraulic actuators. The CAS system includes pitch and yaw rate, angle of attack and dynamic pressure sensors, as well as accelerometers to monitor vertical and lateral acceleration. It is thus able to compute the correct settings for the control surfaces at any combination of speed and g forces.

The CAS also senses the stick forces

Above: A 36th TFW F-15A in formation with an F-5E in the blue-grey camouflage of an Aggressor squadron. The Aggressors simulate MiG-21s for combat training.

applied by the pilot, translating them into electrical signals to the control surface actuators: should the mechanical system fail the CAS would continue to operate the control surfaces. For

Below: Even with a full load of three external tanks, the F-15 is capable of impressive takeoff performance and rapid climb.

Above: Three 405th TTW F-15As in a steep climb over the Arizona desert with engines in full afterburner delivering 11 tons of thrust each.

Right: Performance envelope of the Strike Eagle ground-attack version of the F-15 remains impressive even with external stores.

safety, the CAS is a dual-channel system in which the signals carried by each channel are continuously compared with each other, and if an error greater than a predetermined maximum is detected both are automatically disengaged. The Eagle can be manoeuvred with the CAS off using the mechanical system alone: in this mode, control is reportedly equal to that of earlier fighters, with the CAS providing a marked improvement in handling and effectively intervening to point the aircraft in whatever direction the stick is moved.

The control surfaces themselves are straightforward. The all-moving stabilators act in unison for pitch control and differentially for roll control in conjunction with the ailerons. Being mounted outside the engines, the stabilators could be positioned out of the wing wake without interference from the jet efflux, and at high angles of attack, when the ailerons become progressively less effective, the tail surfaces generate all required roll moments. The twin vertical stabilizers are tall enough to maintain stability at high angles of attack, and the twin booms on which the tail surfaces are mounted are braced to each other via the titanium engine bay assembly to provide a rigid structure for transferring the torsional

loads from the tail to the aircraft.

Modifications to the aerodynamic configuration and control system as a result of flight testing are described in detail in the first chapter. Structural alterations included the clipping of the wingtips to reduce buffeting at high subsonic speeds and high g at around 30,000ft (9,100m); the increased chord on the outer sections of the stabilators to eliminate flutter, producing the notched leading edges of these surfaces; and the doubling in size of the speedbrake.

At the same time, several changes were made to the flight control system, such as the reduction in stick control forces during high-g manoeuvring to make CAS-off control easier. The CAS itself was modified to be less responsive to small, sharp stick deflections, since its original bias towards rapid rolling made the aircraft's response alarmingly jerky during more precise manoeuvres such as formation flying, air-to-air refuelling and target tracking with the gun. Similarly, the aileron-rudder interconnect system was made to disconnect on touch-down to eliminate the accentu-

Right: The F-15 has demonstrated an ability to turn well inside an F-4E, or climb 7,100ft (2,164m) while matching the Phantom's tightest level turn.

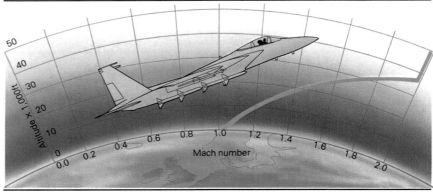

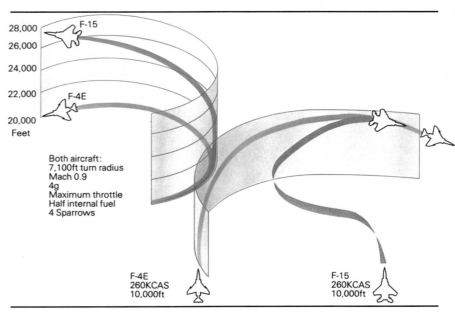

Both aircraft:
7,100ft turn radius
Mach 0.9
4g
Maximum throttle
Half internal fuel
4 Sparrows

F-4E
260KCAS
10,000ft

F-15
260KCAS
10,000ft

Above: Superb performance is matched by a magnificent view from the cockpit: a 49th TFW F-15A is in the background.

Left: A pair of 57th FWW Eagles demonstrate the type's excellent low-level handling qualities over Nellis AFB, Arizona.

ation of weathervaning during cross-wind landings.

While all these problems were being identified and corrected during the flight test programme, the new fighter was demonstrated to a number of journalists during 1974. Clark Martin, of the US journal *Aviation Week and Space Technology*, flew in an F-15B when the aircraft was still subject to a limit of +5.9g: the left afterburner failed to ignite until after liftoff, but the takeoff was still impressive, a 3,300ft (1,000m) ground roll taking 18 seconds to a liftoff speed of 175kt. This compares with a ground roll of only 900ft (274m) for a production single-seater in standard interceptor configuration, when the nose-wheel is rotated at around 100kt and liftoff takes place at 135kt.

Following liftoff the F-15B went into a 50deg climb at 300kt, reaching a height of 14,000ft (4,267m) by the time it was over the end of the 15,000ft (4,572m) runway. During subsequent manoeuvres Clark reported that CAS-off flight was equal to that of earlier fighters, enabling tracking manoeuvres at up to 4g to be carried out at 10,000ft (3,000m) and 350kt. Climb and acceleration were also demonstrated, with a climb at better than 6,000ft/min (1,800m/min) in Military (non-afterburning) power to 32,000ft (9,750m) followed by

acceleration in full afterburner from Mach 0.9 to Mach 1.1 in 10 seconds and Mach 1.2 in 20 seconds.

Another close observer of an early demonstration flight was Captain Robert J. Hoag, Editor of the USAF *Fighter Weapons Review*. Following in an F-4 chase plane, Captain Hoag watched the Eagle lift off after a ground roll of 1,200ft (366m) and reach 10,000ft (3,000m) over a ground track of less than 5,000ft (1,500m). To compare the turning performance of the two aircraft, the F-4 initiated a 5½g turn in full afterburner, starting from a speed of 350-400kt and at an altitude of 12,000ft (3,650m). The Eagle, starting at the same speed and altitude and at a slant range of 6,000ft (1,830m) was able to close to a minimum range on the Phantom's tail within 540deg of turn, using only military power and with no trace of the severe buffeting experienced by the F-4.

Another manoeuvre which particularly impressed Captain Hoag, who was moved to describe the F-15 as a "Superfighter", was a transition from 110kt flight, with landing gear and flaps down, to an Immelmann in full afterburner with gear and flaps up. The transition was immediate, and the Eagle was able to accelerate throughout the manoeuvre.

The implications for combat of the

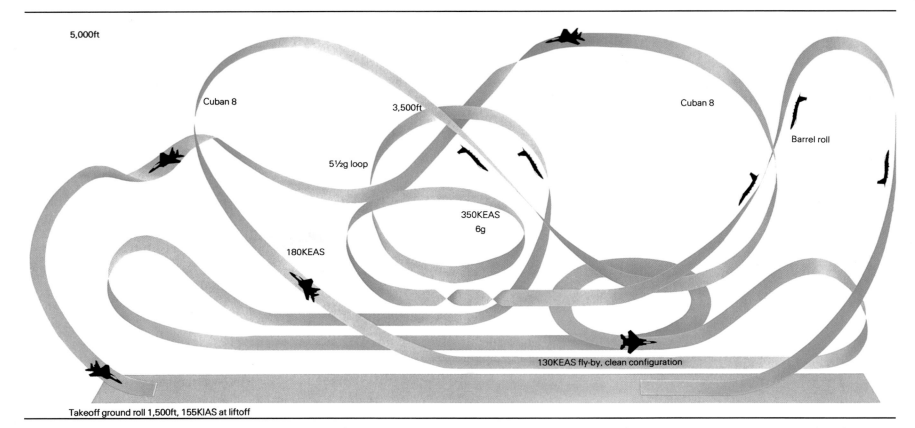

5,000ft

Cuban 8

3,500ft

Cuban 8

Barrel roll

5½g loop

350KEAS
6g

180KEAS

130KEAS fly-by, clean configuration

Takeoff ground roll 1,500ft, 155KIAS at liftoff

Above: Fair-weather flying display given by the Strike Eagle during its public premiere at the 1982 Farnborough Air Show.

power implicit in such demonstrations are obvious. While the Eagle should be able to accelerate out of trouble fairly easily, an opponent would find it extremely hard to get away. The F-15's ability to maintain controllable flight over a wide range of speeds and at angles of attack up to 26deg can enhance the effectiveness of both missiles and guns. And the ability to maintain acceleration at steep angles is a significant advantage against the high-speed, high-altitude MiG-25, allowing the target to be tracked by the radar against a clutter-free background in a snap-up intercept.

Overall, the Eagle's air combat superiority is directly attributable to the high lift and excess power specified in the original requirement. Whereas the pilot of an F-4 must be aware of the need to conserve energy, and will often have to build up energy in combat by diving away into a zoom climb, the F-15 has so much power available that it can accelerate straight into high-g ma-

Below: 36th TFW F-15A touches down with airbrake at full 45deg extension. Early control problems on the rollout were corrected by modifications to the control system.

noeuvres, and sustain them for long periods without losing altitude or airspeed.

Of course, there are other requirements in combat than pure power and manoeuvrability: above all, the pilot must be able to use them effectively. In this respect the bubble canopy and the exceptional visibility it provides is of fundamental importance – according to Captain Hoag, "The pilot feels as if he is riding astride the bird, rather than in it". There is also room for him to twist around in his seat without banging his head against the canopy.

Cockpit layout
The cockpit layout itself was given an enthusiastic welcome. The most frequently used controls are positioned at the top of the centre instrument panel (HUD, UHF radio, Mode 3 IFF and position identification) or on the left console near the throttle (radar controls, fuel jettison, ILS TACAN, landing lights, BIT control panel auxiliary radio and master IFF). Other instruments on the front panel include the air-to-air and air-to-ground weapons monitoring systems, the radar display, standard flight instruments and engine instruments. The right console contains the engine controls, INS control panel and environmental controls. Altogether there are 30 per cent fewer gauges than in an F-4 cockpit, and with the HUD acting as the primary source of flight information and

the communications controls located just below it the time spent looking inside the cockpit is reduced to a minimum.

The pilot is further helped to keep his head up by the location of the main weapon and radar controls on the stick and throttle. With the CAS translating the pilot's inputs into electrical signals, finger and thumb pressure on the stick

Below: Touchdown by a 555th TFS Eagle. Even without a brake parachute the F-15 needs a shorter landing run than the F-4.

is enough to maintain control, while the controls for a number of other functions are also carried on the stick. A trim button allows the aircraft's attitude to be adjusted in pitch or yaw axes; the trigger engages the HUD camera and fires the gun; the weapon release button, depending on the mode selected, will engage the HUD camera, launch a selected missile, release bombs, designate a target or illuminate a target for a Sparrow; another button uncages or cages the seeker heads of heat-seeking Sidewinders or laser-guided bombs; and the air refuelling receptacle re-

lease switch, when the radar is engaged, enables the pilot to engage the radar's boresight or super-search modes. The former commands the radar to scan directly ahead and lock on the first target it detects within ten miles (16km), while in super-search the radar scans the 20deg HUD field of view up to ten miles ahead and locks on any target detected, displaying a box in the HUD to indicate its position to the pilot.

The throttles also carry a variety of controls. Apart from the microphone and IFF transmitter, there is an ECM dispenser switch for releasing chaff or flares, a weapon mode selector for the air-to-air radar mode appropriate to gun, Sparrow or Sidewinder, and the speedbrake control, plus more radar controls. The antenna elevation control allows the radar scan pattern to be adjusted up or down, while the target designator control adjusts the position of the radar scope target acquisition gate, used to designate a target detected in normal search modes.

HOTAS philosophy

The thinking behind the head-up HOTAS (hands on throttle and stick) system of combat is summed up succinctly by Colonel Wendell H. Shawler, Director of the F-15 Joint Test Force, 1973–76: "Everything you need is on the throttle and stick". However, he adds that these functions need to be simplified to avoid confusion during the heat of battle. According to Jack Cranes of MCAIR, addressing the Society of Experimental Test Pilots on the F/A-18 HOTAS system, the average pilot can only use three functions intelligently, wisely and properly. Air-to-air weapon selection on the F-15 is split into three functions: gun, Sidewinder or Sparrow.

Again according to Colonel Shawler, on selecting guns, "you automatically got everything up there (in the HUD)

Right: 36th TFW F-15Cs practise a formation takeoff from a West German autobahn. Nose-up normally takes place when the Eagle reaches a speed of 100kt.

you needed for guns, including short-range radar on your radar selection". The same applies to the two types of AAM. "The fact that you were selecting one of three functions – you got everything you needed. You couldn't do much else – you don't want to. When you start getting all these complexities where you put 50 functions on the stick and throttle, if you select one thing over here, you get three choices there, it gets very difficult." During Colonel Shawler's time HOTAS did not strain the pilot's workload; but later, when all the ECM and EW aspects were added to the one-man cockpit, it did, in his opinion, "put the workload over a lot of people's capabilities".

This view has been echoed by at least one experienced F-15 pilot, Major Dito Ladd, who until transferring to the 527th Aggressors was Chief of Weapons and Tactics with the 525th TFS, 36th TFW. In May 1983 Major Ladd recalled: "There are times when you feel like 'Yeah, I've got this thing whipped, I can take advantage of every opportunity the weapon provides.' That was generally after a period of intense flying. Flying once a day or twice a day over a period of two to three weeks there are times when the airplane can be fun, with one man it can be extremely effective, but it take the time and practice to do it. It's just like anything, you've got to practice."

Right: Two F-15Cs of the 18th TFW take off at sunset from Kwang-Ju air base, Republic of Korea, in April 1982 during one of PACAF's annual Team Spirit exercises.

F-15 Eagle Variants

As the F-15 proved its worth as an air superiority fighter, great hopes were held for it in other roles. It was touted for tactical reconnaissance, the Wild Weasel SEAD (Suppression of Enemy Air Defence) mission. The latter role is long-dead, and the other two appear increasingly unlikely as the years pass. Updates improved its capability as a fighter, but its only real offshoot was the F-15E Strike Eagle. Nor did it emerge in experimental guise; the only exception was the brightly coloured Agile Eagle, a short takeoff and landing/manoeuvre technology demonstrator.

As an air superiority fighter, the development of the F-15 Eagle has been a continuous process. As the F-15A/B it was a dedicated interceptor/air combat fighter, with a very secondary air-to-ground capability. As related earlier, it was plagued with engine problems, one of which resulted in a minor change to its external appearance. The con-di nozzles were encased with augmentor sealing flaps, commonly known as "turkey feathers," the purpose of which was to reduce base drag by ensuring a smooth airflow. Not only did these cause trouble; they increased the time and cost of maintenance in this area. The simple answer was to omit them, exposing the complex system of sliding runners and push rods. This of course increased base drag, but effects on performance were marginal.

Another engine-related problem, apart from durability, which has been

Below: Strike Eagle demonstrates its ability to carry a heavy load of Mk 20 Rockeye cluster bomb dispensers – plus four Sidewinders – in 1981.

dealt with earlier, was that the afterburner was often reluctant to relight. Eagle drivers in mock combat did the obvious thing, and left the engine in minimum 'burner. This naturally burned more fuel, which reduced endurance, making the F-15A/B rather more short-legged than had been anticipated.

From a tactical point of view, this was bad news. A fighter which approached "bingo" fuel while in a furball, was forced to disengage, often while at a tactical advantage. External tanks, widely known as jugs, were not really an option. Firstly, the extra weight, and most particularly drag, reduced performance. Secondly, as a rule of thumb, half the fuel in the jugs was used in getting the other half to where it actually made a difference. Thirdly, jugs sterilised pylons which could otherwise have been used for weaponry, thus reducing combat persistence.

The F-15 had been designed in an era before low-observable technology had made a significant impact on fighter doctrine, with the result that it was slab-sided. There is an American

expression, "When you have a lemon, the best thing to do is to make lemonade!" McDonnell Douglas did precisely this, cobbling together a low-drag conformal fuel tank (CFT) to fit snugly along each side. They hedged their bets by designing it to carry sensors, and also by making it removable, but in practice it became a virtually permanent fixture. Weapons and sensors could be carried along the lower edge of the CFT, which called for extra wiring and plumbing, and this gave rise to the F-15C/D, which differed from the A/B in having a beefed-up landing gear to handle the extra weight.

Fighters have long since been weapons systems: a combination of detection, offensive and defensive avionics all carried in a flying machine. To improve its capabilities, the obvious move is to upgrade the avionics. This could be done in one of two ways: new systems, or by using more sophisticated software. Back in the 1980s the panacea for all ills was, "It's only a software change", but so rapidly did technology advance that

Above: Dive-bombing demonstration by the second development F-15B, 71-0291, in its Strike Eagle configuration in 1980.

software programmes became too complex for this to remain the case.

The first real F-15 update was the Multi-Staged Improvement Plan (MSIP), initiated in 1983. Part I was aimed at the F-15A/B, part II at the F-15C/D. A Programmable Signal Processor (PSP) had been added to the radar, giving enhanced radar performance, and provision for mid-course updating of the AIM-120A AMRAAM, the future medium-range missile for the F-15. In addition, MSIP provided improved ECM and communications.

Right: Command and status, tactical situation, radar, and duplicate of the pilot's HUD displays dominate the aft cockpit of the F-15 AFCD.

Below right: The prototype Strike Eagle strafes a ground target with the 30mm GEPOD. This form of attack is not an economic proposition.

Above: In its new guise of dual-role fighter demonstrator, 71-0291 carries 22 Mk 20 Rockeyes over St Louis in May 1983.

A modified F-15B was flown on February 20, 1991. This carried Cockpit 2000, a central touch-sensitive CRT display some 12.20in (310mm) square, flanked by two 7.9 in (200cm) square screens, all in full colour. These were coupled with a liquid crystal HUD and a helmet mounted display (HMD), and backed

Below: Formation takeoff from Lambert-St Louis, home of MCAIR, with the F-15 dual-role demonstrator in the foreground.

by two Lear Astronautics computers. One uses air-to-air attack management software which combines sensor data and feeds the result to the air combat flight management computer. This last then produces a range of attack profiles in priority order. The pilot then chooses whether to fly a profile manually, or to hook it into the flight control system, in which case the attack is flown automatically. If the target launches a missile, evasive action will also be automatic.

The implications are obvious. What we have here is a robot fighter with a man in the loop. The next step is to put that man in a remote location on the ground. But all this is well in the future; testing was halted for budgetary reasons. Or was it that the USAF was not yet ready for its steely-eyed fighter pilots to be replaced by a computer games expert on the ground? Only time will tell.

For the Eagle, updating continued. A few late-build F-15C/Ds carried the APG-70, but the new and improved APG-63(V)1, which combines com-

ponents from the APG-73 developed for the Hornet E/F with the transmitter and some software from APG-70, was first flown in an F-15C on July 18, 1997. This was being retrofitted in many late-build fighter F-15s from 1999.

Strike Eagle

Whereas the F-15 had a secondary mud-moving capability from the outset, a superior interdictor was needed to replace the elderly F-111. And whereas the latter needed fighter escort, its replacement would have to

Left: The Advanced Fighter Capability Demonstrator equipped with bombs, Sidewinders, forward-looking infra-red pod and long-range ground-mapping radar takes off from Eglin AFB, Florida.

Above: The MCAIR Strike Eagle in its original form, before conversion to AFCD and dual-role demonstrator for USAF trials.

be able to fight its way in and back out again. The increasingly sophisticated range of air to ground weapons available, coupled with the need to operate at night, demanded more than a single crewman could handle. A two-seater was the obvious solution, with a specialist operator in the back seat to handle all the electronic wizardry. In addition, an existing type, for which much of the production cost had already been amortized, was preferred.

There were two front runners. The first two-seater TF-15, tail number 291, which was destined to become the most modified, and almost certainly the most photographed Eagle of all, was used for initial trials. The other main contender was the General Dynamics F-16F, a cranked-wing tailless delta variant of the Fort Worth fighter. While this could carry a huge number of Mk 82 bombs in tandem underwing positions, and had a fuel fraction of 0.40, it had two main drawbacks. It was single-engined, which restricted its size, and therefore its utility as a bomb truck; and, unlike the F-15E, design changes were so extreme as to render it a new aircraft for all practical purposes.

As mentioned earlier, Tornado GR.1 was also considered, probably as a fall-back position. It was never more than a rank outsider, primarily because its air combat capabilities were minimal. (To digress for a moment, several aircraft, including the Harrier, were demonstrated for USAF chief of staff General Allen at RAF Wittering in 1979. At a dress rehearsal, the writer stood in for General Allen, with a piece of paper with four stars on it pinned to his lapel. Freezing, on top of the control tower, a bunch of us stood watching nothing in particular for several minutes. Then station commander Group Captain

Alan Bridges said, with an absolutely straight face, "We have just been watching Tornado, but we can't have it 'til Thursday!")

Tornado's ultra low-level attack profile conflicted with USAF doctrine of medium level attack, covered by heavy ECM. Unsurprisingly, if only because it was closest to the original aircraft, the choice fell on the F-15 in the shape of the F-15E Strike Eagle, or Mud Hen as it was to become affectionately known.

Whereas the original TF-15A, forerunner of the Strike Eagle, looked like an authentic Strike Eagle, what it could not do was to handle the increased weight-lifting capacity. Maximum takeoff weight was increased from the 68,000lb (30,845kg) of the F-15C, to 81,000lb (36,742kg) for the F-15E. Much heavier landing gear was required, and structural stiffening, involving some 60 per cent of the airframe, was needed throughout. Matters were not helped by the fact that operational life was doubled to 16,000 hours. Empty weight increased from 29,180lb (13,240kg) for the F-15C, to 32,000lb (14,515kg) for the F-15E – nearly 10 per cent extra!

Externally the F-15E looked very similar to the F-15D, but under the skin it was a rather different bird. Previously, the engine bays had to be made up of several different components. For the F-15E, extremes of heat and pressure were used to form titanium alloys into complex shapes and curves. Savings were considerable: 240 fewer components; 6,400 fewer fasteners; 25 per cent less weight, and 50 per cent less cost. The engine bays were slightly larger, which at need could accommodate growth in the shape of the much more powerful General Electric F110-GE-229. Then, in August 1991, the

equally powerful F100-PW-229 powerplant entered service.

The APG-70 radar is more flexible and versatile than its predecessor, the APG-63, and has much greater computer capacity. A synthetic aperture mode gives very accurate ground mapping, a degree of target identification, and a ground moving target indicator. Other new modes are terrain following and terrain avoidance. These are backed up with LANTIRN, which gives low level flight and attack capability by passive means.

The accent on low level penetration, typically at 500ft (150m), increased the hazard of birdstrike. To offset this, a new and tough polycarbonate wrap-around windshield was fitted. The "steam-gauge" dial instrumentation of the fighter F-15s was replaced by three colour MFDs, with a wide-angle holographic HUD. In the back seat, the WSO was given four wall-to-wall MFDs, which displayed radar, EW and IR information, aircraft and weapons status, and a moving map. Two hand controllers were provided for the WSO to operate the various systems.

The first F-15E was delivered to the USAF in 1988, and initial operational capability (IOC) was reached in 1989. As related previously, operational baptism came in the Gulf War of 1991, when the Mud Hen performed outstandingly well. Hardened aircraft shelters (HAS) were fine for protecting aircraft against the bombing technology of the 1970s, but much less effective in protecting aircraft against the precision guided munitions (PGMs) of the 1990s. The only value of Iraqi HAS in the Gulf War was that it was impossible to tell in advance which HAS protected aircraft, and which were empty!

Agile Eagle

An adage dating from 1940 stated that the ultimate in air superiority was a tank in the middle of the runway! This was slowly modified into "the ultimate in air superiority is a hole in the middle of the runway!" The Israeli pre-emptive strike in June 1967 demonstrated to the world the vulnerability of fighters that were tied to orthodox bases with long and hard runways. A fighter is only of value in the air; when grounded it is merely a target! The USA, after a short flirtation with VTOL and STOVL, concentrated on short field performance, the rationale being that even if the runway was cut, sufficient stretches would be left usable to support operations.

Takeoff was no particular problem; the fighter could be wheeled out and set up just short of the nearest set of holes, with a usable stretch of concrete in front of it. Landing was a different matter altogether. Given a limited stretch of runway, the fighter had to set down as close as possible to the damaged end, then pull up in the restricted space available. The need was to identify usable stretches of runway, then set down on them.

This was addressed by the F-15S/MTD (Short Landing/Maneuver Technology Demonstrator), which first flew in August 1988. This again was TF-15 291, by now equipped with canard foreplanes and a digital quadruplex FBW system. Runway limits were set at 1,500ft (457m) long by 50ft (15m) wide, with 4.5in (11.43cm) bumps caused by repairs. Conditions for landing were a wet runway at night, a 200ft (60m) cloud base, a 2,600ft (790m) visibility with a 30kt (55kmh) crosswind, and no external landing aids.

Above: Huge radome, the access ladder, and the enormous intakes of the F-15 are its main recognition features from this angle. From astern, the twin fins predominate.

Below: HARM, anti-radar missile, Snakeye bombs, Sparrows and Sidewinders arm the proposed defence suppression Eagle.

This was a tall order. The touchdown point had to be exact, with no margin for scatter. It had to be selected from several miles away, using onboard systems. This called for a carrier-style no-flare touchdown, for which the main gear was redesigned. Having touched down, the fighter then had to stop quickly without being blown off-course (and off the hardstand) by crosswinds.

The key to touchdown lay in the Autonomous Landing Guidance System (ALGS), which used the high-resolution ground mapping feature of the APG-70 to select the landing area. Once selected, the touchdown spot and landing heading were designated, providing steering and elevation data on the HUD. Once on short finals, a perspective of the landing area came up on the LANTIRN display.

At a later stage, thrust vectoring/reversing nozzles were fitted to the F-15S/MTD, tied in with the quadruplex FBW system. These added to braking ability, coupled with canard foreplanes which were actually stabilisers from the F/A-18 Hornet. Deflected to their maximum, they added aerody-namic braking after touchdown.

Demonstrated performance improvements over the F-15A were 38 per cent less distance on takeoff and a 60 per cent reduction in landing roll. In flight, thrust reversal at Mach 1.6 gave a deceleration rate of more than 18kt (33km/sec), down to Mach 0.8 in less than half a minute, while pitch rates were more than doubled. The F-15S/MTD using thrust vectoring might possibly have equalled the Sukhoi Su-37 in "impossible" manoeuvres, but that we shall never know for certain.

On April 21, 1993, NASA test pilot Gordon Fullerton twice landed at Edwards AFB using engine thrust alone for control, commanding flight path and bank angle via two thumbwheel controllers. This technology is however for the next generation; the slab-sided F-15 is one of the least stealthy of fighters, and as such has little future beyond about 2010.

The tremendous increase in all-up weight of the F-15E changed the handling characteristics. Whereas the earlier F-15 was fairly benign at angles of attack above 20deg, it was found that the forebody of the F-15E produced a yawing effect, while the CFTs were destabilising in roll. After the squadrons reported numerous instances of aircraft departing controlled flight, leading to two crashes, a programme called "Keep Eagle" was instituted late in 1992. This resulted in improved flight control system software, Version 7, which was released in August 1994.

This resulted in a direct electric link which could deflect each stabilator dif-

Left: A full-size model of the USAF's ASAT missile ready for loading on an F-15A at Boeing's Seattle facility in August 1982.

Right: Vought ASAT is carried by a Space Command Eagle for vibroacoustic trials as part of the captive flight test programme.

Above: The Boeing-developed ASAT launch pylon incorporates a microprocessor and communications link between missile and aircraft.

Right: The anti-satellite missile would be launched at about 80,000ft (24,400m), and two stages would carry it through to intercept altitude.

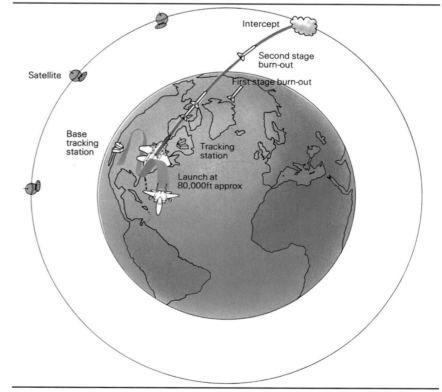

ferentially by up to 32deg in opposite directions, which compared with 12deg on the existing aircraft.

There is a lesson here. No matter how good the computer programmers might be, what matters in the real world is how the aircraft handles. This should be pondered by those who consider that future wars should be fought by robot fighters!

Satellite killer

Another role planned for the F-15 was that of satellite killer. During the Cold War, satellites were seen to have an indirect part to play in any future war, primarily as reconnaissance vehicles, but also as a vital part of a communications and navigation network, notably GPS. The disruption of this was therefore a valid strategic objective. The Soviet Union addressed this problem by using "space mines"; killer satellites which could be manoeuvred to within very close distance of their targets and then detonated. The USA

adopted a very different approach.

In 1979, the Vought Corporation was awarded a contract to develop an anti-satellite missile (ASAT). This was projected to be operational in 1985, but like so many other projects, this date proved to be extremely optimistic.

ASAT was to be carried on the centreline of an F-15. A large weapon, weighing about 2,700lb (1,224kg), it consisted of a first stage based on Boeing's AGM-69 Short Range Attack Missile (SRAM), and a second stage powered by the Altair Thiokol rocket motor which for many years was used as the fourth stage of Vought's launch vehicle. The seeker consisted of heat-homing sensors, coupled with hi-test hydrogen peroxide thrusters for terminal course adjustments.

Initially, two squadrons of F-15s were expected to be deployed in the ASAT role, but after the destruction of a single satellite, which in any case was near its "sell-by" date, the project was dropped.

F-16 Fighting Falcon

Contents

Top: The standard F-16 was powered by a turbofan; the F-16/79 utilised the J79 turbojet. This downgraded variant failed to attract sales.

Above: Norwegian Air Force F-16s routinely carry the Penguin anti-shipping missile, seen here carried on the inboard pylons.

Above right: As part of the five nation mid-life update, this Danish F-16B launches unguided rockets. On the port wing is a data link pod.

Left: An F-16D Viper lays down two parachute-retarded bombs. At low level this ensures that when the bombs go off, the attacking aircraft has managed to get well clear.

Introduction

At the Paris Air Show in 1975, a small and brightly coloured fighter marked its international air show debut with a breathtaking display of manoeuvrability. It was of course the General Dynamics YF-16, flown by Chief Test Pilot Neil Anderson.

Only dimly did observers on the ground comprehend that they were watching the opening of a new era. The F-16 not only set new standards of fighter manoeuvrability, it established a plateau which could not be significantly exceeded for nearly two decades, and even at the beginning of the 21st Century remains hard to beat.

This was no accident. Until that time, fighters had been getting progressively larger, heavier, more complex and less affordable. As a reaction against that trend, the F-16 had been designed as a lightweight, uncompromised close combat fighter, and consisted of, in the words of Pentagon analyst Pierre Sprey, "the smallest possible airframe wrapped around the largest possible engine!" This was coupled with a modest wing loading, relaxed stability, and fly-by-wire, which last gave it the soubriquet of the "Electric Jet".

Austere fighters have never found great acceptance in the West, and the F-16 was no exception. Customers wanted greater capability, and it was soon developed into a multi-role middle-weight. Fortunately the performance and agility penalties of the extra weight proved fairly marginal, and in close combat it became a byword. Adopted by the USAF, it was given the uninspired name of Fighting Falcon, but to the men who fly it, and even the company that makes it, F-16 remains the Electric Jet or, even more commonly, the Viper.

Over its long operational life it has undergone many changes and upgrades, with more powerful engines to handle the added weight, and has appeared in several operational and many experimental versions. It serves with some 20 air forces worldwide, and has seen action with several. A superb 70 to nil air combat record is matched by its air-to-surface capability with both smart and dumb weapons. At the time of writing, production is nearing 4,000, and is scheduled to continue for some time yet. The F-16 will be with us for many years to come.

Development

The F-16 has more multirole capability than any other aircraft in the same weight class currently in service. Originally designed to outfight the MiG-21 Fishbed, it can match the rather later MiG-29 Fulcrum for sheer agility, while remaining a first-class bomb truck. It also has, although to what degree this was deliberate is not known, a small radar cross-section. Moreover it has remained affordable, as many overseas air forces can attest.

In following up the F-86 Sabre of the late 1940s, US fighter designers developed an expensive fascination with the sophistication made possible by improvements in technology. The larger the aircraft, the more capable it became, but while succeeding designs saw massive increases in combat capability, the price was paid in terms of both money and ever-diminishing fleet numbers. From the P-51 Mustang to the F-15 Eagle, each new US land-based fighter was on average 2·4 times more expensive than its predecessor, and Eagle production over 15 years may never reach a tenth of the 15,000 Mustangs built in a third of that time.

This philosophy was challenged briefly in the light of Korean War experience. The F-104 should have ended up a US equivalent of the MiG-21 Fishbed, but like the earlier F-100 evolved into a strike fighter instead of an air-combat fighter. Early models were used in Vietnam for a short time, but the USAF found itself having to combat the agile and lightweight MiGs of the North Vietnamese air force with the heavy and expensive F-4 Phantom – a type originally developed as an all-weather naval interceptor. The subsequent addi-

tion of wing slats and a built-in 20mm cannon enhanced the aircraft's usefulness as an air combat fighter, and the F-4E was to have a long and successful combat career, but the original design had never been intended for dogfighting.

The Vietnam experience

Over North Vietnam, the US pilots found themselves unable to match the kill rates of the Korean War. Instead of a 10:1 or better kill ratio of the earlier conflict, they achieved at best just over 3:1, a figure which steadily fell to still lower values. For a long time, the US services claimed to have maintained permanent superiority over the MiGs, quoting rates of just over unity at worst. In practice, the ratio at times came out slightly in favour of the Vietnamese.

Part of the problem was training programmes which had placed little emphasis on air-to-air combat. The accepted dogma was that the traditional dogfight had a hallowed place in the history of air fighting, but none at all in modern warfare. Even in the early 1940s, the Spitfires and Hurricanes used to defend British skies from the attentions of the Luftwaffe were committed to combat using elaborate pre-planned

tactics which virtually denied the possibility of individual 'free-style' air-to-air engagements. The Luftwaffe pilots had no such illusions, and took a heavy toll of the defenders in early encounters.

With the arrival of the high-speed jet fighter, and the subsequent development of supersonic fighters, the 'no-dogfighting' dogma re-emerged virtually unchanged from its early 1940s RAF form. In view of the speed of the latest warplanes, the firing time available to an attacker was thought to be so small that pilots attempting to dogfight would have little chance of hitting their targets. Long-range combat using air-to-air missiles was thought to be the likely pattern of future combat. In the skies above Korea, Suez, and the Indo-Pakistan border the falsehood of this theory has been demonstrated time and again. In the light of the Vietnam experience it was rejected by the USAF.

As early as 1965 the USAF began concept-formulation studies of new high-performance fighters. These included a heavy 60,000lb (27,000kg) interceptor/air-superiority fighter designated Fighter Experimental (FX), and a lightweight Advanced Day Fighter (ADF). FX would have been heavier

Above: Contrasting styles in fighter design – 15 years separated the first flights of the F-4 Phantom (left) and the YF-16 (right).

than the F-4 Phantom, with twin engines and a variable-geometry wing, while the 25,000lb (11,000kg) ADF design specified a thrust-to-weight ratio and wing loading intended to better the performance of the MiG-21 by a margin of 25 per cent.

The appearance of the Soviet MiG-25 Foxbat fighter in the mid-1960s created a hiatus in USAF future fighter plans. Foxbat posed the threat of the Soviet air force and its Warsaw Pact allies being equipped with Mach 3 fighters at a time when the USAF had only a handful of experimental Mach 3 YF-12 fighter prototypes and no plans for production of aircraft in this performance class. Development of the massive North American F-108 Rapier interceptor had begun in the late 1950s, but this Mach 3 design

Below: Dogfighters old and new in formation provide graphic evidence that Fighting Falcon is hardly bigger than the 1940s P-51 Mustang. Note the 'bubble' canopies.

was cancelled in September 1959, 18 months before the first of two prototypes was due to fly.

Foxbat's Mach 3 capability provoked a redirection of USAF fighter planning. The urgent goal now was to develop a design capable of matching both the existing MiG-21 and the new MiG-25, shifting the emphasis to an FX design – the F-15 – offering a high top speed and long-range missile armament.

Although on 'back-burner', the concept of a lightweight fighter similar to ADF was not dead. Two individuals who did much to keep the concept of a lightweight fighter alive were former fighter instructor Major John Boyd, and Pierre Sprey, a civilian working for the assistant Secretary of Defense for Systems Analysis.

Boyd had already had a strong influence on the FX project and was the inventor of the concept of energy manoeuvrability – a vital element in assessing fighter performance. "Let's pretend that manoeuvrability is an energy problem", he once suggested to a group of thermodynamics students. "When you manoeuvre an airplane you need energy ... you lose energy either in gaining altitude, airspeed or both.

"Normally you lose energy in turning. What happens is that your drag exceeds your thrust, and at that point you have a negative energy rate. That negative rate has to come out of altitude, airspeed or out of a combination of the two. You reach a point, even with your military afterburner, at which drag is greater than thrust. That means you have a negative vector ... you multiply net drag by velocity and that tells you how much energy you're going to have to pump up."

Measuring performance

At first Boyd could hardly believe that this simple idea was a new method of looking at fighter performance. Once he had accepted the fact, he considered how combinations of aerodynamics and engines could be devised to create better aircraft. "You just turn the problem of manoeuvrability around and look at it from a different viewpoint. And the result of that was obvious.... The right thrust-to-weight ratio could give you an important edge over your adversary." Fighter performance could be measured at different combinations of altitude, airspeed and manoeuvring situations in terms of what is now designated Specific Excess Power – Ps in engineering jargon.

Boyd's theory showed that the FX would require an engine with a thrust-to-weight ratio significantly better than that of current designs. The resulting F100 turbofan was not only used to power the F-15, but also created the possibility of a lightweight single-engined design of high performance.

Traditional USAF thinking prior to the

early 1970s equated light weight with short range. To some degree, this was justified in view of the technology of the time. The MiG-21 was a lightweight developed using mid-1950s technology, and the original Fishbed C day fighter gave rise to the quip among export users that it was a 'supersonic sports plane' – an aircraft with very limited range and even more limited payload.

In the late 1960s, Boyd and Sprey devised a 25,000lb (11,340kg) design designated F-XX – a dedicated air superiority fighter of high endurance. Later studies took this weight down even lower to around 17,000lb (7,700kg). The concept met much opposition, since some saw it as a threat both to traditional thinking on the subject of fighters and to the existing F-15 project.

By 1971, Boyd was working for the Air Force Prototype Study Group. Conse-

quently, he was able to push the concept at a time when the idea of competitive flight-testing of prototype designs was returning to vogue after the massive and highly controversial Total Procurement Package contracts of the 1960s which had resulted in the F-111 and C-5 Galaxy.

Main driving force in getting the LWF project off the drawing board and into the experimental shop was Deputy Defense Secretary David A. Packard, who saw the concept of competitive prototyping as a method of reversing the ever-growing cost of new weapon systems. A series of ground rules for such prototyping exercises drawn up by Air Force Secretary Robert C. Seamans specified that funding would be limited, with initial performance goals and military specifications kept to a minimum. Contestants should not be constrained by

Above: The Convair F-106 was built only in small numbers, but the YF-16 from the same Fort Worth plant was the first of more than 4,000.

the existing force structure of the USAF, but should not assume that any long-term production commitment existed.

Two USAF requirements were chosen for prototyping: a medium STOL transport intended to replace the C-130 Hercules, and the lightweight fighter. These resulted in the Boeing YC-14 and McDonnell Douglas YC-15 jet transports and the YF-16 and YF-17 fighter prototypes. Instead of the 'XC-' and 'XF-' designations which would have been traditional for such programmes, the 'Y' (development) prefix was used in order to stress that a mixture of off-the-shelf and experimental technologies were being used.

The first YF-16, serial 72-1567 was rolled out at Fort Worth in December 1973, only 21 months after contract award. Following an 'unofficial' and unplanned first flight on January 20, 1974, it was used to clear the flight **envelope, achieving supersonic speed on its third official sortie. Along with the second prototype it took part in the fly-off against the Northrop YF-17, and was flown against MiG-17 and MiG-21 fighters.**

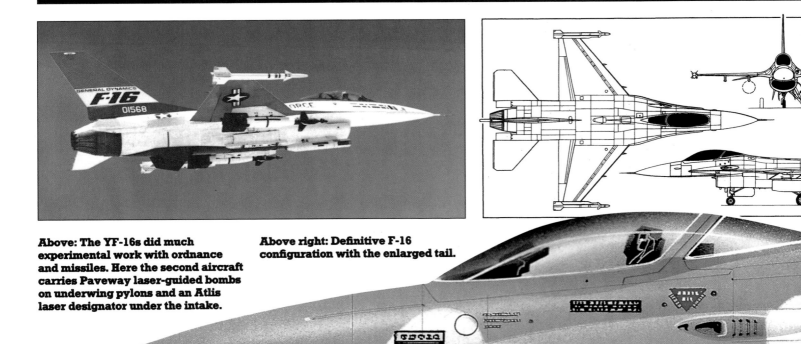

Above: The YF-16s did much experimental work with ordnance and missiles. Here the second aircraft carries Paveway laser-guided bombs on underwing pylons and an Atlis laser designator under the intake.

Above right: Definitive F-16 configuration with the enlarged tail.

Above: When first rolled out the second YF-16 was painted in a blue-on-white camouflage scheme devised by GD. It was later repainted in red, white and blue to match the first aircraft, then in all grey.

Four contracts worth a total of around $100 million were placed early in 1972 under the LWF programme. General Dynamics was given $38 million to develop and fly two YF-16s, while Northrop was awarded $39 million for two prototypes of the rival YF-17. Contracts were also given to Pratt & Whitney for development of a version of the F100 turbofan specifically for single-engined installations, and to General Electric for the new and smaller YF101 engine.

In submitting a Request for Proposals (RFP) for what was now designated the Lightweight Fighter (LWF) to industry in early 1972, the USAF specified three main objectives. The resulting design should fully explore the advantages of emerging technologies, reduce the risk and uncertainties involved in full-scale development and production of a new fighter, and provide the Department of Defense with a variety of technological options available to meet military hardware needs.

Instead of trying to match the 'brochure' capability of Soviet fighters, the USAF decided to optimize the LWF for the likely conditions of future air combat – altitudes of 30,000 to 40,000ft (9,000 to 12,000m) and speeds of Mach 0.6 to 1.6 – with no attempt to equal the performance of the MiG-25 Foxbat. It was designed not for the top right-hand corner of the performance envelope, but for a wide range of flight conditions, and with the emphasis on turn rate, acceleration and range. This combination of parame-

ters would allow the resulting aircraft to intercept and engage not only existing Warsaw Pact types such as the MiG-21, MiG-23 and Su-7, but also more advanced aircraft such as developed MiG-23 versions and the Su-24 Fencer.

The choice of likely operating height would raise a few eyebrows today, when most combat aircraft must fly at treetop height in order to survive, but reflects a time before the surface-to-air missile threat had literally brought the USAF down to earth. Even in the mid-1970s, the concept of flying into hostile airspace at medium altitude under the cover of advanced ECM had still not been abandoned.

Prototype technology
Following industrial submissions by five companies, General Dynamics and Northrop were chosen to develop flight-test hardware, and a contract was awarded to General Dynamics on April 13, 1972. This was a 'cost plus fixed fee' contract worth $37·9 million, and covered the design, construction and test of two prototypes under the USAF designation YF-16, plus one year of flight testing.

Although development and testing of these light fighters was a technology-demonstration programme, the USAF retained the option of carrying on to develop the design into a service aircraft. The contract with GD specified an average flyaway unit cost target of $3.0 million in 1972 dollars, (rather more in

1983 prices), assuming a production run of 300 examples at a rate of 100 per year. Complete design responsibility for the aircraft lay with the contractors, in order to reduce paperwork and maintain the pace of the programme, under the direction of the Aeronautical Systems Division at Wright-Patterson AFB, which monitored both projects throughout subsequent development.

No attempt was made in designing the YF-16 to push individual technological advances: the intention was to produce and test an aircraft capable of being developed into an operational type. New technology was used in in-

Above: According to some critics, the F-16 should have retained the YF-16 configuration shown here – a simple day fighter armed with two AIM-9, a cannon and minimal avionics.

stances where it would have the greatest effect in meeting performance targets, but proven systems and components were retained in areas where such new technology was not required. Components and detail assemblies were designed for ease of manufacture, using low-cost materials wherever possible. Hardware was standardized wherever possible, the design of the air-

Below: In creating the full-scale development F-16s GD engineers increased the areas of the wing, horizontal stabilizers and ventral strakes and re-configured the forward fuselage to accommodate a nose radar. The third FSD aircraft, 75- 0747, flew for the first time on May 3, 1977, and was the first to be fitted with the full avionics and fire-control system. This aircraft was the only F-16 to carry the two-tone dark grey-on-grey camouflage scheme.

AF 01 568

frame often incorporating multi-use parts and assemblies.

Flying advanced technology features on the YF-16 gave the USAF confidence to adopt them in a service aircraft. "If we hadn't put them in the prototype, we'd still be arguing about putting them into a production airplane", F-16 director of engineering Willian C. Dietz told the US magazine *Aviation Week & Space Technology* in 1977. Although high-technology features such as relaxed stability, fly-by-wire control, wing/body blending and strakes, variable camber and the reclining seat were used to improve F-16 performance, these were not seen as high risks in terms of production or maintenance.

Specific cost goals were set at an early stage, and careful studies were carried out to establish areas where a trade-off between cost and performance or operational capability would be acceptable.

Prototype design

Design objective of the YF-16 was to create the maximum agility and manoeuvrability in a small aircraft with minimum avionics capable of conducting air combat operations some 500nm (575 miles/926km) from its own base.

Small size not only dictated design simplicity, but brought a series of other advantages. Factors such as material, detail design and construction being equal, airframe cost is largely dependent on airframe weight, so the move towards a smaller aircraft promised lower costs. At the same time, drag was minimized, allowing a lower thrust setting to be used during aircraft cruise, and increasing the thrust-to-weight ratio possible with any given powerplant. And as experience in Vietnam had shown, the small size of the MiG-17 and MiG-21 made them difficult to detect visually, adding to the problems of aircrew engaging these types in air combat.

One factor which helped focus USAF attention on the virtues of the YF-16 and YF-17 was the Middle East War of 1973. The USAF has always fought its wars under conditions of numerical superiority, but October of that year saw a close ally struggling to win air and battlefield superiority against forces abundantly

equipped along Soviet lines. The need of quantity as well as quality was brought home in a conflict in which one observer estimates that some 40 per cent of the Israeli fighter force was lost, or damaged to the point where it was not available for combat, within the first two days.

One influence on the size of the design was the likely avionics payload. While the LWF requirement specified minimal avionics, the design team recognized that an operational aircraft would probably require a heavier and bulkier payload of electronics. Accordingly, the decision was made not to size the basic aircraft to handle radar-guided missiles such as the AIM-7 Sparrow, but to assume an air-to-air armament of heat-seeking AIM-9 Sidewinder missiles plus a General Electric M61 cannon, while making provisions within

the design to allow Sparrow-class missiles to be incorporated at a later date, should this be desired.

Military requirements specified a load factor of 7·33g while carrying 80 per cent internal fuel. GD decided to increase this figure to 9·0g at full internal fuel, and to increase the service life of the airframe from the normal 4,000 hours to 8,000 hours.

Accepting the fact that fighters invariably end up carrying external fuel tanks, the GD team decided to capitalize on this trend. Assuming that a YF-16 pilot would use externally-carried fuel on the outbound trip to the combat zone, then fight and return on internal fuel, the design team allocated internal fuel volume accordingly, reducing the airframe size. This move shaved 1,470lb (667kg) off the airframe empty weight, and reduced all-up weight by

Above: This head-on view of a YF-16 shows the wing leading-edge strakes and the way the wing is blended smoothly into the fuselage.

3,300lb (1497kg). More importantly, turn rate could as a result be increased by five per cent, and acceleration by 30 per cent.

Before deciding on a configuration for the new aircraft, GD engineers considered the effect of 78 variables, running theoretical analyses and wind-tunnel tests. The latter testing totalled 1,272 hours, and was carried out at speeds from Mach 0·2 up to Mach 2·2, at angles of attack of up to 28deg and at yaw angles of up to 12deg. Parameters identified as having a significant influence on performance included wing sweep, camber and aerofoil section, inlet position and shape, the incorpora-

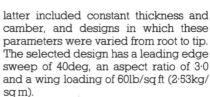

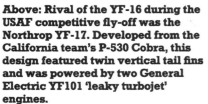

Above: Rival of the YF-16 during the USAF competitive fly-off was the Northrop YF-17. Developed from the California team's P-530 Cobra, this design featured twin vertical tail fins and was powered by two General Electric YF101 'leaky turbojet' engines.

tion of wing/fuselage blending, forebody strakes and canards, plus the number, planform and location of the tail surfaces.

Combat priorities laid down by the LWF requirements were turning performance at Mach 1·2 (demanding low wave drag), turning performance at Mach 0·9 (demanding optimum drag-at-lift), acceleration (requiring minimal wave drag) and maximum lift at Mach 0·8/40,000ft (12,000m) (again requiring optimum drag-at-lift). These conflicting

Below: In creating the production configuration (right), GD engineers slightly increased the dimensions of the original YF-16 (left), and reprofiled the nose section to accommodate the APG-66 radar. This photograph shows the second YF-16 and the first FSD aircraft.

demands made the selection of a wing planform difficult. In many ways, a straight wing fitted with leading edge flaps offered the best compromise, but wave drag was high. Wave drag of a swept wing would have been better, but penalties would have been paid in terms of handling qualities and drag-at-lift.

Previous fighters from the same design stable were the delta-winged F-102 Delta Dagger and F-106 Delta Dart, and the variable-geometry F-111, but neither of these proven technologies seemed right for the new fighter. Delta wings offer high volumetric efficiency, along with low structural weight and wave drag, but suffer penalties in trim drag and drag-at-lift. Variable geometry can give optimum aerodynamic performance in all flight conditions, but imposes problems at weight and balance.

The design finally adopted traded wing loading against aspect ratio to achieve the optimum balance between the conflicting demands imposed by the turn rate and acceleration requirements. Leading-edge sweep angles of 35deg, 40deg and 45deg were tested, along with six aerofoil sections. The

latter included constant thickness and camber, and designs in which these parameters were varied from root to tip. The selected design has a leading edge sweep of 40deg, an aspect ratio of 3·0 and a wing loading of 60lb/sq ft (2·53kg/sq m).

A wing of fixed camber could not have satisfied the conflicting demands of takeoff and landing, subsonic cruise, combat manoeuvring at high G levels and supersonic flight, but the use of variable camber played a major part in maintaining aircraft handling qualities and performance, particularly throughout the likely range of air combat speeds (Mach 0·8 to 1·6). It also allowed the use of a low aspect ratio and a thickness of only four per cent, factors which helped to optimize drag-at-lift and thus transonic manoeuvring.

To achieve this, the YF-16 wing was fitted with leading and trailing-edge flaps: if used throughout the flight envelope, these would help match the wing to changing Mach number and angle of attack. And instead of the slotted pattern of leading-edge flaps often used in other aircraft during takeoff and landing, the YF-16 wing incorporated a plain single-in-chord flap. Flap positions are automatically adjusted by the flight-control system.

Design similarities

At first sight, the competing GD and Northrop designs looked very different, but both made use of moderately swept wings and long root extensions. This was no coincidence, both teams having concluded that the vortexes cast by such extensions at high angles of attack would maintain a good airflow across the wing, even beyond stalling point, thus promising good handling at high angles of attack.

Another area of advanced technology in the YF-16 design was the adoption of wing-body blending. Near the root, the wing's depth is increased to the point where it blends smoothly into the fuselage. Company engineers had originally devised this technique in the late 1940s during studies of jet-powered seaplane fighters, though the definitive Convair YF2Y fighter which flew in 1953 did not in practice use wing-body blending.

Above: Formation take-off by the first and second full-scale development aircraft. The latter sports its third paint scheme – the all-grey finish which replaced the earlier blue-on-white and red/white/blue markings. Both aircraft are fitted with instrumented nose probes.

The technique was also used on the Douglas Skyray and Saab 35 Draken, in both cases providing sufficient internal volume for a substantial payload of fuel.

The YF-16 centre of gravity was located far enough aft to reduce longitudinal stability and increase manoeuvrability. Since lift acted ahead of the c.g., the tailplane was required to push the tail of the aircraft up rather than down in order to maintain level flight. It thus added to the lift rather than subtracting from it as on normal designs. At supersonic speeds, the centre of pressure moved aft, reducing the amount of downward force which the horizontal tail surfaces had to apply.

To 'tame' the resulting flying characteristics, the GD design team had to provide a full-time fly-by-wire stability augmentation and flight-control system to translate the pilot's control demands into movements of the aircraft control surfaces. Without the confidence gained with the YF-16, the Air Force probably would not have adopted a fly-by-wire control system in the production aircraft, a service project director stated in 1977.

In selecting an engine for the new fighter, the GD designers had to consider not only the virtues of single and twin-engined installations, but also the effects of different engine cycles (bypass ratio and pressure ratio). The most obvious candidates were a single Pratt & Whitney F100 or a pair of General Electric YF101s. The former was already under development for use in the F-15 Eagle, and its medium bypass-ratio turbofan design offered high thrust and good fuel economy.

The Fort Worth team did look into the possibility of creating a much lighter aircraft powered by a single YF101, but studies suggested that this would be unable to meet the performance requirements. This approach was in fact to

Right: Experimental 'lizard' camouflage scheme of dark grey, olive drab and dark green worn by two 388th TFW/16th TFTS F-16s, this one a two-seat F-16B, in 1979–80.

be adopted in the late 1970s by Northrop, when the latter company set out to create what eventually became the F-20 Tigershark, but this is a 'shorter-legged' design less able to carry out long-range bombing missions.

The safety factors involved in single and twin-engine designs are more difficult to quantify. Discussing this problem in a technical paper on YF-16 development, Deputy Program Director Harry Hillaker stated "Many evaluations of accumulated accident-rate data have been made with varying conclusions. The number of variables involved in these evaluations make it impossible to arrive at a specific conclusion. I will debate, however, the argument that safety is the primary consideration in determining the desired number of engines." The merits of single versus twin-engined designs are still a subject of debate, and one which was later to play a significant role in persuading some nations to adopt the twin-engined F-18 Hornet rather than the GD fighter.

First flights
The first YF-16 prototype was rolled out at Forth Worth on December 13, 1973, a mere 21 months after GD received the

$37·9 million contract. First flight of the YF-16 took place on January 20, 1974 at Edwards AFB – ahead of schedule and much to the surprise of GD pilot Phil Oestricher and all the technicians watching what should have been a high-speed taxi trial to check pitch and roll response.

As the aircraft gained speed and was rotated into a nose-up attitude, a diverging rolling oscillation built up. Distracted by this, and still relatively unfamiliar with the YF-16's high thrust-to-weight ratio, Oestricher allowed the speed to build up to around 150kt. Realizing that the horizontal tailplane had hit the runway, Oestricher decided that the best way of handling the problem was to get airborne. A brief six-minute circuit followed, and the YF-16 was successfully brought in to a smooth landing.

The subsequent investigation showed that the oscillation experienced during the roll down the runway had been pilot-induced, largely as a result of the gain of the flight-control system. The 'fix' was simple – the gain was reduced by 50 per cent while the aircraft was on the ground, then automatically raised to its full value once airborne.

Above: The moment of liftoff as the third FSD aircraft leaves the Forth Worth runway to begin an avionics test mission. The nose radome carries the normal pattern of probe, while the small black 'teardrop' fairing immediately behind the radome is for a radar-warning receiver.

The official first flight followed on February 2, with Oestricher once again at the controls. The prototype was taken up to 15,000ft (4,500m) with the undercarriage extended. The gear was then retracted, the speed increased to 300–350kt and 2–3g turns carried out. The sortie lasted for 90 minutes. Three days later, Oestricher took the aircraft supersonic for the first time, reaching a top speed of Mach 1·2 and remaining supersonic for five minutes. Manoeuvres at up to 5g were also carried out during this third flight of the YF-16.

By the time that the second prototype joined the programme in May of that year, temporary flying restrictions had been placed on the type following two incidents in which the F100 turbofan had lost power. Both were traced to contamination of the fuel-control valve which had caused this component to

Above: Near-plan view of the third FSD aircraft during a sortie from Edwards Air Force Base. The muzzle port for the 20mm M61 cannon is a prominent feature on the port-side strake. The black-and-white film used has increased the contrast of non-standard markings.

jam at the idle position, but until the problem was cleared up the YF-16 had to remain within 'dead-stick' landing distance of the runway.

To allow spinning and spin-recovery characteristics to be safely explored, along with handling at high angles of attack, a 0·3-scale flying model was flown at Edwards AFB in 1975. Built from glass fibre with an aluminium sub-structure, this was 14ft (4·27m) long, had an 8ft 9in (2·67m) wingspan and was stressed to handle loads of up to 5·5g.

Below: Delivered in November 1977, FSD aircraft No 5 was initially used to explore aircraft handling qualities. It was later assigned to Eglin Air Force Base in Florida to take part in Seek Eagle – a USAF programme to determine the limits of the F-16's weapons carrying capability.

An operational fighter

Even before the second prototype had flown, the LWF programme was no longer just a technology demonstration. In April 1974 US Defense Secretary James R. Schlesinger decided that the successful LWF contender was to be developed into an operational type designated ACF (Air Combat Fighter). As flight testing of the YF-16 and the rival YF-17 continued throughout 1974, pilots from the USAF, US Navy and US government were able to evaluate both types. Trials included air-to-air combat against the A-37B Dragonfly, F-106 Delta Dart, F-4 Phantom and MiG-21. These tests were completed by the end of 1974.

Selection of the YF-16 was announced on January 13, 1975. Secretary of the Air Force John McLucas stated that performance of the GD aircraft had been 'significantly better' during the fly-off, particularly at supersonic and near-supersonic speeds. The YF-16 had also exhibited better acceleration, endurance and turning capability.

An initial development contract awarded by the USAF covered 15 development aircraft – 11 single-seat fighters and four two-seat trainers – and was worth $417.9 million. A separate $55.5 million contract to Pratt & Whitney covered engine development.

The production aircraft was effectively a slightly scaled-up version of the prototype design. The latter had not been fitted with nose radars, and original USAF planning had assumed that the ACF design would carry a small search radar similar in peformance to the Emerson APQ-159 fitted to the Northrop F-5E. The subsequent decision to adopt a more powerful multi-mode set required an increase in nose volume, nose length being extended by 7in (17.8cm), while nose diameter was increased by 4in (10.2cm). The number of access doors on the airframe was increased in the revised design, while the number of weapon stations was increased from seven to nine.

Selection of the YF-16 ended any chance that four NATO countries – Belgium, Denmark, the Netherlands and Norway, all of which were looking to replace their F-104 Starfighters – might adopt the YF-17, although Northrop pointed out that their design had been flown with prototype engines which had clocked up less than 1,000 hours of test running. Production engines would have provided eight per cent more thrust, raising aircraft performance.

The USAF concluded that the GD aircraft outperformed the Northrop design in several areas, although the latter was superior in some respects. Around Mach 0.7, the YF-17 could outturn the YF-16, but from Mach 0.8 upwards the YF-16 was better. The GD aircraft had greater range, and was considered to be closer in standard to a production design in terms of weight, fuel capacity, and thrust-to-weight ratio.

USAF studies suggested that flyaway costs of the F-16 would be some six to seven per cent lower than those of the F-17, and that savings could also be anticipated in development and operation. Engine choice was not a factor in the selection, but the twin-engined design would have consumed 20 per cent more fuel, an important factor as the price of oil continued to rise following the 1973 Middle East War.

US Navy interest

In the meantime, the GD aircraft remained a contender for the US Navy's contemporary NACF (Navy Air Combat Fighter) programme to replace the F-4 Phantom and A-7 Corsair. One configuration proposed by the Fort Worth team was a single-seat design using the fuselage of the two-seat trainer in order to obtain more internal volume for avionics or fuel. The YF-16 had 18cu ft (0.51cu m) of volume for internal avionics, a figure which was reduced in practice to 12.8cu ft (0.36cu m) by the installation of flight test avionics. The new proposal

Above: An international quartet poses on a snow-cleared taxiway – production F-16s in the markings of Norway (bottom left), Netherlands (upper left), Belgium (upper right) and Denmark (bottom right). All are two-seat F-16B versions.

would have provided up to 25cu ft (0.71cu m) of space.

The four NATO nations sent a delegation to the US in May 1974 to discuss possible LWF procurement. At that time the USAF were thinking of ordering 650 fighters, with the US Navy taking a further 800 examples. Selection of the USAF's new fighter was not scheduled until May 1975, but the European air arms wanted a decision by the end of September 1974.

This date was impossible to attain, but the deadline for USAF source selection was brought forward to January 1975 by speeding up the flight test programme. Flight refuelling was used to extend the duration of individual flight-test sorties, while the programme was revamped to avoid unnecessary duplication of flight test conditions. Instead of the two and half years normally required to complete Category 3 flight testing on a new aircraft, the YF-16 and -17 tests were completed in sufficient detail to allow source selection in January 1975, barely a year after first flight. At this point the US Navy, considering that it did not have sufficient data to make a choice, quit the LWF programme to continue its own studies of both aircraft.

Meanwhile the deadline for submission of proposals to the NATO Governments had been extended to January 1975 at the request of the US. The formal F-16 proposal was submitted on January 14, a day after the Swedish proposal (for the SAAB-Scania 37E Viggen) and a day ahead of the French (for the M53 turbofan-powered Dassault-Breguet Mirage F.1E).

The formal decision to adopt the F-16 came as no surprise when announced on June 7, 1975, although many observers noted that Belgium planned to deploy 102 aircraft rather than the anticipated 116. The resulting cost savings were intended to be invested in research and development work directed towards a new West European combat aircraft.

F-16 production

In developing the F-16 from the YF-16, changes were kept to a minimum. Fuselage length was extended by 10in (25.4cm), while the wing area was increased by 20sq ft (1.85sq m), and fitted with two additional hard points. The horizontal tailplane was increased in size, and a jet starter was added to the F100 turbofan.

Assembly of the first full-scale production F-16 began in December 1975, and involved GD in a major modernization of its Fort Worth plant. Since the F-111 programme, the latter (officially USAF Plant 4) had been under-utilized, and had seen no major investment or updating since the 1960s. GD initially hoped to get Department of Defense funding for the modernization needed for the F-16 programme, but the US Government had already decided that it was no longer prepared to finance capital facilities needed for military projects. The Pentagon agreed that the plant would require updating, but expected GD to finance this themselves. By the summer of 1982 the company had invested $70 million, and was planning to spend $25 million more.

In laying out the production line, GD allowed for production of up to 45 aircraft per month. By the end of 1980, production was running at 16 per month and the manufacturer estimated that the current tooling could be used to build another 23–25 per month if required.

Under the 1975 agreement, a total of 348 F-16s for the European partners were to be assembled in Europe, 184 at the Fokker plant at Schiphol in the Netherlands, and 164 by SABCA at Gosselies in Belgium. The four nations are also entitled to offsets of 10 per cent of the dollar value of each aircraft sold to the USAF, and 15 per cent on aircraft sold to other export customers.

The Memorandum of Understanding covering European purchase and co-production of the F-16 ensured that the European companies involved in the project would receive work not only on USAF aircraft but also on Fighting Falcons built for Third World operators. It also stipulated the payment to the US government of a $471,000 research and development levy on the price of each aircraft delivered to the four air arms. The latter figure includes a recoupment charge for F100 R&D.

Preliminary contracts for the F-16 were placed in 1975 with European industry. It is impractical to detail all the suppliers in a programme of this mag-

Left: Demonstration flight by two brand new F-16As of the USAF. In the clean configuration shown here the aircraft could easily outfly the MiG-21 and could cope with the MiG-29 Fulcrum at close quarters. These particular F-16s were delivered in April 1980.

Above: F-16s on the final assembly line at Fokker's Schipol plant in the Netherlands. Co-ordination and control of the multi-national assembly programme was a formidable management task comparable to that of the Apollo space programme.

nitude, but the main contracts were awarded as follows.

Two aircraft assembly lines were set up, one at the SABCA plant at Gosselies in Belgium, where Belgian and Danish airframes are assembled, the other at the Fokker plant at Schiphol-Oost in the Netherlands. At the same time, the Belgian company SONACA – formerly Fairey SA – was reconstituted with new management and was contracted to build the aft fuselage.

Assembly of aircraft for the Netherlands and Norway is handled by Fokker, who also build the centre fuselage, the leading edge flaps, the trailing edge panel and flaperon. Other components such as the vertical fin box and the wing and centreline pylons are built in Denmark by Per Udsen, while the undercarriage is tackled by DAF in the Netherlands, and the wheels by Raufoss in Norway.

European assembly of the F100 engine is handled by the Belgian company Fabrique Nationale, which invested around $35 million in new test cells, machine tools and other equipment. Kongsberg builds the engine fandrive turbine module in Norway, while Phillips in Holland is responsible for the augmentor nozzle module.

Contracts for avionics are widely scattered throughout the four nations. MBLE (Belgium) has overall responsibility for the APG-66 radar, while Signaal and Oldelft (Netherlands) are responsible for the radar antennae and HUDs respectively. Also involved in HUD work are Marconi Avionics in Britain (the original designer of the unit) and Kongsberg. Danish Industrial Group One (Neselco and LK-NES) supply the fire-control computer, the radar displays are built by Danish company Nea Linberg, and Kongsberg handles the inertial navigation system as well as its other contributions.

The creation of European F-16 production facilities was not an easy task. European industry had earlier built the Lockheed F-104G Starfighter, but the latter aircraft was not in USAF service. Since the F-16 is a front-line US warplane, and would be assembled on both sides of the Atlantic, many procedures had to be agreed, standardized and in some cases made the subject of compromise. In the early days of the YF-16 project, paperwork had been kept to a minimum in order to maintain the pace of the programme, but with the adoption of the F-16 by four NATO nations, Fighting Falcon became what is probably the most complex management task that the US Department of Defense has ever undertaken. In 1977 programme director Brigadier General James Abrahamson described the task he faced as "a management nightmare". More than 3,000 suppliers and subcontractors were involved in the international programme, and even under the 998-aircraft production run originally planned some 20,000,000lb

(9,000,000kg) of raw material and three million individual manufactured items were due to cross the Atlantic.

In an ideal world, the F-16 would not have been committed to large-scale overseas production until the design had been frozen and proven, and until the Fort Worth line had ironed out the inevitable production 'bugs'. In practice, however, the aircraft entered production on a similar timescale in both the US and Western Europe, with production facilities being planned before the design was fully refined or production techniques checked out. Not since the days of the original US ICBM programmes had such pressures been placed on project management.

Project management

Since the programme involved contractors in five nations, it was essential to set up procedures under which proposed changes to the design could be jointly discussed and agreed, so that a common standard of hardware would be produced by all of the nations involved. Before components and aircraft could be built, technical standards, acceptance procedures, working practices and even accounting methods had to be jointly agreed. In some cases fundamental differences in procedure and outlook were uncovered.

The US aerospace worker is mobile in outlook, and will tend to 'follow the contracts', working for whatever company needs his services. Two-shift production working is common on large programmes, maintaining production speed and helping to amortize the cost of expensive tooling. In Western Europe, staff are less mobile, with com-

panies placing greater emphasis on long-term workload, and providing greater job security for their employees. Single-shift working is normal, and expensive overtime often frowned upon. It is not uncommon for aerospace plants to shut down completely for anything up to a month during the holiday period.

Such practices may be thought desirable in Europe, but they penalized the performance of the many non-US F-16 contractors. In 1977 it was estimated that European co-production would add over a million dollars to the cost of each F-16 purchased by the NATO air arms. A penalty was also paid in terms of time. As production began, GD estimated the lead time on its Fort Worth line as 24 months, while in the case of the European assembly lines, this rose to 36 months.

In both cases, the end result was increased cost. Unit flyaway price of a USAF F-16 was originally set at $4·85 million in 1975 dollars. The price tag agreed for the NATO aircraft was $6·09 million. Part of this increase was due to R & D levy of $470,000 per aircraft, but the remainder was a reflection of the increased tooling costs and longer lead times.

Methods by which US aerospace suppliers added fixed charges to production costs in order to recover administration and other overhead costs had all been devised to cope with production carried out mostly in the US by US companies. In instances where raw parts might be fabricated in the US, shipped to Europe for finishing, then returned to the US for incorporation within USAF aircraft, normal procedures became distinctly cumbersome.

Above: F-16 centre-fuselage sections on the production line at Fokker's Ypenburg plant in the Netherlands. These sections show how wing/body blending was used by GD engineers in creating the F-16. The central tunnel houses the F100 turbofan.

Bookkeeping was further complicated by the fact that US procurement procedures dictate that the financial records of companies supplying defence hardware be officially audited, but the European companies involved in F-16 assembly were, not unnaturally, reluctant to allow the US government access to detailed financial data. A compromise was devised under which the individual companies were checked by auditors from their own national governments.

Late in 1976, the smooth running of the programme was disrupted when the USAF decided to standardize on the McDonnell Douglas ACES 11 ejection seat without fully consulting the West Europeans.

The NATO air arms requested a total of 18 changes to the F-16. Seven were subsequently cancelled, six were adopted by all five operators and decisions on five more were deferred. These NATO requests added useful facilities to the aircraft, including:
* improvements to the radar to suppress the effects of sea clutter, and to allow a radar image to be 'frozen' on the display
* navigation update capability
* an altitude-hold facility in the aircraft autopilot
* installation of a radar electro-optical video recorder
* improved anti-corrosion treatment

Despite such problems, and the inevitable political haggling over the distribution of offset work, the programme flowed smoothly during the second half of the 1970s. First European co-production contracts were formally signed in July 1976, and the following October saw the first full-scale development aircraft rolled out at Forth Worth, with the first flight following in December.

Full-scale production

The third full-scale development aircraft was used for avionics testing. The radar was delivered two months later, but came with an unexpected bonus – it incorporated a more advanced standard of hardware and software than had been planned – and did not affect the timescale of avionics flight testing.

At the start of 1977 the USAF announced plans to purchase an additional 738 aircraft. Formal authority for full-scale production was given the following October, two months after the first two-seat F-16B flew.

By February 1978 the Belgian production line had opened, followed by

the Dutch line in April. The first F-16 to be delivered to Europe arrived at Gosselies on June 9, 1978, having crossed the Atlantic aboard a USAF C-5 Galaxy. It was used for assembly tests at the SABCA plant. The following month, the first European-built F-16 components – a set of wings – were fitted to a USAF aircraft on the Fort Worth line. The two-way flow of components across the Atlantic had become a reality.

Meanwhile, in the spring of 1978, the US General Accounting Office published a report on the F-16 which drew attention to a number of development problems, including engine malfunctions, structural cracks, minor problems with the radar, and instability at high angles of attack. The report called for the review of the programme and the likely threats which the aircraft would face in service, but pointed out that the problems met to date '... do not seem to be any more severe than those previously experienced in other major systems. And experience with the systems shows that these problems are resolved over time'.

This report attracted some unfavourable publicity for the type, with several knocking reports appearing in print and on TV, but these overlooked the fact that the GAO was to some degree reporting past history. Fixes to many

problems were already at hand.

First flight of a production aircraft from the Fort Worth line took place in August 1978, with the maiden flight of a European F-16 following on December 11, 1978, from Gosselies. This was a two-seat F-16B, and was flown by Neil Anderson and Serge Martin, the latter having spent two weeks on familiarization training at Forth Worth prior to the historic sortie.

Deliveries to the user air arms started in January 1979 when aircraft were delivered from US and European production lines to the 388th TFW at Hill AFB, Utah, and to the FAéB (Force Aérienne Belge, or Belgian Air Force) respectively. In May the first Fokker-built aircraft flew, and four US aircraft completed a four-month series of tests in Europe. A month later the KLu (Koninklijke Luchtmacht, or Royal

Netherlands Air Force) accepted its first F-16s, and in January 1980 deliveries began to the air arms of Denmark, Norway and Israel.

By the end of 1979, the unit flyaway cost of the F-16A was $10·2 million. In numerical terms this may have been far above the $3·0 million originally envisaged back in 1972, but in 1975 dollars was around $4·7 million – well below the USAF 1975 target price of $5·0 million. Until 1980, the F-16 lacked a name. The unofficial use of 'Falcon' resulted in objections by Dassault-Breguet who already used the name for their range of business jets. At a time when the USAF was re-using Second World War nomenclature, the F-16's high performance, long range, bubble canopy and ventral air inlet suggested 'Mustang II' to may observers, but this had been pre-empted by an automobile manufac-

European co-production

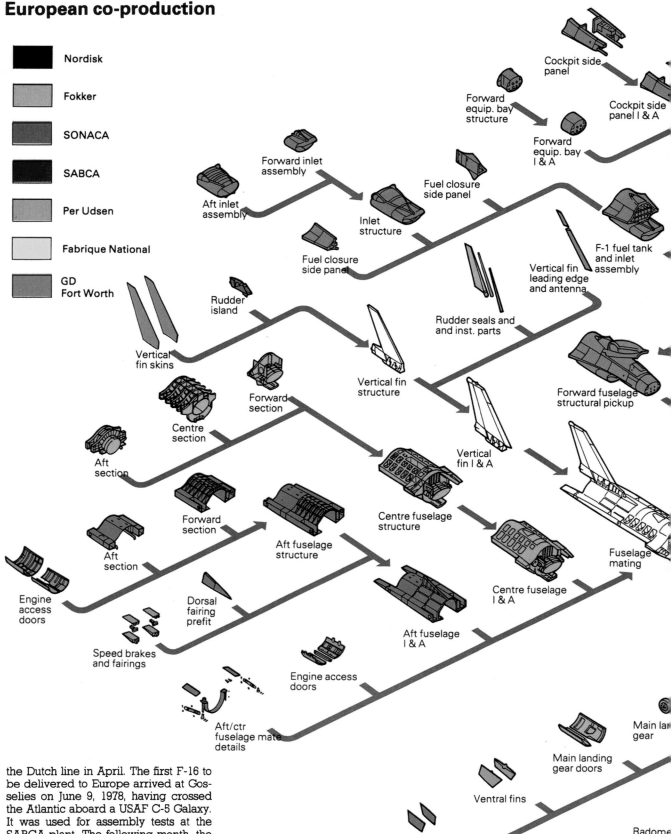

Right: The second European F-16 assembly line is at the SABCA plant at Gosselies, Belgium. Deliveries to the air arms of Belgium and Denmark started in January 1979.

Below: This flow chart shows the principal structural assemblies of European-built F-16s and identifies the major suppliers. The use of European and American components in aircraft built on both sides of the Atlantic involved an immense administrative effort, and European industrial practices were largely responsible for each locally-built NATO aircraft costing a million dollars more than the USAF equivalent. I & A indicates Integration and Assembly.

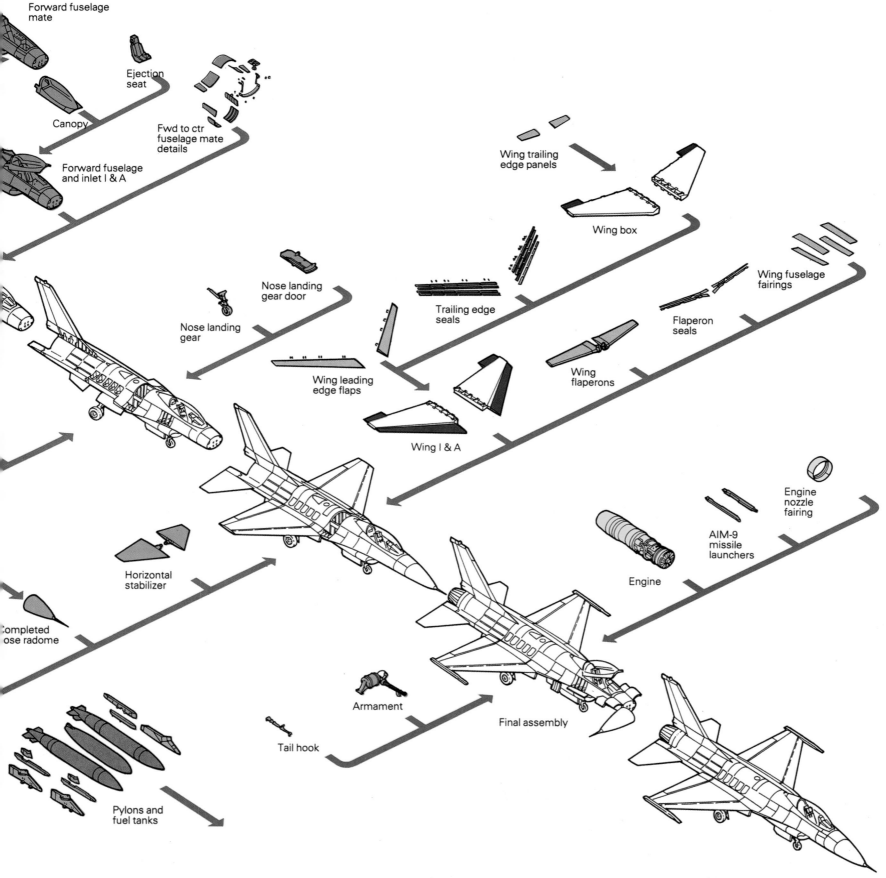

Cockpit structure

Forward fuselage mate

Ejection seat

Canopy

Fwd to ctr fuselage mate details

Forward fuselage and inlet I & A

Wing trailing edge panels

Wing box

Nose landing gear door

Nose landing gear

Trailing edge seals

Wing fuselage fairings

Flaperon seals

Wing leading edge flaps

Wing flaperons

Wing I & A

Horizontal stabilizer

Engine nozzle fairing

AIM-9 missile launchers

Engine

Completed nose radome

Armament

Final assembly

Tail hook

Pylons and fuel tanks

turer. Final choice, made in 1980, was the unimaginative 'Fighting Falcon'.

First phase of the F-16 Operational Test and Evaluation programme was carried out at Hill AFB, Utah, but this was followed by international trials. Nine aircraft took part in the MOTE (Multinational Operational Test & Evaluation) programme, including two from the Belgian and Netherland Air Forces. Six aircraft, plus one of the two reserves and more than 120 personnel, spent six weeks in each of the participating nations during the second half of 1980, so that operating experience could be built up.

Above: Even if the tail markings had been omitted, the extended jet pipe and modified inlets on this two-seater would identify it as an F-16/79, a deliberately-downgraded design compared to the F-16A/B which was released for general export.

Prior to 1980, the number of countries to which the F-16 could be sold was very restricted. In that year the Carter Administration ruled that military aircraft could be developed specifically for the export market, within stringent guidelines. For the F-16, these were that performance, and particularly payload/range, had to be clearly inferior to that of the F-16A. Nor should they be easily upgradable without US assistance.

The solution adopted by GD was to fit a version of the single-spool J79 turbojet, and for this they used one of the original full-scale development two-seater F-16Bs from the USAF. General Electric produced a modified engine, the J79-GE-17X, for the purpose.

The J79 was 18in (46cm) longer than the F100, and in order to keep the

compressor face in the same location the rear fuselage had to be extended by this amount. Fortunately the intake had been designed as a single replaceable component, and it was a simple matter to produce and fit a new inlet, sized to the smaller mass flow of the J79. More difficult was replacing a turbofan with a turbojet. The bypass air of a turbofan insulates the hot core of the engine from the surrounding structure, but for a turbojet there is no such aid. The only possible solution was to use a steel heat shield around most of the engine. While this worked, the weight penalty was almost 2,000lb (907kg), which caused a significant increase to wing loading. Coupled with reduced thrust loading and higher specific fuel consumption, this ensured that with the exception of maximum speed (Mach 2.05), overall performance and agility fell well short of that of the F-16A.

First flight took place on October 29, 1980, and over the next year or so the F-16/79 was evaluated by several nations. But all hesitated before taking such a blatantly second-best fighter.

That they were right was confirmed when the F-16A/B was released for general export.

Onwards and upwards

The development of the Viper through the years has been an almost continual process. Starting as a "Swing Fighter", able to switch from counter air to ground attack with equal facility, it has gone on to cover the spectrum of reconnaissance; close air support/battlefield air interdiction (CAS/BAI); air defence; suppression of enemy air defences (SEAD), previously known as Wild Weaseling; adversary training with both the USAF and USN; and it finally gained a night attack capability. Many years ago, in a soundbite description of the F-16, Fort Worth PR man Jack Isabel paraphrased heavyweight boxing champion Mohammed Ali: "Float like a butterfly; sting like a battleship!"

The F-16 has been built in batches, identified by Block Numbers. Not that this is visible externally; with few exceptions Vipers look very much the same and there is little to distinguish F-

16A/Bs from F-16C/Ds. The early block improvements (1978-1982) were mainly concerned with reliability, maintainability, and ease of production. Block 15 production started late in 1981 (there is always some overlap), and this contained some fairly major changes, part of Multinational Staged Improvement Plan I (MSIP I). This was a move towards greater weapons capability, and involved structural strengthening and extra wiring. The capacity of the central underwing hard points was increased from 2,500lb to 3,500lb (1,134-1,588kg), while hardpoints were also modified to carry AIM-120 AMRAAM, even though this missile was still far in the future. At the same time the engine inlet was strengthened and fitted with hardpoints and wiring to take LANTIRN (Low Altitude Navigation and Targeting with Infra-Red at Night) pods.

The agility of the Viper was largely due to the fact that it had been designed to be unstable, with a wide margin between the centre of lift (cl) and the centre of gravity (cg). In service it had been found that the carriage

of heavy munitions tended to shift the cg towards the cl, making the aircraft more stable and, in so doing, reducing manoeuvrability. To offset this, the stabilators were redesigned and increased in area. Major avionics changes also featured as part of MSIP I.

Block 15 production, which ended in 1987, was followed by an Operational Capability Upgrade (OCU) which lasted until 1997. While this largely involved the avionics suites, it also included compatibility with the Penguin anti-ship missile and the F100-PW-220 engine, which offered greater reliability and service life, if no extra thrust. The final batch of F-16A/Bs for the USAF was completed in 1985, but production of export models, most recently to Block 15 OCU standard, continued for several more years. The one exception is the Taiwanese order, which is built to Block 20.

MSIP II
MSIP II brought into being the first actual designation change: the single seat F-16C and the two-seater F-16D, deliveries of which commenced in July

1984. Externally there was a slight difference; the fin root fairing was expanded forward to house the ALQ-165 Advanced Self-protection Jammer (ASPJ). Ironically the USAF withdrew from this project in July 1990, although ASPJ has been installed on export F-16s, notably those for Korea.

The first F-16C/Ds were Block 25 production aircraft, and apart from ASPJ, they differed mainly in having the Westinghouse APG-68 radar, a much more capable type, with more modes than its predecessor, the APG-66. This was combined with presentation improvements: a wide-angle holographic HUD, and two CRT displays. The Block 25 aircraft were also compatible with AGM-65D Maverick.

Weight growth
With everything bar the kitchen sink hung on it, and more and more black boxes shoehorned into its interior, creeping weight growth was by this time beginning to erode the previously sparkling performance of the Viper. The obvious solution was more power, and this was available in the shape of

General Electric's F110-100, developed from the F101DFE originally intended for the abortive F-14B Tomcat. This developed some 27,600lb (12,519kg) of augmented thrust, an increment of roughly 16 per cent.

One essential was a common engine bay, able to take either power plant with minimal modification. This emerged as the dual Block 30 F-16, powered by the F110, and the Block 32, which retained the original Pratt & Whitney engine. Block 30/32 Vipers, with a common modular intake duct, entered production in July 1986. Both were also fitted with seal-bond fuel tanks.

Most other improvements concerned the avionics, but from the spring of 1987 they were provided with full multi-target AMRAAM capability, and in August of the same year they were fitted out to launch the AGM-45 Shrike anti-radiation missile. This was followed by the AGM-88 HARM, and Vipers were teamed with F-4G Wild Weasel Phantoms to form hunter/killer teams. The Phantom was the hunter,

locating targets then handing off the co-ordinates to the stand-off F-16 killers. Vipers modified for the Wild Weasel role are identifiable by a dorsal spine, as in fact are defence suppression machines in Israeli service.

Still in the future were the Improved Performance Engines (IPE); Pratt & Whitney's F100-229, and General Electric's F110-129, both of which were in the 29,000lb (13,154kg) thrust class. It would however be several years before either became available.

Air defence
Prior to this, in October 1986, the USAF had decided that F-16As would be modified for the air defence role, to be flown by Air National Guardsmen. This was something radically new for what had originally been intended as an austere close combat fighter. A Beyond Visual Range (BVR) capability was needed. BVR was to be provided by AIM-7 Sparrows with continuous wave semi-active homing, with up to six of the smaller and lighter AIM-120A AMRAAM launch and leave missiles when these became available. The

Left: First Fighting Falcon to use the General Electric F110 turbofan (formerly the F101 Derivative Fighter Engine) was the F-16/101. The F110 was developed from the F101 powerplant of the B-1 bomber.

Netherlands Air Force was the first to do so in 1983.

Block 40/42

Some years ago, an Israeli colonel reduced the GD facility at Fort Worth to smoking ruins with a remark to the effect that the F-16 was a jolly good attack aircraft, and that it wasn't too bad as an air combat fighter either! He may be excused on two counts: firstly, he was a helicopter pilot, and secondly, the accent on mud-moving had rather obscured the original design aim. In fact, from time to time proposals have been made for a dedicated attack variant designated A-16, or alternatively carrying the dual-role designation of F/A-16.

The latter was proposed for a CAS/BAI update to Block 30/32 aircraft, but was abandoned in 1992 in favour of using Block 40/42 aircraft, although the F/A designation was not perpetuated. Block 40/42 Vipers, deliveries of which began in May 1989, were equipped to carry LANTIRN, although the first pods were not issued until 1992: the Global Positioning System (GPS); a Digital Terrain System (DTS); and an Automatic Target Hand-off System (ATH). The APG-68 radar was upgraded to become the APG-68(V), with expanded computer capacity, while a few structural tucks and gussets allowed an increase in maximum takeoff weight to 42,300lb (19,187kg). Although at one point touted as the "Night Falcon", with cockpit lighting modified to be compatible with NVGs, this variant remained equally capable by day.

With the entry of Block 40/42, a major change passed largely unremarked. The flight control system, previously quadruplex analogue, became digital. The transition passed with few, if any, real problems, as attested by Fort Worth senior test pilot Steve Barter. This was in direct contrast to some European experiences, as related in later sections.

Recent Blocks

Deliveries of Block 50/52 aircraft began in October 1991. Both batches incorporated IPE powerplants: the GE F110-129 and the P&W F100-229, which gave a healthy thrust increment. The radar was the new APG-68(V5), with a programmable signal processor and VHSIC (Very High Speed Integrated Chip) computing, which allowed data to be extracted from the radar returns which was not otherwise available; notably signature recognition. Other changes were mainly in the avionics field. As from 1996, the Mid-Life Update (MLU) applicable to the F-16A/B, which includes colour liquid crystal displays, makes them inter-operable with Block 50/52 aircraft.

This was followed by the Common Configuration Implementation Programme (CCIP) commenced in 1998, in which all systems in Block 40 and Block 50 aircraft will be brought to a uniform standard, including helmet mounted sights and possibly an agile phased array steerable beam radar, by 2004.

The need for ever-greater external munition loads caused a rethink. These, plus the more powerful IPE propulsion systems, had gradually eroded operational range. The F-15 had overcome this with CFTs; something similar was needed for the F-16. This duly emerged in the shape of the F-16ES (Enhanced Strategic), first flown in 1994, which incorporated 24ft (7.31m) conformal fuel tanks along the upper fuselage, and upper and lower FLIR ball turrets. This not only increases operational radius; it frees hardpoints for ordnance that would otherwise be occupied by jugs. This will be the main change for the so-called Advanced Capability Block 60/62 Vipers.

The rather limited APG-66 radar was modified for the task, while greater range and endurance was provided by the carriage of 600 USgal (2,271 litre) drop tanks. In all, 272 F-16s were modified for the air defence role between February 1989 and early 1992, and designated F-16ADF.

Adversary variant

Whereas the F-5E Tiger II had been well able to simulate the MiG-21 for adversary training, and to a lesser degree the MiG-23, it was totally inadequate to simulate the MiG-29. With few available alternatives, the US Navy selected the F-16C/D as its next adversary fighter. Modified from Block 30 aircraft, with the F110 powerplant, the F-16N, as it was designated, featured minor structural strengthening. This was to withstand the extra stress imposed by the adversary mission, much of which was spent at high accelerations. The M61A Vulcan cannon was deleted and the APG-68 radar was replaced by the APG-66. In the adversary role, they carried an Air Combat Maneuvring Instrumentation (ACMI) pod on one wingtip rail, and a captive

Sidewinder on the other. The designation of the two-seater was TF-16N.

Agile Falcon

Although the General Electric F110-100 had restored the thrust/weight ratio, wing loading had continually increased. This meant that to produce the extra lift needed, the angle of attack for a specific g-loading had to be increased, which at the same time increased drag. While the extra thrust did a good job in enabling Block 30/32 Vipers to turn corners, it was at the same time forcing the wing to operate at ever-decreasing efficiency.

To offset this, Agile Falcon was proposed in 1988. This was to have had a larger wing, with 6ft (1.83m) greater span and with the area increased by 100sq ft (9.29sq m). Of all-composite construction, the new wing would have had a leading edge sweep reduced from 40deg to 38deg, with larger root extensions. To accommodate this, an increase of 15in (380mm) in fuselage length was needed. Such major alterations were deemed unnecessary, and Agile Falcon was cancelled in 1989. However, its memory lingers on in the shape of the Mitsubishi F.2

Above: Fighting Falcon has now flown with the GE J79 turbojet, GE F110 (formerly F101 DFE) turbofan and the standard P&W F100 turbofan.

strike fighter, designed with technical help from Fort Worth, which shows a marked family resemblance to the F-16.

Photo bird

From June 1995, selected Block 30 F-16Cs began to replace the elderly RF-4 Phantom in the tactical reconnaissance role. By now General Dynamics had been acquired by Lockheed Martin, and it was fitted with a customised pod based on that company's Multi-Mission Sensor and Avionics (MMSA) kit, with a FLIR, and a KS-87 camera for Long Range Oblique Photography (LOROP), configured with a framing focal plane array which can "snatch" images during manoeuvring flight, and Sideways Looking Airborne Radar (SLAR). All data gathered is digital, and can be downloaded into a computer for almost immediate analysis. Recce F-16s were not of course a new thing; they had been cleared to carry a variety of reconnaissance pods, and the

F-16 Fighting Falcon
Specifications

Type	YF-16	F-16A	F-16C Block 52
Length	48ft 5in/14.75m	49ft 6in/15.09m	48ft 5in/15.09m
Wingspan	31ft 0in/9.45m	31ft 0in/9.45m	31ft 0in/9.45m
Height	16ft 3in/4.95m	16ft 8in/5.08m	16ft 8$\frac{1}{2}$in/5.09m
Empty Wt	13,595lb/6,167kg	16,285lb/7,387kg	18,600lb/8,437kg
Combat Takeoff	23,810lb/10,800kg	26,536lb/12,040kg	27,500lb/12,474kg
Wing Area	300sq ft/27.87sq m	300sq ft/27.87sq m	300sq ft/27.87sq m
Wing Loading	79lbsq ft-387kg/sq m	88lb/sq ft-432kg/sq m	92lb/sq ft-448kg/sq m
Engine	F100-PW-200	F100-PW-220	F100-PW-229
Max.thrust	23,830lb/10,809kg	23,830lb/10,809kg	29,100lb/13,200kg
T/W ratio	1.00-1.18	0.94-1.08	1.06
V_{max} hi	Mach 2.0	Mach 2.0	Mach 2.0 plus
Ceiling	50,000ft/15,250m	50,000ft/15,250m	50,000ft/15,250m
Climb Rate	50,000ft/min-254m/sec	50,000ft/min- 254m/sec	50,000ft/min- 254m/sec

Users: Abu Dabhi, Bahrain, Belgium, Denmark, Egypt, Greece, Indonesia, Israel, Jordan, Netherlands, New Zealand, Norway, Pakistan, Portugal, Singapore, South Korea, Taiwan, Thailand, Turkey, UAE, USAF, USN, Venezuela.

Early USAF F-16 Units (late 1980s)

Wing	Base	Tail code

Above: Fully laden with external tanks and weaponry, this F-16C of the 422nd TES (Tactical Evaluation Squadron) heads for the range.

Below: Jet pipes of the F110-powered (left) and standard F100-powered (right) versions of the F-16

Tactical Air Command
9th Air Force

56th TTW	Macdill AFB, Florida	MC
363rd TFW	Shaw AFB, South Carolina	SW

12th Air Force

388th TFW	Hill AFB, Utah	HL
474th TFW	Nellis AFB, Nevada	NA, WA

832nd Air Division

58th TTW	Luke AFB, Arizona	LA

US Air Forces in Europe
16th Air Force

401st TFW	Torrejon, Spain	TJ

17th Air Force

50th TFW	Hahn AB, West Germany	HR

Pacific Air Forces
5th Air Force
314th Air Division

8th TFW	Kunsan AB, South Korea	WP

Air National Guard

169th TFG	McEntire ANGB, South Carolina	

Structure

In designing the structure of the F-16, General Dynamics engineers never lost sight of the fact that the end product must be easy to produce. Wherever possible, the attractions of advanced constructional methods such as chemical milling and exotic materials such as titanium and carbon-fibre composites were rejected. Without compromising the performance of the aircraft, the GD team created hardware which would eventually be assembled on four production lines, by Belgian, Dutch, Turkish and US workers, using components built to a common standard by subcontractors on both sides of the Atlantic.

Fighting Falcon may be a high-performance aircraft of advanced aerodynamic form, but in designing its structure the GD engineers eschewed wherever possible sophisticated constructional techniques and materials. The USAF wanted an inexpensive fighter, so a modularized and simplified structural design was adopted.

Despite the aircraft's high performance, some 80 per cent of the structure is manufactured from aluminium alloy. A little less than 8 per cent is made from steel, composites account for less than 3 per cent, and titanium for a mere 1.5 per cent. Around 60 per cent of the structural parts are made from sheet metal, while less than 2 per cent require chemical milling.

The weight savings resulting from the use of advanced technology such as relaxed stability and wing/body blending are very significant, resulting in an empty weight some 1,300lb (590kg) less than would have been the case with a more conventional design. During full-scale development, GD estimated the cost of the F-16 airframe structure as $60 per lb, so this reduction in theory reduced airframe costs by around $80,000.

The development of a military aircraft is often a long saga of ever-increasing takeoff weight. This problem had dogged the F-111, the previous Fort Worth design, but in engineering the production F-16 the GD team maintained rigorous control over weight growth. Between April 1975 and January 1978 the takeoff weight increased by just over 5 per cent from 22,197lb (10,068kg) to 23,357lb (10,595kg), but more than half of this 'fat' reflected increased operational capability, producibility or maintainability.

Fatigue tests

In parallel with the flight-test programme a series of ground fatigue trials were carried out on the fifth development airframe. A test rig set up in a hangar at Fort Worth used more than 100 hydraulic rams to apply stress to an instrumented airframe, simulating the loads imposed by takeoff, landing and combat manoeuvring at up to 10g. By the summer of 1978, this airframe had clocked up more than 16,000 hours of simulated flight in the rig. These tests were carried out at a careful and deliberate pace which sometimes lagged behind schedule.

As the tests progressed, cracks developed in several structural bulkheads. News of this problem resulted in hostile comments in the media, but GD pointed out in its own defence that the cracks had occurred not in flying aircraft but on ground test specimens. If the risk of such cracks during development testing was not a real one, a company spokesman remarked to the author at the time, no-one would be willing to pay for ground structural test rigs. GD redesigned the affected components, thickening the metal, and installed metal plates to reinforce existing units.

Built up from three major sub-sections – nose/cockpit, centre and aft – the fuselage is based upon conventional frames and longerons. The forward manufacturing break point is just aft of the cockpit, while the second is located forward of the vertical fin.

Combined with advanced aerodynamics and the low sfc of the F100 turbofan, the increase in fuselage internal volume created by wing/body blending accounts for the GD fighter's impressive range performance. Some 28 per cent of the weight of a loaded F-14 is fuel, while the equivalent figure for an F-16 is 31 per cent.

Anyone who has seen an F-16 under-

Above: Production aircraft on the Fort Worth assembly line. At this stage the canopy and radome still have protective coverings.

going an engine change cannot help noticing the effect of wing/body blending on the aircraft's internal fuel capacity. Visiting the Fort Worth flight line in 1977, the author was shown an engineless F-16 – one of the development aircraft on the flight line was undergoing an engine change. Looking up through the tail and out through the air inlet, his first reaction was "Where do you keep the fuel?". At first sight it seemed impossible for so much kerosene to be stowed in the limited space which remained.

Wing/body blending was carried out in three dimensions. Seen from the front or rear of the aircraft, the wing gradually blends in cross section with the fuselage, making it impossible to define where the wing ends and the fuselage begins. This blending is varied longitu-

Below: Belgian ground crew prepare an F-16 for flight. The avionics technician needs no steps or ladder in order to work on the radar.

dinally in order to "tailor" the cross-sectional area distribution.

In planform, the wind leading edge also blends with the fuselage thanks to the leading-edge strakes. At high angles of attack, these create vortices which maintain the energy of the boundary air layer flowing over the inner section of the wing. Wing root stalling is thus delayed, and directional stability maintained. Vortex energy also provides a measure of forebody lift, reducing the need for drag-inducing tail trim. Graphic proof of the existence of these vortices may be seen during tight turns if local condensation results in a "contrail" from the strakes. At air shows, the aircraft has been flown with smoke generators whose plumes have clearly shown the trailing vortices. And by keeping the inner-wing boundary layer energised, the strakes allowed a reduction in wing size, aspect ratio and weight – a saving of around 500lb (227kg) in structural weight.

The combination of wing/fuselage blending and variable camber resulted in several advantages, including the additional space provided in a location close to the centre of gravity for internal fuel, avionics and other systems. Without this feature, the F-16 would have been about 5ft (1.5m) longer and the structure some 570lb (259kg) heavier.

Gradually increasing thickness of the wing in the region of the wing root resulted in a stiffer wing than would have been possible with a conventional design. Stiffness was increased by the fact that the lift-increasing manoeuvring flaps allowed a smaller wing of reduced span to be used. The wing structure itself incorporates five spars and 11 ribs. Upper and lower wing skins are one-piece machined components.

Aerodynamic performance

Fineness ratio of the F-16 configuration is lower than the ideal for supersonic flight, but transonic drag is minimized. In conventional designs, wing lift normally falls off at high angles of attack, but the F-16 obtains a useful amount of body lift.

The leading-edge manoeuvring flap and trailing-edge flaperon can be moved at up to 35deg/sec to match Mach number and angle of attack. Maximum speed of movement is matched to the aircraft's ability to respond to changes in pitch, so that flaps and aircraft attitude are always matched.

By shaping the wing aerofoil to match aerodynamic conditions, the moving flaps reduce drag, maintain lift at high angles of attack, improve directional stability, and minimize buffeting. The latter qualities are useful during tight turns in air combat, or while 'jinking' at low level to confuse hostile air defences. The wing is only around 1.5in (3.8cm) deep at the point where the

leading-edge rotary actuator is installed, so the design of this component was a significant challenge.

In the spring of 1982 actuator failures caused the USAF temporarily to ground all F-16s which had exceeded 200 hours of operational flying – 240 of the 400 F-16s in service at that time – for inspection of the wing leading-edge flap. A routine inspection had revealed signs of excessive wear in the actuation mechanism which controls the position of the leading-edge manoeuvring flap. More than 40 aircraft required repair, the remainder being returned to service once this component had been inspected – a process which took around five man-hours per aircraft. As an interim solution pending a definitive 'fix', aircraft were re-inspected every 100 hours.

The vertical stabilizer has a multi-spar and multi-rib structure made from aluminium alloy as is the unit's top cap, but the skins are fabricated from graphite epoxy. The two ventral fins beneath the rear fuselage section are made from glass fibre. Also located under the rear fuselage is a runway arrester hook.

The original pattern of horizontal stabilizer is being replaced by a larger component under the MSIP Phase I programme, details of which are given later in this chapter. Inboard of each are the air brakes. Stowed in the horizontal position when not in use, these are of the split type, the upper and lower sections of which open through an angle of 60deg.

The main undercarriage units retract forwards into the lower fuselage, and the large doors were found to offer a good – although unconventional – mounting location for Sparrow or

Above: By early 1979 the production line in GD's mile-long assembly building was picking up speed. The aircraft nearest the camera was delivered to the USAF in May.

AMRAAM radar-guide missiles. The nose gear is located aft of the intake, so that debris or other foreign objects thrown up by the wheel will not be ingested into the air intake.

The location of the intake is certainly unconventional, but wind tunnel tests showed that the ventral location is subject to minimal airflow disturbance over a wide range of flight conditions and aircraft manoeuvres, since the forward fuselage tends to shelter it from the effects of aircraft manoeuvres. At an angle of attack of 25deg, for example, the air flows into the intake at an angle of only 10deg.

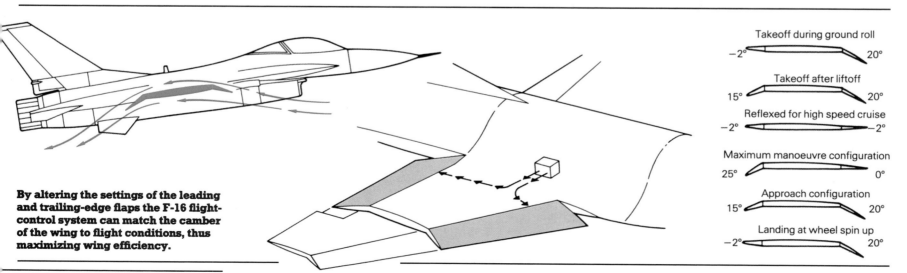

By altering the settings of the leading and trailing-edge flaps the F-16 flight-control system can match the camber of the wing to flight conditions, thus maximizing wing efficiency.

Takeoff during ground roll
−2° / 20°

Takeoff after liftoff
15° / 20°

Reflexed for high speed cruise
−2° / −2°

Maximum manoeuvre configuration
25° / 0°

Approach configuration
15° / 20°

Landing at wheel spin up
−2° / 20°

Critics who predicted in the mid-1970s that the F-16 would suffer a high incidence of engine damage due to FOD (foreign object damage) have been proved wrong. The lower edge of the intake lip is 38in (97.5cm) above the ground, high enough to minimize the chances of small objects or fragments of debris being sucked in. A study of the limited clearance between intake and runway surface on types such as the Boeing 707 (inboard engines) and 737 airliners might have suggested that all would be well, but such obvious comparisons were often overlooked during the wave of F-16 knocking carried out by some 'experts' as Europe was tooling up to build the type.

Conventional wisdom suggests that the complexities of variable geometry are mandatory in an intake for use at Mach 2. Like the creators of the earlier Saab-Scania J37 Viggen, however, the GD engineers ignored the rule book and devised a simple fixed-geometry unit incorporating a boundary-layer splitter plate. This was designed as a single assembly to make future updating easy (a feature later found useful during the development of the turbojet-powered F-16/79 variant). A more traditional variable-geometry intake assembly had been designed, but was destined never to enter service.

In order to reduce the number of spare parts which F-16 units must hold, some components are designed to be interchangeable between port and starboard. These include the horizontal tail surfaces, wing flaperons, 80 per cent of the main landing gear components, and many of the actuator units.

Like any aircraft, the Fighting Falcon is only as good as its pilot. Aircrew assigned to the F-16 are housed in the most sophisticated cockpit that the technology of the early 1970s could devise. Later fighters such as the F/A-18 Hornet may have more advanced electronics, but no other aircraft in the Western world – and probably in the entire world – has the combination of reclining seat and sidestick controller used in the F-16.

Research suggested that a pilot's tolerance could be increased by the use of a reclining seat whose back was tilted at angles of up to 65deg. GD engineers compromised by adopting a tilt of 30deg and by raising the pilot's knees and legs. In terms of providing extra pilot tolerance to high-g manoeuvres the cockpit layout was probably a suc-cess, but the disadvantages of such a configuration seem to have prevented its being used in later designs. Studies carried out by other manufacturers suggest that the raised leg position markedly reduces the panel area which may be used to house displays and instruments.

Good all-round visibility is provided by a canopy whose forward and centre sections are made from a single piece of polycarbonate. An impressive item of plastics engineering, this suffered from 'teething troubles' early in its development. The transparency was required to withstand the impact of a 4lb (1.8kg) bird at 350kt, and passed initial tests with flying colours. Following some minor problems with the canopy protective coating on the YF-16, the USAF modified the latter, but the revised

General Dynamics F-16 Fighting Falcon cutaway

1 Pitot tube
2 Glassfibre radome
3 Planar radar scanner
4 ILS glidescope aerial
5 Scanner drive units
6 Radar mounting bulkhead
7 ADF aerial
8 Forward electronics equipment bay
9 Westinghouse AN/APG-66 digital pulse doppler radar electronics
10 Forward identification light, Danish and Norwegian aircraft only
11 Radar warning antenna
12 Cockpit front pressure bulkhead
13 Instrument panel shroud
14 Weapons systems fire control electronics
15 Fuselage forebody strake fairing
16 Marconi-Elliot wide-angle raster-video head-up display (WARHUD)
17 Side stick controller (fly-by-wire control system)
18 Cockpit floor
19 Frameless bubble canopy
20 Canopy fairing
21 McDonnell-Douglas ACES II zero-zero ejection seat
22 Pilot's safety harness
23 Engine throttle
24 Side console panel
25 Cockpit frame construction
26 Rear pressure bulkhead
27 Ejection seat headrest
28 Seat arming safety lever
29 Cockpit sealing frame
30 Canopy hinge point
31 Ejection seat launch rails
32 Rear electronics equipment bay (growth area)
33 Boundary layer splitter plate
34 Fixed geometry engine air intake
35 Lower UHF/IFF aerial
36 Aft retracting nosewheel
37 Shock absorber scissor links
38 Retraction strut
39 Nosewheel door
40 Forward position light
41 Intake trunking
42 Cooling air louvres
43 Gun gas suppression nozzle
44 Air conditioning system piping
45 Forward fuselage fuel tank, total system capacity 1,072·5 US gal (4,058 litres)
46 Canopy aft glazing
47 Starboard 370US gal external fuel tank (1,400 litres)
48 Forebody blended wing root
49 Upper position light and flight refuelling floodlight
50 Fuel tank bay access panel
51 Rotary cannon barrels
52 Forebody frame construction
53 M61 Vulcan, 20mm rotary cannon
54 Ammunition feed and link return chutes
55 Ammunition drum, 500 rounds

56 Ammunition drum flexible drive shaft
57 Hydraulic gun drive motor
58 Leading-edge flap control shaft
59 Hydraulic equipment service bay
60 Primary system hydraulic reservoir
61 Leading-edge manoeuvre flap drive motor
62 TACAN aerial
63 No 2 hydraulic system reservoir
64 Leading-edge flap control shaft
65 Inboard pylon
66 Pylon fixing
67 Wing centre pylon
68 Triple ejector bomb rack
69 MK 82 500lb (227kg) bombs
70 Oldelft Orpheus reconnaissance pod, Netherlands aircraft only
71 Infra-red linescan
72 Camera ports
73 Reconnaissance pod pylon adaptor, centre line fixing
74 SUU-25E/A flare launcher
75 AN/ASQ aircraft instrumentation system data link transmitter
76 Outboard wing pylon
77 Missile launch shoe
78 AIM-9L Sidewinder air-to-air missile
79 Advanced medium range air-to-air missile (AMRAAM)
80 Aluminium honeycomb leading-edge flap construction
81 Starboard navigation light
82 Static dischargers
83 Fixed trailing edge section

84 Multi-spar wing construction
85 Integral wing fuel tank
86 Starboard flaperon
87 Fuel system piping
88 Access panels
89 Centre fuel tank bay access panel
90 Intake ducting
91 Wing mounting bulkheads
92 Universal air refuelling receptacle (UARSSI)
93 Engine compressor face
94 Pratt & Whitney F100-PW-100(3) afterburning turbofan engine
95 Jet fuel starter
96 Engine accessory gearbox, airframe mounted
97 Gearbox drive shaft
98 Ground pressure refuelling receptacle

design promptly failed its final qualification tests.

This failure triggered off a re-examination of the canopy design and test procedures, and studies of alternative canopy designs. A newer and heavier pattern of canopy was developed in order to ensure adequate resistance to bird strikes. The final design meets all USAF requirements, and offers a level of visibility which must leave MiG-21 and Mirage III pilots drooling with envy. Its high 'bubble' profile may result in some penalty in terms of supersonic drag, but the F100 engine has more than enough thrust to cope. Visibility from the cockpit covers a full 360deg in the horizontal plane, and from 15deg down over the nose through the zenith and back to directly behind – a total of 195 deg. Sideways visibility extends down

Above: A technician examines the forward undercarriage leg of a Belgian Air Force F-16. Note the inlet strut for increased rigidity

to a depression angle of 40deg. The polycarbonate is 0.5in (1.3cm) thick, but its optical quality is high, and the curved surfaces offer minimal distortion of the outside view.

The ejection seat selected for production F-16s was the McDonnell Douglas ACES II (Advanced Concept Ejection Seat) used on the F-15 Eagle. This is a rocket-powered unit with a vectored-thrust STAPAC pitch-control system. Mounted beneath the seat, STAPAC consists of a small vernier rocket motor with a thrust of 235lb (107kg) and a 0.3sec burn time. As the seat leaves the cockpit, a gas generator spins up a pitch-rate gyro. This is uncaged and the vernier motor lit. The latter normally has its thrust axis aligned with the nominal centre of gravity of the seat and its occupant: should the seat pitch forwards

or backwards due to aerodynamic forces or a low or high centre of gravity, the STAPAC vernier will be vectored to apply a corrective force.

ACES II offers zero-zero performance. From a stationary aircraft parked on the ground, it will lift to a height of more than 100ft (30m) and carry rearwards by at least 50ft (15m). Built-in survival equipment includes emergency oxygen, a URT-33C radio beacon, a liferaft and a rucksack.

The Multinational Staged Improvement Plan (MSIP) approved in February 1981 brought in a series of improvements developed under Engineering Change Proposal ECP350. This included modifications to the structure and wiring of the wings to allow the carriage of AMRAAM, the provision of hardpoints on the intake sides to carry

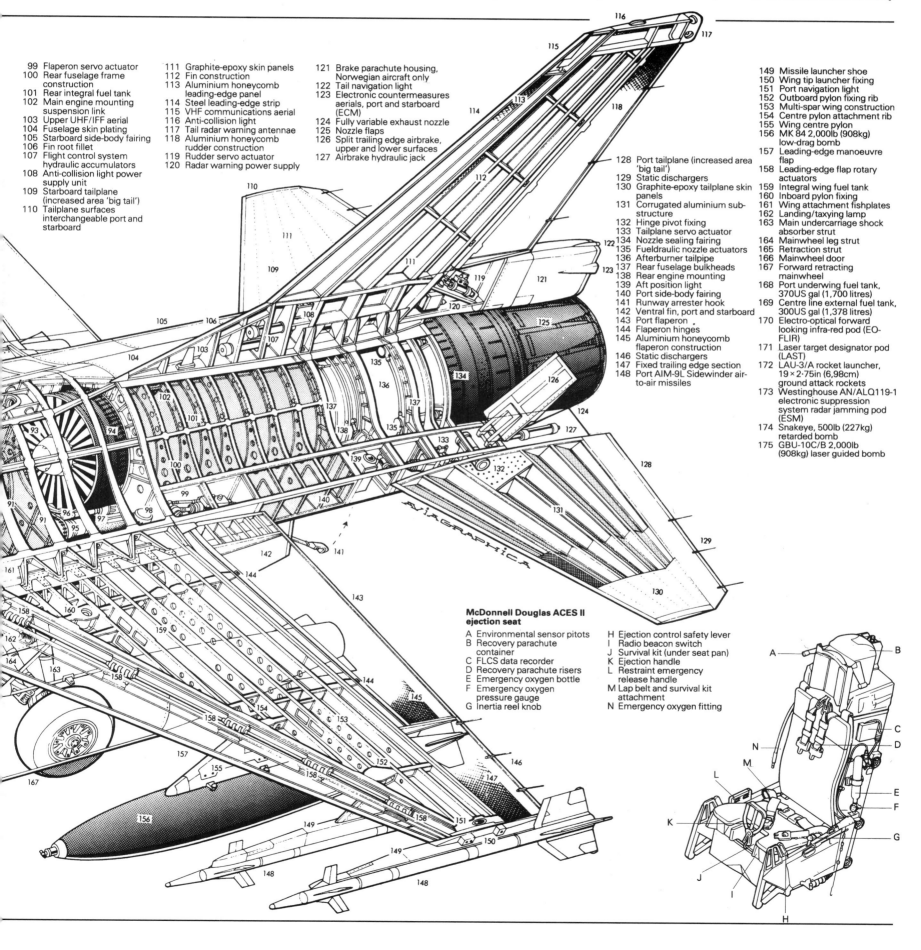

99 Flaperon servo actuator
100 Rear fuselage frame construction
101 Rear integral fuel tank
102 Main engine mounting suspension link
103 Upper UHF/IFF aerial
104 Fuselage skin plating
105 Starboard side-body fairing
106 Fin root fillet
107 Flight control system hydraulic accumulators
108 Anti-collision light power supply unit
109 Starboard tailplane (increased area 'big tail')
110 Tailplane surfaces interchangeable port and starboard

111 Graphite-epoxy skin panels
112 Fin construction
113 Aluminium honeycomb leading-edge panel
114 Steel leading-edge strip
115 VHF communications aerial
116 Anti-collision light
117 Tail radar warning antennae
118 Aluminium honeycomb rudder construction
119 Rudder servo actuator
120 Radar warning power supply

121 Brake parachute housing, Norwegian aircraft only
122 Tail navigation light
123 Electronic countermeasures aerials, port and starboard (ECM)
124 Fully variable exhaust nozzle
125 Nozzle flaps
126 Split trailing edge airbrake, upper and lower surfaces
127 Airbrake hydraulic jack
128 Port tailplane (increased area 'big tail')
129 Static dischargers
130 Graphite-epoxy tailplane skin panels
131 Corrugated aluminium sub-structure
132 Hinge pivot fixing
133 Tailplane servo actuator
134 Nozzle sealing fairing
135 Fuelhydraulic nozzle actuators
136 Afterburner tailpipe
137 Rear fuselage bulkheads
138 Rear engine mounting
139 Aft position light
140 Port side-body fairing
141 Runway arrester hook
142 Ventral fin, port and starboard
143 Port flaperon
144 Flaperon hinges
145 Aluminium honeycomb flaperon construction
146 Static dischargers
147 Fixed trailing edge section
148 Port AIM-9L Sidewinder air-to-air missiles

149 Missile launcher shoe
150 Wing tip launcher fixing
151 Port navigation light
152 Outboard pylon fixing rib
153 Multi-spar wing construction
154 Centre pylon attachment rib
155 Wing centre pylon
156 MK 84 2,000lb (908kg) low-drag bomb
157 Leading-edge manoeuvre flap
158 Leading-edge flap rotary actuators
159 Integral wing fuel tank
160 Inboard pylon fixing
161 Wing attachment fishplates
162 Landing/taxiing lamp
163 Main undercarriage shock absorber strut
164 Mainwheel leg strut
165 Retraction strut
166 Mainwheel door
167 Forward retracting mainwheel
168 Port underwing fuel tank, 370US gal (1,700 litres)
169 Centre line external fuel tank, 300US gal (1,378 litres)
170 Electro-optical forward looking infra-red pod (EO-FLIR)
171 Laser target designator pod (LAST)
172 LAU-3/A rocket launcher, 19×2·75in (6,98cm) ground attack rockets
173 Westinghouse AN/ALQ119-1 electronic suppression system radar jamming pod (ESM)
174 Snakeye, 500lb (227kg) retarded bomb
175 GBU-10C/B 2,000lb (908kg) laser guided bomb

McDonnell Douglas ACES II ejection seat

A Environmental sensor pitots
B Recovery parachute container
C FLCS data recorder
D Recovery parachute risers
E Emergency oxygen bottle
F Emergency oxygen pressure gauge
G Inertia reel knob
H Ejection control safety lever
I Radio beacon switch
J Survival kit (under seat pan)
K Ejection handle
L Restraint emergency release handle
M Lap belt and survival kit attachment
N Emergency oxygen fitting

the LANTIRN electro-optical system, and wiring and structural provisions in the cockpit for the LANTIRN HUD, head-down multi-function displays and other improved avionics.

Load capacity of the centre wing pylons rises from 2,500lb (1,135kg) to 3,500lb (1,590kg). Other modifications prepare the aircraft for the ASPJ ECM system and make provision for a radar altimeter. Control logic of the aircraft environmental control system was also modified to increase system efficiency.

MSIP I modifications

Although the USAF did not expect to take delivery of the new avionics items until the end of 1984, it programmed the associated structural and wiring modifications into the production line in 1981 under the MSIP I programme. These changes added approximately 200lb (90kg) to aircraft weight.

A new horizontal tailplane of increased area is the most obvious external evidence of the MSIP I modifications. Introduced by Engineering Change Proposal 425, this provides the greater control force required to cope with heavy munition loads. When large ordnance loads are carried, aircraft centre of gravity is moved further forward, increasing stability and making the F-16 more difficult to manoeuvre.

The revised tail is easier and less expensive to produce, since its structure does not incorporate titanium. The rising cost and poor availability of this metal led GD to redesign the tailplane spar and pivot in aluminium as part of ECP 425, resulting in a cost saving of 20 per cent. Corrugated aluminium alloy, mechanically fastened to the carbon-fibre skins, replaced the earlier filling of aluminium honeycomb, which was bonded into place. The finished

stabilizer is thicker than the original component, but thanks to the increased span the thickness-to-chord ratio remains unchanged. At the same time, the need for a braking parachute led GD to modify the vertical fin to allow the fitting of this item should customers so desire.

Wherever possible, the design makes maintenance easy. Ground crew working on the F-4 Phantom had to cope with 510 individual lubrication points, 281 fuel line connections, more than 900 individual electrical connectors and 294 avionics units. In the case of Fighting Falcon, lubrication points have been cut to 84, and fuel line connections to 90, while the avionics technicians have only 52 units to deal with. The number of connectors remains high at 841, but these now incorporate silicone grommets, so are easier to service than earlier patterns of connector which were potted (sealed) with rubberized compound after assembly. As a further aid to maintenance, around 60 per cent of the surface of the aircraft is removable, the Fighting Falcon design incorporating 228 access doors. Only four tools are required to open these, and 80 per cent of the aircraft systems are accessible without stands.

Old technology

Some technology from earlier General Dynamics fighters – the Convair F-102 Delta Dagger and F-106 Delta Dart – was used in the F-16 programme. Tests have shown that a fuel tank sealant designated AF-10 Scotchweld which was used on these 1950s designs had a better performance and required less maintenance than the more modern polysulphide rubber-like compounds now in use, and offered cost savings of 25 per cent or more. During tests on F-16 centre-fuselage and aft-fuselage

tanks, the older type of sealant successfully withstood the standard 5psi (0.35kg/sq cm) air-pressure test.

The most drastic structural modification which the Fighting Falcon has undergone was that imposed by the "cranked-wing" F-16XL project, whose delta wing used a planform originally proposed for use on supersonic airliners. Developed in conjunction with NASA's Langley Research Centre, it was intended to offer low drag at high subsonic and supersonic speeds without losing low-speed manoeuvrability. It was of a multi-spar delta design with a leading edge sweep angle varying from 50deg to 70deg. Area was 120 per cent greater than that of the basic wing, while wing weight rose by 2,600lb (1,179kg). Weight was reduced by the use of carbon composite materials for the upper and lower skins. Had

these been made of aluminium alloy, the wing would have been some 600lb (272kg) heavier, an increase that would not have been viable.

During the conversion work, the length of the aircraft fuselage was extended by 56in (1,420mm). This was accomplished by adding two new fuselage sections at the junctions between the three main fuselage sub-assemblies. One 30in (760mm) section was located at the front split point, and a 26in (660mm) section at the rear. This increase in fuselage and wing size allowed internal fuel capacity to be increased by 82 per cent. The latter factor dramatically increased the payload/range performance of the modified aircraft. The F-16XL was intended to carry twice the payload of the F-16 40 per cent further.

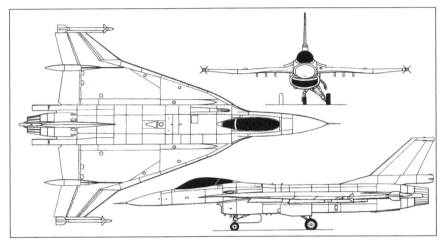

Above: Single-seat version of the F-16XL

Below: The modular design of the basic F-16 fuselage allowed new sections to be spliced in to create the longer fuselage of the F-16XL.

Below right: The first F-16XL was a single-seat aircraft powered by a P&W F100 turbofan and with a wing area increased by 120 per cent.

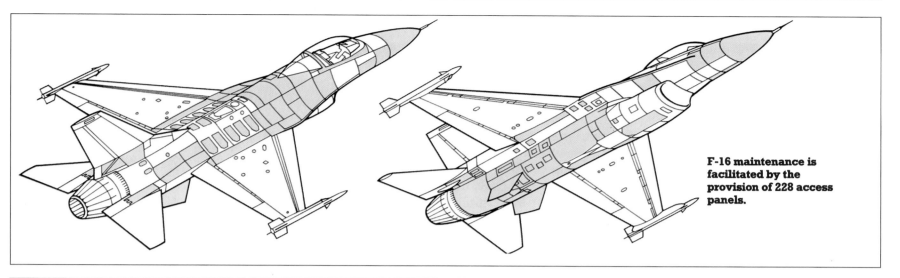

F-16 maintenance is facilitated by the provision of 228 access panels.

Above: A USAF technician removes an access panel from the wing of a 428th Tactical Fighter Squadron F-16 during Exercise Cope Elite 1981.

Right: Although the wing planforms of the F-16/79 (lower) and F-16XL are very different, the fuselage displays a high degree of commonality.

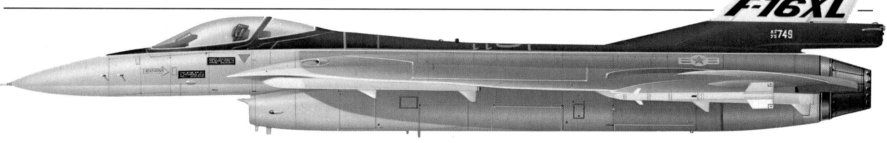

F-16 Fighting Falcon detail comparisons

1. Nose section of the F-16B and D trainers.
2. F-16/AFTI with intake-mounted canards, and dorsal spine containing avionics and instrumentation.
3. Plan view of F-16A and C single-seat versions.
4. Single-seat F-16XL with cranked arrow wing.
5. Tailplane fitted to early production aircraft.
6. Definitive tailplane of increased area.
7. Rear fuselage of F-16/79.
8. Norwegian aircraft have a modified tail fairing which houses a braking parachute.

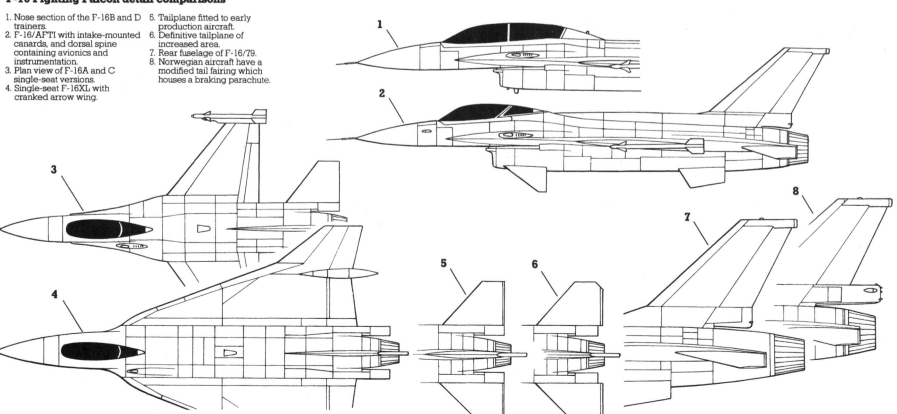

Powerplant

John Boyd's concept of specific excess power demanded a high thrust/weight ratio, which in turn called for a very powerful engine. That selected was the F100 turbofan by Pratt & Whitney, already under development for the F-15. This had problems, and by the time these were solved, galloping weight growth demanded something much better. This finally emerged in the form of the F100-PW-229 and the F110-GE-129, both of which gave a thrust increment in the region of 24 per cent.

Development of the Pratt & Whitney F100 turbofan started in August 1968, when the USAF awarded development contracts to P & W and General Electric for engines suitable for use in the planned FX fighter – later to become the F-15 Eagle. In view of the high thrust-to-weight ratio planned for the new fighter, the resulting engines would have to push the technology of the time to its limits. P&W faced the daunting task of developing a powerplant producing 25 per cent more thrust per pound of weight than the contemporary TF30 turbofan used in the F-111, and twice that of the J75 turbojet used in the F-105 Thunderchief and F-106 Delta Dart.

Both companies built and ran demonstration engines whose light weight, high thrust and low fuel consumption put them well ahead of previous designs. The P&W engine was selected by the USAF for further development, contracts being awarded in 1970. Two versions were originally planned – the F100 for the USAF and the F401 intended to power later models of the US Navy's F-14 Tomcat, though the latter was cancelled when the USN was ordered by the Department of Defense to cut back the size of the planned F-14 fleet.

The F100 is an axial-flow turbofan with a bypass ratio of 0.7:1. It has two shafts, one carrying a three-stage fan driven by a two-stage turbine, the other carrying the ten-stage main compressor and its two-stage turbine. The completed engine is 191in (4.85m) long and, 34.8in (0.88m) in diameter at the inlet, and weighs 3,068lb (1,392kg).

New technologies used in the F100 included powder metallurgy. Instead of forming some metal components in the traditional manner, P&W reduced the raw material to a powder. This could be heated and formed under high pressure to create engine components better able to tolerate the high temperatures planned for the F100 core.

Operating temperature of the F100 turbine was far above that of earlier engines. Successful turbojets of earlier vintage, such as the GE F85 which powers the F-5E, or the GE J79 used in the F-4 and F-104, had turbine inlet temperatures of around 1,800deg F (982 deg C). P&W had achieved figures of just over 2,000deg F (1,093deg C) in the TF30 turbofan, but to meet the demanding requirements of the F100 specification involved temperatures of 2,565deg F (1,407deg C).

Use of such advanced technology resulted in an engine capable of providing the high levels of thrust required by the F-15 and F-16. Maximum thrust is normally described as being 'in the 15,000lb (6,800kg) thrust class' when running without afterburner, and 'in the 25,000lb (11,340kg) class' at full augmentation.

Normal dry (non-afterburning) rating is 12,420lb (5,634kg), rising to a maximum of 14,670lb (6,654kg) at full Military Intermediate rating – the maximum attainable without afterburning. Specific fuel consumption (sfc) – the amount of thrust produced for each pound of fuel burned per hour – is 0.69 at normal rating, 0.71 at Military Intermediate. At full afterburning power, the F100 develops 23,830lb (10,809kg) of thrust at an sfc of 2.17. At this rating, the engine swallows an impressive 860lb (390kg) of fuel per minute.

By the time the F-15 Eagle was ready for its first flight in July 1972, the F100 had completed most of its test programme, meeting 23 out of 24 critical 'project milestones'. Between February and October of the following year, a series of turbine failures dogged attempts to complete the 150-hour run-

ning trial which formed part of the formal Qualification Test. The latter was the most punishing series of tests to which any US military jet engine had ever been subjected, according to P&W. It included 30 hours of running at a simulated speed of mach 2.3, and 38 hours of running at a simulated Mach 1.6.

Following completion of this test, the F100 was subjected to a further series of intensive trials, including 150 hours of running at over-temperature conditions, and a long series of Accelerated Mission Tests. Conducted on the ground, but designed to simulate the stresses of operational service, these were intended to build up running time and detect potential problems. None of these was serious enough to delay the start of F-15 production, and the first

Above: A USAF crewman at Kunsan Air Base in South Korea fuels an F-16. Engines in the F100 thrust class require large amounts of fuel.

Below: At full afterburning thrust, the F100 consumes more than 800lb of fuel per minute. This aircraft is from the 8th TFW, based at Kunsan.

aircraft were delivered to the USAF in November 1974. The F-15 powerplant is designated F100-PW-100 by the company and JTF22A-25A by the USAF.

Despite the obvious merits of the P&W F100 turbofan, including the fact that this engine had already been selected for use on the F-15, GD carried out many studies of the smaller General Electric YF101 engine. The P&W engine was very much a product of late 1960s thinking – a high bypass ratio turbofan offering good and economical performance at its military (dry) rating – while the GE powerplant was a more modern engine with a much lower bypass ratio. Only a small amount of air was ducted past the core in this design, which GE had dubbed a 'leaky turbojet'.

In many ways, the GE engine was more conservatively designed, emphasis having been placed on reliability rather than ultimate performance. GE personnel made no secret of their view that the P&W engine was pushing the technology of the time close to the limits.

Factors considered by GD during the engine evaluation were the weight of the rival powerplants plus the fuel needed for cruise, combat and reserve. The YF-16 design mission included a 500nm cruise to the target area at high subsonic speed, acceleration to combat speed using maximum afterburner, a period of combat in full afterburner involving sustained turns and supersonic and subsonic speeds, then a return to base with a 20-minute sea-level reserve.

Weight calculations

Combined fuel and engine weight for this mission was calculated to be 7,882lb (3,575kg) using a single F100, or 10,234lb (4,642kg) for twin YF101 engines. Two YF101 engines plus installation would weigh 1,024lb (464kg) more than would be the case with a single F100, while an extra 1,328lb (602kg) of fuel would have to be carried. Using the twin GE installation, the F-16 design team would have come up with an aircraft with a mission weight of 21,470lb (9,739kg) instead of the 17,050lb (7,734kg) promised by the P&W engine.

If aircraft weight were kept constant, an F100-engined YF-16 would have a 70 per cent greater mission radius than a twin-YF101 design, GD estimated. Some 90 per cent of this increase was due in roughly equal proportions to the lower engine weight and fuel load required by an F100-powered design, the remainder to reduced drag and airframe weight.

The lower bypass ratio and lighter weight of the F100 installation produced dividends in many areas, GD estimated. Under static conditions at sea level, a pair of YF101 'leaky turbojets' would produce an extra 5,200lb (2,359kg) of thrust, but at Mach 1.2 the turbofan

offered an additional 7,500lb (3,402kg). The difference at 30,000ft (9,000m) and Mach 2 was less marked, but the P&W engine still offered a useful 2,850lb (1,293kg) of extra thrust.

In cruising flight, the big turbofan offered a thrust-to-weight ratio seven per cent better than that of the two YF101 engines, and with a 25 per cent lower fuel flow. At 30,000ft and Mach 2, fuel flow was more evenly matched, but thrust-to-weight ratio was dramatically improved. The P&W engine would consume 6.5 per cent less fuel, but produce a 41 per cent higher thrust-to-weight ratio.

In one instance the F100 turned out to have too much thrust. The residual thrust from an idling F100 was 670lb (304kg) – too high for F-16 operations on icy runways. In theory, this residual thrust could have sent a lightly-loaded

F-16 moving at speeds of up to 50kt, rather too much for taxying. A test programme using the second YF-16 showed that the engine could be adjusted to give a lower idling speed, reducing the taxying speed to a more acceptable figure.

USAF hopes that the F100 would be a mature powerplant by the time the F-16 entered service were dimmed by a series of technical and operational problems. Strikes at two major subcontractors delayed the delivery of engines, while service experience showed that the F100 was wearing out twice as fast as had been predicted. By the end of 1979 the USAF was being forced to accept engineless F-15 airframes, and by the spring of the following year some 30 were in storage. A massive effort by P&W brought the delivery situation under control, but for

Above: To clear the F100 for service, the engine was subjected to the most demanding series of ground tests ever devised for a USAF powerplant.

a long time the F-15 and F-16 fleets remained short of engines.

A modification introduced into the fuel pump of the F100 created problems for the F-15 early in that aircraft's career. In cruising flight, cavitation could begin in the pump, badly damaging the pump vanes. The solution adopted on the F-15 was simple – revert to the original design. In the case of the F-16, a pump failure would be more serious, so Sundstrand developed an

Below: Specifically developed for use in the F-16, the F100-PW-200 has additional anti-stagnation-stall features for single-engine safety.

alternative dual-element pump for this aircraft. This runs at a lower speed, and should one section fail, the other can continue to deliver fuel at a lower rate.

The electronic engine control unit uses the fuel as a coolant. This technique for obtaining 'free' cooling led to problems when the F-15 first entered service. During training missions at Luke AFB, aircraft sometimes had to wait for 45 minutes or more before takeoff, with engines running at idle settings. This gradually heated the mass of fuel in the Eagle's tank to the point where it was no longer cold enough to cool the engine control unit. Given the high temperature of the desert environment at Luke, the unit could not radiate the excess heat away, so tended to overheat, resulting in engine overspeed problems and turbine failures.

Early operational and durability problems with the F100 during the late 1970s were largely overcome by modifications, plus improvements in materials, maintenance and operating procedures. Production of spare parts was accelerated, and field maintenance teams were increased in size.

Part of the problem lay in the fact that the USAF had underestimated the number of cycles which engines aboard such high-performance types as the F-15 and F-16 would actually undergo. (A cycle is defined as the temperature variation experienced in a mission from engine start to maximum power and afterburner, then back to the lower settings used for landing.) In 1977 the service estimated that each engine would undergo 1.15 cycles per flight hour, but in practice the rate was 2.2 for the F-15 and 3.1 for the F-16.

At one time, designers had assumed that the most arduous duty which a jet engine had to face was running for long periods at high power levels. By the late 1960s, research had shown that this was simply not the case. Many failures were due to this type of running, but others were created by the heating and cooling resulting from an engine being run up to high power then throttled back. Technicians dubbed this 'low-cycle fatigue', but had to admit that it was difficult to measure. To aid the design of future engines such as the F100, estimates were made of the average number of thermal cycles to which an engine would be exposed per flying hour. Unfortunately for the F100 programme, these estimates were wrong. In practice, engines were being subjected to far more thermal cycles than the designers had allowed for.

Paradoxically, the additional stress which the engines were receiving was largely due to the F-15 and F-16 being such good aircraft. Given the high manoeuvrability of their new mounts, pilots were flying in a manner not possible on earlier types, pushing the aircraft to high angles of attack and making full use of the extended performance envelope. In the heat of a dogfight, the throttle setting would be changed much more often than on earlier fighters. All this spelled hard work for the engine.

Air combat demands

The F-16 places more strain on the engine than does the F-15, since the Fighting Falcon is used in the demanding air-combat role. P&W studies showed that throttle excursions placed a greater strain on the engine than long runs at a constant setting. Studies involving instrumented test aircraft gathered data on the number of throttle movements and the amount of afterburner use which test F-16s were clocking up, and the company carried out a series of accelerated mission tests to clear the F100 for use in the GD aircraft.

Critical components such as first-stage turbine blades showed signs of distress, condemnation rate during repair being 60 per cent instead of the predicted 20 per cent. Maximum gas temperature was reduced to conserve component life, while R&D funding was concentrated on improvements to reliability rather than increasing thrust. Despite these problems, the F-15 had a better engine-related safety record by the end of the 1970s than any other USAF fighter at a comparable point in its service career.

Another problem which was to dog the F100 during the first years of its service career was stagnation stalling. The compressor blades in a jet engine are of aerofoil section, and, like the wing of an aircraft, can be stalled if the angle at which the airflow strikes them exceeds a critical value. Powerplant stalls are occasional occurrences in most jet engines, particularly in the early stages of development, but the F100 was to prove excessively vulner-

able to stagnation stalling during its first few years of operational service.

Turbofans are prone to a particularly severe type of stall from which recovery is not possible. As the flow of air through the compressor is disturbed, the engine core loses speed, while the combustor section of the engine continues to pass hot gas to the turbine, causing the latter to overheat. If this condition is not noticed, the turbine may be damaged.

Experience with the F-15 showed that in the event of a mild hard start, the pilot might not notice that a stall had occurred, as the loss of acceleration on the twin-engined aircraft was often not sharp enough to indicate to the pilot that one engine had failed. Without a check on the temperature gauge, low-pressure turbine entry temperature could reach the point where damage might occur. To avoid this problem, an audible-warning system was devised for the Eagle. This is not needed on the Fighting Falcon, since a stall of the single engine produces an immediate loss of acceleration.

Some stagnation stalls were found to be due to component failures, but most were linked with afterburner problems. The latter usually took the form of 'hard starts' – virtually mini-explosions within the afterburner. In some cases the afterburner failed to light on schedule; in other instances the burner extinguished. In either event, large amounts of unburned fuel were sprayed into the jetpipe, creating a momentary build-up of fuel. When this was ignited by the hot efflux from the engine core, a pressure pulse was created – the aerospace equivalent of a car backfiring.

Deliberate hard start

A reporter from *Aviation Week* gave this account of a deliberately induced hard start on a test stand: "The force of the auto-ignition was sufficient to rock the heavily sound-insulated concrete test building. A large gout of flame at the afterburner exhaust was seen on the closed-circuit colour-television system." The pressure in the afterburner resulting from a hard start sent a shock wave back up through the fan duct. When this reached the front section of the engine, it could cause the fan to stall, the high-pressure compressor to stall, or, in the worst case, both. It was sometimes possible for a series of stagnation stalls

Above: Dwarfed by the bulk of the McDonnell Douglas KC-10A Extender, an F-16 connects the 'flying boom' to its receptacle during tests of the new tanker/cargo aircraft.

to occur, with each resulting in the afterburner hard start needed to trigger off another.

Stagnation stalls usually took place at altitude and at high Mach numbers, but rarely below 20,000ft (6,100m). Normal recovery method was for the pilot to shut down the engine and allow it to spool down. Once the tachometer showed that engine rpm had fallen below the 50 per cent mark, the throttle could safely be reopened to the idle position, and the F100 would carry out its automatic relight sequence. The F-16 is fitted with a jet-fuel starter, but from a height of 35,000ft (10,700m) a pilot would probably have enough time to attempt at least three unassisted starts using ram air. Critical factor in restarting the engine after a stagnation stall is the low-pressure turbine-inlet temperature. This must fall to 450deg F (232deg C) before the engine can be restarted.

Several modifications were devised to reduce the frequency of stagnation stalls. The first approach taken was to try to prevent pressure build-ups in the afterburner. A quartz window in the side of the afterburner assembly allowed a flame sensor to monitor the pilot flame of the augmentor. If this went out, the flow of fuel to the outer sections of the burner was prevented.

When the F100 engine-control system was originally designed, P&W engineers allowed for the possibility that ingestion of efflux from missiles might stall the engine and a 'rocket fire' facility was designed into the controls. When missiles were fired, an electronic signal could be sent to the unified fuel control system which supplies fuel to the engine core and to the afterburner. The angle of the variable stator blades in the engine could be altered to avoid a stall, while the fuel flow to the engine was momentarily reduced, and the afterburner exhaust was increased in area to reduce the magnitude of any pressure pulse in the afterburner.

Tests had shown that the 'rocket fire' facility was not needed, but P&W engineers were able to use it as a means of preventing stagnation stalls. Engine

Above: A night-time engine test at the Pratt & Whitney plant. The F100 is in full afterburner, and the nozzle has been fully opened to allow the hot exhaust gases to expand.

shaft speed, turbine temperature and the angle of the compressor stator blades are monitored on the F100 by a digital electronic engine control unit, which normally serves to 'fine-tune' the engine throughout flight to ensure optimum performance.

By monitoring and comparing HP spool speed and fan exhaust temperature, the engine control unit is able to sense that a stagnation stall is about to take place, and send a dummy 'Rocket Fire' signal to the unified fuel control system to initiate the anti-stall measures described above. At the same time, a second modification to the fuel control system reduces the afterburner setting to zone 1 – little more than a pilot light – in order to help reduce pressure within the jetpipe.

In an attempt to prevent any pulses coming forward through the fan duct from affecting the core, P&W engineers devised a modification known as the 'proximate splitter'. This is a forward extension to the internal casing which splits the incoming airflow from the engine compressor fan, passing some to the core of the engine and diverting the remainder down the fan duct, past the core and into the afterburner. By closing the gap between the front end of this casing and the rear of the fan to just under half an inch, the engine designers reduced the size of the path by which the high-pressure pulses from the burner had been reaching the core. Engines fitted with the proximate splitter were test-flown in the F-15, but this modification was not embodied in the engines of production Eagles, whose twin engines made the loss of a single engine less hazardous.

When it first flew, the F-16 seemed almost free of stagnation stall problems, but while flying with an early-model F100 engine, one of the YF-16 prototypes did experience a stagnation stall,

Right: Ready for refuelling during a 4,350 mile (7,000km) flight across the United States intended to simulate a transatlantic deployment, an F-16 approaches the boom of a KC-135.

though this occurred outside the normal performance envelope. Three incidents were noted later during flight tests at high angles of attack. All took place at Edwards AFB during low-speed flight tests at high altitude. The first production aircraft to experience a stagnation stall was an FAéB aircraft operating near the limits of the performance envelope. The pilot was able to restart the engine and landed safely.

Given the amount of development work, the stagnation stall problem was soon mastered, although never completely eliminated. To suit the F100 for the single-engined F-16, the USAF decided to adopt the modifications already fitted to the engines of the F-15, plus the proximate splitter.

The original F-16 powerplant was designated JTF22A-33 by the manufacturer and F100-PW-200 by the USAF. It weighs 54lb (24.5kg) more than the original version fitted to the F-15, and incorporates a back-up fuel-control system and a modified cooling system for the control system, which has a hydromechanical back-up.

The improvement in reliability was dramatic. Back in 1976, the F-15 fleet experienced a stagnation stall rate of 11–12 per 1,000 flying hours. By the end of 1981 this had dropped to 1.5 per 1,000 hours thanks to the modifications to the fuel control system and nozzle. Engines fitted to the F-16 fleet (and incorporating the proximate splitter) had an even lower rate – 0.15 per 1,000 hours.

The need for greater engine reliability in the single-seat F-16 has forced the USAF to be cautious when problems emerge. In the summer of 1980, for example, engines in USAF, European and Israeli service were inspected following the discovery of a broken control cable in the wreckage of an aircraft which crashed at Hill AFB during a low-level training flight. This was seen as a precautionary measure for the single-seat aircraft: for the twin-engined F-15 spot checks were deemed sufficient.

Efforts are under way to reduce furth-

F-16 engine comparisons			
Type	**F100-PW-220**	**F100-PW-229**	**F110-GE-129**
Bypass ratio	0.60	0.40	0.76
Max thrust (lb/kg)	23,830/10,810	29,000/13,154	29,100/13,200
Mil thrust (lb/kg)	14,590/6,618	17,800/8,074	17,000/7,711
Weight (lb/kg)	3,200/1,452	3,650/1,656	3,989/1,809
Length (ft/m)	15.92/4.85	15.92/4.85	15.16/4.62
Diameter (ft/m)	3.88/1.18	3.88/1.18	3.88/1.18
Pressure ratio	25:1	32:1	c31:1
Thrust/wt ratio	7.45	7.95	7.30

er smoke output of the F100 as part of a planned component-improvement programme. For example, the combustor has been modified to increase the velocity of the airflow in its front end. This results in improved mixing of air and fuel and leads to more complete combustion and less residual smoke.

Traditional engine-servicing techniques involved replacing critical components at the end of a statistically calculated lifetime. This often resulted in components being removed and scrapped while still perfectly serviceable, giving good safety margins, but at a high cost to the operator. But the USAF wanted engine designers to develop parts with greater tolerance to crack damage so that these could be left in the engine until inspection by non-destructive test (NDT) showed that cracks were starting to develop and a replacement was needed. Life-cycle costs could be cut by up to 60 per cent.

The service's Damage Tolerant Design (DTD) programme involved both Pratt & Whitney and General Electric, and focussed much of its attention on the F100. One of the programme's first achievements was a new pattern of F100 fan disc having five times the life of the original component. Key design elements under DTD were high quality control of the raw material, and the avoidance of shapes and configurations which caused stress concentrations – sharp radii, for example.

The USAF was the first F100 user to take advantage of a warranty scheme offered by P&W in 1980, whereby the company undertook to repair or replace certain high-pressure turbines unserviceable as a result of wear or

mechanical failure at no extra cost to the USAF. Engines covered by the deal were from production lot IX and were due for delivery between February 1981 and January 1982.

To qualify for free treatment, faulty engines would have to have carried out less than 900 equivalents of the TAC engine operating cycle (about two years of normal use) or have developed the fault within three and a half years of delivery. If the HP failure had caused secondary damage to the engine, P&W undertook to cover costs up to 75 per cent of that of a new engine.

Alternative engines

Two things were immediately apparent. The first was that if weight increases continued, much more power would be needed to restore the original performance. The second was that Pratt & Whitney had achieved dominance in the fighter engine market. The latter was not a good thing, as it obviated healthy competition. An alternative engine was badly needed, but the only other manufacturer in sight was General Electric.

In the search for an alternative powerplant for the F-14 Tomcat, which was also in trouble, and the F-16 Fighting Falcon, the US Department of Defense awarded a $100 million contract to General Electric to build five F101DFE (Derivative Fighter Engines) for flight testing. The origins of the F101 lay in the Rockwell B-1B Lancer bomber, coupled with a scaled-up fan and augmentation from the F404 turbofan used to power the F/A-18 Hornet. In passing, it is interesting to note that the F404 was

an exceptionally reliable and stall-free engine. This boded well, especially as General Electric would maintain design expertise in the foreseeable future, to give Pratt & Whitney a viable competitor.

The first F101DFE engine reached full power on December 30, 1979, which was the first day of ground running. During January 1980 it clocked up 60 hours at all power levels. By the end of summer of that year the F101 had completed 430 hours of accelerated mission testing, the equivalent of 1,000 hours of F-16 flying. Since testing had begun, maximum thrust had fallen by less than 2 per cent, while specific fuel consumption in afterburning mode had increased by just over 1 per cent. The F101 was stripped down, found to be in good condition, then rebuilt to undergo further testing. This satisfactorily completed, the engine was then redesignated F110-GE-100, and a substantial order was placed on 3 February, 1984.

The bypass ratio of the F110 was 0.85, and the three-stage low pressure compressor fan has solid titanium blades. The inlet guide vanes have variable trailing edge flaps. Both are individually replaceable. Pressure ratio exceeds 3. The F110 is extremely stall-resistant, and there are no throttle movement restrictions throughout the entire operational envelope, which makes for carefree engine handling.

The nine-stage high pressure compressor has titanium blades in the front sections, changing to stainless steel aft,

Below: A pilot of the 429th Tactical Fighter Wing carries out a pre-flight inspection of his Fighting Falcon's ventral intake.

Above: Final adjustments are made to an F100 turbofan at the Pratt & Whitney works.

Left: Technicians manoeuvre an F100 into the second FSD aurcraft, The multi-flap articulated nozzle is seen here in the open position used when the afterburner is lit. When dry thrust is selected, the nozzle closes to a narrower diameter.

diameter of the fan hub. This allows 8 per cent more air to flow through the fan without changing the inlet diameter, but results in a lower bypass ratio. The three-stage fan has mid-span shrouds on the first two rotors, which gives outstanding resistance to foreign object damage. Pressure ratio is increased from 25:1 to 32:1.

The combustor uses what is known as a "Floatwall" concept, with advanced diffuser technology and more nozzles. Aft of this, the HP turbine varies only from that of its -220 predecessor in using advanced single crystal superalloy to withstand higher operating temperatures. However, the LP turbine was redesigned to match the increased airflow. The afterburner has also been improved, with a greater number of fuel zone segments which give smoother operation during acceleration and deceleration.

Thrust vectoring nozzles are a thing of the future for the F-16, and have great potential, both for short runway operations and for manoeuvre. Several have been flown experimentally.

where both temperature and pressure increase to incredible levels. Aft of this is the annular combustor, which has dual-cone nozzles which inject fuel into 20 scroll cups. These give a contra-rotating swirl effect to the airflow, which produces an optimum fuel/air mix.

The single-stage high pressure turbine has hollow airfoil section blades and vanes, which operate in extreme temperatures. To prevent them from melting or deforming, bleed air from the compressor is used for convection and film-cooling. The segmented sur-

rounding shroud is designed in such a way that it expands with the heat at a constant rate to that of the blades. This allows the clearance between blades and shroud to remain constant. Aft of this is the low pressure turbine, which drives the fan section via an inner concentric shaft. At the extreme rear is the afterburner, with a convergent-divergent nozzle, based on that of the F404.

The F110-GE-100 was followed by the -129 IPE, which has about 80 per cent commonality with its predecessor. The bypass ratio was reduced to 0.76,

and various design changes and new materials, including single crystal turbine blades, have allowed operating temperatures 100deg higher, and greater pressures, which in turn have put the F110-GE-129 firmly in the 29,000lb (13,154kg) category. Another change is a digital electronic control, which offers greatly improved reliability.

Meanwhile, Pratt & Whitney were not watching the grass grow. For their F100-PW-229, they started by streamlining the nose cone while reducing the

Avionics

Advanced aerodynamics and a high thrust-to-weight ratio are not enough to make an advanced fighter. Without its complex payload of avionics 'black boxes', Fighting Falcon would not be able to search for and locate its targets under typically poor European weather conditions, or confuse hostile ground-based or airborne radars. And without the assistance of the complex fly-by-wire flight-control system, the F-16 pilot would probably be unable to cope with the inherent instability of his aircraft. With these systems installed, however, a basic lightweight fighter becomes a formidable multirole combat aircraft.

The austere fighter concept has never been truly successful historically, and the F-16 was no exception. An austere fighter has little future if it can be hacked down by a more advanced aircraft before it can close to visual range, which implies an adverse kill/loss ratio. As former Aggressor pilot Joe Hodges commented: "It sure as hell wouldn't do much for your morale!"

Consequently, as with all current military aircraft, the F-16 has been developed into a weapons system, largely dependent on its black boxes for both attack and survival. Continually upgraded, it has become one of the greatest multi-role fighters of all time, combining the attack and air superiority roles.

Integration of the F-16 avionics makes extensive use of the MIL-STD-1553 multiplexed databus - a significant step forward in avionics design. The significance of computer languages and interfaces may seem obscure, but the complexity of modern warplanes makes standardization of these as important as the standardization of more tangible objects such as fixings, fastenings, connectors and weapon attachment points.

Traditional methods of avionics integration involved the use of bulky and expensive bundles of electric wiring for the distribution of signals and data. Multiplexing is a technique under which various equipments share a common electrical connection on a time-sampled basis - the electronic equivalent of time-sharing an apartment. If the number of times per second during which a signal has access to the electrical connection – databus – is sufficiently high compared with the rate at which that signal may change, the end result will be as acceptable as a fixed piece of wire. Lightweight digital switching electronics may therefore be substituted for heavy and bulky cabling.

Avionics standardization

By specifying an agreed 'code of conduct' for using the databus, MIL-STD-1553 greatly reduces the electronic interfacing problems experienced in earlier digital avionics systems, in which each manufacturer selected his own independent software (computer programs and instructions) as he saw fit.

GD was an enthusiastic supporter of avionics standardization, and all avionics for the F-16 were developed using a common interface and computer language. For the avionics improvements planned as part of the MSIP programme, the company standardized on the latest version of MIL-STD-1553, the Jovial computer language and a new standard interface for stores and stores-management systems.

The APG-66/68 radar

The primary sensor of the F-16 is the Westinghouse (now Northrop Grumman) APG-66 radar for the F-16A/B, and APG-68 radar for the F-16C/D. The latter was a direct development of the former, using high speed processing to enhance performance and to enable more modes, notably air-to-ground, to be included.

Experience during the Vietnam War had shown how enemy aircraft could avoid detection by flying close to the ground, where the clutter experienced on normal pulse radars could hide them from observation. The need to have 'look-down' radar capability forced the adoption of a pulse-Doppler radar, but the traditional high complexity and cost of such equipment made the design of the much smaller APG-66 a difficult task.

In order to carry out a radar-controlled interception, an aircraft requires data on the bearing of the target and its range. Bearing can be measured by means of a highly-directional antenna giving good angular discrimination, but range data can most easily be obtained by pulsing the radar transmitter on and off again at a rate known as the pulse-repetition frequency (PRF). In the simpler types of radar equipment, sufficient time is allowed for one pulse to travel out to the target, be reflected, and return to the radar before the next pulse is transmitted. Engineers describe such radars as low-PRF sets.

Until the 1960s, airborne radars were almost blind when attempting to look downwards to detect low-flying aircraft. The latter were able to hide in the clutter produced by the strong radar echo from the terrain background against which they were being viewed.

Above: Westinghouse engineers install line-replaceable units in a development APG-66 radar to be test-flown in an F-4 Phantom.

Below: Marconi Avionics' holographic HUD begins flight trials in the front cockpit of an F-16B. The large combiner glass gives the unit the wide field-of-view needed for use with LANTIRN.

By the 1960s a new source of microwave power known as a travelling-wave tube (TWT), along with the use of digital signal processors, allowed the creation of pulse-Doppler radars with good look-down performance.

The use of stable and coherent (phase-related) pulses from a TWT allows the radar to measure the Doppler shift in the radar returns from the target – the tiny change in frequency caused by target motion relative to the signal source. Using this technique, the relative velocity of the target against the terrain background allowed the wanted target signal to be extracted from the massive background returns. This technique is known as pulse-Doppler radar.

TWT transmitters cannot match the high levels of power available from the magnetron transmitters used in low-PRF radars, so the designers were forced to use high PRFs in order to illuminate the target with sufficient power. Since each pulse would be transmitted before the previous pulse had completed the round trip out to a distant target and back, each pulse had to be electronically 'labelled' by a low-frequency modulation at the time of transmission.

Medium PRFs

The range data obtained by processing the labelled pulses is of low accuracy, and high PRFs are also poor at detecting targets whose closure rate is low. In the 1970s, therefore, designers of airborne radar turned to medium PRFs. These allow traditional methods of ranging to be used at most combat ranges, while still allowing pulse-Doppler techniques to be used for look-down operation.

Since the PRFs best suited to range measurement are different to those effective against low closing-rate targets, a practical design of medium-PRF set has to switch rapidly from one PRF value to another. This made the design of hardware able to carry out pulse-Doppler signal processing virtually impossible. The solution lay in the use of software-controlled digital signal processing. By making the characteristics of the filter dependent on a computer program (software) rather than physical components (hardware), the designers could contrive near-instantaneous reconfiguration of the filter to match each PRF waveform used by the radar. The first radars to use medium PRFs and digital signal processors were the Hughes APG-63 in the F-15 Eagle and the L.M. Ericsson PS-46/A in the Viggen JA37 interceptor.

Below: The final FSD aircraft was temporarily fitted with a mock-up of an enlarged nose able to house the APG-65 radar used in the F/A-18.

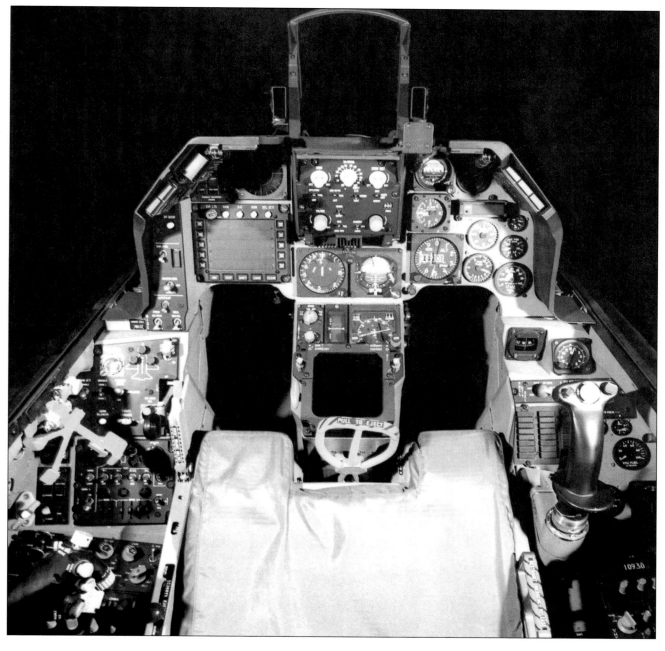

Development contracts for the F-16 radar were awarded to Hughes and Westinghouse, and both companies test-flew prototypes in a competitive evaluation before Westinghouse was awarded the contract for what became the APG-66. The specification was very demanding, calling for a medium-PRF pulse-Doppler set capable of being installed in the modestly-sized nose section of the Fighting Falcon.

The set was initially optimized for the air-to-air role, but air-to-surface modes were also requested soon after the fly-off. To minimize possible delays and cost increases, some compromises in air-to-ground performance were accepted. At high altitudes, for example, radar ground-mapping performance is lower than would have been possible with an antenna optimized for this role.

The APG-66 used in the F-16A/B is a medium-PRF radar (typically 10 to 15kHz). It operates in I/J band and incorporates a 'flat-plate' planar array antenna. Sixteen operating frequencies are available within the band, and the pilot may select between any four. Total weight is 296lb (134kg), and the set occupies a volume of 3.6cu ft (0.1cu m). A mean time between failures of 97 hours has been demonstrated.

Radar operating modes may be selected by the pilot using the throttle, sidestick controller or radar control panel. Like most modern sets, the APG-66 is designed so that all the controls needed during air combat are located

Above: Primary sources of nav/attack data for the F-16A pilot are the HUD (top) and square CRT display (between the pilot's knees).

on the control stick and throttle. When the set is tracking a target, the range scale is switched automatically to reduce pilot workload.

Primary air-combat mode is Downlook, which provides clutter-free indication of low-flying targets. Fighter-sized aircraft may be detected head- or tail-on at ranges of more than 30nm (34.5 miles/55.6km). If the target is flying at a higher altitude than the Fighting Falcon, the pilot may select Uplook mode, gaining a useful 33 per cent increase in detection range.

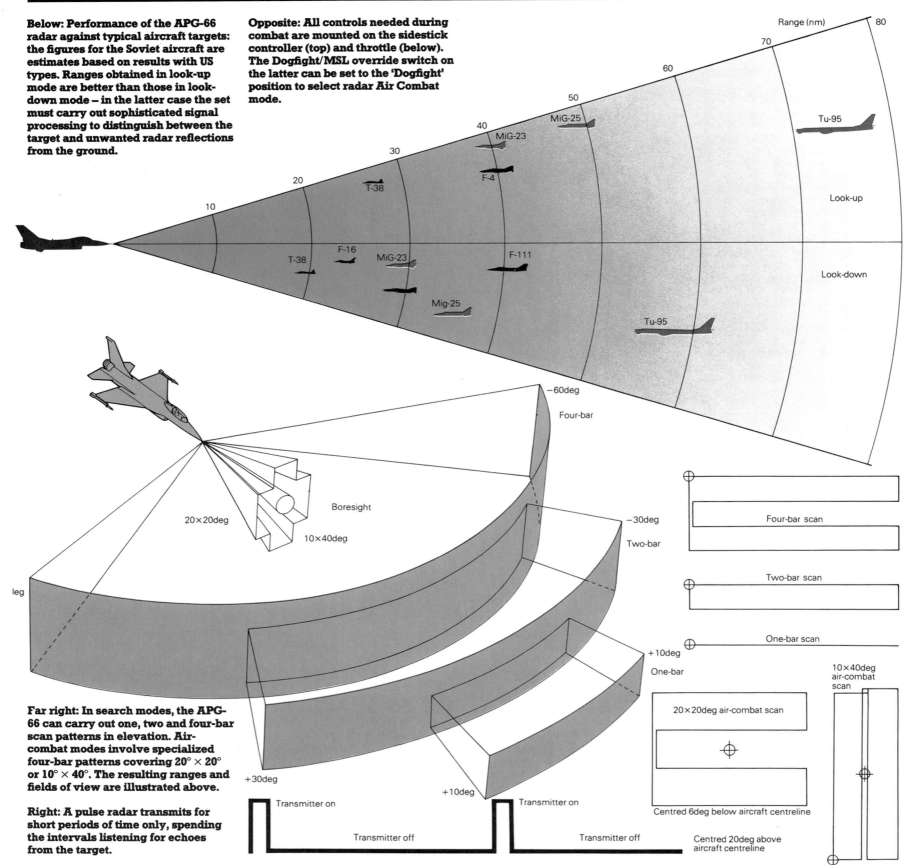

Below: Performance of the APG-66 radar against typical aircraft targets: the figures for the Soviet aircraft are estimates based on results with US types. Ranges obtained in look-up mode are better than those in look-down mode – in the latter case the set must carry out sophisticated signal processing to distinguish between the target and unwanted radar reflections from the ground.

Opposite: All controls needed during combat are mounted on the sidestick controller (top) and throttle (below). The Dogfight/MSL override switch on the latter can be set to the 'Dogfight' position to select radar Air Combat mode.

Far right: In search modes, the APG-66 can carry out one, two and four-bar scan patterns in elevation. Air-combat modes involve specialized four-bar patterns covering 20° × 20° or 10° × 40°. The resulting ranges and fields of view are illustrated above.

Right: A pulse radar transmits for short periods of time only, spending the intervals listening for echoes from the target.

Four modes are available for air-to-air combat. In the Dogfight mode, selected by means of a throttle-mounted switch, the radar automatically scans a 20deg × 20deg field. If the pilot can see the target in his HUD, and the range is less than 10nm, the radar will automatically lock on. If high-g manoeuvres are to be carried out, the area to be searched can be altered to a 40deg × 10deg pattern.

If faced with several closely-spaced targets, the pilot can press the Designate button on his sidestick controller. The radar will then operate in a slim narrow-beam mode, and by manoeuvring his aircraft the pilot can place the beam on to the required target. When he releases the Designate switch, the radar will acquire and track the chosen victim.

Slewable air-combat mode can give the Fighting Falcon pilot the edge during combat manoeuvres. A cursor-control button on the throttle grip allows the scan pattern to be moved to anticipate target manoeuvres. This is particu-larly useful when both aircraft are man-oeuvring in the vertical plane.

Seven modes are provided for air-to-surface use. Air-to-ground ranging is automatically selected during continuously-computed impact point (CCIP) and dive-toss attacks, measuring the slant range to a designated point on the ground.

CCRP attacks

Continuously-computed release point (CCRP) attacks use the set's ground mapping modes. Real-beam ground mapping gives a plan position indicator (PPI) display at 10, 20, 40 or 80nm range, and scan widths of plus or minus 10deg, 30deg or 60deg. This image may be used for navigational updates, the location and detection of ground targets and for direct or offset weapon delivery.

Dedicated sea-surface search modes may be used in the maritime role. Sea 1 is a frequency-agile mode for use against stationary or moving vessels in up to sea state 4, while Sea 2 uses a narrow Doppler notch to detect moving targets in higher sea states, and may also be used to indicate moving targets on land.

Beacon mode also uses a PPI display format. It may be used in conjunction with ground-located radar beacons to take navigation fixes or to carry out offset weapons delivery. In the air-to-air role, this mode is used to locate flight refuelling tankers by interrogating their beacons.

Several auxiliary methods of presenting imagery may be used in these PPI modes. If Freeze mode is selected, the radar carries out a final scan, the image of which is 'held' on the display, following which the radar transmitter is turned off so that the aircraft cannot be detected by passive means. A moving symbol on the display continues to indicate aircraft motion. Expanded-beam real map mode provides an optional ×4 magnification on all PPI modes. The pilot selects the 'patch' to be expanded from anywhere within the radar's scan and range limits.

Highest definition of ground features is given by a special Doppler beam sharpened mode. Usable when the set is ground mapping at ranges of 10 or 20nm, this provides a further ×8 magnification over that in expanded-beam real map mode. Since this mode relies on the processing of Doppler shift, it is only available at angles between 15deg and 60deg off the aircraft's velocity vector. Should the aircraft's subsequent flight path bring the area being viewed to within 15deg of the aircraft centreline, the radar automatically switches to the normal ground-mapping mode. Doppler beam sharpening is likely to be much used when projected specialized off-boresight guided weapons finally enter service.

Development of an effective pulse-Doppler radar of such small size was a formidable technical undertaking, so it was hardly surprising that several problems were experienced during early tests, particularly in look-down mode. Pulse-Doppler radars measure the Doppler shift created by target velocity in order to discriminate between genuine

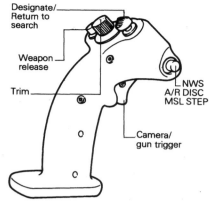

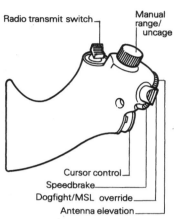

Designate/Return to search — Weapon release — Trim — NWS A/R DISC MSL STEP — Camera/gun trigger

Radio transmit switch — Manual range/uncage — Cursor control — Speedbrake — Dogfight/MSL override — Antenna elevation

Above: If the one-piece canopy were to fail, the combiner glass of the HUD would act as a windshield.

targets and ground clutter. This involves defining a threshold velocity – a speed at which targets must be moving in order to be accepted as valid. Vehicles on West German autobahns often move at speeds of 100mph (160km/h) or more, and were sometimes registered as low-level targets.

During tests over water in Norway, false targets registered on the radar were found to be due to stray radiation from the radar antenna. In designing an antenna, the engineer would like to see all of the signal being directed into the main beam, but in practice some always escapes in the form of sidelobes – unwanted weak beams at an angle to the main beam. A good design will reduce these sidelobes as much as possible, but it is virtually impossible to eliminate them. Radar energy escaping from these sidelobes was being reflected off the water in fjords, creating false targets.

Synthetic imagery

Earlier radars presented a direct radar picture to the operator, who could to some degree use his own skill and experience in deciding which targets were real. Sets such as the APG-66 reduce all radar data to digital form, and present the pilot with a synthetically generated image made up of pre-defined symbols. The screen is free from clutter and is much easier to read than that of earlier types of radar which showed 'raw' data, but the discrimination between real and false targets must be achieved automatically by signal-processing equipment. In the case of the early APG-66 sets, this feature required modification.

During other early trials, the radar

showed poor detection range and low performance in the Doppler beam-sharpened air-to-ground modes. Clearing up these and other 'bugs' took much time and effort, but the situation was under control by the summer of 1979. Modifications were made to the low-power RF circuitry, digital signal processor and system software, and the revised equipment was under flight test and evaluation by the end of 1979.

Improvements to the APG-66 form part of the MSIP update programme. In 1980 Westinghouse was awarded a $25 million contract to begin development of a programmable signal processor (PSP) and dual-mode transmitter for the APG-66. The latter would use low PRFs for air-to-ground work, and medium to high PRFs in air-to-air combat. These modifications were intended to match the performance of the AMRAAM missile, and to improve air-to-ground capability and ECCM performance. The set would also receive track-while-scan and raid-assessment modes. Both new sub-units were designed to occupy the same space as the equipment they replaced.

The design of TWTs able to operate

efficiently over a wide range of PRFs is difficult. Given low or even medium PRFs, the transmitting tube of a radar spends more time silent than transmitting. In engineering jargon, the 'duty cycle' of time 'off' to time 'on' is low. The tube thus has plenty of time to cool between individual pulses, so the designer can work the device hard while it is actually radiating, obtaining high levels of peak power.

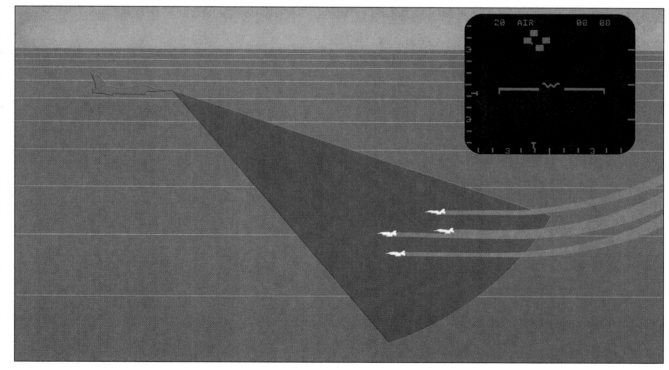

Above right: Primary air-to-air radar mode is Downlook, a medium-PRF search and track mode able to detect low-flying intruders. According to Westinghouse, the set has a low false-alarm rate of less than two per minute. The radar displays use computer-generated alphanumeric and other symbology, to present the pilot with clean imagery, while the effects of clutter and system noise are filtered out by signal processing. Earlier-generation radars presented 'raw' analogue radar imagery to the user, requiring skilled interpretation.

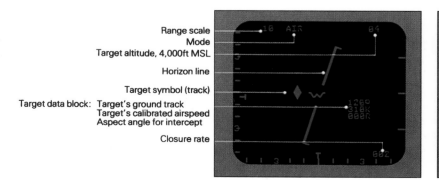

Range scale — Mode — Target altitude, 4,000ft MSL — Horizon line — Target symbol (track) — Target data block: Target's ground track, Target's calibrated airspeed, Aspect angle for intercept — Closure rate

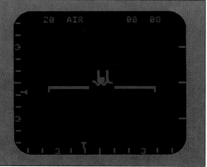

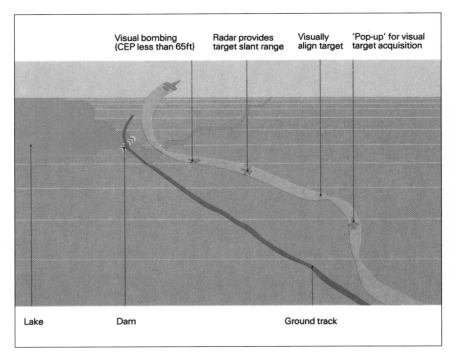

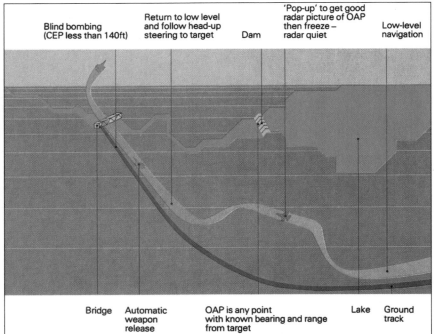

Above: During CCIP (continuously-computed impact point) attacks, the APG-66 radar is used to measure slant range to the target during the final run.

At high PRFs, the tube spends much more of its time transmitting, and has less time to cool down between pulses, involving a duty cycle of 50 per cent or more. As a result, the amount of power which can be extracted in each individual pulse is reduced.

By the time that Westinghouse faced the problem of updating the APG-66, its great rival in the airborne radar business had developed a new type of TWT which made dual-mode operation much more efficient. Working in conjunction with Litton, Hughes had created a TWT able to cope with the high peak-power demands of low- and medium-PRF operation, while still operating efficiently at the high duty cycles required by high PRFs. Long-range detection performance at medium PRFs could now match that at high PRFs.

Radar, operational usage

The first thing to say is that radars have not yet been made idiot-proof; a great deal of skill is needed to get the best out of them. As an example, let us take the APG-68 of the F-16C/D. Early detection is essential, and for this two modes are available: Range While Search (RWS), and Track While Scan (TWS).

Of the two, RWS has the longer

Above right: CCRP (continuously-computed release point) attacks use the ground mapping radar modes. A radar map may be created and 'frozen' during a pop-up manoeuvre.

range. Scan areas are +/-60deg, +/-30deg, or +/-10deg in azimuth, with either 1, 2 or 4 bars in elevation. Bar spacing is 2.2deg in elevation, and has an approximate 50 per cent overlap between bars.

The scan areas of TWS are less: +/-25deg in azimuth with 3 bars, or +/-10deg in azimuth with 4 bars, which gives a much reduced are of search in azimuth. But bar spacing in TWS is 3.3deg which, while it gives greater coverage in elevation, reduces the probability of detection for a target halfway between the bars, compared to the closer bar spacing of RWS.

If the pilot decides to attack when in RWS, he switches to attack mode, generally known as lock-on; he slews the cursor over the selected target indication and designates it. When conditions are right, the radar then automatically switches to Single Target Track (STT) until the attack is either complete or broken off.

TWS is very different. It operates in both manual and automatic modes. In TWS manual, steady contacts are turned into radar files, and the on-screen presentation changes. Designation turns them into full Fire Control Computer (FCC) files, the

priorities of which are determined by the order of designation.

In TWS automatic mode, steady contacts automatically become FCC files, and the nearer contacts are given priority. This means less work for the pilot. Both TWS modes have Multi-Target Track (MTT), which updates each file as the contact is renewed, but neither will allow the radar to be slewed off the priority target, which is indicated with a bug.

If the radar fails to pick up an established contact within about eight seconds (and it must be remembered that radar is not infallible) all it does is to give a high percentage probability of detection; the target indication begins to flash on and off. This is a warning that if the target is not reacquired within a further five seconds it will be lost. The main difference between RWS and TWS is that the former is in real time, whereas TWS is historical, and will extrapolate to fill the gaps. Just sometimes, the TWS picture is not strictly accurate.

Angular resolution of radar is not very good; aircraft in close formation often show up as a single blip on the screen. As an aid to overcoming this, APG-68 features scope expansion modes, in 10, 20 and 40nm (18, 37 and 74km) sectors. These do not show any contacts which are below the resolution limit of the radar; it just makes them easier to see. This is where infra-red comes into its own; it

Right: A wide-angle HUD and two multipurpose CRT head-down displays are the main new features of the F-16C/D cockpit. The HUD was originally intended to be a holographic unit.

has much better angular discrimination. But to return to radar expansion modes, these should be used sparingly, as the "big picture" situational awareness is quickly lost by dwelling on a limited area.

In a multi-bogey situation, the sweep restrictions of TWS may demand a reversion to RWS, in order to cover a larger area. Another possibility is that a hostile aircraft, warned by its RWR that it has been detected, may make a violent manoeuvre which takes it outside the scan limits of TWS. It must be remembered that computers are electronic "idiots", which will do exactly what they are programmed to do, right or wrong. In this case, the computer will continue to extrapolate the track for up to 13 seconds before it vanishes from the screen. And in 13 seconds much can happen!

Can this be avoided? Anticipation is the answer; changes in the velocity vector and closing direction are clues that this may be about to happen. Reversion to RWS from TWS increases the search area, but doing this from TWS auto results in all files dumping, leaving a clear screen. This is a strong argument for using TWS manual rather than TWS auto.

For the terminal portion of the intercept, the F-16 pilot may well want to go STT in order to gain greater tracking capability against a hard manoeuvring target, even though this will probably alert the target via his RWR. There are three ways to go from MTT to STT. At close range Air Combat Mode (ACM) is probably the best option, or otherwise the bugged target can be des-

Right: Like the LANTIRN system itself, the Marconi Avionics holographic HUD is not certain to find a place in future F-16s. The USAF may modify the more conventional F-16C HUD to accept imagery from LANTIRN or other EO systems.

Far right: Standard Marconi Avionics head-up display in an F-16A. The rectangular display seen below and to the left of the HUD control anel is not a radar display but forms part of the Fighting Falcon's sophisticated stores-management system.

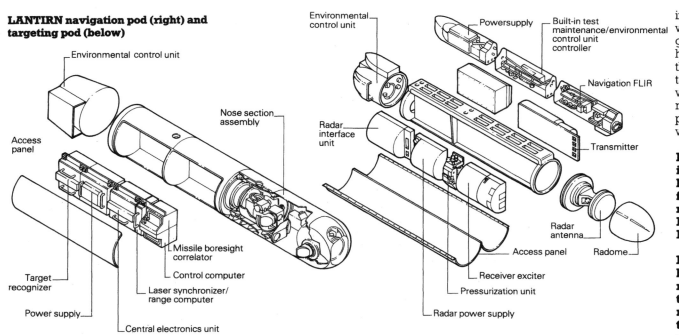

LANTIRN navigation pod (right) and targeting pod (below)

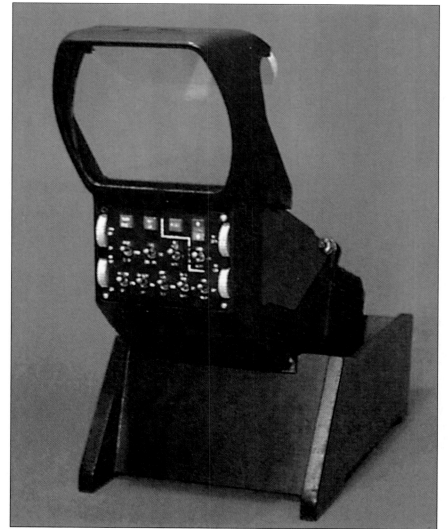

became more sophisticated was often the case, they were difficult to interpret. On the more recent Vipers, full colour liquid crystal displays, including a horizontal situation display, have largely solved this problem, allowing a plethora of information to be shown with maximum contrast. These are available as a retrofit, as well as on new-build aircraft. Helmet-mounted displays, which give high off-boresight missile capability, are planned for the future.

LANTIRN and other sensors

Low Altitude Navigation and Infra-Red Targeting at Night (LANTIRN), developed by Martin Marietta, now Lockheed Martin Tactical Aircraft Systems, gave the F-16 a credible all-weather capability. It consisted of two pods carried on either side of the intake, one for navigation, the other for targeting.

The navigation pod, 6.52ft (1.99m) long and 12in (300mm) in diameter, allowed manual terrain-following flight at selected altitudes, including penetration of the undercast, combined with low probability of intercept signals. It was combined with wide field of view FLIR imagery which, using automatic control of gain, level, focus, and channel balance, provided a "real world" image on the HUD, matching exactly what the pilot could have seen in clear daylight conditions. For low altitude manoeuvring, it could be steered to look into the turn, thus obviating nasty surprises.

The targeting pod, 8.21ft (2.50m) long and 15in (380mm) in diameter, combine laser ranging with a gimballed FLIR sensor for target acquisition and engagement. Multiple fields of view enable the pilot to transition from the HUD to a head down display (HDD) for automatic target acquisition and tracking. At the height of a typical European winter, LANTIRN was designed to quadruple the time in which attack aircraft could operate effectively.

An alternative to LANTIRN carried by some European aircraft is the Automatic Tracking Laser Illumination System (ATLIS). Developed by Martin Marietta in conjunction with Thomson CSF of France, ATLIS is a single pod 8.20ft (2.5m) long and 12in (30mm) in diameter. It contains automatic television trackers, and has a pitch and

ignated on TWS. Another option is to go RWS, and let the radar automatically go to STT when it has the intercept dynamics licked. But whatever the option, be ready to react if the switch to STT from another mode fails. One final point: in TWS, the FCC will hold track files for up to 13 seconds, so if the transfer to STT fails, a quick switch back to TWS should re-establish contact.

If this seems complicated, consider that all the pilot has to do in addition is to fly the aeroplane into an attacking position while maintaining formation integrity, selecting appropriate weaponry, maintaining communications where necessary, planning ahead, while keeping a sharp look-out visually. Simple, isn't it?

Presentation

Presentation of information initially took two forms: a Kaiser monochrome head-down display, and a GEC-Marconi Head-Up Display (HUD). In their crudest form, HUDs

dated from the 1930s, as the earliest reflector gunsights, with a ring and bead focussed at infinity on the sighting glass. Then in the 1950s it was found that other vital flight information could be presented in a similar manner, without interfering with forward view. Still later, GEC-Marconi developed the holographic HUD. This was very much a question of having one's cake and eating it too. Holographic HUDs could be designed to be transparent to all light wavelengths (colours) except one, in this case green. Flight data in green could be reflected back to the pilot whereas all other colours passed through unaffected. Focussed at infinity, the relevant flight and weapons aiming data could be presented without interfering in any way with the "view out of the window".

One exceptional feature of the HUD was a direct result of the canopy design. On the F-16, the canopy is in a single piece, with no

Above: The wide-angle HUD devised for the AFT1/F-16 forms the basis of the F-16C HUD. This design offers the widest field of view possible using conventional optics.

windshield and thus no canopy bow. While this gives unobstructed all-round vision, it has two drawbacks. The first is that there is nowhere on which to hang rear vision mirrors; the second is that, if the pilot has to eject, directly the canopy is jettisoned he is exposed to the full force of the slipstream, possibly at supersonic speeds. In consequence, the HUD has to act as a temporary windshield, and the British company Pilkington, who make the optical components of the HUD, had to ensure that it could withstand the forces involved.

The Honeywell monochrome cockpit displays were good in many ways, but were often difficult to see in bright sunlight. In the case of a cluttered screen, which as sensors

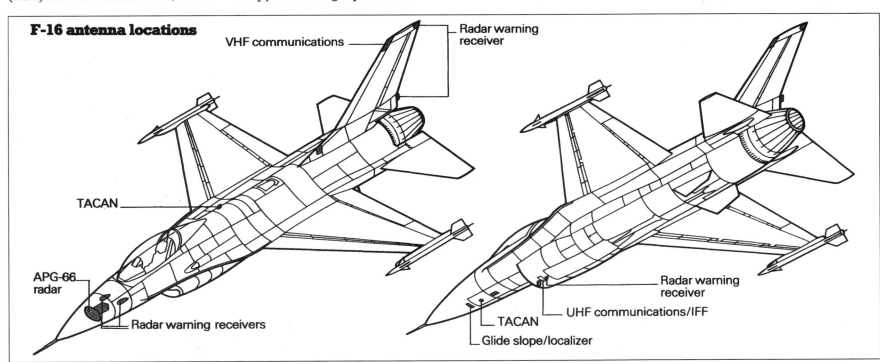

F-16 antenna locations

VHF communications

Radar warning receiver

TACAN

APG-66 radar

Radar warning receivers

Radar warning receiver

UHF communications/IFF

TACAN

Glide slope/localizer

yaw stabilized platform which compensates for aircraft motion. It also contains a laser designator/ranger which allows target handoff to laser-guided weapons.

Israel uses an extensively modified F-16D in the SEAD role. This differs externally from the standard in having a square section dorsal spine, which runs aft from the rear of the canopy. This is used to house the homebrew Elisra SPS-3000 ECM suite. This variant also appears to have been supplied to the Republic of Singapore from April 9, 1999, although whether the ECM suite is the same is an open question.

Navigation
Navigational kit carried includes the Rockwell Global Positioning System (GPS); the Rockwell-Collins ARN-108 Instrument Landing System (ILS); and the Rockwell-Collins ARN-118 Tactical Air Navigation (TACAN) system. The Litton 39 Inertial Navigation System features on early

model F-16s, but was replaced by the LN-93 ring-laser gyro INS by the same manufacturer on later models, while the APN-232 radar altimeter is often featured.

Communications
Standard communications are provided by the Magnavox ARC 164 UHF radio and the Rockwell-Collins ARC-186 UHF radio. For very long range communications, the ARC-200 HF radio is fitted on certain models. Interrogation Friend/Foe (IFF) is the Teledyne APX-101. Data link is via an improved data modem.

Defensive avionics
Even as the knights of old wore armour to protect them against incoming weapons, close-range or

Above: Aircraft cruising at medium altitude should be sitting ducks for hostile defences, but the ALQ-131 pod's noise and deception jammers can counter all known SAM systems.

Above: Main recognition features of the Westinghouse ALQ-131 ECM pod are the full-length ventral gondola and two ventrally-mounted antennae. The red and black markings near the fore and aft-mounted radomes warn personnel to keep at least 15ft (4.6m) away when the pod is transmitting.

Below: In days of old, knights wore armour to protect them against incoming missiles. Protection against modern missiles is largely provided by electronic countermeasures. This F-16A of the 388th Fighter Wing, based at Hill AFB, Utah, carries a Westinghouse ALQ-119 ECM pod on the ventral hardpoint. This is almost certainly the (V)-12 version.

Left: "Lear-Siegler" voice-control system from F-16/AFTI.

Below: Infra-red image obtained from the Oldelft Orpheus recce pod, to be used by RNethAF F-16s.

Above: The USAF has no current plans to deploy a dedicated reconnaissance version of the F-16, but the 6th full-scale development aircraft was flown with a dummy camera pod.

stand-off, so modern fighters wear a form of electronic armour. This takes two forms: detection and warning, and active countermeasures.

The first of these is relatively simple; it consists of detecting hostile radar emissions, classifying them against a pre-stored library of threat signatures, and providing the pilot with an indication of radar type, with its range and bearing. For example, a detection radar poses no immediate threat, although it is obviously undesirable for an aircraft to allow itself to be tracked, especially over hostile territory. On the other hand, it is an advantage for the pilot to know that he is being tracked and from where, since it increases his situational awareness.

The second case is much more complex. If the pilot is being tracked by a radar type which poses a threat, either a surface-to-air missile (SAM), an air-to-air missile (AAM), or by automatic anti-aircraft (AAA) guns, then it is neat to have a system which can automatically counter them. But this is much easier said than done.

The simplest form of ECM is passive, rapid-bloom chaff cut automatically to preset lengths to match the wavelength of the threat radar. By creating multiple false echoes, this tends to swamp the hostile radar screen but, since all chaff released rapidly falls astern of the releasing aircraft, it is of most use against

radars in the rear quadrant, or to cover following aircraft. The F-16 carries the Tracor ALE-40 or -47 haff/flare dispenser. Flares are mainly a measure against heat-homing missiles, or to a lesser degree against IRST systems, but their effective life is short. They also have problems in decoying the so-called "two-colour" systems which operate in two different wavebands using imaging infra-red (IIR), which are much more difficult to spoof.

Radar warning receivers (RWRs) are helpful in that they can display not only the type of radar (and therefore the threat) that they are picking up, but its type, direction, and intensity. The latter gives an indication of range, although this is is not necessarily terribly accurate. But, given a threat type and direction, the pilot can select tactics to defeat it. Gunlaying radars can often be avoided; where this is not possible ECM must be used. In the case of SAM guidance radars, the pilot has an indication where to look; if the SAM can be sighted early enough, it can sometimes be defeated by hard manoeuvre. Most Vipers carry either the Loral ALR-56M or the Dalmo Victor ALR-69 RWR.

Belgian F-16s are fitted with the Dassault Electronique Carapace threat warning system. This is a hybrid system which uses crystal video and super heterodyne receivers, operating in the C-J bandwidth. It couples the antenna array of

ALR-69 with interferometric direction finding, using interception angle techniques, and is stated to be accurate to within one degree.

ECM systems, either internal or pod-mounted, are another matter entirely. Active jamming is an emission and, as such, even if it does not give away the position of the jamming aircraft, it certainly betrays the fact that something hostile is out there, and also its approximate location. Like radar, it says: "This is approximately where I am; this is who I am; and this is roughly what I am doing!" The moral of this story is that active ECM must be used with extreme care!

ECM systems come in two forms, noise and deception. Noise jamming is spread-spectrum, intended to blot out large areas of the radar screen with "white" noise. The problem here is that jammers, particularly pod jammers, are of limited power, and if the hostile radar signal is strong enough, it will "burn through" the jamming. As the old saying goes, two cents worth of ECM will foul up $100 of radar quite easily, but only if the power of the ECM matches that of the radar at the specific range.

Deception jamming is another matter altogether. Basically it consists of one of two things: inserting false returns into the radar, usually via the sidelobes – which in extreme cases can blank out the screen with bogus contacts – or modifying and

retransmitting the return (called range-gate stealing) to produce a false position indication, which, when the actual target passes outside the look-angle/range of the radar, suddenly produces a blank scope!

Back in the 1970s, deception jamming was very effective, but now, nearly 30 years later, against radars with electronic counter counter measures (ECCM) like frequency agility, channel hop, CHIRP and bistatic, to say nothing of remote targeting, in which co-ordinates are provided by AWACS aircraft, other fighters via data link, or ground radar stations, it is much more difficult.

As previously related, the Advanced Self-protection Jammer, ASPJ, or ALQ-169, was proposed for internal carriage by the F-16C/D, and provision for it was made at the base of the fin. But ASPJ was cancelled in 1992 after failing to meet USAF requirements. The manufacturers contested this, and it has since been adopted by South Korea, the first international customer for it. Delivery of the first aircraft so equipped occurred on February 26, 1999. ALQ-169 was also used in extremis by USN Tomcats, and by USMC Hornets over Bosnia.

From 1987, the ALQ-131 jamming pod was carried by F-16A/Bs, and it has been fitted on many export F-16s. From the following year the ALR-69 RWR became standard. Block 50/52 aircraft carry the Loral

This diagram illustrates an automated manoeuvring attack by the AFTI/F-16. During the initial run-in (1) the pilot engages the attack system, then carries out a pop-up manoeuvre (2) to acquire the target and command lock-on. After a period of jinking flight (3) he updates the lock-on (4), then gives the system permission for weapon release (5).

(recently LMAS) ALR-56M RWR, while the Northrop-Grumman ALQ-126 jamming pod entered service shortly after. The ALQ-162 continuous wave jammer is carried by Danish Vipers, while Greece uses the Raytheon ALQ-187. LMAS produced the ALQ-178 Rapport internal ECM system for USAF F-16A/Bs; Rapport III is also used by the Turkish Air Force, and the Israelis have replaced it on recent deliveries with the Elta EL/L-8240. These are the main types of ECM systems. Naturally internal ECM gear is preferable to pods, but much depends on availability, and the budget of the user nation. While it would be nice to be able to compare the capabilities of the various systems, security considerations dictate that this is impracticable in an unclassified source.

Flight control system

From the outset, the F-16 was designed to use a fly-by-wire (FBW) system in which the actuators moving the control surfaces were operated by electrical signals. FBW had been around for a long time; a rudimentary analogue system had been flown on a Tay-engined Viscount airliner testbed in 1952, but it could not be brought to maturity until much greater computer power and miniaturization, brought about by the transistor and the microchip, became available.

As aircraft became heavier and more complex, they tended to become less stable. Computers were introduced into the flight control system to counter this. As a typical example, the F-4 Phantom used stability augmentation systems to improve its flying qualities. Should these cut out for any reason, such as a double generator failure, the bird remained flyable manually, although in this condition it was extremely sensitive to control inputs.

The attitude of the time was that while FBW offered many advantages, not the least in weight-saving, reliability might prove questionable. Therefore a reversionary hydro-mechanical backup system was a sensible precaution in case of emergencies, if only to provide a limited degree (get you home) control.

At a very early stage, the bold decision was taken to use a four-channel (quadruplex) electronic system. This works on a voting system; if one channel gives results which are at variance with the other three, it is bypassed and made redundant. A second channel failure could also be bypassed in the same way, as long as two channels still agreed. One of the possible failure modes involves one or more control surfaces being voted out of the flight control computer loop. In this case, the affected surface(s) would lock in the neutral position.

The weight savings that resulted from the omission of a hydro-mechanical system could be used to house many fail-safe and fail-operative techniques, providing a very high confidence level in the reliability of the system.

This allowed a high degree of relaxed stability to be adopted – a greater margin between the centre of lift and the centre of gravity than had previously been possible. This in turn gave quicker responses to control inputs and correspondingly improved transients between one flight mode and another. It also reduced the amounts of taileron deflection needed to perform high g manoeuvres, or at supersonic speeds.

Another major advantage was that it allowed the horizontal tail to provide extra lift instead of, as in conventional fighters of that era, inducing a download. Initially the tail area was minimised, but later, as we have already seen, it had to be increased again to compensate for trim changes caused by heavy external loads.

Apart from the slight glitch on the unscheduled first flight (as related in the development chapter), the FBW system has been remarkably trouble-free. A slight problem was encountered in August 1981, when faulty valves allowed voltage fluctuations large enough to affect the FCS emergency backup systems, causing uncommanded inputs in all three axes. But this was soon discovered and eliminated. The timing of the F-16 was slightly too early for it to have used digital FBW rather than analogue, but its introduction into later production aircraft was, according to former Chief Test Pilot Steve Barter, almost entirely trouble-free.

Another departure from convention was the use of a sidestick controller, mounted on the right console, rather than the conventional centrally mounted control column. At first, this was a force-transducer, which translated the direction and amount of effort into input commands. This was found to be unsatisfactory, since it limited the "feel" available to the pilot. It was replaced with a new sidestick with a limited amount of movement. The Israelis initially criticised the sidestick on the grounds that an injury to the right arm would prove totally incapacitating, whereas with an orthodox centre stick the aircraft could be flown with the left hand. This criticism has since died away, and other manufacturers have followed the trend.

Armament

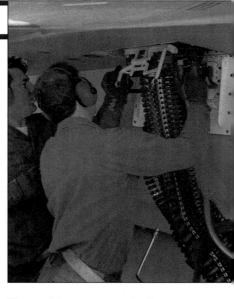

For a small and austere fighter originally armed with just two AIM-9 Sidewinders and a 20mm cannon, the Viper is now cleared to carry a bewildering variety of weaponry. When configured for the air combat arena it can be armed with Sparrow and AMRAAM, the French Magic and Mica, and the Israeli Python series missiles. The range of air-to-surface ordnance, including anti-armour and anti-shipping weapons, is even greater, while it can now deliver conventional bombs and precision munitions against ground targets with deadly accuracy at night.

Despite its age, the General Electric 20mm M61A remains the standard USAF fighter cannon. The service did attempt to develop a caseless 25mm weapon for the F-15 Eagle, but this project bogged down in technical difficulties, so the 20mm seems destined to soldier on well into the 21st Century.

The M61A1 may be a proven weapon, but its adoption in the F-16 resulted in some initial problems. Gun firing from the type was temporarily forbidden in September 1979 following two incidents in which this resulted in uncommanded yawing movements. Gun vibration was found to be affecting an accelerometer in the flight-control system, causing it to feed false data to the control computer, which in turn demanded the yaw.

A simple modification insulated the accelerometer from vibration. Ten aircraft were modified, assigned to Hill AFB, and successfully participated in a Red Flag exercise. The modification was then introduced into production aircraft, and all 106 operational F-16s delivered with the original pattern of accelerometer installation were modified during 1980.

In its F-16A/B form, the Fighting Falcon was armed with AIM-9 Sidewinder missiles for air-to-air combat. Today's Sidewinders are greatly improved versions of the primitive weapon which first entered production in the mid-1950s. Early Sidewinders may not have required the full cooperation of the target during air-to-air combat, but were restricted to use in classical tail-chase attacks in good weather.

With the arrival of second- and third-generation seeker heads, Sidewinder matured into an agile 'dogfight' missile. European F-16s were originally scheduled to carry the AIM-9J – a rebuilt and modernized version of the early AIM-9B or -9C – but the US Government eventually agreed to make the AIM-9L available. This is a highly agile weapon with all-new guidance seeker and proximity fuze. A total of at least 16,000 are likely to be built in the US, and a further 9,000 or more by a European manufacturing consortium.

BVR missiles

In Vietnam, the MiG-17 and MiG-21 interceptors which challenged US warplanes were equipped only with cannon or short-range guided missiles. US pilots could opt to engage targets under beyond-visual-range (BVR) conditions using the Raytheon AIM-7 Sparrow, or close in to engage in a dogfight with guns and AIM-9 Sidewinders. By the time the F-16 was entering service in significant numbers, it faced the threat of aircraft such as the MiG-23 armed with AA-7 Apex long-range missiles. To engage these in a Sidewinder-armed F-16 would put the Soviet pilot in the same position as US aircrew had been in over Vietnam.

Without improvements, the Fighting Falcon stood the risk of becoming the late-1980s equivalent of the Japanese Zero – lightweight and agile but seriously under-armed. Romantics might argue otherwise, but the day of the simple fighter was coming to an end. Testifying before Congress in 1980, Undersecretary of Defense for Research and Engineering William J. Perry described the F-16A as "an incomplete airplane". Detailing the need for BVR combat capability, he said that "we kidded ourselves a little bit on the F-16, thinking we were buying an inexpensive airplane".

As originally planned, the APG-66 radar was not intended to have the capability of handling BVR missiles. What the customer asked for – and Westinghouse delivered – was a multimode set sized for the air-to-air mission but offering the many modes necessary for effective ground attack in the 1980s and beyond.

The definitive solution to the problem was the planned AMRAAM (Advanced Medium-Range Air-to-Air Missile), which was due to enter service in the mid-1980s, but USAF planners considered a number of interim solutions for service in the first half of the 1980s. French missile company Matra could offer a radar-guided version of the R.550 Magic. The US, meanwhile, had already fielded and withdrawn a radar-guided AIM-9C version of Sidewinder and had the technology available to develop an updated version of this as a result of the

Above: 20mm cannon shells are loaded into the magazine of an F-16 at Kunsan Air Base, South Korea. A full load consists of 500 rounds.

Below: The smoke pouring from the F-16 on the target range comes not from the engine but from the 6,000rds/min M61A1 cannon.

Semi-Active Medium Pulse-Repetition-Frequency Seeker Demonstration project carried out at China Lake. Either weapon would have given the F-16 a radar capability, but would have done little to improve the engagement range.

Obvious solutions were the longer-range AIM-7 Sparrow or British Aerospace Sky Flash radar-guided missiles. Although larger than AMRAAM, both missiles could provide the required range but would require modifications to the APG-66 in order to provide target-illumination facilities.

Evaluation of a Sparrow-armed YF-16 was carried out by GD, using company funding, with inert rounds carried on wingtip, underwing and fuselage-mounted pylons. The last location involved the pylon being fitted directly on the undercarriage door, and was used for test firings in November 1977. A test firing of the British Sky Flash missile followed a year later, using pylons in the same location.

The need for interim BVR missiles was questioned by some analysts, who claimed that the problems of target-identification would often inhibit BVR attacks, while the higher cost of the missiles would reduce the amount of live-firing training which would be possible. Adoption of either weapon would have been expensive, and AMRAAM development showed no signs of significant slippage in time-scale, so plans for the older missiles were shelved.

Launch and leave AAMs

The Viper was the first fighter scheduled to carry AIM-120A AMRAAM, a radar-guided launch and leave missile which is currently replacing the AIM-7 Sparrow in US service. Overall dimensions are comparable to those of the earlier weapon,

although at 156.5lb (71kg), launch weight is much less, which enables a relatively small fighter like the F-16 to carry up to six with ease. Maximum speed is comparable at Mach 4, while range is slightly greater at between 30 and 40nm (55-75km).

AMRAAM flies the initial portion of its trajectory under the control of a mid-course inertial guidance unit which can be updated if neccessary by the launch aircraft. In the later stages of flight, the missile switches on its high-PRF radar seeker and homes onto the target. Since this seeker uses active radar, it does not require the launch aircraft to carry a target illuminator antenna or to continue to track the target after launch. If the target attempts to protect itself with jamming, AMRAAM's seeker can be set to operate in a medium-PRF home-on-jam mode during the midcourse or terminal stages of flight.

Hughes and Raytheon developed rival AMRAAM designs in the late 1970s. Each contractor was due to fire ten prototype rounds from F-14, F-15 and F-16 test aircraft. Firings started in 1981, but after only six shots Hughes was declared the winner in December of that year.

The company launched its first test round in February, with the first guided shot (from an F-16) following on August 26. The round scored an almost central hit on a QF-102 target, which burst into flames and crashed. The missile did not carry a warhead. In a series of six design-validation flight tests, AMRAAM scored two direct hits, one near-miss well within the lethal radius of the warhead, and three failures. The design was then modified to take account of the experience gained. Low rate production commenced in 1986.

Over the next few years, AMRAAM tri-

Above: Beyond visual range combat demands that the radar is compatible with the missile, which is the case with the F-16/AIM-120 combination seen here, as an "Electric Jet" launches

als were dogged by failures due to various causes, and only gradually were the problems ironed out. On the other hand, it was almost the only radar homing launch and leave missile in sight, and perseverance was the only possible policy. It was reported that AMRAAM was carried by a few fighters during the Gulf War of 1991, although there were no opportunities for using it. Full scale production began in April 1991, but the price tag precludes its widespread export.

AMRAAM was still far in the future when the Multinational Staged Improvement Programme (MSIP) was approved in February 1981, but the associated Engineering Change Proposal ECP 350 included modifications to the structure and wiring of the F-16 to allow carriage and operation at a later date.

The other launch and leave weapons carried by the Viper have, with one exception, been close-combat heat homers. At first the ubiquitous Sidewinder, the AIM-9L, M and P, filled the slot, but gradually something better was needed. Something with a wider look angle on the seeker; something more agile; something with a larger no-escape zone. There were several options; so widespread had Sidewinder become over the years that most other manufacturers had produced IR missiles which were compatible with Sidewinder carriage. In fact, even the Russian Toropov R-13 and the Chinese PL-2 and PL-5 were for all practical purposes Sidewinder clones.

Two French AAMs have been cleared for use on the Viper: the Matra R.550

AMRAAM. Under an Engineering Change Proposal associated with MSIP, the fighter's wiring and structure allowed for later carriage and operation of the AIM-120.

Magic, and MICA (Missile Intermediat de Combat Aerien) by the same company. Magic 2 has a very sensitive all-aspect seeker which can be slaved to the radar of the parent aircraft, and can manoeuvre at up to 50g, thanks to its combination of thrust vectoring and aerodynamic control surfaces. MICA, °like many Russian weapons, has alternative homing systems, all-aspect IR, and (like AMRAAM) inertial mid-course guidance with J-band active radar terminal homing over the final few seconds. Brochure range is between 27 and 32nm (50-60km).

Israel entered the air combat missile field in 1973 with the Shafrir. This was followed by the much more lethal Python 3, the IR seeker of which has a look angle of up to 30deg about the missile axis. It was used by Israeli F-16s in the Beka'a in 1982, when they claimed several victories. Since then the Python 4 has emerged. This has a two-colour IR seeker and a 60deg off-boresight capability. At 231lb (105kg), it is 20 per cent heavier than Sidewinder, and cannot be carried on the wingtip rails of the Viper. Very manoeuvrable, it is reported to be able to sustain 70g turns – double those of the AIM-9M. Its no-escape zone is reportedly enormous compared to previous generation weapons, but whether this is Israeli propaganda we have no means of knowing.

When, after the unification of Germany, details of the Russian Vympel R-73 became known, it gave the West a horrible shock. Here was the first in-service close combat missile which combined thrust vectoring with

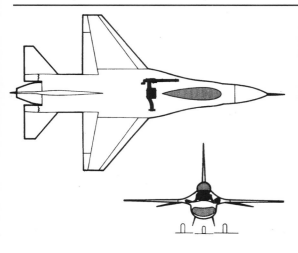

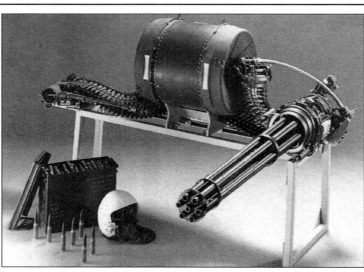

Far left: Location of the M61A1 cannon, ammunition drum and feed in the F-16. GD studies have shown that 30mm DEFA, 27mm Mauser or 30mm Oerlikon KCA could be accommodated should a heavier and more destructive projectile be desired.

Left: In creating the M61 series of aircraft cannon, the Armament division of General Electric revived the rotary principle first devised by the legendary Dr Gatling. This involves rotating the entire barrel assembly: while one barrel is firing, the remaining five are at different stages of the loading/unloading cycle. The result is a very high rate of fire and high reliability.

aerodynamic control to give unparalleled manoeuvrability, combined with an off-boresight launch capability of up to 60deg, using a helmet-mounted sight.

AGM-65 Maverick

The six underwing pylons and single under-fuselage hardpoint of the F-16 allow a heavy ordnance load to be carried, including air-to-surface missiles, 'smart' bombs, tactical nuclear weapons and conventional iron bombs. One of the most important warloads of US F-16s will be the Hughes AGM-65 Maverick used for precision attacks against point targets. This is available in AGM-65A, AGM-65B and AGM-65D forms, which use TV guidance, scene-magnification TV guidance and imaging infra-red (IIR) guidance respectively. The last can be used in day, night or adverse-weather conditions. Currently under development are the AGM-65E laser-guided version and AGM-65F IR-guided variants, but these are intended for use by the US Marine Corps and Navy respectively. All versions use common aft and centre sections and have the same aerodynamic configuration.

More than 26,000 TV-guided rounds were built, demonstrating an 86 per cent hit rate in 1,221 firings. Average miss distance during a series of tests against tank-sized targets was only 3ft (0.91m). A vidicon (TV) seeker in the nose of the missile may be slewed upon its two-axis mounting and used to view the target area. Using a TV image on the cockpit display, the pilot can align the target on the aiming mark, then command lock-on.

AGM-65A has a 5deg field of view, while the AGM-65B Scene Magnification variant has a 2.5deg field of view but can detect targets at longer range thanks to the increased image scale. These early-model Mavericks are not ideally suited to use from single-seat fighters due to the time needed to acquire the target and lock-on the missile seeker. Moreover, visibility conditions in many parts of the world can reduce target detection range to the point where the pilot of a high-speed aircraft no longer has time to operate the weapon. This problem has been appreciated for some time, spurring development of the IR-guided AGM-65D.

Imaging infra-red

The operating principle of the IR version is similar to that of the -65A and -65B, but in this case a thermal image is displayed in the cockpit instead of TV. Two magnifications are provided – wide angle for target acquisition, and narrow angle for final identification and lock-on. One difference is that Maverick operations normally involve using the missile seeker to locate the target: with the IIR version, the seeker may be slaved to or cued by target-acquisition systems such as Pave Penny or LANTIRN.

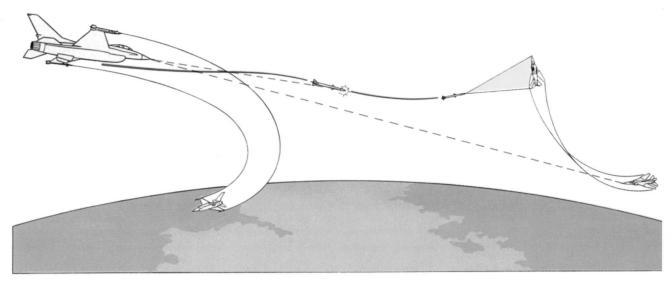

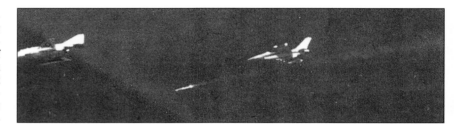

Above: After launching the fire-and-forget AMRAAM missile, the F-16 pilot will be able to turn away. The round will home onto the target during the final stages of flight using an active-radar seeker. Right: Internal arrangement of AMRAAM.

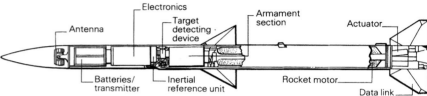

After launch, the round flies a proportional-navigation course, cruising under the impulse given by a solid-propellant rocket motor. All versions of Maverick have roughly the same launch zone. The missile can be launched at dive angles of up to 60deg, while maximum launch altitude varies according to aircraft speed, and generally lies between 33,000 and 40,000ft (10,000–12,000m). Above this height the round would become aerodynamically unstable.

Maximum range varies according to aircraft speed and height – from more than 22nm (25 miles/41km) at Mach 1.2/40,000ft down to around 7nm (8 miles/13km) at Mach 0.5 at low level. At lower altitudes, maximum range is dictated by the loss of kinetic energy during the coasting stage of flight. Above 10,000ft (3,000m) or so, endurance of the thermal batteries used to provide on-board electrical power is the limiting factor. There is no minimum launch altitude, but the minimum launch range is constrained by the limitations of the guidance and the need for the launch aircraft to avoid the exploding warhead.

Right: Destruction of a QF-102 drone by the first guided AMRAAM launch.

Below right: Internal arrangement of the TV-guided Maverick.

Below: Maximum range and height of Maverick launching have been declassified following the export.

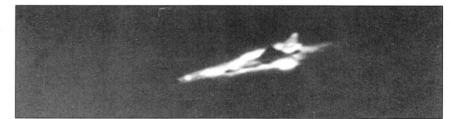

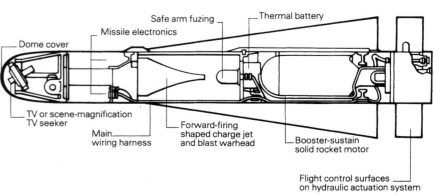

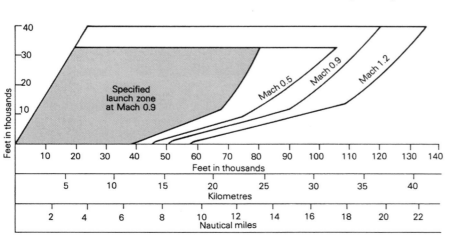

The first full-scale development
F-16B releases a Maverick in a diving
attack. An operational launch at such
altitudes would require massive ECM
protection for the aircraft.

The warhead is a 125lb (57kg) shaped charge unit with good secondary blast effects, and is effective against a wide range of tactical targets including moving or stationary armoured vehicles and trucks; artillery; SAM systems and their associated radars; and aircraft parked in revetments or hardened shelters. The warhead is located aft of the seeker, but the latter incorporates a 'tunnel' to allow the gas jet from the charge to pass freely. (An alternative penetrator/blast-fragment warhead developed for the USN and USMC versions is fitted with selectable fuzing so that it can be set to detonate either on initial impact with the target, or after penetration.)

Maverick requires little modification of the parent aircraft, and can be carried on the three-round LAU-88/A and LAU-88A/A launchers or the single-rail LAU-117/A. A modified version of the LAU-88/A with drag-reducing fairings, including a 'boat-tail' aft section, is intended for use on high-performance aircraft such as the F-16. Drag is reduced by some 45–60 per cent depending on flight profile. Mavericks can be loaded on to the launcher and go/no-go tested as a complete assembly.

Modifications to the LAU-88/A have been devised to allow rapid fire against multiple targets. The modified launcher contains facilities for: ground boresighting all missiles to the 'pipper' of the aircraft sighting system; operating two missiles at the same time, with the seeker head of the second slaved to that of the first; holding the aim of the second round after the launch of the first; and providing a safe time interval between dome cover ejection and missile launch.

One Maverick tactic tested during AGM-65D trials during 1982 involved the use of an F-16 and an F-111 working as a 'hunter-killer' team. Using a belly-mounted AVQ-26 Pave Tack FLIR pod, an F-111F was able to locate and designate a ground target, then use a voice link to call in the Maverick-armed F-16.

A useful alternative to Maverick is a French munition, the AS30L, from Aerospatiale Division Engins Tactiques. Laser guided, it is incredibly accurate. Senior experimental test pilot Joe-Bill Dryden commented that during F-16 compatibility trials it achieved miss distances of about 3ft (less than 1m). It must however be remembered that the results achievable by an experienced test pilot in a no-threat range trial are much better than the average squadron jock can manage in action, especially if he is being shot at. Stand-off range of AS30L is rather less than that of Maverick, but it is much further than would be the case when toss-bombing LGBs while self-designating.

Maximum speed is Mach 1.5, almost half as fast again as Maverick. This, plus the fact that it is rather bigger and more than twice as heavy (1,146lb/520kg as opposed to 485lb/220kg), gives it much more kinetic energy on impact and much greater penetrative power. Combined with a high explosive warhead four times larger (529lb/240kg compared with 126lb/57kg), this makes it considerably more destructive. The Viper is quite happy carrying two AS30Ls. Aiming is via an Atlis II pod carried under the intake, although AS30L works equally well with the US Sharpshooter targeting pod.

Another French weapon cleared for the F-16 is Durandal. This emotive name has several connotations. It was the sword of Roland who held the pass of Roncevalles against the Basques some 1,200 years ago; a French liqueur similar to Drambuie; an early

French jet; and is now a runway-busting bomb! Released at low level, it is braked by parachute and, when nose-down, a rocket motor drives it at high speed through a reinforced concrete runway, after which a 220lb (100kg) HE warhead explodes, breaking up a large area of the surface. Despite reports to the contrary, Durandal has never been used in action by the USAF, since the need to overfly the runway at a minimum height of 185ft (56m) makes the attacking aircraft too vulnerable to ground fire.

Norwegian Vipers carry the Kongsberg Vapenfabrik Penguin 3 anti-ship missile. Derived from a surface-to-surface munition, Penguin 3 carries a 250lb (113kg) high explosive warhead at about Mach 0.8, for a distance of 22nm (40km), varying with the velocity and altitude of the parent aircraft at launch. Unusually for an anti-ship weapon, one variant of Penguin 3 uses infra-red terminal homing, although active radar is another option. It can use remote targeting, often with co-ordinates supplied by a helicopter, and can be programmed to fly a dogleg midcourse to confuse the defenders. Carried on a standard Bullpup pylon, it is 10.44ft (3.18m) long

Top: Two-seat F-16/79 launches a Paveway laser-guided bomb.

Above: The F-16/79 releases iron bombs over a US range. European air arms have long since abandoned medium altitude dive attacks, but the USAF has great faith in ECM.

and 11in (28cm) in diameter.

Other weapons

Back in the bad old days of the Cold War, when the F-16 first entered service, the "worst case" scenario was an all-out attack on the NATO nations in Europe by overwhelming Warsaw Pact forces. As this would have been almost impossible to halt by conventional means (NATO military projections of the era were that the enemy could reach the Channel coast in four days), the question then became not if, but when, do we go nuclear? The Viper, like many other aircraft, was cleared to carry tactical nuclear weapons, chillingly called "buckets of instant sunshine!" Fortunately the threat has long since evaporated, and any question of nuclear-armed F-16s has become academic.

While the maximum load that can be

Above right: Armed with wingtip AAMs, and with bombs on underwing pylons, USAF 388th TFW Fighting Falcons set course on a training mission over a desert range.

Right: Penguin anti-ship missile under the wing of an F-16 of the Royal Norwegian Air Force.

carried by the F-16 is quite outstanding, in action it is very seldom fully laden. In practice, hardpoints are occupied by external fuel tanks, ECM pods, or sensors. The Viper is of course cleared to carry the standard range of "iron" bombs: the Mk 82 of 500lb (227kg); the Mk 83 of 1,000lb (454kg), and the Mk 84 of 2,000lb (907kg). The normal operational load consists of six Mk 82s or a maximum of four Mk 84s, with of course a couple of Sidewinders for self defence.

The Mk 82 can be fitted with Snakeye retarding fins for low-level delivery – these allow the aircraft to get well clear of the impact point – and all can be fitted with a variety of guidance systems. The most common of these is the Paveway series, a laser guidance unit on the nose, coupled with rear control

fins. The target is illuminated by the launch aircraft, by another aircraft, or from the ground. Laser light, reflected off the target, forms a sort of basket shape, at which the guidance system homes. Once the launching aircraft detects the target, via a Pave Penny or similar seeker, it lines up and releases the munition. The one thing to remember is that Paveway has no propulsion system. The bomb can guide a limited amount sideways or down into the basket, but if it is falling short, it is unable to overcome the pull of gravity to correct its trajectory.

A more sophisticated (and more costly) alternative to LGBs is the Rockwell GBU-15, normally applied to the Mk 84. In this case the homing device is either TV or IIR, and it is steered by data link from the parent aircraft. GBU-15 can be launched from low altitude using toss-release, after which it climbs to a point where it can acquire the target. A display on the aircraft shows the image from the seeker, and the operator can then either steer it all the way or lock it on in a similar fashion to Maverick.

Defence suppression

Suppression of Enemy Air Defences (SEAD), looms large in the operational inventory of the F-16, and many weapons are carried for this role. The most important of these are the anti-radiation missiles, which home on the emissions of hostile radars.

First in the field was the AGM-45 Shrike, which was loosely based on Sparrow. Its great weakness was lack of flexibility, and literally dozens of different homing heads, each tuned to a different frequency, were produced. Widely used in Vietnam, its main value was to force hostile emitters to shut down once they knew that a Shrike was

on its way. In the October War of 1973, Israeli Shrikes were effective against Egyptian SA-2s and SA-3s, but failed badly against the SA-6.

Shrike was followed by AGM-78 Standard ARM, a much larger and heavier weapon, with a broad-band seeker. This was still far from ideal, and the next step was the AGM-88 HARM (High-speed Anti-Radiation Missile). In between its predecessors in size and weight, HARM was intended to combine the low cost of Shrike with the sensitivity and large launch envelope of Standard ARM. It used a completely new passive homing system with microelectronic digital techniques. Launch range was short, at 10nm (18.5km), but this was in keeping with its high speed. The relatively short time of flight gave less time for the opposition to detect the launch and shut down before the missile arrived! Even this gave no guarantee of survival; once the emissions cease, HARM continues to home on the last known position.

It is not only the SAM radars which cause problems; the bad guys on the ground with AAA must also be neutralized. From above they have little cover, and are vulnerable to munitions which can cover a large area. The 2,000lb (907kg) bomb is one of these. It can be fitted with a radar ground proximity fuze which detonates it before impact, typically at about 15ft (4.5m). Blast effects apart, it scatters lethal red-hot shrapnel over a wide area. Also effective in this role are cluster bomb units (CBUs). Released from altitude, they open at a pre-determined altitude to scatter small munitions evenly over a wide area. The best of these is the British BLU 755, which not only has better drag characteristics than US weapons, but in service has proved much more reliable.

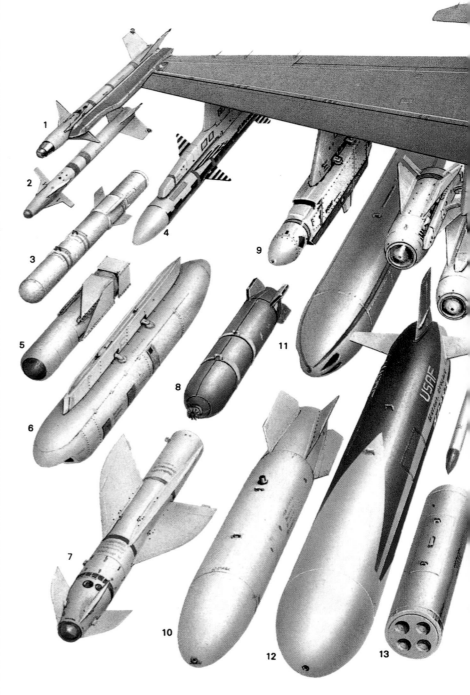

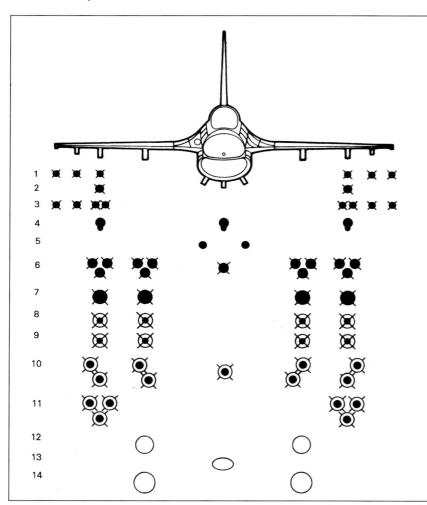

USAF F-16 stores loadings:
1: AIM-9 Sidewinder. 2: AIM-7 Sparrow (proposed). 3: AIM-120 AMRAAM. 4: ALQ-131 ECM pods. 5: Electro-optical/infra-red/terrain-following radar pods. 6: Up to 25 Mk 82 1,000lb (454kg) bombs. 7: Mk 84

2,000lb (907kg) bombs. 8: and 9: Paveway or GBU-15 laser-guided bombs. 10: Up to 17 cluster bombs. 11: AGM-45 Maverick. 12:370gal fuel tanks. 13:300gal fuel tank. 14:600gal fuel tanks.

1 AIM-9L Sidewinder
2 AIM-9J Sidewinder
3 Durandal anti-runway weapon
4 AIM-120 AMRAAM
5 Wasp air-to-surface mini-missile (proposed)
6 Orpheus recce pod (RNethAF only)
7 Penguin Mk 3 anti-ship missile
8 Cluster munition
9 ALQ-131 ECM pod
10 Nuclear bomb
11 GEPOD 30mm gun pod
12 AGM-109 MRASM cruise missile (proposed)
13 SUU-25 flare
14 TV or IIR-guided AGM-45 Maverick
15 SUU-20 practice carrier
16 LAU rocket launcher
17/18 proposed electro-optical, FLIR and radar pods
19 ATLIS II designator pod (trials only)
20 Paveway laser-guided bomb
21 Mk 82 500lb (227kg) general-purpose bombs
22 HOBO 'smart' bomb
23 Mk 84 2,000lb (907kg) general-purpose bomb
24 Mk 82 Snakeye retarded bomb
25 External fuel tank
26 AGM-78 Standard ARM anti-radar missile
27 Mk 83 1,000lb (454kg) bomb
28 Mk 117 750lb (340kg) bomb
29 AGM-45A Shrike anti-radar missile
30 AGM-88 HARM anti-radar missile
31 Radar-detection pod (for proposed Wild Weasel two-seater)

Left: Even with simple iron bombs, the F-16 offers exceptionally accurate delivery. During some trials, diameter of the weapon impact area was only one third of the specified figure.

Right: During low-altitude attacks, the tail fins of the Snakeye 500lb (227kg) bomb open to retard the weapon. The impact point is thus well to the rear of the aircraft, protecting it from blast and debris.

Above: The impressive array of stores carried by, tested on or designed to be compatible with the Fighting Falcon belies the type's original conception as a cheap and simple lightweight fighter.

Right: USAF technicians check 500lb (227kg) bombs on a munition cart, prior to loading them aboard an F-16 during exercise Cope Elite 81. As a result of MSIP modifications, all hardpoints are likely to be cleared to a 9g load factor.

Combat and Deployment

For an aircraft which the USAF was initially not very sure that it wanted, the F-16 Fighting Falcon has done rather well. In service or ordered by over 20 air arms, with nearly 4,000 delivered and orders far exceeding this figure, with production taking place in Europe, Turkey, Korea and Japan (with the FS-2), this small light-weight fighter is an undisputed success story. Nor is this all. It now has a distinguished combat record earned in various parts of the globe with the USAF, Israel, Pakistan, and most recently the Netherlands.

The USAF accepted its first production F-16 on August 17, 1978, and the first delivery to an operational unit followed on January 6, 1979. First unit to be equipped was the 388th Tactical Fighter Wing at Hill AFB, Utah, which built up to its full strength of 102 Fighting Falcons by the end of 1980, and trained aircrew for TAC and export customers.

In the hands of 388th TFW pilots, the Fighting Falcon began to .show its mettle. Three days of war games held at Hill AFB in March 1980 showed how the aircraft could be used to reinforce the NATO Central Front or any other trou-

Below: The long range of the Fighting Falcon allows staging flights from the US to Western Europe without assistance from European-based tankers. On trials, aircraft have flown 2,000nm without refuelling.

ble spot. Refuelling from KC-135 tankers, 12 aircraft carried out a 7,000km (4,350-mile) transit flight lasting 10 hours to simulate overseas deployment, followed by two days of intensive flying.

Despite the sophistication of the new warplane and its avionic systems, the care taken during design and development to ensure reliability and easy maintenance paid off from the beginning, and unit after unit converting to the type found itself clocking up flying hours at a higher-than-predicted rate. In 1979 the average number of hardware failures per flight hour for USAF aircraft was around 1·2, against an eventual goal of only 0·34. During the second half of 1979 the actual failure rate of the F-16s at Hill AFB varied from just under 1·2 down to around 0·75, and this showed signs of falling to the target figure by the early 1980s.

By 1980 the F-16 was displaying impressive reliability. Tactical Air Command, as it then was, had set a standard of 70 per cent for mission capability. Various upgrades, often aimed at improving reliability, followed, and in the Gulf War 11 years later, under true operational conditions, the figure hovered around a remarkable 95 per cent. And this despite five combat losses!

A study carried out in 1976 identified many areas of F-16 operations which would be cheaper than those associated with the earlier F-4. This assumed a typical TAC squadron of 24 aircraft and identified the cost changes (in 1976 prices) detailed in the accompanying table. All other cost such as support equipment and base matériel support were assumed to be unchanged. On this basis the annual operating cost of an F-16 squadron would be 30 per cent less than an equivalent F-4 unit.

Above: Infantrymen watch an F-16 take off during Exercise Team Spirit 82. Fighting Falcons have taken part in many recent exercises.

Fighting Falcon officially started its operational career with the USAF on November 12, 1980, when the 4th Tactical Fighter Squadron – part of the 388th TFW – achieved Initial Operational Capability. In March of the following year this unit took 12 Fighting Falcons overseas for the first time during a month-long deployment to Flesland in Norway. If further proof were needed that the Fighting Falcon was a success, this was provided in June 1981 when seven 388th TFW aircraft won the Royal Air Force-sponsored tactical bombing competition held at Lossiemouth in Scotland, defeating RAF Jaguars and Buccaneers and USAF F-111Es.

Delivery of the 400th aircraft took place in May 1981, the 500th production example following in August of the same year. First USAF pilot to clock up 1,000 hours was Lt Col Dean Stickell of the 16th Tactical Fighter Training Squadron at Hill AFB. He reached four figures of Fighting Falcon flying time in the autumn of 1981, his involvement with the aircraft having begun at Edwards AFB during the type's development and evaluation programme.

Increasing orders

By this time the USAF had 1,388 Fighting Falcons on order, and was talking of ordering a total of almost 1,750 examples for regular Air Force units, plus enough to re-equip the Thunderbirds display team. A possible order to re-equip Air National Guard units was seen as likely to add 600 to 800 further aircraft to the production run. Consideration was also given to storing 150 aircraft in Israel in kit form.

By the summer of 1981 overseas deployment of the Fighting Falcon had begun with the first deliveries to the 8th TFW. Part of the Pacific Air Forces and based at Kunsan in the Republic of Korea, the wing began converting from the F-4D in September 1981. Although a long way from the continental USA, the wing has maintained good operational readiness despite a shortage of spares – a common F-16 problem as more and more squadrons converted to the type. The majority of newly-built components were immediately embodied in new-production aircraft, rather than being shipped to the user as spares. Availability rates of 70–75 per cent were reported early in 1983, partly as a result of earlier Block 10 aircraft being swapped for the then up-to-date Block 15 standard. Basic mission of 8th TFW is strike and interdiction, but air-to-air combat training is also carried out. F-4s released from service at Kunsan were returned to the USA and re-assigned to Air Force Reserve units.

F-16s from USAF Korean bases act as 'friendly enemies' for F-15 units in Japan, allowing USAF aircrew assigned to the latter location to practise dissimilar air combat. During other exercises, techniques have been developed for operating the two types in a co-operative manner. Fighting Falcons can join an F-15 formation to take advantage of the latter's longer-ranged Hughes APG-63 radar and the attrition inflicted by the Eagle's AIM-7 Sparrow missiles in the opening stages of an air combat.

By the spring of 1982, the USAF fleet had exceeded 100,000 flying hours. A total of 345 was in service at that time,

Above: Fighting Falcons often carry a ventral tank, but runway clearance when this store is fitted is clearly minimal.

Comparative annual operating costs
(one TAC squadron of 24 aircraft, 1976$ × 1,000,000)

Element	F-4	F-16
Fuel	4·3	2·1
Training	1·1	0·3
Munitions & missile training	1·1	0·9
Spares	1·8	1·2
Base operating support	1·7	1·3
Depot Maintenance	2·9	2·3
Safety/logistic modifications	0·4	0·6
Military pay & salaries	7·5	5·4
Medical facilities	0·3	0·5

270 with TAC operational units. Deployment of the aircraft to USAFE in West Germany started in December 1982, and the 50th TFW became operational on the type at Hahn Air Base in July 1982.

The first unit to become operational at Hahn was the 313th TFS. Following initial training at Zaragoza in Spain, the unit took its 24 F-16s to Hahn in the spring of 1982. Later that year the 50th TFW and 496th TFS also began re-equipping to bring the Hahn wing up to strength. Aircraft assigned to Hahn were to Block 15 production standard. This includes the larger horizontal tail

Below: The 'bubble' canopy of Fighting Falcon gives good visibility. Even at high angles of attack, the pilot has a clear view over the nose of his aircraft.

Below right: The 388th TFW was the first operational F-16 unit. During Exercise Yellow Alpha in 1980, 18 of its aircraft flew an impressive total of 72 'combat' sorties.

surfaces, and inlet hardpoints for AMRAAM missiles and LANTIRN sensors.

One highly-publicized conversion to the Fighting Falcon was that of the USAF's Thunderbirds display team. The team made no public appearances in 1982 following a four-aircraft crash which killed four members of the group. At that time, the team was using T-38 Talon trainers, but eight F-16s were assigned to the unit in the autumn. Several paint schemes were evaluated before the definitive black/red/white finish was approved. The Thunderbirds completed the transition to the F-16 in November 1982, and were thus able to fly the new type during the 1983 display season.

Starting in October 1982, the US Air National Guard began to deploy the F-16. First ANG unit to re-equip was the

Above: First USAFE Fighting Falcon unit was the 50th TFW at Hahn. Deployment started in December 1982 and was completed in 1983.

169th Tactical Fighter Group at McEntire AFB, which received 24 Fighting Falcons in 1983 as replacements for its A-7 Corsairs. In 1983, another F-16 wing, the 401st TFW, became operational at Torrejon in Spain, followed by the 86th TFW at Ramstein AFB, Germany. First AF Reserve unit to get the F-16, in 1984, was the 466th TFS at Hill AFB, Utah, formely equipped with F-105 Thunderchiefs. As aircraft rolled off the production lines, the Fighting Falcon strength continued to build in USAF ANG and AF Reserve squadrons until the F-16 was numerically the most important aircraft in the inventory.

Above: It is rare to see Fighting Falcons in the clean condition of these Klu examples – even the wingtip rails are empty on the two nearest aircraft.

F-16 sales

Meanwhile, export sales boomed, fuelled by the four European nations which constituted the first overseas customers.

The first European operator to take delivery of the Viper was the Force Aérienne Belge, also known as, in that bilingual country, (French and Flemish) as the Belgische Luchtmarcht, or Belgian Air Force, on January 29, 1979. On January 16, 1981, No 349 Squadron of the FAéB was formally assigned to NATO, and declared fully operational on May 6 of that year. Within two years of the first delivery, the availability rate of Belgian F-16s reached 88 per cent. It was also the first force to use the F-16 as a target tug, with trials held at Solenzara in Corsica.

The next European Viper operator was the Koninklijke Luchtmacht, the Royal Netherlands Air Force, which received its first F-16 on June 6, 1979, although it was April 1981 before 322 Squadron completed conversion training. Fourth was the Kongelige Norske Luftforsvaret, the Royal Norwegian Air Force, which took its first F-16 delivery on January 25, 1980. Norway was of course one of

the few NATO nations to share a common border with the then Soviet Union.

Finally came the Kongelige Danske Flyvevåpnet, whose first delivery took place on January 28, 1980. Esk 727, based at Skrystrup, was declared to NATO on August 26, 1981. GD gave full backup to all four NATO nations; Chief Test Pilot Neil Anderson became one of the few civilians, if not the only one, ever to intercept a Soviet Tu-22M Backfire bomber, although he is reticent as to which air force he flew with.

Non-NATO operators

Prior to this, Iran, which already operated the F-14 Tomcat and the F-4 Phantom, provided a letter of intent for 160 F-16s on October 27, 1976. A letter of intent is of course a statement that the client nation intends to enter into a binding contract. Within three years the Ayatollahs had ousted the Shah and repudiated the deal; not that the USA would have complied in any case. Ironically, the immediate beneficiary was Israel. The major previous supplier of fighters to Israel had been Dassault, but political considerations had by now ruled them out. Production of the Iranian F-16s had begun, and supply of these to Israel posed few problems, apart from various modifications. Deliveries began on July 2, 1980, when the first four left Hill AFB in

Florida for the eleven hour trip, which involved three inflight refuellings.

After this, export orders followed thick and fast. F-16A/Bs were ordered by Egypt, Pakistan, Venezuela, Singapore, Thailand, Indonesia, Portugal, Taiwan, and, in 1999, Jordan and New Zealand. F-16C/Ds have gone to Israel, Egypt, South Korea, Turkey, Greece, and Bahrain, while at home the US Navy ordered it as an adversary aircraft to simulate the MiG-29.

The Osirak strike

The combat debut of the F-16 took place on June 7, 1981. Iraq was building a nuclear reactor at Osirak, near Baghdad. Scheduled for completion in late summer of 1981, the 70MW reactor could have produced sufficient plutonium for five 20kT nuclear devices by the mid-1980s. This capability posed a deadly threat to Israel. It had to be destroyed before it became operational. Too late, and the result would be radioactive contamination of the surrounding area and far downwind.

The distance was great – about 540nm (1,000km) – and a strike involved overflying at least one hostile nation even before reaching Iraq. In-flight refuelling was not an option. Eight F-16A Vipers, in two sections of four, escorted by six F-15s, were assigned to the raid.

Meanwhile, an unexpected prob-

lem occurred. Iranian Phantoms attacked Osirak on September 30, 1980. Although little damage was caused, this alerted the Iraqis to the threat. The defences were immediately strengthened. After a great deal of training, and a couple of postponements, Operation Opera, as it was called, was scheduled for Sunday, June 7, 1981.

The strike force left Etzion AFB in southern Sinai, at 16.00 hours, using minimum afterburner to conserve fuel. They crossed the Gulf of Aqaba at 2,400ft (731m) and 400kt (741kmh), in the process overflying the royal yacht of King Hussein of Jordan. On entering Saudi Arabian airspace, they dropped to 300ft (91m), below the radar. Here they stayed, except for a brief interval when they were forced to climb to avoid a sandstorm. Just before crossing the Iraqi border, the two now empty 370gal tanks were jettisoned.

Once over Iraq, the F-16s accelerated to 500kt (927kmh). At 17.35 Iraqi AAA started to fire. Short of the target, 'burners were lit and the Vipers soared to 10,000f t(3,048m), rolled

Below: From 1988 onwards, these Belgian Air Force F-16s will be joined by a follow-on batch of 44 aircraft destined to replace the present Mirage 5 fleet. Despite an attractive offset package devised by Dassault, the FAéB ordered the GD

F-16 Units, *Desert Shield/Desert Storm* **1990-1991**

Wing	Squadron(s)	Type	Base	Deployed to
347th TFW	69th TFS	F-16C/D	Moody, GA	Al Minhad, UAE
363rd TFW	17th & 33rd TFS	F-16C/D	Shaw, SC	Al Dhafra, UAE
388th TFW	4th & 421st TFS	F-16C/D	Hill, UT	Al Minhad, UAE
50th TFW	10th TFS	F-16C/D	Hahn Germany	Al Dhafra, UAE
401st TFW	613rd TFS	F-16C/D	Torrejon Spain	Incirlik, Turkey
401st TFW	614th TFS	F-16C/D	Torrejon Spain	Doha Qatar, UAE
52nd TFW	23rd TFS SEAD	F-16C/D	Spangdahlem Gy	Incirlik, Turkey
174th TFG	138th TFS	F-16A/B	Syracuse, NY	Al Kharj, Saudia
169th TFG	157th TFS	F-16A/B	McEntire, SC	Al Kharj, Saudia

NB: the last two entries are Air National Guard Units.

Above: Norwegian airfields are snow-covered for much of the year, a factor which caused the RNoAF to request braking parachutes in its F-16s.

inverted, and at five second intervals, straightened up into a 35deg dive, releasing two Mk 84 "iron" bombs at 3,500f t(1,067m).

Of the 16 bombs dropped, 14 were direct hits, 12 of which exploded, devastating the reactor building. Two failed to explode, while the other two undershot, but hit other buildings, killing one French technician. Braving intense AAA fire, the Israeli pilots reached for altitude and set course for home at 600kt (1,112kmh). Not one had been hit.

Vipers at war
The F-16 had already gained a reputation for tack-driving accuracy in training; the Osirak raid was an impressive combat debut for the F-16 as a bomb hauler. Nor did the Israelis neglect its air combat capabilities. The first aerial victory for the F-16 was a Syrian Mil Mi-8 helicopter, downed by cannon fire by a young un-named pilot on April 28, 1981. The first fast jet victim of the Viper was also Syrian, a MiG-21 downed by Amir Nahumi on July 14 of that year.

But these were mere skirmishes. The first major action in which Vipers were involved took place over the Beka'a in Lebanon, in June 1982. In a

textbook action, the Syrian early warning and SAM guidance radars were brought on line by drones, and then systematically destroyed. What survived in the field of detection and fighter control was subjected to intense jamming. As a Soviet Cold War saying went: "Destroy one third, jam one third, and the rest will collapse." And so it proved. Syrian fighters and attack aircraft flew boldly into the area, their radar screens full of "mush", and their situational awareness limited to what they could see "out of the window".

Controlled by Grumman E-2C Hawkeye Airborne Early Warning aircraft, Israeli F-15s and F-16s lurked in the radar shadows cast by the mountains, before hurtling forth to pounce on their prey. The generally accepted kill/loss ratio was 84 to nil, with F-16s credited with 44 aerial victories. Pilot Amir Nahumi accounted for six more Syrian aircraft during this conflict, to become the first, and so far as is known, the only Viper ace.

Further east, the Soviet intervention in Afghanistan had resulted in air operations being undertaken against the rebellious mujahideen, called dushmans (bandits) by the Russians. Both the Soviet and the Russian-equipped air forces were involved. Many mujahideen bases were in Pakistan, and almost inevitably, border violations were frequent. The great difficulty was that in such

Right: The immaculate condition of this Danish Air Force F-16A, its hangar, mobile tool kit and work platforms would satisfy the most fastidious inspecting officer.

Above: Deployment of the F-16 no doubt strained the logistic facilities of the Egyptian Air Force, but will dramatically improve Egypt's technological capability.

mountainous terrain, identifying exactly where the border lay was far from easy.

In all, about 16 aerial victories have been recorded by Pakistani Viper drivers. One, Squadron Leader Khalid, of No 14 Tailchoppers Squadron, is credited with three vic-tories, which is not bad considering that there has been no formal con-flict. The first two came on the morn-ing of September 13, 1988, and were MiG-23s of the Afghan Air Force, fly-ing at 34,000ft (10,363m). The MiGs had deployed IRCM, and Khalid made three fruitless attempts to launch an AIM-9P Sidewinder. At a range of 1.08nm (2km), he over-banked to 130deg, and this time managed to launch. Rolling out, he acquired another MiG (there were four of them), and launched another Sidewinder. Both hit. Khalid's third victory came later – one of six Afghan Sukhoi Su-22s, which was hit by two Sidewinders.

Another victory of great interest was scored by Squadron Leader Ather. In the late summer he was vec-tored against four Sukhoi Su-25s in full Soviet markings. Ather, at 18,000ft (5,486m) and about 1.6nm (3km) astern, launched an AIM-9L at a Frogfoot flying at 24,000ft (7,315m). On impact, the Frogfoot broke in two, and the pilot ejected. He was Alexandr Rutskoi, who later became a Major General and Vice President of Russia!

Vipers in the Gulf

Desert Shield and *Desert Storm* saw the largest ever overseas deploy-ment of the F-16. No Viper air combat

Below: One result of the Soviet invasion of Afghanistan was clearance for Pakistan to receive US warplanes – F-16s rather than the A-7 Corsair IIs originally requested.

Above: As US/Israeli relations grew more strained following the Osirak raid and 1982 invasion of Lebanon, the supply of further F-16s to the IDFAF was repeatedly embargoed.

victories were recorded in *Desert Storm*, primarily due to lack of opportunity. In what few chances arose, the USAF F-15C Eagles assigned to gaining air superiority simply elbowed everyone else out of the way, including the USN Tomcats.

In any case, the F-16 was mainly used as a bomb truck, and for defence suppression. A total of 249 Vipers flew over 13,450 sorties – more than any other type – with an astonishing 95.2 per cent mission-capable rate. In all, F-16s delivered about 20,000 tons of ordnance during the conflict; about one fifth of the total. Most of this consisted of "iron" bombs, but a considerable number of smart weapons were used. Just one point here: deliveries of AGM-65 Maverick against multiple targets proved to be a "very busy" process, in which pilots quickly became "maxed out"!

With "iron" bombs, the accuracy to which the USAF had become accustomed simply did not happen. In fact, on one occasion a whole squadron of F-16s, briefed to attack a runway, managed to miss it. Now a runway is a pretty large target, so how could this possibly happen?

The cause lies in the parameters of weapons clearance used in the carriage and testing phase. Virtually all air-to-ground weapons have a carriage limit of Mach 0.95. While a few weapons have oscillation or flutter problems at speeds higher than Mach 0.95, or even fuzing limitations, most do not. Many can in fact be carried, and released, at supersonic speeds, with no problems. The restriction here stems from the budget available for testing. There is no immutable law which states that air-to-surface munitions cannot be carried and released at supersonic speeds; it is just they have not been tested above Mach 0.95.

The main factor in the Gulf War was that in order to avoid the worst of the ground fire, release heights were in

excess of theoretical levels. When making diving attacks, the F-16 picked up too much speed and, in the Gulf, weapon release speeds were often in the Mach 1.05-1.10 region. While the fact that no aircraft were lost due to ordnance malfunction at supersonic speeds proves that such releases are perfectly feasible, accuracy suffers. Flow-field effects

change dramatically in the transonic region, and the data in the weapons aiming computer, which is only calibrated up to Mach 0.95, becomes increasingly in error. Forcing the computer to guess does nothing for delivery accuracy with conventional "iron" bombs.

In the Gulf War, Kuwait and Iraq were divided into "kill" boxes, each about

30nm(56km) square. The F-16s were given a target within the designated box. If it could not be found, the Vipers were free to attack any other target within their box. This was not always so good. Spotting individual vehicles from 20,000ft (6,096m) altitude, at a slant range in the region of 5nm (9.25km), was close to impossible. Iraqi camouflage was good; anything obvious was

Right: Painted with temporary US markings and loaded with external tanks, a Fighting Falcon begins the long trip which will end some 11 hours later in delivery to the Israeli Defence Force – Air Force.

almost certainly a dummy.

F-16s, other than those employed on the SEAD (Wild Weasel) mission, often worked with "Pointer" Vipers, so-called from their call-sign. Pointers consisted of a pair of F-16s of the 388th TFW orbiting over the kill box, one searching for targets with binoculars while the other covered him. They carried up to six Mk 82s, or CBUs, with which to mark the target.

The 138th TFS F-16As of the ANG were given the pod-mounted GAU-5/A Pave Claw 30mm cannon for ground strafing, but flaws in the software made it inaccurate. It was withdrawn after only one day. F-16s of the 388th TFW used LANTIRN in the Gulf, but generally they operated at altitudes too high for it to be really effective. The Weasel Birds carried a variety of weapons; Shrike and HARM, low drag (slick) Mk 82/84 84 bombs, and CBU-5H/CBU-87 cluster bombs. While this does not sound too impressive, the Viper was described as "the backbone" of the USAF tactical fighter force.

Eight F-16s were lost as a result of the Gulf War. An engine fire in a 33rd TFS aircraft caused Richard Seizer to eject safely on September 30, 1990. The first Viper combat losses were two F-16Cs of the 614th TFS, on January 20, 1991. Mike "Cujo" Roberts, flying "Clap 4", fell victim to a SA-2 over downtown Baghdad, while the jet of former Aggressor Jeff "Tico" Tice was hit by an SA-3 on the

egress. Losing fuel and hydraulic fluid, he headed homewards, but was forced to eject deep in Iraq. Both pilots became PoWs.

Four days later another F-16 pilot succumbed to ground fire. He ejected over the Persian Gulf, and was rescued by an SH-60B helicopter from the guided missile frigate USS *Nicholas*.

The fourth F-16 victim was Scott "Spike" Thomas of the 17th TFS, on February 17. Hit by ground fire, he ejected 40nm (22km) inside Iraqi territory, but was rescued by a US helicopter. The fifth and last F-16 victim was William Andrews of the 10th TFS, who was reportedly hit by a shoulder-launched SA-16. Efforts to rescue him resulted in the loss of a UH-60 Blackhawk helicopter, and he became a PoW. A single post-war loss occurred on February 21, when an F-16 flamed out during in-flight refuelling.

Post-Gulf action

Even after the end of the Gulf War, Saddam Hussein's Iraq continued to be a thorn in the side of the West. Air exclusion zones were established by the West over northern Iraq to protect the Kurds, and over southern Iraq, to protect the Shi'ite Marsh Arabs. Violation of these led to more clashes, in which the F-16 played a significant part.

On December 27, 1992, two Iraqi MiG-23s from Al Kut AB, entered the

southern exclusion zone. Ignoring warnings, they turned to confront patrolling F-16s, one of which launched an AMRAAM from a range of 3nm (5km), to score the first victory with this missile. The remaining MiG-23 speedily departed in the direction of Iran.

This was followed on January 19, 1993, by an AMRAAM shootdown of a MiG-25 Foxbat over the northern exclusion zone. Attacks on Iraqi ground targets, usually SAM batteries, were also frequent at this time. Since then, Iraqi intransigence has ensured that sporadic attacks have continued; Operation *Desert Fox* was implemented on December 16, 1998, and later that month HARMs were launched by F-16Cs.

The first five months of 1999 saw 41 attacks on Iraqi targets, virtually all of them radar and/or SAM sites, in which F-16s participated at least 18 times, often in the SEAD role. And the end is not yet in sight.

Balkan Vipers

The civil war caused by the breakup of the former Republic of Yugoslavia saw bitter fighting. The UN intervened with Operation *Deny Flight*, imposed on April 12, 1993. Almost a year later, on February 28, 1994, it was violated by six Serbian Jastreb J1 light attack aircraft. They were detected shortly after taking off, by a NATO E-3A orbiting high over the Adriatic. The Jastrebs having ignored

three warnings, two F-16s were cleared to engage them, and the leader downed three, one with an AMRAAM, the other two with Sidewinders. A Sidewinder launched by the other F-16 missed. Two more F-16s now joined the fray, and another Jastreb fell to a Sidewinder. Contact was lost, and only regained as the two survivors exited Bosnian air space. Nor were Bosnian operations confined to air denial. On several occasions Bosnian Serb targets were bombed, and one F-16 fell to a SAM. With first Croatia and then Bosnia more or less pacified, in 1999 the spotlight turned to Kosovo. The F-16 force available for operations was international; the USAF and Turkish elements were reinforced by Norwegian, Netherlands, Belgian, Danish and Portuguese Vipers.

Hostilities began on March 24, and the first air victory of the campaign was a MiG-29, brought down by a Netherlands F-16A using an AMRAAM from head-on – the only Viper victory of the conflict, and the first by a Netherlands pilot in well over half a century. After a couple of days, the Serbian pilots ceased to try to contest the air. F-16s flew combat air patrols, SEAD, and straight attack missions. The only F-16 loss of the conflict was a Viper of the USAF 555th FS which suffered engine failure on May 2. The pilot ejected safely, and was rescued within two hours. A few weeks later, hostilities ceased.

Top left: Israeli Fighting Falcon in its delivery paint scheme. Squadron insignia added to the aircraft since then are deleted from all official photographs.

Middle: F-16A of the 35th TFS, 8th TFW – the 'Wolf Pack' – from Kunsan Air Base, South Korea. Note the wolf's head insignia, which appears on both sides of the fuselage.

Left: Royal Norwegian Air Force F-16s are finished in an overall grey paint scheme, and carry the fuselage national markings below the aft section of the canopy.

Below: The black randome on this Royal Netherlands Air Force F-16A of 308 Sqn identifies the aircraft as an early production example. Under the Pacer Loft programme these are being updated to Block 15 standard.

Performance and Handling

When it was first demonstrated at Le Bourget in 1975, the F-16 was the total close-combat fighter, able to outmatch anything in the sky in one versus one combat. But one versus one is a peacetime training exercise, and has little to do with war. Gradually it evolved into an extremely capable warplane, and if weight increases have eroded its agility, it still handles remarkably well, as many pilots will attest.

A lightly loaded F-16 with full internal fuel has a thrust-to-weight ratio of just over 1:1 in full afterburner. Working with the lightweight YF-16 prototypes, GD test pilots carried out pre-takeoff engine and system checks at 80 per cent power. Application of full afterburning power would have caused the wheels to slide.

Fighting Falcon begins its take-off roll with the wing leading and trailing-edge flaps positioned 2deg up and 20deg down respectively. After brake release, the aircraft quickly picks up speed. Rotation is usually at around 125kt, liftoff at around 140kt.

When Robert Ropelewski of *Aviation Week* flew the F-16B for the first time in 1979, GD Chief test pilot Neil Anderson was able to demonstrate the takeoff performance: "Anderson ... rotated the nose upwards, stopping at 60deg pitch as the aircraft began climbing out". Given the 30deg reclining tilt of the Fighting Falcon ejection seat, this climb angle meant that the torsos of the two pilots were literally horizontal. The F-16 can climb vertically, but this would result in the pilot hanging head-down in his seat.

"Acceleration continued, even in that attitude", reported Ropelewski, "the aircraft passing through 170kt about 30 seconds after brake release. A wing-over manoeuvre was used to level the aircraft at around 8,000ft (2,450m) altitude, still within the length of the Carswell (AFB) runway. A USAF Northrop T-38 chase aircraft which had started its takeoff roll on the same runway five seconds after the F-16 was just lifting off the runway below."

When the undercarriage is retracted the leading edge changes to 20deg down, while the gain of the flight-control system is doubled to reach its normal flight value. (The 50 per cent reduction while on the ground was incorporated as a result of the inadvertent first flight of the original YF-16 prototype). Throughout the mission the flight-control system remains at full gain, except when the door which covers the refuelling receptacle is opened. The latter operation reduce the control response in pitch and roll by an amount designed to make the aircraft 'less nervous', during the approach to the tanker, refuelling and subsequent separation.

One of the most novel features of the F-16 cockpit is the sidestick controller used in place of the traditional control column. This is located on the starboard side of the cockpit, and incorporates an adjustable armrest mounted on the cockpit wall. This is essential in high-g flight conditions, and includes an optional wrist rest which may be folded back against the wall if not required.

The original pattern of sidestick controller did not move, but was force sensitive only. Although effective, this scheme provided no indication to the pilot of when maximum input was being demanded. To avoid sprained wrists in the excitement of high-g manoeuvres, the USAF decided to allow the definitive design of stick a few millimetres of movement to provide the required degree of 'feedback' to the pilot. The rudder pedals have around 0.5in (1cm) of movement.

The flight-control system ensures that the pilot cannot over-stress the aircraft. No matter how hard he operates the controls, the angle of attack and load factor are limited, ensuring that he cannot demand more than 26deg angle of attack or 9g load factor.

In practice, the 9g figure is probably close to the limit that the human body can take while performing a useful military mission. In conventional cockpits, pilots often experience tunnel vision – commonly known as grey-out – at levels of around 6 or 7g, but the semi-reclining seat of the F-16 seems to extend this limit by up to 2g. *Aviation Week*'s Robert Ropelewski noted no vision problems at manoeuvres of 8g or more, despite having had grey-out at around 7g in other aircraft.

Above: Even in dry thrust the F-16 is capable of impressive aerobatics. In combat, the added impetus of the afterburner offers the pilot 'brute force' solutions to any desired manoeuvre, while his opponent might have to conserve energy.

Right: The superb visibility of the F-16's canopy is illustrated by this view of aircraft from the 8th TFW. If the pilot looked round he would be able to see his own vertical stabilizer.

The brisk acceleration of the F-16 is a feature which has attracted much comment from pilots. Neil Anderson quotes one of the USAF pilots who tested the YF-16 as saying that flying the F-16 was '... like riding on top of a telegraph pole. Every time you light the afterburner, you are a little nervous that it is going to run out from under you'.

Any feeling that the pilot rides on top of the Fighting Falcon rather than within it is heightened by a bulbous canopy large enough to allow the pilot to look over his shoulder and observe his vertical stabilizer and see whether or not he is leaving a contrail. Pilots used to the more traditional pattern of low-drag canopy used on such aircraft as the F-4 or A-7 are likely to feel somewhat exposed. At relatively modest bank

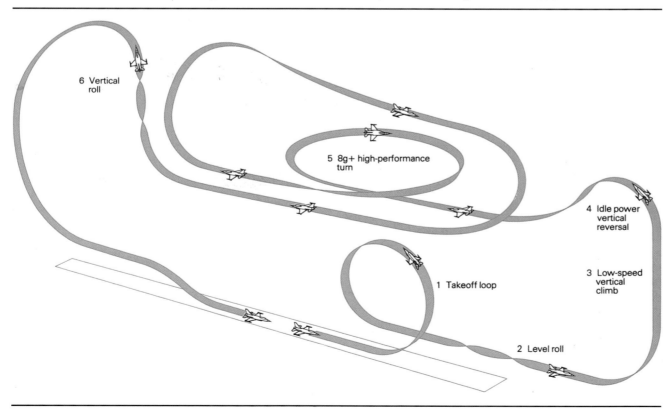

1 Takeoff loop
2 Level roll
3 Low-speed vertical climb
4 Idle power vertical reversal
5 8g+ high-performance turn
6 Vertical roll

Above: Neil Anderson (left), Chief Test Pilot at General Dynamics, played a major role in the F-16 programme. Colleague James McKinney (right) flew the aircraft during the 1979 and 1981 Paris Air Shows.

Left: This composite diagram illustrates some of the manoeuvres flown by the F-16 at Farnborough and Paris Air Shows during the late 1970s.

angles the pilot is able to look vertically downward at the terrain below, while the absence of canopy frames in the forward field of view removes the reference points by which pilots instinctively position the horizon during normal flight. During initial Fighting Falcon sorties, new pilots are recommended to fly by instruments until they become accustomed to the external view.

In high-speed cruise the wing leading and trailing-edge flaps are positioned 2deg above centre. Should the pilot attempt maximum-rate manoeuvres, the leading edge will move to 25deg down and the trailing edge will move to neutral. Vortexes generated by the leading-edge strakes play a significant part in improving the handling of the Fighting Falcon, producing improved

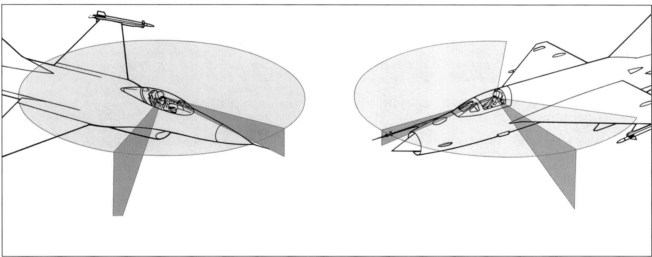

Above: Visibility from the cockpit of the F-16 is greatly superior to that from the MiG-21bis.

Left: F-16B two-seater flies an impressive-looking 9g climbing turn.

airflow over the wings and vertical tail. Lift, pitch and directional stability are all improved, while buffet intensity is reduced. Hard manoeuvring at high supersonic speeds can result in some buffeting, according to GD, but for most of the performance envelope Fighting Falcon is buffet-free. Transition through the transonic region is smooth, with only a slight buffeting as speed is increased through Mach 0.95.

Maximum speed
In the first edition of this work, author Doug Richardson bewailed the fact that full performance details had not been released by June 1983. Fortunately, with the passing of time, this has been corrected. Performance envelopes for both the F-16A and F-16C, with two wingtip Sidewinders, a full bag of gun ammunition, and 50 per cent internal fuel, show a maximum speed of Mach 2.05 at altitudes between 30,000 to 40,000ft (9,144-12,191m) for the A

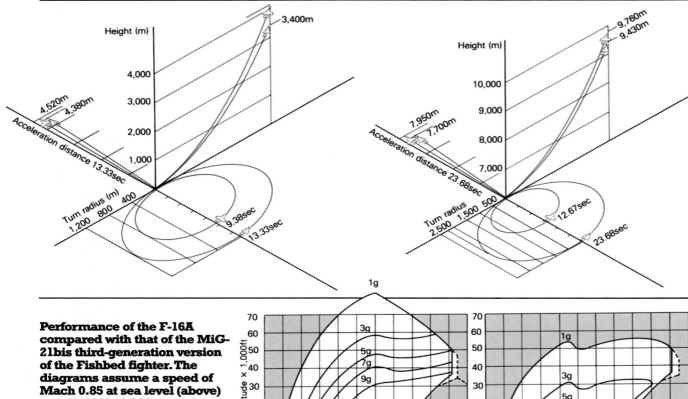

Performance of the F-16A compared with that of the MiG-21bis third-generation version of the Fishbed fighter. The diagrams assume a speed of Mach 0.85 at sea level (above) and 20,000ft (6,000m) (right). In all cases turning performance, acceleration and rate of climb are superior to those of the MiG.

Above: The instantaneous manoeuvre envelope of the Viper is seen here. It varies considerably according to subtype and warload.

Above: Sustained manoeuvre envelopes are naturally more restricted than those for instantaneous manoeuvre. As seen, sustained 9g is limited.

model, and 30,000 to 46,500ft (9,144-14,173m) for the C model with the IPE engine, either the F100-PW-229 or the F110-GE-129.

This is not an absolute limit; it is an engine dynamic pressure limitation. The F-16 is red-lined at 800kt (1,482kmh) calibrated air speed (KCAS) and exceeding it by any significant margin can lead to a serious engine failure!

It is not that the F-16 will not go any faster; it will. But not ever just for fun, or to see how fast it can go. Vipers powered by the original F100-PW-200 could only be forced past 800 KCAS in a dive, but the latest models with IPE engines will go past 800 KCAS as though it isn't there. But at the end of the day we are talking about a combat aeroplane, and the carriage of external stores automatically limits maximum speed. With most air-to-ground ordnance, the limit is Mach 0.95, although when in air-to-air configuration the F-16 is well supersonic. So, is the ability to exceed the placard limit by 50 KCAS or more of any practical use?

The answer is yes. When at "Winchester" (all munitions expended) and with something nasty like an Su-27 Flanker trying to intercept, the extra speed, used judiciously, might mean the difference between escape and failure.

At sea level, the envelope shows 800 KCAS, which is actually 800kt (1,482kmh) true air speed (TAS), which is Mach 1.21. The final point before we leave the subject of speed is that Vipers with IPE engines can supercruise, i.e., maintain supersonic speed without afterburner. However, this is only Mach 1.05 to 1.08.

Ceiling

The operational ceiling of all F-16s is generally stated as 50,000ft (15,239m). This is at variance with performance envelopes with show roughly 76,000ft (23,164m) instantaneous for both the F-16A and C, 57,500ft (17,525m) sustained for the F-16A, and 61,500ft (18,744m) sustained for the F-16C. So why a 50,000ft limit? There are two reasons. The highest altitudes quoted have been attained by test pilots wearing full pressure suits. Squadron pilots do not wear pressure suits, and exceeding the limit by any significant amount is asking for trouble. Secondly, at very high altitudes, manoeuvre perfor-

mance is lost; even roll rate slows dramatically. Nor is there a valid operational reason to take the F-16 up this high.

Climb and acceleration

Climb rate is the fashionable 50,000ft/min (254m/sec), which is the par-for-the-course brochure number given for almost every modern fighter. It is generally assumed to be the initial climb rate that can be achieved by hauling upwards from sea level at Mach 0.9. Of course, at any other combination of speed and altitude, it varies considerably. There is however an approximate relationship between climb rate and acceleration. Let's have some really good numbers for the F-16C, carrying two AIM-9 Sidewinders and two AIM-120 AMRAAM, with 50 per cent internal fuel!

Starting down at 5,000ft (1,524m), acceleration from 260kt (481kmh) (Mach 0.4) to 650kt (1,205kmh) (Mach 1.0) takes 21 seconds, an average of 18.57kt (34.41kmh) per second; a real kick in the back! Up at the more usual operational altitude of 15,000ft (4,572m), acceleration from 313kt (580kmh) (Mach 0.5) to 751kt (1,392kmh) (Mach 1.2) takes 35 seconds at an average of 12.51kt (23.19kmh) per second. The reduction in acceleration is in part due to drag, which increases in proportion to the square of the speed, and in part due to the steep transonic drag rise. Up at 30,000ft (9,144m), the reduction is even more pronounced. Going from 530kt (982kmh) (Mach 0.9) to 942kt (1,746kmh) (Mach 1.6) takes all of 59 seconds at 6.98kt (12.94kmh) per second. Of course, all these times can be bettered by nosing down and unloading. They are all closely comparable with, or in most cases better than, the equivalent figures for the MiG-29, F/A-18 Hornet, and the Mirage 2000C.

Right: Contrails forming from the strakes of this F-16 trace the path of the vortexes passing over the wing. These streams of energized air greatly enhance flying qualities.

Turning

The F-16 set a new trend in fighter performance; the ability to sustain a 9g turn, albeit in a small portion of the envelope. This is rather larger for the F-16A than the C model, extending from about Mach 0.72 to Mach 0.97 at sea level, and peaking at about 7,000ft (2,133m) at Mach 0.85. The 9g instantaneous manoeuvre envelope (instantaneous manoeuvre being the acceleration which can only be held with the loss of speed, altitude, or both) is much larger, extending out to V_{max} and in places over 30,000ft (9,144m).

There follows sustained turn rates for the F-16C configured as before with four AAMs. At 5,000ft (1,524m) and Mach 0.5, sustained turn is 16deg/sec with a g-loading of about 4.75 – on a par with the MiG-29 and the F/A-18. At Mach 0.7 this increases to 17deg/sec at roughly 7g, and to 18deg/sec at Mach 0.9 and 9g, where it has a slight but definite advantage over the other two fighters. At Mach 1.2 it turns

at 9deg/sec at nearly 8g, an area where it beats the other two fighters.

At 15,000ft (4,572m), it sustains 12deg/sec at Mach 0.7, again at about 4.75g, and 13deg/sec at Mach 0.9 (approx 6.5g) – closely matched in both areas by Fulcrum, Hornet, and the Mirage 2000C. At Mach 1.2, 9deg/sec (6+g) it is a decided superiority, while at a storming Mach 1.5 it still sustains 5deg/sec at about 6g. Surprisingly, it is matched at this point by the Mirage 2000.

Finally, up at 30,000ft (9,144m), the F-16C can manage 7deg/sec at both Mach 0.7 and 0.9, at 2.75 and 3.5g respectively, falling to 6deg/sec at Mach 1.2 (c4g), and 4deg/sec at Mach 1.6 (4.5g). At this altitude it has little if any advantage over its rivals in sustained turning.

What, if any, is the value of sustained turning? Fighter pilots hold mixed views on this. One school of thought is, first, that in a confused close combat situation, what is needed is the absolute

Above: Despite its relatively large wing area, the Fighting Falcon offers pilots a smooth ride at low altitudes and high air speeds, essential qualities for the strike role.

maximum that the fighter can provide, and this generally calls for instantaneous rather than sustained manoeuvre, and, second, that the only time the latter would ever be seen is in transit between one extreme and the other. This being the case, its greatest value would be down among the weeds, where there is no altitude to trade for energy. Accelerations of 9g are widely regarded as defensive in nature; the physiological effects on the pilot detract from his flying and weapons aiming skills, quite apart from the danger of g-induced loss of consciousness (g-loc). On the other hand, sustained turn is a great thing to have while jockeying for position at the start of an engagement, since it allows energy levels to be maintained.

Handling
In 1994, Geoff Roberts of *AirForces Monthly* magazine went to Carswell AFB in Texas to fly the F-16. Geoff was extremely experienced, having flown Meteor night fighters, Javelins, Jaguars, Tornados, you name it, for the RAF. In his spare time he had also flown a Spitfire of the Battle of Britain Memorial Flight, something that few are ever trusted to do. Accompanied by F-16 senior test pilot Joe Sweeney, Geoff rotated at 145kt (269kmh), followed by a 55deg nose-up climb to just below 18,000ft (5,486m).

These were his impressions. "During the short time that we had been climbing I had time to become reasonably familiar with the pressure stick in the pitching plane, and a left turn allowed a brief intro-

Right: The Thunderbirds aerobatic team have flown F-16s since 1983, and no replacement is yet in sight. They are USAF's equivalent to Britain's Red Arrows.

duction into the lateral control of the aircraft. Here it was extremely sensitive and I found it very easy to overbank.

"I was invited to input full-scale lateral deflection – or, to be more precise, full lateral pressure on the stick. A very rapid roll ensued.... Stopping this roll precisely where desired was very tricky but might have something to do with slower reactions. (Geoff was 62 at the time!)

"Aerobatics were a delight.... I found that 3,000ft (914m) was quite adequate for a loop at around 15,000ft (4,572m) and 300kt (556kmh) entry speed.... Barrel rolls were not at all demanding.

"I am now an ardent fan of the F-16 which is a very impressive and effective aeroplane in a variety of roles. Every air force should have some, and quite a number do. That said, I'd just as soon prefer them to be on our side!"

Below: Without its electronic fly-by-wire system the F-16 would not be controllable.

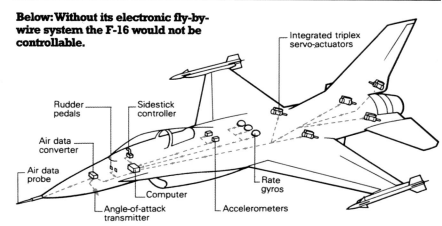

Experimental Variants

Having developed a fighter that set new standards in performance and manoeuvrability, General Dynamics, now Lockheed Martin, were not content to rest on their laurels. They actively sought, and are still seeking, ways of capitalizing on the original design to produce a fighter for the future. Whether or not they will succeed remains to be seen.

Having produced a fighter which could outmanoeuvre all previous and contemporary types, the obvious next step was to modify it perform the previously impossible. Relaxed stability and a computerized flight control system were the tools used.

The *raison d'étre* of a combat aircraft is to bring its weapons to bear efficiently and accurately. Back in the 1970s, this was done by pointing the nose of the aircraft accurately in the general direction of the target. Extreme accuracy in both azimuth and elevation was needed for air-to-air and air-to-ground gunnery. Rather less accuracy was needed for air-to-

Below: First F-16 to explore the strange world of decoupled flight movements was the YF-16/CCV. A series of 87 flights by the rebuilt prototype in the mid-1970s paved the way for the more recent AFTI/F-16.

air missiles and "smart" air-to-surface weapons; the more accurate the aim, the less work the missile tracking system had to do to connect. "Dumb", or even laser guided air-to-surface ordnance called for directional accuracy.

Conventional manoeuvre rather complicated matters. If the aircraft needed to edge to one side to line up on a ground target, the aircraft first had to bank in that direction, then reverse and level out very precisely to aim. Achieving the correct balance between angle of bank and course was far from easy, and made great demands on piloting skill. A flat skid to one side or the other was not an option; control became far too inaccurate. The question then became, could this be avoided?

It could of course, but only by abandoning traditional flight modes. An aircraft could be made to change its flight path without changing its atti-

tude. The aerodynamics were complicated, but not impossible. When strafing a ground target, if the initial heading was not quite right, it could be made to "sidestep". In a head-on guns pass at a slightly higher opponent, it could be pointed upwards, enabling it to shoot without risking a mid-air collision. By the same token, the nose could be pointed sideways without the fighter ending on a collision course with its opponent. There were many variations on this theme, which was called decoupled flight.

Control-Configured Vehicle
The USAF Flight Dynamics Laboratory came up with the concept of a Control-Configured Vehicle (CCV), and in the mid-1970s one of the YF-16 prototypes, 01567, was rebuilt as part of this programme. As we have previously seen, relaxed stability is the distance between the cen-

Above: The FloTrak wrap-around may look clumsy if not downright agricultural, but trials have shown that with its aid an F16 could be towed across waterlogged ground, or taxied over a rough field.

tre of lift and the centre of gravity. This was as good a starting place as any, and the distance was made variable by modifying the fuel system to allow greater control over the centre of gravity. Extra and unconventional control surfaces were also needed, and canard surfaces appeared beneath the intake on either side of the nosewheel. The flight control system was reprogrammed to provide unconventional modes.

GD test pilot David Thigpen took the YF-16/CCV aloft on 16 March 1976, to explore the problems. For normal flight, it was conventionally controlled, but the unconventional modes could be switched in when required. The YF-16/CCV could gain or lose elevation by using direct lift; move laterally (sidestep) by using direct sideforce; or yaw, pitch, or roll independently of the flight vector.

Near-disaster struck on 24 June, when the YF-16/CCV lost power on the final approach. David Thigpen brought it down short of the runway, but the hard landing collapsed the landing gear. Six months elapsed before repairs were effected and testing resumed.

The flight test programme was completed by the end of July 1977, after 125 hours in 87 sorties. Tremendous advances in mission effectiveness were established, but no further action was taken. The reason given was that while highly skilled and experienced test pilots could handle the decoupled flight modes, they were beyond the abilities of the average squadron jock.

Advanced Fighter Technology Integration

Advances in computer technology and high-speed integrated systems suggested that the problems of decoupled flight could be overcome. In December 1978, GD was awarded a contract to modify one of the FSD aircraft (No 750) as a test bed for the Advanced Fighter Technology Integration (AFTI) programme.

The AFTI F-16 was fitted with the same inlet-mounted canard surfaces as the F-16CCV, but externally it differed in having a dorsal spine, used to house the flight test equipment. Internally it differed in having a triplex (three channel) digital FBW control system, able to handle fully decoupled manoeuvres.

Changing from a quadruplex analogue FCS to a triplex digital system was not easy, and the first flight was delayed while the software was debugged. It eventually took place on 10 July 1982, and after three sorties from Fort Worth, it was flown to Edwards AFB to begin a two-year test programme. The first year explored decoupled flight modes, as well as checking handling over a large portion of the flight envelope. Only then was the new digital FCS proved. But, as with the F-16CCV, it was found that while decoupled manoeuvres improved combat capability in the hands of experienced test pilots, they were beyond the ability of the normal squadron pilot, who, it was judged, would have difficulty in performing

Below: First F-16 to explore the strange world of decoupled flight movements was the YF-16/CCV. A series of 87 flights by the rebuilt prototype in the mid-1970s paved the way for the more recent AFTI/F-16.

adequately while, for example, being forced hard against the cockpit side during side-force manoeuvres. This did not however deter the Japanese in their FS-2 requirements.

SCAMP

One of the major tactical fighter requirements of the near future is supercruise – the ability to maintain supersonic speed for extended periods with using fuel-prodigal afterburning. This is far from a new idea. GD carried out studies for the Supersonic Cruise And Manoeuvring Project (SCAMP) between 1976 and 1980. In mid-1981, two FSD F-16s were assigned to Fort Worth to be rebuilt to the proposed new configuration, with the designation F-16XL.

This was radically new – a cranked-wing tail-less delta. Designed by NASA, and optimised for supersonic

cruising, the wing had a 70deg swept leading edge inboard, with reduced sweep of about 50deg outboard. This had several effects; it more than doubled the wing area, which greatly reduced the wing loading, which increased the instantaneous manoeuvre potential.

A factor for supersonic flight was that the ratio of wing thickness to its chord (t/c ratio) had to be low; typically around 5 per cent. The chord – i.e., the length across the wing from front to back, parallel to the fuselage – was extremely long on the delta planform adopted; consequently the depth was considerable. The extra volume thus made available was used for fuel tankage, allowing a massive 80 per cent increase in internal fuel capacity. The YF-16 had originally been designed with what was then considered to be the optimum fuel

Above: Seen from this angle the F-16/XL bears a distinct resemblance to Fort Worth's biggest delta – the Convair B-58 Hustler. Note how the stores are mounted close to the underside of the wing.

fraction – i.e., the ratio of fuel weight as against the normal takeoff weight in fighter configuration – of 0.30. The F-16XL was of course much heavier than the standard Viper, and the increased fuel load resulted in an exceptionally high fuel fraction of 0.38.

On the new wing, leading edge extensions (LEX) did not really exists as such, and the wing commenced further back, level with the rear of the canopy, curving outwards before raking back at a very sharp angle on the inboard section. Spanwise flow was obviously a problem, and to overcome this small fences were located

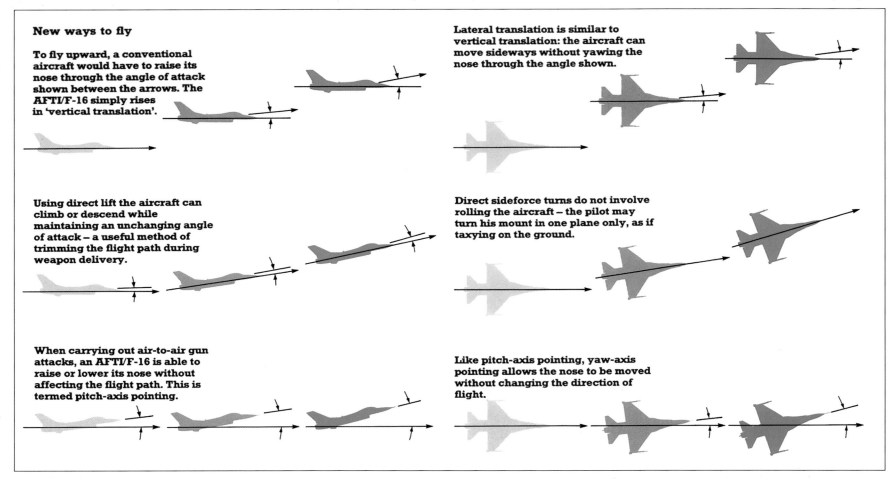

New ways to fly

To fly upward, a conventional aircraft would have to raise its nose through the angle of attack shown between the arrows. The AFTI/F-16 simply rises in 'vertical translation'.

Lateral translation is similar to vertical translation: the aircraft can move sideways without yawing the nose through the angle shown.

Using direct lift the aircraft can climb or descend while maintaining an unchanging angle of attack – a useful method of trimming the flight path during weapon delivery.

Direct sideforce turns do not involve rolling the aircraft – the pilot may turn his mount in one plane only, as if taxying on the ground.

When carrying out air-to-air gun attacks, an AFTI/F-16 is able to raise or lower its nose without affecting the flight path. This is termed pitch-axis pointing.

Like pitch-axis pointing, yaw-axis pointing allows the nose to be moved without changing the direction of flight.

at the change in angle between the inboard and the outboard leading edge, with aerodynamic fairings – the so-called "Kuchemann carrots" – behind them and projecting past the trailing edge. The inboard leading edge section was fixed and cambered; large slats occupied the outboard leading edge. Two-piece flaperons occupied the trailing edge. Sidewinder launch rails were retained on the wingtips.

On the standard F-16, the horizontal tail surfaces had been carried by shelves; these were retained on the F-16XL but with a refined shape. The fuselage was stretched by 4ft 8in (1.42m) and the height of the fin

increased by 11in (28cm).

GD test pilot Jim McKinney took the F-16XL on its first flight on 15 July 1982, reaching a V_{max} of Mach 0.9 and an altitude of 30,000ft (9,144m) – an acceleration of 3g and an angle of attack of 20deg. Rather surprisingly, angles of attack at takeoff and landing were lower than those of traditional deltas: 8deg and 10deg respectively. McKinney reported that the ride of the F-16XL was much more "solid" than that of the standard Viper.

He did however have one very exciting moment while checking roll response at a very high calibrated airspeed. While making a maximum

roll input to port, he hit a hefty patch of turbulence. The exceptional loading broke the bell crank connecting the starboard flaperon to the actuator, with a noise like "a cannon going off in the cockpit"! The flaperon snapped back over centre and checked the roll, although so violently that it broke off the vertical fin cap and two-thirds of the starboard missile rail. Handling his stricken bird very gently, McKinney brought it in to a safe landing.

The two-seater F-16XL, hopefully redesignated F-16F, was a rebuild of the FSD aircraft previously damaged in a landing accident. Ground proof-load tests suggested that the aft

wing spar of this aircraft would fail at about 85 per cent of the planned loading, so the aluminium centre section was replaced by a steel component. Powered by the General Electric F101DFE (Derivative Fighter Engine), it first flew from Fort Worth on 29 October 1982 with Alex Wolf in the front seat and Jim KcKinney in the back.

Tests showed that the F-16F could supercruise only while using afterburning and, despite its huge fuel capacity, its endurance in this

Below: The F-16 that never was – the forward-swept wing demonstrator proposed to DARPA in the mid-1970s.

regime was judged to be inadequate. While the large wing area reduced wing loading, it increased empty weight, and the addition of an extra 2.67 tons of fuel aggravated the situation by reducing thrust loading. In consequence, sustained turn capability was far inferior to that of the standard bird.

It was not all bad news. As a bomb-hauler it could carry an equal load over a tactical radius half as great again, while its long wing chord allowed most of its bombload to be carried in drag-reducing tandem configuration. With 12 Mk 82 500lb (227kg) bombs mounted on low-drag pylons, it could manage Mach 1.2, which was better than average.

After 798 sorties totalling 940 flying hours, the F-16F test programme terminated in August 1985, with no possibility of service adoption. One of the reasons given was that the F-16F largely duplicated the F-15E mission. In 1989 both aircraft were returned to flight status to investigate boundary layer flow at supersonic speeds for NASA; these tests continued into the mid-1990s.

The project arose one final time in 1995, when Lockheed Martin, as GD had now become, proposed the Falcon 2000 for the USAF, as an alternative if the JSF programme was cancelled.

VISTA/NF-16D

The ability to simulate the flying characteristics of new aircraft makes for a valuable research tool. Prior to 1991 this had been done by a single Lockheed NT-33A, modified by Calspan. Delivered in 1951, this was by far the oldest aircraft in the active USAF inventory, and was long overdue for replacement. The F-16, in this case 86-0048, fitted with the F110-GE-100 engine, was the obvious candidate to become the Variable Stability In-flight Simulator Test Aircraft (VISTA).

The VISTA/F-16 was based on the unique configuration of the Israeli F-16Ds, with a square-section dorsal spine, which provided space for the variable stability and data acquistion

systems. Volume for up to four Hawk simulation computers was made by removing the gun and ammunition drum. The evaluation pilot occupies the front seat, with a removable variable-feel centre stick. The rear cockpit is occupied by the safety pilot, who has normal flying controls and can take over if anything goes pear-shaped in the front seat.

NF-16D/MATV

It was not long before the VISTA F-16 was used for something radically different. Many years earlier, German aircraft designer Wolfgang Herbst had become frustrated by the conventional limits of aerodynamic manoeuvrability, in which manoeuvre was limited by the amount of lift supplied by the wings at various speeds. He evolved the concept of supermanoeuvrability, in which aircraft could manoeuvre at speeds well below their normal stall, the so-called post-stall regime, by using thrust vectoring. This concept had been tried and proven by the Rockwell/MBB X-31. Now it was time to try it on an established fighter, rather than a purely experimental type.

The NF-16D/Vista was fitted with the General Electric Axisymmetric pitch/yaw-Vectoring Engine Nozzle (AVEN), which first flew from Fort Worth on 2 July 1993. Integrated with the FCS, with no extra controls needed, AVEN provided in the region of 6,000lb (2,722kg) side-force at an angle of 17deg, which was achievable in less than one third of a second. Evaluated at Edwards AFB between July 1993 and March 1994, it achieved pitch rates of 50deg/sec, a stabilized angle of attack of 83deg, and a transient angle of attack of +/-180deg, in which it was actually flying backwards. These enabled totally unconventional manoeuvres to be performed, out-classing the capabilities of conventional machines.

There were initially instability problems in the roll and yaw axes between 35-50deg angle of attack, but these were corrected with software changes in the DFCS, aided by

nose chines which reduced asymmetric forebody vortex generation. An anti-spin parachute was fitted but, interestingly, this was never used. Jim Henderson, of the 422nd Test and Evaluation Squadron at Edwards, commented that in one versus two (F-16) engagements, you could be offensive all the time, quickly killing one bandit before engaging the other. As a retrofit, this would greatly anhance the combat capabilities of Vipers, and the Israelis, at least, are known to be interested.

Above: Powered by the F110-GE-100, the Variable Stability In-Flight Simulator (VISTA) NF-16D has a square-section dorsal spine to house various systems. The rear cockpit is occupied by the safety pilot.

Below: Offered as a STOVL technology demonstrator to meet a US Navy requirement, the E7 is the most drastically modified F-16 proposed to date. Powerplant would be a single GE F110 turbofan.

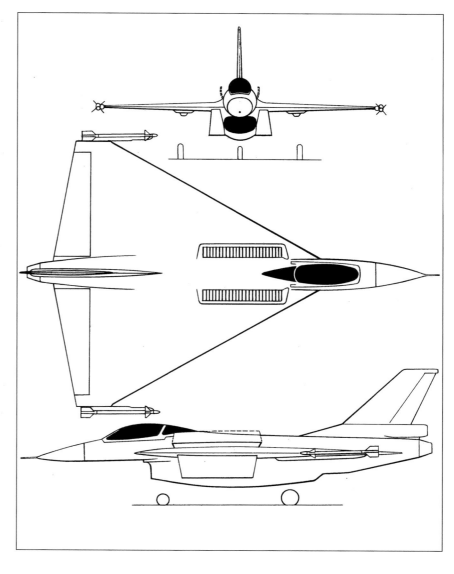

F/A-18 Hornet

Contents

Top: The huge leading edge wing root extensions, and the fact that the outward canted fins are set forward, are the main features of the Hornet.

Above: The Royal Australian Air Force was one of the first customers for the Hornet, because versatility and range were primary requirements.

Above right: The two-seater F/A-18F, tail hook deployed, comes in for a landing aboard a carrier. The Super Hornet is the latest variant.

Left: The F/A-18 Hornet has for all practical purposes replaced the F-4 Phantom, the A-7 Corsair II, and to a degree the F-14 Tomcat in the US Navy.

Introduction

Criticism of Western fighter designs has been a growth industry for more years than I care to remember, largely because of the inability of the experts to predict accurately the form that future war in the air will take. Thus the first homing missiles were expected to put an end to manoeuvring close combat and make guns redundant: in fact, whereas it had often been possible to evade a gun attack by accelerating out of range, the reach of the new weapons made such a course distinctly unwise; the ability to turn hard became more rather than less necessary, in order to make the missile work hard to catch the target and increase the chances of failure. Manoeuvre may start at longer ranges, but is more vital than ever before.

The F-18 has received more than its fair share of criticism. It is not as capable as the F-14 in the fleet defence role; it is inferior to the F-16 in close combat; it lacks the range of the A-7; and so on. Yet the Hornet had the task of replacing not one but two types in the US Navy inventory, the A-7 Corsair and the F-4 Phantom – and the latter, the

most versatile and capable fighter of its generation, is a particularly hard act to follow.

It should not be forgotten that almost every fighter ever built has sooner or later been festooned with ordnance and asked to do something for which it was not originally designed. The fact that the Hornet has rather more provision than usual for weapons delivery built in from the outset must be a major point in its favour. It must also be remembered that all modern fighters are the result of a series of compromises.

The F/A-18 Hornet, derived from the Northrop YF-17 light fighter, was a trend-setter. It had the first "glass cockpit", in which CRTs replaced conventional dial instruments. Although designed for the dual role, its air combat qualities were not compromised. Manoeuvre capability is superior to most other fighters of its generation, while its medium range combat capability is outstanding. It has of course undergone various upgrades, and the latest variant will enter service in 2001.

Development

Speaking on June 30, 1981, Vice Admiral Wesley L. McDonald, US Navy, addressed the critics of the F/A-18 programme: "After seven years of design, development, open testing and intensive study, the capability of this aircraft is well understood. While some factions have been criticizing legitimate problems that typically are not known until much later in service, others have been fixing those problems. Today, no significant discrepancies remain . . ." While these comments certainly seem justified, the Hornet's origins can be traced back beyond those seven years to Northrop design studies of the 1960s.

The first half-century of air warfare saw fighters grow larger, faster, heavier, less manoeuvrable, much more versatile, and vastly more expensive. No nation has an unlimited defence budget, and with the increase in costs came a diminution in fleet size. The trend firmly established itself: fewer aeroplanes, but of greater capability. As combat aircraft grew more expensive, attempts were made to break out of the vicious circle of rising costs with such aircraft as the lightweight Folland Midge and its Gnat derivative. But a main argument against the concept was that the number of young men with both the desire and the ability to fly complex fast jets was not large; it made little sense to equip them with anything less than the very best. This attitude was fine for the wealthier industrial nations, but not so good for the others.

An early, and very successful example of an austere lightweight fighter was the F-5 Freedom Fighter, manufactured by the Northrop Corporation. As early as 1954, a Northrop team toured both Europe and Asia, sounding out the defence needs of many nations. Their findings led to the development of the N-156, later to become the F-5, as a private venture.

Basically, the fighter force that a nation thinks it needs and the fighter force that it can afford are two different things. Force size and quality are limited by capital outlay, maintenance costs and skilled manpower resources, while the number of fighters available for action at any one time is governed by force size and maintainability. The F-5 was designed to offer supersonic performance as a fighter and a secondary strike capability, coupled with the simplicity, reliability and maintainability to provide a high sortie rate. Its sole concession to complexity was in the use of two engines, an early example of systems redundancy, although its fuel costs were assessed as less than half those of the single-engined F-104. It first flew on July 30, 1959.

The United States Defense Department ran a Military Assistance Program (MAP) to help the smaller aligned nations acquire suitable defence equipment. On April 25, 1962, the DoD designated the F-5 as the MAP all-purpose fighter, which effectively meant that it could be supplied to friendly nations on very advantageous, heavily subsidized terms. As a result the F-5 was to see service with the air arms of more than two dozen countries.

Right: This unusual planform view of the prototype Northrop YF-17 high over the Mojave desert shows many of the unique features of this fighter. The cut-outs in the LEX, through which the ground can be seen, the sharply swept, high aspect ratio horizontal tailplanes and the forward set of the vertical tail surfaces are all clearly apparent.

With the F-5 an ongoing project, it was time to look to the future. Northrop had no way of knowing how long the F-5 would stay in production, and that 35 years later it would still be in the process of up-grading, even though the superior F-20 failed to attract customers. Every aspect of aviation tends to be evolutionary rather than revolutionary. Northrop had identified a market need and filled it; the obvious next step was to consider a successor.

This meant staying in the export market rather than trying to produce a fighter for US service, and involved special considerations, the main one being technical and manufacturing participation by the main customer countries. By allowing the customer to have a hand in producing the aeroplane, the deal could be made much more attractive, as much of the money spent would benefit indigenous industry. The overall cost had to be attractive, both in capital outlay and in terms of operational life expenditure. The aeroplane would have to be mission-capable; while it could hardly approach the standards of the superfighters then under development, it would have to do a convincing job for the money. Cost-effectiveness was not a term current at the time, but this was the aim. In the event, the success of the cheap but potent F-5 has probably proved a hindrance to early sales of the new fighter. Finally, any deals with foreign countries had to be politically acceptable to the DoD; the United States was hardly likely to countenance sales to a friendly country which was likely to use the equipment in a conflict with another friendly country.

Left: An early picture of the YF-17. The small strakes on the nose cone have not yet been added.

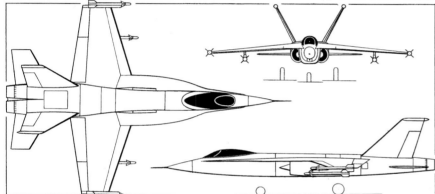

Above left: The Northrop F-20 Tigershark is, like the Hornet, descended from the F-5A, which the F-20 closely resembles.

Left: Development stage – the P-530 Cobra. The early requirement for Mach 2 capability is reflected in the Starfighter-like fuselage shape and the half cones to the inlets.

Below: F-5E of the 425th TFTS. The success of Northrop's earlier lightweight fighter has probably inhibited sales of the company's F-18L.

In the mid-1960s, Northrop initiated discussions with F-5 users and other interested parties to determine their requirements. They also postulated the most likely threat, and as many of the early F-5 operators were members of NATO, the discussions took on a distinctly European aspect. The fighter threat at that time was of course the Soviet-designed MiG-21, which was in service in large numbers with the Warsaw Pact countries: the projected threat was its successor, expected to be a simple, cheap, lightweight air superiority fighter, likely to enter service in the mid-1970s.

From the requirement studies emerged five basic missions: interception, air superiority, reconnaissance, close support and interdiction. These roles have conflicting requirements and an aircraft optimized for any one of them would be compromised in the others to a greater or lesser degree.

Lee Begin takes charge

Back in 1956, Northrop's Lee Begin, Jr., had made the first drawing of the N-156, later to become the F-5. Now, ten years later, he took charge of the Northrop project office team whose function it would be to translate ideas and requirements for the new fighter into hardware. Early studies showed that optimization for air superiority would result in the minimum compromise for the other roles. This was hardly surprising, as the aerodynamic requirements of an air superiority fighter themselves demand a great deal of compromise.

The role requirements are: (1) high rate of climb; (2) fast acceleration; (3) high turn rate combined with small turn radius; and (4) good transient performance (i.e., the ability to change the direction of flight rapidly). Items (1) and (2) require a high thrust/weight ratio, plenty of specific excess power (P_s) and the lowest possible drag, all of which are achieved by wrapping the smallest possible body around the largest possible engine. Item (3) demands a low wing loading which in turn calls for a relatively large wing (with its attendant weight and drag), plenty of P_s, and a high aspect ratio. Item (4) is conferred by good performance in pitch, and particularly in the rolling plane, with a fast rate of roll and rapid roll rate acceleration. This calls for a relatively small wing with a low aspect ratio. The art is to produce the best compromise between these conflicting requirements.

By 1967 the decision had been taken to design a Mach 2 air superiority fighter with secondary capability in other roles. The potential market was assessed at about 3,000 aircraft, of which the Northrop share could be about one-third, and the main types the new fighter could be expected to replace were the F-5, the Lockheed F-104 Starfighter and the Dassault Mirage III.

Gradually the outlines of what was to become the P-530 Cobra emerged. The original 'paper aeroplane' formulated in 1966 clearly showed its F-5 ancestry. The wing was of similar shape although greater in area, and featured a small leading edge extension (LEX) at the root, although it was high mounted. The engine inlets were set forward, just behind the cockpit, while the vertical and horizontal tail surfaces were almost identical. By the following year, larger LEX had been added, and the inlets were now positioned beneath the wings, which had developed a taper on the trailing edge from a point at about one-third of the span to the fuselage.

YF-17 configuration: seven stages of development

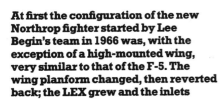

1966:
high wing,
forward inlets

1967:
larger leading edge
extension (LEX),
underwing inlets

1968:
larger LEX,
twin tailfins

1969:
contoured LEX,
larger tail

1970:
refined fuselage,
shorter inlets

1971-72:
P-600
twin-engined
lightweight fighter

1974:
P-630
projected derivative

1973:
YF-17 prototype

1971-72:
P-610
single-engined
lightweight fighter

1974:
Cobra development

At first the configuration of the new Northrop fighter started by Lee Begin's team in 1966 was, with the exception of a high-mounted wing, very similar to that of the F-5. The wing planform changed, then reverted back; the LEX grew and the inlets shortened; twin fins appeared, then were moved forward, while the horizontal tail altered shape; and gradually the various features were refined. Aircraft design is evolutionary rather than revolutionary, and this illustration clearly shows how the YF-17 grew from the original F-5.

The most radical departures in layout came in 1968. The wing had reverted almost to its original shape, while the LEX had been extended much farther forward. They were now definite strakes rather than mere extensions, and their function was to generate large vortices across the upper surface of the wing which would inhibit the spanwise movement of the boundary layer air across the wing surface to give better handling qualities at high angles of attack (AOA). They also provided a destabilizing effect at transonic and supersonic speeds as the wing centre of lift moved aft, thus reducing trim drag. Finally the LEX served as compression wedges, reducing the intake Mach number by lowering the local AOA at the intakes. Running along the inside edge of the LEX were cut-outs, or slots. The purpose of these was to draw off the stagnant fuselage boundary layer air before it could be ingested by the engines, and expel it into the low pressure area above the wing roots.

Tail redesign

The tail had undergone the most radical changes. The horizontal surfaces were more sharply swept than before, and were of increased area, but the single fin and rudder had vanished, to be replaced by small twin vertical surfaces canted outwards, set above the engines at the extreme rear of the fuselage. Wind tunnel tests proved this layout unsatisfactory, and in 1969 the design showed that the LEX had been contoured, and the vertical tail surfaces were much larger, and had been moved forwards on the fuselage to a position where they overlapped both the trailing edge of the wing and the leading edge of the horizontal tail. This position produced some area rule effect, and good lateral stability was provided by the vortices from the LEX impinging on the fins, which were canted outwards at the startling angle of 30deg to obtain maximum benefit.

To achieve a thrust/weight ratio close to or exceeding unity, the two engines were required to have a static thrust in afterburner of about 12,000lb (5,445kg) each. The two main contenders for the supply of the engines were Rolls-Royce, with the RB.199, and General Electric with their new GE 15. General Electric agreed to develop their engine specifically for the Cobra, and the GE 15, later to become the YJ101-GE-100 was chosen. The twin-engined configuration

selected was a follow-on from the F-5, giving extra safety and reducing operating costs due to attrition. Much controversy surrounds the twin versus single engine debate; it was erroneously but widely believed that the engine-related attrition rate for a twin-engined aircraft was much less than that of a single-engined type.

By 1970 the P-530 Cobra looked much as the F-18 does today. The engine inlets had been shortened and the vertical tail surfaces were not canted at quite such an extreme angle. Meanwhile Northrop had set up other design teams. One team produced a layout for a single engined variant, the P-610, while another team, for reasons best known to the manufacturers, came up with a design called the P-600, almost identical to the P-530.

Unlike many fighters designed earlier, the Cobra always featured guns as part of its armament. At one stage two 20mm M39 revolver cannon were featured, but the final choice was the six-barrel General Electric M61, mounted under the nose. Wingtip launch rails were provided for Sidewinders, although theoretically the choice of missile was left to the customer, and seven hardpoints were provided for the carriage of up to 16,000lb (7,260kg) of stores. A one-piece bubble canopy gave the pilot excellent all-round vision.

By 1972 Northrop had invested a great deal of money in the Cobra project. More than 4,000 hours of wind tunnel testing had been completed and nearly 750,000 engineering man hours expended. Now they needed partners to further the programme who would be prepared to invest $100 million in the construction and testing of two pre-production machines, and whose requirements would total between 300 and 400 Cobras. The pre-production machines would allow the customer to evaluate the aeroplane before placing a firm order, and the initial payment would be offset against the total cost of the order. Provision had been made to allow the Cobra to be split up into production packages to share manufacture between customer nations, and both Holland and Norway

Right: The use of ultra-violet light allows the photography of airflow patterns formed in the wind tunnel. This picture of a YF-17 model on test, taken nearly a year before the first flight, shows the vortices formed by the LEX leading edge extensions.

were showing interest, but the vast capital expenditure involved in replacing a major portion of a nation's air force makes it a political and financial as well as a military issue. In practice, politicians become both military and financial experts and the resulting hot air delays the proceedings.

Hard lessons

Meanwhile wars had been fought and lessons learned. Vietnam 1965-1972, the Middle East wars of 1967 and 1969-70 and the Indo-Pakistan conflict of 1971 had all involved much air fighting, and one thing had become evident: close combat, the old-fashioned dogfight, was still very much a part of air warfare. The F-4 Phantom, arguably the most capable aircraft of its era, had found itself hard pressed by the comparatively cheap, lightweight Soviet designs. One of the truisms of air combat is "Don't fight the way your opponent fights best", but the Phantom often had no choice.

The historical record had until that time shown that the fastest fighter possessed a clear advantage in combat, both in attack and in defence. Until the Korean War, the difference between combat cruising speed and maximum speed rarely exceeded 15 to 20 per cent, but with the advent of Mach 2 capable fighters the difference became a factor of between two and three. Consequently, the advantage passed from the fastest aircraft in terms of capability to the fastest moving aircraft at the time of engagement. Over Vietnam, this was often the defending MiGs. The attempt to find an answer took two forms: better weapon systems with reliable beyond-visual-range (BVR) kill capability, and fighters which could beat the MiGs at their own game.

Two men who played a large part in developing the latter concept were defence systems analyst Pierre M. Sprey, and USAF Colonel John Boyd. Col. Boyd is well known for formulating

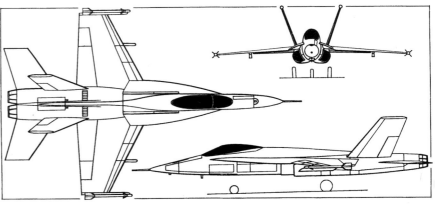

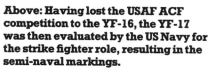

the concept of energy manoeuvrability, and perhaps less so for his development of a flying technique to counter roll reversal by using rudder instead of aileron, 'setting the hook' as he called it. Their early studies centred around a design for a dedicated air superiority fighter, and priorities were established from the lessons of the past. The most obvious lesson was that the majority of air victories were the result of a surprise attack, so the problem became a question of how best to achieve surprise. Part of the answer lay in keeping the fighter small and therefore difficult to see. This was at the time almost heresy. The latest US fighters were the Grumman F-14

Tomcat and the McDonnell Douglas F-15 Eagle, both very capable, colossally expensive and extremely large.

Doubts were beginning to surface as to whether the established trend was the correct one. There could be little doubt that however capable a fighter was, it would stand little chance in close combat if heavily outnumbered by simple, austere (and cheap) fighters. This was in fact borne out by later Red Flag exercises, where the big super-fighters performed wonderfully well in numerically small engagements but achieved a kill ratio in multi-bogey combats barely in excess of 1:1 against F-5Es of the Aggressor Squadrons.

Above: Having lost the USAF ACF competition to the YF-16, the YF-17 was then evaluated by the US Navy for the strike fighter role, resulting in the semi-naval markings.

Below: Trailing smoke, a YF-17 lifts off the runway. Compare the flimsy landing gear and single nose wheel with the beefy-looking undercarriage subsequently added to the F-18.

Below left: Three-view drawing of the YF-17, showing the basic configuration finalized in 1973.

Below: The P-600 differed from the YF-17 in wing and tailplane planform, and in the cant angle of the fins.

Below right: The two YF-17s were later redesignated F-18L by Northrop for evaluation purposes.

Bottom right: The hooded aspect of the YF-17, which inspired the name Cobra, is seen at takeoff.

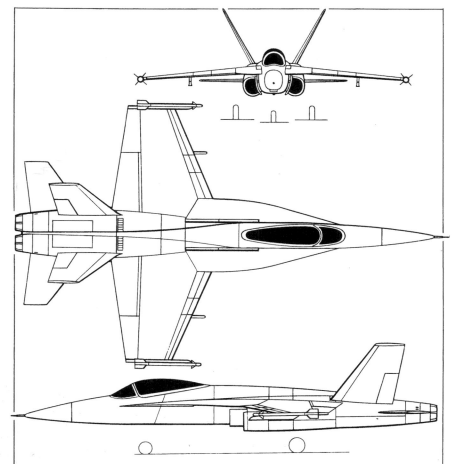

F/A-18 Hornet

By 1971, Major Boyd was working for the Air Force Prototype Study Group, and was in a position to push the light fighter concept. At the same time, the Department of Defense resorted to the time-honoured custom of ordering prototypes which could be evaluated by flying against each other. Prototyping was regarded as a systems management technique to be pursued as a possible method of achieving continuing technical superiority cheaply, or as the jargon has it, 'in an austere funding environment'. It can be summarized as "let's see the goods before we buy".

LWF requirement
On January 6, 1972, the USAF issued a request for proposals for a lightweight fighter (LWF). Little in the way of performance minima was specified, thus freeing the designer to concentrate on the main requirements, which were to demonstrate exceptional manoeuvre and handling capability in the transonic regime. In short, the LWF was to be designed for greatest effectiveness in the middle of the flight performance envelope.

A minimum load factor of 6.5g was specified, along with limited avionics for navigation, communications and fire control for guns and missiles. The new design had to demonstrate advanced technology while keeping both weight and cost down.

LWF proposals were submitted by Boeing, Ling-Temco-Vought, General Dynamics and Northrop. The Northrop proposal was based not on the P-530 but on the virtually identical P-600. On April 13, 1972, the field was narrowed to two, contracts being placed with General Dynamics and Northrop, worth $38 million and $39 million respectively. Each was to build two prototype fighters for evaluation. They were to be technology demonstrators, and no Air Force requirement was to be presumed. A cost limit of $3 million was set based on a procurement of 300 aircraft in Fiscal Year 1970 terms. This allowed the competing design teams to make cost/performance tradeoffs, rather than be forced to keep tweaking the performance up a little to meet firm specification requirements, usually at disproportionate cost.

Bearing the Air Force designation YF-17, the first Northrop prototype was rolled out on April 4, 1974, its maiden flight took place on June 9, and it was followed into the air by the second prototype on August 21 of the same year. It had taken nearly eight long years, but the concept had finally made the transition from paper aeroplane to flyable hardware. The YF-17 was a single-seat fighter powered by two afterburning General Electric YJ-101 low bypass ratio turbojets, each rated at about 15,000lb (6,800kg) static thrust. The wings were set in the mid-fuselage position with 5deg of anhedral, and were of trapezoidal planform reminiscent of the F-5, with an area of 350sq ft (32.52m^2), a 20deg sweep at quarter-chord, with LEX and slots as drawn for on the P-530. Variable camber was featured, in the form of leading edge manoeuvring flaps and plain trailing edge flaps which deflected automatically as a function of AOA and Mach number.

The fuselage had grown to about 4ft (1.22m) longer than the P-530, and narrow strakes had appeared on both sides of the nosecone. The pilot sat on a Stencel Aero 3C ejection seat, which was raked back at an angle of 18deg. The bubble canopy gave excellent rearward visibility although this was somewhat negated by the airbrake when extended, this being located on top of the fuselage between the twin fins, which were canted outwards at about 20deg, rather less than those of the P-530. The all-moving tailplane showed most changes, being mounted low on the rear

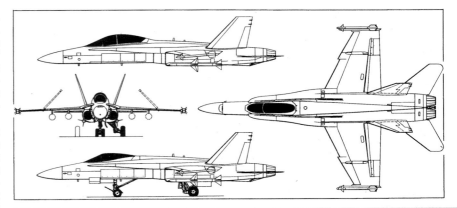

Above: The first prototype F-18 on an early flight demonstrates its variable camber wing.

Top: Hornet 1 looks rather weary after nearly four years of test flying. Navy and Marine Corps markings are on opposite sides.

Right: Hornet 3, the carrier suitability trials aircraft, flies over USS *America* on October 30, 1979, prior to making the first deck landing. During the next four days Hornet 3 carried out what the US Navy called, "the most successful sea trials in naval history", including 32 catapult launches.

Left: The original configuration of the F-18, plus a profile of the two-seat TF-18. The notched wing and tailplane leading edges are McDonnell Douglas innovations, along with the arrester hook and folding wings needed for carrier operations, and the altered tailplane planform.

Below: A contrast in prototypes. The YF-17 (left) is noticeably smaller and less chunky than the Hornet 3, and while both aircraft carry Sidewinders on wingtip rails, the F-18 also carries two Sparrows under the fuselage.

fuselage and swept more sharply than on the Cobra, while its span had increased to 22.21ft (6.77m) and its aspect ratio had risen considerably. Fly-by-wire (FBW) systems operated ailerons, rudder and tailplanes, with mechanical pitch and roll backup for the tailplane.

The YF-17 retained the nine external store stations of its predecessor and its air-to-air armament consisted of a Sidewinder mounted on a rail on each wingtip, and the M61 cannon mounted high in the nose instead of underneath as formerly. Avionics were basic: an air-to-air ranging radar by Rockwell Interna-

tional with a small phased array antenna; the Litton Industries LN-33 Inertial Navigation System (INS); a Teledyne transponder; and a gunsight head-up display (HUD) by JLM International. The clean takeoff weight had been held down to 23,000lb (10,430kg), which gave a very favourable thrust/weight ratio. Considerable weight savings had been achieved by redesigning the undercarriage, which on the Cobra had been intended for rough field operations and was consequently more rugged and heavier than necessary for runway operations.

In the air, the YF-17 performed well. During flight tests it demonstrated a top speed of Mach 1.95 (there was no requirement for Mach 2 and considerable weight and complexity savings had been achieved by using fixed inlets), a peak load factor of 9.4g, a maximum altitude of 50,000ft (15,250m), and a sea level rate of climb exceeding 50,000ft/min (254m/sec). Handling was excellent: the YF-17 could achieve AOA of up to 34deg in level flight, and 63deg AOA was reached in a 60deg zoom climb, while the aircraft remained controllable at indicated speeds right down to 20kt (37km/h). Northrop were consequently able to claim that their contender had no AOA limitations, no control limitations, and no departure tendencies. It was certainly an impressive performance.

A decision was taken in April 1974 that the LWF was no longer to be just a technology demonstrator, but that the successful contender would be developed into a USAF Air Combat Fighter (ACF). The general reasoning was that basic commitments demanded more fighters than the number of F-15s or F-14s that could be purchased with the funds available, so a nucleus of expensive high-technology fighters was to be supported by austere and much cheaper ones. This became known as the hi/lo mix, in which the fighter force was to have adequate

numerical strength containing a significant level of high technology.

The flight test programme for the ACF contenders was rushed through in a few months instead of the normal two years. Formal evaluation took place towards the end of 1974, and the result was announced on January 13, 1975: the new air combat fighter for the USAF would be developed from the General Dynamics YF-16. The contest had been far from a walkover and the YF-17 had proved superior in some regimes, but the award had gone to its single-engined rival.

Navy fighter requirement
Meanwhile another potential market had emerged. Back in 1971 the US Navy had become concerned at the cost of the F-14 Tomcat, which had caused both rate of procurement and total number to be restricted to the extent that the Navy could not afford the number of Tomcats that it deemed necessary. Furthermore, the ageing Phantoms and Corsairs would need to be replaced in the not too distant future, and various alternative solutions were examined, including a cheaper F-14, a navalized F-15 and improved F-4s. A group called Fighter Study IV discussed and rejected these alternatives, formulating instead the requirements of a new Naval Air Combat Fighter with a secondary attack capability, known as VFAX (fighter/attack experimental aeroplane) and to be armed with both the short range Sidewinder and the medium range Sparrow. It was anticipated that this would be a totally new design, but Congress decreed that the USN should study derivatives of the ACF contenders.

Below: Maiden flight. Carrying dummy Sparrows and Sidewinders, Hornet 1 lifts off the runway at Saint Louis on November 18, 1978, with McDonnell Douglas Chief Test Pilot Jack Krings at the controls.

Northrop, inexperienced in the particularly demanding requirements of carrier-based fighter design, teamed up with McDonnell Douglas, makers of the very successful Phantom, and the result of this collaboration was a navalized version of the YF-17, known initially as the Northrop P-630 and later as the McDonnell Douglas Model 267. In retrospect, it seems probable that Congress had in mind the use of a common type by both Air Force and Navy, with cost savings resulting from a large order. The precedent had been set years earlier by the F-4 Phantom, which was designed for carrier operations and went on to form a major part of the USAF inventory.

Navy assessment

The US Navy took a long, hard look at both the ACF contenders. Quite apart from the constraints imposed by carrier operations, their requirements differed considerably from those of the Air Force. The F-16 was a close combat dog-fighter *par excellence*, whereas the Navy needed a machine that could be used to modernize both fighter and attack squadrons. In particular, fitting out a fighter to carry the medium-range Sparrow was a major task. The procurement limit set for the Tomcat was sufficient to equip only 18 of the 24 squadrons in the Carrier Air Wings, leaving a further six to be modernized, plus 12 US Marine Corps fighter squadrons, as well as six Navy and Marine reserve squadrons to be re-equipped. In addition, there were 24 front-line and six reserve attack squadrons then flying the A-7 Corsair, which would need new aircraft

from the early 1980s. Allowing an annual attrition rate of 4.5 per cent, the result was a total requirement of 800 aircraft.

To fulfil the dual roles, the Navy needed a fighter which could easily be adapted to carry the Sparrow, and which could equally easily be converted for the attack role. The original P-530 had been designed as a strike fighter, so there were few problems in that direction. But the Navy, unlike the Air Force, carried out most of their missions over the sea. Engine malfunction leading to the loss of the aeroplane was bad enough, but over the sea it was also likely to cause the loss of a hard-to-replace piece of software – the pilot. General Dynamics had teamed with LTV (Vought) to produce a navalized variant of the YF-16, but the two engines of the Northrop/McDonnell Douglas fighter offered better safety, and this was a major factor in influencing the Navy's decision, although the YF-17 was also able to demonstrate better carrier recovery performance than its rival. A further consideration was that the design had more multi-mission potential.

The choice of the future F/A-18 as the Navy's new fighter/attack aeroplane was announced on May 2, 1975. A frequent accusation against the Navy during the following years was to be that they had bought the loser in the ACF competition. Of course, they had, but they had also bought the aeroplane that they considered was better suited to their needs. A comparison of USN requirements with the projected figures for the new fighter, now redesignated F-18, shows how closely they matched (see table). The only serious shortfall in the figures was

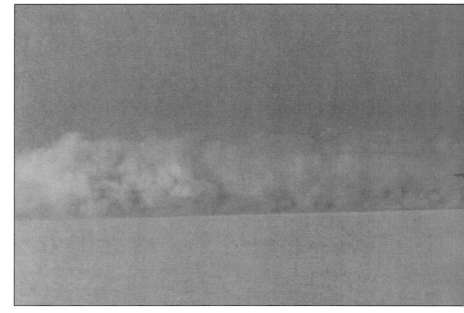

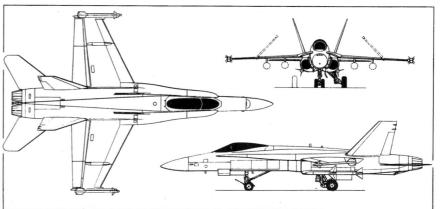

US Navy VFAX requirement/projected F-18 comparative data		
	VFAX	**F-18**
Vmax dry power	Mach 0.98-1.0	Mach 0.99
Acceleration Mach 0.8-1.6	80-110 seconds	88.3 seconds
Combat ceiling (000ft/000m)	45-50/13.72-15.25	49.3/15.03
P_s, Mach 0.9/10,000ft (3,050m)	750-850ft/sec 229-259m/sec	756ft/sec 230.5m/sec
Buffet-free sustained load factor	5.0-5.5g	6.6g
tructural load factor	7.5g	7.5g
Single-engine climb rate	500ft (152m)/min	565ft (172m)/min
Minimum approach speed (kt/km/h)	115-125/212-230	131/241
Escort fighter radius (nm/km)	400-450/737-829	415/765
Strike radius (nm/km)	550/1,013	655/1,027

on minimum approach speed, but it was felt that this could be improved.

McDonnell Douglas, with the McDonnell Aircraft Corporation's extensive background of designing carrier fighters, became the main contractor for the F-18, with Northrop as a major subcontractor, the construction work being split approximately 60/40. At the same time, Northrop were to develop a land-based version of the fighter for the export market under the designation F-18L and, in the event of orders being placed, the work share was to be reversed. One thing was certain: the naval F-18 would be a much heavier beast than the YF-17, and more powerful engines would be required. This was resolved on November 21, 1975, when General Electric received a letter

contract to proceed with the new F404, a developed and uprated version of the YJ-101. McDonnell Douglas received their letter contract on January 22, 1976, for the Full Scale Development (FSD) batch of 11 aircraft, nine single- and two twin-seaters: the first flight was scheduled for July 1978.

Adapting a land-based fighter to become carrier-capable is a very complicated process, and the aircraft also had to be fitted out to meet the Navy's dual-role mission requirements. Provision had to be made for the carriage of Sparrow missiles together with a compatible fire-control system, and all-weather avionics. A Hughes multi-mode radar was selected, and the nose had to be fattened by 4in (10cm) to accommodate the antenna, but no lengthening was needed.

Above: Dust billows up behind Hornet 3 as it carries out one of a series of cross-wind landing trials at Edwards AFB, California, during the summer of 1980. The flaps and ailerons are right down, and the stabilators are deflected to their maximum extent. A total of 119 landings were made in crosswinds of up to 30mph (48km/h).

Left: The Hornet after several fixes. The notches in the wing and tailplane leading edges have disappeared, as has almost all the slotted area in the wing root leading edge extensions.

Above: Hornet 3 aboard the aircraft carrier USS Dwight D. Eisenhower in February 1982. The complexity of the main landing gear, which retracts rearward while rotating through 90deg in order to avoid the Sparrow positions, is clearly apparent.

Below: The third FSD Hornet steps delicately (or so it seems) from the edge of the flight deck. As the weight comes off the wheels, the main gear takes on a totally different appearance (compare this view with the picture above).

To meet the long-range patrol requirements, provision for an extra 4,460lb (2,023kg) of fuel had to be made, bringing the total internal fuel capacity to 10,680lb (4,844kg) – compared with the 6,400lb (2,903kg) of the YF-17 – in four fuselage tanks plus an extra tank in the inboard section of each wing. A further 2,000lb (907kg) of fuel could be carried in drop tanks, and provision was made for in-flight refuelling.

For carrier operations a nosegear towbar and an arrester hook were added, and the undercarriage was redesigned to cope with the extra weight and the high stresses of catapult takeoffs and arrested landings, while to save space below or on deck, the outboard wing panels were made to fold. Alll these changes involved additional weight, bringing the projected gross weight of the F-18 to 33,580lb (15,232kg) at this stage, compared with the 23,000lb (10,433kg) of the YF-17. Considerable structural strengthening was required to cope with both the stress of catapult launching and arrested deck landings, or 'traps', and the weight increases. These modifications took the wing loading past acceptable limits. In consequence the wing area was increased from the 350sq ft (32.52m²) of the YF-17 to 400sq ft (37.16m²). This was done by increasing the span by 2.5ft (0.76m), and extending the chord by adding to the leading and trailing edges.

Much attention was paid to improving the carrier approach characteristics. The aerodynamic shape of the LEX was refined, and they were extended further forward on the fuselage, with a consequent increase in area. The deployment angles of the leading and trailing edge flaps were increased from 30deg to 45deg, and the ailerons were programmed to droop at a maximum angle of 45deg in low-speed flight. The hori-

Left: Stropped up on the catapult ready for launch. The rudders are toed in at a 25deg angle to provide a nose-up moment at takeoff.

zontal tail surfaces, or stabilators, changed shape yet again, to give a lower aspect ratio than before, and a snag was added to the leading edges of both the wing and the stabilator to generate high energy air and reduce spanwise drift during carrier approaches.

It was predicted that these improvements would reduce the approach speed to 125kt (230km/h), at an AOA of 6-7deg, giving the pilot an excellent view over the nose. This compared very favourably with the Phantom, which approached nose-high at an AOA of 13-14deg. It was also anticipated that operation with very heavy payloads in zero wind over deck (WOD) conditions would be possible, and that the WOD requirements at maximum loads would be very low.

Cost and complexity

Another important factor that influenced final design, and one by no means unique to the Hornet, was the sheer complexity of modern fighters. This had a knock-on effect, as complexity caused costs to soar and greatly increased the lead time from design inception to service entry. Soaring costs also reduced procurement levels, increasing the temptation to soldier on with the existing equipment for a few more years, and this in turn increased the operational life of fighters already in service to unprecedented levels – the life span of the Phantom, for example, has already exceeded 40 years. As a result, the production Hornet was designed to have a very long service life of 6,000 flying hours, including 2,000 catapult launches and 2,000 traps. Low procurement levels also meant that fighters had to be designed to fulfil more than one role, which put survivability and maintainability at a premium. In time of war, a prime requirement is a high sortie rate. The Hornet was therefore designed for high survivability and extreme ease of maintenance, while its dual role was stressed by the unofficial but widely used F/A-18 designation.

At the same time, a single-seat aircraft was being asked to supplement the two-seat Tomcat, and replace both the single-seat Corsair and the two-seat Phantom. This was a hard act to follow, and the question was very frequently posed as to whether one man could handle the workload. McDonnell Douglas rose to the challenge and, in a *tour de force* of cockpit design, took the experience and technology gained on the F-15 and improved on it by a considerable margin. The hands on throttle and stick (HOTAS) concept was adopted, with all the controls necessary for the combat mission placed on either the throttle or the control column. This appears to have been remarkably successful, although it does seem to demand from the pilot some of the qualities of a concert pianist. Information is presented on three cathode ray tube (CRT) displays, thereby eliminating at a stroke most of the hordes of dials that cover the dash and side consoles of most modern fighters. Information is called up at a touch of a button; the clever bit is hitting the right button.

First flight

The F-18 made its maiden flight on November 18, 1978, only four months late. Flown by McDonnell Douglas chief test pilot Jack Krings, the first Hornet, Bu. No. 160775, resplendent in a white, blue and gold paint scheme, lifted off the runway at Lambert Saint Louis International Airport at shortly after 1100 hours local time. The flight, during which no problems were encountered, lasted 50 minutes, and a speed of 300kt (550km/h) and an altitude of 24,000ft (7,300m) were recorded.

After the initial flight test phase at Saint Louis the first Hornet moved to the Naval Air Test Center (NATC), NAS Patuxent River, Maryland, for the FSD test programme, which was to last from January 1979 to October 1982. This was not to be without its tribulations but, after all, that is what test programmes are for. The eleven FSD aircraft and their functions are shown in the accompanying table.

Above: Hornet 6 in orange and white high-visibility livery. This aircraft was used for high AOA and spinning trials, for which the gaudy paint job was an asset.

Right: Different-coloured AIM-9s – port red, starboard white – assist aspect identification on film of the high AOA and spin tests.

Below right: Hornet 7 takes on fuel from a KA-3 tanker. The US Navy uses the probe and drogue system for in-flight refuelling rather than the USAF's boom and receptacle.

Full Scale Development roles

Aircraft	Bu. No.	Test function
Hornet 1	160775	Flight test and flutter
Hornet 2	160776	Propulsion and performance
Hornet 3	160777	Carrier suitability and ECS
Hornet 4	160778	Structural flight test
Hornet 5	160779	Avionics and weapon systems
Hornet 6	160780	High AOA and spinning
Hornet T1	160781	Armament and systems
Hornet 7	160782	Armament and systems
Hornet 8	160783	Performance and systems
Hornet T2	160784	Accelerated engine service test
Hornet 9	160785	Maintenance engineering

Previous test programmes had been carried out at a variety of locations, depending on which function was under test, but in the case of the F-18 the new Principal Site Concept was applied, with almost all flight testing taking place at Patuxent River. Apart from logistical advantages, this provided the opportunity for Navy and McDonnell Douglas personnel to work closely together, both in the air and on the ground, thus ensuring full naval participation in design improvements. The test programme called for no fewer than 3,257 test flights and involved two shifts, six days a week for both the Navy and the main contractor and the principal subcontractors. By mid-1981 over 3,500 flight hours had been logged in more than 2,600 flights.

The gestation period of the Hornet was surrounded by controversy. Some of this, mainly political in nature, was caused by the cost increases attendant upon the development of a lightweight fighter (a term thought to be synonymous with cheap) into a capable middle-weight. Unfortunately the Hornet's development period coincided with a period of high inflation and this had the effect of making things look much worse than they were. The vast sums being spent had the effect of making the programme highly visible, and a considerable amount of speculation took place as to whether it would be cancelled.

With hindsight it appears unlikely that cancellation was ever a possibility, although alternative programmes were kept constantly under review. Potentially more damaging were the questions raised by the test programme itself. Certain technical problems and performance shortfalls emerged, some of which led to vociferous criticism, not only from the press and the politicians, but also from sections of the military whose personal prejudices ran counter to the F-18 concept.

An underlying cause was the proposed dual role of the new fighter. The F-4 Phantom, originally developed as a fleet defence fighter, had been turned into the greatest multi-role aircraft of its time. It had, however, been found wanting in the close combat arena, and there was a subsequent stress on the air superiority fighter role. Now here was McDonnell Douglas taking the *losing* fighter in the ACF competition and fitting it out to become not only a fighter but an attack aircraft as well. This gave some people the impression of a retrograde step, especially in view of the doubts that had been raised about the ability of one man to cope with the workload. Finally, there were those in the Navy who felt that the aircraft had been foisted on them by the DoD decision that the choice had to be made between the contenders in the Air Force competition, rather than commissioning a purpose built design. With this background, the Hornet had many detractors from the outset.

Early test flights confirmed that the nosewheel lift-off speed was unacceptably high, at 140kt (258km/h), and Hornet 3 (Bu. No. 160777) was modified to overcome this problem. The snag in the leading edges of the stabilators (a modification made by McDonnell Douglas) was

filled in, and a software programme change was made which automatically 'toed-in' the rudders 25deg at takeoff, while the weight was still on the wheels, providing a downward moment aft of the rotation axis. These modifications reduced the nosewheel lift-off speed to an acceptable 115kt (160km/h).

Hornet 2 (Bu. No. 160776) showed performance deficiencies which caused considerable acrimony. Navy Preliminary Evaluation (NPE) 1 revealed a shortfall of 12 per cent in specific range in cruise conditions, and a lesser but still significant shortfall in combat conditions, while acceleration from Mach 0.8 to Mach 1.6 at 35,000ft (10,670m) took longer than the 110 seconds predicted. A number of contributory causes were found. The engines were early standard,

with performance levels below those subsequently achieved. The leading and trailing edge flaps were automatically actuated, and a programming fault had set the angle between two and three degrees too low to achieve optimum cruise performance. A software change cured this particular problem. There were also a number of faults in the environmental control system.

When all the changes had been made the shortfall on range reduced to 8 per cent, this being due to unanticipated drag. As a result, a Hornet was tufted to assess the airflow patterns on its surface. The slots in the LEX were found to cause a considerable proportion of the excess drag, and on Hornet 8 they were filled in for further tests. This did not cause the anticipated adverse effect on the airflow

into the intakes and became a standard fix, along with two further drag reducing modifications: the wing leading edge radius was increased, and a fairing was installed over the environmental control system efflux under the fuselage to direct exhaust air rearward instead of straight out across the airstream. These fixes increased the range, but had little effect on the acceleration problem.

On the credit side, the engine response was excellent, the transition from flight idle to full afterburner taking less than four seconds, and afterburner lightup was satisfactory, being demonstrated at 45,000ft (13,700m), and 150kt (276km/h). Slight deficiencies in specific fuel consumption (sfc) were shown, but these were partially corrected by a change to the main fuel control.

Above: The dropping of objects from an aircraft in flight is a process fraught with peril: here an empty fuel tank is successfully discarded. For this series of trials in December 1980, Hornet 7 is equipped with a camera on the tailhook assembly and three more on each wingtip. In the event, the elliptical-section drop tank was replaced by a conventional tank.

Top: The seventh FSD Hornet built was the first two-seater, T1. Initially wearing white, blue and gold livery, it is seen here on October 26, 1982, in orange and white at NATC Patuxent River. Behind it are Hornet 6, also in high-visibility finish, and Hornet 3 with wings folded and Sidewinders still in position on the wingtips.

Below: Hornet T2 in US Navy low-visibility grey finish. Although the fuel capacity of the two-seater is reduced, it remains fully combat-capable.

The range shortfall was to have serious repercussions. The Navy specification called for a range of 444nm (818km) in the fighter role and 635nm (1,170km) for attack missions. As at November 1979, the range limits had been set at 404nm (745km) in the fighter and 580nm (1,068km) in the attack configurations. Additional fuel tanks were not an acceptable solution, since the initial specified weight of 20,146lb (9,138kg) had already been exceeded by 1,962lb (890kg). An excess of 1,600lb (762kg) was considered acceptable, and a weight reduction programme was instituted to save 341lb (155kg), although this was not to take effect until the 123rd aircraft.

The most serious problem of all concerned rate of roll, which was well below the specified rate of 180deg/sec. Figures released early in 1980 gave the achieved roll rates as 185deg/sec at Mach 0.7, 160deg/sec at Mach 0.8, and 100deg/sec at Mach 0.9, all at 10,000ft (3,050m). At 20,000ft (6,100m) the roll rate was on specification at Mach 0.9, but as velocity increased so roll rate diminished. Analysis and observation showed the problem to have two main causes, namely flexing of the outer wing panels,

and roll damping with the wingtip Sidewinders in place: when the outboard aileron was deflected in the transonic speed range, the wing bent in the opposite direction to counter the aileron action. The leading edge could actually be seen curling up from the cockpit!

The solution was a compound one. The snag in the leading edge, which incidentally did not feature in the YF-17, was eliminated, and the trailing edge box was strengthened to increase torsional stiffness, at the same time strengthening the trailing edge box into the wing root. This involved using monolithic graphite material instead of the sandwich in the inner wing and aluminium in the outer section. The trailing edge spar was also thickened, together with its webs and caps, while the ailerons were extended outboard to the wingtips, increasing their area by 36 per cent, and differential movement of the leading and trailing edge flaps was introduced. The differential horizontal authority of the stabilator was also increased. A spin-off effect of the increased aileron size was a 7kt (13km/h) reduction in the undesirably high carrier approach speed.

The Hornet encountered certain other problems during the test programme. The No. 4 fuel cell in the fuselage was very prone to leakage, and only a redesigned and strengthened cell cured the problem. Structural testing also revealed some flaws, details of which are given in the following chapter.

Carrier suitability trials

Hornet 3 (Bu. No. 160777) was slated for carrier suitability trials. After extensive testing at Patuxent River, during which over 70 catapult launches and 120 arrested landings were made, Navy test pilots Lt. Cdr. Richards and Lt. Grubb flew out to the USS *America* for initial sea trials during the late afternoon of October 30, 1979. During the next four days the Hornet carried out what were later described as "the most successful sea trials in Naval Aviation history". Between them, the two pilots carried out 32 catapult launches and traps, plus 17 touch-and-go landings, or 'bolters', and demonstrated vertical descent rates of 19.5ft/sec (5.9m/sec). Serviceability was 100 per cent throughout the trials, with no hold-ups recorded, and general characteristics, including deck handling, were

recorded as excellent. Most catapult launches were made using intermediate power although full afterburner was used during two. The on-board auxiliary power unit (APU) was used for starting the engines, thereby keeping the 'yellow stuff' on deck to a minimum.

However, on its return from the trials Hornet 3 blotted its copybook when, arriving at NAS Oceana, it suffered, of all things, a landing gear failure. The fault lay in the centering mechanism to the main gear axle, which was experiencing a higher than predicted stress level. A new dual-chamber shock strut had to be developed, and this cured the fault.

This same aircraft was detached to Edwards AFB in California during the summer of 1980 for crosswind landing tests, and a total of 119 landings were made in crosswinds up to 30mph (48km/h). On March 17, 1981, Hornet 3 was again in trouble when, after a high sink rate approach at Patuxent River, the end of the fuselage-mounted rod on one of the main gears pulled out of the side

Below: In the attack role, FLIR and LST/SCAM pods replace the Sparrows on the fuselage mountings.

Above: Hornet 8, assigned to performance and systems tests, poses for the camera during IFR trials in May 1981. The refuelling probe can be seen extended, and the tanker is, slightly unusually, a USAF KC-10 with drogue gear.

Left: The ninth single-seat Hornet to be built was the first to receive the low-visibility grey finish. Seen here in fighter configuration, it is unusual in having no FSD number on the tailfin.

Below: With a payload of four Mk 84 1,000lb (454kg) slicks, this aircraft – also shown opposite – demonstrated the Hornet's attack range with the simulated attack on the Pinecastle range, 620nm (1,150km) from NATC Patuxent River, in September 1981.

brace actuator. After touchdown, the gear moved outboard and collapsed, causing damage to the flaps, wingtip, and engine intake.

The first fully automatic hands-off landing was made at Patuxent River on January 22, 1982, with McDonnell Douglas test pilot Peter Pilcher at the controls. This was the Hornet's first flight carrying the automatic landing system, and it is believed that this was the first time a fully automatic landing had been made on an initial flight. On January 26 Navy pilots started using the system, and by August of that year sufficient experience had been gained for the second batch of sea trials to be made, this time aboard the USS *Carl Vinson*. Two Navy pilots shared 63 catapult launches and traps, and numerous bolters, with various load combinations both by day and by night

Weapons trials

Other tests were going well, and the air-to-air and air-to-ground weapons trials were particularly successful. The first live missile firing was carried out by Hornet 5 (Bu. No. 160779) during December 1979, with McDonnell Douglas test pilot Bill Lowe at the controls, and the Sidewinder passed within 2.5ft (0.76m) of the BMQ-34 radio controlled target, well within lethal range. By October 1980 eight missile firings with both Sidewinder and Sparrow had been carried out against radio-controlled drone targets, with a 100 per cent success rate. No fewer than five of the eight missiles scored direct hits.

The ground and air firing tests of the M61 cannon also proved satisfactory. The ground tests involved firing the complete 570-round magazine in one long burst, while in the air tests six short bursts were used to empty the magazine. Both the 4,000 and 6,000 rds/min modes were used, and firing the gun was found to have no detrimental effect on either radar tracking or engine operation. The gun position above the nose was suspect, since it was thought that it might interfere with air to ground visual tracking at night, and that the accumulation of gas particles on the windscreen might degrade night visibility, so another test involved firing at a flare on a one-man liferaft on a cloudy night. No tracking difficulty was encountered, and no problems were caused by the gas particles.

Nor was the attack capability of the Hornet neglected. After early release trials of various stores, following which it was found necessary to move the store racks 5in (12.5cm) forward due to a flutter problem, one of the batch of nine pilot production Hornets (Bu. No. 161248) took off from Patuxent River bound for the Pinecastle Range Complex near Orlando, Florida, some 620nm (1,150km) away. It carried four Mk 83 1,000lb (450kg) bombs, two AIM-9 Sidewinders and three 315US gall (1,192lit) external tanks, with a Martin-Marietta laser spot tracker and Perkin-Elmer strike camera (LST/SCAM) pod on the right inlet position, a Ford Aerospace forward looking infra-red (FLIR) pod on the left inlet and a full load of 570 20mm cannon shells in its magazine. The Hornet's gross takeoff weight was 48,253lb (21,900kg), and after depositing its ordnance on target it returned in just over three hours with 1,600lb (726kg) of fuel remaining.

One change that was found necessary involved the drop tank designed specifically for the Hornet. Manufactured from spun fibre impregnated with aluminium, it was elliptical in cross-section to give better ground clearance, but the stresses imposed by catapult launches and traps proved too much, and it was replaced by a cylindrical tank holding an extra 15US gall (57lit) of fuel.

Left: A crowded deck on 'Connie' by day, with two Hornets on the catapults and a further four from VX-5 spotted, with wing tanks but no weapons

The cockpit also saw changes; colour MFDs replaced two of the original monochrome ones, while the third was adapted to suit a Smiths Srs 2000 digital moving map display. A new ACES zero/ zero seat, capable of returning to the vertical following a low- level ejection at angles far removed from the vertical, replaced the previous model.

The next upgrade, to allow night and all-weather low level attack, was first flown on a two-seater F/A-18D, on 6 May 1988. This carried the Hughes AAR-50 Thermal Imaging Navigation Set (TINS), supplemented by the Loral AAS-38 NITE HAWK FLIR targeting pod. Unlike the USAF LAN-TIRN pod, TINS cannot be steered to "look into" the turn, so the pilot wears Night Vision Goggles (NVGs), with which the cockpit lighting is compatible.

Whereas two-seater Hornets normally have orthodox control columns and throttles in the rear seat, the Night Attack F/A-18D operated by the USMC has had them removed. The back-seat is occupied by a naval flight officer, who operates the nav/attack systems with two hand controllers. Like the pilot, he has three displays, but these are decoupled, allowing them to be operated independently of what is happening up front.

The empty weight of the F/A-18C had naturally increased, although the margin was small; barely 1,170lb (531kg), and increased weaponry had raised the normal takeoff weight by another 1,100lb (499kg). This was offset by more power in the shape of the F404-GE-402, first flown in September 1991. A smokeless engine, this was rated at 17,600lb (7,983kg) thrust with full augmentation. An increase in inlet size was needed to handle the greater mass flow, making the first visible external change.

The next upgrade for the F/A-18C/D was the radar. Deliveries to the US Navy of Hornets with the APG-73 began in May 1994. Based on APG-65, the main difference is in the speed and capacity of the processors, increasing receiver sensitivity which improves resistance to hostile countermeasures and also mode capability. For example, it gives better resolution in ground mapping modes and improved discrimination in raid assessment mode.

Super Hornet

In the late 1980s, prior to the demise of the Soviet Union, stealth had become the new buzzword. The proposed replacement for the elderly A-6 Intruder was the futuristic triangular A-12, under development by McDonnell Douglas and General Dynamics. But the A-12 was pushing the state of the art a mite too far, and after a truly spectacular cost over-run, it was cancelled. As an insurance, McDonnell Douglas studied a radical Hornet upgrade.

This duly became the Super Hornet which, although it bore a superficial resemblance to earlier models, was for all practical purposes a new aircraft. To avoid frightening the bean counters of the General Accounting Office (GAO) further with a new project (the A-12 had been a terrible shock for them), the single-seat F-18E and the two-seat F-18F Hornet designations were retained to show them that this was a mere upgrade of a tried and proven type. There was just enough truth in this to be convincing.

In appearance, the F-18E is the big brother of previous Hornets. Wing area is increased by 100sq ft (9.29sq m), span by 4ft 4in (1,32m), and root depth by 1in (25mm). It varies slightly in planform in having a dogtooth leading edge, included to increase aileron roll authority. This is similar to that of the original FSD aircraft, but which was later eliminated. The LEX area has

---

The General Electric F404 engine, despite being a relatively new design, was one of the success stories of the programme. As a previously untried engine it was subjected to an accelerated test programme – referred to as the 'Hornet Hustle' – involving Hornets T2 (Bu. No. 160784) and 9 (Bu. No. 160785). In just 55 flight days the two Hornets flew 116 missions, totalling just short of 150 flying hours, and on three occasions Hornet T2 achieved six flights a day, a remarkable performance. The F404 was found to have excellent throttle response, to be virtually stall-free, and to have little trouble relighting in flight.

High alpha

While initial service entry of the F/A-18A/B was straightforward, the sheer capability of the aircraft led to unforeseen problems. Unlike the F-16, the fight control computer of which limited it to an angle of attack of 26deg, the Hornet had no such alpha restriction; up to 55deg could be reached, although rudder authority was lost due to it being blanked by the wings, and roll rate was greatly reduced.

The troops, delighted with the agility of their new mount, pushed it hard.

The first sign of trouble was when structural cracks were discovered in some fuselage mainframes. What had happened was that strong vortices from the LEX had impinged on the canted fins, causing unpredicted side forces. Many Hornets were grounded, and others had flight restrictions imposed, while a fix was sought.

At first local structural strengthening was applied, but as flight time accumulated, this was shown to be inadequate. The final solution was pure Heath Robinson (Rube Goldberg to our American readers). A small metal flange was fixed to the rear upper surface of each LEX. At high angles of attack, this modified the vortices in such a way as to alleviate the aerodynamic side forces imposed on the fins. No more was heard of the problem, which now appears to have been solved satisfactorily.

F/A-18C/D

The pace of modern technology is such that a fighter has barely entered service before at least some of its equipment has

started to near obsolescence, although perhaps fortunately this applies more to avionics, which are more easily replaced than engines and airframes. The F/A-18 was no exception. The first operational Hornet squadron achieved initial capability in January 1983; the prototype F/A-18C began flight testing in September 1986, and deliveries began a year later.

External differences between the A/B and the C/D are minimal – a few excrescences here and there to house aerials and antennae. Initially at any rate, all changes between the two concerned the avionics and weapons fit. An improved high-speed mission computer with a larger memory gave AMRAAM compatibility for the first time. Another weapon new to the Hornet was AGM-65F Maverick, which uses Imaging Infra-Red (IIR) homing, which has an automatic target acquisition facility, allowing first pass attacks on multiple targets. Various other avionics gadgets were hidden beneath the skin, and provision was made for internal carriage of the ALQ-165 Advanced Self-Protection Jammer (ASPJ), although this was eventually cancelled in 1992.

Right: Bu. No. 161248, first of the pilot production batch, and the Hornet that flew the Pinecastle strike demonstration, turns low over the water as if to line up for a deck landing, though as the hook is not down this is hardly likely.

Below right: A swarm of Hornets over the Mojave desert, as Naval Air Test and Evaluation Squadrons VX-4 from Point Mugu and VX-5 from China Lake join forces. All are single-seaters and all carry centreline tanks, while the rearmost aircraft also has wing tanks. Some carry Sidewinders while others have bombs on the wing pylons.

been increased by almost 40 per cent in order to maintain full manoeuvre capability at more than 40deg angle of attack, and there are spoilers on the upper surfaces to act as speed brakes and to increase nose-down pitch authority.

The area of the horizontal tail surfaces was increased by 36 per cent and that of the fins by 15 per cent. The greatest increase of all was 54 per cent to the rudder area, while rudder deflection was upgraded from 30deg to 40deg, adding to high alpha control.

Although a high proportion of composites were used, and the proportion of aluminium alloy fell dramatically, a substantial weight increase was inevitable. Greater power was needed, and this was provided by the latest engine derivative, the F414-GE-400, with a rated maximum thrust of 22,019lb (99,88kg). Few alterations were needed to install this, the main one being larger intakes to accommodate the increased mass flow. These were totally revised, with a raked trapezoidal configuration, with certain stealth features.

The fuselage was extended by 2ft 10in (0.86m), and provision was made for 3,000lb (1,361kg) more internal fuel, while a few "affordable" stealth measures, such as saw-tooth doors and panels were incorporated. RCS of the F-18E is stated to be similar to that of the F-16, at about 12.8 sq ft (1.19sq m). The dorsal speed brake of the earlier models was deleted; spoilers on the LEX are supplemented for landing by aerodynamic braking by rudder and flap deflection. Empty weight increase was 5,400lb (2,450kg) while maximum takeoff weight grew 11,600lb (5,262kg) to 63,500lb (28,803kg).

First flight of the Super Hornet took place on 29 November 1995, with project test pilot Fred Madenwald at the controls. On 14 February 1996 it was delivered to the Super Hornet Integrated Test Team at NAS Patuxent River, and the remaining six prototypes followed in quick succession.

Carrier compatibility trials were successful; the F-18E demonstrated its ability to land aboard with a substantial load, rather than have to jettison unexpended ordnance to get down to its maximum carrier landing weight. But, at this point, a serious problem was discovered. Deceleration which involved reducing angle of attack between 15 and 23deg at high subsonic speeds caused a rapid uncommanded roll of up to 30deg, described as "a bit alarming". It was caused by flow separation over the outer wing panel with asymmetric bursts. This was clearly unacceptable, and various fixes were sought. The final solution was a slotted fairing over the wing fold which allowed air to flow either way through the wing fold hinges.

Production Super Hornets began operational evaluation with VX-9 at NAWS China Lake in May 1999, which at the time of writing is still continuing. Even before this, the Fleet Replacement Air Group VFA-122 was established at NAS Lemoore on 15 January, and initial operational capability (IOC) is scheduled for 2001.

Hornets in Desert Storm			
Unit	Carrier	Base	Service
VFA-151	CV-41 USS Midway	n/a	USN
VFA-192	CV-41 USS Midway	n/a	USN
VFA-195	CV-41 USS Midway	n/a	USN
VFA-81	CV-60 USS Saratoga	n/a	USN
VFA-83	CV-60 USS Saratoga	n/a	USN
VFA-82	CV-66 USS America	n/a	USN
VFA-86	CV-66 USS America	n/a	USN
VFA-15	CVN-71 USS Theodore Roosevelt	n/a	USN
VFA-87	CVN-71 USS Theodore Roosevelt	n/a	USN
VMFA(AW)-121	n/a	Sheik Isa	USMC
VMFA-212	n/a	Sheik Isa	USMC
VMFA-232	n/a	Sheik Isa	USMC
VMFA-235	n/a	Sheik Isa	USMC
VMFA-314	n/a	Sheik Isa	USMC
VMFA-333	n/a	Sheik Isa	USMC
VMFA-451	n/a	Sheik Isa	USMC
409 Sqn	n/a	Doha, Qatar	CAF
439 Sqn	n/a	Doha, Qatar	CAF

Structure

A modern fighter is a series of compromises, and trade-offs have to be made between many conflicting requirements. The transition from lightweight air combat fighter to middleweight multi-role carrier fighter and attack aircraft was not an easy one, with additional weight and the demands of carrier operations having to be accommodated without degrading performance. The Hornet has convincingly demonstrated a high degree of operational flexibility and, just when it appeared that it had run out of growth capability, it was reborn as the Super Hornet.

The Hornet is unusual in that it was developed by one company from a prototype designed and built by another. The Northrop YF-17 Cobra, designed as a lightweight fighter, was rightly judged to have more development potential for carrier operations than the rival F-16 Fighting Falcon. But as Northrop had no experience in the demanding field of naval fighters, the McDonnell Douglas Aircraft Company of St. Louis, its long tradition of carrier jets including the F-4 Phantom, was awarded design leadership in the navalization of the YF-17. MCAIR, as the company was known before being acquired by Boeing, took 60 per cent of the work; Northrop became responsible for 40 per cent.

Joint manufacture

McDonnell Douglas builds the forward fuselage and cockpit, wings, stabilators and landing and arresting gear, while Northrop manufactures the centre and aft fuselage sections, the splice between them, and the vertical fins. The joined fuselage sections, complete with all their associated plumbing and systems, are then shipped to Saint Louis for final assembly by McDonnell Douglas, who, with their carrier fighter background, retain overall responsibility for stress analysis. Major systems such as hydraulics, fuel, engines, environmental control, and secondary power are the responsibility of Northrop, while the

Right: The structural flight test Hornet pictured in June 1979. Without paint the various materials are visible: the black areas are graphite/epoxy composites while the dark grey patch on the fin is titanium.

Below: A different view of the same aircraft. The composite areas under the LEX are access panels for the avionics LRUs.

crew station, avionics and flight control systems are down to McDonnell Douglas.

Both companies used full scale and very accurate engineering development jigs to work out the precise routings and positions of the plumbing and sub-systems within the airframe. A land-based version, the F-18L, was developed and marketed by Northrop, but without success. Had this gone ahead, the main contractor/subcontractor relationship would have been reversed, with Northrop taking project leadership with a 60 per cent share of production.

The original Hornet contract was for eleven FSD aircraft, comprising nine single-seaters and two twin-seaters, plus one fatigue test and one static test airframes. Based on a purchase of 800 aircraft, the cost was predicted at $5.9 million each in Fiscal Year 1975 terms, including the cost of engines and avionics which were to be supplied

through separate government contracts. Unfortunately, the cost was to escalate out of all proportion during the next few years, a period of very high inflation, and both politicians and the popular press were heard calling for cancellation.

In all fairness, the same vociferous protests had greeted just about every new American fighter project during the previous ten years, the F-111 being the outstanding example. A type of perverse logic seemed to prevail: if it was cheap it must automatically lack capability, whereas if it was capable it must be either too expensive or too complicated to work properly, and the slightest setback was blown up to assume the proportions of a major disaster. Fortunately, more sober counsels prevailed and a total of 1,377 Hornets, including the 11 FSD aircraft, were ordered for the US Navy and Marine Corps, although the USN stated that their actual requirement was for 1,845 aircraft, despite unit costs

Above: An unusual close-up belly view of FSD Hornet 7 taken during armament and systems trials in February 1980. The ECM fairings under the intakes and the chaff and flare dispensers show up well.

having risen to over $20 million in the interim. The rate of production had reached seven Hornets a month in December 1983 and continued into the late 1990s. The aircraft was then replaced by the F-18E/F Super Hornet, scheduled to remain in production until 2015.

Technically, the Hornet structure represents a transitional stage in fighter design. By weight, 49.6 per cent of the airframe is made up of aluminium, while steel accounts for 16.7 per cent, titanium 12.9 per cent and advanced composites 9.9 per cent. These proportions compare interestingly with the Air Force F-15 and F-16, which are at extremes of the scale. The F-15 contains by weight only 37.3 per cent aluminium and 5.5 per cent

steel, but 25.8 per cent of titanium, whereas the F-16, which deliberately avoided high technology materials, contains about 80 per cent of aluminium, just under 8 per cent steel, and only 1.5 per cent titanium and less than 3 per cent of advanced composites.

The use of advanced composites in the Hornet was, until the advent of the AV-8B Harrier II, more extensive than in any other operational fighter. Although contributing just under 10 per cent of the total weight, graphite epoxy composite material covers approximately 40 per cent of the surface area of the Hornet. Light in weight, of high strength, fatigue resistant and, most important in a carrier environment, corrosion resistant, it is used in the wing skins, trailing edge flaps, ailerons, stabilator, fin and rudder surfaces, most maintenance access doors, and the airbrake.

The fuselage is a semi-monocoque basic structure incorporating differential area ruling, with reduced area above the wings and increased cross-sectional area below them, both of which help to generate positive lift and reduce lift-induced drag. The forward position of the fins was also selected partially for its area-rule effect. The fuselage structure is mainly of light alloy, with machined aluminium fuselage frames. The engines are located in the extreme rear of the fuselage, with titanium firewalls between them. The engine bay face is formed by the production break between the rear and centre fuselage sections. The pressurized cockpit in the forward fuselage section is of fail-safe construction and is mounted above the nosewheel bay, which is probably longer in proportion to fuselage length than in any other aircraft. The 'barn door' type hydraulically actuated airbrake is mounted between the twin fins, and is of graphite epoxy material.

Two-dimensional inlets
Mach 2 was not a specified requirement, so the engine inlets are two-dimensional external compression types, allowing savings in weight and complexity. They also have a small radar cross-sectional area, thus reducing the risk of head-on detection. The inlets are preceded by 5deg fixed ramps, solid at the front and perforated just in front of the inlet proper

Right: Conventional materials and composites are combined in the Hornet's airframe for optimum strength and lightness. Graphite/ epoxy composites cover 40 per cent of the surface area while accounting for under 10 per cent of structural weight. Titanium is used far more widely than in the F-16 but less than in the F-15.

in order to dispose of the sluggish boundary layer air from the ramp face. The only moving parts on the intakes are the bleed air doors, which exhaust upwards into the LEX flow field.

The wings are of cantilever construction, set in the mid-fuselage position with slight anhedral. Typically Northrop in their trapezoidal shape, they feature variable camber and, at first sight rather outlandish-looking, leading edge extensions (LEX). This combination, known as a hybrid wing, confers excellent manoeuvrability in the subsonic/transonic flight regime, and really outstanding high-AOA capability, rather better even than the vaunted F-16. The main wing construction is a six-spar machined aluminium alloy torsion box, with graphite-epoxy wing panels. The box is attached to the fuselage by six dual-fork attachment lugs.

Control surfaces
The variable camber is achieved with full-span leading edge flaps which have a maximum extension angle of 30deg, and single-slotted trailing edge flaps, actuated by Bertea hydraulic cylinders, with a maximum angle of 45deg. Computerized automatic actuation sets the optimum angle for the prevailing flight conditions, whether manoeuvre or cruise. The ailerons, with Hydraulic Research actuators, can also be drooped

to an angle of 45deg, thus acting as full-span flaps to give low landing approach speeds, and the ailerons and flaps also provide differential movement for roll. The wing loading is modest and the variable camber gives the good gust response characteristics necessary for the attack role. The leading edge flaps and the ailerons have aluminium skinning, while the trailing edge flaps are of graphite epoxy. The wing fold essential for carrier stowage comes at the inboard end of each aileron, with a titanium hinge and an AiResearch mechanical drive, and a Sidewinder launch rail is carried on each wingtip.

Above: Small is beautiful in the close combat arena, and this head-on shot demonstrates the Hornet's small presented area.

Below: The work split between McDonnell Aircraft Company, Saint Louis, and the Northrop Corporation in California is approximately 60/40. As shown in the diagram, Northrop's contribution (shown in red) comprises the rear fuselage and fins, which are shipped to Saint Louis for final assembly with the MCAIR-built forward fuselage, wings, stabilators and landing gear.

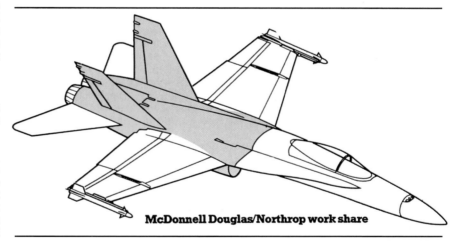

McDonnell Douglas/Northrop work share

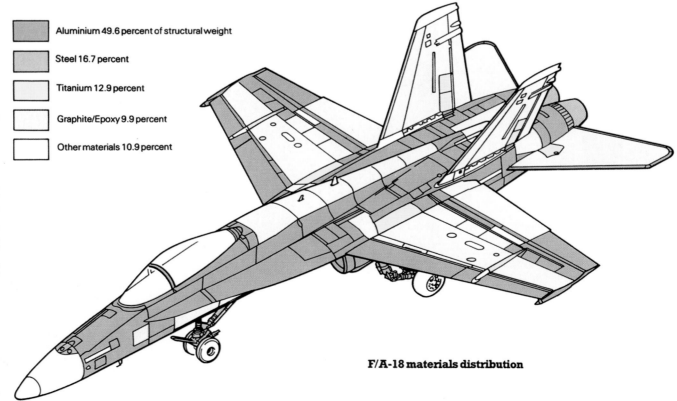

Aluminium 49.6 percent of structural weight

Steel 16.7 percent

Titanium 12.9 percent

Graphite/Epoxy 9.9 percent

Other materials 10.9 percent

F/A-18 materials distribution

Above: A VFA-125 Rough Raiders Hornet is prepared for a mission. The elliptical section drop tank being fitted gave greater deck clearance, but was unable to take the stresses of ship-based flight.

The most remarkable feature of the wing is the LEX, which extends forward past the cockpit. It acts as a giant vortex generator which scrubs the wing clean of slow-moving boundary layer air and permits controlled flight at AOA exceeding 90deg, although it should be noted that engine thrust is needed to maintain control of the aircraft in these regimes. The LEX also increases maximum lift by up to 50 per cent, and reduces lift-induced drag, supersonic trim drag and buffet intensity. Furthermore, it acts as a compression wedge to reduce the Mach number at the engine inlet face, and reduces the angle of the air entering the inlet by 50 per cent of the AOA.

Each LEX contains empty space that nothing other than fluid would fit into, but if the space were used for fuel it would be too far ahead of the centre of gravity, and damage would cause fuel spillage into the engine intake, which is undesirable to say the least. The LEX cannot house cannon without bulges spoiling the airflow, but one use has been found: the Hornet boarding ladder is integral, and retracts neatly into the underside of the left-hand LEX.

The Hornet's all-moving tailplanes, or stabilators, are unusual in that their span exceeds 50 per cent of the wing span, apparently to give adequate roll control as tailerons, where the effectiveness of the ailerons is insufficient. They are actuated by National Water Lift servo-cylinder hydraulic units, acting collectively for pitch and differentially for roll

Right: January 1982, and VFA-125 deploy to Yuma for ACM. A couple of adversary aircraft can be seen in the background, as can an AV-8A Harrier in hovering flight.

control. Like many modern fighters with engines mounted at the rear, the Hornet is close-coupled, and the pitch rates achieved have been described by Navy pilots as 'unbelievable'. The stabilators are constructed from aluminium honeycomb clad with graphite epoxy, but with aluminium leading and trailing edges, reinforced with titanium near the pivots.

Tail configuration

The twin fin and rudder arrangement has two outstanding advantages, in that it reduces or eliminates the effect of body vortices at high AOA, and also presents a smaller radar cross-sectional area than a single fin of the same total area seen from side-on.

The fins are of cantilever structure, with a six-spar torsion box connected to

six fuselage/fin attachment frames with integral lugs. They are skinned with graphite epoxy, with titanium leading edges and detachable glass fibre tips. The mid-fuselage location and outward cant was selected to avoid blanketing by the fuselage at high AOA and also to avoid the possibility of biplane interference at low forward speeds. Titanium panels cover the rudder hydraulic actuator positions, and the rudders themselves are of one piece aluminium with graphite-epoxy skinning.

The retractable tricycle undercarriage is manufactured by Cleveland Pneumatic, and accounts for a great deal of the steel used in the Hornet, while the wheels and brakes, which are of the multi-disc type, are by Bendix. The nosegear consists of a forward retracting

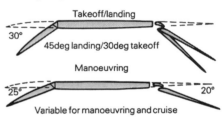

Above: The Hornet's wings feature variable camber, and computerized actuation which alters the section automatically to give optimum performance in all flight conditions. Variable camber also reduces gust response and improves the ride quality at low level and high speed.

twin nosewheel, with a shuttle arm for catapult launching and a long drag strut extending rearward. Nosewheel steering is accomplished by an Ozone hydraulically actuated unit. The main gears have single wheels that retract rearward, turning through 90deg to stow horizontally in housings under the engine air ducts. The Sparrow missile positions are in the direct retraction path and must be avoided, resulting in heavier and more complex gear. The aircraft is designed for a maximum descent rate of 24ft/sec (7.32m/sec), a vertical speed of just over 16mph (25km/h). The tyres are made by B. F. Goodrich, and are size 22×6.6-10, 20-ply, on the nosegear, and 30×11.5-14.5, 24-ply, on the main gear. Pressures are 350psi (24.13 bars) all round for carrier

operations, while for land-based operations the pressures are 150psi (10.34 bars) for the nosewheel and 200psi (13.79 bars) for the main gears.

The Hornet was the first production aeroplane to fly with a quadruple (four channel) digital fly-by-wire (FBW) control system. FBW is generally accepted as indicating pilot control of aircraft movement by means of electrical impulses, rather than pilot control of the position of the control surfaces. The pilot, using (in the Hornet at any rate) orthodox stick and rudder movements, signals his requirements to the flight control computer and lets the electrons worry about the vulgar details of flying the aeroplane.

This gives a close approximation to what is called 'carefree manoeuvring', leaving the pilot to concentrate on carry-

ing out the mission without the distraction of having to fly the machine to its limits while being careful not to overstep the mark, which inevitably uses up some of his mental capacity. The quadruplex system works on a 'vote': if one system fails, the other three, being in agreement, vote to overrule it. If a second system fails, then providing that two systems still agree, FBW still works. As a last resort, the Hornet retains direct electrical back-up to all control surfaces, and for extreme emergencies there is direct mechanical back-up to the stabilators only.

Duplicate hydraulics

The hydraulic system is duplicated, and the two systems are routed separately as far as possible. This was a direct result of experience in Vietnam with the Phantom, which had duplicate hydraulic systems running side by side. Consequently, a hit in the right (or wrong) place took out both systems. The hydraulic reservoirs contain a level sensing system which detects leaks and automatically closes the faulty section down, leaving the rest of the system fully operative.

The air conditioning and environmental control is by Garrett AiResearch, and the electrical power system is by General Electric. One safety feature is that no electrical power is needed for either fuel feed or transfer. A fire detection and extinguishing system is also incorporated: detection triggers a warning light in the cockpit. The extinguishing system consists of a pressurized container situated between the engine firewalls, and is actuated by the pilot through three entirely separate systems, one to the left-hand engine and its

Above: FSD Hornet 3 is lined up for a catapult launch from USS *Dwight D. Eisenhower* in February 1982. In an unladen condition the Hornet launches in military power, without using afterburner.

AMAD (airframe mounted accessory drive), with separate outlets to both engine and AMAD; a similar arrangement to the right-hand engine; and a third outlet to the APU (auxiliary power unit).

In the transition stage between the YF-17 and the F/A-18, the overall size of the aircraft was increased by some 12 per cent to accommodate 4,400lb (1,997kg) of extra fuel to meet the Navy's mission requirements, and to accommodate a larger, 28in (71cm) radar antenna, the minimum size that could meet the 35nm (64km) search range specified, in the nose. Meeting carrier requirements caused a disproportionate increase in weight, and the larger and more powerful F404 engines replaced the YJ101s. The wing loading had grown with the extra weight; the wing itself was enlarged by an extra 50sq ft (4.65m²), and McDonnell Douglas added snags to act as additional vortex generators to the leading edges of both wings and stabilators. These were subsequently removed, as previously related.

As well as growing rather larger in overall dimensions and considerably heavier, the Hornet was designed to have a service life one-third longer than that of the two aircraft that it was to replace – 6,000 hours as opposed to the 4,500-hour lives of the Phantom and Corsair. Accordingly, a very demanding static strength and fatigue testing programme was instituted for the airframe, which by the summer of 1981 had exceeded the proposed 6,000-hour lifetime, and which was finally taken to a total of 12,000 hours, including 4,000 simulated catapult launches and the same number of simulated arrested landings.

Left: Hornet 3 apparently preparing to demonstrate a high sink-rate arrested landing, to judge by the excessively high angle of attack on the final approach to the flight deck of *Dwight D. Eisenhower*.

Static tests included maximum 11.25g symmetrical pull-ups, rolling pull-outs at up to 9g, and engine mount loadings exceeding 11g. Testing for 9g excursions was set at a rate of 27 per 1,000 hours, a far more demanding rate than the 10 per 1,000 hours stipulated for the F-15. These tests are structurally demanding, none more so than the drop test, of which 100 were carried out, at descent rates of up to 24ft/sec (7.32m/sec) on the main gear. Every fourth drop test was a simulated in-flight engagement, nosegear-first landing at descent rates of up to 27ft/sec (8.23m/sec).

It was hardly surprising that some failures occurred, but finding fault is the purpose of a test programme. If no failures were anticipated, the costly test and development programme could be eliminated. If no failures were to be found, then perfection would have been achieved, and the test programme would still have been worthwhile for the high confidence level gained. Fortunately, none of the failures was particularly serious, and the causes were eliminated fairly easily.

After approximately 300 spectrum hours of fatigue testing a fatigue crack developed in bulkhead No. 453. Investigation established that this was due to secondary bending, and the thickness of the metal in the affected areas was increased to give extra stiffness.

Much later, after 2,428 spectrum hours

Right: Main gear retraction is complicated by the positions of the Sparrow missiles. The gear retracts rearward and rotates through 90deg for stowage in their housings under the engine air ducts.

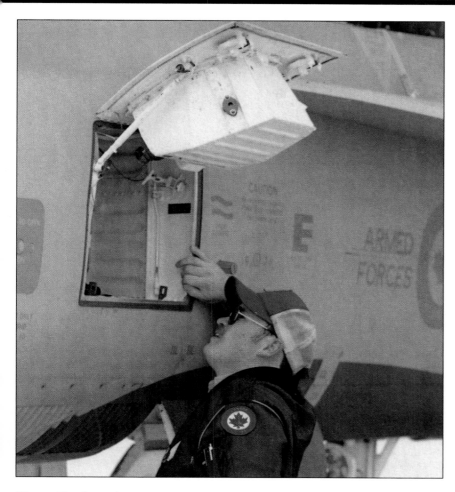

Above: The Canadian Armed Forces were the first foreign purchasers of the Hornet, with an order for 148 aircraft. A Canadian ground crewman peers intently into the gun mechanism access panel.

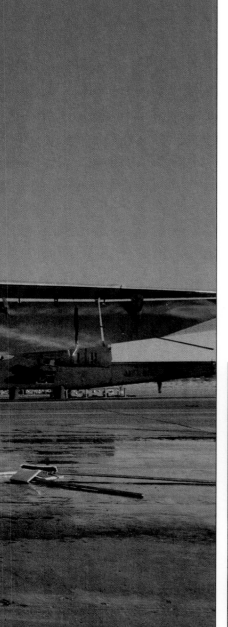

Left: A two-seat Hornet is given a thorough wash, with intakes and AOA vanes protected by covers. Note the boarding ladder extended from its stowage in the LEX.

Below: A Canadian Armed Forces two-seat CF-18 in the hangar with the avionics bay access panels open. The avionics are LRUs and designed for rapid substitution.

³⁄₁₆in (5mm) diameter holes which had been drilled in the bulkhead to hold a hydraulic line swivel link fitting. In this case, the fix was to discontinue drilling these holes and attach the fitting to the bulkhead by a different method. Other minor defects included fatigue cracks found after 2,702 hours of fatigue testing in the leading edge flap drive lugs, which were redesigned to incorporate shorter pins, while a failure in the leading edge flap transmission was fixed by increasing the thickness of the wing gear, which had the effect of reducing the concentration of stress at that point. It should be pointed out that this is by no means a catalogue of disasters, but the sort of minor events that occur in any test programme.

One of the greatest assets of a military aeroplane is a high sortie rate: it must be able to 'get up and go' as often as possible, and not be grounded by footling defects. Reliability is a key factor in achieving this state of affairs, but equally important is maintainability, which was a fundamental consideration in the design of the Hornet. No fewer than 307 access doors are incorporated in the surface, with the selection of the type of door fasteners being based on the anticipated frequency of access. Quick release latches are used on over 53 per cent of the door areas. The approach was to obtain positive locking with no special tools needed, and no locking wire, thus reducing the ever-present danger of foreign object damage, or FOD. Almost all the access doors are accessible from deck level; only 30 require the use of work stands to reach them.

Avionics black boxes are situated at chest height and only one deep, so that extracting a failed unit will not involve the removal and subsequent replacement of a serviceable unit. The black boxes are Line Replaceable Units (LRUs) and are designed for on-the-spot substitution, so that while the old unit is pulled out and taken back to the workshop for repair a new one is slotted into its place with a minimum of fuss. The radar is track-mounted and can be rolled out for ease of access and maintenance; the windscreen hinges forwards to allow access behind the instrument panel; and the ejection seat can be removed for servicing and replaced without affecting the canopy rigging.

Both avionics and consumables are covered by Built-In Test Equipment (BITE). The engine APU can provide power for check-out of all systems without the engines running and without the need for an external power source, and a fault causes a caution light to come on in the cockpit. The pilot then calls up information on the failure on his cockpit multimode display. In the nosewheel well, a position pioneered on the F-15, where it is easily accessible to the deck crew but

(approximating to 4,000 hours of aircraft life), a crack was discovered in the bulkhead which holds the main landing gear uplock system. This was caused by an error during the manufacturing process resulting from a tooling problem. A quarter-inch (6mm) diameter hole had been drilled slightly out of position. To correct this a half-inch (13mm) diameter hole had been drilled and plugged, and the new hole had then been drilled in the correct position, through the plug, creating a weakness. Only the first eight Hornets had been affected by this error before the tooling was corrected, and fatigue testing was suspended for nearly two weeks while McDonnell Douglas evaluated the use of bonding material on both sides of the affected part of the bulkhead.

At the same time, further minor cracks were found in the No. 453 bulkhead. These emanated from a group of four

sheltered from the elements, is the Maintenance Monitor Panel (MMP), which pinpoints systems failures visually. Equipment is fitted with 'fail' flags which provide confirmation that repair or replacement is needed when the relevant access door is opened.

For speedy pre-flight checking, deck crews have access to a separate consumables panel which indicates critical fluid levels on a 'go/no go' basis. Without this there would have to be a time-consuming series of checks on such things as engine oil, APU oil, drive system oil, hydraulic fluid, radar coolant, liquid oxygen, fire extinguishing fluid, and liquid nitrogen for cooling the seeker heads of the Sidewinders. Servicing points are so distributed as to minimize the risk of deck crew getting in each other's way. Significant maintenance data is recorded in flight by the Maintenance Signal Data Recorder, which measures data on the engines, avionics, and structural strain gauge and makes it available at the end of the mission in the form of a print-out.

Reliability demonstration

A formal reliability demonstration was completed in November 1980, comprising 100 flight hours in 50 flights. Only 12 failures were recorded, three of which were avionics related, and only two of which affected the satisfactory performance of the mission. This compared very favourably with the Navy's requirements, which were a Mean Time Between Failures (MTBF) of 3.7 hours against a demonstrated performance of 8.33 hours, and an ultimate target of 90 per cent probability of mission success against a demonstrated 96 per cent. The mean time for repair was 1.8 hours and the direct Maintenance Man Hours per Flight Hour (MMH/FH) figure was 3.4.

Maintainability checks were held at various points in the development programme. After 1,200 flying hours the planned level of unscheduled MMH/FH was 8; the Hornet demonstrated 7.47, and at 2,500 flying hours the target of 5 MMH/FH was easily bettered, the Hornet recording 3.62. The guarantee for Fleet Supportability evaluation is 3.35 MMH/FH; this was eventually bettered by a wide margin.

The Hornet compares very favourably with other USN aircraft. In the year between July 1982 and June 1983, the MMH/FH figure for production Hornets was 2.62, while comparable figures for other machines were 4.54 for the A-7E Corsair, 5.17 for the A-6E Intruder, 5.6 for the F-4S Phantom, and 5.86 for the F-14 Tomcat. During the same period, the Hornet's Mean Flight Hours Between Failures (MFHBF) was also remarkable, production aircraft turning in a figure of 2.1 against 0.7 for the Corsair, 0.6 for the Intruder, 0.8 for the Phantom and 0.6 for the Tomcat.

A further maintenance bonus results from the fact that the Hornet is to replace both the Phantom and the Corsair. Regardless of whether the Hornet is the F-18 fighter or the A-18 attack variant, it remains essentially the same aircraft, and only 4,000 different support items need to be stocked to maintain it. An all-Hornet air wing will dramatically reduce the spares inventory, not so much in terms of total quantity of items stocked, although the demonstrated reliability and maintainability of the McDonnell Douglas fighter will do much to reduce this, but in the number of types of spares. A current mixed air wing of Phantoms (12,500 support items) and

Corsairs (8,000 support items) is something of a logistical nightmare. The all-Hornet air wing will show a reduction in the number of components to be stocked of the order of 80 per cent.

The Hornet is constructed in stages, with individual sections being fabricated separately before being brought together in a predetermined order for final assembly. The rear and centre fuselage sections are constructed in Northrop's Hawthorne plant, then put together before being shipped to the McDonnell Douglas factory in Saint Louis for final assembly. The vertical fins are also manufactured in Hawthorne. The other major sections are the wings,

stabilators, forward fuselage and cockpit and the landing gear.

Aluminium sheet structures are automatically drilled and routed, while heavier aluminium structural sections are formed in a gigantic two-storey machine manufactured by the Hydraulic Press Manufacturing Co, which can exert a pressure of up to 7,000 tons (711,000kg). Components which will undergo high stress, fatigue, or high temperatures, such as the stabilator pivots or engine firewall linings, are made of titanium. A process known as super-plastic forming/diffusion bonding shapes titanium sheet, which is made plastic by a combination of temperatures

Above: A contrast in styles. The enlarged LEX, canted fins and small fixed intakes are the major points of difference displayed by a two-seat F-18 alongside the same manufacturer's fourth pre-production F-15 Eagle.

of 1,650deg F (900deg C) and pressures of 250psi (16.8 bars), while the world's largest profile milling shop cuts the finished components from forgings using computer controlled machines.

Pipe bending is also computerized, and coloured plastic caps on the open ends of the tubes prevent contamination prior to assembly. The electrical wiring is installed in pre-made bundles during

McDonnell Douglas F/A-18 Hornet cutaway

1 Radome
2 Planar array radar scanner
3 Flight refuelling probe, retractable
4 Gun gas purging air intakes
5 Radar module withdrawal rails
6 M61A1 Vulcan 20mm rotary cannon
7 Ammunition magazine
8 Angle of attack transmitter
9 Hinged windscreen (access to instruments)
10 Instrument panel and cathode ray tube displays
11 Head-up display
12 Engine throttle levers
13 Martin-Baker Mk 10L 'zero-zero' ejection seat
14 Canopy
15 Cockpit pressurization valve
16 Canopy actuator
17 Structural space provision for second seat (TF-18 trainer variant)
18 ASQ-137 Laser Spot Tracker
19 Wing root leading edge extension (LEX)
20 Position light
21 Tacan antenna
22 Intake ramp bleed air spill duct
23 Starboard wing stores pylons
24 Leading edge flap
25 Starboard wing integral fuel tank
26 Wing fold hinge joint
27 AIM-9P Sidewinder air-to-air missile
28 Missile launch rail
29 Starboard navigation light
30 Wing tip folded position
31 Flap vane
32 Leading edge flap drive shaft interconnection
33 Starboard drooping aileron
34 UHF/IFF antenna
35 Boundary layer bleed air spill duct
36 Leading edge flap drive motor and gearbox
37 Engine bleed air ducting
38 Aft fuselage fuel tanks
39 Hydraulic reservoirs
40 Fuel system vent pipe
41 Fuel venting air grilles
42 Strobe light
43 Tail navigation light
44 Aft radar warning antenna
45 Fuel jettison

46 Starboard rudder
47 Radar warning power amplifier
48 Rudder hydraulic actuator
49 Starboard all-moving tailplane
50 Airbrake
51 ECM antenna
52 Radar warning antenna
53 Formation lighting strip
54 Variable area afterburner nozzles
55 Afterburner duct
56 Engine fire suppression bottles
57 Arrester hook jack and damper
58 Port all-moving tailplane
59 Afterburner nozzle actuator
60 Tailplane pivot bearing
61 Arrester hook
62 Tailplane hydraulic actuator
63 General Electric F404 afterburning turbofan engine
64 Engine digital control unit
65 Formation lighting strip
66 Engine fuel system equipment
67 Port drooping aileron
68 Single slotted Fowler-type flap
69 Aileron hydraulic actuator
70 Wing fold rotary actuator and gearbox
71 Port navigation light
72 AIM-9P Sidewinder air-to-air missile
73 Leading edge flap rotary actuator
74 Port leading edge flap
75 Airframe mounted engine accessory gearbox, shaft driven
76 Leading edge slat drive shaft
77 Auxiliary power turbine
78 Flap hydraulic jack
79 Twin stores carrier
80 Outboard stores pylon
81 Aft retracting mainwheel
82 Mk 83 general purpose bombs
83 AIM-7 Sparrow air-to-air missile
84 Mainwheel shock absorber strut
85 Inboard stores pylon
86 Main undercarriage pivot bearing
87 Hydraulic retraction jack
88 Radar equipment cooling air spill valves

89 External fuel tank
90 Air conditioning system heat exchanger
91 Radar equipment liquid cooling units
92 AAS-38 forward looking infra-red (FLIR) pod
93 Boundary layer splitter plate
94 Air conditioning system water separator
95 Centreline fuel tank
96 Forward fuselage fuel tanks
97 Avionics equipment bay
98 Liquid oxygen converter
99 Nose undercarriage hydraulic retraction jack
100 UHF antenna
101 Retractable boarding ladder
102 Forward retracting nosewheels
103 Nosewheel steering unit
104 Landing/taxiing lamp
105 Carrier approach lights
106 Catapult strop link
107 Control column
108 Rudder pedals
109 Gun gas vents
110 Ammunition feed mechanism
111 Pitot head
112 UHF/IFF antenna
113 Radar equipment module
114 Formation lighting strip
115 Forward radar warning antenna
116 Radar scanner tracking mechanism

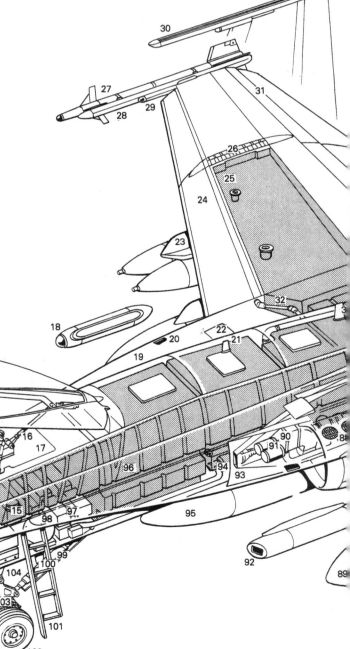

Above: Worker participation is encouraged as the 100th Hornet shipset manufactured by Northrop is officially handed over. The placards remind the workforce of their importance to the project.

the build-up of each section, as are fuel and hydraulic lines. The fuselage, wings and empennage come together at final assembly and the systems are connected and checked. The final stages are the installation of the avionics and engines. After a comprehensive ground check, the aircraft is rolled out ready for its first flight in the hands of a company test pilot.

One production process not touched upon so far, and one which the Hornet utilized more than any other production aircraft before the advent of the Advanced Harrier, is carbon fibre composite material, in this case graphite epoxy. Composites possess high strength to weight and stiffness to weight ratios, have unique flexibility qualities and low thermal conductivity, and are extremely resistant to corrosion and fatigue. In certain applications they can be stronger than steel, stiffer than titanium, and, very significantly, lighter than aluminium. They consist of carbon/graphite or other high-performance fibres bound in epoxy resin or other matrix. In their fibre form they show near-perfect crystalline structure, and it is the parallel alignment of the crystals along the filament axis which provides the great strength and stiffness. The Hornet uses a total of 1,326lb (597kg) of graphite epoxy, giving a weight saving of 25 per cent which, coupled with strength in certain applications plus corrosion resistance, makes the extra cost involved worthwhile.

Although McDonnell Douglas has the world's largest facilities for making aircraft parts from advanced composites – more than 500,000sq ft (46,500m^2) of floor area – only 55 of the Hornet's 220 graphite epoxy panels are made there. This is partly due to the highest concentration of composites occurring on the sections made by Northrop.

Super Hornet

Main gear retraction on the basic Hornet was extremely complex, due to the need for the wheels to clear the Sparrow missiles carried semi-conformally along the outside of the intakes. In the past, undercarriage weaknesses had manifested themselves, in one incident resulting in the death of Hank Kleeman, the first pilot to score a victory with the F-14 Tomcat, a Libyan Su-22. With the replacement of the rather large and ungainly AIM-7 Sparrow by the much smaller and far more lethal AIM-120 AMRAAM, and a completely modified inlet and duct, this could be rectified. A simplified but stronger (to handle the increased weight) and surprisingly, rather lighter, main gear was designed.

Steel and titanium alloy components remained much the same, as did the design acceleration factor of 7.5g. The extensive use of graphite (carbon) epoxy panels on the wing, centre and rear fuselage, and tail surfaces, reduced the weight ratio of aluminium alloy from 50 to 29 per cent. The use of graphite epoxy was also reported to materially reduce RCS but, when one considers that radar emissions can pass through the material and be reflected back from the internal structure, this is not very convincing. Stealth qualities are also reportedly improved by the use of serrated door edges and carefully realigned panel joins. As previously mentioned, the intakes were the subject of a major revision to accommodate greater mass flow.

Composite problems and repairs

The most highly stressed composite panels are the wing skins, and these have titanium inserts, with the metal bonded and tapered into the panel at the root. Sheets of composites are carefully laid on top of each other to get the orientation correct, then bonded in an autoclave under heat and pressure. To cut single ply thickness, a 1,000 watt carbon dioxide (CO_2) laser is used, able to achieve speeds of up to 5-7in/sec (12.7-17.7cm/sec). For multiple ply cuts, a reciprocating 2in (51cm) carbide blade is used, able to cut slightly faster.

Battle damage repairs to composite materials tend to be much more difficult than repairs to the traditional aluminium skinning. Whereas the latter can be patched with a piece of metal and a few rivets, the former is more complex. Delamination is the main problem – separation of the plies that make up the material. If this is serious, the only course is to replace the component completely. For less serious damage, a "band-aid" patch is the answer, while the Israeli method is to cut neatly around the damaged area, then insert a rubber bung! Where the damaged area is too large for this to be done, it can be patched with titanium, usually at the cost of compromising low observability.

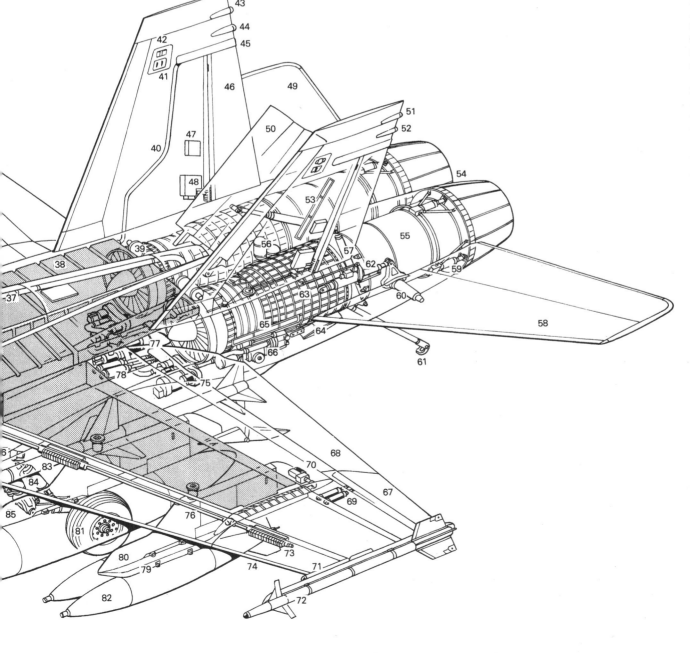

Powerplant

The evolution of the Hornet's General Electric F404 low-bypass turbofan was closely linked with that of the aircraft itself. Starting out as the YJ101, developed specifically to power the Northrop P-530 Cobra and designed for economy and reliability rather than ultimate performance, it first took to the air along with the prototype YF-17 in June 1974. When the Northrop lightweight fighter was upgraded into the McDonnell Douglas F/A-18 strike fighter for the US Navy, the engine grew with the project, gaining in size, weight and thrust to become the F404-GE-400 and finally the F414-GE-400.

The Northrop design concept for a light-weight fighter was twin-engined from the outset. Two engines conferred a lower attrition rate and greater safety, but carried built-in penalties of their own. The structure to contain them was perforce more complex than that of a single-engined fighter, and therefore heavier, and more weight would be added by the duplication of fuel and other engine-related systems. Another penalty which is often overlooked is that two engines have twice the potential to go wrong, and double the amount of servicing and maintenance needed. Ideally then, the engine needed to be simple and easily maintainable, and to have exceptional reliability. At the same time, it had to give the high thrust to weight ratio and rapid throttle response essential for fighter operations.

The choice of engines originally lay between the Rolls-Royce RB.199 and the General Electric GE15. General Electric agreed to develop their engine specifically for the new Northrop fighter, and the choice was made, not that it ever seemed very likely that an American aircraft manufacturer would design a new product around a British engine. Redesignated J101, the new powerplant was first seen in public at the Paris Air Show in May 1971. The GE15 had incorporated technology from the F101 turbofan, then under development to power the Rockwell B-1 supersonic bomber, and many of the ideas were carried over into the J101.

Emphasis in design of the J101 was placed on reliability rather than ultimate performance. Cost was naturally an important consideration, and the 'design to cost' concept was treated as part of the technology of the engine. Although bearing the J prefix used to denote a turbojet, it was in fact a turbofan engine, albeit with a very low (0.2) bypass ratio. General Electric described it at this stage as a continuous-bleed turbojet, with the excess delivery from the low-pressure (LP) compressor being discharged around the core. For this reason it was semi-facetiously referred to as a 'leaky turbo-jet'.

Turbofan advantages

In pure turbojets, the afterburner and efflux nozzle is exposed to the super-heated exhaust gases from the turbine. In a bypass engine, or turbofan, while some of the bypass air mixes with the core exhaust and is burned in the afterburner, the remainder is used to cool the engine external skin and nozzle, and no secondary flow for cooling the engine or exhaust nozzle is required, thereby considerably reducing complexity, drag, weight and cost. A further advantage is gained during afterburning in that the bypass air is still relatively rich in oxygen, whereas the core exhaust has already passed through the engine where much of its oxygen has been consumed.

The J101 was a physically small engine, 12ft 1in (3.68m) long and with a maximum diameter of 2ft 8½in (0.83m).

With three low-pressure and seven high-pressure compressor stages, it achieved a compressor pressure ratio exceeding 20:1, and an annular combustor eliminated the smoky exhaust trails that war has shown lead to MiG pollution. It featured just two turbine stages, one high- and one low-pressure, and a variable converging-diverging nozzle. Its static thrust rating was 9,000lb (4,082kg) at full military power, and 15,000lb (6,800kg) with full afterburner, which gave it a thrust/weight ratio in the region of 8:1.

The J101 was made up of seven major modules, a feature which greatly facilitated ease of repair and maintenance. At the front was the LP compressor, a three-stage axial flow design. Variable inlet guide vanes regulated the engine air flow. Behind it came the HP compressor, of seven stages, which had been developed from the F101 turbofan. Some of the stages featured variable geometry to ensure efficient operation. Under the HP compressor was positioned the electrical-hydro-mechanical engine control module, designed to provide stall-free operation regardless of any rate of throttle movement anywhere in the flight envelope and thrust range. Between the HP compressor and the HP turbine came the combustor.

The next module in line was the single-stage HP turbine driving the HP compressor. Both the blade design and cooling in this stage were derived from the F101. Then came the LP turbine

Above: This head-on view of the F404-GE-400 augmented turbofan strikes the essential keynote of simplicity. From the outset, the accent has been on reliability rather than ultimate performance.

which drove the LP compressor at the front of the engine. This featured convection cooled blades, and convection cooled vane segments brazed into pairs on the nozzle. Finally there was the afterburner module, the design of which was based on that of the tried and proven J85, as used in the F-5E. This had an annular pilot flame holder, and a single-stage main fuel distributor provided smoothly modulated thrust variation.

Having the advantage of using proven technology from the F101, development of the J101 was comparatively rapid, so that initial component testing occupied just 14 months. Testing of the first core engine began in March 1972, and the first complete engine test took place during the following July. In the meantime, the USAF had issued its request for proposals for the LWF, an Air Force contract following at the end of April 1972, and the Y prefix, denoting pre-production was added. The engine thus became the YJ101-GE-100.

Simulated flight testing, carried out at the Arnold Engineering Development Center at Tullahoma, Tennessee, covered the performance envelope from high altitude to sea level supersonic speed, and various speed/AOA combi-

Above: The J101 low bypass ratio turbofan was developed to power the Northrop YF-17. It is often forgotten that for the fly-off against the YF-16 the YF-17 was using early development engines. The J101 was designed for ease of maintenance, with seven modules.

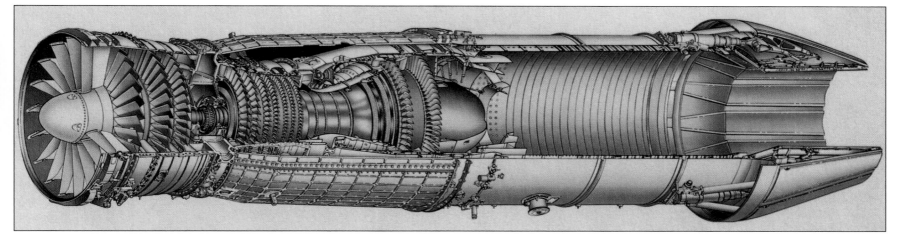

Above: Cutaway view of the F404, showing the simplicity of the layout by comparison with earlier turbojets. Accessories are mounted on the airframe rather than the engine, so it is not 'handed'.

nations. The Prototype Preliminary Flight Rating Test (PPFRT) was completed in December 1973, using a single engine, in just 101 test hours, and the USAF cleared the engine for unrestricted operation throughout the entire flight envelope. The YJ101 first flew in the YF-17 prototype on June 9, 1974.

Altogether, seven engines were used in the short YF-17 flight test programme. A total of 302 flights, amounting to 719 flight hours, were clocked up, during which the YJ101 proved to be remarkably fault-free, not one engine-related delay being recorded. Peacetime

Below: An F404 engine on the test rig. Accelerated mission oriented testing condensed the operational mission cycles, concentrating on areas of maximum stress. Each AMT hour represents five flight hours.

operations are considerably more arduous for an engine than those flown in war. Not only do training sorties tend to last longer, but at least one, and possibly several combats may be simulated, whereas on a war mission none at all may occur. Reliability in peace and survivability in war are the keynotes.

It should be remembered in this context that for the ACF competition the YF-17 was using what was to all intents and purposes an experimental engine, while the rival General Dynamics YF-16 was powered by the Pratt & Whitney F100 engine already developed for the F-15. In fact, the Fort Worth company did consider using two YJ101s in their machine, but the YF-16 was a rather smaller aeroplane than the YF-17, and the weight and drag penalties of accommodating two engines were shown by design studies to be unacceptable. As we have seen earlier, the single-engined design was declared the winner of the competition.

The YF-17's two engines and larger airframe were to prove a blessing in disguise. Although the ACF competition had been lost, the YF-17 was considered

by the Navy to be the most suitable aeroplane for development to meet their multi-role requirement. But to turn a lightweight fighter into a carrier-suitable, multi-mission machine was obviously going to promote it into the midleweight class, and more thrust would be needed if a dramatic and unacceptable reduction in the new fighter's performance was to be avoided.

Upgrading the J101

The obvious answer was to upgrade the YJ101, which so far had proved outstandingly successful. The result was the F404-GE-400, the F designation acknowledging that it was a turbofan rather than a turbojet, although it was at first referred to as an augmented turbojet, while the number in the 400 range denoted that the project was funded by the US Navy. The new engine was very similar to the YJ101, but scaled up by about 10 per cent and with the bypass ratio increased to 0.34, still less than half the ratio of the F100. Corrosion-resistant materials, essential to counter the salt-laden environment of carrier operations, were used throughout.

The F404, at 13ft 2in (4.01m), was 13in (34cm) longer than the YJ101, and the fan diameter was increased by one inch (2.5cm). The mass airflow was raised about 10 per cent to 140lb/sec (63.5kg/sec) and combined with a 50deg F (28deg C) increase in turbine inlet temperature, and the pressure ratio was increased to 25:1. The thrust ratio remained at 8:1. These improvements resulted in a dry thrust of 10,600lb (4,800kg) and a maximum afterburning thrust of 16,000lb (7,250kg). This put it in the same thrust class as the General Electric J79, used to power the ubiquitous Phantom among other aircraft, which could reasonably be described as the F404's predecessor.

To see how far engine technology had progressed in 20 years, a brief comparison is in order. In achieving comparable thrust, the F404 was, at 2,121lb (962kg), barely half the weight and two-thirds the length of the J79. A 25:1 pressure ratio achieved with just ten stages compared very favourably with the 13.5:1 ratio of the J79's 17 stages, while the total number of components per engine was just 14,400 against 22,000.

The small size of the F404 contributed directly to the weight saving: fewer parts, only three structural frames and sumps, with their attendant lubrication systems, and just five main bearings. Yet weight reduction, although important, was not the only consideration, because the F404 could have been made lighter still. As with the YJ101, design to cost was an integral part of the programme and in several areas weight was the trade-off to keep cost down. Typically, these were the use of solid rather than hollow compressor blades, cast rather than fabricated structures, and solid metal rather than honeycomb material in casings and ducts. Steel was also used instead of titanium where the substitution was found cost-effective.

Powering a carrier fighter is the most demanding role for an engine in the entire aviation spectrum. It must be both reliable and durable, able to withstand not only the thrust and environmental changes encountered in the fighter mission, but also the repeated stresses of catapult launches and arrested landings, for which a design factor of 11g was built in. Furthermore, the deck idle thrust must be very low, so as not to cause embarrassment to either the pilot or deck-handling crew in a crowded area.

The development programme for the F404 was the most comprehensive for an engine ever. While components were originally scheduled to undergo some 5,000 test hours, in the event about 8,000 hours were clocked up, and 14 development engines underwent more than 13,000 factory test hours over a period just short of five years. The first F404 engine test took place in January 1977, a month ahead of schedule, and quickly demonstrated the required sea-level performance, and the first of six engines arrived at the Naval Air Propulsion Test Center (NAPTC) at Trenton, New Jersey, shortly afterward. Nine engines were delivered in 1978 and a further 24 in 1979. PPRFT took place in May 1978, and the first flight, in Hornet 1, in November of the same year; the Model Qualification Test (MQT) was completed in July 1979; and the first production engine was handed over in January 1980.

Engine test modes
Testing took place in three basic modes. The Simulated Mission Endurance Test (SMET) duplicated the throttle movements and power settings used in the fighter and attack missions. Three tests were held, each of 750 hours, approximating to three years of operational service. The Accelerated Mission Test (AMT) used the SMET missions as a

Above: The nozzles of the F404 are variable, with a 12-petal external cover. Here they are shown in the fully closed flight idle position.

basis, condensing the operational cycles and concentrating on the areas where damage was most likely to be caused. Each AMT hour represented five hours of operational usage, so that the 2,000 plus hours of AMT logged in the development programme represented more than 10,000 flight hours. Finally, Accelerated Service Testing (AST), the so-called Hornet Hustle, was flown by Hornets 9 and T2. The AST was a 1,000-hour programme, the first half of which was flown by McDonnell Douglas test pilots and the remainder by Navy pilots. The flight programme was very intensive: on three separate occasions, Hornet 9 flew six sorties per day.

F404/J79 comparison

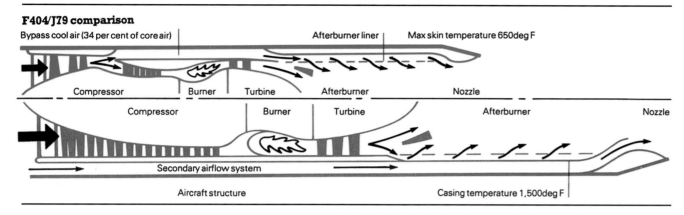

Left: Comparison of the F404 (top) with the J79, used to power the F-4 and F-104. Comparable thrust is achieved for half the weight and two-thirds the length of the earlier engine.

Below left: The auxiliary power unit (APU) gives the Hornet a self-starting capability and also provides power for systems checks from internal sources.

Below: Engine fires are extinguished by selective discharge into any of three areas: starboard engine and AMAD, port engine and AMAD, or the auxiliary power unit.

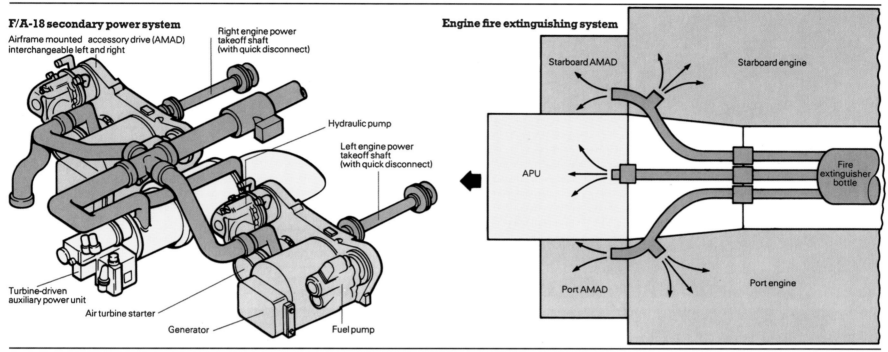

F/A-18 secondary power system

Engine fire extinguishing system

The F404 flight test programme proved remarkably trouble-free. The engine was shown to be extremely stall-resistant at high AOA and various combinations of yaw and sideslip, and no compressor stall was experienced in the first 300 flights from Patuxent River. This was in part due to the careful integration of the airframe and inlet design, particularly the LEX, with the engine. The LEX reduced the angle of the airflow into

Below: The lack of requirement for Mach 2 performance allowed simple fixed inlets to be used, with a saving in both weight and cost.

the inlets to approximately half the angle of attack. Some stalls, afterburner blow-outs, and engine flameouts were later experienced at AOA of between 50deg and 90deg, but the stalls quickly corrected themselves and both engine and afterburner were found to relight automatically. The engine was also found to be wonderfully responsive, accelerating from idle to full afterburner in less than four seconds, and throttle slams from flight idle to maximum power and back were tested and found to cause no problems.

All this is not to suggest that the F404 was entirely fault-free. The specified acceleration time from Mach 0.8 to Mach 1.6 was not achieved, although the Hornet showed that it could match even F-15s in drag races up to Mach 1.2. Certain shortfalls were revealed in specific fuel consumption – the amount of fuel burned per unit of thrust per hour – but although these could only partially be compensated, this was not felt to be particularly serious. The sfc of the F404 at military power is 0.85lb per pound of thrust per hour. Other engine-related problems were a single case of a No. 4 bearing failure, and turbine blade fractures, which are described in the previous chapter.

One fault was discovered as a result of a small power loss to both engines in the same aircraft, following relight tests. With the engines stripped down, the blades of the HP turbine were found to be worn approximately 20 mil (0.5mm). Checks made on other engines revealed a wear range of between 4 and 8 mil (0.1-0.2mm). It was concluded that a temperature difference between the blades and the casing had caused rubbing and resultant wear. As the performance of both the affected engines was still above specification, no action was taken and they were re-installed.

Much more serious was the engine failure that led to the loss of Hornet T2 on September 8, 1980. The LP turbine disc suffered a catastrophic fracture and flew to pieces, causing irremediable damage. The casing of the F404 is designed to retain fractured turbine blades, which are, after all, a fairly common failure with any engine, but great lumps of a 90lb (41kg) metal disc revolving at very high speeds contained far too much kinetic energy to be stopped. Parts of the disc were not recovered, which hampered the investigation into the cause of the crash.

At that time, 33 flight test engines had been delivered. The discs in 12 of these had been formed with conventional castings, while the remainder had been manufactured by a 'fine mesh' powder metallurgy process known as hot iso-static forming developed by General Electric. In this process the raw material, called Rene 95, was reduced to a powder before being poured into a mould where it was subjected to extreme heat and pressure, the end result being known as '60 mesh'. The failed LP turbine disc was of 60 mesh, and turbine discs of this material were replaced immediately pending the results of the enquiry.

The findings were inconclusive, due to the fracture having occurred in a part of the disc that was never found, but it was thought that either a flaw in the material or a defect in the manufacturing process was responsible, and that the incident could be described as a 'worst case' event. General recommendations included redesigning all F404 rotor parts for maximum life. The turbine disc was to be strengthened, and holes formed between the existing holes to reduce stress concentration. The isostatic forming and forging process was not fully understood; in an on-going technology programme the process had been refined still further to produce '150 mesh' which tests showed to have four times the reliability of 60 mesh, which was used in all further engines.

Maintainability

Ease of maintenance is another facet of reliability. In line with the entire Hornet concept, the F404 engines were designed for maximum maintainability. One feature carried over from the YJ101 was the modular construction, which allowed entire sections to be replaced rapidly with a minimum expenditure of manhours. It will be readily appreciated that in the cramped confines of an aircraft carrier at sea, both manpower and space is at a premium.

Special consideration was given to rapid engine changes. Unlike most twin-engined designs, there are no left and right engines on the Hornet; any engine can be fitted on either side. This was achieved by mounting engine accessories on the airframe instead of on the engine. The engine has only ten connections, or interfaces, with the aircraft and can be changed without special equipment being used, 'within the shadow of the aircraft'. Large engine bay doors under the rear fuselage open inward toward the centreline, exposing everything that needs servicing, all of which are mounted on the underside quadrant of the engine. The engine is changed by lowering it vertically out of the bay. With practice, a four-man team can complete an engine change in 20 minutes, although demonstration teams have often beaten this figure.

Servicing has been made particularly easy. There are no scheduled overhauls; just what is called 'on-condition' maintenance, which means putting right what

Left: The F404 was designed in seven modules for ease of repair and maintenance. The engine is suspended vertically to allow the modules to be disconnected.

Below: Engine removal only takes place when remedial action is necessary, or when a module reaches the end of its scheduled life. With practice, a four-man crew can change an engine in less than half an hour, and any engine can fit either side.

needs attention. The necessity for this is established by an In-Flight Engine Condition Monitoring System, or IECMS, in which trained electrons whiz about the engine to check that all is well. Faults are displayed in the form of flags in the cockpit to warn the pilot, and read-outs for maintenance personnel. Engine removal therefore only takes place when a fault is recorded that requires remedial action, or one of the modules has reached the end of its scheduled life.

Borescope inspection

Apart from the IECMS, each engine contains 13 ports to allow internal inspection by borescope, although only nine of these are accessible with the engine installed. The F404 should require workshop maintenance less than twice for every 1,000 flight hours, and the target mean time between maintenance actions is 175 flight hours. This compares well with the corresponding figures for the J79, which are 3.1 per 1,000 hours and 90 hours respectively. The mission abort rate for the F404 is once every 2,000 hours.

Engine accessories, called line-replaceable units, are placed on the underside of the engine and are replaceable through the engine bay door. Each engine has an Airframe Mounted Auxiliary Drive (AMAD) System, which drives a fuel pump, a hydraulic pump, and a 40kVA General Electric VSCF generator.

An unusual feature of the Hornet is that the pilot can climb aboard and start the engines just as though he were in a car

Left: Care and concentration as the engine dolly is positioned ready for the start of an engine change. Such changes are done 'within the shadow of the aircraft' as a matter of routine – an important consideration at sea.

vents and dumps are located on the top of the fins. In-flight refuelling can be used to increase the range; a retractable probe is located in a compartment at the top of the starboard side of the nose, just ahead of the cockpit.

A slight problem encountered with the Hornet's fuel system during the FSD programme was that the specification requirement of 10 seconds of normal engine operation at negative g was not being consistently achieved. The Parker jet pumps, mounted in a small reservoir designed to trap sufficient fuel for 10 seconds of negative g operation, tended to pump air pockets trapped in the fuel as readily as the fuel itself. The remedy was to replace the jet pumps with Sundstrand turbine-driven fuel boost pumps, which would not suck air.

The F404-GE-400 was capable of still greater things, as was evidenced by its selection for the abortive Northrop F-20 Tigershark and the far more successful Swedish JAS 39 Gripen, both of which demanded considerably more thrust. In USN service the next step was the F404-GE-402, rated at 17,600lb (7,983kg) maximum thrust and 11,925lb (5,409kg) thrust in military power. This was achieved by using monocrystal turbine materials to allow greater turbine entry temperatures, modified electrical hydro-mechanical control schedules, and ceramic matrix composites in the afterburner secondary flaps and seals.

Much more power was demanded for the larger and heavier Super Hornet, and this was provided by the F414-GE-400, rated at 22,019lb (9,988kg) maximum, and 14,011lb (6,355kg) military thrust. The core was evolved from the F412 developed for the cancelled A-12, with a larger fan: a new low pressure turbine, and an afterburner developed by GE for the F120 which would hopefully power the F-22. With a pressure ratio of 30:1 and a thrust/weight ratio of 9:1, it also featured a Full-Authority Digital Control (FADEC) unit.

The F414 needed a 16 per cent increase in mass airflow, which was in part provided by new trapezoidal intakes. The first fan stage had removable blades as a bird-strike-tolerant feature, while the second and third stages featured combined blade/discs (blisks) to reduce weight and cost.

(well, almost), which saves a lot of ground support equipment, or 'yellow stuff', from cluttering up the carrier deck. The secret lies in the Garrett AiResearch Auxiliary Power Unit, or APU, which is mounted on the aircraft centreline just ahead of the twin engine bays, and is accessible through a quick-release door on the underside of the fuselage. It is a compact unit, weighing 112lb (51kg), and it develops 200hp (150kW).

The APU is started from the cockpit by battery power. It then supplies high-pressure air to the turbine starter to start the engine. Once one engine has been started, a power shaft drives the AMAD and thereby the pumps and generator,

Below: Flaps down for the photo call, an F-18A Hornet lights the afterburner for the benefit of the camera. The nozzles are small by present-day standards and are a direct aid to reducing the risk of detection.

so that cross-bleed air can be used to start the second engine. Of course, the engines can always be started from an external power source if necessary.

The APU has another valuable function. By disengaging the accessory drive from the engines, all the aircraft systems can be run independently of either the engines or an external power source. This enables a full ground checkout to be made of all systems that require electrical power, hydraulic power, fuel pressure, or cooling, entirely from the Hornet's own resources. The APU can also be used to supplement air conditioning on a very hot day when engine bleed air proves insufficient for both the environmental control and avionics bay cooling systems.

Fuel system

Internal fuel is contained in four fuselage and two wing tanks, which are self-sealing and protected by foam in the wing

and fuselage voids. Shaft-driven motive flow boost pumps in each AMAD unit pump fuel from the main wing and fuselage tanks to the engine feed tanks. The fuel, either JP-4 or JP-5, is supplied to the engines from separate feed tanks which interconnect for cross-feeding and are self-contained and self-sealing to provide a 'get you home' facility if the main tanks are damaged. The only fuel lines to enter the engine compartments are a main feed to each engine fuel control. This minimizes the chance of a broken or damaged fuel line spilling fuel into the hot engine compartment.

The total internal fuel capacity is 11,000lb (4,990kg) which can be augmented by three external tanks each containing 350US gall (1,324lit), bringing the maximum fuel load to approximately 17,800lb (8,075kg). A single refuelling point on the left side of the front fuselage is used for both ground refuelling and purging the fuel system, while the fuel

Avionics

It is not enough for a modern fighter to have outstanding performance and handling qualities. It also needs clever systems for target location, weapons delivery, threat detection, navigation and communications if it is both to survive and to carry out its mission successfully. Current technology allows very sophisticated systems to be designed small enough to fit a single-seat aeroplane, and the Hornet's cockpit is a *tour de force*, presenting the information in such a manner that one man can fly the demanding spectrum of missions required of an aircraft designed for both fleet defence and long-range attack.

At the heart of the Hornet's complex avionics system is the cockpit, where all the information comes together for use by the pilot. Much of the controversy surrounding the aircraft has been based on quite justifiable doubts as to whether one man could handle all the information to be thrown at him and still fly the mission successfully. Previous Navy fighters, the F-4 Phantom and the F-14 Tomcat both had two-man crews, and they could be pretty hard-pressed at times.

The challenge to McDonnell Douglas was formidable: to take the Northrop YF-17 lightweight fighter and dress it out as a carrier-borne multi-role combat aircraft involved a tremendous increase both in the complexity of the systems and in the amount of information that would need to be presented. The Hornet had to be able to replace both the Phantom and the Corsair, and also to supplement the Tomcat in the fleet defence role; the systems and instrumentation requirement for all these tasks was enormous. Moreover, the ejection seat, raked back at an angle of 18deg as compared with the 15deg of the F-15's seat, brought the pilot's knees higher, reducing the instrument panel and console area available to only about 60 per cent of the usable area in the F-15 cockpit, but with more systems to control and display.

Starting from scratch

To design an effective cockpit, McDonnell Douglas started with the proverbial clean sheet of paper. Mission analysis was the first step. Whether flying an air-to-air or air-to-ground mission, the pilot would have up to three different air-to-air weapons, a combination chosen from more than two dozen air-to-ground weapons, all the aircraft systems and about 250 switchology functions to handle. Originally, the A-18 version was to have a moving colour map display that was not required in the F-18, while the Marine Corps wanted one UHF and one VHF radio in their aircraft rather than the two UHF sets that were to be the standard Navy fit. These differences were resolved by fitting moving map displays in all Hornets and adopting the Navy radio fit as standard.

Mission analysis identified three main workload areas: (a) weapon and sensor management during combat, in which time was critical; (b) communications, navigation, and identification (CNI) systems management throughout the entire flight spectrum, with special emphasis on carrier operations in conditions of poor visibility; and (c) systems mode management and miscellaneous requirements, which were usually not time-critical, but still occupied valuable console space as well as units of the pilot's mental capacity.

Cockpits of other aircraft were studied, in particular the company's own F-15, and work done as part of the US Navy Advanced Integrated Modular Instrumentation Systems programme

Above: Hornet pilots have been known to describe the cockpit as being "out of Star Wars". The displays reflected in this pilot's visor heighten the impression.

Top: The planar array antenna of the Hughes APG-63 radar is quite small, a fact made apparent by this assembly line photograph.

Right: One-man operability is the keynote of the Hornet cockpit layout. Information is called up as required on the CRT displays at the touch of a few of the surrounding buttons.

was examined, as was the cockpit proposed by McDonnell Douglas for the Model 263 VFX contender. McDonnell Douglas had also been building a large simulator complex which had been extensively used during the design stage of the F-15. The simulator was heavily involved during the design and development of the Hornet, not least for the cockpit layout, in which both test and service pilots could try out proposed systems and suggest improvements.

The final solution lay in more intensive use of computer-aided controls and displays than on any previous aeroplane. The time-critical combat weapon and sensor management was achieved via the hands on throttle and stick (HOTAS) concept pioneered on the F-15. A pilot in combat usually flies with his left hand on the throttle(s) and his right hand on the control column: using HOTAS, all necessary switches for weaponry or essential data displays are mounted on one or the other of these controls. The pilot is therefore able to control the necessary weapons, sensors or displays without moving his hands away from either control, and without taking his eyes off either the target or the head-up display (HUD). Management of the CNI functions was incorporated in the up-front control (UFC) panel located in the centre of the dash, while systems mode management is accomplished by switches surrounding three head-down cathode ray tube (CRT) displays.

Cockpit displays

The most striking aspect of the Hornet cockpit is the almost total lack of dials and conventional instrumentation. Prominent are the three 5in (12.7cm) square CRTs on the instrument panel. These are linked to the two mission computers and also the HUD. The HUD is of the twin-combiner type, with a comparatively wide 20deg×20deg field of view; its optics are located behind the CNI panel, and it is the main flight instrument for both weapon delivery and navigation, including both manual and automatic carrier landing modes. Data such as speed, heading, attitude, AOA, altitude, g loading, steering commands and cues for attack are projected either

as symbols or in alpha-numeric format on the combiner glass and focussed at infinity, so that the pilot is enabled to assimilate the information without losing sight of the target or the carrier deck.

CRTs were chosen for the three headdown displays (HDDs) for their sheer versatility in showing different kinds of information in a small space. It is easier and quicker for the pilot to assimilate the information that he requires than from a conventional presentation because flight, sensor and weapon information are all grouped conveniently together on the CRT display. This has had the effect of allowing the conventional armament panel and more than a dozen electro-mechanical servoed instruments

of dubious reliability to be deleted from the aircraft cockpit. CRTs also offer the best combination of contrast and resolution, two conflicting requirements, in bright sunlight.

Two CRTs are set high on the instrument panel; the multi-function display (MFD) on the right, and the master monitor display (MMD) on the left. Manufactured by Kaiser Aerospace, they are identical and interchangeable units: in the event of a failure of one, their functions could be interchangeable in flight and the mission would not have to be aborted. Each contains symbol generators, capable at need, depending on the complexity of the modes, of driving two or three displays, while the HUD can be driven by either. Each CRT has 20 push-button controls around its perimeter, which allow different operating modes or stored programs to be called up, and the software-programmed display processors can operate all the computerized displays. Between them, they have the added advantage of allowing the pilot to select the information he wants and present it where he wants it.

The MFD is the primary sensor display for radar attack and radar mapping information, and the digital computer gives a processed and clutter-free presentation. Also presented in an alpha-numeric format is flight information such as speed, attitude, weapon status, altitude etc. The symbology can be either cursive or TV raster (525 or 875 lines). The MMD is the primary warning, electro-optical and infra-red sensor and armament display, as well as projecting cautionary and advisory information on the aircraft systems.

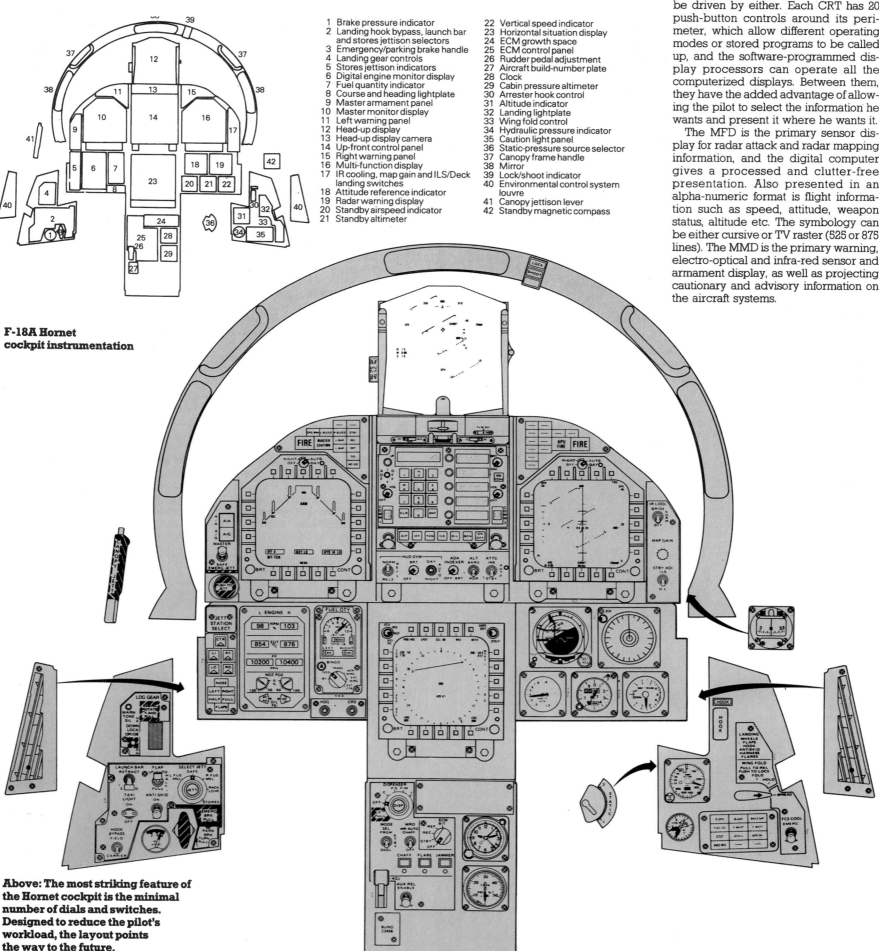

1 Brake pressure indicator
2 Landing hook bypass, launch bar and stores jettison selectors
3 Emergency/parking brake handle
4 Landing gear controls
5 Stores jettison indicators
6 Digital engine monitor display
7 Fuel quantity indicator
8 Course and heading lightplate
9 Master armament panel
10 Master monitor display
11 Left warning panel
12 Head-up display
13 Head-up display camera
14 Up-front control panel
15 Right warning panel
16 Multi-function display
17 IR cooling, map gain and ILS/Deck landing switches
18 Attitude reference indicator
19 Radar warning display
20 Standby airspeed indicator
21 Standby altimeter
22 Vertical speed indicator
23 Horizontal situation display
24 ECM growth space
25 ECM control panel
26 Rudder pedal adjustment
27 Aircraft build-number plate
28 Clock
29 Cabin pressure altimeter
30 Arrester hook control
31 Altitude indicator
32 Landing lightplate
33 Wing fold control
34 Hydraulic pressure indicator
35 Caution light panel
36 Static-pressure source selector
37 Canopy frame handle
38 Mirror
39 Lock/shoot indicator
40 Environmental control system louvre
41 Canopy jettison lever
42 Standby magnetic compass

F-18A Hornet cockpit instrumentation

Above: The most striking feature of the Hornet cockpit is the minimal number of dials and switches. Designed to reduce the pilot's workload, the layout points the way to the future.

Left (from left): The Hornet's primary cockpit displays are the master monitor display (MMD), horizontal situation display (HSD), head-up display (HUD) and multi-function display (MFD). Functions of the MMD and MFD are interchangeable, and either can drive the HUD.

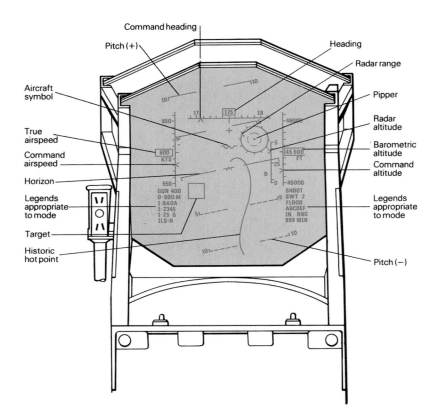

Command heading

Pitch (+)

Heading

Radar range

Aircraft symbol

Pipper

Radar altitude

True airspeed

Barometric altitude

Command airspeed

Command altitude

Horizon

Legends appropriate to mode

Legends appropriate to mode

Target

Historic hot point

Pitch (−)

F/A-18 head-up display symbology

and a further seven on the stick, but experience gained on the F-15, which also uses HOTAS, plus extensive simulator tests, and, of course, the rapidly mounting flight time of the Hornet itself, has shown that the use of HOTAS lies well within the abilities of the average pilot. In this connection, it should be noted that not all the functions will be needed at once, but just a few at a time to meet the needs of the moment. Incorrect mode selection is always a potential problem, but the error becomes instantly apparent on the feedback on the visual displays, and corrections can be made almost instantaneously.

Only three of the HOTAS switches are primary to air combat; others are secondary, or are related to carrier landing functions. The primary switches are the Air-to-Air Weapons selector and the Automatic Lock-on selector on the stick, and the Target Designator control on the left-hand throttle. It should be remembered that the Hornet has two engines and therefore two throttles; while the throttles are so shaped as to be operated as a single control, there can be no guarantee that this will always be the case.

The Air-to-Air Weapons selector has three positions for selection of Sparrows, Sidewinders or guns as appropriate. The selection cues the radar automatically to the nominal parameters for the weapon chosen for range and azimuth, elevation and pulse repetition frequency. This has the added advantage of allowing the pilot to vary his search pattern by altering the weapon selected. For long-range work, Sparrow is selected and the radar automatically enters range-while-search

in digital form using mechanical drum counters. A departure for the Navy is the use of white cockpit lighting at night. In the unlikely event of complete power failure or loss of displays, standby instruments are located at the bottom right of the dash. They consist of pneumatic airspeed, altitude, and vertical speed indicators, and a gyroscopic Attitude Director Indicator.

HOTAS control
Not quite as way out as the displays, but still very advanced, is the HOTAS concept, which gives the pilot control of the major sensors, weapons, and displays without removing his hands from the throttle and stick; which of course is where he wants them in the heat and confusion of combat. No longer is he reduced to groping in the cockpit to find the correct switch while trying to maintain visual contact with a distant opponent.

The HOTAS system looks at first sight as though the pilot will need the manual dexterity of a concert pianist to operate the ten switches mounted on the throttles

Left: Typical HUD symbology, showing all the information the pilot needs as he closes on his target. Among the data displayed are range, height, speed and weapon selected — in this case the gun, which is shown as having 400 rounds remaining.

Below: The original Ferranti combined map and electronic display unit on which the Hornet horizontal situation display is based. A coloured film map is projected on the screen, and additional navigation information can be displayed as required.

At a lower level, below the UFC panel, is a third CRT. This is the horizontal situation display (HSD), based on the British Ferranti system but repackaged and licence-built in America by Bendix. It consists of a coloured, film-projected moving map acting both as a horizontal position indicator and as a display for attack information such as time/range to target, Tacan steering and INS waypoint steering commands, and it updates position as required. It also presents electronic warfare and threat indications. The HSD has push-button controls in the same manner as the MFD and MMD, which call up the information requested. An ingenious feature of the HSD is that it has a lens system that effectively forms an aperture 10in×7in (25.4cm×17.8cm) for the pilot to see the display in bright lighting conditions as though it were hooded. At night, the pilot can lean slightly forward, which effectively removes the aperture to a point outside his line of vision and prevents him being dazzled by the display. Almost every avionic system is linked to the three CRTs, as described below in connection with the specific functions.

Situated between the MMD and MFD, and below the HUD, is the up-front display, which deals with CNI functions. Supplied by McDonnell Douglas Electronics, it is so positioned that only a slight glance down from the HUD is necessary. The bottom row of buttons, reading from left to right, select autopilot, Identification/Friend or Foe (IFF), Tactical Air Navigation (TACAN), Instrument Landing System (ILS), Data Link, and Beacon, with an on/off switch on the extreme right. Just above, at extreme left and extreme right, are the switches controlling the two UHF radios. Other switches control the Automatic Direction Finding (ADF) system and essentials such as brightness, volume, etc.

The main area of the panel is taken up with a keyboard and electronic readout panels. The pilot selects a function and the readout panels display the options on that particular function; the desired option(s) are selected and the data is entered via the keyboard. The UFC panel then automatically clears, ready for further use. All controls are within easy reach of either hand, and with practice numerous CNI functions can be performed under instrument conditions.

The remaining instruments are nearly, but not quite, standard. Master warning lights are used to indicate that all is not well, but the detailed information on the malfunction appears immediately in a corner of either the MMD or the MFD. Engine and fuel state data is presented

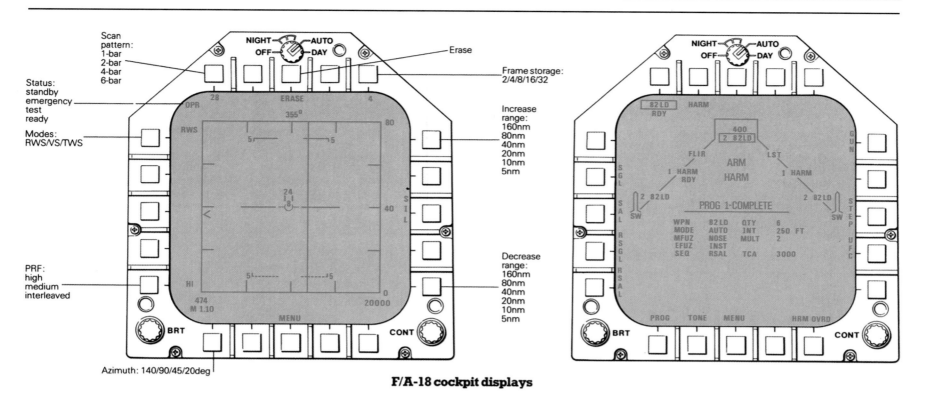

F/A-18 cockpit displays

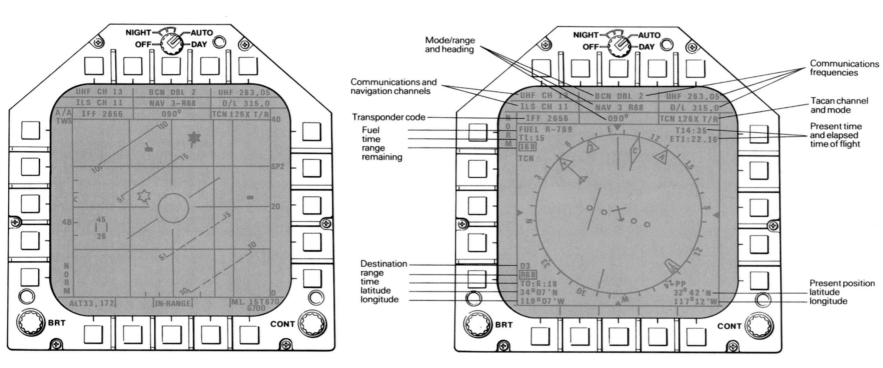

mode, out to a maximum of 80nm (147km). For Sidewinder, the search range automatically switches to 20nm (37km), with four-bar elevation scans and plus or minus 70deg in azimuth; while for guns, the search range reduces to 5nm (9km), with six-bar scans and plus or minus 45deg in azimuth. A check on the weapon selected is given on the HDDs.

The Automatic Lock-on selector is also three position and offers three modes for visual lock. These take the forms of: (1) a 3deg boresight circle on the HUD for pinpoint fly to lock-on; (2) a 20deg circle on the HUD, which gives rapid search and target acquisition within the HUD field of view; and (3) a vertical scan racetrack which opens off the top of the HUD. This is used for off-boresight lock-on, and the acquisition method used for a visual target is for the pilot to roll his aircraft until the target appears to be positioned directly above the centre of the front canopy arch. Tightening the turn then pulls the target (relatively speaking) down into the radar acquisition area, or even better, into the HUD field of view.

In all these modes target lock-on is automatic and is displayed on both the HUD and the MFD, and a 'shoot' symbol comes up on both displays when the electrons are satisfied that a satisfactory firing solution has been achieved for the weapon selected. Back-up is supplied by flashing light indicators for both lock and shoot on the top right-hand quadrant of the canopy arch. This is particularly useful when the off-boresight mode is being used, as the pilot will be visually tracking the target at a high angle-off well outside the HUD field of view in many cases.

The Target Designator Control (TDC) mounted on the left throttle is an isometric/force transducer switch which moves the designator symbol on the displays in any direction. To describe its function as simply as possible, if the pilot wishes to alter a radar mode or function, whether it be range, elevation, scan, mode, azimuth or whatever, he uses the switch to move the TDC brackets on the displays to cover whichever parameter he wishes to change, then operates the switch until the desired parameter appears. Alternatively, he can slew the brackets to cover a target symbol then, by pressing the button, designate and lock on to it. The TDC can also be used to alter the line of sight of the infra-red and laser sensors if they are carried.

Other combat-related components of the HOTAS system are the gun/missile trigger and air-to-ground weapon

Above: Typical cockpit displays. Top left is the radar display for the range-while-search mode, using high PRFs out to a distance of 80nm (147km). Top right is a stores management display, showing a bomb release programme for the six Mk 82 LD bombs; Harm and Sidewinder are also indicated. Bottom left is air-to-air track-while-scan radar mode, while bottom right is a sample horizontal situation and mission data display.

Below: Fighter pilots have always needed to fly with one hand on the throttles and the other on the control column, but as weapons and sensors grew more complex this became more difficult to achieve. The solution, pioneered on the F-15 and subsequently adopted for the F-18, is for all time-critical functions to be mounted on these controls, using the HOTAS (hands on throttle and stick) approach pioneered by the F-15.

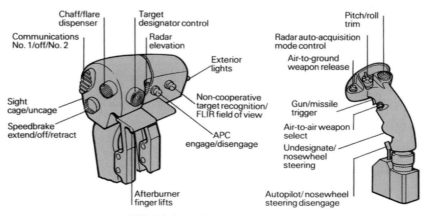

F/A-18 throttle and control stick

release switch which are mounted on the control column; the airbrake control; the infra-red seeker head cage/uncage button for the Sidewinders, which automatically slaves the IR sensor to the line of sight of the radar; a three-position communications selector switch; the three-position chaff/flare dispenser switch; and the radar elevation control, which are all on the left-hand throttle; and the non-co-operative target recognition/FLIR field of view control on the right throttle. Non-combat related functions are the autopilot/nosewheel steering disengage switch; the nosewheel steering cancel switch; and the pitch and roll trim, which are all on the control column; and the automatic power compensator engage/disengage switch (part of the automatic carrier landing system); exterior lighting switch; and finger lifts to engage ground idle power, all mounted on the throttles.

The pilot sits on a Martin Baker SJU-5/A ejection seat which is based on the tried and proven Mk 10. It provides a zero speed, zero altitude escape capability, and is effective up to 600kt (1,110km/h). Excellent all-round visibility is provided by a tear-drop shaped canopy made of laminated acrylic plastics. Visibility is possibly not quite as good as from the F-16, but there is little in it, and it is certainly good enough to make Fishbed and Flogger drivers suck their teeth. Oddly enough, two different manufacturers are involved, PPG Indus-

tries making the windshield while the canopy itself is from Swedlow.

The Hornet is more than just an aeroplane; it is a fine example of an integrated weapons system, and it is difficult to single out any one item as being particularly outstanding, especially as the degree of integration is such that almost everything seems interlocked with everything else. Having said that, the AN/APG-65 radar, manufactured by the Hughes Aircraft Company Radar Systems Group, is a fine piece of kit containing many advanced features never before incorporated in a tactical aircraft. The requirements were stringent: to produce a radar which lacked nothing in the air-to-air modes, and was equally good for navigation and air-to-ground functions; to be one-man operable and small enough to fit a medium-sized fighter; to be easily maintainable; and to have an unprecedented level of reliability, with a target MTBF of no less than 106 hours. Proposals were originally submitted by both Hughes and Westinghouse, with the Hughes design being selected at the end of 1977.

APG-65 radar
The APG-65 is a coherent pulse-Doppler radar operating in the X-band (8-12.5GHz), which is fairly standard for airborne radars as it requires a fairly small antenna – an important consideration when space is restricted, as it always

is in fighters. Coherent pulse-Doppler radar dates back to the late 1950s, when the travelling wave tube (TWT) was developed.

The function of the TWT is to increase the level of power of a signal that is fed into it. Essentially, a radar sends out massive signals and gets minute ones back in return, and the more powerful the signal transmitted, the better the return. Using a signal from a continuously running coherent oscillator, the TWT produced pulses suitable for radar in which every pulse is exactly in phase with the preceding and following pulses. This enabled the Doppler shift – the observable frequency change when the range between the transmitter and the receiver is altering – to be used in radar for the first time.

One immediate advantage was that for the first time a low-flying aircraft could be detected against the ground returns, or radar echoes from the surface, since a moving target gives a shift in frequency returns which makes its echo different from the echoes bouncing back from the ground. Digital computers then sort out the echoes that are different. Most returns are likely to be shown to be moving in conformity with the flight path of the radar-carrying aircraft, and as these are in most cases the echoes from the ground, a threshold can be established, the unwanted returns filtered out, and only those which are not showing a Doppler shift which is in conformity with

the flight path are presented on the radar display. These are likely to be targets.

In the air-to-air mode, the system contains two weaknesses. There is little point in detecting a horse and cart simply because it is moving, so a bottom limit must be set to the velocity of non-flight-path-conformal echoes. This is usually about 90mph (144km/h). Consequently, slow-flying machines such as helicopters can be filtered out, while very fast moving surface vehicles can be acquired. Furthermore, an aircraft flying at a right angle to the flight path is also likely to be filtered out, as its relative velocity will not exceed the threshold limit. Of course, this only applies to a radar searching downwards against the ground clutter; against a clear sky background it will not apply.

Pulse repetition frequency
A fundamental choice to be made with pulse-Doppler radar is the pulse repetition frequency (PRF). The range is wide: 100,000 transmitted pulses per second and upwards is classed as high PRF, while 1,000 pulses per second is low PRF. In between these extremes comes medium PRF, which, as we shall see, is very useful. High PRF has one great advantage: the greater the number of transmitted pulses per second, the higher the average power radiated, and the higher the average power, the greater the detection range. A high PRF waveform is also excellent at detecting a target coming in head-on with a high closing speed, but it is not so good at detecting targets with a low closure rate, such as would be encountered from the tail-on aspect with a low overtaking rate. Neither is it much good at measuring range; although a low degree of frequency modulation (FM) can be impressed on the pulse as a sort of identity tag, ranging information gained in this manner is not very accurate.

The inaccuracy inherent in measuring range in the high PRF mode stems from the short time lapse between each pulse. It is difficult to tell which pulse has engendered which echo, and ambi-

Left: The APG-65 radar runs out on rails for ease of access. The antenna uses electric drive, and the WRA modules are apparent.

Below: Much of the flight testing with the APG-65 radar was carried out by this specially modified T-39D Sabreliner. The picture at left is also of this aircraft.

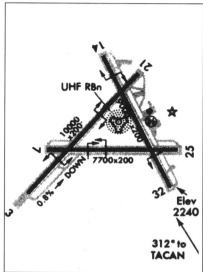

Above: Doppler beam sharpening techniques give excellent ground mapping resolution. Compare the upper picture of a DBS patch mode map with the airfield layout below it. Computer techniques are used to give a vertical picture.

guities arise in consequence. Low frequency PRF has much better ranging capability, the time lapse between pulses enabling a return to be received from a considerable distance before the next pulse is transmitted, which removes the ambiguity of high PRF.

A compromise solution of medium PRF was first used operationally in the F-15 radar, the APG-63. Medium PRF confers many advantages in the medium-range detection and accurate tracking of small, high-speed targets, the accuracy being sufficient to enable data for weapons delivery to be processed. In the APG-65, a medium PRF waveform is interleaved with high PRF. The medium PRF used is not a constant waveform, but a series of PRFs in the medium band. This in practice gives good average solutions to the problems posed by the varying velocities of different targets. The PRF variation is accomplished by the programmable gridded TWT.

The use of rapidly varying PRFs was made possible by the use, for the first time on a production fighter, of a programmable signal processor, which has the staggering ability to perform up to 7.2 million operations per second; what are called real time calculations. This allows incoming echoes to be sampled and analyzed to adjust and set the processing boundaries. Range gate and filter configurations are pre-programmed on software, unlike those of the APG-63, which give a fixed choice of selections. On the

Right: The USM-469 Radar Test System for the APG-65 radar installed at NAS Lemoore, California.

Below: The WRA modules in the APG-65 are designed for speed and ease of replacement in the field.

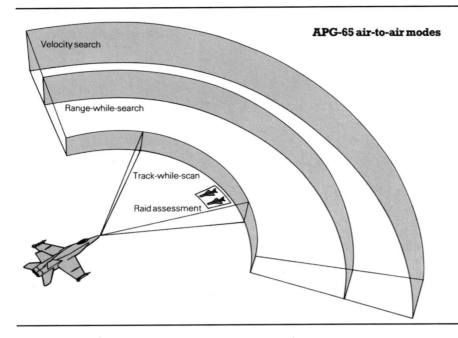

APG-65 air-to-air modes

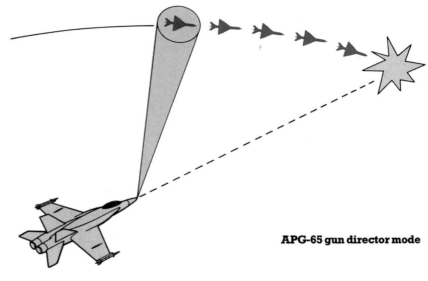

APG-65 gun director mode

Hornet, if new modes are needed due to the requirements of new weapons or changes in the nature of a threat, or existing modes need modification, a software change will suffice.

The APG-65 is, considering its capability, remarkably small. It weighs just 340lb (154kg) excluding the rack, and its volume, excluding the antenna, is only 4.49cu ft (0.127m³). It contains approximately 14,000 parts, compared with the 27,000 parts of the AWG-9 on the Tomcat, and on test it has exceeded its MTBF guarantee of 106 hours, which compares remarkably well with the in-service figure of 8.2 hours for the AWG-9. Modular for easy maintenance, like so much of the Hornet, it consists of five primary subsystems which are all known as weapon replaceable assemblies (WRAs).

Radar servicing

As in all the other systems, BITE is incorporated, and can detect 98 per cent of potential or actual failures and indicate in which WRA the malfunction exists. Any WRA can be substituted in 12 minutes. One great advantage of the WRAs is that they are all digital, and need no special alignment or adjustment when being fitted. For servicing, the dielectric radome (by Brunswick) swings open to the right, and the APG-65 can be run out on an extending track; the radar is fully operable even with the track extended.

The antenna is a fully balanced, low side-lobe slotted waveguide planar array, using direct electric drive, thus saving the weight and complexity of a hydraulic system. The transmitter contains the X-band gridded TWT, which alone among the WRAs is liquid-cooled to reduce both the necessary voltage and the thermal stresses, both of which reductions contribute to reliability. All other WRAs are air-cooled. The radar data processor stores instructions for the different operating modes on a floppy disc unit with a 256K 16-bit word capacity; on demand, the instructions are transmitted to a 16K capacity solid-state memory, which controls the operation of the radar.

The digital signal processor is the key element in the radar: without its real-time handling of the masses of incoming information, the entire sequence would fail. The receiver/exciter unit converts the incoming signals from analog to digital form; it consists of low-noise field effect transistor (FET) amplifiers, which give great reliability for low cost, a low-noise exciter with multiple channels, and the analog/digital converter.

The APG-65 carries out a great deal of work on its own programs, but the net

Above: Velocity search detects long-range closing targets; range-while-search detects all-aspect targets; and track-while-scan follows ten targets, displaying eight.

Above right: Gun director mode uses pulse-to-pulse frequency agility to track targets and set the correct lead for a gun attack.

Right: Three air combat manoeuvre modes are available, all of which provide automatic lock-on to the first target acquired. Top is boresight acquisition, centre is vertical acquisition, used against either a higher or a turning target, while bottom is head-up display acquisition, which covers the area directly ahead of the HUD and locks on to the first target detected. A 'step-through' facility is provided to allow the pilot to reject targets successively until he acquires the one he wants.

results still have to be presented to the pilot on the cockpit displays, partly with symbology and partly in alpha-numeric form. Gone are the days when the raw data was presented on the CRT in analog form, and the pilot or a second crew member had to exercise a great deal of expertise in deciphering what it all meant.

We have seen that the APG-65 is a very sophisticated piece of kit: precisely what can it do? Its mission modes fall into three basic categories, air-to-air, air-to-ground, and navigational functions, which also contain some capabilities that we have not so far examined. Air-to-air modes are:

Velocity search. This mode utilizes high PRF for long-range detection. As we have seen, high PRF works best at long range on rapidly closing targets. The priority for this mode is early detection of targets that are likely to pose a threat within a timespan measured in minutes, rather than those that are heading in an entirely different direction and will not become a threat unless a radical change of course is made. The information is presented to the pilot as azimuth and velocity only, in other words the direction the target is coming from, and how fast it is approaching.

Range while search mode uses both high and medium PRF waveforms to detect targets at all aspects and relative velocities out to about 80nm (150km) range. The high PRF pulses are FM coded for ranging while the medium PRF utilizes the range gate filtering incorporated in the PSP. The purpose of range while search is to detect anything out there, regardless of aspect, heading, velocity, or threat potential.

APG-65 air combat manoeuvre modes

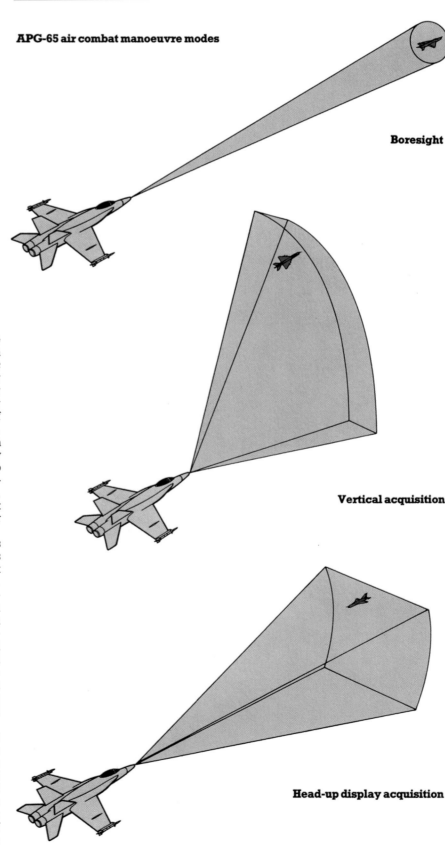

Boresight

Vertical acquisition

Head-up display acquisition

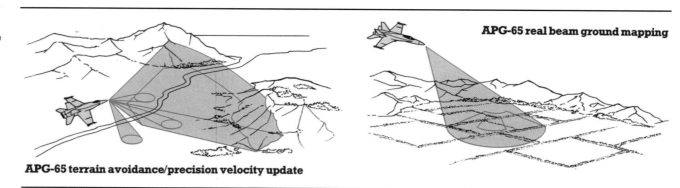

Right: The terrain avoidance mode coupled with precision velocity update confers a first-pass blind strike capability in the attack mode.

Far right: Doppler beam sharpening improves ground mapping; sector mode uses a 19:1 sharpening ratio, while patch mode uses a 67:1 ratio.

Below: High-resolution radar mapping modes greatly simplify navigation as well as target location and identification.

APG-65 real beam ground mapping

APG-65 terrain avoidance/precision velocity update

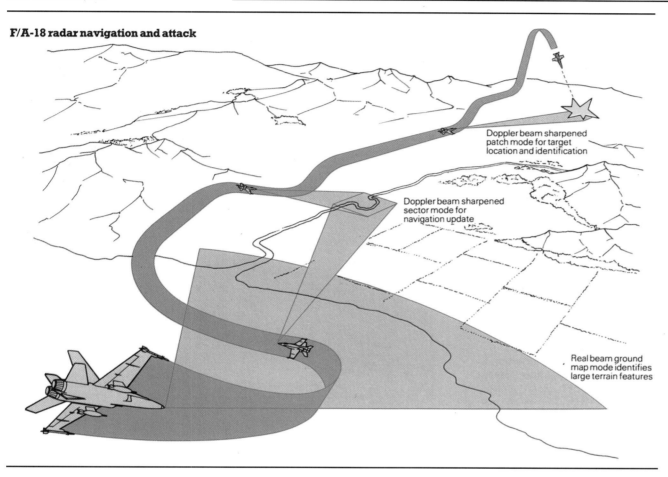

F/A-18 radar navigation and attack

Doppler beam sharpened patch mode for target location and identification

Doppler beam sharpened sector mode for navigation update

Real beam ground map mode identifies large terrain features

Track while scan is a medium PRF mode used during the closing phase at ranges below 40nm (75km). While not in the same league as the Tomcat's big AWG-9, the APG-65 has the more than useful ability of maintaining files on the tracks of ten separate targets, while displaying the eight most likely ones to the pilot, eight being considered the maximum number, in terms of workload, that the pilot can cope with. The aspect, altitude, and speed of the highest priority target, i.e., the greatest threat, is also displayed.

At some future date, the Hornet is to be equipped with the launch and leave AIM-120 AMRAAM (Advanced Medium Range Air-to-Air Missile). When this happens, it will provide the Hornet with the capability of engaging separate targets simultaneously.

Single target track mode is automatically cued on the HUD when the target comes within range while the radar is in the range while search mode. The pilot then switches to STT mode, which uses two-channel monopulse angle tracking able to follow the target through most manoeuvres, although computer logic is needed to extrapolate 180deg turns and Split-S and Immelmann type manoeuvres by the target. Provided only that the antenna gimbal limits are not exceeded, the radar should not break lock in the STT mode. Attack steering commands and data for weapon launch are shown on the HUD, while the velocity, aspect and altitude of the target are displayed on the MMD.

In addition to target tracking, the system continually computes launch parameters, and 'shoot' cues are displayed when a firing solution has been achieved. A special high pulse rate provides illumination for the semi-active radar homing (SARH) AIM-7 Sparrow missiles. As the range reduces to below 20nm (37km) the pilot has the option of using the heat-seeking Sidewinder, and uncaging the seeker head with the throttle-mounted switch slaves the IR sensor to the line of sight of the radar. A visual check of which target has been acquired, essential in a confused tactical situation, is provided on the HUD.

Raid assessment mode has been developed to solve the perennial problem of hostile aircraft flying in such close formation that radar discrimination is insufficiently sensitive to be able to separate them. In consequence, they appear on the display as one target. This is a matter of particular concern in the NATO defence area, and also the Middle East, where such 'bunching' tactics were brought to a fine art in 1973. In essence, the raid cannot be hidden, but the single blip gives no clues as to the composition of the force, and there-

fore allows no intelligent guesses to be made as to its intentions until the moment it splits up, which is generally far too late for effective counteraction to be taken.

The raid assessment mode, effective at ranges of up to 30nm (55km), provided that the enemy formation has a minimum separation between aircraft of about 500ft (150m), uses Doppler beam sharpening techniques based on expanding the area around a single target return to give increased resolution, which in turn should allow the radar to separate the individual components of a formation.

Air combat manoeuvre modes
These break down into three forms.
Boresight utilizes a narrow 3.3deg beam placed on a target which is within the boresight axis, or centreline, of the radar-carrying aircraft, the time-honoured method of pointing one's nose at the enemy, although in a manoeuvring engagement this is really of most use in the traditional pursuit attack from astern.
Vertical acquisition scans an arc 5.3deg wide by 60deg above boresight

and 14deg below, once every two seconds, and is most useful for tracking a target when either the tracking aircraft or both it and the target are in a hard turn. The pilot rolls the Hornet into the same plane of motion as the target, positioning the target above the centre of the canopy arch. Vertical acquisition is most useful when both aircraft are turning hard with the target less than 60deg angle-off.
Head-up display acquisition is the third air combat mode. This scans the 20deg by 20deg field of view of the HUD, which is plus or minus 10deg in azimuth, and 14deg above boresight to 6deg below in elevation, once every two seconds.

In all these modes, which can be used over ranges varying between 500ft (150m) and 5nm (9km), the radar locks on to the first target acquired automatically, with visual cues indicating lock and shoot appearing on the CRT displays, the HUD, and via flashing lights on the canopy bow. Despite the automatic acquisition of targets, the pilot can always reject them in turn until he reaches the one he really wants; alternatively he can designate the target with the moveable cursor.

Gun director mode can be used for ranges of less than 5nm (9km) and the radar provides position, range and velocity data on the target, which drive the gun aiming point, or pipper, on the HUD. Glint, or erratic changes in the apparent radar centre of the target, which can under some circumstances move off the target altogether, is overcome to a large degree by the use of pulse-to-pulse frequency agility. This method also provides very accurate data for lead-angle prediction, simplifying high angle-off shooting; the pilot places the pipper on the target and presses the trigger. A conventional sight is used as back-up in the event of a malfunction.

The air-to-ground modes are no less impressive. In particular, the long-range surface mapping, using high resolution modes never previously incorporated in a tactical aircraft, is outstanding. To identify large geographical features from long distance, necessary, for example, when approaching a hostile coastline, the **real beam ground mapping** mode is used. This combines low PRF with pulse compression to confer long range, and non-coherent pulse to pulse frequency agility to avoid glint. The mode provides a rather crude small-scale radar map of the terrain ahead, from which large features such as river

Right: Pilot's eye view of the vertical acquisition mode. A target is seen (left) off to the right and turning. The pilot rolls his aircraft (centre) into the plane of motion of the target by positioning his aircraft in such a way as to make the target appear to be above the centre of his canopy bow. Acquisition should be automatic, but if a firing solution can not be achieved he tightens the turn, causing the target to appear to move down into the HUD. In this mode, the 5.3×74deg arc is scanned every two seconds.

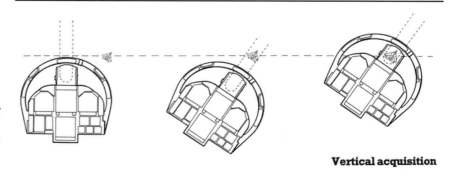

Vertical acquisition

estuaries can be readily identified. In all the ground-mapping modes, the display presentation is computer-adjusted to present the map from a vertical viewpoint rather than from the shallow angle obtained from the aircraft, which would give a distorted view and make recognition of features much more difficult. Other ground mapping modes give better resolution over smaller areas by using doppler beam sharpening (DBS). In the **DBS sector** mode, a beam sharpening ratio of 19:1 is used, while the **DBS patch** mode utilizes a 67:1 ratio.

Terrain avoidance mode is used for low-level strikes in poor visibility. An automatic terrain-following system would of course be far better but this is not a built-in capability; instead, terrain avoidance shows the pilot where the ground is, and it is then up to him to avoid it. Two sets of data are presented; one is the ground profile along the velocity vector of the aircraft (the direction in which it is travelling, which is not necessarily the same as the direction in which it is pointing), while the other shows the ground profile at a preset level below the direction of travel. Obstacles projecting through this preset level of clearance are clearly shown on the displays, which allows avoiding action to be taken. In a dive the terrain along the direction of travel is displayed, but in a climb the display shows the terrain parallel to the ground. This prevents the pilot from levelling out too soon in the event of there being a peak ahead of him.

Precision velocity update is another radar capability. It can be used to provide the Doppler input to the computer for weapon delivery, and also to improve navigation by updating the inertial platform of the INS for velocity errors. It also provides for in-flight alignment, although the demonstrated accuracy of the Litton ASN-130 INS, at 0.5nm per hour (far better than the specification requirement), is such that little correction is likely to be needed.

A carrier fighter perforce spends much of its time flying over water, and anti-shipping strikes are part of its func-

tion. To detect ships, **sea surface search** mode can be selected, although tracking is not a feature of this function. Radar clutter from the surface of the sea varies considerably according to the sea state (how rough it is). When the sea surface search mode is selected, the radar first samples the sea state. This is then analyzed by computer and a filter threshold is established to filter out the background clutter and present only those returns that do not conform, which are likely to be ships.

Other air-to-ground modes are concerned with ranging and attack. Either fixed or moving targets may be attacked, using two-channel monopulse angle tracking combined with coherent frequency agility, and ranging on designated targets is accomplished by one of two methods, depending on whether the depression angles are large or small. For large depression angles, split-gate range tracking is used, and monopulse tracking is used if the depression angles are small. A designated target is automatically acquired in this mode, which can also be used to provide ranging information when the target is designated by laser or infra-red means.

The outstanding reliability of the radar is no accident: from the outset it was a primary requirement, since it is obviously of little use to have the most capable radar in the world if it spends half its time in the repair shop. Simplicity of design was primary, as was an intensive test programme. Comprehensive testing during production is also used to detect potential or actual faults (infant mortality is the manufacturer's term) with both high and low temperature and exacting vibration conditions an integral part of the highly automated tests.

The specified requirement of 106

Right: View from the seat of the Sperry Operational Flight Trainer. Simulation is playing an increasingly important part in training pilots on new types. The realism here is excellent, apart from the fact that the pilot is not wearing gloves.

hours MTBF was met in June 1983, a whole year ahead of schedule. At this time, the requirement for the development stage achieved was only 85 hours MTBF, but as Hughes Program Reliability Manager Terry Rostker explained: "After we met that requirement, we decided to continue the test at our own risk to show that the radar can meet the mature system requirement of 106 hours MTBF (equivalent to 148 hours of failure-free running in the test chamber). At 149 hours, we stopped the tests to analyze the results and to review them with McDonnell Douglas and the Navy. Then an additional 54 hours of test were run to validate the highly successful demonstration."

The tests were stringent, to say the least. Each radar was sealed in an environmental chamber and subjected to a series of nine-hour operational cycles. Each nine-hour segment consisted of 90 minutes of cold soaking at −65deg F (−54 deg C), followed by a further 90 minutes at −40deg F (−40deg C). The set was then switched on and allowed to warm up for just six minutes, before being continuously operated for six hours at temperatures of up to 160deg F (71deg C).

In line with the overall maintenance-free concept of the Hornet, the APG-65 requires no regular maintenance inspections, calibration, or adjustment. Only when a malfunction manifests itself does it receive any attention.

New radar

The capability and flexibility of the APG-65 was confirmed by the fact that it did not start to be replaced until May 1994, more than a decade after entering service. The Hughes APG-73 became operational with late production batches of the F/A-18C/D. It is also the radar of choice for the Super Hornet. Based on its predecessor, the main improvements stem from tripled processing speed and memory capacity, made possible by technical advances in the interim.

By increasing receiver sensitivity, the ratio of listening to sending time is increased many times. This not only makes the emissions harder to detect, coupled with improved frequency agility it makes them much more difficult to jam. Existing modes are enhanced – notably air-to-surface such as sea search and ground mapping. In the air-to-air modes, it allows multiple launches of AMRAAM, improved angular discrimination in raid assessment mode, and greater non-co-operative target recognition.

Greater capacity gives significant growth potential, and a terrain-following mode is planned. In the future, a fixed active electronically scanned array

Above: Air combat is simulated in the Hughes Weapons Tactics Trainer, in which the fledgling Hornet pilot spends about 50 hours. Consisting of two domes, each containing a Hornet cockpit, the WTT enables trainees to fly against each other or the computer.

Left: The first night landing is one of the less dull moments in a Navy pilot's life. Simulated carrier landings and takeoffs, coupled with emergency procedures, ensure that the pilot is as well prepared as possible.

Right: Like all USN and USMC combat aircraft, the Hornet is equipped with the ALE-39 countermeasures dispenser system. A total of 30 rapid-bloom chaff, flare and jamming cartridges are carried in each of the two dispensers mounted just behind the inlets on the underside of the Hornet's fuselage.

(AESA) antenna will be added. This will give multiple beam steering, allowing different modes to be used at the same time, and a much lower probability of intercept, while detection ranges will at least double. Planned for service entry in 2005, this will give greater operational flexibility.

Cockpit changes
Cockpit displays have also been improved. As noted earlier, the original film-based moving map has been replaced by the Smith's Srs 2000 colour digital map system, shown on the HSD; on the Super Hornet this is a flat panel active matrix Liquid Crystal Display (LCD). Also on the Super Hornet, the push-button operated up-front control panel located directly below the HUD has been replaced by a monochrome touch-sensitive screen. The HUD itself is now the Kaiser AVQ-28. A raster type, it is compatible with FLIR imagery.

With the increasing age of the only dedicated all-weather attack aircraft in the USN inventory, the A-6 Intruder, the need to operate at night gradually took on increasing importance. This was reflected in both the F/A-18D Night Attack Hornet operated by the USMC, and the introduction of GEC night vision goggles on USN aircraft, to allow the use of which the cockpit lighting had to be made compatible. For more accurate navigation, the existing TACAN was supplemented by the Global Positioning System (GPS) in which a series of satellites are interrogated to give previously unthinkable accuracy, while the original Litton ASN-130 Inertial Navigation System (INS) was replaced by the same company's ASN-139 ring laser INS. This not only gave greater precision, it needed far less time to set up prior to takeoff. Another black box that remains in place is the Automatic Carrier Landing System (ALCS), albeit with software changes to accommodate the greater weight and slightly different approach characteristics of the Super Hornet.

Defensive avionics
As Sir Winston Churchill once said, "...it is sometimes necessary to take the enemy into account!" Sensors like radar are all very well for offensive action, but the Hornet pilot also needs prior warning of any nasty surprises that his opponent might be planning, and the means to defeat them electronically.

Radar warning was provided by the Itek, latterly Hughes, ALR-67, currently in the (V)3 model. This not only locates but identifies threat radars by comparing their signatures against a stored library, before presenting them on a cockpit display, complete with approximate range and bearing. Threats are assigned priority, and if the threat is serious (i.e., a SAM guidance radar) it is accompanied by an audible warning, while countermeasures are taken automatically.

Above: In the attack role the Hornet carries the AAS-38 FLIR pod on the port Sparrow station. Using thermal imagery, this produces a picture on the cockpit MMD of terrain or targets at night. Definition is remarkably sharp, as evidenced by this series of pictures of a US Navy amphibious assault ship.

With the cancellation of the ALQ-165 ASPJ in 1992, the Hornet was left with the Lockheed-Sanders ALQ-126B internal deception jammer, which deployed methods such as range-gate stealing. But these are active measures, with emissions that can be homed upon. The alternative, apart from flying in company with a dedicated ECM aircraft such as the EA-6B Prowler, is to deploy passive countermeasures. At first this was the Tracor ALE-40 chaff and flare dispenser, but the Super Hornet will carry four Tracor ALE-47 dispensers, giving far longer and more intensive ECM and IRCM endurance.

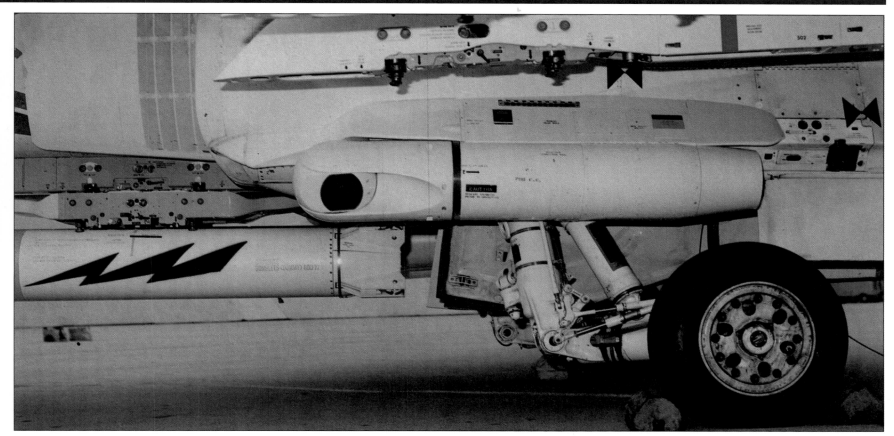

Above: The FLIR pod in position on FSD Hornet 7. The optical head rotates and swivels automatically to follow a designated target.

The other, and most recent counter-measures are air-launched decoys. The Brunswick ADM-141 Air-Launched Decoy (TALD) entered US Navy service in 1986, and was widely used by in the Gulf War of 1991. Unpowered, and with a glide ratio of 10:1, it was launched from medium altitudes and pre-programmed to follow a flight path comparable to that of an attacking aircraft. Three variants were developed: a defence saturation version with active RF amplifiers and a "reflective lens" system; a chaff TALD to mask the strike force; and an IR TALD for missile training.

More recent is the Raytheon ALE-50 towed radar decoy. Streamed several hundred yards astern, this is pro-grammed to reproduce the radar signa-ture of the actual aircraft that it is protect-ing. Optimized against monopulse radars, its purpose is to lure SAMs and AAA away from "mother", causing them to detonate well astern, far outside their normal lethal radius. Naturally the towed

Below and below right: The LST/SCAM pod occupies the starboard fuselage station. The crewman is fitting the pod's WRA-203 centre section.

decoy is ineffective against AAMs launched from ahead, and little better against AAM attacks from astern.

Trials revealed a problem, however. The ALE-50 towed decoy was mounted between the engine nozzles. When deployed, heat from the afterburners melted the towing cable. Even in mili-tary power, the engine efflux heat melted the insulation and shorted out the system.

The solution was to add a bracket to hold the cable away from the exhaust, but even then manoeuvres will be restricted to below 6.5g in military power, and a limited time at 2.5g with maximum thrust. The genuine article will use fibre optics, but the general effects are expected to be the same.

Attack avionics
The days when a pilot peered through his windshield, identified a target, and lobbed a bomb in its general direction, are long gone. In its attack incarnation, the F/A-18A/B carried two pods on what would otherwise have been its Sparrow stations.

To port was the Ford Aerospace (lat-terly Loral) AAS-38 FLIR targeting pod, named NITE HAWK in 1991. To locate the target, the pilot initially selects a 12deg x 12deg field of view along a line of sight which can be varied between 30deg up and 150deg down. The former

enables the pilot to scan well ahead when diving; the latter is used either to keep the target in view when in a steep climb, or to look astern. He can also roll up to 540deg in either direction before the system gives up and sulks.

Televisual presentation is at actual size on the MMD, and is shown the right way up (i.e., as the pilot would actually see it) regardless of the evolutions of the seeker head. Once the target has been identi-fied, the field of view can be closed down to 3deg x 3deg, giving image magnification of about four times. The auto-tracker is then engaged and feeds data to the mission computer, which in turn calculates weapons release solu-tions. AAS-38A can also be used to update navigation by focusing on a bridge or another fixed feature of pre-cisely known location.

For the Night Attack Hornet, NITE HAWK was supplanted by the Hughes AAR-50 NAVFLIR or, as it was later des-ignated, TINS (Thermal Imaging Navigation Set). Longer (6ft 6in/1.98m as compared to 6ft/1.83m), of smaller diam-eter (10in/25cm against 13in/33cm), and much lighter (214lb/97kg compared to 380lb/172kg), TINS consisted of four Weapon Replaceable Assemblies (WRAs): the FLIR sensor; the electronics unit; the thermal control unit; and the pod adaptor. Field of view was 191/2deg x 191/2deg. A "staring" system (i.e., for-

ward-looking with no angular adjust-ment possible), it presented either a black-hot or white-hot image as pre-ferred, onto the Kaiser AVQ-28 HUD, with a 525-line raster video format. At first this caused problems, as there was a slight discrepancy between the image por-trayed and the real world. While this was dangerous in low-level flight under cer-tain conditions, it was quickly resolved. Unlike the USAF LANTIRN pod, TINS cannot be steered to "look into" the turn; consequently at night the pilot had to wear GEC NVGs, costing about $50,000 dollars.

The starboard position was occupied by the Martin Marietta Laser Spot Tracker/Strike Camera (LST/SCAM) pod. This had a dual function. First, it could search for, acquire, and then track laser-coded energy from a remotely designated target, which gave a first-pass strike capability in adverse weather. Once acquired, the LST passed target mission data to the mission computer, which in turn pro-vided aiming and weapons release data onto the HUD. Secondly, a Perkins-Elmer panoramic camera covered the target before, during and after the attack, for damage assessment. In 1993, the ASQ-173 replaced the origi-nal LST/SCAM, able to actually desig-nate targets directly rather than rely on remote designation.

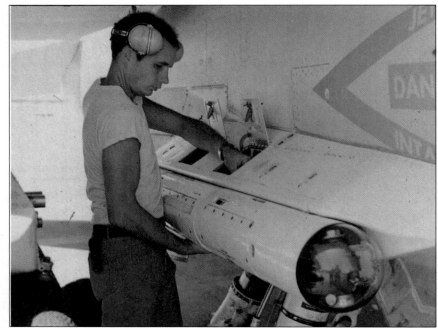

Armament

Like its insect namesake, the Hornet carries a vicious sting. In the air-to-air role it can carry up to six AIM-120 AMRAAM and four AIM-9 Sidewinder missiles. For the air-to-surface mission it is cleared to carry virtually every weapon in the US Navy inventory. But where it really scores is as a multi-role fighter, able to switch from one task to another in mid-mission if necessary.

Despite the return to fashion of the aircraft gun, missiles are the primary weapons of the modern fighter in air-to-air combat. Missiles have a chequered history, and have been the source of many misconceptions and misunderstandings. Before examining the weapons relevant to the Hornet, perhaps we should take a brief overview of the entire subject.

For a start, the term 'guided missiles' has found wide currency in the argot of aviation. This is a misnomer. Very few missiles are in fact guided, which term implies positive control by the firer, and the air-to-air missiles carried by the Hornet certainly do not come into this

Below: A Canadian Armed Forces CF-18 carries eight BL-755 cluster bombs on its four underwing pylons.

category. Homing missiles, or target-following missiles would be a more accurate description.

To digress briefly, missiles that can manoeuvre to follow their targets seem to have caused a certain amount of confusion in the United States in their early days, as the first manoeuvring air-to-air missile in the world to enter service, the AIM-4 Falcon, was originally allotted an experimental fighter designation as the XF-98. There was, of course, some justification for this; Hughes Aircraft had for all practical purposes created a small pilotless kamikaze aeroplane!

A myth widely disseminated in the early days of homing missiles was that they would obviate the need for manoeuvring combat between fighters. Future air encounters were to be fought at long range, with the victory going to

the side which detected the enemy earliest, got into position first, deployed the longest-ranged weapons and had the best countermeasures. War in the air was to become a war of technology: the new missiles would manoeuvre unerringly in tracking down their targets, and they could not be out-run except at the very limit of their range, and then only in the unlikely event of their being detected in time. But as Admiral of the Fleet Lord Fisher commented at the start of the century, "The best scale for an experiment is 12 inches to the foot!" And so it was to prove: experience was to show that the elaborate theorizing had been almost entirely wrong.

Let us take a brief look at the characteristics common to almost all homing missiles. They are rocket-propelled, and are accelerated to a very high speed

Above: Close-up of the large and drag-inducing twin store rack and pylon as armourers practice bombing up a Hornet at sea. The bombs do not yet have fuzes attached.

within a few seconds, after which they coast along, gradually losing speed until finally control is lost, when they either explode at the end of their run or fall harmlessly (from the opposing pilot's viewpoint) to the earth. For most of their travel they are too fast to be outrun, so, leaving aside countermeasures for the moment, evasive action is the only recourse.

In the long-gone days when guns were the only effective air-to-air weapon, a standard method of evasion was to dip the nose of the aircraft and accelerate away out of range. Against

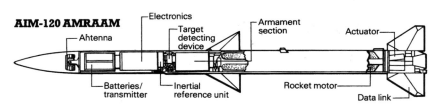

missiles, with effective ranges measured in miles, this was futile. The new homing missiles had not ended manoeuvring combat; rather, they had made manoeuvre much more important. Yet the missiles were supposed to be able to out-manoeuvre the fighters. This idea appears to have arisen from the fact that some missiles were advertised as being able to perform 30g turns, whereas fighters were designed to a limit of 7g or a little over.

There are three ways of measuring turning ability. One is in multiples of acceleration, or g; a second is in terms of radius of turn, measured in linear distance; while the third is in rate of turn, expressed in degrees per second. As turning performance is a function of speed, the number of gs that can be pulled is largely irrelevant. The quoted 30g is for a very high velocity only, and as the velocity of the missile decays, so does its ability to manoeuvre. In this it is like an aircraft, but a much more extreme case.

Missile versus aircraft
Colonel John Boyd's concept of energy manoeuvrability applies to missiles exactly as it does to fighters. A missile travelling at Mach 4 at the tropopause and describing a 30g turn would have a radius of turn of about 14,600ft (4,450m) and a rate of turn slightly exceeding 14deg/sec. By comparison, a fighter flying at its 'corner velocity' – the point where its turning ability is best, or about 400kt (737km/h) – can turn on a radius of only 8,180ft (2,494m) with a mere 2g acceleration, and achieve a turn rate of 16deg/sec at 6g. Naturally, the missile does not necessarily have to match either the turn radius or turn rate of its target, as it can cut the corner, but having to manoeuvre bleeds off energy and reduces its further capability, while at the same time the difficulties of tracking are greatly multiplied. This, of course, applies to a missile coming in from the stern quadrant of the target; from any other direction an energetic manoeuvre may easily take the target outside the missile's flight envelope.

Missiles perform simple tasks best, so the role of the pilot of the target aircraft is to make himself as difficult to hit as possible. Discounting countermeasures for the moment, he does this by generating as much angle-off as he can and hopefully puts himself outside the missile's reach. If he either knows or suspects that the missile tracking him is a heat-seeker, he will attempt to shield his hot exhaust behind the cooler body of his machine.

To summarize, missiles are not yet ten feet tall. Like aeroplanes, they have clearly defined flight performance

Above: FSD Hornet 7 launches a Sparrow during early armament trials at NAS Patuxent River. Sparrow confers a BVR kill capability.

Right: AMRAAM is a launch-and-leave missile using inertial guidance for the midflight phase and active radar terminal homing.

envelopes, and a pilot under attack will often survive if he can draw it either beyond the limits of the envelope or out toward the boundaries where it will perform less well. The really clever part is knowing when he is under attack, particularly from BVR (beyond visual range) missiles.

While missiles have flight performance envelopes, these are conditioned to a large extent by the relative speeds and aspects of the launching aircraft and its target, so that performance data that is generally available must be qualified. For example, speed is generally stated in terms of Mach number, but many factors affect this, including the velocity of the launching aircraft and the altitude at launch. Ideally, the launching fighter should be flying as fast as possible at launch to impart as much of its own velocity, and thus energy, to the missile, in this way maximizing the total energy of

Right: Target speed and relative heading vary an air-to-air missile's launch envelope considerably – by 10nm in this example.

Below: Three types of missile homing: AMRAAM (top), Sparrow (centre) and Sidewinder.

the missile at motor burn-out. This in turn will increase range and also kill probability (P_k), especially with BVR weapons.

Launch at low altitude will not only reduce the speed of the launching aircraft, and thus the amount of extra energy that it can impart, but also the maximum velocity of the missile. The air at low level is denser, creating more drag, and the higher pressure on the backchamber of the missile will decrease thrust. Maximum speed data for missiles should therefore be viewed

with caution, as, for the same reasons, should flight-time and range.

Still other factors affect speed and range. An obvious example arises in the case of a missile being launched at a target high above, when the missile has to use a considerable portion of its energy in lifting itself to a great height, instead of propelling it as far and as fast as possible, although this is to a small extent offset by the benefits of falling air pressure on the backchamber and reducing drag as the altitude increases and the air gets thinner.

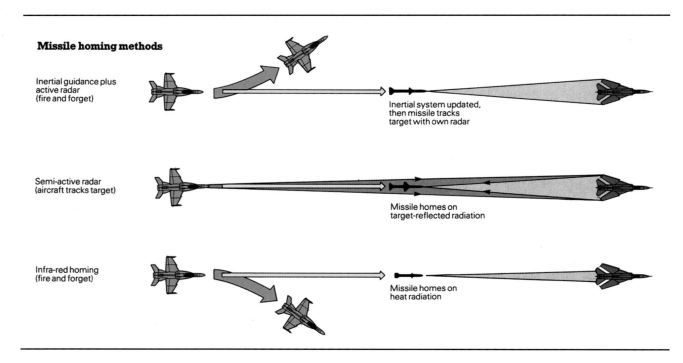

Missile homing methods

Inertial guidance plus active radar (fire and forget)

Inertial system updated, then missile tracks target with own radar

Semi-active radar (aircraft tracks target)

Missile homes on target-reflected radiation

Infra-red homing (fire and forget)

Missile homes on heat radiation

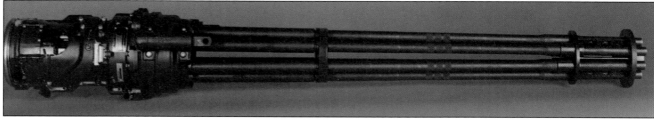

Above: Ears protected against noise and heads helmeted against hard edges, armourers reload a Hornet's M61 Vulcan cannon.

Right: The six barrels of the M61 give a maximum rate of fire of 100 rounds per second and help achieve a high degree of reliability.

Range is generally stated in terms of distance, which is a fixed measurement, generally given at the tropopause (36,090ft/ 11,000m). But, since a missile is launched from a dynamic aircraft at a dynamic target, this can be very misleading. If we compare hypothetical cases of head-on and stern-on attacks, using a missile with a flight time of 30 seconds and a static range of 20nm (37km), given a target velocity of Mach 1 in both cases, and provided that the radar acquisition and homing system is up to the task, the missile can be launched against the head-on target while it is still 25nm (46km) away. From astern, the maximum range reduces to a mere 15nm (28km), to give it an outside chance of overhauling the target. The difference is the distance that the target moves during the missile time of flight. Launch ranges are therefore almost infinitely variable, depending on the dynamics of the situation – comparative velocities, aspects, headings, and of course, relative altitudes.

AIM-7 Sparrow
Sparrow was the primary air-to-air weapon of the early Hornets. A semi-active radar homer, it was the first missile to give beyond visual range (BVR) engagement capability. Sparrow was far from new; it originated almost 50 years ago as Project Hot Shot for the US Navy, as a bomber destroyer. Continually upgraded and improved, it was one of the biggest missile programmes in history, with more than 50,000 built.

M61 hit probability

Above: A MiG-21 at 500kt (921km/h) and 90deg angle-off should be hit at least four times by an accurately aimed burst from a Vulcan.

Right: The close proximity of the M61 cannon and the radar equipment in the nose of the Hornet required some very clever design work to damp antenna vibration down to an acceptable 30 g during gun firing.

F-18 nose gun and radar installation

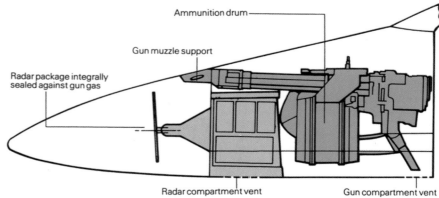

Ammunition drum

Gun muzzle support

Radar package integrally sealed against gun gas

Radar compartment vent

Gun compartment vent

It first saw service in Southeast Asia, where it was widely expected to cut a deadly swathe through the North Vietnamese Air Force. Unfortunately this was not to be. The problem was reliable identification at ranges beyond the visual, and after a couple of "own goals" it was restricted to visual encounters only. The introduction of "Combat Tree", a MiG IFF interrogator, in the final full year of the war, reduced the risks, but this notwithstanding, Sparrow failed to fulfil its early promise.

There were several reasons for this. In the urgency of combat, many missiles were left hanging on aircraft until, as one observer commented "they almost rusted in position!" The US Navy often

treated Sparrows as just another munition, rolling them across the deck before mounting them on the aircraft and fitting their aerodynamic surfaces. This was no way to treat a system dependent on delicate electronics, and failures were many. The record shows that in Vietnam, the October War of 1973, and the Beka'a action of 1982, Sparrows were launched on 632 occasions. They were credited with just 73 victories: 11 per cent! Further research showed that *only four* of these were true BVR kills; the rest were all gained from within visual distance!

In theory, the fact that the launching fighter had to continuously illuminate its opponent with radar to use SARH

Sparrows was of little consequence. A single opponent was in no position to shoot back, at least until guns range was reached, by which time it might easily have been destroyed. But if there were several opponents...! With the radar locked onto a single target, the fighter was electronically blind to all other adversaries. And with a closing speed possibly in excess of 1,000nm (1,8531kph), more than one nautical mile every four seconds, close combat would quickly be joined with the survivors of the enemy formation. This was not a good idea, especially as the Sparrow had a rather long minimum range, typically half a mile, during which it could neither arm itself nor

manoeuvre.

The situation deteriorated still further with the advent of all-aspect heat homing missiles. Previously these could be used only from the rear quadrant, homing on the hot exhaust plume, but all-aspect seekers could home equally well on aerodynamic hot spots on the airframe. This gave rise to a "shoot-out at the OK Corral" scenario. If an opponent managed to launch an all-aspect heat-seeker shortly before he was destroyed by a SARH missile, there was a fair chance that the attacker would also be hit. Swapping one for one was no part of the game plan, and other means were sought.

AIM-120 AMRAAM

What was needed was a launch and leave, also known as a fire and forget, missile. Heat homers filled this requirement for close combat, but lacked range. They could of course have been given longer legs, but the problem was that they lacked discrimination. To date, no-one has ever produced a missile seeker that could tell the difference between white stars and red. In a confused, multi-bogey scenario, a heat missile will switch targets if a better opportunity presents itself. Back in the bad old days of the Cold War, where the "worst case" scenario was an all-out conflict in Europe between NATO and the Warsaw Pact, a medium range heat-seeker was not a good idea.

The requirement was a BVR missile which could be locked onto its target at launch, have its course updated during its time of flight, then use terminal homing for the final intercept phase. In addition, the ideal was a salvo of missiles that could be launched against multiple targets almost instantaneously. This had already been done with the Tomcat/Phoenix combination, but this was unaffordable in the context of tactical fighters.

The solution was AIM-120 AMRAAM, a lighter weapon than Sparrow, allowing more to be carried for a given takeoff weight, but of similar length. As related elsewhere there were however development problems, and full scale production did not start until April 1991. Fairly agile "off the rail", the AIM-120 uses active radar terminal homing, which cuts in as the missile closes to within about 10nm (18km) of the target. This also means that if necessary AMRAAM can be used as an all-aspect close combat weapon.

At medium range, the great advantage of AMRAAM is that the launching fighter does not have to switch its radar to attack mode, usually known as locking on. The target, alerted by its RWS, will probably realise that it is under surveillance, but unless it has an advanced missile approach warning system, may not know that it is actually under attack. Hornets now routinely carry AMRAAM in the counter-air mission.

AIM-9 Sidewinder

Like Sparrow, Sidewinder started out as a bomber-destroying missile using infra-red seeking to home on the hot exhaust plumes from astern. As IR is intrinsically more accurate than radar homing, the warhead could be relatively small, minimising both diameter and weight. Range was short, and this combination allowed it to be simple and cheap (about $2,500 a copy). From dead astern, launched at a non-manoeuvring (i.e., bomber-type) target, at high altitude, contrasted against a clear and cold sky background, it was extremely reliable.

Fortunately, the war for which it was designed failed to materialize, and

Above: FSD Hornet 8 during gun firing trials in April 1980. Unusually for a modern fighter, the cannon is located just above the aircraft centreline. This is as close to the ideal position as the radar allows.

Sidewinder came to be used against tactical aircraft, which unless the initial approach was made unseen, were far less co-operative. In practice, Sidewinder was easy to use. The pilot pointed his aircraft at the foe and energized the missile seeker head. As it started to

Below: A Hornet of VMFA-314 Black Knights lets fly with a Sidewinder from the starboard wingtip rail. Previously equipped with F-4Ns, the Black Knights converted to the Hornet in March 1984 and are assigned to CVW-13 on USS Coral Sea.

rally was a daylight-only weapon. The USAF was not interested, but operational trials began late in 1991. However, the limitations proved too great, and it was cancelled.

By the late 1980s, Sidewinder had begun to look rather long in the tooth. Its designated successor was the European-developed Advanced Short Range Air to Air Missile (ASRAAM), but this was so long delayed that the US services lost interest. They then suddenly realised that even the latest Sidewinders were badly outclassed by the Russian Vympel R-73 in look angle, in agility, and (aided by a helmet-mounted sight – HMS – system) in off-boresight capability.

A programme was instituted to match the Russian weapon with an improved Sidewinder, the AIM-9X. Seeker performance targets included a minimum low level acquisition range in ground

Left: FSD Hornet 7 configured for the attack mission, with three Paveway laser-guided bombs and an AGM-84 Harpoon on pylons, Sidewinders on the wingtips and fuselage FLIR and LST/SCAM pods.

acquire a likely heat source, he heard a growl in his earphones, which rose to a strident note as it locked on. A quick check to make sure that the target was within range, then a squeeze of the trigger launched the Sidewinder on its way.

There were operational problems to overcome. Early variants were easily distracted by alternative heat sources – the sun, sunlight reflected from clouds or snow, or even hot spots on the ground. Nor could it "see" through cloud. It was, and still is, a limited weapon in many ways, although it complemented Sparrow very well.

As the years passed, it was developed through many variants. The initial 11deg/sec tracking was increased to 20deg/sec, the seeker look angle rose from 25deg to 40deg, and brochure range was extended from 1.72nm (3.2km) to about 9.5nm (17.7km). Increased capability was matched by increased cost, but even then it remained affordable in quantity. A total far in excess of 100,000 has been produced.

In service, Sidewinder did have an unexpected effect on fighter tactics. The advent of "magic missiles" which were able to follow their targets, was widely expected to end manoeuvre combat. In practice, just the opposite happened. If a fighter pilot spotted an opponent closing on him from behind, but still at a distance, a standard evasive tactic was to drop the nose and accelerate away out of range. The long reach of the Sidewinder (compared with cannon) made this distinctly unprofitable; the best move was to turn hard and try to get outside the look angle of the seeker, or inside the turn radius of the missile. Rather than eliminate manoeuvre combat, Sidewinder made manoeuvre more imperative than ever!

All variants up to the AIM-9J were rear quadrant only weapons, and while the J was reported to have limited all-aspect capability, this was marginal at best. It was generally considered that if the pilot of the target aircraft knew that his opponent was behind him, assuming that he had sufficient energy manoeuvrability, he could deny a valid Sidewinder shot, or stand a good chance of defeating it if it was launched.

The breakthrough came with the AIM-9L, or Lima, as it was known. With an argon-cooled, fixed reticle tilted mirror seeker, this was the first Sidewinder to have a genuine all-aspect capability.

Above: FSD Hornet 4, the structural test prototype, photographed in August 1981 carrying four Mk 84 2,000lb (907kg) on wing pylons. Blue and white Sidewinders are carried for attitude identification.

Right: Close-up of the underwing pylons, the nearer mounting a pair of Mk 82 slicks on a twin store carrier. Underwing stores carriage is a cumbersome business.

Further upgrades followed, many of them rebuilds from earlier variants.

Developed for the US Navy, the AIM-9R was a particularly interesting version, as it used a visible-wavelength imaging seeker in lieu of the standard IR reticle head. This gave a longer acquisition range and greater resistance to counter- measures, but natu-

clutter of 3.5 nm (6.5km), rising to 7nm (16km) in clear air at altitude. HMS compatibility was specified, and sufficient data processing capacity to discriminate between the target and the latest flare decoys. US Naval Air Systems Command short-listed two companies in December 1994, Hughes Missile Systems, and Raytheon. After an intensive period of evaluation, Naval Air Systems Command issued an EMD contract on 13 December 1996, and F/A-18Cs test-fired two AIM-9Xs in the summer of 1999. Low-rate production is expected to start in 2001, with operational capability two years later.

Gunfighter Hornet

About four decades ago, improvements to the then generation of missiles were such that many fighters were designed without an internal gun. The general attitude was that not only was a gun badly outranged by the new wonder weapons, it was relatively ineffective in the interception mission which was perceived as the main role of the fighter. Close combat was widely thought to be a thing of the past, reducing guns to unnecessary ballast. Not only the West followed this trend; a surprising number of Russian fighter designs were equally gunless.

There was of course a secondary reason. The low thickness/chord ratio of wings designed for Mach 2 made them unsuitable for mounting guns, while the nose was usually occupied by a large and rather delicate radar, which did not take kindly to the vibration caused by cannon fire in close proximity. Another factor was that the ingestion of gun gases tended to have undesirable effects on the engine. This posed the problem of where to put a gun. It was in some ways much easier to omit it altogether.

Combat experience soon showed the error of this thinking. In the skies over North Vietnam, missile-armed Phantoms often found themselves disadvantaged by gun-armed MiGs which, flying under close ground control, often appeared "out of the weeds" within minimum missile range. Then, in 1967, the Israeli Air Force scored a resounding victory over their Arab opponents, claiming 58 victories, all with cannon-fire. The myth of the all-missile fighter promptly evaporated.

By the time the Hornet emerged, there was really only one aircraft gun in sight. This was the 20mm M61A1 Vulcan cannon by General Electric, which had already been selected for the F-14 Tomcat, the F-15 Eagle, and the F-16 Fighting Falcon. It was large, with six rotating barrels, and able to spew out 100 rounds each second.

The best place to put the gun is always on the centreline, where the recoil causes no asymmetric loading. But in the new generation of fighters this was simply not possible; the radar took priority. The F-16 was even smaller than the F/A-18, and the gun was mounted in the inner edge of the LEX, with its magazine in the centre fuselage aft of the cockpit. But for the Hornet, this solution was simply not possible, since the carefully contoured lines of its LEX would be spoilt, with a consequent loss of the aerodynamic benefits.

With no alternative, the designers chose to mount the gun high in the nose, behind, but in close proximity to, the radar. Both it and its magazine were

Right: A Hornet of VFA-113 Stingers en route to the Leach Lake range in California (top). After releasing two Mk 82 slicks in a shallow dive (centre), the aircraft banks away (bottom), showing the empty racks.

Above: The BL-755 cluster bomb unit is not a new weapon, but it still had to be cleared for use by the Hornet. This Canadian CF-18 carries eight, with cameras attached in five positions to record the drop.

pallet-mounted for easy access and changing. With some trepidation, they then tackled the vibration problem.

Ground firing trials showed that the vibration level at the top of the planar antenna could reach a totally unacceptable 400g. Hughes overcame this problem by putting four antivibration mounts onto each bulkhead at the front and rear of the radar. This allowed the radar assemblies to "float" between the bulkheads, and damped the vibration down to a mere 30g. While this still sounds a lot, it was deemed acceptable.

Only the position of the muzzle, on top of the nose and immediately ahead of the pilot, was still suspect. During night firing, muzzle flash would appear to be in the perfect position to interfere with the pilot's night-adapted vision. A night-firing trial was held with a flame float as the target, and the pilot reported that he had no trouble in tracking it. Not that a flame float is a fair trial,

but the gun is almost entirely a daytime weapon, either for strafing surface targets or for air combat. The other fear, that sticky gun gases, flowing back over the canopy, would goo it up, proved largely unfounded.

The M61 is a very old weapon in concept, but very reliable, with an average stoppage rate of just one round in 10,000. Looked at the other way, this is once every 100 seconds at full rate, but this is still far better than the previous generation of gasoperated revolver cannon could achieve. Part of its reliability is due to the fact that it is externally powered. The rifled barrels rotate anticlockwise (looking in the direction of fire), and the fact that there are six of them helps to dissipate the heat, reducing wear and giving longer barrel life. Muzzle velocity is 3,400ft/sec (1,036m/sec).

The tremendous rate of fire demands a linkless feed, and the magazine capacity of 570 rounds allows about six seconds of firing at maximum rate, or more likely eight or nine short bursts. M50 series ammunition is used, and while by modern standards this has poor ballistic qualities and lacks hitting power, the Vulcan can put a lot of

lead into the air in a very short time. At full firing rate, the shells leave the muzzle at 34ft (10.36m) intervals, and this distance reduces marginally during the time of flight. Let us assume a MiG-29, crossing at an angle of 90deg, in plane to the firer, at a speed of 500kt (927kmh). It travels its own length in just 0.063 seconds, but given a true aim, and the Vulcan at full rate, it will be stitched about six times. This is a very extreme example, but you get the idea.

A criticism of the Vulcan heard in some quarters is that it takes time to wind up to the full rate of fire. In fact it takes just three tenths of a second, and another half second to wind down again. This argument, proposed by Pentagon analyst Pierre Sprey in a paper entitled "First Rounds Count", is that the first placement of the pipper tends to be the most accurate; after that it tends to wander off. Therefore the Vulcan is still winding up to speed when the aim is truest. But the opinion of many very experienced fighter pilots is that this is no big deal; it would take four M39 revolver cannon (which hit full rate instantly) to exceed the output of a single M61 in a half-second

burst. And where could four M39s be fitted into a Hornet?

In fact the shortcomings of the M61 are fully appreciated, and a new lightweight cannon is under development for the Super Hornet. The gun is of less importance than it was even 20 years ago, but it still has relevance. Essentially it is a weapon of the last resort; instantly available, with a snapshot capability that cannot be matched by any missile, current or projected. Short on range and of limited destructive power it may be, but an adversary ignores its presence at his peril.

Finally, the only effective countermeasure against the gun is manoeuvre. The radar may be solid with jamming, and heat decoys may render IR missiles useless, but the gunarmed fighter will always possess the means to shoot his opponent from the sky. Provided of course that he can get in close and bring his nose to bear!

Air-to-surface weapons
The load-carrying capacity of the Hornet was originally stated to be 17,000lb (7,700kg) on nine hardpoints, although this was later reduced to 13,700lb (6,214kg). The

Above: One of the principal anti-ship weapons carried by the Hornet, the AGM-65F variant of Maverick uses imaging infra-red homing.

F/A-18E/F has two extra hardpoints, increasing the maximum carrying capability to 17,500lb (7,938kg). But here we are talking theory; it is rare for any combat aircraft to depart on a mission at anything like the maximum weight to which it has been cleared.

Below: Another weapon test carried out by the CAF Aerospace Engineering Test Establishment, this time involving unguided rockets.

The reason for this is simple; the weapons load is optimized for the target to be attacked. In many cases, for example defence suppression missions with HARMS and CBUs, the weapons carried are considerably lighter than the hardpoint limits. Also, there is little point in carrying extra weapons, which may degrade performance, on the off-chance that a target of opportunity might just present itself.

To digress for a moment, consider that in the air combat role the F/A-18E/F Hornet can carry 10 AIM-120 AMRAAMs plus two Sidewinders. Twelve on-board potential kills, not counting the gun! This gives excep-

tional combat persistence, exceeding even that of the Russian Su-27 Flanker.

The Hornet has been cleared to carry virtually every air-to-surface weapon in the USN inventory, depth charges and torpedoes excepted. The two wingtip rails are dedicated to Sidewinders for self-defence; they cannot be used for any other munitions. They have a secondary value: they act as aerodynamic endplates, helping to stem outboard air flow.

When long range or endurance is required, the centreline and two inner wing hardpoints are wet; they can be used to carry jettisonable fuel tanks which add 6,435lb (2,920kg) of fuel. The four inner wing points can carry multiple ejection racks (MERs), supplemented by a triple ejection rack (TER) on the centreline. These allow a total of 19 Mk 82 bombs each with a nominal weight of 500lb (227kg) to be carried. The MERs and TERs however induce high drag, and their use is operationally restricted. A typical load would more likely be four Mk 83s of 1,000lb (554kg) and six Mk 82s.

The drag penalties of MERs and TERs arises not only from the racks, or from the weapons considered individually, but also from the interference drag they cause in combination. In flight, the airflow accelerates past the bombs and their racks, reaching a maximum velocity just ahead of their maximum width. Consequently, clusters of bombs grouped close together on an MER impinge upon each other's and the rack's accelerated airflow, and interference drag results. This not only affects aircraft performance, but also bombing accuracy, as the drag-induced forces tend to impart pitching and yawing moments to the weapons at the moment of release, especially with attack speeds of about 600kt (1,100kmh).

Operational handling of the bombs is simple. The ground crew load the weapons and make the fuze code settings. The pilot then checks the loadings on the MMD, and sets up to three delivery programmes on the attack computer. Even these are not immutable; both the pro-

grammes and the weapon's status can be changed in flight.

The usage and delivery methods of laser guided bombs (LGBs), Snakeye retarded bombs, and Rockeye CBUs have been dealt with in earlier sections, as have fuel/air weapons – the so-called "poor man's nukes". A variation on the LGB, intended to increase range while overcoming the limitations imposed by gravity drop was the AGM-123 Skipper II. Like the Paveway series, this was a bolt-on kit with a power source. It was widely used in the Gulf War in 1991.

The previous generation of smart bombs have their drawbacks. TV guidance cannot be used at night, while laser and IR guidance can both be foiled by fog and precipitation. A guidance system was needed which could be used around the clock, in virtually any weather conditions.

This resulted in the Joint Direct Attack Munition (JDAM), low rate production of which began in May 1997. Like the Paveway series, GBU-30 is a bolt-on addition to Mk 83 and 84, and BLU-109 and -110 dumb bombs. Designation is GBU-31 for the 2,000lb (907kg) weapons and GBU-32 for the 1,000lb (454kg) bombs.

The guidance system consists of a Rockwell-Collins GPS coupled to an extremely accurate but affordable Honeywell INS, able to detect and adjust for wind changes during the trajectory. Accuracy is less than that of an LGB, but a test programme in 1996/1997 demonstrated an average accuracy of 31ft 6in (9.6m), which for blind bombing, without sight of the target, is incredibly good. Typically JDAMs can be dropped from up to 15nm (28km) away.

In passing, it should be mentioned that a weapon first used in early 1999 can also be carried by the Hornet. This is the Advanced Unitary Penetrator (AUP). This is the BLU-116A, which is virtually identical to the BLU-109, but has twice the penetration against targets hardened with reinforced concrete. The basic munition can be used with laser guidance, the GBU-15 and AGM-130, or with the JDAM GPS/INS system.

While the Hornet has been

cleared to carry "special weapons", the B.57 or B.61 nukes, it seems unlikely that these will ever be used for real, unless of course Saddam Hussein or some other megalomaniac develops and uses them, in which case retaliation in kind will become unavoidable. Deterrence is still, as it always was, the name of the nuclear game.

Other simple weapons are the Canadian CRV-7 rocket and pods of unguided folding-fin rockets, notably the LAU-97. But the latter is a short-range weapon that involves duelling with the ground defences. In the current climate of opinion, a multi-million dollar fighter should never be risked against cheap and cheerful ground-launched anti-aircraft weapons. By the same token, the French Durandal runway-busting bomb, the delivery parameters of which make the delivery aircraft vulnerable to ground fire, will never be used.

Air-to-surface missiles

AGM-62 Walleye, produced by Martin Marietta from 1966 to 1978, is one of the oldest air-to-surface guided weapons in the US Navy inventory. An unpowered glide bomb, with a warhead based on the Mk 84, it uses TV guidance, with a gyro-stabilized Vidicon camera in the nose. Range depending on release altitude is 30nm (56km). Walleye is released in the general direction of the target, and signals from the TV camera received via a dedicated data link pod on the Hornet produce a target image on a cockpit display. The pilot then locks the Walleye onto it and monitors its progress, guiding it manually if necessary. After extensive use in the Gulf War, few Walleyes are thought

to remain in stock.

The problem with unpowered bombs is that they cannot stretch their glide; Sir Isaac Newton does not permit the laws of gravity to be broken. Locking onto the target is all very well, but if the required glide angle is too shallow, the weapon will inevitably fall short. This makes some form of power essential.

The direct successor of Walleye was AGM-65 Maverick. Powered by a solid-fuel rocket motor, Maverick has gone through several variants. The US Marine Corps now uses the AGM-65E with laser guidance and a 300lb (136kg) blast/penetration warhead, while the US Navy has selected the AGM-65F, with imaging infra-red (IIR) homing, fine-tuned to increase effectiveness against ships at sea. Under development is a millimetric radar homing variant. Speed is high subsonic, and range when launched from sea level is between 0.6 and 8.5nm (1-16km), or double this distance when launched from altitude.

The preferred anti-shipping missile carried by the Hornet is AGM-84 Harpoon. A long range (59nm/110km) weapon, it is powered by a small turbojet which gives it high subsonic speed over the water. Steering commands are pre-programmed into the strapdown inertial navigation system prior to launch, and these can include multiple doglegs to confuse the opposition. A radar altimeter determines its height over the water, and at a predetermined point it switches to active radar, or in some cases, IR seeking, which automatically locks onto to the target. During the final phase of the approach it pops up, then dives vertically onto the target.

US Navy F-18 ordnance loads

Weapon	Armament Station								
	1	2	3	4	5	6	7	8	9
Air-to-air missiles									
AIM-9G/H/L Sidewinder	1	2						2	1
AIM-7F Sparrow		1		1		1		1	
Air-to-surface missiles									
AGM-65E/F Maverick		1	1				1	1	
AGM-88A Harm		1	1				1	1	
Conventional weapons									
Mk 82 LD/HD		2	2		2		2	2	
Mk 82 LGB		1	1				1	1	
Mk 83 LD		2	2		1		2	2	
Mk 83 LGB		1	1				1	1	
Mk 84 LD		1	1				1	1	
Mk 84 LGB		1							
Mk 20 or CBU-59/B Rockeye		2	2		2		2	2	
BLU-95 FAE-II (fuel-air explosive)		2	2		2		2	2	
AGM-62 Walleye		1						1	
Walleye data link pod					1				
Practice bombs									
Mk 76/Mk 106 dispensers		1	1		1		1	1	
BDU-12/20		1	1				1	1	
BDU-36		1						1	
Rocket launchers									
LAU-10D/A, -61A/A or -68B/A		2	2				2	2	
Special weapons									
B57 or B61		1						1	

This not only makes it very difficult to defend against; it can penetrate deep into the bowels of the target ship before detonating, thus maximizing damage.

A Harpoon derivative is AGM-84E Standoff Land Attack Missile (SLAM). It is 25.5in (65cm) longer than Harpoon and 200lb (91kg) heavier. Range is of the order of 60nm (110km). SLAM uses a modified version of the Harpoon mid-course guidance system coupled to a GPS receiver. The IIR seeker of the AGM-65D Maverick is used for

Above left: Defence suppression is a task that an air arm ignores at its peril. Here, the first firing of an AGM-88A Harm by an F-18 is carried out by FSD Hornet TF1 over Wallops Island test range in October 1983.

Left: The cameras carried during separation trials show up clearly on wingtips, in Sparrow positions and under the rear fuselage as an inert B61 'special weapon', designated BDU-12/20, falls clear of FSD Hornet 7.

terminal guidance, passing target imagery back to "mother" via data link. Once lock-on has been achieved, the attack becomes fully automatic. From 1997, SLAM ER (Expanded Response) entered service. This has a maximum launch range of 150nm (278km), an improved warhead and, in future, an automatic target recognition system.

The sophistication of modern ground-based counter air defences has put a premium on remote attack, allowing ordnance to be released from well outside SAM range. The proposed solution was the AGM-154 Joint Stand-Off Weapon (JSOW), developed by Raytheon. An all-singing, all-dancing munition, it uses a variety of navigation/target acquisition systems, a variety of warheads, and can be either a glide or a powered weapon.

Range of the powered JSOW exceeds 108nm (200km), whereas the unpowered versions can reach out to 40nm (64km) from high altitude but only 12nm (22km) from low altitude. Although the unpowered version has been used against Iraqi air defence sites in the late 1990s, it has been criticised for not offering significantly more stand-off capability than current weapons.

AGM-154A is a soft-target weapon with BLU-97 submunitions, while the AGM-154B is anti-armour, with BLU-108 submunitions. Both use GPD/INS homing. AGM-154C has a unitary warhead, with an autonomous IIR terminal guidance sensor. In the late summer of 1999, the US General Accounting Office stated that effectiveness of the B and C variants would be less than projected, due to a limited ability to hit moving targets, or targets where the geographical co-ordinates are not known in advance.

SEAD

With the EA-6 Prowler due for retirement, the Hornet is the obvious replacement in the Suppression of Enemy Air Defences (SEAD) role. Hornet has long carried the AGM-45 Shrike, of Vietnam vintage; Standard was built in only limited quantities, and the successor is the AGM-88 High speed Anti-Radiation Missile (HARM). Its function is to seek and destroy hostile ground radars, operating in three modes: self-protect, target of opportunity, and prebriefed.

In the self-protect mode, the Hornet's RWR detects threat emissions, the mission computer assesses threat priorities and feeds the necessary data to the missile, all in milliseconds, whereupon HARM can be launched and will home on the emissions selected. In target of opportunity mode, the seeker operates automatically. In prebriefed mode, HARM is launched from within range, and in the general direction of known hostile ground radars. If one comes on line and starts to emit, HARM will immediately start to home on it. If emissions cease during the missile time of flight, HARM will continue to home on its last known position, whereas if nothing happens, HARM will detonate in midair at the end of its run.

Above: Some idea of the wide variety of stores that the Hornet can carry is given here, though the list is by no means comprehensive. The operational use of TERs is restricted because of the high degree of drag they induce in flight.

F/A-18 Hornet stores options

1 AIM-9L Sidewinder AAM
2 AIM-9J Sidewinder AAM
3 AGM-65 Maverick ASM
4 AGM-62 Walleye ASM
5 AGM-109 Harpoon anti-ship missile
6 Drop tank, 315US gall (262 Imp gall, 1,192lit)
7 B57 tactical thermonuclear bomb
8 Durandal anti-runway weapon
9 SUU-20 practice dispenser
10 ASQ-173 laser spot tracker/strike camera (LST/SCAM) pod
11 AIM-7 Sparrow AAM
12 AGM-88A Harm anti-radar missile
13 Gun port
14 M61A1 Vulcan 20mm cannon with 570-round ammunition drum
15 GBU-10E/B Paveway II Mk 84 2,000lb (907kg) laser-guided bomb (LGB)
16 AAS-38 forward-looking infra-red (FLIR) pod
17 Mk 84 2,000lb (907kg) low-drag (LD) general-purpose bomb
18 Three Mk 82 500lb (227kg) low-drag (LD) 'slick' general-purpose bombs on TER (triple ejection rack)
19 Mk 82 high-drag (HD) 'Snakeye' retarded general-purpose bomb
20 M117 750lb (340kg) general-purpose bomb
21 Stores carrier
22 Data link container for Walleye guidance or flight test monitoring
23 CBU-59/B or Mk 20 Rockeye antitank cluster bomb
24 Two Mk 83 1,000lb (454kg) low-drag (LD) general-purpose bombs
25 LAU-61A/A rocket pod
26 LAU-68B/A rocket pod

Hornets in service

On June 30, 1981, Vice Admiral Wesley L. McDonald, US Navy, gave his verdict on the Hornet's value to the service: "The versatility of the F/A-18 to effectively perform both the fighter and the attack missions provides the battle group commander with options never before available. When in a defensive posture, the Hornet will counter either air or surface threat. Offensively, it will provide both fighter escort and a survivable ordnance delivery vehicle with finite accuracy. This force multiplication effect is not available with any other aircraft in the world . . . All indications are that the Navy/Marine team has a superb machine in which to move forward into the future. He was right!

Experimental squadrons VX-4 and VX-5 were the first USN units to fly the Hornet, but the first true Hornet squadron was VFA-125 – the Rough Raiders – which was commissioned at NAS Lemoore, California, on 13 November, 1980. VFA-125 was a fleet-readiness squadron, charged with training both ground and air crew for the operational units. As such, it had at its peak a far greater complement than a normal squadron, with a total strength of 60 Hornets, a high proportion of them two-seaters, 75 officers, including 30 pilots, and about 600 enlisted men. It converted operational squadrons to the Hornet at a rate of four per year. A second fleet-readiness squadron, VFA-106 Gladiators, was commissioned at NAS Cecil Field, Florida, in April 1984. Although a third, dedicated Marine squadron was reported to be planned for MCAS Yuma, Arizona, this was never activated.

The Rough Raiders were a unique mixed Navy and Marine Corps outfit. Their first commanding officer was Capt. James W. Partington, USN, and the executive officer was Lt. Col. Gary R. VanGysel, USMC. Their backgrounds were, as one might expect with a dual-role aircraft like the Hornet, dissimilar. Captain Partington had extensive attack experience flying Skyhawks and Corsairs, while Lt. Col. VanGysel was a very experienced Phantom driver. At first the squadron build-up was slow. The first Hornet arrived on 19 February, 1981, and was followed by two more aircraft from the pilot production batch. The first full-scale production Hornet did not arrive until September, and by the end of the year, the Rough Raiders had eight Hornets.

Approximately 150 of the Hornets on order were two-seat TF/A-18As, about one in every nine of the total order and, following the precedent of the F-15 and F-16, they were redesignated F/A-18Bs.

Later two-seaters became F/A-18Ds and Fs. The two-seaters are fully combat-capable, although carrying less fuel; they are slightly short on range compared to the single-seater. They feature an extended canopy, with the rear seat set 6in (15cm) higher than the front seat to give the guy in the back good visibility, and the rear cockpit is identical to the front except that it does not have a HUD. The second seat displaces a fuel tank, and the TF/A-18A carries 600lb (272kg) less fuel internally. Any performance differences between the two are marginal.

By August 1981 the VFA-125 pilots had reached the stage in their training where they were ready for Air Combat Manoeuvring (ACM) experience, despite the fact that at this point only three Hornets had been assigned to the squadron, and these had to be shared between 16 pilots. ACM is an unproduc-

Above: Two F-18As and two TF-18As of the Rough Raiders in a neat formation during the deployment to MCAS Yuma in January 1982.

tive exercise when carried out between fighters of the same type as the only difference is that of pilot quality, so adversary aircraft were provided in the form of an A-4 Skyhawk of VA-127 (the Cylons), from NAS Lemoore, and an F-5E Tiger II from the US Navy Fighter Weapons School (usually known as 'Top Gun') at NAS Miramar, near San Diego.

An adversary aircraft is a type selected for its performance similarities to known or likely 'threat' aircraft. The Skyhawk represents the MiG-17 while

Below: A Hornet of VFA-125 takes the wire aboard USS *Constellation* during the Rough Raiders' first carrier qualifications in October 1982.

the F-5E doubles for the MiG-21. In most cases, adversary aircraft wear Warsaw Pact camouflage, with Soviet-style 'buzz numbers' on the nose. Adversary pilots are trained in Soviet techniques and tactics, and with their specially chosen aircraft simulate the most realistic threat possible for training purposes.

The four-day exercise consisted entirely of one versus one encounters. The adversary pilots, both very experienced men, were as keen as anyone to see what the Hornet could really do, especially after all the controversy that had surrounded it. They were most impressed, Major George Stuart of the USMC describing the Hornet as being as capable as any aircraft in the inventory, while Lt. John C. Forrester, USN, felt afterwards that there was no comparison between the Hornet and the two adversary types. He was also impressed by the fact that the Rough Raiders, although inexperienced on the type, had reached such a high level of competence, the sign of an easy aeroplane to fly.

The next stage was a ten-day deployment to MCAS Yuma with five Hornets in November 1981, followed by an extended deployment, also to Yuma, by nine Hornets, lasting from January 5-27, 1982, to complete ACM training for the initial batch of 16 pilots assigned to VFA-125, and to finalize the ACM syllabus for the squadrons to be trained on the Hornet. The advantage of Yuma is that it has an electronically instrumented range able to track up to eight aircraft at a time, while simulating and assessing missile firings and recording the proceedings on video tape. The entire mission is then replayed to the pilots on their return. Skilled debriefers beware! This elaborate system, produced by Cubic Corporation's Defense Systems Division in San Diego, rejoices in the acronym of TACTS/ACMI (Tactical Aircrew Combat Training System/Air Combat Manoeuvre Instrumentation). Electronic pods are attached to the participating fighters: these emit signals

which are received by a network of solar-powered antennas on the ground for transmission back through a series of micro-wave relay stations to a mobile recording centre. The combats can then be reconstructed and evaluated.

The bulk of the opposition for the second deployment was provided by Skyhawks of the Cylons, although Top Gun Skyhawks, Canadian F-5s from No. 433 Squadron, and Tomcats from VF-51 and VX-4 also participated. The anti-Tomcat sorties were flown one versus one, while the others were generally multi-bogey encounters at odds of up to three to one against the Hornet. The multi-bogey engagements pressurized the Rough Raiders into using their systems capability to the full, whereas in one versus one encounters there is always a tendency to close quickly to visual range, then stay visual.

Naturally, the Hornet did not win every encounter – there is no aircraft/pilot combination in the world capable of pulling that off – but the results achieved left the Rough Raiders full of enthusiasm for their mount. Navy Lt. Phil Scher of the Cylons hitched a ride in the back seat of a Hornet during one exercise. An experienced adversary pilot who had previously flown against the Tomcat, Eagle, and Fighting Falcon, he commented afterwards: "From close up, I can honestly say that the F/A-18 is magic. I don't think that there are many airplanes, if any, that are capable of physically beating the Hornet in the air."

Shoot-out at Yuma
Questions that are frequently posed are, how good is the Hornet in the air-to-air arena, and how would it shape up against the F-16? The following account of an engagement that took place during the second Yuma deployment in part answers the first question.

Through Telegraph Pass at 420kt (774km/h), two F/A-18 Hornet jet fighters enter the range, level at 'Angels one-five', and scan the early morning sky for

the enemy. Hornet One's radar locks on to a target. He transmits:

"Contact . . . a single . . . on the nose at 15,000ft (4,570m)."

Hornet Two climbs to 25,000ft (7,620m) to gain an offensive position. Suddenly the radar blip separates.

"We've got two . . . the wingman is splitting high and left," replies Hornet Two. "I'm showing 1,000kt (1,840km/h) overtake."

Above: A Hornet of VFA-125 photographed at high altitude. The strangely foreshortened effect is a result of distortion caused by the canopy of the A-7 camera ship.

Below: Hornets of VMFA-314 Black Knights prepare to launch during their first sea deployment in July 1983. The Black Knights are assigned to CVW-13 aboard USS Coral Sea.

Above: In military power only, a clean Hornet of VMFA-323 Death Rattlers leaves the flight deck. The Hornet can be flown off the catapult 'hands-off'. VMFA-323 partners VMFA-314, VFA-131 and VFA-132 as part of the air wing embarked on *Coral Sea*.

Left: As a direct result of combat experience, pilots of modern fighters have an unobstructed view to the rear. The Hornet is comparable to any in this respect, as this view of a TF-18A back-seater shows.

Below: Pilot's eye view astern as a Hornet climbs gently away from the carrier it has just left in December 1982. It can be seen that blind spots, potentially so dangerous in air combat, have been reduced to a minimum.

"Six miles . . . in the box . . . four miles, tally-ho," replies Hornet One. "It's an A-4, shoot, shoot!"

"Fox One," calls Hornet Two, and the computer sends the simulated missile on its way to a lethal kill. As Hornet Two pitches back to assist, he hears Hornet One call a shot on the remaining bogey. The computer scores the shot as a miss as the bogey pilot hauls his aircraft into a vision-dimming 6g turn. Hornet Two manoeuvres into a cover position while Hornet One strives to regain the offensive advantage.

"Fox Two," calls Hornet One. "Good kill" is the call over the radio from the computer monitor station. Both aircraft turn west and 'bug out' in full afterburner, streaking towards 'good guy' country at the pass. The entire fight is over less than 30 seconds after the pilots initially sighted each other.

Pilots and aircraft

It may, of course, be argued that this exercise involved adversary aircraft which were far inferior to the Hornet and was therefore an unfair match. On the other hand, adversary pilots are men of high experience and ability levels, who do not do the job to be beaten and thus bolster their opponent's confidence; they play to win. Despite the discrepancy in the hardware, pilot ability historically always has been, and for the foreseeable future will continue to be the dominant factor in air fighting. Better technology helps a lot, but it is not the be-all and end-all.

In a contest between the Hornet and the Fighting Falcon, with pilots of equal ability, the result appears to be wide open. At the time of writing, the Hornet's weapon system is superior, and the Fighting Falcon has no effective answer to the 'shoot-in-the-face' capability conferred by the AIM-7 Sparrow. It then becomes a question of tactics. Initially, the Hornet pilot should try to keep his energy levels high and maintain his distance, taking Sparrow shots from any angle as opportunity offers, thus forcing the F-16 to manoeuvre hard to evade and deplete his energy. If this succeeded, the Hornet could then close for a heat missile or gun shot. In one versus one close combat, the contest would be fairly even.

It is the author's opinion that transient performance is more important than sustained turning ability. While no fighter in the world can match the sustained turn ability of the F-16, the pitch rate and the high AOA capability of the Hornet are believed to be better than those of the F-16, so that pilot ability would be the dominant factor in any contest between the two, and especially the ability of each pilot to use the strong points of his machine, which, rather surprisingly, is not always the case. For example, an Aggressor Squadron F-5E versus F-16 combat in 1982 saw the austere Northrop fighter achieve a good attacking position, whereupon the F-16 pilot evaded by a series of 9g loops which the F-5E was unable to match. The Aggressor pilot later commented: "I just flew around a while and waited for him to get tired!" This was not a good example of the use of sustained turn.

Multi-bogey combats

It must be remembered that one versus one combats are just peacetime training; they are not war. In war, multi-bogey combats are the norm, and they are, regardless of technical superiority, a great leveller. Leaving aside the BVR attack capability of the Hornet, one would expect the results of a multi-bogey contest between the F-16 and the Hornet to come out about equal, given equal numerical quantities. Given equal cost quantities, the cheaper F-16 would have a slight edge, but there are limits to the cost quantity equation. Given equal cost quantities, the austere F-5E is probably the greatest of them all, but procurement levels would be so high that pilot standards would have to drop to fill the empty cockpits. Moreover, the equal cost quantity argument, if carried to extremes, also involves the acceptance of an adverse kill ratio, which would be counterproductive due to the effect on morale. But to return to the Hornet, it may be fairly assumed that in the fighter role, it will perform extremely creditably.

The built-in reliability and maintainability of the Hornet paid handsome dividends during the second Yuma detachment. Originally, 288 sorties were planned, an average of 1.5 per aircraft per day. In the event, a total of 326 sorties exceeding 400 hours flight time were carried out, and every sortie had full systems operable. Only one sortie had to be cancelled, when a minor fault caused a 20-minute delay, which was enough to prevent the pilot from arriving at the range at his allotted time. Each Hornet averaged 44.7 hours of flight time during the deployment, and the remarkably low average of 11 MMH/FH was recorded. Not one fuel leak or hydraulic failure occurred during the deployment, a stark contrast to the Hornet's predecessor, the F-4 Phantom, of which it is often said, with some justification, that if it doesn't leak, it must be empty. The air combat training syllabus was satisfactorily finalized, and two months later a three-week deployment to NAS Fallon, in Nevada, served a similar function for the attack training syllabus.

Performance analysis

The original specification deficiencies either have been cured or do not seem to worry the pilots. The slow roll rate is now up to about 220deg/sec, about as much as a pilot can reasonably handle. The Hornet still does not accelerate from Mach 0.8 to Mach 1.6 in the required time, which was to give maximum energy at missile launch, but it is faster up to Mach 1.2 than virtually anything else, having beaten even the F-15 in 'drag races' up to this speed, and as hardly any air combat is likely to take

place at speeds exceeding Mach 1.2, the pilots consider this deficiency to be unimportant.

The Hornet has attracted a lot of flak over its range capability, but many of the comparisons drawn seem suspect, especially those involving the Corsair. Fuel flow management and close attention to flight profiles for the attack mission have produced improvements, and although a Hornet in the attack configuration does not have the radius of action of the Corsair that it replaces, the difference is reportedly less than 10 per cent. The Hornet's far greater survivability due to its vastly superior performance is considered by the pilots to be more than an adequate trade-off for a reduction in maximum range.

From the staff point of view, an operational evaluation in 1982 stated that the unrefuelled capabilities of the Hornet cause a reduction in the stand-off range of a battle group, an important consideration in the event of an action against a Soviet fleet equipped with SS-N-12 or SS-N-19 surface-launched anti-shipping missiles with a range of 300nm (550km). Nevertheless, it appears that the criteria for the Hornet should not be performance comparisons against other types, but how well it performs its allotted role.

In the final analysis, theoretical ranges attainable at certain speeds under precise conditions with defined weapon

loads are irrelevant. With the attack role specifically in mind, the only question worth asking is, can the Hornet deliver a worthwhile load at a sufficient distance (not necessarily greater in either case) with greater accuracy and a greater margin of survivability than the aircraft that it is to replace? In the air combat role, the question becomes, can the Hornet perform both as an interceptor and close combat fighter in an effective manner without being outclassed by the opposition? In both cases, the answer must be an unqualified yes. The pilots genuinely praise the Hornet's handling qualities, although with neutral speed stability the control column does not have a lot of 'feel', and a certain amount of care must be taken to avoid overstressing the airframe. Maximum lift, achieved at about 35deg AOA, can be reached with a one-handed pull on the stick, while to reach higher AOA two hands are needed. The aircraft is almost spinproof, while if it does depart controlled flight, recovery is simple. It is stable in both roll and yaw, and is a good gun platform up to 30deg AOA.

Carrier qualification

A further milestone in finalizing the Hornet training syllabus was reached between September 27 and October 4, 1982, when the Rough Raiders completed their first carrier qualification operations aboard the USS *Constella-*

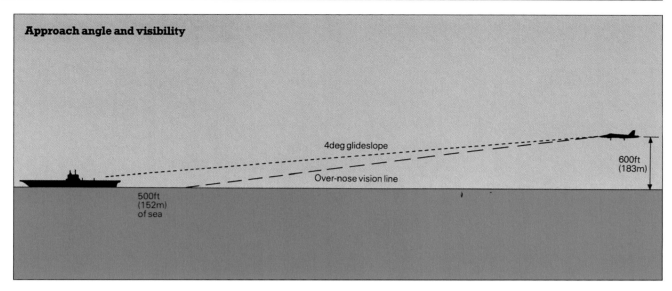

Approach angle and visibility

4deg glideslope

Over-nose vision line

600ft (183m)

500ft (152m) of sea

Above: The Hornet has a low AOA on the final approach, and the excellent visibility over the nose simplifies landing on a carrier deck to a considerable degree.

tion. Six pilots using two single-seat Hornets logged ten bolters as well as 57 day and 24 night traps during this period, and no problems were encountered.

Catapult launches are regarded as easy. The Hornet taxis to the cat, and the launch bar, which is attached to the nose gear, is positioned in the shuttle on the catapult track. The pilot makes his final checks, then waves to the catapult officer that he is ready to go. The Hornet is trimmed to fly 'hands off', though it is normal for the pilot to put his left hand on the throttle to prevent it slipping back under the 4g acceleration as the catapult fires.

Landing is carried out either manually or automatically. For a manual landing the pilot sets up the speed, line-up and glideslope. 'On-speed' is taken from the aircraft's instruments, while line-up is judged from the centreline on the carrier

Below: The carrier suitability trials Hornet launches from a 6deg ski-jump ramp at NATC Patuxent River. The attitude of the main gear suggests that a fair proportion of the aircraft's weight, though not yet all of it, has been transferred to the wings.

deck. The glideslope, an angle of about 4deg, is taken from the Fresnel Lens, which is a series of directional lights on the carrier: the pilot watches the mirror of the Fresnel Lens and the correctness of his approach is shown by the colour of the light reflected in the mirror, an orange light indicating that the glide-slope is correct. At touch-down the throttles are advanced to full military power; if the hook misses the wires the Hornet flies right on past the carrier and tries again.

The automatic system is different again. At a set distance out on the approach the pilot couples his ACLS to the ACLS SPN-42 system on the carrier. This transmits signals to the Hornet's auto-pilot which guide the aircraft straight on to the carrier deck, making due allowance for deck motion. The throttles are controlled automatically in this mode by the Hornet's approach power compensator (APC).

Training syllabus

The pilot training syllabus evolved by VFA-125 lasts five months, a little longer than the course for maintenance personnel, and consists of four phases: transition, air-to-air, air-to-ground, and carrier qualification. Instruction begins in the brand new Hornet Learning Center at Lemoore, where computer-assisted

Left: Final checks are carried out as one of the VMFA-314 Hornets prepares to launch from the catapult aboard USS *Constellation* during carrier operations in July 1983.

Below: Deck crew cluster round Hornets of VMFA-314 as they get ready to launch. The coloured vests indicate the various functions to which the individual crewmen are assigned – purple and a white 'F' identify the fuelling team.

audio-visual techniques cover procedures, switchology and systems operation, and the fledgling Hornet pilot then progresses to the simulators. The first of these is the Part-Task Trainer (PTT), consisting of simplified Hornet cockpits, in which familiarization with HOTAS is begun and the manipulative skills needed to operate the controls is acquired. Then comes the Operational Flight Trainer (OFT), which simulates actual flight from takeoff to landing by means of three visual displays and uses a g-suit/g-seat buffet system for extra realism. OFT training covers both airfield and carrier takeoffs and landings, the complete instrument syllabus, and emergency procedures.

Then comes the Weapons Tactics Trainer (WTT), consisting of two 40ft (12.2m) domes with a cockpit in each and seven televisual projectors. The WTT, in which each student will spend an estimated 50 hours, provides advanced air-to-air radar training and ACM practice. Each dome can be operated solo, or combined into a 'twin-tub' to allow the pilots in each dome to 'fly' against each other. The projectors generate a realistic earth/sky backdrop on the inside of the domes on which target, missile and gunfire images are also generated. After sufficient time has been spent in the simulators, flight training begins. This consists of around 70 sorties, supplemented by the simulators as necessary, followed by a further 20 sorties for carrier qualification.

Operational squadrons

The first operational Hornet squadron was VMFA-314, the Black Knights, commanded by Lt. Col. Peter Field, who had played a major part in the Hornet FSD programme at Patuxent River. The Black Knights were part of the Phantom-equipped 3rd Marine Air Wing based at MCAS El Toro, California, and the inaugural ceremony took place on January 7, 1983, at El Toro. At a press conference immediately afterwards, Lt. Col. Field had a number of points to make about the Hornet in reply to questions from reporters.

The first concerned the accuracy of weapons delivery, which was described as better than ever before, with a weapon system "literally out of Star Wars". The second point concerned the sheer pleasure of flying the Hornet. This contrasts with the Phantom, which has never been regarded as an easy aeroplane to fly and requires a lot of concentration. The third point concerned the maintainability of the Hornet, with MMH/FH reduced to one-third of the figure for the Phantom. He commented that the squadron had achieved more flight hours over a given period with their first four Hornets than they had been used to getting from their full complement of 12 Phantoms. Later in the year, the Black Knights participated in Red Flag 83/5 at Nellis AFB, where they flew as aggressors, clashing with Air Force F-15s and F-16s. Unfortunately, the details are still classified at the time of writing.

The Black Knights were followed on to the Hornet by their fellow squadrons of the 3rd MAW, VMFA-323 and VMFA-531, and the Navy was not far behind, VA-113 Stingers commencing training for the Hornet on March 26, 1983. They became operational in August of the same year, a full two months ahead of schedule. The Stingers were previously equipped with Corsairs, and their commanding officer, Cdr. William Pickavance, was quick to comment that for years the squadron had needed fighter escort, whereas they now had an aircraft with an excellent self-defence capability.

Hornet Squadrons: USN and USMC Hornet Units, Summer 1999				
Squadron	**Name**	**Type**	**Tail Code**	**Carrier**
VFA-15	Valions	F/A-18C/D	AJ	Roosevelt
VFA-22	Redcocks	F/A-18C/D	NH	Vinson
VFA-25	Fist of the Fleet	F/A-18C/D	NK	Lincoln
VFA-27	Chargers	F/A-18C/D	NF	Kitty Hawk
VFA-34	Blue Blasters	F/A-18C/D	AA	Washington
VFA-37	Bulls	F/A-18C/D	AC	Enterprise
VFA-81	Sunliners	F/A-18C/D	AA	Washington
VFA-82	Marauders	F/A-18C/D	AB	Kennedy
VFA-83	Rampagers	F/A-18C/D	AA	Washington
VFA-86	Sidewinders	F/A-18C/D	AB	Kennedy
VFA-87	Golden Warriors	F/A-18C/D	AJ	Roosevelt
VFA-94	Mighty Shrikes	F/A-18C/D	NH	Vinson
VFA-97	Warhawks	F/A-18C/D	NH	Vinson
VFA-105	Gunslingers	F/A-18C/D	AC	Enterprise
VFA-106	Gladiators	F/A-18A-D	AD	FRS
VFA-113	Stingers	F/A-18C/D	NK	Lincoln
VFA-115	Eagles	F/A-18C/D	NK	Lincoln
VFA-122	Flying Eagles	F/A-18E/F	NJ	FRS
VFA-125	Rough Raiders	F/A-18A-D	NJ	FRS
VFA-131	Wildcats	F/A-18C/D	AG	Eisenhower
VFA-136	Knight Hawks	F/A-18C/D	AG	Eisenhower
VFA-137	Kestrels	F/A-18C/D	NE	Constellation
VFA-146	Blue Diamonds	F/A-18C/D	NG	Stennis
VFA-147	Argonauts	F/A-18C/D	NG	Stennis
VFA-151	Vigilantes	F/A-18C/D	NE	Constellation
VFA-192	Golden Dragons	F/A-18C/D	NF	Kitty Hawk
VFA-195	Dambusters	F/A-18E/F	NF	Kitty Hawk
VMFA(AW)-224	Bengals	F/A-18D	WK	Unassigned
VMFA-251	Thunderbolts	F/A-18C/D	AB	Kennedy
VMFA-312	Checkerboards	F/A-18C/D	AB	Kennedy
VMFA-314	Black Knights	F/A-18C/D	NE	Constellation
VMFA-323	Death Rattlers	F/A-18C/D	NE	Constellation
VX-9	Vampires	F/A-18A/F	XE	Unassigned

Two of the biggest controversies about the Hornet appear to have been largely silenced since its operational debut. The first concerned the multi-role capability insofar as it affected the pilot. Some pilots are natural air fighters, while others really enjoy moving mud. The opinion has been widely held that never the twain should meet, and while units had specialist roles, pilots tended to be assigned to squadrons where their natural bent could best be utilized. Reports from the squadrons appear to indicate that interchangeability appears to be working, although doubts will continue to exist for some time yet. Of course, a squadron contains more pilots than aircraft, so it seems logical that if the split between natural fighter and natural attack pilots is about even, then the nature of the mission can be allowed to affect the allocation of the pilots within certain limits.

Solo mission capability

The other doubtful area has been whether one man can fly the type of mission that has come to be regarded as the prerogative of the two-seater. The general opinion of those who fly the Hornet appears to be that the advanced avionics, and especially the cockpit, enable one man to perform satisfactorily, although this verdict is not unanimous. Some former Skyhawk and Corsair pilots would prefer a back-seater to help with the workload, despite, or perhaps because of their previous experience. It is, however, accepted in the Hornet squadrons that this is a minority opinion. As the old saying goes, "Combat is the ultimate, and the unkindest, judge."

At least 40 USN and USMC squadrons are planned, although this number, as well as the total planned procurement of the Hornet, may change if Navy and Marine Corps mission requirements are revised. The Hornet has largely supplanted the F-14 Tomcat in the fleet air defence role and, as from 1999, *Constellation, Kitty Hawk, John S. Stennis, Carl Vinson, Abraham Lincoln, John F. Kennedy, Enterprise,* and *George Washington* deploy only a single

squadron of Tomcats, with three squadrons of Hornets. The sole exceptions are the *Theodore Roosevelt* and the *Dwight D. Eisenhower*, which have two Tomcat squadrons.

At one time the US Navy and Marine Corps planned to have at least 40 Hornet squadrons in service, but this has been reduced in recent years. Hornets will almost certainly replace the remaining Tomcats as the latter reach the end of their useful lives, and it seems probable that an EW Hornet based on the F/A-18F will replace the elderly EA-6B Prowler, although this will be a hard act to follow. But in another ten years or so, many Hornets will be replaced by the proposed Joint Strike Fighter, always assuming this goes ahead.

The success of the ski-jump in assisting the Harrier to take off, which on the face of it appears to offer something for nothing in terms of aerodynamics and power, caused the USN to examine its applications for conventional machines. In the mid-1980s Hornet ski-jump trials were held at NAS Patuxent River, but operationally the concept was not pursued.

Export Hornets

Even as the USN and USMC were building up their Hornet stocks, many other nations sought to upgrade their strength. Air defence was the primary requirement, but an all-rounder with a credible all-weather attack capability was a very attractive proposition.

In the 1980s, the main competition came from the General Dynamics F-16 Fighting Falcon and the Dassault Mirage 2000. Both were single-engined, and both were more affordable than the Hornet in terms of acquisition and operating costs. In the export field, this was a built-in headwind for the all-rounder from St. Louis, and only where the national operational requirements were most demanding, and quality more important than quantity, was it successful.

The first export customer for the Hornet was the Canadian Armed Forces, which placed a substantial order in the summer of 1980. Factors influencing the Canadian decision were the sheer size of the country and the nature of the terrain. Airfields were few and far between; weather conditions were often extreme. Two engines were considered to give a better safety margin in those days, although in recent years reliability has improved to the degree that the difference is marginal. Finally, the Hornet was considered to have more growth potential than its rivals.

The Canadian CF-188 differed from its US counterpart in detail. A 600,000-candlepower spotlight was mounted on the port side of the forward fuselage; a standard CAF item used to visually identify other aircraft at night. A different ILS was fitted, the ACLS omitted, and the standard USN sea survival gear was replaced by a cold-weather land survival outfit.

Another feature of the CF-188 is the

Above: Two CF-18B two-seaters of the CF take on fuel from a CC-137 tanker. Flight refuelling is essential for the Canadian Forces, given the vast size of the country. Dummy canopies are painted on the undersides of all Canadian CF-18s for aspect deception of opponents in combat.

dummy canopy painted on the underside of the fuselage. Matt black, but with irregular patches of gloss to give the impression of highlights, this was the brainchild (and patent) of American aviation artist Keith Ferris. The idea is to give aspect deception, to make an opponent think that the CF-188 is doing something that it isn't. Opinions on its effectiveness are divided; one school of thought is that if you are close enough to see it, you are too close to be fooled. Others maintain that it poses a collision hazard, so it obviously works some of the time.

The first CF-188s were delivered to

Right: The Royal Australian Air Force has ordered a total of 75 Hornets to replace three squadrons of Mirage IIIs. Among the distinctive features of the RAAF Hornets are the IFF antennae under the nose.

Cold Lake, Alberta, on 25 October 1982, and the first Canadian Hornet unit formed was No 410 Operational Training Squadron, whose pilots had been through the VFA-125 syllabus. There are two Canadian Hornet Wings: No 4 with three squadrons at Cold Lake, and No 3 with two squadrons at Bagotville, Quebec. Although the A/B variants, they have been continually upgraded over the years, and hope to retrofit the APG-73 radar before long.

Like Canada, Australia has a large and inhospitable land-mass to defend, but much of their flying is done over water, with maritime surveillance one of their priorities. As with Canada, the main opposition was provided by the F-16, and once again the Hornet won out through the factors of twin-engined safety, better growth potential, and superior avionics.

The first two Hornets for Australia were delivered to RAAF Williamtown from NAS Lemoore in California, a distance of 6,672nm (12,364km) in a record-breaking non-stop flight of 15 hours. They were accompanied by a KC-10 Extender, and refuelled in midair 13 times in total. In theory only four refuellings were necessary, but for safety reasons they were kept topped well up.

The remaining Australian Hornets were assembled in-country. They differ from USN standard in not having catapult launch equipment, and the ACLS was replaced by a conventional ILS. They have indigenous TACAN, IFF and fatigue monitoring systems, an aural gear down warning system, and an HF radio for long distance communications. Finally, they have a landing light.

Considerable upgrading is planned: the APG-65 radar will be replaced by

Above: The first Swiss-assembled Hornet seen on its first flight in October 1996. It took a long time for the thrifty Swiss to decide on the Hornet, but given their needs it was the right choice.

Below: Four two-seater F/A-18Ds for the Malaysian Air force seen at Lambert St. Louis just prior to their departure to Butterworth AFB in August 1998.

the APG-71, and a GPS navigation system, an improved mission computer, a new RWR and ECM dispenser are all scheduled. AMRAAM will replace Sparrow and ASRAAM, with a helmet-mounted cueing system, will replace Sidewinder.

The third Hornet operator was Spain, which selected the type on its superior avionics. The first Spanish EF-18, as it was designated, arrived in 1986 and deliveries were complete by 1990. Spain has since taken delivery of another batch against delays with Typhoon. They are based at Torrejon, Moron, and Zaragosa.

Switzerland was impressed by the docile handling and superb radar/avionics which it felt was suitable for operations in such a mountainous country, but then paused to re-evaluate. After some considerable delay, the first Swiss Hornet arrived in 1996, and No 16 Squadron was commissioned that year at Payerne.

Swiss F/A-18C/D models, powered by F404-GE-402 engines, are virtually straight off the shelf, but with a couple of unusual modifications. In Switzerland the

Hornet is used for air defence only, and their aircraft are thus devoid of air-to-surface kit. But the ensuing weight savings were eaten up by the use of titanium fuselage bulkheads instead of aluminium alloy, which increases airframe life by another 2,000 hours. The Swiss are not known for rapid aircraft replacement, and this looks like a typical example of Helvetian thrift. Almost certainly the Swiss will still be operating Hornets in 2030, long after they have been retired elsewhere.

The ALQ-165 ASPJ is fitted, which implies more faith in the system than the US services had (another bargain?), while the use of liquid oxygen, regarded as a hazard in tunnel shelters, has been replaced by an On-Board Oxygen Generation System (OBOGS).

Hard on the heels of neutral Switzerland came almost equally neutral Finland. As a near neighbour of the Russian Federation, Finland has always been careful to be even-handed in military aircraft acquisition, operating a mix of Russian and Western types. When the Suomen Ilmavoimat received its first

Hornets, on 7 November 1995, it became the first air arm to operate an advanced American fighter side by side with MiGs, although as the MiG-21bis was phased out soon after, this was of short duration.

Like the Swiss, the Finns operate the F/A-18C/D in the air defence role only, and also like them their Hornets carry the ALQ-165 jammer. The engines are the F404-GE-402, with the APG-73 radar. The climate of Finland is fairly extreme, and one of the reasons given for the selection of the Hornet over its competitors was that the Ilmavoimat was impressed by its performance in the equally harsh climate of Canada.

The first Ilmavoimat Hornet unit was HavLLv (Fighter Squadron) 21, based at Tampere/Pirkkala, which is also the home of the Hornet conversion unit. It was followed by HavLLv 31, based at Kuopio/Rissala in 1996. Like the Swedes, the Finns have a tradition of off-site basing, and in August of that year this unit notched up a notable first when its Hornets operated from a stretch of road. One notable difference from the USN aircraft is that Finnish Hornets are fitted with

Below: Leading edge root extensions prominent, a Spanish EF-18 launches from Aviano in Italy for a combat air patrol over Kosovo as part of Operation *Allied Force*. The only loads are "jugs" and AAMs.

Martin-Baker seats, partly for commonality with existing equipment, at a reported saving of $800,000.

At the time of the invasion by Iraq, the Al Quwwat Al Jawwiya Al Kuwaitiya (Kuwait Air Force) had 40 F/A-18C/Ds on order, one of the selection criteria having been that the Hornet was at least a match for the Iraqi MiG-29 in air combat, and far superior in the attack role. The order was fulfilled shortly after the end of the Gulf War, replacing the A-4 Skyhawks and Mirage F.1s previously operated.

Malaysia was the next Hornet operator, with eight F/A-18Ds to provide an single squadron attack force in conjunction with 18 MiG-29Ns in the air superiority role. Malaysian Hornets are powered by F404-GE-402 engines, and are fitted with the APG-73 radar. The first Malaysian Hornet was delivered on 19 March 1997.

Thailand ordered Hornets in May 1996, but their offer was conditional upon part payment in cash, part in goods. While this was initially accepted by McDonnell Douglas, notwithstanding the trend for Thai cuisine, it took an awful lot of frozen Thai chicken to pay for a single Hornet. The order was cancelled.

At the end of 1999, several nations are evaluating the Hornet, including former Warsaw Pact members. Whether any orders will emerge remains to be seen, but Chile has expressed an interest in the F/A-18E/F to counter Peruvian MiG-29s.

At the first rumblings of conflict in the Gulf in 1990, the US Marines were quickly on the scene; four Hornet squadrons arrived at Bahrain in late August 1990, and started to fly air defence missions. They were supplemented on 7 October by the Canadian 409 Squadron at Qatar on 7 October. But action only commenced on the first day of Desert Storm; 17 January 1991.

It was the first daylight attack of the war; seven F/A-18Cs of VF-81 Sunliners launched from USS *Saratoga,* based in the Red Sea. The target was an airfield, H-3, nearly 550nm (1,019km) from the carrier, in western Iraq. The strike was scheduled as a four-ship, which was just as well, since three Hornets had to withdraw because of loss of cabin pressurization, loss of communications, and failure to transfer fuel from centreline tanks, respectively. Not a good start.

The Sunliners carried four Mk 84 bombs, a nominal load of 8,000lb (3,629kg); two Sparrows and two Sidewinders, plus a 330gal centreline tank. This load was well within the Hornet's maximum. Attack formation was line abreast. As they closed to within 30nm (56km) of H-3, an E-2C Hawkeye AEW aircraft warned them – "Bandits on your nose, 15 miles" (28km). The Hornets switched to air-to-air mode, and soon all four detected the incoming Iraqi fighters and locked onto them.

They were four MiG-21s in port echelon, supersonic at Mach 1.2. Most

Above: A considerable effort was made to sell the Hornet overseas. This 1980 photograph shows an early prototype, with unfilled LEX slots and notched wing leading edge, in Swedish Air Force markings.

favourably placed were Hornet pilots Mark Fox and Nick Mongillo. Fox stated: "I shot a Sidewinder first. It was a smokeless missile, and I thought at first I had wasted it because I couldn't see it tracking towards the MiG. I fired a Sparrow. The Sidewinder hit though, followed by the Sparrow. The first missile actually did the job, and the Sparrow flew into the fireball."

Meanwhile Mongillo had launched a Sparrow at the second MiG. It connected. The two surviving Iraqi MiGs fled. With switches reset air-to-ground, Fox and Mongillo went on to bomb the target. The dual role fighter had finally proved its worth. As Mark Fox commented: "I do believe we're the only guys to kill anybody while carrying 8,000lb of bombs!" The record was however rather spoiled when Spike Speicher of VF-81 was shot down by an SA-6 missile and killed while on a defence suppression mission earlier that same day.

Defence suppression (SEAD) was a major task for the Hornet during *Desert Storm,* with AGM-88 HARMs the preferred weapon, backed by CBUs and LGBs. The attack mission was far from

Right: A United States Marine Corps Hornet refuels from a USAF KC-135R tanker during the Gulf War of 1991. Note that the tanker boom is fitted with a drogue to allow US Navy and Marine aircraft to take on fuel.

easy. As described by Steve Pomeroy of VMFA-333: "Lousy weather, pitch black, low overcast so you can see all of the AAA and surface-to-air missiles coming up through it, but you can't physically see the target. We can acquire the target based on radar predictions. You're looking through the head-up display, showing slant range, elevation. You've told the computer where the target is, and the weapons are released based on that information".

Faced with intense ground fire, the Hornets ingressed and bombed from considerably higher altitudes than those they used during training. This reportedly gave acceptable levels of accuracy, but we should remember the F-16 experience, in which release speeds exceeded those for which the attack computer had been programmed, leading to much greater inaccuracy. The LST/SCAM also failed to perform as well as expected during the conflict.

Another task, to which USMC two-seater F/A-18Ds were assigned, was as Fast-mover Air Controllers in high threat areas. These located targets and called in strike aircraft. When the strikers arrived, they marked the targets with unguided rockets.

Hornet Gulf War losses were minimal – an F/A-18C of VFA-81 on 17 January and an F/A-18A of VFA-87 on 5 February. Both pilots were killed. Four Hornets were lost to non-combat causes, two of them in a mid-air collision between USMC aircraft on 8 March.

Right: A United States Marine Corps Hornet refuels from a USAF KC-135R tanker during the Gulf War of 1991. Note that the tanker boom is fitted with a drogue to allow US Navy and Marine aircraft to take on fuel.

Specifications

	YF-17	F/A-18A	F/A-18C	F/A-18E
Wingspan	35ft 0in (10.67m)	37ft 6in (11.43m)	37ft 6in (11.43m)	44ft 8½in (13.63m)
Length	56ft 0in (17.07m)	56ft 0in (11.43m)	56ft 0in (11.43m)	60ft 1¼in (18.32m)
Height	14ft 6in (4.42m)	15ft 3½in (4.66m)	15ft 3½in (4.66m)	16ft 0in (4.88m)
Wing area	350sq ft (32.52sq m)	400sq ft (37.16sq m)	400sq ft (37.16sq m)	500sq ft (46.45sq m)
Empty weight	17,000lb (7,711kg)	21,830lb (9,902kg)	23,000lb (10,433kg)	29,574lb (13,415kg)
Normal takeoff weight	23,000lb (10,433kg)	34,700lb (15,740kg)	36,970lb (16,769kg)	46,200lb (20,956kg)
Engines	2 x YJ101-100	2 x F404-400	2 x F404-402	2 x F414-400
Max thrust each	14,000lb (6,350kg)	16,000lb (7,258kg)	17,700lb (8,029kg)	22,000lb (9,979kg)
Internal fuel		10,860lb (4,925kg)	10,860lb (4,925kg)	14,400lb (6,532kg)
Loadings at normal takeoff weight/max power				
Thrust	1.22	0:92	0.96	0.95
Wing	66lb/sq.ft (321kg/sq m)	87lb/sq ft (424kg/sq m)	92lb/sq ft (451kg/sq m)	92lb/sq ft (451kg/sq m)
Performance				
V_{max} hi	Mach 1.95	Mach 1.7	Mach 1.7	Mach 1.8 plus
V_{max} lo	n/a	Mach 1.01	Mach 1.01	Mach 1.01
Operational ceiling	50,000ft (15,239m)	50,000ft (15,239m)	50,000ft (15,239m)	50,000ft (15,239m)
Climb rate	50,000ft/min (254m/sec)	50,000ft/min (254m/sec	50,000ft/min (254m/sec	n/a
Internal fuel	n/a	10,860lb (4,926kg)	10,860lb (4,926kg)	14,400lb (6,532kg)
Range varies with payload and flight profile				

Bosnia to Kosovo

The break-up of the artificial state of Yugoslavia in the early 1990s was followed by bloody civil war. A United Nations peace-keeping force was sent in, followed on 14 July 1993 by Operation *Disciplined Guard,* to provide air cover for six UN security zones. Among the first aircraft to arrive at Aviano in Italy were eight Hornets of VMFA(AW)-533 Hawks, closely followed by six USN aircraft from the USS *Theodore Roosevelt.* All were equipped with the Loral AAS-38 NITE HAWK pod, which was in the process of replacing the LST/SCAM, and which allowed autonomous laser designation.

Since then, Hornets have been almost permanently on station as Operations *Deny Flight* and *Provide Promise* followed. Spanish Hornets also participated. For much of the time there was little action, but they were there and ready. When F-16 pilot Scott O'Grady was shot down on 2 June 1996, the Hawks, by now on the second deployment to the theatre, provided much of the cover during the rescue operation.

As the threat intensified, the Hawks were fitted with the ALQ-165 ASPJ, and other squadrons soon followed suit. Operation *Deliberate Force* saw the Bosnian Serb anti-aircraft forces reduced to impotence by massive air strikes, and peace talks commenced at Dayton, Ohio.

Balkan belligerence did not cease; it merely shifted south to Kosovo. At this point NATO, rather than the UN, took a hand. Peace talks having failed, NATO was left with no alternative but to commence massive air strikes against selected Serbian targets. In Operation *Allied Force,* which began on 24 March 1999, Canadian and Spanish Hornets, as well as American F/A-18s, flew from Aviano, while the Hawks, on their third deployment, operated from Taszar in Hungary. It took 72 days of gradually increasing force, but finally the rump of the Yugoslavian state backed down.

America's Stealth

Contents

Top: The design of the Lockheed F-22A Raptor is a tradeoff between stealth, performance, and agility.

Above: The angular shape of the Lockheed F-117A Nighthawk arose from the need to deflect radar pulses away at an angle, rather than straight back to the sender, reducing detection probability.

Above right: The Northrop B-2A seen on its first flight on 17 July 1989. With no vertical surfaces it relies on split speedbrakes/ailerons for lateral control, as seen here.

Left: The Lockheed Martin X-35 Joint Strike Fighter contender, seen here in US Marine Corps markings. The combination of stealth, STOVL, and affordability, poses problems.

Warplanes

Introduction

Many years ago, a book and film series featured "The Invisible Man!" The hero was an extraordinary crime fighter, who exploited the fact that he could not be seen, and therefore was very difficult, if not impossible, to oppose. Taken to its logical conclusion, an invisible army would be invincible. As for an invisible air force – this concept occurred to the Austrians in 1912, long before the outbreak of the Great War. In those days the only means of detection was visual, and so they replaced the linen coverings of their aeroplanes with transparent Cellon. This was not very successful. Cellon was much heavier than doped linen which reduced performance; nor did it stand up to the ravages of weather. The engine and pilot could not be concealed, while reflections from its surface defeated the object of the exercise.

In 1916, the German Luftstreitkräfte experimented with a couple of Fokker E.III Eindeckers covered in Cellon, with equally dismal results. The idea was right but its time had not yet come.

Visual detection against small (i.e., fighter-sized) aircraft was generally limited to between two and six nautical miles (3.75-11km). Radar detection could increase this to between five and ten times. Radar, and to a lesser degree infra-red invisibility, thus became far more important. There were two ways to achieve this: either to build the aircraft with radar absorbent materials (RAM), which could soak up the incoming impulses and convert them to heat, or to deflect them away at an angle. The former was quite simple, if not terribly effective; the latter was extremely difficult. The main problem was predicting the best deflection angles, which only became possible with advanced computers. For all practical purposes, the SR-71 Blackbird was first generation stealth; the faceted F-117A was of the second generation; while the curvaceous B-2A, with no vertical surfaces, was of the third generation.

America's Stealth Warplanes

Designing a stealth aircraft requires elimination at best, or minimising at least, the visual, radar, thermal and acoustic signatures. Working towards these goals, US designers have for decades been attempting to create the ultimate stealth warplane (and missile), and have battled against a combination of compromises essentially made up of stealth requirements versus performance and mission stipulations, and cost. That they have developed the world's most stealthy combat aircraft to date, in their B-1B, B-2A, F-117A, F-22A and JSF designs, is a tribute to their ingenuity. It remains to be seen whether funds will be made available for them to make further strides toward perfecting the art.

In any form of conflict, invisibility has traditionally been the greatest advantage, conferring as it does, surprise. Its first manifestation was the ambush, in which troops lay concealed until the last minute. Night attack was another, in which the cover of darkness allowed troops to approach undetected, although this demanded a force with a high level of training to be effective. It was inevitable that the concept of invisibility should be applied to air warfare.

Initially, the only two detection signatures were visual and aural. In the early stages, little could be done about the latter, but, since sound lagged behind the aircraft as a compound function of its height, speed, aspect, and distance from the detector, "aural stealth" was not very effective. And as aircraft speeds increased, it became ever less so.

The primary detection signature was visual. As early as 1912, the Austrians experimented with transparent cover-

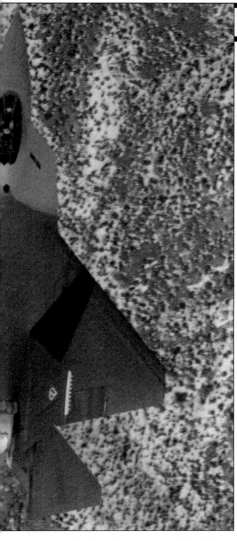

Left: In designing the F-22A Raptor, Lockheed chose to combine speed and agility with a variety of stealth features, which include airframe shape and two-dimensional thrust-vectoring nozzles.

ings, while the first ever stealth fighters were three German Fokker Eindeckers in 1916. There were however problems with weight and the effects of rain, while on a cloudy day, the stealth effect was minimal. There was little future for an overweight fighter that could only be used in clear conditions.

The next step was camouflage. Pale blue undersides made aircraft more difficult to see against the sky, although pale pink was used on high-flying RAF reconnaissance Spitfires. But, as aircraft spent most of their time on the ground, colour schemes were adopted which helped them blend into the background. This underside-topside contrast continued into the 1980s. It was finally dropped because when attack aircraft at low level reefed into a hard turn, they displayed a flash of pale belly, visible to other aircraft miles away. Attack aircraft were consequently given camouflaged undersides as well. Air combat fighters took to wearing all-over air superiority grey, combined with lo-viz national markings.

This did not altogether suit the fighter fraternity, who in a confused, close combat, multi-bogey engagement, needed to immediately identify brothers who were in trouble, to warn them. Even as the all-red aircraft of the Red Baron had been instantly identifiable, they felt that in close combat this was an asset rather than a liability. A German adage from 1944 stated that if aircraft were camouflaged they were British; if they were silver they were American; if you couldn't see them at all, they were German!

There are two sides to the invisibility coin: one is reduction of visual signature; the other is deception. Possibly the first trial of the latter was carried out by the ranking surviving German ace of World War I, Ernst Udet, who experimented with a tinplate rear gunner on the back of his Fokker D.VII in 1918, although with what practical result is not known.

In 1942, an RAF Whitley was fitted with lights along the leading edges of its wings, to reduce visibility when attacking U-boats. While this was perceived to offer certain advantages, it never became operational. In more recent times, experiments with airframe lighting have also taken place, the idea being to highlight the airframe to the same level as the background. As it did not enter service, it can be assumed that the benefits of this system are outweighed by the disadvantages.

American aviation artist Keith Ferris produced two schemes for aspect deception – a dummy cockpit painted on the underside, and a countershading scheme. The former is used by the Canadian Armed Force Hornets. Opinions on effectiveness vary; some, like former Aggressor Major Joe Hodges, say that if you are close enough to see it you are too close to be fooled. Others state that in close combat exercises it is a collision hazard, implying that it works at least some of the time.

Countershading, which was used in the famous AIMVAL/ACEVAL exercises in the late 1970s, was also aimed at aspect deception. The idea was that if one wing was visible, the other was not. The general conclusion was that countershading worked well with a fighter wings-level at high noon, but at any other time it was not a viable proposition.

Hours of darkness

In the first few months of World War II, the RAF were made aware that the attrition attendant upon daylight bombing was unacceptable. They consequently reverted to night raiding, as did the Luftwaffe in late 1940. Aircraft undersides were painted matt black, to defeat hostile searchlights, although strangely the albedo, or reflectivity, often made them appear white when illuminated. But seeking darkness for protection against visual detection gave rise to the next two detection methods.

Radar, the emission of electronic pulses reflected from the target aircraft, gave much better results. But this gave rise to the whole new field of electronic countermeasures (ECM). These took two forms, active, and passive. Active ECM involved the broadcasting of signals on the same wavelength as that of the radar, blotting out the true return. It could also be used to blank out communications between night fighters and their controllers. As active ECM became more sophisticated, deception measures were used to provide false radar indications.

Active ECM had an inherent flaw. It was an emission, and as such its direction

Below: Developed from the Lockheed Skunk Works' A-12 interceptor, the SR-71 strategic reconnaissance aircraft was the first "modern" stealth aircraft (first flight almost 40 years ago!). Its most obvious stealth features were inward-canted fins and chines from the nose to the leading edge. In and under the skin were a host of other RCS-reducing measures. Whether these were succesful or not is academic: the SR-71's Mach 3+ cruising speed and high-altitude capability rendered it essentially invulnerable to interception.

could be homed upon. This was put to good use by the Luftwaffe, who used it to home on RAF ground-mapping radars such as H$_2$S, which was carried by heavy bombers. But even broad-band jamming revealed the approximate direction of its source, which enabled night fighters to be vectored in its general direction. Long after Word War II, RAF Lightning fighters could "home on jam" in this way, waiting only until the blanked-out quadrant started to move around the screen, which indicated the relative movement of a jamming source close at hand. At this point the pilot could look "out of the window" with a fair chance of seeing the intruder.

Passive ECM took two forms. The first was releasing bundles of Window (British), Chaff (American), Doppel (German), or Giman-Shi (Japanese) from the aircraft, or by homing on hostile radar emissions. By whatever name, chaff consisted of metallised strips cut to half the size of the wavelength of the detection radar, or dipoles. Released in clouds, chaff gave false target indications, although as they quickly lost speed, discriminating radar operators could tell the difference. In modern times, chaff is most effective against missiles, which naturally do not carry discriminating radar operators.

The second form of passive ECM, albeit with more deadly intent, consisted of homing on airborne radar emissions. The use of this by Luftwaffe fighters has been mentioned, but it was not a one-way street. Luftwaffe fighter radars could be homed upon by RAF night fighters, using a device called Serrate. But as with all such passive systems, this was directional only, with no range capability. To be effective, ranging was needed, and this could only be supplied by airborne radar.

For most of World War II there was no system that could differentiate between roundels, swastikas, and white stars; therefore visual identification had to be made prior to launching an attack. In the final few months of the war, a device called Perfectos (many British systems were named after cigars) entered service. This was able to trigger the German Identification Friend/Foe (IFF) system, and thus confirm that a contact was indeed German. This gave the Luftwaffe night fighter pilots an interesting choice – leave IFF switched on and be shot down by an RAF Mosquito, or turn it off and be shot down by "friendly" Flak. Most chose the latter as the least lethal option!

Positive identification by an IFF interrogator was near perfect, but difficult to achieve in practice. Not until 1972 did the USAF gain access to the Russian IFF system; when it did, an interrogator codenamed Combat Tree was introduced on Phantoms of the 432nd TRW in Vietnam, with a fair degree of success.

The final detection system used in World War II was infra-red, or heat-homing. Used only by the Luftwaffe, this took two forms: active, in the shape of an infra-red searchlight, and a passive sensor. The former was so range-limited that it was virtually useless. The latter needed many years of development before it reached operational maturity; its time was yet to come.

Modern times

Moving on two decades from the end of the war, aural detection was of importance to helicopters only, while visual detection had become of far less import in the main combat arena. Fighter-sized targets were all but invisible at 7-8nm (c13km), whereas radar could reach out to 10 times this distance. "Invisibility" was thus far more a question of invisibility to radar than to visual acquisition, even with electro-optical aids such as TISEO. On the other hand, radar emissions, or even radio communications, could quite easily give the game away. They could announce: "This is what I am; this is where I am; and this is what I am doing!" Low-observability, or stealth, could very easily be compromised by any form of electronic emission.

Next in importance was the infra-red or heat signature. There was little point in minimising radar and communication transmissions if the aircraft could be detected by other means. And while IR had no ranging capability, two widely spaced ground stations could possibly track an aircraft, or a formation, by the heat signature, using simple triangulation.

Stealth measures

The requirements of a stealth aircraft, or as our French friends quaintly put it, "le furtif", are primarily a low radar signature, minimized active use of radar, reduced communications, and a small heat signature. If it is optimised to fly at night, then its visual signature hardly matters; if by day its visual signature is of less importance than that of its radar cross-section (RCS). Thermal signature (IR), comes a poor second.

It is not widely understood that size has only a remote bearing on RCS. The keynote is reflectivity: how much electronic energy is returned to the emitter. Shaping is all-important. If one throws a ball against a wall at an angle, it will bounce off at a similar angle but in the other direction; i.e., a ball thrown at 30deg will bounce off at 120deg from the thrower. Radar is a bit more complicated, but the same general principle applies.

Radar is dependent on its emissions returning to the receiver, however attenuated. But if the emissions are deflected away from the target at an angle which ensures that few if any will be bounced back in the original direction, radar stands little if any chance of establishing a firm contact. This is the main principle of stealth. However good countermeasures may be, the ideal situation is not to be detected in the first place.

First generation stealth

Strategic reconnaissance, with its operational need to penetrate hostile territory undetected, and to egress unharmed with its valuable intelligence, was the obvious first choice for stealth technology. Careful shaping was used on the Lockheed A-12 and its successor, the SR-71 Blackbird. Chines from the nose to the leading edge, wing-body and wing-

Below: The most radical aspect of the B-2 is that it has no vertical surfaces. The leading edges, carefully shaped for stealth, are covered with dielectric (radar-transparent) material, behind which are wedges of radar-absorbent honeycomb, designed to trap and dissipate radar emissions.

nacelle blending, and inward-canted fins were the obvious external signs, while radar absorbing materials (RAM) were extensively used. RAM takes two forms: matrixes of various kinds, notably pyroceramics, and paint. The latter contains ferrites – tiny iron balls – which convert the incoming radar energy into heat, although these are effective only over a limited range of radar frequencies.

Under the skin, corner reflectors were used in the chines and the wing leading edges. These were carefully angled to trap incoming electromagnetic energy inside them, and were filled with pyroceramic RAM. The A-12/SR-71 avoided interception by combining extreme altitude and extreme speed with low observable features. Extreme altitude put it beyond the reach of most interceptors and SAMs; extreme speed reduced the tracking time of enemy radars, and also the reaction time available to the defences. Stealth measures reduced both the latter even more.

Radar detection range is essentially a function of the fourth root of the radar cross-section. Tremendous reductions in RCS are needed to produce a significant effect on detection range; for example, an order of magnitude (one tenth) will give a range reduction of about 44 per cent, say from 50nm (93km) down to 28nm (52km). While this is well worth having, an order of magnitude reduction takes some achieving.

Below: The Lockheed Martin X-35 full-scale mock-up, contender for the Joint Strike Fighter (JSF). Among the design requirements were a high level of stealth, including internal missile carriage, combined with a demanding radius of action.

Above: While it proved the stealth concept, the F-117 had its failures in combat. In the Gulf War its infra-red sensors could not penetrate cloud or rain, and many were the times when a Nighthawk arrived over its target, only to find it socked in. The only alternative was to return with its munitions unexpended. Nor could the type ever be used by day; visibility from the cockpit is atrocious, while its performance is best described as pedestrian. If sighted by a conventional fighter, it would be a dead duck.

Rockwell B-1B Lancer

Conceived at a time when the "worst case" scenario was all-out war between East and West, with ICBMs and SLBMs providing first and second strike capabilities, respectively, the strategic bomber looked to be an anachronism. Even armed with stand-off weapons, it appeared vulnerable to fighter and SAM defences. But the operational flexibility of the manned bomber could not be denied. After several false starts, the end result was the B-1B manned penetrator. The Soviet Union thought that was a good idea, and developed a B-1B clone: the Tu-160 Blackjack.

Way back in the early 1960s, when the "worst case" scenario was an all-out nuclear war between NATO and WARPAC, the role of the strategic bomber was called into question. Far more flexible than intercontinental ballistic missiles (ICBMs) or submarine-launched ballistic missiles (SLBMs), the bomber could be recalled after launch; it could be deployed forward as a statement of national resolve; it was able to switch targets as required. But could it penetrate an increasingly lethal air defence system?

Soviet SAM systems of the era, primarily the SA-2, codenamed Guideline, were perceived to be very effective at medium and high altitudes, to the point where the only argument was whether its probability of kill was 80 or 90 per cent. The USAF B-58 Hustler had an unprecedented Mach 2 dash speed over the target but, this notwithstanding, it was withdrawn from service in 1970. The Mach 3 B-70

Valkyrie was cancelled. The Boeing B-52 Stratofortress, workhorse of Strategic Air Command, was switched to low level (below the radar) penetration in about 1963, as were the V-Force (Victors and Vulcan) bombers of the RAF.

Studies of the period showed that the best chance of successful penetration of a heavily defended area lay in high subsonic speed at low altitude combined with Mach 2 performance at high altitude to reduce transit time through lightly defended areas. Variable-sweep wings were selected to combine economical cruising with high-speed low level penetration. North American Rockwell, designers of the Valkyrie and soon to become Rockwell International, were awarded a contract for a new strategic bomber – the B-1.

First flight took place at Palmdale, California, on 23 December, 1974, and what the Air Force called "probably the most successful flight test programme of all time" was begun. Be that as it may, the B-1 was cancelled by President Carter on 30 June, 1976, in favour of the new "wonder weapon", the cruise missile, although the existing B-1 prototypes were retained as research vehicles for the Bomber Penetrator Evaluation (BPE) programme.

A definite USAF need was for a multi-role aircraft, able to deliver conventional bombs and mines, as well as nuclear weapons. With no alternative in prospect, the B-1 programme was reinstated by the Reagan administration on 2 October, 1982. Beefed up to carry an extra 82,000lb (37,195kg) of payload, to have longer range and a lower RCS than the original article, it was ordered into production on 20 January, 1983.

Contemporary reports credited the B-52 with an RCS of 1,070.6sq ft (99.5sq m), while the original B-1 was credited with an RCS varying between one twentyfifth and one thirtyfifth of this. Rumour control now kicked in, crediting the B-1B

AMSA 1967

By 1967 the Advanced Manned Strategic Aircraft layout depicted here had emerged from a plethora of radical designs. The fuselage is a broad lifting body, while the fully swept angle of the wing is a truly remarkable 75°.

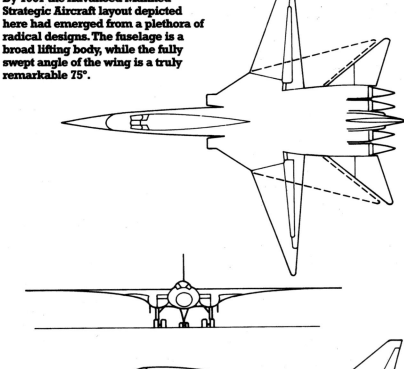

B-1A first prototype (74-0158)

All B-1As were finished originally with white anti-flash paint, but this made them far too visible at low level.

U.S. AIR FORCE

Left: Condensation ripples from the trailing edge as the third B-1, seen here in polished natural metal, nears the contrail belt. Distinct vortices can be seen arising from the wing glove seal area.

as having an RCS with an order of magnitude less than the B-1 – something like that of a starling! This was of course horse manure.

The sleekly contoured B-1 has since been credited with an RCS of 107.6sq ft (10sq m); almost an order of magnitude less than that of the B-52, while in 1999 the B-1B was reported as having an RCS "slightly larger than the F-16", probably about 26.9sq ft (2.5sq m). This reduction was achieved in three ways: extensive use of RAM, a fixed, phased array radar antenna, and revised engine intakes.

The Mach 2 requirement had been dropped for the B-1B, which allowed less complicated and more stealthy intakes to be used. The lips were raked horizontally at a steep angle, the ducts were made serpentine to prevent hostile radars looking straight down their throats at the compressor faces, while guide vanes and baffles were used to deflect incoming emissions.

RAM is of course wavelength-limited but, since the main threat to low level penetration was expected to be fighters, the RAM was tailored to the standard fighter wavelength – the 3cm I/J band. It was applied to fore and aft canted internal bulkheads (which were also a stealth feature), around the glove vanes, the front of the wing fairings, spoilers, flaps and horizontal stabilizers.

The use of a fixed, phased array radar was an innovation, the first of its type to enter service anywhere in the world. Whereas the B-1 had mounted two planar array radars in its nose, the Westinghouse APG-164 had only one, and that was canted steeply downwards as a stealth measure. Automatic terrain-following was essential for low-level penetration, but electronic beam steering, coupled with intermittent rather than continuous emissions, gave a significantly reduced probability of intercept.

The B-1B carries two specialized avionics suites, one offensive (OAS), the other defensive (DAS). The OAS is a raft of systems concerned with such things as navigation, communications, target acquisition, and munitions management and status.

Left: In-flight refuelling enabled the B-1A to maximise payload/range performance by taking off with its maximum bomb load, then topping up fuel to maximum flying weight.

40158

Left: The first operational B-1B is handed over to SAC at Offutt AFB, Nebraska, on 27 June 1987. The foreplanes which give ride control at low altitude are clearly seen.

The DAS is a unified fully automatic system, the ALQ-161, with the specialist operator acting as a monitor and systems manager. Its function is to listen, detect, classify, prioritize threats and initiate countermeasures. The latter is of course a two-edged sword: ECM begun too early simply confirms to the opposition that something nasty is out there, when detection might not yet have been achieved. The DAS is also linked to the Westinghouse ALQ-153 tail-warning radar. An active emitter does not seem a good idea under these circumstances, but it was the only way to detect a fighter carrying out a visual, non-radar attack from the rear quarter.

Alas, the DAS concept as applied to the B-1B was ahead of its time, and failed to reach maturity. While attempting to cover the entire spectrum of possible radar threats, the I/J band – commonly used by fighters – was neglected, possibly because it was felt that stealth measures against this wavelength were adequate. More problems were encountered when the DAS interfered with other systems

Rockwell International B-1B cutaway

1 Radome
2 Multi-mode phased array radar scanner
3 Low-observable shrouded scanner tracking mechanism
4 Radar mounting bulkhead
5 Radome hinge joint
6 In-flight refuelling receptacle, open
7 Nose avionics equipment bays
8 APQ-164 offensive radar system
9 Dual pitot heads
10 Foreplane hydraulic actuator
11 Structural mode control system (SMCS) ride control foreplane
12 Foreplane pivot fixing
13 Front pressure bulkhead
14 Nose undercarriage wheel bay
15 Nosewheel doors
16 Control cable runs
17 Cockpit floor level
18 Rudder pedals
19 Control column, quadruplex automatic flight control system
20 Instrument panel shroud
21 Windscreen panels
22 Detachable nuclear flash screens, all window positions
23 Co-pilot's ejection seat
24 Co-pilot's emergency escape hatch
25 Overhead switch panel
26 Pilot's emergency escape hatch
27 Cockpit eyebrow window
28 Ejection seat launch/ mounting rails
29 Pilot's Weber ACES 'zero-zero' ejection seat
30 Wing sweep control lever
31 Cockpit section framing
32 Toilet
33 Nose undercarriage drag brace
34 Twin landing lamps
35 Taxiing lamp
36 Shock absorber strut
37 Twin nosewheels, forward retracting
38 Torque scissor links
39 Hydraulic steering control unit
40 Nosewheel leg door
41 Retractable boarding ladder
42 Ventral crew entry hatch, open
43 Nose undercarriage pivot fixing
44 Hydraulic retraction jack
45 Systems Operators' instrument console
46 Radar hand controller
47 Crew cabin side window panel
48 Offensive Systems Operators' ejection seat (OSO)
49 Cabin roof escape hatches

50 Defensive Systems Operator's ejection seat (DSO)
51 Rear pressure bulkhead
52 External emergency release handle
53 Underfloor air conditioning ducting
54 Air system ground connection
55 External access panels
56 Avionics equipment racks, port and starboard
57 Cooling air exhaust duct
58 Astro navigation antenna
59 Forward fuselage joint frame
60 Air system valves and ducting
61 Dorsal systems and equipment duct
62 Weapons bay extended range fuel tank
63 Electrical cable multiplexes
64 Forward fuselage integral fuel tank
65 Electronics equipment bay
66 Ground cooling air connection
67 Defensive avionics system transmitting antennas
68 Weapons bay door hinge mechanism
69 Forward weapons bay
70 Weapons bay doors, open
71 Retractable spoiler
72 Movable (non-structural) weapons bay bulkhead to suit varying load sizes
73 Rotary dispenser hydraulic drive motor
74 Fuel system piping
75 Communications antennas, port and starboard
76 Starboard lateral radome
77 ALQ-161 defensive avionics system equipment
78 Forward fuselage fuel tanks
79 Control cable runs
80 Rotary weapons dispenser
81 AGM-69 SRAM short-range air-to-surface missiles
82 Weapons bay door and hinge links
83 Port defensive avionics system equipment

84 Fuselage flank fuel tanks
85 Defensive avionics system transmitting antennas
86 Port lateral radome
87 Port navigation light
88 Wing sweep control screw jack
89 Wing pivot hinge fitting
90 Lateral longeron attachment joints
91 Wing pivot box carry-through
92 Wing sweep control jack hydraulic motor
93 Carry-through structure integral fuel tank
94 Upper longeron/carry-through joints
95 Starboard wing sweep control hydraulic motor
96 Wing sweep control screw jack
97 Starboard navigation light
98 Wing sweep pivot fixing
99 Wing root flexible seals
100 Aperture closing horn fairing
101 Flap/slat interconnecting drive shaft
102 Fuel pump
103 Fuel system piping
104 Starboard wing integral fuel tanks
105 Leading edge slat drive shaft
106 Slat guide rails
107 Slat screw jacks
108 Leading edge slat segments (7), open
109 Wing tip strobe light
110 Fuel system vent tank
111 Wing tip fairing
112 Static dischargers
113 Fuel jettison
114 Fixed portion of trailing edge
115 Starboard spoilers, open
116 Spoiler hydraulic jacks
117 Single-slotted Fowler-type flap, down position

118 Flap screw jacks
119 Flap guide rails
120 Wing root housing fairings
121 Dorsal spine fairing
122 Wheel bay dorsal fuel tank
123 Main undercarriage leg strut
124 Port main undercarriage, stowed position
125 Wheel bay avionics equipment racks
126 Fuselage lateral longeron
127 Wing root housing
128 Engine bleed air ducting
129 Ventral retractable air scoop
130 Fuel cooling heat exchanger
131 Heat exchanger spill air louvres
132 Rear rotary weapons dispenser
133 Control ducting
134 Tailplane longeron
135 Wing glove section tail fairing
136 Starboard wing fully swept position
137 Starboard engine exhaust nozzles
138 Longeron joint
139 Automatic stability and control system equipment (SCAS)

B-1B Lancer, Weapons Load

Nuclear gravity	Internal	External
B-28	12	8
B-43	12	14
B-61	24	14
B-83	24	14
Nuclear guided		
AGM-69 SRAM	24	14
AGM-86B ALCM	8	14
Conventional		
Mk 82	84	14
Mk 84/BLU-109	24	14
GBU-29/30 JDAM	24	n/a

and sensors, causing the B-1B to be dubbed "the world's first self-jamming bomber!" The best one can say is that the DAS was not a success. It is scheduled for upgrading in 2003, while eight Raytheon ALE-50 towed radar decoys are currently carried.

Weaponry

As would be expected for a strategic bomber designed for the Cold War, the B-1B carries a formidable weapons load. For maximum penetration, internal loads only would be carried for stealth reasons, although external weapons might be used to clear defences out of the way when inbound to the target. A very heavily defended target would have stand-off weapons allocated. Internal weapons are carried on rotary launchers.

Nuclear weapons are no longer considered a viable option in today's climate of opinion, but the B-61 and B-83 nuclear gravity weapons would have been the preferred choice if the Cold War had become hot. Gravity weapons could be released between 150ft and 50,000ft (56-15,240m), parachute-retarded to allow the B-1B to escape its effects, and fuzed for either. The yield of the B-83 varied between 10 and 500 kilotons, while that of the B-61 was one megaton.

The Boeing AGM-69 Short Range Attack Missile (SRAM) was a defence suppression weapon with a 200 kiloton warhead. Rocket-propelled, its speed and range varied with the altitude and speed of the launching aircraft – between Mach 2.8 and Mach 3.2, and 30 to 90nm (56-167km). A total of 24 are carried on

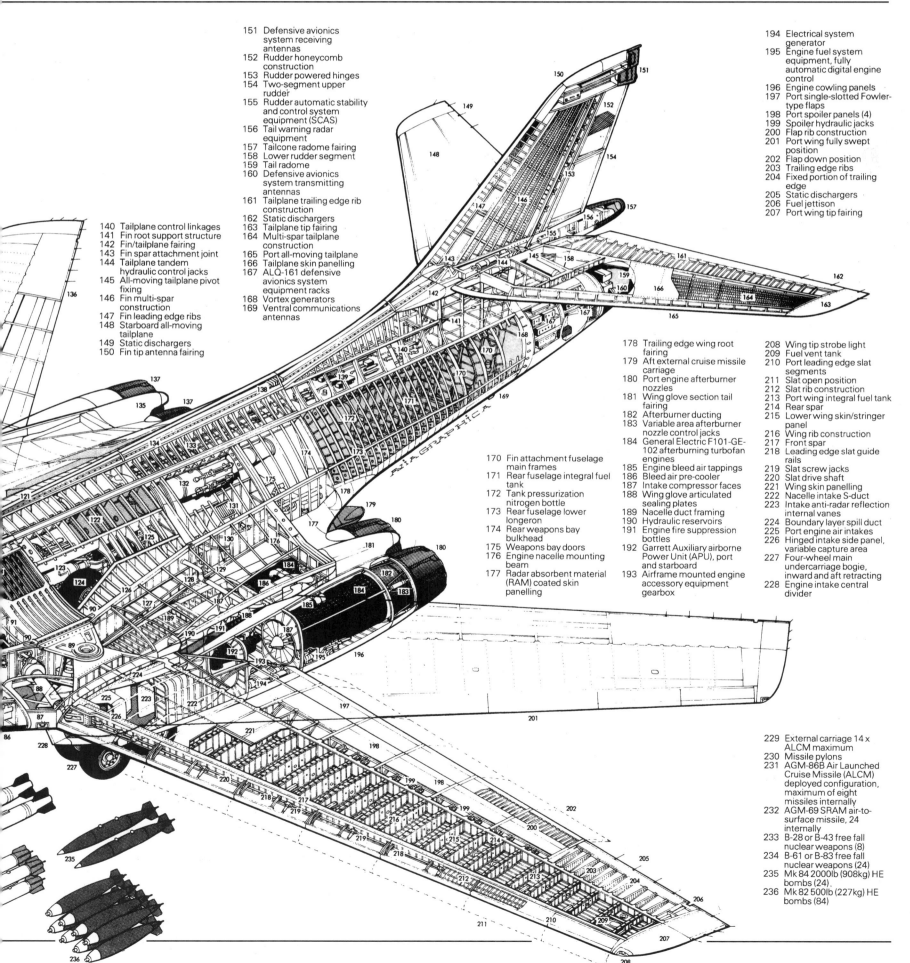

151 Defensive avionics system receiving antennas
152 Rudder honeycomb construction
153 Rudder powered hinges
154 Two-segment upper rudder
155 Rudder automatic stability and control system equipment (SCAS)
156 Tail warning radar equipment
157 Tailcone radome fairing
158 Lower rudder segment
159 Tail radome
160 Defensive avionics system transmitting antennas
161 Tailplane trailing edge rib construction
162 Static dischargers
163 Tailplane tip fairing
164 Multi-spar tailplane construction
165 Port all-moving tailplane
166 Tailplane skin panelling
167 ALQ-161 defensive avionics system equipment racks
168 Vortex generators
169 Ventral communications antennas

140 Tailplane control linkages
141 Fin root support structure
142 Fin/tailplane fairing
143 Fin spar attachment joint
144 Tailplane tandem hydraulic control jacks
145 All-moving tailplane pivot fixing
146 Fin multi-spar construction
147 Fin leading edge ribs
148 Starboard all-moving tailplane
149 Static dischargers
150 Fin tip antenna fairing

170 Fin attachment fuselage main frames
171 Rear fuselage integral fuel tank
172 Tank pressurization nitrogen bottle
173 Rear fuselage lower longeron
174 Rear weapons bay bulkhead
175 Weapons bay doors
176 Engine nacelle mounting beam
177 Radar absorbent material (RAM) coated skin panelling

178 Trailing edge wing root fairing
179 Aft external cruise missile carriage
180 Port engine afterburner nozzles
181 Wing glove section tail fairing
182 Afterburner ducting
183 Variable area afterburner nozzle control jacks
184 General Electric F101-GE-102 afterburning turbofan engines
185 Engine bleed air tappings
186 Bleed air pre-cooler
187 Intake compressor faces
188 Wing glove articulated sealing plates
189 Nacelle duct framing
190 Hydraulic reservoirs
191 Engine fire suppression bottles
192 Garrett Auxiliary airborne Power Unit (APU), port and starboard
193 Airframe mounted engine accessory equipment gearbox

194 Electrical system generator
195 Engine fuel system equipment, fully automatic digital engine control
196 Engine cowling panels
197 Port single-slotted Fowler-type flaps
198 Port spoiler panels (4)
199 Spoiler hydraulic jacks
200 Flap rib construction
201 Port wing fully swept position
202 Flap down position
203 Trailing edge ribs
204 Fixed portion of trailing edge
205 Static dischargers
206 Fuel jettison
207 Port wing tip fairing

208 Wing tip strobe light
209 Fuel vent tank
210 Port leading edge slat segments
211 Slat open position
212 Slat rib construction
213 Port wing integral fuel tank
214 Rear spar
215 Lower wing skin/stringer panel
216 Wing rib construction
217 Front spar
218 Leading edge slat guide rails
219 Slat screw jacks
220 Slat drive shaft
221 Wing skin panelling
222 Nacelle intake S-duct
223 Intake anti-radar reflection internal vanes
224 Boundary layer spill duct
225 Port engine air intakes
226 Hinged intake side panel, variable capture area
227 Four-wheel main undercarriage bogie, inward and aft retracting
228 Engine intake central divider

229 External carriage 14 x ALCM maximum
230 Missile pylons
231 AGM-86B Air Launched Cruise Missile (ALCM) deployed configuration, maximum of eight missiles internally
232 AGM-69 SRAM air-to-surface missile, 24 internally
233 B-28 or B-43 free fall nuclear weapons (8)
234 B-61 or B-83 free fall nuclear weapons (24)
235 Mk 84 2000lb (908kg) HE bombs (24).
236 Mk 82 500lb (227kg) HE bombs (84)

Above: A busy scene at Palmdale, with assembly work on the first B-1B finally approaching completion. An interesting detail evident here is the nacelle fairing between the starboard engine effluxes.

Right: The B-1B crewman gives scale to the massive twin-wheel main gear leg of the B-1B. The Lancer was designed for deployed operations from bare-base airfields.

Below: Cutaway of the definitive B-1B engine, General Electric's F101-GE-102. Almost identical to the earlier -100 in appearance, it features greater durability and is slightly heavier.

three internal rotary launchers, each with eight weapons stations. In theory all eight SRAMs on a single launcher could be pre-targeted and launched within 45 seconds.

Ironically, one of the main weapons carried is the AGM-86 cruise missile, which originally caused the cancellation of the B-1A. Propelled by a small jet engine at high subsonic speed, and with a range of some 1,300nm (2,500km), its accuracy is such that it can be used for precision attacks. A sophisticated INS

and terrain contour matching (Tercom) guidance system allow it to compare the terrain over which it is flying against pro-files stored in the computer memory.

The AGM-86 was originally to be car-ried in the three 15ft (4.57m) weapons bays, but during the development stage its length increased by nearly one third. To accommodate it internally, the bulkhead between the front and middle bays was made removable. The standard warhead is 2,000lb (907kg) of high explosive,

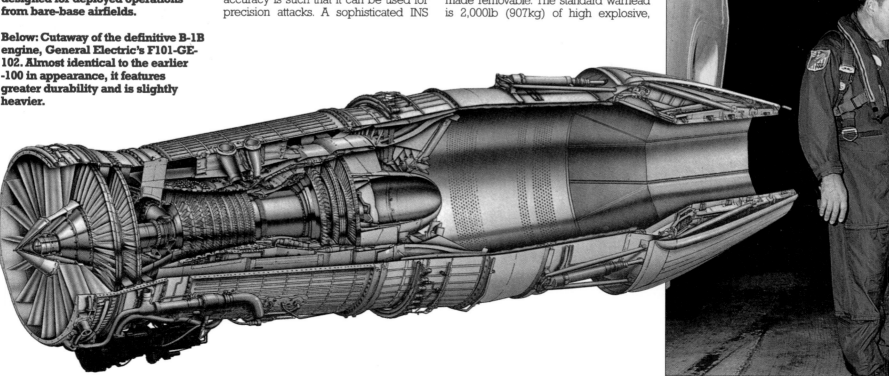

Above: A closeup of the front of a B-1B engine nacelle, showing how well the engine compressor face is shielded from hostile radar emissions. In this pre-installation picture, the variable lips are constricted into a normal in-flight position.

Below: Low observables technology has been applied to the intakes, resulting in a serpentine duct with angled guide vanes and baffles to deflect or trap radar energy. Heated vanes are shown in red. These are an anti-icing measure.

B-1B intake layout

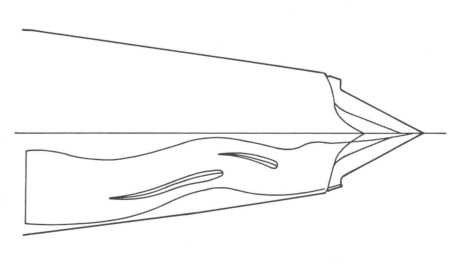

although others, including a 200 kiloton nuclear warhead, are available for special needs.

The latest weapon carried by the Lancer is the Joint Direct Attack Munition (JDAM), a guidance system for conventional bombs which uses a combination of GPS target information and INS to achieve outstanding accuracy at low cost and under any weather conditions. An upgrade to the B-1B is scheduled to be complete by 2001, enabling JDAM, JSOW, and other weapons to be carried.

In service

Unusually for such a large aircraft, the Lancer has a control column rather than a yoke, which led to stories that it handled like a fighter. While it is responsive for its size, the inertia of 200 or so tons ensures that it flies like a bomber. Sweeping the wings back and forth calls for rapid transfers of fuel to ensure that the centre of gravity stays within limits; this is done automatically.

In all, 100 aircraft were produced, enough for four Bomb Wings: the 96th at Dyess in Texas; the 28th at Ellsworth in South Dakota; the 319th at Grand Forks, North Dakota; and the 384th at McConnell, Kansas. Strategic Air Command (SAC) took delivery of its first B-1B on 7 July, 1985, and assigned it to the 96th BW. The slow buildup had begun. But shortly after, the Soviet Union dissolved, taking with it the main threat. SAC did not long survive its traditional adversary, and its successor, the newly created Air Combat Command, was an altogether different force with a different philosophy.

The B-1B was belatedly named Lancer.

Left: The phased array antenna of the APQ-164 radar is canted down to reduce its radar reflectivity. Although in this picture it looks movable, it is fixed, and the radar beam is steered and pointed as required by electronic means.

Right: The Eaton ALQ-161 defensive avionic system comprises no fewer than 107 separate units dispersed around the aircraft to give comprehensive coverage. It is designed to detect and defeat known and projected threats.

Below left: The pilot's console is dominated by the central CRT, which in this instance apparently shows the aircraft to be in a gentle turn at low level. There is no HUD, but the CRT is set only just below the pilot's normal line of vision.

Below: A B-1B test drops an inert B61 nuclear round during weapons trials. However simple the process of dropping a bomb from an aircraft may appear, it must be checked out if disasters are to be avoided.

ALQ-161 defensive avionic system configuration

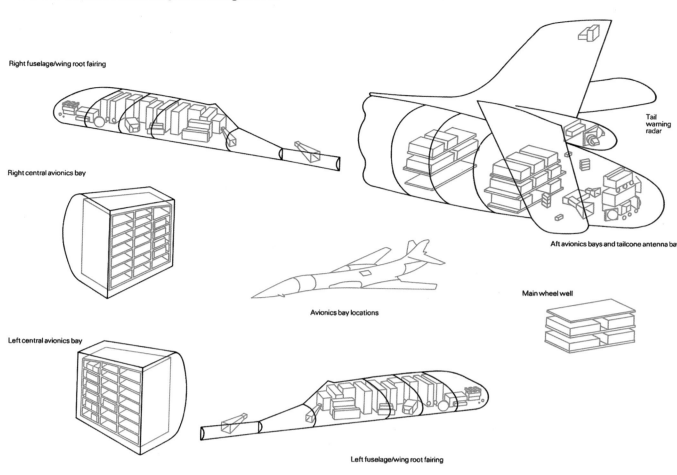

Right fuselage/wing root fairing

Right central avionics bay

Left central avionics bay

Left fuselage/wing root fairing

Avionics bay locations

Tail warning radar

Aft avionics bays and tailcone antenna bay

Main wheel well

A trifle too late, since within the USAF B-One had been corrupted to Bone, and this name stuck. By this time the Gulf War of 1991 had been fought and won, but the Bone took no part in it. Its further history was troubled by changes within the Air Force structure. The 96th BW was inactivated on 1 October, 1993, and its component units passed to the 7th Wing. The 28th BW remained at Ellsworth, with a third squadron added, but the 319th at Grand Forks was inactivated on 16 July, 1994. At McConnell, the 384th BW became the 384th Bomb Group, which in turn was inactivated, to be replaced by the Kansas Air National Guard. This was a culture shock for the Guardsmen; they had previously flown F-16s!

Switched to more conventional means of attack, the B-1B crews started to make long deployments. The most spectacular of these was when two aircraft of the 28th BW left Ellsworth in 1993. Having crossed the Atlantic at high altitude, they overflew Holland and Germany at low level, before climbing back up. After more than 24 hours aloft, they recovered to Diego Garcia in the Indian Ocean. Following just a single day's rest, they returned to Ellsworth via the Pacific, having circumnavigated the globe.

Not until November 1998 did the Lancer finally go to war, when four aircraft were deployed to Oman for operations against Iraq. In December it was used during Operation *Desert Fox*, when it delivered Mk 82 iron bombs on a Republican Guard barracks at Al Kut from medium to low levels, devastating it.

Action in the Middle East was followed by action in the Balkans. On 1 April, 1999, five Lancers of the 28th BW arrived at RAF Fairford for Operation *Allied Force* against Yugoslavia, and two of them flew their first missions that same night. As in *Desert Fox*, the standard load was 84 500lb (227kg) unguided bombs. The conflict ended on June 10. Not one B-1B was so much as scratched, but they had used their ALE-50 towed decoys.

Specifications		
Dimensions	**B-1A**	**B-1B**
Length	151ft 2in/46.07m	145ft 9in/44.42m
Height	33ft 7in/10.23m	33ft 7in/10.23m
Span (15° sweep)	136ft 8in/41.65m	136ft 8in/41.65m
Span (67½° sweep)	78ft 2in/23.83m	78ft 2¾in/23.83m
Wing area	1,950sq.ft/181.16m²	1,950sq.ft/181.16m²
Weights		
Empty (approx)	172,000lb/78,019kg	192,000lb/87,090kg
Max takeoff	395,000lb/179,192kg	477,000lb/216,367kg
Max weapons load	115,000lb/52,164kg	125,000lb/56,700kg
Power		
Engines	4xF101-GE-100	4xF101-GE-102
Max thrust	30,000lb/13,608kg	30,780lb/13,962kg
Mil thrust	17,000lb/7,711kg	17,000lb/7,711kg
Performance		
Speed hi	Mach 2.22	Mach 1.2
Speed lo	Mach 0.85	Mach 0.8
Range unrefuelled	5,200nm/9,636km	5,600nm/10,378km

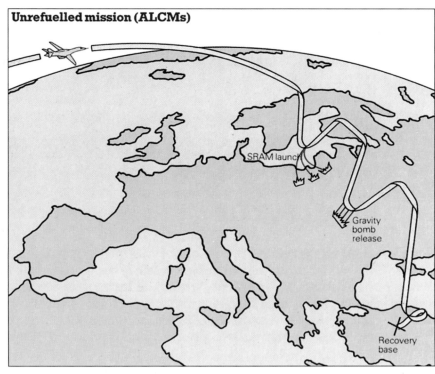

Unrefuelled mission (ALCMs)

Left: Seen here at RAF Fairford in May 1999, is Bone 86-097 of the 28th BW. This was one of five aircraft which attacked targets in Serbia with 84 Mk 82 500lb bombs.

Left bottom: No fewer than 84 Mk 82 500lb bombs cascade from a B-1B during range trials. The locations of the triple bomb bays are evident.

Above: A B-1B at the International Air Tattoo at RAF Fairford in 1997. Bone deployments to Europe are rare; few could have guessed that less than two years later the type would fly operational missions from this field. This was however not its combat debut; that was flown from Oman against Iraq in December 1998, devastating a Republican Guard barracks at El Kut.

Above: Increased range, low observability and a more diverse payload were key features of the LRCA – subsequently the B-1B – so that the new bomber would be able to penetrate air defences at low level in support of theatre forces in Europe. Air-launched cruise missiles are still a weaponry option, but these now have conventional rather than nuclear warheads.

Below: Wings fully swept, a Bone overflies the Nevada desert in 1985. Fast low level penetration, coupled with high subsonic transit to the war zone at high altitude, were the keys to its strategic usage in the nuclear role. But as a conventional bomber, it has dropped its ordnance from medium altitudes, using the Global Positioning System and other means to obtain a high level of accuracy with old-fashioned iron bombs.

F-117 Nighthawk

With the SR-71 and the B-1B, low observables were only an aid to penetrating a hostile defensive system. The former relied mainly on its overwhelming speed and altitude performance to evade interception, while the latter was designed for a "brute force" approach, staying under the radar where it could, jamming where it couldn't, and taking out defence systems with nuclear missiles when all else failed. An aircraft that could penetrate undetected would be even better. The Lockheed "Skunk Works" set to work.

Have Blue

In 1974, the US Defense Advanced Research Projects Agency (DARPA) asked five military aircraft manufacturers to study the possibility of producing a fighter with a significantly reduced radar signature. Surprisingly, in view of the development work done on the YF-12 fighter variant of the A-12/SR-71, Lockheed was not one of them. This was soon changed, and the company became an active participant.

The starting point dated back 100 years; Scotsman James Clerk Maxwell had produced a set of mathematical formulae, later refined by German Arnold Johannes Sommerfeld, which predicted the way in which given geometrical shapes would reflect electro-magnetic radiation. Then, in 1962, a Russian physicist, Piotr Ufimtsev, published a paper on diffraction which simplified things a little.

He concentrated on the electro-magnetic currents formed at the edge of geometric shapes. It was still all very complicated, but computers of the era were improving all the time, in speed and in calculating power.

The breakthrough came from retired Lockheed mathematician Bill Schroeder. As the equations were too complex to apply to anything other than simple flat shapes, he conceived the idea of creating a three-dimensional aircraft shape using a limited number of two-dimensional triangular plates. This would keep the number of calculations within reasonable bounds. With the plates angled to deflect incoming radar energy away from its source, a truly low RCS might be achieved. The remaining problem was: could such a shape be made to fly?

The ball then passed to software engineer Denys Overholser, whose team then created a computer programme to calculate the RCS. This was low – very low indeed – and the initial results were borne out by empirical tests on a model.

In April 1976, Lockheed was declared the winner of the DARPA competition, and the previously unclassified project was made top secret and transferred to the Air Force Special Projects Office. The Skunk Works then built two small technology demonstrators under the codename Have Blue.

Development was shrouded in secrecy, and test flying was carried out at the secure facility at Groom Lake, starting early in 1978. Lockheed test pilot Bill Park made the first flight.

Have Blue was small, 38ft (11.58m) long, with a span of just 22ft (6.71m). Powered by two General Electric J85 turbojets, it weighed about 12,000lb (5,443kg). Wing sweep was an incredible 72.5deg, which had several drawbacks. Payload/range performance was poor, climb was sluggish, and high sink rates developed quickly as speed decayed during landing approaches.

The windshield was a V-section, similar to that of the F-106 Delta Dart, which did nothing for a head-up display and, like the Convair fighter, probably produced annoying reflections from the instrumentation. The engine intakes were located above the wing roots, while the exhausts

Above: The strange facetted shape of the F-117 Nighthawk has foiled the efforts of many aviation artists and photographers as seen here. Even with landing lights on, it is very difficult to visualise correctly.

Above left: An F-117, accompanied by a Northrop T-38 chase plane, comes in to land. As no conversion trainer was built, a chase plane flown by an experienced Nighthawk driver was an eminently sensible safety precaution.

Left: A Have Blue prototype. Very small, and with less facetting than the definitive F-117A, it differs mainly in the inward canted fins and rudders, which actually increased the infra-red signature.

were flattened to reduce IR signature. Another measure to reduce IR signature was counter-productive. Two inward-canted fins were supposed to shield the exhaust plume from above; in fact, by reflecting the heat downwards, they had the opposite effect and made Have Blue

much more detectable from below.

A jet aircraft could hardly limit itself to the confines of Groom Lake; nor could all testing be done at night. To confuse out-side observers, the proof of concept air-craft were painted irregularly in motley shades of blue and grey, designed to

Top: Toadlike, this disruptively camouflaged early F-117A crouches menacingly on the apron. Its flat engine exhausts are designed to minimise its IR signature. As can be seen, the fins and rudders are now canted out, unlike Have Blue.

Above: The incredibly high sweep of the Have Blue prototypes is seen here, as is the fact that the under-side is facetted, unlike the F-117, which is completely flat. Handling was extremely difficult, with high sink rates at low speeds.

Above: An F-117A of the 37th Fighter Wing based at Tonopah in Nevada. The view from the cockpit is very poor to the front and side, and non-existent astern. In daylight it would be a dead duck if caught by a fighter.

make it difficult to discern their true shapes from the ground.

Although little information has been released, it is known that the Have Blues were not easy to fly. The first crashed on 4 May, 1978. Bill Park had got into a high sink rate situation and touched down very hard, which damaged the starboard main gear. After a second abortive approach he ejected, sustaining serious injuries in the process. The problem was officially attributed to a fault in the analogue fly- by-wire software. The second aircraft, which first flew on 20 July, was lost in July 1979, after a hydraulic problem.

Whatever the handling problems, the low observables were outstanding, although the need for total attention to detail was highlighted on one occasion when a Have Blue was detected from 50nm (80km) away as it flew towards the White Sands radar range. The fault arose from a panel on the underside, three screws on which had not been sufficiently tightened, allowing it to stand proud by less than 0.12in (3mm)! This was the classic example of tiny items being more important than actual physical size when large reductions in RCS are sought. But, hiccups such as this apart, Have Blue was judged a success.

Senior Trend

The Air Force wasted little time; an engineering development contract for a full-scale stealth fighter was awarded to

Lockheed on 16 November, 1978. Its code name was Senior Trend.

At first, Senior Trend was expected to be nothing more than a rather larger but otherwise identical Have Blue, but lessons learned from the earlier programme were incorporated. Wing sweep was reduced to 67.5deg, increasing aspect ratio and significantly improving handling. The inward canted all-moving fin assemblies were replaced by an outward-canted V-shape, located on the central spine of the aircraft. Other external differences were a flat windshield, necessary for a HUD but at a slight penalty in stealth; other external changes in the cockpit were dictated by scale. A more steeply sloped nose of a revised shape to house forward and downward-looking IR sensors, and a laser target designator, was essential. Contrary to expectation, almost all the aircraft surface was of aluminium alloy, rather than composite materials, with RAM coating.

There were no prototypes; the first five Senior Trends acted as flight test vehicles, and design changes found necessary were to be implemented on the production line, or made the subject of a retrofit. In fact, one major design change did occur during production; the fin area was found to be far too small, so larger fins were fitted from a very early stage.

As a risk reduction measure, many off-the-shelf components were used. The engines were the tried and proven General Electric F404s, produced in a non-afterburning variant designated - F1D2. The environmental control system came from the C-130 Hercules; brake hydraulics were taken from the Gulfstream III bizjet, and the ejection seat from the F-16. Also from the F-16 came the digital quadruplex FBW system,

Above: The Nighthawk raided targets in Iraq with impunity during Desert Storm. Seen during Desert Shield, these examples were protected from the extreme climate of Saudia by hardened air conditioned shelters.

albeit with suitably modified software.

This was particularly important. The quest for stealth meant that many of the usual tradeoffs between performance and handling had been ignored. Senior Trend, with its flat underside, and an upper shape best described as looking like a cubist jelly mould, was unaerodynamic and draggy; in flight it spilled vortices in all directions, and would have been impossible to control by conventional means. But as the late Ben Rich, former head of the Skunk Works, commented, the capabilities of modern computers were such that they could even have made the Statue of Liberty fly!

The first of an eventual 59 aircraft made its maiden flight from Groom Lake on 15 June, 1981, piloted by Hal Farley. Serial number 780 was painted in a disruptive camouflage scheme; like Have Blue, most of its initial test flying had to be conducted in daylight. Succeeding flight test aircraft were painted grey, but then the edict came down from on high that they were to be black. As Ben Rich recalled: "The Skunk Works plays by the Golden Rule; he who has the gold sets the rules!"

It had been known that Senior Trend would be unstable in pitch and yaw, but it soon became clear that it was even worse than predicted. American pilots, never at loss for a pithy expression, dubbed it the "Wobblin' Goblin"! When the aircraft was finally revealed to the public many years later, this was vigorously denied, but Farley, speaking at a

symposium of the Society of Experimental Test Pilots in 1990, commented: "About the only thing it didn't do was fall on its tail while standing on its wheels!" A lot of work on the FBW software finally tamed the handling to the point where average squadron jocks could cope with it.

Other problems were that it generated little sideforce with sideslip, which meant that the standard lateral accelerometer could not be used, and probes had to be developed to overcome this. The first fins and elevons suffered from flutter, and the original metal fin assemblies were eventually replaced with composite units, while stiffening was added around the structure to the outboard elevon actuators. Finally, icing trials showed that the wire grilles over the intakes, sized to defeat radar, were prone to clog up. The solution in this case was to heat the grilles.

Programme secrecy

One of the enduring mysteries of the stealth fighter is that it was able to maintain its cloak of secrecy for so many years, even after operational units had been formed. While this was carefully orchestrated by the Air Force, thousands of Lockheed employees knew about the project, but said nothing. It was a remarkable performance.

In part, secrecy was aided by disinformation. In the mid- to late 1980s, rumours started to surface about a new stealth fighter commonly thought to be the F-19, due to an unexplained gap in numbering between the McDonnell Douglas F/A-18 Hornet and the Northrop F-20 Tigershark. Seemingly authoritative sources depicted it as looking something like the Space Shuttle, and members of

the public actually reported seeing it.

It is of course always possible that Senior Trend was to have been the F-19, but it was finally revealed as the F-117; another mysterious designation, since the "century series" had been dropped many years before. Firstly it was not, nor ever could have been, a fighter; an A for attack prefix would have been far more accurate. Secondly it was speculated that the gap between the end of the "century series" and F-117 had been filled by redesignating Russian types, of which the USAF had several. It finally transpired that F-117 was derived from a callsign in the early test and evaluation days. Whatever the reason, it was a great red herring; guaranteed to confuse and confound not only the potential enemy, but the general public too! The final USAF masterstroke came in November 1988 when they released a photograph of the F-117. This was taken from an angle which totally defeated the world's best illustrators. Without exception, when they prepared the plan view, they made the wing sweep far too shallow!

Even though the first F-117 was not due to reach the Air Force until 1982, Tactical Air Command (TAC) made provision well in advance. They formed the 4450th Tactical Group at Nellis AFB in October 1980. The 4450th TG was actually composed of several units, the first of which was P-Unit, activated in June 1981, equipped with 20 A-7D Corsairs, and commanded by Gerry Fleming. The SLUFs, as the Corsairs were known, fulfilled a dual purpose. Not only were they a plausible cover, allowing the 4450th TG to pose as an A-7 trials unit, they also enabled pilots to stay proficient on fast jets. The latter was important, since the buildup of F-117s was slow, and pilot

hours were low. It has also been suggested that the SLUFs flew chase missions on the F-117s, but the very concept of chase missions at night is highly improbable. P-unit was later redesignated the 4451st Test Squadron, which became operational in January 1987.

Q-Unit was the oldest F-117 outfit. Formed in September 1982 under Al Whitley, it was later redesignated 4452nd "Goatsuckers" Test Squadron, a training and conversion unit. Next was I Unit, activated in July 1983 under Sandy Sharpe,

which became the 4450th Night Stalkers Test Squadron. Finally, Z Unit, later to become the 4453rd Test and Evaluation Squadron, the Grim Reapers, was formed in October 1985 under Roger Locher. Locher was a particularly interesting character. As an F-4 backseater, he flew with three victory pilot Bob Lodge in Vietnam, was shot down on 10 May, 1972, and set a record evasion time of 23 days. On his return to the US, Locher trained as a pilot.

Pilot selection was exhaustive; a minimum

Top: This head-on view clearly shows the unusual cockpit shaping and the gridded engine inlets. The latter are designed to prevent hostile radar emissions from reaching the face of the compressor.

Above: Front and side views clearly show the non-aerodynamic shape of the Nighthawk. But, as Skunk Works chief Ben Rich said, "We could even make the Statue of Liberty fly!"

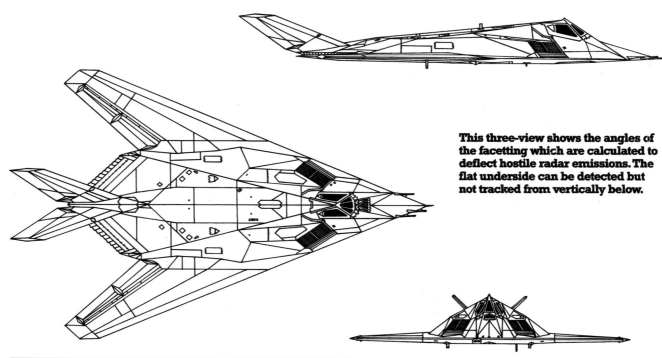

This three-view shows the angles of the facetting which are calculated to deflect hostile radar emissions. The flat underside can be detected but not tracked from vertically below.

Right: The cockpit of the F-117A is reminiscent of an advanced video game, apart from incoming data link. This is the only information the pilot has during the mission. His left knee holds mission data; his right knee carries the map of the target area and its environs.

Below right: Four Nighthawks line up for a mission at Tonopah AFB in the featureless Nevada desert. The cockpit workload is high, as much depends on achieving a time over target accurate to within seconds.

of 1,000 hours on fast jets was required, combined with a steady temperament. This was essential; all F-117 sorties were at night, including first flights on type, and there was no two-seater conversion trainer available, only many hours of simulator time.

The 4450th TG was theoretically based at Nellis, but was actually at Tonopah, way out in the boonies. It received its first F-117 on 2 September, 1982. Tonopah was developed for the purpose at great expense, with a 12,000ft (3.66km) main runway, individual shelters for all F-117s, which, it had been found, reacted badly in the rare event of rain, and the most intense security of any USAF base. Before Senior Trend went public in November 1988, the shelter doors at Tonopah could not be opened until half an hour after sunset, and even then not until all interior lights had been turned off. Ground operations were mainly conducted by torchlight.

Personnel were flown in and out of Tonopah from Nellis at five-day intervals; for the pilots the switch from Hawk to Owl at such short intervals was fatiguing. Then, once the night pattern was established, pilots had to avoid being around at sunrise, since dawn threw their already stretched biorhythms out of kilter. As Ben Rich commented: "You would have thought you were at a vampire convention as daybreak approached – watching all the night workers scurrying to their blacked-out rooms before they were caught by the sun!"

In such a demanding regime, accidents were inevitable. The very first machine to fly went down near Groom Lake on 21 June, 1982, although Lockheed test pilot Ken Dyson survived. Former Aggressor pilot Ross Mulhare was not so lucky when he flew into a hillside near Bakersfield, California, in July 1986. Only a massive security operation, combined with disinformation as to type, concealed the fact that this was a top-secret stealth aircraft. Then on 14 October of the following year, Mike Stewart augured into gently sloping desert terrain near Tonopah. Like Mulhare, he was also unlucky. No reason, other than possible pilot fatigue, was apparently found for these two crashes.

There were however elements of farce in some incidents. One pilot (no name, no packdrill) landed safely, only to spot smoke appearing from somewhere underneath as the runway lights were dowsed. A quick call for help, and he prepared to evacuate the cockpit, switching off all lights as he went.

This made the night terribly dark. With a muttered, "This is going to hurt" (it did), he slid over the angular surfaces to the ground, then removed himself to a respectable distance. As his eyes grew accustomed to the starlight, he saw movement. He had forgotten to apply the parking brake, and his jet was slowly rolling backwards down the slope.

What to do? There were no large rocks handy to use as chocks so he tore off his parachute harness, folded it suitably, and stuffed it behind the nosewheel. With the aircraft halted, he once again removed

himself to a respectable distance. Oncoming lights then heralded the approach of fire engines, ambulances, and sundry other vehicles at top speed. Suddenly realising that he was directly in their path, he initiated Plan B. He legged it rapidly to the side of the runway.

All's well that ends well, and so it proved. The smoke was from an overheating section in the environmental control system, and indicated nothing seriously wrong. Both man and bird lived to fly another day, although naturally the pilot came in for his fair share of leg-pulling.

Ready for war

The 4450th TG achieved Initial Operating Capability (IOC) on 28 October, 1983,

but this was, quite frankly, marginal. Only eight pilots had been declared combat-ready; few weapons had been cleared for use; and thermal tiles around the jet efflux were giving problems. Speed was limited to Mach 0.8, and the black jet was alpha-limited to 4g. This was far less than had been planned, but fortunately fixes were fairly quickly found.

Once the veil of secrecy was lifted from the F-117, daylight flights, notably the first sorties of a pilot on type, could be made. This eased the strain of conversion considerably. A second effect was that the SLUFs could be dispensed with; they were replaced by eight Northrop T-38 Talon supersonic trainers. Not only did these allow pilots to maintain proficiency,

they could be used as chase planes to monitor first-timers in the F-117.

On 5 October 1989 the 4450th TG was redesignated as the 37th Tactical Fighter Wing (TFW), under command of TAC's 16th Air force. The 4450th TFS became the 415th TFS Night Stalkers; the 4451st TS became the 416th TFS Ghostriders, and the 4452nd TS became the 417th TFS Bandits. The evaluation phase now finished, it was now fully operational. The 4453rd TS, its evaluation task now complete, was disbanded.

Sensors and weapons

There was just one problem with stealth aircraft; if they were undetectable by air traffic control, civilian or military, they

Right: A Nighthawk off a deserted part of the Californian coastline. From this angle, the flat engine effluxes, designed to promote rapid mixing of exhaust gases with the ambient air, are clearly visible.

Below right: An armed Dutch F-16 Viper formates with an F-117A on one of the latter's rare excursions to Europe. As can be seen, the chunky Lockheed attack aircraft is not very much larger than the fighter. But operationally they are very different, as the F-117 is extremely specialised.

were potential collision hazards. To transit through friendly controlled airspace, radar reflectors were fitted, to make the F-117 detectable by conventional means.

Uncompromised stealth brought other problems. No emitters such as radar could be used. How best then to navigate accurately to the target and attack it? A very accurate ring-laser gyro with an hourly error measured in metres rather than miles was part of the answer. It was later coupled with GPS. Combined, the F-117 could be over the target with a precision of a second or two.

This sort of accuracy was essential for two reasons. Firstly, a multi-aircraft attack on targets in the same area (the classic case was downtown Baghdad) on a dark night with no radar, carried with it an inherent collision risk. Secondly, the instant that the first bombs explode, the defences will open up with barrage fire. However ineffective this may be, it distracts the pilots a little. Being under fire is generally reckoned to triple the miss distance achieved under benign range conditions. Also, the inevitable flashes do nothing for the imaging infra-red search capability. The ideal is for all bombs to be on their way down before the defences are alerted.

Target detection was the next problem. The F-117 was fitted with two IR sensors, one forward-looking, the other downward-looking. The former could, in clear weather, pick up the target from way back, while the latter would take over as the target was neared. Initially, difficulties were encountered in handing over the target from one sensor to the other. In a dive-toss attack, this could involve several handovers between the two sensors, but, as the F-117 is at its best and most stealthy when flown straight and level, this was no great problem. Initial picture quality was far from good, but this was largely cured by new hardware.

Then there is weapons aiming. There would be little point in being able to sneak past the defences undetected, only to have to rely on less than accurate weapons. The F-117 uses laser self-designation. The Gulf War of 1991 saw it hailed as a marvel of sheer accuracy, and among other things it was hailed as the winner of the "bombs down chimneys" competition. The truth was rather more prosaic. Laser guidance is laser guidance, regardless of the platform from which it is used, and the same inaccuracies apply. If the Nighthawk has an advantage in bombing accuracy, it is that its unobserved approach allows the pilot to take a rather more careful aim, undistracted by anything the local air defences hurl up at him.

And what of the weapons? For stealth reasons these had to be carried internally, and in such a moderate sized aircraft the available volume is limited. The standard load consists of two GBU-10 Paveway IIs, or two GBU-27 Paveway IIIs; both are laser guidance systems fitted to 2,000lb (907kg) Mk 84 bombs. Paveway III is the more accurate of the two.

At the point of weapons release, the bomb bay doors, which have serrated edges as a stealth measure, snap open.

The bombs then swing down on trapezes and are released, after which the bomb bay doors snap shut once more, minimising the time during which RCS is compromised. The pilot then continues to designate the target until impact. Of course, two smaller weapons can be carried, but this seems pointless. The Black Jet is best when carrying its full warload capacity.

Nighthawk at war

The F-117 made its combat debut on 21 December, 1989, as part of Operation *Just Cause*, the invasion of Panama. It had previously been precluded from the bombing of Libya in 1988, which was carried out by England-based F-111s.

Just Cause seems to have been selected as an easy option, as the air defences were virtually non-existent.

The climate of world opinion at that time had already become anodyne; wars were only acceptable if casualties were minimal. The task was neutralize the garrison of the Panamanian Army at Rio Hato by dropping 2,000lb (907kg) bombs within 150ft (46m) of the barracks. A Mk 84 makes a very loud bang; its blast effects are considerable. The level of confusion caused rendered the garrison ineffective, giving US air-dropped forces a walkover.

Six F-117s, two of which were reserves, set off from Tonopah 2,600nm (4,818km) away and, after multiple refuellings,

arrived over Panama. What ensued can only be described as a foul-up. The barracks were obscured by low cloud, while the prevailing wind was in a direction not forecast. Of the two Rio Hato attackers, lead pilot Greg Feest switched his attack to the right of the barracks, not the left .as briefed, and informed his number two accordingly. Lead then fouled up and bombed on the left side of the barracks as originally planned. His wingman offset his bomb to the left, and missed the target area by almost 1,000ft (305m). It was an inauspicious start, aggravated by controversy about targeting. Even this was difficult to support, given the veil of secrecy surrounding the type.

On 12 July, 1990, the 59th and final F-117 was delivered to the USAF.

Desert Storm

Coalition operations against Iraq in 1991, saw the Nighthawk emerge with an enhanced reputation. On 17 August, 1990, Al Whitley, the first USAF pilot to fly the F-117, assumed command of the 37th TFW. Within 48 hours, 21 F-117s of the 415th TFS left Tonopah and staged through Langley, Virginia. On the following day, 18 of them took off and set course for the Middle East. After multiple in-flight refuellings, they arrived at Khamis Mushait in Saudi Arabia. High in the mountains, the climate of Khamis Mushait was very similar to that of Tonopah, to the point where it was called Tonopah East!

Khamis Mushait could have been made to order for the F-117; maybe it was. Hardened shelters housed two F-117s each, and a long runway, necessary because of the high touch-down and takeoff speed of the Nighthawk, was

available. (To digress, when the F-117 made its first European appearance at the Paris Air Show in the following year, runway arrester gear was installed prior to its arrival. Fortunately it was not needed.) The 415th TFS Nighthawks were reinforced by another 18 F-117s of the 416th TFS on 4 December.

For the F-117, the war started at 0251 on 16 January, 1991, when Greg Feest dropped a 2,000lb (907kg) LGB on a radar centre 65nm (120km) southwest of Baghdad. It had been speculated that some of the lower-frequency Iraqi early warning radars might just have been able to detect the Nighthawk; these could then have vectored defending fighters into the area on the offchance of making a visual sighting. Consequently, Iraqi EW radars were high on the list of target priorities.

Not long after Feest's attack, other F-117s arrived over Baghdad, and rained bombs down on defence, communications, and command targets. At first the night sky was quiet; only with the first

bomb explosions did the defences really light up. Pilot Ralph Getchell described the scene as "like Las Vegas", while Greg Gonyea of the 416th TFS called it "flying through a popcorn popper!" It was however all barrage fire; unable to detect and track the Nighthawks, all the Iraqis could do was to pump stuff up in the hope that some of it might just connect. It was a vain hope; the night sky is a very big place, and not one F-117 was so much as scratched.

Raids continued, and with the effectiveness of stealth now established, six more aircraft, this time from the 417th TFS, were deployed to "Tonopah East" on 26 January, making the total 42. Between them, they flew 1,271 combat sorties, about one third of them over Baghdad itself, and delivered more than 2,000 tonnes of munitions. Average mission length was 5½ hours, involving several in-flight refuellings. The F-117 was also less profligate of resources than other types; it needed no dedicated fighter escort and no defence suppression air-

craft, with the secondary effect of needing fewer tankers. On the other hand, mission planning needed very careful integration; as the Black Jet was not detectable by Allied radar, and could thus not be monitored and controlled by AWACS, it had to be kept well separated from conventional strikes.

While it proved the stealth concept, the F-117 had its failures. The infra-red sensors could not penetrate cloud or rain, and many were the times in the Gulf War when a Nighthawk arrived over its target, only to find it socked in. The only alternative was to return with its munitions unexpended. Nor could the type ever be used by day; visibility from the cockpit is atrocious, while its performance is best described as pedestrian. If sighted by a conventional fighter, it would be a dead duck.

Nighthawks since the Gulf

The reorganization of the USAF in the early 1990s saw the abandonment of the word "Tactical", and the 37th TFW become the 49th FW, now based at

Left: Flight refuelling is essential for Nighthawk missions to extend the range and endurance required. But its stealth qualities, including the lack of an onboard radar, cause problems in finding a tanker.

Right: A Nighthawk seen outside its nest of hardened shelters at Khamis Mushait air base during the Gulf War. This base became known as Tonopah East, due to its similarity to the base in the Nevada desert!

Below right: The primary weapon of the Nighthawk was a 2,000lb (907kg) laser guided bomb, seen here about to be loaded into the internal bay of an F-117. Internal carriage is essential for stealth.

Holloman, New Mexico. On 21 February, 1999, 12 F-117s deployed to Aviano in Italy to support Operation *Allied Force* over Kosovo and Serbia. Little was released about stealth operations, but on 27 March an F-117 was shot down. The Yugoslavs claim that it fell to a SAM; other sources quote conventional AAA. Conventional wisdom states that if something is unrepeatable, it must have been a fluke. On 4 April, another dozen F-117s arrived at Spangdahlem in Germany as backup, but this was their final deployment in that theatre.

Upgrades

Like any other military aircraft nearing the end of its second decade of service, the F-117 has undergone its share of updating. The Operational Capability Improvement Programme (OCIP) was carried out in stages. Stage 1 was the replacement of the three original Delco computers with LMAS AP-102s, similar to those used by the Space Shuttle. This gave a quantum leap in capability. Stage 2 was a revised cockpit, with Honeywell colour MFDs which could be used to display FLIR/DLIR imagery. The redundant FLIR screen was replaced by a digital moving map display.

OCIP 2 also introduced two new gadgets: a Pilot Activated Automatic Recovery System (PAARS), in which a single switch could recover the aircraft into straight and level flight from any attitude, and a Flight Management System. By tying the autopilot to the navigation computer, this could put the aircraft over the target to an accuracy of less than one second. After the Gulf War, GPS was added. New coatings were also introduced, while IR signature was greatly reduced.

Despite various proposals, notably a carrier aircraft, F-117 production ceased in July 1990, and will not be restarted. There are several reasons for this. Reduction in force sizes means that such a mission-limited and payload/range-limited aircraft is not a viable proposition for the future. Also, stealth has moved on a generation. Finally, it must be considered that a single advance in detection technology might invalidate stealth overnight. Two possibilities exist; one is that the problems of bistatic radar may be overcome; the other is ultra-wide-band radar, currently used to detect underground pipes. Its current range is only about 5.5nm (10km), but an order of magnitude increase could render current stealth technology redundant. The question then becomes: new stealth or no stealth?

Specifications

Lockheed Martin F-117 Nighthawk

Dimensions Span	43ft 3¹/₂in/13.35m
Length	65ft 11in/20.09m
Height	12ft 5in/3.79m
Wing area	913sq.ft/84.82m²
Weights	
Empty weight	30,000lb/13,608kg
Max takeoff weight	52,500lb/2,381kg
Power	2xF404-GE-F1D2 turbofans
Thrust (installed)	9,720lb/4,409kg
Fuel capacity	c18,300lb/8,300kg
Performance	
Max speed	Mach 0.85
Landing speed	180kt/334kmh

Left: The 37th Tactical Fighter Wing was redesignated the 49th Fighter Wing, based at Holloman AFB in New Mexico. Aircraft from this unit flew against Serbia in 1999.

B-2 Spirit

The Northrop Grumman B-2 Spirit is the world's most advanced bomber, and represents the latest generation of stealth warplanes to enter service. As such, it bears no resemblance to the angular Lockheed Martin F-117 Nighthawk, but is a reversion to the flying wing configuration which has been around almost as long as manned powered aviation.

June 1995. The writer was driving in the environs of Paris, heading for Le Bourget for the Paris Air Show, when the rush hour traffic unaccountably started to slow. Across to the left, the B-2 was gently cavorting, displaying its unmistakable lines. As B-2 watching and driving were incompatible activities, the traffic gradually came to a halt, probably the first time that any aeroplane had ever stopped the Paris rush hour traffic.

The B-2 had taken off from its

Below: June 1995 and B-2A No 88-0329 Spirit of Missouri touches down at Le Bourget on its first deployment to Europe. Note the rake angle on the main gear doors as seen here.

American base, crossed the Atlantic, carried out a practice bombing mission over the Vliehors range in Holland, and then lobbed in at Le Bourget for its first official visit to Europe, staying on the ground for about two hours, albeit with engines running.

It was a curious sight. We have all seen photographs in which it looks like a two-dimensional cardboard cutout painted black. Well, from some angles, that is exactly how it looks! With a new crew on board, it took off again, and made several low passes at low speeds in rather gusty conditions. To an observer on the ground, it appeared to be a mite unstable in pitch, although Northrop-Grumman staff assured me that the pilot was merely demonstrating control responsiveness.

The B-2 made its second public appearance in Europe at Farnborough 1996. *Spirit of Washington*, flown by mission commander and former A-10 pilot Frank Cavuoti, and pilot Darryl Davies, made a couple of passes in the distance. It was stated that the B-2 was so secret that it was not allowed to land but, since it had been on the ground for two hours at Le Bourget, this was simply unbelievable.

Originally, 100 B-2 Spirits were to be ordered, but in practice barely 20 entered service. The standing joke was that once the USAF had run out of Whisky, Gin, Brandy, Rum and Tequila, etc., they quickly ran out of spirit names, and this determined the number of aircraft ordered.

Above: First flight of the Northrop B-2A Spirit, on 17 July 1989; with Bruce Hinds of Northrop and Colonel Richard Couch at the controls, it flew to Edwards from Palmdale.

Development

The flying wing had long been seen as the ideal aerodynamic shape, since the entire structure contributed to lift. In the early days of manned powered flight, the main attribute was stability. In 1913, J. W. Dunne exhibited his D.8 tail-less swept wing biplane at Deauville, France. Pilot Commandant Felix (a Frenchman, naturally) astonished spectators by leaving the controls and walking out on the lower wings.

Other notable flying wings were the

Right: The most notable feature of the B-2A is the lack of vertical surfaces. The chined leading edge near the nose is a stealth feature, as are the set-back engine intakes.

Right: The B-2A seen on its eighth test flight. In peacetime it must carry a radar reflector, without which the aircraft would become a nightmare to traffic controllers.

Westland Pterodactyl, the German Horten series, and, in 1947, the Armstrong Whitworth AW.52 jet. In the USA, John D. Northrop was the leading exponent of flying wings. Far more aerodynamically efficient than conventional layouts, they promised equal payload/range for lower weight and less installed power. The propeller-driven XB-35 was followed by the eight-jet YB-49. The latter was not adopted by the USAF for two main reasons: it was inherently unstable in the days when stability augmentation systems were new and untried, nor could it match the speed of the conventional Boeing B-47 Stratojet. With the cancellation of the YB-49 programme, John Northrop left the industry. Many years passed before the company he founded ventured back into the bomber business.

In 1974, Northrop was one of the companies asked by DARPA to investigate stealth, and in the following year was, with Lockheed, one of the two finalists for Have Blue. Northrop's model had a diamond-shaped planform and a large dorsal engine inlet. From the front, the RCS was acceptably small, but much larger from some other angles. Nor did Northrop have the RAM technology to match its rival.

While Lockheed was awarded the Have Blue contract, DARPA approached Northrop about a project codenamed Assault Breaker, a battlefield surveillance aircraft designed to detect tanks and other ground assets. Survival was an even bigger problem, since the aircraft would need to loiter in the vicinity of the battlefield for extended periods, while using radar.

The need to use radar emissions seemed to negate the project from the outset, but the Hughes company was already working on two useful features, Low Probability of Intercept (LPI), and antennae with reduced radar reflectivity. If this could be made to work properly, the Assault Breaker concept was viable. Meanwhile Northrop set to work to design a low observable airframe. Whereas the approach for Have Blue and the later Senior Trend was to minimise head-on and tail-on RCS by scattering the incoming energy away in a few "spikes", Northrop needed to provide a low RCS from any angle. It was a tall order.

The shape that finally emerged looked

Right: A partial view of the engine effluxes shows that they are shielded from prying ground radars and IR seekers, and to a lesser degree from airborne sensors.

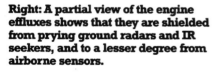

Below: Three-views show the very simple lines of the Spirit, the angles carefully calculated to defeat hostile radar emissions, giving the familiar double-W shape to the wing trailing edge.

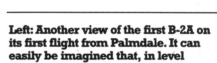

Left: Another view of the first B-2A on its first flight from Palmdale. It can easily be imagined that, in level flight at operational altitude, it would visually appear as little more than a thin straight line.

Below: The B-2A production line at Palmdale, with the lead aircraft more than half covered with walk mats to prevent skin damage.

like an inverted Victorian bath, with flat sloping sides with a rounded top and front, flaring into an abrupt chine towards the bottom. Small straight wings, steeply canted ruddervators, and a deep-set dorsal intake rounded out the picture. Rather than be deflected away, incoming radar emissions tended to flow around it.

The capacious fuselage contained a Hughes battlefield surveillance radar which could be rotated internally, to look out of first one side, then the other. Data linkage was installed on the reverse side, to provide near-real-time intelligence to friendly forces. A single prototype was ordered in April 1978 with the codename Tacit Blue. It did not enter service, and its main value was in giving Northrop entry into the exclusive world of low observables. But whereas Lockheed had gone for the faceted approach, the Northrop Corporation had tried (and to a large degree succeeded) by using compound curves.

Birth of a bomber

While the Carter administration had cancelled the B-1A, it was still aware of the need to replace the elderly B-52 fleet. At much the same time, it initiated studies for what later became known as the Advanced Technology Bomber (ATB). Lockheed's submission was codenamed Senior Peg and, while the study remains classified, it is believed to have been an enlarged and stretched F-117. The

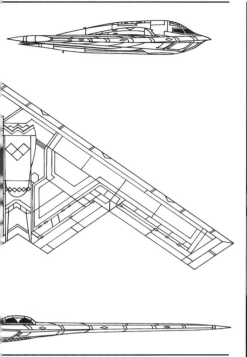

Right: The engine inlets are shaped to deflect radar emissions, and are located above the wings to conceal them from ground radars or from lower flying aircraft. A serpentine duct and RAM does the rest.

Below: Anti-radar construction of the wing leading edge and the outboard trailing edge can be seen. As yet there is no counter to the B-2A.

Northrop submission was a flying wing design codenamed Senior Ice. The flying wing configuration, because it lends itself to the ideal "flat plane", is also a useful platform for the use of low observables.

Once again we must remember that the Cold War was at its height, and that the Soviet Union would have been a formidable foe. A bomber penetrator was

badly needed, but the B-52 had been more or less relegated to the role of cruise missile carrier, while the F-111 was too short-legged. Viable options were few.

Meanwhile, Ronald Reagan assumed the presidency, and the vital decision fell to his administration. While the ATB held great promise, it was also a very high-

risk programme. Rushing it into service to replace the B-52 could have been a recipe for total disaster. The result was a "belt and braces" compromise: build 100 B-1s, with improved stealth qualities, quickly; and follow these at a later date with 132 ATBs. The relaxed time frame for the ATB was expected to minimise technical risks.

The ATB contract was awarded to Northrop on 20 October, 1981. It covered full-scale development, and six aircraft plus two static test airframes. Much has been made of Northrop's previous experience with flying wings, but after an interval of nearly three decades, this seems a dubious advantage. It has also been stated that greater computer power enabled the company to use compound curves rather than the Lockheed faceted approach, but this is denied.

Tweaks

The design had not been frozen at the time of the order. The cockpit, weapons bays and engines were neatly packaged towards the centre of the aircraft, while much of the massive wing area housed fuel. Digital fly-by-wire was used, even though the ATB had neutral stability. Mission tradeoffs dictated a moderate leading edge sweep angle and a surprisingly modest aspect ratio.

But changes were just around the corner. Firstly, SAC decided that it wanted a multi-mission aircraft, which meant enlarging the weapons bays. Then the threat projection boffins decided that the Soviets might in the future produce very powerful radars which could give a useful detection range even against stealth aircraft. SAC's answer was to guard against this by the time-honoured method of very low, under-the-radar penetration, using terrain masking.

This had not been foreseen by the designers. Low level penetration was not a good idea for a bomber with a large wing area and a modest wing loading. The flight control computer could cope with the rapid changes required by gust alleviation, but the control surfaces themselves were poorly placed to counter continuous bumps at low level. An unacceptable level of structural flexing would ensue.

Stiffening the airframe was the simple solution, but this was calculated to involve a weight penalty of about 4.5 tons. This was avoided only by extensive redesign. The outer wing sections were made shorter and thinner, with only two control surfaces instead of three, while

the outboard centrebody sections were extended aft and provided with two elevons each. This gave the now familiar double-W trailing edge.

However, it was not all bad news. A new form of radar absorbent structure for the leading edges required less depth for the same effect. This allowed quite major changes, most of them for the better. Wing sweep was reduced by two degrees, while the single wing spar and the cockpit moved forward. This in turn allowed the engine inlets to be moved aft, which simplified the intake ducts and structure, with a considerable weight saving. Not until 1984 did the ATB pass its final preliminary design review. At last production could start in earnest.

Into the air
The B-2 was designed and built under conditions of almost total secrecy, which incidentally added an enormous amount to its cost. Rumours abounded that it would be a flying wing, but there was no confirmation of this. Progress was slow, in part because the B-1B programme was eating up much of the available funding, and not until 22 November, 1988, was it finally unveiled, in front of an invited audience at Palmdale, California. The view was from the front aspect only; the planform, the sawtooth trailing edge, and the engine effluxes remained concealed, although an enterprising photographer overflew the area and obtained planform pictures, bending rather than actually breaking the security regulations.

First flight took place nearly eight months later, on 17 July, 1989. The delay was caused by the fact that at roll-out, AV-1 lacked many essential parts and systems, including engines. The roll-out seemed premature. But why?

Three possible solutions present themselves. Firstly, with the programme seriously delayed, it was felt necessary to present evidence of tangible progress to Congress and to the US taxpayers. Secondly, maybe it was felt that the total security blackout could not be kept in place for much longer, and early roll-out thus pre-empted a leak. Finally, the Tu-160 Blackjack, the Russian equivalent of the B-1B, but rather larger, had entered limited service during late 1987. Early roll-out of the B-2 may just have been used to convince the Russians that the programme was further advanced than in fact it was. Or maybe the reason was a combination of all three!

Piloted by Northrop's Bruce Hinds and Colonel Richard Couch, commander of the B-2 Combined Test Force, AV-1 flew from Palmdale to Edwards AFB, a trip lasting 2 hours 20 minutes, during which the landing gear remained down. But even now progress remained slow; in the first 11 months only 16 flights, totalling 67 hours, were logged. AV-2 lagged; its first flight did not take place until 19 October of that year.

In 1989, Congress decreed that full-rate production would not be funded until the first stage of stealth testing had been passed. As full RCS tests were not scheduled to finish until the summer of 1991, this imposed yet more delays. The complexity of the aeroplane, which had much to do with the sheer precision of forming its outer skin, required a production time of five years. This decision had also delayed the five development B-2s and the six production articles already authorized. AV-1 was well under way, but work on the other 11 was slowed down. This attracted uninformed adverse comment from the media, which had already done much to rubbish the B-1B. Much of this centred on early Northrop flying wings, which had little relevance to the B-2 project.

B-2 details
The most radical aspect of the B-2 was that it had no vertical surfaces. This was an important stealth measure. The directional control function was assumed by the split outboard wing control surfaces, which acted as ruddervators, turning the aircraft by increasing drag on one side or the other. There was one problem with this; the surfaces became effective only when deployed at more than five degrees – the angle needed to take them outside the boundary layer flow over the wing – and in normal flight they were opened to this angle. This naturally compromised stealth, and operationally it was proposed to make course changes by using differential engine thrust.

The leading edges, carefully shaped for stealth, were covered with dielectric (radar-transparent) material, behind which were wedges of radar-absorbent honeycomb, designed to trap and dissipate radar emissions. The wing itself consisted of a single titanium spar, with a titanium carry-through box in the centre-section, surrounded by all-composite construction. The rest of the wing skin structure was composite. As this could not be allowed to deform under aerodynamic loads, thus compromising stealth, it was made very stiff, up to 0.91in (23mm) thick in places. The wing structures are also integral fuel tanks.

Constructionally, the B-2 was a new generation. No mockup was built to ensure that everything fitted where it should; it was all computer-generated, and surface tolerances were a fraction of a millimetre; for sheer accuracy, this was far beyond anything previously attempted.

This was made even more difficult by the use of compound curves; hardly a single surface on the B-2 has a constant radius, while all edges are either serrated or match the angles of main surfaces. The engine intakes are close inboard above the wings, are S-shaped to conceal the compressor face from ahead, and have hydraulically-actuated doors on the upper surface to provide extra air for low-speed conditions, taxying, and idling.

The engines are four General Electric F118-100 unaugmented turbofans, mounted within the wing depth. The fairings aft of the intakes are aerodynamic only. The exhausts are two-dimensional as in the F-117, deflected slightly upwards, cooled by bypass air and mixed with chlorofluorosulphuric acid to prevent contrails.

From outside, the cockpit transparencies seem very large. The reason for this becomes apparent when one examines the roof ejection hatches for the ACES II ejection seats. The normal crew is two men, and these are placed well back from the windows. Without such large transparencies, the view would be unduly limited and, to pilots used to fighters, it still appears so. There is a seat available for a third crew member, but so far this has been found unnecessary. "Glass" cockpit displays are the norm.

The B-2 has been stated to handle like a fighter, but this was also said of the B-1B. Speaking to the B-1B chief test pilot at Le Bourget many years ago, the writer was told that while the B-1B was responsive, it took a while for the controls to overcome the inertia of such a heavy aircraft. This is almost certainly the case with the B-2. On the other hand, at normal operational speeds, the B-2 is extremely responsive, as in-flight refuelling trials have demonstrated.

Weaponry
The B-2 has two internal weapons bays equipped with either racks or rotary launchers, located entirely within the wing depth, and not, as first reported, in the dorsal hump aft of the cockpit. These could carry up a theoretical load of 50,000lb (22,680kg) of conventional munitions. In practice, this consists of 80 Mk 82 500lb (227kg) or 16 Mk 84

2,000lb (907kg) iron bombs. GBU-87 CBUs or GBU-30 (JDAM) munitions are other options, as is the Raytheon AGM-1254 JSOW. The nuclear load is 16 B-83 or 20 B-61 "beasties", although in the current political climate this is no longer a realistic option.

Spirit in service

Compared to the Fairchild Republic A-10 Thunderbolt II and the Rockwell B-1B Lancer, which received official USAF names so late as to be almost a symbol of belated remorse, the B-2 was named Spirit at a relatively early stage. In fact, the limited number of B-2s which entered service were named after US States.

The B-2 was designed to be stealthier against a much wider range of frequencies than the F-117, including VHF, used by Russian early warning systems. This increased the problems by at least an order of magnitude but, at the end of the day, the B-2 proved to be the most survivable aircraft in the USAF inventory. At the Farnborough Air Show in 1996, British Aerospace (BAe) claimed to have detected the B-2 quite easily; however, since it was in comfortable visual range, how valid was this? It must be remembered that the aircraft, flown by former A-10 pilot Frank Cavuoti, needed to be painted by air traffic control in the area, and had been given an enhanced radar signature. This was also a useful countermeasure to prevent potential enemies gaining actual performance numbers on the bird. The Hughes APQ-181 radar low probability of intercept (LPI) radar has 21 modes, all to do with ground mapping and target finding, which, tied in with GPS, allows it to strike accurately in any weather conditions.

The first and only B-2A unit is the 509th Bombardment Wing, based at Whiteman AFB, Missouri, which has individual shelters for each aircraft.

Spirit at war

The combat debut of the B-2 took place on 24 March, 1999, when aircraft of the 509th BW attacked targets in Yugoslavia. Missions lasted up to 31 hours. By May 5, using the callsign Darth (Vader), they dropped more than 500 GBU-30 JDAMs – over 450 tons of munitions using the GPS targeting system. The B-2A has now earned itself the soubriquet of "combat proven".

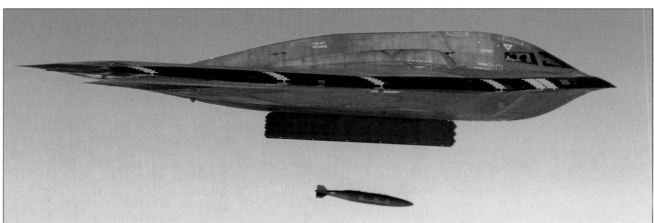

Above left: A view of one of the two capacious internal weapons bays of the B-2A. While these could carry a load of 50,000lb (22,680kg) on rotary launchers, the most likely warload is less, about 40,000lb (18,144kg).

Top right: A B-2A drops a GAM-113 deep penetration weapon, also seen at left. This is effective against buried and hardened targets, but is extremely specialised, needing very precise aiming.

Above centre: The GBU-30 JDAM is the weapon of choice for the B-2A, and about 500 were dropped on Yugoslavia in the spring of 1999, using the GPS targeting system. This amounted to over 450 tons of munitions.

Above: the serrated edges of the bomb-bay doors of the Spirit are clearly visible as this example launches a Mk 84 2,000lb (907kg) conventional bomb during trials.

Specifications: Northrop Grumman B-2A Spirit

Dimensions Span	172ft/52.42m
Length	69ft/21.03m
Height	17ft/5.18m
Wing area	5140sq.ft/477.52m²
Weights Empty weight	153,700lb/69,718kg
Normal takeoff	336,500lb/152,635kg
Weapons load	50,000lb/22,680kg
Internal fuel	180,000lb/81,647kg
Power Propulsion	4xF118-GE-100
Military thrust	19,000lb/8,618kg
Performance Vcruise	Mach 0.85
Ceiling	50,000ft/15,239m
Range	6,000nm/1,112km

Production and deliveries

Air vehicle	Serial	Delivered	Spirit of
1001(AV-1)	82-1066	17 July 1989	
1002(AV-2)	82-1067	19 October 1990	Arizona
1003(AV-3)	82-1068	18 June 1991	New York
1004(AV-4)	82-1069	17 April 1992	
1005(AV-5)	82-1070	5 October 1992	Ohio
1006(AV-6)	82-1071	2 February 1993	Mississippi
1007	88-0328	August 1994	Texas
1008	88-0329	December 1993	Missouri
1009	88-0330	August 1994	California
1010	88-0331	December 1994	South Carolina
1011	88-0332	October 1994	Washington
1012	89-0127	February 1995	Kansas
1013	89-0128	September 1995	Nebraska
1014	89-0129	November 1995	Georgia
1015	90-0040	January 1996	Alaska
1016	90-0041	December 1995	Hawaii
1017	92-0700	July 1996	Florida
1018	93-1085	May 1996	Oklahoma
1019	93-1086	August 1996	Kitty Hawk
1020	93-1087	August 1997	Pennsylvania
1021	93-1088	December 1987	Louisiana

ATF/F-22

During the World War II, a fighter pilot who had previously been rhapsodising about his mount could within a matter of weeks be bitterly complaining about its shortcomings. Such were the vagaries of fighter design of that era. Over the past half-century, all that has changed is the length of time involved for technology to take a leap ahead. This has posed problems. Looking a few months ahead is a far cry from looking two decades or more into the future. Yet this has to be done. The two main questions are: what and how? The USAF answer was the F-22 Raptor.

Concept definition studies for an Advanced Tactical Fighter (ATF) commenced in 1983. At that time, the F-15 had been in service for just eight years, but as combat aircraft had become ever more capable, so their design and development times had lengthened. At the time, the Soviet Union still posed the major threat, with conventional war in Europe (with its potential for nuclear escalation) as the "worst case" scenario. It was known that the Russians had a new generation of fighters coming along (the MiG-29 and Su-27) and, while little firm intelligence was available about them, it was safer to overestimate their capabilities than to underestimate them. This being the case, it was unclear how long the USA could hold its technological lead. It was time to look to the future.

Below: By 1986 the appearance of the Lockheed ATF had changed greatly. Laterally raked intakes appeared, much smaller canards were now located high and aft of the cockpit, and the fins were much more steeply canted.

Tactical air operations fall into two main categories – defensive and offensive. The latter is by far the most difficult. Tactical fighters have to operate in the teeth of ground and air defences, they are exposed to strong and persistent jamming of both sensors and communications, while the fuel gauge determines when action must be broken off, usually at a most inconvenient moment. Yet it is almost always necessary to carry the fight to the enemy; defensive actions might stave off defeat, but rarely if ever do they win wars.

The main problem was, how best to operate effectively over hostile territory without incurring unacceptable losses? Clearly, the traditional fighter virtues of speed, acceleration, rate of climb, and agility, had to be maintained in a new tactical fighter, together with a superior weapons system. It also had to be affordable in adequate quantities; the lessons of the F-14 and F-15 acquisition programmes were still fresh.

The USAF addressed the problem on two fronts; stealth and speed. Stealth might not allow totally undetected penetration of hostile air space, but it could delay it by a significant amount. This in turn would give a first shot, first kill capability, in any encounter with enemy fighters.

In conjunction with this, speed would reduce the reaction time available to the defences, crimping in the already reduced radar detection and missile envelopes still more. The next question was exactly how fast? One thing was certain: high subsonic speed was not enough. Supersonic speed was fine, but involved using afterburner, and that had two drawbacks. It could not be sustained for long without the aircraft running out of fuel. Also afterburner was a giant heat source in the sky; it compromised stealth, and made a marvellous target for heat-seeking missiles. This was not the object of the exercise.

The ideal was supersonic flight without the use of afterburner, or supercruise, as it came to be known. But there was little point in increasing cruising speed by small amounts; operationally the difference between Mach 0.95 and Mach 1.05

Above: An artist's impression of the Lockheed ATF contender released in 1985 shows a chined nose similar to that of the SR-71, a fairly orthodox delta wing with canard foreplanes, and vectoring engine nozzles.

would be marginal. What was needed was a significant increase; possibly approaching 50 per cent, or something of the order of 250kt (463kmh) extra.

Studies showed that a speed of Mach 1.4 was about the minimum for clearing six o'clock, reducing vulnerability to any sort of attack from astern, while significantly shrinking radar and SAM envelopes. Obviously it was a case of the faster the better. Now, if this sort of speed could be reached and sustained without 'burner, fuel consumption would be drastically lowered, and combat endurance proportionately increased. The latter was particularly important; stealthy aircraft have to carry all their fuel internally; in combat, drop tanks are not an option.

There were other advantages in being able to cruise in this speed regime for

Right: Were the Lockheed artist's ATF impressions of 1985 and 1986 deliberate disinformation? The YF-22 seen here shows no sign of a tail-less canard delta; only the thrust-vectoring nozzles remain.

extended periods. If an engagement looked probable, conventional fighters would have to select afterburning and accelerate hard to increase their energy state, whereas the supercruiser was already there. If necessary, the ATF could always use its own afterburners, in which case it had a head start. Maximum speed requirement was initially Mach 2.5. This could be handy when homeward bound out of missiles, to quote but one instance. The required operational radius on internal fuel had to be rather better than that of contemporary fighters; a figure of 700nm (1,297km) was widely quoted.

In the event of the expected war, airfields would have been prime targets. The ability to operate from short fields or damaged runways was another early requirement for the new fighter; the specified limit was 2,000ft (610m).

While the operational philosophy was detect first, shoot first, kill first, there could be no guarantee that the fight would not close to visual range. While all fighter design consists of a series of compromises, stealth, however important, could not be allowed to compromise close combat agility.

Contracts and competition
On 31 October, 1986, the Air Force

Below: The losing ATF contender was the Northrop/McDonnell Douglas YF-23. A more radical design than the YF-22, its outstanding features were the trapezoidal wing planform and steeply canted ruddervators.

Right: Were the Lockheed artist's ATF impressions of 1985 and 1986 deliberate disinformation? The YF-22 seen here shows no sign of a tail-less canard delta; only the thrust-vectoring nozzles remain.

Below: The losing ATF contender was the Northrop/McDonnell Douglas YF-23. A more radical design than the YF-22, its outstanding features were the trapezoidal wing planform and steeply canted ruddervators.

Secretary announced that two companies had been selected to build two demonstration/validation prototypes each. Unsurprisingly they were Lockheed and Northrop, the leaders in stealth technology. Such a huge and potentially difficult contract called for partners in the enterprise. Lockheed teamed with Boeing and General Dynamics; Northrop with McDonnell Douglas, perhaps a predictable pairing in view of their shared work on the F/A-18.

It had been obvious that the thrust needed for the required level of supercruise would demand more powerful engines than then existed. Engines always take longer to develop than airframes; so contracts had been placed for technology demonstrator engines in September 1983, with General Electric for the YF120, and with Pratt & Whitney for the YF119. These were to box and cox on the prototypes: one of each airframe powered by one of each type engine. Once all four prototypes had been successfully flown by the manufacturers, an exhaustive evaluation would take place, the results of which would determine which type would be selected for the USAF.

By now the specification had been firmed up. Gross weight was not to exceed 50,000lb (22,680kg), which in fact proved the hardest part. Minimum supercruise was to be Mach 1.4 to 1.5. With two thirds internal fuel, ATF had to be able to manage 6g turns at Mach 2.5 at 30,000ft (9,144m), while sustained load limits of +9g/-3g with 80 per cent fuel were demanded. At high altitude, Soviet air defences were sparse, and an

Above: Roll-out of the first F-22A on 9 April 1997. It was officially named the Raptor at this high profile ceremony, supplanting the previously suggested Lightning II. First flight took place on 7 September 1997.

operational ceiling of 70,000ft (21,335m) had once been quoted, but this was now relaxed to become sustained 2g turns at 50,000ft (15,239m). Above this level, pressure suits would have been needed. Down among the weeds, acceleration from Mach 0.6 to Mach 1 was to take 20 seconds; or from Mach 0.8 to Mach 1.8 in 50 seconds at 30,000ft (9,144m). The short-field performance remained as previously stated at 2,000ft (610m); take-off was not too bad, but landing could be attained only with the help of thrust reversing.

As the years passed, some things changed. First to go was thrust reversing. Then, as the Soviet Union melted away, the Mach 2.5 requirement was relaxed. This greatly simplified intake design; moveable ramps were difficult to reconcile with stealth.

Meanwhile, engine development was moving fast. While turbofans are far more economical than turbojets, the latter give much more thrust in the thin air at high altitudes. With this in mind, General Electric tried to have the best of both worlds by using a variable-cycle engine, acting like a turbofan when needed, but with the bypass cut out to make it a turbojet at high altitudes. Pratt & Whitney took the simpler route; a turbofan with very high operating temperatures.

Right: A bench trial of the Pratt & Whitney F119 afterburning turbofan as selected for use by the F-22A. This has a two-dimensional vectoring nozzle, but differential movement with two engines gives roll control.

Northrop YF-23

The first prototype YF-23 to fly took to the air from Edwards AFB on 27 August, 1990. Piloted by Paul Metz, it climbed to 25,000ft (7,620m) with ease, forcing the F-15 flying chase to use afterburning just to keep up. It was a promising start, marred only by the port main gear door opening slightly during a gentle left turn. This caused the flight to be terminated early.

The YF-23 really looked like a vision of the future. The wing planform was diamond-shaped, with 40deg of leading edge sweep matched by 40deg forward sweep on the trailing edges, with cropped tips. In what virtually amounted to a butterfly tail, all-moving ruddervators were splayed out at an acute angle. As one would expect in a low-observables aircraft, all leading and trailing edges were at matching angles.

The wing leading edges contained a single-piece slat, while the trailing edges featured outboard ailerons and inboard flaperons. The unorthodox planform gave unique advantages, with a combination of enormous area, low wing loading, and a low aspect ratio. The extremely long chord inboard allowed depth where it was most needed, which simplified the structure and provided wing/body blending over a high proportion of the fuselage length. Such a vast

Top: From this angle, features such as the single-piece transparency to the cockpit, including the sawtooth leading edge, the chined nose and trapezoidal intakes raked laterally and vertically, are clearly seen.

Above left: Both YF-22 prototypes formate on a KC-135 tanker for in-flight refuelling during the ATF evaluation. The far aircraft carries a spin recovery parachute, an essential aid for high alpha trials.

Above: The primary reason for the selection of the YF-22 over the YF-23 was that it had superior high alpha performance. Here one of the YF-22 prototypes launches itself vertically skywards.

area is however at variance with super-cruise requirements.

The nose had chines which led back to the wing leading edges, possibly acting as a vortex generator in lieu of leading edge extensions. By shedding vortices at high angles of attack, this also improved yaw control. The cockpit transparencies were a strange blend of compound curves. Trapezoidal intakes under the wing curved upward to the engine compressor face, with the engines themselves (in this case YF119s) housed in overwing "humps", exhausting into shallow troughs open at the top, with sawtooth ends, vaguely reminiscent of the B-2A. Concentrating on stealth, Northrop had chosen not to use thrust-vectoring nozzles which, we must agree, are decidedly unstealthy. A double internal weapons bay was located just aft of the nosewheel, but few details are available.

The second YF-23, powered by the YF120-GE-100, first flew in the following October. In all, the two Northrop prototypes flew 50 sorties for a total of 65.2 hours during the evaluation period. The YF119-powered aircraft reached a supercruise speed of Mach 1.43. This is believed to have been significantly exceeded by the GE-powered machine, but the actual figure was immediately classified.

Also during the evaluation period, the YF-23 reached a speed of Mach 1.8 and an altitude of 50,000ft (15,239m), a stabilized angle of attack of 25deg, and what Vietnam veteran Paul Metz called "The best gun tracking to 4g I've seen!" The results of stealth tests are naturally classified information.

Lockheed YF-22

Flown by Dave Ferguson, the first YF-22 took to the skies on 29 September, 1990, powered by two YF120-GE-100s. It was slightly disappointing after the futuristic Northrop fighter. Chunky and workman-like in appearance, it resembled nothing so much as an F-15 extensively redesigned for stealth. But, on reflection, that could be no bad thing!

The wing planform was rhomboidal; a 48deg swept leading edge with cropped tips, with a modest forward sweep of 17deg on the trailing edge. Wing area was 12.5 per cent less than that of the YF-23, which made it better for the super-cruise requirement (less drag), but it was still more than one-third larger than that of the F-15, with a corresponding impact on wing loading. The single piece leading edge slats were unusual in that they ran all the way out to the tips, with a strange V-shaped junction inboard where they met the fixed portion of the leading edge.

Ailerons outboard and flaperons inboard occupied much of the trailing edges.

Tail surfaces were fairly orthodox, with outward canted all-moving fins – set slightly forward on the fuselage in the manner of the Hornet – and outboard-mounted tailerons, the leading and trailing edges of which conformed to the wing angles.

Like the YF-23, the nose of the YF-22 was small, sized to house a phased array low probability of intercept radar. The front fuselage was V-shaped below the midpoint, sharply rounded at the junction between the two sides. The upper surface of the nose was domed, with complex curvatures. Like the YF-23, the single-piece canopy canted inwards, more or less completing a diamond cross-section, and sloped steeply down at the back. Serrated edges maintained the low observable profile, as they did on all other doors and hatches.

Whereas previous stealth aircraft, the F-117 and the B-2, had their intakes located on the upper surface of the wing, for a fighter this was unacceptable, due to pressure losses. Every last bit of power had to be screwed out of the engines, and this demanded underwing intakes, as Northrop had also recognized with the YF-23.

The intakes of the YF-22 were trapezoidal in section and raked back horizontally to match the leading edge angle. Since the Mach 2.5 requirement had been dropped, they were plain, with RAM-lined horizontal serpentine ducts. Splitter plates diverted the boundary layer air from the forebody, dumping it into the low pressure area above the wings. From the rear aspect, the YF-22 was less stealthy than the YF-23, in that it featured two-dimensional thrust vectoring nozzles. Lockheed's design approach had stressed all-round capability – performance, agility and stealth – whereas Northrop had given stealth priority. It was a demonstration of how different aircraft could be in conforming to a common specification.

During the evaluation phase, the two YF-22s flew 74 sorties, totalling more than 91 hours. Mach 1.8 was exceeded, while an impressive supercruise speed of Mach 1.58 was achieved, although afterburning was used to reach a high initial Mach number before it was cancelled, and the speed allowed to stabi-

lize. Shock waves impinging on the tailerons caused them to lose authority at speeds in excess of Mach 1.4, but thrust vectoring more than compensated for this. In high angle of attack testing, the YF-22 reached 62deg at an equivalent air speed of about 60kt (111kmh), with control authority still in reserve.

Decision time
By April 1991, all four airframe/engine combinations had met the specification. The selection ultimately fell on the Lockheed YF-22 powered by the Pratt & Whitney F-119, and was apparently made on the basis of least risk, it having the most mature technology. The official Engineering/Manufacturing/Development (EMD) contract was awarded to Lockheed in August 1991. This covered the completion of design work, manufacture of production tools, and 13 aircraft, two of which were to be static test tools. This was later cut to seven single-seat F-22As and two twin-seat F-22Bs.

Development
Even during the evaluation phase, the design was being refined, and was not finally frozen until March 1992. In the search for reduced drag, improved manoeuvrability, and reduced RCS, the following changes were made. The wingspan was increased by 18in (460mm) while leading edge sweep was reduced to 42deg. Both were achieved without altering the wing area. Wing root thickness was reduced, while twist and camber were modified, and the shape of the two-piece flaperons revised. The final wing alteration was to scarf the tip, to give better look angles to threat and missile warning antennae, which were located to give all-round coverage.

The tailerons were also modified; the leading edge sweep was changed to match that of the wings and given a broader chord, while the inboard trailing edges were aligned with the booms on which they were carried. The huge fin/rudder assemblies were also reduced in size, by 14in (355mm) in height and 20sq ft (1.86sq m) in area. They were also used as speed brakes, using differential movement, which allowed the conventional dorsal speed brake to be eliminated.

Keeping within the specified 50,000lb (22,680kg) weight limit eventually proved to be impossible. Given the requirement for supercruise, with all fuel and munitions carried internally, the ATF was inevitably a large aircraft; it could hardly have been otherwise.

Initially RCS was larger than anticipated, while other problems arose, which was only to be expected with such a radically new design. RCS was reduced by minor changes: drain holes were reduced from 227 to 44; large access panels were reduced from 62 to 43; while the number of sawtooth angles on panel leading edges was also reduced. The front fuselage was revised in detail; the nose was given a new and slightly blunter shape, which not only reduced RCS but improved radar performance. Other changes were made to the inlet ducts, to give greater concealment to the compressor faces.

The cockpit was moved slightly forward to give the pilot a better view "out of the window", and the canopy made sleeker. Unusually, the nosewheel was modified to retract aft rather than forward; in the previous position, the airflow helped to force it down when being extended.

These measures resulted in an overall reduction in length by 25in (63.5cm); at the same time the engine inlets were moved back 18in (45.7cm), mainly as a weight-saving measure, but this was also found to improve stability, and also gave a better view from the cockpit sideways and downwards.

The selection of the Pratt & Whitney engine made the GE-powered prototype redundant, and it was grounded to serve as an engineering mockup. This left only one aircraft to carry out the flight test programme. Then, with this about 90 per cent complete, disaster struck.

Left: The F-22 cockpit simulator concentrates on uncluttered data presentation, although the HUD looks complicated to the untrained eye as a missile is launched.

Above: The preferred weapon of the Raptor is the AIM-120 AMRAAM, the first trial launch of which took place in 1990. Up to six "cropped" AIM-120Cs can be carried.

On 25 April company test pilot Tom Morgenfeld was scheduled to explore supersonic flight characteristics, when the telemetry – the radio link between aircraft and ground, providing data from a number of sensors – failed. Telemetry allowed instant analysis of the flight, the profile of which could then be modified in the light of results. With this out of action, there was little point in continuing the flight, and Morgenfeld aborted and returned to Edwards AFB.

Having just refuelled, the aircraft was still well above its maximum permitted landing weight. The standard procedure was to burn off the excess fuel, which Morgenfeld attempted to do with a series of low altitude passes along the runway. Unfortunately, on the second pass, when the landing gear was raised and afterburning engaged, the YF-22 produced an uncommanded pitchup. While Morgenfeld corrected instantly with forward stick, the thrust vectoring system, which should, according to the manual, have been locked in the fixed position, tripled its authority, resulting in a very sharp pitchdown.

Keeping up with such fast oscillations is beyond the ability of any pilot. In Vietnam, the F-105 had been prone to pilot- induced oscillations, and the corrective measure was known as the JC manoeuvre. The pilot let go the controls; muttered "OK Jesus, you've got her", and waited for the oscillations to damp out. But this was only feasible with plenty of ground clearance. Poor Tom had no such

option, and his control inputs always lagged the aircraft. After seven seconds of behaving like a roller-coaster, the YF-22 hit the runway gear up, fortunately at a flat angle. It skidded along the runway for more than a mile, and caught fire. Morgenfeld was only slightly injured, but the aircraft was damaged beyond repair. The cause was a software anomaly in the quadruplex digital FBW system.

Lightning II to Raptor
Naming aircraft is a ritual of acceptance for the USAF, and delay implies a lack of faith in the product. Compared to the drawn-out process of finding names for the A-10, F-16 and B-1B, naming the ATF was by contrast conducted in almost indecent haste. At first it was unofficially known as the Lightning II, a tribute to a World War II Lockheed fighter that was a "turkey" against the Luftwaffe, but was very successful against the Japanese. This name did not last; on April 9, 1997, the Lockheed F-22A was officially named Raptor, a bird of prey, by General Richard Hawley, head of Air Combat Command.

The occasion was the rollout of the first EMD aircraft, No 4001. This aircraft first flew on 7 September of that year, piloted by Paul Metz. If success is measured by the ability to be in the right place at the right time, Paul Metz must be high on the list. A Wild Weasel pilot in Vietnam, he demonstrated the Northrop F-20 at Farnborough in 1984. Then, as previously recounted, he became chief test pilot for the YF-23 in the Northrop/McDonnell Douglas partnership. He then emerged as chief test pilot for Lockheed/Boeing/GD on the F-22A. This must truly make him one of the world's most gifted test pilots.

Raptor details
The Raptor has three internal weapons bays, one ventral, and one on either side, aft of the inlets. Up to six "cropped" AIM-120C AMRAAMs or two AMRAAMs and two JDAMs can be carried in the main bay. At launch, the doors snap open and the weapons are pneumatically expelled through the boundary layer air. Each side bay carries a single AIM-9 Sidewinder, which is swung outwards on a trapeze launcher before release. Internal weapons bays and trapeze launchers are far from new in the USAF; they were used more than three decades ago by the Convair F-102 and F-106. A possible alternative counter-air weapon is the BAe/Matra/Boeing Meteor AAM, in which Boeing became a partner on October 20, 1999. For close range work, the M61A2 fast-firing cannon is carried, although the maximum rate of fire of this is 4,000 rounds/minute.

Whereas previous fighters had computers for separate tasks, the approach for Raptor was much more integrated. Two Raytheon computers – each with the power of a Cray supercomputer, able to process up to seven billion bits per second – handle everything. Production aircraft now have triplex digital FBW in lieu

of the quadruplex system in the YF-22. The idea was to create an aircraft which could, to a large degree, think for itself. The incredible complexity of the programming has however caused glitches. A Society of Experimental Test Pilots presentation in 1998 drew the following comment from one of the Raptor team: "It throws tantrums, and will sometimes refuse to let pilots open the canopy. You shouldn't really complain about being stuck in the cockpit of the world's best fighter... but when it's 110deg F outside...!"

The Raptor cockpit has four active-matrix liquid crystal displays, two up-front displays, a wide-angle HUD, and an integrated control panel. A helmet-mounted sight is a certainty for the future. A side-stick controller is used, full of buttons, as are the throttles on the left, which give more than 60 time-critical functions. Pilot's Associate is also used, which gives aural advice on the tactical situation, while speech recognition reduced the manual workload. Pilot situational awareness has been stressed in the F-22.

The radar is the APG-77, an active array fixed antenna radar which, by minimising the send/receive ratio, and selectively using multiple pencil beams, has a low probability of intercept. Tilted backwards as a stealth measure, the antenna has greater capability looking up than

looking down while deflecting incoming emissions away. All modes are geared to presenting information to the pilot in an easily assimilable manner.

Rather more important is the LMAS ALR-94 EW suite, which monitors hostile emissions, and which includes an infrared missile launch detector. This displays threat indications on a moving map, allowing the Raptor to thread its way between the defences without being detected, and gives voice warnings of hostile missile attacks. Perhaps the one major item missing is an IRST detector, but this will almost certainly be added later.

What of the future? The production aircraft has already demonstrated a Mach 1.5 supercruise, and this may well be pushed up to Mach 1.6 before long. Four Raptor wings are scheduled to replace F-15s, with initial operational capability for the first squadron set for late in 2004. Doubtless the mission capability will be expanded and, with the development of thrust vectoring, it may prove possible to eliminate the fin/rudder assemblies to improve stealth.

The Raptor has just one enemy that might defeat it – the US General Accounting Office, where the "suits" hold sway, and which finds difficulty in understanding the price of national defence and freedom. They could still force its cancellation.

Specifications: Lockheed Martin/Boeing F-22A Raptor	
Wingspan	44ft 6in/13.56m
Length	62ft 1in/18.92m
Height	16ft 5in/5.00m
Wing area	840sq.ft/78.04m²
Empty weight	31,670lb/14,365kg
Max takeoff weight	55,000lb/24,948kg
Engines	2xF119-PW-100
Max thrust	c35,000lb/15,876kg
Internal fuel	25,000lb/11,340kg
Max speed	Mach 2 plus
Supercruise	Mach 1.58 plus
All other performance figures are classified	

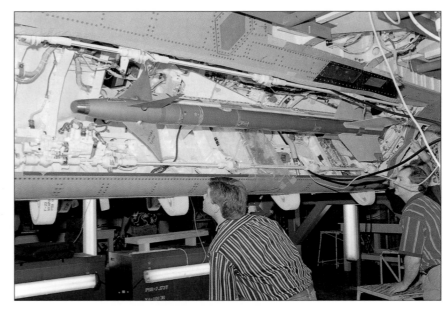

Right: The carriage of external stores is not compatible with stealth, so weaponry must be carried internally. Here engineers check the fit of an AIM-9M Sidewinder, which swings out on a trapeze prior to launch.

From this angle the reverse sweep of the fins, which matches that of the wing trailing edge, is the most obvious stealth feature. Note the side weapons bay.

Joint Strike Fighter

One thing has always been obvious: economies of scale result in lower unit prices. The more aircraft produced, the less the acquisition price will be, as development costs are amortised against production. It therefore makes economic sense to produce an aircraft which will suit as many user requirements as possible. But the problem lies in the compromises inherent in meeting the requirements of several services. This is the built-in headwind that the Joint Strike Fighter (JSF) has to overcome.

JSF started life as the Joint Advanced Strike Technology (JAST) fighter. JAST originated in 1986 as a combined British/American study, to replace Royal Navy Sea Harriers and USMC AV-8B Harrier IIs with a more capable supersonic Advanced Short Takeoff Vertical Landing (ASTOVL) aircraft. There were

Below: The chin inlet of the X-32 seen here can be drooped to aid pressure recovery in thrust-borne flight. Any other method would be incompatible with supersonic speed.

several ways of going about this, and various concepts were explored.

Lift engines in the forward fuselage combined with an afterburning vectored thrust engine for conventional propulsion, as used by the Russian Yak-141, was the most basic solution. But lift engines occupied volume that would have been better used for other things; in conventional flight they became just so much dead weight and complexity.

Plenum chamber burning was an alternative. This consists of using an afterburning-style system in the front

nozzles. While this allowed the proven Harrier-style four-poster, or even better a three-poster engine configuration, to be used, the problems were extreme. Ground erosion and hot gas recirculation and ingestion would rob the aircraft of much of its "go anywhere" capability. Also, the Harrier engine, with its oversized compressor, needed to feed the front ducts, was ill-suited for supersonic flight. A different approach was needed.

By 1990, the ATF was coming along fast, and the USAF, mindful of the way that its twin needs of quality and quantity had

Above: The Boeing JSF proposal is the X-32, seen here in this computer-generated image. This configuration has since been supplanted by a more orthodox wing and tail layout.

been met by the F-15 and F-16, started to show interest, as did the US Navy, which was then considering a navalized ATF as a Tomcat replacement.

At this point, the Advanced Research Projects Agency (ARPA) commenced the X-32 study for a Common Affordable Light Fighter (CALF). With four services

Right: The three-piece lobsterback vectoring tailpipe of the Pratt & Whitney F119 derivative engine for the JSF. This was designed by Pratt & Whitney together with Rolls-Royce.

Below: The McDonnell Douglas JSF was to have diverted the thrust of its main engine into two rotating nozzles, backed by a lift engine, for thrust-borne flight, with the main engine reverting to a straight-through configuration in normal flight. This was judged too risky.

Below: The Lockheed Martin X-35 in its USAF conventional takeoff and landing configuration. In many ways it resembles a scaled-down F-22A with a single vectored nozzle.

Bottom left: Head-on view of the X-35 mockup, in which the stealth features are readily apparent. The likeness to the Raptor is even more marked from this angle.

Bottom centre: The Pratt & Whitney Low Observable Axi-symmetric Nozzle could be used on USAF and USN JSF's, as these have no vertical takeoff or landing requirements.

Bottom right: The US Marine Corps variant of the X-35. This service demands an ASTOVL capability, to give it the operational flexibility currently provided by the Harrier.

Below: ASTOVL capability is provided for the USMC and RN JSF variants by a shaft-driven lift fan just behind the cockpit, combined with a three-piece lobsterback main nozzle.

interested, and the prospect of export sales, the potential market was assessed as at least 3,000 aircraft. The potential for economies of scale was enormous, enhanced further by the use of advanced technologies developed for the ATF. In particular, the same basic engine would be used, modified for vertical lift where necessary.

In 1993 a technology validation programme was commenced with Britain as a partner. The demonstrator was to be single-engined, with a maximum empty weight of 24,000lb (10,886kg). Other requirements were a high level of stealth, including internal missile carriage, a demanding radius of action, and an LPI active array radar.

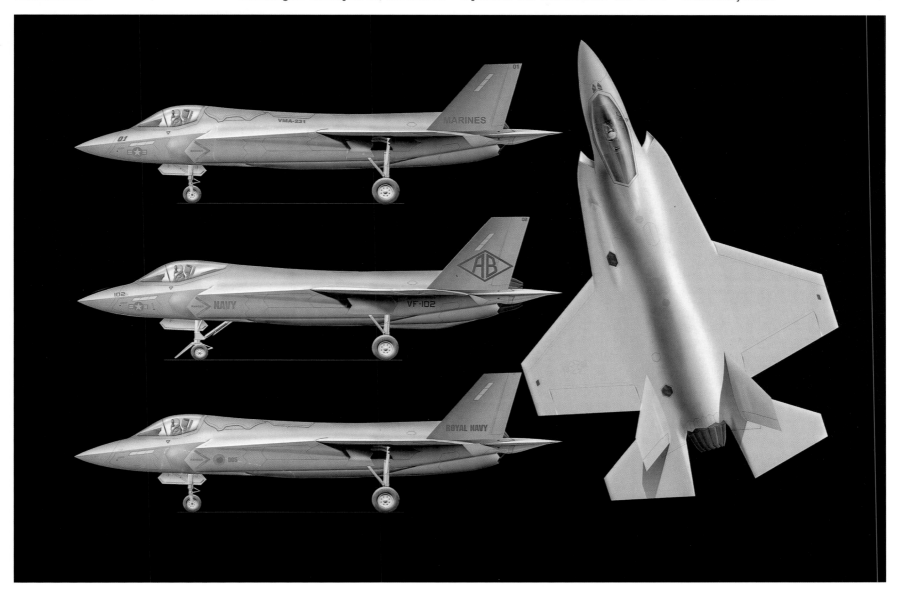

Three consortia entered, led by Boeing, Lockheed, and McDonnell Douglas, with whom BAe were teamed. The engine contractors were General Electric and Pratt & Whitney. Both collaborated with Rolls-Royce on ASTOVL requirements.

As could have been predicted, different service requirements now started to emerge. Conventional Takeoff and Landing (CTOL) was favoured by the USAF and the USN, whereas the USMC and RN demanded ASTOVL. This called for some difficult compromises, although the USAF relented a little by indicating that it might take up to 200 ASTOVL aircraft (of a requirement for 2,036) to give some austere base deployment capability. Other service differences were a beefed-up structure for carrier operations, and flight refuelling receptacles for the USAF but probes for the USN.

The contenders

McDonnell Douglas was eliminated in November 1996 on the grounds of high technical risk. It had the flat butterfly tail of the YF-23, and a wing planform reminiscent of the F-101 Voodoo. MACAIR had favoured a lift engine behind the cockpit, and a clamshell to divert the main engine thrust into two rotating nozzles for takeoff and landing. On transition to wing-borne flight, the exhaust would be switched back through the main nozzle.

The Boeing JSF proposal, now designated X-32, started out with a cropped rhomboidal wing shape, steeply canted ruddervators, and no horizontal tail surfaces, although these have since been added, and a fairly orthodox swept wing adopted.

Power is a modified Pratt & Whitney F119, with the bypass ratio increased to 0.60, located amidships. The afterburner and a two-dimensional vectoring nozzle are set well aft. In ASTOVL mode the latter is closed, diverting the thrust to two rotating nozzles directly under the centre of gravity. This is fairly close to the Harrier in concept, but needs powerful reaction jet controls for thrust-borne flight. In conventional flight the rotating nozzles are faired in, both to preserve stealth and to minimise drag. This arrangement blocks the natural place for the main gears, which instead retract into wing housings. A chin intake is used; this drops down to improve pressure recovery at low speeds.

While both X-32s (CTOL and ASTOVL) are 45ft (13.72m) long, the span, at least on the original planform, varied. On the ASTOVL it was 30ft (9.14m), to fit RN carriers without wing folding, while that of the CTOL variant was 36ft (10.97m). Empty weight is about 22,000lb (10,000kg), with the carrier fighter about 1,984lb (900kg) heavier. The impact of the revised planform is not known.

The Lockheed Martin consortium, since joined by Northrop Grumman and BAe, is now constructing the X-35. In many ways it resembles a scaled-down F-22, which is hardly surprising.

The engine is the Pratt & Whitney F119-611, modified with a larger fan section. For the CTOL variants, a stealthy axisymmetric nozzle is used, but for ASTOVL the system is radically different. At the hot end, a three-piece lobsterback vectoring nozzle is used.

The other component of vertical lift is a shaft-driven fan located just behind the cockpit. This is engaged and disengaged via a multi-layer clutch and gearing system, which was first ground tested in late 1999. The basic advantage of the lift fan is that the airflow through it is low-energy and low-temperature, minimising ground erosion and hot gas ingestion. Disadvantages are weight and complexity, and wasted fuselage volume.

The length of both X-35s is 50ft 10in (15.50m) and span is 32ft 10in (10m). The

wing area of 540sq ft (50.2sq m) is dictated by carrier approach requirements, and high lift devices occupy both leading and trailing edges. Predicted weights (CTOL) are 21,600lb (9,798kg), ASTOVL 23,000lb (10,433kg), with the carrier fighter probably similar.

First flights of both the X-32 and X-35 are scheduled for 2000, with the winner due to enter service seven years later. But will, in the present climate, the JSF ever reach service? That it will be needed in the long term can hardly be doubted. But will the accountants agree?

Above: A computer-generated image of the X-35 launching a pair of cropped AIM-120C AMRAAMs. As these must be carried internally for missions where stealth is needed, it is obvious that its counter-air persistence will be limited.

Above left: The engine proposed for JSF is the Pratt & Whitney F119-611, differing from the original F119 in having a larger fan section. It is seen here on the test rig with what appears to be a long extension jet pipe and standard nozzle.

Top left: How the X-35 would look in Royal Navy service. However the smoky trail from the missile would be counterproductive, while it is unlikely that two bandits would leave contrails as depicted. But how else could this be illustrated?

Top right: A US Navy JSF in close combat with what looks remarkably like a MiG-29. Small, stealthy, and with thrust vectoring giving enhanced agility, there is little doubt that the X-35 could become a formidable fighter in years to come.

Above: Simulated carrier recovery, as a US Navy X-35 comes aboard. It differs from the USAF variant in having a strengthened structure for deck landings, a tail hook, and a retractable flight refuelling probe rather than the USAF receptacle.

Harrier

Contents

Top: A Sea Harrier FRS.51 of the Indian Navy Air Squadron 500, first based on the carrier *Vikrant*, ex HMS *Hercules*. *Vikrant* has been replaced by *Viraat*, ex-HMS *Hermes* of Falklands fame. The land base is Dabolin.

Above: Low over the water, and apparently in a steep turn, this Harrier GR.5 launches an AIM-9L Sidewinder from an underwing pylon. This missile, which was successful in the South Atlantic, is scheduled to be replaced by ASRAAM.

Above right: A Sea Harrier FRS.1 photographed shortly after the end of the South Atlantic War in 1982, streams fuel from a vent pipe. It carries two Sidewinder training rounds, but combat experience saw this quickly increased to four.

Left: The Harrier GR.5 differs from previous variants in its bulged cockpit canopy and an extra pylon under each wing for an IR missile carried for self-defence. The GR.5 was quickly supplanted by the GR.7.

Introduction

The story of the Harrier is without parallel. It began with a rather unwieldy scheme conceived by a Frenchman for vectoring jet thrust not only backwards, to achieve high forward speed, but also downwards, to make the aircraft rise vertically off the ground. Engine designers at Bristol translated the concept into a more elegant solution: a new type of aircraft engine able in one neat package to provide lift, thrust and even inflight braking. But the British, into whose lap the concept fell in 1957, had just been shortsighted enough to predict that the RAF was never going to need any more fighters or bombers. Future wars were going to be fought exclusively with missiles, which seemed a more attractive option because they were cheaper.

Despite these extraordinary circumstances, the completely new idea of a single-engined "jump jet" managed to survive. This was because American money paid for three-quarters of the engine, and one man – Sir Reginald Verdon Smith – said his company would pay for the remainder. A little later, Sir Sydney Camm at Hawker Aircraft managed to persuade his board to pay for two prototypes of the novel P.1127 aircraft his team had designed. And in June 1960, four years from the start, British officials actually thawed enough to sponsor the P.1127 itself, provided that it was understood it was purely for research, and had nothing to do with such a taboo subject as a future combat aircraft!

With the passage of a complete decade, reason returned. The P.1127 was developed into the Harrier, which gave its users greater tactical flexibility than could have been conferred by any other type. At the time, this primarily meant off-site basing, with Harrier squadrons located forward, close to the front line, and away from the airfields which would have made such easy targets. But, while Harriers could be based in woodland clearings, or in farmyards, using barns as hangars, the difficulties of resupply would be enormous. On the ground, fuel tankers and ammunition trucks, traversing poor quality farm roads, would be vulnerable to enemy air attack. Air resupply could only be via helicopter, but in turn demanded vast resources to keep the Harrier units operational. Later thinking settled for urban basing, using supermarkets as hangars and their car parks as landing strips, with the added advantage of good road access.

Slightly earlier, the MoD announced that British carrier aviation was no more; since it felt that all British naval actions would be carried out near the British Isles, fleet defence would be carried out by the RAF! The Royal Navy did manage to order a new type of ship called a "through-deck cruiser", ostensibly a helicopter carrier, but obviously a Harrier-carrier.

The rest is history. Sea Harrier fighters were developed, and won the South Atlantic campaign in 1982. Without them the Falkland Islands would have been irretrievably lost to Argentina. The US Marines picked up the ball, developing the AV-8B and the dedicated fighter variant AV-8B Plus. The next step in ASTOVL inevitably seems to be the stealthy Joint Strike Fighter (JSF).

The Jump Jet

In the mid-1950s the aeronautical world was becoming increasingly occupied with ideas for lifting fixed-wing aircraft vertically off the ground with the thrust of jet engines. For the next ten years every possible arrangement was studied, and more than 30 different schemes were actually flown. It is ironic that one of the least favoured of them should, after many years of fighting against not only the predictable ignorance, entrenched positions and totally closed minds, but also self-imposed political problems peculiar to Great Britain, eventually have won through to show the world that you can have airpower without either airfields or giant carriers.

The self-imposed political problems stemmed from the now notorious *White Paper on Defence* of April 1957, which stated in the clearest terms that Britain's Royal Air Force was "unlikely to require" any more fighters or bombers – ever! Indeed, the phrase was interpreted in even stronger terms, to the extent that all combat aircraft programmes for the RAF were cancelled, excepting only the Lightning interceptor, which, said the Minister "has unfortunately gone too far to cancel". The very mention of future combat aircraft was enough to damage the career of officers or civil servants, and there was absolutely no point in anyone in the aircraft industry coming up with a new design.

It so happened that, just over a year earlier, Michel Wibault had put the finishing touches to a proposal for a combat aircraft unlike anything seen previously. One of the most famed French designers between the wars, Wibault had the vision to see that the numerous new NATO airfields being built in the 1950s might eventually become vulnerable to attack by nuclear missiles. Immovable, and littered with costly warplanes, they would present the ideal target. After much thought he came to the obvious conclusion: the only way to make airpower survivable is to divorce it from airfields.

Various VTOL (vertical takeoff and landing) aircraft already existed. Some were tail-sitters, pointing skywards, while others were flat-risers with swivelling engines or some other arrangement for obtaining both lift and thrust. Wibault devised a strange solution in which a gas turbine drove four large centrifugal compressors through gearboxes and shafts. Around each blower was a delivery casing – variously called a snail, a scroll, a diffuser or a volute – which could be rotated through 90°. With the four nozzles pointing downwards, the result was lift; with the nozzles facing rearwards, the result was thrust.

Wibault named his aircraft a Gyropter. He was not bothered about whether it should be a fighter or an attack aircraft; in the mid-1950s NATO was becoming interested in VTOL for both purposes. He was concerned with the basic principles, such as the need for the resultant VTOL lift force to pass through the aircraft CG (centre of gravity). He also knew that aircraft able to hover, a condition in which ordinary control surfaces are useless, have to have an extra control system using RCVs (reaction control valves) at the extremities, fed by compressed air. To drive his blowers he picked the Bristol Orion, with a sea-level

potential of 8,000hp, as the most powerful turboshaft engine available, though the portly shape of his aircraft, and its relatively low-energy jets, precluded it from being supersonic.

Wibault failed to get much reaction from the Armée de l'Air or US Air Force, so he next took his proposal to the MWDP (Mutual Weapons Development Program) office in Paris. This was the agency through which a bountiful USA funded promising European military projects unsupported by their own nations. The MWDP director, Col Johnny Driscoll, USAF, was intrigued. Two years earlier he had supported the Bristol

Right: Typical of many free-flying rigs of the 1960s, this German VTOL helped in developing the VAK 191B strike fighter. Note the four RB162 lift jets, fed from two fuel drums amidships, and the wind anemometer!

Orpheus, which was unwanted in Britain, and this had been the engine choice for all the contenders in the NATO light strike fighter competition, which was won by the Fiat G91. He asked the man behind the Orpheus, Bristol Aero-

Above: The pioneer free-flying jet VTOL device was the first Rolls-Royce TMR (thrust-measuring rig), popularly called The Flying Bedstead. The two Nene engines supplied air for four reaction control nozzles.

Right: A Harrier GR.3 of RAF No 1(F) squadron recovers to its ship during Operation Corporate in spring 1982. It was the inherent simplicity of the single-engine vectored-thrust concept that enabled it to produce invaluable no-airfields airpower.

Engines technical director Stanley (later Sir Stanley) Hooker, to review Wibault's proposal. Hooker criticised the clumsy shafts, gearboxes, compressors and rotatable scrolls, but strongly favoured the use of a single engine for both lift and thrust, in a flat-rising jet. He showed the idea to his friend, the great Theodore von Kármán, who instantly said "Ah, vectored thrust" – today a common term.

Hooker took the scheme back to Bristol and handed it to his team: Charles Marchant, Gordon Lewis, Pierre Young and Neville Quinn. It did not take these brilliant young engineers long to come up with a scheme that retained the benefits while eliminating the drawbacks. Instead of bevel gears and transverse shafts to four blowers they pro-

posed a single 1·5:1 reduction gear to drive two stages from the LP (low-pressure) compressor of the new Olympus BOl.21 turbojet, discharging through left and right vectoring nozzles. From this projected engine, the BE.48, further work gave the BE.52, in which the Orion was replaced by the lighter, simpler and cheaper Orpheus. Next, the BE.53 was produced by making the big front compressor an integral part of the engine, with a single front inlet, the inner part of its airflow going to supercharge the core engine and the outer part being discharged through the vectoring nozzles.

Fortunately Wibault was delighted at the transformation of his idea, and in December 1956 he and Lewis jointly applied for a patent for the first aircraft to

look vaguely like a Harrier. This historic patent drawing not only showed two cold fan nozzles and two hot rear jet nozzles but it also featured contra-rotating spools and PCB (plenum-chamber burning). Making the HP (high-pressure) and LP spools rotate in opposite directions almost cancelled out the previously very large gyroscopic forces caused by the spinning masses in the engine, which in hovering flight would otherwise have caused severe problems. PCB is the vectored-thrust equivalent of afterburning or reheat, in that by burning extra fuel upstream of the cold and/or hot nozzles the thrust can be greatly increased for short periods. PCB was for the moment put on one side, to avoid its potentially thorny develop-

ment problems. Without it the BE.53 would only give about 8,000lb (3630kg) thrust, but the immediate objective was to get something built and tested.

By great good fortune Driscoll's successor at MWDP, Col Willis (Bill) Chapman, was an enthusiast for VTOL. In the subsequent period of nearly 30 years the USAF has consistently stuck its head in the sand whenever it is asked what would happen if the many hundreds of Soviet missiles currently targeted on NATO airfields (including all those in the USA) were ever to be fired. In 1956, however, it was still possible to keep an open mind, and Chapman positively raced to find money to pay 75 per cent of the development bill of the BE.53. Equally quickly, Sir Reginald Verdon Smith, chairman of the Bristol Aeroplane Co (parent of the engine firm), agreed to finance the remainder, as he had done previously with the Orpheus. This was the crucial decision that got the whole project started.

Hawker gets involved

Sadly, Wibault died at this juncture, and never saw his idea bear fruit. Another casualty was Maj Gerry Morel, brave French member of the British SOE who succumbed to his wartime treatment by the Gestapo and Vichy police. Director of the Société Franco-Britannique, he played a leading role in launching both the Orpheus and Pegasus, and as agent for Hawker he hosted Sir Sydney Camm at the 1957 Paris airshow just before he died. Camm said he had been watching the Rolls/Ministry VTOL schemes, with numerous special lift jets, with increasing disbelief. Morel asked him if he had seen the BE.53. On return to Kingston Camm sent a famous letter: "Dear Hooker, what are you doing about vertical takeoff engines?"

At the time Camm was immersed in trying to turn the Mach 2 P.1121 into the twin-engine, two-seat P.1129 to meet the TSR.2 requirement. Jet lift was a second-

Above: Seemingly perhaps the most attractive way to build a jet VTOL, the tilting-engine aircraft still poses many problems. Germany's VJ101C had six RB145 engines, two in the fuselage and two twin tip pods, and reached supersonic speed.

Below: When the Hawker P.1127 was being designed the only VTOL with official sponsorship in Britain was the Short SC.1, a slow five-RB108 aircraft (four for lift, one for thrust) which carried out a vast amount of fundamental research.

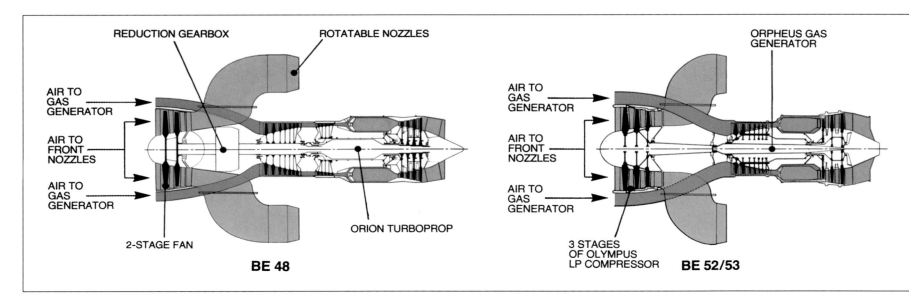

REDUCTION GEARBOX
ROTATABLE NOZZLES
ORPHEUS GAS GENERATOR
AIR TO GAS GENERATOR
AIR TO FRONT NOZZLES
AIR TO GAS GENERATOR
2-STAGE FAN
ORION TURBOPROP
BE 48
AIR TO GAS GENERATOR
AIR TO FRONT NOZZLES
AIR TO GAS GENERATOR
3 STAGES OF OLYMPUS LP COMPRESSOR
BE 52/53

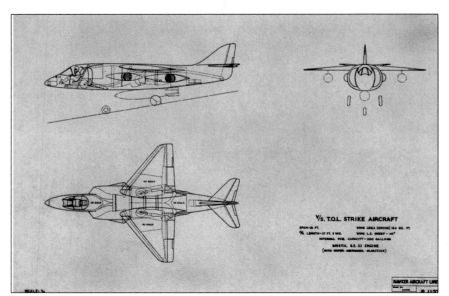

Top: An original company drawing from Kingston of the first of the P.1127 project studies. The words WITH WATER METHANOL INJECTION have been deleted by the designer. Note the conventional landing gear.

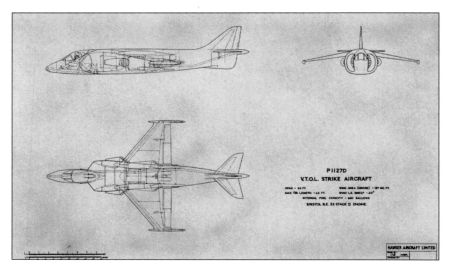

Above: The P.1127D was the aircraft actually built, and at company risk. This drawing, dated 20 September 1959, conforms closely to the first prototype, XP831, which began its hovering trials at Dunsfold in 1960.

ary matter, and in any case 8,000lb of lift from an engine based on the Orpheus seemed, in Camm's book, a typical engine-maker's overstatement. Hooker sent along the first BE.53 brochure, and Camm passed it to two of his best young engineers, Ralph Hooper and John Fozard. On 28 June 1957, in the same month as the Paris airshow, Hooper signed the first Hawker vectored-thrust drawing. As the jetpipe was not deflected, only the cold front jets were aligned with the CG, and the aircraft had to be STOL (short takeoff and landing), not VTOL. It was a rather slow three-seat battlefield surveillance aircraft. A little later it was refined into a two-seat support aircraft with lateral inlets. Meanwhile, down at Bristol the engine was developed into the BE.53/2, the first

Pegasus, with mirror-image fan blading, to give contra-rotating spools to cancel out gyroscopic torques, and with the hot jetpipe bifurcated to a second pair of vectored nozzles.

Now the hare-brained scheme was suddenly looking plausible. As the P.1129 project became bleaker (because the RAF kept increasing the TSR.2 demands), so did the jet-lift work become more important. In August 1957 the first P.1127 brochure described a new aircraft designed around the Pegasus, with the four nozzles disposed around the CG under a high wing. This time it was a single-seater for attack and reconnaissance, and as it was a true VTOL it had air-bleed RCVs for control in hovering flight. Col Chapman was pleased with the proposal, but thought

the range too short to be of real value to NATO air forces. Bristol raised the thrust to over 11,000lb (4990kg) by substituting the high-airflow HP compressor of the Orpheus 6, the result being the Pegasus 2. In early 1958 MWDP put up 75 per cent of the money for six of these engines, Bristol agreeing to pay the other 25 per cent, while Hawker Aircraft agreed to fund continued aircraft design and testing.

In the Pegasus 2 the engine had become a neat turbofan with the original bent pipe nozzles replaced by short nozzles with multiple cascade vanes to guide the flow. Bypass ratio was set at about 1·35, to match the thrusts from the cold and hot nozzles, and one major change was that the bleed power for the RCV nozzles was taken through stainless-steel pipes from the HP spool, Hooper having found that bleeding cooler fan air through aluminium pipes needed such enormous airflow that the pipes would not fit inside the wings! As there were only small gyroscopic effects, Camm was hopeful that complex triply-redundant three-axis autostabilization would not be needed. Hugh Conway, former managing director of Shorts and well up in the SC.1 autostab problems, later became managing director of Bristol Siddeley Engines. He gave a long briefing to Camm on what had to be done. After he had gone, the Hawker boss said "We are only ignorant buggers here at Kingston, and don't understand all that science. We'll leave the P.1127 simple, and let its pilots fly it".

The company-funded P.1127

The last major changes to the P.1127 were to adopt bicycle landing gear, with the wingtip outriggers made shorter by sharply sloping the wings down to 12° anhedral, the wing being placed above the fuselage so that it could be removed in order to change the engine. By mid-1958 Hawker Aircraft were busy testing models to investigate the novel airflows with sucking at the inlets and blowing at the four nozzles angled in various directions. In June 1958 the Ministry of Supply permitted tests to be done in government tunnels, and later extensive research was done at NASA in the United States, largely because the P.1127 was such an interesting aircraft. In March 1959 the Hawker Siddeley board boldly decided to fund two P.1127 prototypes, and work on these went ahead at high speed. By this time both the RAF and RN were daring once again to consider manned aircraft, including VTOL. Unfortunately, at the same time, Rolls-Royce, pushing its multiple lift-jet concept, announced collaboration with Dassault of France on a VTOL Mirage.

This seriously damaged the prospects of the P.1127. Having no home market, it was dependent on NATO, whose offices

were already funding three-quarters of the vital engine. But the French made it clear they would have nothing to do with a British project, especially in view of Dassault's programme. To cut an extremely long and involved story short, while by April 1959 the RAF was at last openly thinking about a Hunter-replacement in the class of the P.1127, NATO had begun to plan a more ambitious scheme for a VTOL supersonic aircraft to meet NBMR-3 (NATO Basic Military Requirement 3). The latter resulted in a plethora of submissions from companies throughout the NATO aircraft industries, most of them as international collaborative projects. Hawker proposed a grossly stretched supersonic P.1127, the P.1150, powered by an uprated Pegasus with PCB.

NATO upgraded the NBMR-3 specification in its final form in March 1961, and the resulting Hawker submission was the P.1154 powered by the completely new Bristol Siddeley BS.100 engine of 33,000lb (14970kg) thrust. In April 1962 the P.1154 was declared the "technical winner" of the competition, but to appease France the rival Mirage IIIV was said to be "of equal merit". Moreover France predictably said it would never

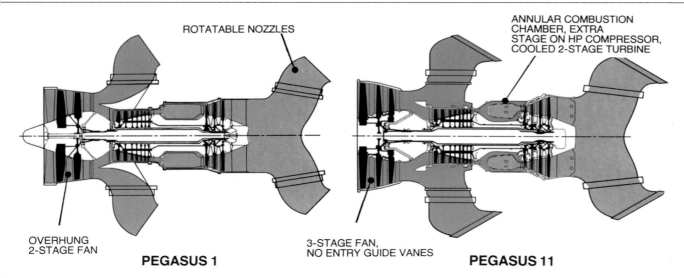

ROTATABLE NOZZLES

ANNULAR COMBUSTION CHAMBER, EXTRA STAGE ON HP COMPRESSOR, COOLED 2-STAGE TURBINE

OVERHUNG 2-STAGE FAN

PEGASUS 1

3-STAGE FAN, NO ENTRY GUIDE VANES

PEGASUS 11

Evolution of the Pegasus

Simplified drawings showing how the first Wibault-derived scheme devised at Bristol, the BE.48, evolved over a decade into today's Harrier engine. The first two drawings, the BE.48 and 52/53, are slightly falsified in that the two inlets to the gas generator were actually at the top and bottom of the engine, while the front nozzles were on the sides. The significance of the colours is that magenta shows the hot portions of each engine, and blue the cooler elements. In today's Pegasus 11 the front nozzles discharge 110°C jets at 1,200ft/s (366m/s) and the rear 670°C jets at 1,800ft/s (549m/s).

accept any candidate but the Mirage IIIV, which it would continue to develop. This caused the whole NATO house of cards to collapse, and eventually the IIIV along with it, but it left both the RAF and RN looking for aircraft in the class of the P.1154. Eventually versions of the big supersonic Hawker aircraft were developed for both customers, but the RN did all it could to damage the programme by insisting on the maximum number of differences. Eventually the RN pulled out in February 1964, buying long-takeoff Phantoms (which it soon lost as the result of the 1965 decision to phase out British carriers). The RAF P.1154 was simply cancelled by the government in February 1965. The reasons were purely political, but, to explain the decision to the public, Prime Minister Wilson said that the P.1154 "will not be in service in time to serve as a Hunter replacement".

Below: The only serious rival to Hawker's V/STOL programme in the early 1960s was Dassault of France, which followed the Rolls-Royce formula (also supported by the British official establishment) in having a battery of separate lift engines. This was the first nine-engined Balzac.

More Phantoms were bought, which in fact cost more than the predicted P.1154 price and were available no sooner (and of course Hunters are still serving today in many air forces).

At the time, the cancellation of the P.1154 appeared a mistake of great magnitude, and certainly the decisions by the RN and the British government were taken for erroneous and very short-sighted reasons. Looking on the bright side, the British services were left with a nucleus of officers who understood a little about V/STOL, and industry was left with a wealth of experience. In any case, while the big supersonic V/STOLs were all the rage, the original Pegasus-powered subsonic programme had made great progress, though without any obvious eventual production application.

Bristol Siddeley Engines ran the first Pegasus 1 at Patchway in September 1959. Rated at 9,000lb (4082kg), this used LP bleed air for aircraft control and was for ground running only. The Pegasus 2 ran in February 1960, and at first all that Bristol could promise Kingston was 10,000 lb (4536kg). Hawker experimental pilot Hugh Merewether had been invited by NASA to fly the Bell X-14

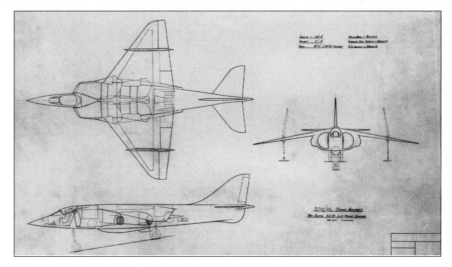

Above: Not previously illustrated, the Hawker P.1132 was an amazingly advanced aircraft for August 1958. It would have had two BE.53 engines, handed left and right to discharge on the outboard side of the engine only. Even at 1958 thrust ratings these would have allowed a gross weight of 29,000lb, the same as today's Harrier II, as well as transonic speed. This "STO/VL" was not built.

Below: Dated 30 September 1961, this drawing shows the P.1150/3 which was planned to meet the NATO NBMR-3 competition.

Bottom: The initial form of P.1154, which succeeded the P.1150/3 in the NBMR-3 contest. Later this impressive machine was further developed for the RAF, only to be cancelled in 1965.

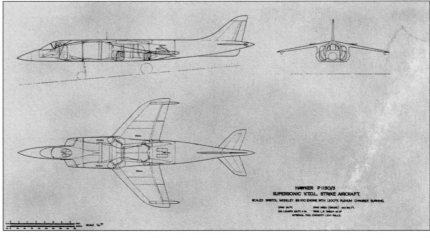

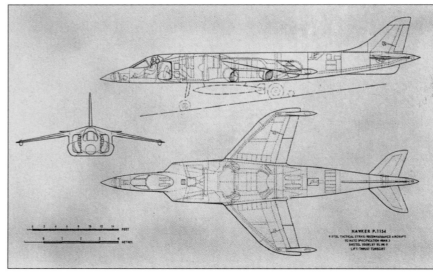

with vectored jets, and in making a vertical landing (VL) he ran out of roll power, even though both jets were at high power, and damaged the aircraft. Extra RCV power seemed a good idea for the P.1127, but it would mean even less thrust for lift, and Hawker's estimate of the first P.1127's empty weight was about the same as the promised engine thrust. Fortunately another 1,000lb (454kg) was then forthcoming from the installed engine, and in August 1960 it was cleared at 11,000lb (4990kg) for 30 min of VTOL or 20 hours of conventional flight.

By this time the two P.1127s were visible at Kingston, and to avoid embarrassment at having them emerge with no serial number the Ministry had at last coughed up some money in June 1960 and drafted a contract, both aircraft meeting experimental requirement ER.204D which was written around them. Serial numbers XP831 and 836 were allocated. Meanwhile, because the excess thrust for lift was so small, it was recognised that recirculation of hot efflux gas back into the engine inlets had to be avoided, so Hawker's airfield at Dunsfold was fitted with a special grid designed to channel gas well away from the aircraft. Hooker suggested to Camm that perhaps the first flight should be in the conventional (runway) mode, to check handling qualities. Camm snapped back "All Hawker aircraft have perfect handling qualities, the first flight will be a VTO"!

Testing begins

Ground running of XP831 began on 31 August 1960. Large bell-mouth inlets were fitted for these initial trials, and the aircraft carried the minimum of removable equipment. For hovering, in October, it was positioned over the grid with loose tethers to heavy weights. Even the wheel doors were removed, and the radio replaced by an intercom link. Chief test pilot A. W. "Bill" Bedford may even have wondered if the weight of plaster on his broken leg (gained as a car passenger in Switzerland) would prove the last straw, but on 21 October 1960 he got daylight under the wheels of the small prototype that was to lead to a new era in aviation.

There were problems, but also solutions. At rest the aircraft naturally tipped over on to one outrigger; always, on the next liftoff, there was inadequate RCV power with the Pegasus 2 to bring the wings level, so the aircraft would skid sideways across the grid and slew around in yaw. Again, inadequate RCV power made it impossible, even with full rudder, to stop the aircraft pirouetting

tail-on to any wind, because of the powerful momentum drag in the inlets. And the tethers themselves caused great difficulty, so that Merewether said his task was "like trying to learn to ride a bike by riding down a narrow corridor".

On 19 November 1960 the hated tethers came off, and Bedford said it was "like freeing a bird from a cage". Free hovering proved most successful, and with progressive increases in engine thrust the missing removable items were replaced. A further improvement in RCV control came when, instead of having a swivelling rear pitch jet, the tail installation comprised separate pitch and yaw RCVs. But when high-speed taxi tests began it was found that the main gear hung lower than the outriggers, giving undue freedom in roll; poor nosewheel steering was combined with severe shimmy of the freely castoring outriggers, and the latter began leaving wavy lines of black molten rubber across the Dunsfold runway.

These problems were fixed by locking the outriggers and increasing their extension so that both touched the ground together. XP831 was sent to the RAE at Bedford, and after further high-speed runs Bill Bedford made the first conventional flight on 13 March 1961, far out-accelerating the chase Hunter. On 7 July 1961 the second aircraft opened its flight programme in the conventional mode from Dunsfold, and soon demonstrated speeds of well over 500 knots (576mph, 927km/h) at low level. By December 1961 this machine had gone on to pull 6g in sustained turns, reach over 40,000ft (12.2km) and achieve Mach 1.2 in a shallow dive. Then, because of a

Left: The first photograph of the first prototype P.1127, taken outside the Dunsfold hangar in August 1960 before the serial XP831 had been painted on. Later doors and other items were taken off to save weight

Below: Hawker Siddeley paid for this fully equipped ground-running pen long before there was any suggestion of Ministry funding. The picture was taken as the 2,000lb/sq in air bottles were starting the engine.

fault in the construction of the moulding, the glassfibre left front engine nozzle came off in the air. Bedford tried to land at RNAS Yeovilton, but when he lowered the flaps he entered a roll which could not be arrested, and he had to eject. A few days later a farmer arrived at Yeovilton with the missing nozzle, and though this facilitated diagnosis it took years before really satisfactory front nozzles were achieved. Eventually, though they do not really "need" such material, they were made of steel like the hot rear nozzles.

On the whole, flight development of the first two examples of this radical aircraft had been remarkably smooth, and there had been no need for any significant alteration to the aircraft or engine. This early phase was completed on 12 September 1961 by the achievement of complete transitions. Aircraft XP381 was either lifted off in VTO, accelerated forwards to high speed and then brought back to a VL, or taken off in the conventional mode, slowed in the air to the hover and then accelerated again for a rolling landing. In October 1961 operations were made from grass and other rough surfaces, and an especially important development was the start of STO trials, the nozzles being vectored down to 50° or 55° after a quick acceleration to about 60 knots.

In November 1960 the Ministry had funded four further P.1127s, actually calling these "development aircraft" as if they might be for something more than pure research. Soon there were plenty of detail differences as these came into use and, along with XP831, were progressively modified. Among the new features were a kinked wing leading edge giving increased chord at the tips, a row of upper-surface vortex generators to prevent wing drop at high Mach numbers, improved outrigger gears without pointed-nose fairings, Küchemann streamwise wingtips, modified tailplanes with greater area and 18° anhedral, improved RCV fairings and, for a time, inflatable rubber inlet lips that could be puffed up to a large radius for hovering and deflated to give a sharp lip for high-speed flight. Variable-radius inlets are needed for all jet V/STOLs, but a good scheme has never been devised. Rubber simply failed to stand up to high-speed flight.

Design improvements
Back in 1959 attitudes in the RAF and the Ministry had been changing. The TSR.2 project was well under way, and the Air Staff felt they could test the situation by writing a requirement for General Operational Requirement 345 for the simple Hunter replacement, which might well be a V/STOL. Though many officers scorned the P.1127 for its puny capability and lack of Mach 2 speed, some saw the possibility of future development. This obviously hinged upon what Hooker's team could do at Bristol, and they were already busy fitting the HP turbine with aircooled blades. This enabled gas temperature to jump from 977°C to 1,177°C, giving higher thrust. When combined with a new three-stage fan without inlet guide vanes, an annular combustor and other improvements, the result was the Pegasus 5, which soon gave 15,500lb (7030kg).

This at last enabled Hawker to design an improved P.1127 able to carry a little warload as well as fuel, but it is very doubtful that anything more would have happened – apart from the NATO fixation on much heavier supersonic V/STOLs – had not the United States come to the rescue a second time. Larry Levy, a wealthy American, had joined MWDP in Paris and had the vision to see

that what was wanted was for NATO actually to get some service experience in, to see how jet V/STOLs could be operated in the field. He had the political clout to persuade the American, British and Federal German governments to fund a Tripartite Evaluation Squadron. Originally each nation was to put up the money and pilots for six aircraft, but – against German advice – this was cut to three on British pressure for economy. By early 1962 the RAF had given up GOR.345, and with it any hope of using a simple Pegasus-engined aircraft, deciding instead to go all out for Mach 2 with the P.1154. Despite this, the TES survived, because other nations were involved, and the aircraft were ordered by the newly created British Ministry of Aviation (formerly Ministry of Supply) on 21 May 1962.

The improved aircraft were called Kestrels. Powered by the Pegasus 5, they featured a new swept wing, with a thicker centre section causing a hump in the fuselage, which had first flown on XP984, the final P.1127. In its ultimate form this wing had small dogtooth discontinuities and extended-chord outer sections. A better relationship between the nozzles, wing and aircraft CG was obtained by splicing in extra fuselage sections above the front nozzles and below the rear nozzles (in effect moving the wing aft, as well as lengthening the

Right: Taken in 1964, this photograph shows the fifth P.1127 after it had received streamwise wingtips, inflatable inlet lips, eleven vortex generators on each wing, and the odd kinked-anhedral tailplane.

Flying controls

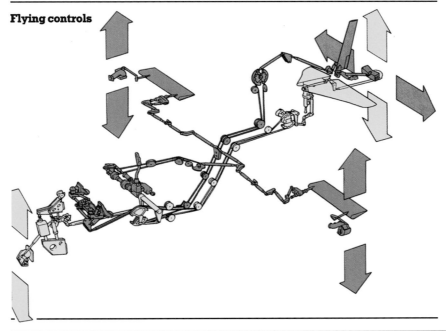

Left: If one had to put one's finger on a single aspect of the Harrier that has led to today's hard-won success it would surely be simplicity. Here the basic flight-control system is seen, and uniquely the normal stick and pedals operate not only the aerodynamic surfaces but also, and at all times, the RCVs (reaction control valves). As the engine nozzles are selected to angles at which powered lift becomes important, so do the RCVs come into effective operation, supplied with high-pressure engine bleed air to give thrust as shown by the large arrows. There is no change in control "feel".

Below: Not many photographs were taken of XP836, the second P.1127. This was chiefly because the glassfibre left front engine nozzle, clearly seen here, was made with an inherent structural weakness which led to nozzle separation in late 1961.

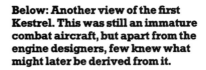

fuselage) and giving a sharper bifurcation to the jetpipe to move the hot nozzles forwards. By this time the hot nozzle fairings were all of the rectangular "spade" type instead of the "pen nib" type originally used, the flaps were extended in to the wing root, and toe-operated wheel brakes were standard. The Kestrels also had main-gear doors stressed for use as airbrakes, ventral strakes, taller fins, and eventually all had a substantially larger tailplane with a 16° anhedral and a kinked leading edge.

XS688, the first Kestrel but not quite up to full standard, flew on 7 March 1964. The TES was formed at Dunsfold under Wg Cdr D. McL. Scrimgeour, RAF, on 15 October 1964, and from April 1965 operated at RAF West Raynham and various unprepared dispersed sites in the neighbourhood. Its pilots were drawn from the RAF, Luftwaffe, USAF, USN and US Army. Two came from the latter service, though it had no hope of operating high-speed jets, whereas the Marines were not included despite their intense interest. The Kestrels had the pitot head on the fin, as in late P.1127s, and instead of a long nose probe a forward oblique camera was fitted. Under each wing was a pylon intended to carry a wide variety of stores, but these hardly ever carried anything during TES flying except 100gal (455lit) drop tanks, though on other occasions Kestrels dropped practice bombs.

Altogether 938 sorties were flown by the TES prior to disbandment in November 1965, roughly 24 missions per aircraft per month, with a total of some 600 hours. Takeoffs were made from concrete, tarmac, grass, compacted soil, various plastics and rubber sheets, aluminium sheet, glassfibre sheet, a portable pad constructed from interlocking aluminium planks, and plenty of surfaces covered with wartime PSP (pierced steel planking). Except for a US pilot who tried a rolling takeoff with the parking brake on, there was no serious incident, and the

Above: One of the first air-to-air pictures of the first Kestrel, taken in March 1964 with Dunsfold's Hunter T.7 two-seat chase aircraft in attendance. Rubber lips were fitted.

Below: Another view of the first Kestrel. This was still an immature combat aircraft, but apart from the engine designers, few knew what might later be derived from it.

general opinion was extremely favourable. One of the most important benefits was that the TES got used to operating without a fixed airfield with centrally heated brick-built accommodation, which air forces had taken for granted since 1945.

Following TES use, six Kestrels went to the USA. By this time the USAF had decided it preferred airfields to V/STOL and chose to regard them as quaint foreign devices, despite their new US joint-service designation of XV-6A; according to *Aviation Week* it was "trying to think what to do with them". NASA, on the other hand, used XV-6As both at Dryden and at Langley for serious research, and found them valuable tools limited only by the 50-hour overhaul life on each engine.

This limited life was constantly being improved at Bristol, where, even if no funding had been forthcoming, Hooker's team would have kept on cranking in improvements. By early 1964, when no

Kestrel had flown and all attention was focussed on the BS.100 engine for the P.1154, Bristol Siddeley was well advanced with a greatly improved Pegasus, the Mk 6, which first ran a year later. Its titanium fan handled substantially greater airflow, the combustion system was further improved with vaporizing burners and water-injection for short periods at enhanced power, both HP turbine stages were aircooled, two-vane hot nozzles were fitted, the fuel system was again revised and a life recorder was added. Despite its greatly increased thrust of 19,000 lb (8618kg), the Pegasus 6 was lifed at 300 hours.

The P.1127 (RAF)

This outstanding performance by the engine company, which had already more than doubled the thrust of the Pegasus with more yet to come, at last made it obvious that a Kestrel successor could fly useful combat missions. Though there continued to be factions within the

Left: Large grab-holds near the front nozzles identify this as an XV-6A, a Kestrel in the USA (actually aboard CV-62 USS *Independence*), seen in May 1966 during carefully measured carrier suitability evaluations.

RAF that scorned any Pegasus-powered subsonic aircraft, those who took the trouble to examine the possibilities came up with surprising results. Thanks to its economical engine even the Kestrel had demonstrated mission radius and endurance as good as the best Hunter, and with the Pegasus 6 it was possible to combine this with a warload considerably greater than the Hunter could carry. In any case, V/STOL capability means that aircraft could be dispersed into front-line bases not only untargetable by missiles but also close to the enemy, thus enabling weapons to be carried in place of external fuel. It is fortunate that the CAS (Chief of the Air Staff), Sir Thomas Pike, took pains in 1962-3 to keep the Pegasus aircraft alive in parallel with the big BS.100-powered machines, and in 1963-5 his successor, Sir Charles Elworthy, did likewise.

When the Labour government took office in October 1964 it had campaigned partly on the fact that it would do away with British military aircraft. It informed the Air Staff that two of the three main programmes would be cancelled (later the third went, also). One of the first casualties was the P.1154. The Air Staff had seen this coming and began writing a new requirement, ASR.384, for a simple replacement for the Hunter in the tactical attack and reconnaissance roles, derived from the P.1127. The aircraft itself became known as the P.1127(RAF), but eventually was named Harrier, a name previously picked for the P.1154 and, back in 1927, for a Hawker bomber powered by an earlier Bristol engine, the Jupiter.

In a nutshell the proposal was that Hawker should produce an improved Kestrel powered by the Pegasus 6, and pack into it whatever avionic items from the P.1154 might fit. Even this fall-back proposition was only won with difficulty. Prime Minister Wilson, still professing to hate British planemakers, refused to sanction any suggestion of a possible production programme. The best deal the RAF could get was that the Ministry, which had just been renamed the Ministry of Technology (Mintech), would fund a small development batch. Then a decision would be taken on whether the P.1127(RAF) was worth putting into service.

Mintech came through with an order for six development aircraft, XV276-281, only two weeks later, on 19 February 1965. By this time Sir Sydney Camm had been Chief Designer for 40 years, and he had handed over the reins to John Fozard as Chief Designer P.1127(RAF). In 1966 Camm passed peacefully away on his local golf course, so like Mitchell with the Spitfire he never saw his last creation get into production. But for "Foz" and his design team it was a time of hectic action. Compared with the P.1154 the P.1127(RAF) was supposed to be easy, but it was not possible just to put the new engine and combat equipment into a Kestrel. Many parts of the airframe had to be redesigned, and it all had to be done in a very short time indeed, because first flight date had been fixed for 31 August 1966.

Left: The first military unit to fly the Harrier was No 1(F) squadron, RAF, which converted during 1969. This photograph shows a 1 Sqn GR.1 over the disputed territory of Belize, which this handful of aircraft have protected for over ten years.

The Harrier

When the "P.1127(RAF)" was at last allowed to be produced, after cancellation of the much more powerful P.1154(RAF), it bore the stigma of appearing superficially to be a second-best alternative. Because it was small and subsonic, many of the Air Staff still doubted that it would be of much real value, a belief heartily echoed by the USAF which by this time (1965) had ceased to show much interest in V/STOL because it could not see beyond supposed percentage penalties. It needed real dedication for the Hawker engineers to produce the Harrier right first time, and to a very challenging timescale.

While the P.1154 lived, nobody in the RAF was particularly interested in the smaller V/STOLs powered by the Pegasus. After the issue of ASR.384 and the contract for a development batch (DB) of six aircraft, the simplistic belief of many in high places was that the P.1127(RAF) already existed in the Kestrel; all that was needed was to install the Pegasus 6 engine and the extra equipment items that its power made possible. The team at Kingston knew better, but even they did not immediately realize that they would have virtu-

Below: G-VSTO was a production Harrier GR.1, XV742, which in 1971 was painted in glossy epoxy camouflage and civil registration, with HSA logo on the fin. It was used as a demonstration aircraft pending completion of the company's own G-VTOL.

ally to start again with a different air-frame. In fact, the redesign changed well over 90 per cent of the drawings.

Airframe

For reasons already emphasized, the P.1127s and Kestrels had been made as light and simple as possible, but the P.1127(RAF) had to meet full service requirements. The structure had to be stressed to higher factors, the symmetric limit being 7·8g at maximum weight. The weights were all going to be considerably increased, yet the landing gear had to be stressed for more severe landings, with rates of descent to 12ft/s (about 3·66m/s). The entire airframe had to be designed for a safe life of 3,000 flight hours, to a most severe mission load spectrum, virtually all at very high speed at the lowest possible level, which meant demonstrating 15,000 hours on a speci-

men. Low-level jets suffer severely from the birdstrike problem, and though this mainly affected the inlet and engine it also meant the windscreen had to withstand the nominal 1lb (0·45kg) bird at 600 knots (1111km/h).

The wing managed to retain the original main structural box, which comprises two triangular boxes joined on the aircraft centreline. Upper and lower skins are machined from heavy plate to provide integral stiffening, and the inboard portion of the box on each side forms a sealed integral fuel tank, each of 172·5gal (784lit) capacity. The wing is tiny, because it was originally designed for high-speed flight, and low-level attack aircraft need the smallest possible wing in order to have minimum gust response, and thus give the pilot an acceptably smooth ride in rough air even at full throttle. Despite this small size, the extra

Above: Completion of a NATO exercise in Norway, in temporary winter camouflage, highlights the way RAF Harriers have operated around the clock for 15 years.

lift of the wing on short rolling takeoffs is important in enabling more fuel or weapons to be carried, and later still the RAF took a leaf from the book of the US Marine Corps and studied the Harrier as an air-combat fighter, where a larger wing would show to advantage.

In any case, the wing differs greatly from that of the Kestrel. The section profile did not alter, remaining an NPL (National Physical Laboratory) "peaky" section with a generous nose radius, with thickness/chord ratio varying from 10 per cent at the root to 5 per cent at the tip. The leading edge was again redesigned, with extended chord outboard

Below: A Harrier GR.1 of RAF No 20 Sqn, shown with gun pods attached but otherwise in the clean configuration. Subsequently the appearance was markedly altered by the addition of the LRMTS on the nose and the RWR installation at the tail. No 20 Sqn later re-equipped with Jaguars.

Left: Taken in 1963, this picture shows the first Kestrel being built (the same aircraft is shown airborne on p.10). The integral-tank wing sits on the fuselage above the engine.

and initially a double kink leading to the inboard section; later this was replaced by a single dogtooth some way inboard of the inner small fence. Vortex generators were also needed. The Kestrel had finally had ten on each wing, but the Harrier began with four and ended with a row of 12.

Below: Slinging test at Dunsfold to demonstrate compliance with the requirement to hoist the aircraft with maximum fuel, weapon load, and pilot in the cockpit. If dropped from this height, the landing gear would absorb the energy.

More significant was the need to preserve longitudinal stability with full external stores, because this was before the CCV (control-configured vehicle) technology had matured sufficiently for an unstable fighter to be attempted. The specified stores loading was two pylons under each wing, rated at 1,200lb (544kg) inboard and 630lb (286kg) outboard. To retain adequate CG margins it was necessary to move the aerodynamic centre of the wing to the rear, and the obvious way to do this was to add area outboard. In fact, two tips were designed, both added immediately outboard of the outrigger gears. The normal tip can be unbolted and replaced by a larger tip giving extra span for improved cruising efficiency, and thus greater range for ferrying.

As before, the ailerons and plain flaps are of bonded aluminium honeycomb construction, both being hydraulically driven and the ailerons being positioned by Fairey powered flight-control units. Previously Fairey and Dowty had alternated for the contracts for the P.1127, Kestrel and P.1154. Despite Camm's dislike of clever devices, autostabilization was provided, but in a simple form with limited authority on pitch and roll only, without duplication. A light bobweight was added, and later the yaw axis was also brought in, but flight with autostab switched off is no problem. Hovering in gusty conditions is easier than with a helicopter, because the mean density of the Harrier exceeds 25lb/cuft (400kg/m³) and it needs little pilot input.

In solving the thorny problems of longitudinal control it was found that, aerodynamically, the final Kestrel tailplane shape could do the job, though with increased trim range. Structurally, it was back to the drawing board, because even with the Pegasus 5 the Kestrel tailplane had vibrated frighteningly during ground running, with jets aft, becoming a blur with 6in amplitude at a frequency of about 13Hz! To permit running with engine nozzles aft, the TES had had to anchor the tailplanes to the ground to meet the stipulated life of 1,000h. With the Harrier the required life was trebled, and engine power greatly increased, yet the final tailplane came out weighing 211lb (95·7kg), only 32lb (14·5kg) more than before. One of the many remarkable successes of Harrier flight development was to clear the aircraft with all combinations of external stores with impeccable handling up to AOA (angle of attack) exceeding 20°, despite the destabilizing effect of some 30,000 jet horsepower blasting a few inches beneath the tailplane.

Though closely related to that of the Kestrel, the fuselage was completely redesigned, with room for many extra items and stressed to much greater loads. A few items, such as Tacan and the nav/attack computer (avionics are described later), were fitted into the small nose, along with an F.95 oblique camera looking diagonally ahead on the left side. The seat became a Martin-Baker rocket-assisted H.9 or 9D, mounted on the sloping rear pressure bulkhead of the cockpit, which has the modest dP (pressure differential) of 3·5lb/sq in (24kPa). Though a flat front windscreen was required, for good view directly ahead, rear and aft vision were compromised by retaining a low--mounted seat and a canopy level with the top of the fuselage. There is a small rear-view mirror, but the view is limited both by the fuselage itself and the large inlets on each side. The canopy, opened manually along sloping tracks, contains MDC (miniature detonating cord) to shatter the acrylic moulding a split second prior to ejection.

The centre fuselage was restressed to carry two gun pods, as alternatives to belly strakes which, first used on the Kestrel, help to increase pressure on the undersurface in low-altitude hovering. In addition there is a centreline hardpoint for stores of up to 1,000lb (454kg). Two fuselage bulkheads, Nos 9 and 11, are stressed above the left inlet for a large oblique inflight-refuelling probe, which is attached on the rare occasions when it will be needed. Fuel is carried in five modest tanks, all integral with the structure: 51·5gal (234lit) each side aft of the inlets, 39gal (177lit) each side between the nozzles and 104gal (473lit) above the main-gear bay immediately behind the wing. Under the wing, immediately behind the engine, is the titanium drum containing 50gal (227lit) of demineralised water for injection into the engine combustor to restore thrust during VTOL operations on a hot day.

The rear fuselage was redesigned to house the main avionics bay and lox (liquid oxygen) container, with the associated air-conditioning bay immediately to the rear, served by a ram inlet in the base of the fin. The cockpit air-conditioning was located immediately behind the seat, in the space between the inlet ducts, with two projecting ram inlets in the dorsal surface and the system exhaust ejecting into the inner faces of the two inlet ducts.

Like other areas the inlets were again redesigned. Not only did the Pegasus 6 need a greater airflow, but this time there had to be a definitive inlet able to give acceptable efficiency at all speeds from flying tail-first up to over Mach 1, while at the same time withstanding severe birdstrikes on the inlet lip and on the curving wall which forms the inner skin of the forward tanks. By this time it was evident that the problems of any flexible variable-radius lip were not going to be solved quickly, if ever, so as well as reshaping the duct itself the problem of variable geometry focussed attention on metal mechanical systems. The final answer was a very short, sharply curved duct with a strong lip having the same peaky aerodynamic profile as the front of the wing, and provided with six suck-in auxiliary doors around the outside of each duct, mating with six more doors on the inner wall. The boundary-layer bleed slit on the inner wall, first used on the Kestrel, was enlarged and reprofiled to reduce drag and airflow distortion.

Unfortunately, no way could immediately be found to avoid distortion of the inlet airflow caused by the six auxiliary doors, which while admitting a large extra airflow caused cross-stream flow and turbulence and reduced pressure recovery. Further distortion was inevitably caused by the stream of hot air on the inner wall from the cockpit air-conditioning heat exchanger. While five of the six DB (development batch) aircraft had the inlet as described, a better configuration was eventually finalized after the DB drawings had been com-

British Aerospace Harrier GR Mk 3 cutaway

1 Pitot head
2 Laser Ranger and Marked Target Seeker (LRMTS)
3 Windscreen washer reservoir
4 IFF aerial
5 Yaw vane
6 Windscreen wiper
7 Pilot's head-up-display (HUD)
8 Martin-Baker Mk 9D, zero-zero ejection seat
9 Boundary-layer air exhaust ducts
10 Cockpit air-conditioning system
11 Engine oil tank
12 Twin alternators
13 Engine accessory gearbox
14 Auxiliary power unit (APU)
15 Starboard wing pylons
16 Starboard wing integral fuel tank
17 Aileron power unit
18 Starboard navigation light
19 Roll control RCV (reaction control valve)
20 Outrigger wheel fairing
21 Starboard aileron
22 Hydraulic reservoir
23 Plain flap
24 Anti-collision light
25 Water tank
26 Water filler cap
27 Flap jack
28 Rear-fuselage fuel tank
29 Emergency ram-air turbine
30 Turbine release control
31 Equipment bay air-conditioning system
32 HF aerial tuner
33 HF notch aerial
34 Starboard all-moving tailplane
35 Rudder control linkage
36 Total-temperature probe
37 Forward radar warning receiver
38 VHF aerial
39 Rudder
40 Rudder trim tab
41 Yaw control RCV
42 Rear radar warning receiver
43 Pitch control RCV
44 Port all-moving tailplane
45 Tail bumper
46 Tailplane power unit
47 UHF aerial
48 Control system linkages
49 Twin batteries
50 Chaff and flare dispensers
51 Avionics equipment racks
52 Airbrake hydraulic jack
53 Liquid-oxygen converter
54 Hydraulic-system nitrogen pressurising bottle
55 Airbrake
56 Fuel jettison
57 Aileron hydraulic actuator
58 Port aileron
59 Aileron/roll RCV mechanical linkage
60 Hydraulic retraction jack
61 Outrigger wheel leg fairings
62 Port outrigger wheel
63 Roll RCV
64 Port navigation light
65 Bleed air ducting
66 Rocket pack
67 Outboard wing pylon
68 Aileron control linkage
69 Port wing integral fuel tank
70 1,000lb (454kg) GP bomb
71 Rear (hot stream) swivelling exhaust nozzle
72 Inboard wing pylons
73 Mainwheels
74 Pressure refuelling connection
75 Ammunition tank
76 Main undercarriage hydraulic jack
77 Fuselage flank fuel tank
78 30mm Aden cannon
79 Forward (fan air) swivelling exhaust nozzle
80 Engine monitoring and recording equipment
81 Ventral gun pod, port and starboard
82 Hydraulic-system ground connectors
83 Forward fuselage fuel tank
84 Rolls-Royce Pegasus Mk 103 vectoring-thrust turbofan
85 Supplementary air intake doors (free-floating)
86 Nosewheel
87 Landing/taxiing lamp
88 Nosewheel hydraulic jack
89 Hydraulic accumulator
90 Boundary-layer bleed air duct
91 Ejection-seat rocket pack
92 Engine throttle and nozzle control levers
93 Instrument panel
94 Control column
95 Rudder pedals
96 Pitch feel and trim actuators
97 Inertial platform
98 Pitch RCV
99 Camera port
100 Camera
101 Transponder
102 LRMTS protective "eyelids"

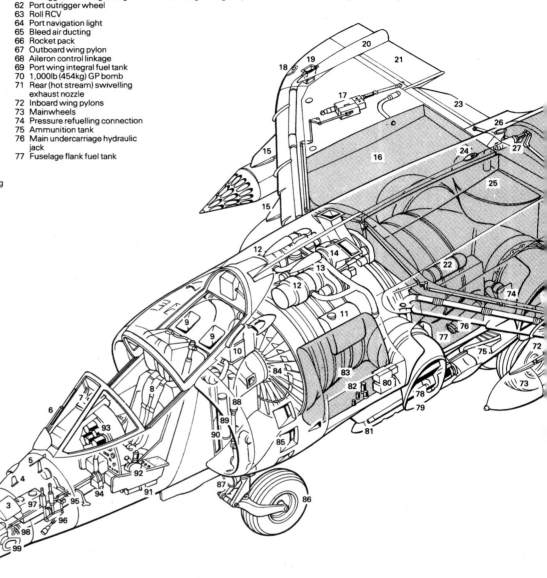

Above: AV-8A Harriers for the US Marine Corps on the line at Kingston in 1971. Because the wing is removed on each engine-change the fuselage and wing were virtually completed before the two came together at the flight-test airfield at Dunsfold, near Cranleigh, Surrey.

mitted to manufacture. Thus, the production Harrier has a superior inlet system, outwardly distinguished by having eight large doors forming an almost continuous auxiliary-inlet ring. After flight development this system was made to behave almost perfectly over a range of inlet airflow angles and engine throttle rates equalled by very few other jet aircraft.

The last major development effort concerned the landing gear, which even in the Kestrel had been only passable rather than good. The primary objective of much greater energy absorption was met chiefly by increasing oleo stroke, without significantly increasing the loads to be absorbed at the attachments. Weak and spongy nosewheel steering was curable, but problems with excessive freedom in roll remained. In fact in early DB aircraft the heelover angle in turns worsened from 1·5° to 3·5°. The first of the six aircraft just made the due date, 31 August 1966, with a brief hover by Bill Bedford. Later, in fast runway operations, the unsatisfactory lateral stiffness on the ground became obvious, and in 1967 the decision was taken to redesign the main oleo into what was called the self-shortening form. On alighting, the new leg collapsed almost without resist-

ance for the first 7·0in (178mm), by which time the outriggers were firmly on the ground. From that time on the landing gear, and all ground behaviour, has been better than that of most normal aircraft. Bay doors were arranged to close after extension of the gear to keep out foreign matter disturbed by the jets. Tyre pressures are typically 90lb/sq in (620kPa), or slightly higher for two-seat versions; this is fine for off-runway operations, and not much more than a quarter of the figure for the main gears of an F-15.

Powerplant

In many respects the Pegasus is unique. Conceived by Bristol Aero-Engines, developed by Bristol Siddeley and finally put into production after the takeover by Rolls-Royce, it is not only totally new in conception but it even broke much new ground in its basic design. The first time it was seen by the public it was doctored to resemble a conventional civil turbofan, the BS.58 (though bulges at the sides confirmed the rumours of vectored thrust with lateral nozzles) and even this looked novel with its inlet face completely devoid of any struts or inlet guide vanes (IGVs). Instead the front face of the engine comprised the first stage of the

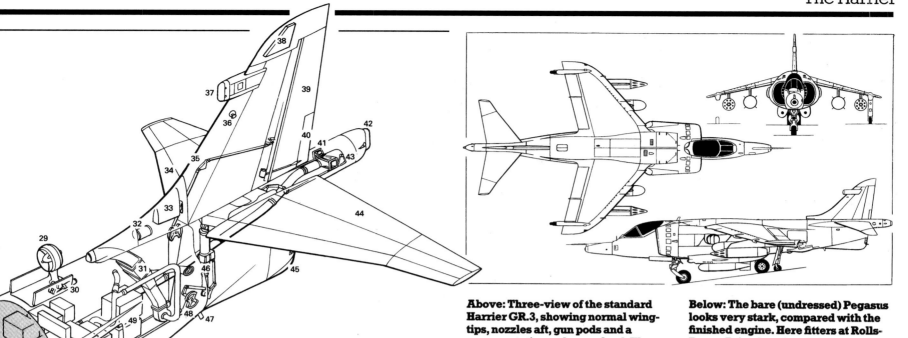

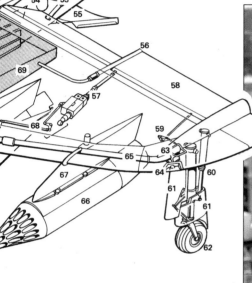

Above: Three-view of the standard Harrier GR.3, showing normal wing-tips, nozzles aft, gun pods and a representative ordnance load. The position of the retracted outrigger gear is shown by a broken line in the side elevation. LERX wing-root extensions flew on one GR.3.

Below: The bare (undressed) Pegasus looks very stark, compared with the finished engine. Here fitters at Rolls-Royce Bristol are installing the GTS (gas-turbine starter) on top of the intermediate casing of a Pegasus 11 Mk 103 for a Harrier GR.3 of the RAF. Engine weight is 3,113lb (1412kg).

Above: Disposition of operational equipment in the Harrier GR.3, with shading showing the location of internal fuel. It is not yet possible to publish a similar illustration showing the Zeus active ECM system which is due in the late 1980s.

fan itself, though today most turbofans are built this way.

Dr Hooker's team were able to do away with IGVs because of the onward march of gas-turbine aerodynamics. IGVs had been needed in earlier engines to swirl the incoming air in the direction of rotation of the moving blades downstream, in order that the Mach number of the flow past the outer parts of the blades should always be well below 1. The development of thin, sharp-edged blades of so-called lenticular form enabled Mach number at the tips to go well into the supersonic region, up to about 1·5. Once the flow was supersonic, there was no point in having IGVs. Their omission saved engine length, weight and cost, improved resistance to bird-strikes and made it possible to eliminate all inlet anti-icing systems.

A further innovation, bold at the time but today commonplace, was to make the entire fan overhung, in other words to cantilever it ahead of the front bearing. The fan's light weight, large diameter and enormous airflow made vibration a problem, and there was bound to be severe vibration because of the extremely short inlet ducts, which in turn stemmed from the fact the engine had to be centred around the aircraft CG. The main resonant blade frequencies thus had to be kept outside the running speed range, and this was achieved by fitting snubbers (mid-span shrouds) to the blades, so that they all touched each other. This also solved the problem of distortion of static pressure distribution downstream of the fan, where it discharges into a plenum chamber which feeds the two front nozzles. The production engine has three stages of fan blades, all made in Hylite 45 titanium alloy in place of the Pegasus 3's aluminium, and all with snubbers.

In the same way, the need to split the hot gas downstream of the turbines and discharge it through left and right nozzles demanded a sharply bent exhaust duct, and this induced vibration in the LP turbine blades. The method of attack was rather similar, in that all blades in the second HP and both LP stages were drilled near mid-span and heat-resistant wire laced through to give an anti-vibration link joining all blades in each stage. (Today, in the AV-8B, new shrouded LP blades are used instead, avoiding the loss in efficiency of the gas flowing past the wires.)

There are many other technically interesting parts of the Pegasus, including the combustion system which, in sharp contrast to the original Orion and Orpheus, has a fully annular chamber with vaporizing burners. The latter were among the technologies inherited when Armstrong Siddeley joined Bristol to form Bristol Siddeley, and after careful tests the Bristol team were not too proud to admit that the Coventry firm's idea was superior. As a result the Harrier's combustion has generally been perfection, and its absence of visible smoke adds to its elusiveness which is a great bonus in warfare.

All other aspects of the Pegasus, however, pale into insignificance compared with the underlying need to vector the entire engine thrust through 98·5°. No other engine of such power has ever been thus vectored, nor fitted with four nozzles. It was clear from the start that the four nozzles simply *had* to move in unison, in the same way that the wings have to stay fixed to the fuselage. Moreover, with thrust often much greater than the total weight of the aircraft, the angles of the nozzles had to be controlled accurately. Thus, all four nozzles had to move together and, in any setting, all four had to be positively locked.

The final scheme adopted is to bleed HP air, the same 400°C supply as that fed to the RCVs, and use it to power two motors driving a differential gearbox in such a way that, if either motor jams, the other continues to drive but at half-speed. From this gearbox the scheme echoes the Wibault concept, in that a drive shaft along the underside of the engine is geared to two cross shafts. Instead of then using further gears, Hooker wisely elected to use chains. The chain drives have proved to be totally reliable, light and free from backlash or other problems. Credit for the air servo-motor goes to the Plessey company, though the entire system was produced by Hawker. It is controlled by a single lever in the cockpit, which is the only control in the Harrier cockpit not found on normal aircraft. It can drive the nozzles at rates up to 100°/s. As explained later, the system eventually matured as an extra flight trajectory control for use in air combat.

Systems

The flight control system in a V/STOL aircraft really has to comprise two systems, one for use in V/STOL flight and the other, the conventional system, for use only at speeds sufficiently high for

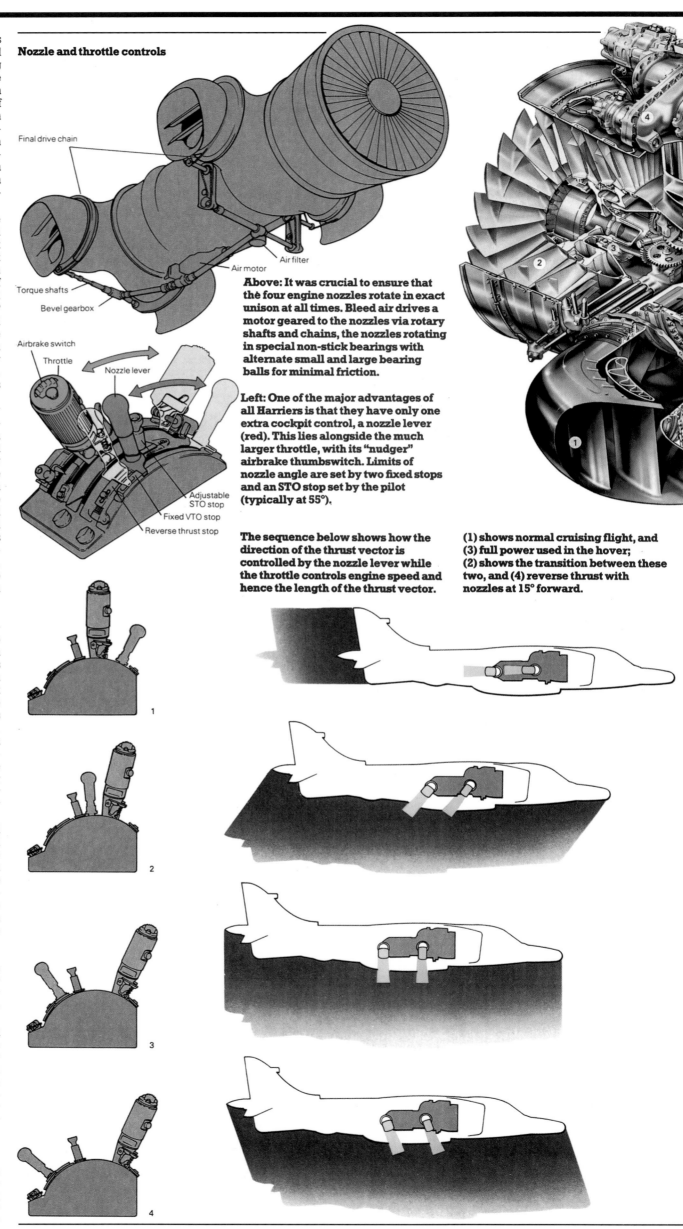

Nozzle and throttle controls

Final drive chain

Air filter

Air motor

Torque shafts

Bevel gearbox

Airbrake switch

Throttle

Nozzle lever

Adjustable STO stop

Fixed VTO stop

Reverse thrust stop

Above: It was crucial to ensure that the four engine nozzles rotate in exact unison at all times. Bleed air drives a motor geared to the nozzles via rotary shafts and chains, the nozzles rotating in special non-stick bearings with alternate small and large bearing balls for minimal friction.

Left: One of the major advantages of all Harriers is that they have only one extra cockpit control, a nozzle lever (red). This lies alongside the much larger throttle, with its "nudger" airbrake thumbswitch. Limits of nozzle angle are set by two fixed stops and an STO stop set by the pilot (typically at 55°).

The sequence below shows how the direction of the thrust vector is controlled by the nozzle lever while the throttle controls engine speed and hence the length of the thrust vector.

(1) shows normal cruising flight, and (3) full power used in the hover; (2) shows the transition between these two, and (4) reverse thrust with nozzles at 15° forward.

1

2

3

4

Rolls-Royce Pegasus 11 (Mks 103 and 104 visually similar)

1 Steel front nozzle
2 Three-stage titanium fan
3 Front (ball) bearing
4 Gearbox carrying engine-driven accessories and (7)
5 GTS exhaust
6 GTS inlet duct
7 GTS (gas-turbine starter), also
serving as APU (auxiliary power unit)
8 Eight-stage titanium HP compressor (rotates in opposite sense to 2)
9 Fuel manifolds
10 Annular combustor with vaporising burners
11 Two-stage HP turbine with aircooled blades
12 Two-stage LP turbine driving fan
13 Nimonic rear nozzle
14 Nozzle final-drive chain
15 Double-ended bevel gearbox
16 Thermal insulation

Though the Rolls-Royce Pegasus may appear complicated, in fact it is an amazingly simple and neat engine, and dramatically better than the vectored-thrust schemes that led to it. Contra-rotating LP and HP spools are used in order almost to eliminate any gyroscopic couple from the large spinning masses, which could lead to control problems in a small hovering aircraft.

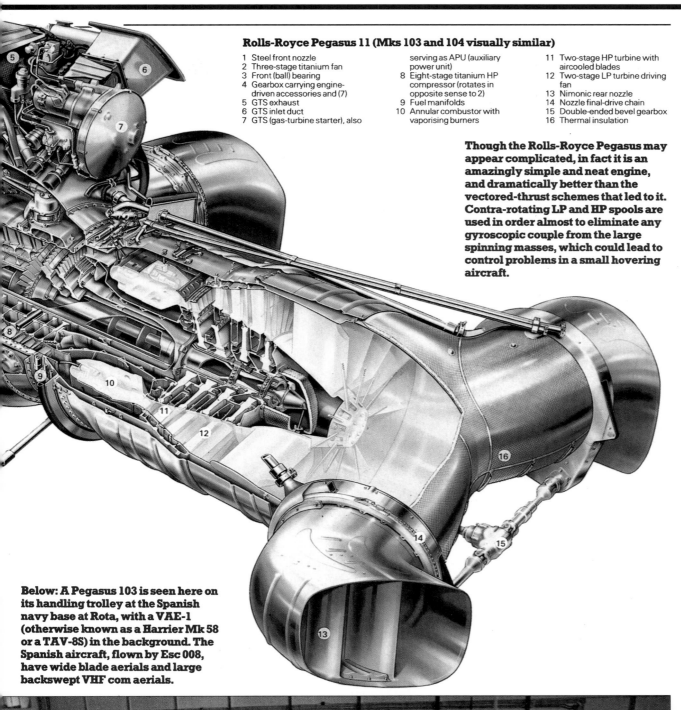

Below: A Pegasus 103 is seen here on its handling trolley at the Spanish navy base at Rota, with a VAE-1 (otherwise known as a Harrier Mk 58 or a TAV-8S) in the background. The Spanish aircraft, flown by Esc 008, have wide blade aerials and large backswept VHF com aerials.

ordinary control surfaces to be effective. As already noted, the conventional system is fully powered and irreversible, apart from the rudder which has a trim tab and manual drive. The horizontal tail is made up of left and right "slabs" without elevators, and it resembles that of the F-4 Phantom in having a large angular movement and marked anhedral. Roll is controlled solely by the small ailerons, though partly because of the short span the rates of roll are good.

At low speeds and in hovering flight the RCV system is progressively energized. There is no sudden transfer from one system to the other; the aerodynamic surfaces continue to be deflected, but as speed is reduced down to the hover, so does the RCV system progressively and smoothly take over. The linkages to the RCV system are, in fact, driven from the local conventional flight-control circuits. The ailerons drive roll RCVs at the front of the outrigger gear fairings. The rudder drives the yaw RCV in the projecting tail end of the fuselage. The tailplane drives the nose-down pitch RCV at the tail, while the nose-up RCV under the nose is driven directly from the stick.

The RCV system is not brought in by q-feel (dynamic pitot pressure) or an airspeed sensor, but simply according to the position of the main engine nozzles. When the nozzles are fully aft, the master shut-off valve under the engine HP compressor delivery is closed; thus, though pilot flight-control demands move both the aerodynamic surfaces and the RCVs, the latter's shutters open and close without any compressed air emerging. As soon as the engine nozzles move away from the fully aft position, the master shut-off valve begins to open. Rapidly the supply pressure in the stainless-steel pipes builds up until, when the engine nozzles are at about 20°, the master valve is fully open. Pilot control demands now result in the aerodynamic surfaces being accompanied by extremely powerful blasts from the associated RCVs.

It might not be appreciated just how powerful the RCV system has to be. The air supply is at 400°C (750°F), almost a dull-red temperature, and at a nozzle exit pressure of 150lb/sq in (1034kPa). The RCVs are heat-resistant steel, with convergent nozzles opened or closed by shutters sealed by sliding carbon bearings. In action, each RCV emits a supersonic jet moving at about 1,700mph (2740km/h). At full control demand the Harrier RCV system is transmitting energy at a rate of several thousand horsepower.

The early P.1127s had a constant-bleed system for the RCVs, and pilot demands merely shut down some valves and opened others wider. Such a system would be unacceptable in the Harrier, for the loss in available engine thrust would be serious, quite apart from denuding the engine turbines of air pumped by the compressor, thus increasing gas temperature. The Harrier instead has a demand system. When the pilot's cockpit controls are centred, no air is consumed. Stick and rudder movements open the appropriate RCVs progressively, to give a smooth and natural aircraft response. Particular effort was needed to perfect the roll RCVs, and achieve exactly the right "gearing", in terms of matching roll response to pilot stick deflection. The roll RCVs are especially interesting in that each is cunningly made to blast air either upwards or downwards, depending on the pilot demand, thus doubling the roll control power in comparison with that from a unidirectional RCV installation.

Most secondary power functions in the Harrier are served by the hydraulic system. This is duplicated, energized by two engine-driven pumps to a pressure of 3,000lb/sq in (20.69MPa). It serves the flying control system, flaps, landing gear and doors (the latter closing with gear down), airbrake, adaptive anti-skid wheel brakes, windscreen wiper and the jack which extends the RAT (ram-air turbine). The latter, normally retracted in a box in the top of the rear fuselage, can be extended to provide emergency system pressure. It provides ample power for flight control, but in view of the special nature of the Harrier, and the demanding nature of a dead-stick (engine off) landing, the RAT is being removed from RAF Harriers. In emergency, hydraulic items can be moved by stored nitrogen pressure.

Electrical power is generated as AC (alternating current) by two 12kVA alternators projecting ahead of the accessory gearbox above the engine fan case. TRUs (transformer/rectifier units) convert some power to DC, part of which charges the two batteries. The latter, in the rear fuselage, provide power to start a Lucas gas-turbine APU (auxiliary power unit), which is mounted on the rear of the accessory gearbox where it fits above the Pegasus plenum chamber. It can be started from the cockpit in the most extreme climatic conditions, and makes the Harrier completely independent of any ground power. Among other things it drives a 6kVA alternator for ground servicing and stand-by, and also serves as the starter for the Pegasus. The APU draws in air from a rectangular inlet in the top of the fuselage and discharges exhaust from a second flush aperture nearby.

Pilot oxygen is supplied from a Normalair-Garrett lox converter of 1gal (4·5lit) capacity. Like other system components, this is located in the rear fuselage, in this case immediately above the airbrake.

Fuel tankage in the airframe has been described, and it can be supplemented by two drop tanks carried on the "wet" (plumbed) inboard wing pylons. Originally the Harrier was cleared with combat tanks of 100gal (455lit) or ferry tanks of 330gal (1500lit), the latter seldom being needed in European service. During Operation Corporate (see later chapter) new tanks of 190gal (864lit) size were also flown, though these are not used by the RAF. The ground pressure-fuelling connection is immediately ahead of the left rear engine nozzle. The flight-refuelling probe, roughly 10ft (3m) in length, is attached above the left inlet and coupled to the inflight-refuelling valve in the aircraft fuel system. The probe is inclined upwards and outwards so that its tip is easily visible to the pilot. Finally, the large airflow and power of the Pegasus tend to give a false idea of the Harrier's fuel consumption. In the worst condition, hovering at full weight at sea level, fuel burn is 220lb (100kg)/min. This is one-sixth that of an F-4 Phantom on take-off.

Avionics

When the P.1127(RAF) was rather suddenly invented, upon cancellation of the P.1154(RAF), there was no background of an RAF OR (operational requirement) or official specification. As time was pressing, the Air Staff merely issued ASR.384 as a re-issue of the most recent

Right: Taken during an actual RAF low-level training sortie, this photograph shows how the pilot can look simultaneously both at the HUD display and at the scene ahead. The Harrier is diving into the valley.

Above: The cockpit of an RAF GR.3, showing the traditional dial instruments. The HUD and head-down moving-map display are on the centre-line; left are flight instruments with the weapon panel below.

Harrier GR.3 Cockpit Layout

1 Pilot display unit
2 Flying instruments
3 PDU controls
4 Weapon control panel
5 V/UHF controls
6 Throttle and nozzle box
7 Hand controller
8 F.E. 541 NDC (navigation display computer) unit
9 Engine instruments
10 Fuel instruments
11 F.E. 541 NDC control
12 Centralised warning system panel
13 Tacan controls
14 Voice recorder
15 IFF (identification friend or foe) controls

Left: Though well-known, this is still the best photograph yet taken of SNEB rockets being fired from an RAF Harrier. This Ministry of Defence (RAF) picture dates from GR.1 days. The photographer was looking almost straight up at the diving aircraft, firing on a ground target.

draft of OR.356, which was the document covering the P.1154(RAF), but with the radar omitted and the mission numbers down-graded to suit the anticipated mission capability of the smaller, subsonic Pegasus-powered aircraft.

The radar was omitted because it would have been extremely difficult to include it, there was no mention in ASR.384 of air combat missions, and the equipment itself did not yet exist (the supplier, Ferranti, had not even been awarded the full development contract). Apart from this item, much of the P.1154(RAF) avionics suite was written in without change, notably including the INAS, HUD and NDC.

The INAS (inertial navigation attack system) is the Ferranti FE.541, which because of its NBMR-3 application was actually designed for the P.1154(RAF). Its basis is the inertial platform in the nose, bolted to the cockpit front pressure bulkhead, which feeds positional information to the IMS (inertial measurement system) and present-position computer, which in turn feeds position information to the NDC (navigation display computer) and trajectory information to the WAC (weapon-aiming computer). The NDC is also called a projected map display, because its main display is a circular screen on which is projected optically a 35mm cassette containing a selected topographic map covering typically 800nm (921 miles, 1483km) north/south and 900nm (1,036 miles, 1668km) east/west.

There are two other inputs to the NDC. One is traditional Tacan, the long-established radio navaid which gives R-theta (radius and bearing) information from an interrogated ground station. The other is the Sperry C2G gyrocompass, providing an additional source of heading information. Present position is at the centre of the NDC, and the pilot himself has inputs in the form of buttons on the NDC, and a separate pistol-grip hand controller with a rolling-ball input and white "fix" button, which is depressed as the aircraft overflies a point whose position must be recalled or which must later be regained.

The third major avionic item specified at the start was the HUD (head-up display). This was designed by a small firm called Specto, which was taken over by Smiths Industries. It receives height and speed information from the ADC (air-data computer) and cockpit HUD control panel (and, after this item had been fitted, the LRMTS, as described in the next chapter). The HUD provides basic flight guidance information for all modes of flight, including a vital cue showing any tendency to sideslip at speeds too low for natural weathercocking by the fin, as well as the primary steering information for all air-to-ground or air-to-air attacks.

A HUD camera was specified to record the display as a training aid, and other basic avionics included HF, VHF and UHF radio, and IFF (identification friend or foe). Tactical VHF was also called for, but in fact this was never fitted until it appeared on AV-8 series aircraft of the US Marines and Spanish Navy.

After delivery, two very important extra items changed the appearance of Harriers of the RAF. These, the LRMTS and RWR, are described in the next chapter. EW (electronic-warfare) installations are also discussed there, and in the account of Operation Corporate.

Weapons

No internal weapons were called for. Like the P.1154(RAF) the Harrier was to rely solely on externally carried stores, though the supersonic predecessor's emphasis on guided missiles (such as Red Top and AS.30) was replaced by simpler weapons thought more appropriate to a tactical battlefield situation: bombs, rocket pods, and external gun pods. Hawker designed the pods to accommodate a single Aden Mk 4 gun of 30mm calibre together with its ammunition. The ammunition box accommodates 100 rounds, and 130 can be accommodated without causing feed problems if the capacity of the feed chutes is utilized. For minimum aircraft drag the firing aperture at the front of the pod is covered by a frangible cap, blown off by the first round. These pods have a useful effect as LIDs (lift-improvement devices), and when removed are replaced by thin strakes serving the same purpose.

Details of weapon loads are given in a diagram. The maximum weight of external loads can reach 9,000lb (4082kg), but the limit for normal operations is 5,300lb (2400kg). For the reconnaissance mission, the centreline fuselage pylon can carry a Hawker pod housing five optical cameras, two left and two right oblique F.95 Mk 7s and a forward F.135. Since the Falklands campaign RAF Harriers have carried AIM-9 Sidewinder self-defence AAMs.

Below: Selected weapons carried by the RAF and US Marine Corps, the American stores being in brackets.

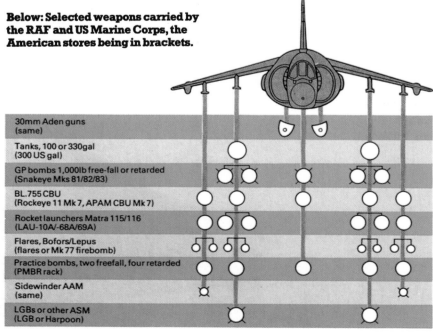

Weapon									
30mm Aden guns (same)									
Tanks, 100 or 330gal (300 US gal)									
GP bombs 1,000lb free-fall or retarded (Snakeye Mks 81/82/83)									
BL.755 CBU (Rockeye 11 Mk 7, APAM CBU Mk 7)									
Rocket launchers Matra 115/116 (LAU-10A/-68A/69A)									
Flares, Bofors/Lepus (flares or Mk 77 firebomb)									
Practice bombs, two freefall, four retarded (PMBR rack)									
Sidewinder AAM (same)									
LGBs or other ASM (LGB or Harpoon)									

Harrier in Service

Since April 1969, Harriers have flown well over a million operational hours, almost all under conditions of peculiar severity. Unlike other aircraft, a fair proportion of this time has been spent at full throttle in hovering flight, balanced on four thunderous jets which often kick up debris from the ground. Yet FOD (foreign object damage) has been less than that for many conventional aircraft, and even the birdstrike problem has been no worse than for other low-level attack aircraft. Furthermore, it was hoped that the Harrier would have advantages in air combat, leading to suggestions that all future fighters would one day have vectored thrust.

XV276, the first of the six DB prototypes, made its first hover on 31 August 1966. Subsequent development was most successful, and progressed from a simple unpainted aircraft with a long nose probe, no guns or pylons, six blow-in inlet doors and four vortex generators on each wing, to aircraft indistinguishable except to a real expert from the first production Harrier GR.1 (GR, ground attack and reconnaissance). The latter aircraft, XV738, was the first of 60 ordered in early 1967, sufficient to equip an OCU (Operational Conversion Unit), a front-line squadron in Britain and another in RAF Germany.

In the course of 1967 numerous carry-trials flights at Dunsfold proved various external stores, and the process gained momentum in 1968 with five aircraft at the Aeroplane & Armament Experimental Establishment, Boscombe Down. Indeed, it has never stopped, and even today new weapons and EW fits are being cleared both in Britain and in the USA. Among the early clearances was the AIM-9B Sidewinder AAM, envisaged as a light self-defence weapon. Photographs of the installation, on the outboard pylons, were taken in January 1968; but no provision was made for it in RAF Harriers, so in Operation Corporate 14 years later the trials had to be flown as a crash programme!

In early 1968 Hawker Siddeley Aviation hosted the media at Dunsfold. Though it was a new experience to witness a pirouetting display by seven jump jets, many of the pressmen failed fully to appreciate that they were witnessing the start of a new era in warfare

Above: A brace of RAF Harrier GR.3s on a training mission in 1980 from 233 OCU, Wittering. Individual aircraft letters are in pale blue above the fin flash. Aircraft L, on the right, is probably XV807. Each aircraft is carrying two tanks and two practice-bomb carriers.

Right: When new this Harrier was designated as a Hawker Siddeley AV-8A, or Harrier Mk 50, and it is shown in its original markings in service with VMA-231. Note the big tactical VHF mast above the fuselage, the bolted-on probe and the light practice bombs carried in tandem.

Above: This US Marine Corps Harrier was the fourth to be built and the third to be delivered (on 12 March 1971), but it was photographed in July 1982 after updating to AV-8C standard. For most of its career it has served with VMA-513.

Above left: Four AV-8As of the US Marine Corps – probably from VMA-513, though this is not certain – en route to air/ground rocket firing during a practice deployment to MCAS Yuma, Arizona. Attacks would be made in 20° dives.

in which airpower can be provided with neither airfields nor aircraft carriers. Bob Lickley, assistant managing director, reported good results with dropped stores, dry contacts with Victor K.1A tankers, ceiling climbs to beyond 50,000ft (15·24km) and the company's offer to sell Harriers at "£750,000 to £1 million, depending on quantity and equipment". He also announced further growth in thrust of the Pegasus, all of which could be translated into greater fuel or weapon loads.

During 1968 a massive effort was made to perfect the nav/attack system, which in some respects was new to British experience and at the time was fully competitive with anything flying elsewhere. Even in 1967, when it worked properly, accuracy of the basic inertial system degraded at less than 1nm (1·15 miles, 1·85km) per hour, and weapon delivery accuracies were the best ever achieved with RAF attack aircraft, and similar to results with the contemporary

F-111. By autumn 1968 the main advance had been reliability and consistent performance. Several important trials were also flown from ships, following earlier experiments with P.1127s, as related in the next chapter.

Enter a customer

Overseas interest in the Harrier was in some places intense, though in most cases without the slightest thought of purchase. The only serious acquisition interests were shown by a few navies, and in any case Hawker Siddeley's main marketing effort was a low-key one aimed at educating military aviators whose usual understanding of vectored-thrust V/STOL was based on deeply rooted misconceptions. It was certainly a great surprise when, at the 1968 Farnborough air show, a commissionaire at the Hawker Siddeley chalet announced that at the door were three officers of the US Marine Corps who would like to fly a Harrier!

In fact, the Marines had been looking at the Harrier for eight months. One of the Corps' basic needs is effective airpower over a beach-head where its tough "Leathernecks" might be making an assault on a foreign shore. It had the choice between helicopters and total reliance on the giant carriers of the US Navy. The best helicopter seemed to be the Lockheed AH-56A Cheyenne, incredibly complex and costly and yet seemingly vulnerable because of its modest speed. For eight years a further alternative had been sought in SATS (short airfield for tactical support), but this meant the beach assault had to

arrive complete with shiploads of aluminium planking, gas-turbine catapults, arrester installations and much more, as well as a complete Seabee construction battalion to fasten it all together. There had to be a better answer.

From the 1950s, largely because of the unswerving belief of Col, later Gen, Keith B. McCutcheon, the Corps had decided that the future lay with a V/STOL, when the technology matured. Though the Marines had played no part in the TES, they had carefully studied the six XV-6A (Kestrel) aircraft which from 1966 flew from Edwards, NASA-Dryden, NASA-Langley and the Naval Air Test Center at Patuxent (Pax) River, where Marine pilots at last flew them. In April 1966 an XV-6A flew from the LPD (assault ship) USS *Raleigh*, and for the first time the Marines began to wonder if the little Hawker jet might not represent the germ of something they could use. There was no doubt it had all the performance they wanted, and it had the most flexible basing possibilities anyone could wish. But not until 1968 was it clear that the more powerful version, the Harrier, might be able to do a useful job in the close-support mission.

Thus, despite the outpourings of the uninformed media, whose universal view in the United States was "the Harrier couldn't carry a box of matches across a football field", Gen Leonard C. Chapman, Commandant of the Corps, ordered that the British aircraft should be thoroughly evaluated. Brig-Gen Johnson came to England with two outstanding pilots, Col (later Gen) Tom Miller and Lt-Col Bud Baker. The Minister of Technology granted each Marine pilot ten flights, and their searching evaluation confirmed that the Harrier could do rather more than the popular American – and, in fact, world – opinion, and was close to being the ideal air weapon that the Corps had long dreamed of. It quickly drew up plans for a buy of 114 aircraft, sufficient to support four 20-aircraft squadrons plus training and attrition.

At Christmas 1968 the Marines announced their interest, and that they had received Department of Defense (DoD) approval for an initial buy of 12 aircraft to get the programme started. Funds for these were slashed from the DoD budget in the final rounds of Congressional cuts in January 1969, but this was only a temporary setback. A line

item in the FY70 (Fiscal Year ending 30 June 1970) budget was $58 million for 17 new F-4J Phantoms. The Marines willingly gave up these aircraft and used the money to pay for the initial 12 Harriers, which received the US designation AV-8A. They were to be made in Britain, and as nearly as possible copies of the RAF Harrier. Subsequent AV-8As were to be licence-built in the USA, and Baker and Miller visited all the chief American aircraft companies. Instant interest came from Douglas, which saw the AV-8A as the replacement for its own A-4 Skyhawk. But the California company had just come under the control of MCAIR (McDonnell Aircraft of St Louis). To everyone's surprise, not only did Sandy McDonnell express support, but he even got the British V/STOL project transferred to MCAIR! A 15-year agreement was signed with Hawker, not only for making the AV-8A but also for mutual exchange of all subsequent vectored-thrust V/STOL data and drawings. Pratt & Whitney signed with Rolls-Royce in October 1971 for joint future development of the Pegasus, under the US designation F402, with an option on a manufacturing licence.

In October 1969 the US Navy (on behalf of the Marines) and in January 1970 the USAF carried out evaluations of Harriers at Dunsfold. Both reports were highly positive, despite the tragic death on 27 January 1970 of Major Charles R. Rosberg, USAF, who got into uncontrollable roll during the tricky narrow band of airspeeds accelerating away from a VTO, when a flat turn or yaw is dangerous. This was the first fatal accident to any Hawker jump jet.

One of the changes specified in the AV-8A was the new Pegasus 11, with increased mass flow, improved water injection and turbine cooling and further revisions to the fuel control. This went into production as the Mk 103 for the RAF and Mk 803 for the AV-8A, but in fact these engines were too late for the first ten AV-8As which were delivered with Mk 802 (Pegasus 10) engines. Another obvious change was clearance with American ordnance, and the USMC

Below: Rising above the solid century-old ironwork of St Pancras station, London, XV744 was a very new GR.1 when it took part in the transatlantic race to New York City in May 1969. It had 100gal tanks, probe and bolt-on ferry wingtips.

interest in air combat prompted the obvious carriage of AIM-9 Sidewinder missiles. Though these had been fitted to a P.1127(RAF) at the A&AEE, the wiring was never installed. Amazingly, after the wiring to fire Sidewinders had been designed and fitted for the AV-8A, the RAF insisted that it should be specially *omitted* from its own Harriers, thereby causing a "crash" modification programme in April 1982! The Marines planned to replace the Aden guns at an early date, but these soon built up such a fine reputation they have remained in use to this day, even though they do not fire standard US ammunition. American communications radio, IFF and certain other avionic items replaced British equipment, an armament safety switch isolating the weapon circuits whenever the main landing gear oleo was compressed was fitted, and a direct manual throttle for use in emergency was also specified.

While the AV-8A programme got under way, deliveries began of Harrier GR.1s to the RAF. The first aircraft, XV738, had flown on 28 December 1967. Carriage and weapon-release trials and nav/attack refinements occupied 1968, and in January 1969 the first RAF unit, the

Harrier Conversion Unit, was formed at Dunsfold. The first delivery to an operational squadron, appropriately No 1 Sqn, based at Wittering, took place on 18 April 1969. On paper No 1 had actually received XV741 and 744 on 9 April, but both were diverted to take part in the transatlantic air race held in May. They were fitted with ferry tips, 100gal (455lit) tanks and refuelling probes and flew from the centre of London to the centre of New York and back. The first takeoff, from a disused coal-yard at St Pancras station, was notable for the amount of coal-dust blown over assembled dignitaries. The NY pad was a site at the Bristol Basin, in mid-Manhattan, so named because it had been filled with rubble from bombed buildings in Bristol, home of the Pegasus! Times for the 3,490 miles (5616km) were 5h 57min westbound, the best of any competitor, and 5h 31min eastbound.

Entry into service

QFIs (qualified flying instructors) who had completed Harrier conversion at Dunsfold then trained pilots of No 1 Sqn, followed in due course by Nos 4, 20 and 3 (in that order) forming a wing in RAF Germany at Wildenrath, the total RAF buy having been increased as listed in the Appendix. In early 1970 the HCU was restyled 233 OCU (Operational Conversion Unit) and moved to Wittering. It was true to RAF form that all the early Harrier conversion was done without the benefit of a dual two-seater, though this had been studied at Kingston since 1960. Some of the early two-seat P.1127 studies were novel, but reflected the unusual problems of putting a second cockpit in such a tight-knit V/STOL with four nozzles disposed around the CG. It was

Below: XZ146, an RAF two-seater, seen at Dunsfold in 1978 after it had been updated to T.4A standard with RWR and LRMTS. Curiously, it still has the original short fin. The same machine is seen above in its final paint scheme.

Below: Here XZ146 (see below) is shown resplendent in the markings of RAF No 4 Sqn, based at Gutersloh and carrying guns and bomb pods.

Below: In contrast, USMC 159380 is seen serving with VMA(T)-203 with the definitive tall fin, but of course no RWR, LRMTS or gun pods.

eventually clear that the only solution was a direct stretch of the fuselage with tandem seating.

When the RAF got round to drafting a requirement (ASR.386) for a two-seat Harrier, it made life harder by demanding that the aircraft should be able to take its place in the operational inventory, flown from the front seat with normal fuel and weapons. It was by no means certain that this was achievable, but once a contract for two two-seat development

Right: G-VTOL, the British Aerospace civil demonstrator, churning up the desert during a rolling vertical landing on an overseas trip in 1973. This aircraft has full "airways" avionics, and can go at short notice anywhere in the world.

aircraft (XW174-5) had been received in 1967, work began in earnest. It was only rendered possible by the continued dramatic increases in thrust of the engine, because a two-seater was clearly going to be appreciably heavier.

It is simple to list the design changes in producing the two-seat Harrier T.2 (T = trainer), but in fact it was no simple task. The nose, with pupil cockpit, was cut off and moved 47in (1·19m) forward. The instructor cockpit was inserted in the gap, at a level some 18in (457mm) higher than the pupil. To provide room for the rear seat and pressure bulkhead, the cabin air-conditioning system was removed from its previous location immediately behind the seat. It was replaced by a new system, of greater capacity matched to the volume of the dual cockpits, packaged in the large new fairing behind the canopy. The latter was redesigned as a single large framed structure hinged open along the right side. To reduce the pitch moment the F.95 camera and inertial platform were moved from the nose to a location under the rear seat, immediately in front of the nose gear. To maintain control power, the forward RCV was brought even further into the nose, being moved forward by 56in (1·42m). To balance the destabilizing effect of the larger nose the entire tail was moved 33·3in (846mm) to the rear, and the vertical fin enlarged by mounting it on an extra root section 11in (279mm) high. The ventral fin was changed in shape and enlarged. The fuselage tailcone was lengthened, partly to increase the moment arm of the pitch/ yaw RCVs and partly to house ballast to counter the extra mass ahead of the CG. This ballast, and the instructor seat, are removed when the aircraft is flown as a single-seat combat aircraft. The horizontal tail was not altered, apart from adding shot-filled tubes near the tips to damp resonance caused by the fact that the long fuselage has a natural frequency that is a sub-harmonic of that of the tailplane. Thus, ground crew must be careful never to bolt a single-seat tailplane on a two-seater.

The first two-seater flew on 24 April 1969, but this crashed from fuel-control contamination and the real development was done with XW175. There were few problems apart from inadequate yaw (weathercock) stability at high AOA (angle of attack). This proved a most intractable problem, taking until the late summer of 1971 to cure. By this time pro-

1 Classical dispersed operation

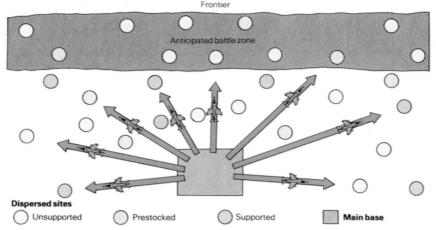

Frontier

Anticipated battle zone

Dispersed sites
○ Unsupported ○ Prestocked ○ Supported ■ **Main base**

2 Operations from unsupported sites

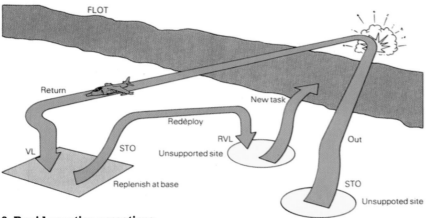

FLOT

Return
Redeploy
New task
VL   STO   RVL   Out
Unsupported site
STO
Replenish at base
STO
Unsuppoted site

3 Rapid-reaction operations

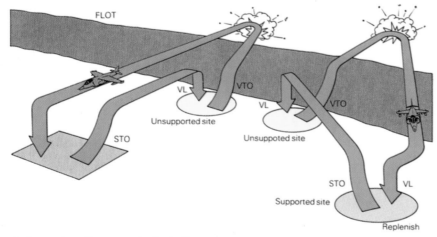

FLOT

VL   VTO
VL   VTO
Unsupported site   Unsupported site
STO
STO   VL
Supported site
Replenish

4 Operations from prestocked sites

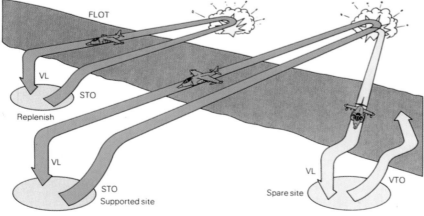

FLOT

VL
STO
Replenish
VL
VL   VTO
STO   Spare site
Supported site

1 In the classical pattern Harriers work from a main base near the land battle but disperse away from it in emergency or whenever the need arises. This stylized plan view shows a front-line area dotted with the three kinds of dispersed site.

2 Here the main base has been heavily attacked and is being used only as a logistics centre. The unsupported sites are bare plots used as "ground loiter" positions close to the FLOT (forward line of own troops). Pilots are summoned by radio communications.

3 This is the "cab rank on the ground" concept, which among other things saves fuel compared with the cab rank method of 1944. Note that one dispersed site here is big enough for an STO, which gives more payload or mission endurance.

4 Here there is no main base, and all operations are from prestocked sites (with fuel, weapons and a few support personnel) or supported sites (which also have full frontline servicing and briefing facilities, and radio communications).

Above: Harrier GR.3s of RAF No 1(F) Sqn temporarily in removable Arctic camouflage while on detachment to RNorAF base Bardufoss in 1979. The occasion was a NATO exercise called, appropriately, Cold Winter.

duction T.2s were in service, and many were modified with the final cure, which, after several adjustments, is a broader vertical tail with 18in (457mm) extra height, together with automatic opening of the airbrake to 26° whenever the horizontal tail is commanded to large negative angles.

Prolonged further trials, including carriage of stores, were flown with the first production T.2, XW264, which first flew on 3 October 1969. Subsequent details of production mark numbers, serials and numbers built are given in the Appendix at the back of the book. The RAF uses the two-seaters for pilot conversion at 233 OCU and on each Harrier squadron for weapon-delivery instruction, instrument ratings and various other checks. From 1971 the two-seaters greatly eased conversion problems, improved general proficiency standards and enabled inexperienced first-tour pilots to join Harrier squadrons.

Units in operation

Operational flying was approached in easy stages. An early overseas deployment was No 1 Sqn's armament practice camp at RAF Akrotiri, Cyprus, in March 1970, when a great deal of live firing at ground targets was combined with a long transit flight, but without using air refuelling. Then followed a busy round of off-base operations in various climates, Tacevals (tactical evaluations) in which the operational performance of a unit is numerically assessed in simulated frontline conditions, introduction of a succession of aircraft improvements, and solution of some of the major operating problems, other than the intractable one of birdstrikes. At first "everything but the kitchen sink", and sometimes that too, was taken to each dispersed site in order to make things as much like a well-equipped airfield as possible. Though NATO has never attempted to emulate

the Warsaw Pact air forces in spartan dispersed-site exercises, at least the RAF Harrier squadrons have acquired great experience in how to sustain high-intensity operations for a week or more without going near an airfield and with the minimum of special equipment. Even so, such an exercise still needs eight C-130 loads, not counting fuel.

No 20 Sqn converted from Harriers to Jaguars in 1977, and Nos 3 and 4 were brought up to 18 aircraft each and relocated at Gutersloh, nearer East Germany than any other NATO airfield. Both units have scored maximum possible marks in many exercises, including NBC (nuclear, biological, chemical) simulations. On most exercises each Harrier has flown an average of from four to 12 combat missions a day, with full briefings and complete changes of weapons and other "consumables", but without inertial realignment. In Exercise Oak Stroll in 1974 a total of 24 serviceable aircraft flew 1,121 missions in nine days, while in Big Tee (Tee = Tac eval exercise) in the same year No 1 Sqn flew 364 missions in three days with 12 aircraft, one machine flying 41 sorties. The CO said "Try *that* with an F-teen jet!"

The STO technique

Very soon it was obvious that the optimum type of mission is STVOL (short takeoff, vertical landing), the STO greatly increasing possible weapon loads for a given mission radius. The technique could hardly be simpler: the aircraft is lined up with the park brake on, the ASI bug (marker on the rim of the airspeed indicator) is set to a pre-computed takeoff speed, such as 140

knots, and the nozzle angle stop locked at 50°. The throttle is then moved to 55 per cent, brakes released and the throttle slammed to 100 per cent. A quick glance to check that full power has been obtained, and then, as the needle rotates past the bug, the nozzle lever is quickly whipped back to the stop. The Harrier leaps off the ground, gear is retracted and, as the aircraft climbs away on a mixture of engine thrust and wing lift, the nozzle lever is inched forwards, at the same time raising the flaps, until at about 180 ASI the aircraft is fully wingborne. At speeds up to 400 ASI, with nozzles aft, a Harrier out-accelerates everything else in the sky.

Above: Taken in 1971, this picture shows the lavishly equipped kind of hide with which RAF Harrier units played early in the aircraft's career. In a real war hides might be more spartan, and less visible.

Curiously, in view of its major extra capability of vectored-thrust V/STOL, the Harrier is in almost all respects simpler to fly than other tactical combat aircraft. As explained in a later chapter, it can operate when all other jets are grounded. It can also be operated from small pads, platforms and heaving ship decks by pilots who have never even seen a ship previously. (The very

important ski-jump technique appears in the next chapter.) The one standard departure from the STOVL operating routine comes when operating from unprepared surfaces, in which case an RVL (rolling vertical landing) is made, touching down with as much forward speed as the available run allows – typically 40 ASI – to minimise FOD (foreign-object damage) and recirculation of jet gas.

Below: An early GR.1 on Ministry trials in 1971, hovering near a simulated blasted runway while laden with guns, tanks, rocket launchers and recon pod.

From the earliest days of the P.1127 great attention has been paid to the increased importance of reingestion and FOD in V/STOL aircraft. Flow patterns round a hovering Harrier in ground effect are complex, and strongly modified by the extremely high energy supersonic blasts from the RCVs, but the underlying pattern is that there are four slightly divergent pillars from the main engine nozzles which spread out on impact across the ground. Jet temperatures are roughly 100°C for the front nozzles and 600°C for the rear (the RCV jets are at around 300°C), but absence of smoke means that the only way to see the jets is by "heat haze" light refraction. Air

Comparative mission radii that can be flown by a conventional attack aircraft (red) and a Harrier GR.3 (blue), in all but the last case with 5,000lb (2268kg) bombload. When available runway shortens, Harriers win out.

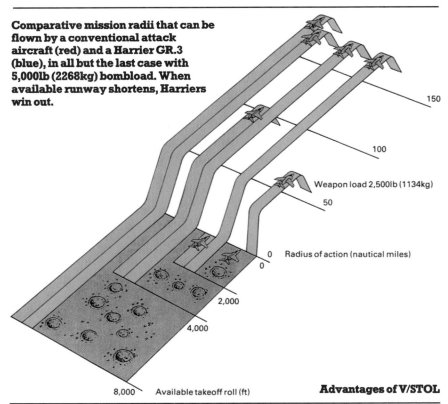

Advantages of V/STOL

and gas spreads outwards along the ground, rapidly losing energy, but the flows spreading inwards, for example from the two left-hand nozzles, almost immediately meet the mirror-image flow from the other side of the aircraft. The only place to go is up, resulting in a fountain jet rising vertically and striking the belly of the aircraft. This might seem advantageous, like the fountain that supports the ball at a shooting gallery, but in fact the high-velocity flow round the fuselage tends to act like the air flowing over the curved surface of a wing and suck the Harrier downwards. It is the designer's task to arrange strakes and dams to contain this flow, rather like the design of an air-cushion vehicle, to create a high-pressure area that will more than overcome the suck-down and instead add to the lift.

RAF Harriers and related aircraft have a simple LID (lift-improvement device) in the form of the two gun pods. These break up the impacting flow and, even though it can freely escape past the landing gears to front and rear, create a region between the pods where pressure is significantly above atmospheric. When the pods are removed, their effect is achieved by fitting strakes along the belly in the same locations.

FOD is an enormous subject. One aspect is birdstrikes, which cause significant attrition of low-flying aircraft everywhere that there are birds. Peculiar to the Harrier is FOD caused by poor operating procedures, which at the least can leave the aircraft covered in dirt blasted from the ground, and at worst can write off the engine fan, or the complete engine, or the complete aircraft. Despite its large fan and sea-level airflow of 432lb (196kg)/s, the Pegasus is a tough engine, and the Hylite fan blades stand up particularly well to most FOD, but at the same time it is essential for all Harrier personnel, especially pilots, to bear the problem in mind.

This is especially important when operating from unprepared sites. The Harrier obviously needs to be as self-sufficient as possible, and though (surprisingly) ladders are still deemed essential for cockpit access, various changes have made the RAF aircraft normally independent of ground services. Electrical power has been considerably uprated, both by fitting the Mk 2 version of the Lucas APU, with electrical output raised from 1·5kVA to 6kVA, while the original pair of engine-driven 4kVA alternators have given way to the 12kVA machine which was fitted to the AV-8A from the start.

One reason for wanting more electrical power has been the introduction of

additional equipment. Of course, the recon pod consumes a little power, and this is often carried by No 4 Sqn. All RAF Harriers in front-line service have since the late 1970s also carried two items that alter the appearance of the aircraft. One is the RWR and the other the LRMTS.

New equipment

The LRMTS (laser ranger and marked-target seeker) occupies the thimble extension on the nose. The Ferranti 106 laser, similar to that fitted to the Jaguar, is a Nd-YAG type which can be fired actively as a super-accurate measuring device which can be aimed by either the nav/attack system or the pilot within a 20° cone ahead. It provides target range, range-rate and angles, presented on the HUD. In the passive (MTS) mode it detects and locks on to any target illuminated with Nd-YAG (IR "black light") by friendly troops, providing the same weapon-guidance information as before. The ground illuminator and airborne receiver can be coded together to avoid spoofing IRCM (IR countermesures) or false lock-ons.

The RWR (radar warning receiver) is the MSDS ARI.18223, a typical 1960s-style installation which warns the pilot if his aircraft is being illuminated by a hostile radar. It covers the E to J frequency bands, of wavelengths from 15 down to 1·5cm, and receives at two aerials (antennae) mounted at the tail, that near the top of the fin leading edge covering the 180° facing ahead and that at the tip of the tailcone covering the 180° to the rear. The installation is rudimentary, the warning in the cockpit being merely a four-sector display which illuminates any 90° sector in which a hostile emitter is operating, and indicates its frequency band. Audible warning can also be given. In later aircraft the RWR is linked with an EW installation, but until May 1982 nothing had been provided to protect RAF Harriers. This subject is dealt with in the chapter on Operation Corporate, where EW protection was suddenly needed.

While these items were being retrofitted, more powerful engines became

Right: LRMTS with the lid off, a Ferranti picture showing the nose laser of a GR.3 and particularly laying bare the gimballed optical system of Cassegrain-telescope type.

British Aerospace Harrier GR.3

Below: The RAF Harrier GR.3 is here illustrated with a selection of its ordnance. The very advanced Wasp missile (shown with a tube launcher) will not now be selected for use by the RAF. In the Falklands, GR.3s were fitted with the Royal Navy rocket launcher, with 36 tubes of 2in calibre (see pages 38-9).

1 AIM-9B Sidewinder AAM (for the Falklands campaign the improved AIM-9L, now in production in Europe, was quickly made available, and a twin carrier was also cleared for use)
2 Hunting JP.233 dispenser (short type)
3 Lepus flare
4 Drop tank, 100gal (455lit); for the Falklands conflict a 190gal (864lit) pattern was quickly cleared for use
5 Wasp ASM launching pod (12 round)

6 Wasp ASM (unloaded); development of this weapon has recently been suspended
7 Practice-bomb dispenser with bombs installed
8 BAe reconnaissance pod with horizon-to-horizon optical cameras, forward oblique and various low-level cameras, plus BAe D type 401 IR linescan
9 Gun pod (one of two) containing 30mm Aden and ammunition
10 Ammunition, typically 120-130 rounds per gun, maximum being 150

11 Two Matra retarded bombs, 882lb (400kg)
12 ML twin carrier with two GP bombs, 1,000lb (454kg)
13 Rocket launch pod and rockets; one common type is Matra 155 with 18 tubes of 2·68in (68mm) for SNEB rockets
14 GBU-13/18 Paveway II smart (laser-guided) bomb which was based on the British 1,000lb (454kg) free-fall bomb
15 Hunting BL.755 cluster bomb, 611lb (277kg), (contains 147 bomblets in seven bays)

Right: Almost all RAF Harrier flying in Europe has been from airfields. Here XV738, the very first RAF Harrier (also illustrated opposite) is making a rolling takeoff with 3 Sqn.

Below: A standard RAF Harrier GR.3, XZ134 was one of the final batch of 12 aircraft ordered in 1974 (later buys were for attrition). It flies with 3 Sqn at RAF Gutersloh.

Below: AV-8A No 159241 was delivered in 1974 to Marine Corps squadron VMA-231, and is shown here in today's toned-down national markings. Home base is MCAS Cherry Point, NC.

available. The Pegasus 102, production mark of the Pegasus 10 which had run in 1969 at 20,500lb (9299kg), introduced a higher turbine entry temperature and was a field modification. The uprated aircraft became the GR.1A and T.2A. The Pegasus 103 (Pegasus 11), rated at 21,500lb (9752kg), became available in 1972, and by 1976 had replaced all earlier engines. The mark numbers were changed to GR.3 and T.4, while new two-seaters fitted with the Mk 103 from the start were styled T.4A.

Clearly one of the shortcomings of first-generation Harriers, especially those of the RAF, has been a lack of any EW (electronic warfare) capability. The addition of a rudimentary RWR gives 360° coverage of hostile emitters, but what does the pilot do about it, except perhaps perform a smart change of course or start jinking? In the Falklands war we saw the embarrassing spectacle of chaff bundles being jammed in under the airbrake and between bombs and their ejector-release units! Now at last even the existing GR.3s are to get a proper EW kit, and as MSDS (Marconi Space & Defence Systems) estimates the potential order (with RDT&E and all spares) as worth "£100 million plus", each

installation must be costed at more than the original price of the Harrier GR.1! GEC-Marconi, latterly British Aerospace (BAe), provides the electronic warfare system known as Zeus on RAF aircraft, which includes a radar warning receiver, pulse-Doppler missile approach warner, electronic jamming, and chaff/flare dispensers. Zeus was carried from the start by Harrier GR.5/7s; the latter also carries ASRAAM missiles for self-defence.

As noted earlier, the USMC specified the Pegasus Mk 803 (export 103, also called F402-RR-401) but had to accept temporary installation of the Mk 802 (export 102, or F402-RR-400) in the first ten AV-8As. Deliveries began on 26 January 1971, and in late 1972 all AV-8As were cycled through NAS Cherry Point to bring them up to definitive standard. This included not only the Dash-401 engine but also the back-up manual fuel control, which was later added to RAF engines, for control following a bird-strike and consequent surge and flame-out. The planned American licence production never materialized because of the funding in small annual batches, in

the teeth of opposition by Congress, which made transfer of production prohibitively costly. Thus, to the 12 FY70-funded aircraft were added 18 funded in FY71, 30 in FY72 and 30 in FY73. This left 24 for FY74, but in fact plans changed.

At the start the Marines suffered encouragingly low attrition, but after three years the rate increased sharply. Almost all incidents appeared to reflect on the pilot rather than the aircraft, and after prolonged enquiries it was decided that the AV-8A was a mount for ex-fighter pilots, who in the initial stages had been selected exclusively, rather than ex-helicopter pilots, who were finding it very hard to stay mentally abreast of what was happening. While the pilot selection procedures were tightened and training patterns revised, the decision was taken to buy some two-seaters in the final batch. Fearful of Congress withholding funds, the Marines

Below: RAF No 4 Sqn is the only unit which routinely carries out reconnaissance missions, using the multisensor pod on the centreline. These GR.3s were on a mission from Wildenrath in May 1983. Aircraft letters come yellow, orange or red.

Left: Marine Corps No 158385, the second AV-8A to be built, was delivered to VMA-513 on 5 February 1971 and is seen here on the deck-edge elevator of USS *Guam* during the AV-8A's first sea deployment.

stuck 100 per cent to single-seaters in the first four increments, and only felt safe in buying trainers in the final year. Extra costs of the two-seaters and various weapon clearances ate into the budget so that in the final year, instead of 24, only 20 aircraft could be afforded. These comprised 12 AV-8As and eight two-seaters, which were expected to be called AV-8Bs but instead received the designation TAV-8A.

Marine modifications

Modifications kept being made to the Marine aircraft, as a result of operating experience. Though the value of the INS was not in doubt, the Marines wanted a rough-and-ready nav/attack system needing no warm-up/alignment time and less skilled maintenance, and in 1973 the FE.541 system was replaced by a Baseline nav/attack system comprising the HUD fed with data from a Smiths IWAC (interface/weapon-aiming computer) which usually provides CCIP (continuously computed impact point) steering markers for air/ground visual delivery. Another change was to replace the Mk 9D seat by the American Stencel SIII-S3, on national policy grounds, and another was to fit a non-toppling attitude/heading reference system. Hawker had also fitted tactical VHF radio to many AV-8As, and to all two-seaters, with a large inclined aerial mast above the fuselage. The two-seaters are specially equipped with both tactical VHF and UHF, for use in the Airborne Tac Air Commander role in control of ground forces.

The first combat unit, formed in April 1971, was VMA-513 at Beaufort (pronounced Bewf't) MCAS in South Carolina, under Bud Baker. This squadron did many of the weapon trials at China Lake and Point Mugu, both in California. Next came the remaining units of Marine Air Group 32, all at MCAS Cherry Point, North Carolina: VMA-542, VMA-231 and training squadron VMA(T)-203. All have operated intensively from every kind of site or ship, including carriers (CV-42 *Franklin D. Roosevelt*), assault ships or Landing Platform, Helicopter (LPH-3 *Guam* in particular) and LHAs (Landing Helicopter Assault). It is largely because of Marines experience that Harriers made more than 13,000 missions from ships at sea before there was an accident of any kind, as noted in the next chapter.

In early 1970 Col Baker asked a fellow Marine, Capt Harry Blot, to be project officer for developing ACM (air-combat manoeuvring) with the AV-8A. Blot quickly decided the basic aircraft had excellent handling, a good engine that kept going in all combat situations, and an excellent thrust/weight ratio, but was penalized by its high wing-loading and poor rear view. Blot was under the impression that Viffing (VIFF, vectoring in forward flight) was common practice in RAF squadrons. In fact, Hugh Merewether had briefly toyed with "cracking the nozzles" at various speeds in the first 1127(RAF), and so had at least two RAF test pilots, but it was strictly absent from RAF Pilots Notes. Oddly, there had never been a deliberate attempt to see how well the Harrier

Left: Activity aboard USS *Guam* in 1974 as AV-8As of VMA-542 fly training missions. Each AV-8A is clean, without even guns, but inflight-refuelling probes are installed, for A-4 "buddy" contacts.

Defensive Break by Harrier

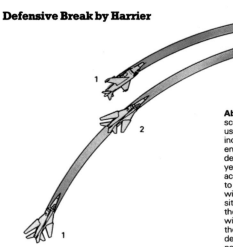

Right: In these three sets of artwork the Harrier appears as an RAF GR.3, but in fact the drawings are based on originals stemming from the US Marine Corps, who pioneered the use of Viffing as an extra advantage in combat.

could look after itself if intercepted, but this is just what Blot was asked to do with the AV-8A.

Test sorties at the US NATC (Naval Air Test Center) were at a premium, so he decided to go straight to the limit: achieve 500-kt speed and then slam the nozzles to 98°! In his own words: "The airplane started decelerating at an alarming rate, the magnitude of which I could not determine because my nose was pressed up against the gunsight . . . the violence of the maneuver had dislodged me from the seat, and I was now straddling the stick, with my right hand extended backwards between my legs trying to hold on for dear life . . ." This was the start of the discovery that the Harrier can be a most difficult opponent in close combat.

The point has already been made that the Harrier is very small, smokeless and an odd shape, so that it is peculiarly difficult for an enemy to see at a glance what it is doing. Its IR signature is low and diffuse. On top of these factors, its ability to Viff was obviously worth exploring. NASA ran fresh trials with an XV-6A, while Blot organized computer simulations which showed, discouragingly, that Viffing would entail such loss in energy as to nullify any gains in manoeuvre. The computer program was then loaded into the twin-dome ACM simulator at MCAIR in St Louis, and this showed a very different picture. Most of it was impressive, but at low speeds there were results that conflicted with Blot's findings. He was, in particular, told that no aircraft could turn in the way he reported, while harsh demands at low speeds resulted in end-over-end tumbling resulting in a crash. Blot went back to NATC and spent many sorties carefully approaching these computer situations. He found that the uncontrolled tumbling was an error in the simulation, while the turn-rate discrepancy resulted from the actual aircraft being able to achieve a form of blown-wing effect, due to the pumping action of the jets, which with skill could result in turns that no other aircraft could equal.

Tests were also run in Britain, notably at the RAE, but the RAF has shown only marginal interest in ACM and its Harriers try to avoid combat, which is not part of their mission. The US Marine Corps, however, not only found exciting possibilities but even succeeded in getting British Aerospace (as Hawker Siddeley became on 1 January 1978) and Rolls-Royce to remove two limitations on Viff potential. The nozzles were modified with greater strength and a higher-

Above: The simplest of all Viff scenarios is when engine thrust is used to reduce turn radius or increase normal acceleration. In this engagement the Harrier RWR detects the enemy astern, but not yet in firing range (1). The Harrier accelerates, while pulling enough g to prevent the enemy from getting within firing parameters. This is the situation from (2) until at position (3) the faster enemy has just come within firing range. At the latter point the Harrier pilot performs his unique defensive break, pulling maximum normal acceleration and adding Viff. There is no way the enemy can avoid overshooting, and he then becomes an easy close-range target (4). Variables are numerous, one being that at (3) the Harrier pilot could even set the nozzles to 98·5° for more violent deceleration; another is that at (4) the half-roll may not be necessary, especially if AAMs are used.

Climb and Flip by Harrier

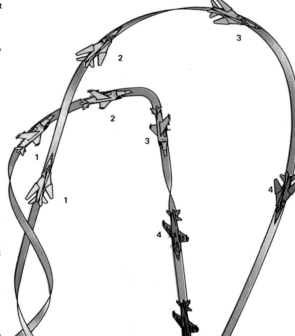
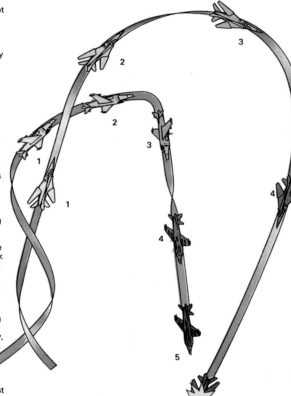

Right: In this so-called "climb and flip" the Harrier performs one of its numerous "impossible" manoeuvres, which are now part of the routine air-combat repertoire of all experienced US Marine Corps Harrier pilots. The sequence begins with the Harrier (whose trajectory is indicated by a blue line in all these illustrations) and its adversary (red line) climbing in a steep spiral and losing speed, the enemy close behind and eager to get within firing parameters before the Harrier can pull one of its tricks. From this position (1), with the enemy in close trail, the Harrier pilot using light stick forces pulls well past the vertical (2) and, as the speed bleeds away through the 200-knot level, he adds a small nozzle angle (3). The Harrier very quickly flips to a 90° nose-low attitude. The enemy has no option but to follow a semi-ballistic arching curve to end up going steeply downhill. Still travelling quite slowly, the Harrier goes into full reverse (4). There is no way the enemy can avoid going on down past what seems to be a Harrier stopped in mid-air. When the enemy gets to position (5) he presents the simplest possible target, for guns or AAMs.

Harrier as the Attacker

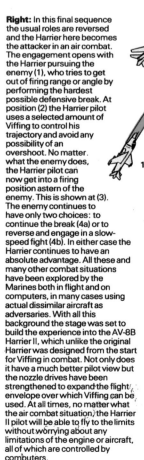
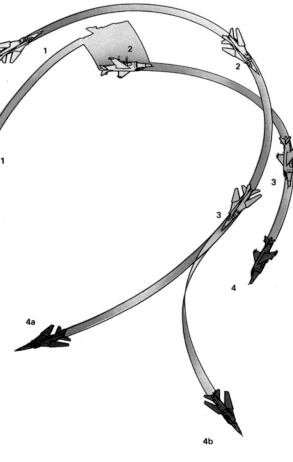

Right: In this final sequence the usual roles are reversed and the Harrier here becomes the attacker in an air combat. The engagement opens with the Harrier pursuing the enemy (1), who tries to get out of firing range or angle by performing the hardest possible defensive break. At position (2) the Harrier pilot uses a selected amount of Viffing to control his trajectory and avoid any possibility of an overshoot. No matter what the enemy does, the Harrier pilot can now get into a firing position astern of the enemy. This is shown at (3). The enemy continues to have only two choices: to continue the break (4a) or to reverse and engage in a slow-speed fight (4b). In either case the Harrier continues to have an absolute advantage. All these and many other combat situations have been explored by the Marines both in flight and on computers, in many cases using actual dissimilar aircraft as adversaries. With all this background the stage was set to build the experience into the AV-8B Harrier II, which unlike the original Harrier was designed from the start for Viffing in combat. Not only does it have a much better pilot view but the nozzle drives have been strengthened to expand the flight envelope over which Viffing can be used. At all times, no matter what the air combat situation, the Harrier II pilot will be able to fly to the limits without worrying about any limitations of the engine or aircraft, all of which are controlled by computers.

power drive, while the engine was provided with a combat plug, a screw-in turbine temperature control fuse, that for 2½ minutes allows the engine to give full power in wingborne flight, instead of a maximum of 75 per cent. This removed all restrictions on Viffing, at all speeds, attitudes and altitudes, without ever having to keep an eye on instruments. The potential discovered is described by Blot, now a general, as "absolutely eye-watering". It has been utilized to the full in the AV-8B.

In the mid-1970s the US Marine Corps began working on a major CILOP (conversion in lieu of procurement) programme to update surviving AV-8As for continued use through the 1980s. The scheme was put into operation at Naval Air Rework Facility, Cherry Point in 1979. It was planned to rework 60 aircraft, but the figure was cut by budget pressures to only 47, and these have been upgraded to AV-8C standard. The chief task is an airframe audit and rework under a SLEP (service life extension programme) for a further 4,000 hours flying. The LIDs of the AV-8B Harrier II (described later) are installed to enhance payload/range. Surprisingly, no laser or other weapon delivery system is installed, but EW gear is vastly augmented. The ALR-45 radar warning receiver is installed, with aft-facing aerials in the tailcone and forward-facing on the wingtips. A Goodyear ALE-39 dispenser for chaff, flares or jammers is installed in the rear equipment bay. An Obogs (on-board oxygen generation system) similar to that described in the AV-8B chapter is installed, and new radios include a new UHF and the KY-58 secure voice transmission system. AV-8C conversions are supported by kits from BAe Kingston-Brough division and MCAIR St Louis.

The plane in Spain

There is another operator of regular Harriers: the Spanish naval aviation, or Arma Aérea de la Armada. The Franco government began discussions in 1972, and, following a demonstration by chief test pilot John Farley which showed that the wooden deck of the old carrier *Dédalo* would barely get warm, far less burst into flames, a requirement was announced for 24 V/STOLs and an initial order was placed for six single-seat Harrier Mk 55s and two two-seat Mk 58s. Because it was feared a possible British Labour administration would tear up the deal, the order was placed via Washington and MCAIR, the aircraft being shipped to St Louis for final assembly and delivery as AV-8S and TAV-8S machines with BuAer numbers. They were assigned to Escuadrilla 008, with Spanish designation VA-1 Matador and, for the trainer, VAE-1. In 1977 a repeat order was placed for five more single-seaters. They are broadly to AV-8A standard, but with a broad VHF blade aerial for communicating with helicopters at sea. Operations from *Dédalo* and shore base Rota, near Cadiz, have been most successful and the new carrier, *Principe de Asturias* operates 12 Harrier IIs. The Matadors have since been sold on to Thailand.

Left: A pair of VA-1 Matadors of the second batch, alias Harrier Mk 55 or AV-8S, seen at BAe Dunsfold in company with G-VTOL.

Sea Harrier

Harriers of all kinds have operated from more ships, of more diverse types, than any other aircraft in history. Certainly no other aircraft comes close to the Harrier in logging over 13,000 missions from ship decks before there was a single incident involving damage to an aircraft. This chapter describes the special multirole Harrier developed for operations at sea. It can be based on large carriers, small carriers with ski jumps, small carriers without ski jumps, surface warships with a flat pad 80ft by 50ft (24m×15m), and also on container ships which 48 hours previously had no military equipment on board.

The greatest virtue of air power is flexibility, and this is no more so than when it is deployed at sea, where it can be switched to any part of the world very quickly. The conventional aircraft carrier is probably the highest value target of all, but the STOVL Harrier permits air operations from something less than this. Back in

Below: Taken in the post-Falkland period in late 1982, this photograph shows a Sea Harrier FRS.1 streaming fuel from the jettison pipes. It has Training Sidewinder missiles installed.

February 1963 the P.1127 ran a programme of demonstrations from the carrier HMS *Ark Royal*, test pilots Bedford and Merewether discovering that operations from a deck were, they said, "simpler than from an airfield."

It may be that, in pursuing an elusive commonality with the RAF in 1963-64, and seeking the Mach 2 V/STOL P.1154RN, the Royal Navy was biting off more than it could chew. There would probably have been major problems in operating these heavy and expensive machines, though it is doubtful if they would have cost more than their replace-

ment, the Spey-Phantom, which needs a large ship with full catapult and arrester gear. But the abrupt decision of the 1966 Labour government to terminate British fixed-wing airpower at sea, and to cancel the new carrier (CVA-01) then in design, brought a totally new situation. It is difficult for a service to argue against Government cuts in defence. If Their Lordships had said "What would we do if Argentina invaded the Falklands?" the Defence Minister in 1966 would have replied, in effect, "We really cannot concern ourselves with such unlikely eventualities!" So the fixed-wing Fleet

Above: Royal Navy No 809 Sqn was assembled at short notice by Lt-Cdr (now Cdr) Tim Gedge, and here most of its beautifully painted aircraft are seen immediately before departure from Yeovilton.

Air Arm wound down to a full stop, and, after a while, saddened and perturbed people all over Britain stuck labels in their cars saying FLY NAVY.

By the late 1960s P.1127s, Kestrels, XV-6As and Harriers had demonstrated the complete absence of hassle in operating from many warships, some with nothing but a small helicopter pad, in various sea states with winds gusting to 40kt and with the ship doing anything from full speed to being at anchor. Several major shipbuilding companies were studying "Harrier carriers", with displacements down to a mere 6,000 tons, and without the need for catapults and arrester gear. The British Admiralty, having been informed that there would be no more fixed-wing seagoing airpower, and that there would be no replacements for the ageing fleet carriers *Ark Royal* and *Eagle*, was clearly faced with a lunatic situation. The government view was that future maritime airpower would be provided by the land-based RAF, a service already overextended and unable to operate except around the shores of Britain! The US Navy could not be relied upon to provide airpower for purely British actions around the world, and the only possible, and obvious, alternative was to deploy a specially developed maritime version of the Harrier from a new class of V/STOL ship. Special ships were clearly indicated, though the V/STOL aircraft could also operate from simple helicopter pads on existing warships. The Admiralty was kept continuously updated on Hawker Siddeley's Maritime Harrier studies, yet, if the official story is to be believed, the decision was taken in 1968 to deploy a new class of V/STOL carrier – known as a "through-deck cruiser"

Below: One of the third batch of production Sea Harriers, this FRS.1 is depicted with a single victory symbol. It later destroyed a second Mirage in the South Atlantic war while serving with 809 Sqn.

Left: France has long eyed the Harrier, and especially the Sea Harrier, with extreme interest. Here an RAF GR.1 is seen aboard the *Jeanne d'Arc*, a most useful ship of over 12,000 tons displacement, in October 1973. Sea Harriers would have fit this ship ideally, but ultimately no orders were forthcoming, probably due to politics.

Above: In 1971 RAF No 1(F) Sqn took their Harrier GR.1s aboard HMS *Ark Royal*, trying to assist a stupid political scheme whereby, in the absence of such ships, the RAF would provide air cover for the Royal Navy! No 1 has enough to do in connection with warfare on land, but the trials on this ship were impressively simple.

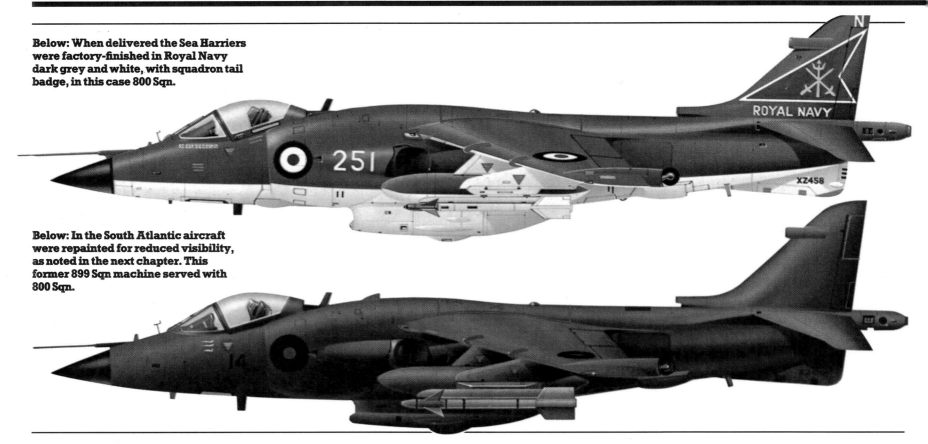

Below: When delivered the Sea Harriers were factory-finished in Royal Navy dark grey and white, with squadron tail badge, in this case 800 Sqn.

Below: In the South Atlantic aircraft were repainted for reduced visibility, as noted in the next chapter. This former 899 Sqn machine served with 800 Sqn.

(TDC) to avoid any hint that it might be used for the forbidden fixed-wing aircraft – which was to be designed *for helicopters only*. This is so beyond belief that it could be discounted, were it not for the fact that the initial form of TDC ship was indeed not optimised for fixed-wing V/STOL operation!

Part of the trouble was that, like many air staff at that time (1968-72), the RN Air Warfare department totally overlooked the air defence capability of the Harrier because it had (an official quote) "too short an endurance" and did not fly at Mach 2. Indeed, when RAF No 1 Sqn received an unprecedented clearance to go aboard RN carriers and fly combat

missions (which the squadron did in March 1970, without the slightest trouble), the author was advised by an RN spokesman that "Of course, this idea that the fleet might be defended by Harriers is laughable!" Despite this, Hawker was asked by MoD to modify No 1 Sqn Harriers for shipboard operation by adding tie-down shackles to the outrigger gears and add a relay to the nosewheel steering so that, whenever the anti-skid brakes were switched off, the nosewheel steering would be engaged, preventing the aircraft from pirouetting round on a rolling deck. The RAF had plenty of other tasks for 1 Sqn – which could well have been wiped out on the

first day of a war, anyway – and in any case looked askance at the whole idea of a Maritime Harrier. The "light blues" doubted the ability of such an aircraft to intercept supersonic "Backfires", judged its ship to be costly and vulnerable, and feared that resurrection of naval airpower would result in cutbacks in the RAF's own budget. Meanwhile, the "dark blues" were not only mentally locked-in to the concept of Big Ship airpower but still wanted highly supersonic speed and a backseat crew-member.

Thus in true British fashion, the environment was confused and unfavourable. Despite this a few farsighted and dogged individuals, mostly at Kingston, kept on studying the possibilities for what in 1971 was called the Maritime Support Harrier. Though the RN Ship Department at Bath was well into the design of the TDC ship, its form was still somewhat fluid and there was no official requirement for it to carry any aircraft except helicopters. As for the MS Harrier, this too was fluid, because Hawker and MCAIR were busy with a next-generation aircraft, the AV-16 family, powered by the more powerful Pegasus 15 and in some forms capable of supersonic speed on the level. It was partly because of this vision of increased performance that, in early 1971, the RN Air Warfare staff began to consider an MS Harrier seriously; but the whole situation was made academic by the fact that there was no money.

The "Through-Deck Cruiser"

From the start of the TDC ship design it had been policy that these ships would serve in an ASW (anti-submarine warfare) role, act in a command/control role for both naval and air forces, and "make a contribution to area air defence". When the author asked what the latter meant he was told that it was interpreted as meaning a requirement for the Sea Dart SAM, and as finally designed a twin launcher for this missile represented virtually the only armament of these large and costly vessels! But at some time in late 1971 the Admiralty not only made a case for a Maritime Harrier but got

Treasury permission for it, and this not only resulted in a rethink of the TDC ship but also enabled Hawker to authorize a firm design programme. Rather than being an AV-16, the Maritime Harrier was to be a minimum-change Harrier, and when the Naval Staff Target for its previously forbidden new jet was issued in August 1972 it was seen to be written round the Harrier GR.3 with the minimum of alterations.

At last there was a programme for a V/STOL and a ship to carry it. Vickers received the contract for the first ship in April 1973, with a planned commissioning date of 1980. The TDC designation was gradually replaced by others:

Left: An unusual formation off the Devon coast in 1981 made up of Sea Harriers of 899 Sqn (lead aircraft, tail code VL for Yeovilton), 801 (nearest, code N for HMS *Invincible*) and 800 (tail code H for HMS *Hermes*).

long-range shore-based aircraft; (R) sea search of at least 27,000sq miles (70000sq km) in one hour at low level; and (S) at least 250nm (463km) radius (depending on mission profile) carrying a wide range of anti-ship or ground-attack stores, with accurate delivery.

In fact, mission radius and load were already known to depend on the takeoff run available, as with any other fixed-wing machine, and in the early 1970s a further major variable came into the picture: the ski jump. Before describing this, it is worth noting that by 1972 the Hawker test pilots had deeply explored Harrier operations from ships and come up with basic operating rules. If mission load is not important, the fastest reaction time, typically 90s from initiation of engine start to wingborne flight, is achieved with a VTO, and this also burns the least fuel (a matter of a mere 100lb, 45kg, to wingborne flight, compared with over 1,000lb (454kg), for an F-14). VTO enables aircraft to be spotted only 30ft (10m) apart, gives least sensitivity to ship motion and hardly ever requires the captain to alter course or speed. STO, on the other hand, enables heavier loads to be carried for any given radius, and a 500ft (152m) run with 30kt (55km/h) WOD (wind over the deck) gives exactly double the mission load that can be lifted from VTO. It was found that the ideal deck markings were white "tram lines" just 7ft (2·13m) apart, and that the takeoff clearway need be no more than 38ft (11·6m) wide. Harriers can line-up nose to tail and takeoff at full power with nozzles pointing aft. As for landings, these were always VL, and not only simpler but safer than using conventional carrier aircraft which hit the wires at 120kt (222km/h) relative speed.

official documents since 1980 have called these ships Command Cruisers, ASW Cruisers, AS Cruisers and CAHs (for Carrier, Assault Helicopter). At Kingston, Hawker received the development study contract for what was called the Naval Harrier. As studies had been going on in depth for several years previously, and money (equated with time) was tight, the job should have been completed quickly. Sadly, funding was

Below: The island of HMS *Hermes* shelters XZ450, the first Sea Harrier to fly, on board for operational trials in the Irish Sea in October and early November 1979.

administered in trickles, and often dried up entirely, and the planned go-ahead was delayed until January 1973, when an order for 24 aircraft was arranged. This was then delayed until June, when a complete review of the UK's defence commitments put the whole programme back into the melting pot. At last Hawker were advised in December 1973 that the go-ahead had been agreed, and would be announced the following week. What actually happened was a "fuel crisis", soaring inflation and industrial unrest. In 1974 there were two General Elections, a series of Defence Cuts and a near-total loss of hope. Then on 15 May 1975, as chief test pilot Farley and chief designer

(Harrier) Fozard were on short finals at Dunsfold in the company Dove, the tower advised them "The BBC has just announced they're ordering 24 Sea Harriers!"

Designation of the aircraft is Sea Harrier FRS.1, for fighter/reconnaissance/strike. This versatility has rarely been attempted in any one aircraft, and it was not so much making the best of a bad job as the result of prolonged tests to establish the missions that can be flown from a small deck. The three roles actually spelt out in the Naval Staff Target were: (F) a 400nm (741km) radius of action at altitude carrying guns and Sidewinders against any ship-based or

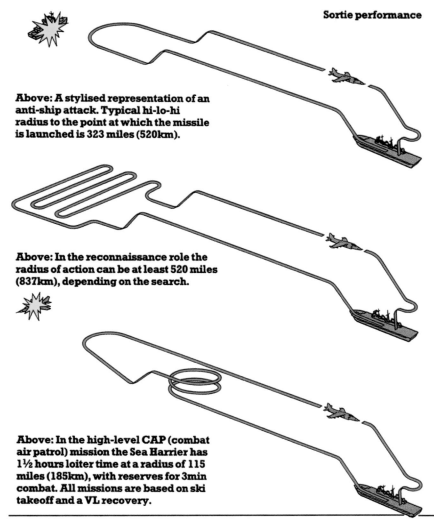

Sortie performance

Above: A stylised representation of an anti-ship attack. Typical hi-lo-hi radius to the point at which the missile is launched is 323 miles (520km).

Above: In the reconnaissance role the radius of action can be at least 520 miles (837km), depending on the search.

Above: In the high-level CAP (combat air patrol) mission the Sea Harrier has 1½ hours loiter time at a radius of 115 miles (185km), with reserves for 3min combat. All missions are based on ski takeoff and a VL recovery.

Left: The DB (development batch) GR.1 Harrier XV281 made the first ski jump trials at the RAE Bedford, beginning with the ramp set at 6° on 5 August 1977. Here 281 goes off the end in the spring of 1978 with the ramp set at 15°, which is close to the best angle for operational use.

All this had been worked out in detail, and remains valid, and one particular series of trials was to take off at lower and lower airspeeds to investigate the limiting value of ASI and AOA, so that in any situation the maximum safe weapon load or minimum safe deck run could be assessed. Unlike a runway takeoff, the aircraft is instantly out of ground effect as it runs off the edge of the deck. On the other hand, it can be allowed to sink, because the deck is something like 50ft (15m) above the sea. But there is not a lot of time or space, and if total engine failure were to occur as the aircraft left the deck, it would go into the sea in 2½s, barely time for the pilot to eject. The dynamics of carrier flying have been studied by many people, some of whom in the mid-1940s were convinced landing gears could be replaced by flexible decks, while others believed it would help if the deck moved relative to the ship! Vectored thrust introduced a new situation, and an officer studying for an MPhil thesis at the University of Southampton came up with an answer whose importance is matched by its elegant simplicity.

Lt-Cdr Doug Taylor RN wrote his thesis on the subject of V/STOL operations from confined spaces – not necessarily ships – and showed that if the takeoff surface ends in an upward curve, great benefits ensue. As in any STO departure, there is a choice between length of run (for any given wind) and mission load. Taylor calculated that leaving with a trajectory inclined upwards at about 10° would add an upwards velocity component that would counter the "fall" resulting from insufficient airspeed, and thus compensate for an initially inadequate combination of jet thrust plus wing lift to balance the weight. In other words, the Harrier could start its flight with deficient lift (resulting from either too much mission load or insufficient STO run). Over the next ten seconds or so the thrust component from the nozzles set at 50° accelerates the aircraft to about 35kt (65km/h) higher airspeed, by which time there is no lift deficiency, and from this point on the aircraft can climb away normally. The big advantages are that it is possible either to take the air with a much heavier load or at greatly reduced airspeed, the entire initial trajectory is much higher above the sea or ground, and in the event of engine failure there is much more time in which to assess the situation and eject. In the case of a ship launch in severe weather, a ski ramp ensures a positive upwards trajectory even in the worst case of the ship pitching bows-down into the sea.

It is a yet further grave reflection on the British Official Establishment that from 1972 until mid-1975 there was very little support for the ski-jump idea, even though – at considerable expense –

Hawker had done extensive studies and model tests which fully confirmed the most sanguine predictions. Indeed, the ruling view in the Admiralty was that such a disturbing idea was unwelcome, to the extent that Fozard called the ship experts "The Flat Deck Preservation Society". Doggedly, the first ship was built with a flat deck and a Sea Dart launcher bang in the bows on the centre-line, so that a ski ramp would obstruct its arc of fire!

Ski-jump – at last!

In 1976 Hawker at last managed to get the MoD to fund the construction of a ski ramp for research on land, and this was built by Redpath Dorman Long at RAE Bedford. The first ski launch was made by P.1127(RAF) XV281 on 5 August 1977 at an exit angle of 6°. Subsequently this aircraft and others, including two-seaters, made 367 launches at angles up to 20°, at which angle the landing-gear oleos were just bottoming with the 4g vertical acceleration. Over 100 pilots had a go – they queued up – and Harriers took the air at 100kt (185km/h) below the normal STO speed of 142kt (263km/h)!

Not least of the many good features of this brilliant idea was that no aircraft modifications whatsoever were called for. This was doubly welcome, because the Sea Harriers had really become quite new aircraft, and in any case were,

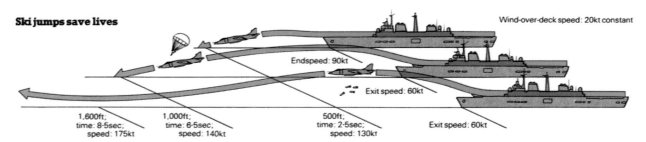

British Aerospace Sea Harrier FRS.1 cutaway

1 Pitch RCV (reaction control valve)	8 Windscreen wiper
2 Pitch feel and trim actuators	9 Instrument panel
3 Inertial platform	10 Pilot's head-up-display (HUD)
4 IFF aerial	11 Martin-Baker Mk 10H zero-zero ejection seat
5 Yaw vane	12 Boundary-layer air exhaust ducts
6 Rudder pedals	13 Cockpit air-conditioning system
7 Control column	

14 Engine oil tank
15 Alternator
16 Engine accessory gearbox
17 Auxiliary power unit (APU)
18 Starboard wing pylons
19 Starboard wing integral fuel tank
20 Aileron power unit
21 Starboard navigation light
22 Roll control RCV
23 Outrigger wheel fairing
24 Starboard aileron
25 Hydraulic reservoir
26 Plain flap
27 Anti-collision light
28 Water tank
29 Water filler cap
30 Flap hydraulic jack

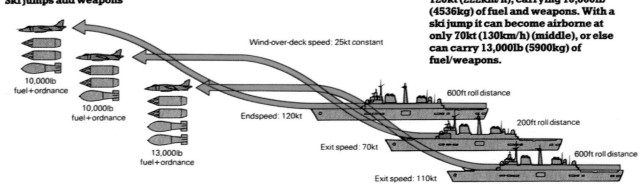

Ski jumps save lives

Wind-over-deck speed: 20kt constant

Endspeed: 90kt

Exit speed: 60kt

1,600ft; time: 8·5sec; speed: 175kt

1,000ft; time: 6·5sec; speed: 140kt

500ft; time: 2·5sec; speed: 130kt

Exit speed: 60kt

Above: Even though failure of the nozzle drive happens much less often than once in 10,000 launches, it is a factor to be reckoned with. In takeoff – jets aft – from a flat deck (top) the pilot has to eject, but has barely enough time to realize it before he hits the sea. With a ski jump at maximum weight he has almost three times as long (centre drawing). Alternatively, by smartly jettisoning external stores, he can even climb away despite the failure.

Below: Another, quite unrelated, benefit of the ski jump is that it enables a Sea Harrier either to carry a bigger load or to use a much smaller deck. In the traditional flat deck (upper ship drawing) the aircraft goes off the end after a run of 600ft (180m) at a speed of 120kt (222km/h), carrying 10,000lb (4536kg) of fuel and weapons. With a ski jump it can become airborne at only 70kt (130km/h) (middle), or else can carry 13,000lb (5900kg) of fuel/weapons.

Ski jumps add weapons

Wind-over-deck speed: 25kt constant

10,000lb fuel + ordnance

10,000lb fuel + ordnance

13,000lb fuel + ordnance

600ft roll distance

200ft roll distance

600ft roll distance

Endspeed: 120kt

Exit speed: 70kt

Exit speed: 110kt

Below: A simple cutaway showing the main items of fuel, on-board equipment and weapons of the Sea Harrier FRS.1.

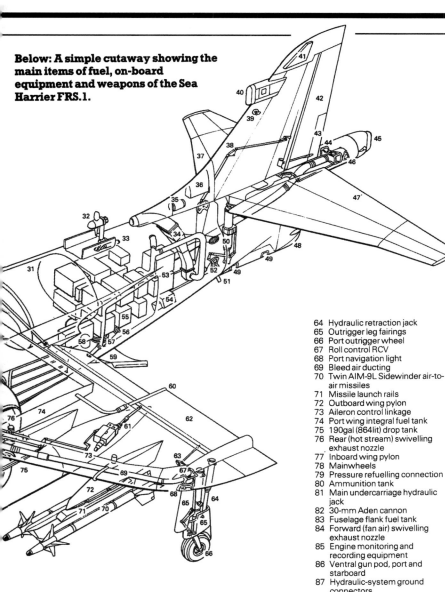

64 Hydraulic retraction jack
65 Outrigger leg fairings
66 Port outrigger wheel
67 Roll control RCV
68 Port navigation light
69 Bleed air ducting
70 Twin AIM-9L Sidewinder air-to-air missiles
71 Missile launch rails
72 Outboard wing pylon
73 Aileron control linkage
74 Port wing integral fuel tank
75 190gal (864lit) drop tank
76 Rear (hot stream) swivelling exhaust nozzle
77 Inboard wing pylon
78 Mainwheels
79 Pressure refuelling connection
80 Ammunition tank
81 Main undercarriage hydraulic jack
82 30-mm Aden cannon
83 Fuselage flank fuel tank
84 Forward (fan air) swivelling exhaust nozzle
85 Engine monitoring and recording equipment
86 Ventral gun pod, port and starboard
87 Hydraulic-system ground connectors
88 Forward fuselage fuel tank
89 Rolls-Royce Pegasus Mk 104 vectoring-thrust turbofan
90 Supplementary air-intake doors, free floating
91 Nosewheel
92 Landing/taxiing lamp
93 Nosewheel hydraulic jack
94 Hydraulic accumulator
95 Boundary-layer bleed air duct
96 Pitot head
97 Radar hand controller
98 Ejection-seat rocket pack
99 Engine throttle and nozzle control levers
100 Doppler radar
101 Radar scanner
102 Radome, folded to port
103 Ferranti Blue Fox radar

31 Rear fuselage fuel tank
32 Emergency ram-air turbine
33 Turbine release control
34 Equipment bay air-conditioning system
35 HF aerial tuner
36 HF notch aerial
37 Starboard all-moving tailplane
38 Rudder control linkage
39 Total-temperature probe
40 Forward radar warning receiver
41 VHF aerial
42 Rudder
43 Rudder trim tab
44 Yaw control RCV
45 Rear radar warning receiver
46 Pitch control RCV

47 Port all-moving tailplane
48 Tail bumper
49 Radar altimeter aerials
50 Tailplane power unit
51 UHF aerial
52 Control system linkages
53 Twin batteries
54 Chaff and flare dispensers
55 Avionics equipment racks
56 Airbrake hydraulic jack
57 Liquid-oxygen converter
58 Hydraulic-system nitrogen pressurising bottle
59 Airbrake
60 Fuel jettison
61 Aileron power unit
62 Port aileron
63 Aileron RCV mechanical linkage

like the new ships, delayed by industrial unrest and other factors quite unconnected with the aircraft itself. The original build standard had been discussed in 1972, but it was not finalized until after the go-ahead in 1975.

Almost all the changes were confined to the front end, which was completely redesigned. Apart from this the main differences were: substitution of aluminium alloy for magnesium or Mg-Zr alloy to avoid sea-water corrosion (the only items not changed were the nose and outrigger wheels and the engine gearbox); a 4in (100mm) increase in fin height, mainly from building in the RWR as an extra section; addition of an emergency wheel-brake system; various system changes, including a liquid oxygen converter of a different make; addition of lashing lugs to the nose gear; increase in tailplane nose-up travel by 2°; increase in wingtip RCV roll power for use in turbulent ship wakes; and a switch to the Mk 104 engine, still a Pegasus 11 but with complete anti-corrosion protection and an uprated gearbox drive for a 15kVA alternator to supply the greater electrical loads. To facilitate checking engine thrust prior to launch it was planned to add a hold-back link to the main gear, secured to a hydraulic snubber below deck and severed by the pilot via a release button on the nozzle lever, but this was never fitted.

Above: The family relationship imparted by Sir Sydney Camm is obvious as one of Yeovilton's Hunter T.8M Blue Fox radar trainers formates with a Sea Harrier of 899 Sqn. Every Sea Harrier pilot trains on the Yeovilton T.8Ms.

The aircraft nose, however, is totally new, and aesthetically vastly improved. The chief alterations are addition of a multimode radar, installation of a totally different nav/attack system, and accommodation of the extra avionics and cockpit panels by raising the entire cockpit 11in (279mm), which automatically improves pilot view. Cockpit displays were completely redesigned.

Never before had so much mission capability been built into so small an aircraft, and this is combined with the ability to operate from almost any warship, in any weather, with only one man on board and with no external assistance or ground power supplies. The avionics were therefore a major challenge, and the result has proved to be an excellent compromise that has scarcely needed any alteration.

Blue Fox radar
As it is by far the largest sensor, the radar can be dealt with first. Ferranti was the logical supplier, because of its major involvement with the RAF Harrier and its work on the P.1154 radar. In fact the Blue Fox radar was derived more nearly from the Seaspray fitted to Navy Lynx helicopters, but considerably augmented. Operating in I-band, it is a neat modular 186lb (84kg) package, aircooled and installed in a nose which hinges 180° to the left to reduce aircraft length. There are four main mission operating modes: search, with a B-type (sector) scan, PPI, multi-bar (raster) or single scan; attack, with intercept and lead/pursuit or chase in the air-combat mission, and weapon-aiming via the HUD in anti-ship or surface attack; boresight, for quick ranging on targets of opportunity; and xpdr (transponder) for immediate identification of friendly targets. Two two-seat Hunters were rebuilt as T.8M radar trials aircraft, later serving with a third conversion as Sea Harrier radar trainers at Yeovilton. A P.1127(RAF), XV277, was flown in 1974 with a metal mock-up nose. While this was satisfactory aerodynamically, it would not have been adequate to house the desired radar dish. This was the factor that drove the Kingston designers to adopt the raised cockpit configuration.

Left: One of the first ski-jump takeoffs by a Sea Harrier FRS.1 in early 1980 from the newly commissioned HMS Invincible, whose ramp is limited to 7° by the location of the Sea Dart SAM launcher (seen, unloaded, on the left). The aircraft has two tanks and three practice bomb carriers.

The nav/attack system installed in the Sea Harrier bears little resemblance to that of the Harrier. It reflects the ship-based environment, which, for example, imposes inertial alignment problems, and the unusual spread of missions. Two digital computers are used, one 20k (20,000 words) WAC (weapon-aiming computer) associated with the HUD and used to provide symbology and weapon-aiming graphics, and an 8k navigation computer which ties together that series of equipments and feeds a nav control/display panel on the right console. Navigation inputs come from: a Ferranti all-attitude TGP (twin-gyro platform) which, while avoiding most INS problems, provides a continuous measure of aircraft attitude and acceleration; a Decca 72 doppler radar and Sperry flux valve, which provide independent ground speed and heading inputs and monitor the TGP; and Tacan, UHF homing, an I-band transponder and an ADC (air-data computer). Even at sea the system takes only 2min to align, and provides: present position as a lat/long or tactical grid reference; range, bearing, course-to-steer and time to any of ten waypoints (any of which can be assigned a velocity, because it might be a ship); estimates of time remaining on task, derived from fuel contents and flow-meter readings; range/bearing to a Tacan station or an offset position; groundspeed/track and wind-speed and direction; and immediate update by pilot input by overflying a known waypoint, radar fix or Tacan.

An improved cockpit

Designing the cockpit to accommodate an exceptional amount of display information in a small space was a real challenge, but it has proved popular with pilots and very easy to learn. Thanks to the raised position, the side consoles are wider than in the Harrier, yet more panel space has also been provided ahead. The latest miniaturized displays are used, examples being the row of CWS (centralized warning system) lights around the coaming. The HUD is newer than that of the GR.3, with a larger display linked to the programmable computer interfacing with numerous weapon-aiming and navaid equipments. On return to the ship the approach and landing are assisted by MEL Madge (microwave aircraft digital guidance

Above: British Aerospace Dynamics is now in production with the Sea Eagle long-range anti-ship missile, two early examples of which were flown on the first Sea Harrier, XZ438, during carry trials in 1981.

equipment) which can feed through the WAC to the HUD. The main radar display is to the right, and the pilot has a hand controller at the rear on the left console.

Not only does the seat's elevated position give a better all-round view, but the canopy is bulged at the sides. View to the rear compares favourably with that in most other fighters, and with gear extended the pilot can look across the inlet ducts and check the outrigger gears, which cannot be seen in a GR.3. The seat itself is the latest Martin-Baker type, the Mk 10H, one of the rocket-assisted zero/zero variety (usable at zero height and zero airspeed), and its main parachute is deployed in 1·5s, compared with 2.25s for the Mk 9D of the GR.3. Ahead of the flat bulletproof windscreen is a yaw vane, centred instead of offset as in the GR.3, and the reconnaissance and strike camera is relocated to look out of the right side of the nose. Another addition is a radar

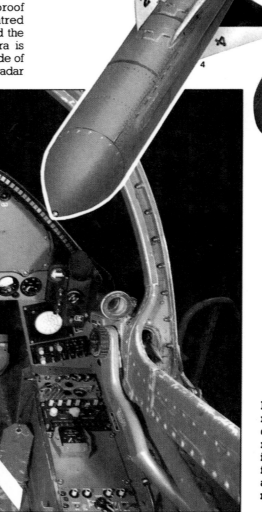

Left: A Sea Harrier cockpit. On the right side of the main panel the radar display (here blanked off for security reasons) replaces the engine/fuel instruments of the GR.3, and basic flight instruments occupy the central area which in the GR.3 is filled by the moving-map display.

British Aerospace Sea Harrier FRS.1

Below: Artwork showing stores normally carried by the Sea Harrier. Item No 8, the reconnaissance pod, could easily be carried, as it is by RAF Harriers, but is not currently required by the Royal Navy. Several other stores could readily be cleared for use.

1 Matra 550 Magic AAM (used by Indian Navy)
2 AIM-9L Sidewinder AAM
3 AIM-9B Sidewinder AAM
4 Sea Eagle ASM
5 Harpoon ASM
6 100gal tank (190gal, 864lit, is now used)
7 Lepus flare
8 Reconnaissance pod
9 30mm Aden gun pod
10 30mm ammunition
11 1,000lb (454kg) GP bomb
12 Matra retarded bomb
13 ML twin carrier with Matra 155 launchers
14 RN 2in (50·8mm) rocket launcher
15 BL.755 cluster bomb

Above: Three-view drawing of a BAe Sea Harrier FRS.1. The position of the nosecone containing the Blue Fox radar main unit when folded back is shown in dotted outline.

Right: Elements of the Ferranti Blue Fox multimode radar, with the mechanically steered aerial (antenna) mounted in its yellow transport cradle. In front are the cockpit push-button and pistol-grip hand controllers.

Below: A selection of stores carried by Sea Harriers. Inboard wing stations have a maximum capacity of 2,000lb (907kg), twice that of the outboard stations.

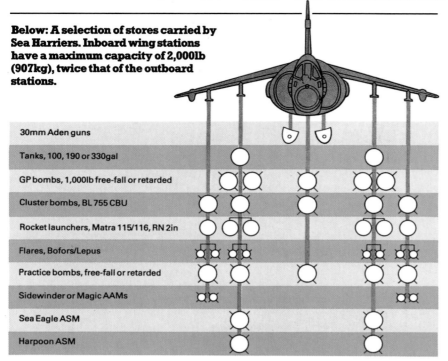

- 30mm Aden guns
- Tanks, 100, 190 or 330gal
- GP bombs, 1,000lb free-fall or retarded
- Cluster bombs, BL 755 CBU
- Rocket launchers, Matra 115/116, RN 2in
- Flares, Bofors/Lepus
- Practice bombs, free-fall or retarded
- Sidewinder or Magic AAMs
- Sea Eagle ASM
- Harpoon ASM

altimeter, with display prominent on the main primary panel fed by aerials recessed in the ventral fin similar to those of the AV-8C.

RWR and armament generally is the same as for the GR.3, though the pylons were strengthened. Weapons, however, have always been different and more diverse, including Sidewinder AAMs, RN 2in (50·8mm) rocket pods and anti-ship missiles. No wiring is provided for a reconnaissance pod.

The original plan was to go ahead with the 24 production aircraft, but in May 1978 the plan was changed, ten additional Sea Harriers being ordered and the first three being earmarked as special trials aircraft (XZ438-440). Because of the complexity of their instrumentation, these aircraft were overtaken by XZ450, the first of what had become 31 production aircraft, and despite delays due to industrial unrest this flew in its primer paint on 20 August 1978. Two weeks later, in Fleet Air Arm livery, it did ski jumps from a new 15° sagging-catenary ramp built by Royal Engineers at the Farnborough airshow using standard Fairey MGB (medium girder bridge) components. The first instrumented aircraft, XZ438, flew on 30 December 1978, and subsequent progress was rapid. XZ451, with Modex number 100, was delivered to RNAS Yeovilton on 18 June 1979, the IFTU (Intensive Flying Trials Unit), No 700A Sqn, commissioned there on 19 September, and a month later an extremely successful sea trials programme was flown from HMS Hermes in the Irish Sea.

Subsequently 700A became 899 Harrier HQ Sqn, with Nos 800 and 801 Sqns as the combat units, the plan being to assign one to each Command Cruiser: Invincible, Illustrious and Ark Royal. By sheer chance it was decided to retain the old carrier Hermes for Sea Harrier training, despite a decision to send her to the breakers' yard in 1982 on the commissioning of Illustrious. After much argument it was decided to carry out a refit in late 1979 and fit her with a 12° ski ramp. How momentous this narrow decision would be, could not be dreamed of.

Overseas sales

Subsequent RN work-up of the Sea Harriers is discussed in the next chapter. Meanwhile, navies around the world continued to watch the progress of these unique aircraft with growing interest. India remained at the top of the list of serious potential customers, and Australia planned to buy HMS Invincible in 1983 (though remaining undecided about fast V/STOL jets). The first customer to follow the RN's lead did, in fact, turn out to be India, which had long used Hawker (Armstrong Whitworth) Sea Hawks from INS Vikrant. In July 1972 John Farley flew the company demo two-seater, G-VTOL, to give requested demonstrations from the ageing carrier despite the 30°C steamy monsoon atmosphere. Farley flew 22 times in two days, and, when he left, the Indian Navy was totally sold on this amazing aircraft. It placed an order for six Sea Harrier Mk 51 single-seaters, and two two-seat Mk 60s, for delivery in 1983.

During the Falklands war the Indian

Left: XZ492 of No 800 Sqn flying over HMS Hermes in 1981, with AIM-9B Sidewinders, tanks and guns. At that time Hermes was earmarked for immediate scrapping; nobody could foresee how vital she would later be.

Navy team at British Aerospace watched for a sudden speed-up on their aircraft, indicating that they were being rushed through for delivery to the Royal Navy instead. This never happened, and the first Mk 51, bearing the white tiger badge of No 300 Squadron, was handed over at Dunsfold on 27 January 1983. Pilots and ground staff were trained at Yeovilton before the first FRS.51s flew out to *Vikrant* in late-1983. Differences between the Mk 51 and the RN FRS.1 are minor; for example a gaseous oxygen system is fitted, and the AAM is the Matra Magic.

Today the Sea Harrier is a formidable and exceptionally versatile warplane, and it has been proved so in exceptionally tough circumstances. The original Harrier FRS.1 has been updated, and the BAe/Marconi Blue Vixen multi-mode pulse-Doppler radar, which has Track-While-Scan, Multiple Target Sort, and

Above: XZ457, aircraft "713" of 899 Sqn at Yeovilton, destroyed two Mirages and a Skyhawk but is seen here over Somerset in company with a newly-acquired Harrier T.4(RN), the Royal Navy's two-seat trainer version.

Right: Had all Sea Harrier FRS 2s been new-build aircraft, the radar nose would have been more shapely, and its wing rather larger. But, as many were converted from the FRS.1, this was not possible.

Threat Prioritization, now gives BVR capability with four AM-120 AMRAAM missiles, rather than the Sidewinders that were its initial armament. This makes it a hunter rather than a defender. Other updates include MFDs and HOTAS controls. Other air-to-air weaponry includes ASRAAM, and twin 30mm cannon pods.

Left: Now intensively used by the Indian Navy's No 300 Sqn, IN601, the first Sea Harrier FRS.51, is seen here in primer paint and temporary SBAC registration G-9-478 on its first flight on 6 August 1982. A month later it was at the Farnborough Air Show (see above).

Above: Externally there are few differences between the Indian Navy FRS.51 and the regular FRS.1, apart from the white tiger badge of 300 Sqn. Internally a gaseous oxygen system is fitted, and the Indian Navy's AAM is the Matra 550 Magic.

Operation Corporate

The recovery of the Falkland Islands from the occupying forces of Argentina was quite unlike any other campaign in the history of human conflict. Operation Corporate was mounted at very short notice, and involved all the armed forces of the Crown in a land/sea/air war utterly unlike anything for which those forces had been trained, and in a remote and inhospitable part of the globe some 4,000 miles from the nearest friendly base! The success of the entire operation depended upon the Sea Harrier, later joined by the RAF Harrier, both of which at the start were unproven weapon systems.

The refusal of a group of Argentine scrap-metal dealers to leave British territory on South Georgia gave a clue that a direct confrontation was possible, and on 31 March 1982 Admiral Sir John Fieldhouse RN, who had just returned to Britain from Exercise Springtrain in the Mediterranean, was ordered to begin preparing Task Force 317, of which he was to be overall Commander. Indeed, he had ordered Rear-Admiral "Sandy" Woodward to prepare a detachment before he left Gibraltar. Immediately plans were put into action involving all the fighting services.

Crucial to the possible retaking of the islands was airpower, because Argentina possessed powerful fighter and attack brigades within both its air force and naval aviation. Thanks to the decision of the British government in 1966 there was no seagoing British airpower whatsoever, except for the small force of Sea Harriers, which had barely settled down and whose pilots were mostly inexperienced. Even this force had only come into existence in the teeth of opposition from defence officials and the Treasury.

At RNAS Yeovilton, Somerset, were the three Sea Harrier squadrons: 800 (Lt-Cdr Andy Auld), 801 (Lt-Cdr Nigel Ward) and the HQ unit 899 (Lt-Cdr Tony Ogilvy). To make things more difficult, 801 were on leave on the day of mobilization (2 April) and 800 were due to go on leave at mid-day! Each had an establishment of five aircraft, but 899 was split up to augment the two first-line squadrons, so that on 5 April, with spare aircraft added to the establishment, HMS Hermes, the Task Force flagship, sailed from Portsmouth with 11 Sea Harriers of 800 Sqn which had landed on an already

Above: An aircraft of No 800 Sqn on the slippery deck of Hermes in a force 10 gale. In the background are the flagship's "goalkeeper" (Broadsword) and, on the skyline, Invincible.

overcrowded deck, and a few miles out a 12th landed on. The brand-new HMS Invincible was almost as crowded, and among her air units was 801 Sqn with eight aircraft. Among the mountains of stores, all loaded in less than three days but which were to sustain a campaign lasting three months, were the newest and best Sidewinder AAMs, the AIM-9L. Not previously used by the RN, though in production by a European industrial group, AIM-9L has a completely new guidance system, more powerful control fins and a high-power warhead.

The unknown quantity

Thus, from the start, the Task Force had a small air component equipped with a unique aircraft which, though it was rela-

tively new and untested in battle, promised to be outstandingly versatile. In particular, it was expected to be able to intercept and destroy attacking Argentine aircraft, including the Mach 2 Mirage and Dagger – all are called Mirages here, for simplicity – which in low-level attack are extremely subsonic. By an accident of geography the Falklands are at such a distance from the several large mainland airbases that, while low-level attacks by the Argentine aircraft were perfectly capable of being

Above: Unusually approaching from dead astern, a Sea Harrier recovers aboard Hermes at twilight. One Sidewinder has been fired, but tanks are retained. All touchdowns are vertical.

mounted, there would not be a lot of fuel to spare, especially if afterburner was used. At the same time, the Task Force was going to stand off at a considerable distance, and the Sea Harriers likewise were not going to have much time on station either. Not least, the Argentine aircraft were several times more numerous. Put another way, the total embarked force of 20 British fixed-wing aircraft was so small that even a single combat loss was going to be significant.

At an early stage it was clear that more aircraft would be needed. There were other Sea Harriers and pilots, and there were also the Harriers of the RAF, and preparations were made to bring as many into the South Atlantic as the two flat-top ships could accommodate. Lt-Cdr Gedge was ordered to form a third Sea Harrier squadron, and he immediately located Sea Harriers at Boscombe, Dunsfold and other locations, though none was in front-line condition and almost all were in various stages of refit, rebuild, special trials or still being completed by the maker. All were urgently hurried through to the latest combat-ready state – without, incidentally, commandeering a single one of the FRS.51 aircraft building for the Indian Navy. Lt-Cdr Gedge just managed to scrape together an adequate number of Sea Harrier pilots, including some on exchange posting in Australia and the USA. By April 30 Gedge had formed 809 Sqn, though he had to import two RAF

Below: This profile shows XV787, first flown on 9 September 1970 and heavily engaged on combat missions with 1(F) Sqn in the Falklands in 1982. Note the chin transponder and Paveway LGB.

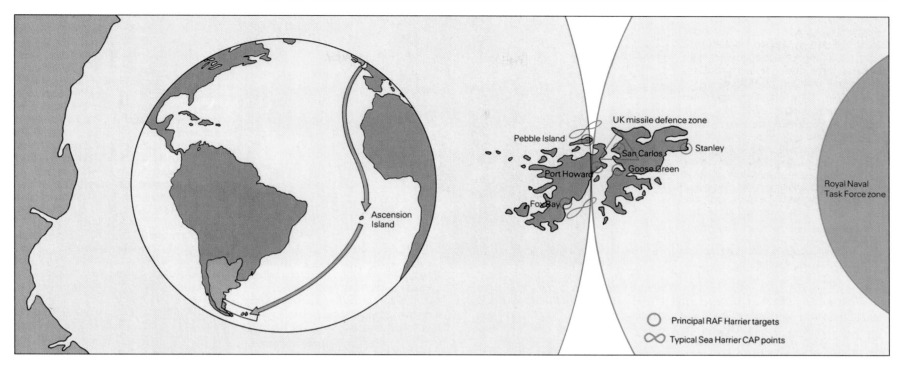

Above: An overall idea of the geography is provided by these two maps, one of the globe superimposed on a larger-scale map of the Falklands. The former emphasizes the colossal distance from Britain, as far as New York to New Zealand. The local map shows a 400 nautical mile radius from Argentina in red and a 200 nm radius from the Task Force in blue.

Right: Sea Harrier XZ498 of No 800 Sqn makes a VL aboard *Illustrious* in Falklands waters in 1983. During the war she served with 801 on *Invincible*.

Harrier pilots who had Lightning interceptor experience, and he also had to leave two aircraft behind to carry on essential development and training.

The eight aircraft of the new squadron were to a slightly later standard than other Sea Harriers, and they later had twin Sidewinder launchers and 190gal (864lit) tanks. They were factory-painted in a shade of light "barley" grey which RAE experts calculated would blend in best with winter South Atlantic environments. The other squadrons had left Britain painted in standard dark sea grey with white undersides, with bold unit insignia on the tails. Clearly they had to be toned down for warfare, and the decision was taken to paint the undersides the same colour as the top, to apply Type B (red/blue) roundels and low-contrast black serial number and Modex numbers, and no other markings. The repainting was done on the journey south. *Invincible*'s modern air-conditioning enabled spray-painting to be used, but in *Hermes* 800 Sqn had to be laboriously painted by hand.

Back at Yeovilton No 809 readied itself for combat, the two hijacked RAF pilots quickly learning how to use the Blue Fox radar and launch over a ski jump. The flight-refuelling probes were fitted, and on 31 April/1 May the whole squadron flew out to Ascension Island. All aircraft refuelled a total of 14 times from Victors, though few pilots had ever made an AAR (air/air refuelling) contact before. As in all such deployments the objective was to keep all tanks nearly filled, so that, if the next refuelling were to fail for any reason, the aircraft could still fly to a friendly airbase. At Ascension the newly formed squadron parked awaiting a ship, and every possible crevice and hole was taped over to keep out the wind-blown volcanic grit and sand.

By Easter, 3 April, the decision had been taken to commit RAF No 1 Sqn (W/C Peter Squire), with the Harrier GR.3, but in this case much remained to be done. The prime mission was expected to be air defence, for which the RAF Harrier units were initially neither trained nor equipped. Many aircraft modifications were required, and as with the RN units the situation was compounded by the squadron's planned imminent departure for a major exercise in Canada. S/L Bob Iveson, a No 1 Sqn flight commander, was sent to Liverpool to study a large and fast container ship, *Atlantic Conveyor*, and report on her suitability as a Harrier ferry. It was clear she could carry the aircraft as deck cargo, but no flying would appear possible, and there were major problems with personnel accommodation.

She had been laid-up at Liverpool, but was quickly readied, and while still at Liverpool a Sea Harrier carried out deck trials; but she had to sail, jammed with stores, on 23 April without any fixed-wing aircraft aboard. By this time the Harriers, 14 in number, had already been substantially modified. The largest task was to insert along the wings the wiring for Sidewinders on the outer pylons. Launch rails for these missiles were added, and the complete installation was tested with live firings from Llanbedr on the Aberporth range. In the interest of ordnance commonality the aircraft was cleared to use the RN rocket launcher, housing 36 rockets of 2in (50·4mm) calibre instead of the usual RAF Matra 115 which takes 18 (or 19 if the centre tube is used) of 68mm. Another new weapon cleared in a hurry was the Mk 13/18 Paveway II LGB (laser-guided bomb), which was thought to be particularly appropriate to the GR.3 since this aircraft has a compatible 10·6 micron laser. Under the nose a blister appeared covering a transponder added to enhance the GR.3's response to the ship aircraft direction radars. Also to be cleared for use were the big 330gal (1500lit) drop tanks, which were to be needed on the long flight south.

A "marinised" GR.3
Apart from these modifications, all the GR.3s were put through an environmental protection programme, as many holes and joints as possible being sealed to prevent salt-water ingress even if waves were to break over the aircraft. Where ingestion could not be prevented, new drain holes were provided. Lashing-down lugs were added to the outrigger gears, and other changes were made to facilitate shipboard operation. Meanwhile, Ferranti Ltd had worked around the clock updating Finrae (Ferranti inertial rapid-alignment equipment) to ready the GR.3's INS immediately prior to each mission. The trolley-mounted package was based on the FIN 1064 (updated Jaguar) INS, and continuously provided north and horizontal references over long periods. Three Finraes were flown to Ascension and taken aboard *Atlantic Conveyor*, and the final software program was sent via communications satellite direct to the South Atlantic.

It had been planned for each pilot of No 1 Sqn to qualify by making three takeoffs over the ski ramp at Yeovilton, but it was evident after a few attempts that there was "nothing to it", and a single launch apiece was sufficient. Close air combat was another matter, and every pilot put in intensive DACT (dissimilar

Above: A tradesman of RAF No 1(F) Sqn together with the pilot use the Finrae to align the inertial platform of a Harrier GR.3 prior to a sortie from HMS *Hermes* in May 1982. The Sea Harrier in the rear had different navaids and did not need Finrae.

Below: *Atlantic Conveyor* steaming south in early May 1982, with six Harriers and eight Sea Harriers. Only the former really needed the protective bags, and one Sea Harrier of 809 was parked fully fuelled and armed on the bow spot.

air-combat training), including air combat against Mirages of l'Armée de l'Air and Super Etendards of l'Aéronavale. Then the first group of nine Harriers flew from Wittering to St Mawgan, Cornwall, and from there went on to Ascension on 3-5 May. Each was met five times by Victors, the procedures again providing for diversion to a friendly base should the next AAR fail to top up because of malfunction. Typical flight time was 9h 15min, easily a record for any Harrier in RAF service. Not for the first time the RAF resolved to rethink the traditional "relief tube" and rubber bottle, with a Velcro slit in the immersion suit.

At Ascension three of the aircraft were temporarily commandeered to provide local air defence. The other six air-taxied across to the moored *Atlantic Conveyor*, each making a VL on the newly added VTOL spot in the bows, then turning aft and taxiing down a narrow canyon left between walls of two-high containers – which provided the only protection against the sea – to a

marshalled spot, where the aircraft were parked and wrapped in Driclad envelopes. Few of the pilots had been aboard a ship before. The ship also took aboard the eight Sea Harriers of 809 Sqn, and various helicopters. The final Sea Harrier was parked at readiness on the VTOL spot, for local defence. On 18 May *Atlantic Conveyor* passed lat 52°S and closed with the Task Force, whereupon the GR.3s, freed from their garments, air-taxied across to *Hermes*. This time their pilots experienced a deck pitching and rolling in what were soon to be recognized as normal South Atlantic conditions. Meanwhile 809 put six aircraft on *Hermes* and two on *Invincible*, though later this squadron had four on each ship as planned.

In late May five more GR.3s, completing No 1's total of 14, were flown out to Ascension. Four were taken aboard the *Contender Bezant*, a Ro-Ro ship whose conversion had caused major problems. The remaining aircraft, plus the three now released from defending Ascension, flew all the way south to the Task

Force, one pair on 1 June and the other pair on 8 June. This time the landlubber pilots viewed 4,000 miles (6440km) of cold ocean with anxiety. There was no question of there being any possibility of diversion to any land base whatsoever, and for the last 800 nautical miles (1500km) they were entirely alone, and though they could use Tacan they had to preserve radio silence. To cap it all, one pair arrived on the deck of *Hermes* in the middle of an Argentine air attack.

On its way south the original Task Force had launched CAPs (combat air patrols) with increasing frequency. These ranged out as far as 120 miles (193km), usually to the south-west, and as the TEZ (the 200-mile, 322km Total Exclusion Zone) was approached a lot of flying was done at night. In any case, with the onset of winter, daylight gradually shortened to a narrow band between about 1100 and 1730 local time, and weather progressively worsened. Much of the hardest action, in late May and June, took place with gale-force winds, mountainous seas, and everything on

deck being covered in condensation which froze at night. Towards the middle of June it snowed heavily. For much of the time cloud base was at 200ft (90m) and occasionally it was half this, with visibility typically being half a mile (800m) with high winds. Under these conditions the Harriers and Sea Harriers experienced no special difficulty, whereas conventional carrier-based aircraft in a similar situation would not have been able to fly at all.

Meeting the "Argies"
Contact with what had become the enemy was made on 25 April when a Sea Harrier of 801 intercepted an FAA (Fuerza Aérea Argentina) 707 on long-range reconnaissance looking for the Task Force. It was outside the TEZ and, the rules of engagement at that time being restrictive, it was not attacked.

The first combat missions were flown by 12 aircraft from *Hermes* at dawn on 1 May. With top cover provided by 801 from *Invincible*, nine Sea Harriers made a carefully planned low-level attack on Port Stanley airfield, which had been bombed on the previous night by a Vulcan. The first four came in at 520kt (963km/h) at 100ft (30m) with variously fuzed 1,000lb (454kg) bombs to hit the SAM and gun defences, attacking in a forwards toss. This went well, the air-burst weapons being seen to explode directly over their targets. Four of the other five aircraft each had three BL.755 cluster bombs, for use against aircraft and support areas, while the fifth had three 1,000lb (454kg) with contact fuzes. All aircraft also had two tanks and the

gun pods. Despite intense ground fire, only one aircraft was hit, taking a 20mm shell through the fin. The holes were quickly repaired with Speedtape (adhesive-backed aluminium tape). The three other Sea Harriers from *Hermes* hit Goose Green, again encountering intense hostile fire.

During the daylight hours of 1 May, several pairs of Sea Harriers encountered Argentine Mirages and Daggers, many of which launched AAMs. For the most part these were elderly Matra 530s, which fell short without posing a threat, but an Israeli-built Shafrir forced pilot Martin Hale of 800 Sqn to take hard evasive action before it broke lock. Earlier, Nigel "Sharkey" Ward, CO of 801 Sqn, had intercepted three T-34C Turbo-Mentors, forcing them to jettison their bombs and escape into cloud. Following them, Sharkey almost collided with one, missing it by a few feet.

The first Sea Harrier success of the day came during the afternoon when Paul Barton and Steve Thomas encountered two Mirages. Barton manoeuvred into the vital six o'clock position and launched a Sidewinder, destroying the Mirage of Carlos Perona. Meanwhile Thomas launched a Sidewinder at the leading Mirage. Its pilot, Garcia Cuerva, broke hard towards cloud, but the missile followed and detonated close by. Badly damaged, and streaming fuel from perforated tanks, Cuerva sought sanctuary at Port Stanley, only to be shot down by "friendly" ground fire. Further successes followed that day: a Dagger fell to Bertie Penfold of 800 Sqn, and a Canberra to Al Curtiss of 801 Sqn.

Left: On 8 June 1982 Marshall of Cambridge flew the first C.1(K) tanker version of the RAF Hercules, which can operate from Stanley. Here a "Herc tanker" refuels an RAF Harrier GR.3 over the South Atlantic in 1983.

Below: Hosing down the flight deck of the Task Force flagship shortly after the Argentine surrender, when the worst of the blizzards were over. In the theatre all Sea Harriers on *Hermes* were administered by 800 Sqn.

Harrier Force Deployed

Sea Harrier	Harrier GR.3	Method of Transit
12	0	Embarked in UK, HMS *Hermes*
8	0	Embarked in UK, HMS *Invincible*
8	6	Flown UK to Ascension Island, embarked *Atlantic Conveyor*
0	4	Flown UK to Ascension Island, flown to 52°S, vertical landing on HMS *Hermes*
28	**10**	**Total**
0	4	Flown UK to Ascension Island, embarked *Contender Bezant*, flown off to Port Stanley having arrived after ceasefire

Harrier Force Missions

Sorties	2,000+ South of Ascension Island
	1,650 within Total Exclusion Zone
Combat Missions	**Sea Harrier:**
	1,100+ CAP sorties
	90 offensive support
	GR.3:
	125 ground attack and tactical reconnaissance
Flying Rate	approx 55 hours/aircraft/month
	up to 10 sorties/aircraft/day
	3-4 sorties/pilot/day
	up to 10 hours/day in cockpit
Pilot/aircraft ratio	1.2 initially
	1.4 later
Aircraft availability at beginning of each day	95%
Operational loss rate/sortie	0.38%
Overall loss rate/sortie	0.61%
Known successful ejection attempts	100%

Harrier Force Losses

Reason	Sea Harrier	Harrier GR.3
Air-to-Air combat	0	0
Ground Defences	2	3
Slid off deck	1	0
Hit sea after take-off	1	0
Collided or flew into sea	2	0
Total	**6**	**3**

Having established a measure of superiority, it was three weeks before the Sea Harrier added to its air combat account.

Few days were to be as busy as this, and losses began with Lt Nick Taylor, who was killed by AAA at Goose Green on 4 May. By mid-May the Sea Harriers had completely covered the islands with photo reconnaissance, and on 20 May the first RAF Harriers also got into action. The pilots of No 1 Sqn were, on the whole, far more experienced in low-level attack missions, and though they had looked forward to flying air defence sorties, the Royal Navy took the view that this was best left to the Sea Harriers. It was therefore decided that the GR.3s should be rewired to carry offensive stores outboard and they subsequently took over most of the low-level attack and reconnaissance, leaving the Sea Harriers to fly CAP and other air-defence duties.

GR.3s join in

Prior to the arrival of the GR.3s, the Sea Harrier pilots had decided to fly attack missions by day and night using a mix of medium level bombing and low-level tosses. The RAF Harriers worked almost exclusively at the lowest possible level, and, because even with the help of the surviving Finrae (two went down with the sunk *Atlantic Conveyor*) navigational accuracies could not quite equal those achieved with stationary alignment on an airfield, it was decided to navigate and attack visually wherever possible.

The first mission by No 1 Sqn, tasked on 20 May, was a strike against fuel and oil dumps at Fox Bay. Led by the CO, with both his flight commanders, S/Ls Bob Iveson and Jerry Pook, the tight formation made a single pass at low level straight over the target and used BL.755 CBUs (cluster bomb units). There were many secondary explosions, culminating in a giant fireball. Subsequently the GR.3s flew 125 sorties on attack and reconnaissance, the latter using the centreline pod. Three aircraft were lost, all due to ground defensive fire, which was usually intense and caused so much aircraft damage as to depress serviceability below the amazing figure of "above 99.9 per cent" set by the Sea Harriers.

The three losses were: XZ963, 21 May, hit by Blowpipe missile at Goose Green,

Above: Flying practice continued on the journey south in April 1982. Ready for the first real mission aboard *Hermes* are 1,000lb retarded bombs, AIM-9Ls and Mk 46 AS torpedoes for the ship's Sea King HAS.5 helicopters.

F/Lt Jeffrey Glover ejected and captured (the only British PoW); XZ998, 27 May, hit by two large-calibre shells when at high speed at below 100ft supporting 2 Para near Goose Green, S/L Iveson losing flight control and hydraulic pressure, the aircraft then catching fire, arresting dive by vectoring nozzles but finally having to eject, evading capture and being picked up by Royal Marine flying Army Gazelle over two days later; XZ972, 30 May, after flying through heavy fire on 19 previous missions took several hits at low level when attacking a helicopter landing site west of Stanley and began losing fuel rapidly, and though S/L Pook thought his chance of survival poor because of loss of radio he was in fact accompanied by his wingman who had alerted *Hermes*, and when Pook ejected 45 miles (72km) short of the ship he actually heard the

Sea King that was waiting to collect him.

Pook was only off operations for one day, because of a stiff neck, and in the closing stages he was one of the GR.3 pilots to use smart LGBs against difficult point targets. The hills around Port Stanley enabled all such attacks to be made behind cover, the Harrier approaching on the far side of Mounts Harriet, Tumbledown, or Two Sisters and lobbing the weapon in a toss over the summit. On two occasions the FAC (forward air controller) fired the Ferranti designator too soon and the LGB failed to achieve lock, but on all other FAC-designated smart attacks there was a direct hit. This weapon would have been valuable on many earlier attacks, almost all of which were against small targets that were exceedingly difficult to locate, but it might have been difficult to set up a friendly designator and a good launch trajectory. On at least one occasion, over Stanley airfield, an LGB failed to lock-on when designated by a GR.3's own laser. On some occasions attacks on heavily defended point targets were made at just above ground level by groups of

GR.3s directed by a Sea Harrier overhead at much higher altitude who could see the target and send minor course changes.

In the whole of Operation Corporate the RN Sea Harriers flew 2,376 missions for a total of 2,675·4 hours. Seldom, if ever, has so much depended on so few aircraft. Despite the appalling weather, aircraft averaged 55 hours per month, flying 6 to 10 sorties per day. It was common for pilots to fly two combat missions without leaving the cockpit, and the serviceability never fell below 95 per cent. HMS *Invincible*'s aircraft flew 99.97 per cent of the tasked sorties, losing only

Sea Harrier Air Combat Victories

Victim	AIM-9L Sidewinder	30mm cannon	Total
Mirage/Dagger	11	0	11
Skyhawk	7	1 1/2 [1]	8 1/2
Canberra	1	0	1
Pucara	0	1	1
Hercules	1/2	1/2	1
Puma helo	0	0	1 [2]

[1] Shared with ground fire
[2] Crashed while evading

Destroyed on ground

By Sea Harrier

Victim	30mm cannon	CBU	Total
A-109 helo	2	0	2
Islander	0	1	1
Pucara	0	1	1
Puma helo	0	1	1

By Harrier GR.3

Chinook helo	1	0	1
Puma helo	2	1	3

Range varies with payload and flight profile

part of one sortie through unserviceability. Operations continued at a high intensity in conditions far below peacetime limits, and were assisted by local extensions given to various component lives, including the complete engine, and by allowing interchange between Harrier and Sea Harrier engines and fuel system components.

After the shock of meeting the Sea Harrier on 1 May, the Argentine FAA and CANA (naval air arm) avoided any clash with "the Black Death" for three weeks. Despite this, there was no let-up in round-the-clock CAPs, and sadly two aircraft, XZ452 and 453, flown by Lt-Cdr John Eyton-Jones and Lt Alan Curtis, disappeared on 6 May while on CAP in very bad weather; almost certainly they collided in cloud. On 24 May ZA192 hit the sea shortly after takeoff on a stormy night, Lt-Cdr G. W. J. Batt being killed. On 29 May ZA174 slid off the rolling icy deck of HMS *Invincible* while moving forward for the next takeoff; Lt-Cdr Mike Broadwater ejected and was picked up by a Sea King. The sixth and last loss was on 1 June when 801's air-warfare instructor, F/Lt Ian Mortimer, RAF, was shot down by a SAM while at 15,000ft (4572m) in XZ456. Mortimer was snatched from under the noses of the enemy in an amazing night search/rescue mission lasting nine hours.

A lull in Argentine air activity followed. On 9 May two Sea Harriers of 800 Sqn took off to attack Port Stanley

airfield, only to find it socked in with cloud. As they turned away, they picked up a radar contact about 60nm (111km) out to sea. On investigating, they found the intelligence trawler Narwal and attacked it with bombs and cannon fire. It sank next day. A week later, the Argentine supply ships *Bahìa Buen Suceso* and *Rio Carcaraña* were abandoned after being bombed and strafed by Sea Harriers of 800 Sqn. Then on 22 May the patrol boat *Rio Iguazu* was strafed and set on fire.

Black Death

Argentine pilots, both Air Force and Navy, had dubbed the Sea Harrier the "Black Death", and concentrated on keeping well clear of it if possible. After the first "Black Buck" Vulcan raid on Port Stanley airfield, the only Argentinean air superiority squadron had been withdrawn to protect the mainland against possible raids. Only rarely did its aircraft appear after this, leaving the attack squadrons to fend for themselves as best they could.

On 21 May, coincidentally Navy Day in Argentina, the Task Force landed at San Carlos Water. This provoked a strong reaction and heavy fighting. Sea Harriers accounted for five Skyhawks and four Daggers on this day, with a Pucara as an added bonus. Another Dagger fell on 23 May, and three more on the following day. This was in addition to losses to ground fire.

Above: The Task Force flagship returned to Portmouth on 21 July, to a welcome that was deeply moving. Sea Harriers urgently needed at Yeovilton were flown off from the Bay of Biscay, but six were ranged on deck, together with the entire ship's company.

An epic action on took place over Choiseul Sound on 8 June. Four Skyhawks of Grupo 5 flying at zero feet attacked landing craft at dusk. Visibility was very poor. Nearly two miles (3.2km) above them were a pair of Sea Harriers of 800 Sqn, flown by David Morgan and David Smith. Seeing the attackers, which were at first misidentified as Mirages, they launched themselves down in a power dive. Pulling out astern of the Skyhawks, Morgan launched two Sidewinders in quick succession. Both connected, and he then sprayed cannon fire at the remaining two, with no effect. Out of ammunition, he then pulled vertically up to give Smith his chance. Another Sidewinder struck home. The fourth Skyhawk was widely reported to have hit the sea during evasive action but, in fact, its pilot Hector Sanchez punched off his external tanks, poured on the coals, and escaped into the gathering gloom. The Sea Harrier was credited with 22 air victories in the South Atlantic.

In late May Nos 11 and 59 Sqns Royal Engineers constructed an FOB (Forward

Operating Base) at Port San Carlos. It comprised an 850ft (259m) strip made of MEXE aluminium planking, with taxi and parking loops at one end where fuel was stored in large flexible pillow tanks. The FOB was not used for reloading ordnance, but it enabled Harriers and Sea Harriers to put in almost twice as much time on CAP or cab-rank attack patrol by eliminating the round trip of some 400 miles back to the ship to refuel. One GR.3 sank through a joint in the metal matting, the nose gear going in up to the landing light. Using RE heavy lift gear the aircraft was bodily wrenched free; then it went straight back into action. On another occasion W/C Squire was making the authorized slow approach, with gear down and landing light on to avoid being engaged by British Rapiers, when his jet blast lifted a section of matting which struck his aircraft, XZ989. The impact drove the nozzles to the aft position, and the Harrier hit the ground hard, careered through the strip, severing it, and continued up a nearby hill and over the brow before coming to rest in a Rapier crew's slit trench. The runway was quickly repaired.

Throughout the campaign nobody was more impressed by the performance of the Harrier and Sea Harrier than the men who flew and maintained them. Over 2,000 sorties had been flown, in the harshest conditions imaginable, and each day aircraft availability for both types together averaged better than 95 per cent. Unserviceability lost less than 1·0 per cent of the planned missions, despite the fact that virtually every aircraft took damage from ground fire. Many aircraft, mainly RAF Harriers because of their low attack tasking, took numerous hits from calibres up to 20mm yet were operational on the next day. one GR.3 was hit in the RCV hot-air duct near the tail. On its approach to *Hermes* with nozzles down, the rear end quickly cooked up until it was almost red hot, but XW919 was back in action 36h later; a performance that seems to typify the achievement of these aircraft during this arduous campaign.

Left: Removing the protective nosecap from one of the newly added AIM-9Ls on a GR.3 of No 1 (F) Sqn at the forward base at San Carlos. Note the badge of HarDet (Harrier Detachment). Even in operations from this land site the INS was seldom used, aircraft using dead-reckoning and the pilots's eyeballs.

Harrier II

The latest brochures feature the Boeing AV-8B Harrier II and Harrier II Plus. Boeing? The Harrier was designed and built in England by Hawker, latterly British Aerospace. Yet most of the world now looks upon it as American. It all started back in 1969, when McDonnell Douglas of St. Louis concluded a licence agreement for the AV-8A for the US Marine Corps. Since then, they have virtually taken over the project. Granted, the RAF now flies the Harrier GR.7 and the Royal Navy the Sea Harrier FRS.2, but most Harriers are built in the USA as the AV-8B Harrier II, and the dedicated fighter variant AV-8B Plus, which has been exported to Spain and Italy.

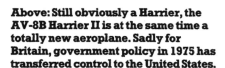

By 1971 the Harrier was in production for the RAF and the almost identical AV-8A for the US Marine Corps. Though a few dissenting voices were still heard, which for reasons of ignorance or vested interest claimed that jet V/STOL was not cost/effective, or immature, or merely "foreign", it was obvious to any thinking person that it represented the dawn of a new era in aviation. So Hawker and MCAIR, and Rolls-Royce and Pratt & Whitney, did the obvious and began studying advanced developments of both the Harrier and its Pegasus engine.

Unlike previous aircraft, the Harrier and its Pegasus engine are intimately integrated. Quite apart from the patent situation, no other engine could provide both thrust and lift, and as the future of the Harrier appeared to depend crucially upon the provision of more of both of these factors, the foundation for the Advanced Harrier appeared to be a more powerful Pegasus.

Rolls-Royce Bristol decided to build a demonstrator engine to show the kind of performance possible with a few modifications. The new engine proposed was given the designation Pegasus 15, but the demonstrator was an intermediate engine using the existing Pegasus 11 core and adding only the proposed Pegasus 15 fan, with a diameter increased by 2¼in (57mm) to handle a significantly increased airflow. The Pegasus 15 was aimed at 24,500lb (11113kg) thrust, so the Bristol team were pleased when the lash-up demo engine gave a figure of 24,900lb (11295kg) on its first testbed run in May 1972. Hawker and MCAIR felt safe in assuming 25,000lb (11340kg) in their aircraft studies.

Not least of the encouraging aspects of the Advanced Harrier was that this time there appeared likely to be four major launch customers: the RAF, Royal Navy, US Marine Corps, and US Navy. The latter had decided to deploy a major force of advanced V/STOL fighters aboard its Sea Control Ships, which in many ways were to be like the Royal Navy's *Invincible*. A Joint Management Committee was set up at government level with representatives of the civilian defence ministries (Mintech for Britain), the four customer services and the four main industrial partners. Hawker at Kingston produced the P.1184 and P.1185 project studies. MCAIR produced the AV-8C (not today's AV-8C), a minimum-change Harrier development with a long-span swept wing based on Douglas work with NASA's Richard T. Whitcomb with a supercritical profile matched to Mach 0·92 cruise (and originally studied for a developed DC-9). Such a wing could house more fuel and greatly increase STO lift, besides having enough span for numerous stores pylons. All the studies featured a raised cockpit with all-round view, and of course the inlets had to be enlarged, though it was just posssible to squeeze the Pegasus 15 into the existing size of fuselage.

The AV-16 design

Though Hawker and MCAIR collaborated closely, and had growing technical teams at each other's plants, they pursued their studies independently. By 1973, after agonizing evaluations, it had been decided to let the Pegasus fan grow a further half-inch, to get 25,000lb (11340kg) with lower turbine temperature and thus achieve long low-cost life, even though this meant a redesign of the fuselage. The AV-8-Plus also introduced a further improved high-airflow elliptical-lip inlet provided with a second row

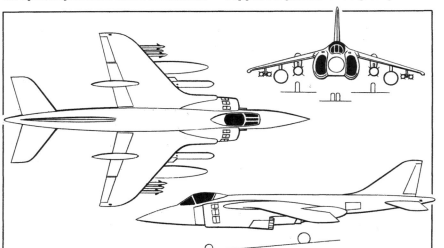

of suck-in auxiliary doors. Both teams also began to discover ways in which local modifications could increase VTO or STO lift without any appreciable penalty. Wisely, both judged that the right course was to modify the proven Harrier as little as possible, and to do so only when a major gain appeared possible with small technical risk. Both adopted the designation AV-16, meaning twice the capability of an AV-8.

Unfortunately, some customers, including both navies, kept harping on the supposed primitive simplicity of the

Above: Still obviously a Harrier, the AV-8B Harrier II is at the same time a totally new aeroplane. Sadly for Britain, government policy in 1975 has transferred control to the United States.

basic Harrier – which in fact is why it has survived and succeeded – and on the apparent advantages for naval missions of a highly supersonic V/STOL. The US Naval Air Systems Command asked both airframe companies how they would design such a machine, and Hawker dusted off its latest series of S (for supersonic) family of studies. These featured a PCB-boosted four-poster engine, of the kind described in the final chapter, which in turn pushed the main gears out into the wing as in the P.1154RN. The wing itself was naturally not only unlike that of a Harrier but utterly unlike that of the AV-8-Plus, which far from yielding

Left: Shown with an assortment of tanks and weapons in the plan and head-on views, the S-6 was one of the "might have been" supersonic designs studied at HSA Kingston in 1973-4.

Below: A direct plan view emphasizes the more obvious new features of the AV-8B, especially the new wing. Low-visibility markings highlight the APU (GTS) inlet and exhaust apertures.

supersonic speed would actually make the aircraft slower. Thus, the AV-16 S-6 had a well-swept wing of low aspect ratio and very low thickness/chord ratio, with broad streamwise tips and long root extensions. High-altitude Mach number was 1.95.

With a PCB thrust of 34,500lb (15650kg) the attractions of such a machine were obvious, and it would probably have met with the approval of

the US Navy, which did not wish to bother with a mere "warmed over" version of the existing Harrier. But the likely costs were already daunting, inflation was beginning to bite, and the only really definite and urgently concerned customer, the Marine Corps, was horrified at the idea of such a complete redesign and merely wanted a more capable subsonic bomb truck. At the time it seemed tragic that, because of

narrow-minded conflict of interest and perhaps also the sheer diversity of possible aircraft, the idea of a really big two-nation, four-customer programme was by 1973 falling apart.

It was especially disheartening to lose the US Navy, because in terms of numbers this was potentially the No 1 customer. On 13 October 1972 Navair, the Naval Air Systems Command, awarded a major V/STOL development contract

Above: This unusual 1981 formation of AV-8B 161396 and an AV-8A 159255 shows the much greater volume available in the new nose and cockpit areas. Another contrast is the lateral area of the twin under-fuselage strakes.

to North American Rockwell for the extremely advanced and complex XFV-12A. This was expected to hover in August 1974 and make transitions a month later. We are still waiting for the XFV-12 to fly, and in fact the whole project fell so short of prediction it was abandoned in 1980. But its very existence could easily have caused MCAIR to look for easier lines of business, and it is to the credit of Sandy McDonnell – who inherited from his uncle a very tough and canny business sense – that instead of dropping the rejected AV-16 the St Louis company continued to believe that it was the right way to go.

To offer encouragement, in 1973 the US Marine Corps issued a formal requirement for such an Advanced Harrier, and MCAIR and Hawker began doing joint studies, which culminated in a submission to the US and British governments of an "AV-16A" on 13 December 1973. It had the MCAIR long-span super-critical wing, the Pegasus 15 engine, and numerous lift-improving detail refinements throughout the airframe. But

Left: Never has an aircraft programme of recent years started out so good on paper yet proved so great a disappointment as the US Navy Rockwell XFV-12A, abandoned in 1980.

factors outside the programme were casting a deepening shadow. One was the continuing uncertainty of what the customers wanted. Only the Marines simply wanted an AV-16A. The RAF wanted an Advanced Harrier whose major improvements could be retrofitted to its existing Harriers, and on this count the MCAIR wing and Pegasus 15 engine were both non-starters. The Royal Navy had by this time become committed to the design that became the Sea Harrier. Worst of all, inflation was beginning to bite, and not only was the development cost of the AV-16A and its engine put at $1 billion but this was expected to double because of inflation by the time the aircraft entered service.

Increasingly the meetings dwelt on problems rather than progress, and what seemed to be the *coup de grâce* was the announcement of the British government on 19 March 1975 that: "There is not enough common ground on the Advanced Harrier for us to join in the programme with the US". In fact, this was not true, because one aeroplane will now serve both countries, but that particular government simply wanted to cut defence spending and was delighted to latch on to any project that seemed to be in difficulties. In the United States Navair cancelled its sponsorship of the AV-16A due to lack of funds. The Navy itself had already picked the XFV-12A, and terminating the "foreign program" pleased a lot of partisan Congressmen.

Pegasus 15 abandoned

Though this was the low point in a protracted story, the crunch in 1975 did allow each airframe partner, if it chose to, to press ahead with its own unfettered studies for its own customers. Both quickly came to the same conclusion regarding the Pegasus 15. It is possible that, had PCB development never been shelved by Rolls-Royce following cancellation of the P.1154, a 34,500lb (15650kg) PCB Pegasus 15 would have been funded in 1975, with dramatic long-term results. But the Mk 15 engine alone was costed at $600 million to US qualification, and, when it was found that this equated to $200,000 per pound of extra thrust, the whole project seemed not worth while. The crucial decision was taken to abandon any immediate major Pegasus development, and concentrate on the airframe instead. Navair funded a study of Pegasus alternatives, carried out jointly by Pratt & Whitney and Rolls-Royce, which suggested: 1, the Pegasus 104, as later adopted for the Sea Harrier; 2, the Mk 104 with internal

changes to improve maintainability and give a TBO (time between overhauls) of 1,000h; 3, the Pegasus 11D with small internal changes giving 800lb (363kg) more thrust; and 4, an 11D with 1,000h TBO. Not submitted, Rolls also studied the 11D+ with increased temperature and 22,500lb (10206kg) thrust.

For a possible Advanced Harrier for the Marines, Navair picked the second choice above, the improved Mk 104 with 1,000h TBO, and with virtually all the detail improvements aimed at improving ease of maintenance and reducing total costs over perhaps a 20-year period rather than at increasing performance. Despite this, MCAIR had already shown in 1975 that by airframe modifications alone, the payload/range capability of the AV-8A could be at least *doubled*!

MCAIR were in any case determined to continue Advanced Harrier development for the Marines, and in 1975 had put a growing technical team on the job. It could have elected to go it alone, but wisely chose to continue collaboration with Hawker, who retained liaison engineers at St Louis and played a significant part in the design of what by 1975 had become the AV-8B. Before the end of 1975 MCAIR had completed the basic project design, and had already carried out extensive test programmes. One of the latter was to rebuild a crashed AV-8A to look broadly like the AV-8B, and this impressive non-flying demonstration aircraft was rolled out as early as 7 August 1975.

The obvious new feature of the AV-8B was the wing. This was a refined version of the Whitcomb supercritical wing, designed by an MCAIR team under T. R. Lacey. Its chief new feature is that, in one of the boldest structural decisions for many years, its entire primary structure is carbon-fibre composite (called graphite composite in the USA), and it is the largest carbon item in any aircraft, excepting the Rockwell B-1 horizontal tail. On any count it is larger than the Harrier wing, with span over 30ft (9·1m) and a much deeper cross-section, the average t/c (thickness to chord) ratio being 10·5 per cent compared with 8·5. Thus it can accommodate almost twice as much fuel as the original wing, 4,950lb (2245kg) compared with 2,834lb (1285kg), besides giving far greater STO lift and providing for three pylons on each side. It has eight spars, each with an undulat-

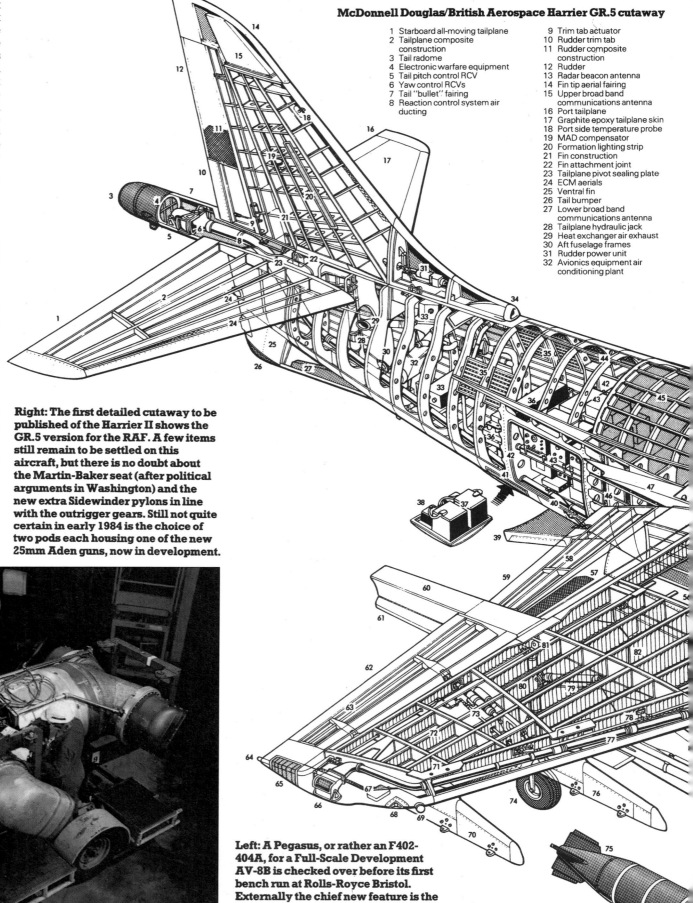

McDonnell Douglas/British Aerospace Harrier GR.5 cutaway

1 Starboard all-moving tailplane
2 Tailplane composite construction
3 Tail radome
4 Electronic warfare equipment
5 Tail pitch control RCV
6 Yaw control RCVs
7 Tail "bullet" fairing
8 Reaction control system air ducting
9 Trim tab actuator
10 Rudder trim tab
11 Rudder composite construction
12 Rudder
13 Radar beacon antenna
14 Fin tip aerial fairing
15 Upper broad band communications antenna
16 Port tailplane
17 Graphite epoxy tailplane skin
18 Port side temperature probe
19 MAD compensator
20 Formation lighting strip
21 Fin construction
22 Fin attachment joint
23 Tailplane pivot sealing plate
24 ECM aerials
25 Ventral fin
26 Tail bumper
27 Lower broad band communications antenna
28 Tailplane hydraulic jack
29 Heat exchanger air exhaust
30 Aft fuselage frames
31 Rudder power unit
32 Avionics equipment air conditioning plant

Right: The first detailed cutaway to be published of the Harrier II shows the GR.5 version for the RAF. A few items still remain to be settled on this aircraft, but there is no doubt about the Martin-Baker seat (after political arguments in Washington) and the new extra Sidewinder pylons in line with the outrigger gears. Still not quite certain in early 1984 is the choice of two pods each housing one of the new 25mm Aden guns, now in development.

Left: A Pegasus, or rather an F402-404A, for a Full-Scale Development AV-8B is checked over before its first bench run at Rolls-Royce Bristol. Externally the chief new feature is the long zero-scarf front nozzle. The heavy blue plate around it is test gear.

AV-8B structural materials

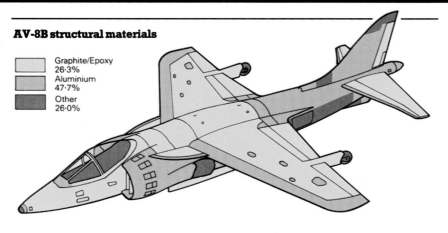

- Graphite/Epoxy 26·3%
- Aluminium 47·7%
- Other 26·0%

Above: Another far from obvious new feature of all Harrier II aircraft is the widespread use of graphite composite.

The 26·3 per cent by weight equates to about 40 per cent by volume, because of the low density of this material.

ing (sine-wave) web, yet the switch to carbon and deeper profile enables the new wing to weigh 330lb (150kg) less than an equivlent all-metal wing.

The leading edge is now swept at 36° instead of 40°, and is a simple aluminium alloy structure which after flight development has only a single outboard fence. The trailing edge is totally new. While the RCVs are right at the tip, for maximum roll power, the outrigger landing gears have been moved inboard between the ailerons and flaps, reducing track to 17ft (5·18m) for easier manoeuvring and with the leg fairings replaced by doors. Inboard are the enormous double-slotted flaps which in the STO mode are extended to 62° and react powerfully with the wing circulation induced by the angled nozzles.

MCAIR and NASA conducted prolonged tests to rearrange the nozzles, wing and flaps to obtain the most favourable circulation around the inboard wing in STO. This work also led to new longer zero-scarf front engine nozzles which give 200lb (91kg) more thrust. It is planned to switch to titanium, saving 50lb (22·7kg). This wing/flap/nozzle improvement provides the largest of the many increments in STO lift, no less than 6,700lb (3039kg) on a 1,000ft (300m) run.

The new engine inlets were further refined to increase airflow and reduce drag, and the geometry of the double row of auxiliary inlet doors improved. Eventually, at the seventeenth production AV-8B, it was found possible to use large single doors. These increase VTO lift by 600lb (272kg), but instead of this

33 Avionics equipment racks
34 Heat exchanger ram air intake
35 Electrical system circuit breaker panels, port and starboard
36 Electronic warfare equipment
37 Chaff and flare dispensers
38 Dispenser electronic control units
39 Ventral airbrake
40 Airbrake hydraulic jack
41 Formation lighting strip
42 Avionics bay access door, port and starboard
43 Avionics equipment racks
44 Fuselage frame and stringer construction
45 Rear fuselage fuel tank
46 Main undercarriage wheel bay
47 Wing root fillet
48 Wing spar/fuselage attachment joint
49 Water filler cap
50 Engine fire extinguisher bottle
51 Anti-collision light
52 Water tank
53 Flap power unit
54 Flap hinge fitting
55 Titanium fuselage heat shield
56 Main undercarriage bay doors (closed after cycling of mainwheels)
57 Flap vane composite construction
58 Flap composite construction
59 Starboard slotted flap, lowered
60 Outrigger wheel fairing
61 Outrigger leg doors
62 Starboard aileron
63 Aileron composite construction
64 Fuel jettison
65 Formation lighting panel
66 Roll control RCV
67 Radar warning signal processor
68 Starboard navigation light
69 Radar warning aerial
70 Outboard pylon
71 Pylon attachment joint
72 Graphite epoxy composite wing construction
73 Aileron power unit
74 Starboard outrigger wheel
75 BL755 600lb (272kg) cluster bomb (CBU)
76 Intermediate pylon
77 Reaction control air ducting
78 Aileron control rod
79 Outrigger hydraulic retraction jack
80 Outrigger leg strut
81 Leg pivot fixing
82 Multi-spar graphite wing construction
83 Leading-edge wing fence
84 Outrigger pylon
85 Missile launch rail
86 AIM-9L Sidewinder air-to-air missile
87 External fuel tank, 300US Gal (1135lit)
88 Inboard pylon
89 Aft retracting twin mainwheels
90 Inboard pylon attachment joint
91 Rear (hot stream) swivelling exhaust nozzle
92 Position of pressure refuelling connection on port side
93 Rear nozzle bearing
94 Centre fuselage flank tank
95 Hydraulic reservoir
96 Nozzle bearing cooling air duct
97 Engine exhaust divider duct
98 Wing panel centre rib
99 Centre section integral fuel tank
100 Port wing integral fuel tank
101 Flap vane
102 Port slotted flap, lowered
103 Outrigger wheel fairing
104 Port outrigger wheel
105 Torque scissor links
106 Port aileron
107 Aileron power unit
108 Aileron/air valve interconnection
109 Fuel jettison
110 Formation lighting panel
111 Port roll control RCV
112 Port navigation light
113 Radar warning aerial
114 Port wing reaction control air duct
115 Fuel pumps
116 Fuel system piping
117 Port wing leading-edge fence
118 Outboard pylon
119 BL755 cluster bombs (maximum load, seven)
120 Intermediate pylon
121 Port outrigger pylon
122 Missile launch rail
123 AIM-9L Sidewinder air-to-air missile
124 Port leading-edge root extension (LERX)
125 Inboard pylon
126 Hydraulic pumps
127 APU intake
128 Gas turbine starter/auxiliary power unit (APU)
129 Alternator cooling air exhaust
130 APU exhaust
131 Engine fuel control unit
132 Engine bay venting ram air intake
133 Rotary nozzle bearing
134 Nozzle fairing construction
135 Ammunition tank, 110 rounds
136 Cartridge case collector box
137 Ammunition feed chute
138 Fuel vent
139 Gun pack strake
140 Fuselage centreline pylon
141 Zero scarf forward (fan air) nozzle
142 Ventral gun pack (two)
143 Aden 25mm cannon
144 Engine drain mast
145 Hydraulic system ground connectors
146 Forward fuselage flank fuel tank
147 Engine electronic control units
148 Engine accessory equipment gearbox
149 Gearbox driven alternator
150 Rolls-Royce Pegasus 11 Mk 105 vectored thrust turbofan
151 Formation lighting strips
152 Engine oil tank
153 Bleed air spill duct
154 Air conditioning intake scoops
155 Cockpit air conditioning system heat exchanger
156 Engine compressor/fan face
157 Heat exchanger discharge to intake duct
158 Nose undercarriage hydraulic retraction jack
159 Intake blow-in doors
160 Engine bay venting air scoop
161 Cannon muzzle fairing
162 Lift augmentation retractable cross-dam
163 Cross-dam hydraulic jack
164 Nosewheel
165 Nosewheel forks
166 Landing/taxiing lamp
167 Retractable boarding step
168 Nosewheel doors (closed after cycling of undercarriage)
169 Nosewheel door jack
170 Boundary layer bleed air duct
171 Nose undercarriage wheel bay
172 Kick-in boarding steps
173 Cockpit rear pressure bulkhead
174 Starboard side console panel
175 Martin-Baker Mk 10 ejection seat
176 Safety harness
177 Ejection seat headrest
178 Port engine air intake
179 Probe hydraulic jack
180 Retractable inflight-refuelling probe (bolt-on pack)
181 Cockpit canopy cover
182 Miniature detonating cord (MDC) canopy breaker
183 Canopy frame
184 Engine throttle and nozzle control levers
185 Pilot's head-up-display (HUD)
186 Instrument panel
187 Moving map display
188 Control column
189 Central warning system panel
190 Cockpit pressure floor
191 Underfloor control runs
192 Formation lighting strips
193 Aileron trim actuator
194 Rudder pedals
195 Cockpit section composite construction
196 Instrument panel shroud
197 One-piece wrap-around windscreen panel
198 Ram air intake (cockpit fresh air)
199 Front pressure bulkhead
200 Incidence vane
201 Air data computer
202 Pitot tube
203 Lower IFF aerial
204 Nose pitch control air valve
205 Pitch trim control actuator
206 Electrical system equipment
207 Yaw vane
208 Upper IFF aerial
209 Electronic warfare equipment
210 ARBS heat exchanger
211 MIRLS sensors
212 Hughes Angle Rate Bombing System (ARBS)
213 Composite construction nose cone
214 ARBS glazed aperture

being at the cost of poorer high-speed behaviour the drag in cruising flight is actually reduced. Another very large contribution (1,200lb, 544kg) to VTO lift is furnished by the greatly improved LIDs (lift-improvement devices), which were devised jointly by BAe and MCAIR. Even the mid-1975 AV-8B mock-up had strakes added to the gun pods, with the inter-pod space boxed in by a hinged surface upstream – called a dam, but looking like an airbrake – which when tested on an AV-8A not only increased low-altitude lift by 1,220lb (533kg) but also reduced hot-gas reingestion and lowered inlet temperature by 20°C.

As well as being modified in shape, the complete forward fuselage, horizontal tail, rudder and the removable panels covering the top of the fuselage were all redesigned in carbon fibre. An incidental advantage is the elimination of tailplane resonance problems, and this is hoped to extend also to the proposed TAV-8B two-seater. As for the cockpit, this has been raised 10·5in (267mm) and provided with a giant circular-profile canopy giving an outstanding all-round view. The cockpit is descibed later. The whole nose was greatly enlarged, to provide additional space for avionics and other equipment, and the front windshield was increased in size and made a single curved piece of very thick multi-layer stretched acrylic, with deicing but no wiper.

These were the chief improvements proposed by MCAIR for the AV-8B, which continued at full pressure at St Louis, assisted by NASA, though not yet funded by the Navy. By early 1976 another damaged AV-8A had been rebuilt with many AV-8B features, including the wing, flaps, LIDs and engine inlets, and initially put through engine-running and lift interaction tests resting on tall supports out of doors. By September 1976 it was in the giant 40×80ft tunnel at NASA's Ames Research Center. This full-scale model, whose wing was made

Below: Aerodynamicists festoon prototype aircraft with tufts to explore airflow and look for flow breakaway. Here a YAV-8B, 158394, has tufting covering the entire top and bottom of both wings. Inboard stores are Snakeye bombs.

Above: The third FSD aircraft, seen here near St Louis in April 1982, was the first to be fitted with LERX at the wing roots. This photograph illustrates the excellent visibility from the cockpit; the pilot is head up during air-to-air and air-to-ground combat.

of aluminium and wood, completed 319h of testing, and smaller models completed over 4,000h in perfecting the new high-lift features of the AV-8B.

Funding is authorized

In March 1976 William P. Clements Jr, the US Deputy Secretary for Defense, announced agreement in principle to a programme for 342 AV-8B aircraft for the Marine Corps, comprising two YAV-8B prototypes, four FSD (full-scale development) prototypes and 336 production machines. Later the 336 were to be divided into 12 pilot production, 18 limited production and 306 full production. Limited funding was authorized, including cover for the two prototypes, and a complete test example of the new wing. To save time and cost the two

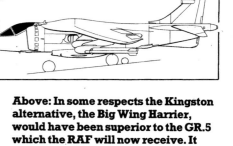

YAV-8Bs were rebuilt AV-8As, Nos 158394 and 158395. These incorporated the complete new wing, with carbon (graphite) structure; but not yet incorporating production-style manufacturing methods, as well as the new inlets, and LIDs, but retaining the original tailplane, forward fuselage, cockpit and internal systems. The first YAV was completed 53 days ahead of schedule and at 188lb (85·3kg) under the calculated empty weight, so that it weighed almost exactly the same as a regular Harrier. AV-8B

Above: In some respects the Kingston alternative, the Big Wing Harrier, would have been superior to the GR.5 which the RAF will now receive. It was particularly designed for higher speed and better manoeuvrability.

Project Test Pilot Charley Plummer lifted off from the concrete apron at Lambert St Louis airport for the first time on 9 November 1978.

In March 1979 ski takeoffs began from the Fairey-built MGB 12° ramp which had been purchased by the US Navy and airlifted from Farnborough to Pax River. A month later, in April 1979, MCAIR was awarded the long-awaited contract for the four FSD aircraft, and a long-lead contract for $35 million to begin preparation for production. At the same time it was by this time all too evident that the AV-8B was still tainted with the hated label "foreign" in influential sections of Congress. Though it had no historical precedent, the Carter administration decided to put the screws on the RAF to buy the AV-8B rather than the home-grown Big-Wing Harrier by making a full go-ahead on the AV-8B contingent upon export sales. Many partisan things were said, and certainly there existed a powerful lobby who wanted all the Navy vote to be poured into the colossal and escalating funding-trough of the F/A-18A Hornet (from the same contractor) and major ship programmes. SecDef Harold S. Brown called the F/A-18A-only choice a "more efficient" solution, overlooking the fact that a distant Marines beachhead might offer no conventional airbase. Another DoD spokesman called the AV-8B "an inefficient project that consumes funds needed for overall force modernization".

Probably the most serious result of the three years of delaying tactics for political ends was an increase in the estimated US price for the programme of no less than £920 million, due solely to infla-

Above: BuAer No 158394, the first YAV-8B, caught by the camera in a tight turn over the Patuxent River runways in early 1982. Note the two cine cameras under the rear fuselage, aft of the old Aden-shape gun pods.

tion. Had the RAF simply bought the AV-8B at the start there might have been no delay at all, but the British situation was not easy to resolve. The RAF's needs continued to be for an improved Harrier able not only to fly far and fast at the lowest possible level, in the face of bad weather and intense hostile electronics and ordnance, but also to dogfight when necessary against agile opponents. Air Staff Requirement 409 stipulated various numerical parameters, including a maximum speed not less than that of the GR.3 and a sustained turn-rate of 20°/s. Hawker (BAe from 1978) strove to meet all the RAF's needs, and also to do so with changes which could be retroactively applied to existing RAF Harriers. It succeeded on all counts, with its proposed Big-Wing Harrier, produced to MoD study contract in 1978-80 and noteworthy for a fully swept long-span (over 34ft) wing made in metal and not only retrofittable but also with a high-speed profile for low drag and high manoeuvrability. Prominent at the roots of the leading edge were LERX (leading-edge root extensions) to add area at high AOA and create strong vortices, and thus delay the onset of flow separation from above the wing. They have a deliberate destabilizing effect and, seen in various forms on most modern air-combat aircraft, they enhance manoeuvrability. Tested on a GR.3 (XV277) they enabled pilots to pull 1g extra at any given engine thrust.

The Big Wing Harrier proposed many other new features, and would have had no fewer than ten stores attachments on the wings alone. BAe thought it at least as saleable as the AV-8B, which was slower than the GR.3 and missed meeting the RAF turn rate by miles with a limit of under 14°/s. It therefore produced brochures to try to convince governments, notably the British, that it had the better product and that it would be better for Britain to have the whole of an initially modest RAF programme, with a big export potential, than a minor share of the AV-8B. The decision was agonizing, but the carpet was rather pulled from under BAe when the Minister of Defence announced in 1980 that "the Big Wing is unlikely to be any part of an improvement programme for the GR.3". Though deadlock appeared to continue, in fact BAe very reluctantly came round to the view that half a cake is better than the whole of a non-starter, and in January 1981, as the new Reagan administration took office in Washington, BAe recommended acceptance of the AV-8B as the most commercially viable solution.

At last the Minister of Defence announced in July 1981 that the AV-8B would be bought for the RAF, with an expected total of 60 aircraft. Much fewer than the original Harrier buy, this will equip new squadrons to serve alongside GR.3 units, the latter aircraft being given a major mid-life update. At once there was what previous SecDef Brown had

Below: AV-8B No 5, the first true production Harrier II, in the St Louis plant with F-15s in the rear in April 1983. Note the double row of inlet doors, which have now been replaced by single doors of improved form.

called "a new situation", and an MOU (Memorandum of Understanding) was signed on 24 August 1981 authorizing full-scale development. MCAIR and BAe decided on the family name Harrier II. The deal at the industrial level finally thrashed out is: for all US and 75 per cent of third-country sales, MCAIR is prime contractor with BAe a subcontractor; for all UK and 25 per cent of third-country sales, BAe is prime, with MCAIR a subcontractor; actual split of airframe work is about 60 MCAIR to 40 BAe; and systems and equipment are split about 80 US to 20 UK. The engine is a far better deal for Rolls-Royce, which merely has to relinquish up to 25 per cent of the production content to Pratt & Whitney, and for the Marine Corps buy only.

One advantage of the delay in launching full-scale development was that it was possible to crank in numerous further updates to both the aircraft and engine. The latter progressed from the YF402-RR-404, used in the YAV-8B aircraft, to the F402-404 with an improved 1st fan stage with wide-root blades to permit higher rpm, a higher-output gearbox and a new bulkhead matched to the production AV-8B. This was cleared at 21,700lb (9843kg) in 1980, and in the same year running began on a further improved sub-variant, the Dash-404A, with a revised swan-neck (intermediate casing) with a more efficient air path, and an increased-capacity No 2 bearing. In the same year, 1980, testing began of the full production engine, the F402-RR-406, with the shrouded LP turbine, triple interstage labyrinth seals, improved HP turbine cooling and a forged combus-

Above: The "pretty" FSD aircraft, 161397, on test from St Louis in April 1982 with gear extended and a touch of airbrake. LERX and LIDs are installed.

tion-chamber outlet. The Pegasus is amenable to uprating, and the 11-61 (F402-RR-408) on late-build USMC AV-8Bs pumps out 23,850lb (10,818kg) of thrust. The RAF Harrier GR.7 is powered by the Pegasus 11-21 Mk 105, rated at 21,750lb (9,866kg), while RN Sea Harriers are fitted with the navalized Mk 104 or 106 of broadly comparable performance.

The advantage of composites
The first of the four FSD aircraft flew in Plummer's hands at St Louis on 5 November 1981. All four were flying by June 1982, and two further airframes were built for structural testing, a novel feature of the AV-8B being that as no fatigue is yet known in carbon composite structures the wing and tailplane should have unlimited life. By July 1982 the fatigue specimen had completed 24,000h, equal to two planned lifetimes each of 12,000 flying hours. Further work led to the introduction of improved structural manufacturing and test methods, such as accurately cutting out large numbers of stacked carbon composite plies (laminates) simultaneously, and automatically traversing an ultrasonic scanner over the entire wing skins to check on perfect inter-laminate bonding.

More fundamental have been the improvements to the on-board systems. Nobody was ever totally satisfied with the original Harrier stability and control which in one band of airspeeds during a

AV-8B avionics aerials (antennas)

This diagram shows the locations of the main avionics aerials of the Marines' AV-8B. Many, but not all, will be common to the RAF Harrier GR.5.

transition could lead via a yaw and involuntary roll to complete loss of control. The Harrier II has a new high-authority SAAHS (stability and attitude-hold system) with a pitch/roll autostabilization computer and an electronic interface to the front RCV. Longitudinal and lateral margins are greatly improved, and with SAAHS operative throughout the flight envelope the pilot workload is greatly reduced, and anxiety virtually eliminated. Writing in *Rolls-Royce Magazine* the AV-8B Program Manager at Pax River, Maj Richard H. Priest, commented "It sounds good, but how does that translate when I'm trying to land on a 72ft by 72ft pad in the trees, or on a pitching deck on a dark night? I lower the nozzles and begin deceleration. I quickly realise that almost no lateral stick inputs are required, and the classic AV-8A nose wander is just not there any more. Continuing the decel to hover I am again impressed by the rock-steady feel of the aircraft, and how cool the engine is running under these demanding conditions.

Reducing the power to descend to about 15ft I wait for the cobblestoning [random attitude disturbances] to begin, but it never occurs." In fact, so effective are the LIDs that AV-8B pilots just let the aircraft mush down on to the air cushion, where it refuses to sink any further until the power is brought back.

In production AV-8Bs propulsion management is handled by a Fadec (full-authority digital electronic control) produced by the new group DSIC (Dowty and Smiths Industries Controls). The AV-8B is the first production application for a Fadec, which again reduces pilot workload and any peaks in turbine gas temperature. As part of a far-ranging five-year NASA research programme into AV-8B stability and vectored-thrust aircraft behaviour generally, which will spin-off into future fighter designs, it was planned in 1984 to integrate the throttle and nozzle controls into a single cockpit control, so that the pilot could fly in true Hotas (hands on throttle and stick) style, without ever having to move his left hand from one control to another. The idea is simple, but execution has proved difficult, as the VAAC Harrier has demonstrated flying from Boscombe Down. It is more likely to enter service on STOVL variants of the Joint Strike Fighter.

The NASA study had further tasks, including the refinement of simulator models to develop new navigation and guidance concepts for use in bad weather, including essentially blind landings impossible with other combat aircraft.

System improvements

Typical of system improvements throughout the aircraft, the Harrier II flap control system is digital FBW (fly by wire). It is self-monitoring, and controls the two electrohydraulic power units, each of which can push with 30,000lb (13·6 tonnes) to move the flaps at 7°/s down to 25° and at 64°/s from 25° to 62°. In earlier Harriers breakage of the torque tubes linking the flaps could cause flap asymmetry and force the pilot to eject. With the Harrier II the flap system can suffer any kind of failure and even shut down, yet the pilot can still fly the aircraft. The system also controls droop of the two ailerons, which improves lift in STO or at high AOA, and eliminates the need for the pilot to adjust flap setting in flight. Other major system improvements include constant-frequency AC electrics, an updated inertial navigation system (ASN-130 in the AV-8B, a GEC-Marconi FIN 1075 in the GR.7) and an Obogs (on-board oxygen-generating system) which passes engine bleed air through filter beds which remove everything but the oxygen, as it is needed.

Left: The original planning cockpit used in defining the standard for the Harrier GR.5. The head-down moving-map display is on the right, and the MFD on the left is shown in the stores readout mode.

Below left: An early AV-8B simulator (July 1979), though with a cockpit not very different from those in today's production aircraft. Here the RAF moving-map display is replaced by the panels for fuel and ALE-39 ECM.

It goes without saying that the Harrier II cockpit is totally new. A great deal was fed in from the F/A-18A programme, including a large MFD (multifunction display) on the left and a prominent and easily used UFC (up-front control) for CNI (com/nav/ident) which incorporates a fibre-optic data converter. Above the UFC is the large Smiths Industries HUD, with dual combiner glasses, and on the right is a fuel panel and another controlling the Goodyear ALE-39 chaff/flare dispenser in the rear fuselage (in the GR.5 the RAF plan to have a moving-map display here instead). The armament control panel is low on the left, below the MFD.

At present all Harrier IIs have an approximately similar Hotas system, the stick and throttle grips including the following control functions: SAAHS control, air start, manoeuvre flaps (for combat), com selection, sensor selection, sensor cage/uncage, slew control/designation, weapon selection, weapon release, gun firing and aircraft trim. Viffing for combat will later be added to this impressive list. Pilot view is superb, and unlike the original low-canopied Harrier the pilot can sit well upright yet still find that the HUD is dead centre in his forward FOV (field of view). Previously, pilots sat as high as possible to try to see out, and then could not get down to use the HUD; "Harrier hunch" became famous throughout the Marine Corps. With the second-generation aircraft there is no need to hunch, and all controls also are comfortably situated without need to move the body.

Above: This drawing depicts an RAF Harrier GR.5. Stores shown include GP bombs, BL.755 CBUs and Lepus flares. LIDs strakes are fitted, though the expected gun pod is the new 25mm Aden. The RWR installation is the same ALR-67 as used by the US Marine Corps, with forward-facing aerials on the wingtips, though a different RWR may be selected.

The primary weapons delivery sensor for the Harrier II is the Hughes ASB-19(V) Angle Rate Bombing System (ARBS). Located in the tip of the nose, this comprises a laser spot tracker (LST), and a TV contrast tracker, working together. They can be locked onto any surface target, and thereafter continuously feed the appropriate angular rate of change information to the HUD and, if it is set to attack mode, to one of the MFDs. The picture from the TV seeker can be magnified six times onto one of the MFDs for greater clarity and discrimination.

The laser receiver also detects and locks onto any target illuminated by a correctly coded off-board laser, ground-based or air. There would be little point if a whole flight of Harriers attacked the same target; a sophisticated system of pulse coding ensures that there is no confusion over which target belongs to which aircraft. This allows first pass attacks to be made.

Bombs are usually dropped using Auto-Weapons Release (AWR) mode, controlled by the weapons computer. As a fall-back position they can be aimed manually, aiming with either the Continuously Computed Impact Mode, widely known as the "Death Dot", with manual release as the pipper moves through the target, or by using a depressed sightline mode. The use of LGBs or AGM-65 Maverick air-to-surface missiles has been described elsewhere in this volume; the methods are the same regardless of which aircraft is the user. ARBS had one primary failing; it was a daylight-only system.

This was soon corrected. The next step was to make the Harrier II night-capable. This was done by both major services; the US Marine Corps wanted the Night Harrier, while the RAF converted the GR.5 into the GR.7, making the fastest transition between types the latter service had seen since World War II.

One of the greatest problems of night operations is making sure that aircraft in the same target area do not get in each other's way, with the attendant risk of a mid-air collision. The mission computer was given a time over target facility, with the ability to regulate speed to suit. This was aided by the addition of Global Positioning System (GPS) data from 1992.

The next problem was to be able to see and identify the target at night. This was done by mounting a CEC-Marconi Forward- Looking Infra Red (FLIR) sensor above the nose. The image from this can be projected onto the HUD,

almost exactly matching the "real world" view out front, always assuming that anything could be seen at all. The HUD of course continues to present its usual information. The FLIR picture is repeated on one of the MFDs, and a switch on the throttle can change this from "white hot" to "black hot" as required.

The FLIR is complemented by GEC Nightbird Night Vision Goggles (NVGs), which work on a light enhancement principle which gives a green picture. This is essential; since the FLIR is fixed, unlike LANTIRN, the NVGs allow the pilot to "look into" the turn, thus avoiding potentially nasty surprises.

Moonlight gives the pilot "almost" daytime picture quality, although the NVGs have no depth, and lack of definition makes obstacles such as power lines difficult to see. Their field of view is limited to about 40deg, and their use has been described as like "looking through a pair of cardboard toilet roll tubes!" But, for all that, they do give a fair amount of night capability. One final point on NVGs: as they weigh just over 2lb (1kg), they are a potential hazard if ejection is needed. The Martin Baker Mk 12 zero altitude, zero forward speed seat has been modified to include the automatic jettison of the NVGs on RAF Harrier GR.7s. This option is not available on USMC Harrier IIs, with the result that NVGs cannot be worn by their pilots during takeoff and landing.

The RAF GR.5 was always intended to be modified to carry FLIR, and the GR.5a actually carried the wiring for this. Most GR.7s are actually modified versions of the GR.5 and 5a.

Defensive armament

Both Marine Corps and RAF Harrier IIs routinely carry two AIM-9 Sidewinders for self-defence, although these are scheduled to be replaced with ASRAAM with the RAF in the near future. Guns feature largely, both as an air-to-air weapon of the last resort, and for strafing ground targets, although duelling with ground defences at low level is widely regarded as being neither a very practical nor an economic proposition.

The guns are carried in underfuselage pods, which are shaped to act as LIDs. The gun carried by USMC Harriers is the General Electric GAU-12, a 25mm five-barrel Gatling type with a rate of fire of 3,600rpm. Unusually, a single gun is carried in the left hand pod, with 300 rounds of ammunition in the right hand pod and

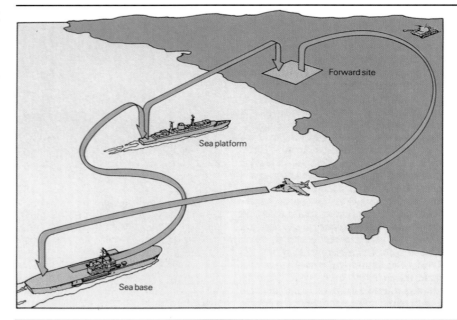

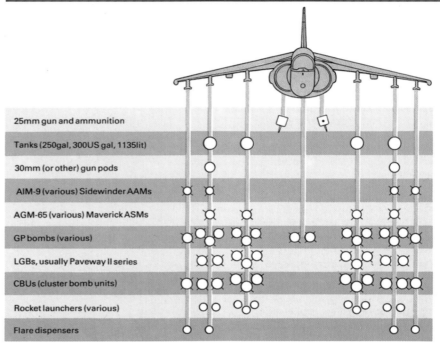

25mm gun and ammunition							
Tanks (250gal, 300US gal, 1135lit)	○	○				○	○
30mm (or other) gun pods	○						
AIM-9 (various) Sidewinder AAMs	☒ ☒					☒ ☒	
AGM-65 (various) Maverick ASMs	☒ ☒	☒ ☒			☒ ☒	☒ ☒	
GP bombs (various)	○○○ ○○	○○	○○	○○	○○○	○○ ○○	
LGBs, usually Paveway II series	☒☒ ☒	○☒ ☒			○☒ ☒	☒☒ ☒	
CBUs (cluster bomb units)	○○○ ○○	○○			○○○	○○ ○○	
Rocket launchers (various)	○○	○○○			○○○	○○	
Flare dispensers	○ ○					○ ○	

mechanically fed across from one side to the other. The RAF proposed two 25mm Aden revolver cannon, with a lesser rate of fire. Although several are believed to have entered experimental service the project foundered on excess weight and was cancelled. As at the beginning of year 2000, no replacement is in sight.

Fighter Harriers

In its early years the Harrier was never seriously regarded as a potential air

superiority fighter. For one reason, it was firmly subsonic. For another its wing loading was definitely on the high side, restricting its turning capability. At the time, much was written about Vectoring In Forward Flight (VIFF) enabling it to perform unorthodox manoeuvres which conventional fighters could not follow. While this was basically true, VIFF manoeuvres were too imprecise to be of much use. Peter Day of No 1 (F) Sqn, the first man to receive a 3,000 hour Harrier patch,

Harrier II mission profiles

Left: Simplified mission diagram showing AV-8B operation from sea bases against land targets. The very flexible Harrier family could do a VTO or, as shown on a *Tarawa* class ship, an STO. A brief visit is made to the helicopter pad of a surface warship, followed by a VL at a forward site on land, before returning to the original ship.

Right: Here a selection of possible AV-8B shore-based missions is shown. A rolling takeoff would usually be made wherever possible, and certainly at the main base (unless rendered totally unusable). The forward sites would if possible be camouflaged, and most would probably offer only a very restricted run. Tanks imply hostile ground forces.

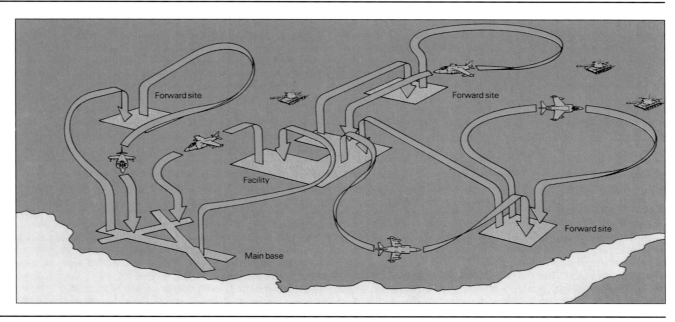

Left: Early Harriers were largely daylight-only aircraft but the need to operate at night rapidly became of extreme importance. The result was the Night Attack Harrier II.

presented by Harrier test pilot Duncan Simpson, commented that, while it was useful to nibble off a few degrees of angle to obtain a firing solution, large amounts of VIFF merely served to deplete energy.

The South Atlantic War of 1982 was the proving ground for Harrier fighters, when subsonic Sea Harriers frequently defeated supersonic Mirage IIIs and Daggers. As previously mentioned, the Sea Harriers flew many dissimilar air combat sorties prior to their departure,

some against 527th Aggressor Squadron F-5Es and, it must be stated, they did not always win. This was not the story told by Sea Harrier commander Sharkey Ward, although he did generously allow that on one occasion the then Aggressor commander (not named, but actually Bob Mendell) fought him to a draw. On the other hand, the publicity arising did nothing for Argentinean morale.

For the Royal Navy, the lessons of the South Atlantic War were threefold.

Firstly, the Sea Harrier radar was inadequate for the task. Secondly, medium range AAMs with BVR capability were required. Thirdly, two AAMs were simply not enough.

The British solution was the Sea Harrier FRS.2, or F/A.2, as rebuilt FRS.1s were designated. This carried a GEC-Marconi Blue Vixen multi-mode pulse-Doppler radar, and was armed with four AIM-120 AMRAAM missiles. Had it not been for the fact that most FRS.2s were to be rebuilt FRS.1s, it

could also have had a bigger wing, giving greater manoeuvrability.

The American solution was predictably more exotic. The prime purpose of the Harrier for the US Marines was close air support for amphibious operations. The reaction of the average "grunt" was: "Fine, park one next to my foxhole!" But, for air superiority, the Marines were forced to rely on the US Navy. What they really needed was their own air superiority fighter.

Externally similar to the AV-8B, the new aircraft had a slightly bulged radome which held the Hughes APG-65 multi-mode pulse-Doppler radar as used by the F/A-18 Hornet (for details of which see the relevant section). This differed only in having a slightly smaller diameter radar antenna. Air-to-air armament consisted of up to six AIM-120 AMRAAM, or two AMRAAM and four Sidewinders. It could also double in the air/ground role. This was the AV-8B Harrier II Plus, which first flew on September 22, 1992. The RAF pencilled in the designation GR.9 for a similar machine, but this now looks most unlikely to emerge.

Harriers all have two-seater conversion trainers. In the RAF these have been given even numbers, T.2, T.4, and T.10, etc. US Harriers are the TAV-8A and TAV-8B.

Far left: An assortment of wing-mounted or centreline stores (not the gun pods) carried during Navy Board of Inspection and Survey trials. In front are a Sidewinder training store, and AIM-9L and a pair of AIM-9Ns.

Left: Weapon release trials from Patuxent River in October 1982, using the third aircraft, included this set of two triplets of inert Snakeye retarded bombs. Delivery accuracy has been consistently excellent.

Below: The slightly bulged radome, which houses a Hughes APG-65 multi-mode pulse-Doppler radar, albeit with a cropped antenna, marks this as a Harrier II Plus. Seen here with AIM-120 AMRAAM and AIM-9N Sidewinder

air-to-air missiles, the Harrier II Plus was designed to give the US Marine Corps a measure of air superiority over the beachhead, not-withstanding the absence of supersonic flight capability.

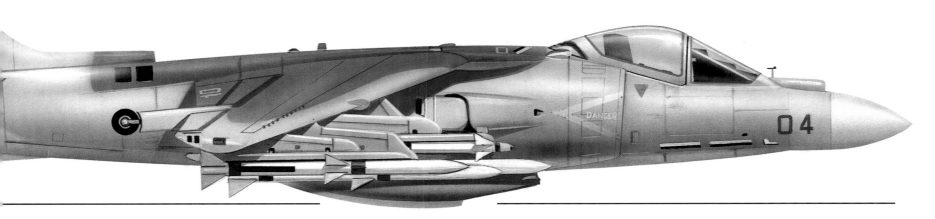

War and Peace

Initially, the Harrier concept was intended to lead to a multi-mission STOVL fighter, the Hawker P.1154, a twin-engined design with Phantom capabilities. This was some thirty years ago, and would have involved plenum chamber burning. With hindsight, this was far ahead of the state of the art at that time, and would almost certainly have involved a costly cancellation. By contrast the Harrier has been a success story, mainly because its aims were limited to the achievable.

The success of the Harrier and Sea Harrier in the South Atlantic in 1982 set a precedent which was underlined in the Gulf War some nine years later. Some of us were surprised when no RAF Harriers were deployed for Operations *Desert Shield* and *Desert Storm,* when heaps of Jaguars and Tornados were sent to the theatre. What we did not realise was that the GR.5/7 had not then been cleared for many of the weapons that it was later to carry. But the deficit was made good by the US Marine Corps, which was well ahead in weapons clearance for the AV-8B.

First to arrive were VMA-311 from

Below: Today's GR.3? Sure, but what other aeroplane – anywhere in the world – can deploy real airpower without needing any kind of airfield or carrier? This aircraft from 233 OCU demonstrates the aerodynamics – using rainwater – of a rolling VL.

MCAS Yuma and VMA-542 from MCAS Cherry Point, on 19 August, 1991. The former had a rough night crossing; it was a dark and stormy night, with "St. Elmo's fire" all around the aircraft. Eleven in-flight refuellings saw them arrive at Rota in Spain, before flying on to Bahrain. From Bahrain, VMA-311 moved to King Abdul Aziz Airfield. This was a bare-bones facility, and the troops set up a base in the car park of a nearby soccer stadium. Shortly after, they were joined by VMA-542. Next in theatre was VMA-331 from Cherry Point, deployed aboard the assault ship USS *Nassau.*

A second wave of AV-8Bs arrived on 22 December, headed by VMA-231. This squadron had been based at Iwakuni in Japan. Prior to departing, they had painted the inside of their intakes gloss white to neutralize the "black hole" effect of Harriers seen from head-on. Shepherded by KC-10 tankers, they staged to the Middle East via Wake

Island, Hawaii, Yuma, Cherry Point, and Rota. The total distance was more than 15,600nm (28,900km), but this route was dictated by logistics. The final accession of strength was a detachment of six AV-8Bs from VMA-513 aboard the assault ship USS *Tarawa.*

The field at King Abdul Aziz was by now a very crowded place, with 60 AV-8Bs plus other aircraft. To make the most of the Harrier II's quick reaction capability, a forward operating location was set up near Tanajib, within minutes of the Kuwaiti border. This could hold up to a dozen Harrier IIs.

Initially the Marine AV-8Bs were scheduled to be held back during Phase I of *Desert Storm,* but on the first morning four VMA-311 aircraft on quick reaction alert were called in to take out Iraqi artillery positions shelling Khafji. On the following day, the force commenced to "prepare" the battlefield. Often they were guided in by forward air controllers

Above: Some people might get the idea McDonnell Douglas was trying to corner the market in advanced combat aircraft. The chief point that emerges from this June 1982 formation picture is the relatively small size of the Harrier II, compared with the F-15 (nearest) and F/A-18 (furthest).

(FACs) in OV-10s, or sometimes by fast-mover F/A-18Ds. Most attacks were made from medium altitude, with a fairly steep dive used to line up on the target, pulling out at about 6,000ft (1,829m) to minimise the time spent in the lethal zone of Iraqi light AAA.

At first, a single Sidewinder was carried for self-defence but, since it became apparent that the Iraqi air threat was virtually non-existent, these were left off. The normal weapons load was four or six Mk 82 or Mk 83 bombs, or Rockeye CBUs. Strafing with cannon was widely used. In all, 86 Harrier IIs flew 3,380

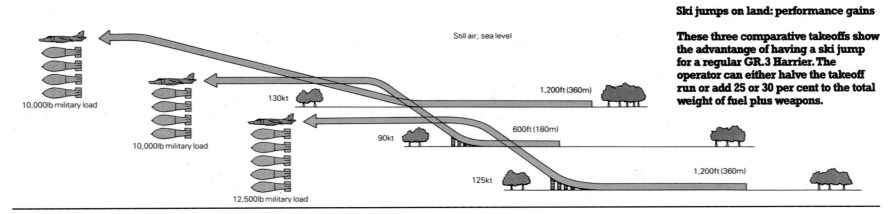

Ski jumps on land: performance gains

These three comparative takeoffs show the advantage of having a ski jump for a regular GR.3 Harrier. The operator can either halve the takeoff run or add 25 or 30 per cent to the total weight of fuel plus weapons.

Still air; sea level

10,000lb military load

130kt

10,000lb military load

90kt

12,500lb military load

125kt

1,200ft (360m)

600ft (180m)

1,200ft (360m)

combat sorties and delivered nearly 27,000 tons of ordnance, most of it unguided. Five Harrier IIs were lost in action; two pilots were killed, two taken prisoner, and one was rescued. Given the hazardous nature of close air support, this loss rate, barely one tenth of one per cent, was remarkably low.

Post-Gulf War Harrier action

British Harriers have since had their share of active service. HMS *Ark Royal* sailed for the Adriatic on 14 January, 1993 with six Sea Harrier FRS.1s of 801 Sqn aboard, to cover peace-keeping operations in Bosnia. During the following year, Serbian active aggression increased,

Below: The US Marine Corps received 27 new-build Harrier II Plus, and has remanufactured more than 72 of its original AV-8Bs to II Plus standards. Spain and Italy have both ordered the type for carrier usage.

and NATO air forces intervened. On 16 April, 1994, two Sea Harriers were tasked to bomb Serbian tanks but, hampered by bad weather, they ran in very low. Too low in fact; one was hit by an SA-7 shoulder-launched missile. The pilot ejected safely and was rescued.

Another milestone was the first operational deployment of the Sea Harrier FRS.2 on 26 January, 1995, with 801 Sqn aboard HMS *Illustrious*. The career of the FRS.1 ended a month later, when HMS *Invincible* returned from the Adriatic with 800 Sqn.

Meanwhile, back in the Middle East, eight Harrier GR.7s left Laarbruch in Germany in April 1993 for Incirlik in Turkey, replacing Jaguars in the international force over northern Iraq. Used mainly for armed reconnaissance, this deployment was largely uneventful. Recalled to Gioia del Colle in Italy in mid-1995, they were soon in action over Bosnia as part of Operation *Deliberate*

Right: G-VTOL, the company demonstrator, has been used for hundreds of ski-jump takeoffs to show potential customers there really is nothing to it. Here it is using the RAE Bedford ramp which is set at 20°. The development of mobile, land-based ramps must be a priority for the future.

Force. In this they were joined by *Invincible's* new Sea Harrier FRS.2s, making their combat debut.

After a quiet spell, the Balkans pot boiled over again in March 1999. In a bid to stop ethnic cleansing in Kosovo, NATO launched air strikes against selected Serbian targets. The Harrier contingent was a detachment of eight GR.7s of No 1 Sqn, based at Gioia del Colle, joined by the Sea Harriers of 800 Sqn in mid-April, which flew combat air patrols.

Initial results by the GR.7s proved disappointing, as bad weather and high

Above: Sea Harrier FRS. Is recovering aboard *Hermes* in May 1982, with an RFA oiler and plane-guard Sea King in the background. At the time of writing no Sea Harrier has ever been damaged in recovering aboard its ship.

humidity proved a problem to their sensors. At first Harriers failed to find their allotted targets and aborted their missions. But, while results improved with practice, this seems to indicate that a GPS-linked system is needed.

Spanish Harriers

The first export customer was Spain, which received six AV-8S single-seaters and two TAV-8S two-seaters in 1975/76. This of course was the baseline AV-8A, and the recipient was Escuadrilla 8a, based at Rota. Renamed Matador, they were deployed aboard the carrier *Daedalo*. This deployment was sufficiently successful to persuade the Spanish Navy to invest in a new carrier with a 12deg ski-jump. Completed in 1985, this was the *Principe de Asturias,* and was matched by an order for 20 EAV-8Bs, plus a two-seater. The first of these arrived in October 1987. By March 1993, 12 aircraft had been delivered to Esc 9a, although one had been lost in an accident. The remaining eight aircraft were to be the fighter variant EAV-8B Plus, with those already delivered to be retrofitted to this standard. Matadors have contributed to operations over Bosnia, flying from the *Principe de Asturias*.

Indian Harriers

The Indian Navy has a long tradition of using Hawker carrier fighters; Sea Hawks took part in the war of 1965, flying from the carrier INS *Vikrant,* which had originally been laid down as HMS *Hercules*. The initial order, placed in 1978, was for six Sea Harrier FRS.51 and two two-seat conversion trainers. These

were all delivered by March 1984. Then, in 1987, India bought HMS *Hermes*, of South Atlantic fame, and commissioned her as INS *Viraat*. In all, 23 Sea Harrier FRS.51s and four conversion trainers have been delivered.

Italian Harriers

For decades the Italian Navy had no mandate to operate fixed wing aircraft, but behind the scenes parliamentary wheeling and dealing finally saw this reversed. It was not a moment too soon; the aircraft carrier *Guiseppe Garibaldi* had been completed in 1985; theoretically it was a helicopter carrier, but...! With the proper clearances the Italian Navy ordered 16 AV-8B Plus fighters and two two-seater TAV-8Bs in 1989.

The first five aircraft were completed in the USA and worked up at MCAS Cherry Point, from where they were brought home in triumph in 1994 by *Garibaldi*. The rest have since been delivered, and are operational from Grottaglie. Their international debut was in support of UN operations in Somalia in 1995.

Thai Harriers

The Royal Thai Navy had long had ambitions for seaborne air power. The first step was the purchase of a carrier from Spain. This duly emerged as the RTNS *Chakri Naruebet*, a *Principe de Asturias* class vessel with the unlikely addition of a royal suite on board. It was delivered on 4 August, 1997. By this time, the original Spanish Matadors were surplus to requirements, even though they had many years of life remaining, and these were also refurbished and supplied to Thailand, to equip 301 Sqn.

Transfer of the jets took place on 24 October, 1996, and shortly after, Thai pilots began converting onto type at Rota. With seven single-seaters and two two-seater jets on board – all that remained of the original Spanish com-

plement – the new carrier arrived home on 4 August, 1997. The land base of 301 Sqn is U-Tapao.

Ski-jump

The ski-jump has increased Harrier capability but apart from allowing relatively heavy loads to be carried from fairly small ships, what other uses has it? One fairly obvious proposal was to use it to allow tactical fighters to be operated from damaged airfields, since a very short takeoff run was needed. In this connection, the US Navy experimented at Patuxent River with launching conventional (i.e., non-thrust vectoring) tactical fighters such as the Hornet and Tomcat, from ski-jumps. It was quickly established that this was a practical proposition; all they had to do was to arrive at the base of the ramp at a certain critical speed.

The inherent possibilities in this were never developed. A permanent ski-jump would quickly have become a prime target; the alternative was a mobile, quickly set-up ski-jump. One apparently very sensible suggestion was that the ideal would be to use hardened shelters as the base for permanent ski-jump ramps, giving plenty of them on every airfield so equipped at minimal cost.

However, this was not pursued. Nor was it a practical proposition to haul mobile ski-jumps to forward airfields, which the US Marines would have liked. Apart from any other consideration, the ability to lift a greater weight of munitions from a forward operating location would have compounded the difficulties of resupply!

Ironically, the main beneficiary of the ski-jump appears to be the Russian Navy. Navalized variants of the MiG-29 Fulcrum and the huge Su-27 Flanker can both be launched from ski-jumps in the bows of carriers, thus enabling them (bearing in mind that the Russians only moved into the "blue-water" carrier fleet

in recent times) to bypass the traditional catapult launch. This simplified their task immeasurably.

Small ship operations

The Harrier has been touted as being compatible with any ship which is able to operate a helicopter, the theory being that a Harrier can set down on, and lift off from, any helicopter pad that can accommodate its physical dimensions. This was a straightforward extrapolation of the World War II CAM-ships, which could launch a single Hurricane to drive away enemy shadowers. However, the Hurricane was a one-shot aircraft; it could not be recovered, and at the end of its fuel was forced to ditch.

As with the Hurricane, launching the Sea Harrier from a small ship was no big deal; the difficulty lay in recovery. Let us consider the oft-quoted case of Sea Harrier pilot Ian Watson. In June 1983, he became low on fuel far out over the Atlantic, having "lost" his carrier. Having sighted a small (2,300-ton) Spanish merchant ship, he managed to land on it with minimal damage. While this is often quoted as a classic example of small ship operations, the following must be borne in mind.

Having "lost" a much larger carrier, how much easier would it be to "lose" a smaller ship! Then, while Watson managed to land successfully, how would he have fared at night, or in poor weather? The standard procedure for landing on a "Harrier carrier" is to make an approach offset to port, come to the hover level with it, then move across before descending vertically to the quite large and roomy flight deck.

Night approaches to a small ship are quite a different matter. As the ship pitches and rolls, the pilot tends to follow the movement of the ship, which often takes him out of phase and stands a fair chance of landing him in the water.

Systems have been developed for helicopters which can minimise the risk but, even so, the time inevitably comes when the Harrier must move into the turbulent area behind the ship's superstructure, while the precision demands of landing on a helicopter-sized pad become extreme. As BAe test pilot Heinz Frick commented: "...you need a lot of skill to land an aircraft on a small ship. In rough weather it can be practically impossible!"

Takeoff is not without peril either. The critical time comes when the Harrier is not quite flying, but nor attached to the deck. What was needed was a device that could secure the Harrier at these critical moments. Thus was born the Skyhook concept.

Skyhook

Aware of the problems of operating from small ships in adverse weather conditions, BAe evolved a truly Heath Robinson (Rube Goldberg to our US readers) system, called Skyhook. The idea was first formulated in 1981, and developed into a crane which could reach out and grab a hovering Harrier and lower it gently to the deck. At launch it would raise it clear of the deck, then hold it in position until the Harrier was ready to fly!

In a sea state of Force 6, a vessel travelling at 15kt (28kmh) would pitch at up to plus or minus 7deg, roll at up to plus or minus 15deg, while vertical deck movement might reach 16ft (5m). These were the limits that Skyhook was designed to handle.

Skyhook's detractors justifiably argued that, towards the end of the 20th Century, against a modern tactical or strategic air threat able to launch anti-shipping missiles from extended ranges, a single Sea Harrier could achieve little in the fleet air defence role, especially as the days of unarmed shadowers were long gone. This was one of the most potent arguments against carrying a single aircraft on a small ship.

As envisaged, it was a complete package to carry four Sea Harriers and two Sea King helicopters in below-decks hangars, with two cranes (two for safety). The latter were normally stowed on deck, to be extended as needed. An active control system on the crane, triggered by inertial motion sensors and powered by hydraulic rams, ensured that its pick-up head was space-stabilized – i.e., moved straight ahead at the speed of the ship regardless of how much the latter pitched and rolled.

The pick-up head contained a simple parallax hover sight, with two horizontal and one vertical lines in a single plane, and two horizontal index markers near the pilot. These gave clear guidance information to the Sea Harrier pilot, allowing him to move inboard to the correct distance from the ship, at the correct height, with the exact fore-aft correlation in a 10cu ft (0.28 cu m) volume. This apparently was quite feasible, even with the early Harriers, which were slightly twitchy in the hover.

Trials were flown at Dunsfold by Heinz Frick, who found little difficulty in maintaining position within the required limits. We must of course remember that he was a fully trained test pilot. The capabilities of a "squaddie" were not tested.

Once in position "in the box", an imaging infra-red system in the Skyhook head measured the exact angle and distance of the aircraft, by viewing a pattern of IR-absorbing patches. Once the clever electrons were satisfied, the pick-up probe was extended, making contact in about one second. When this was achieved, the pilot reduced power, and hydraulic jacks on the probe locked, pulling the Harrier up into the docking cradle.

At this point the Skyhook control officer swung the Sea Harrier inboard and lowered it to the deck, where it could be refuelled and rearmed. Then two options were possible. One school of thought favoured an optimised Sea Harrier with no landing gear. This would have had two immediate effects. The weight saving arising would have lowered the admittedly high wing loading, improving not only manoeuvrability but also warload carriage in the hover, making for a more effective warplane. It would also have demanded the use of preloaded trestles on board ship, with the required munitions ready, and automatically raised into position, including 30mm gun pods.

Below decks, the trestle carrying the Sea Harrier would have been automatically moved into the hangar, while another took its place, thus easing onboard handling problems. The downside of this was that a great deal of flexibility would have been lost when the time came for the wheel-less Harrier to transfer to a shore base.

To return to Skyhook, it was then automatically programmed to take the replacement Harrier topside, hoisting it and swinging it outboard while reverting to the space-stabilization mode. During this time the pilot carried out his cockpit checks. When satisfied, he signalled that he was ready for launch, and, checking that the nozzles were in the hover position, he applied power. As Skyhook sensed a negative load, it disconnected and withdrew rapidly upwards. At this point the pilot turned away from the ship and commenced to accelerate into wingborne flight.

Skyhook was a system that could have provided limited fleet air defence on a shoestring for many of the world's navies. But, like many other bright ideas, it was stymied by the end of the Cold War. And the question mark that always hung over it was: could it really have been used by

Right: If any of the local farmers around Dunsfold had been watching these early experiments in 1982 they might indeed have thought Kingston-Brough Division were mad. G-VTOL proved that, from the pilot's point of view, the Skyhook concept is "a piece of cake".

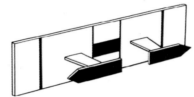

The hover sight

Below: A sequence showing how aircraft capture by the BAe-promoted Skyhook is envisaged. The guidance display – simplicity itself – is carried on the end of the Skyhook. It uses parallax to allow the pilot to formate his aircraft correctly in the contact window.

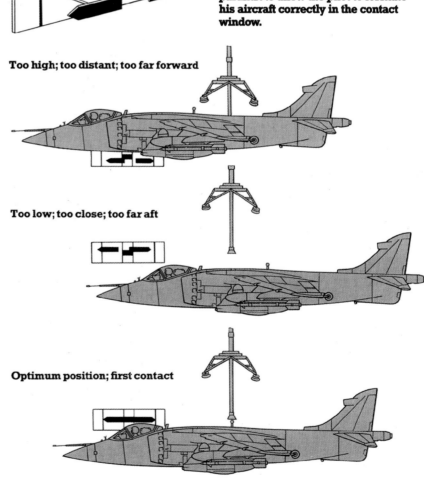

Too high; too distant; too far forward

Too low; too close; too far aft

Optimum position; first contact

Locked in place

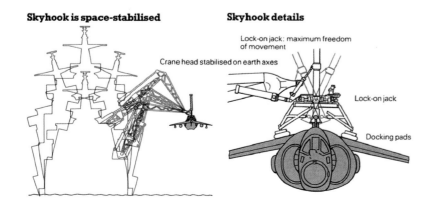

Skyhook is space-stabilised

Crane head stabilised on earth axes

Skyhook details

Lock-on jack: maximum freedom of movement

Lock-on jack

Docking pads

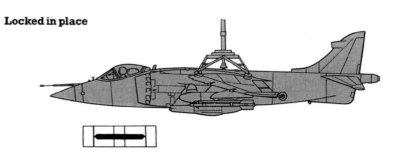

Specifications

	Harrier GR.7	Sea Harrier FRS.2	AV-8B Harrier II	AV-8B Harrier II Plus
Span	30ft 4in/9.25m	25ft 3in/7,70m	30ft 4in/9.25m	30ft 4in/9.25m
Length	47ft 1in/14.35m	46ft 5in/14.15m	46ft 4in/14.12m	47ft 9in/14.55m
Height	11ft 8in/3.56m	11ft 10in/3.61m	11ft 8in/3.56m	11ft 8in/3.56m
Wing area	230sq.ft/21.37m²	201sq.ft/18.67m²	230sq.ft/21.37m²	230sq.ft/21.37m²
Empty weight	13,971lb/6,337kg	14,585lb/6,616kg	15,060lb/6,831kg	14,867lb/6,744kg
Max TO weight	29,750lb/13,495kg	26,200lb/11,884kg	31,000lb/14,062kg	31,000lb/14,062kg
Engine	Pegasus Mk 105	Pegasus Mk 106	F402-RR-408	F402-RR-408
Thrust	21,550lb/9,775kg	21,550lb/9,775kg	23,850lb/10,818kg	23,850lb/10,818kg
Intl Fuel	7,759lb/3,519kg	5,050lb/2,291kg	7,759lb/3,519kg	7,759lb/3,519kg
V_{max}	583kt/1,075kmh	635kt/1,177kmh	570kt/1,056kmh	602kt/1,115kmh
Ceiling	35,000ft/10,667m	c45,000ft/13,715m	35,000ft/10,667m	c45,000ft/13,715m
Radius	471nm/873km	400nm/741km	471mn/873km	c600nm/1,112km

Right: The PCB rig at Shoeburyness during test operation. The water spray visible is to cool ground-based instrumentation during the initial running-up test phase. Note PCB flames visible in front nozzles.

ordinary squadron pilots?

SCADS
Rather more pedestrian in concept, if easier to operate, was the Shipborne Containerized Air Defence System (SCADS). This had its origins in the "Woolworths" carriers of World War II, in which flight decks were fitted to suitably sized transports to give a modicum of air cover to convoys.

The modern trend in seaborne transport is the container ship. In layout similar to the tanker, with a large deck area and the superstructure well aft, the container ship normally carries much of its cargo at deck level, in ISO standard containers. Each container is 8 x 8 x 40ft (2.4 x 2.4 x 12m).

The ideal starting point is a ship of some 30,000 tons which is capable of 25kt (46kmh). The containers could house fuel, munitions and spares, sufficient to last six Sea Harriers and two Sea King ASW helicopters for a minimum of 30 days. They could also provide temporary accommodation for support personnel, and for defensive weaponry.

Quickly convertible to its role of ersatz aircraft carrier, the container ship could have proved a valuable tool in naval power projection. The way ahead was shown in the South Atlantic in 1982 by the ill-fated *Atlantic Conveyor*, which ferried RAF Harriers south, with a Sea Harrier spotted for local air defence. Only after the RAF Harriers had hover-taxied to their allotted carriers was the *Atlantic Conveyor* sent to the bottom by an Exocet missile. Given anything like the defensive systems allotted to warships, this almost certainly would not have happened.

What was clearly needed was an evaluation of container ships as ad hoc aircraft carriers, although in peacetime the major problem is obtaining the consent of their owners! However, what should be borne in mind is the sheer flexibility provided by the Harrier/Sea Harrier.

The future
What does the future hold for the Harrier? The honest answer appears to be, not a lot, although it will remain in service for many years to come. Supersonic variants have been under consideration for nearly four decades, but nothing has emerged. The future of STOVL combined with stealth appears bright, if (and it is a very big "if") the Joint Strike Fighter ever enters service. What we must remember is, that against all the odds, against the best that Dassault and Yakovlev could produce, it was the Harrier that led the way!

Harrier Operators

Unit	Type	Base
Royal Air Force		
1 Squadron	Harrier GR.7/T.10	Cottesmore
3 Squadron	Harrier GR.7/T.10	Cottesmore
4 Squadron	Harrier GR.7/T.10	Cottesmore
20 (R) Squadron	Harrier GR.7/T.10	Wittering
Royal Navy		
800 Squadron	Sea Harrier FRS.2	Yeovilton
801 Squadron	Sea Harrier FRS.2	Yeovilton
899 Squadron	Sea Harrier FRS.2/T.8	Yeovilton
US Marine Corps		
VMA-211 Wake Island	AV-8B	Yuma
VMA-214 Black Sheep	AV-8B	Yuma
VMA-223 Bulldogs	AV-8B/AV-8B Plus	Cherry Point
VMA-231 Ace of Spades	AV-8B/AV-8B Plus	Cherry Point
VMA-311 Tomcats	AV-8B Yuma	
VMA-513 Nightmares	AV-8B Yuma	
VMA-542 Tigers	AV-8B/AV-8B Plus	Cherry Poin
VMAT-203 Hawks	AV-8B/TAV-8B	Cherry Point
VX-9 Vampires	AV-8B	China Lake
NWTS(CL) Dust Devils	AV-8B	China Lake
Spanish Navy		
Esc 9	EAV-8B/EAV-8B Plus	Rota
Indian Navy		
INAS 300/SHOFTU	Sea Harrier FRS.61/T.60	Dabolin
Italian Navy		
Gruppo Aerei Imbarcati	AV-8B Plus	Grottaglie
Royal Thai Navy Air Division		
301 Squadron	AV-8S/TAV-8S	U-Tapao

Above: The Rolls-Royce Pegasus 11-61 powers the Harrier II Plus. Seen here is the oversized compressor, needed for slow speed and hovering flight, and four rotating vectoring nozzles which are a unique Harrier feature.

SCADS ship layout

Below: SCADS (shipborne containerized air-defence system) is something that in the early 1980s is highly exciting, but it is almost certainly by no means the only bright idea to be triggered off by vectored thrust. This diagram shows how any modern container ship could be adapted so that, at less than 48h notice, it could be converted into an operating base for the world's most versatile combat aircraft. There are an unlimited number of ways in which Harriers and ships can be wedded, but SCADS appears in 1984 to be very hard to beat – whatever the budget!

Europe's

Contents

Top: The quadrinational EF 2000 Typhoon is the most capabable if the most expensive of the new birds.

Above: In service since 1982, the Mirage 2000 is still a very potent warplane. Relaxed stability and fly by wire were used to overcome the worst drawbacks of the tail-less delta configuration.

Above right: The diminutive shape of the Saab JAS 39 Gripen conceals a capability closely comparable to that of the F-16. Ordered by South Africa, it is expected to sell well.

Left: The Dassault Rafale, seen here during carrier trials. It is stated to be "good around the boat", though approach angle of attack seems a bit high by current standards.

New Fighters

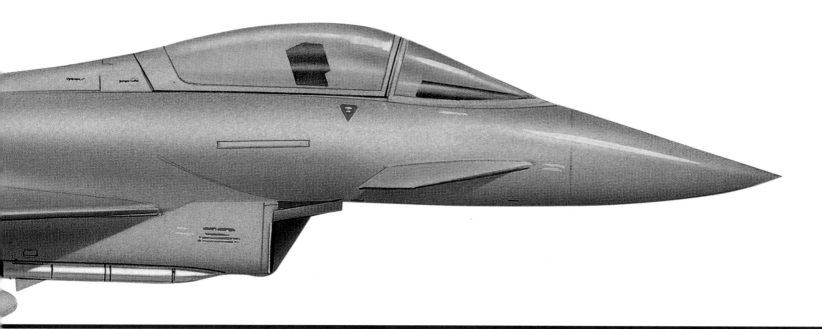

Introduction

In the mid-1970s, the "worst case" scenario was a conventional invasion of Europe by the Soviet Union and its Warsaw Pact allies. The overwhelming numbers available to the Eastern Bloc, both in the air and on the ground, gave little hope of the West stemming the tide without recourse to nuclear weapons.

Air superiority over the battlefield was essential, but how best to gain it? The superb American F-14 Tomcat and F-15 Eagle, which entered service in 1973 and 1974 respectively, completely outclassed the opposition. But they were unaffordable in the quantities needed. Adverse odds of between 5:1 and 10:1 would quickly create confusion, and confusion degrades technology very quickly indeed. The USA adopted a "belt and braces" solution, seeking to redress the numerical imbalance with much simpler fighters, the F-16 and the F/A-18. But where did this leave the Europeans, with their much smaller defence budgets?

Britain and Germany had previously bought the American

Phantom, but this was now getting long in the tooth. The British, with their special requirement of operating autonomously far out over the North Sea, developed the Tornado F.3, a very specialised and capable interceptor, but a turkey in close manoeuvre combat.

France operated the Mirage F.1, a conventional and rather pedestrian fighter by the standards of the day, and the Anglo-French Jaguar attack aircraft.

Sweden had a record of producing unorthodox fighters and specialised in off-field basing. Its primary combat aircraft was the Viggen, a canard cranked delta, but with the canards intended to improve short field performance rather than manoeuvrability.

The other two important European nations were Italy and Spain. The former flew updated but ancient F-104S Starfighters, while the Spanish operated Phantoms and Mirage F.1s, and later bought a few F/A-18 Hornets.

A whole new generation of European fighters was needed.

Europe's New Fighters

The USAF has always been a "Rich Man's" air force. Who else could have afforded not one, but four, Aggressor Squadrons to provide dissimilar air combat training? Which other nation could have poured money into low-observable technology, leading to the F-117 and the B-2, to say nothing of the F-22? Certainly not European nations. Their path has been more predictable. Affordability has been the keynote; top quality stealth is an expensive commodity, and therefore it has been traded against performance and manoeuvrability. This has resulted in similar configurations being adopted for the latest generation of European fighters.

All four of the latest generation European fighters – Mirage 2000, Rafale, Gripen and Typhoon – use delta wings, as did the abortive Israeli Lavi, unlike their American and Russian counterparts. The clever bit is how they managed to overcome the inherent faults of the delta wing. The triangular, or delta-shaped wing, offers many advantages to a high performance fighter. It combines a sharp leading edge sweep, good for acceleration and for supersonic flight, with a large wing area and consequently low wing loading for manoeuvre. Unlike most wing configurations, it has no clearly defined point of stall, and in descending manoeuvres can be controlled at quite low airspeeds. The long chord inboard gives considerable wing depth, which not only keeps the thickness/chord ratio low, which is necessary for supersonic flight, but provides ample space for fuel tanks and other equipment such as the main landing gear. It is also simple to construct. To obtain the greatest benefits in terms of internal volume, a tail-less delta is optimum, as this provides the longest chord and the greatest depth of wing.

There are however drawbacks. The larger the wing area, the higher the drag, due to the larger wetted area. In supersonic flight the centre of lift moves aft, which causes a tendency to pitch nose-down. The broad chord of the delta tends to increase the distance of the aft movement, which needs correspondingly more compensation.

In a tailed aircraft, this is offset by using the tailplane to produce a download which, while it restricts supersonic manoeuvrability, is widely regarded as acceptable. In a tail-less delta, the download can only be offset by an upward deflection of the trailing edge control sur-

Left: The first EF 2000 Typhoon to be powered by the definitive Eurojet EJ 200 turbofans, afterburners lit, lifts off the runway. In March 2000 Greece ordered 60 Typhoons, the first export order of the type.

Below, far left: Where the desert meets the land: Rafael B.01 shows its semi-circular intakes to advantage, a compromise between the side and chin intakes, with bulged fuselage as the compression wedge.

Below centre: Showering steam and spray in all directions, Sweden's JAS 39 Gripen diminutive fighter takes off from a widened stretch of roadway, which is part of the national dispersed basing scheme.

Below: Well-armed French-built Mirage 2000-5 of Taiwanese Air Force heads skyward with a full bag of air-to-air missiles. Faced with a threat from the People's Republic of China across the water, the Mirage 2000-5 may oppose the Su-27.

faces, which increases drag just when this is least wanted.

Maximum lift on a delta wing is achieved at a relatively high angle of attack. While this should theoretically make takeoff and landing speeds quite low, in fact it does nothing of the sort, as the angle of attack is so high that the rear end would be scraping along the runway long before minimum flying speed was reached. Nose-up pitch control was

achieved by deflecting the trailing edge elevons (surfaces that double as ailerons or elevators) upwards. This also increased drag when it was least needed, and reduced lift when it was most needed. The same effect was visible on landing, when the fighter had to be brought in at speeds well above the stall if unacceptably high sink rates were to be avoided. Inevitably takeoff and landing speeds were higher, and ground rolls were longer than they

would have been with a conventional tailed layout.

While increased angle of attack gives increased lift (at least up to a certain point), it also increases induced drag – i.e., drag due to lift. Very quickly, total drag starts to exceed the thrust available from the engine. This is known as getting on the back of the drag curve, where the lines subtended from available thrust and increased drag cross over. At this point,

speed bleeds off alarmingly. At altitude, the answer is to drop the nose and convert altitude into energy. But on the landing approach this is not a good idea. The ground is far too close!

In manoeuvre combat, the same thing applies. Hard turns tend to bleed off speed at a tremendous rate, although in close combat this can be used to force an opponent cleverly trapped at six o'clock, to overshoot.

Dassault Mirage 2000

The Dassault Mirage 2000 is unusual in that instead of being designed to meet an official specification, the specification was written around the aeroplane. The original requirement was for the Super Mirage, with a performance to closely match the F-15. It soon became obvious that this would be unaffordable, and Dassault started work on a cheaper alternative. When the Super Mirage was cancelled, the Mirage 2000 was waiting in the wings. First flown on 10 March 1978, it was an instant success.

In the early postwar years, the Paris-based Dassault company produced a rather pedestrian family of conventional jet fighters. The threat at this time was the nuclear-armed fast jet bomber, and the problem of interception was paramount. Studies showed that the tail-less delta configuration was optimum for the top right-hand corner of the flight performance envelope, where speed and altitude were maximised. The result was the Mirage III.

Judged by its contemporaries, the Mirage III was a fairly ordinary fighter. Then, the miracle happened. In the fighter world, the *imprimatur* is "combat proven!" Acquired by Israel, more or less by default, at a time when the latest British and American fighters were embargoed, the Mirage IIICJ gained an enviable reputation against Arab-flown MiG-17s, -19s and -21s. The MiG-21 in particular was rated as a formidable opponent – fast, agile, and with jack-rabbit acceleration. That the dominant factor was pilot quality was largely ignored by the rest of the world; the kudos fell to the Mirage III, which was subsequently bought and operated by over 20 nations.

The French were however under no illusions. The successor to the Mirage III was the Mirage F.1. This had a conventional swept-wing and tail, with a combination of slats and flaps which more than offset the much heavier wing loading. Approach speed was almost one third less than that of the Mirage III, while at most speed/altitude combinations the F.1 could out-turn its predecessor, while bleeding off much less energy in the process.

The next projected Dassault fighter was the Super Mirage. Again, this was of conventional layout, and its specified performance rivalled that of the American F-15. However, the Super Mirage proved unaffordable, and studies of a cheaper alternative were commenced in 1972. By this time, the advantages of relaxed stability with a computerized fly-by-wire system were becoming realised, and Dassault felt that this would largely offset the disadvantages of the tail-less delta configuration.

The result was the Mirage 2000, which first flew on 10 March 1978. A tail-less delta, it appeared very similar to the Mirage III, but beneath the skin it was completely different. Full-span leading edge slats on the wing leading edges, and full-span two-piece elevons to the trailing edges gave automatic variable camber, as used on the F-16. Computer-controlled, these were now a practical proposition and, rather than producing downloads at the most undesirable times, could be configured for extra lift in most flight regimes. The flight control system was analogue quadruplex fly-by-wire, later converted to digital.

Leading edge sweep was 58deg, and careful wing-body blending reduced wave drag. It also reduced radar cross section, but this was incidental. The rear of the canopy was faired into the fuselage, reducing drag at the cost of a marginal reduction in rearward visibility. Composite materials were used extensively to save weight, while limiters on the quadruplex FBW system gave carefree handling, as anyone who has seen Dassault test pilot Patrick Experton doing his yawing, pitching straight run, doing everything but bring up his breakfast, will testify.

To improve high angle of attack handling still more, small strakes on the outside of the intake ducts were used to create vortices to clean up the airflow over the upper surface of the wings.

One unusual feature for the era was that, at a time when most designers were concentrating on agility rather than absolute performance, both Dassault

Left: The warload on this Mirage 2000-5 consists of four MICA and two R550 Magic AAMs. Also carried are two external fuel tanks shaped for supersonic flight. High speed and altitude are its forte.

and *L'Armée de l'Air* settled for the top right hand corner of the flight performance envelope: maximum speed and maximum altitude. Interception, particularly of the fast and high-flying Russian MiG-25 reconnaissance aircraft figured high in the list of priorities. This was a primary reason for reverting to the tailless delta configuration.

The engine was also optimised for this regime; the SNECMA M53 was a single spool turbofan with a low bypass ratio and a moderate compression ratio, at a time when fighter engine designers were concentrating on two-spool turbofans. The M53 was more nearly a continuous-bleed turbojet than a turbofan, but it was very efficient at supersonic speeds at high altitude. As in all fighter design, this was a compromise. At subsonic speeds at low altitude, specific fuel consumption is relatively high.

The M53 has been cleared for Mach 2.5, although the Mirage 2000 airframe is restricted to Mach 2.2 by kinetic heating. This could however be exceeded if ever higher speeds became necessary to effect an interception. It has typical Dassault variable inlets – semi-circular, with translating half-shock cones known as "souris", or mice!

Mirage 2000 in service

The first Mirage 2000s entered service with *l'Armée de l'Air* in November 1982. This was the 2000C, with a two-seater conversion trainer, the 2000B. The first production batch of 37 aircraft carried the Thomson-CSF RDM radar and were powered by the SNECMA M53-5 engine, but subsequent production articles were fitted with the more capable Thomson-CSF/Dassault Electronique RDI radar and the M53-P2 turbofan. This was optimised for the interception mission, using very high Pulse Repetition Frequencies (PRFs) to give unambiguous range and velocity data in search mode against distant targets. Against typical fighter-sized targets from head-on, typically with an RCS of 53.8sq ft (5m2), maximum range was stated as 65nm (120km). Against tail-on targets, or in look-down mode, this reduced to 30nm (56km).

That modern fighters are essentially weapons systems was also recognized. The Mirage 2000C was never going to be able to catch a reconnaissance Foxbat at its extreme altitude/speed range, so the extra performance needed was built into the radar/missile combination, the missile in this case being the Super 530D. The radar could provide guidance against very high flying opponents using a "snap-up" mode, with an altitude differential of at least 19,686ft (6,000m), enough to compensate for the disparity in aircraft performance. Other weapons carried were the Matra Magic heat-homer, and two 30mm DEFA 553 or 554 revolver-type cannon with 125 rounds each, although the latter did not feature on two-seaters.

Next came the export model, the Mirage 2000E, which was first delivered in 1984. While this had the M53-P2 turbofan, the radar was the RDM. A multi-mission aircraft, this could carry a variety of air-to-surface weaponry and reconnaissance kit. Like the 2000C, it also had a two-seat version, the Mirage 2000E/D.

Whereas in pre-FBW days the large wing area and load loading of the delta configuration had made its gust response poor at low level, giving a poor quality of ride, computerization was now in a position to remedy this. The next Mirage 2000 was the N (for *nucleaire*). First flown on 3 February 1983, the 2000N was a dedicated two-seater, with a guy in the back to handle the nav/attack systems. Intended to replace the elderly Mirage IV, this was optimised for low level penetration with an *Air-Sol Moyenne Portée* (ASMP) stand-off nuclear store with a 300KT yield. Two Magic 2s were carried for self-defence. The Dassault Electronique Antilope V radar provided automatic terrain-following, and was coupled with the Sagem INS and TRT radar altimeter. GPS has since been added, giving a high level of navigational accuracy.

A conventional air-to-surface attack was the obvious next step, and this duly emerged as the Mirage 2000D, which first flew in February 1991. Based on the 2000N, this was dedicated to all-weather attack with conventional weapons, dumb or smart. The radar was the Antilope 50, optimised for the non-nuclear air-to-surface mission.

The most radical advance came in October 1990, when the Mirage 2000-5 first took to the air, although almost six years passed before the first one was delivered. The Mirage 2000 had followed the trend for Hands On Throttle And Stick (HOTAS) and a "glass cockpit" with three multi-function displays. But with the Dash 5, Dassault introduced the APSI cockpit. This had no fewer than five colour displays. At the top is of course the Thomson-CSF wide angle HUD with a 30deg by 20deg field of view. Immediately below this is the innovatory "head level" display, which shows radar, FLIR, or laser imagery, so positioned that it is in the pilot's line of vision.

Below this, on either side of the dash, are two colour multi-mode displays, and below these and centrally mounted is the synthetic tactical display, also in colour. The radar for the Mirage 2000-5 is the pulse-Doppler multi-mode Thomson-CSF RDY Detexis, which not only gives greater range and capability in the air superiority role than its predecessor, but has more and better air-to-surface modes. While the French are understandably coy about its capabilities, it is known that it can detect up to 24 targets while assigning priorities and tracking the eight which the computer assesses as the greatest threats, while continuing to scan the area. Combined with the Missile Intermediat Combat Aerienne (MICA), this gives a multiple target engagement capability.

Defensively, the Mirage 2000-5 has an integrated internal countermeasures suite, which obviates the need for external pods. This consists of a Serval radar warning receiver, a *Caméléon* jammer, and a *Spirale* chaff/flare dispenser. From 1995, Matra *Samir* missile launch warning systems, based on infra-red detection of heat sources, have been progressively retrofitted. When activated, these give an aural warning, and a visual indication of the threat quadrant. The Mirage 2000-5 entered service with *l'Armée de l'Air* on December 30 1997.

Next in succession was the Mirage 2000-5 Mk II. This was essentially an export variant with a night attack capability using the Thomson Optronics *Nahar* FLIR for navigation and the Damocles targeting pod. Air-to-surface weapons carried include Marconi laser guided bombs, and the BAe/Matra *Black Shaheen* cruise missile, with a maximum range of 135nm (250km). The first customer for the Mk II was Greece, which placed an order in May 1999 for delivery in 2001. One final variant is the Mirage 2000-9. This is essentially the Mk II, but with a new INS and larger cockpit displays, for the United Arab Emirates.

Performance and manoeuvrability

The author first saw the Mirage 2000 demonstrated at the Farnborough Air Show, 1984, when its greatest rivals were the Northrop F-20 Tigershark and the General Dynamics F-16 Fighting Falcon. His immediate reaction was that it was a flying speed brake, able to decelerate in hard turns so rapidly that it could force an opponent to overshoot.

Like most modern fighters, the Mirage 2000 is stressed for loadings of +9g/-4.5g, although the FBW system can be over-ridden to allow the maximum of 13.5g if necessary. Not that the duration of this could be other than very brief! Maximum roll rate at subsonic speeds is a very rapid 270deg/sec, while pitch rates are also very fast. Instantaneous turn rate varies between 20-30deg according to altitude, but sustained turn rate is less, as one would expect given the modest thrust/weight ratio.

The F-16 set new standards in fighter manoeuvrability, and has been for many years the yardstick against which all other fighters are judged. So how does the Mirage 2000 compare? The following figures were provided by Dassault.

The immortal insigne of the Cigognes (Storks) on its fin, this Mirage 2000C shows classic Dassault lines, with translating side intakes coupled with a tailless delta wing.

Optimised for the top right hand corner of the flight performance envelope, one would obviously expect the two litre Mirage to be superior in this regime. And so it proved. Maximum speed of Mach 2.2 plus at the tropopause could not be matched by the Fort Worth fighter; nor could the operational ceiling of 57,500ft (17,526m) as against the F-16's 49,500ft (15,088m). By the same token, the Mirage ran out the winner in terms of acceleration from Mach 0.9 at the tropopause. After two minutes at maximum power, the French fighter had attained Mach 1.85, and after three minutes it was at Mach 2.17. The figures for the F-16 were Mach 1.75 and Mach 1.86 respectively.

It is however only fair to state that a document issued by Fort Worth shows that in acceleration from Mach 0.4 to Mach 1.0, the F-16 is significantly better, which (given the respective thrust loadings) is only to be expected. Another factor is that Mirage 2000 fuel consumption in all flight regimes is considerably lower, in part due to a smaller engine. What we have to remember here though is that we are comparing actual fuel used rather than sfc. Never compare cabbages with kings!

In instantaneous turn at 15,000ft (4,572m), the Dassault figures show the Mirage 2000 to be 4deg/sec better at Mach 0.7, but could only match the F-16 from Mach 0.9 to Mach 1.5. On the other hand, notwithstanding its huge wing area, the Mirage 2000 holds up well in the preferred arena of the F-16 – sustained turning. At 5,000ft (1,524m) it lags the Texas fighter by only 2deg/sec between Mach 0.5 and Mach 1.2. The same margin prevails at 15,000ft (4,572m) until Mach 1.5 when it becomes level pegging; while at 30,000ft (9,144m) there is little or no difference between the two fighters from Mach 0.7 to Mach 1.6.

Any discussion of which is the better fighter of the two is fairly pointless. Much depends on initial position at the start of the engagement; even more on respective pilot quality, and to a degree, the ability of the opposing weapons systems. In 1995 Geoff Roberts of *AirForces Monthly* magazine flew the Mirage 2000-5 from Istres. What he was most impressed with was the rapidity of spot rolls, essential in combat for changing direction quickly. And this was with two external fuel tanks on! He also commented that rolls were much easier to control precisely than had been the case with the F-16, which he had flown a year or so earlier.

Weaponry

As previously noted, most Mirage 2000s carry two 30mm DEFA 553 or 554 cannon. Two guns may be unusual, but with only 125 rounds per gun, and a relatively slow (vis-a-vis the M61) rate of fire. Maximum effective firing range is about 2,953ft (900m), but the optimum is 1,640ft (500m). The gunsight gives an aiming dot on the HUD, enclosed in a circle which unwinds with range in an anticlockwise direction. A figure to the left of this indicates how many rounds are left.

Initially the primary air-to-air weapon

Left: Unique to the cockpit of the Mirage 2000-5 is the look-level display just beneath the HUD. This allows the pilot to assimilate information without ceasing to look "out of the window".

Below: The two-seater Mirage 2000D conversion trainer, showing the typically Dassault semi-circular intakes with translating shock-cones which make it capable of Mach 2 plus at altitude.

Right: The SNECMA M53-5 is a simple single spool turbofan with a low bypass ratio (making it more nearly a continuous bleed turbojet) and a moderate compression ratio, best at high altitude and speed.

Below right: A Mirage 2000N with an ASMP nuclear store on the centreline, low over southern France. France sets great store on nuclear deterrence, and the 2000N will replace the ageing Mirage IV.

of the Mirage 2000 was the Matra Super 530D (D = Doppler). A semi-active homer, it had large surfaces to add to the body lift normally used by AAMs, which increased its utility in the thin air of the stratosphere. Maximum brochure speed was Mach 4.6, and range 22nm (41km). It was large – 12ft 5in (3.80m) long and 10.35in (265mm) in diameter – and heavy, 584lb (265kg).

For close combat, the Matra R550 Magic 2 was the preferred weapon. Similarly sized to Sidewinder, but rather shorter ranged, it was for all practical

Right: Even with three external fuel tanks on board, the Mirage 2000 is extremely agile. Roll rate is very fast, while control is very precise, even more so than the F-16.

purposes interchangeable with the American missile. How well it would compare in the arena of battle remains to be seen, although Magic has its advocates.

More recently, MICA has entered service. A French AMRAAM equivalent, it uses inertial midcourse guidance, followed by active radar homing terminal homing. IR homing is another option. Like the US missile, MICA is fairly small and light compared to previous medium range AAMs. Unusually it uses a combination of aerodynamic surfaces and thrust vectoring for control. The latter enables it to manoeuvre hard shortly after launch, giving a very short minimum range. Brochure speed is Mach 3.5, while maximum range is 27nm (50km).

The typical air-to-air load would be four MICA with two Magic 2s, or six MICA. Air-to-surface weapons loads include up to 18 551lb (250kg) dumb bombs; three 2,200lb (1,000kg) dumb or laser-guided bombs; up to 18 BAP 100 or Durandal anti-runway bombs; six Beluga or 18 BAT 120 CBUs; and a couple of Exocet anti-ship missiles or AS 30L laser-guided missiles. Other possible stores are Armat anti-radar missiles, or unguided rocket pods. ASMP is of course only carried by Mirage 2000Ns.

To summarize, Mirage 2000 is a superb multi-role aircraft. It flew air defence missions in the Gulf War of 1991, although (like the RAF Tornado F.3) it failed to make contact with the enemy. It has also flown combat air patrols and attack missions over Bosnia and Kosovo. In recent years it has been overshadowed by its more modern French stablemate, Rafale.

Specifications: Dassault Mirage 2000-5	
Dimensions	
Span	29ft 11in/9.13m
Length	48ft 1in/14.65m
Height	17ft 1in/ 5.20m
Wing area	441sq ft/41sq m
Aspect ratio	2.03
Weights	
Empty	16,535lb/7,500kg
Max takeoff	23,942lb/10,860kg
Power	1 x SNECMA M53-P2
Max thrust	21,375lb/9,696kg
Mil thrust	14,400lb/6,350kg
Intl fuel	7,055lb/3,200kg
Performance	
V_{max} hi	Mach 2.2 plus
V_{max} lo	Mach 1.2
Operational ceiling	59,058ft/18,000m
Climb rate	58,000ft/min-295m/sec, or 4 min to 49,000ft (14,934m)

Left: A Mirage 2000 launches a MICA over the test range. While MICA is the French equivalent of AMRAAM, the huge smoke trail at launch is a non-stealthy attribute which can reveal the attack.

The simple lines of the Mirage 2000 are revealed in this three-view of the Mirage 2000-5. Externally similar to the Mirage IIIC, variable camber and fly by wire make it far more capable.

Left: The Mirage 2000 has done very well in the export market and serves with eight air forces worldwide. The extinct volcano makes a very dramatic backdrop to this desert-camouflaged aircraft.

Above: Abu Dhabi is one of the export customers for the Mirage 2000; the two aircraft nearest the camera are desert-camouflaged Mirage 2000EADs; the far machine is a two-seater Mirage 2000DAD.

Right: Loaded for bear, this Mirage 2000-5 of l'Armée de l'Air carries four Super 530D medium range AAMs under the fuselage and two R550 Magic dogfight missiles outboard on the wings for close combat.

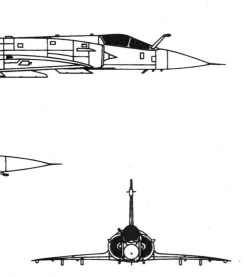

Saab JAS 39 Gripen

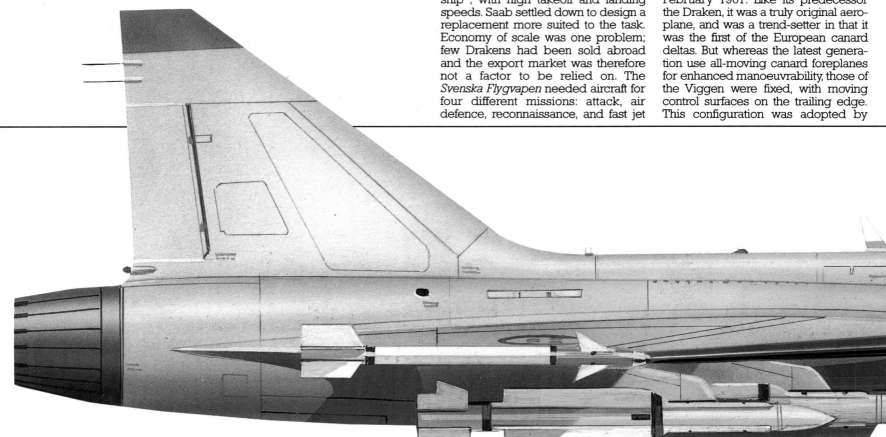

With a population of barely one quarter of that of the United Kingdom, and a defence budget to match, it is truly amazing that Sweden has not only managed to produce a series of top quality indigenous fighters, but is now in the process of entering the export market. The latest is the JAS (Jakt/Attack/Spåning) 39 Gripen; a small canard delta which is not only already in service in Sweden, but has been ordered by South Africa.

Sweden is a proud and independent nation. Neutral throughout World War II, it was determined later to preserve its neutrality, whatever the cost. This was not easy. Sweden has a small population and consequently a small gross national product from which to finance its defence needs. To aggravate the situation still more it had long borders. The threat against which it had to guard was not Norway to the west, nor Denmark to the south, nor even Finland to the east. It was the Soviet Union, which despite its communist heritage had openly stated that it was bent on world domination. In this it was more imperialist than any of the European empire builders had ever been.

In the early post-war period, military aviation was still relatively simple and affordable, even though the advent of the jet engine had opened up a whole new vista. Many nations tried to stay in the ball game – notably Argentina with the Pulqui series; Egypt; Spain; Israel (desperate to survive as a nation) with the Kfir, Dagger and Lavi; India with the indigenous Marut fighter-bomber and latterly the LCA; while the vast resources of China were turned to reverse-engineering Russian types.

Given the odds, Sweden appeared to have little chance of surviving in the "big boys" league of Britain, France, the USA and the Soviet Union. Yet the Swedish military aviation industry not only survived, but flourished. Over the past half-century, it has made Sweden self-sufficient in "home-brew" tactical fighters, a process that continues into the 21st Century.

In the jet era, it all started with the J.21R, a jet variant of the J.21 propeller-driven pusher fighter. This was followed by the J.29 Tunnen, a simple and basic swept-wing fighter, then the transonic A.32 Lansen, more or less a Hunter equivalent. Next came the revolutionary J35 Draken tail-less double delta, which was designed by the simple process of arranging the engine, the cockpit, and the necessary black boxes into a compact mass, then drawing the outline of a fighter around them.

One of the paramount needs of warfare is security of base. Given a population of a mere 14 million, the *Svenska Flygvapen* could not afford an effective fighter defence with an effective airfield defence system. Instead they chose to disperse their air assets as best they might.

The Swedish solution, in a large, heavily wooded, and under-populated country, was to set up what amounted to semi-permanent forward operating locations in remote areas. Specially selected and strengthened stretches of road were used for takeoff and landing, with the aircraft dispersed under the trees. Also well concealed were command and communication buildings, fuel and ammunition dumps, and limited maintenance facilities. This was made possible by the fact that for the most part Swedish forests were coniferous, providing cover all year round. It was assumed that a period of international tension would precede a surprise attack, and that this would allow timely dispersed deployment.

This view was reinforced by the Israeli pre-emptive strike against Arab airfields in June 1967, which succeeded in grounding a high proportion of the Egyptian Air Force from Day 1. There is an old saying: "All's fair in love and war!" As Lt Col "Boots" Boothby, USAF (ret), observed: "Pearl Harbor was the Day of Infamy; the Israeli pre-emptive strike was a great tactical victory. It all depends whose side you're on!"

The J.35 Draken was not ideally suited to dispersed basing. It was a "hot ship", with high takeoff and landing speeds. Saab settled down to design a replacement more suited to the task. Economy of scale was one problem; few Drakens had been sold abroad and the export market was therefore not a factor to be relied on. The *Svenska Flygvapen* needed aircraft for four different missions: attack, air defence, reconnaissance, and fast jet

training. If these missions could be combined in a single airframe the home market could make this an economic proposition.

The new aircraft also needed to be optimised for dispersed basing, and for this short takeoff and landing runs were needed. Of these, landing was the main problem. In winter, ice and snow made the stretches of road used as runways very slippery. What was needed was something that approximated to naval carrier operations: an approach system leading to a precise touchdown point, using a brutal no-flare landing with a sink rate rather more than most land-based fighters could handle. Once on the ground, reverse thrust would limit the landing run, as on icy surfaces, conventional brakes would be of little use.

The closely contemporary Harrier might have proved an even better solution to the short field dilemma, but at this point it was a very expensive aeroplane for what it could do, and it was firmly subsonic. Sweden wanted a supersonic aircraft, preferably Mach 2 capable, for the air defence role. Also, they were firmly committed to independence.

The result was the Viggen, the prototype of which was first flown on 8 February 1967. Like its predecessor the Draken, it was a truly original aeroplane, and was a trend-setter in that it was the first of the European canard deltas. But whereas the latest generation use all-moving canard foreplanes for enhanced manoeuvrability, those of the Viggen were fixed, with moving control surfaces on the trailing edge. This configuration was adopted by

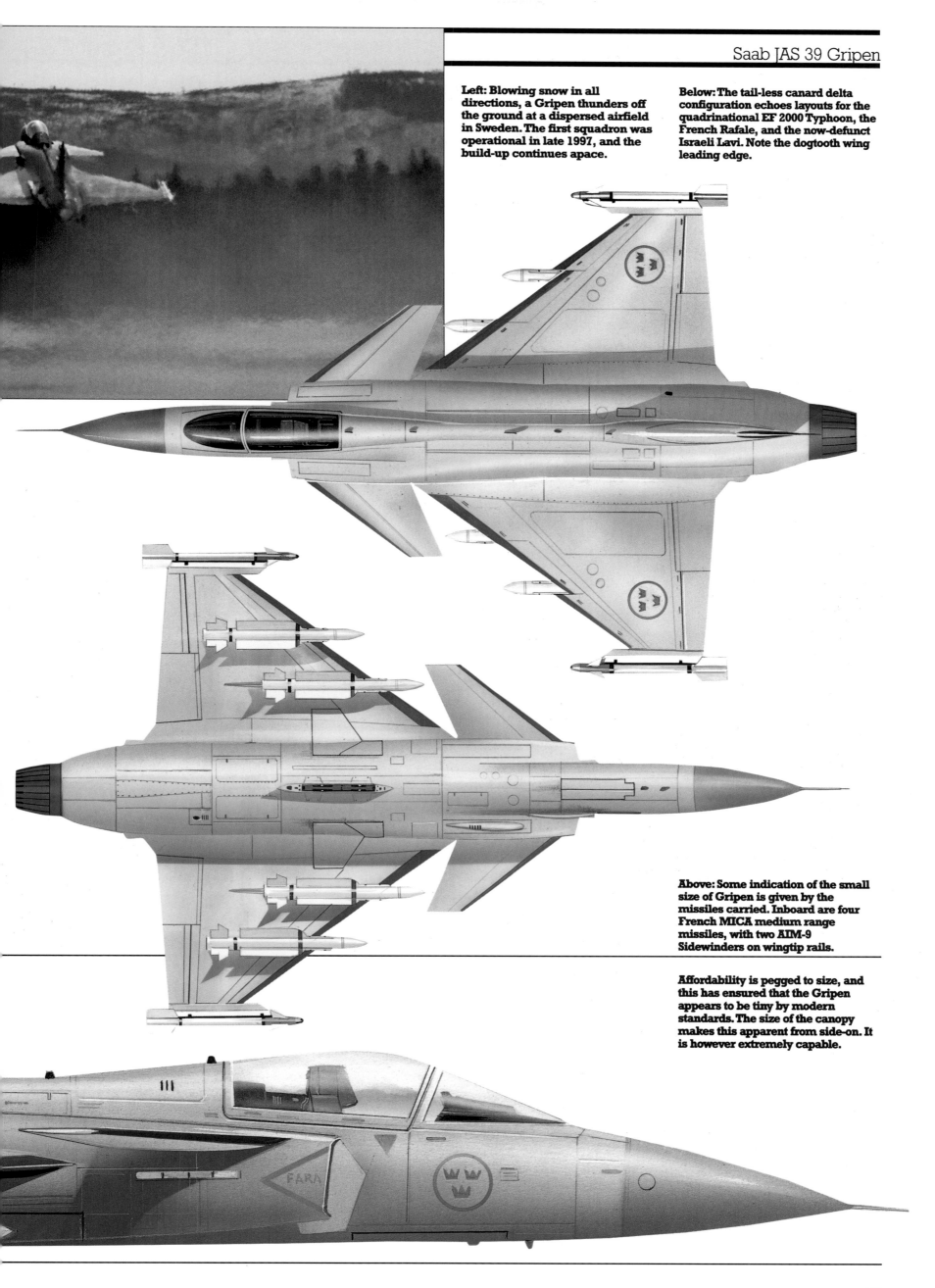

Left: Blowing snow in all directions, a Gripen thunders off the ground at a dispersed airfield in Sweden. The first squadron was operational in late 1997, and the build-up continues apace.

Below: The tail-less canard delta configuration echoes layouts for the quadrinational EF 2000 Typhoon, the French Rafale, and the now-defunct Israeli Lavi. Note the dogtooth wing leading edge.

Above: Some indication of the small size of Gripen is given by the missiles carried. Inboard are four French MICA medium range missiles, with two AIM-9 Sidewinders on wingtip rails.

Affordability is pegged to size, and this has ensured that the Gripen appears to be tiny by modern standards. The size of the canopy makes this apparent from side-on. It is however extremely capable.

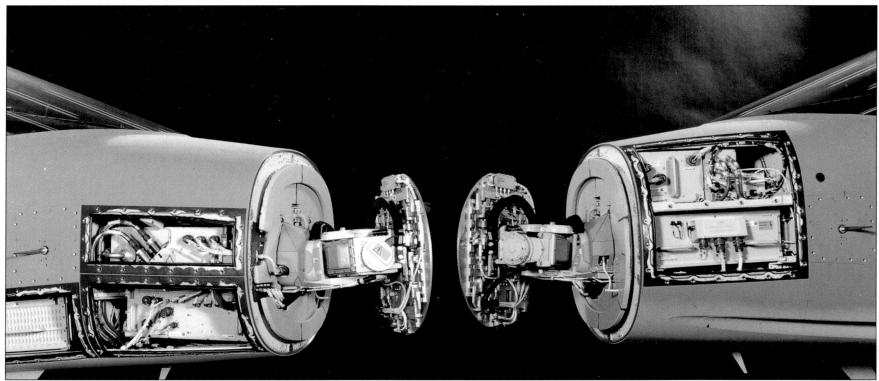

Saab to improve short-field performance, with a flat landing approach, and for no other reason. This was in fact outstanding – a takeoff roll of 1,312ft (400m) and a landing roll of 1,640ft(500m). In other respects, the Viggen, in its main variants of JA.37 (fighter) and AJ.37 (attack), was fairly ordinary. It was unfortunate that Viggen was slightly ahead of its time; a few years later and relaxed stability and FBW could have made quite a difference.

By 1979, a successor was under consideration. It needed the latest technology: FBW, relaxed stability, a high thrust/weight ratio with moderate wing loading, composite construction, a modern multi-mode radar, and all the avionics goodies. But it also needed to be affordable. Although at one point evaluated by NATO against the Mirage F.1 and the F-16, Viggen had not achieved a single export sale, and the new type might also fail to sell. The new aircraft had to be a multi-role type, to replace Viggen in all its functions but, as there is a link between weight and cost, to be affordable in sufficient numbers it had to be smaller, even though the payload/range had to be at least equal. Studies appeared to indicate that advances in technology would make possible a lightweight fighter with full capability.

The new fighter was designated JAS (*Jakt, Attack, Spåning*) 39, and a consortium consisting of Saab-Scania, Volvo Flygmotor, Ericsson, and FFV Aerotech was formed to design and produce it under the name of *Industri Gruppen JAS*. The fighter variant took precedence; attack and reconnaissance were secondary. The first step was to establish a target weight.

With this done, the search was on for a suitable engine. As with both the Draken and the Viggen, this would be a licence-built foreign type, developed and optimized by Volvo. Three possibilities were considered: the American Pratt & Whitney PW 120 and General Electric F404, which had been selected to power the F/A-18 Hornet, and the RB.199 from the European consortium Turbo-Union as used in Tornado. Elastic variants were considered, with maximum thrust moved up or down. None was perfect.

The PW 120 was too large and heavy,

Above left: The computer-controlled cockpit displays consist of a wide angle, diffractive optics HUD, and three monochrome head- down displays. The centre one shows flight data superimposed on an electronic map.

Left: A planar array antenna is used in the Ericsson PD- 05/A pulse-Doppler radar. Performance details have not been released, but maximum detection range is expected to be at least 50nm (93km).

Above: One of the air-to-surface weapons cleared for Gripen is the AGM-65 Maverick, carried on underwing pylons, which gives a precision stand-off capability. Sidewinders provide self defence.

Above: The optimum chin inlet was abandoned due to marginal ground clearance, and side inlets were adopted by default. This was one of the penalties of small size when operating in winter conditions.

Below: The almost obligatory weapon "shopping list". Here we see MICA and Skyflash AAMs with Sidewinders on wingtip rails, AGM-65 Maverick ASMs, DWS 39 dispensers, rocket pods, and RBS-15F missiles.

while the extremely economical if complex three-spool RB.199 had too high a bypass ratio to be really suited to the air superiority mission. Finally, the F404 lacked sufficient thrust to power what had to be a single-engined high performance fighter. However, it had already proved itself to be extremely tough and reliable and it had considerable development potential. Increases in mass airflow, and higher turbine entry temperatures were calculated to significantly increase thrust. It was therefore selected to be developed by GE and Volvo as the RM12.

By now, many configurations had been studied, including a forward-swept wing, and a more or less conventional swept wing and tailplane layout but with a dorsal engine intake. At high angles of attack, this was not a good idea. But gradually the JAS 39 Gripen emerged as we now see it. At one point, a chin intake on the lines of the F-16 was studied, but rejected for a variety of reasons. Firstly, it mean that the nose-wheel leg was located well aft, giving an unacceptably short wheelbase, with potential ground handling problems. Secondly, it imposed restrictions on the length of the centreline stores that could be carried. Ground clearance would have been very limited, and (given the requirement for dispersed basing) would have been vulnerable to foreign object ingestion. With no Mach 2 requirement, fixed intakes could be used, and these were eventually located on the fuselage sides. While this was not ideal, the F404 had already demonstrated that it was very tolerant of disturbed airflow.

Right: For short landings, Gripen uses aerodynamic braking, using its canards with its speedbrakes to pull up in a short distance. This is essential for off-site basing.

Below: The Swedes claim small size is a stealth asset, but this applies more in a visual encounter than in a BVR radar engagement. How stealthy it really is remains to be seen.

A delta wing planform was adopted, set in the mid position, mainly to optimise wing/body blending, but with the additional advantage that it provided plenty of clearance for external stores. The dogtooth leading edge has two flaps, and two elevons make up the trailing edge.

All-moving canard foreplanes were mounted on the outsides of the intake ducts; these filled a dual purpose in that tilted at a steep angle after touchdown they provided aerodynamic braking, also a download which increased the effectiveness of the main braking system. No attempt was made to use thrust reversing, although at some future date a thrust vectoring nozzle and a more powerful engine such as the EJ200 are probable.

Off-basing has since been modified to a new system – Airbase 90. As with the Harrier, the difficulties of deployed basing were extreme. Airbase 90 consists of a conventional airfield, with all its support systems, but surrounded by a network of short strips of road typically five in number, from which aircraft can be operated, connected by a system of taxiways. Airbase 90 ensures that all aircraft are widely dispersed and concealed, and yet are within reach of centralized maintenance.

The cockpit of Gripen has followed modern trends, with HOTAS, a wide angle HUD, three MFDs, and a steeply raked Martin Baker ejection seat. This, like much else, has been imported, as being cheaper to buy "off the shelf"

rather than develop from scratch. Radar is the Ericsson PS-05/A pulse-Doppler type with modes similar to those of the American APG-68, and with a probable detection range of 50nm (93km) although no performance details have been released.

Development and service
The prototype first flew on 9 December 1988, piloted by Stig Holmstrom. Prior to this, Stig had spent about 1,000 hours in the simulator. On landing he commented that while the Gripen flew well, the FBW control system was rather too sensitive. This was perhaps not all that surprising. Although the Swedish consortium used the American company Lear Astronics, the direct leap to triplex digital FBW was

still a big one, even with triplex analogue backup. And computer prediction of how a totally new fighter type will behave in the air is still an imperfect art.

Just weeks later, flaws in the software manifested themselves in a dramatic fashion. As Lars Rådeström came in to land, he was caught by a freak crosswind. Unable to regain control he hit the runway hard, slewed off it, and came to rest inverted. Fortunately his most serious injury was a broken elbow.

The software control laws were extensively modified, and when the flight test programme resumed in May, Gripen was reported to be much more stable. It made its international debut at Farnborough Air Show 1992, albeit with a rather muted display, and all seemed to

be going well. By this time, Gripen was behind schedule and it failed to appear at the Paris Air Show the following year.

On 8 August 1993, Lars Rådeström flew a public display over Stockholm. During a shallow turn, the Gripen made some large uncommanded movements which the test pilot was unable to correct. "Feeling", as he said afterwards "like butter running down a hot potato" he ejected as it performed what looked like a "Cobra" manoeuvre, then crashed, fortunately missing spectators on the ground.

This was a major setback, and once again the software was scrutinized. New P.11 flight control software was developed, but it was not cleared for use until 22 March 1995. It was then incorporated in production aircraft later that year.

Like most modern aircraft, Gripen has a two-seater operational trainer, the JAS 39B. To make space for the second seat, the fuselage was lengthened by 27in (70cm), the internal gun was deleted, and internal fuel reduced.

The first Gripen unit was F.7 Wing at Såtenäs, with 2 Attackflygdivisionen declared operational in November 1997, and 1 Attackflygdivisionen almost a year later. The next unit was F.10 Wing at Angelholm, which was under training in mid-1999. The Gripen conversion unit is based at Såtenäs, and is scheduled to convert two squadrons a year for a total of 12 by 2006.

The future
Future Gripen variants may well have

more powerful engines, such as the EJ 200 developed for Typhoon. Thrust vectoring is another possibility. Marketing has never been a Swedish strong point, but in 1996 an agreement was reached with BAe that they would handle Gripen sales in countries where they already had experience, especially those in hot climates.

Gripen has been demonstrated in Eastern Europe, where cost is critical. Its main opponent is predictably the F-16. Its current price is little more than half that of Rafale and about two thirds that of Typhoon, which makes it an economic proposition. Many countries have expressed interest, but the only firm order to date is from South Africa.

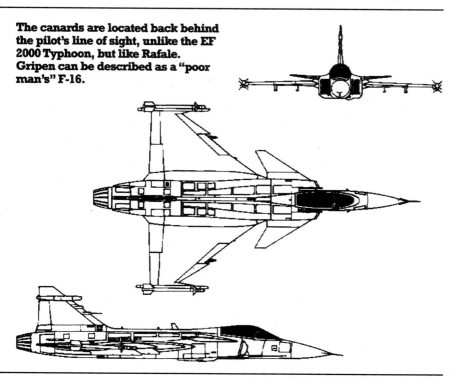

The canards are located back behind the pilot's line of sight, unlike the EF 2000 Typhoon, but like Rafale. Gripen can be described as a "poor man's" F-16.

Specifications: JAS 39 GRIPEN	
Dimensions	
Span	27ft 7in/8.40m
Length	46ft 3in/14.10m
Height	14ft 9in/4.50m
Wing area	c275sq ft/25.54sq m
Aspect ratio	2.76
Weights	
Empty	c12,346lb/5,600kg
Takeoff	c19,224lb/8,720kg
Intl fuel	5,000lb/2,268kg
Power	1xVolvo/GE RM12 turbofan
Max thrust	18,105lb/8,212kg
Mil thrust	12,141lb/5,507kg
Performance	
V_{max} hi	Mach 1.8
V_{max} lo	"supersonic"
Ceiling	50,000ft/15,239m
Climb rate	c50,000ft/min (254m/sec)
Armament	1 x 27mm Mauser BK 27 cannon
	2 or 4 AIM-120 AMRAAM or Meteor
	2 or 4 ASRAAM or Sidewinder

Below: The first two-seater Gripen conversion trainer, the JAS 39B – with lengthened fuselage, internal gun deleted, and internal fuel capacity significantly reduced.

Below right: a JAS 39 Gripen soars skywards with a mixed ordnance load. These include a single Maverick and two anti-shipping missiles carried on the inboard wing pylons.

Dassault Rafale

In the late 1970s, the perceived wisdom was that the agile fighter was the way to go. The European nations had two choices: they could buy American, or they could develop their own. The latter course was taken by Britain, France, Germany, Italy and Spain. Complete agreement proved impossible; France, with an eye on the export market, wanted a smaller and cheaper aircraft. In the end the Dassault company unilaterally produced what finally emerged as the Rafale.

In the late 1970s, several European nations, influenced by the superb dual role capability of the F-16, polished their respective crystal balls and looked to the future. The threat then, and for more than another decade, was the Warsaw Pact, fronted by hordes of cheap and cheerful fighters and attack aircraft, but already there were ominous signs that the Soviet Union was developing a whole new generation of fighters which would match the best the West had to offer. While these would take time to mature and enter service, the future looked bleak unless something superior could be developed as a matter of urgency.

France's Mirage 2000 was limited by its size, which in turn was determined by the fact that it was single-engined. Many years before, Dassault had scaled up the Mirage III to become the Mirage IV, a twin-engined nuclear strike aircraft. Now they applied the same process to the Mirage 2000 – two SNECMA M53 engines, and a wing area some 79 per cent larger. This was the Super Mirage 4000, first flown from Istres on 9 March 1979 by Chief Test Pilot Jean-Marie Saget.

Compared to the Mirage 2000, the Super Mirage 4000 flew higher and farther, and climbed faster than its single-engined sibling. Externally the only real difference was that the Super Mirage 4000 had all-moving canard foreplanes; internally the systems of the Mirage 2000 were largely duplicated, although a world first was the use of a composite fin structure as a fuel tank. The Super Mirage 4000 was first seen in public at the Paris Air Show in 1979, where it showed remarkable agility for such a large aircraft. But l'Armée de l'Air had no requirement for it, and the projected customer, Saudi Arabia, bought F-15s instead. It did however serve a useful purpose later, in proving FCS and canards for what became Rafale.

France goes it alone

By 1983, the air forces of Britain, France, Germany, Italy and Spain had more or less agreed on the specification for a new agile multi-role fighter. France, intransigent as ever, demanded design leadership on the grounds that Dassault was more experienced with delta wings than any other company – which, although true, was not particularly relevant – and industrial leadership on the basis that Dassault could handle the complex problems of a multi-national project more efficiently than the other companies, which was optimistic, to say the least. In all fairness, it must be said that Dassault had over the years demonstrated the ability to take critical decisions more quickly than most, but whether they could carry their partners along with them was open to doubt.

Design leadership by Dassault would for all practical purposes have committed the European partners to a rather smaller aircraft than they really wanted, which in turn would have resulted in the French SNECMA M88 turbofan being by far the most suitably sized engine. To a large degree, Dassault could also have tried to impose the use of French avionics. This was clearly unacceptable.

Matters were not helped by a demand for 46 per cent of production by Dassault, leaving only 54 per cent to be apportioned between the other four nations. Even when this outrageous claim was reduced to 31 per cent, it did nothing to mollify the other participants. The other factor was that France authorized the production of two Avion de Combat Experimentale (ACX) demonstrators in April 1983, although in the event only one was built. This was followed shortly after by authorization for the SNECMA M88 turbofan, thus giving Dassault a head start over their erstwhile partners, who were now potential rivals.

The main reason that Dassault wanted a smaller aircraft than the other partners was cost, which is closely related to weight. A cheaper aircraft would be easier to export.

Above: Originally conceived as a dedicated air superiority fighter, Rafale has largely become a two-seater attack aircraft. On the export market it has been a failure.

This was not a major factor with the other European nations, and it was hardly surprising when they declined. By 1985, France had been elbowed out, with no option but to unilaterally develop the ACX. This would not only give them the aircraft that they specifically wanted but, by producing flyable hardware before their competitors, it would give Dassault a head start in the export market. The Mirage 2000C had only the previous year achieved initial operational capabil-

In planform Rafale is very similar to the EF 2000 Typhoon, the JAS 39 Gripen, and the now-defunct Israeli Lavi. It is strange that the USA has avoided the canard delta.

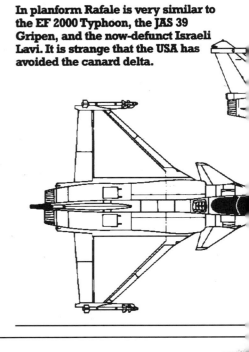

This side view of Rafale armed with MICA and Magic missiles depicts the two-seater Rafale B, intended to replace the Jaguar while reducing the single pilot workload.

ity with l'Armée de l'Air, and the production lines would be kept busy with this until the new fighter was developed.

The ACX was to be a multi-role aircraft with significant air combat capability. Its first task was to replace the already obsolescent F-8 Crusaders in the fleet air defence role for l'Aeronavale, for which it had to be carrier compatible. Unless a "home-brew" product was available, and there was no way in which the Mirage 2000 could have been adapted for carrier operations, the only alternative would have been to buy F/A-18 Hornets.

Next, ACX was to replace the Jaguars of l'Armée de l'Air, and at much the same time, the Super Etendards of *l'Aeronavale*. Only when this was com-

plete, many years in the future, would it start to replace the Mirage 2000 in the air defence role.

Development
The ACX, later named Rafale, or Squall, first appeared as a technology demonstrator. The first public indication of it had been a model at the Paris Air Show in 1985, decked out in a black and gold livery. As this was similar to a current racing car sponsored by a tobacco company, the irreverent Brits dubbed it the "John Player Special!" This was not well received by Dassault, who adopted a white colour scheme with red and blue trim for the first Rafale prototype.

The two-spool definitive engine, the

SNECMA M88, was still under development, and the prototype, Rafale A, was powered by two General Electric F404-400 turbofans by default. Dimensionally it was slightly larger than the definitive article. First flown on 4 July 1986 by Dassault Chief Test Pilot Guy Mitaux-Maurouard, Rafale A was an instant success. In a display of Gallic hubris, it was taken to 36,000ft (9,144m) and Mach 1.3, and put through 5g turns – a marked departure from first flights by other manufacturers.

The design of the engine inlets was innovative, combining the first class pressure recovery characteristics of the Mirage 2000 side inlets with the high angle of attack efficiency of a chin intake. With no Mach 2 requirement these were

Above: Rafale M, the Aeronavale carrier fighter redesignated F.1, optimised for fleet air defence, which will carry four radar-homing MICA and two IR MICA missiles.

of fixed geometry, and by constricting the front fuselage beneath the cockpit a segmental inlet was formed beneath a large but streamlined bulge. The bulge held sharply swept all-moving canard foreplanes, set well aft of the cockpit where they caused no obstruction to visibility, and rather higher than the wing.

The delta wing was set in the mid position, with a small leading edge root extension inboard, and cropped at the tips to hold missile rails, as with the Swedish Gripen. The trailing edge was swept forward slightly and filleted at the junction with the fuselage. Rafale A had three-section leading edge slats and three-section trailing edge elevons; on subsequent aircraft both slats and elevons were reduced to two sections.

The American-style bubble canopy was not copied; like that on the Mirage 2000, the transparency tapered into a dorsal spine which ran the full length of the fuselage, ending in a bullet fairing which housed ECM equipment and the drag 'chute. A sharply swept fin and rudder was of similar shape to that of the Mirage 2000, with the same VOR horizontal aerials, and a SPECTRA ECM housing near the top.

The wings and fin are almost entirely made of carbon-fibre composite material, including the trailing edge control surfaces,

Left: From this angle the unique inlet of the Rafale is shown to advantage. It is a compromise between the traditional Dassault side inlets and the chin position.

Above: "Good around the boat" is how former Super Etendard, now Dassault test pilot Yves (Bill) Kerhervé described the navalized Rafale. But the angle of attack is high by USN standards.

Below: Like the Mirage 2000, Rafale has a "glass cockpit", with a moving map "look-level" display beneath the wide-angle holographic HUD. A side-stick control with HOTAS follows the traditions of the F-16.

Left: Unlike the M53 of the Mirage 2000, the two SNECMA M88-3 engines of Rafale are twin-spool turbofans. These will be followed by the -4, which has a modified low pressure compressor and afterburner.

and much of the fuselage is also clad in this material. Kevlar is used at the nose and at the rear, while small amounts of aluminium lithium are also present. The canards and the leading edge slats are made of diffusion-bonded titanium alloy. The twin nose-wheel and single main wheels retract forward. They can withstand sink rates of up to 10ft/sec (3m/sec).

The maritime Rafale is of course rather heavier, about 1,345lb (610kg), than its land-based counterpart, since not only is it stressed for the much higher sink rate of 20ft/sec (6m/sec) but it has to withstand catapult launches and arrested landings. The beefed-up landing gear also varied from its land-based counterpart in having the nose wheel able to pivot through 360deg when being towed, or through plus/minus 70deg with the pilot steering it. The nose leg incidentally has a jump strut to aid takeoff. Both types carry tailhooks, and while the carrier machine was originally to have had wing folding, this was abandoned when it was found that the composite construction of the wing would be weakened by the insertion of hinges and folding gear. Unlike the land-based variant, it has an integral boarding ladder.

Inevitably, the initial flight test programme fell on Rafale A. It first appeared in public at the Farnborough Air Show 1986. During the following year it bettered its specification speed of Mach 1.8 by attaining Mach 2 at 42,653ft(13,000m), while at Farnborough '88 it demonstrated a sustained turn rate of 24deg/sec, albeit at low speed. Just prior to this, it had demonstrated a minimum flying speed of 80kt (148kmh) a maximum speed at low altitude of Mach 1.14, and a stabilized angle of attack of 32deg.

Rafale A was also used for initial carrier trials, and made dozens of dummy approaches to the deck of the carrier Clemenceau. Not stressed for carrier landings, and with no tailhook, it still managed to demonstrate an approach speed slightly slower than that of the Super Etendard, although the angle of attack was, by normal standards, on the high side at 16-18deg. This apart, Dassault test pilot Yves "Bill" Kerhervé, a former l'Aeronavale pilot, described Rafale as "good around the boat!"

Powerplant

SNECMA (Société Nationale d'Etude et de Construction de Moteurs d'Aviation) is the only French fighter engine company, and has a long history of successful engines. As mentioned in the section on the Mirage 2000, the M53 was a continuous-bleed turbojet, optimised for the top right-hand corner of the envelope, whereas the M88-2 developed for Rafale was a true turbofan.

Advanced technology was used, with cooled microcrystalline vanes in the high pressure compressor, and powder metallurgy, which allows very high operating temperatures. A three-stage low pressure compressor is followed by a six-stage high pressure compressor. The combustion chamber is annular, and both high and low pressure turbines are single-stage. Pressure ratio is a massive 25.5:1, and the turbine entry temperature is 1,577deg Celsius.

The M88-2 was first flown in Rafale A, replacing one of the F404s, and has since been used for Rafale prototypes, one of which has reportedly supercruised. A speed of Mach 1.4 has been mentioned, but this seems to be gilding the lily. The production aircraft is powered by the -3,

with a modified low pressure compressor, while for the future the still more powerful -4 will have a revised low pressure turbine and afterburner.

Towards service

The first M88-powered Rafale, C.01, took to the skies on 19 May 1991. It was followed by the first Aeronavale prototype, M.01, on 11 December of that year, although it was almost two years before it made its first arrested landing on the carrier Foch. Rafale C was the air force single-seater, while Rafale B was the two-seater for the same service, and flew on 30 April 1993. Then there was Rafale D (discret - stealth), although apart from the use of radar-absorbent materials and a gold-filmed canopy, there was little movement in this direction. But, in the meantime, requirements were changing.

Firstly, the dissolution of the Warsaw Pact and Soviet Union had removed the main threat, putting Western defence budgets into disarray, which caused Rafale progress to slow tremendously. It was at this point that the most urgent l'Armée de l'Air priority became the replacement of its Jaguar fleet. Meanwhile, the Gulf War had been fought and won, with French Jaguars flying many missions. This clearly showed one thing: the workload of an attack pilot was unacceptably high. The benefits of a specialist weapons systems operator were undeniable, and as a result, whereas most Rafales were originally to be single-seaters, the vast majority of l'Armée de l'Air Rafales were now to be two-seaters. This was at the cost of a slight increase in weight, and a small reduction in internal fuel capacity.

More recently, the lettering sequence for Rafale subtypes has been changed. Rafale M has now become Rafale F1, optimised for fleet air defence and air combat, with delivery of the first production aircraft taking place in late 1999. This will be followed in 2000-2002 by the improved Rafale 1.1, with Magic IR missiles replaced by IR MICAs. The main l'Armée de l'Air type will be the two-seater Rafale F2, which should enter service in 2004, and which will have an automatic terrain-following capability. Further in the future are the F3 and F4, in 2006 and 2008, respectively. These will have improved air combat capabilities, with a helmet-mounted sight, and the ability to fly the SEAD mission. By 2015, Rafale should have replaced most French tactical aircraft currently in service.

Radar and avionics

The Rafale radar selection and progress was far from easy. At first it was to be the Thomson-CSF RDX, but this soon ran into extreme problems. Electronique Serge Dassault then offered their Antilope 60, but this also proved unsuitable. Eventually, at the end of 1988, the two companies formed a consortium, Groupement Interét Economique (GIE) to crack the problem with a new radar – Radar du Bord du GIE (RBG). But full scale development did not begin until 29 November 1990, a serious delay.

At much the same time, the radar was again renamed Radar á Balayage Electronique deux plans, or RBE.2. This was chosen to reflect the fact that instead of a moveable antenna, that of RBE.2 was fixed, using electronic scanning in two different planes. This was a notable first in a European fighter. Then, in 1998, GIE gave way to Thomson-CSF Detexis when the two companies officially merged.

The fixed phased array antenna consists of about 25,000 diodes which effectively provide two "lenses", one vertical, the other horizontal. A polarizing filter then gives extremely accurate and instant beam shifting in several directions, which allows different modes to be used simultaneously, with minimal side-lobes. Range is stated to be rather greater than that of the Mirage 2000-5 radar, with search mode look down at 54nm (100km). Few hard facts have been released, although it is said to be able to detect and track "several dozen" targets, while in combat mode it allows simultaneous attacks on four targets. But its greatest advantage, apart from sheer flexibility, is that it has a low probability of intercept – a stealthy radar!

RBE.2 is under development for the air-to-air role, and has limited air-to-surface capability. The latter, including terrain-following, will be added in time for the F.2 Rafale in 2003, with a much improved version for the F.3 to come, funding permitting.

The radar is backed by a device known as Optronique Secteur Frontale (OSF), jointly developed by Thomson-CSF and SAGEM. This is a combined two-waveband IRST, FLIR, and laser rangefinder. Two small sensors ahead of the windshield work in unison, the one on the left handling surveillance, tracking and lock-on, while the other concerns itself with identification and analysis. Under perfect weather conditions, maximum IR range is said to be up to 70nm (130km), but this seems optimistic. The laser ranger should be effective out to 12nm (22km).

A comprehensive threat warning and self-defence suite is also carried. This is SPECTRA (Systeme pour la Protection Electronique Contre Tous les Rayonnements Adversés). First flown in 1998, this internal system detects and jams hostile radars, and warns of missile launches and laser detection. Slaved to the other nav/attack systems, it gives all-round coverage by sensors at the top and the base of the fin, in fairings ahead of the canards, at the front and rear of the wingtip missile rails, and on each side of the intakes.

Rafale also mounts the usual navigation and communications systems, including data link for remote targeting. The flight control system is of course FBW, with three digital and one analogue system as backup. Interestingly, the Aeronavale version also has auto-launch and carrier approach software modes, one of the functions of the latter being to automatically hold a steady 16deg angle of attack.

The cockpit

The crew position of Rafale is state of the art. The ejection seat on Rafale A was raked back at 32deg, but the definitive article is the SEMMA (licence-built Martin-Baker) Mk16, with a rake angle of 29deg. Naturally it has zero/zero capability. The wrap-around windshield is backed by a starboard-hinged canopy transparency, as on the Gripen. As previously mentioned, the transparencies are gold-filmed as a stealth measure.

HOTAS is of course obligatory but, unlike the Mirage 2000, a sidestick controller is used. Both this and the twin throttles are mounted relatively high, while the former has an adjustable wrist rest, which aids control during high-g manoeuvres. Voice control is used for some non-critical functions, such as radio operating; ironically the language used is English, presumably as an export feature.

Displays are very similar to those of the Mirage 2000-5 – a holographic HUD and three MFDs, two of which are touch-sensitive liquide crystal screens, which flank the radar display. For the future a helmet-mounted display is projected, which will provide target acquisition and designation data. This will allow missile launches at high off-boresight targets, limited only by the look angle of the missile seeker. OBOGS, an On-Board Oxygen Generating System, is used, reducing at least one logistics problem.

Weaponry

Originally a gun was to have been mounted on the side of the left engine duct, but this was later transferred to the other side. A 30mm GIAT (formerly DEFA) 791, it is a seven-chamber revolver cannon with four different selectable firing rates (300, 600, 1,500 or 2,500 rounds per minute) and a high muzzle velocity of 3,363ft/sec (1,025m/sec). Probable capacity is 125 rounds, which would give firing times of 25, 12, 5, and 3 seconds respectively. If this doesn't sound a lot, consider that it represents at least three bursts at a fleeting target.

Rafale carries 24 hardpoints, with one less on the naval F.1. The primary air-to-air weapon is MICA, a French AMRAAM equivalent, supplemented by the R550 Magic 2 heat homer. Up to nine AAMs can be carried, although a typical load would be six MICA and two Magics. At some future date, Magic will be replaced by a heat-seeking MICA. The French weapons are interchangeable with the US AMRAAM and Sidewinder missiles, as a necessary aid to the potential export market.

Many air-to-surface weapons have been cleared for use, although some, such as Durandal, are unlikely ever to see action. Apart from US weapons, such as Harpoon and Maverick, which have been described elsewhere, the Norwegian Penguin and French Exocet and AS 30L anti-ship missiles may be carried; Beluga CBUs and various LGBs are also on the list. More recent are APACHE (Arme Propulsée á Charge Ejectables) stand-off submunition dispenser, with a range of up to 75nm (140km), and SCALP (Systéme de Crosiére conventionale Autonomé á Longue Porté de precision) which will use GPS guidance and have a range of more than 216nm (400km) with either submunitions or a single unitary warhead, at least two of which can be routinely carried.

In 1999 former BAe test pilot Chris Yeo evaluated the two-seater Rafale which was laden with three 2,000 litre external tanks, two SCALPS, each weighing 2,866lb (1,300kg) and four MICA AAMs, a heavy load for a relatively small fighter. He found that it was easy to fly precisely, and that roll rate, even with such a load, was about 150deg/sec. He was

Above: An air-to-surface load of two Apache stand-off munitions dispensers is supplemented by two MICA medium range and two Magic dogfight AAMs. Extended range is given by three massive drop tanks.

Below: An R 550 Magic demonstrates its manoeuvrability at launching by turning hard across the nose of its parent aircraft on the range at Cazaux. The ability to manoeuvre hard after launch is vital.

impressed.

Five of Rafale's hardpoints are plumbed for tanks, and it seems almost certain that the F.1 will be adapted to use buddy tanking, even though this halves the force available. The only viable alternative is for l'Aeronavale to buy used KA-6Ds from the USN.

Specifications			
	Rafale A	**Rafale F.1**	**Rafale F.2**
Dimensions			
Span	36ft 9in/11.20m	35ft 9¼in/10.90m	35ft 9¼in/10.90m
Length	51ft 10in/15.80m	50ft 2½in/15.30m	50ft 2½in/15.30m
Height	17ft 4in/5.30m	17ft 4in/5.30m	17ft 6¼in/5.34m
Wing area	506sq ft/47sq m	495sq ft/46sq m	495sq ft/46sq m
Weights			
Empty weight	20,943lb/9,500kg	21,319lb/9,670kg	19,973lb/9,060kg
Max takeoff	n/a	47,399lb/21,500kg	47,399lb/21,500kg
Power	2xF404-GE-400	2xSNECMA M88-3	2xSNECMA M88-3
Max thrust	16,000lb/7,258kg	19,558lb/8,871kg	19,558lb/8,871kg
Mil thrust	10,600lb/4,808kg	10,950lb/4,967kg	10,950lb/4,967kg
Int fuel	9,921lb/4,500kg	9,900lb/4,491kg	c9,500lb/4,309kg.
Performance			
V_{max}	Mach 1.8	Mach 2	Mach 2
Ceiling	c50,000ft/15,239m	54,957ft/16,750m	54,957ft/16,750m
Climb rate	c50,000ftm/254ms	60,000ftm/305ms	60,000ftm/305ms
Loadings	n/a	+9/-3.6g	+9/-3.6g

Eurofighter Typhoon

Three nations, Britain, Germany and Italy, had many years before they combined to produce the Panavia low level interdictor. Multi-national projects had the theoretical advantage of economy of scale due to large production runs, while keeping indigenous industry abreast of the latest technology. The original three were joined by Spain in the Eurofighter consortium (although France dropped out) to produce what finally emerged as the EF 2000 Typhoon, to replace Phantoms, Mirage F.1s, Jaguars, Starfighters, and eventually the Tornado F.3.

In the late 1970s, the primary fighter used by Britain, Germany and Spain was the F-4 Phantom, which by then was getting a bit long in the tooth. Of the other NATO nations, Italy operated the even older and less capable F-104 Starfighter; four of the smaller European nations – Belgium, Denmark, Holland and Norway – had acquired the F-16 as a dual role fighter; while Portugal, in the extreme west of Europe, could afford nothing better than the A-7 Corsair for air defence. France, although aligned with NATO for mutual defence, was not a member, and in any case, was in the process of launching the Mirage 2000.

Prior to this, the old friend of the author, Lt Col Lloyd "Boots" Boothby, USAF (ret), had come up with one of his most famous sayings: "The Russians and North Vietnamese are not our enemies; they are our adversaries. Our enemies are the politicians in Washington!''

He might well have added the accountants and treasury officials. The latter, the traditional enemies of those who would defend their countries, and who, left to their own devices, would declare the bayonet the most cost-effective of weapons in terms of purchase price plotted against the potential number of usages, had to agree that the economies of scale arising from a multi-national project were worth having. The scene was set for a huge new fighter project, with every major nation in Europe, with the exception of non-NATO and independent Sweden, as participants.

International co-operation

The situation was not entirely clear-cut. In the event of a NATO war with the Soviet Union, Britain would have been charged with providing air cover to transatlantic convoys bringing reinforcements from the USA. For this the RAF would need a specialized interceptor, able to operate autonomously far out over the North Sea, and the Iceland/Faroes gap, in the face of severe ECM. Having evaluated the F-14 Tomcat (too expensive), and the F-15 Eagle (inadequate for such a specialized mission), the RAF had settled on an air defence variant of Tornado, and was pushing this hard.

On the other hand, the RAF had Phantoms, Jaguars and Harriers based in Germany, and these, in the event of war, would be in the front line. The unique qualities of the Harrier made it irreplaceable, but the Phantom, designed more than 20 years earlier, was not the best air superiority fighter in the world, while the Anglo-French Jaguar, although a decade

younger in concept, was a dedicated attack aircraft. By the time a new multi-role fighter could be developed, it too would be ripe for replacement.

In the event of hostilities, Germany was first in the firing line. The trinational Tornado IDS, then entering service, was outstanding in the interdiction role, but the primary air defence fighter was the F-4F Phantom. Italy also had Tornado IDS, but with the antiquated Starfighter for air defence. Spain operated both Phantoms and Mirage F.1s but, looking into the future, they needed something better. As it happened, they bought the F/A-18 Hornet as an interim solution. The position of France has been outlined in the previous section.

The tri-national Tornado had pointed the way to European co-operation, and produced, in the face of much ignorant and ill-informed criticism from the press and politicians, an outstanding interdiction/strike aircraft. The obvious course was a European consortium similar to that which produced Tornado, but with France and Spain added.

Four nations agreed on a baseline

fighter with a minimum empty weight of 20,943lb (9,500kg), but the French described this as a "platinum card" option, and tried to force a smaller and lighter design on their partners. As described in the section on Rafale, this was unacceptable, as were French demands, and in August 1985, Britain, Germany, Italy and Spain decided to go ahead, with France being left out in the cold.

By this time, Dassault were well ahead, and Rafale A was demonstrated at Farnborough 1986. But meanwhile, the other nations had not been standing still. The three original Tornado partners (Spain at this time was still on the fringes of the project) had agreed on the European Fighter Concept – a canard delta – as the Agile Combat Aircraft (ACA). Then, in 1983, Germany, the biggest and most obstructive fly in the ointment in the entire programme, which they continued to be even into the 1990s, pulled out.

The Germans did return to the fold in August 1985, when they signed the Turin Agreement, which committed the then

Above: July 1998 saw two of the seven development aircraft, DA 2 and DA 4, both assembled at Warton in England, in the air. Nearest the camera is DA 4, the first two-seater conversion trainer.

three nations to a project definition phase for an agile air superiority fighter with an empty weight of 22,046lb (10,000kg), a wing area of 538sq.ft (50sq m), and two engines of about 20,000lb (9,072kg) thrust. Spain became a signatory a few weeks later, and the Eurofighter company was formed to develop it.

Experimental Aircraft Programme

Meanwhile BAe and Aeritalia of Italy had continued alone, and cobbled together a technology demonstrator, the Experimental Aircraft Programme (EAP). Superhuman efforts saw EAP not only fly some three weeks before the Farnborough Air Show of 1986, piloted from Warton by Dave Eagles, but allowed it to appear at the show to give the impression that, while Rafale, making its international debut, might be ahead, the

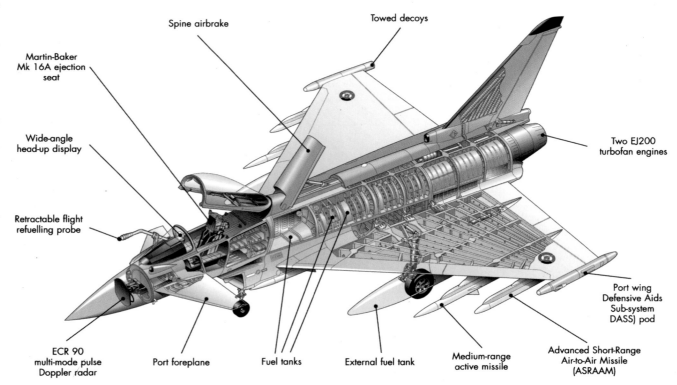

Spine airbrake · Towed decoys · Martin-Baker Mk 16A ejection seat · Wide-angle head-up display · Two EJ200 turbofan engines · Retractable flight refuelling probe · Port wing Defensive Aids Sub-system DASS) pod · ECR 90 multi-mode pulse Doppler radar · Port foreplane · Fuel tanks · External fuel tank · Medium-range active missile · Advanced Short-Range Air-to-Air Missile (ASRAAM)

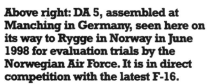

Above right: DA 5, assembled at Manching in Germany, seen here on its way to Rygge in Norway in June 1998 for evaluation trials by the Norwegian Air Force. It is in direct competition with the latest F-16.

margin was small. The truth was that Rafale A was much nearer to a production fighter than was EAP

EAP had a cranked delta wing, swept at 57deg inboard and 45deg outboard. The cropped tips were left plain, without missile rails. A quadruplex FBW system controlled wing cambering as a function of airspeed and angle of attack, with split leading edge slats and trailing edge flaperons. This maximised the lift/drag ratio in manoeuvring flight while minimising the shock wave in supersonic level flight.

The canards were set well forward,

Below: The "smiling" chin intake is stated to be a stealth measure. Its lower lip automatically droops at high angles of attack to improve pressure recovery to the EJ 200 afterburning turbofan engines.

The greatest difference between Typhoon and Rafale or Gripen is the location of the canard foreplanes. Set well forward, Typhoon's give a much longer moment arm.

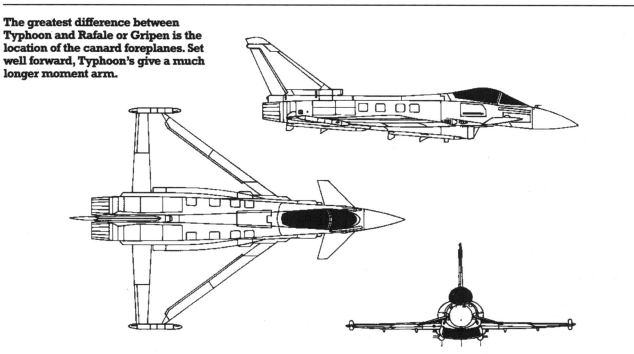

unlike those of Gripen and Rafale, to give the greatest possible moment arm for maximum leverage at high angles of attack. This position was criticised for obscuring the pilot's view "out of the window", but studies showed that only rarely did opponents pop up in positions where they would be masked by the canards, and, even then, they could not be hidden for long, especially during manoeuvring flight, with the canards continually deflecting. In any case, the radar and IRST were the main detection sensors; visual acquisition was secondary. The chunky fuselage had a chin intake, the lower lip of which could be drooped at low airspeeds or high angles of attack to improve airflow into the inlets. The two-

piece canopy was faired into a dorsal spine which ended in a huge Tornado-style fin, which extended almost halfway along the fuselage. Not for nothing is Tornado known as "the mighty fin!" The spine just aft of the canopy doubled as a speed brake.

The projected weight of the aircraft demanded an engine specifically sized for it, and a consortium consisting of Rolls-Royce (Britain), MTU (Germany), FiatAvio (Italy), and ITP (Spain) was set up to develop it as Eurojet Turbo GmbH. But, as previously stated, engine development is an even longer process than that of the airframe. Consequently EAP was powered by two Turbo-Union RB.199s as used on Tornado. Although a compromise

solution, this allowed the flight performance envelope to be thoroughly explored in the course of 259 sorties.

What's in a name?
It is an unfortunate fact that, in the present age, image takes on undue importance. Politicians and popular press are always quick to make cheap points if it suits their agenda to do so, and an extremely costly and high-profile programme such as the European Fighter Aircraft (EFA) can easily become a target for criticism. This had been amply proven with Tornado, which for years laboured under the title of the Multi-Role Combat Aircraft (MRCA). The letters were all too easily converted to "Must Refurbish Canberras Again", or

even worse, "Mother Riley's Cardboard Aeroplane"! But not until Tornado finally entered service and proved itself to be an outstanding combat aircraft, were the knockers silenced.

This was not a British phenomenon; almost all American combat aircraft had been similarly rubbished during the development phase. The French, aware of this, disarmed much of the criticism by using emotive names from the outset, notably with Rafale.

Eurofighter as a company name was pretty anodyne, but the addition of EFA for the aircraft did nothing to improve matters. In 1992, it was renamed Eurofighter EF 2000, making it officially the Eurofighter Eurofighter 2000, a public relations disaster of the first magnitude, especially as the 2000 bit had long been pre-empted by the final Mirage. As a purely personal opinion, had EFA been named Spitfire 2 in 1988, it would have drawn much less flak from the great unwashed. Even the Germans would hardly have objected; the author has yet to meet a World War II German flyer who does not jump at the chance of having his photograph taken while standing by, or in the cockpit of, the original bird.

The naming deficiency was not resolved until 1998, when EF 2000 officially became Typhoon, in part because the German Taifun was essentially similar. While this was a natural follow-on to Tornado, Germany objected strongly on the grounds that in World War II RAF Typhoons had killed many Germans. The author also objects, on the grounds that as the original Typhoon was a failure as a fighter, although it later became a very successful close air support aircraft, the name was hardly worth perpetuating. The same goes for the German Bf 108 *Taifun;* an undistinguished four-seater communications aircraft. Surely Tempest would have been better! But be that as it may, EF 2000 is now the Typhoon.

Development
Although at first only seen in artists impressions, Typhoon gradually changed and developed from EAP. Trials of the latter showed that the maximum coefficient of lift (CL_{max}) changed non-linearly as the centre of gravity moved aft in supersonic flight, reducing the amount of instability. A relaxation of supersonic agility requirements saw a straight leading edge introduced. The elongated canopy was replaced by a bubble type, and the huge Tornado-style fin and rudder was replaced by a much smaller all-moving vertical surface, with an ECM housing near the top, and a bullet-shaped fairing appeared low on the trailing edge.

The all-moving fin was soon supplanted by a traditional and rather larger fin and rudder assembly, although not as large as that of EAP, with an air scoop at the base. The ECM housing vanished, to be replaced by pods on the cropped wingtips. The size of the foreplanes was reduced, while a change in forward fuselage section, from ogival to circular to house a larger radar antenna, produced an upward-curved "smiling" intake. This was at first stated to be a stealth measure, but in fact curved inlet ducts, combined with RAM tiles, shield the compressor faces from prying hostile radars, with

Above left: The tall and angular fin doesn't look quite right, but the alternative was twin fins with much greater weight and complexity. The nosewheel is set a long way back.

Left: DA 3, the first Typhoon to be assembled in Italy. This angle shows the flaps and slats which provide variable camber, and the strake/step below the cockpit canopy.

RAM paint used in other regions.

While little has been released, the RCS target for Typhoon was between one quarter and one fifth of that of a conventional fighter, and this is a contractual obligation. This puts its RCS at a bit less than that of the F-16 when in clean condition. But the carriage of external stores will do nothing to help matters.

Close-coupled canards as used on Gripen and Rafale caused vortices which served to "clean up" the airflow over the wing, but the relatively long distance between Typhoon's canards, which in any case are canted downwards, and its wing, reduces this effect. To compensate, small strakes are mounted on each side of the cockpit, where they double as steps.

The wing is almost entirely carbon composite construction, with multiple carbon-fibre spars bonded to the undersurfaces. The fin/rudder assembly and the front fuselage are of similar construction, while the centre and aft fuselage are skinned with composites. Quality problems with the ultra lightweight aluminium lithium, scheduled to be used on the chin intake, wing and fin leading edges, and other places, caused this to be replaced with a conventional aluminium alloy. Titanium alloy is used for the canard foreplanes, around the engines, and for the outboard flaperons, which have to withstand the heat of missile launches from the outboard pylons.

Progress was slow until 1992, when Germany, financially hit by reunification, seized on the disappearance of the Soviet threat as an excuse to query the necessity of Typhoon. For a while, the project looked like foundering. Only with a reduced specification did it go ahead. As one respected commentator observed, the two main problems faced by Typhoon have been Germany and Germany. It was therefore mortifying to the other partners when the first flight of DA.1, on 27 March 1994, took place at Manching with German test pilot Peter Weger at the controls. That this need not have occurred was demonstrated ten days later when Chris Yeo hauled the BAe-assembled DA.2 off the runway at Warton.

Both DA.1 and DA.2 were powered by Turbo-Union RB.199 Mk 104Es. The first Typhoon to fly with EJ 200 engines was DA.3, from Caselle in Italy on 6 June 1995, piloted by Napoleone Bragagnolo. Since then, DA.1 and DA.2 have been retrofitted with the EJ 200, and all seven prototypes have flown with this engine.

Power

EJ 200 is a two-spool turbofan with a thrust/weight ratio of 9:1, an overall pressure ratio of 26:1, and a bypass ratio of 0.4:1. The three-stage LP compressor and five stage HP compressor are driven by single-stage turbines, with a single airspray can annular combustor. The afterburner consists of 15 burners with fuel vaporizers, radial fuel manifolds, and air-cooled radial gutters, which give extreme flexibility.

The baseline engines are rated at 20,250lb (9,185kg) wet thrust and 13,500lb (6,124kg) in military. For the future, increasing the fan pressure ratio to 4.6:1 and the mass flow by 10 per cent should give 23,288lb (10,563kg) and

16,200lb (7,348kg) respectively. In a second development phase, with improvements to the HP spool, increases of 30 percent may become possible. The Spanish company ITP, responsible for the "hot end" of EJ 200, successfully ground-tested a variable thrust nozzle in 1998. This will almost certainly be incorporated at some future date.

Flight control system

Digital quadruplex FBW is now so commonplace that it is largely taken for granted. According the former F-16 chief test pilot Steve Barter, the transition from analogue to digital FBW was accomplished without undue difficulty. If Dassault has had any difficulty with the Mirage 2000 or Rafale, they have kept it very quiet, as

have the Russian Mikoyan and Sukhoi design bureaux. Two very public accidents betrayed the fact that, even with US assistance, all did not go well with Gripen, while even the world's most expensive fighter, the F-22 Raptor, came to grief.

It was therefore greatly to the credit of Eurofighter that they actually admitted to having problems with Typhoon's FCS, even though it gave the politicians and "popular" press a stick with which to beat them. To paraphrase Dr Johnson: "The peasants in full pursuit of the technocracy!"

The problems were twofold: how best to handle the non-linear aerodynamic qualities of an unstable canard delta, and how to cope with massive changes in the

centre of gravity caused by the carriage and release of a large range of external stores, many of them heavy. This has however since been overcome, and works well. A major feature, and this itself caused problems, was carefree handling. While it is possible to set aerodynamic limits via the FCS, where air combat is concerned, slight overshoots must be permitted. Only this allows the pilot to take his aircraft to the limit aggressively, otherwise he is restricted as he approaches the limit. The Typhoon FCS allows the pilot to over-ride the preset limits in extremis, but these circumstances will be rare indeed.

Cockpit and avionics

Typhoon has a modern "glass cockpit"

Above right: 'burners blazing, a Typhoon blasts off the runway. Note the drooped slats on the leading edge, which give the impression of curvature, and the wingtip pods.

Right: Eurojet EJ 200 was tailored for the specific needs of Typhoon. A two-spool turbofan, it will almost certainly be given a vectoring nozzle in the future.

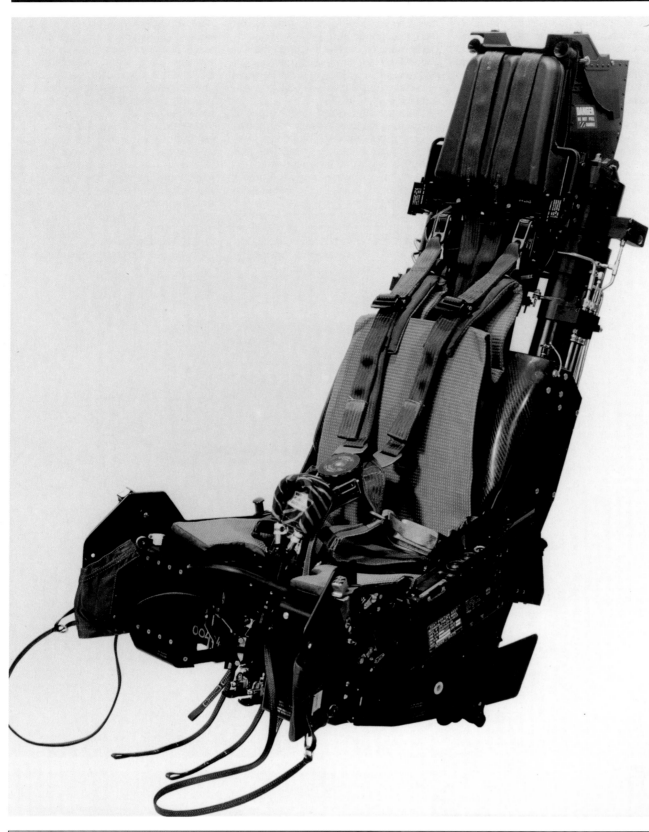

with HUD and MFDs. The Martin Baker Mk 16A seat has a mere 22deg rake; the better to allow a good view over the nose. HOTAS is of course obligatory, but an orthodox central control column is preferred to the sidestick.

Radar is the European Collaborative Radar 90 (ECR90), developed by Marconi/Fiat/DASA/Indra. At an early date, the decision was made not to go for a fixed phased array antenna, but to take existing technology to its limits with a moveable planar array. As stated, the choice was first generation electronic scanning against final generation conventional scanning. The main advance is the use of data-adaptive scanning, which permits the target tracking function to control the antenna scan pattern, which in turn demands a very agile antenna. Virtually everything is automatic, to reduce pilot workload. ECR90 was based on the existing Blue Vixen. It has three modes: air-to-air; air-to-surface; and navigation. A low transmit/receive ratio not only increases the probability of detecting low RCS targets,, it reduces the chance of detection by hostile systems.

ECR90 is supplemented by a FIAR/Pilkington Infra-Red Search and Track (IRST) system, with a sensor mounted on the port side of the front fuselage. This has two functions – scanning, and FLIR. It operates in two wavebands, 3 and 11 microns, and is therefore a "two-colour" system. For air combat, it will be fully integrated with the radar.

Finally, there is the Defensive Aids Sub-System (DASS). This provides integrated threat detection and warning, and automatic deployment of countermeasures, including towed radar decoys from wingtip pods. Ultra-violet missile launch warners would have been nice to have, but at first a rearward-looking active radar system will be deployed. RAF aircraft will carry a laser warning sensor under the nose. Secure Data Link for

remote targeting, and Helmet-Mounted Sights, will be standard.

Weaponry

A 27mm Mauser cannon with 150 rounds is carried in the starboard wing root. Trials have shown that 27mm is optimum, giving the best combination of hitting power and ballistic qualities. Typhoon has 14 hardpoints. The typical air-to-air load will be four AIM-120 AMRAAM, a missile previously discussed, carried semi-conformally beneath the fuselage, and six ASRAAM. ECR90 can also pro-

vide continuous-wave homing for SARH missiles such as Skyflash. This is not simply to use up surplus stocks; there is still a place for SARH missiles in the modern inventory. F-15s operating in defence of Kosovo carried two, the reason being that when AMRAAM goes active, it is a little bit "iffy" as to which target it will select. By contrast, SARH missiles do not deviate from the target selected.

In future, Typhoon may well use an advanced form of AMRAAM, or the European Meteor, which uses ramjet propulsion to give not only long range

but manoeuvrability towards the end of its trajectory, vastly increasing the no-escape zone.

ASRAAM was originally to have been a Sidewinder replacement. A wingless missile with control fins at the tail, it is faster and more agile than the US weapon. The seeker is a staring (i.e., fixed) focal plane array, gimballed to give up to 90deg off-boresight coverage, cued by a helmet-mounted sight. Thermal imaging allows it to select the most vulnerable point on the target. It is also stated to have an "over-the-shoul-

der" aim capability, but this is guaranteed to make wingmen uneasy.

Typhoon will carry the full range of current air-to-surface ordnance, with the addition of the Storm Shadow cruise missile, which is virtually identical to the French SCALP, and ALARM, the BAe anti-radiation missile first used in the Gulf War.

Typhoon is scheduled to enter service with the RAF, the *Luftwaffe,* and the Italian and Spanish air forces. To date the only export order is for Greece, but Norway is confidently expected to be the next export customer.

Specifications		
Eurofighter Typhoon		
	EAP	**EF 2000 Typhoon**
Dimensions		
Span	36ft 7$\frac{1}{2}$in/11.17m	35ft 11in/10.95m
Length	57ft 6in/17.53m	52ft 4in/15.96m
Height	18ft 1$\frac{3}{4}$in/5.53m	17ft 4in/5.28m
Wing area	538sq ft/50sq m	538sq ft/50sq m
Weights		
Empty Weight	22,046lb/10,000kg	24,240lb/10,995kg
Max takeoff	34,000lb/15,420kg	50,706lb/23,000kg
Power	2xRB199 Mk 104D	2xEJ200
Max thrust	16,500lb/7,484kg	20,250lb/9,185kg
Mil thrust	n/a	13,500lb/6,124kg
Internal fuel	9,500lb/4,309kg	11,000lb/4,990kg
Performance		
V_{max} hi	n/a	Mach 2 plus
Ceiling	n/a	c60,000ft/18,287m
Climb rate	n/a	c60,000ft min/305m sec

Above: The Martin-Baker Mk 16A ejection seat, raked back at 22deg, has been selected for the Typhoon. The angle is a compromise between resisting the g forces at high alpha and the best view over the nose.

Below left: DA 3 is seen here over the Italian Alps. It can be armed with four Sparrows or AMRAAM, and two Sidewinders. Possible future weapons will include the medium range Meteor and the close combat ASRAAM.

Above left: Typhoon has a typically modern "glass cockpit", with coloured multi-function displays surmounted by a wide-angle holographic HUD. Supplemented by a helmet-mounted sight, it is a formidable system.

Below: First Typhoon to fly was DA 1 from Manching in Germany, on 24 March 1994, followed 10 days later by BAe-assembled DA 2. This was in some ways unfortunate, as Germany had caused many delays in the project.

MiGs

Contents

Top: The MiG-23, NATO reporting name Flogger, was once the numerically most important fighter in the Soviet inventory, but has been phased out.

Above: A MiG-25A Foxbat interceptor lines up on the runway for a night mission, in typical Russian winter conditions. The Foxbat in the foreground is not ready to fly, as is shown by ice on the upper surfaces.

Above right: East meets West in this picture of an Egyptian Air Force MiG-21bis carrying an American AIM-9 Sidewinder beneath the port wing. The clearance between the ground and the ventral drop tank is marginal.

Left: The MiG-29 Fulcrum is the Russian equivalent of the American F/A-18 Hornet, with perhaps a bit of the F-16 thrown in. But, despite its fearsome reputation, it has failed to score in three conflicts.

Introduction

In 1893 a primitive factory was founded in the outskirts of Moscow, to make bicycles and other tubular metal products. Gradually it progressed to making automobiles, then, in 1909, aeroplanes. World War I stimulated aircraft production; from making 180 in 1914, it made 492 prior to the revolution in late 1917. Most were foreign designs, Farmans, Nieuports, Moranes, etc. In 1918, the factory became "State Aircraft Factory No 1!"

The first indigenous Soviet aircraft to be produced was the R-1, designed by Nikolai Polikarpov in 1923. This was followed in 1927 by a two-seater trainer, the U-2, better known in the West as the PO-2. Incredibly, this aircraft not only served throughout the Great Patriotic War as a nuisance raider; it even became infamous in the Korean War as "Bedcheck Charlie". But in its early days State Aircraft Factory No 1 was engaged primarily in producing aircraft designed by others.

Meanwhile, two gifted designers, Artem Ivanovich Mikoyan and Mikhail Iosifovich Guryevich had emerged. In late 1939 they formed the MiG Opytno Konstruktorskoye Byuro (OKB – Experimental Construction Bureau). Their first efforts were the MiG-1 and MiG- 3 high altitude fighters. These were largely unsuccessful, and for the remainder of the Great Patriotic War the factory was engaged in building aircraft designed by other OKBs, including Ilyushin, Petlyakov, and Yakovlev.

The MiG OKB first rose to prominence in the late 1940s with the swept wing MiG-15, which gained an enviable reputation in the Korean War. For many years after, the MiG OKB produced a series of jet fighters which were used world-wide in a series of conflicts. Since 1962, State Aircraft Factory No 1 built MiG-21, MiG-23 and MiG-29 fighters. In more recent times it became the Moscow Aircraft Production Organization (MAPO), responsible for marketing MiG fighters around the world.

The MiG Family Develops

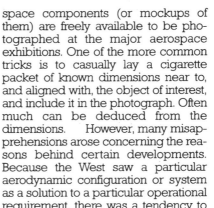

The aircraft design and production system in the old Soviet Union was completely different from that of the West. The OKBs were given a specification drafted by the armed forces, which they tried to meet in every respect. Prototypes were then built and evaluated, but once a selection had been made, production was allocated to whichever factory had sufficient and suitable capacity. The aircraft designation stemmed from that of the OKB, and for years had little relevance to the factory of origin.

Since 1990, the Russians have pursued a policy of openness. This has allowed the West to know more about their combat aircraft than had been the case for the preceding four decades. But old habits die hard. Even now, with the Cold War over for 10 years, a degree of disinformation still persists, which makes it difficult, but not impossible, for outsiders to make correct judgements on current Russian aircraft. This is why the reader may on occasion find apparently contradictory statements in what follows. But things were once much worse.

While East and West were subject to the same laws of propulsion and aerodynamics, careful study of photographs often revealed valuable information (although it tended to be fairly imprecise on dimensions, and consequently for weights). Where new Russian military aircraft were concerned, this was either via satellite photography or by covert photography from the ground. In the latter case, more detail was available, but the sky background gave nothing against which to assess dimensions, unless of course the pilot's helmet was visible. But even this gave only rough approximations.

To digress for a moment, many aerospace components (or mockups of them) are freely available to be photographed at the major aerospace exhibitions. One of the more common tricks is to casually lay a cigarette packet of known dimensions near to, and aligned with, the object of interest, and include it in the photograph. Often much can be deduced from the dimensions. However, many misapprehensions arose concerning the reasons behind certain developments. Because the West saw a particular aerodynamic configuration or system as a solution to a particular operational requirement, there was a tendency to believe that the Russian adoption of such a solution was prompted by similar operational reasons to those of the West. Just sometimes this was correct, but in other cases it was far from the truth, leading to the most awful intelligence misappreciations, the consequences of which may often be seen in what follows.

The other main difference is that whereas Soviet fighter design was always dominated by official operational requirements, the West has tended to be led by technology. This has inevitably led to a race between rival aircraft companies, which of

MiG Fighter Specifications:

Type	MiG-21bis	MiG-23B	MiG-27K	MiG-25PD	MiG-29M	MiG-31
Span	23ft 5¾in/7.154m	25ft 6¼in/7.78m	45ft 9¾in/13.97m	45ft 11¾in/14.12m	37ft 3in/11.36m	44ft 2in/13.46m
Length	48ft 2¼in/14.70m	50ft 4¼in/15.35m	50ft 9¾in/15.49m	64ft 9½in/19.75m	57ft 0in/17.37m	74ft 5in/22.69m
Height	14ft 9in/4.50m	14ft 4in/4.37m	14ft 4in/4.37m	18ft 6in/5.64m	15ft 6in/4.73m	20ft 2in/6.15m
Wing area	247.6sq.ft/23m²	368sq.ft/34.16m²	369sq.ft/34.16 m²	661sq.ft/61.4m²	409sq.ft/38m²	663sq.ft/61.6m²
Power	1xR25-300	1xAL-21F-300	1xR-29B-300	2xR-15BD-300	2xRD-33K	2xD-30F6
Max thrust	19,840lb/9,000kg	25,353lb/11,500kg	25,353lb/11,500kg	24,692lb/11,200kg	19,400lb/8,800kg	38,580lb/21,820kg
Mil thrust	8,796lb/3,990kg	17,637lb/8,000kg	17,637lb/8,000kg	19,400lb/8,800kg	12,125lb/5,500kg	20,944lb/9,500kg
Intl fuel	5,000lb/2,260kg	9,920lb/4,500kg	9,269lb/4,204kg	76,965lb/34,920kg	9,978lb/4,526kg	36,045lb/16,350kg
Normal TO weight	19,230lb/8,725kg	40,995lb/18,600kg	39,890lb/18,10 0kgt	80,953lb/36,720kg	37,038lb/16,800kg	90,389lb/41,000kg
Wing loading	78lb/ft²/379kg/m²	111lb/ft²/ 544kg/m²	108lb/ft²/ 530kg/m²	122lb/ft²/ 598kg/m²	91lb/ft²/ 442kg/m²	136lb/ft²/ 666kg/m²
Thrust loading	1.03	0.62	0.64	0.61	1.05	0.85
V_{max} hi	Mach 2.05	Mach 2.35	Mach 1.70	Mach 2.83	Mach 2.30	Mach 2.83
V_{max} lo	Mach 1.06	Mach 0.91	Mach 0.91	Mach 0.98	Mach 1.23	Mach 1.23
Climb	45,275ftm/230msec	n/a	n/a	n/a	64,945fpm/330mps	c41,000fpm/208mps
Ceiling	57,418ft/17,500m	54,957ft/16,750m	n/a	67,917ft/20,700m	55,777ft/17,000m	67,589ft/20,600m

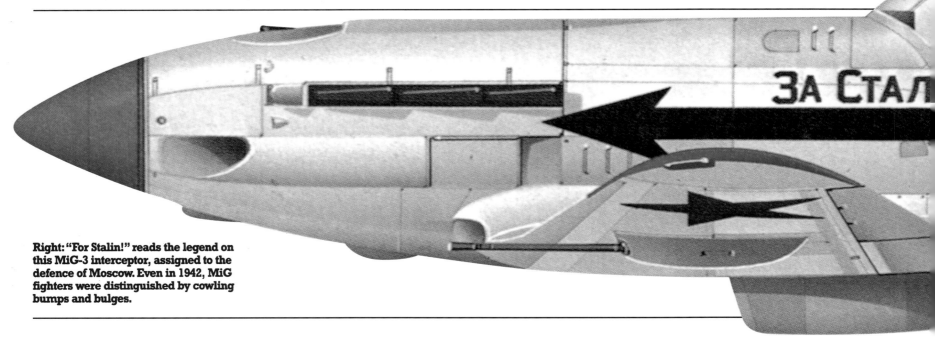

Right: "For Stalin!" reads the legend on this MiG-3 interceptor, assigned to the defence of Moscow. Even in 1942, MiG fighters were distinguished by cowling bumps and bulges.

Left: Artem I. Mikoyan, photographed in March 1966. Aged 34 when the MiG bureau was founded, he headed it until he literally died at his drawing board in 1970. The status and influence of leading Soviet engineers such as Mikoyan is almost unbelievable in Western terms.

Right: First design from the MiG bureau was the MiG-1, a high-altitude fighter whose stubby lines indicated a concern with weight reduction and high performance.

Right below: These MiG-3s seem to be split into elements of three, with lead aircraft and wingmen distinctively marked. Rigid tactics compensated for expertise lost in pre-war purges.

course are totally responsible not only for design, but for manufacture. At times the result has been that the boundaries of technology have been pushed a little too hard, with unsatisfactory results. The classic example of this was the defensive avionics system of the Rockwell B-1B, which to a degree was aimed at a projected threat which never materialized. General Bedwell of US Air Force Systems Command is on record as saying that while 95 per cent of the targets were achieved, the remaining 5 per cent were so far out of sight as to be economically unattainable.

Another example was the Western development of look-down, shoot-down radar/missile combinations. Now this actually worked. The USAF and USN actually had such systems in service before a viable Soviet low level threat emerged. The Soviet procurement system did not lend itself to meeting an anticipated threat, only a real one.

There is of course a third factor. Modern Russian combat aircraft first appeared in public in the West at the Farnborough Air Show in 1988, in the shape of the then largely unknown and intriguing MiG-29. Unfortunately, overheated imaginations in the Western press gave rise to some totally potty speculation as to its capability. The much-hyped tail slide was for example presented as a valid combat manoeuvre by the Russians and, to give them full credit, they kept a straight face while

Right: One can only wonder what happened to the German-derived engines of the pre-production MiG-9 when the pilot discharged the mighty 37mm Nudelman-Suranov NS-37 fowling-piece on the intake splitter.

doing so. The fact is that the Russians have a well-developed sense of humour, and at least some of them took full advantage of Western credulity, a situation which persists to the present day.

The OKB within the system
At the top of the heap is the Defence Ministry, responsible for procurement. Next down is TsAGI, the Central Institute of Aerodynamics and Hydrodynamics, which takes the basic requirements and makes recommendations as to the optimum configuration. This is the reason why certain Russian fighters appear to have been turned out of the same jellymould, varying only in size and detail. Classic examples are the tailed delta MiG-21 and Su-9, and more recently the MiG-29 and Su-27. Not that either of these pairs are identical; they just have rather similar layouts, devised to solve common problems.

The task of the OKBs is to take the basic recommendations and turn them into flying hardware. On occasion, two OKBs have competed for the same project, but this was regarded as wasteful. Of course, the Americans have often produced competing designs for a competitive flyoff, the most notable example being the light fighter competition between the General Dynamics YF-16 and the Northrop YF-17, which was won by the former. At the time of writing, the Joint Strike Fighter competition is in full swing, with Boeing and Lockheed head to head. But in what was the Soviet Union, this situation hardly ever occurred, and in the straitened economic climate at the beginning of the 21st Century, not at all.

The MiG-15
What put the Mikoyan and Gurevich OKB into a commanding lead in the Soviet fighter industry stemmed from sheer chance. The main problem was the lack of a decent turbojet engine. While in 1945 the USSR had captured more than their share of German aircraft engineers, the German jets were far behind the West in fields such as metallurgy and high temperature technology. Catching up could not be done overnight; by comparison with British and American aircraft, the early Russian jets were turkeys.

The impasse was broken by the British Labour Government, who in September 1946 agreed to supply Russia with samples of the Rolls-Royce Nene and Derwent engines. Now while both were centrifugal flow engines, a configuration which was subsequently overtaken by the axial flow engine, the Nene was the most advanced jet engine of its time in the world. The fact that it was already nearing the limit of its potential was hardly relevant; it was the best and, reverse-engineered by Klimov as the RD-45, it was adopted for the swept-wing MiG-15.

First flight of the prototype took place on 30 December 1947 with test pilot V.N. Yuganov at the controls. It was designed as a bomber destroyer, optimised for high speed, a high rate of climb, and a high ceiling, with heavy cannon armament. After various modifications it was accepted for service in August 1948.

Bomber destroyer or no, the MiG-15 established a formidable reputation in the skies of Korea between 1951-53. Mainly flown by Russians, it demonstrated a clear superiority in altitude and climb performance over the

Above: A North Vietnamese MiG-17F under attack by US Navy F-8 Crusaders on December 14, 1967. In such low-level engagements subsonic speed was no handicap.

Above right: The MiG-15UTI – known under the NATO reporting system as 'Midget' – was the standard trainer for Soviet fighter pilots for decades until the introduction of the Aero L-39. This example was photographed after being overhauled in Prague for the Iraqi Air Force, which used the type into the late 1970s.

Above far right: Under Project Moolah, the USA offered asylum and money to any pilot defecting with a MiG-15. The project was successful, and analysis and testing of the MiG-15 helped to define tactically important modifications to the F-86 Sabre, such as the importance of the all-moving "flying tail" for high-speed pitch control. (See below right for original markings.)

Right: This Shenyang FT-5 (Chinese two-seat trainer version of the MiG-17PF), photographed at its Pakistan AF base in March 1981, illustrates the generally high quality of workmanship apparent on most of the south-of-the-border 'bootleg' MiG designs.

American F-86 Sabre, which was powered by an axial-flow jet engine. The Americans, and the handful of RAF pilots who flew with them on exchange tours (notably John Nicholls, later Air Marshal Sir John, who became the RAF VCAS) were not amused by the fact that the MiG-15 was powered by what was essentially a British engine.

Having said this, the Sabre did manage to establish a combat superiority over the Soviet fighter, in that its han-

Below: The MiG-15bis, in bright red and pale blue colour scheme, was used by the Moskovsky Okrug PVO aerobatic display team – the Red Falcons – and flown at early Aviation Day demonstrations in the mid-1950s.

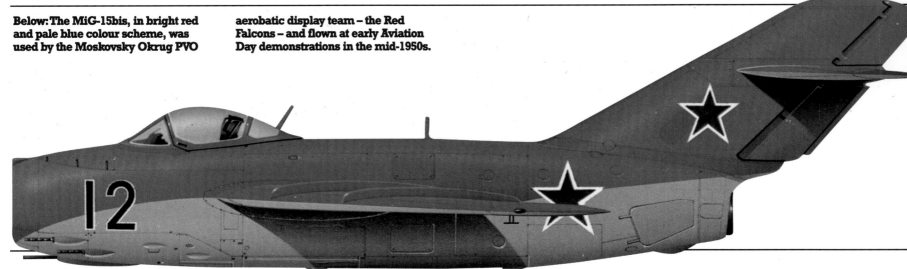

Below: The MiG-15 made its combat debut in the markings of North Korea, but usually flown by Chinese or Soviet pilots. This MiG-15bis was flown to Kimpo, near Seoul, South Korea, by Snr Lt Kum Suk No of the Korean People's Army Air Force, on September 21, 1953, and evaluated by the US Air Force.

dling was far better, giving greater manoeuvrability in close combat. Also it was supersonic in a dive. The best the MiG could manage was Mach 0.92, and its handling left much to be desired. Its advantages were that it had a much higher ceiling, which allowed it to take the initiative, and a rate of climb at high altitude which left the Sabre standing.

The MiG-17

The MiG-15 was gradually improved in a series of stages, finally evolving into the MiG-17. This had a larger wing with a compound leading edge sweep, and in its first major MiG-17F variant (F = forsirovanni = boosted) had an afterburning VK-1F engine. This was still a centrifugal flow engine, and it could not quite push the MiG-17F past Mach 1 in level flight. Other variants were the MiG-17P, with the RP-1 Izumrud (Emerald) radar in the nose, giving it limited adverse weather capability; and the MiG-17PF, which carried four K-5 radar homing missiles. In all, nearly 40 nations operated

Top: A MiG-19PF with Izumrud radar and the inevitable external tanks. Not a large aircraft, the MiG-19 weighs about as much as an A-4 Skyhawk, but with its twin engines it is significantly more powerful.

Middle: All-round vision hood, two heavy cannon and effective airbrakes made the MiG-19 a fairly effective dogfighter, by the standard of the day.

Above: The potential handling problems of the MiG-19's highly swept wing were countered by the use of very large wing fences. One wag suggested that their function was to prevent the airflow from defecting to the tips.

Right: Tyres smoke gently as a Pakistan AF Shenyang F-6 – a Chinese reproduction of the MiG-19 – touches down. The relatively large external tanks are common to all of the small, powerful MiG designs.

Left: A radar-equipped MiG-17PF 'Fresco-D' interceptor on final approach. The intake bullet houses the conical scan search element of the Izumrud radar, and the bulged lip contains the ranging set. The large area of the wing is apparent.

for the Mikulin engine design bureau, and shortly after to head his own OKB, had developed an axial flow turbojet, at first designated VRD-5, later the TR-3A, then the AL-5. With a seven stage compressor, this produced 11,464lb (5,200kg) static thrust. The only Soviet engine in sight to promise supersonic flight, it was adopted for the I-350 project in June 1950.

The I-350 had a wing leading edge sweep of 57deg, with four fences on each side. Aspect ratio was startling for the time, 2.63. Piloted by Grigoriy Sedov, it nearly came to grief on its first flight on 16 June 1951, when the engine flamed out as it was throttled back prior to landing. Six more flights served to demonstrate that the engine was too unreliable for service.

The I-350 was replaced by the SM-2, powered by two AM-5A turbojets. Of similar configuration to its predecessor, it was first flown by Sedov on 24 May 1952. Problems were immediately encountered. At high angles of attack the high-set tailplane was blanketed by the wake from the wings. The cure for this was to relocate it to the base of the fin. This still proved inadequate, and instability in pitch caused it to be moved further downwards, to a mid-fuselage position. Spoilers were added in front of the ailerons to improve roll rates, while a powered flight control system was introduced which incorporated artificial "feel". Wing fences were reduced to two. But while the SM-2 could reach Mach 1.19, this was only in a dive. It needed afterburning AM-9B turbojets to make it a truly supersonic aircraft.

The MiG-19

The first flight of the MiG-19 prototype took place on 5 January 1954, some six months after the North American F-100 Super Sabre. It could reach Mach 1.3 at altitude, and climb rate was an

outstanding 35,435fpm/180msec. It was ordered into production on 17 February 1954, and first deliveries were made, NATO reporting name Farmer, in March 1957.

Operational variants included the radar-equipped MiG-19P; the MiG-19PM, armed with four K-5M beam-riding radar-homing missiles; and the high-flying MiG-19SV. Vladimir Ilyushin, then serving as a military test pilot, took part in evaluating the high altitude equipment needed. The MiG-19 was also reverse-engineered in China as the Shenyang J-6, while in the 1980s a greatly modified attack variant, the Nanchang Q-5, NATO reporting name Fantan, was produced. This had a "solid" radar nose housing Western avionics, and cheek intakes.

The MiG-19 took part in the Middle East Wars, flying for Egypt, where it made little impression on Israeli pilots. As Israeli ace Oded Marom commented after shooting one down in the Six Day War, "You never saw such a miserable aircraft as a MiG-19, like a big cigar. Fat fuselage, short wings like a bug, and it flew the same – like a bug!" As the J-6 it also flew for Pakistan against India. In 1971, J-6 pilot Sayed Sa'ad Hatmi brought down two Sukhoi Su-7s and a Hunter to add to his two Sabre victories in 1965, to become Pakistan's second air ace. The J-6 also saw action over North Vietnam in the later stages of the war, where aces Le Than Dao and Nguyen Duc Soat scored some of their victories in the type. Its agility surprised many American fighter pilots.

The MiG-19, probably the first fighter in the world to have a thrust/weight ratio in excess of unity at combat weight, remains in service at the turn of the century, although the Q-5 (A-5 in its export version) is purely an attack aircraft. It is currently operated by: Albania (F-6); Bangladesh (A-5); China People's Republic Liberation Army (about 2,500 J-6 and 500 Q-5), Navy about 300 J-6 and 100 Q-5); Egypt (F-6); Iran (Revolutionary Guard F-6); Myanmar (A-5); North Korea (F-6); Pakistan (A-5 and F-6); Somalia (F-6, probably unserviceable); Sudan (F-6); Tanzania (F-6); and Zambia (F-6).

the MiG-17, NATO reporting name Fresco, and it took part in most of the "brushfire" conflicts around the world over the next three decades. Notably it was involved in the Middle East conflicts against Israel, and in Vietnam against the USAF and USN. North Vietnamese pilots Nguyen Van Bay, Le Hai, and Luu Hai Chao, are credited with becoming aces on the MiG-17. It has been licence-built in Poland and Czechoslovakia, and by the People's Republic of China as the Shenyang J-5.

It remains in service with Albania (F-

5); the People's Republic of China (F-5), the major user, which retains about 500 in the Liberation Army Air Force and 100 in the Navy; Congo; Ethiopia; Guinea; Guinea-Bissau; Madagascar; Mali; North Korea (F-5); Pakistan (FT-5, training only); Somalia, although these are probably non-operational; Sudan (F-5); and Tanzania (F-5).

Supersonic MiGs

The next step was to produce an aircraft capable of supersonic speed in level flight. A.M. Ly'ulka, chief designer

MiG-21 'Fishbed'

Small and austere, the combat record of the MiG-21 appears to indicate that it is a complete turkey. It has been on the wrong end of a beating in three wars in the Middle East, in Vietnam, and in the Gulf War of 1991, and did little to redeem itself for India against Pakistan. The design is elderly, dating from 1956, and the avionics are basic. Condemned by the West as a "boy racer" fighter, it was bought by no fewer than 49 nations, participated in more wars than any other fighter, and nearly 50 years later remains a prime candidate for upgrading.

Once the physical and psychological barrier of Mach 1 had been breached, aerospace technology advanced at a gallop. The 1950s saw all previous records for speed and altitude shattered. They were a time of serious work on near-hypersonic aircraft, airborne nuclear power, radical chemical fuels and previously undreamt-of weapons and sensors. It was also the decade in which the Cold War between East and West froze solid.

The Soviet Union's development of nuclear and thermonuclear weapons, and the Korean War of 1950-53, set the international tone for the decade, and there was very little change in the atmosphere from 1950 to 1960. The mood was one of sullen confrontation, and East and West both armed themselves – almost exclusively – for total war.

The 1950s concept of total war was not the same as today's. Nuclear weapons still had to be delivered by subsonic bombers, far more susceptible to interception than today's missiles. The total number of warheads on either side was smaller, because nuclear weapons were difficult and expensive to produce,

and so large that only a handful could be carried on one aircraft. Moreover, the public at large was kept blissfully unaware of the hazards of radioactive fallout. For these reasons, it was felt that non-nuclear combat could still be important, even in the case of an all-out thermonuclear exchange. Another difference between the 1950s and the two subsequent decades was that defence against nuclear attack was considered to be feasible and essential.

Neither the Soviet Union nor the United States, however, could afford to maintain vast land forces while racing to develop new systems for strategic attack and defence. The US had moved to consolidate its alliances in Europe, leading to the establishment of the North Atlantic Treaty Organization in 1949. In 1955 a 'Treaty of Friendship, Mutual Assistance and Cooperation' was signed in Warsaw by the USSR and six other East European states, ostensibly as a defensive response to NATO; in fact, the Warsaw Pact formalized relationships which had existed since the establishment of Communist governments in Eastern Europe in the aftermath of the war. In both cases,

there was a need for conventional weapons to equip these forces, as well as the Soviet and US units that would be based alongside them.

In the USA, the advance of technology had driven the air-defence interceptors and tactical fighters apart by the early 1950s, to the point where the aircraft designed for one mission were incapable of performing the other, even with adaptation. The Soviet Union, however, continued to require all-purpose fighters in the mould of the MiG-15, MiG-17 and MiG-19.

The strategic bomber threat

Several factors influenced Soviet planning for advanced fighters in the early 1950s. One was the rapid expansion of the USAF force of jet bombers. In just four years of production, starting in 1952, the USAF built the staggering total of 2,000 Boeing B-47s, whose Mach 0.9 cruising speed rendered the MiG-15 and MiG-17 impotent, and the MiG-19 of marginal usefulness. The low-time B-50 bombers which the B-47s replaced were converted into tankers; together with the availability of bases in Britain and else-

Above: The small size of the MiG-21F is apparent in this view. The design of the canopy was influenced by that of the Folland Gnat; it formed a blast shield to protect the pilot in the event of ejection.

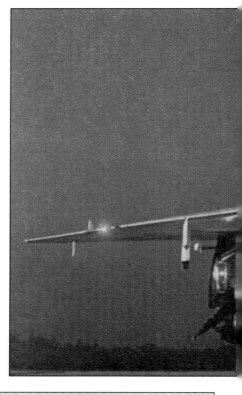

Below: Czech-built MiG-21Fs, produced at the Aero factory near Prague and designated S-107, can be distinguished from otherwise similar Soviet-built machines by the lack of a glazed rear section to the canopy.

Bottom: The Tumansky R-11 was a remarkable engine. The two-spool powerplant has a high thrust/weight ratio, and contains only 3,500 parts, fewer than the much smaller J85, thanks to good basic design.

Below: A pristine S-107 (MiG-21F). Note that the port gun has been removed, making way for additional electronics. The combined pitot boom and yaw/pitch sensors is a standard piece of equipment.

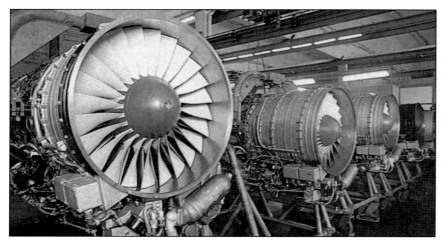

Mikoyan Ye-2A prototype

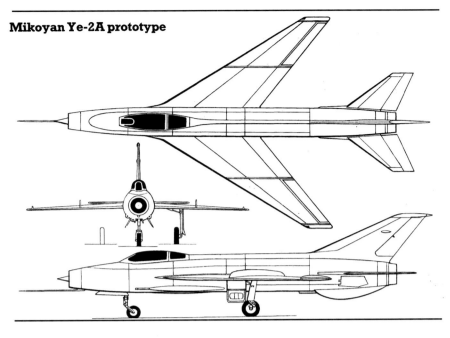

Above: The aerodynamic configuration of the Ye-2A was based on a thin-winged MiG-19. The less conventional delta-winged Ye-5, with a lower empty weight, proved to have better performance in all respects.

Below: Through ingenious design, it proved possible to fit a radar in the already tightly packed airframe, creating the MiG-21PF. Note the oversize, low-pressure tyres common to all MiG-21s.

Above: a MiG-21F of the DDR Luftstreitkrafte slows down for the camera, displaying its three small ventral airbrakes. The aircraft in the background is a later model, with a broader fin and relocated brake chute.

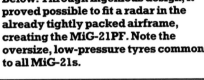

where, this made the B-47's relatively short range very much less important. B-47 attacks could be expected from almost any direction. Meanwhile, the intercontinental B-52 was well advanced in development. As well as adding a truly global dimension to the jet bomber threat, it would carry more extensive countermeasures than the B-47 and would cruise at higher altitudes.

Combat experience in Korea was also important. While the kill/loss ratio had been heavily in favour of the USAF (probably about 4:1, rather than the 10:1 claimed at the time) there was little dispute that the basic design of the MiG-15 had proved sound. A few small but significant items of equipment, and much better training and experience, had decided many engagements. In terms of performance and firepower, the MiG-15 had held its own against the much larger F-86. Korea also demonstrated that tactical air warfare could still come down to a close-range, turning engagement, and that absolute performance, including speed, acceleration and rate-of-climb, was important; an aircraft with the advantage in performance gave its pilot

the initiative in starting or ending an engagement.

Basic Soviet military doctrine, however, introduced a complication into the conception of any new Soviet fighter: numerical superiority was vital. Western Mach 2 fighters were, without exception, more complex and more expensive than their subsonic and transonic predecessors. There were fewer of them, and they needed more maintenance. Such a development would have been unacceptable to the Soviet front commander, who then as now considered numbers first and technical quality second. Resolving the dilemma by increasing the resources devoted to fighter production was out of the question; bomber production took absolute priority, and it would be years before the Soviet strategic strike force attained parity with Strategic Air Command.

The requirement

The solution was to issue a requirement in late 1953, calling for a fighter with Mach 2 speed, and a service ceiling close to 66,000ft (20,000m) – both figures based on what was necessary to engage a B-52 – but demanding that the aircraft be little bigger than a MiG-17, and actually smaller than a MiG-19. Moreover, the aircraft had to carry a range-only radar, air-to-air missiles and a pair of heavy cannon, and it had to possess conventional flying characteristics, good manoeuvrability and reasonable field performance.

By the standards of the time this was a very stiff requirement indeed. The small size was the root of most of the problems it posed. Many of the components of the aircraft were basically fixed in size and weight; the pilot, seat and cockpit enclosure, the radar and radio equipment, the guns and the missiles were examples. They tended to make a fixed contribution to the weight and drag of the aircraft, and some of them imposed other constraints, such as the cockpit, which required a minimum cross-section forward of the wing. The main reason why Western designs had grown in weight and size was to reduce the weight and drag of these fixed items as a proportion of the total-aircraft figures.

The call for high supersonic speed compounded the difficulties. The aircraft was to be small, its internal fuel capacity would not be great, and it accordingly

Left: Details apparent on this S-107 include the ogival centrebody and the large vertical wheel wells. Note the large Fowler flaps, fully extended for take-off. The aircraft may be taking off on dry thrust in order to conserve its limited supply of fuel.

could not afford an oversized engine. An efficient supersonic configuration was vital. The Area Rule called for a smooth, and not excessive, variation in cross-sectional area from nose to tail, and the need to reduce wave drag meant that the fuselage must be as slender as possible. Neither was readily compatible with a light, efficiently packed airframe of small overall dimensions.

The new fighter would be single-engined – there is no evidence that any other layout was considered. The development of the Tumansky RD-9 had built up experience in small, light, powerful turbojets to the point where the design of a slightly larger engine would not present too many problems, and a single-engined aircraft would have a more slender, lighter rear fuselage than a twin of the same size.

The overall layout of the aircraft was strongly influenced by the aerodynamicists at the MAP's Central Aero-Hydrodynamics Institute (TsAGI). At that time TsAGI's influence was at its zenith, and its technical authority was such that its recommendations were almost read as law. However, TsAGI itself was

Left top: Each Soviet fighter regiment contains two or three two-seaters for conversion training. In this scene at a SovAF base, a MiG-21U 'Mongol-A' taxies out for a training mission, with an Su-7 following it.

Left: The MiG-21PFM featured plain, blown flaps. These were less efficient on take-off than the original Fowler flaps, so provision was made for the execution of flapless, rocket-assisted short take-offs.

Below: MiG-21FL was the designation of this subtype, built by HAL at Nasik. It was basically similar to a late-production MiG-21PF, but had an export-model radar and a more powerful version of the R-11 engine.

strongly influenced by the success of the earlier MiG fighters, whose mid-set wings and circular-section fuselages may have been less than ideal from the systems-packaging standpoint, but were aerodynamically straightforward and contributed to low drag and uncomplicated handling. Under TsAGI control, the MiG trademarks appeared on everything from cruise missiles to the Mya-4 heavy bomber.

Another feature which was probably assumed from the start was the inlet design. All previous Soviet fighters and prototypes had featured nose intakes, so the adoption of any other configuration would have meant a simultaneous move into a new internal geometry and a new speed range. The design has advantages of its own: it mandates long, gradually curved ducts, which tend to generate few surprises; the inlet itself is free from problems caused by wakes and vortices from the airframe or gun gas ingestion; and the air enters the inlet as it has to enter the engine, equally distributed in a circular pattern. The two main drawbacks are that such a layout takes up a large volume in the forward fuselage, and makes it almost impossible to install an engine with greater mass flow at a later date.

Planforms for supersonic flight were many and various in the early 1950s. Thin, moderately swept wings, tailless deltas, ultra-thin straight wings and other layouts were all being tried, with varying degrees of success, but most of them were ruled out for the new Soviet fighter by the terms of the requirement. Medium sweep angles were limited to about Mach 1.5 with contemporary powerplant technology; tailless deltas and F-104-type thin wings would not have achieved the necessary runway performance with existing technology.

Alternative solutions
TsAGI proposed two solutions. One was to modify the MiG-19 wing for a higher Mach number; the other was a new layout, combining a sharply swept delta wing with a tailplane. The basic delta

had been flown in 1949, on the Convair XF-92A prototype, and despite its outlandish appearance it had shown itself to be free of vices or surprises. Its drag was little higher than that of a swept wing, but it offered much more volume, had more area for the same weight, and was inherently stiff. Its main disadvantage was that it replaced the normal tailplane; at low speed, instead of flaps lifting the aircraft, the delta wing had up-elevon weighing it down. The delta also generated its maximum lift at very high angles of attack, which were impractical for conventional aircraft. Finally, the fact that the relatively short trailing edge had to provide all the pitch and roll forces for the aircraft, with a short moment arm, made the delta less manoeuvrable than a conventional aircraft.

Adding a conventional tail relieved many of the problems and produced a layout with inherently good stability and handling. In particular, the delta's ability to maintain stable airflow up to high angles of attack – as a result of vortices shed by its sharply swept leading edge – was retained. This was important for a fighter, because it meant that the ailer-

Right top: A Yugoslav Air Force MiG-21PFM, fresh from its regular overhaul. Soviet support practice relies on frequent major overhauls, conducted at factory-type rates.

Right: The introduction of the Mach 2, radar-equipped MiG-21PF was a major step forward for the non-Soviet Warsaw Pact forces. This example is a member of a single regiment of MiG-21PFs supplied to Romania.

Below right: The second-generation MiG-21s were the first to have radar, a major omission from the original. Note that the HAL aircraft, built later than the Soviet types, has a GP-9 gun pack housing a twin-barrel GSh-23.

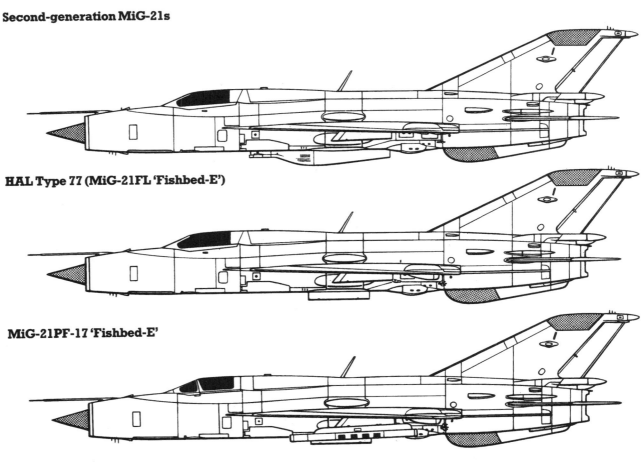

Second-generation MiG-21s

HAL Type 77 (MiG-21FL 'Fishbed-E')

MiG-21PF-17 'Fishbed-E'

MiG-21PFM 'Fishbed-F'

ons remained effective at virtually all times, and the pilot could pull very hard manoeuvres without worrying about losing lateral control.

The only serious limitation of the layout was that its short span, thin section and high sweep militated against high wing loadings. Even with large and effective flaps, the TsAGI-type tailed delta would not be a champion weight-lifter, and growth potential would be limited. (The West's only tailed delta, the A-4 Skyhawk, carries heavy external loads, but has a thicker, slatted wing.) However, future growth beyond the scope of the requirement was not something which the Soviet system considered important.

In early 1954, the MAP directed the MiG bureau to build prototypes of the small supersonic fighter with both swept and delta wings. A near-parallel programme, also started in 1954, called for swept-wing and delta-wing prototypes of very similar configuration, but larger. Clearly, MAP was concerned that the MiG-17 sized aircraft might not meet all the requirements, particularly the evolving needs of the PVO.

The challenge facing the MiG bureau was to fit all the components of an advanced fighter aircraft into the close confines of the TsAGI configuration. This was done with considerable ingenuity, and work on the new prototypes – all designated with the Soviet letter written as E, but pronounced Ye - forged ahead. To a Western eye, the internal layout of the new aircraft would have seemed random and disorganized, and the exterior appearance untidy. However, the nature of the design becomes much clearer when the packaging problem is considered.

The core of the design was a new engine from the Tumansky bureau, the R-11. This was a two-spool design, with a three stage low pressure compressor and a five stage high pressure compressor, giving a pressure ratio of slightly less than 9. Specific fuel consumption using afterburner was in the region of 2.20; in military thrust it was 0.94. With a weight of 2,462lb(1,117kg), it provided a thrust/weight ratio of 5.53, which was quite exceptional for the time. It was achieved partly by straightforward, economical design – the engine was outstandingly simple, with a total of only 3,500 different parts – and partly by deliberately sacrificing durability.

The latter aspect is important. In Soviet terms, reliability is distinct from durability. Reliability directly affects the performance of the weapon in combat, and there is nothing to be done if a critical failure occurs in action. Absolute reliability is the goal. Durability, on the other hand, is something which is only vital to a certain degree. In Western terms, an engine which must be returned to a large maintenance depot,

stripped, disassembled and checked and repaired where necessary every 250 hours is an abomination. In the Soviet Union, a time between overhauls (TBO) of 250-300hr is not uncommon, and the reasoning behind this fact is interesting.

Maintenance logistics
As noted in the previous chapter, the combat units are not expected to worry about fixing their aircraft and engines, beyond the most elementary maintenance (which is made as easy as possible, with plenty of small, quick-opening panels for routine inspections). Instead, they run them for their allotted lifetimes and exchange them for newly overhauled equipment, fresh from the maintenance depot. The conservative TBOs mean that unscheduled removals are rare, and the engines need little inspection in service. The logistics system is geared to handle all the overhaul work and the traffic in repaired components, and generally works smoothly because nearly all the work is scheduled.

In fact, the TBO requirement is set by the needs of the Front commander. He knows that his logistic system will not work smoothly in wartime; essentially, he needs enough time on the weapons he has available to fight the war. Assuming that, at any given time, his fighter engines will have an average of half their

TBO left, the target TBO is twice as many hours as the fighter is expected to fly in the course of the main offensive.

In the case of engines, the short TBOs make it possible to achieve higher thrust/weight ratio and better fuel consumption. Both these figures improve with increasing engine pressure ratio, but this also means higher temperatures in the engine. Much of the advanced and expensive technology in Western engines is devoted to achieving long life with high temperatures; Soviet metallurgy is not quite as advanced as that of the West, but engine performance is closely comparable because long TBOs are not required.

Given the size of the R-11, the fuselage design of the MiG prototypes was built up around the engine and its inlet trunk, which was split vertically just behind the inlet lip and merged just ahead of the engine. Structurally, it was basically similar to the earlier MiGs. The wings were separate – being removable for transport and repair, as MAP requires – and attached by lugs and bolts to high-strength forged steel ring-bulkheads with stainless-steel fittings. These bulkheads were the heart of the aircraft. The inlet ducts, and the main fuel tanks between them, fitted inside the ring. The rear fuselage bolted to the rearmost bulkhead, and the forward fuselage –

Above left: An unusual interim (or possibly, updated) MiG-21PF with the early narrow-chord fin, later braking-chute arrangements and provision for rocket-assisted take-off.

designed around the pilot's seat, the electronics bay and the inlets – was attached to the front. The nosewheel bay served a dual purpose, providing access to the lower electronics bay; a single bonnet-like panel ahead of the windscreen hinged forward to give access to the upper part of the bay.

Internally, the design reflected the need for minimum cross-section, with a number of notable features. In the nose, a single aluminium panel on each side extended from just behind the inlet to the leading-edge wing root, and from the cockpit sill to the lower part of the fuselage; it formed both the side of the fuselage and the outer wall of the inlet duct. Neither of the small, thin-section wings would accommodate the landing gear without the use of small high-pressure tyres, but these would have been operationally unacceptable because of the requirement to operate from quickly prepared strips or cleared tundra. A fuselage-mounted gear, however, would have had too narrow a track. The answer was an ingenious inward-retracting

Right: The number of early-production MiG-21PFs, codenamed 'Fishbed-D', with the same narrow-chord fin as the MiG-21F, was not large. This example was assigned to a display team, possibly formed by the Moscow Air Defence District.

Right: The third-generation MiG-21, represented by this Yugoslav MF, was a major advance. The mix of air-to-air and air-to-surface weaponry shown on this aircraft was theoretically possible, if unusual. The outboard pylons were plumbed for fuel tanks.

Above: A mixed Polish Air Force formation containing three MiG-21PFMs and (furthest from camera) an early MiG-21PF. Operationally, the aircraft were interchangeable.

Above: A well-used early-model MiG-21PF of the Polish Air Force. The prominence of the rivets is due to the use of steel rivets, which are prone to surface corrosion.

gear, in which the wheels were attached to the legs by a complex but sturdy mechanical linkage. As the legs folded into the wing, the wheels remained in a near-vertical position and retracted into the fuselage sides between the main bulkheads.

New design trademark

Because the wheels were a little too large for the space available, the designers added small bulges in the fuselage and gear doors above and below the wheel wells. This proved to be the start of a design trademark. Soviet designers, unlike their Western counterparts, never seem too afraid of adding small bulges in the skin to ease a problem of internal design, to add strength or simplify construction, or to avoid having to enlarge the overall cross-section. They do nothing for the looks of the aircraft, but cause very little extra drag, especially toward the rear, where the airflow over the skin is already broken up.

The design of the stabilizer also deserves special note. The aim was the

slimmest possible rear fuselage, but the aerodynamic configuration called for an all-moving stabilizer at mid-height, in line with the wings. On the MiG-19 the stabilizer was set at the top of the fuselage, and the two halves were deeply rooted in the structure; that would not be possible with the new aircraft, because the jetpipe was in the way. Both stabilizers would have to transmit their loads separately into the side of the fuselage.

The solution was to adopt the same geometry as used for the MiG-19. The trunnions on which the tail pivoted were angled in line with the sweepback at half-chord. In Western designs, the trunnions are usually at 90° to the fuselage; the MiG method carries the loads into the fuselage further forward, so that the main load-bearing structure can be shortened. The tailplanes were linked by bellcranks and rods (one bellcrank accounts for another pimple on each side) to the single actuator and the artificial-feel system, in the leading edge of

the fin. This layout also placed the stabilizer and rudder actuators close to the engine ancillaries, reducing the length of the hydraulic system.

That much was common to the two different versions. The swept wing was based on the MiG-19 structural design, with two spars and ribs at right angles to the leading edge. The delta featured a full-span swept main spar, supported by two unswept booms forming another structural box. Large, area-increasing Fowler flaps were fitted to the trailing edge of the delta wing.

The first in the series to fly was the swept-wing Ye-50, on 9 January 1956, piloted by V.G. Mukhin. It was powered by the Mikulin AM-9Ye turbojet rated at 8,377lb/3,800kg static thrust, supple-

mented by the Dushkin S-155 rocket motor, which was first used on 8 June. On its 18th flight on 14 July, it was destroyed on after landing short of the runway. A third prototype was lost when it caught fire at high altitude in 1957. Pilot N.A. Korovin did not survive.

The mixed-power, swept-wing Ye-50 was discontinued in favour of the tailed delta configuration powered by a single afterburning turbojet, which was pioneered by the Ye-4 and Ye-5. First flown in May and June 1956, respectively, these appeared at the Tushino Aviation Day that year, where Western observers failed to recognize their small size, and assessed them to be dimensionally about the same as the similar planform Sukhoi Su-9, which also appeared there.

Below: Two Soviet MiG-21PFMs, ready to roll on a night intercept training mission. With reheat used for take-off, the operational radius will not be substantial.

Bottom: Another unusual variant: an early-model MiG-21PFMA, fist of the third generation, delivered to Czechoslovakia before the GSh-23 internal gun was available. The anti-ingestion strakes are also absent.

Another misconception of Western intelligence was that the swept-wing Ye-2, NATO reporting name Faceplate, had entered mass production, while the delta-winged Ye-5 Fishbed had been abandoned. In fact the reverse was true!

In fact, it was the Ye-5 that was

Left: In what appears to be a full pressure suit, this Polish MiG-21PFM pilot prepares for a high altitude flight. Dominating the dashboard is the hood which shields the radar screen from bright sunlight.

Left middle: The spartan cockpit of a MiG-21MF. Note the robust ejection handles and the reliable, low-maintenance toggle switches, protected by metal rings from inadvertent operation.

Bottom: A Soviet pilot poses for the camera with his MiG-21MF. The boom-mounted pitch and yaw sensors, absent from the second-generation types and the PFMA, made a comeback on this and later versions.

selected as the basis for the production aircraft, mainly because its thicker wing gave it more internal fuel capacity, at the end of 1956. Neither type had shown any serious aerodynamic vices; the problems that were encountered affected the Ye-2A and Ye-5 equally. The two most serious of these concerned engine/inlet matching and the flight control system.

Problems with the first true supersonic inlet in the Soviet Union were not surprising. The design was classically simple, a derivative of the conventional blunt-lipped circular inlet used on earlier MiGs; that design worked well up to Mach 1.4, but shock-waves formed from the lip generated an increasing amount of drag at higher speeds. The Ye-2A/Ye-50 inlet had a sharp lip, and a pointed central cone. The aerodynamic function of the inlet cone was to form a shock wave – the primary shock – ahead of the inlet aperture, decelerating the air (relative to the aircraft) before it entered the inlet. This type of inlet is simple, and works well under test conditions; the problem with the original Ye-2A/Ye-50 inlet was that it had no variable geometry

Mikoyan MiG-21MF 'Fishbed-J' cutaway

1 Pitot-static boom
2 Pitch vanes
3 Yaw vanes
4 Conical three-position intake centrebody
5 'Spin Scan' search-and-track radar antenna
6 Boundary layer slot
7 Engine air intake
8 Radar ('Spin Scan')
9 Lower boundary layer exit
10 Antennas
11 Nosewheel doors
12 Nosewheel leg and shock absorbers
13 Castoring nosewheel
14 Anti-shimmy damper
15 Avionics bay access
16 Attitude sensor
17 Nosewheel well
18 Spill door
19 Nosewheel retraction pivot
20 Bifurcated intake trunking
21 Avionics bay
22 Electronics equipment
23 Intake trunking
24 Upper boundary layer exit
25 Dynamic pressure probe for q-feel
26 Semi-elliptical armour-glass windscreen
27 Gunsight mounting
28 Fixed quarterlight
29 Radar scope
30 Control column (with tailplane trim switch and two firing buttons)
31 Rudder pedals
32 Underfloor control runs
33 KM-1 two-position zero-level ejection seat
34 Port instrument console

35 Undercarriage handle
36 Seat harness
37 Canopy release/lock
38 Starboard wall switch panel
39 Rear-view mirror fairing
40 Starboard-hinged canopy
41 Ejection seat headrest
42 Avionics bay
43 Control rods
44 Air conditioning plant
45 Suction relief door
46 Intake trunking
47 Wingroot attachment fairing
48 Wing/fuselage spar-lug attachment points (four)
49 Fuselage ring frames
50 Intermediary frames
51 Main fuselage fuel tank
52 RSIU radio bay
53 Auxiliary intake
54 Leading edge integral fuel tank
55 Starboard outer weapons pylon
56 Outboard wing construction
57 Starboard navigation light
58 Leading edge suppressed antenna
59 Wing fence
60 Aileron control jack
61 Starboard aileron
62 Flap actuator fairing
63 Starboard blown flap
64 Multi-spar wing structure
65 Main integral wing fuel tank

66 Undercarriage mounting/pivot point
67 Starboard main wheel leg
68 Auxiliaries compartment
69 Fuselage fuel tanks Nos 2 and 3
70 Mainwheel well external fairing
71 Mainwheel (retracted)
72 Trunking contours
73 Control rods in dorsal spine
74 Compressor face
75 Oil tank
76 Avionics pack
77 Engine accessories
78 Tumansky R-13 turbojet (rated at 14,550lb/6,600kg with full reheat)
79 Fuselage break/transport joint
80 Intake
81 Tail surface control linkage
82 Artificial feel unit
83 Tailplane jack
84 Hydraulic accumulator
85 Tailplane trim motor
86 Tailfin spar attachment plate
87 Rudder jack
88 Rudder control linkage
89 Tailfin structure
90 Leading edge panel
91 Radio cable access
92 Magnetic detector
93 Tailfin mainspar

whatsoever, and could not accommodate the full range of speeds and altitudes of which the aircraft was capable.

Adjustable inlet

The solution was an adjustable three-position centre-body, automatically controlled according to airspeed, which allowed the airflow to be matched to the flight conditions and the needs of the engine. Also, the area of the basic inlet was reduced to avoid compressor stalls, while to aid in starting, relighting and low-speed flight, small auxiliary suck-in doors were added just below the wing leading edge. A final addition was a spill door on each side of the nose, to relieve excessive pressure in the inlet. Meanwhile, a programme of research into more efficient Mach 2 inlet configurations got under way, using modified MiG-19s.

The control problem was essentially one of systems design. In pursuit of light weight and efficiency, the MiG OKB had provided only a single hydraulic system, with manual back-up for the rudder and ailerons and a standby electrical system

for the stabilizer. The first pre-production prototype, the Ye-6, was lost after the engine stalled, and the standby stabilizer control proved inadequate; after that, the system was redesigned around dual hydraulics. The modified aircraft was cleared for production in 1957, as the MiG-21, and deliveries started in the following year.

The first true prototype of the MiG-21 was the Ye-6, which took to the air in 1956. Meanwhile Mikulin had fallen from grace, and his bureau had been taken over by and renamed for Sergei Tumansky. The AM-11 which powered the Ye-5 became the R-37F, which was then developed into the R-11F-300 production article.

The Ye-6/1 demonstrated a level speed of Mach 2.05 at altitude, but on 28 May 1958 a violent compressor stall at about 59,000ft (18,000m), damaged both the

Right: Simple, proven construction methods are used in the MiG-21. Note also how components that do not fit the fuselage shape are accommodated in fairings and conduits.

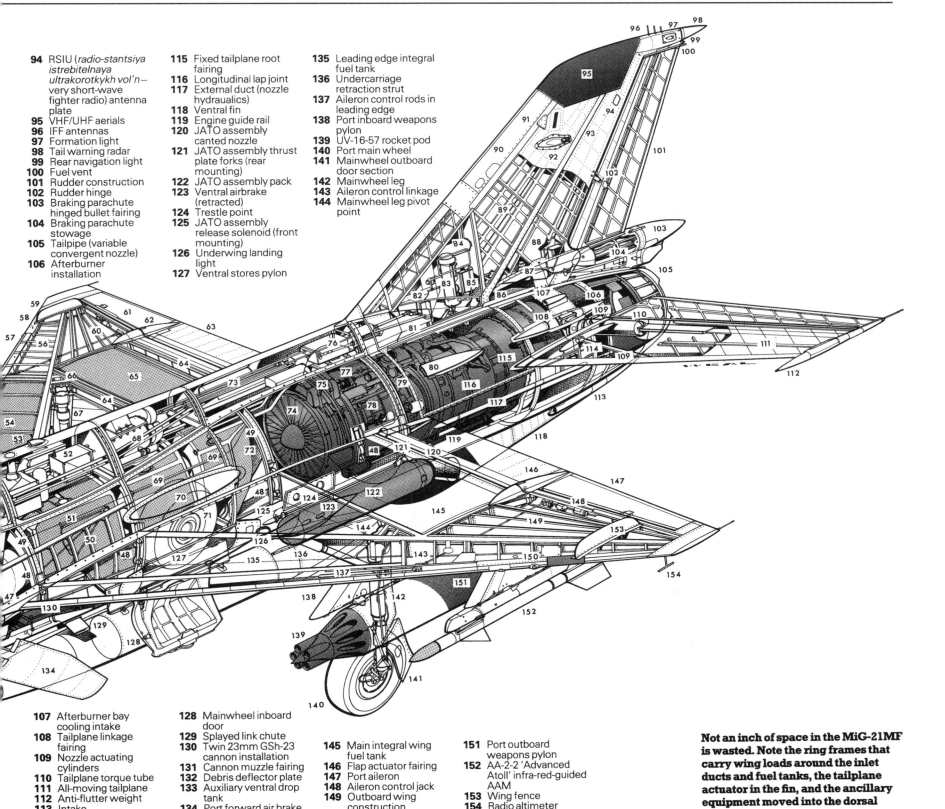

94 RSIU (*radio-stantsiya istrebitelnaya ultrakorotkykh vol'n* — very short-wave fighter radio) antenna plate	115 Fixed tailplane root fairing	135 Leading edge integral fuel tank
95 VHF/UHF aerials	116 Longitudinal lap joint	136 Undercarriage retraction strut
96 IFF antennas	117 External duct (nozzle hydraualics)	137 Aileron control rods in leading edge
97 Formation light	118 Ventral fin	138 Port inboard weapons pylon
98 Tail warning radar	119 Engine guide rail	139 UV-16-57 rocket pod
99 Rear navigation light	120 JATO assembly canted nozzle	140 Port main wheel
100 Fuel vent	121 JATO assembly thrust plate forks (rear mounting)	141 Mainwheel outboard door section
101 Rudder construction	122 JATO assembly pack	142 Mainwheel leg
102 Rudder hinge	123 Ventral airbrake (retracted)	143 Aileron control linkage
103 Braking parachute hinged bullet fairing	124 Trestle point	144 Mainwheel leg pivot point
104 Braking parachute stowage	125 JATO assembly release solenoid (front mounting)	
105 Tailpipe (variable convergent nozzle)	126 Underwing landing light	
106 Afterburner installation	127 Ventral stores pylon	

107 Afterburner bay cooling intake	128 Mainwheel inboard door	
108 Tailplane linkage fairing	129 Splayed link chute	
109 Nozzle actuating cylinders	130 Twin 23mm GSh-23 cannon installation	145 Main integral wing fuel tank
110 Tailplane torque tube	131 Cannon muzzle fairing	146 Flap actuator fairing
111 All-moving tailplane	132 Debris deflector plate	147 Port aileron
112 Anti-flutter weight	133 Auxiliary ventral drop tank	148 Aileron control jack
113 Intake	134 Port forward air brake (extended)	149 Outboard wing construction
114 Afterburner mounting		150 Port navigation light

151 Port outboard weapons pylon	
152 AA-2-2 'Advanced Atoll' infra-red-guided AAM	
153 Wing fence	
154 Radio altimeter antenna	

Not an inch of space in the MiG-21MF is wasted. Note the ring frames that carry wing loads around the inlet ducts and fuel tanks, the tailplane actuator in the fin, and the ancillary equipment moved into the dorsal spine to make room elsewhere.

fan and the duct. Unable to relight the stricken engine, and rapidly losing the hydraulic control systems, test pilot Vladimir Nefyedov attempted a forced landing, using the emergency electrical flight control system. He failed. The aircraft overturned on touchdown and caught fire. Nefyedov, badly burned, died within hours.

Proven inadequate, the emergency electrical system was replaced by a backup hydraulic system on all later machines. The Ye-6/2, which featured wingtip missile rails, was flown by veteran test pilot Kostantin Kokkinaki. The Ye-6/3, which first flew in December 1958, was modified during the following year, and given the designation of Ye-66, which even the MiG OKB later described as "fanciful". It set new world speed records, in one of which Mach 2.35 was briefly attained.

The first production aircraft was the extremely basic MiG-21F, which flew in 1958. Powered by the R-11F-300, it was fast, agile, and simple. Internal fuel was a mere 3,946lb (1,790kg), a fuel fraction of 0.26 at normal takeoff, which gave it an extremely limited radius of action. But, since it was essentially a point defence fighter, this mattered little.

Weaponry consisted of two 30mm NR-30 cannon with 60 rounds apiece, with radar ranging linked to the gunsight. At this point there were no provisions for AAMs; the only other air-to-air weapons were unguided rockets in pods, for the destruction of heavy bombers. Various

air-to-ground stores, rocket pods or bombs, could also be carried. Only 40 MiG-21Fs were built.

Next was the MiG-21F-13, which was the main early production variant. This had provision for two R-3S heat-seeking missiles similar to the AIM-9B Sidewinder, mounted on underwing pylons rather than the wingtip rails previously tried. The R-3S (K-13A/ AA-2 Atoll) was, like the AIM-9B Sidewinder, limited in range, look angle, and manoeuvrability, and had a rear-aspect-only homing capability; the preferred target was the hot engine exhaust plume.

As a weight-saving measure one of the cannon was deleted, and the other held only 30 rounds. Internal fuel was increased by 18 per cent, bringing the fuel fraction up to a respectable 29 per cent. A little way into the production run, the fin was made shorter and broader to improve longitudinal stability. The cockpit environmental control system was better, while an autopilot, beacon receiver, radio compass, and the Sirena 2 radar warning receiver were added. The MiG-21F-13 was built in large numbers in the Soviet Union, license-built in Czechoslovakia and India, and reverse-engineered in China as the J-7.

Regardless of its operational limitations, the MiG-21F-13 was exported world-wide. Stressed for 7g, which was about par for the course at that time, handling was benign even though the controls were heavy, which was actually an advantage in that it made the aircraft

almost impossible to overstress. It offered the then fashionable Mach 2 cachet at an affordable price, even though to approach Mach 2 in a MiG-21 was to risk running out of fuel. What test pilots can achieve is a far cry from the capabilities of the ordinary squadron jock! Rumour control even stated that when low on fuel, the centre of gravity would pass out of limits and render the aircraft uncontrollable. This was effectively refuted when one or two wheels-up landings were made after running out of fuel.

MiG-21P, -PF and -PFM

The MiG-21P was the first variant to be solely armed with AAMs – four R-3Ss, with the remaining cannon deleted. Fitted with a TsD-30T radar, with search, acquisition, tracking and firing modes, it was also equipped for automatic ground control. Load limit was increased to 7.8g; short field performance was boosted by larger wheels and rocket-assisted takeoff; and the dorsal spine was enlarged to carry extra fuel. The series was terminated in favour of the MiG-21PF in June 1960. The MiG-21PF was yet another gunless fighter. Powered by the R-11F2-300 turbojet, rated at 13,492lb (6,120kg) maximum thrust, it had a wider air intake, which in turn gave space for the RP-21 Sapfir radar in the larger translating shock cone. An even larger dorsal spine allowed internal fuel to be increased still more. In all other respects it resembled the MiG-21P, with larger wheels, etc., although the ASP-5ND gyro gunsight was replaced by the PKI-1 collimating sight. The MiG-21PF was in large-scale production between 1962 and 1968.

A downgraded "monkey" variant was supplied to India as the MiG-21FL. This was powered by the R-11F-300 turbojet, with Sapfir radar replaced by the more basic R-2L.

All modifications were accompanied by weight increases. Wing loading gradually crept up, from 61lb/sq.ft (298kg/m2) to 70lb/sq.f t(340kg/m2) in the MiG-21 PFL. To improve low speed handling, air drawn from the high pressure compressor was used for flap blowing on the MiG-21PFL. The engine was again marginally upgraded to accommodate this; the R-11F2S-300 was rated at 13,613lb (6,175kg).

Structural tweaks increased the load limits to 8.5g; the chord of the fin was lengthened to give greater lateral stability; while the new KM-1 ejection seat allowed a revised windshield and canopy to be used. The RP-21M radar provided semi-active radar guidance for R-3R homing missiles, giving an all-aspect attack capability, while a 23mm twin-barrelled GSh-23 cannon in a GP-9 pod could be carried on the centreline. The MiG-21PFS saw the Fishbed transition from a simple day fighter to one with limited adverse weather capability.

Developed in parallel were the MiG-

21R reconnaissance variant, and the very similar MiG-21S interceptor. Rather heavier than the MiG-21PFM, both had reduced performance. The MiG-21S was replaced in production by the MiG-21SM. This had the much more powerful R-13-300 turbojet developed by the Gavrilov bureau, rated at 14,308lb (6,490kg) maximum thrust. The Arab-Israeli Six Day War of 1967 had clearly shown that missile-only fighters were a mistake, and the SM carried an integral 23mm twin-barrelled GSh-23L cannon in addition to two each of R-3R and R-3S missiles. The RP-22 Saphir-21 radar and SPO-10 RWR were combined with the new ASP-PFD gunsight, optimised for manoeuvre combat. But to squeeze everything else in, fuel capacity was reduced.

To detail every Fishbed variant would be prodigal of space; only major versions can be listed. The MiG-21M was a "monkey" variant for export, but surprisingly the MiG-21MF virtually amounted to an update of the -21M to -21SM standard. The main difference was greater accent on air-to-surface capability; structural strengthening allowed maximum takeoff weight to be increased to 20,732lb (9,400kg), with an ordnance load of 2,866lb (1,300kg). Air-to-air armament consisted of two each of R-60R and R-60T missiles. But as the airframe had been developed, so the view from the cockpit had deteriorated. This was partially offset by the introduction of the TS-27AMSh rear-view periscope.

The final Russian variant was the MiG-21bis, production of which took place at Gorki between 1972 and 1975. Externally almost identical to the MiG-21MF, it was powered by a completely new engine, the R-25-300. Compression ratio was almost double that of the R-11, and mass flow was much greater. Maximum thrust was 15,653lb (7,100kg), with military thrust 9,039lb (4,100kg). The two-stage afterburner was fully modulated, and at supersonic

Left: The multi-role MiG-21MF had a less obtrusive radar display than the pure interceptor versions. The prominent master caution panel, above and to the right of the radar scope, is also noteworthy.

Below left: The unguided rocket has been a favourite Soviet weapon since the 1940s, providing great firepower and reasonable accuracy without sophisticated aiming systems. This is a UB-16 pod (16 S-5 57mm rockets).

Below: An unusual feature of this MiG-21MF is that the inboard wing pylons have been removed.

Below right: The spine profile identifies this aircraft as a MiG-21bis, known to NATO as 'Fishbed-L'. This aircraft has a similar gunsight to the MiG-21MF; later versions have a true head-up display.

MiG-21 stores options

1 AA-2-2 'Advanced Atoll' radar-guided air-to-air missile (compatible with 'Jay Bird' radar)
2 UB-16-57 rocket pod
3 57mm rockets
4 500kg general-purpose bomb (a total of 48 types of free-fall bomb, including nuclear, napalm, chemical and fuel-air explosive types, are qualified for use on the MiG-21)
5 108Imp gal (490lit) drop tank; 176Imp gal (800lit) and 286Imp gal (1,300lit) tanks also available
6 GP-9 pack (GSh-23 gun and ammunition)
7 23mm ammunition (normal load 200rds)
8 Reconnaissance pod with forward plus three lateral oblique cameras, IR linescan printer and ECM chaff dispenser
9 AA-8 'Aphid' IR-homing air-to-air missile
10 AA-2 'Atoll' IR-homing air-to-air missile
11 ECM jammer pod

MiG-21 weapons provision and avionics

1 GSh-23 cannon with 200rds ammunition
2 Centreline pylon, capacity 500kg (1,100lb)
3 Inboard wing pylon, capacity 250kg (550lb)
4 Outboard wing pylon
5 'Spin Scan' radar
6 'Odd Rods' IFF antennas
7 Main avionics bay
8 HF notch antenna, ILS
9 Radar altimeter
10 VHF/UHF antenna
11 Radar warning receiver
12 VHF communications and data link antenna

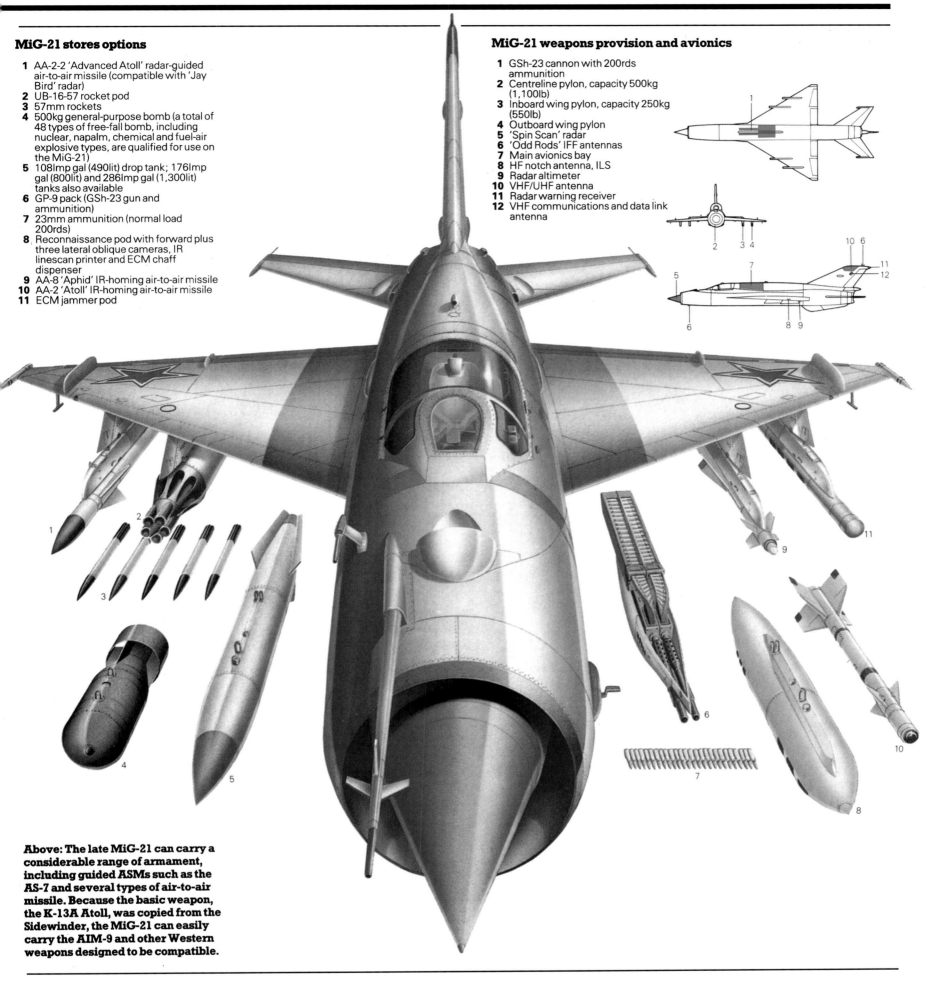

Above: The late MiG-21 can carry a considerable range of armament, including guided ASMs such as the AS-7 and several types of air-to-air missile. Because the basic weapon, the K-13A Atoll, was copied from the Sidewinder, the MiG-21 can easily carry the AIM-9 and other Western weapons designed to be compatible.

speeds had a special feature which increased thrust to 21,825lb (9,900kg) below 13,124ft (4,000m) for a maximum of three minutes.

Trainers

Like most high performance fighters, the MiG-21 has had its share of two-seater conversion and operational trainers. To make space for the second seat, internal

Left: The MiG-21bis line at Nasik. Note that the spine is one of the last elements added to the basic fuselage structure, which is common to all MiG-21s. An in-service MiG-21M is being overhauled on the left.

Below left: The rear fuselage of the MiG-21bis, looking aft from the transport break joint. Auxiliary air ducts are visible. Note the deeper, stronger frames around the final jetpipe, which carry the tailplane loads.

Below: Points of interest on the very powerful R-25 engine – this is a HAL-built example – include the neatly packaged accessories and the engine's simplicity: there is no variable geometry whatsoever.

Mikoyan MiG-21SMT 'Fishbed-K'

The hump-backed MiG-21SMT 'Fishbed-K' was a long-range interceptor, and was the first version to be seen with four missiles. It was not produced in very large numbers, and formed a bridge between the third and fourth generations.

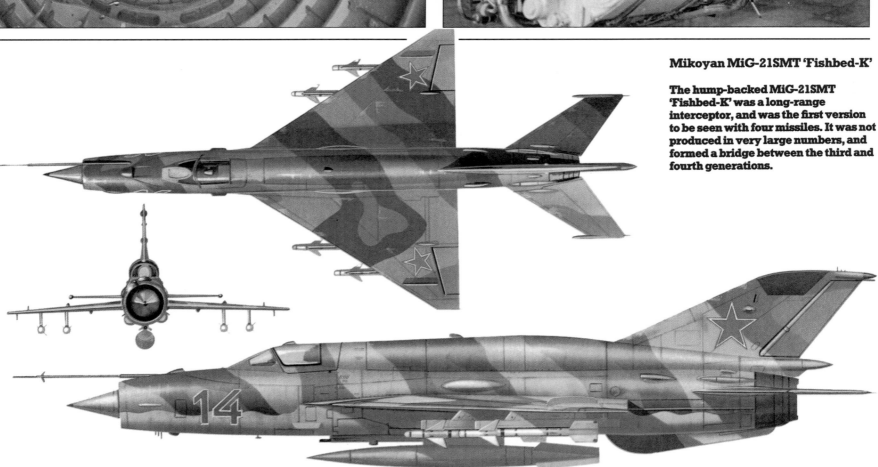

cannon have been omitted and fuel reduced. The first two-seater MiG-21U, based on the MiG-21F-13, was flown by Piotr Ostapyenko on 17 October 1960. It was followed in 1966 by the MiG-21US, which had blown flaps, the R-11F2S-300 turbojet, and the wide chord fin of the MiG-21PFM. Finally, the MiG-21UM varied only from its predecessor in the avionics fit. All were stressed for just 7g.

Chinese Fishbeds

In 1961, the People's Republic of China negotiated a licence to build the MiG-21F-13, but before details could be finalized diplomatic relations between the PRC and the USSR were broken off. The Chinese then set about the massive task of reverse engineering what became the J-7 (J = Jian = fighter).

The first flight of the J-7 (F-7 for export versions) took place on 17 January 1966, piloted by Ge Wenrong, and production commenced at Chengdu in the following year. Since then the J-7 has been continually modified and updated to the point where, although it is still unmistakeably a MiG-21 in origin, it is for all practical purposes a new aircraft. The enlarged dorsal spine which featured on late model Russian Fishbeds was however not adopted.

The current production article is the F-7MG, the most distinguishing feature of which is a cranked leading edge to the delta wing. The trailing edge has a slight forward sweep outboard, and has automatic manoeuvring flaps. Otherwise it retains the pitot inlet and shock cone of earlier models, the cone housing the Marconi Super Skyranger radar.

The most widely exported version is the F-7M Airguard. It is powered by a Liyang WP-13F turbojet rated at 13,448lb (6,100kg), and has a mainly Western avionics fit, initially with the GEC-Marconi Super Skyranger radar, but since replaced in some models by the FIAR Grifo. Typical weapons fit is up to four AAMs – the Chinese PL-2, -5 or-7, or Western Sidewinders or Magics. Two 30mm cannon with 120 rounds are mounted internally.

Airguard was to have been followed by the Super-7, a radically modified variant developed in cooperation with Grumman. A "solid" nose housing the Westinghouse APG-66 multi-mode radar, the General Electric F404 turbofan, fed by fixed geometry cheek intakes, and a wrap-around windshield and single piece canopy made it appear a very different bird. But American participation was cancelled following the Tiananmen Square massacre in 1989, and the Super-7 lapsed.

It was later revived with Russian assistance, specifically MiG-MAPO, and considerably redesigned became the FC-1. First flight was reported to have taken place early in 1997. It retains the radar nose and cheek intakes; the radar has not yet been chosen, but will probably be a Russian type.

The engine is the Klimov RD-93 afterburning turbofan, rated at 17,985lb (8,158kg). The most radical external changes are strakes to the wing leading edges; shelves on each side of the fuselage which carry control runs and also the horizontal tail surfaces; and a differently shaped vertical tail surface. Wingtip missile rails have been added, and the internal gun is a twin- barrelled GSh-23. The FC-1 is expected to enter service in 2003.

Upgrades

Something in the region of 12,000 Fishbeds have been built, and production continues in China. Of this vast total, something like 3,000 are still in service with over 40 nations, more than half of which are front line equipment with a dozen or so states. This makes the MiG-21 and its derivatives a prime target for upgrading, although the age and condition of the airframes remains a significant factor.

During the Great Patriotic War, the life expectancy of a Soviet fighter was a mere 80 flying hours. This was the maximum it could be expected to survive in the combat zone. The same attitude continued into the uneasy peace; the Soviet OKBs designed aircraft for war, with a good-enough standard of finish but a very short, by Western standards, safe fatigue life.

Soviet MiG-21 production ended in about 1975, by which time steady development had increased the fatigue life to about 2,100 flying hours. At a very low

Left: The Super-7 seen here was to have had American engine and avionics. More recently it has been revived with Russian assistance as the FC-1, powered by the RD-93 turbofan.

Below left: The Chengdu F-7MG derived from the MiG-21 remains in production. The wing leading edge is cranked, while the trailing edge has reverse sweep outboard.

Below: The export version of the F-7 is the Airguard, which has mainly Western avionics and the GEC-Marconi Super Skyranger radar. It is compatible with Western AAMs.

Bottom: A "glass cockpit", HOTAS and a new HUD are features of the MiG-21-2000, an upgrade offered by Israel Aircraft Industries which includes the Elta EL/M 2032 radar.

(again by Western standards) utilization rate, this gave a service life of about 20 years. This could however be extended considerably by a degree of structural refurbishing. But where the original design concept was to provide a platform to bring simple weapons to bear effectively, this function was to a degree supplanted by clever avionics and even cleverer weapons. At the same time, the single- role fighter was largely replaced by a multi-role machine.

Apart from on-going development by Mikoyan, and later Chengdu, the first stage in a MiG-21 upgrade programme was carried out by British Aerospace, which from the late 1970s to the early 1980s provided Egyptian MiG-21s with several items of Western avionics. This was however fairly small beer to what was to come.

At the Paris Air Show in 1993, MiG-MAPO revealed the MiG-21-93. This was fitted with the Kopyo multi-mode radar, an IRST sensor, provision for a helmet-mounted sight, and chaff/flare dispensers in the wing roots. The cockpit was modernized, with multi-function displays and HOTAS, and most of the original avionics were replaced. The Thomson-CSF Detexis EWS-21 RWR was an optional extra. Air-to-air armament consisted of four R-77 or R-27R/R-27T medium range AAMs, or four R-73 dogfight missiles. For air-to-surface operations the X-25MP Kegler anti-radiation missile could be carried, as could the X-31A or P anti-ship missile, or two KAB-500KR TV-guided bombs. Replacing the engine with the RD-33 is another option.

MiG-MAPO followed this with the MiG-21-98, aimed at older variants, for which it is to receive a smaller radar to fit in the shock cone. This upgrade will include better avionics than the -93, and a "glass cockpit" based on that of the MiG-29SMT.

Israel has long been noted for reducing MiG-21s to scrap, so it was a reversal of fortune to find Israel Aircraft Industries (IAI) offering the MiG-21- 2000 upgrade. This proposal was different in that it started with a structural life extension programme, which made a lot of sense, coupled with an optional increase in fuel capacity. The radar offered was the Elta EL/M 2032 pulse-Doppler multi-mode type, which has been claimed in some quarters to be superior to the APG-73 of the F/A-18C/D Hornet. Given the restrictions in antenna diameter imposed by the shock cone, this is difficult to believe.

Even with a wrap-around windshield and one-piece canopy, the view from the cockpit is not all that good. It is cramped by any standards; the present writer, of average height and build, tried it for size and felt like a cork in a bottle when the canopy was lowered. On the other hand, HOTAS and two MFDs give the appearance of modernity.

Multi-role is the accent of the MiG-21-2000; it can carry two EW pods and a reconnaissance pod, or three Griffin LGBs. In the air-to-air role, the standard fit is four Python 3 AAMs.

The fourth major upgrade scheme is the Israeli/Romanian Lancer, produced by Elbit and Aerostar, responsible for avionics and airframe/engine, respectively, designed for the MiG-21MF. Aerostar virtually remanufactures the airframes for a zero-life product. The avionics are designed around the EL/M-2032 radar, and the black boxes are specified by the customer.

Fishbed at war

The operational debut of the MiG-21 took place in 1963, when in Egyptian and Syrian service it clashed with Israeli fighters. These early encounters were inconclusive, although Mirage IIICJ pilot

Yoram Agmon managed to damage a Syrian MiG-21 in April 1965. More than a year later, on 14 July 1966, he managed to destroy a Syrian MiG-21 north of Galilee. It was an inauspicious start for the Russian fighter. Other losses followed, and on 16 April of that year an Iraqi Fishbed pilot defected to Israel, allowing them to thoroughly evaluate it. This gave the Israelis a tremendous tactical advantage.

Arab-flown MiG-21s had a poor record against the Israelis, not that their mount was that inferior to the Mirage IIICJ; their training and aggression were not in the same league. The Six Day War of June 1967 saw them take a beating in air combat against determined opponents.

Right: MiG-21PFs were the main subtype used in North Vietnam; had a cannon-equipped version been available earlier, the Vietnamese pilots might have been even more successful in air-to-air combat against their USAF and US Navy adversaries.

Below: A once-unthinkable formation: an F-16 and an A-10 of Tactical Air Command with a MiG-21 and a MiG-15UTI. The Soviet aircraft are in Egyptian service; the occasion was the Bright Star 82 joint exercise.

Above: Despite its poor quality, this photograph, released by the US DOD and State Department in March 1985, shows that Cuba has received the updated MiG-21bis, with its generally improved combat capability.

Left: One modified MiG-21PFM airframe became the 'Fishbed-G', a low-speed, fixed-gear testbed for the jet-lift Stol concept and a predecessor of the 'Faithless' Stol fighter. Note down elevator on the approach.

The War of Attrition followed from the middle of 1969. Still the Egyptian MiG drivers were unable to make inroads, and in April 1970 Soviet "volunteers" arrived to help. A confrontation could not be long delayed, and in July it occurred.

The Israeli set up an ambush with four Mirages as bait. Much lower, beneath the radar cover, lurked four more Mirages and four Phantoms. All the Israeli pilots were hand-picked. Twenty Russian-flown MiG-21s were scrambled to intercept, the Israeli escort zoom-climbed to meet them, and a huge dogfight took place. Five Russians went down, for no Israeli losses. The Egyptians were pleased, since the Russians had proved no better than themselves. Again, the deciding factor was pilot quality. The War of Attrition ended just eight days later.

Meanwhile the war in Southeast Asia had been in full swing for several years. In theory, the North Vietnamese MiG-21s were outclassed by the Phantoms of the USAF and USN. In practice it wasn't like that. The difference was the comprehensive radar coverage and ground control of the North Vietnamese, which allowed them to track targets and position their fighters for a devastating surprise attack. Far from home, the American fighters were largely reliant on their on-board systems.

Guided by ground control, the North Vietnamese MiG-21s approached at low level to a favourable position astern. Once there they zoom-climbed to altitude before making an often lethal supersonic pass from six o'clock. The American kill/loss ratio was often adverse. It must be stated here that the USAF and USN had abandoned close combat training, which left them at a distinct tactical disadvantage.

To reverse the trend, the USAF conceived Operation Bolo, a carefully planned ambush, early in 1967. Led by World War II ace Robin Olds, this partially succeeded; the Phantoms claimed seven MiG-21s for no losses. While this made the North Vietnamese more careful, in the seven months from August 1967 they accounted for 18 USAF aircraft while losing only five in return. Meanwhile, in December 1971, Indian Air Force MiG-21s clashed with Pakistani F-104A Starfighters for the first time. The Russian-built fighter showed itself capable of out-turning and out-accelerating the American-built fighter, shooting down four at low level without loss. This was its finest hour!

A hiatus in the fighting over North

Egyptian Air Force Mig-21PF 'Fishbed-D'

Egyptian Air Force MiG-21PF 'Fishbed-E'

Egyptian Air Force MiG-21RF 'Fishbed-H'

Egyptian Air Force MiG-21MF 'Fishbed-J'

North Vietnamese Air Force MiG-21PFMA 'Fishbed-J'

Vietnam from 1968 ended in early 1972, and the air war continued until January 1973. In this time, 41 MiG-21s fell to Phantoms, the vast majority of them to the AIM-B Sidewinder. The ranking North Vietnamese ace was MiG-21 pilot Nguyen Van Coc, with nine victories scored between 1967 and 1969, including two reconnaissance drones.

In the Middle East, the October War of 1973 was yet another defeat for the MiG-21, as was the Beka'a action in 1982, when opposed by American-built F-15s and F-16s. The final major war in which the MiG-21 took part was the Gulf War of 1991. On 17 January 1991 two F-7s were downed by Hornets, and on 6 February two MiG-21s were downed by F-15Cs. Since then, the only Fishbed losses have been to ground fire.

The combat record of the MiG-21/F-7 makes it look like a turkey. But as always, pilot quality is the deciding factor. Given modern radar and avionics, it might yet prove itself. The final factor is the quality of the opposition.

The Fishbed is in service with Afghanistan, Albania, Algeria, Angola, Azerbaijan, Bangladesh, Bulgaria, Cambodia, China, Congo, Croatia, Cuba, the Czech Republic, Egypt, Ethiopia, Guinea, Guinea-Bissau, Hungary, India, Iran (Republican Guard), Iraq, Laos, Libya, Madagascar,

Left: India has both built and operated a variety of MiG-21s, including these HAL-built MiG-21Ms.

Below: In October 1973, a MiG-21 is destroyed by cannon fire from an Israeli F-4E Phantom. Despite good performance on paper, the Soviet fighter's own gun has not proved as lethal as the M61 carried by later models of the F-4.

Above: Non-Soviet pilots have praised the MiG-21 for its straightforward handling and ruggedness. In this ground-to-air photograph an Indian pilot shows off a specially marked display aircraft.

Bottom: The MiG-21 configuration was adapted for a series of larger aircraft, culminating in the Ye-166 testbed for high-Mach propulsion technology.

Mali, Myanmar, Nigeria, North Korea, Pakistan, Poland, Romania, the Slovakian Republic, Sudan, Sri Lanka, Syria, Tanzania, Vietnam, Yemen, Zambia and Zimbabwe.

Left: Yugoslav Air Force MiG-21PFMAs – the examples shown here are early models without an internal gun – in a tunnel-type underground hangar. More often, MiG-21s are protected by dispersal and their ability to use sod runways.

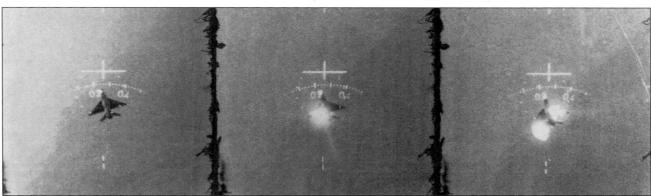

MiG-23/27 'Flogger'

Few fighters of the 1960s have been built in such large numbers as the very fast and predatory-looking MiG family of swing-wing fighters that carry the NATO codename 'Flogger'. With no direct equivalent in the West, the MiG-23 and MiG-27 represent a uniquely Soviet approach to the tactical fighter problem: powerful, quite large and remarkably simple to build in quantity. It was the last of these qualities that shocked the West, making the types far more readily affordable than any Western fighter of comparable capability, and allowing them to be deployed with unprecedented speed.

In the early 1960s, it seemed that almost every air arm in the world was taking delivery of new and advanced equipment. Genuine Mach 2 performance, the province of a very few aircraft in the late 1950s, was beginning to reach the squadrons. In the Frontal Aviation inventory, the MiG-21 was well established in production, the radar-equipped versions were entering service, and the merits and deficiencies of the type were clearly appreciated in the Soviet Union if not in the West.

Western fighters of the 1960s thoroughly outclassed their Soviet counterparts, not only in payload and range but also in operational equipment: more effective air-to-air missiles, carried in larger numbers; air-to-air radars large enough to detect and track targets beyond visual range, and guide missiles on to them; improved navigation equipment permitting routine operations beyond the range of ground control. The pinnacle of fighter design at that time was the US Navy's new F-4 Phantom: compared with the contemporary MiG-21PF, the Phantom carried four times as many missiles and eight times as many bombs, could pick up targets three or four times as far away and, in theory, could shoot them down before coming within range of their weapons.

While the supremacy of numbers is paramount in Soviet military doctrine, the related discipline of 'military-technical art' concerns the technical quality of military equipment. It involves the identification of the most important factors in weapon performance, and the standards which must be met to ensure that an opponent does not enjoy some

overwhelming advantage due to technology. At the same time, military-technical studies single out performance standards which are less important, and can be sacrificed in the interests of easy production.

It was clear in the early 1960s that some of the deficiencies of the existing MiG-21 could become critical by the end of the decade. An aircraft in the class of the F-4 would have some vital advantages: the 'first look', because of its radar, the 'first shot', because of its long-range missiles, and, importantly, the ability to accept or decline an engagement, because of its higher performance. Against the MiG-21, the F-4 would be able to fight when the circumstances were favourable and show discretion at other times. It should be noted that in Vietnam, the MiG-21 showed up well when circumstances were in its favour; on the few occasions when F-4 units mounted an aggressive fighter sweep, the kill-to-loss ratio was heavily in favour of the F-4.

As the new fighter requirement made

Below: The MiG-21DPD was strictly a low-speed test aircraft, with a fixed landing gear. The lightweight, compact lift engines were probably developed by the Kolesov bureau.

its way through the system, this type of comparison helped define the most important qualities of a new type. A basic building block was the ability to detect and engage targets beyond visual range (BVR), calling for a long-range search and tracking radar and reliable radar-guided missiles. Like the F-4, the new fighter would carry shorter-range IR-homing missiles for close combat.

Performance requirements
The new type was to be faster in level flight, climb and acceleration than the MiG-21, while greater range would also be desirable; although no dramatic increase in the internal fuel capacity, as a fraction of clean gross weight, was demanded, it could be assumed that the MiG-21's CG problem would be avoided and general advances in design would provide a further improvement. The MiG-21 was judged correctly to be more manoeuvrable than most of its contemporaries, so no increase in sustained or instantaneous turn rates was required.

Above: A MiG-23M and flight-suited aircrew photographed at a base in the cis-Carpathian Military District. The aircraft carries a centreline fuel tank, with very little ground clearance on this version.

Right: An excellent sequence showing the first swing-wing MiG, the Ye-231 (or Ye-23-1). The original and much cleaner configuration of the prototype is clearly visible.

Below: The MiG-21DPD was part of a complete V/Stol technology programme. Together with the Yak-36, it led to the operational Yak-38, as well as the Ye-230 prototype.

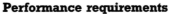

Soviet V/Stol fighter development

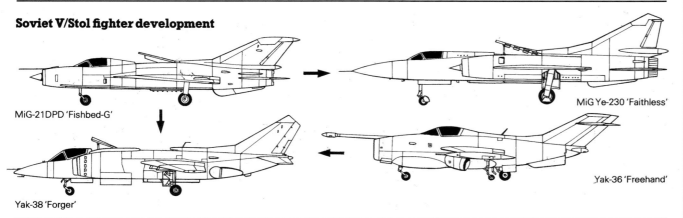

MiG-21DPD 'Fishbed-G'

MiG Ye-230 'Faithless'

Yak-38 'Forger'

Yak-36 'Freehand'

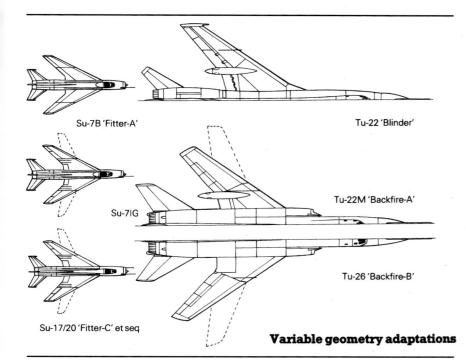

Su-7B 'Fitter-A'

Tu-22 'Blinder'

Su-7IG

Tu-22M 'Backfire-A'

Su-17/20 'Fitter-C' et seq

Tu-26 'Backfire-B'

Variable geometry adaptations

Above: One TsAGI VG configuration was intended for adaptations of existing aircraft, such as the Su-7 and Tu-22. The Su-7IG and Tu-22M test/evaluation types led to the definitive Su-17/20 series and the Tu-26.

Below: The wing of the Ye-231 prototype was cleaner and smaller than that of the subsequent production aircraft; the main part of the vertical fin was the same size, but the dorsal fin was noticeably smaller.

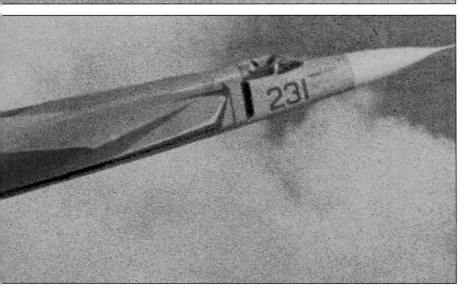

Field performance was also pegged at MiG-21 levels. The final requirement was – as usual – that the size and cost of the aircraft be kept to a minimum. The requirement was probably issued by the TsKB in late 1963 or early 1964.

It must have been clear that the requirement would probably have to be met by a new aircraft. The most advanced Soviet fighters under development were the PVO's new interceptors, the Mikoyan Ye-26 (MiG-25) and the Sukhoi Su-15. The Mach 3, short-range MiG-25 was far too specialized for the FA, and while the Su-15 might have seemed superficially close to the requirement in terms of flight performance, capacity for avionics and weapons and size, it was a specialized PVO weapon. Its radar was optimized for counter-countermeasures performance rather than range, it was heavily dependent on maintenance facilities and it needed too long a runway. The same objections applied to the series of tailed-delta MiG prototypes developed between 1959 and 1962.

The requirement was tougher than it might appear at first sight. The speed and payload targets, coupled with a limitation on field lengths, eliminated the straightforward tailed delta. The classic Western compromise would have been a thin-section, moderately swept wing, as on the F-4, Mirage F.1 and Crusader. The MiG OKB was already developing an aircraft, the Ye-26, with such a wing, but it does not seem to have been considered for very long in the case of the new FA aircraft. The reason for this probably lies in the basic design trades: the speed requirement would have driven the wing loading upward to the point where the field-length target was out of reach.

The solution was to evaluate what were, at the time, two radically new technologies which promised to relieve the aerodynamic problems involved in attaining high speeds without long runways. One was variable sweep, the other was propulsive lift.

The latter, as applied to a basically conventional supersonic fighter, was not

New variable geometry fighters

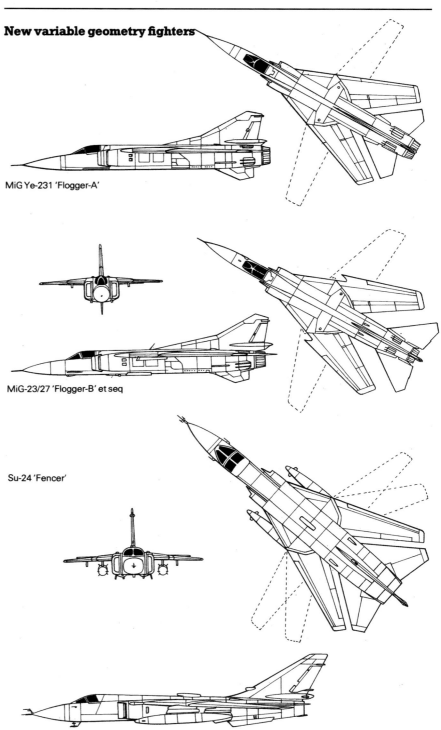

MiG Ye-231 'Flogger-A'

MiG-23/27 'Flogger-B' et seq

Su-24 'Fencer'

Left: This view shows clearly how the prototype's stabilizer, further forward than that of the production aircraft, fits neatly into the overall planform so that the wing and stabilizer tips align when the wing is in the fully swept position with the leading edge at an angle of 72°.

Above: TsAGI developed a neat planform for new VG aircraft such as the Ye-231, which featured a simple wing/fuselage junction and, unlike most Western layouts, had room for a high-capacity stores pylon under the glove. Modified for the production MiG-23, it was retained for the Su-24.

Left: A MiG-23M 'Flogger-B' in the initial production configuration. The heavy glove pylons are associated with the big AA-7 'Apex' missile, and shoes for the older AA-2 'Atoll' are carried on the belly pylons.

quite unique to the Soviet Union, being evaluated almost in parallel by Saab in the early days of the Viggen programme. The fighter would be equipped with two or three small lift jets mounted vertically in the fuselage, slightly forward of the CG and exhausting through variable louvres in the belly. On takeoff and landing, these engines would provide a vertical thrust equal to between a third and a half of the total weight of the aircraft, reducing the need for lift. All things being equal, the aircraft would take off and land more slowly.

There was a further benefit. As the speed of an aircraft is reduced from its maximum, it is given more 'up elevator' to raise the nose, increase the wing's angle of attack and maintain lift for level flight. The elevator (or stabilizer) is generating an increasing amount of downward thrust, and the wings have to provide more lift to compensate for this force. Supersonic combat aircraft tend to have short tails, for reasons of weight and drag. The stabilizer is working with a short lever, and the downforce must be higher; look at any supersonic combat aircraft on take-off or on the approach, and you can see the stabilizer angled sharply nose-down, and thrusting the whole aircraft towards the ground.

In the jet-lift-assisted fighter, the lift-jets would provide a powerful and drag-free force to raise the nose, being ahead of the CG. At low speeds, the stabilizer could actually be used to lift the tail, and yet the aircraft would remain stable. In effect, the lift-jets allowed the area of the stabilizer to be added to that of the wing, rather than subtracted from it. The potential reduction in landing and takeoff speed was very large indeed, and – apart from the extra internal

Right: MiG-23U trainers are attached to each operational regiment. They have a back-up combat mission, but are compromised operationally by having a much less effective radar than the single-seat variants.

Below right: Photographed around 1975, this MiG-23M has a full complement of operational equipment including the IRST (infra-red search and track) set under the nose. The black panel ahead of the IRST forestalls reflection problems.

Below: The basically clean and straightforward lines of the MiG-23 – a direct result of the Soviet emphasis on ease of production – are very apparent on what appears to be a factory-fresh MiG-23M.

volume occupied by the lift engines – the fighter could retain an uncompromised supersonic configuration with a small-area, low-drag wing and no complex high-lift devices.

The other formula considered for the new FA fighter, variable sweep, was more familiar in the West. TsAGI was entirely familiar with the history of variable sweep, although it had never been tested in the Soviet Union. The concept

was little younger than the swept wing itself, having been first studied as soon as the unfavourable low-speed characteristics of the swept wing were detected. It had been tried on two manned aircraft in the USA, with indifferent results, mainly because it was thought necessary to slide the entire wing root fore and aft to keep the wing's aerodynamic centre in the same position.

British research work into Sir Barnes Wallis' Swallow concept pointed the way to eliminating this complication, by moving the pivot points away from the centreline and tapering the moving panels. Finally, in the late 1950s, John Stack's work at NASA's Langley Research Center showed that a fixed-root, outboard-pivot variable-sweep wing was within the state of the art and could be provided with effective aerodynamic controls.

Right: Even with the aid of top and side periscopes, the instructor's view from the MiG-23U rear cockpit is less than panoramic. Most performance monitoring is presumably carried out via instruments.

This work was thoroughly documented and discussed, and formed the starting point for TsAGI's investigations. Another source of inspiration was the General Dynamics F-111, revealed in mid-1964 but doubtless known to the Soviet Union before that time.

VG benefits

Although 'variable sweep' is an accurate description of the mechanical functioning of such a wing, some of its benefits and implications are connected with the fact that the aerodynamic shape of the wing changes in other ways as it swings back. The term coined by NASA – 'variable geometry' or VG – is not mere verbosity, but is more complete and accurate. The wing not only has variable sweep, but also variable span and variable thickness, all being significant.

Varying the sweep angle itself has certain benefits. Some high-lift devices work best on a virtually unswept wing. Highly swept wings, on the other hand, have some advantages: they have low drag at very high speeds, because the wing lies behind the main shock wave from the nose, and are relatively little affected by gusts in high-speed, low-level flight. Wings with more than 60° sweep have very poor low-speed be-

haviour, and such sweep angles are practical only with VG.

VG also means variable span. A long-span wing generates more lift for takeoff, and less induced drag – drag due to lift – in medium-speed cruising flight. At higher speeds, the drag due to the size of the wing, and Mach effects, become more important, and a shorter-span wing is more efficient. To some extent, too, a VG wing has variable area, because part

of the trailing edge retracts into the fuselage or glove as it sweeps back. This increases the wing loading, reduces high-speed drag and improves the aircraft's low-level, high-speed ride.

As the wing sweeps back, its chord – measured parallel with the centreline – increases. Its physical thickness stays the same, so its aerodynamic thickness, defined as the ratio of thickness to chord, is reduced. Thick wings generate more lift at low speeds, thin wings produce less drag at high speeds, and the VG aircraft gets the best of both worlds again.

VG complications

It was these qualities that made VG attractive in the early 1960s, and made it the basis for so many design studies. Its implementation presented some challenges, however. Stability and control were complicated by the gross changes in aerodynamic shape: in particular, the aerodynamic centre (AC) of the aircraft tended to move aft with the sweeping of the wing, and moved further aft at supersonic speed, threatening to cause high trim drag. The rearward AC shift affected pitch stability as well, making the size and the position of the stabilizer more critical than ever. Lateral (roll) and directional (yaw) stability were also

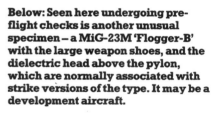

Above: The 'Flogger-E' was first observed in Libyan service, and is generally considered to be an export version, but this aircraft carries Soviet markings. Probably, a substantial number of these cheaper versions serve with Soviet units oustide the Western theatre.

Below: Seen here undergoing pre-flight checks is another unusual specimen – a MiG-23M 'Flogger-B' with the large weapon shoes, and the dielectric head above the pylon, which are normally associated with strike versions of the type. It may be a development aircraft.

affected to some degree. Structurally, the chief problem was the design of small pivot mechanisms that would be completely reliable and yet would carry some of the highest loads in the airframe.

All the problems connected with AC shift could be reduced by moving the pivot points further outboard, and this also reduced the loads on the pivots because more of the flight loads were carried on the fixed part of the wing. But there were costs involved with this approach. Chiefly, the benefits of VG were reduced along with the risks.

TsAGI studies of these problems produced two different VG planforms. One was similar to that of the F-111, with a few variations which, without greatly affecting performance, made it easier to integrate into an aircraft design. The pivots were slightly farther apart, the distance between them being 22 per cent of the total span, rather than 17 per cent, and the maximum sweep angle, measured from the pivots, was slightly smaller.

As a result of these two differences, much less of the TsAGI wing actually retracted into the fuselage when it was swept back, and the fixed root or 'glove' was shorter than that on the F-111. This made the design of the fuselage less difficult, by reducing the size of the cut-out and cavity needed to accommodate the wing, made the glove shape compatible

Above: Ordnance fit on this MiG-23M appears to include dual AA-8 shoes, with provision for another store, under the gloves, an AA-2 shoe under the starboard belly pylon and a bomb rack to port.

with conventional inlets, and increased the span of the glove just enough to provide room for a high-capacity stores pylon. Another difference was a larger gap in plan view between the wings and the stabilizer, but like the F-111, and unlike later VG designs, the wings and stabilizer were at the same level.

The other layout produced by TsAGI

was originally intended for use on modified versions of swept-wing aircraft, and was based on an Su-7 planform, the pivots being set at 30 per cent span. This layout formed the basis for the Su-20/22 and the Tu-22M 'Backfire' bomber, both originally derived from fixed-geometry designs, but worked well enough to be adapted for the completely new Tupolev 'Blackjack' strategic bomber.

It was the more ambitious, F-111-style planform that was evaluated for the new tactical fighter, alongside the propulsive-lift concept. The decision to do so was almost certainly taken during 1964, and represented a significant break with

Western practice. In the West, VG was regarded as a feature of complex, expensive aircraft, and was used only where its perceived cost and complications were needed to meet specific mission requirements. TsAGI and the TsKB, however, intended to implement VG as cheaply as possible, using it to increase the mission efficiency of a basic tactical combat aircraft and thereby contain its size and cost.

The Mikoyan OKB espoused two different concepts to give reduced runway performance – jet lift and variable sweep. The former was never intended to produce vertical takeoff and landing as with the Harrier; it was simply a way of reducing takeoff and landing runs. The resulting aircraft duly emerged as the MiG-23PD (Podyomne Dvigatyeli – jet lift) prototype 23-01, using the tailed delta configuration of the MiG-21. Two Koliesov RD-36-35 lift jets rated at 5,181lb (2,350kg) apiece were mounted in mid-fuselage, set at a slight forward angle and fed via a rearward-hinged louvred door. A movable ventral grid beneath the nozzles allowed the pilot to adjust the thrust angle, giving a degree of reverse thrust on landing.

The main propulsion unit was the Khachaturov R-27-300, fed by semi-circular intakes on each side of the fuselage, with half shock cones as in the

Mikoyan MiG-23MF 'Flogger-B' cutaway

1 Pitot tube
2 Radome
3 'High Lark' J-band radar scanner dish
4 Radar dish tracking mechanism
5 'Swift Rod' ILS antenna
6 Avionics cooling air scoop
7 Radar and avionics equipment bay
8 Ventral doppler antenna
9 Yaw vane
10 Dynamaic pressure probe (q-feel)
11 SRO-22 'Odd-Rods' IFF antenna
12 Armoured windscreen panel
13 Head-up display
14 Instrument panel shroud
15 Radar head-down display
16 Instrument panel
17 Rudder pedals
18 Angle of attack transmitter
19 IR sensor housing
20 Nosewheel steering unit
21 Torque scissor links
22 Pivoted axle beam
23 Twin aft-retracting nosewheels
24 Nosewheel spray/debris guard
25 Shock absorber strut
26 Nosehweel doors
27 Hydraulic retraction jack
28 Control column
29 Ejection seat firing handles
30 Wing sweep control lever
31 Engine throttle control lever
32 Pilot's ejection seat
33 Electrically-heated rearview mirror
34 Ejection seat headrest
35 Upward hingeing cockpit canopy cover
36 Canopy jack
37 Starboard air intake
38 Canopy hinge point
39 Screw-jack-actuated adjustable boundary layer splitter plate
40 Boundary layer bleed air holes
41 Port engine air intake
42 Intake internal flow fences
43 Retractable landing/ taxying lamp (port and starboard)
44 Temperature probe
45 Variable-area intake ramp doors
46 Boundary layer bleed air ejector
47 Avionics equipment bay
48 ADF sense antenna
49 Boundary layer air duct
50 Forward fuselage fuel tank
51 Ventral cannon ammunition magazines
52 Ground power connections
53 Intake suction relief doors
54 Weapons system electronic control units
55 SO-69 Sirena 3 radar warning antennas

56 Fuselage flank fuel tanks
57 Wing glove fairing
58 Starboard Sirena 3 radar warning antennas
59 Jettisonable fuel tank (176Imp gal/800lit capacity)
60 Nose section of MiG-23U Flogger-C tandem-seat trainer
61 Student pilot's cockpit
62 Folding blind flying hood
63 Rear seat periscope (extended)
64 Instructor's cockpit
65 MiG-23BN Flogger-F dedicated ground attack variant
66 Radar ranging antenna
67 Laser ranger nose fairing
68 Raised cockpit canopy
69 Armoured fuselage side panels
70 Wing leading edge flap (lowered)
71 Starboard navigation light
72 Wing fully forward (16° sweep) position
73 Port wing integral fuel tank (total internal fuel capacity 1,265Imp gal/5,750lit)
74 Full span plain flap (lowered)
75 Starboard wing intermediate (45° sweep) position
76 Starboard wing full (72° sweep) position
77 Two-segment spoilers/lift dumpers
78 Non-swivelling jettisonable wing pylon (wing restricted to forward swept position)
79 Wing glove sealing plate
80 Wing pivot bearing
81 Wing pivot box carry-through unit (welded construction)
82 VHF antenna
83 Wing sweep control screw jacks
84 Fin root fillet
85 Rear fuselage fuel tank
86 Tumansky R-29B afterburning turbojet
87 Afterburner duct cooling air scoop
88 Cut-back fin root fillet (Flogger-G)
89 Tailplane control and hydraulic equipment bay
90 Starboard all-moving tailplane
91 Tailfin
92 Short wave ground control communications antenna
93 UHF antenna
94 ILS antenna
95 Sirena 3 tail warning radar
96 ECM antennas
97 Tail navigation light
98 Static discharger
99 Rudder
100 Rudder hydraulic actuators
101 Brake parachute housing
102 Split conic fairing parachute door

103 Variable area afterburner nozzle
104 Fixed tailplane tab
105 Static discharger
106 Port all-moving tailplane
107 Afterburner nozzle control jacks (6)
108 Tailplane pivot bearing
109 Tailplane hydraulic jack
110 Airbrakes (4), upper and lower surfaces
111 Airbrake hydraulic jack
112 Afterburner duct
113 Ventral fin, folded (undercarriage down) position
114 Ventral fin control jack
115 Lower UHF antenna
116 Ventral fin down position
117 Engine accessory equipment bay
118 Wing root seal
119 Port spoilers/lift dumpers
120 Flap guide rails
121 Port plain flap
122 Fixed spoiler strips
123 Static discharger
124 Port navigation light
125 Leading edge flap (lowered)
126 Port wing integral fuel tank
127 Wing pylon mounting rib
128 Extended-chord sawtooth leading edge
129 Port mainwheel
130 Mainwheel door/debris guard
131 Shock absorber strut
132 Hinged axle beam
133 Articulated mainwheel leg strut
134 Hydraulic retraction jack
135 Fuselage stores pylon
136 Twin missile launcher
137 AA-8 'Aphid' short range air-to-air missile
138 GSh-23L twin-barrel 23mm ventral cannon pack
139 Gun gas venting air scoop
140 AA-2 'Atoll' air-to-air missile
141 Fuselage centreline pylon
142 Ventral fuel tank (176Imp gal/800lit capacity)
143 Wing glove pylon
144 Missile launch rail
145 AA-7 'Apex' long range air-to-air missile

Mirage III. Flap blowing as used on most later MiG-21 variants was incorporated, bleeding air from downstream of the final compressor stage. First flown on 3 April 1967 by Piotr Ostapyenko, it was shown in public at Domodedovo in July of that year.

The variable-sweep article, the MiG-23/11, was slightly later in timing. First flight, by Mikoyan chief test pilot Alexsandr Fedotov, took place on 10 June 1967. It used the same engine, with the slight difference that the nozzle area was adjustable, but the cheek intakes were nearer rectangular in shape, with variable ramps instead of half shock-cones, fronted by splitter plates. Throttle control was linear, certainly a first for Mikoyan, and unlike most Western types, when to engage afterburner the throttles had to be rocked outboard through detents.

Power for the wing sweep was provided by a hydraulic worm wheel and screw arrangement, controlled by a lever on the front port console, unlike the trombone slide arrangement of the F-111. Three sweep angles were provided – 16deg, 45deg, and 72 deg – for take-off/landing and economic cruise, manoeuvre, and high speed and low level respectively. Four-section leading and single-slotted trailing edge flaps were linked to give maximum lift at min-

imum sweep. To avoid wing twisting at high speeds, two-section spoilers were used instead of ailerons. A roll commanded in one direction caused the spoiler on that side to be deflected, while the opposite taileron was also moved. At maximum sweep the spoilers were automatically locked, and roll con-

Above: India is a major operator of the 'Flogger' family, with three variants in service: the MiG-23BN strike fighter, MiG-23M fighter and the MiG-27M, the last-named being built at Nasik by HAL and bridging the gap between the MiG-21 and MiG-29.

trol was provided entirely by the differentially moving tailerons.

The steeply raked fin was supplemented by a ventral strake for extra stability at high Mach numbers and high altitudes. Too large to permit adequate ground clearance, this was hinged to fold to starboard when the wheels were lowered. A twin-wheel nose gear retracted aft, while single wheel main gears retracted into the fuselage.

Fedotov was immediately enthusiastic about the prototype, testing the full range of wing sweep angles on only the second flight, and reaching Mach 1.2 on the third. On 9 July 1967 he demonstrated it at Domodedovo, when it was assigned the NATO reporting name of Flogger. But once again, Western intelligence fouled up, and the designation was thought to be the MiG-25. As we shall see in the next section, this caused all sorts of problems.

The wing design however proved inadequate in certain areas. This led first

Below: Rugged simplicity of construction is a hallmark of the MiG-23 design. Note in particular the robust forgings which form the heart of the design. Also, large access panels are almost absent; these are not required by Soviet maintenance philosophy.

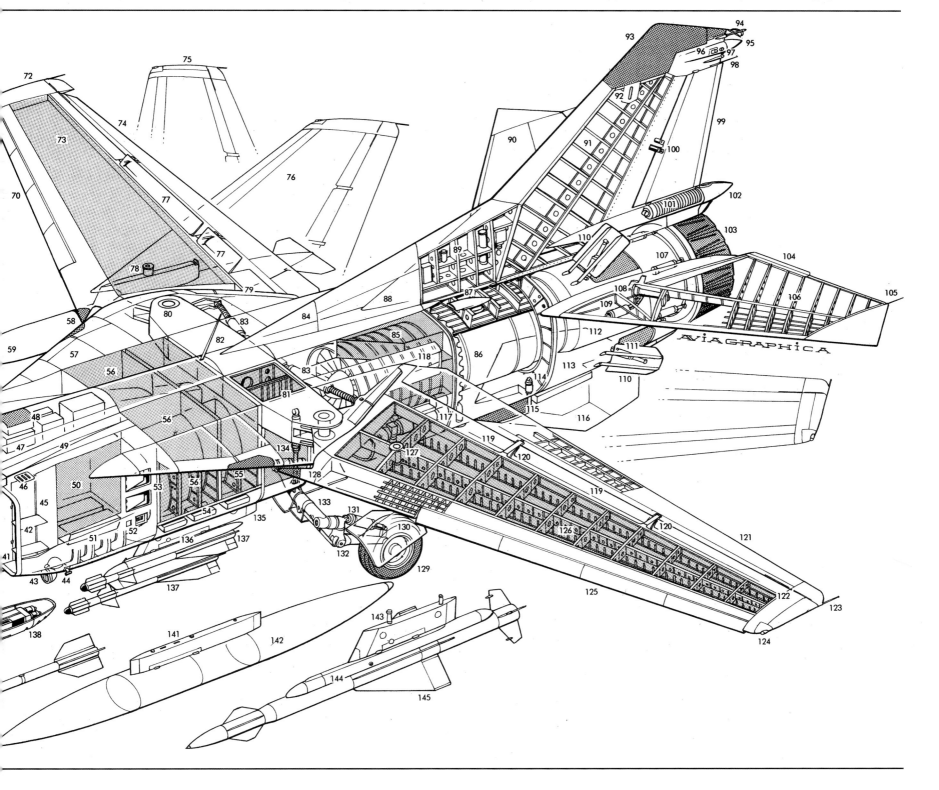

to the type 2 wing, then to the type 3 wing. The chord of the type 2 wing was increased on the fixed leading edge, giving significantly greater area, and produced a dogtooth at the junction with the wing glove. At the same time it increased the sweep angles by 2deg 40min. Minimum sweep thus became 18deg 40min intermediate sweep became 48deg 40min; and maximum sweep became 74deg 40min. For the sake of simplicity, neither the manuals nor the sweep angle indicator on the dash were changed, even though the figures were now incorrect. The type 3 wing, which appeared on production aircraft from 1973, differed only from the type 2 wing in having leading edge flaps, as per the original.

MiG-23S

The first production Flogger was the MiG-23S, first flown by Fedotov on 28 May 1969. The uprated R-27F2M-300 turbojet, rated at 15,212lb (6,900kg) military and 22,046lb (10,000kg) maximum thrust, was used by the MiG-23S and by the MiG-23UB two-seater combat trainer. However, it lacked the thrust to achieve the initial design goals, and was therefore no more than an interim type. Another shortfall was the proposed Sapfir-23 radar, which was not ready in time. In default, the Sapfir-21 was installed, but this limited its weaponry to four R-3R or R-3S AAMs. This was of course in addition to the twin-barrelled GSh-23L cannon. Only 50 MiG-23Ss were built, between mid-1969 and the end of 1970.

The R-27F2M-300 was a simple twin-spool turbojet with a mass flow of 209lb (95kg) per second; specific fuel consumption of 1.9lb/lb (kg/kg) maximum, reducing to 0.95lb/lb (kg/kg) military; with a five stage LP and a six stage HP

Top: Czech Air Force MiG-23BNs are similar to those supplied to India. Clearly visible on the nearer aircraft is the armour plate – almost certainly titanium – applied to the sides of the cockpit.

Above: Apparent in this view of an Indian Air Force MiG-23BN is the improved downward view provided by the attack fighter's shorter, wedge-shaped nose. The head-up display combiner is also visible.

Left: Medium sweep probably gives the best compromise between speed and agility. This sequence shows that the overwing spoilers are used to aid roll control up to fairly high speeds.

compressor. This compared well to the final American turbojet in widespread use, the General Electric J79, although it must be stated that the J79 was a much earlier design, with 17 compressor stages. The R-27F2M-300 was thus shorter, about the same weight, and delivered about 23 per cent more thrust. In accordance with Soviet practice, it had a much shorter time between overhauls, and all in all, was a much simpler piece of machinery. However it lacked the necessary thrust to meet the design goals in full, and was therefore only an interim type.

MiG-23UB

The decision to build a two-seater trainer variant of the Flogger was taken very quickly, in contrast to usual Soviet practice. A further departure was to give it a limited combat capability. To accommodate the second cockpit, internal fuel was reduced by some 397lb (180kg), which was partially compensated by an extra tank in the rear fuselage. The normal view "out of the window" of the Flogger was poor; it has been compared to that of a tank driver, although a slight exaggeration has crept in there. The instructor in the rear cockpit was given a periscope to improve forward visibility. First flown in May 1969 by Mikhail Komarov, production began in 1970. The MiG-23UB was produced in Irkutsk until 1978.

Structural features

Structurally, the new type followed MiG-21 practice, with a mix of conventional light alloy and high-strength steel. MAP's production organization continued to display a fondness for massive forging presses, and these were used to make the key bulkheads, the wing carry-through structure and the spars.

The inlets were of the vertical-ramp type, but were based on the design developed by the central propulsion bureau, TsIAM, for the new Sukhoi Su-15. A primary splitter wedge performed the dual function of clearing off the turbulent air close to the fuselage and forming the primary shock wave ahead of the inlet aperture. Hinged to the rear of this plate was a movable ramp, back-to-back with another ramp inside the inlet. The two ramps moved outward to narrow the inlet at high speed, while boundary-layer flow adhering to the inlet ramp was drawn through tiny perforations in the ramp and vented overboard. Simple in function, these inlets had been shown to work well at speeds up to Mach 2.4 At low speeds, two suck-in auxiliary doors in each inlet wall provided additional airflow.

The main landing gear was unique. Each levered-suspension unit was attached to a massive beam, pivoted close to the aircraft centreline and shaped to fit in the space between the inlet duct and the fuselage side. As the gear retracted, the beam swung upward into the fuselage side, and the wheel folded downward to lie behind and parallel to the beam. While heavy and complex in itself, the gear design took up very little volume in the fuselage and incredibly little of the valuable area on the surface, while clearing both wing and centreline stores and providing a wide track for ground stability. Its only drawback was that it was rather short, giving the aircraft a tail-down, waddling gait and failing to provide more than minimal ground clearance for under-fuselage stores.

Left: There was little that could be done to rectify the MiG-23's lack of all-round vision, but side mirrors and a roof periscope on the canopy frame are a partial solution.

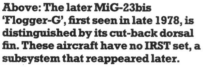

Above: The later MiG-23bis 'Flogger-G', first seen in late 1978, is distinguished by its cut-back dorsal fin. These aircraft have no IRST set, a subsystem that reappeared later.

Below: The MiG-23 cockpit is basically simple and features a large number of single-message caution and warning captions. Critical radar and weapon data is displayed on the HUD.

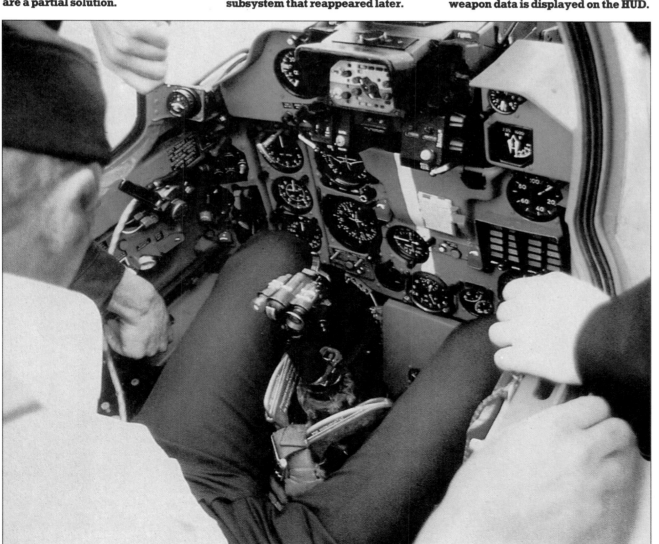

Above: Landing after its demonstration in Sweden, a MiG-23bis deploys its brake chute. The more level ground attitude of the later version, with its revised landing gear, is notable.

Below: An Indian Air Force MiG-23BN rolls out after landing. The brake parachute is used routinely, but it is interesting to note that neither spoilers nor airbrakes are deployed.

Above: Indian Air Force MiG-23BN climbs out with full afterburner. The variable inlets and fully variable nozzle of this version are of little use in its normal operating regime – high subsonic speed at low level.

Below: Wings fully aft and throttle fully forward, a MiG-23bis pulls up during a display in Sweden. The stable pattern of precipitation along the leading edge shows that the notch is doing its job and preventing tip stall.

Left: Illustrating the Soviet Union's confidence in its allies is this export-model 'Flogger-E' of the Libyan AF, with the radar/missile system of the MiG-21MF. One Libyan MiG-23 pilot crashed in Italy, probably while trying to defect.

MiG-23M/MiG-23MF/MiG-23MS

The first major production variant was the MiG-23M, initially with the type 2 wing, and later retrofitted with the type 3 wing. It was powered by the definitive engine – the Khachaturov R-29-300, rated at 28,660lb (13,000kg) maximum, and 18,298lb (8,300kg) military thrust. More complex than its predecessor, but still basic by Western standards, it was just under 4.5in (110mm) longer and just under 6in (148mm) narrower, but weighed some 838lb (380kg) more. This was the powerplant which first gave Flogger its most acclaimed tactical advantage – its "jackrabbit" acceleration.

Flogger was not the best-turning aircraft around; in fact its turning ability has been compared to that of a tram. USAF F-5Es of the Aggressor Squadrons were able to match its agility with ease during dissimilar air combat training, but when it came to acceleration they were not in the same league.

At this point, perhaps we ought to consider fighter tactics. Since 1916 there had been two schools of thought – performance versus agility. Superior performance allowed the pilot to force combat on an inferior opponent; it also allowed him to decline combat and depart when circumstances were unfavourable. Superior agility gave the advantage once close combat was joined. More than 50 years later the same argument still applied.

Previous Soviet air superiority fighters, as opposed to interceptors such as the Su-15, had traditionally been more agile than their opponents. The classic example had been the MiG-21 versus the Phantom in Vietnam, in which the lightweight "sports car" had been generally able to outmanoeuvre the heavyweight American weapons systems.

By playing to their strengths – performance, acceleration and thrust – the Americans had generally managed to get the better of their more agile opponents. The MiG-23 represented a sea-change in Soviet thinking in that it sacrificed agility for performance. The truism that the dominant factor in air combat was surprise had become widely accepted on both sides of the East/West divide, and performance gave the best chance of achieving surprise. The doctrine became one of high-speed slashing attacks: blow through, then reposition for a second run. As the Americans put it; speed is life! The MiG-23 was the first Soviet tactical fighter to subscribe to this doctrine, equipped as it was with beyond visual range (BVR) missiles and tremendous acceleration. It was also much larger and heavier than its predecessor, the MiG-21.

By now the Saphir-23-Sh radar was available, and this allowed the BVR R-23R missile to be carried. Two was the normal load, plus two R-23T or R-13M heat-homers – two on hardpoints beneath the wing gloves, the other two beneath the fuselage. These were backed by a TP-23 IR sensor and the ASP-23D fire control system. A variety of air-to-surface weaponry was also cleared for use.

Internal fuel capacity was increased using a fourth tank in the rear fuselage, while three drop tanks with a total capacity of 1,359lb (616kg) could also be carried. The MiG-23M first flew in June 1972, and spawned two export versions. These were the MiG-23MF, which had "monkey" avionics, and was armed with R-3 AAMs, and the MiG-23MS, powered by the R-27F2M-300 turbojet.

MiG-23ML

First flown in 1976, the MiG-23ML was a completely upgraded Flogger variant. Normal takeoff weight was reduced by omitting the fourth fuselage tank, while dry power was increased with the Khachaturov R-35-300 turbojet. This was derived from the R-29-300, but with pressure ratio increased to 13.1:1. Maximum thrust remained the same, but military thrust was rated at 18,850lb (8,550kg).

The MiG-23ML differed from the MiG-23M in having three-section trailing edge flaps, an upgraded flight control system, the Saphir-23ML radar and TP-23M IR sensor, and the ASP-17ML sighting system. Two more underfuselage hard points were incorporated, while the dorsal fin was shortened. In 1978, MiG-23MLs visited Rheims in France, without their IR sensors, and without switching on their radars. This caused a minor sensation in the West, when every NATO pilot was clamouring for an air test as the Floggers crossed West Germany, in an attempt to get a close look at the potential opposition. Production of the MiG-23ML continued until 1981.

MiG-23P/MiG-23MLD

The MiG-23P was a specialized interceptor variant modified for the mission with automatic guidance from ground stations tied to the autopilot by data link, a similar system to that used by the Su-15/21 and the MiG-25. A three-dimensional flight path, which included speed and firing parameters, was included in the system.

The MiG-23MLD was essentially a MiG-23ML retrofitted with a gadget which automatically actuated the leading edge flaps according to a combination of speed, altitude, and attitude. It also included RWRs and chaff launchers. Some aircraft were fitted with a missile combat simulator for training purposes.

MiG-23B, MiG-23BK, MiG-23BM, MiG-23BN

Even as Flogger entered service as an air superiority fighter, the Soviet Frontal Aviation had a requirement for a light attack fighter. Big though the Flogger might be, it was not in the same league as the Su-7 and its derivatives, and thus qualified. The other main requirement was economical mass production. In essence it was to be an equivalent of the Anglo-French Jaguar, a subsonic fighter-bomber with a limited self-defence capability. But the subsonic restriction was quickly abandoned to allow the aircraft to exit from hostile airspace quickly. Supersonic capability also permitted a greater degree of self-defence against fighters using heat missiles.

First flown by Piotr Ostapyenko on 20 August 1970, the MiG-23B was vastly different to previous variants. It was powered by the Saturn Ly'ulka AL-21F-300 turbojet, rated at 25,353lb (11,500kg) maximum and 17,637lb (8,000kg) military thrust. This single-shaft engine was selected as a cheaper and simpler alternative to the Khachaturov turbojet. The Saphir radar was replaced by the PrNK Sokol-232 nav/attack system, and the nose silhouette was modified to the Outkonos (duckbill) shape. Armour plating was used to protect the cockpit against ground fire; inert gas was forced into the fuel tanks as they emptied to protect gainst explosions; and a comprehensive suite of ECM devices was fitted. Only 24 were built, but these were continuously upgraded.

The MiG-23BN was powered by the R-29B-300 turbojet similarly rated to the AL-21F-300, but apart from this and the Sokol-23N nav/attack system they were identical. The BK and BM differed only in their avionics fit. Maximum speed at alti-

MiG-23 stores options

1 Tactical air-to-surface missiles
2 AA-8 'Aphid' (R60) air-to-air missiles
3 GP-9 pack (23mm GSh-23 and ammunition)
4 176 Imp gal (800 lit) centreline fuel tank
5 AA-2 'Atoll' IR-homing air-to-air missile

High speed and a heavy armament are the MiG-23's strong points. While AAMs are the primary armament, anti-radiation missiles and other air-to-surface weapons not requiring specific guidance systems can also be carried.

MiG-23 combat avionics

1 'High Lark' radar
2 Main avionics compartments
3 Sirena 3 radar warning receiver
4 VHF antenna
5 HF notch
6 VHF/UHF antenna
7 'Swift Rod' ILS antenna
8 VHF omnidirectional range antenna
9 Not known
10 Laser ranger and marked target seeker

MiG-23 stores provision

1 GSh-23 with 200rds ammunition
2 Centreline pylon for 176 Imp gal (800lit) fuel tank
3 Fuselage pylon, capacity 1,650/2,200lb (750/1,000kg)
4 Wing glove pylon, capacity 2,200lb (1,000kg)

tude in clean configuration was Mach 1.7; at sea level this reduced to Mach 0.91. Radius of action at low level with four 551lb (250kg) bombs and a full bag of external tanks was 324nm (600km).

However, the MiG-23B series was a disappointment in the attack role, its main weaknesses being the engine and the nav/attack system. Its main importance was that it formed the springboard to the purpose-designed MiG-27.

MiG-23M operational equipment

The new MiG-23M was a fully operational aircraft, with a full range of equipment. The nose was occupied by the Saphir-23-Sh radar, manufactured by Kunyavskiy, which was given the NATO reporting name of 'High Lark'. A pulse-Doppler radar working in X-band, it had limited look-down capability and a tracking range of 30nm (55km). Emissions from the original 'High Lark', recorded by Western electronic intelligence assets, were considered to be suspiciously similar to those of the Westinghouse AWG-10 fitted to the F-4J Phantom; some F-4Js had been lost over Vietnam in 1967-68, and it has been suggested that the original 'High Lark' owes a great deal to the recovered AWG-10 specimens. In any event, the 'High Lark' was a respectable performer for its time, with some ability to detect low-flying targets against ground clutter. (This 'look-down' capability must be distinguished from 'look-down, shoot-down'; 'High Lark' cannot guide a missile on to a low-flying target.)

In consideration of the changes in the fighter mission, and the possibility that the new fighter might operate beyond the range of ground control, the MiG-23 became the first Soviet fighter to feature a long-range navigation system, in the form of Doppler. Beneath the nose of the MiG-23M was a prominent housing with an optically flat glass front. This housed the TP-23 infra-red search and track sensor, an area in which the Soviet Union was starting to establish a commanding lead over the West.

Other antennas, built into the nose, the tailfin tip, the gloves and the tips of the

Above: One of a batch of photos taken at Tripoli in 1975, which revealed the existence of the 'export' MiG-23.

Right: Points of interest in this nose-to-nose confrontation between MiG-23BN and Jaguar at an Indian Air Force base include the similarity of the forward fuselage design, the much larger inlets (and greater power) of the MiG, and the Soviet type's short, stout landing gear.

claws, betrayed the presence of defensive and communication systems. The large dielectric panel at the tip of the fin housed the datalink antenna; a rear-facing bullet on the fin, and forward-facing antennas on the wings, probably housed the Sirena radar-warning receiver (RWR) system. The three differently shaped vertical aerials of the 'Odd Rods' IFF system spouted ahead of the windshield, and bow-and-arrow antennas, reported to be part of the 'Swift Rod' instrument landing system, were carried on the nose and fin. In the lower fuselage was an array of 20 small holes; their purpose is not known for certain, but they may well have been dispensers for flares and chaff cartridges, used as last-ditch missile decoys.

From the outset, the MiG-23 was designed to carry an internal GSh-23 cannon. (Interestingly, the Ye-230 had appeared at Domodedovo in 1967 with an accurate mock-up of the gun pack, before the weapon itself was known in the West.) The installation was similar to that of the MiG-21PFMA and subsequent variants, as discussed in the previous chapter.

The primary armament of the new fighter was to comprise the new R-23 and R-60 air-to-air missiles, designed for medium range and visual range combat, respectively. Given the NATO reporting name of AA-7 Apex, the R-23R, using

Right: Egypt took delivery of a number of MiG-23 export models – fighters and MiG-23BNs – before its rift with the Soviet Union. Some of the aircraft seen here may still be in service, at a well concealed airfield on Nellis AFB, Nevada.

SARH guidance, was the first Soviet venture into BVR combat. Some 22 per cent longer than the American Sparrow, it was however of slightly smaller diameter but marginally heavier, and with a slightly lighter warhead. Its range, at just under 15nm (27km) was however far less. As missile specialist Doug Richardson commented, Soviet missile propulsion technology of the era was "stone age!"

While the figures are far from impressive, it must be remembered that for the USSR the R-23R was a first generation SARH missile. The Americans, far more advanced in this field, achieved a probability of kill (Pk) of only about 8 per cent over Vietnam with Sparrow. Hardly any of these were true BVR kills; most launches took place from within visual distance, and the unreliability of the system caused many pilots to ripple-fire Sparrows in pairs, in the hope that at least one would work as advertised.

This was a far cry from the results achieved in trials, but the hurly-burly of combat is a far cry from the sterile white-glove conditions of the test range, where failures were often declared a "no-test!" In the world of war, there is no such thing as a "no-test". But somehow the Soviet missile designers had to stay in the race, and to do this, they had to start somewhere. For them, the starting point was the R-23R.

Like the early Sparrows, Apex had the rather long minimum range of almost one nautical mile (1.8km). Prior to this the missile had not armed itself; nor could its guidance system start to work. It was however rather better than nothing.

In common with Soviet interceptor-borne missiles, the R-23 was carried in two versions, one with infra-red homing and one with semi-active radar homing. The missiles could be released separately or in sequence, complicating the opponent's countermeasures problem and increasing the chances of a hit. One advantage of the TsAGI VG configuration was that it provided space below the gloves for the substantial pylon which this weapon required.

The other missile developed for the MiG-23 was the Molniya R-60, NATO reporting name AA-8 Aphid. A tiny dog-fight weapon, it is barely three-quarters the length of a Sidewinder, 7mm less in diameter, and weighs less than half as much. Its 7.7lb (3.5kg) warhead makes it little more than a guided cannon shell. When one considers that the Sidewinder warhead, which is nearly three times as heavy, has often been found to lack lethality, one wonders what the Soviet Union hoped to achieve with such a small weapon, apart from sheer manoeuvrability.

Homing is by IR, and contrary to normal Soviet practice there is no radar homing variant. This is understandable; a radar antenna in a body diameter of less than 4.75in (12cm) would have such a limited range as to be practically worthless.

Missile deployment

Production of the MiG-23 seems to have run ahead of the development of the new missiles. When the type was first observed in East Germany, in the course of 1973, it was seen to be carrying launch rails for K-13-type missiles. The new weapons probably entered service in the Soviet Union in the mid-1970s, and were kept away from the less secure areas of Eastern Europe and the Baltic until the early 1980s. Initially, the glove pylons each carried a single R-23, and the belly pylons each mounted one R-60; dual launchers for the R-60 or K-13-class weapons have been seen on the glove pylons, replacing the R-23 rail; also, twin R-60 rails can be fitted to the belly pylons. While the MiG-23 can in theory carry eight short-range missiles, two R-23s and four R-60s seem to constitute the normal armament.

MiG-23 as a threat

The MiG-23 does appear to have been easy to fly, although not all the systems worked as well as they might. A Russian Flogger driver based in what was East Germany once told the author that the only time he and his wingman pulled off a perfect practice interception was when they were called away from a party to an alert. Perhaps vodka affects the memory!

The MiG-23 was fast, heavily armed, and had a respectable range, but NATO observers were not, to begin with, very disturbed by its arrival. It was clearly not in the class of the new US fighters then under development, and was generally more comparable with the F-4. As 1973 gave way to 1974, however, Western economies recoiled under the impact of the oil embargo and subsequent price rise, and defence plans everywhere came under budgetary pressure. Meanwhile, the number of MiG-23s in the field continued to increase at an ever faster rate, and the West started to take notice.

It soon became clear that the MiG-23 was an outstanding achievement in producibility, even by Soviet standards. This did not result from any single breakthrough, but from the fact that ease of production was a priority at all stages of design. The TsAGI VG planform, for example, was designed to be compatible with a simple fuselage and simple inlet design. The strength of the structure primarily relied on a few components of high-tensile steel, reinforcing the straightforward riveted-alloy airframe. The inlet was a proven design that had been demonstrated to perform properly without a complex control system. Khachturov's engine used advanced design in the aerodynamics to reduce the number and cost of the individual stages. This philosophy was carried right through the airframe.

By the end of 1973, MiG-23 production was probably running at 150 aircraft a year. While the MiG-21 still offered superior manoeuvrability, and would be retained for the tactical air defence mission, the newer fighter was far superior to the MiG-21 and Su-7 in any role that involved long range or an appreciable warload. With sizeable fleets of such obsolescent types in being, the opportunity to carry out a rapid replacement programme, and to reply firmly to NATO's flexible response strategy, could not be missed. It was decided to accelerate production of the MiG-23 to unprecedented levels.

MiG-23 in action

As a fighter, the MiG-23 has been largely unsuccessful, and was withdrawn from Russian service in 1997, after only brief service over Afghanistan in the 1980s. It was also used by Iraq in the long-running war against Iran, although no details of it being involved in air combat have so far emerged. This is hardly surprising; air encounters were extremely rare.

On 4 January 1989, two Libyan MiG-23s attempted to intercept two USN Tomcats over the Gulf of Sirte. The Tomcats attempted to sidestep, but within seconds the Libyan fighters, obviously under ground control, turned back towards them, intent on closing the range. Against aircraft armed with BVR missiles this was worrying to the US pilots; yet the Tomcat leader held off as long as possible before attacking. Finally a decision could no longer be deferred; missiles were launched, and both Floggers were shot down. The entire engagement took barely five minutes from start to finish.

The MiG-23 has taken part in just two large-scale conflicts, emerging from neither with any credit. The first was the Beka'a action of 1982, when in a matter of days the Israelis claimed an 84 to nil victory ratio against Syria. About 36 of these were MiG-23s, although it must be admitted that they were up against much more modern F-15s and F-16s, and that their ground control had effectively been blinded. Two more Syrian MiG-23s were lost to F-15s on 20 November 1985, in the final clash between Syria and Israel.

More recently, the Gulf War of 1991 saw eight Iraqi Floggers downed by USAF F-15s, six with Sparrows, two with Sidewinders. The record shows that they put up little resistance, not that it would have done them much good.

The jury is still out on whether the MiG-21 was a turkey; there is less doubt about the MiG-23, especially since unlike the earlier fighter, there is little or no demand for upgrading.

Strike variant

At the same time, a more extensive revision of the design was carried out, to produce an optimized strike aircraft. To reduce empty weight, at the cost of operationally useless Mach 2+ capability, the new type was fitted with simple fixed inlets and a shorter, lighter nozzle, while its payload was increased through a number of modifications. To increase the under-fuselage capacity, the fuselage weapon pylons were moved from the underside of the fuselage proper to the inlet ducts, making it possible to carry larger stores; new landing gear support beams increased ground clearance so that a large store or a drop tank could be carried on the centreline; and a small rack was added on each side of the rear fuselage. These racks are usually described as mountings for auxiliary take-off rockets, but in fact carry additional stores, or flare or chaff dispensers.

For long-range missions, non-swivelling hardpoints were provided for two more 175gal (800lit) fuel tanks under the wings; the tanks would be used at the brakes were enlarged to handle the higher gross weight of the new type, and were covered by bulged doors. Almost certainly, the new type introduced the Tumansky R-29 engine, uprated by 15 per cent over the R-27.

Another important change was the provision of a new gun, a six-barrelled Gatling type weapon of 30mm calibre, which could spew out heavy shells, each weighing 0.84lb (380 grammes), at the rate of 90 per second, with a muzzle velocity of 2,789ft (850m) per second. However, this impressive performance was rather spoilt by lack of firing time. A full magazine held only 260 rounds, giving a single burst of less than three seconds, or perhaps four short bursts. The GSh-6-30 was mounted ventrally, close to the centreline.

Strafing

The success of the Il-2 Sturmovik in the Great Patriotic War had given the Russian a fixation about the effectiveness of strafing ground targets. This despite the fact that the relatively short range of the gun brought a multi-million rouble aircraft well within the envelope of sophisticated modern but relatively cheap ground defences, making a duel of this nature hardly an economic proposition!

Apart from the fixed GSh-6-30 cannon, the MiG-27 could carry two SPPU-22-01 gun pods, each with a twin-barrelled cannon. These differed from Western pods in that they could be depressed in flight. A constantly changing downward angle, cued automatically by a combination of air speed, speed over the ground (from Doppler), altitude, and the extremely accurate Fone laser ranger, would achieve a much greater concentration of fire on a ground target than could be achieved by using conventional fixed guns. Provided only that the initial aim was accurate, this would give a much greater potential for scoring hits,

Mikoyan MiG-27 'Flogger-D'

The MiG-27 is a fully developed, extended-range strike version of the family. Excess weight – including the variable inlets and nozzle – is removed and replaced by extra fuel, more weapons and additional avionics. Virtually all the aircraft of this type have been delivered to Soviet units.

with consequently greater lethality.

In all, the MiG-27 could carry a maximum of 8,815lb (4,000kg) of external stores on seven stations, although on most missions two or three of these would be occupied by external tanks. For self-protection, two R-3S (also known as the R-13M) AAMs could be carried. The range of "smart" bombs cleared for use included the Zvezda Kh-23 command-guided weapon, NATO reporting name AS-7 Kerry, and the Vympel Kh-29 (AS-14 Kedge), which uses either laser or TV guidance according to model. The range of dumb weapons includes 240mm S-24 rockets, UB-32-16 rocket pods, and up to 22 iron bombs of sizes ranging from 110lb (50kg) to 1,102lb (500kg). Tactical special weapons were another option.

Avionics included the PrNK-23 nav/attack system, the SAU automatic flight control system, the SPS-141 IR jammer, the RI-65 voice warning system covering 16 parameters, the SG-1 RWR, and of course the Fone laser rangefinder.

Increased payload, structural changes and, above all, provision for stand-off ASMs made the new variant a very different machine from the fighter versions, or the original strike aircraft. Accordingly, it received the designation MiG-27. Its arrival in East Germany, in mid-1975, came as a total and unpleasant surprise to NATO; even worse, the 16th Air Army had four regiments of this highly effective strike aircraft by the end of the year. It was a quantum jump in capability over the Su-7, and its appearance threatened to end NATO's large margin of qualitative superiority over the Warsaw Pact.

Some, but by no means all, of the improvements incorporated in the MiG-27 were applied to the MiG-23BN, which became the export-model ground-attack variant of the family. Something of a mongrel, it had the Mach 2.3 propulsion system of the original MiG-23, but with no search radar it was virtually useless in the high-altitude air-to-air regime. Most of the advanced avionics appear to be missing, including those connected with advanced ASMs, the structure is similar to that of the MiG-23 and the less effective GSh-23 gun is retained. MiG-23BNs delivered to Warsaw Pact air forces have the same small nose antenna fairings as the MiG-27; these may be command antennas for the AS-7, or part of another earlier-technology ASM system. Some Soviet units also operate this type.

The MiG-23BN served a multiple purpose. Despite its simplified systems, it is an effective 'bomb truck', and is easier and cheaper to produce than the more complex MiG-27. The retention of variable inlets seems paradoxical, but it does mean that the same basic airframe can be changed to a fighter configuration at the final assembly stage if national needs require it.

The new variants were identified by NATO in order of observation; the MiG-23U trainer was 'Flogger-C'; the MiG-27, 'Flogger-D'; the 'export model' MiG-23, 'Flogger-E'; and the MiG-23BN became 'Flogger-F' for Middle East and other export customers, and 'Flogger-H' in its WarPac version.

With the introduction of the MiG-27, a second State Aircraft Factory was brought into the programme, and production surged ahead. By the late 1970s, the Soviet Union was estimated to be building more than 500 MiG-23s and MiG-27s per year. The type was exported throughout the Middle East, to Cuba and to Vietnam, and production of the MiG-27M was licenced to HAL in India, deliveries starting in 1979. The MiG-23S was supplied not only to Frontal Aviation, but also to the PVO, providing some measure of capability against low-flying aircraft and replacing many obsolescent types.

It should be remembered, though, that not all of the aircraft delivered were of the top-grade types. Neither the MiG-23M nor the MiG-27 was confirmed to be in use outside Soviet units – with the exception of the East German Luftstreitkraefte (LSK), which was under full-time Soviet command – until the early 1980s, when India and Syria acquired the MiG-23M. At its peak, about 3,000 Floggers were in Soviet service, making it easily the most numerically important type. But almost as it entered service, the new breed of American superfighters made it obsolescent. It is perhaps noticeable that the Soviet Union, instead of screwing every last ounce of capability from what quickly became a proven design, as was their wont, failed to develop the MiG-23 series as fully as they had the much earlier, and far more basic, MiG-21. Instead, they concentrated on the next generation, the MiG-29 and Su-27.

This was a tacit admission of failure. Variable-sweep had been a false dawn. Adopted to give a combination of short runway capability, high performance, and low gust response for high speed penetration at low level, the penalty of high wing loading, leading to poor manoeuvrability, had compromised the Flogger as a fighter. It had been outclassed by superior technology – variable camber, relaxed stability, and fly-by-wire. Its greatest strength

Left: An excellent view of a MiG-27. Note the electro-optical and electronic installations above the glove pylons, nose laser rangefinder, ventral six-barrel Gatling gun, 'scabbed-on' cockpit armour and rear-fuselage stores pylons.

Far left: Apparent in this view of a MiG-27 are the repositioned pylons, bulged wheel bays and taller main landing gear.

was ease of production, which allowed it to enter service quickly and in great numbers.

The West however played the quality versus quantity card; the generation of fighters which entered service was vastly superior. They were of course concerned about being ground down by superior numbers, but no-one ever seemed to approach from the opposite direction. What of the Russian viewpoint?

To go up against Western fighters such as the F-14 and F-15, to say nothing of the F-16 and F/A-18 in an antique like the MiG-23, would have been a nightmare. For a Russian pilot to have gone into action knowing for certain that his radar was outranged, making it equally certain that he would be detected and shot at while still beyond the effective range of his own missiles; expecting to be blown away while still trying to close to visual distance, but knowing that even if he did so he would have been easily outmanoeuvred, was not conducive to a confident state of mind. MiG-25 pilot Viktor Belenko, on learning of the long-range lethality of the Tomcat, asked what were the best tactics to use against it. The answer was cold comfort; that once the range had been closed, the Tomcat would lose many of its advantages! The unanswered question was how!

For both East and West, morale was the problem. The West was faced with fighting against heavy odds; the East against far superior technology. For the Russians, it was a question of losing the battle, in terms of exchange ratios, but winning the war.

Flying the Flogger

An indication of the stability of the Flogger was granted to the West on 4 July 1989. The pilot, Colonel Nikolai Skiridin, having taken off from Kolobrzek in northern Poland, experienced engine problems shortly after takeoff and ejected. Trimmed to climb, the aircraft crossed the whole of Germany, much of Holland, and almost all of Belgium, accompanied by F-15s of the USAF, before running out of fuel and crashing near Wevelgem.

Then on 11 October 1989, a Syrian defector, Abdel Bassem, sneaked past the Israeli defences and landed at a civilian airstrip. While this did not go down well with the Israeli High Command, it did at least present them with a flyable MiG-23ML, which they quickly evaluated. Brief Israeli conclusions were that it could take off in a very short distance, could out-accelerate the F-16, but was extremely heavy on the controls. The advanced Saphir radar had no cockpit screen; all indications were displayed direct on the HUD.

More recently, Ben Lambeth, of the US think-tank Rand Corporation, flew the MiG-23UB, called krokodil by Russian pilots. Takeoff was 10deg nose-high, and liftoff came at about 140kt (259kmh). His first impression was of the poor view from the cockpit – he was in the front seat. Angle of attack was red-lined at 18deg, and departure and pro-spin tendencies were vicious. Corner velocity – the speed at which the turn rate is maximised – was about 430kt (797kmh), rather on the high side. Roll response was slow, stick forces were heavy, and Lambeth

assessed the turning capability as something between the F-104 and the F-105. In fact, very poor. The "feel" of the Flogger was somewhere between the Tornado and the unslatted Phantom. To summarize, it was no real match even for the Phantom, while against the next generation of Western fighters it was a non-starter.

Flogger in service

Approximately 1,500 MiG-23/27s remain in service with 17 nations worldwide, although in many cases they are in storage. They are: Algeria; Angola, where they have suffered from SAMs fired by UNITA; Belarus; Bulgaria; Cuba; Ethiopia; India, a major operator with over 400 examples including the MiG-27 Bahadur; Iraq; Kazakhstan; Libya; North Korea; Poland; Romania; Syria; Turkmenistan; Ukraine; and Yemen.

Below: Another photo showing the extensive range of sensors carried by the MiG-27. The four-bomb armament carried here is probably little more than a practice load.

Bottom: The MiG-27 HUD is similar to that of the MiG-23. The canopy has no central frame; this may mean that the ejection seat is designed to break through the transparency.

MiG-27 stores options

1 FAB-250 550lb (250kg) general-purpose bomb
2 FAB-500 1,100lb (500kg) general-purpose bomb
3 Tactical air-to-surface missile

4 AA-2-2 'Advanced Atoll' air-to-air missile
5 23mm Gatling gun and ammunition
6 1,100lb (500kg) low-drag bomb
7 176Imp gal (800lit) centreline fuel tank

The most heavily armed member of the series, the MiG-27 can carry and launch most of the new tactical ASMs and smart weapons introduced by Soviet forces over the past ten years.

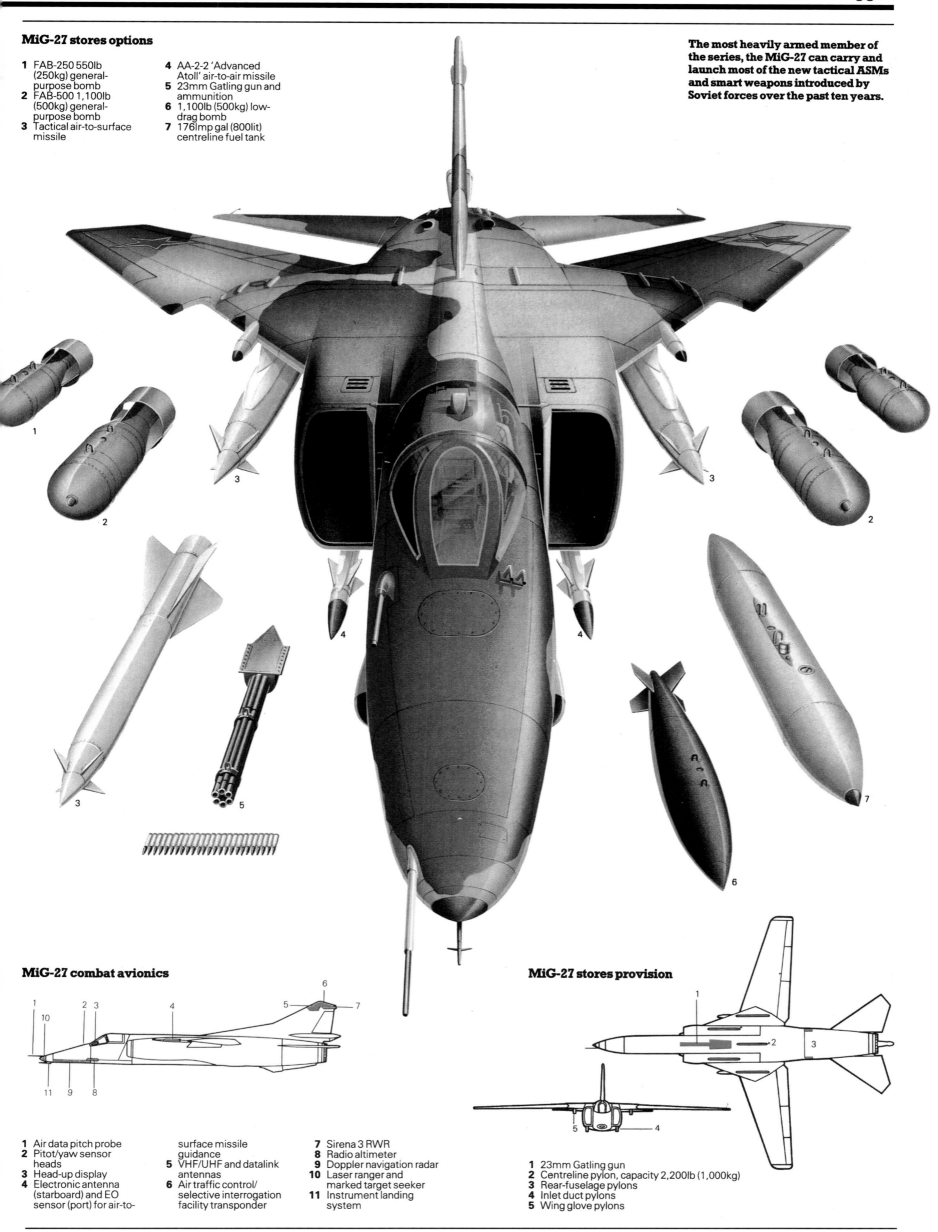

MiG-27 combat avionics

MiG-27 stores provision

1 Air data pitch probe
2 Pitot/yaw sensor heads
3 Head-up display
4 Electronic antenna (starboard) and EO sensor (port) for air-to-

surface missile guidance
5 VHF/UHF and datalink antennas
6 Air traffic control/selective interrogation facility transponder

7 Sirena 3 RWR
8 Radio altimeter
9 Doppler navigation radar
10 Laser ranger and marked target seeker
11 Instrument landing system

1 23mm Gatling gun
2 Centreline pylon, capacity 2,200lb (1,000kg)
3 Rear-fuselage pylons
4 Inlet duct pylons
5 Wing glove pylons

MiG-25 'Foxbat'

The MiG-25, NATO reporting name Foxbat, became an aerial bogeyman to the West for many years, mainly due to a series of intelligence misappreciations. It was however a really remarkable feat of engineering, given the Soviet technology of the era. The best analogy is Spitfire performance achieved with the doped linen, bracing wires and wooden frame of the Sopwith Camel! The Soviet designers used what was available and what they knew would just about work. The result was an outstanding single mission interceptor, and the fact that Western intelligence construed it as an air superiority fighter should not detract from its undeniable virtues.

The MiG-25, NATO reporting name Foxbat, was a uniquely Russian solution to what at first appeared to be an intractable problem – how to intercept the ultra fast, ultra high-flying Lockheed A-12 reconnaissance aircraft, the ancestor of the SR-71 Blackbird. It involved stretching contemporary Soviet technology past what had previously been considered possible. Its performance was such that Western intelligence jumped to the conclusion that the Soviet Union had made a quantum advance in technology.

From mid-1956, American U-2s had conducted reconnaissance overflights of the Soviet Union. At 70,000ft (21,335m) they were beyond the reach of the defences, and the USSR could make little fuss without revealing their own impotence. This situation could not last, and finally, on 1 May 1960, they managed to down one of the intruders. But the Americans had already foreseen that this time would come, and had initiated Project Oxcart, an aircraft which could sustain speeds in excess of Mach 3 at altitudes of up to 85,000ft (25,907m). Although Oxcart was not officially revealed until 1964, Soviet intelligence became aware of it in 1960. This posed them the problem of how best to intercept an aircraft some 16 miles (26km) high and covering the ground at 28nm (52km) each minute.

The Mikoyan OKB set to work. As the recipe for jugged hare begins, first catch your hare. This was easier said than done. Close, preferably automated, ground control was needed to steer the interceptor towards the target. But, for this to be effective, the interceptor had to have an outstanding rate of climb and ceiling, plus exceptionally high speed. At Mach 3 and over, an astern conversion was out of the question; the best option was collision course from the front quarter, or at worst, from abeam. This in turn demanded a long range radar which could operate in the face of ECM, and large radar homing missiles. These had to be large because in the attenuated air at very high altitude blast effect would be quickly dissipated. They also had to bring down the target consistently; there could be no second chance.

Propulsion

The first problem was the propulsion unit. Mikulin and Tumanskiy took as a basis the high-altitude-optimised R-15K used by the Jastreb reconnaissance drone. To achieve the speed and rate of climb required, the design was compromised to the point where it manifested extremely poor efficiency at low altitudes and subsonic speeds.

The result was the R-15-300, a basic single spool engine with only five compressor stages. This gave a low pressure ratio by conventional fighter standards, but was necessary if turbine entry temperature limits were not to be exceeded in high speed flight. At the top end of the range, the pressure ratio was quite exceptional. Another feature was water/methanol injection. Fed from tanks in the fins, it cooled the air, helping to increase thrust while keeping temperatures within limits. The engine was backed by a huge afterburner, with four injection manifolds – three concentric flameholders, and a con-di nozzle. For all practical purposes, this put the engine into the turbo-ramjet class, essential since afterburning would be used for most of the interception. The R-15-300 was first flight-tested in Ye-150 and Ye-152 prototypes, which were in effect overgrown MiG-21s.

The baseline engine was the R-15B-300, rated at 22,509lb (10,210kg) maximum and 16,535lb (7,500kg) military. While this did not provide an exceptional thrust loading in the pure fighter sense of the word, it was the ultra-high altitude performance that counted, and in this regime it was exceptional.

Fuel was the next problem. With full 'burner continually used for takeoff, climbout, and the interception, combined with inefficient operation on the subsonic return to base, consumption was going to be horrendous. The only possible solution was to design the aircraft as a flying fuel tank, in order to max-imise capacity. External tanks were not a viable option; all they would have done was to reduce performance, and this could not be considered. A special high-density fuel, T-6, was developed, but even with this, internal fuel weight was an enormous 32,120lb (14,570kg). As this was used, the centre of gravity was constantly changing, and to compensate, an automatic fuel transfer system was needed. This was a first for the MiG OKB.

The heat barrier

One of the greatest problems of trisonic flight was aerodynamic heating. At Mach 3, at an ambient temperature of 0deg Celsius, the friction of the atmosphere rushing past the nose would raise the temperature to 300deg Celsius, with other exposed parts of the airframe heating up accordingly. This was bad news. The standard airframe material duralumin (a stiff aluminium alloy) started to soften at above 130deg Celsius. For all practical purposes this ruled out its use for all but a few non-critical applications.

The Americans used titanium alloy for the A-12 and SR-71. Almost as strong as

Above: A MiG-25R 'Foxbat-B' undergoing flight-line inspection. The sharp waisting of the fuselage between the inlets is very clear in this view, as is the gradual widening of the upper ramps from front to rear.

steel, it was however considerably lighter. It was a difficult metal to handle and weld, but US technology was sufficiently advanced to cope. The USSR had no such option. It was considered, but with the exception of a few small and simple areas, such as the wing leading edges and around the tailpipes, it was rejected.

The result was Hobson's choice – nickel steel. In part this decision was forced by a totally unexpected factor, a dearth of riveters. But there was no shortage of welders, and welded steel showed many advantages, notably for the integral fuel tanks. Welded tanks would be less prone to leaks, especially as high temperature sealants, essential for riveted tanks, simply did not exist at that time. All that had to be established was that welded steel tanks could cope with aerodynamic flexing, and with the stresses imposed on landing, without rupturing. This was finally confirmed, and design proceeded. The welded steel fuel tanks occupied 70 per cent of the total volume.

There were of course other heating problems to be overcome. Initially the canopy plexiglass simply melted, and a new material had to be developed. The environmental control system kept the pilot cool, but the new canopy material remained much too hot to touch. Similar

Right: One of the Ye-26 prototypes takes a bow over Domodedovo on July 9, 1967. Note the vertical fins, much smaller than those adopted for the production MiG-25. The nose is black, but there is probably no radar inside.

Right middle: Although it has a new radar, the 'Foxbat-E' has the same AA-6 missiles as the older aircraft. The appearance of the nose is slightly changed, because the new radome is closer to an ogive than a cone, and is shorter than that of the original

Below right: The MiG-25 'Foxbat-E' has been produced by fitting older airframes with the more effective and less compromised radar of the MiG-23bis, together with a similar IRST system.

Below: Lt Viktor Belenko's MiG-25 rests in the overrun area at Hakodate airport, in northern Japan, following its pilot's defection. It was the largest single windfall of technical intelligence in the superpowers' history.

problems applied to the dielectric materials.

Naturally the engine was a significant heat source, and this had to be contained. The solution was a steel shield plated with silver 30 microns thick, and wrapped with fibreglass. Other precious metals were also tried, notably gold and the rare element rhodium. All were far too expensive.

Airframe
Its big and brutal appearance apart, the MiG-25 was fairly conventional. A massive nose, to accommodate a large and powerful radar and a lengthy electronics compartment, was flanked by twin steeply raked variable engine inlets. The cockpit, set deep into the fuselage, was faired back into a dorsal spine. The rear view was appalling, but at speeds in excess of Mach 2 this was irrelevant.

Not easily seen from photographs is that the wing leading edge had compound sweepback, 42.5deg inboard to the half-span point, reducing to 41deg outboard. Shoulder-mounted, at first it had zero dihedral, and extra longitudinal

stability was given by downward-canted winglets on the tips on the first prototype, and triangular endplates on the first seven preproduction aircraft. These were later scrapped in favour of 5deg of anhedral, with anti-flutter weights on the wingtips. A full-chord fence was fitted at about the midpoint, with a much smaller one further outboard. Control surfaces consisted of blown flaps over a third of the trailing edge and two-section ailerons. Two hardpoints were fitted under each wing.

All-moving tailerons were set low, beneath the wing line. These moved in unison for pitch control, and differentially for roll. Twin fin/rudder assemblies, of typically MiG shape with cropped tips, were set well aft, and canted outwards, assisted by ventral strakes. Dorsal and ventral speed brakes completed the external picture.

As work continued, the thought occurred that the new MiG aircraft would have reconnaissance applications, in addition to interception, and in fact it was the reconnaissance Ye-155R-1 prototype that first flew, on 6 March 1964. This pro-

vided several valuable lessons for the interceptor. Canard foreplanes had been fitted to this machine to provide a degree of destabilization in certain flight regimes, but in practice these were found to be of little value, and were abandoned. This series of test flights also saw anhedral introduced, and the abandonment of the wing endplates. The chord of the ventral fins was also reduced; they had a disconcerting habit of grounding. Piotr Ostapyenko took the Ye-155P-1 into the air for the first time on 9 September 1964. Problems were encountered, and only slowly solved, with the tailerons and ailerons. The fin area was increased in size. Then, when a single missile was launched at high speed, a dangerous asymmetry arose. This was eventually cured by automatic trimming. The short engine time between overhauls was far from satisfactory but at first little could be done about this.

Records and myths
On 16 March 1965, Alexsandr Fedotov set new world speed records for the 1,000km (625-mile) closed circuit with

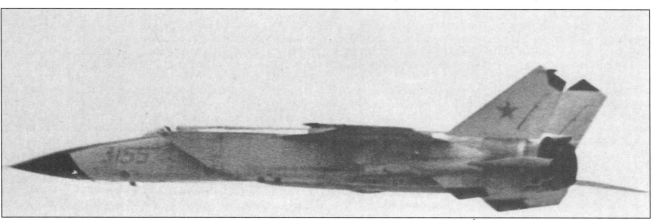

Above: This was the first photograph released in the West to show the MiG-25 carrying the two-stage AA-6 'Acrid' missile. Semi-active radar-homing weapons are carried on the outer pylons, and IR-homers inboard.

Left: The truck by the left-hand MiG-25U carries all the diagnostic equipment for the type, tools for routine maintenance and a ground power unit, and also acts as a tug.

the best efforts of Israeli Peace Jack (specially modified) Phantoms to intercept. Speeds generally were of the order of Mach 2.5, although on one occasion a Foxbat was tracked over Sinai at Mach 3.2. This aircraft barely made it back to base, its engines wrecked by overspeeding. It was not appreciated at the time that this was the inevitable consequence of exceeding the engine limit of Mach 2.83, and Mach 3.2 was thus considered to be a normal operational capability by the West. Between 4 June and 25 July 1973, the Ye-266 set a hatful of new records. These included time to altitude for 20,000, 25,000 and 30,000m (65,620, 82,025 and 98,430ft), the latter in 4min 4sec, and an absolute altitude figure of 118,913ft (36,240m), the latter set by Fedotov. These were of short duration; the McDonnell Douglas Streak Eagle recaptured them for the USA in January and February 1975, only to lose them again to the Ye-266M in May. This gave the Foxbat myth an added boost, but worse was to come.

Shortly after Foxbat squadrons had been deployed to Poland, Soviet reconnaissance units had deployed a new drone. These were tracked by radar at speeds of Mach 2.8 at 90,000ft (27,431m) to North Atlantic ports and back. It was assumed that these were Foxbats, and that their operational radius was at least 650nm (1,205km). Wrong again!

2,205lb (1,000kg) and 4,410lb (2,000kg) payloads at Mach 2.185. As setting records is an expression of national pride, using specially modified aircraft, this caused little reaction in the West. Then on 5 October 1967, Mikhail Komarov reached Mach 2.808 over a 500km (312-mile) closed circuit, while on the same day, Alexsandr Fedotov reached an absolute altitude of 98,355ft (29,977m) with a payload of 2,000kg. Now the West really did start to take notice!

At this point, myth took over. Western intelligence simply could not credit that the Soviet Union would build a single

mission interceptor to counter the A-12/SR-71; instead they assumed that the Foxbat was a true air superiority fighter, with all that entailed. Another factor muddied the waters. Having confused the MiG-23 with the MiG-25, they assumed that the latter was being mass-produced in large numbers. "Mirror-imaging" produced a picture of an all-titanium fighter with advanced turbofan engines, fully manoeuvrable, and with a combat radius of about 600nm (1,100km). Finally, it was assumed that the huge radome held a large and effective pulse-Doppler multi-mode radar. In the eyes of the West, Foxbat assumed the

status of an aerial bogeyman; a tactical fighter outclassing anything the West had to offer!

It was this imagined threat which caused the performance specification of the F-15 Eagle to be set so high as to be unattainable. But even with what the Americans were able to achieve, the F-15 became the best fighter in the world for more than two decades. And all thanks to faulty intelligence!

Matters were not helped by events in the Middle East between October 1971 and 1973. Reconnaissance Foxbats based on Cairo overflew Israel at 80,000ft (24,400m) with impunity, despite

The myth was finally laid to rest on 6 September 1976, when Viktor Ivanovich Belenko defected from his base at Sakharova to Hakodate in Japan, bringing with him the MiG-25 Foxbat. A windfall for Western intelligence, they soon uncovered its secrets. The use of nickel steel rather than titanium had caused them to underestimate its empty weight by a significant margin. At the same time they discovered that it was not built for manoeuvre combat; with half internal fuel used it was limited to no more than 5g, and at maximum takeoff weight this fell to about 2.5g. Combat radius on a full 'burner intercept mission was just 160nm (296km) while ferry radius was little over 1,000nm (1,853km).

One of the biggest surprises of all was the radar. Smertch-A was not designed for long range detection; that was the province of ground control. Instead, it was optimised for accurate targeting in the face of heavy ECM. Instead of transistors, it used old-fashioned thermionic valves. To burn through hostile jamming the output was tremendous, of the order of 600kW, and it was reputed to be able to kill a rabbit at 200 paces. Whatever the truth of this, it was a court-martial offence to switch the radar on beforewell after takeoff.

Weaponry

The production MiG-25P typically carried two Bisnovat SARH R-40R and two heat-homing R-40T missiles, NATO reporting name AA-6 Acrid. Twice the weight of Sparrow, and with large aerodynamic surfaces to provide lift and control in the thin air of the stratosphere, these huge weapons are credited with a range of 38nm (70km) SARH and about 16nm (30km) for IR. Speed for both is stated to be Mach 4.5, although the warhead weight is no more than that of

Mikoyan MiG-25 'Foxbat-A'

Features of the MiG-25's shape which are frequently overlooked – the straight wing leading edge, the slender 'neck' of the forward fuselage between the inlets, and the tapering inlet lips – are apparent in this old but generally accurate drawing.

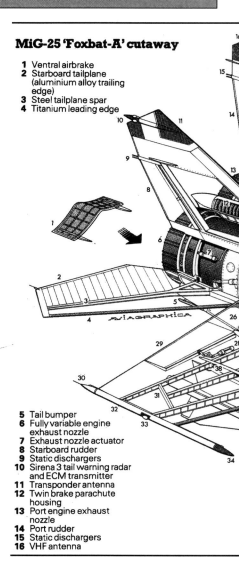

MiG-25 'Foxbat-A' cutaway

1 Ventral airbrake
2 Starboard tailplane (aluminium alloy trailing edge)
3 Steel tailplane spar
4 Titanium leading edge
5 Tail bumper
6 Fully variable engine exhaust nozzle
7 Exhaust nozzle actuator
8 Starboard rudder
9 Static dischargers
10 Sirena 3 tail warning radar and ECM transmitter
11 Transponder antenna
12 Twin brake parachute housing
13 Port engine exhaust nozzle
14 Port rudder
15 Static dischargers
16 VHF antenna

Sparrow.

MiG-25PD Foxbat E

The MiG-25P was succeeded by the improved -25PD from 1978. This was powered by two R-15BD-300s, rated at 24,692lb (11,200kg) maximum and 19,400lb (8,800kg) military thrust. Service life was extended in stages to 1,000 hours. The now-compromised Smertch-A radar was replaced by the Kirpichev Saphir-25, which had a tracking range some 50 per cent greater and better look-own capability. A TP-26Sh1 IRST was added beneath the forward fuselage, as was a large auxiliary fuel tank. From 1979, all Soviet Air Force MiG-25Ps were upgraded to the new MiG-25PD standard.

Weaponry was also improved; the improved R-40TD and R-40RD became the standard fit; alternatively two R-40TDs could be combined with four short range R-60Ms.

MiG-25R, RB, and others

First flown on 6 March 1964 by Alexsandr Fedotov, the MiG-25R-1 went through all the early modifications described for the interceptor variant.

Left: Apparent in this view of a Libyan MiG-25 are the three propulsion nozzles of the AA-6 missile, which have passed unnoticed in all previous publications. The two small nozzles on the sides of the missile, between the wings, are probably the exhausts of the cruise motor, the booster being in the tail.

Below left: The planform of Foxbat was very simple. The steeply raked engine inlets are reminiscent of the A-5 Vigilante, while the change in leading edge angle is barely visible. Anti-flutter weights on the wingtips are typical of the Mikoyan OKB.

Unarmed, and reliant on sheer performance allied to ECM for survival, it carried two rotating oblique and one fixed vertical camera in nose bays that formerly housed the radar. The revised nose had two camera ports on each side. Production commenced in 1969; in that same year it was decided to give the aircraft a bombing capability.

This resulted in the MiG-25RB. The requirements were to cruise for extended periods at Mach 2.35, and to reach Mach 2.83 with a full external bomb load. The latter was to consist of up to 10 FAB-500T conventional bombs, or a single nuclear store. Accuracy then became the problem. Hitting targets with conventional weapons from supersonic speeds and altitudes above 65,620ft (20,000m) was, and probably still is, impossible. The results achieved during trials have not been released.

Later reconnaissance Foxbats carried sideways-looking airborne radar (SLAR); these were notably the MiG-25RBK, RBS and RBV, differing only in the equipment carried. Then there was the electronic intelligence variant, the MiG-25RBF, and the MiG-25BM defence suppression aircraft, armed with four Kh-58 anti-radar missiles. Finally, and inevitably, such an advanced machine demanded a two-seater conversion trainer. This emerged as the MiG-25PU and -25RU. A second cockpit was inserted in what had been the radar and avionics bay in the nose, and unusually the instructor took the front seat. Neither of the aircraft had combat capability.

Foxbat in service

We saw earlier that reconnaissance Foxbats successfully overflew Israel in the 1970s. Just occasionally Soviet MiG-25Ps managed to scramble into position to deny overflights to SR-71s, although Viktor Belenko is on record as saying that he could never get near them. As a fighter, the Foxbat's record is undistinguished. At least three Syrian MiG-25s have been shot down by Israeli F-15s, and two Iraqi MiG-25s fell to USAF F-15s during the Gulf War.

An estimated 350 MiG-25s remain in the inventories of Algeria, Armenia, Azerbaijan, India, Iraq, Kazakhstan, Libya, Russia (where they have been largely supplanted by the MiG-31), Syria, and Turkmenistan. How many remain serviceable is an open question.

Below: Groundcrew give scale to the heavyweight MiG-25, its tall verticals and mighty afterburners. One man is standing on the stabilizer, a testimony to the type's rugged construction.

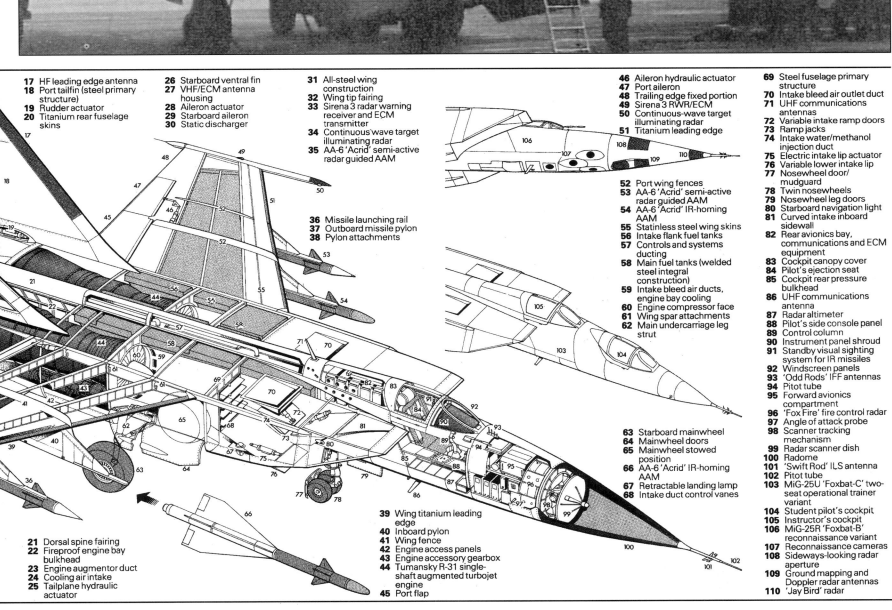

17 HF leading edge antenna
18 Port tailfin (steel primary structure)
19 Rudder actuator
20 Titanium rear fuselage skins
21 Dorsal spine fairing
22 Fireproof engine bay bulkhead
23 Engine augmentor duct
24 Cooling air intake
25 Tailplane hydraulic actuator
26 Starboard ventral fin
27 VHF/ECM antenna housing
28 Aileron actuator
29 Starboard aileron
30 Static discharger
31 All-steel wing construction
32 Wing tip fairing
33 Sirena 3 radar warning receiver and ECM transmitter
34 Continuous wave target illuminating radar
35 AA-6 'Acrid' semi-active radar guided AAM
36 Missile launching rail
37 Outboard missile pylon
38 Pylon attachments
39 Wing titanium leading edge
40 Inboard pylon
41 Wing fence
42 Engine access panels
43 Engine accessory gearbox
44 Tumansky R-31 single-shaft augmented turbojet engine
45 Port flap
46 Aileron hydraulic actuator
47 Port aileron
48 Trailing edge fixed portion
49 Sirena 3 RWR/ECM
50 Continuous-wave target illuminating radar
51 Titanium leading edge
52 Port wing fences
53 AA-6 'Acrid' semi-active radar guided AAM
54 AA-6 'Acrid' IR-homing AAM
55 Stainless steel wing skins
56 Intake flank fuel tanks
57 Controls and systems ducting
58 Main fuel tanks (welded steel integral construction)
59 Intake bleed air ducts, engine bay cooling
60 Engine compressor face
61 Wing spar attachments
62 Main undercarriage leg strut
63 Starboard mainwheel
64 Mainwheel doors
65 Mainwheel stowed position
66 AA-6 'Acrid' IR-homing AAM
67 Retractable landing lamp
68 Intake duct control vanes
69 Steel fuselage primary structure
70 Intake bleed air outlet duct
71 UHF communications antennas
72 Variable intake ramp doors
73 Ramp jacks
74 Intake water/methanol injection duct
75 Electric intake lip actuator
76 Variable lower intake lip
77 Nosewheel door/mudguard
78 Twin nosewheels
79 Nosewheel leg doors
80 Starboard navigation light
81 Curved intake inboard sidewall
82 Rear avionics bay, communications and ECM equipment
83 Cockpit canopy cover
84 Pilot's ejection seat
85 Cockpit rear pressure bulkhead
86 UHF communications antenna
87 Radar altimeter
88 Pilot's side console panel
89 Control column
90 Instrument panel shroud
91 Standby visual sighting system for IR missiles
92 Windscreen panels
93 'Odd Rods' IFF antennas
94 Pitot tube
95 Forward avionics compartment
96 'Fox Fire' fire control radar
97 Angle of attack probe
98 Scanner tracking mechanism
99 Radar scanner dish
100 Radome
101 'Swift Rod' ILS antenna
102 Pitot tube
103 MiG-25U 'Foxbat-C' two-seat operational trainer variant
104 Student pilot's cockpit
105 Instructor's cockpit
106 MiG-25R 'Foxbat-B' reconnaissance variant
107 Reconnaissance cameras
108 Sideways-looking radar aperture
109 Ground mapping and Doppler radar antennas
110 'Jay Bird' radar

MiG-29 'Fulcrum'

The MiG-29, NATO reporting name Fulcrum, is a true heir to the MiG-21 in that no-one can agree whether it is a top-class fighter or a turkey. Its flying and weaponry qualities seem to indicate the former, but its combat record by the beginning of the 21st Century has been abysmal. Designed to counter the American 'teen series of fighters, it has done little to inspire confidence that it could, although its off-boresight missile capability and helmet-mounted sighting system have caused no little dismay in the West.

Above: The MiG-29SM Fulcrum is a second generation aircraft, with increased internal fuel capacity, quadruplex analogue fly-by-wire in pitch but triplex analogue FBW in roll and yaw. It also carries the superior N-019M radar combined with a "glass cockpit".

Like the USA, the former Soviet Union had paid close attention to events in the limited wars that abounded in the 1960s and '70s. Again like the Americans, the Russians concluded that the dogfight was not dead, BVR combat was not a panacea, and that manoeuvre combat was an essential part of the future. The MiG-23 had the advantage in BVR combat against the F-16, but not against either the F-15 or F/A-18. Then when, as it inevitably would, the fight closed to knife range, it was badly disadvantaged against all three. In this scenario, agility became paramount. With this in mind, TsAGI produced aerodynamic recommendations for the configuration of an agile close combat fighter, which at the same time lacked nothing in performance. This resulted in the superb Sukhoi Su-27 Flanker, described in detail in the next section, and the MiG-29 Fulcrum tactical fighter, and explains why they have a certain family likeness, even though they differ considerably in detail.

The Legkiy Frontovoy Istrebityey (LFI – frontline light fighter) project was launched in the early 1970s. Development took time, and not until 6 October 1977 did the prototype take to the air, piloted by Alexsandr Fedotov. In all, the MiG OKB needed 19 prototypes to develop the engine, an augmented turbofan, and to get the configuration right. The aircraft first came to the attention of the West when it was photographed by a US satellite at Ramenskoye in November 1977, when it was given the reporting name of Ram-L. The limitations of satellite photography (or was it disinformation?) were exposed over the next few months when a mass of speculation, including dimensions, was released by the West, all of which was inaccurate.

The second prototype flew in June 1978, but was lost shortly after due to an engine fire, making MiG future chief test pilot Valeriy Eugenievich Menitsky the first in a distinguished line of Fulcrum ejectees. He was followed by Fedotov, who parted company with the fourth prototype on 31 October 1980, also as a result of engine problems. Not until June 1983 did the MiG-29 start to reach the operational units.

The West got its first real look at the MiG-29 in July 1986, when six Soviet

Left: The huge con-di nozzles of the widely spaced Klimov RD-33 turbofans, which give a static thrust of 18,298lb (8,300kg) in afterburner. The RD-33 is however short on operational life.

Below: In profile the similarities of the MiG-29 to the Su-27 are very apparent. However, the styling of the vertical tail surfaces is that of the Mikoyan OKB, beyond a remote shadow of a doubt.

aircraft visited the Finnish air base at Kuopio-Rissala. But while photographs became available for the first time, this visit served only to increase speculation; firm information was not forthcoming. Then, at the Farnborough Air Show in 1988, not one, but two MiG-29s appeared, one of them the previously unknown MiG-29UB two-seat conversion trainer, flown by Anatoliy Nikolaevich Kvochur and Roman Petrovich Taska'ev respectively, the latter with Yuri Ermakov in the back seat. What was more, brochures were available. For the first time, authoritative figures were available for dimensions and weight!

The flying demonstration confirmed that the Fulcrum was in the same general manoeuvre class as the F-16, but what really caught the imagination of many observers was the tail slide. Kvochur pulled his fighter into a vertical climb and cut the power. In a full stall, it slid backwards for a couple of seconds before the nose was allowed to fall through and power was restored. There appeared to be no tendency to drop a wing, and the MiG-29 was obviously under full control throughout

Mikhail Romanovich Waldenberg, at the time chief designer of the MiG OKB, later stated that this was a valid combat manoeuvre designed to break a pulse-Doppler radar lock. While there could be no doubt that this would work, as it would reduce the relative velocity of the Fulcrum to below the velocity screening threshold of the average pulse-Doppler radar, was any pilot seriously going to sacrifice all his energy-manoeuvrability in a combat situation? And then take forever to get it back? The only possible conclusion was that the tail slide was no more than a spectacular air show trick. This was just the first move in a Russian attempt to exploit the gullibility of far too many Western observers.

Fulcrum details

The most radically different feature of the MiG-29 was the fact that its underslung engine nacelles were widely spaced, and that from the midpoint there was no clearly apparent fuselage, just a Tomcat-like pancake. The engines ran "straight-through" from intake to nozzle. This configuration was adopted for the Tomcat to avoid problems with the TF30 turbofans, which were known to be extremely sensitive to disturbed airflow. Although it has never been confirmed, in view of the loss of two prototypes due to engine problems, it seems probable that a similar solution was adopted for the Klimov RD-33 turbofans of the MiG-29.

The RD-33 was a two-spool afterburning turbofan with a bypass ratio of 0.47 – slightly on the high side for a fighter engine – and a 13 stage compressor giving a pressure ratio of 20:1. Maximum static thrust was 18,298lb (8,300kg), giving a thrust/weight ratio in excess of unity at combat weight, while military thrust was 10,891lb (4,940kg). Like all Russian engines of the era, it was short on operational life, with just 400 hours between overhauls.

One feature really caused raised eyebrows. The intakes, which had variable ramps to allow a maximum speed of Mach 2.3, also had top-hinged perforated doors which closed when the aircraft was on the ground. Louvred vents above the intakes supplied most of the air in this condition. Speculation ranged from the practical: was this to starve the engines of air and thus reduce residual thrust when taxiing on icy runways (a known problem with the F-16), to the absurd: was it a stealth measure to stop hostile radar from reaching the compressor face?

The question was resolved by Mikhail Waldenberg; it was an anti-FOD measure to prevent the ingestion of ice or small stones on takeoff from semi-prepared runways! Simple answers are best! It was however possible to fly at up to 432kt (800kmh) with the doors closed, and angle of attack limited to 22deg. The only practical reason for this would be to prevent bird ingestion in low level flight, although this has never been confirmed.

The wing has the moderate leading edge sweep angle of 42deg, and a relatively high aspect ratio. Leading edge root extensions are followed by three-piece computer-controlled manoeuvre flaps, while the trailing edge carries slotted flaps with ailerons outboard. The pancake area is stated to supply some 40 per cent of the total lift, in which it is similar to the Tomcat.

Right: The large leading edge root extensions, the moderate wing sweep and aspect ratio, the widely spaced engine nacelles with twin fins, and the louvred doors for the engine intakes, are the salient features.

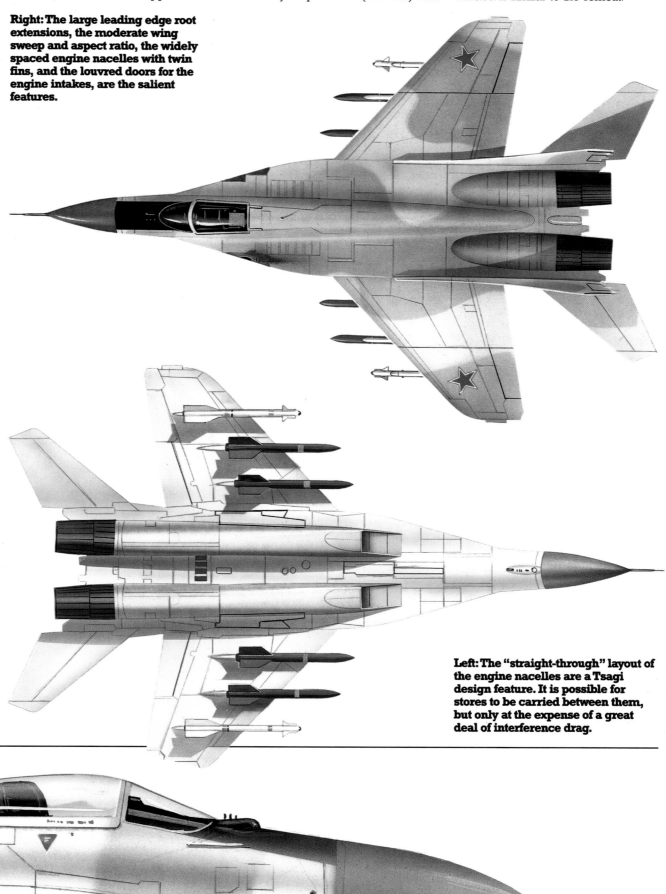

Left: The "straight-through" layout of the engine nacelles are a Tsagi design feature. It is possible for stores to be carried between them, but only at the expense of a great deal of interference drag.

Above: The "potato masher" control surfaces of the R-77 "Amraamski" as seen on this Fulcrum at Farnborough 1994 are unique. These should give a credible BVR capability.

All-moving tail surfaces are mounted on booms outside the engine nacelles and have a leading edge sweep of 50deg, while the twin fins are of typical Mikoyan shape, with dual sweep and cropped tips. The leading edges of these carry forward onto the upper wing surfaces and, while they have no apparent aerodynamic purpose, are used to house flare dispensers.

The twin nose wheel is located aft of the cockpit and retracts forward. Originally it was set almost under the pilot's seat, but this was changed. The single wheel main gears retract forward into the wing roots, with the wheels turning through 90deg to lie flat above the legs.

In one respect the MiG-29 Fulcrum A was the last of the dinosaurs. The flight control system was hydraulic rather than FBW, although it contained some advanced features, including an angle of attack limiter set at 26deg. This can of course be over-ruled by an experienced pilot, but this is not recommended for the average squadron jock. Construction is largely conventional, with a combination of steel and aluminium lithium, and a limited amount of composite construction.

As would be expected, the cockpit display was old-fashioned "steam-gauge", although the ejection seat, raked back at 10deg, was the Zvezda K-36DM. This was a great advance on the KM-1 seat that had saved Menitsky and Fedotov, and was demonstrated in spectacular fashion at the Paris Air Show in 1990 when Anatoliy Kvochur lost control after a low level birdstrike and ejected. One of the most interesting points was the SUV fire control unit.

This linked the Phazotron N-019 Zhuk radar to the KOLS-29 IRST which combined a laser ranger. The latter gave very precise ranging, while the IRST tracked the target accurately. If the target disappeared into cloud the radar, cued by the IRST, automatically cut in, and vice versa. This made the 30mm Gryazev/Shipunov GSh-30-1 single-barrelled cannon embedded in the port wing root exceptionally accurate. With a firing rate of 1,800 rounds/min, the magazine capacity of 150 rounds gave only five seconds of firing time.

Missile armament at first consisted of six R-60 AAMs, a mix of SARH and IR homers, or two medium range R-27Rs and four short-range R-60s. The R-60s were later supplanted by the extremely agile R-73, NATO reporting name AA-11 Archer. Using a combination of thrust vectoring and aerodynamic controls, this small missile could be used up to 60deg off-boresight.

The brochure for the Zhuk radar states a maximum detection range of 43nm (80km) against fighter-sized targets, plus/minus 90deg off boresight, and up to 27nm (50km) range against targets in the rear hemisphere. It does seem however that a little hype had crept in here, as users have since criticised it as lacking search angle. Unlike contemporary Western radars, it lacked multiple tracking and multiple target engagement capability. One tremendous advance was however a helmet-mounted sight, which allowed R-73s to be launched at high off-boresight angles, obviating the need to point the fighter at the target, and posing extreme tactical problems for opponents.

Fulcrum variants
A two-seat conversion trainer, the MiG-29UB, was the obvious first move. Fulcrum was already short on internal fuel, and reducing this still more to make room for the second seat was not a viable option. By removing the radar, space was made to extend the double cockpit forward, although the optronics system was retained, together with the cannon. The MiG-29UB prototype was first flown by A.G. Fastovets on 29 April 1981, and entered production during the following year.

MiG-29S/MiG-29SE
The first modification addressed the two basic failings of the original – short range/endurance, and multiple target engagement. The dorsal spine was enlarged to increase internal fuel capacity, while two underwing hardpoints were plumbed for tanks. Five-section leading edge flaps replaced the previous four; while the improved

N-019M radar not only allowed simultaneous engagement of two targets, but was compatible with the new Vympel R-77 active radar AAM, which was quickly dubbed Amraamski in the West. The MiG-29SE was an export version, with downgraded avionics.

MiG-29M
The MiG-29M was the second generation Fulcrum, in that it had a fly-by-wire control system. This was quadruplex analogue in pitch, but triplex analogue in roll and yaw. The official

Below: This "fish-eye" lens view of a MiG-29 was taken at Chalovskiy AFB near Moscow, July 1988. It shows clearly the engine intake louvres in the wing root extensions.

explanation for this was that analogue systems were simpler to develop than digital (although the contemporary Su-27 used a digital system).

Other changes were equally radical. The intake blanks were replaced by mesh guards as on the Su-27 (see next section); the overwing intake louvres were scrapped, and the magazine capacity was reduced to 100 rounds. This allowed an increase in internal fuel, albeit at the price of greater vulnerability. Ruptured tanks would spill fuel straight into the intakes.

Below: The cramped and cluttered cockpit of the MiG-29. Prominent is the Zvezda K-36D ejection seat that saved the life of Mikoyan test pilot Anatoliy Kvotchur.

The wings were also structurally modified to increase tankage, which now became one third greater than that of the original. A new aerofoil section with a sharp leading edge, and ailerons extended out to the tips, improved handling at high angles of attack. A modified speed brake and larger horizontal tail surfaces, with a notched leading edge, were other external changes.

Less obvious were the new Klimov/Sarkisov RD-33K turbofans, rated at 19,400lb (8,800kg) maximum and 12,125lb (5,500kg) military thrust, which demanded enlarged and modified intakes to handle the greater mass flow. They were equipped with full-authority digital engine control (FADEC) to give optimum perfor-

mance in all flight regimes.

An upgraded radar, the Phazotron N-010 Zhuk, provided ground mapping, improved air-to-air capabilities, including track while scan up to 10 targets, and far better navigation modes. The cockpit was also upgraded; the seat was raised to give a better view over the nose, and two multi-function displays in addition to the HUD were incorporated.

First flown on 25 April 1986 by Valery Menitskiy, the MiG-29M failed to be adopted for service, probably because even better variants were coming along fast.

MiG-29K

Russian ambitions for a "blue-water" navy resulted in the MiG-29K (K = korabelniy = carrier) variant. A strengthened main gear to withstand the no-flare strain of carrier landings, and a beefed-up rear section with a tail hook were needed. Wing area was increased, and wing folding incorporated. A retractable refuelling probe was fitted on the port side of the nose; in all other respects the aircraft was similar to the MiG-29M.

First flown by Takhtar Aubakirov on 23 June 1988, it was used for deck trials in November 1989 on the *Admiral Kuznetsov*, using a ski-jump takeoff. It was however found much inferior to the Su-27 in the carrier fighter role, and was abandoned.

MiG-29SMT

First revealed at Mosaero in 1997, the MiG-29SMT (the T stands for toplivo = fuel) is the latest in the line. Based on the MiG-29S, it has a modern avionics system with large colour liquid crystal displays, and is to a degree compatible with Western avionics systems should they be required. On 22 April 1998, the Russian Air Force announced that 300 MiG-29s would be upgraded

Above: Le Bourget 1989. The MiG-29 is about to hit the ground (centre) while pilot Anatoliy Kvotchur can be seen (left) under his brolly!

to SMT standard, which would give them a credible multi-role capability.

Fulcrum in service

The stuff of myth and legend, Fulcrum has to date seen action with three air arms. In the Gulf War of 1991, five Iraqi MiG-29s were downed by F-15s, four of them with Sparrows. Then in February 1999, two Eritrean MiG-29s were shot down by Ethiopian Su-27s. On that occasion the pilots on both sides spoke Russian! On 24 March of the same year, Yugoslav (Serbian) MiG-29s of the 127th Fighter Aviation Squadron based near Beograd rose to oppose NATO forces in the Kosovo conflict. They were first intercepted by four F-16As of the Netherlands, one of which launched an AIM-120 AMRAAM for the first Dutch aerial victory since World War II. Shortly after, two Fulcrums were downed by USAF F-15s. On the following night, two more MiG-29s were shot down on the Bosnian border by F-15s. The combat record of Fulcrum is therefore 0:12, which is hardly impressive.

At least 1,300 MiG-29s are currently in service, more than half with Russia and the Ukraine. Other users are: Belarus, Bulgaria, Cuba, Eritrea, Germany, Hungary, India, Iran, Kazakhstan, Malaysia, North Korea, Peru, Poland, Romania, Slovakia, Syria, Turkmenistan, Uzbekistan, Yemen, Yugoslavia. The USAF has acquired enough for a complete squadron from Moldavia, which were expected to be used for Aggressor training, but the silence on these has since been deafening.

MiG-31 'Foxhound'

By the early 1970s, a new threat to the Soviet Union was emerging – salvos of cruise missiles at high and low levels, launched by elderly B-52 bombers of the USAF. There was also the Rockwell B-1 to be considered, although whether this would ever enter service was at that time doubtful. The requirement was for a very fast interceptor with long range and endurance, able to destroy small targets far above or well below its own altitude while operating autonomously. This was a tall order.

In accordance with the standard Soviet philosophy of screwing the last ounce of capability from a proven design, the MiG OKB started with the MiG-25. But while this met the high speed, high altitude requirements, it was sadly lacking in other departments. It was too short-legged; was firmly subsonic near the ground; its radar was inadequate for anything but the main task; and its operational philosophy of semi-automatic interception under close ground control reduced the pilot to little more than a systems manager, responsible for takeoff, missile launch, and return to base, while monitoring fuel status and other systems.

More economical engines would, given its huge internal fuel capacity, provide adequate range. Structural modifications could overcome the low-level speed restrictions, but a whole new radar and weapons system with a true look-up/shoot-up, look-down/shoot-down capability was needed. This in turn demanded a specialist operator, for whom space had to be found.

Power

Engine development began in 1972, taking as a base, rather surprisingly, the core of the Soloviev D-30 series of commercial turbofans. The result was the Aviadvigatel D-30F6, which was flight tested on two Ye-155M prototypes.

The D-30F6 is a twin-spool turbofan with a bypass ratio of 0.50. Five LP and 10 HP compressor stages, both driven by two-stage turbines, provide a compression ratio of 21.3:1, forward of the 12 flame cans in the combustion chamber. Much of the construction is titanium alloy, and very sophisticated air cooling is used to offset the maximum turbine entry temperature of 1,660K. But the most remarkable feature is the extremely long afterburner, with its concentric spray rings. One of the primary identification features of the MiG-31 is the extent that the huge nozzles protrude behind the tail.

Using the same high density T-6 fuel as the MiG-25 engines, the D-30F6 produces 34,171lb (15,500kg) maximum and 20,944lb (9,500kg) military thrust. Even more remarkably, specific fuel consumption figures are 1.9 and 0.73lb/lb (kg/kg), respectively; rather better than those of the RD-33 which powers the MiG-29. Engine limiting speed is Mach 2.83, which also defines the maximum aircraft speed at altitude. At sea level it is limited to Mach 1.23, which is still excellent.

Airframe

The Ye-155MP, piloted by Alexsandr Fedotov, first flew on 16 September 1975, but four years of testing were needed before the MiG-31, NATO reporting name Foxhound, entered production. While the basic Foxbat configuration was retained, under the skin it was a very different bird. Whereas the composition by weight of the MiG-25 had been 80 per cent nickel steel, 8 per cent titanium alloy and 11 per cent aluminium alloy, technological advances reduced the steel content to 50 per cent while increasing the titanium content to 16 per cent and the aluminium content to 33 per cent. Excluding the radome and transparencies, composite content was virtually nil. In theory this gave a significant weight saving, but in practice it was more than offset by other changes. Installation of the D-30F6 engines needed considerable modification, including the enlargement of the intakes to handle the increased mass flow. To allow supersonic flight at low level, the wing box was strengthened with a third main spar. Other small tucks and gussets were added, increasing the maximum operating load factor from 4.5g to 5g at supersonic speed. Small leading edge extensions were added to the wing root, and four-piece titanium flaps occupied the whole of the leading edge, while flaps and ailerons took up the entire trailing edge.

The fuselage was lengthened to accommodate the second seat, but did the poor unfortunate backseater have a good view "out of the window"? Oh dear, no; with the exception of a couple of small transparencies on each side his canopy was solid metal, probably as a reminder to keep his mind on his work. Not that the pilot's view was much better; apart from a rear view mirror he had no vision at all past the 3-9 o'clock line, while the canopy above his head was also solid. This last was of course no great problem; if there is one direction in which a pilot of any nationality cannot look while wearing a bone-dome, it is straight up! It must however be stated that at the Mach 2.35 supersonic cruise speed of Foxhound, rearward vision is a luxury rather than a necessity.

To increase range and endurance still more, "wet" fins housed more fuel, bringing the internal maximum fuel weight to a massive 36,035lb (16,350kg). At the same time, a crude and angular flight refuelling probe was fitted on the port side, just ahead of the cockpit.

The fuel system at first caused many problems. In 1979 a brilliant piece of flying allowed a dead-stick landing to be made after fuel starvation took out both engines. Imagine a dead-stick landing in a 46 tonne aircraft with a wing loading of more than 136lb/sq.ft (670kg/m2)! Some feat! Then on 4 April 1984, MiG OKB chief test pilot Alexsandr Fedotov and his

Below: The MiG31 is heavier than the MiG–25, but its overall dimensions are about the same. The plan view shows that the length of the main fuselage has been considerably increased – the tailpipes (which are actually longer than shown) have been extended aft, and the inlets forward – while room has been made for a second cockpit by widening the fuselage.

Left: The MiG-31, NATO reporting name Foxhound, is obviously a descendant of Foxbat, the main differences being the second seat for the weapons systems operator, and the extended nozzles for the Aviavdigatel D-30F6 turbofans.

These drawings were based on early US DoD illustrations, and some details differ from the production aircraft (eg, no solid cockpit portion shown, and shorter nozzles than actual). However, they show an aircraft directly derived from the MiG-25. In detail, the aircraft may differ more substantially from its predecessor, reflecting its lower design speed and greater range.

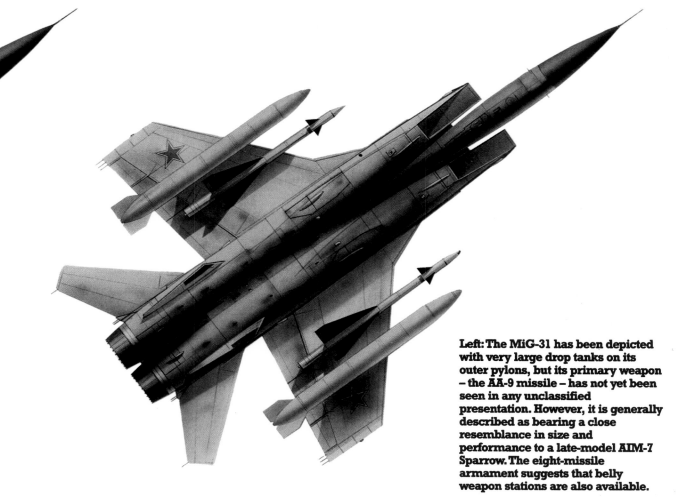

Left: The MiG-31 has been depicted with very large drop tanks on its outer pylons, but its primary weapon – the AA-9 missile – has not yet been seen in any unclassified presentation. However, it is generally described as bearing a close resemblance in size and performance to a late-model AIM-7 Sparrow. The eight-missile armament suggests that belly weapon stations are also available.

backseater Valeriy Zaisev, died in a crash following a total systems failure.

The final major change was a typically Russian solution to a typically Russian problem. Foxhound was even heavier than its predecessor, which caused difficulties in taxying across anything but hardened surfaces. The twin-wheel main gear bogies were so configured that the wheels were offset, thus spreading the load on ground with suspect bearing pressure both longitudinally and laterally. This reduced the chances of it becoming bogged down.

Avionics and weaponry

Foxhound radar was the Phazotron S-800 Zaslon, NATO reporting name Flash Dance. At first thought to have a hydraulically controlled planar array antenna, this was revealed in 1991 as being a fixed phased array antenna, with two-axis electronic beam steering. According to MiG OKB chief designer Rostislav Belyakov, Zaslon has been in service since 1983, the first phased array fighter radar in the world by far.

Believed in the West to operate with old-fashioned phase shifters, by the end of 1999 far outclassed by the latest technology, the S-800 allows tracking of up to 10 targets while providing a simultaneous attack capability against four of them. Search area is 70deg on either side of the boresight line in azimuth, and plus 70deg up and 60deg down in elevation. Russian sources also state that it has an astern search capability, although this is hard to believe, since it would probably involve microwaving the crew! Operational usage envisages four Foxhounds more or less in line abreast,

Above: Foxhound carries four Vympel R-33 (AA-9 Amos) and four R-77 (AA-11 Archer) dogfight missiles. The R-33, the Russian equivalent of the AIM-54 Phoenix, combines inertial midcourse guidance with active radar.

roughly 108nm (200km) apart, all using the radar in search mode, with all in contact via data link. This would cover a frontage of about 486nm (900km), and with an effective range against fighter-sized targets of 108nm (200km), reducing to about 65nm (120km) in look-down mode, would make it difficult for a hostile aircraft or cruise missile to slip past undetected. On detection, flight lead would assign targets to individual Foxhounds in the formation for attack. The much earlier F-14 could launch a simultaneous attack on six targets, although these were limited to a narrow sector of sky. The spread of targets for Zaslon was stated to be much wider, including simultaneous shoot-up and shoot-down. As with all recent Russian fighters, the radar is supplemented by an IRST, in this case retractable and mounted ventrally.

Mikoyan chief test pilot Valeriy Menitsky has categorically stated that this radar has capability against stealth aircraft, but refused to be drawn as to ranges and against which types. The effect of this was rather spoiled when the present writer later questioned the incumbent chief test pilot Roman Taska'ev, who among other things has the distinction of being the first pilot to fly

Foxhound over the North Pole, on the subject. He replied: "How should I know? We have no stealth aircraft against which to test it!" Yet another example of Russian disinformation?

Unlike Foxbat, Foxhound carried an internal cannon – the six-barrelled 23mm GSh-6-23, with 260 rounds, located in a fairing above the starboard wheel well. The main weapon is of course the long range Vympel R-33, NATO reporting name AA-9 Amos. Like its US counterpart, the AIM-54 Phoenix, it uses inertial mid-course guidance, coupled with active radar terminal homing. The same diameter as Phoenix, it is believed to have slightly shorter range. Like its predecessor, Foxhound has virtually no manoeuvre capability for close combat.

Foxhound variants

The first proposed upgrade was the MiG-31M, the prototype of which first flew in 1986. Externally the cockpit was reshaped; the original windshield and quarterlights were replaced by a single curved transparency, but the view from the back seat was reduced to two small clear vision panels. The dorsal spine running aft from the cockpit was deepened and broadened. This allowed internal fuel capacity to be increased to a massive 39,683lb (18,000kg). The depth of the wing fences was reduced, and small tubular pods, presumably holding ECM and communications kit, appeared on the tips. Fin height and rudder area were increased slightly. Digital FBW

flight controls replaced the previous hydraulics.

A bulged radome housed the improved Zaslon M radar, which was stated to double existing detection ranges, giving around 216nm (400km) against an AWACS-sized target, and the definitive weapon was to be the SARH/AR-homing R-37, coupled with Amraamski for medium range work. The original circular tactical information display in the rear cockpit was replaced by three multi-function displays (MFDs), one of which is thought to be a moving map display.

A serious incident during the flight test programme occurred on 9 August 1991. A mechanical aileron control failure resulted in an uncommanded roll to port. Vladimir Gorbunov, a test pilot with the Ministry of Aircraft, managed to hold straight and level flight using full right stick and rudder. But at low speed on the landing approach the situation worsened. With no options left, he went with the roll and, when inverted, pushed into a climb, then pulled when the aircraft came right side up, and used differential engine power to assist control. Gradually he gained height, and once clear of the built-up area he and his back-seater ejected.

The MiG-31M was not adopted for service, almost certainly because the Russian economy had virtually collapsed, making it unaffordable.

Just as the USAF had modified an F-15 to destroy satellites, so the Soviet Union commenced similar trials with the MiG-31. Two aircraft were completed in 1987, and tests continued for several years.

Designated MiG-31/07, this differed from the standard in having endplates on the wingtips, curved leading edge extensions, and only a single underfuselage hardpoint for a large weapon.

First revealed in August 1998 the MiG-31BM was fitted out for the defence suppression mission. Little is known about this except that in addition to its air-to-air armament of R-33s and R-77s, it carried two anti-radiation missiles, a Kh-58 under the starboard wing and a Kh-31P under the port wing.

Foxhound in service

Initial operating capability was first achieved by the 786th Air Defence Fighter Regiment at Pravdinsk in 1983. The breakup of the former Soviet Union and the ensuing financial difficulties caused a cutback in interceptor strength, and currently about 300 are believed to remain in Russian service, with a further 20 in Kazakhstan. By 1996, Foxhound crews averaged a mere 19 hours per year; the accident rate grew while unserviceability meant that barely one fifth were available for operations at any one time. Today, it seems probable that Foxhound has been withdrawn from Russian service, but this has yet to be confirmed.

Below: The Phazotron S-800 Zaslon radar, which entered service with Foxhound in 1983, was the first operational fighter radar in the world with a phased array antenna and electronic beam steering.

Mikoyan 1.42

On 29 February 2000, the Mikoyan 1.42 fighter technology demonstrator lifted off from the runway at Zhukovsky and climbed to about 3,280ft (1,000m). Flown by RSK-MiG chief test pilot Vladimir Gorbunov, it circled twice with its wheels unretracted in the modest speed range of 270-324kt (500-600kmh) before landing after just 18 minutes. It had been delivered to Zhukovsky, and in December 1994 high speed taxi trials were made. Then funding ran out, and it languished on the ground for the next five years. Then late in 1999, the Mikoyan OKB became part of the RSK organization, which is now funding the initial flight testing.

Above: The flattened nose houses a modern phased array radar which is stated to have a multiple target engagement capability.

Below: The 1.42 has a canard delta configuration, and has been stated to be superior to the F-22 in some areas. But this is hard to credit.

A fifth-generation fighter to equal the American F-22 had long been rumoured. Design actually started in 1986, but it was a long time before the 1.42MFI (MultiFunksionalny Istrebitel - multi-role fighter) became visible as flying hardware. In the interim, it has been shielded by disinformation and confusion. The Mikoyan OKB chief Rostislav Belyakov was the source of many outright untruths about this machine, many of which have been perpetuated until the present day.

In 1994, the first, and so far as is known the only, prototype 1.44 was delivered to Zhukovsky. In December of that year, Roman Taska'ev carried out high-speed taxi trials, but without ever lifting the aircraft into the air. Officially, the problem was lack of funding, although it must be noted that this did not prevent Sukhoi from flying the S-37 Berkut (see next section).

At the Paris Air Show in 1997, Ivan Bourtko of MiG-MAPO claimed that the 1.42 had flown, and that it would be demonstrated at Mosaero later that year. It wasn't! But in January 1999 it was revealed to the world, although still firmly on the ground. It was then announced that it would fly in March, and following this, late in 1999. Neither date was met, and its prospects looked poor.

The 1.42 is a canard delta, with the wing in the mid position, and outwardly canted fins mounted on the wings which have moveable ventral surfaces directly below them. Small control surfaces on the wings inboard of the fins appear to act as elevators. The wings have no root extensions, and the canard surfaces, mounted slightly higher, have an inboard dogtooth.

The twin Lyulka AL-41F afterburning turbofan engines are reputed to have a maximum thrust of 40,500lb (18,370kg), and at military power will give super-cruise. The square chin intakes do not look very stealthy, but have serpentine ducts with radar-absorbent coatings. They are of course variable geometry, to allow for speeds well in excess of Mach 2. The nozzles, which are thrust vectoring, are ceramic-coated to reduce IR signature.

Composites are widely used, and the main missile armament is carried internally in a bay between the engines, a radical departure for Russian fighters. Radar is the pulse-Doppler phased array article widely known as the N-014. Stores – bombs, fuel tanks and missiles – can also be carried beneath the wings, albeit at a penalty in stealth.

From close up, the usual Russian "good-enough" finish is apparent, which is not compatible with low observability.

However, the MiG OKB had stated that the 1.42 is to have plasma shielding against hostile radar emissions. So what is plasma shielding? On re-entry, the early space capsules were surrounded by ionized particles, which caused a temporary radio blackout. The Russians are known to have been working for some time to reproduce this effect electronically, although no results have been released. Obviously they cannot afford to cut off the radar emissions and communications of their own aircraft, so the problems seem extreme.

Nor is that all. A leading American expert on stealth has commented that plasma shielding is possible eventually, but not in his lifetime! Also, it will demand a "significant" amount of power to achieve, possibly as much as 25 per cent of engine output. The prospects do not look good.

Russia's Sukhois

Contents

Top: The huge but extremely capable Su-27 Flanker was the first Russian fighter to challenge MiG supremacy.

Above: Speed, agility, range and endurance, coupled with combat persistence provided by first 10, then later 12, AAMs, are the keynotes of the Su-27 Flanker, which is in some ways superior to the F-15.

Above right: One of the two Su-20 Fitters supplied to Germany by the Egyptian Air Force for evaluation. The Su-17/20/22 were variants of the Su-7 with variable-sweep wings.

Left: The Su-24 Fencer was widely held by Western intelligence to be a clone of the American F-111, but this was a misappreciation. In many ways it was much less capable.

Introduction

For decades following the Korean War, MiG was synonymous with Soviet fighter in the West. Of the more famous Soviet design bureaux, Lavochkin, Polikarpov and Petlyakov had lapsed, Ilyushin and Tupolev had moved into the world of heavy aircraft, while Yakovlev had waned into semi-obscurity. From the Western viewpoint, Mikoyan and Gurevitch, with the MiG-15, -17, -19, -21, -23 and -25, was the fighter design OKB. Less apparent was the fact that the OKB of Pavel Sukhoi was designing first class fighter and attack aircraft throughout this period, with a brief interval between 1949 and the death of Stalin in 1953, when the Sukhoi OKB had been closed down following a prototype crash.

One thing was evident: whereas MiG fighters were widely exported, and their deeds in limited wars were equally widely acclaimed, Sukhoi was producing excellent interceptors for home defence, and also attack aircraft. The former failed to enter combat in their designed role, and thus gained no plaudits and glory. The latter were merely bomb trucks, and were overshadowed by the air superiority MiG fighters. The Su-24 Fencer, widely regarded as an F-111 equivalent in the West, gained a certain notoriety, but this was largely the result of a misappreciation by Western intelligence.

The era finally ended with the advent of the superb Su-27 (NATO codename Flanker), which entered service in 1986. For all practical purposes an F-15 Eagle equivalent, and in some areas superior to it, Flanker was the top of the range Russian product, far better than the MiG-29 Fulcrum.

Sukhoi Fighters

Pavel Osipovich Sukhoi was commissioned in 1917, and completed his aerodynamic training after the Civil War. After working on heavy bombers, he set up his own Opytno Konstruktorskoye Byuro (Experimental Construction Bureau – OKB) in 1938. During the Great Patriotic War, his designs were overshadowed by those of Lavochkin, Ilyushin, and Yakovlev. The early post-war period saw the Soviet Union move into the jet age (with an unwarranted amount of help from the British Labour Government of the time, which supplied details and samples of the latest engines). With this, the Sukhoi and Mikoyan and Gurevich (MiG) OKBs moved out of the shadows. But when in 1949 a fighter prototype broke up in mid-air, the Sukhoi OKB was closed down. Not until after the death of Stalin in 1953 could it be reformed, by which time the MiG OKB had established an ascendancy in Soviet fighter design. Many years passed before Sukhoi managed to reverse the trend.

The resurgence of the Sukhoi OKB first became evident at the Aviation Day at Tushino on 24 June 1956, when three prototypes previously unknown in the West were displayed. All were large; all were single-engined. Western intelligence, abetted by Soviet disinformation, became terribly confused, and it was some time before the three were positively identified. At the time, this was par for the course. One was the Su-7, which

was remarkable for the 62deg leading edge sweep of its wing. First flown by A. Kochetkov (on loan from the Lavochkin OKB) on 8 September 1955, this was assigned the NATO reporting name of Fitter. It was the first Soviet aircraft to feature a slab tail and a translating nose cone to optimise pressure recovery at supersonic speeds, even before the MiG-21!

The second was the Su-9, a tailed delta

first flown by V. Makhalin on 26 May 1956, which was assigned the reporting name of Fishpot B. This also had a pitot nose with a moving cone-shaped centrebody.

Below left: Almost identical to the MiG-21 in appearance, the Su-11 all-weather interceptor was a larger aircraft altogether. Used only by PVO-Strany in the air defence role, it saw no active service.

The third, assigned the name Fishpot A, was also a tailed delta, but with a chin inlet surmounted by a large radome. Of the three, only Fishpot A failed to enter

Below: The Su-9 Fishpot B and Su-11 Fishpot C were supplanted in the air defence role by the Su-15 Flagon, seen here carrying two R-98MR AAMs. The "solid" nose allowed a far more capable radar to be carried.

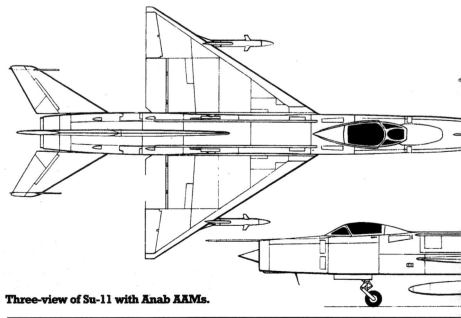

Three-view of Su-11 with Anab AAMs.

Left: An Su-7 streams its braking parachute on landing, framing another Fitter waiting to take off. Short field performance was not good.

The Su-7 Fitter entered service with Frontova Aviatsiya, the Soviet tactical air force, as a dedicated attack aircraft. With two Nudelman-Richter NR-30 cannon installed in the wing roots, and an unimpressive payload/range capability, it was exported to many Soviet-aligned countries. Its sharply swept wing did nothing for short field performance; rotation speed was 194kt(360kmh), and the take-off run was nearly 7,900ft(2,400m) on a hot day, although this could be improved by using rocket-assisted takeoff. It saw action with the Indian Air Force (where its huge size caused it to be dubbed the "Whale") against Pakistan, and with more than one Arab nation against Israel. Iraq is believed to still have a few, as has North Korea, but their operational value is now very dubious.

By contrast the Su-9 Fishpot B was intended as an all-weather interceptor, for which the tailed delta configuration with a 53deg leading edge sweep was then considered optimum. The delta wing had lower supersonic wave drag, which resulted in a slightly higher maximum speed. Designed to the same aerodynamic requirements as the MiG-21, it was however considerably larger. It carried no cannon, and its main armament consisted of four first generation K-5 (NATO reporting name Alkali) radar beam-riding missiles. Radar was the S-band R1L, NATO name Spin Scan.

Fishpot B entered Soviet service in 1959, but like the Su-7 it had a small internal fuel capacity, which for all practical purposes confined it to local area defence. Unlike the Su-7, it had no provision for rocket-assisted takeoff; for home defence it could rely on the availability of large paved runways.

Below right: Despite its size, the Su-7 Fitter had a poor payload/range capability. Known in the Indian Air Force as the "Whale", it could however outfly the MiG-21 at low altitude, although only after 'burner was lit.

production. All were powered by afterburning turbojets designed by Lyul'ka, a teaming that has endured almost unbroken until the present day.

Greatest Russian test pilot
On 4 September 1962, an Su-9 variant known as the T-431 piloted by Vladimir Sergeievitch Ilyushin, son of the famous aircraft designer, reached an absolute altitude of 94,658ft (28,852m). Exactly two months later, Vladimir set new sustained speed/altitude records of 1,305mph/1,133kt/2,100kmh (Mach 1.975) at 69,455ft (21,169m) over a 15.6 mile (25km) course near Zhukovsky.

Major General Ilyushin, as he later became, wears the Hero of the Soviet Union Star. A small leprechaun of a man, with a ready wit, he was quickly promoted to chief test pilot for Sukhoi, in which position he probably made more maiden flights of important (i.e. successful) jet fighters, than any other pilot in the world. He retired as chief test pilot only after making the first flights in both the deeply flawed Su-27 Flanker A, and the outstanding Su-27 Flanker B, to become Deputy Designer-in-Chief of the P.O. Sukhoi machine building factory. A friend of the author, he has contributed greatly to this section.

Further Sukhoi developments
The Soviet Union had a reputation for screwing the last ounce of capability from proven designs. The Su-9 Fishpot B was supplanted by the Su-11 Fishpot C, which first flew in 1961. In appearance almost identical to its predecessor, it was fitted with the more powerful Lyul'ka AL-7F-1 turbojet, which could push it to Mach 2 at altitude. Radar was the X-band Uragan 5B, NATO reporting name Skip Spin, and only two AAMs were carried. These were the far more potent and longer ranged R-98MR and R-98MT, NATO reporting name Anab, with SARH and IR homing, respectively. Neither the Su-9 nor the Su-11 were made available for export. Having been the backbone of the Soviet air defence force for many years, Fishpots were finally retired from service in the 1980s.

Not only was the Fishpot series short-legged, other performance was nothing outstanding, and its radar and armament was inadequate. Something better was badly needed. This duly emerged in the shape of the Su-15, NATO reporting name Flagon.

The first requirement was for a longer ranged and more powerful radar, which in turn demanded a larger antenna. This forced the abandonment of a radar antenna in the translating shock cone in favour of side inlets, which could provide a much larger "radar nose". The need for much greater endurance than its predecessors called for increased fuel capacity, and the result was a twin-engined single-seater.

At the Soviet Aviation Day in 1967, Vladimir Ilyushin demonstrated the new interceptor. A tailed delta like its predecessors, it was the first really effective all-weather air defence fighter produced by the Soviet Union. Powered by two afterburning Tumansky R-13F-300 turbojets, it was theoretically capable of Mach 2.5 and had a service ceiling of 65,600ft (20,000m).

Much of its structure was similar to that of the Su-11. The wing area was small, giving the high wing loading of 108lb/sq.ft (527kg/m²), but for the interception mission, speed, acceleration and rate of climb were much more important than manoeuvrability. Like the contemporary MiG-25, the flight control system was linked to ground control via the autopilot.

Early models carried the Uragan 5B radar, but this was later supplanted by the X-band Twin Scan, with a maximum range of about 30nm (56km). Four AAMs, generally the R-98MR and R-98MT Anab, were routinely carried, although in the later stages two R-23R Apexes or two Molniya R-60 Aphids replaced two Anabs. Very much a "hot ship", Flagon was reported to be very responsive to the controls, although unforgiving if mis-

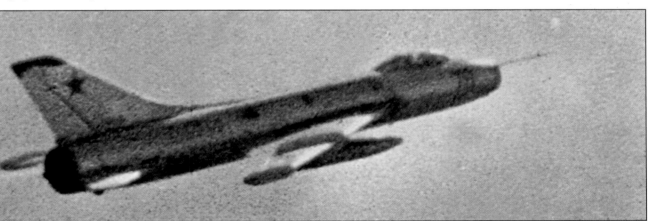

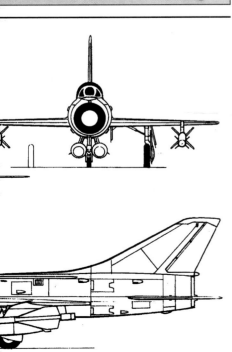

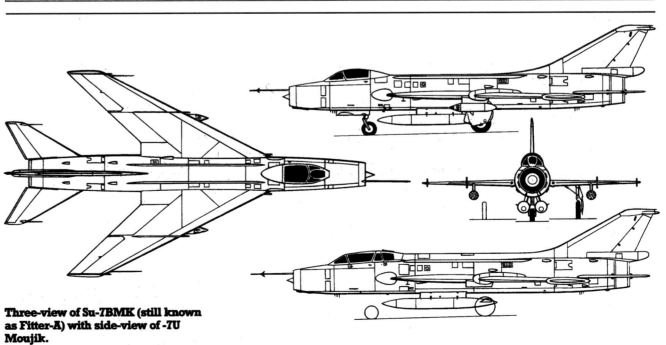

Three-view of Su-7BMK (still known as Fitter-A) with side-view of -7U Moujik.

Left: An Su-20 Fitter of the Polish Air Force is seen here with inlet spill doors fully open for takeoff. The variable-sweep wing section is set well outboard, while the only stores visible are external tanks.

Right: This almost plan view shows the Su-17 at minimum sweep angle, with drop tanks carried just inboard of the pivot, unfortunately masking its rather clumsy join. As can be seen, the wing pivots well outboard.

handled. In this it was similar to the American F-104 Starfighter. It was also reported to use flap-blowing, also like the American fighter. The approach speed of 216kt (400kmh) was very high, and called for precise judgement on landing, while a similar rotation speed needed a long takeoff run.

A later variant had increased wing area, produced by the simple expedient of reducing leading edge sweep outboard while retaining the same span, to give a cranked delta configuration. This became the Su-21 Flagon, with improved handling. Like most fast jets, Flagon had a two-seater combat training version, at a small penalty in internal fuel capacity. Viktor Belenko flew the Su-15/21 prior to defecting in the MiG-25 Foxbat.

The main reason why Sukhoi air defence fighters remained in the shadow of their MiG counterparts was that they were never exported. Therefore they had no opportunity to distinguish themselves in combat. Flagon did however become infamous for shooting down two Korean airliners, the first near Murmansk in 1978. Hit by three bursts of cannon fire, it made a wheels-up landing on a frozen lake, with one passenger dead and others injured. The other was the ill-fated Flight KAL 007 which strayed over Sakhalin; it was destroyed by a missile with great loss of life, an incident that incurred the condemnation of the world. Flagon began to be replaced by the Su-27 Flanker during the 1980s, but a few remained in service as late as 1993.

The Fitter series
The Su-7 Fitter A previously mentioned was an enormous attack aircraft, the nearest Western equivalent of which was the Republic F-105 Thunderchief, although the Russian fighter had no internal weapons bay. It was tailored around a huge Lyul'ka afterburning turbojet, one

Below left: A Polish Air Force Su-20 thunders down the runway on takeoff, its wings at minimum sweep. The Su-20/22 were export versions; the Frontal Aviation aircraft was the "full-up" Su-17.

of the operational problems of which was that the afterburner took 6-7 seconds to light, a disadvantage in a combat emergency.

As previously noted, short-field performance and payload/ range were poor. The former was largely due to the wing design, the exceptionally sharp (62deg) sweep of which needed a heavy structure and developed maximum lift at an excessive angle of attack, while the relatively small area gave a high wing loading. Although available, rocket-assisted takeoff was prodigal of scarce resources, and aggravated the logistics problems of forward basing. Yet contemporary Soviet doctrine demanded that attack aircraft operate from semi-prepared airfields.

The simplest answer to this requirement was the use of a variable-sweep wing, which by reducing takeoff speed and approach speed on landing meant that less runway was need from which to operate. Whereas the Americans made full use of variable sweep to enhance performance and to increase manoeuvrability, the Russians used it almost entirely for a combination of short field performance and high speed.

While in the West the Su-7 was widely regarded as a turkey, it had virtues of its own. At low level, it could out-accelerate even the MiG-21 and, unlike the latter, it was supersonic at low altitude in clean condition, and climbed "like a rocket". It was also very stable in a low-level attack run, unlike the MiG-21. Stall was benign, marked only by an increasing sink rate, while spin recovery was easy. Also it was very resistant to battle damage. Given these strengths, the Su-7 was considered worthy of further development.

To avoid major modifications, the wing pivots were set well outboard, rather further than the optimum position, but this was dictated by the location of the main gear mountings. It had however the

Below: This is the Ly'ulka-engined Su-17U Fitter G two-seate trainer, with an enlarged vertical fin and ventral strake. The instructor pilot in the rear seat has raised his periscope for takeoff.

advantage that the change of trim with wing sweep angle was minimized. The fixed inboard section retained the single-slotted trailing edge flaps; the movable outboard trailing edge section consisted of single-slotted flaps with ailerons outboard. The junction of fixed/moving wing was marked by a large fence, with a smaller fence inboard of it. Pretty it was not, but it worked.

The first flight of technology demonstrator S-22I, with Vladimir Ilyushin at the controls, took place on 2 August 1966. This became the Su-17 Fitter B, powered by the AL-7F1-250 turbojet. The first production aircraft appeared in 1968. Weapon load was 6,614lb (3,000kg), with 6,173lb (2,800kg) of internal fuel. Short field performance and payload/range were improved a little, even though weight had increased.

Fitter B was followed in 1972 by the Su-17M Fitter C, the first mass-produced version, powered by the AL-21F-3 turbojet, which gave 17 per cent more thrust. Weapons load was increased to 8,818lb (4,000kg), and internal fuel to 8,003lb (3,630kg) to give a much more credible operational capability. It was the same old story: if performance is improved, the aircraft can obviously carry more!

The Su-17M was followed by the Su-20, an export ("monkey") version, with downgraded avionics and weapons capability. Another export variant was

the Su-22, powered by the Tumansky R-29B-300 turbojet. Nav/attack avionics were fairly basic in Fitter C; it was followed into Soviet service by the Su-17M2 Fitter D, which was produced between 1975-79. This had a slightly longer nose, with a Fon-1400 laser ranger in the shock cone, a DISS-7 Doppler navigation radar, and an improved gunsight. In all, 15 variants appeared before production ceased in 1990, including two two-seater combat trainers. The most advanced of all was the Su-17M4 Fitter K, the export version of which was the Su-22M4.

Typical weapons include the laser-guided Kh-25ML Karen and its radio command-guided Kh-25MR variant; the laser-guided Kh-29L Kedge and its Kh-29T TV-guided counterpart; and the Kh-25MP Kegler anti-radiation missile. Unguided bombs and rockets, and SPPU-22-01 gun pods can also be carried. Interestingly two of the latter can be mounted to fire rearwards. This would have two purposes: to distract ground defences after the aircraft has overflown them, and just possibly for convoy strafing. No details of the sighting system have been released for this mode. Internal guns are two NR-30 cannon as for the Su-7, although for two-seater combat trainers one of these is omitted. For self-defence against fighters, two R-60 Aphids could be carried on swivelling pylons beneath the underwing panels.

Other external stores include the KKR-1 reconnaissance pod, with three cameras and a flare dispenser, with electronic warfare kit in later versions. Guidance pods are needed for various smart weapons, and drop tanks are required to supplement the meagre internal fuel fraction of 0.23. Flight refuelling is not an option, although this has been proposed as an upgrade.

Fitters in action
The combat debut of the Su-7 came in the Arab-Israeli Six Day War in 1967. Mainly in Egyptian service, it achieved little. Over the next seven years it did not much more than provide targets for the Israelis. Top-scoring Israeli ace Giora Epstein claimed an Su-7 on 7 June 1967. He downed another Su-7 with cannon fire during the War of Attrition, and two more with Shafrir AAMs on 18 October 1973, then two Su-20s later that afternoon, the fifth and sixth of his eventual 17 victories. The Fitter did prove it could bite back, however. In the Indo/Pakistan War of December 1971, the PAF claimed a total of 15 Indian Fitters shot down; the IAF counterclaimed that no Fitters were lost, although several were damaged. While most missions flown were in support of the ground forces, "Mad Mally"

Malhotra of No 32 Squadron turned on an intercepting PAF F-6 (MiG-19) with cannon fire. The PAF later admitted the loss of an F-6 on this day.

Fitters next became the object of world attention on 19 August 1981, when two Libyan Air Force Su-22s intercepted two F-14 Tomcats of the US Navy over the Gulf of Sidra. It was no contest, even though one of the Su-22s launched the first missile. Within less than a minute, Sidewinders had accounted for both Fitters.

The most recent adventures of the Su-7/17/20/22 family took place during the Gulf War of 1991. Their ground attack role notwithstanding, four Fitters, actual type not ascertained, were downed by Sparrows launched from F-15s on 7 February 1991. These victories were followed by two more Su-22s downed by Sidewinders on 20 and 22 March, respectively. In all, 44 Su-20/22s are believed to have defected to Iran during the conflict.

Fitters were phased out of Russian service in the mid-1990s but about 550 remain in service with 15 air forces. This has spawned a lively market for upgrades. The Su-22M5 is on offer with a "glass cockpit" and HOTAS, and a mix of Russian and French technology. If adopted, this will give Fitters a credible air-to-air capability for the first time. Currently the shock cone in the nose houses a Klon-54 laser rangefinder. This would be replaced by the Phathom radar, jointly developed by Phazotron and Thomson-CSF. Although believed to have limited performance by modern standards, and certainly the antenna must be small to fit the shock cone, it will allow the use of BVR missiles. A helmet-mounted sight is another possibility.

Fitters currently serve with Afghanistan, Azerbaijan, Bulgaria, the Czech Republic, Iran (with the Revolutionary Guard), Iraq, Libya, North Korea, Peru, Poland, Slovakia, Syria, Turkmenistan, Uzbekistan, Vietnam, and Yemen.

Above left: Seen here launching an AS-7 Kerry beam-riding air-to-ground missile, the scoop intake at the base of the fin identifies this as the Su-17M4 Fitter K, first seen by the West in late 1984.

Below left: Strolling out to their aircraft prior to an exercise, the pilots give scale to this very big fighter. Blue 71 and the aircraft behind it are two-seaters. The air sensor boom is extremely strong.

Above: A Libyan Arab Air Force Su-22 seen here with supersonic drop tanks and K-13 heat-seeking AAMs. Two of these tangled with USN Tomcats over the Gulf of Sidra in 1981; both were shot down by AIM-9 Sidewinders.

Below: The leader of this formation of Polish Su-22M4 Fitter Ks peels off, exposing its large wing glove and awkward-looking junction. For such a limited design, it is remarkable that upgrades are proposed.

Sukhoi Su-24 'Fencer'

The Soviet Union has often been accused of copying Western ideas. The truth was more prosaic. Tactical thinking on both sides of the Iron Curtain often tended to follow similar lines, with the result that approximately similar aircraft emerged from the process. It must however be stated that the openness of Western society meant that in most cases the USSR knew what was projected at quite an early stage, and could evaluate, borrow and counter Western ideas.

When the existence of the Su-24, given the NATO reporting name of Fencer, was first revealed, at first Western commentators tended to dismiss it as a clone of the General Dynamics F-111, which it lagged by about five years. The two aircraft were in fact quite similar: twin engines; variable sweep wings; and a two-man crew side by side.

Their respective origins were however quite different. The F-111 was originally intended to be an all-singing, all-dancing multi-role aircraft, as capable as an interceptor and a carrier-borne fleet air defence fighter as a low level penetrator and interdictor. It was to utilize the very latest "state of the art" technology.

By contrast, the 1961 requirement which resulted in the Su-24 was comparatively modest. It was to replace the elderly and firmly subsonic Ilyushin Il-28 and Yakovlev Yak-28 tactical bombers with a supersonic low level penetrator, capable of a five minute dash "under the radar" at 650ft (200m) at Mach 1.14. Specifically, it was expected to be developed from the Su-7.

Early Western intelligence appreciations considered Fencer to be smaller than the General Dynamics aircraft; in fact it was slightly larger and heavier. Given the size and weight of both, it was inevitable that they should be twin-engined. Variable sweep wings? These entered widespread use among Russian aircraft over the next few years, unlike the

USA, which had just two. It is of course just possible that the side-by-side seating layout was influenced by the F-111, but it would hardly have been possible without a huge radome, which naturally influences the width of the forward fuselage. Of course, such a layout actually aids crew co-operation, while helping to reduce fuselage length, but most fast jet pilots like to have an all-round view "out of the window". On balance this may have been a mistake.

As the record shows, the F-111 was an unmitigated disaster as an interceptor and as a carrier fighter, and was ordered solely as a tactical interdictor and, in its FB-111 variant, a strategic penetrator. Even then its early record was troubled.

Below: An early artist's impression of the Su-24 Fencer released by the Department of Defense. Wings are at medium sweep, and all in all, this portrayal is remarkably accurate.

Many problems arose from the very advanced technology used, which in some cases was insufficiently mature.

Fencer development

Initial progress was slow, and not until August 1965 was an official order placed for a prototype. At that time, vertical lift was regarded as a possible way of solving the short field performance problem, and this solution was experimented with using an Su-15 with three lift engines

Above: Another Department of Defense artist's impression, showing the near simultaneous launch of two large AAMs, probably the AA-5 Ash. However, this was never carried.

mounted amidships. This was promptly assigned the reporting name of Flagon B, although it never entered service. This gave a short rolling takeoff, and results were apparently good enough for it to be publically demonstrated at Domodedovo in 1967, which showed official confidence in the concept.

The prototype T6-1 was delta winged, as was the almost exactly contemporary British TSR.2, designed for much the same mission, but later cancelled. The T6-1 had

Below: Shown here for comparison, two F-111As of the 430th TFS, 474th TFW, over the Nevada desert. While the similarities are obvious, the differences are much less so.

four Koliesov lift engines in the fuselage. On 2 July 1967, it was flown for the first time by Vladimir Ilyushin (who else?).

Lift engines were all very well, but they occupied too much volume and added far too much weight, reducing the payload/range equation. The compromise solution, as with the later Fitters, was variable sweep, with high aspect ratio to reduce takeoff and landing speeds, and also to provide economical cruising, and low aspect ratio for high speed and high

acceleration. This was combined with high wing loading which gave low gust response at low altitudes. Sukhoi test pilot Eugeny Frolov commented to the author that the high wing loading made Fencer the most difficult to handle of all the Sukhoi fast jets.

Be that as it may, Sukhoi were able to design a "proper" variable-sweep wing, with pivots in the optimum position and control surfaces to suit. This was a huge stride after the lash-up used for the Su-17 family, although it was not a Soviet "first". The variable-sweep MiG-23 had already flown on 10 April 1967.

Some 30 months passed before the new Sukhoi, the T6-2IG (*Izmeyaemaya Geometriya* – variable geometry), fol-

lowed the T6-1 into the air on 17 January 1970, with the same pilot, Ilyushin, at the controls. Four leading edge sweep angles were provided: 16deg, giving an aspect ratio of 5.64 for takeoff, landing, and economical cruise; 35deg and 45deg intermediate settings; and 69deg, giving an aspect ratio of 2.11 and low gust response for high performance flight.

Misappreciations

As was so often the case, Western intelligence overestimated the performance of Fencer, assuming that it had been built to Western standards, and was for all practical purposes an F-111 clone. To make matters worse, they misidentified it as the Su-19! V_{max} at high level was stated as

Mach 2.18, whereas in fact it was a comparatively pedestrian Mach 1.35. V_{max} at low level was given as Mach 1.2, which was almost correct. But both of these figures were for the clean condition; no combat aircraft in those days ever flew clean – there was no point in charging around the sky with no ordnance! Take for example the F-111: fully laden it was firmly subsonic, while its operational ceiling was barely 15,000ft (4,572m). Much the same restrictions applied to the Su-24!

Another misappreciation was that the Soviet Union had developed economical turbofans, but this was not the case. Fencer was actually powered by two Saturn/Lyulka AL-21F-3 turbojets, which made a nonsense of Western payload/range calculations; at low level, on internal fuel only, the operational radius of Fencer was a mere 216nm (400km), rising to 302nm (560km) with drop tanks. But this notwithstanding, Fencer was regarded as a major threat by the West, mainly due to its low-level penetration capability.

Fencer details

The Su-24 has a rectangular fuselage, fronted by a large radome. Side inlets with fixed ramps feed the engines. Early production models featured variable ramps, which naturally caused the West to seriously miscalculate maximum speed.

The shoulder-mounted wing gloves are swept at 69deg, with the main moving part of the wing able to vary between this and a minimum sweep of 16deg, which keeps the approach speed to a moderate 124kt (230kmh). Aspect ratio varies between 2.11 and 5.64. Four section retractable slats occupy the whole of the leading edge (three-section in later models), with two-piece double-slotted flaps on the trailing edge, amended to three-piece flaps on later aircraft.

Two intermediate wing sweep settings are used: 35deg for subsonic cruise, and 45deg for maximum agility, not that the Su-24 could ever have been very agile in the fighter combat sense, with a combat wing loading in the region of 133lb/ft2 (650kg/m2), but it had to be able to line up on target very quickly.

Its wings have no ailerons; roll control is provided by differentially moving stabilators, supplemented at low speeds by spoilers on the upper wing surfaces, which can "dump" lift as required. These can also be used to reduce the landing run. The slim fin and rudder assembly is supplemented by two fixed ventral strakes. In accordance with Russian practice for tactical aircraft, twin-wheel main gears with low pressure tyres are used to give a rough-field capability. These retract forward into the lower part of the fuselage behind the intake ducts, turning through 90deg to lie flat. The forward sections of the main gear doors also double as speed brakes. The nose leg also has a double wheel, although this retracts aft, and is fitted with what is most easily described as a mudguard to prevent stones and other debris being sprayed up into the intakes.

The large radome houses separate attack and terrain-following radars. These are the Orion-A air-to-surface radar, with a maximum range of 81nm (150km), and the Relyef terrain-following radar, the latter linked to the flight control system.

Left middle: From Fencer B onwards the rear fuselage exhaust shrouds were re-profiled to a more rounded shape, and a much larger braking parachute housing was fitted.

Left: One of the first pictures of the Su-24M, (Fencer D), covertly taken in East Germany. From this angle the main difference is the lengthened and reshaped radome.

Vladimir Ilyushin commented to the writer that this was rather better than the kit carried by the F-111! Relayed to Neil Anderson, who had done much of the test flying of the F-111 TFR system, including hair-raising trips down the Grand Canyon at night, this drew the comment: "Well, it ought to be.... It was a much later system than we had!"

Other internal nav/attack systems are the DISS-7 Doppler navigation radar; the Kaira-24 laser/TV sighting system; and short and long range radio navigation aids. Various other items are carried in pod form, of which more later. The whole has eventually become integrated as the PNS-24MK Tigre, which enables the aircraft to automatically fly a pre-programmed route and deliver its ordnance accurately on target. Had the operational radius of Fencer been what the Western analysts had calculated, it would have been a formidable aircraft indeed.

The cockpit is roomy, although less so than the F-111, but the displays are strictly "steam-gauge" dials. Initially the ejection seats were the limited KM-1M, but were soon replaced by the Zvezda zero/zero K-36M, then the rocket-boosted K-36D, which has not only since become standard on Russian aircraft, but has attracted interest from the USAF.

Service and variants

The Su-24 was officially commissioned into the Soviet Air Force in February 1975, having attained initial operational capability during the previous year. Early examples had no integrated self-protection system; instead they relied on Sirena, and later Beryoza, radar warning systems.

The first flight of the Su-24M, Fencer D, which had fixed inlets and a fence on the wing glove, took place on 24 June 1977. It carried new smart weapons, a new integrated nav/attack system, and the BKO-2 integrated self-protection system, comprising the Beryoza RWR, Mak IR missile launch warner, and the SPS-162 Geran active response jammer, together with APP-50A chaff/flare dispensers.

The Su-24M has a fuselage lengthened by 29.5in (75cm), and has provision for flight refuelling. Production examples started to leave the factory in the summer of 1979. The export version is the Su-24MK (K = Kommercheskiy – commercial), which has minor differences in the communications and IFF kit. It also lacks the wing glove fences, and in most cases, IFR.

Flight refuelling greatly increases payload/range capability since it allows takeoff with reduced fuel and more ordnance, topping up from a tanker once airborne. The Russians are not noted for their tanker fleet, but Fencer has a buddy/buddy capability. The main problem with this is that it halves the number of strike aircraft available.

Next on the scene was the Su-24MR Fencer E, a dedicated reconnaissance variant. This retains the Relyef terrain-following radar, but the Shtyk side-looking radar has replaced the Orion. Kaira-24 has been replaced by the AP-402A panoramic camera, and the Aist-M TV camera and Zima IR scanner have been installed under the fuselage. Other equipment is carried in pods – the Shpil-2M laser or Tangazh Elint, and the Efir-1M radar reconnaissance system. The Su-24MR has no attack capability; it carries two R-60 Aphid AAMs for self-defence.

The final Fencer, the Su-24MP Fencer F, is an EW variant distinguished by a narrow longitudinal fairing under the nose. This carries a comprehensive EW suite, part internally and the rest in pods. The Russian equivalent of the EF-111, only eight Su-24MP aircraft were built, serving with the 118th EW Regiment. The fact that so few were built indicates that it was probably not a success.

Fencer made its combat debut on 21 April 1984, when it made medium-level attacks (about 18,045ft/5,500m) on Afghan rebels. Results in this and subsequent attacks were inconclusive. No losses were incurred, but in more recent times at least one has fallen to Chechen ground fire.

Ordnance

Fencer D has eight hardpoints – four beneath the fuselage, one each beneath the wing gloves, and one each swivelling under the outboard wing sections, with a maximum capacity of 17,637lb (8,000kg) for Fencer D. A six-barrel 23mm cannon, the GSh-6-23 with 500 rounds, is carried internally in the starboard fuselage.

In its strike role it carries TN-1000 and TN-1200 tactical nuclear weapons. The full range of dumb bombs and CBUs has been cleared for use, while the anti-radiation Kh-58U Kilter, Kh-25MP Kegler, Kh-31P Krypton and many other smart weapons, including the Kh-59 Kazoo, are all in the Su-24 inventory.

Nearly 900 Fencers serve with various air forces, about half with what was originally the Russian *Frontova Aviatsiya* (Frontal Aviation), although it is gradually being phased out in favour of the Sukhoi Su-30. Other users are: Algeria, Azerbaijan, Belarus, Iran (with 24 ex-Iraqi Su-24s); Khazakstan, Libya, Russia *(Aviatsiya Voenno-Morskogo Flota* – Naval Aviation); Syria; Ukraine (the second largest user with about 230 aircraft); and Uzbekistan.

Left top: The Su-24 Fencer C can be distinguished from Fencer B by the larger square-topped fin with an EW aerial on the tip. Other EW aerials are located the intake sides.

Below: If photographs of this poor quality were all the DoD had to go on at the time, it is little wonder that serious misappreciations were made by Western intelligence.

Below middle: Fencer C flying in clean condition. From this angle, the EW aerial pods on the intake sides are clearly visible, just ahead of the wing glove root.

Bottom: Large wing fences at the junction between glove and wing proper mark this as an early Su-24M. Another identification feature is the ventral EO sensor housing.

Su-25 'Frogfoot'

Once again we have a direct comparison with an American aircraft; the Su-25 Frogfoot, familiarly known in its own service as the Grach (Rook), was designed for much the same close air support and the anti-armour role as was the American Warthog, otherwise known as the Fairchild Republic A-10A Thunderbolt II, although as we shall see, operational priorities differed considerably.

Russia has a tradition of producing heavily armoured ground attack aircraft, notably the Ilyushin Il-2 and Il-2m3 Shturmovik in the Great Patriotic War. These were notoriously difficult to shoot down. On many occasions they survived multiple attacks by German fighters, and although damaged, returned to base. Survivability was the keynote.

The *Luftwaffe* responded with two dedicated attack aircraft, the Henschel Hs 129 tank destroyer, and the Ju 87G, which was armed with two 37mm gun pods. By contrast, the Western Allies used two main fighter types, neither of them terribly suitable for the task, in the close air support role – the American P-47 Thunderbolt and the British Typhoon. Both relied on sheer speed to survive; neither armour nor survivability was a factor.

After World War II, the concept of a survivable close air support aircraft fell into abeyance. Not until more than two decades later, during the Vietnam conflict, was it revived. How this resulted in the A-10A we have already seen. With the US project underway, the Soviet Union started to con-

sider a similar concept. Like the USA, they commissioned prototypes from two design bureaux, Sukhoi and Ilyushin, to be evaluated against each other.

Ilyushin produced the Il-102, a large, twin-engined, low-wing machine with, amazingly, a gun turret in the tail remotely controlled from what can only be described as a semi-submerged "mid- upper" position similar to that of the Bristol Beaufort. Unseen by the West until 1992, its appearance gave rise to speculation that the Ilyushin OKB had drawn heavily on the Il-40, NATO reporting name Brawny, of early 1950s vintage. Little is known about the Il-102 except that it was powered by fighter-type turbofans, probably RD-33s, and was approximately 50 per cent heavier than its Sukhoi rival. The Il-40 had failed to enter service, and the Il-102 followed its predecessor into oblivion, the most likely reason for which was that it was simply far too costly.

With commendable foresight, the Sukhoi OKB had in fact commenced design studies a year or more before the requirement that

led to Frogfoot was issued. They thus had a head start over their rivals. Also, Soviet requirements differed appreciably from those of the USA. They were more concerned with close air support than with tank-busting; therefore the lack of a monster cannon was less serious. Frogfoot carries a non-standard twin-barrel 30mm GSh-2-30 cannon with a mere 250 rounds. It is non-standard in that its installed weight is almost double that of the usual fighter weapon, which implies a very high muzzle velocity with perhaps a non-standard round.

Another major difference was the utility or otherwise of long loiter time or extended range. With no economical turbofan available, Sukhoi settled for what they had. The prototypes were powered by two RD-9 tur-

Below: Czechoslovakia was the first export customer for Frogfoot, back in 1985. On the partition of the country into the Czech Republic and Slovakia, the surviving Su-25Ks and two-seat UBKs were shared.

bojets, replaced in production models by two Tumansky-Gavrilov R-95Sh turbojets, non-afterburning variants of the R-13-300 used to power the MiG-21. Unlike the Warthog, these were mounted closely on each side of the fuselage. Internal fuel capacity was less than two-thirds that of the American aircraft, while with no long oversea deployments envisaged no flight refuelling probe was fitted.

Frogfoot development
The first flight of the Su-25 took place on 22 February 1975, inevitably with Vladimir Ilyushin at the controls. In appearance it was very similar to the Northrop A-9, the loser in the American AX competition. This was of course a classic example of similar require-

Bottom: The export model Su-25 is the K, seen here in Czechoslovak markings. The wingtip pod is in fact a split "crocodile-type" speed brake designed to hold the speed constant in a diving attack.

ments resulting in similar solutions. Whereas the twin fins and rudders of the A-10 were seen as a significant advance in survivability, the single fin unit of the Su-25 featured a two-section rudder, giving a measure of redundancy.

The only major change to the prototypes, apart from the new engine type, was a larger wing, with the aspect ratio enlarged from 5 to 6.85, slightly more than that of the Warthog, which was probably undertaken to improve sustained turning. The state acceptance trials ran from 26 April 1978 to 30 December 1980, including a two-aircraft deployment to Shinand in Afghanistan between 16 April and 5 June 1980, and production began in earnest. The first unit to become operational on type was the 200th

Below: Frogfoot carries all its external stores on underwing pylons, eight of which can be seen here, as can the high aspect ratio wing. Optimised for manoeuvrability, the leading edge sweep angle is modest.

Independent Attack Air Flight, based at Sital-chai in Azerbaijan.

Frogfoot details

The Frogfoot (also known as *Grach* = Rook) is dimensionally rather smaller than the Warthog, but surprisingly, when one considers the weight of the gigantic Avenger cannon carried by the American aircraft, its empty weight is only marginally (3 per cent) less. This appears to indicate that it is stuffed rather fuller with kit than is the Warthog, with a commensurate increase in vulnerability. It is difficult to imagine that its armour protection would be sufficiently heavier than that of the American aircraft as to account for the difference. The Warthog, with its accent on redundancy is, as World War II fighter ace Jim Lacey once described the Hurricane, a collection of non-essential parts. The Su-25 does not approach this to the same degree.

The shoulder-mounted wing of the Grach is long and slender. It is swept at just under 20deg, and features a dogtooth. The entire

Left: The Sukhoi Su-25 Frogfoot A is to a degree the Russian equivalent of the American A-10A Warthog, but with close air support rather than tankbusting a priority its design is very different.

leading edge is occupied by five-section leading edge slats. The straight trailing edge has two-section flaps inboard on each side, with ailerons outboard. Compared to the A-10, the wing area is 35 per cent less, giving a significantly higher wing loading at normal takeoff weight and combat weight, although aspect ratio is marginally higher.

Pods on the wingtips contain hydraulically operated split speed brakes at the rear, which open automatically at the optimum attack speed of 372kt (690kmh). The pods also contain retractable landing lights, and SPO-15 radar homing and warning system antennae, together with navigation lights.

Installed power for the production Rook is marginally more than that of the Warthog, giving a lower power loading, essential for low-level manoeuvrability. The Rook is also nearly a third faster than the A-10A at ground level, which adds considerably to its survivability. Internal fuel is more than 50 per cent less, and while Frogfoot has never even begun to approach the loiter time of the A-10, in accordance with Soviet combat doctrine this is not important. Service ceiling is also much lower, but for a close air support aircraft this hardly matters.

Like its American counterpart, the Su-25 has its cockpit enclosed in a titanium "bathtub". Instrumentation comprises old-fashioned "steam-gauge" dials. Other protection is extensive: the engines are enclosed in stainless steel bays, steel armour panels are used to protect the fuel tank bay, while a hinged armoured panel protects the pilot's head in the event of an attack from astern.

Like all modern combat aircraft, Frogfoot is a "foam jet", its fuel tanks filled with reticulated polyurethane foam which, while it marginally reduces capacity, greatly reduces the chance of an explosion when hit and penetrated by hostile fire. Control runs are hydraulically operated rods rather than the cables preferred on the A-10.

Frogfoot in service

Forward basing was an essential part of Soviet philosophy, and Frogfoot was designed to "stand alone" for several days on semi-prepared airfields. For this it carries four pods in a special package of spares and replenishments, etc. This does not however relieve it of servicing requirements, and technical personnel have to be on hand. A major difference with the USAF is that whereas their crew chiefs are senior NCOs, in Russia they are all commissioned officers. This is widely regarded as a protective measure against the pernicious influence of vodka among NCOs and other ranks.

Frogfoot was first seen in the West at the Paris Air Show in 1989, flown by Oleg Tsoi and Anatoly Ivanov, the latter in the two-seater Su-25UT. The display consisted mainly of rather gentle vertical manoeuvres, with limited throttle movement, possibly because throttle "slams" were not permitted. According to Eugeny Frolov, Frogfoot is extremely easy to handle, and in fact the two-seater trainer variant did not fly until 6 August 1987, more than 12 years after the first flight of the prototype. Almost certainly the two-seater was developed to aid export sales to Third World nations with little or no jet experience.

The former Soviet Union was a landlocked empire surrounded by potential enemies. One of the greatest threats was the US Navy, which was able to project air power

anywhere in the world at short notice. To counter this, the Soviet Navy started to build a "blue-water" fleet, with aircraft carriers. Like the Germans before them, they were obliged to use carrier aircraft converted from standard land-based types. The *Hindenburg* was to carry navalized Bf-109 fighters and navalized Ju-87 Stukas. Similarly, the Russian carrier *Tbilisi*, later renamed *Admiral Kuznetsov*, was to carry either MiG-29 Fulcrums or Su-27 Flankers for fleet air defence, and the Su-25 Frogfoot for attack. The two-seater seen at Paris carried an arrester hook, presumably for carrier operations; on 1 November of that year the first Frogfoot landed on *Admiral Kuznetsov*.

The obvious question is, how would the Su-25 have fared in the carrier strike role? The obvious answer is, not very well; it was too slow, and far from sufficiently stealthy. It could only have been effective in covering sea-borne landings against Third World powers, a scenario where the Soviet Navy had no experience.

Tankbuster

The Sukhoi Su-25T, first flown on 17 August 1984 by Alexander Isakov, is an anti-armour export variant. It features the Voshkod nav/attack system, with night capability, and the I-251 optical tracking system. It is anticipated that this variant will act as lead aircraft for formations of Su-25Ks. It carries up to 8,818lb (4,000kg) of ordnance, the main part of which is 16 Vikhr anti-tank missiles, and has significantly more internal fuel than the standard Frogfoot. It also has a vastly improved self-protection system.

The combat debut of the Su-25 came in Afghanistan on 18 June 1981, when the 200th Independent Attack Air Flight was deployed to Shinand. Against the Muhajideen it was relatively ineffective, as the USAF had found with fast-mover jets when operating against the Viet Cong.

Several Su-25s were lost to US-made Stinger missiles during the conflict, and more to Pakistan Air Force F-16s following border violations. The fact is that the Frogfoot was being used for counter-insurgency operations for which it was not designed, nor entirely suitable.

Iraq also used the Su-25 in the Gulf War of 1991, although "used" is hardly the right word. While they were never sent into action, seven are believed to have arrived in Iran, while two were shot down by F-15s using Sidewinders while en route, on 6 February 1991. Since then the Frogfoot has also been used against Chechnya, where further losses have been sustained.

More than 600 Su-25s are currently in service, operated by Algeria, Angola, Armenia, Azerbaijan, Belarus, Bulgaria, Czech Republic, Eritrea possibly, Georgia, Iraq, Kyrgystan possibly, North Korea, Peru, Russia, Slovakia, Tajikistan, Turkmenistan, Ukraine, and Uzbekistan.

Left: The Klon-PS laser rangefinder and target designator can be seen in the nose, as can the muzzle of the 30mm GSh-2-30 cannon.

Right: The Frogfoot is stated to be very easy to fly and conversion to type poses no problems. There is however a two-seat combat trainer.

Below: The modified contours of the nose, together with the new shapes beneath the fin, mark this as the Su-25TM, a dedicated anti-armour machine. The missile is an R-60.

Below right: Frogfoot losses over Afghanistan resulted in extensive survivability measures being taken, but despite this, further losses have ensued over Chechnya.

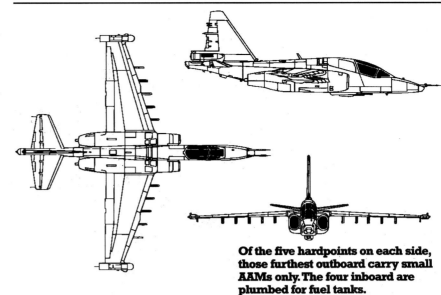

Of the five hardpoints on each side, those furthest outboard carry small AAMs only. The four inboard are plumbed for fuel tanks.

The Flanker

The keynote of fighter design is threat and counter-threat. The MiG-25 Foxbat was designed to intercept the Lockheed A-12/SR-71 series, but with Foxbat wrongly perceived by Western intelligence as an air superiority superfighter, the USA produced the outstanding F-15 Eagle to counter it. This in turn posed problems for the Soviet Union, which needed something which could give them parity. TsAGI provided aerodynamic recommendations, adopted by both Mikoyan and Sukhoi. In the latter case, this led to the Su-27 Flanker.

The programme for the *Perspectivnyi Frontovoi Istrebitel* (Future Tactical Fighter) was initiated in 1969, at about the time when the F-15 was selected as the winner of the FX competition. While

Below: A satellite photograph taken from high over the Ramenskoye test centre in 1979 showed the outline of a previously unknown fighter. It was given the NATO reporting name of Ram-K as a temporary measure.

this was well in advance of the first flight of the F-15, enough information was available via the open Western press to indicate its potential capabilities to the Soviet Union. Both the Mikoyan and Sukhoi OKBs offered proposals, and in 1971 the Sukhoi T10 project was selected for further development.

The T10 was huge, slightly larger than even the F-15, which was hardly surprising given the range and performance minima required. Its was expected to be able to outfight the F-15, and also the F-14 Tomcat, which was only marginally easier, bearing in mind that the US Navy fighter could give the Eagle a hard time in close combat in the lower speed ranges. It had to carry a large radar for long-range detection, and a huge bag of BVR and close combat AAMs. It was to be powered by two turbofan engines widely spaced to allow a "straight-through" airflow. The Soviets had obviously heeded the engine problems encountered by the General Dynamics American F-111, and adopted the solution employed by the Grumman F-14 Tomcat!

The T10-1 was the first Russian fighter to employ fly-by-wire, albeit with neutral rather than relaxed stability. Sukhoi had gained experience in this technique with the experimental S-100 high speed research aircraft in 1972. For the T10-1, they used a triplex analogue system in pitch, with mechanical backup.

The Sukhoi T10 was twin-engined, had wings of moderate sweep and fairly high aspect ratio, with leading edge root extensions, curved tips, and two fences on each side. The slab stabilizers were set below the wing level, and moved differentially, while the high aspect ratio square-topped twin fins and rudders were mounted above the engines and, like those of the F/A-18 Hornet, set well forward to minimise the effects of blanketing at high angles of attack. On certain prototypes, these were canted outwards, again like those of the Hornet.

On 20 May 1977, five months earlier than the MiG-29 Fulcrum, our old friend Vladimir Ilyushin opened the throttles, lit the afterburners, and sent the T10-1 hurtling down the runway at Zhukovsky and into the air. It is believed that this was the flight which was filmed from the ground, and later appeared on Soviet television, although not until December 1985. For some considerable time, the grainy images from this were the best available in the West. The Russians, always masters of disinformation in the military aviation field, had scored again.

Alas, the new fighter was not a success. Directional stability at speed in excess of Mach 2 was marginal, and there were other handling, flutter, and aileron rever-

sal problems. Drag was higher than predicted, whilst the Ly'ulka AL-21-F3 engines were not only underpowered, even though the dry (military) thrust was greater than that of the definitive engine. It also gave a much higher specific fuel consumption than forecast, causing a serious deficiency in range.

The second prototype, T10-2, crashed on 7 May 1978 as a result of a fly-by-wire failure. The pilot, Eugeny Soloviev, ejected outside the parameters of the seat, and did not survive. To compound the problems, operational studies showed that the T10 was very inferior to the F-15 in most departments.

The first intelligence concerning the new fighter reached the West in 1979, after it had been photographed by an American satellite. Initially it was given the reporting name of Ram-K, after Ramenskoye, now Zhukovsky, where it was first seen. Its existence caused a flurry of speculation, and at first it was thought to have variable-sweep, which indicates the limitations at the time of of satellite photography. Little could observers have known that it was a near-disaster. Even the use of the more powerful and definitive Saturn-Ly'ulka AL-31F turbofans in the T10-3 prototype from 23 August 1979 made little difference. Something far better was needed. Equally it had to be based on the T10, as a new start was not practical.

Back to the drawing board

The result was an almost total redesign. According to Ilyushin, only the centre-section remained the same. Even the cockpit was increased in size. Externally the main differences were that the vertical tail surfaces, made taller, were now mounted outboard on booms, but internally it was a very different bird. The "beaver tail" was replaced by an extended "sting". The nosewheel was moved aft, while retractable mesh grids were introduced over the intakes as an anti-FOD measure. Wing area was increased, with squared-off tips.

Not until 20 April 1981 was the T10S-1, otherwise known by the OKB as the T10-7, ready for flight, and once again the pilot was Vladimir Ilyushin. Even then the delays had not seen fixes for all the prob-

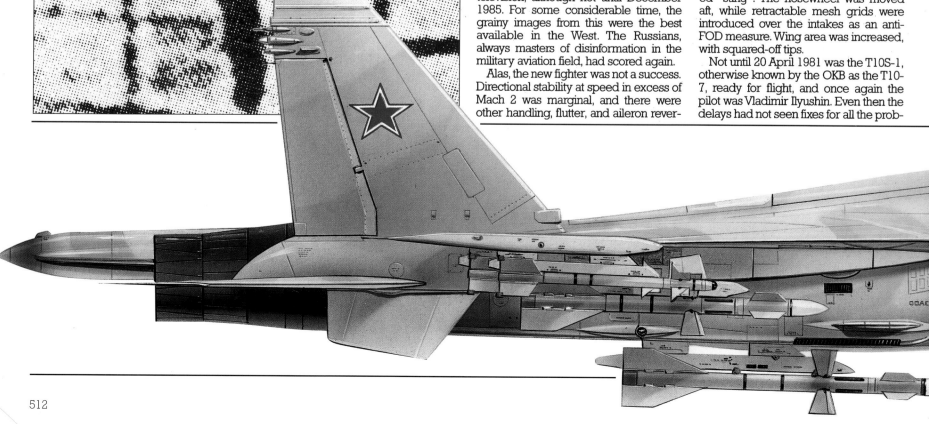

Left: Not until 1987 did the West get a good look at an operational Su-27, when one was photographed by the crew of a Norwegian P-3 Orion over the Barents Sea. The missiles carried are R-27 Alamos.

Right: Very heavily armed even in its basic version, the number of hardpoints has been increased to 16 on the latest models. Here we have R-27s, both radar and heat homing models, and R-60s.

lems; on 3 September of that year a fuel system failure of the T10-7 saw Vladimir eject unharmed, although the aircraft was destroyed. Little more than three months later, on 23 December of that year, the leading edge slats, which had been introduced on the T10-5, separated in flight. The ensuing crash killed test pilot Alexsandr Komarov. When Nikolai Savodnikov attempted to duplicate Komarov's flight, he lost what was reportedly almost the whole of the port wing, but managed to get the remnants of his stricken aircraft down in one piece.

Redesigned and strengthened, this problem was overcome, but further problems with the flight control software, the fuel system, and the radar, delayed service entry until 1986. The fuel system was, to say the least, different. Western fighters traditionally used a combination of flight refuelling combined with external tanks (jugs) to extend ferry range and/or combat radius. The Soviet Air Force was not noted for its tanker facilities, which were basic and minimal; nor was it expected to perform long-range overseas deployments. Yet, given the huge size of the Soviet Union, extended range was an obvious operational requirement. Whereas the Mikoyan OKB settled for two separate designs, the MiG-29 tactical fighter and the MiG-31 interceptor, the solution adopted by Sukhoi was to pack every available space with fuel, albeit at the expense of a measurable increase in vulnerability. The problem then became keeping the centre of gravity between limits, using automatic transference of fuel between tanks.

For the normal tactical mission, only the standard amount of fuel would be carried, but on sorties where extended range was required, the maximum would be used. This resulted in an overload condition, where g was strictly limited. While it has never been confirmed, a rapid fuel dump facility was needed to get the aircraft down to normal fighting weight if combat was joined.

As a rule of thumb, half the fuel in external tanks is needed to get a fighter to the point where it actually extends range. Other considerations are that the jugs increase the radar cross-section, making the fighter more readily

Above: The lines of the Su-27 are very simple and clean. The wingtip launch rails are shown carrying the R-73 agile dogfight missile, but in more recent variants these have been replaced by Sorbtsiya ECM pods.

The view from the highset cockpit is first class, and while the IRST sensor just in front of the windshield looks obtrusive, in practice it does not obstruct forward vision in the slightest.

The aerodynamics of the Su-27 were carefully refined to give neutral stability.

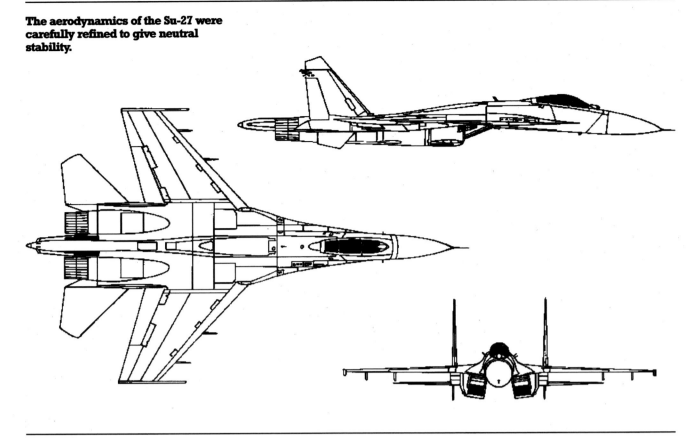

detectable by radar, while they also sterilize hardpoints that could otherwise be used for ordnance. The Sukhoi solution was ingenious in that it largely avoided both problems.

The record breakers

The original Ram-K had since been given the NATO reporting name of Flanker A; its successor, the T10S, now the Su-27, became Flanker B, and this achieved initial operational capability in 1984. This was followed on 7 March 1985 by the debut of the first two-seat combat trainer, the Su-27UB. Apart from the second seat, the Su-27UB differed mainly in having taller fins. Only a marginal reduction in fuel capacity was made, and for all practical purposes it was fully combat capable. While this was standard procedure in the West, it was a first for the Soviet Union.

It was in 1986 that the West was really forced to sit up and take notice. A stripped Flanker, actually the T10-13, designated P-42, set a hatful of new time to altitude records between 1986 and 1988, that had been previously held by the F-15 Streak Eagle.

The P-42 was, like the Streak Eagle, stripped of all weapons pylons, operational equipment, radar, and even paint. The radome was replaced by a metal fairing. Piloted by Viktor Pugachev and Nikolai Savodnikov (Vladimir Ilyushin had finally retired from test flying; high-gs are wearing on the system), the P-42 reached 9,843ft (3,000m) in just 25.373 seconds on 27 October 1986. While this was barely 8 per cent faster than the Streak Eagle, it was however a significant improvement. On 15 November of that year Pugachev reached 19,686ft (6,000m) in 35.07 seconds, beating the Streak Eagle by 2.28 seconds. Sadovnikov later achieved 44.176 seconds to 29,529ft (9,000m) and 55.542 seconds to 39,372ft (12,000m) in a single sortie; beating the Streak Eagle by more than 10 per cent and 4 per cent, respectively. Then, in 1988, the P-42 reached 49,215ft (15,000m) in just 70.33 seconds – beating the Streak Eagle's record for that time to height by more than 10 per cent. This served notice on the USAF that the Russians had managed to better the F-15 in some areas, and that the technological gap, once estimated at 15 years, was closing.

The P-42 went on to set many new records for short takeoff and landing, and several class records with and without payload. It now stands in the museum at Zhukovsky. Another pre-production machine, the T10-20, was converted to break the 500km (800-mile) closed circuit record. So far as is known, the attempt was never made.

Su-27 in public

Blurred satellite pictures and grainy TV images apart, Flanker now started to emerge from the shadows. The Su-27 started to intercept Norwegian aircraft over the Barents Sea, which allowed it to be photographed at close range. This was highlighted by an incident on 13 September 1987, when a Norwegian P-3 Orion maritime patrol aircraft came into slightly too close contact with the Russian fighter. So close did the Flanker come that its port fin tip was hit by the outboard starboard propeller of the Orion. Little damage was caused to either aircraft, and both returned to base safely. It did however allow Western observers to have a very close look at the type, not that this permitted anything more than

Left: It was this particular Su-27, Bort No 388, with which the Cobra manoeuvre was first performed in public at Le Bourget 1989, flown by test pilot Viktor Pugachev.

Right: The massive radome, with the
IRST seeker just ahead of the windshield, and the sharp-edged chines
to the wing roots, are the salient
features from this angle.

speculation.

The arrival of two MiG-29s at the
Farnborough Air Show in 1988 was a
breakthrough for the West. At the time,
"rumour control" had it that Flankers
might appear in the near future, but no-
one really believed it. Fulcrum possibly,
as this was being widely touted for
export, but Flanker – never! Russian tactical fighters had on occasion appeared in
the West, but previous major Russian air
defence fighters, such as Fishpot and
Flagon, had never even been considered!

Then, with virtually no advance warning, not one but two Flankers appeared at
the Paris Air Show in 1989, the Su-27 and
the two-seater Su-27UB, flown by Viktor
Pugachev and Eugeny Frolov, respectively. An indication of their outstanding
range was given by the fact that they had
flown unrefuelled from Moscow! And,
whereas in 1988 Westerners had been
given only limited access to the MiG-29s
and their pilots, at Paris the Russians
could hardly have been more helpful. To
the absolute amazement of the writer, he
was positively encouraged into the cockpit of the Su-27UB, with Deputy Chief
Designer Konstantin Marbashev and an
interpreter perched precariously on the
access ladder (it was a long way up), and
encouraged to ask difficult questions.
While not all of them were answered in
full, it was an encouraging start.

Dimensionally, the Su-27 was seen to be
even larger than either the Foxbat or the
Eagle. In a complete break with Russian
tradition, the all-round view from the
roomy cockpit was superb. An attempt at
HOTAS had been made, the centrally
mounted control column and the twin
throttles were liberally festooned with buttons and switches although the instrumentation was old-fashioned "steam gauge"
dials. Rather ironically, a parked F-16 was
straight in the centre of the HUD, just
where the gunsight would be.

A suggestion that multiple target tracking was possible passed without comment at this point, although this was almost
certainly the case. One thing Flanker did
not have at this stage was a multiple target
engagement capability, although this was
soon to be rectified. From outside the Infra
Red Search and Track (IRST) sensor,
mounted just ahead of the windshield,
appeared to be obtrusive, but from the
cockpit it was unnoticeable.

The future was also discussed. A mid-
life update with a "glass cockpit" and
improved avionics was in prospect, and a
carrier-compatible naval Flanker was
under development. The Russian designer would not however be drawn on the
subject of thrust-vectoring nozzles;
Sukhoi's interest was neither confirmed
nor denied.

Whereas Fulcrum was the last of the
Russian "iron birds", Flanker was the first
of the new generation, with analogue FBW
allied to neutral stability; a thrust/weight
ratio at takeoff weight in fighter configuration of 1.14; a maximum speed of Mach
2.35; automatic variable wing camber;
and an angle of attack limit of 30deg.

It was this that really set the cat among

Above right: Two-seater Flankers
have a distinct hump to accomodate
the second cockpit, while the fins are
taller, with squared-off rather than
cropped tips.

Right: Photographed by a NATO
aircraft, this Su-27 totes a range of R-27
AAMs. These are the extended range
ER/ETs and medium range R/Ts,
respectively Alamo C/D and A/B.

**Left: The Su-30MK can carry a large
variety of weapons – four R-73 and one
R-27 AAMs; a Kh-29T, a Kh-31, and a
Kh-59M make up the ASM load; while a
KAB-500 LGB and a multiple loaded
bomb rack are also carried.**

the pigeons. Have you ever heard a collective gasp from several tens of thousands of people? This is what happened
on day one, when Viktor Pugachev performed the "Cobra" maneuvre in public
for the first time. Starting from level flight
at what appeared to be quite a moderate
speed, he suddenly hoiked the big fighter onto its tail, for a brief moment passing
an angle of attack of 100deg, before
pitching back into a slight nose-down
position. We all thought he had dropped
it! But no – it was performed on every day
of the show, under complete control.
Eugeny Frolov also performed the
Cobra, demonstrating that the two-seater
lacked nothing in agility.

Western commentators immediately
assumed this to be a valid combat
manoeuvre, signifying pointability for a
missile shot, and also a means of forcing
an overshoot in a close combat situation.
As the present writer is on record as saying at the time, no spatial displacement
was evident, therefore the Cobra could
not be used to avoid a missile shot, while
if the attacker was in gun range, all it did
was to present the largest possible planform target. Of course, if the attacker was
close, the most likely outcome was a
mid-air collision! This notwithstanding, a
great deal of rubbish eventually found its
way into print on the subject. What was
the truth? Some seven years later, the
writer questioned Sukhoi test pilot
Eugeny Frolov. His answers were
unequivocal.

*"For my first Cobra I was given priority
for the rear seat in a two-seater flown by
Mr. Pugachev. For the pilot it is quite easy;
you pull back on the stick before switching
off the FBW (and with it the angle of attack
limiter), so there's no great problem. I first
flew the Cobra in public at Le Bourget in
1989. At first we regarded this manoeuvre
as a showpiece, but as we thought more
and more about combat requirements
(inspired by Western media comments)
we started to improve and refine it."*

This was a far cry from the official
Sukhoi line purveyed to the writer by
Konstantin Marbashev, that the Cobra
was a valid combat manoeuvre.
Eugeny's comment makes it quite clear
that this was not initially the case,
although the Sukhoi OKB quickly saw
the potential and started to develop it.
On the other hand, it must be recognized that no Western fighter had ever
demonstrated a similar manoeuvre. It
was however an interesting fact that the
Russians who, like the Germans, had
never been noted for giving aircraft
emotive names, quickly adopted the
NATO reporting name of Flanker as
their own, and more than that, in future
years, issued lapel pins showing the Su-
27 superimposed on a snake with the
legend "Cobra!" This despite the fact
that Sukhoi publicists insist that the name
of the aircraft is Blue Lightning, even
though in Russian service it is more
widely known as the *Zhuravlik* (Crane), a

**Above left: Folding wings are a
feature of the navalised Flanker D
(Su-27K), and these operate even with
AAMs on the hardpoints. Nearest is
an R-27T (Alamo B) heat-homer; the
other two are R-73 Archer heat-
homing agile dogfight missiles.**

**Left: The Su-35 Super Flanker which
varies by having all-moving canard
foreplanes mounted on lengthened root
extensions. The Su-35 also had relaxed
stability, the first of its breed to do so.**

name derived from its long "neck" and slightly drooped radome.

Flanker details

The Su-27 Flanker B is, as previously described, huge. It is powered by two Saturn/Ly'ulka AL-31F (F = *forsirovanni* = afterburning) turbofans, with a four-stage low pressure compressor, a nine-stage high pressure compressor, an annular combustor, and single stage high and low pressure turbines, with a fully variable con-di nozzle. These provide a thrust/weight ratio well in excess of unity.

Like the engines of the MiG-29 the AL-31Fs are widely spaced, apparently a TsAGI recommendation. The huge inlets are rectangular in section, raked back at a steep angle, but reverting to vertical for the bottom few inches to minimise spillage drag. They are optimised for speeds well in excess of Mach 2 by three-stage variable ramps, while retractable titanium mesh guards protect the compressor faces from FOD in the form of birds, stones, or ground mechanics! The wide spacing of the engines give a Tomcat-type pancake effect to the rear fuselage. Base drag was minimised by a long tail "sting".

The wings are of simple planform, with a 42deg sweep on the leading edges and sharp-edged leading edge extensions, now ogival in section, rather than plain. Aspect ratio is rather greater than that of the F-15, giving better potential sustained turning at the marginal expense of roll rate. Late production aircraft have wingtip ECM pods similar to those of the Typhoon.

The wing fences of the Flanker A are long gone. Full-span leading edge slats are supplemented by trailing edge flaperons, while the differentially moving horizontal stabilizers are supplemented by vertical twin fins and rudders set back and carried on booms outboard of the engines. A speed brake similar to that of the F-15 is mounted dorsally.

As previously noted, the fuel overload of a massive 22 tonnes, reduces the need to carry jugs, leaving all 10, or on later models 12, external hardpoints, free for ordnance. In the air-to-air role, weaponry consists of up to four extended range R27ER/ET Alamo C/D and six R27R/T medium range AAMs. This gives greatly increased combat endurance, compared with the eight AAMs routinely carried by Western fighters. For close combat, these could be supplemented by R-73 Archer IR missiles, with HMS aiming. A 30mm Gryazev/Shipunov GsH-301 cannon is located in the starboard wing root with 150 rounds, the sighting system tied into the radar and the IRST, with laser ranging.

The RLPK-27 radar, with an enormous antenna, has a search range of 130nm (244km) range and a tracking range of 92nm (170km). Initially it could track up to 10 targets simultaneously and engage two. The IRST has an effective range of 27nm (50km) in the frontal hemisphere, given suitable atmospheric conditions, but the laser ranger, while accurate at close quarters, is much less. Large though it may be, the Sukhoi Su-27 Flanker is considered by far the greatest and most versatile Russian fighter of the 20th Century.

The double wheel nose gear retracts forwards rather than aft as in Flanker A, while the single wheel main gear retracts forward to lie flat in the wing roots. As with every successful Russian aircraft, Flanker was developed into a plethora of variants. As is standard Russian practice, fighters were given odd numbers; attack aircraft, interdictors, and bombers were given even numbers. This was also the case with the Su-27, which was developed for a variety of roles.

The first variant was the two-seater Su-

Right: The Flanker cockpit is roomy if rather cluttered. Old-fashioned dials are now being replaced by a "glass cockpit", and experiments are being made with a sidestick control to replace the conventional column, which has HOTAS as seen here.

27UB Flanker C two-seater operational trainer, with the second seat set high to give a good all-round view. A slightly longer fuselage and taller fins were the keynotes of this variant. Only a small reduction in fuel capacity was needed to make space for the second seat and, unlike most Russian two-seater conversion trainer aircraft, the Su-27UB is fully operationally capable. Since 1986, two-seater production has been concentrated at Komsomolsk. The export variant, the Su-27SK, is a "monkey" aircraft, lacking many advanced avionics and ECM systems. In this it parallels the single-seat export Su-27SK, which lacks the Pallad electronic jammer, while other systems are also downgraded.

Following the revelations at Paris in 1989, Western observers awaited Farnborough 1990 with bated breath. The writer was determined to interview Viktor Pugachev, but the Sukhoi test pilot spent much of his time in the cockpit, with a huge queue at the bottom of the ladder. Unwilling to waste time waiting, with no guarantee of success, I walked away, beneath the giant bird. And there, just a few paces away, was a large gold-braided hat. Underneath it, smiling broadly, was the diminutive figure of Vladimir Ilyushin in person, clad in full Russian Major General's uniform complete with the red ribbon and gold star of a Hero of the Soviet Union! He was totally ignored by the reporters dutifully waiting for Pugachev! If only they had known...!

Vladimir was a veritable mine of information, about both Flankers past and Flankers future. He confirmed that the mid-life update would consist of a "glass cockpit", improved radar and avionics, and a flight refuelling probe. He told me that the T10-24 prototype, which commenced flight trials in 1985, was fitted with all-moving canard foreplanes, the main purpose of which was to improve short-field performance by allowing a flatter approach on finals. This aircraft had been briefly fitted with a single thrust vectoring nozzle in 1989, as a technology demonstrator.

For the future, Vladimir predicted a two-seater "command" aircraft, able to control interceptions and strikes, and a dedicated strike aircraft to replace the ageing Su-24 Fencer, which it was now revealed, was not in the same league as the even older American F-111.

Su-33 (Su-27K) Flanker D

In the final years of the Soviet Union, global power projection was a priority, to match the US Navy carrier fleet. Great oaks from little acorns grow, and so it was for the Soviet Navy. They had to start somewhere! Initially their fixed wing carrier aircraft was the Yakovlev Yak-38 which was capable of a short rolling takeoff and a vertical landing. Powered by lift-jets, with a vectoring main propulsion jet, the Yak-38, NATO reporting name Forger, was for all practical purposes an inferior Harrier. In the air defence role it was a non-starter, while its attack capabilities were totally outclassed by the contemporary generation of US carrier aircraft. Something better was badly needed, and a navalized Flanker was developed for the mission.

This was the Su-33, service designation Su-27K, (K = *korabelnyi* = carrier), NATO reporting name Flanker D. Experiments commenced on 28 August 1982, when T10-3, piloted by Nikolai Sadovnikov, took off from a dummy flight

deck at Saki in the Ukraine. To bypass the difficulties of catapult launching, the Soviet Navy decided to explore the possibility of using a ski-jump as pioneered by Britain's Royal Navy with its Sea Harrier. One was built at Saki; the first ski-jump takeoff took place on 25 September 1984 using T10-25.

The canard-equipped T10-24, piloted by Viktor Pugachev, was first flown in May 1985. Progress was slow; fully automatic landing trials did not begin until 1987, while the first proper prototype, T10-37, only flew in August of that year. The first real deck landing, on the carrier *Tbilisi*, later renamed *Admiral Kuznetzov*, took place on 1 November 1989, piloted by Viktor Pugachev. Nearly two more years passed before service pilots began to fly the type, and not until October 1994 was it formally accepted by the Russian Navy.

Externally Flanker D differs from Flanker B in several aspects, notably the canard surfaces. Wing folding, essential in the limited space of carrier lifts and hangars, involved using a full-span trailing edge flap and aileron, split at the wing fold. The horizontal tail surfaces were also made to fold, as was the much shorter tail "sting", which has an arrester hook beneath it. Unable to launch from the deck with a full bag of ordnance and fuel, Flanker D is forced to rely on flight refuelling, the probe for which is mounted just ahead of the cockpit on the port side, causing the IRST seeker to be relocated to starboard. With no dedicated carrier-borne tanker aircraft available, it has to resort to the Sakhalin "buddy" refuelling pod; topping up after takeoff. This, as mentioned elsewhere, effectively halves the strike force available.

One further detail: the original Flanker was designed for rough-field operations;

consequently its landing gear did not need beefing up for carrier operations. Structurally, like all naval aircraft, it makes greater use of anti-corrosion materials than its land-based counterparts.

Su-27M and Su-35 Super Flanker

First flown on 28 June 1988 as the T10M-1 prototype, the Su-35 was designed as an advanced air superiority fighter. Its manoeuvrability was enhanced by moving from the neutral stability of the Su-27 to positive (relaxed) instability, something that was helped by having "wet" fins, moving the centre of gravity aft. A quadruplex digital FBW system was proposed, although this did not become mature until 1996, while the extensive use of composites and welded aluminium lithium reduced weight. For the record, lithium is the only known metal light enough to float in water. Differentially moving canard surfaces, square topped fins, and wingtip pods housing ECM jammers, completed the picture, and the Sukhoi brochure described the Su-35 as having a triplane configuration (shades of the Red Baron!).

It was in this variant that the predicted "glass cockpit" finally emerged, with four multi-function displays. Two different radars are reported to be in contention – NIIP's N-011M phased array radar, which is stated to have a maximum search range of 216nm (400km) and can track up to 20 targets and engage six simultaneously, and Phazotron's Zhuk-PH, also a phased array type of similar performance. Development problems have however occurred; the in-service date continues to slip, and the current situation is confused.

It was in the Su-35 that Eugeny Frolov first demonstrated a new manoeuvre, the "Hook", which was in essence a horizontal

Left: A completely new front end, with side-by-side seating, toilet and galley, marks the Su-34 theatre bomber dubbed Platypus by the West (previous designations: Su-27IB, Su-27KU, Su-32MK, Su-32FN).

Cobra and, if anything, even more spectacular. Progress was however not all honey; in April 1996 Oleg Tsoi had a double FCS failure while flying weapons release trials. Approaching the range, he experienced bank oscillations of increasing magnitude, with cockpit warnings. Instructed to jettison the ordnance and eject, he instead chose to return to the airfield at Akhtubinsk, in Kazakhstan, some 81nm (150km) away, using the "rigid link" backup system. Unstable without the analogue system, Tsoi had problems on landing his sick bird; the port undercarriage leg collapsed and he veered off the runway, ending in a field. Fortunately little damage was caused.

More embarrassingly, at Farnborough in 1994, Su-35 pilot Vyacheslav Averianov overshot the runway on landing after a validation flight. Damage was minor. Averianov was to have a much more dramatic escape at Paris in 1999, when flying the Su-30MKI with thrust vectoring he spiralled into the ground, then bounced back up using full power before ejecting unharmed.

Su-30M, Su-30MK, Su-30MKI

First flown on 30 December 1989, the Su-30M is a two-seater attack aircraft, based on the Su-27UB, with which it is externally almost identical, and has a significant air defence capability. Like the Su-27K, it has provision for a flight refuelling probe. The avionics are supplemented by an augmented navigation system, and a tactical data exchange system which allows the Su-30 to "hand off" targets to other aircraft during the course of the mission. The variant to which Vladimir Ilyushin referred as a "command" aircraft, is actually an Su-30 with a dedicated interception radar, and no air-to-ground capability. In this role, the crew act as fighter controllers in a multi-bogey scenario.

The Su-30MK can also be used in the SEAD (Suppression of Enemy Air Defences) mission, carrying Kh-31P Krypton anti-radiation missiles, cued by the SPO-32 Pastel RWR pod which is carried on the front hardpoint between the engine intakes. This pod also contains the SPS-161 jammer, which is extra to the other self-protection systems.

The Su-30 is thus a long range interceptor; the Su-30M is an attack aircraft for export, with no smart weapon capability (and to date no takers); the Su-30MK is a multi-role export variant. This leaves the Su-30MKI, which is being acquired by the Indian Air Force as a deep penetrator. It has canard foreplanes, and will be updated with a Phazotron phased-array radar, and eventually, thrust vectoring, with Saturn Ly'ulka AL-31FP turbofans. Final delivery of the "full-up" Su-30MKI is scheduled for 2000, although whether this date will be met is open to doubt. The People's Republic of China, which already operates the single seat Su-27SK, is also interested in what would become the Su-30MKK in Chinese service.

Su-27IB (Su-34) Platypus

The Su-27IB (Istrebitel Bombardirovschik – fighter-bomber) first flew on 13 April 1990, piloted by Anatoliy Ivanov. It differs from previous Flankers mainly in having

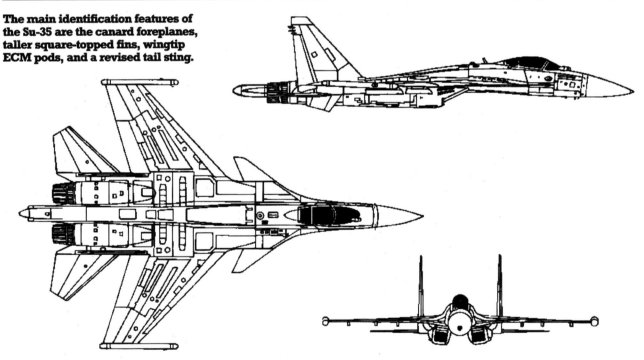

The main identification features of the Su-35 are the canard foreplanes, taller square-topped fins, wingtip ECM pods, and a revised tail sting.

Left: Dorsal speed brake extended, Eugeny Frolov brings his Su-37 in to land at Farnborough in 1996 after a virtuoso aerobatic display which included the Super Cobra and Kulbit.

a completely new front section with side-by-side seating. The cockpit is protected from ground fire by a 17mm titanium alloy "bathtub" and, unusually, is high enough for the crew to stand and stretch during a long flight. Other unusual features are a small toilet and galley aft of the crew position, which indicate that range and endurance, especially with flight refuelling, allow strategic missions to be flown.

The flattened section chined nose gives it the duck-billed appearance which caused it to be dubbed "Platypus" by the West. The chines extend to the leading edge extensions which in turn give onto canard foreplanes. Intended primarily to replace the Su-24 Fencer, the engine intakes are of fixed geometry, limiting maximum speed, not that this matters too much for an interdictor.

Sukhoi excelled in the confusion stakes with this variant. Having started out as the Su-27IB, it was identified in 1992 as the Su-27KU carrier trainer, then in 1994 as the Su-34, before appearing at Paris in 1995 as the Su-32FN. This was stated to be a shore-based maritime aircraft with a radar optimised for sea search, and anti-shipping and anti-submarine weaponry detection devices, including sonobuoys.

In its long range strike version, range is stated to be 2,159nm (4,000km) on internal fuel only, giving an operational radius probably in excess of 700nm (1,300km). This can of course be extended by flight refuelling, preferably from dedicated tankers, making endurance in the region of six to eight hours. The phased array Leninets radar has a full terrain-following capability, with many ground mapping modes. It is backed by INS and the GLONASS satellite navigation system.

One area of difference between the original Su-27IB and the Su-34 is the main gears, where tandem twin wheels have replaced the former single wheel. Sorbtsiya-S ECM pods now occupy the wingtips, displacing the former missile rails, and the tail sting has been lengthened and canted upwards. It is believed to house a rear-looking radar which is not only a warning system, but can be used to launch rearward-firing R-73 AAMs at a pursuer. One of the main problems here is that of positive target identification. R-73 is a visual range weapon but, as the rearward view from the Platypus is abysmal, total certainty will be hard to establish.

Sukhoi Su-37

The manoeuvrability of conventional fighters had always been dependent on aerodynamic limits, primarily the lift generated. Thrust vectoring – using the engines for control at speed/altitude combinations where ailerons and tailerons lost effectiveness – seemed a possible answer. Pioneered by Dr Wolfgang Herbst of MBB, and tested by the Rockwell/MBB X-31, this was at first called post-stall manoeuvrability; later it became supermanoeuvrability.

Sukhoi had been experimenting with thrust vectoring since the late 1980s, but the greatest difficulty was integrating it into the flight control system. A whole heap of new laws had to be developed. The basic design of Flanker did not help; the long tail sting effectively limited nozzle movement to pitch only.

The Su-37, as it was designated, first flew on 2 April 1996, piloted by Eugeny Frolov. It is powered by two Saturn Ly'ulka AL-37FU afterburning turbofans with hydraulically powered nozzles which can be vectored through 15deg above or below horizontal. The AL-37FU has an entirely new advanced technology four-stage low pressure compressor, followed by a nine-stage high pressure compressor. Output is 32,000lb (14,515kg) maximum, and 18,740lb (8,500kg) in military power.

The Su-37 was first seen in the West at Farnborough in 1996. At Le Bourget a year earlier, the writer had asked Eugeny what he had in mind for it. Quietly, he said that he would have to fly the aircraft first to see what it could do, adding that he did not think that I would be disappointed.

I was not! First the "Super Cobra", in which he pulled the big fighter to an angle of attack of 135deg, recovered to nose-up vertical using thrust vectoring, hung apparently stationary for between four and six seconds, then kicked the nose back down into level flight. This was followed by the "Kulbit", or somersault. From an entry speed of 189kt (350kmh), Eugeny pulled up as though for a Cobra, but kept going until he was completely inverted. He then stabilized for a couple of seconds, then dropped the nose downwards to recover 30deg nose low and with just 32kt (60kmh) on the clock. If these figures seem very precise, my source was the pilot himself. It was an amazing demonstration of pointability. But whether the Su-37 will enter service remains to be seen.

Su-27KUB; Su-33UB

Broad hints about a carrier-compatible "Platypus" had been around for many years, but not until 29 April 1999 did it take to the air. Flown by Viktor Pugachev and Sergei Melnikov, it varies considerably from the original. The duck-bill nose has gone, replaced by a circular section radome, apparently as a result of a change in radar to the N-014 used by the Su-35. Wing span and area are both significantly increased, while adaptive direct lift control surfaces keep the approach speed of what is a huge carrier aircraft within manageable limits.

By September 1999 the Su-27KUB had commenced dummy deck landing trials, and was expected to graduate to carrier compatibility trials aboard the *Admiral Kuznetsov* by the end of the year.

Flanker has seen little active service to date, although at least one has been lost to Chechen ground fire. In air combat, two Eritrean MiG-29s were shot down by Ethiopian Su-27s on 25 and 26 February 1999. No details of these encounters are available, except that the pilots of both sides spoke Russian.

Flanker users

The following nations either already operate the Su-27 and its derivatives, or (*) expect to receive them in the near future: Algeria*, Armenia*, Belarus, China (People's Republic), Ethiopia, India, Kazakhstan, Russia, Syria*, Ukraine, Uzbekistan, Vietnam.

Sukhoi Specifications

Type	Su-17M4 Fitter K	Su-24M Fencer D	Su-25 Frogfoot
Dimensions			
Span max/min	44ft 11in/13.68m/32ft 11in/10.03m	57ft 10½in/17.64m/34ft/10.37m	47ft 1in/14.36m
Length	62ft 5in/19.02m	80ft 6in/24.53m	50ft 11½in/15.53m
Height	16ft 10in/5.13m	20ft 4in/6.20m	15ft 9in/4.80m
Wing Area	414sq.ft/38.49m² - 375sq.ft/38.45m²	594sq.ft/55.17m² - 549sq.ft/51.02m²	324sq.ft/30.10m²
Aspect ratio	4.86-2.88	5.64-2.11	6.85
Weights			
Empty	23,457lb/10,640kg	49,207lb/22,320kg	20,235lb/14,530kg
Normal takeoff	36,156lb/16,400kg	79,299lb/35,970kg	32,023lb/14,530kg
Max takeoff	42,989lb/19,500kg	83,554lb/39,700kg	38,647lb/17,530kg
Power	1xAL-21F-3A turbojet	2xAl-21F-3A turbojets	2xR-95Sh turbojets
Max thrust	24,692lb/11,200kg	24,692lb/11,200kg	n/a
Mil thrust	17,196lb/7,800kg	17,196lb/7,800kg	9,921lb/4,500kg
Intl fuel	8,311lb/3,770kg	21,715lb/9,850kg	6,614lb/3,000kg
Performance			
V_{max} hi	Mach 1.77	Mach 1.35	Mach 0.82
V_{max} lo	Mach 1.02	Mach 1.15	373kt/691kmh
Ceiling	49,871ft/15,200m	54,137ft/16,500m	22,950ft/7,000m
Climb rate	n/a	n/a	11,400ftm/58msec
Range	756nm/1,400km*	1,350nm/2,500km*	999nm/1,850km*

* with external tanks

Sukhoi Specifications

Type	Su-27 Flanker B	Su-35 Flanker	Su-27KUB Flanker
Dimensions			
Span	48ft 3in/14.70m	48ft 3in/14.70m	52ft 6in/16m
Length	71ft 11in/21.94m	72ft 10in/22.20m	69ft 6in/21.18m
Height	19ft 6in/5.93m	21ft/6.40m	n/a
Wing area	668sq.ft/62.04m²	668sq.ft/62.04m²	753sq.ft/70m²
Aspect ratio	3.48	3.48	3.66
Weights			
Empty	36,112lb/16,380kg	40,565lb/18,400kg	c41,006lb/18,600kg
Normal takeoff	51,015lb/23,140kg	56,659lb/25,700kg	n/a
Max takeoff	62,391lb/28,300kg	n/a	c100,000lb/45,360 kg
Power	2xAL-31F turbofans	2xAL-35F turbofans	2xAL-35F turbofans
Max thrust	27,558lb/12,500kg	30,865lb/14,000kg	30,865lb/14,000kg
Mil thrust	16,755lb/7,600kg	17,637lb/8,000kg	17,637lb/8,000kg
Intl fuel	20,723lb/9,400kg*	24,039lb/10,904kg *	24,039lb/10,904kg*
Performance			
V_{max} hi	Mach 2.35	Mach 2.35	Mach 1.70
V_{max} lo	Mach 1.14	Mach 1.14	Mach 1.06
Ceiling	59,058ft/18,000m	59,058ft/18,000m	n/a
Climb	60,000fpm/305msec	60,000fpm/305msec	n/a
Range	1,512nm/2,800km	2,160nm/4,000km	2,000nm/3,700km
AAMs carried	10	14	n/a

* is overload internal fuel. Normal capacity is 7,496lb/3,400kg less.

Sukhoi S-37 Berkut

For years, "rumour control" had indicated, with the aid of the occasional model in the Russian Pavilion at the Paris Air Show, that Sukhoi were interested in forward sweep. To a large extent this was discounted. The Grumman X-29 had explored the concept, but the project faded after 1992 without so much as a hint of official interest. Forward sweep seemed to have gone the way of the dodo!

Then, on 25 September 1997, Sukhoi test pilot Igor Votintsev thundered down the runway at Zhukovsky and lifted the S-37 *Berkut* (Golden Eagle) into the air. Features included canard foreplanes, semicircular inlets topped with chines, outward canted fins, and forward-swept wings with a 20deg leading edge angle!

Now, forward-sweep has certain aerodynamic advantages. It provides greater manoeuvrability at low speeds and high angles of attack, and allows a smaller and lighter wing for the same performance. There are however several unanswered questions.

Why, when Sukhoi were so heavily engaged in exploring supermanoeuvrability with vectored thrust, did they bother to produce this extremely expensive company-funded demonstrator? Why did it carry the red stars of the old Soviet Union rather than the modern Russian national insignia? And, disinformation apart, why was it touted as a prototype fighter when it was obviously nothing more than a technology demonstrator? Why was it given a Russian Navy paint job (dark blue), rather than an Air Force finish? And, finally, why was it given the emotive name of *Berkut,* when no previous Sukhoi fighter had been given such a privilege? Was it simply to grab the attention of the media?

While none of these questions has been answered, an insider's view was provided for the writer by Vladimir Ilyushin. He stated quite categorically that it was an experimental aeroplane for high angle of attack research, and also of advanced systems, and carried no weapons. While an IRST housing is clearly visible in front of the cockpit, this indicates only that parts of previous aircraft were used to reduce costs. Whereas the engines were at first stated to be the Aviadvigatel D-30F6 as used on the MiG-31, the rated thrust of 27,560lb (12,500kg) exactly matches that of the Saturn Ly'ulka AL-31F. So which is it? Finally, internal fuel is a mere 8,818lb (4,000kg), giving a fuel fraction of 0.17 – about half what one would expect on a prototype fighter!

The flight test programme has been proceeding very slowly, and only 30 months after the first flight has it been announced that the S-37 has exceeded Mach 1. Test pilot Igor Votintsev has stated that supersonic handling is "easy and stable".

Above: Between 1946 and 1950 Soviet designers experimented with forward sweep, using full-scale gliders launched from "mother" aircraft such as the Tu-4, and their behaviour recorded and filmed. This example was designed by V.P.Tsybin.

Left: However good FSW actually is, the angle of attack on finals appears rather excessive, running the risk of grounding the rear end. In this and many other pictures, Berkut appears to be dark green, but the actual colour is Russian Navy blue.

Below: The Sukhoi S-37 Berkut FSW demonstrator has obviously borrowed its nose section and fins from the Flanker production line. The semi-circular intakes are however very different, as are the canard fore-planes and horizontal tail surfaces.